"Masterfully integrating clinical and experimental research on memory and trauma, Brown, Scheflin, and Hammond provide the most comprehensive review to date of trauma treatment and the law. This book is essential reading for all mental health professionals and attorneys involved with trauma survivors."

—MARLENE STEINBERG, M.D.

Associate Professor of Psychiatry

University of Massachusetts Medical Center and Research Affiliate, Yale University School of Medicine

Author, *Handbook for the Assessment of Dissociation*

"We must continue to grapple with the complexities surrounding the recovered memory issue; we must advance a more informed approach to those struggling to make sense of their lives in the therapy room and the courtroom. This constructive and informative book moves us in that direction.

"*Memory, Trauma Treatment, and the Law* is important reading for those in the clinical, research, and legal arenas who deal with recovered memory issues as well as for those interested generally in the cross-fertilization of knowledge between psychological specialties. It brings together state-of-the-art material on the science of memory, the treatment of trauma, and the interests of the legal field. It is truly an essential resource."

—JUDITH L. ALPERT, PH.D.

Professor, Department of Applied Psychology

Faculty, Postdoctoral Program in Psychotherapy and Psychoanalysis

New York University

"The authors have written an extraordinarily comprehensive, balanced, and state-of-the-art book that is essential reading for anyone who would avoid becoming ensnared in the thicket of the recovered memory debate."

—ROBERT I. SIMON, M.D.

Clinical Professor of Psychiatry and Director, Program in Psychiatry and Law

Georgetown University School of Medicine, Washington

"In a painfully and often irrationally divided field, Brown, Scheflin, and Hammond's masterwork is a superb guide for the perplexed. Encyclopedic in its scope and exceptionally thorough and rich in its details, this landmark book will represent the standard of science and care for many years to come."

—ONNO VAN DER HART, PH.D.

Professor, Department of Clinical Psychology and Health Psychology

Utrecht University, The Netherlands

"This book is a scholarly, lucid, thoughtful examination of trauma, memory, hypnosis, and the law. It turns the cold light of research onto key areas of the heated 'memory wars,' leading to conclusions that are fair and sensible. The writing is spirited but logical. The authors add more light than heat to an area that is crucial to the future of psychotherapy."

—DAVID SPIEGEL, M.D.

Professor of Psychiatry and Behavioral Sciences

Stanford University School of Medicine

"No serious scientist or practitioner in the fields covered by this comprehensive book can be considered knowledgeable unless they are familiar with its contents. It is the best single-source state-of-the-art overview available."

—MELVIN A. GRAVITZ, PH.D.

Past President, American Society of Clinical Hypnosis

Past President, Division of Hypnosis, American Psychological Association

"Few areas of law are more controversial than those surrounding delayed memories. This book sets the standard as the definitive work on the subject by furnishing a comprehensive analysis of the issues and indispensable information for members of the legal and mental health professionals. *Memory, Trauma Treatment, and the Law* is a great book."

—SOL GOTHARD, J.D., M.S.W., ACSW

Judge, Fifth Circuit Court of Appeal

State of Louisiana

"The authors have created an excellent resource showing the impact of research, clinical practice, and litigation on each other. It is encyclopedic in scope, examining the evolution of current controversies in memory research, hypnosis, trauma treatment, and related matters; yet it is concise and rich in detail and case material, illuminating a path through this complex terrain for the therapist concerned with ethical practice, such as competence and informed consent, and the many pitfalls of diagnosing and treating patients with trauma."

—THOMAS F. NAGY, PH.D.
Clinical Faculty, Department of Psychiatry
Stanford University School of Medicine

"This book provides clinicians, lawyers, researchers, and judges with an encyclopedic overview of what science actually knows about such complex issues as how children process overwhelming experiences, how trauma affects memory, the nature of suggestibility, the promises and limitations of hypnosis, and appropriate standards of care of individuals with suspected trauma histories. Since the debate about these issues has been characterized by much passion and little attention to the data, it is marvelous to see a book like this, a triumph for the voice of reason."

—BESSEL A. VAN DER KOLK, M.D.
Professor of Psychiatry, Boston University School of Medicine
Visiting Professor, Harvard University
Director, HRI Trauma Center

"*Memory, Trauma Treatment, and the Law* is a monumental volume without peer. Brown, Scheflin, and Hammond have rendered a thoughtful, comprehensive, and even-handed examination of the scientific foundations of clinical and legal practice in this area. This book should be a well-thumbed reference in the library of every attorney, therapist, researcher, and policymaker."

—KEN POPE, PH.D., ABPP
author of *Recovered Memories of Abuse: Assessment, Therapy, Forensics*

"Acrimony and bias have characterized the debate about the impact of trauma on memory. At last a reasoned, balanced text has appeared that provides a thoughtful, well researched examination of all of the issues related to this debate. This book is a must read for clinicians, forensic psychologists, and memory researchers as well as legal professionals working with cases involving allegations of repressed memories or false memories.

"The authors are to be commended for the breadth and depth of research found in this book. Most importantly, the authors have provided a conceptual framework for the memory-trauma debate that has the potential to bridge the differences that have so negatively affected this area of research and practice."

—JOHN C. YUILLE, PH.D.
University of British Columbia

"In an age when advocacy ignores science and controversy obscures knowledge, now comes the essential source for an unbiased and complete review of the science on this important topic. If every psychotherapist and lawyer were to have only one book on the topic, this should be that book."

—JON R. CONTE, PH.D.
Professor, University of Washington

A Norton Professional Book

MEMORY, TRAUMA TREATMENT, AND THE LAW

Daniel Brown

Alan W. Scheflin

D. Corydon Hammond

W. W. NORTON & COMPANY

New York • London

The authors are grateful to the following for permission to redraw and reproduce figures 3.1, The University of Chicago Press; 3.2, Academic Press; and tables 17.1, Brunner/Mazel, Inc.; 17.2, Martha L. Rogers, Ph.D.; 17.3 and 17.4, Kluwer Academic Publishers; guidelines from *Clinical Hypnosis and Memory*, pp. 34–35, American Society of Clinical Hypnosis.

Printed in the United States of America

First Edition

The text of this book is composed in Goudy Old Style and Gill Sans.
Desktop composition and book design by Justine Burkat Trubey.

Library of Congress Cataloging-in-Publication Data

Brown, Daniel P., 1948–
Memory, trauma treatment, and the law / Daniel Brown,
Alan W. Scheflin, D. Corydon Hammond.
p. cm.
"Norton professional book".
Includes bibliographical references and index.
ISBN 0-393-70254-5
1. Child sexual abuse—United States. 2. Psychology,
Forensic—United States. 3. Psychotherapists—
Malpractice—United States. 4. False memory syndrome.
5. Recovered memory. I. Scheflin, Alan W. II. Hammond,
D. Corydon. III. Title
KF9323.B76 1998
364.15'36—dc21   97-25902
CIP

W. W. Norton & Company, Inc., 500 Fifth Avenue, New York, NY 10110
http://www.wwnorton.com

W. W. Norton & Company Ltd., 10 Coptic Street, London CW1A 1PU

1 2 3 4 5 6 7 8 9 0

To our wives—Marushka, Jamie, Melanie—for giving us our best memories, none of them false and none of them repressed.

To our children—Jeremy and Gabriel, Hallie, Matthew and Erin—for keeping us mindful of our obligation to pass on a better world, one worthy of their goodness, which has inspired our lives.

About the Authors

‖‖‖‖‖‖‖‖‖‖‖‖‖‖‖

DANIEL BROWN, PH.D. received his B.S. from the University of Massachusetts and his Ph.D. from the University of Chicago. He is an Assistant Clinical Professor in Psychology at Harvard Medical School, an Adjunct Professor at Simmons School of Social Work, and Director of The Center for Integrative Psychotherapy, Cambridge, MA, a psychotherapy private practice, continuing education sponsoring organization, and forensic consultation group.

Dr. Brown has taught hypnotherapy for 26 years. He has written three books on hypnotherapy, including a standard textbook, *Hypnotherapy and Hypnoanalysis* (1986) and two books one specialized topics, *Hypnosis and Behavioral Medicine* (1987) and *Creative Mastery in Hypnosis and Hypnoanalysis* (1990). He has also co-authored two books on human development. *Human Feelings* (1993) synthesizes developmental research and clinical observations on emotional development in children and adults, and *Transformations of Consciousness* synthesizes Eastern and Western views on self development.

As an expert on trauma, memory, and suggestibility, Dr. Brown has testified in numerous cases involving alleged psychological damages associated with posttraumatic stress and dissociative identity disorders and in malpractice cases involving alleged implanted false memories. He served as Guest Co-editor of the *Journal of Psychiatry and Law* (Summer 1996 issue) to prepare a special edition on current scientific research in response to the recovered memory debate.

ALAN W. SCHEFLIN holds a B.A. with High Honors from the University of Virginia (1963), a J.D. with Honors from the George Washington University Law School (1966), an LL.M. from the Harvard Law School (1967), and an M.A. in Counseling Psychology from Santa Clara University (1987). He has taught in the Law School and the Philosophy Department at the Georgetown University Law School, and has been a Visiting Professor at the University of Southern California Law School.

Professor Scheflin has authored approximately three dozen articles, book chapters and book reviews. His co-authored second book, *The Mind Manipulators* (1978), was published in more than a dozen countries. *Trance on Trial* (1989), his co-authored third book, received the American Psychiatric Association's 1991 Manfred S. Guttmacher Award as the year's most outstanding publication on forensic psychiatry. His co-authored fourth book, *Clinical Hypnosis and Memory: Guidelines for Clinicians and for Forensic Hypnosis* (1995), received the Society for Clinical and Experimental Hypnosis Arthur Shapiro Award for "Book of the Year" for 1995.

Professor Scheflin has testified before Legislatures, and has been judicially recognized in federal district court as an expert on mind and behavior control, and in state court as an expert on suggestion and suggestibility, memory, and hypnosis. He has delivered invited addresses to all of the major professional hypnosis organizations in this country and several in other countries. He has also addressed the American Psychiatric Association, the American Orthopsychiatric Association, and the American Psychological Association, as well as other professional mental health and legal organizations.

Professor Scheflin is the Forensic Editor of the *Journal of the American Society of Clinical Hypnosis*, an Advisory Editor of the *Cultic Studies Journal*, and a Guest Co-Editor of the *Journal of Psychiatry and Law* (Summer 1996).

In 1993, Professor Scheflin received the Irving I. Sector Award in honor of his service to the American Society of Clinical Hypnosis. Professor Scheflin currently holds a tenured teaching position at the Santa Clara University School of Law.

D. CORYDON HAMMOND, PH.D., ABPH, is the past president and a fellow of the American Society of Clinical Hypnosis (ASCH). The ASCH honored Dr. Hammond with a Presidential Award of Merit in 1989 for "creating significant publications which have contributed to the advancement of knowledge in clinical hypnosis." He also received their Irving Secter Award in 1990, and the Thomas P. Wall Award for Excellence in the Teaching of Clinical Hypnosis in 1994. He has chaired ASCH workshops in the U.S. and Canada, as well as annual and scientific meetings.

Dr. Hammond is Professor of Physical Medicine and Rehabilitation and Co-director of the Sex & Marital Therapy Clinic at the University of Utah School of Medicine. His work in psychology has focused on the treatment of psychological and medical disorders with hypnosis and biofeedback. He is a diplomate of the American Board of Psychological Hypnosis, the American Board of Family Psychology, and the American Board of Sexology.

He has published over 60 professional journal articles, chapters, or reviews, and six other books, including a leading clinical hypnosis textbook, the *Handbook of Hypnotic Suggestions and Metaphors*. He coordinated a national task force on hypnosis and memory, establishing new standards in that area, and is the primary author of *Clinical Hypnosis and Memory: Guidelines for Clinicians and for Forensic Hypnosis*. This volume was honored with the Best Book of the Year Award by the Society for Clinical and Experimental Hypnosis. Dr. Hammond is an associate editor of the *American Journal of Clinical Hypnosis*, and for many years was an advisory editor for the *Ericksonian Monographs*.

Dr. Hammond also facilitated the creation of the credentialing program for the ASCH and is the primary author of their national *Standards for Training in Clinical Hypnosis*. He has been the past chair of the board of trustees of the ASCH Education and Research Foundation. Dr. Hammond has also served in the leadership of the University of Utah Summer School on Alcoholism and Other Drug Dependencies for 25 years.

Acknowledgments

This book began several years ago when the first two authors were conducting a weekend training seminar in Boston. At that time, the false memory debate was highly acrimonious, and further complicated by an absence of solutions. Proper education and training, as well as the development of useful guidelines, seemed appropriate to help eliminate the legitimate concerns raised by false memory advocates. The first two authors agreed that a presentation of the science of memory was essential, as was the articulation of the latest developments in trauma treatment. Furthermore, because false memory issues were being debated in legal confrontations, a full explanation of legal matters would be essential.

At this time, the second and third authors had independently agreed to write something on the topic of forensic hypnosis. Almost the entire scientific literature on the subject had developed since 1985, but it had not yet been collected and analyzed in a single source.

It seemed quite sensible for these two projects to be combined. Our goal was to inform ourselves and others as to what the scientific literature had to say about the crucial topics of memory, trauma, and hypnosis. The extensive research that we conducted altered our views over time and gave us the opportunity to provide a comprehensive text that clinicians, researchers, lawyers, and judges would use when dealing with recovered memory issues.

In the last few years we have conducted extensive interviews with researchers, clinicians, patients, ex-patients, lawyers, and judges. We thank everyone for their generosity and frankness. We have also had the opportunity to appear in court as expert witnesses, sometimes in favor of the false memory position and sometimes against it, depending upon the individual facts of each case.

Our reading of the scientific literature has led us to a carefully considered moderate position. On the one hand, we reject the legitimacy of certain excess that false memory advocates have identified and we have spoken out against therapists whose preexisting biases cause them to shape their patients' memory reports according to these beliefs. We accept the fact that under certain conditions "implanting memories," or what we would call "obtaining false belief reports," may be possible.

On the other hand, the science concludes that "repressed" memories are real and that they are no less accurate than memories continuously recollected. Furthermore, there appears to be a separate memory processing system for memories that are traumatic. Thus, we believe that the great benefit of the false memory controversy has been not only to make therapists and patients aware of a form of extreme therapy that should not be practiced but also to alert clinicians and researchers to a form of extreme pseudoscience that has been used to attack trauma therapists. Pseudoscience at both extremes must be tempered and corrected. "Recovered memory" therapy must be stopped, but so too must the extreme unscientific positions that appear in the attacks on such therapy.

The manuscript of this book has undergone five rounds of peer review and three rounds of legal review. We have benefitted enormously from these independent reviews and have been quite willing to listen to the sage advice received from these reviewers. Over the years, this manuscript has undergone at least seven major revisions and constant updating. Our goal has been to present the science and the controversies with all due fairness.

We have countless people to thank for their contributions to this book. Edward Frischholz provided detailed comments on chapters 8 and 10, and Onno van der Hart made numerous insightful corrections and additions to chapter 13.

We would especially like to thank Karen Olio and Ken Pope for the many articles and Internet bulletins they sent our way so that our knowledge of the evolving scientific literature was always kept up to date. Lawrence Lifson and Bessel van der Kolk, co-course directors of the annual Trauma conference at Harvard Medical School, and Lawrence Lifson, course director of the annual Psychiatry and Law conference at Harvard Medical School, provided us with a yearly forum to present our evolving ideas to a diverse professional audience. A special thanks goes to Jamie Caploe for her assistance in editing many of these chapters. A debt of gratitude is owed to Valerie Wall of the American Society of Clinical Hypnosis Press first for believing in this book enough to agree to publish it, and then for her graciousness in allowing us to find another publisher when the book became too big for the new ASCH Press to handle.

Dr. Brown wishes to thank those members of his group private practice who made comments on various drafts of this manuscript—Deborah Block, Larry Rosenberg, Judy Osher, and Liz Rice-Smith. He is especially appreciative of the generosity of Michael Murphy and Nancy Lunney, who provided him with the "Little House" at Esalen Institute in Big Sur, CA, for a monthlong writing retreat, during which a number of these chapters were composed.

Professor Scheflin would like to thank Dean George Alexander, his teaching partner, colleague, and friend for over two decades. Dean Alexander's persistent demand for accuracy and proof has had a vital impact on the development of the manuscript. His legal opinions on many of the topics have also been highly beneficial to us. Many of the students in our law and psychiatry course over the years have contributed extremely helpful independent research on these issues, including a 1997 paper by Michael Kowalski awarded first prize in a writing contest sponsored by the American College of Legal Medicine. Professor Cynthia Bowman of Northwestern University School of Law also deserves special recognition for her brilliant article in the *Harvard Law Review* and for the constant stream of e-mails that kept us up-to-date on legal cases and theories. A huge round of applause is due for the research librarians at the Santa Clara University School of Law—Prano Amjadi, Kendra Anderson, Barbara Friedrich, Delores de la Fuente, and Mary Hood—for finding the most obscure references we requested. Many thanks to Dean Mack Player for recognizing the importance of this project by permitting a reduced teaching load during the time this book was nearing completion. My special colleagues at the law school, Dennis Lilly, Kerry Macintosh, John Bush, and Leslie Griffin, know how much I owe to them. As always, the most special thanks are reserved for family—my parents Helen and Murray Scheflin, my brother Larry, his wife Toni, my nephew Scott Scheflin, my in-laws Bob and Jeanne Caploe, and my brothers and sisters-in-law, for their unwavering emotional support.

Dr. Hammond would like to thank V. Alton Dohner, M.D., and Donald Price, Ph.D., for their advice and assistance.

We warmly express our profound appreciation to Susan Barrows Munro, our editor at Norton, for taking such good care of our manuscript. Her encouragement and belief in this book, her courage and willingness to publish on this controversial and litigious subject, her personal attention and diligence about demanding changes when necessary—all without question finally brought these chapters together to become a whole and better book. Working with Susan was a real joy. We wholeheartedly thank her for all her help.

Finally, we would like to acknowledge our many clinical and forensic clients, and others like them, whose suffering constantly reminded us of the importance of completing this book.

Contents

||||||||||||||||||||

MEMORY,
TRAUMA TREATMENT,
AND THE
LAW

1

The False Memory Debate

INTRODUCTION

The 1990s have witnessed an intense professional, legal, and public controversy about the accuracy and credibility of recovered memories of childhood sexual abuse. On one side of the debate are researchers and clinicians who assert that an individual traumatized as a child can be partly or fully amnestic for the trauma for some significant period of time and then later recover accurate memories, either spontaneously or in the context of psychotherapy. On the other side are researchers and clinicians who assert that claims about recovered memories of abuse are partly or fully fictitious and, for the most part, are the product of therapeutic suggestions about alleged traumatic events that never really happened but which the patient comes to accept falsely as fact (Yapko, 1994a, p. 34).

At the heart of the controversy are two important factors: science and politics. Much of the debate has in fact been political, but each side's position has been justified by the claim that it represents the true scientific view. Armstrong (1994) says, "Rarely . . . [does the] professional literature address the issue as a political one" (p. 179), and yet the seemingly scientific debate is at times intensely political—with a "fundamentalist spin" (p. 7). The political portion of the debate is relatively simple to understand; the science is relatively complex.

The political battle pits two different ideological positions against one another. On one side are those persons who believe that children are generally accurate when they report having been abused, and adults are generally accurate when they claim that they have recovered memories that had been repressed of physical and/or sexual abuse suffered when they were young. On the other side are those persons who believe that children are highly suggestible, thereby making their reports of abuse highly questionable, and that severely traumatized children do not repress memories that they later discover as adults, so these memories are actually "false beliefs" and probably implanted by therapists.

For a variety of reasons, the debate has become savage. Zealots on both sides have staked positions so radical that intelligent discussion and scientific inquiry have been difficult, if not impossible. These "squeaky wheels" have received the media oil. Voices of moderation in the middle have not attracted the same media attention. Advocates at one extreme essentially claim that therapists are brainwashers, while extremists on the other side counter that false memory adherents are pedophiles and pedophile protectors. From the very beginning, the debate has been characterized by a viciousness unparalleled in the annals of contemporary scientific disagreements. Because of the zealotry, science has taken a back seat. In its place have been wild and inaccurate articulations or "hyperbole" and "rhetorical devices" (Myers, 1994) that have served, not as science, but as emotional sound bites for a gullible media.

It is our purpose to set the record straight about what the science can tell us. We cannot claim to be immune from the divisiveness that has hampered intelligent discussion regarding false memory matters, but we can point out that we have all at one time or another testified as forensic experts on both sides of the issue. In some cases, we have been highly critical of the conduct of therapists working with traumatized individuals. In other cases, we have been critical of the excesses and overgeneralizations that sometimes accompany the false memory position.

In our view, there is much that both sides have in common, if only intelligent dialogue could replace name-calling and animosity. As the late brilliant attorney Louis Nizer cogently observed, "mud thrown is ground lost" (1966, p. 178).

What do both sides have in common? Quite a lot. No one gains when therapists use unduly suggestive techniques that cause patients to remember things that never happened and cause those patients to disrupt families by accusing innocent people of heinous acts. No one gains when real victims of child abuse are disbelieved and told their memories are false. No one gains if children are always believed or always disbelieved when they talk about abuse. If both sides were to work together to eliminate unduly suggestive therapy and to learn how to retrieve the most accurate memories, everyone would profit.

It is in the spirit of shifting the acrimonious debate away from the political and back to the scientific that this book has been written. We ask and answer one fundamental question—what does science tell us? Unlike the world of politics, the answers science provides are not simple sound bites designed to influence public opinion.

When the debate turns to the science, two fundamental subjects are involved: (1) *memory* and (2) *therapeutic influence*. The first question to be answered is: can memories of abuse be recovered after a long delay? This phenomenon has been referred to as "delayed recovery of memory" or "repressed memory" (Loftus, 1993), "suspected repressed memory" or "illusory memory" (Lindsay & Read, 1994), "exhumed memory" (Kihlstrom, 1993), or "dissociative memory" (Spiegel & Scheflin, 1994).

We will use the term *recovered memory* as a reasonably neutral term throughout this book because it does not presume the operation of the specific defense mechanism like repression or dissociation.

Central to answering this question is the relationship between recovered memories and memory accuracy. Some researchers and clinicians have assumed that all memory for trauma that is later recovered is essentially accurate, while others have claimed that individuals may all too readily come to believe a memory for events that never really occurred. While this debate reflects a wider controversy within memory science about trace and constructionist theories of memory, the current debate, what we will refer to as the *false memory controversy*, is quite specific. It is about two related concerns: (1) the reliability of children's accounts of being molested, and (2) the reliability of adult recall of childhood trauma, primarily of childhood sexual abuse. Both concerns raise even more fundamental questions about the reliability of memory in general and the extent to which it can be socially influenced.

The second essential ingredient of this scientific debate concerns the impact on memory of *therapeutic influence*. While trauma therapists generally see part of their role as facilitating the retrieval of heretofore inaccessible trauma and abuse memories, the historical accuracy of those memories has been less important than healing the patient's psychological distress about them. False memory advocates have stated that therapists, in their zeal to uncover trauma memories, have in fact implanted them, wittingly or unwittingly.

At the core of the debate is the role therapeutic influence plays on memory. In particular, there is concern about whether recovered memories of sexual abuse have been implanted by overzealous therapists (Yapko, 1994a). Others (Spanos, 1994) believe that memories of childhood trauma recovered in psychotherapy are "primarily fantasy constructions" (p. 18). Loftus (1993) has been a main spokesperson for this position, arguing that memories can be "manufactured" or "created" in adults in the laboratory (Loftus & Hoffman, 1989) and also created while they are in therapy (Loftus, 1993).

A parallel debate currently exists over the investigation of allegations of childhood sexual abuse, with some researchers and clinicians taking the position that children rarely lie about abuse except under very specific circumstances (Goodman, Bottoms et al., 1991), while others claim that false allegations frequently exist as a product of poorly conducted child abuse investigations (Ceci & Bruck, 1995; Gardner, 1991; Underwager & Wakefield, 1990). Whether we consider recovered memories in adults or allegations of sexual abuse in children, the controversy is essentially the same—the accuracy or inaccuracy of the memories of abuse.

HISTORICAL INFLUENCES

Janet and Freud

Clinicians and researchers who are somewhat removed from the controversy have been puzzled by the intensity of the disagreement among their professional colleagues, especially the personal attacks on outspoken advocates and the astounding increase in lawsuits. It is especially important to set this heated debate within its historical and cultural context. As Yapko aptly has remarked, "Our culture plays a significant role in shaping our beliefs about abuse and victimhood" (1994a, p. 41). Various historical and cultural trends have converged to create and shape the character of the memory debate.

Modern treatment of traumatized patients, as well as patients suspected of having been traumatized, began about a century ago with the pioneering studies on hysteria by Charcot (1887) and Janet (1889) and Breuer and Freud (1893–1985). Janet directed a laboratory for the study of hysteria under Charcot at the Salpêtrière in France. He presented his theory of hysteria in the landmark book, *L'Automatisme Psychologique* (1889). These ideas have recently been translated and summarized in van der Hart & Friedman (1989) and in van der Kolk, Brown, and van der Hart (1989).

According to Janet, traumatization is an outcome of the inability to cope effectively in the face of some real threat. Some emotions, such as the feeling of complete and extreme helplessness, become intensified in response to the threatening situation. These "vehement emotions" interfere with normal memory processing and consciousness. They cause a "disaggregation" or "dissociation" of ordinary consciousness so that independent nuclei of consciousness are split off from ordinary awareness and/or voluntary control. One consequence of dissociation is that the overall field of consciousness is narrowed. Another consequence is that the split-off traumatic content of memory remains active in the form of "subconscious fixed ideas" or "automatisms." These automatisms have the potential of becoming activated in certain situations and of drastically influencing (1) conscious experiences, in the form of somnambulistic states, attention and concentration difficulties, and hysterical conversion reactions (paralysis, contractions, seizures), and (2) memory, in the form of amnesia or hypermnesia.

The objective of treatment, according to Janet, was to help the patient process the traumatic memories and integrate them into conscious awareness. Janet conceived treatment as unfolding in three stages (van der Hart, Brown et al., 1989). The first stage entailed establishing rapport and helping the overwhelmed patient achieve stabilization. In the second stage, hypnotic methods, including hypnotic dreaming and automatic writing, were used to uncover and help the patient integrate traumatic memories and associated affects into consciousness. Sometimes this might be accomplished by direct hypnotic suggestion for symptom reduction. Other times traumatic memories could be neutralized through a gradual process of accessing and working through memory fragments, from least to most threatening. Sometimes the beliefs and associated affects associated with the traumatic event could be directly transformed by hypnotically suggesting "substitute" neutral and/or positive beliefs and affects. Finally, once memory integration was more or less complete, Janet assisted his patients in achieving a stable identity and helped to enhance their ability to function.

Janet believed that hysterical symptoms function as a sort of defense, i.e., to keep the memories out of conscious awareness. In this sense, Janet saw hysteria as "in part a disorder of memory processing or a phobia of memory" (van der Kolk, 1989, p. 372). The primary goal of treatment was to use hypnosis to facilitate memory processing and integration so that the symptoms would disappear, even if the final outcome meant some degree of memory distortion. Insofar as memory integration led to symptom reduction, Janet did not concern himself with whether or not a patient's resultant memory for the traumatic event was accurate or inaccurate. His willingness to use methods such as substitution implies that symptom reduction took primacy over memory accuracy.

Janet and Freud developed their understanding of hysteria within the same intellectual Zeitgeist. They shared a "fundamental idea that memory lies at the root of neurosis" (Kihlstrom, 1993) and that the recovery and integration of memories were necessary for symptom reduction. They also, at least at first, shared the belief that these memories outside of conscious awareness originally came from genuine traumatic experiences.

Breuer and Freud first summarized their clinical investigations of hysteria in their famous document, *Studies on Hysteria* (1893). Like Janet, Breuer and Freud came to believe that hysterical symptoms in their adult female patients were caused by real-life traumatic events, usually by childhood sexual molestation, often within the family. This view came to be known as "the seduction theory." Like Janet, Breuer and Freud asserted that uncovering the memories of traumatic sexual seduction was a necessary focus of treatment because "hysterics suffer mainly from reminiscences" (p. 7). In Freud's early work, hypnosis was the "royal road" to accessing these memories of childhood seduction. Breuer and Freud summarized their treatment philosophy in the famous dictum, "Cessante causa cessat effectus [when the cause ceases the effect ceases]" (Kihlstrom, 1993). Thus, memories associated with childhood sexual abuse persisted and manifested their secrets in the form of hysterical symptoms for many years, until brought into consciousness and worked through with early psychoanalytic methods such as hypnosis and dream interpretation.

Later, Freud dramatically changed his views on the cause of hysterical symptoms and abandoned his earlier seduction theory. In "Three Essays on Infant Sexuality" (1905/1953), and in subsequent papers, Freud developed his oedipal theory. He no longer believed that most hysterical patients were victims of real sexual molestation; rather, he came to believe that most of the memories of sexual abuse reported by hysterical patients were largely fantasy productions derived from the oedipal conflict. Nevertheless, Freud insisted that these imagined seductions were as emotionally compelling to the patient

as real sexual molestation would be, even if the seduction had not actually occurred.

It is important to appreciate that the current false memory controversy is by no means a new controversy. Freud's earlier seduction theory and later oedipal fantasy theory represent within one clinician's writing both positions in the current memory debate. The historic controversies surrounding Freud's radical shift in thinking about whether hysterical symptoms were associated with real or imagined childhood sexual trauma did not come to an end with the publication of *Three Essays*. While psychoanalytic thinkers for the next fifty years rarely challenged Freud's authoritative position that most of the memories for childhood sexual abuse reported in psychoanalysis were fictional, the controversy became reactivated within psychoanalytic circles in particular, and later within the public domain and the media, with the publication of two important works—Rush's pioneering critique of psychoanalysis in "The Freudian Coverup" (1977) and, more directly, Masson's (1984) *The Assault on Truth: Freud's Suppression of the Seduction Theory*.

Masson, a psychoanalyst with access to the archives of Freud's unpublished papers, argued that Freud did, indeed, reject the seduction theory, but not primarily because of accumulating scientific evidence against it. Rather, it was his own fears that led him to publicly reverse his position. Freud became disturbed about the professional and societal implications of his seduction theory because acknowledging its validity would necessitate an admission of widespread childhood sexual molestation within Victorian society, particularly within the Victorian family. Masson argued that Freud simply did not want to pursue the negative career implications of the seduction theory, with its potential to reveal the underbelly of Victorian society.

Masson also noted that Freud's seduction theory was poorly received by his male colleagues. Freud was definitely ambitious and knew that any opportunity he might have in professional circles depended upon his good name in medical circles. His "Aetiology" paper was not well received by his influential and highly judgmental male peers. To win back their confidence in him, Freud knew he had to reverse his stance on childhood sexual abuse. But how could he do it and still save face? He found the solution in the oedipal explanation.

With the publication of Masson's startling book, an old debate became reactivated, now situated in a new context. Concurrently, sophisticated clinical theories about assessment and treatment of post-traumatic stress disorder (PTSD) and dissociative identity disorder (DID) emerged. As some historians have said, contemporary interpretation of history often tells us more about the current interpreters' stance and culture than about history per se. In that sense, we learn much in the reaction to Masson's book about the increasing polarization of contemporary views on PTSD and DID, and very little about which of Freud's theories was "right."

Trauma experts generally assert that Freud's seduction theory exposes the extent to which genuine childhood sexual abuse existed then—and exists now—in Western industrial society (e.g., Calof, 1994). Some contemporary trauma experts have gone so far as to assert that "the phenomenological presentation of oedipal material is markedly different from sexual abuse memories" (Davies & Frawley, 1994, p. 89). Skeptics within the traditional psychoanalytic community and within the wider mental health field, as well as cognitive scientists, assert that there is very little evidence to support the seduction theory. Kihlstrom (1993), an accomplished memory scientist and an advocate of the false memory position, reminds us that most of Freud's data supporting the seduction theory come from Freud's interpretation of his patients' dreams, which is rather indirect evidence. Kihlstrom believes that after Freud formulated the seduction theory he developed a confirmatory bias and "pressured patients to produce memories that conformed with his expectations." In other words, Kihlstrom believes that the reports of sexual seduction were iatrogenic (false positives).

Kihlstrom's speculation, though interesting, proves too much. One might equally argue that the oedipal fantasy in turn also functioned for the older Freud as a confirmatory bias so that he failed to understand and correctly identify cases of genuine childhood sexual abuse (false negatives) and simply passed these patients off as having oedipal fantasies. The bottom line is that we need corroborative data to know how extensive childhood sexual abuse was in Freud's era. Contemporary professionals who champion either the seduction or the oedipal theories tell us more about where they stand on the current false memory controversy than about the validity of either of Freud's theories.

The evidence that does exist supports the view that child abuse was widespread and known to medical men throughout Europe. Masson (1984) notes that doctors and alienists were familiar with the fact that large numbers of children routinely arrived at the morgue with physical evidence of abuse and torture. Indeed, medical lectures were held at the morgue and the children's bodies were used for medical demonstrations. In his important book, *Child Abuse and Moral Reform in England 1870–1908*, Behlmer reports that the scandal of physical and sexual child abuse grew to such unacceptable social proportions that moral reform movements began in many countries to protect children from these often domestic abusive situations. Medical doctors knew that the abuse was occurring, but they kept silent. In general, child-rearing practices were harsh, with many manuals instructing parents to break the will or spirit of the child in order to obtain obedience and suppress the child's innate sinfulness. Children were also physically exploited for their labor.

The social movements that began in the last century to protect children attracted the attention of the courts and important government officials. Child protective agencies were created to save children from conditions of abuse. Indeed, as Behlmer (1982) documents, child abuse was well-known and plentiful in the Victorian era, and afterwards. Ironically, it is not the existence of child abuse during Freud's era that needs explanation; rather, it is, as Behlmer (1982) observes, "the curious decline of public interest in child abuse between 1914 and the early 1960's" (p. 225).

Child Abuse Investigations

Why did public concern about child abuse decline after World War I? Behlmer (1982) concludes that the "material and psychological wounds of two world wars and protracted economic crisis tended to divert humane attention on both sides of the Atlantic." Also, the creation of child protective service agencies probably convinced the public that the problem was being solved.

The modern era of child abuse concerns began in the 1950s when American radiologists were first able to make connections between skeletal lesions in babies and the likelihood that the lesions were parentally inflicted. Though the technique now existed to prove child abuse, doctors did not use it for that purpose until the appearance in 1962 of the seminal article by C. Henry Kempe, a University of Colorado Medical School pediatrician, which outlined what he called the "battered child syndrome" and provided detailed medical data about the trauma of child abuse. In this classic article, Kempe and his associates also made the point that doctors and trained medical personnel, despite the physical evidence in front of them, were emotionally unwilling to believe that parents could brutalize their children and were further unwilling to start asking pertinent questions of the parents or report to the police. The silence of the medical profession, Kempe argued, contributed to the continuation of the abuse.

Kempe's articulation of why medical personnel, who feel exclusive loyalty to the patient, ignored massive evidence of child abuse may indirectly shed light on the severe rejection Freud experienced when he raised the subject in 1896. Physicians then, and continuously until the late 1960s at the earliest, knew the truth, but they maintained a conspiracy of silence (Hechler, 1988).

At the time Kempe's article appeared in July 1962, the *Journal of the American Medical Association* predicted that "the battered child syndrome will be found to be a more frequent cause of death than such well recognized and thoroughly studied diseases as leukemia, cystic fibrosis, and muscular dystrophy, and it may well rank with automobile accidents and the toxic and infectious encephalites as causes of acquired disturbances of the central nervous system."

Kempe's article inspired an avalanche of writing about child abuse and resulted in a positive shift in medical thinking about child abuse issues. The down side, however, was the dissemination of an attitude that abuse was a "disease" like other medical illnesses (Armstrong, 1994). Nevertheless, for the next decade, the proper role of medical personnel in cases of child abuse was frequently discussed. By the end of the 1960s, a medical profile of child abuse had been formulated and child abuse itself was viewed as a medical, as well as a social, problem.

The social libertarian climate of the 1960s assisted in the public willingness to do something about child abuse. Inquiry into childhood sexual abuse was given a strong push by the passage of the first wave of child abuse legislation. By 1966, every state except Hawaii, which soon followed, had enacted statutes mandating physician reporting of suspected child abuse. By the mid-1970s, other professionals were also listed as mandated reporters, and the definition of abuse broadened beyond physical and sexual abuse to include neglect and emotional maltreatment.

If childhood sexual abuse was the "last frontier" of abuse to be explored by the mid-1970s (Sgroi, 1975), the passage of the federal Child Abuse Prevention and Treatment Act in 1974 (Gardner, 1992; Myers, 1994) opened up a whole new industry of child savers. This act provided for mandatory reporting by professionals of suspected childhood sexual or other abuse by a caregiver. Professionals were granted immunity from prosecution for reporting, but were subject to strong penalties for failure to report abuse. Every state now has some sort of mandated reporting law.

A second important feature of this Act was to provide funding incentives for each state to develop programs in the areas of (1) assessment and treatment of victims of childhood sexual abuse and (2) the investigation and prosecution of offenders. Child protection agencies, social service agencies, and justice system personnel were given official sanction and extensive legal authority to investigate allegations of childhood sexual abuse. The creation of multidisciplinary teams and the evolution of prevention programs followed. The number of abuse allegations doubled in the first seven years and then doubled again in the next six years after this Act became law (Myers, 1994).

Unfortunately, however, guidelines for assessing allegations of childhood sexual abuse were not available in the late 1970s and early 1980s. Thus, child abuse investigators working for social service and law enforcement agencies were required to investigate large numbers of cases with little or no formal specialized training. Training programs on how to conduct a child abuse investigation were virtually nonexistent (Gardner, 1992). Individual child abuse investigators were given a great deal of authority in their attempts to substantiate reports of childhood sexual abuse, as well as considerable autonomy in conducting the investigation. Inferior investigative methods and excesses were not uncommon. To make matters worse, statutes were repeatedly amended to broaden the types of professionals included and the scope of the abuse to be reported. Every state now requires reporting by mental health professionals (Kalichman, 1993).

One unfortunate consequence of the failure to develop standards for childhood sexual abuse investigations and treatment in the first decade was a significant shift in objectives away from what the Act was intended to address. Whereas the original focus had been on identifying and providing appropriate interventions for children at risk, "Increasingly child protection is viewed within a legal formula where finding fault is the major goal" (Conte, 1991, p. 13). The child abuse investigator often had two conflicting tasks: (1) to assess risks and provide a clinical intervention, and (2) to decide whether or not the allegations were valid. In that sense, Gardner has attacked child abuse investigators as "validators." Dawes (1994) points out that the policy statement of the American Academy of Child and Adolescent Psychiatry explicitly mandates clinicians to "decide . . . whether or not any sexual abuse occurred" (p. 165). Excesses in child abuse investigations do occur. Defense attorneys have pointed out that such investigations are conducted with the "presumption of guilt" (Hechler, 1988, p. 55), so that due process may be violated.

Another unfortunate consequence of unregulated child abuse investigations was that highly idiosyncratic and often excessive interviewing techniques were utilized, which sometimes included systematic leading and misleading questions, and even direct coercive tactics, to confirm preexisting biases that the interviewer held about the allegations in question (Ceci, 1994; Ceci & Bruck, 1995; Gardner, 1992; Hechler, 1988). These sloppy methods caused harm in many directions. First, they compromised the integrity of the children by manipulating their reports through suggestion, thereby providing a way for perpetrators to escape prosecution. By using a defense strategy that the interviewing methods were invalid, lawyers could argue that the reports could not be trusted, and, still worse, that the minds and memories of the children had been contaminated beyond repair, thus preventing the gathering of reliable evidence by any means. Second, sloppy interviewing techniques were

likely to increase the rate of false accusations of abuse that never occurred, thereby damaging innocent parties (Ceci & Bruck, 1995).

Excesses in interviewing tactics also provided the fuel to false memory advocates, who could offer transcripts of highly suggestive child abuse interviews as evidence to support their arguments that children were simply not credible witnesses in many child abuse cases (Bruck & Ceci, 1995; Ceci & Bruck, 1995). Some of the more outspoken critics of these child abuse investigative practices have claimed that such techniques readily lead to the significant rise in false allegations (Gardner, 1992; Underwager & Wakefield, 1990). On a more positive note, a variety of groups more recently have developed better guidelines for conducting child abuse investigations in a manner that minimizes suggestive influences (e.g., Bull, 1995; Hoorwitz, 1992; Yuille, 1988). Standardized interview protocols are being developed for conducting child abuse investigations (Hechler, 1988; cf. chapter 17 of this volume for a review of these protocols). Moreover, major research programs were developed to find out how fallible and suggestible children's memory for alleged abuse indeed was (for review cf. Ceci & Bruck, 1993). The results of the enormous amount of research presently underway should help in the development of more accurate and reliable interviewing techniques.

Twentieth-Century Psychiatry

The false memory controversy is the outcome of at least two independent fields of professional inquiry headed on a seemingly inevitable collision course. The first field is the rapidly evolving and quite diverse subject of trauma research, treatment, and investigation. This includes professional trauma treatment, the increased interest in dissociative disorders, and indirectly, the self-help recovery movement and child abuse investigations. The second field is the equally rapidly evolving domain of academic cognitive and memory science and its recent transformation into an applied science. These trends are set against the backdrop of wider social movements, most notably feminism, the disintegration of the nuclear family, the development of the child protection movement, the drastic changes in mental health practice, and the increased litigiousness, which has altered the concept of "responsibility" in the search for "deep pockets." Each of these forces has contributed to shaping the character and intensity of the false memory controversy as it now stands.

The Rise of Trauma Therapy

Freud's original rejection of the seduction theory had a dampening effect on the study of trauma and abuse lasting until World War II. The era following the war was marked by a number of important works on treatment of war neurosis (Grinker & Spiegel, 1945; Watkins, 1949), Holocaust survivors (Krystal, 1968; Neiderland, 1968), and civilians suffering from crises, natural disasters, and accidents (Lindeman, 1944).

Professional interest in the effects of trauma and its treatment was sparked again as a consequence of the Vietnam War. By the mid 1970s, a clinical conception of traumatization was emerging that was most clearly articulated in Mardi Horowitz's *Stress Response Syndromes* (1976), in which the modern concept of posttraumatic stress disorder was delineated. The basic elements of Horowitz's biphasic model of posttraumatic adjustment included an alternation between intrusive reexperiencing and a general numbing of responsiveness. This biphasic model became the foundation for the diagnosis of PTSD incorporated into the third edition of *DSM* in 1980.

With respect to recovered memories of childhood sexual abuse and ritual abuse, feminist writers have depicted modern Western culture as having gone through three eras—the Age of Denial (up until the 1970s), the Age of Validation (from the late 1970s up to 1990), and the Age of the Backlash (from 1990) (Armstrong, 1994). During the late 1970s, the "conspiracy of silence" (Butler, 1978) about widespread childhood abuse, including childhood sexual abuse, came to an end. The impetus to speak out about childhood sexual abuse was largely fueled by important studies, first on sexual behavior (Kinsey et al., 1953), and then on rape trauma (e.g., Brownmiller, 1975; Burgess & Holmstrom, 1974). Each of these areas of inquiry began and gained momentum against the backdrop of the rise of the feminist movement. Toward the close of the 1970s, the prevalence of terrorization and abuse of chil-

dren was brought starkly into public awareness with the sensationalized Chowchilla school bus kidnapping in 1976 and the careful attention paid to the lasting effects of this trauma on the children (Terr, 1979, 1983a).

By the late 1970s, things suddenly changed. As the culture became increasingly sensitized to violence against women and children, the stage was set to bring the issue of childhood sexual abuse out of the closet and onto center stage. What helped set the stage was the landmark clinical studies on physical abuse of children (Green, 1980; Helfer & Kempe, 1968; Kempe et al., 1962), and also the early pioneering work on domestic violence (Gelles, 1974; Gelles & Straus, 1988; Walker, 1979). A surprising number of important books on childhood sexual abuse appeared, like Butler's *Conspiracy of Silence* (1978), Foreward and Buck's *Betrayal of Innocence* (1978), Meiselman's book on *Incest* (1978), Armstrong's *Kiss Daddy Goodnight* (1982), Justice and Justice's *The Broken Taboo* (1979), and Herman's *Father–Daughter Incest* (1981). While these books clearly delineated the familial dynamics of incest and its psychological consequences, a number of sociological theories, appearing shortly after, began to paint a picture of just how prevalent incest was within American and European families. These surveys described prevalence rates of 19.2% (finkelhor, 1979) and 38% (Russell, 1986), respectively, of women in America, and 32% of women in The Netherlands (Draijer, 1988), who reported that they had been sexually victimized by the age of 18.

As the impact of these studies was felt within the professional mental health community, and then among the general public, thinking about the long-term effects of incest began to evolve into a formulation of the diagnosis of PTSD. Gelinas's (1983) article in *Psychiatry* recast incest sequelae in terms of posttraumatic stress symptoms. Summit's paper "Childhood Sexual Abuse Accommodation Syndrome" (1983) and Rieker and Carmen's (1986) paper on the "disconfirmation and transformation of sexual abuse" describe how sexually abused children significantly distort their perception and memory for trauma so as to preserve the attachment relationship with the intrafamilial perpetrator and the rest of the family.

Toward the end of the 1980s and into the 1990s, the literature reflects attention to individual differences in response to incest, with an increasing appreciation of the variable long-term psychological effects of incest and the identification and prediction of a range of psychopathological outcomes (Briere & Conte, 1993; Brown, 1990; Kendall-Tackett et al., 1993).

During this same era, significant advances in treatment began to emerge, along with broad-based works outlining a general model for the treatment of PTSD associated with such diverse events as war, rape, incest, physical abuse, torture, and accident victimization. Following Horowitz's seminal work (1976) on phase-oriented treatment of PTSD, a number of subsequent works began to delineate the rationale and stages of treatment of PTSD. A remarkable consensus began to emerge about the stages of treatment (Brown & Fromm, 1986; Courtois, 1988; Herman, 1992; Parson, 1984; Sgroi, 1989). Part of the impetus for the evolving consensus in trauma treatment was the establishment of the Society for Traumatic Stress Studies in 1985 and the publication of its journal, *Journal of Traumatic Stress*, which became a forum for mental health professionals to share information, research, and clinical knowledge.

Historically, the phase-oriented model of treatment traces its roots back one hundred years to Pierre Janet, who described three general stages in the overall treatment of trauma and dissociation: (1) stabilization, (2) memory processing, and (3) rehabilitation (van der Kolk et al., 1989). While modern phase-oriented treatment of PTSD has generally preserved Janet's basic outline of the stages of treatment, its emphasis is different. One very important implication of the phase-oriented approach to treatment is that it is not narrowly focused on abuse. Among contemporary trauma experts there is a reasonable consensus that rapid uncovering and classical abreaction are contraindicated because they may be harmful (Brown & Fromm, 1986; van der Hart, 1991).

Another important difference between earlier and contemporary treatment of trauma is that uncovering and integration of traumatic memory have now been set within a wider treatment frame, in which symptom stabilization, coping enhancement, and self development serve as necessary prerequisites to memory processing. The primary goal of treatment is *not* the uncovering of traumatic memory per se, but

self and relational development (Brown & Fromm, 1986). The stereotype of memory recovery techniques that false memory advocates sharply criticize is rarely *the* central treatment focus in professional phase-oriented trauma treatment. Although memory integration plays a role in the overall treatment frame, it is balanced against a substantial focus on stabilization and self/relational development.

As phase-oriented trauma treatment has evolved, the question arises: trauma treatment for whom? Because a portion of the overall trauma population remembers the trauma, while another portion does not, are the treatments essentially the same for each group? The problem lies in whether or not memory uncovering/integration is indicated for both groups. While experts within the trauma field have generally applied the same phase-oriented treatment model to both groups, false memory advocates, largely from outside the trauma treatment domain, have recently challenged this view. Some have argued that memory recovery should not be done under any circumstances with patients who are amnestic for trauma (Ofshe & Watters, 1994).

The Resurrection of Dissociative Disorders

This same era also saw a resurgence of interest in dissociative disorders, especially study of multiple personality disorder (MPD). Early intense interest in MPD at the turn of the century steadily declined over the next 75 years. As the tide turned, early pioneers like Cornelia Wilbur, with her famous case, Sybil (Schreiber, 1973), and others like George Greaves (1980) and Phil Coons (1980) were influential in revitalizing professional interest in MPD so that it was included in the third edition of *DSM* (1980). As more professionals documented cases of MPD, an informal network evolved, culminating in the establishment of the International Society for the Study of Dissociative Disorders in 1984. Since then, a number of clinical and research papers have appeared on the diagnosis and clinical features of MPD (Boon & Daijer, 1993; Kluft, 1982; Lowenstein, 1991; Putnam, 1989), its relationship to trauma (Putnam, 1989; Spiegel, 1984), and its treatment (Kluft, 1982, 1984 a, b, 1988a; Ross, 1989; Sachs, Braun, & Shepp, 1988; Sachs, Frishholz, & Wood, 1988; van der Hart et al., 1993).

The rise of MPD from virtually no cases to hundreds of cases in just over a decade has aroused the skepticism of false memory advocates, but they do not speak with a uniform voice on this subject. Some members of the Advisory Board of the False Memory Syndrome Foundation appear to have no quarrel with the existence of MPD, and at least one has made a persuasive argument for the creation of a new dissociative disorder called "pseudo-identity disorder" (West, 1994). Others consider MPD to be completely iatrogenic—on the order of past lives and alien abductions (Ofshe & Watters, 1994). The dramatic rise in the number of diagnosed MPDs has been given an iatrogenic interpretation by some false memory advocates.

The simple explanation may be that the simultaneous expansion of interest in hypnosis and in the dissociative disorders, right after psychoanalysis had peaked, meant that more clinicians were focused on dissociation. Because hypnosis is one of the more prominent and profound methods of exploring dissociation, the rise of interest in hypnosis, especially Ericksonian hypnosis in the 1970s, naturally led to an increased interest in hypnotic phenomena, including amnesia and dissociation. As Zeig (1985) noted: "Ericksonian methods are probably the fastest-growing field of psychotherapy in the Western world."

As seriously dissociated patients began to report more and more severe and extremely sadistic stories of abuse, a crisis of credibility was inevitable. This was clearly articulated in Jean Goodwin's article on "Credibility Problems in Sadistic Abuse" (1994). Several dozen inpatient units specializing in the treatment of patients with severe dissociative disorders began to emerge in the 1980s. Because these units are somewhat selective for the most severely disturbed patients with dissociative disorders, it is not surprising that by the late 1980s papers began to emerge on the phenomenon of ritual abuse; with those publications, the debate about credibility intensified.

In the 1980s, there was a great revival of interest within professional circles and popular culture regarding childhood sexual abuse and also dissociative disorders. The 1980s could be characterized as the Age of Validation (Armstrong, 1982). As one scholar of popular culture has said, "Anyone who asserts that the topic of incest is still concealed in a 'conspiracy of silence' is ignoring what has been happening in popular culture" (Victor, 1994, p. 6). "Hidden traumatic memories" had become the culturally specific "idiom of distress" for modern American society (Kenny, 1995, p. 454).

The Cognitive and Memory Sciences

The scientific study of memory has undergone a major revolution since the late 1960s. Modern scientific study of memory began just about a century ago with Ebbinghaus's classical studies on memory for nonmeaningful material. Serial learning has been the main focus of memory research for almost 70 years. In a radical break with the Ebbinghaus tradition, Neisser and others initiated a number of research projects on memory for meaningful material. Memory science became a science in search of relevance, starting with the first conference on the Practical Aspect of Memory in 1976 (Gruneberg et al., 1978). Studies began to emerge on personal memory (Brewer, 1986), especially the scientific study of autobiographical memory, and memory for major news events, or flashbulb memories (Brown & Kulik, 1977). Major symposia took place on the application of memory science to the study of everyday memory (Gruneberg et al., 1978, 1989). Several new journals appeared, like *Applied Cognitive Psychology*. The memory science of the 1970s was rapidly becoming an applied science.

The first major area of application for the applied memory science was the law, namely, memory for eyewitnessing crimes. Throughout the 1970s and 1980s, Elizabeth Loftus and others developed their scientific careers through extensive laboratory investigation of memory accuracy and memory suggestibility as applied to eyewitness testimony. Loftus's *Eyewitness Testimony* (1979a), Wells and Loftus's *Eyewitness Testimony: Psychological Perspectives* (1984), and Ceci, Ross, and Toglia's *Children's Eyewitness Testimony* (1987) are representative of work done in this area with both adult and child eyewitnesses.

By the late 1980s, most memory scientists had an appreciation for the constructive nature of human memory and for the problem of memory accuracy in certain applied areas, including eyewitness testimony, police lineup identification, and ordinary memory for personal life experiences. The fact that many distinguished memory scientists joined the

Scientific Advisory Board of the False Memory Syndrome Foundation in the early 1990s seemed a natural outcome of memory science's transformation into an applied science. Studying memory of patients in psychotherapy has been an inevitable extension of applied memory science into a new, and much needed, area of application, especially since the study of memory for eyewitnessing crimes and making proper identifications had already peaked by the mid 1980s.

CONTEMPORARY CULTURAL TRENDS

The Self-Help Movement

Within the wider popular culture, developments parallel to the changes in the scientific community were occurring in the 1980s. Given voice by the women's movement, popular testimonials and exposés on rape (Brownmiller, 1975; Russell, 1975), incest (Armstrong, 1978; Bass, 1980; Rush, 1980; Sanford, 1980; Sisk & Hoffman, 1987), and child pornography (Lederer, 1980) appeared in the mass literature. Grass-roots self-help groups for adult children of alcoholics, women seeking empowerment, incest survivors, and, shortly thereafter, multiple personality patients and survivors of ritual abuse were formed throughout the country. These self-help groups were natural extensions of the proliferation of twelve-step programs, beginning with Alcoholics Anonymous and expanding into Narcotics Anonymous, Overeaters Anonymous, and Sex and Love Addicts Anonymous. Based on the same essential recovery model, groups began to appear for adult children of alcoholics (Black, 1981) and codependence (Schaef, 1986; Woititz, 1983).

Manuals provided guidelines for how to start self-help groups (e.g., Ernst & Goodwin, 1981). These books presented a model for survivors of abuse to speak out (Bass & Davis, 1988). Eventually, these self-help manuals became referred to as "incest resolution therapy" (cf. Haaken & Schalps, 1991) and "recovered memory therapy" (Ofshe & Watters, 1993), because all of them were characterized by a loosely held set of common assumptions about the value of uncovering and facilitating abreactions of traumatic memories and affects and breaking the

silence in the form of telling the trauma story. Networks with informal newsletters for abuse survivors and self-help groups inevitably followed. For patients with severe dissociative disorders, likewise, popular firsthand accounts began to appear, like *Michelle Remembers* (Smith & Pazder, 1980) and *When Rabbit Howls* (Chase, 1987).

This was also an era when many survivors began to offer their services to help other survivors, sometimes informally and sometimes in the form of somewhat structured counseling services. The number of self-professed abuse therapists, with or without professional training and supervision, greatly increased.

The movement to license substance abuse counselors and masters level psychologists across many states in the 1980s coincided with the emerging self-help recovery movement. Many of these self-help abuse therapists were given the official stamp of professionalism. The outcome of these trends was what Ofshe and Watters (1993) have called the "institutionalization of recovered memory therapy" by the end of the decade. With this institutionalization and professionalizing of a mass of recovery therapists, who for the most part lacked the broad-based training in human development, personality, psychopathology, and social systems that is characteristic of professional training in the psychiatric, psychological, and social work disciplines as a step toward independent licensure, a curious polarization developed between self-help recovery therapy practiced by lay healers and the sophisticated phase-oriented treatment models followed within the mental health licensed professions.

Therapists associated with the self-help recovery movement are more likely to frame their treatment narrowly, primarily around recovering memories of abuse and "breaking the silence" within the wider community. This approach differs somewhat from the model of phase-oriented treatment evolving within the mental health profession, where trauma treatment is set within a wider framework of symptom management, coping enhancement, correcting cognitive distortions, and facilitating self and relational development.

Ironically, two quite contradictory movements created the popularity of self-help groups. First, the victimization movement, which provided "abuse excuses" in place of responsibility, was sweeping across the country (Dershowitz, 1994). Shifting responsibility was also the major theme of the law of torts, which regulates fault and compensation for harm. In court, lawyers argued for shifting losses from victims to deep pockets on ever expanding "foreseeability" theories that were prevalent from the late 1960s to the mid 1980s. Out of court, newly emerging victims sought solace from a second movement—the "empowerment" movement. Just as a new class of victims was being identified, a new creed to fight for "empowerment" emerged. Victims could share their distress in victims groups, or they could attempt to shrug off the past in empowerment groups. Either way, self-help groups filled a growing social need. However, certain excesses in the recovery movement, such as an almost "revivalist" promise of recovery through groups and workshops, may have only served to have survivors view themselves as "enjoying lengthy ill health and even lengthier recovery," thus further marginalizing surviving women (Armstrong, 1994).

Another sign of the enormous popularity of the recovery movement was John Bradshaw's writings and workshops on "the inner child," which spread throughout the country like a new religious movement in the late 1980s. According to Bradshaw (1988), everyone comes from a dysfunctional family. Thus, the definition of trauma, narrowly defined by mental health professionals in *DSM-III* (American Psychiatric Association, 1980), expanded its domain within popular culture. Virtually anyone could claim to have been "traumatized" as a child and seek ever more readily available options of diverse recovery therapies, groups, workshops or workbooks. As Yapko has remarked, "The criteria for defining oneself as an abuse victim in this society keeps expanding so as to include potentially anyone" (p. 87).

Wider Social Movements

Yapko also says, " . . . the epidemic of allegations of child sexual abuse does not exist independently of the culture in which the allegations are made" (1994a, p. 19). The contemporary memory debate needs to be seen against the background of the wider social movements from which it arises. The rise of the women's movement on a popular level and increasingly sophisticated feminist theories of culture

on an academic level have played a major role in giving survivors of rape, childhood sexual abuse, and sadistic abuse (largely women) an increasingly strong voice in society. Feminist theorists have focused their social critique on a patriarchal social structure (Grand, 1995b; Herman, 1981). The essential question raised by them is: what kind of society would allow a large percentage of its female children to be physically and/or sexually victimized by the time they reached adulthood?

The statistics are indeed grim. According to Kalichman (1993), even with documented massive underreporting:

> Child maltreatment constitutes one of the great social maladies of our time. In 1991, 2,694,000 cases of child abuse and neglect were reported in the United States, an average statewide increase of more than 6% over 1990, and more than a 40% increase nationally since 1985. . . . The majority of reports involve neglect (45%), but physical abuse accounts for 25% of reports, sexual abuse for 15%, and emotional maltreatment for 6% of reports. (p.2)

While the feminist challenge has been directed primarily at the patriarchal social structure, wider changes within the culture have challenged the very structure of the American nuclear family. A popular view of the 1950s was that child abuse was largely a function of either a broken home (Robins, 1966) or the culture of poverty (Lewis, 1966). By the mid 1980s, it was becoming increasingly clear that childhood sexual abuse (e.g., Kempe & Kempe, 1984) and domestic violence (Walker, 1979) were very representative of the American middle-class and upper-middle-class family.

Haaken (1994) has argued that the false memory controversy is the outcome of, and expression of, this challenge to the American middle-class family. Child abuse investigations by social service agencies constitute major inroads into the sanctity and privacy of the American family. One anthropologist, for example, has argued that child abuse investigations entail a kind of "resocialization" of an isolated incestuous family, with the demand that it enter into the wider community and adhere to its social norms around acceptable standards of child-rearing (Phelan, 1987). Haaken believes that the great professional proliferation of interest in childhood sexual abuse during the 1980s became a major challenge by the professional community to parental authority over child-rearing. Implicit in the professional message were standards for good parenting.

A similar challenge was occurring within the self-help community, culminating in the proliferation of adult child of alcoholics and inner child workshops, and popular literature in the late 1980s. The implication of the codependent and inner child messages was that the once sacred American middle-class nuclear family of the 1950s had become the dysfunctional American family of the 1980s. According to Haaken, the rapidly growing appeal of the False Memory Syndrome Foundation to middle- and upper-middle-class parents is that it gave voice to their resistance to the professional and popular challenges to the authority of parents, as well as providing a simple explanatory model for the rebellion of their children. The False Memory Syndrome Foundation attack is directed primarily at therapists because therapists symbolize the pervasive message within the culture that all problems in life arise from dysfunctional parenting. Haaken believes that parents have become increasingly afraid that their children's loyalty is switching from them to therapists, who the children claim understand them better and who also help them to understand how dysfunctional their relationship with their parents really had been.

Haaken sees the Freyds, the founders of the False Memory Syndrome Foundation, as paradigmatic of a larger generational struggle. The manifest struggle is between a daughter, Jennifer Freyd, who alleges to have recovered memories of childhood sexual abuse by her father, and her parents, who claim that the allegations are false and were suggested by an incompetent therapist. The latent struggle, according to Haaken, is between a mother defending her vision of the seemingly normal American middle-class family and a daughter saying that it is dysfunctional. The problem is, according to Haaken, that both sides have a point. Even though childhood sexual abuse does happen all too often in seemingly normal families, allegations of childhood sexual abuse are not always about childhood sexual abuse. Sometimes, according to Haaken, they are symbolic expressions of a wide range of other complaints about family behavior that contributes to "the inju-

rious side of feminine development in the culture." The symbolic switch has been necessary because childhood sexual abuse has been the "only official story" of damage to women's development that has been socially sanctioned.

A further challenge to parental authority began in the late 1980s with the application in court of the delayed discovery doctrine (Ennis et al., 1995). Beginning in the state of Washington with *Petersen v. Bruen* (1990), allegations of harm caused by childhood sexual abuse by an adult plaintiff were heard by the court despite the fact that the normal statute of limitations had expired. The court accepted the argument that the plaintiff had repressed all memories for the abuse and could not have brought action prior to the discovery of the abuse and its causal relationship to the alleged psychological damages. Over the next few years, the delayed discovery doctrine was applied in many other states by courts or legislatures (Spiegel & Scheflin, 1994). Victims of alleged childhood sexual abuse were not only finding their voice in the self-help movement, but also rapidly gaining legal clout to take action against alleged perpetrators.

The rapid increase in malpractice suits against therapists for allegedly implanting false memories of abuse is in part a backlash by parents against children who have challenged their parental authority in the courts. It is indeed no accident that the concept of *repression* has become so central to the false memory argument. Its pivotal importance as a means to extend the rights of victims of childhood abuse in the legal system would have to be challenged by the parents on scientific grounds before courts would reverse the trend favoring children. If repression could be shown to be an unscientific concept, the delayed discovery doctrine would no longer assist the alleged adult victims in holding alleged abusers accountable in the courts.

Grand (1995b) sees the false memory movement as a symptom of "the historical trend toward discrediting victims" (p. 258). She wishes to "contextualize" the memory debate and "to articulate the archaic patriarchal assumptions that implicitly organize the current formulations of such phenomena." She believes that the "unquestioned judgment of the father" underlies the false memory debate, in that the fundamental assumption in the debate is that:

parental memory and judgment is superior to the memory and judgment of the accuser . . . it is the parental construction of history, not the adult child's construction of history, that defines truth. (p. 264)

Grand believes that memory science has been misused as a political tool to reassert parental authority:

finally, patriarchal bias is evident in the ubiquitous unidirectional challenge to patient memory. . . . Research on the fallibility of memory is utilized to cast doubt on accuser memory alone. Thus, what appears to be merely science qua science is actually functioning in the service of colonization. Parental memory is implicitly viewed as exempt from memory deficits and the suggestive influences that discredit accuser memory. (p. 267) . . . One never reads a research study that equally applies findings about the suggestibility of memory to accused and accuser alike. (p. 268)

Yet even in the context of her feminist critique of the false memory movement, Grand is ready to concede that false—or what she prefers to call "confabulated"—memory is a genuine phenomenon that happens under very specific conditions. According to Grand, confabulated memories occur primarily in patients who have a "developmental arrest" in their ways of acquiring knowledge and knowing the truth and/or who have a deep, often dissociated hatred of parental authority. Women who grow up within the context of patriarchy are disempowered. Thus, their knowledge of the world is limited to what is "received from external authority" and what "can only be known intuitively" (p. 271). Confabulated memories are unlikely to occur in individuals who have developmentally more advanced ways of knowing, such as the ability to engage in "deliberate analysis" or the ability to integrate the "inner voice of intuition" with "thoughtful analysis and objective knowledge" (p. 272). Moreover, those whose false belief about abuse that never occurred are prone to enact "dissociative malice" that, while not arising from abuse, legitimately arises from "a genuinely destructive family system" characterized by disempowerment and marginalization (p. 286).

Larger economic trends have fueled both sides

of the false memory controversy. In a market-based economy, mental health professionals are under increasing pressure to abandon a general practice model in favor of marketing certain specialties, of which abuse treatment is just one example (Haaken & Schlaps, 1991). In the climate of the current debate about managed care, therapists for economic reasons have often been forced to narrow their therapeutic focus in treating trauma patients beyond what a phase-oriented treatment model requires. Therapists may try to justify a limited number of sessions for stabilization, or for rapid memory integration, to meet the demands of third-party insurance carriers for time-limited treatment.

Self-help abuse treatment, meanwhile, has become its own "growth industry" (Gardner, 1992), which offers services to the public competing with professional mental health practice for increasingly limited financial resources. The danger inherent in these economic trends is that the evolving consensus around a more broad-based, phase-oriented model of trauma treatment has been seriously compromised. Professional trauma treatment is in danger of becoming eclipsed by the stereotype of "recovered memory therapy" that false memory advocates accuse it of being.

On the other side of the debate, false memory advocacy has been accused of becoming its own type of growth industry. Some academic memory researchers have discovered considerable profits in offering expert testimony concerning the recovered memory controversy. Moreover, plans for widespread filing of malpractice suits against "recovered memory" therapists has the potential for opening up a rather large pot of insurance money for accused families and recanting patients, as well as opening up a whole new area of application for lawyers who stand to make comfortable salaries regardless of the outcome of each case. Even settlements encourage the filing of additional suits.

An even larger social trend has shaped the false memory controversy. America is embroiled in rapid social change, in which the dominant patriarchal culture has become destabilized. Anthropologists have done extensive research on how revitalization movements typically proliferate during times of rapid social change and shifts in the authority of a dominant culture (Harris, 1974; Myers, 1909; Wallace, 1956). The rise of evangelical religious movements, cult movements, and interest in past lives, alien abductions, etc., in the past two decades stand as symptoms of rapid, and resisted, social change. Kihlstrom (1993) views past lives and alien abduction reports as "other forms of repressed memories." These phenomena are best viewed, in our opinion, not as forms of repressed memories, but as symptoms of larger social anxieties and a search for meaning in the increasingly dehumanized world of mass technological society.

Jeffrey Victor (1993) has viewed allegations of Satanic ritual abuse as an outgrowth of these larger social anxieties. He believes that, at the level of popular culture, any given social group has symbolic forms through which it communicates "social anxieties." These symbolic forms include the oral transmission of myths, folktales, and legends in traditional culture and urban legends and rumors in contemporary popular culture. These rumors are orally transmitted and appear over and over again in very different geographic locations. Most city dwellers, for example, have heard the story of alligators in the sewer system. According to Victor, the stories of Satanic ritual abuse are like the story of the alligators in the sewer system, in that these various versions of Satanic stories convey "shared anxieties" about consensually affirmed threats (p. 60). In that sense, the Satanic ritual abuse stories function for a changing American society much like the Jewish conspiracy idea functioned for the Germans in the transition from an economically failed democratic state to the rise of Nazism.

According to Victor, Satanic rumors are transmitted primarily through an oral tradition, especially in conjunction with popular books like *Michelle Remembers* and *When Rabbit Howls*. When these books are talked about at self-help groups, much in the same way ghost stories are told at camp, the stories continue to spread. They are also transmitted in the mass media and through a network of therapists. While Victor is skeptical that these stories ever depict genuine memories of extreme abuse, he believes that they are diagnostic of widespread social anxieties. They offer a shared externalized conspiracy explanation for a society under rapid social change, if not decline. Victor's point is not that therapists are implanting such memories in their patients, but that Satanic ritual abuse narratives are a product of the interaction between patient and therapist, both

of whom are members of a larger society and in this sense share the same social anxieties.

THE RISE OF THE FALSE MEMORY SYNDROME FOUNDATION

In 1984, parents who claimed to be falsely accused of sexually abusing their children formed an organization to attack the excesses arising from the unchecked growth and power of the child protection agencies. The group formed largely as a reaction against the failed large-scale investigation and prosecution of daycare staff in Jordan, Minnesota, after a number of children at the center made graphic ritual abuse allegations. This case attracted national attention because of poor investigative techniques and questionable prosecution practices (Hechler, 1988). The group named VOCAL (Victims Of Child Abuse Laws) immediately began to grow in numbers and political clout. The tone and agenda of VOCAL have been expressed by an accused father, Richard Wexler (1990), in his book *Wounded Innocents: The Real Victims of the War Against Child Abuse*:

> The war against child abuse has become a war against children. Every year, we let hundreds of children die, force thousands more to live with strangers, and throw a million innocent families into chaos. We call this "child protection." . . .
>
> We have turned almost everyone who deals with children in the course of his or her work into an informer, required to report any suspicion of any form of child maltreatment, and we have encouraged the general public to do the same. We have allowed such reports to be made anonymously, making the system a potent tool for harassment.
>
> We allow untrained, inexperienced, sometimes incompetent workers to label parents as abusers and even to remove children from their homes entirely on their own authority. (pp. 175–176)

The establishment of the False Memory Syndrome Foundation was, like VOCAL a decade earlier, the outcome of American middle-class family members accused of sexual abuse. While we may never know the historical truth of what happened in the Freyd family, its story illustrates the wider cultural tensions. In December of 1990, after her second therapy session, Jennifer Freyd allegedly recovered memories of childhood sexual abuse. In that session Jennifer is said to have expressed anxiety about an upcoming visit by her parents. Her therapist routinely had asked her if she had ever been sexually abused, but the subject was not pursued in that session. Following the session, however, Jennifer had a series of flashbacks and soon recovered memories of the alleged abuse. She claimed that her father had sexually molested her from when she was three until she was 16 years old, when she went away to college. Her father, Peter, a mathematics professor, denied the allegations. Her mother, Pamela, an educator, became increasingly disturbed about the rupture in the relationship between parent and child. The distressed parents eventually came to the conclusion that the allegations must have been made up in Jennifer's therapy.

In 1991, Pamela Freyd published an anonymous account, "How Could This Happen?" It was disseminated generally across the United States and ultimately also found its way overseas. Within a year, the true identity of the author of the pamphlet was widely known.

Although Jennifer did not sue her parents and did not publicly proclaim them to be molesters, her parents founded the False Memory Syndrome Foundation (FMSF) in 1992. Since then, one family's struggle has become the lightning rod for the most acrimonious debate in the field of psychotherapy. In a mere five years, the FMSF has gained approximately 3,000 dues-paying members, and about 18,000 allegedly falsely accused families have contacted FMSF (P. Freyd, 1996). The Freyds had hit a sensitive nerve, and they discovered that they were far from alone.

The FMSF continues to attract an impressive Scientific Advisory Board and has disseminated information to the media across the world on the potentially suggestive nature of psychotherapy and the dangers that can ensue. The FMSF also assists a network of lawyers who are advising accused parents on their legal rights, sometimes including ways to sue therapists who have allegedly implanted false memories. Currently, there are an estimated 800 malpractice suits against therapists concerning memory issues, with many more expected to follow (Taub, 1996, p. 186).

How do we understand the sudden success of the FMSF? From a wider social perspective, the FMSF represents a backlash against increasing accusations about the dysfunctional nature of the American middle-class family, particularly against therapists who symbolize parent-blaming (Haaken, 1994). From the narrower perspective of childhood sexual abuse, the FMSF represents two extremes—the painful agony of those accused without due process, but also a potentially clever legal defense for justly accused perpetrators. The problem, of course, is in accurately knowing the proportions of alleged abusers that are genuinely or falsely accused.

The reason the FMSF has gained such popularity so quickly is that it has served as a conduit for a number of very different interest groups: (1) falsely accused parents who are seeking due process, (2) genuine perpetrators who need support in "science" for their legal defense, (3) memory scientists in search of a new area of practical application beyond eyewitness research, (4) researchers on coercive persuasion and brainwashing who now have a wider arena than the cult phenomenon, (5) clinicians who are uncomfortable with the excesses in treatment inherent within the stereotype of self-help trauma treatment, (6) sociologists, anthropologists, and historians seeking to understand the transformation of contemporary American society and popular culture, and (7) by a logical psychiatrist's.

For the most part, Jennifer Freyd remained silent after her initial private allegations against her father. However, after personal material about the family struggle was sent to the members of the committee that would decide Jennifer's promotion as a professor of psychology at a well-known university, Jennifer spoke publicly. In a videotaped talk at a professional conference in Ann Arbor, Michigan, on August 7, 1993, Jennifer, herself a scientist specializing in memory, wondered why the media had chosen to believe that her father's memories of no abuse were true, when her father had a record of treatment for alcoholism, and yet disbelieved her own memories, despite the fact that she is a well-respected memory researcher (Freyd, 1993). Jennifer was puzzled as to why her parents' cry of victimization eclipsed her father's documented history of alcoholism and her own allegations of being a victim.

Jennifer (Freyd, 1993) wondered about the ethics, and the dual relationships, created by some FMSF Board members:

> . . . Harold Lief was my mother's psychiatrist for many years. He explained to me that he did not believe I was abused because in the early 1980s, when he met with my father once or twice in order to admit him to Silver Hill for treatment for alcoholism, he learned that my father's erotic fantasies were "entirely homoerotic." Now, I won't count it an ethical blunder to make the unfounded argument that a man with homoerotic fantasies in a heterosexual marriage is incapable of molesting his prepubescent daughter, but I do wonder about the ethics of telling the daughter of his patient such information. . . .
>
> Board members Orne and Wakefield were also names my parents first mentioned to me in therapeutic, not collegial roles. For instance, Orne was consulted by Lief about my father and I understand that this consultation included sessions with my father. . . . In psychology, at least, there are very specific ethical codes about dual relationships that would seem to be violated in these cases. (p.26)

Jennifer further reported her frustration at the reason so-called experts refused to believe her—nice men don't do such things with children. The *San Francisco Examiner* quoted a FMSF board member as follows:

> "Nobody wants to have anal intercourse with a two-year-old, except someone who is insane," said Dr. Paul McHugh, chief of psychiatry at Johns Hopkins University. . . . "But now I'm seeing all these men with fine records, stable lives, marriages intact, their children with fine school records, and they are being accused of the most horrible and violent acts." (Salter, 1993, p. A-18)

McHugh's position, as we have seen, reflects the attitude shared by medical personnel who, for almost a century, refused to acknowledge the extent of child abuse. As Jennifer (Freyd, 1993) correctly responds, there is no profile of a molester and "apparently 'normal' people can indeed engage in gruesome actions" (p. 4).

After a four-hour nonobjective presentation of the issues by *Frontline*, a PBS documentary show, a letter was received by the network from William Freyd, the brother of Peter and the uncle of Jennifer. William Freyd, a corporate executive, sides with his niece against his brother, thus reinforcing Jennifer's accusations against her father. In the letter William Freyd (1995) states:

> There is no doubt in my mind that there was severe abuse in the home of Peter and Pam, while they were raising their daughters. Peter said (on your show, "Divided Memories") that his humor was ribald. Those of us who had to endure it remember it as abusive at best and viciously sadistic at worst.
>
> The False Memory Syndrome Foundation is a fraud designed to deny a reality that Peter and Pam have spent most of their lives trying to escape. . . .
>
> That the False Memory Syndrome Foundation has been able to excite so much media attention has been a great surprise to those of us who would like to admire and respect the objectivity and motives of people in the media. Neither Peter's mother (who was also mine), nor his daughters, nor me have wanted anything to do with Peter and Pam for periods of time ranging up to more than two decades.

On the other side of the family, Peter and Pamela Freyd have consistently and completely denied the allegations against them and they have have worked tirelessly to aid families who claim to have been falsely accused. Their exposure of shoddy therapy is an important social contribution, and their directing attention to the deficits of memory has already led to intense scientific scrutiny of how memory actually works.

Naturally, Peter and Pamela Freyd are innocent until proven guilty in a court of law. Unfortunately, the factual issues in the Freyd family have never been fully presented and debated, leaving each side reasonable room to reach opposing conclusions. We are saddened by the double blow that has fallen on this family—disruption and loss of privacy. Because there is no substitute for family, it is our hope that this one will eventually mend.

Whether Peter and Pamela are innocent or guilty, the need for an organization like the FMSF is beyond dispute. It is important to keep in mind that there are three aspects to the FMSF that must be kept separate: (1) the guilt or innocence of Peter and Pamela Freyd, (2) the value of the FMSF as an independent organization apart from its founders, and (3) the views disseminated by the FMSF Scientific Advisory Board. Even if it were established that Peter and Pamela Freyd were guilty of the accusations against them, the FMSF and the scientific views it espouses would have to be considered on their own terms.

The FMSF has served two valuable social functions. First, the organization has called public attention to a form of bad therapy that clearly exists and clearly harms patients and their families. Unduly suggestive therapy techniques, as well as therapists who seek (and find) child abuse wherever they look, must be stopped. Scheflin (1994) has reported an example:

> Some months ago I was called to testify as an expert in a case involving a woman's accusation that her estranged husband had molested their three-and-a-half-year-old daughter. A therapist who saw the daughter confirmed the mother's claim.
>
> My investigation turned up no evidence to support the mother's claim, not even a statement from the alleged victim. In fact, the young girl showed no hesitations, negative feelings, or troubling impressions about her father. Based on this and other evidence, I concluded that the accusation was false. I suggested the father's attorney ask the therapist whether she had ever seen a child in therapy who was not abused. The therapist answered that she had not.
>
> Once it was clear that the therapist considered *every* child she saw to be abused, the case against the father evaporated.

Because some therapists are so prone to see child abuse everywhere, the therapy that they practice may essentially work as a self-fulfilling prophecy. A patient who comes with no memories of having been abused as a child may leave that therapy firmly convinced that many family members were repeatedly abusive and that the patient has "forgotten" these abusive acts. Therapists may receive aid and comfort in these matters from poorly run state or local child protection agencies. For example, in the case just discussed by Scheflin (1994), what should have

been a happy ending was marred by further developments. In a passage edited out of the published article, Scheflin noted that "After the case was over, I learned that my conclusions had been correct. It turned out that the County officials knew before trial, and still know, that if they want to get a diagnosis of child abuse, they should send the child to this therapist." Thus, we have conspiracy of professionals, all of whom may be well-intentioned, that will continue to cause terrible harm to innocent children and families.

In addition to calling public attention to these abuses of therapy and child protection, the FMSF also serves another valuable function as a support group for persons falsely accused of abusive acts. In its role as a support group, the FMSF has given much needed hope, guidance, and legal advice to falsely accused parents, relatives, and strangers. Had the FMSF not been founded by the Freyds, another group would have had to have been created to serve this important function.

Apart from the Freyds themselves, and the FMSF as an independent organization, it is also important to consider the the work of the Scientific Advisory Board established by the FMSF. In this book we do not attempt to develop, pass judgment on, or resolve the personal issues dividing the Freyd family, and we acknowledge the good work accomplished by the FMSF. Our main concern is with the science espoused by those persons serving as FMSF scientific advisors. The task is hampered by the fact that the Scientific Advisory Board is composed of many specialists whose views are not in agreement concerning basic issues, such as the validity of multiple personality disorder or repressed memory.

The original FMSF scientific position was moderate and sensible. As stated in the very first *FMS Newsletter* (December 5, 1992) on page 1:

- People can have false memories.
- Under certain conditions, people can get others to remember things that never happened.
- Memory does not work like a tape recorder. People don't just store an event and play it back later as a true copy of previous events.
- What is recalled in a memory is partly a function of current emotions and concerns. What

people remember depends on things that they are currently thinking about and emotions they are currently feeling.

- A person or professional can have fixed expectations, hence seek to validate them.
- The way a question is asked can influence what a person remembers or says he or she remembers.
- Any person, including a therapist, may unknowingly suggest ideas to a patient.
- Hypnosis, sodium amytal, massages, dream interpretation, self-help books, or participation in survivor groups will not increase the accuracy of recall.
- Vividness, detail, and emotional affect are not reliable indicators of accurate memory.
- Most people cannot remember anything that happened before a certain age, approximately two years. Any memory of events much before that time is almost certainly a reconstruction based on later events and should be viewed with skepticism as to its literal factuality. The evidence of very early childhood memories is very controversial.
- The term *repression* refers to a *theory* about active suppression of memories with later recovery in psychotherapy. Freud's claim was that impulse and desire are repressed—not memories. It is unlikely that most traumatic events are repressed. The entire status of the theory is very controversial.

From this modest set of premises the FMSF's Scientific Advisory Board began to draw ever wider, and ultimately more controversial, conclusions. The more controversial assumptions or claims made by at least some members of FMSF's Scientific Advisory Board and/or by attorneys associated with the FMSF include: dissociated amnesia for childhood sexual abuse does not exist; recovered memories are necessarily inaccurate; recovered memories of childhood sexual abuse or ritual abuse are necessarily caused by therapeutic suggestion; psychotherapy is a form of coercive persuasion; dissociative identity disorder does not exist and is the iatrogenic product of psychotherapy; and professional trauma treatment is a form of memory recovery therapy.

Because of the extremely successful mobilization of social resources against the problem of childhood sexual abuse (Myers, 1994), the 1980s were characterized by the development of assessment tools for the identification of abuse, phase-oriented trauma treatment, the emergence of the self-help recovery movement, and the widespread investigation of allegations of childhood sexual abuse. Childhood sexual abuse had become the "default option" (Kihlstrom, 1993).

The 1990s have been characterized as the Age of the Backlash (Armstrong, 1994; Hechler, 1988; Myers, 1994) and as "the great incest massacre" (Armstrong, 1994). Myers (1994) defines backlash as "a strong adverse reaction to a political or social movement," in this case against the child protection movement. Finkelhor says, "In the late 1980s, after a period of almost exclusively favorable media attention, child protection became more controversial." finkelhor reminds us that this backlash does not so much represent an "organized opposition group" as it does a loosely defined social trend or "counter-movement" (Myers, 1994, pp. 1, 6–7), although the so-called "backlash" may constitute several very different movements such as: (1) the skepticism about children's allegations of sexual abuse, and (2) the skepticism about adult recovery of memories of childhood sexual abuse.

Some see the False Memory Syndrome Foundation as a well-organized political opposition group. Herman (1994) has pointed out that the rapid increase in complaints about false allegations by parents and in the number of recanted claims of abuse since 1992 corresponds very closely with the establishment of the FMSF. What interest groups constitute the FMSF? According to finkelhor (1994), the main interest groups fueling the backlash are: (1) parents and daycare operators who were accused of and investigated for abuse allegations; (2) attorneys who have developed child abuse allegations and therapy malpractice as specialties; (3) the news media; and (4) scientists and clinicians.

Because the FMSF has disseminated information widely and vigorously, the accusation has been made that the FMSF is "suggesting" to patients that abuse claims were made up in therapy. This accusation is the equal and opposite complaint that memory scientists make when they accuse therapists of suggesting false memories of abuse. In suggestive patients, post-event suggestions can be accepted from *any* source, and FMSF post-event information is no exception.

Nevertheless, the FMSF has become an important vehicle for changing societal attitudes about childhood sexual abuse and about psychotherapy. As Bass and Davis (1994) point out in the second edition of *The Courage to Heal*, the first edition of their book was well received when it first came out in 1989. It was several years before it became the center of the false memory controversy. The new edition of *The Courage to Heal* includes historical documentation of the emerging backlash. The authors hope that victims of genuine abuse do not lose their own voice in the face of a crisis about the authors' credibility.

Because the agendas of the FMSF are complex and the motivations of its members and advisors diverse, it is important that the reader appreciate that much of the false memory controversy is not a scientific debate, especially given the fact that much of the current debate is based on rather "indirect" evidence (Schooler, 1994). The false memory controversy is a complicated social debate motivated by a number of diverse special interest groups who have found a common idiom for social criticism, all set within a culture desperately wanting to preserve some semblance of traditional family values over and against the encroachment of social service and therapeutic trends that have challenged the sanctity of American family structure and the success of parenting.

2

|||||||||||||||||||||

The Contours of the
False Memory Controversy

THE ESSENCE OF THE
MEMORY DEBATE

This chapter will describe the basic arguments in
the memory debate, which essentially centers
around three issues:

1. Is memory fallible? How accurate or inaccurate is memory? How complete or incomplete
   is memory?
2. Does therapy assessment and/or treatment
   contribute to the distortion of, or enhancement of, memories for abuse?
3. Does therapy help or harm patients with
   known or suspected trauma for abuse?

Is Memory Fallible?

The debate about the accuracy of memory needs to
be understood within the wider context of memory
theory. Advocates of a *trace theory* of memory (e.g.,
Penfield, 1958; Semon, 1904) view the human
memory representation as a more or less exact copy
of an event. According to the extreme end of this
view, memory is like a video recorder or movie cam-
era, and retrieval merely involves playing back the
tape or film (Reiser, 1980).

Starting with Bartlett's pioneering work on

memory for complex narratives (1932), and appearing again in contemporary information processing
theories on memory (e.g., Neisser, 1967), a
constructivist theory of memory has become the dominant paradigm since the 1970s. Constructivist thinkers argue that every time something is remembered
it is reconstructed. While each successive recall may
preserve the gist of the memory, some portion of
the details will inevitably be different on each occasion.

Most of the memory researchers who have studied the eyewitnessing of crimes and, more recently,
the relation between memory and psychotherapy
(notably Loftus, 1979a,b, 1993; Loftus & Ketcham,
1994; and Kihlstrom, 1993, 1994a,b), are situated
firmly within the Bartlettian constructivist tradition
of memory. Loftus and Ketcham (1994) consider
memories to be "creative blendings of fact and fiction" (p. 5).

On the other hand, a significant portion of
trauma clinicians adhere to some sort of trace theory
of memory. Terr (1994), as the title of her recent
book, *Unchained Memories*, implies, advocates what
is essentially a trace theory of traumatic memory,
although she agrees that memory for the details of
the traumatic events is often quite distorted due to
the operation of psychological defenses. Yapko
(1994b) found that about one-third of clinicians in
a survey of therapists' beliefs about memory assumed

that the mind functions like a computer, accurately recording events as they actually occurred. Kihlstrom has been critical of trauma therapists who believe that traumatic memories get "triggered" by external stimuli, in that the concept of triggering implies a trace theory. He says, "memories aren't triggered at all, they are reconstructed" (Kihlstrom, 1993).

Many others adhere to a *partial reconstructive* theory of memory (Brewer, 1986). According to this view, the gist of important personal experiences is accurately retained but peripheral details are not (cf. Bartlett, 1932). Many contemporary trauma specialists have accepted this position (e.g., Bass & Davis, 1994; Brown, 1995a; Christianson, 1992a,b; Harvey & Herman, 1994).

This debate between trace and reconstructive theories of memory has been waged as a battle between two opposing camps. Which side you are on—"false memory" or "recovered memory"—is the first, and often the last, question asked in this debate. Polarization, as well as the felt need to be decisively in one camp or the other, has splintered the memory and therapy communities. Careful evaluation of the scientific research and clinical experience demonstrates that this is the wrong question. The opponents are not really talking about competing *theories* about memory, but, rather, about different *types* of memory.

Most of the research supporting the constructivist theory of memory is derived from studies on normal memory processing, typically with volunteered college students as subjects. As some have argued, these data may not be so readily generalizable to patients with posttraumatic stress symptoms (van der Kolk, 1993). The essence of Horowitz's information processing model of trauma is that trauma, by definition, disrupts normal information processing (Horowitz & Reidbord, 1992). In that sense, a traumatic memory may be frozen in time. To the extent that it remains unprocessed, it may not be subject to the reconstructive tendencies of normal memory processing. Recent neurobiological studies support Horowitz's view that traumatic memory is processed differently from ordinary memory (Bremner et al., 1995a; Rauch et al., 1996).

The controversy about the accuracy or inaccuracy of memory is reducible to two essential issues: (1) the fallibility of memory, and (2) the suggest-

ibility of memory. To put this point another way, we can say that human memory is subject to *omission errors* (fallibility) and *commission errors* (suggestibility).

There is a great deal of scientific evidence relevant to the question of *memory fallibility*. Most of the data come from research on the relationship between memory performance and emotional arousal. Typically, experimental subjects are exposed to either an emotionally arousing or a non-arousing control condition, following which the memory for the event is measured. The typical outcome measure is the total amount of information about the situation that is retained, and differences found between experimental and control groups serve as the measure of differential memory performance in the emotionally arousing and non-arousing situations. Depending on how the experiment is constructed, the results typically reveal either a decrement or an increase in memory performance in the emotionally arousing condition relative to the control condition (Christianson, 1992b; Deffenbacher, 1983). While it is generally accepted that emotional arousal affects memory performance, with either a decreased or increased memory for the details of the original situation, these data have often been cited in eyewitness research and expert testimony in support of the view that memory for an emotionally arousing and/or traumatic situation is fallible (Loftus, 1979a,b, 1993).

In other words, memory scientists assert that in emotionally arousing situations, and possibly traumatizing situations, the individual is likely to make a greater number of omission errors, i.e., remember less total information about the event. Other memory scientists have pointed out that emotionally aroused subjects often insert erroneous details into the memory (commission errors). Lindsay and Read (1994), for example, remind us that normal subjects typically make a number of errors in everyday autobiographical memory, and that autobiographical memory is particularly prone to errors even in the absence of emotional arousal. Moreover, Loftus has drawn upon a body of data on childhood amnesia to argue that adults who allegedly recover memories for specific events that go back to the first year or two are making claims that go against everything memory scientists know about amnesia for early childhood events (Loftus, 1993).

The upshot of these arguments by memory scientists is that clinicians working with patients with known or recovered memories of abuse should expect that the information about past events in question, especially with respect to memory for personal autobiographical memories, is prone to significant omissions and errors. This is even more likely if the event was emotionally arousing and happened in the very remote past, especially the early years of life. Loftus and Ketcham (1994, p. 135) argue that therapists have a duty to patients "to critically assess the "historical truth" of memories recovered in therapy.

Furthermore, these memory scientists warn clinicians not to confuse memory accuracy with confidence, emotionality, or vividness of detail, because numerous studies have shown that experimental subjects can be highly confident about erroneous memories or report memories that have a compelling emotional impact and are quite rich in detail yet are quite erroneous. Loftus, Korf, and Schooler (1989), for example, found that there is no significant relationship between the belief in a memory and its accuracy or inaccuracy. Not only did subjects tend to hold strong beliefs about inaccurate memories, but they were also reluctant to accept that the memory was in error when they were given feedback about the memory performance.

On the other side of the argument, advocates of the trauma accuracy position have pointed out that most of the conclusions drawn about memory fallibility are based upon research with normal college students who watch slides or films, and these results are not readily generalizable to traumatized patients with posttraumatic stress symptoms. Moreover, some of this same research data suggest the opposite conclusion by finding that there is an increased memory performance for an emotionally arousing situation, at least for the gist of the arousing event (Christianson, 1992b). So, it cannot be readily assumed from the available data that memory for trauma per se is fallible, although it may be (Brown, 1995a). Furthermore, advocates of the trauma accuracy position have pointed out that the great preponderance of available studies on emotion and memory are limited to the measurement of memory performance for minor details, not for the gist of important events, and to the extent to which memory for trauma is about life events of major con-

sequence, the laboratory findings simply may not be relevant to memory for trauma (Brown, 1995a; Olio, 1993; Olio & Cornell, 1994; Yuille & Cutshall, 1986).

Trauma accuracy advocates assert that memory for abuse is fixed in time and is generally accurately retained, even if the details are subject to distortion and ordinary, normal memory errors (Olio, 1993; Olio & Cornell, 1994; see discussion between Ellen Bass and Elizabeth Loftus in Loftus & Ketcham, 1994, p. 209; Terr, 1994). The problem, as trauma accuracy advocates see it, is that the traumatic memories are sometimes less accessible, though they may be more accurate than nontraumatic memories if properly retrieved.

The debate about the *accessibility of memories for trauma* essentially is about the *completeness* of the available memory. Advocates of the trauma accuracy position have argued that a significant subsample of the overall group of traumatized individuals fail to remember trauma for a significant duration of time and then later recover the memory either spontaneously or in psychotherapy. *Amnesia for trauma* has been reported to sometimes follow physical abuse, childhood sexual abuse, rape, homicide, and other traumas. The concept of amnesia for trauma, or traumatic dissociation, is critical to the debate, because it is used to justify psychotherapeutic memory processing as part of a comprehensive phase-oriented treatment and sometimes to justify more narrowly applied memory recovery techniques. Advocates for the false memory position, who use the term *repression* rather than traumatic amnesia, have argued that the scientific evidence for repression is overstated (Garry & Loftus, 1994; Kihlstrom, 1993; Loftus, 1993). Trauma accuracy advocates, in turn, have argued that the false memory advocates have failed to take into consideration extensive clinical and experimental literature on dissociation and dissociated memory and have instead misleadingly cast the debate in terms of repression (Calof, 1994).

The disagreement focuses on three points. First, an "unresolved debate" about the *base rates* for traumatic amnesia exists (Lindsay & Read, 1994, p. 25). In the studies on childhood sexual abuse, for example, the base rates for partial and full amnesia for childhood sexual abuse range from the low of 4.5% to a high of 82% across studies. Regardless of how difficult it is to obtain reliable base rates of amnesia for trauma across studies, *every* study documents some subgroup of traumatized patients who are amnestic. Bass and Davis correctly say that, "the fact that people experience amnesia for traumatic events is—or should be—beyond dispute" (1994, pp. 40–41).

Second, there is a disagreement about the *definition of amnesia,* because reports of amnesia generally range along a continuum from complete amnesia, to partial amnesia (which can take several forms: (1) recall of some memories for the abuse then recall of others at a later point, (2) fragmented memories for specific episodes, or (3) recollections of memories without emotional impact or any relationship to current symptomatology), to no amnesia (Harvey & Herman, 1994). False memory advocates, using the term "repression" rather than "traumatic amnesia" (Garry, Loftus, & Brown, 1994; Lindsay & Read, 1994; Loftus, 1993; Loftus & Ketcham, 1994; Ofshe & Watters, 1993, 1994), argue that "repressed memories . . . did not exist until someone went looking for them" (Loftus & Ketcham, 1994, p. 141). It is true that rates of amnesia for trauma vary considerably depending on how amnesia is defined.

Third, there is disagreement about the *mechanisms* of amnesia, ranging along a continuum of repression, dissociation, denial, splitting, and normal forgetting. False memory advocates have sometimes pigeonholed the debate into one about massive repression (Loftus, 1993) or "robust repression" (Ofshe & Watters, 1993). They have reminded us that failure to remember trauma may not always be due to repression, but, rather, to other environmental and developmental factors (Kihlstrom, 1993), and sometimes to simple, normal forgetting of remote events (Loftus, 1993) or motivated avoidance (Ofshe & Watters, 1993). The extreme repression hypothesis defines repression as a highly selective, involuntary complete loss of memory for a traumatic life experience, along with loss of awareness that the memory is lost, followed by recovery of the memory intact after a very long retention interval (Loftus & Ketcham, 1994; Ofshe & Singer, 1994; Ofshe & Watters, 1994). Proponents of this view see robust repression as distinct from traumatic amnesia.

Trauma accuracy advocates have sometimes been puzzled by this aspect of the memory debate because many clinicians readily concede that a variety of defensive operations, of which repression is just one example, may be operative in causing amnesia for trauma. In detailed case examples, Terr (1994) mentions repression, denial, suppression, dissociation, displacement, splitting, and sometimes simple forgetting as contributors to amnesia for trauma. Spiegel has written extensively from a theoretical perspective on how dissociative mechanisms contribute to amnesia for trauma (Spiegel & Cardena, 1991; Spiegel & Scheflin, 1994). Putnam et al. (1995) have shown that major dissociative conditions are associated with more severe abuse. The trauma accuracy advocates argue that, apart from the problem of accessing a traumatic memory, the memory influences information processing, mood, behavior, and interpersonal relations (Spiegel & Scheflin, 1994).

So why, then, does the debate persist more narrowly around the concept of repression and not more appropriately around the more general issue of amnesia for trauma? The answer to this question is complex, and more political than scientific. From a forensic point of view, as we shall see in chapter 16, the concept of repression is critical to discussion of the delayed discovery rule, which operates to suspend the statute of limitations barrier to the bringing of lawsuits (Spiegel & Scheflin, 1994). From a scientific point of view, false memory advocates have cited Holmes's (1990) critical review pointing out that the laboratory evidence accumulated over 60 years in support of the clinical concept of repression is less than impressive. From a political standpoint, it is easier to mount an attack on a psychoanalytic concept than on a physiological concept.

If the notion of repression is destroyed, an attack may be launched on the clinical justification for uncovering suspected traumatic memories and on the forensic justification for applying the delayed discovery rule in childhood sexual abuse cases. Thus, while some advocates of the false memory position believe that the "substantive controversy turns on the validity of the concept of repression" (Ofshe & Watters, 1993), advocates of the trauma accuracy position argue that this reductionistic position grossly oversimplifies the variety of factors contributing to amnesia for trauma, as well as the often reported variations in amnesia for trauma.

Is Memory Suggestible?

The second controversy about the accuracy of memory is about the *suggestibility of memory*. Advocates of the false memory position have argued that at least a significant sub-sample of patients are suggestible, and that clinicians who treat patients with known and recovered memories for abuse need to be mindful of the suggestive influences operative in the therapeutic interaction. Otherwise, the clinician may iatrogenically suggest memories for events that never really occurred. Ceci and Loftus (1994), two experts on memory suggestibility in children and adults, respectively, note that "memory for non-events is far from rare" (p. 354), especially if the suggested false information is plausible and repeated. The essential argument of the false memory advocates is that therapists sometimes "implant" false memories of abuse in their patients, and the patients accept and believe these fantasies as if they pertained to genuine abuse in the past. According to Loftus (1993), and Loftus and Ketcham (1994), suggestions of false memories for abuse come from two sources— the psychotherapy relationship and educational materials, e.g., books, lectures, the news media— although others have argued that the suggestive role of self-help books has been overemphasized (Ennis et al., 1995).

The research data on memory suggestibility cited as evidence of therapeutic implantation of memories for abuse come from three sources. First, there is a large body of data on post-event misinformation suggestibility. Loftus with adults and Ceci with children, along with many other memory scientists, have conducted numerous studies for over two decades on misinformation suggestibility. Typically, experimental subjects are shown a stimulus event in the form of a slide show or video of an emotionally arousing or non-arousing situation. After viewing the stimulus event, the subject is asked a series of questions or reads a narrative about the event, some parts of which are accurate and some of which are misleading. When the subjects' memories are tested, some subjects incorporate the misleading post-event misinformation into the report about the original event. This phenomenon is known as *misinformation suggestibility*. (The scientific literature on this subject will be reviewed in chapter 8.) The magnitude of misinformation suggestibility depends on

many factors, such as the type of misinformation given, the age and personality of the subject, the degree of the uncertainty about past events in question, the duration of time between the original event and memory retrieval, the conditions of memory retrieval, and the source of the misinformation.

Authorities on misinformation suggestibility, including Loftus, Ceci, Lindsay, and Read, have attempted to generalize these findings to psychotherapy, especially to "recovered memory" therapy. They assert that clinicians who ask patients about suspected traumatic events for which patients are uncertain may be unwittingly "implanting" ideas of abuse that never happened. The danger of suggestion here is, in their view, especially great when the patient is uncertain about the abuse, the abuse is thought to have happened in the remote past, and the patient is repeatedly questioned about the suspected past abuse.

The second source of memory suggestibility data is extensive research on pseudomemory production in high-hypnotizable subjects. Hypnotizable subjects are prone to accept hypnotic suggestions for events that never happened and under certain conditions believe that these fictitious events actually happened. The phenomenon is known as *hypnotic pseudomemory production*. The rate of pseudomemory production in high-hypnotizable subjects may be remarkably high, under certain conditions, though pseudomemory production is not especially remarkable in low-hypnotizable subjects.

Advocates of the false memory position have argued that the use of hypnosis with patients runs the risk of implanting false memories for abuse (Lindsay & Read, 1994; Ofshe, 1992; Ofshe & Watters, 1993, 1994), although this statement is quite misleading, since the research on hypnotic pseudomemory production has shown that it is primarily hypnotizability, not a formal induction or a particular hypnotic procedure, that is the risk factor for pseudomemory production. In other words, the issue is more a matter of the trait of hypnotizability (the way high-hypnotizable subjects process information that makes it harder for them to distinguish between fantasy and memory production) than a matter of a given hypnotic procedure or even of hypnosis itself. (The science exploring hypnotic pseudomemory production is developed in chapter 10.)

The third source of memory suggestibility data is from research on *interrogation procedures,* and on *coercive persuasion,* otherwise known as *brainwashing* or *thought reform.* Some advocates of the false memory position have conducted extensive research on interrogation techniques by police, and others have studied coercive tactics, ranging from communist thought reform programs to contemporary mind control in religious, political, and therapeutic cults. From this data, false memory advocates conclude that memory recovery therapists sometimes use a combination of hypnosis and social influence tactics to persuade clients to accept beliefs as memories of abuse that never happened (Ofshe & Watters, 1993, 1994).

Still other researchers on hypnosis and motivated social influence, including Nicholas Spanos (1994) and Michael Yapko (1994a), have argued that a combination of hypnosis coupled with leading or misleading interview techniques can produce fantasies and fictitious narratives in therapy. These fantasies go beyond the recall of childhood sexual abuse to the belief that the patient has memories for past lives or for UFO abductions. Spanos and Yapko make the point that if patients can be led to believe in the historical truth of these fantastic improbabilities, it is even simpler to implant false beliefs about plausible occurrences, such as childhood sexual abuse.

Regardless of the type of suggestibility cited, advocates of the false memory position have drawn upon each of these areas of suggestibility effects to construct their argument that therapists have been implanting false memories for abuse. Advocates for the trauma accuracy position have countered with several rebuttals. First, while it may be appropriate to hypothesize that false memories *can* be produced through therapeutic influence, it is premature to generalize the findings from other sources to therapy because, as of now, there are *no* studies on suggestive influences in therapy per se (Brown, 1995a).

Second, while advocates of the false memory position assert that completely fictitious events can be implanted ("construct entire events" [Loftus, 1993 p. 531]; "fantasize entire complex scenarios" [Spanos et al., 1994, p. 433]; "entirely false memories" [Ofshe & Watters, 1993]), advocates of the trauma accuracy position caution that most of the research data, at least on the misinformation effect,

pertain to misleading suggestions for peripheral details and not for central actions or complex realities (Olio & Cornell, 1994). Furthermore, others using research designs simlar to those used by Loftus to investigate misinformation suggestibility have found that the misinformation suggestibility effect may not be readily generalizable to therapeutic suggestions of false memories (Pezdek & Roe, 1994).

While it is tempting to view therapists as having the power to choose which past reality they wish to implant or remove, like Arnold Schwartzenegger in the movie *Total Recall,* there is in fact very little *direct* evidence to support the view that a therapist can and will implant a complete memory or an even more elaborate reality construction in a therapy patient. Most of the anecdotal cases cited by each side probably contain inaccurate statements of what really happened, because it is very difficult to know what really happened based on a memory report alone. Thus, supporters believe what they want to believe—false memory advocates believe recanters and disbelieve patients, while trauma advocates hold the opposite beliefs. Alpert (1995b) notes:

> At least some memory scientists fervently promulgate the view that the abuser is now the therapist who pursues buried memories. . . . Although there are no laboratory studies of memory suggestibility in psychotherapy, this is nevertheless believed. These memory scientists seem to imply that the victims are no longer the ones who are molested but rather the ones who are falsely accused. (p. 6)

Third, trauma advocacy supporters have countered that statements about "memory creation" and "memory implantation" constitute a distortion or misrepresentation of the research on misinformation suggestibility (Brown, 1995b). A number of careful studies have shown that the data supporting the view that the original memory representation is fundamentally altered by post-event suggestions are rather thin, although such alteration can occur in a small subgroup of patients under certain conditions. A greater portion of the variance of reports of false information is attributed to contextual factors or social influence. The point is that those who argue that false recovered *memories* for abuse are sometimes "created" by therapeutic situations may not be wrong. Their argument, however, may be premature and is certainly overstated based on the available data.

A more useful set of questions may be:

1. Under what conditions do false reports occur in psychotherapy?
2. How many of these false reports are attributed to personality factors, extensive social influence, and/or contextual demands?
3. Under what conditions are these reports indicative either of less stable social compliance or more internalized enduring changes in the original memory representation?

A central point in the debate about suggestibility of memory is the controversy about *base rates* of genuinely false memories for trauma recovered in psychotherapy. Advocates of the false memory position usually assert that the base rates of false memories for abuse created in psychotherapy are quite high. Some have suggested that an "epidemic" of false allegations is emerging in this country (Yapko, 1994a, p. 19), and that false allegations are "happening far more frequently than we might like to believe" (p. 32). Frankel (1993) speaks of the "growing momentum" of false allegations brought about by therapy. Loftus and Ketcham (1994) speak of "the epidemic of [false] repressed memories" (p. 84). Lindsay and Read (1994) state "many people in North America have come to believe that they were sexually abused as children when in fact they were not" (p. 283), basing their claim on the sheer number of accusations that patients are making against alleged perpetrating parents. Lindsay and Read add, however, that we "don't know how common illusory memories are but the number may be large" (p. 29). Advocates of the trauma accuracy position assert that such statements are overstated speculations. They are quick to point out that there are no independent cases of false memory syndrome (Grand, 1995b; Pezdek, 1994). The only data-based study to test the base rates of false memory syndrome found that only 3.9%–13.6% of women with recovered memories met some but not all of the false memory diagnostic criteria (Hovdestad & Kristiansen, 1996).

One of the major problems with base rates in the false memory controversy is the willingness of some false memory advocates to believe virtually every recanter and to disbelieve virtually every accuser. In this regard, they commit the same error they accuse therapists of committing, only in reverse. Therapists, they claim, are wrong to believe all of their patients' statements about abuse. But these false memory proponents automatically believe the claims of recanters and disbelieve the claims made by therapy patients. This political stance naturally slants the data in favor of big numbers of false memories. While there can be no doubt that there are true recanters, it is also a fact that there are recanters who, having been subjected to social influence processes, withdraw correct allegations. Similarly, it would be unwise for therapists to believe everything their patients tell them about abuse, but it would also be unfair and unprofessional to disbelieve all accounts, even those allegations that strain credulity.

Suppose a 35-year-old man walks into a therapist's office and presents symptoms of depression. He claims that he is having trouble receiving his full Veterans' Administration benefits, and that he cannot keep a job or hold a serious romantic relationship together. In fact, he says he has no relationships, no real contact with family or friends. The therapist asks why this is so, and the patient responds that he is a victim of government mind control. Should the therapist believe this story? Should the therapist disbelieve the story? When asked for details, the man says that he was working at a top secret Army facility in France 15 years earlier when some important documents were found missing. He was accused of stealing the documents and was hypnotized and given truth serum and a lie detector test, all of which failed to establish any evidence of guilt. He was then attacked by the French police in a gun battle with Army police, and then taken by Army police officers to an old mill where a "greenish" looking man sat him down in a chair and asked him if he had taken the documents. When he said "no," he suddenly found himself on the floor, in a corner of the room, with his head exploding like shooting stars. From that moment on, he has never been the same. Would you believe this story? Should the therapist automatically disbelieve it?

The story is true, except that the man, James Thornwell, went to a lawyer rather than a therapist. The lawyer filed a Freedom of Information Act request with the Army for relevant documents. Before the documents arrived, Thornwell was interviewed by Scheflin and Opton (1978), who recorded his statements. Months later, several thousand pages of documents arrived from the Army, which validated everything Thornwell had described, even the names of personnel involved. Although there was some distortion in reference to the names, it is not clear that Thornwell ever learned the names accurately at the time. In one of the documents from that time, Army officials discuss the "problem" of Thornwell's excellent memory if he should make public statements. The Congress of the United States awarded Thornwell approximately half a million dollars as compensation, and his story was presented on CBS's 60 Minutes show. An accurate made-for-TV movie entitled Thornwell still plays on late-night television.

It is virtually impossible to collect data on which recovered memories are factual or fictitious (Brown, 1995a). Using recanters as evidence of a false memory is not scientifically sound unless there is control for two factors. First, the actual truth must be known in order to say with assurance that the recanter did have false memories that had been implanted or suggested by the therapist. Second, the recanters must not be highly suggestible individuals who have simply accepted post-event leading and misleading information that they have had false memories implanted. Thus, while it is appropriate to raise questions in scientific and public forums about the incidence of false memory production in psychotherapy, the highly speculative nature of such claims merits appropriate restraint and caution.

Therapeutic Assessment and Treatment

Does therapeutic assessment and/or treatment contribute to the distortion or the enhancement of memory? Advocates of the false memory position have criticized therapists who claim that they can identify cases of childhood sexual abuse from a checklist of warning signs and symptoms (Ceci & Loftus, 1994; Loftus, 1993; Loftus & Ketcham, 1994; Ofshe & Watters, 1993; Pope & Hudson, 1995a,b; Yapko, 1994a). As examples of such questionable assessment procedures, they cite popular books like The Courage to Heal (Bass & Davis, 1988), Secret Survivors (Blume, 1990), and Repressed Memories (Fredrickson, 1992). These books list signs and symptoms of sexual abuse. Even if the profession agreed upon a list of signs and symptoms, the lists provided by these authors are so broad that very few people are actually excluded. Aside from the existence of the lists and their overinclusiveness, false memory advocates also point to the fact that the lists provide no legitimate avenue of escape. According to these authors, if you remember abuse, then you must have been abused; but if you do not remember abuse, you still may have been abused. Indeed, the more you don't remember, the greater the likelihood that the abuse occurred. The patient has no way to deny abuse under this logic. At best, the patient is left with "I cannot say for sure." Given this therapeutic perspective, overprediction of abuse is inevitable and the possibility of having patients develop beliefs about abuse that never happened is more likely.

As Haaken and Schlaps (1991) say, "incest becomes the unifying event around which symptomatology and emotional experiences are organized" (pp. 39–40). Linking adult presenting symptoms with a history of childhood sexual abuse for which the person may be amnestic has a long history, going back to Janet and Breuer and Freud. While it is generally accepted that childhood sexual abuse may cause certain symptoms in adults, it cannot be readily assumed that such symptoms in adults necessarily imply childhood sexual abuse. Lindsay and Read (1994) correctly challenge the logic here by noting that "knowing that A causes B does not imply that every example of B was caused by A" (p. 311). The question is whether the childhood sexual abuse explanation is the correct explanation for a given patient's symptoms. Yapko (1994a), for example, says that childhood sexual abuse cannot be identified from a symptom checklist because symptoms are "general enough to fit almost anyone" (p. 13). A number of studies have shown that the long-term sequelae of childhood sexual abuse are highly variable (Briere, 1988; Brown, 1990; Kendall-Tackett, Williams, & finkelhor, 1993) and that childhood sexual abuse accounts for only a portion of the variance of symptoms and other problems for which adults enter psychotherapy (Ceci & Loftus, 1994; Nash, 1994). Ceci and Loftus assert that no single symptom is manifest in the majority of adult survivors of childhood sexual abuse and that a significant number of survivors are relatively asymptomatic.

Pope and Hudson (1995a,b) have applied strict methodological criteria to demonstrate that none of the available studies meets sufficient methodological criteria to be able to establish a clear causal relationship between adult symptoms and childhood sexual abuse. However, their review did not include the recent Widom and Morris 20-year prospective study (1997), which meets the Pope and Hudson criteria and firmly establishes a causal relationship between adult psychopathology and childhood sexual abuse.

Trauma advocates also link current dissociative pathology to earlier traumatic experiences (Calof, 1994; Cardena & Spiegel, 1993; Chu & Dill, 1990; Davies & Frawley, 1994; van der Hart & Friedman, 1989; van der Hart & Horst, 1989; van der Hart & Nijenhuis, 1995; van der Kolk & van der Hart, 1989), although Tillman, Nash, 1994 and Lerner (1994) in their critical review have demonstrated that there is perhaps no clear linear relationship between traumatic events and the development of dissociative pathology. At best such a relationship is complex and multidetermined.

Similar controversies exist with respect to the linkage of trauma and eating disorders. A number of reports have documented a relationship between childhood sexual abuse and the subsequent development of an eating disorder (Bulik, Sullivan, & Rorty, 1989; Folsom et al., 1989; Hall et al., 1989; Lacey, 1990; Oppenheimer, et al., 1985; Root & Fallon, 1988; Ross, Heber, et al., 1989; Sloan & Leichner, 1986; Steiger & Zanko, 1990; Stuart et al., 1990). Pope and Hudson (1992), however, have critically reviewed these studies and claim that the better controlled studies fail to demonstrate a higher prevalence of eating disorders in the childhood sexual abuse group relative to control groups, although their conclusions are dependent upon the strictness of the methodological criteria used to evaluate the available research.

Therapists who rely too heavily on a cookbook approach run the risk of falsely discovering repressed memories of some sort of disguised abuse, and they increase the likelihood that both patient and therapist alike will unwittingly come to accept the abuse explanation and organize the unfolding treatment around it (Lindsay & Read, 1994). Moreover, narrowing the focus to childhood sexual abuse runs the risk of missing the complexity of the issues and failing to address other significant current life problems (Ceci & Loftus, 1994), sadistic impulses (Ganaway, 1989), masochistic fantasies (Newman & Baumeister, 1996), or impairments in self and relational development (Davies & Frawley, 1994; Haaken & Schlaps, 1991; Hedges, 1994).

The false memory advocates claim that some memory recovery therapists make a diagnosis of childhood sexual abuse very quickly, often within the initial intake session, and sometimes they even diagnose over the telephone without seeing the patient (Yapko, 1994a). Indeed, it was the awareness of these telephone diagnoses that led Yapko to begin writing his well received book.

The main therapeutic error, according to the false memory advocates, is telling the patient during the initial evaluation that he or she is, or may be, a survivor of childhood sexual abuse. This emphatic statement, from a highly prestigious, credible source, who is presumed to be acting in the patient's best interests, may be highly persuasive in implanting a *suggestion*, especially if the patient has no memory for the abuse and has never considered that his or her symptoms are in any way associated with abuse (Loftus & Ketcham, 1994; Yapko, 1994a). The therapist may genuinely believe that abuse is the *only* way to explain the symptoms. The therapist, in supplying the patient with this explanatory model for the presenting symptoms of distress, is also providing an excuse for not taking full responsibility for one's own life. Defense lawyers for generations have been using a "blame the victim" defense that includes, as a subpart, the "abuse excuse" (Scheflin, 1995).

Advocates of the trauma accuracy position have responded that the false memory arguments minimize the importance of understanding symptoms and reduce everything to memory and suggestibility. Bass and Davis have countered:

> There is a lot more to determining whether someone is a survivor than a single memory. The "false memory" argument hinges on the assumption that an assessment of a childhood sexual abuse is based solely or primarily on memory . . . [but] fail[s] to explain the presence of symptoms. A therapist cannot induce you to jump out of your skin every time someone comes up behind you. (1994, p. 35)

Thus, while it certainly may be the case that general symptom checklists may be overused and misapplied, the sensitive clinician must also be alert to a "disguised presentation of PTSD" (Gelinas, 1983). Davies and Frawley's interpretation of the wide variety of symptoms asociated with childhood sexual abuse is "that being sexually abused affects every realm of a child's life" (1994, p. 37). In other words, the risk of making a false positive does not justify making a false negative. Exactly how a clinician finds the middle ground between the extremes of failure to recognize disguised PTSD and getting the patient to accept a suggestion for an incorrect explanatory model for abuse is very difficult.

The real issue here involves a treatment plan—whether or not, under what conditions, and when the clinician communicates to the patient his or her index of suspicion that a disguised abuse presentation may exist. In phase-oriented trauma treatment, memory integration is rarely the initial focus of treatment. Because the initial goal is typically symptom stabilization and coping enhancement (Brown & Fromm, 1986), the question as to whether these symptoms are generally associated with disguised abuse memories typically is not the central concern until later in the treatment. Treatment can proceed without premature disclosure on the issue and without initially suggesting that the patient may have been abused and have not known it. Early on in treatment, helping the patient "learn to live with doubt" (Yapko, 1994a, p. 172), over and against the patient's need for a coherent explanatory model, may make sense. Later in treatment, there may be a certain "clinical utility" to exploring suspected abuse themes, without regard to their veracity (Lewis, 1995; Nash, 1994). It may help the patient to construct a compelling personal narrative that makes sense even if it's not accurate (Nash, 1994, pp. 356–357). This may be a useful clinical goal so long as both patient and therapist understand that the abuse explanation may have narrative truth but not historical truth (Spence, 1982).

A related controversy has to do with the preparation of a formal diagnosis. Lindsay and Read (1994) are critical of the overuse of the diagnosis of the posttraumatic stress disorder (PTSD) for patients presumed by therapists to have a disguised abuse presentation, but for whom no abuse history is known. According to *DSM-IV*, there must be a known stressor to make a diagnosis of PTSD. Clinicians sometimes assume that the presence of intrusive reexperiencing, generalized numbing, and physiological reactivity justifies a PTSD diagnosis, with the rationale that the patient's memory for the presumed abuse is inaccessible to consciousness. Making such a diagnosis of PTSD carries an implicit, and sometimes explicit, suggestion of trauma.

Likewise, many false memory advocates have criticized what they believe to be the overuse and outright suggestive use of the diagnosis of multiple personality disorder (MPD) (Ofshe & Watters, 1994), now called dissociative identity disorder (DID) in *DSM-IV*. They cite the great increase in cases of MPD in the past decade as an example of the "treatment-oriented diagnostic bias" (Frankel, 1993, p. 954), and are especially skeptical when the diagnosis is first "confirmed" in hypnosis (Ganaway, 1989).

On the question of the legitimacy of the MPD condition, advocates of the false memory position disagree with one another. Some advocates take the extreme position that a diagnosis of MPD is always an iatrogenic product of hypnotic suggestion and "leading diagnostic interviews" (Dawes, 1994; Ganaway, 1995; McHugh, 1993; Merskey, 1992; Ofshe & Watters, 1994; Spanos, 1994), or a failure of the therapist to recognize the patient's misuse of self-hypnosis (Ofshe & Watters, 1994, p. 217). For these researchers, malpractice actions may be called for in any case where MPD is diagnosed. Other advocates of the false memory position accept the legitimacy of MPD, but observe that, even where it is the correct diagnosis, it cannot be assumed that MPD is necessarily associated with abuse (Ganaway, 1995). Others have argued that, although multiplicity may be a legitimate diagnosis, current treatment approaches run the risk of reinforcing a type of "false consciousness," in which the patient redefines his or her identity around the diagnosis in a way that undermines development and individual freedom and responsibility (Hacking, 1995).

Advocates of the trauma accuracy position assert that the presence of intrusive reexperiencing symptoms, generalized numbing symptoms, and physiological reactivity raises a legitimate index of suspicion, even if a traumatic stressor is not known.

In these cases, the correct diagnosis is posttraumatic stress symptoms (PTSS), along with an appropriate treatment focus on stabilization. While trauma accuracy advocates concede that temporary, situation-specific multiple identity enactments might be created in the laboratory with hypnosis (Spanos, 1994), no one has ever demonstrated the laboratory creation of MPD as a diagnosable clinical disorder. Trauma accuracy advocates also claim that many MPD patients keep their alter personalities covert and that some patients will disclose alter personalities *only* with structured interviews and/or hypnosis (Kluft, 1982). They note that MPD patients are not dumb. If the patient senses or knows the therapist does not believe in MPD, the patient will not exhibit those symptoms. Thus, the condition does not present to such a therapist and the therapist's disbelief in MPD becomes a self-fulfilling prophecy.

Once again, the controversy boils down to this: does the risk of suggesting false positives justify false negatives (fish, in press; Nash, 1994)? How does the clinician weave between falsely suggesting multiplicity and failing to diagnosis it? The argument that MPD can be iatrogenically suggested overstates what the available data support.

The essential argument of the false memory advocates is that therapists, or at least certain kinds of therapists, are iatrogenically creating false memories of abuse that never really occurred (Lindsay & Read, 1994; Loftus, 1993; Loftus & Ketcham, 1994; Ofshe & Watters, 1993, 1994). Moreover, it has been argued that uncovering memories in itself distresses the patient and may cause harm. As Loftus describes a case of alleged therapeutically suggested false memories, "The memories had actually created the trauma" (p. 18). Loftus (1993), in an *American Psychologist* article that has received wide exposure, speaks about "therapist's suggestions" in general, without further qualification, thereby implying that therapy in general is a problem.

Ofshe and Watters (1993) at least make it clear that they are limiting their criticism to "recovered memory therapies," and Haaken and Schlaps (1991) discuss "incest resolution therapists." In that sense their comments seem to address the self-help trauma movement more than the professional practice of phase-oriented trauma treatment, although Ofshe and Watters (1994) include some professional trauma treatment specialists, notably Courtois (1988) and Herman (1992), in their classification of recovered memory therapy. Lindsay and Read (1994) and Kihlstrom (1993) focus their criticism on those therapies that use "extensive memory recovery techniques," either by self-help therapists or by professionals.

Few of these advocates of the false memory position ever cite the major writings on phase-oriented treatment of trauma, so it is unclear whether they simply do not know the professional literature on trauma treatment or whether they know this literature and are exempting it from their concerns. Because it is never exactly clear just how these loosely defined recovered memory therapies compare to the standard, phase-oriented treatment of trauma, we do not know to what extent the false memory criticisms are indeed applicable to professional, phase-oriented trauma treatment. If they wish to limit their concerns to certain therapies, it is misleading, as Loftus has done, to speak about "therapist's suggestions," because, even if not intended, the statement implies a general indictment of the profession of psychotherapy. Yapko (1994a) attempts to handle the problem by limiting his criticism to those therapists who suggest abuse, although the argument then becomes rather circular. In any event, we are left with the very real problem that the exact nature and definitional boundaries of the suggestive therapies are less than adequately defined in the false memory literature.

THE FALSE MEMORY MODEL

There is, however, consensus on *how a therapist can create false memories for abuse.* There is within the false memory literature a consistent model for the mechanisms by which patients can come to believe memories for abuse that never really occurred. The six-part false memory model consists of the following elements:

1. Suggestions of abuse
2. Therapists' beliefs
3. Confirmatory bias
4. Memory recovery
5. Specific memory recovery techniques
6. Suggestive therapy procedures

Suggestions of Abuse

As we have seen, the process of suggestion begins during the initial intake evaluation in which the therapist is said to make the *suggestion of abuse* to the patient, either explicitly through offering an explanation of warning signs and various symptoms, or implicitly in the form of a PTSD or DID diagnosis. Most advocates of the false memory position are careful to say that such therapists for the most part are not intentionally making abuse suggestions. Yet, while the therapist may "unwittingly suggest ideas" (Loftus, 1993, p. 530) and may be "suggestive without being aware of doing so" (Lindsay & Read, 1994, p. 19), the patient may be sufficiently misled. As Yapko (1994a) explains:

> Therapists generally offer their suggestions benevolently in the genuine belief that they will truly help a client (p. 95) . . . [and] genuinely come to believe the signs of abuse are present and that the history of abuse is the only explanation that accounts for the client's symptoms. (p. 116)

When a therapist communicates to a patient who has no memory for abuse that the therapist believes the patient has been abused, it has a priming effect, in that it "directs the patient to be attentive to the abuse and adopt abuse as a frame-of-reference to interpret the information" (Victor, 1994, p. 7). Frankel (1994) sees the false memory problem as the result of a "purposeful search for a history of such trauma" (p. 332). Such an idea can become "a unifying event around which symptomatology and emotional experience are organized" (Haaken & Schlaps, 1991, pp. 39–40).

Years ago, Jerome Frank's classic book *Persuasion and Healing* (1961) described how therapy succeeds by offering a cohesive explanatory model to a patient, without regard for whether the offered belief system is true or false. This theme has been amplified by some false memory advocates into a distinction between narrative truth and historical truth (Spence, 1982, 1987, 1994a), coupled with the claim that recovered memory therapists are helping patients who have no memory for abuse to construct entirely new identities as abuse survivors (Kihlstrom, 1993; Yapko, 1994a), and then to enact their victim role with others (Ofshe & Watters, 1993, 1994).

Therapists are led to make these suggestions of abuse by their own past history and their own set of beliefs about trauma, memory, abuse, and hypnosis.

Therapists' Beliefs

Patients are most vulnerable to adopt abuse as a new frame of reference with therapists who have *a countertransference overidentification with abuse,* and/or *a certain set of erroneous beliefs about abuse and trauma.* The improper use of suggestions of abuse is likely to be common, according to Haaken and Schlaps (1991), with therapists who "share a common history of sexual abuse" (p. 44). For these therapists, abuse is likely to be seen as the cause of many adult problems, and evidence for abuse may be found even in total repression of any memories.

Ganaway (1995) has criticized some therapists for what he believes to be their "fascination for and indulgence in the phenomenology of multiplicity." These therapists are likely to "discover" DID in patients and fail to correctly identify other areas of psychopathology. Some of these therapists actually claim to be suffering from DID themselves, which, they claim, enhances their skill in recognizing it in others. Many therapists will make the MPD diagnosis because it is trendy, the latest fashion in psychopathology.

Most of the false memory advocates implicate a *therapist's beliefs* as playing a central role in the suggestive processes, especially when the therapist has considerable "certainty" that abuse has occurred (Yapko, 1994a, p. 163). According to Yapko, when a therapist has a "unwavering belief" (p. 120), "one way or another he or she communicates . . . the message to the client" (1994, p. 118). Ofshe and Watters (1993) say, "The therapist's expectations predict the direction of treatment" (p. 9).

How do the therapist's fixed beliefs about abuse contribute to false memory production? By persuading the patient to accept the therapist's opinion as fact. Some advocates of the false memory position argue that the therapist's beliefs are accepted, as the literature on persuasive attitude change demonstrates, when an idea is offered by a highly *"credible" source* (Yapko, 1994a) who is often an *"authority figure"* (Victor, 1994) whom the patient sees as acting in his or her best interests. Dawes (1994) comments on how authoritative beliefs and statements may lead to false beliefs about childhood sexual abuse:

> "Knowing" within ten minutes from the way a client walks that she was an incest victim as a child can easily lead a psychologist to ask questions that suggest to her that she must have been a victim. This suggestion in turn can lead the client to reinterpret inaccurately recalled instances of benign behavior toward her as indicative of abuse, which can lead her to conclude that abuse occurred when it didn't—perhaps based on a fully reconstructed memory of such abuse. (pp. 31–32)

Other advocates of the false memory model have argued that the "heightened bond and increased dependence on the therapist" make the patient more suggestible (Ofshe & Watters, 1994, p. 113). In addition, they argue that the patient is overly suggestible because the patient is trying to give the therapist what he or she wants to know, to please the therapist, much like the experimental subject who responds to *demand characteristics* inherent in experimental situations (Ofshe & Watters, 1993, p. 10). Yapko has added that, because the patient is "uncertain" about the source of his or her distress and has a significant "need to know," the patient is apt to rely on the therapist to provide a frame of reference (1994a, p. 101).

Confirmatory Bias

Once introduced into therapy, fixed beliefs about suspected abuse may exert a continuous influence on the therapeutic process. Drawing on Dawes's polemical attack on the unscientific basis of most psychotherapeutic practices (1994), several false memory advocates have criticized what they believe to be a "*confirmatory bias*" operative in the therapist's mind (Ceci & Loftus, 1994; Lindsay & Read, 1994; Loftus, 1993; Yapko, 1994a). Loftus (1993) defines a "confirmatory bias" as a "tendency to search for evidence that confirms their hunches rather than searching for evidence that disconfirms" (p. 530). Kihlstrom speaks of the *tally argument*, i.e., the therapist only believes what tallies with his or her assumptions about the suspected abuse.

Whereas the confirmatory bias and tally arguments are usually made about psychotherapists who believe abuse has occurred when the patient fails to

report it, a comparable argument has been made when patients actually report or communicate suspicions of abuse to therapists. Frankel (1993) criticizes the "unquestioning acceptance" of these abuse accounts (p. 957). Lindsay and Read (1994) believe that it is a mistake for the therapist to avoid any expression of doubt about the patients' reports as if this would be harmful to the treatment. They feel that "unqualified acceptance" helps create a mind set in the patient that lowers memory monitoring criteria. Unless there is some "disconfirmation," the patient may unwittingly be cued that it is all right to guess about matters of uncertainty. Consequently, the patient will more readily confuse fantasy productions with factual memory than would normally be the case.

Therapists are not immune from the tendency everyone has to give added weight to information or arguments that support preexisting beliefs, and to discount information that contradicts those beliefs. The failure to understand how this tendency operates and to account for it when doing therapy contributes to false reports honestly believed.

Memory Recovery

Another central element of the false memory model is that *memory recovery* leads to false memories for abuse. The definition of memory recovery ranges from general to specific. Ceci and Loftus (1994) refer in general to "memory work" as the "royal road to false memory." Frankel (1993) refers not to a specific set of techniques as much as to a consistently narrow treatment focus, what he calls the "persistent encouragement to recall past events" (p. 954). Loftus and Ketcham (1994) speak of "the internal and external pressure to remember" (p. 25) and the encouragement "to stockpile memory" (p. 27). Yapko (1994a), likewise, addresses his concerns to "A therapist who hunts relentlessly for a hint of sexual abuse" (p. 18). Ceci (1994) criticizes therapists who "pursue their memory work in a persistently suggestive manner" (p. 47). Loftus (1993) believes that memory recovery techniques place the treatment focus squarely on memory reconstruction. She says:

> The therapist convinces the patient with no memories that abuse is likely, and the patient

obligingly uses reconstructive strategies to generate memories that would suggest that conviction. (p. 528)

Ofshe and Watters (1994) refer to any psychotherapy that assumes that current symptoms are caused by past experience as the "etiological model of therapy" (p. 47), and any attempt to focus on the past as necessarily suggestive, even though it may help the patient make sense (although not accurately) of the symptoms.

Specific Memory Recovery Techniques

Certain *specific memory recovery techniques* have been targeted under the false memory model. Ofshe and Watters (1993) address their criticism to the "extensive use of memory recovery techniques [like hypnosis, dream work, and guided imagery] . . . that encourage guesses, speculation and confabulation" (p. 9). Elsewhere, they describe "the process of helping the client imagine scenes of abuse," the outcome of which is to "effectively destroy the patient's ability to distinguish between imagined events and memory" (1994, p. 89, 108). Lindsay and Read (1994), likewise, say that "extreme forms of memory recovery therapy" like hypnosis, dream interpretation, guided imagery, journaling, and body memories "constitute an extraordinarily powerful suggestive influence" (p. 326). In his more recent work, Lindsay (1995) has come to the conclusion that "there is little need for prolonged and multifaceted searches for hidden memories" under any circumstances (p. 287). Yapko adds focus on body memories and past lives to the list of special memories recovery techniques. Loftus and Ketcham (1994) state the general false memory opinion that these methods blur the distinction between imagination and memory (p. 158). The trouble with these methods, according to false memory advocates, is that they are "potentially suggestive" (Ceci & Loftus, 1994), in that they encourage active exploration of fantasy and speculation in a context in which the criteria for distinguishing between fantasy and factual memories are unclear. Excessive use of these methods may increase the possibility that the patient will accept a false premise of abuse as factual.

Suggestive Therapy Procedures

Another dimension of the false memory model deals with "*suggestive therapy procedures*" (Yapko, 1994a, p. 41). Yapko, with extensive clinical experience in hypnosis, describes how the therapist's presuppositions function as indirect suggestions (p. 119). Sometimes therapists make outright "process suggestions" that allow patients to fill in the blanks (p. 105). Ofshe, whose background is in studying thought reform, talks about the effects of "explicit suggestions of abuse." He views memory recovery therapy as something akin to brainwashing, in that therapists sometimes resort to "more powerful persuasive tactics" (Ofshe & Watters, 1993, p. 15), including "interpersonal pressure and old fashion propaganda" (p. 7) and hypnosis. For Ofshe (1992) it is a *combination* of hypnosis and other "dissociation-inducing" techniques, coupled with the application of social influences, like interrogation techniques, that leads to false memory production, especially if the suggestions are "constantly reinforced" (p. 134). Patients are said to "internalize the idea of abuse, redefine their life histories around the idea, and to recast . . . identity" as abuse survivors (Ofshe & Watters, 1994, pp. 6, 15). Haaken and Schlaps (1991) likewise warn about the "enormous pressure to work on the incest" (p. 43).

Ofshe and Watters (1993) describe the stages of the false memory model: they start with the therapist's expectations. Then the patient is persuaded to agree that abuse probably occurred. Memory recovery techniques are introduced that encourage guessing and fantasy in memory. These memories are repeatedly verbalized until the patient accepts that he or she has been abused. Finally, the patient greatly embellishes and elaborates upon the memory and holds it with great confidence, even though the event never happened.

Advocates of the trauma accuracy position remind us that there have been virtually no scientific studies of suggestive influences in psychotherapy per se (Brown, 1995a). The entire argument is based on "indirect evidence" (Schooler, 1994) and so is quite speculative. Moreover, while the above arguments offer a lot useful hypotheses about suggestive influences in psychotherapy, there is as yet no consistent theory about how and under what conditions therapy may be suggestive. The problem with the false memory model is that it overstates the case.

The history of psychotherapy outcome research has undergone a similar process. Early research tried to show whether therapy was effective. Now it has become clear that simple "yes" or "no" answers satisfy simple minds but do not contribute much to our understanding of psychotherapy outcome. A more appropriate and accurate, but vastly more complicated, question is: what type of therapy is effective with what type of patient with what presenting problem in what context with what method and with what therapist? Likewise, a more appropriate question for the memory debate would be: what type of therapy conducted by what type of therapist matched with what type of patient in what kind of treatment relationship and in what context and using what specific techniques is more, or less, likely to contribute to the generation of false memories for abuse?

With respect to the specific types of suggestive influences the false memory advocates describe— beliefs, confirmatory biases, memory recovery techniques, and the use of suggestion and coercive persuasion—trauma advocates argue that there is little evidence that therapists' beliefs necessarily influence patients' beliefs specifically about abuse, although they may.

Moreover, when false memory advocates criticize the use of memory recovery techniques, especially hypnosis, they overstate the data (e.g., Ofshe & Watters, 1994, chapter 7), because the research has demonstrated that hypnotic procedures contribute very little to the variance of pseudomemory production, unless those techniques are used improperly. As we will see in chapter 10, most of the variance of hypnotic pseudomemory production is accounted for by two variables: (1) the trait of "hypnotizability," and (2) the therapy relationship as a social influence variable. Specific hypnotic procedures contribute very little to pseudomemory production. It is misleading and erroneous to say that hypnosis or hypnotic procedures necessarily contribute to the production of pseudomemories, any more than any other request for memory information does. Hypnotic procedures have a variety of uses with traumatized patients (Brown & Fromm, 1986) and are useful specifically for memory reconstruction, at least under certain circumstances (e.g., Gravitz, 1994).

Some researchers who are more favorable to the false memory position cite data supportive of the hypothesis that hypnosis contributes to false memory production. However, only about a quarter to a third of the surveyed therapists reported ever using hypnosis to recover memories (Lindsay & Poole, 1995; Poole, Lindsay, Memon, & Bull, 1995). Other false memory advocates say that indirect suggestions and coercive persuasion are operating in psychotherapy, but they offer no systematic descriptions of just how and to what extent suggestive influences actually operate. It is certainly true, however, that a confirmatory bias can play a role in psychotherapy, may influence the therapy process, and may even contribute to false memory production. But it is equally true that a confirmatory bias can operate for advocates of the false memory position, who work with alleged perpetrators and recanters and use their claims as evidence of false allegations of abuse. In other words, a recanter who now claims that abuse was simply suggested in psychotherapy may have been subject to other post-therapy suggestive influences through association with false memory advocates or in group meetings with other recanters. The argument of suggestive influences necessarily goes both ways. While it is certainly important to conduct careful scientific studies on suggestive influences in psychotherapy, it is equally important to conduct studies on suggestive influences operative in the false memory movement.

THERAPISTS CAUSE HARM

Another argument of the false memory advocates is that therapists who suggest abuse that never happened can cause harm to innocent parties, typically to family members when the alleged perpetrator is a family member. Some, however, have also argued that the emotional pain of memory recovery therapy is in itself harmful (Ofshe & Watters, 1994, p. 114). Dawes (1994) has complained that the consequence of "unwarranted assertions" about childhood sexual abuse can "weaken people's trust in their own autonomy" (p. 35) and "reinforce feelings of incompetence" (p. 184). Haaken and Schlaps (1991) warn that preoccupation with incest can foster overdependency and fixation upon the victim role, at the expense of enhancing self and relational development. Hedges (1994) warns that the counter-transference tendency to believe abuse memories as historically true diverts attention from recognizing and working through early transference patterns; readily believing the patient constitutes a "collu[sion] with resistance" (p. 80).

The primary complaint is that memory recovery therapists encourage patients to disclose their illusory memories of abuse to other family members and to confront their perpetrator in and out of court (Yapko, 1994a). As Dawes states, "Where is the evidence that simply learning to blame, or hate somebody is therapeutic?" (1994, p. 185). Abuse allegations have been made based solely on recovered memories without any corroborative evidence (Loftus & Ketcham, 1994). Yapko describes how "the alleged abusers' world goes up in flames with the first hint of accusation" (p. 26). The entire family is trapped in a conflict of loyalties, and often the family spins apart in different directions, with some members refusing contact or communication with other members. Yapko draws an analogy between a family falsely accused and losing a child to a religious cult. He asserts that "confrontation is not an absolute necessity for the recovery to take place" (1994a, p. 173). Kihlstrom (1993) likewise censures the trend in which, "these therapeutic processes are no longer confined to the consultant room: catharsis often involves confronting the parent or other figures who allegedly perpetrated the abuse." Ofshe and Watters (1993) claim that false memories produced by therapists "have devastated thousands of lives" (p. 4).

Some advocates of the trauma accuracy position do believe that confrontation with the alleged perpetrator is a necessary condition to recovery in that it holds the perpetrator accountable (Bass & Davis, 1988). Many advocates of the trauma accuracy position, however, concede that in the great majority of cases encouraging confrontation or relational cut-offs does more harm than good, because patients are often retraumatized in the process (Giaretto, 1976). Disclosure is never useful as an attempt to become more clear about memories, and premature disclosure is sometimes a resistance to therapeutic work. Most responsible therapists, therefore, are conservative about confrontations and cut-offs. In fact, one of the few available data-based studies on victims confronting alleged perpetrators of childhood sexual abuse found that "therapists did not advise or encourage early confrontation" (Cameron, 1994, p. 13). However, a limitation on family contact sometimes is clinically indicated in a malevolent family constellation where the patient's safety may be a primary question (Gelinas, 1995).

DISTINGUISHING BETWEEN TRUE AND FALSE REPORTS

It is very difficult to evaluate allegations of abuse based on recovered memories of abuse alone. Advocates of the false memory position criticize those therapists who readily assume that if a patient reports memory for abuse it must be genuine. They assert that our index for suspicion should be raised when therapists base their beliefs on questionable criteria such as: (1) the fact that the memory was prompted by external circumstances and does not involve conscious or direct recall (Yapko, 1994a), (2) the emotionality, confidence, and vividness of the detail of the memory (Lindsay & Read, 1994), and (3) the fact that the memory was retrieved using memory recovery techniques. How do we tell whether memories recovered and reported in these ways are genuine or fictitious? In addition, these advocates assert that it is erroneous to assume that there "must be some measure of truth in the allegations, even if they have been exaggerated or otherwise distorted" (Yapko, 1994a, p. 129). Kihlstrom (1993) says, "the vagaries of memory are such as to make it impossible to get at the truth by remembering alone," and Ceci and Loftus note that "there is no Pinocchio test" for recovered memories (1994, p. 356). Ceci (1994) and others have conducted research demonstrating that even experts on psychotherapy and law are unable to distinguish between genuine and false memory reports. Therefore, false memory advocates assert that such recovered memories should not be taken seriously unless there is independent corroboration (Frankel, 1993; Ganaway, 1995; Kihlstrom, 1993; Yapko, 1994a). In rebuttal, Harvey and Herman (1994) have stated that independent corroboration is often available, but is overlooked by false memory advocates. Price (1995) says, "False [in false memory syndrome] appears, though, to signify nonverification, rather than objective truth" (p. 289). It simply means that the evidence was insufficient to validate the allegation. Moreover, Pope (1996) reminds us that the diagnosis of a "false memory syndrome" implies that the abuse memory in question has been independently corroborated as false. Yet, advocates of the false memory position rarely offer any direct evidence other than hypothetical arguments of therapeutic suggestion to vindicate those saying they have been falsely accused of abuse. The demand for independent corroboration goes both ways.

Some extreme advocates of the trauma accuracy position do believe all patient reports for abuse without question. Most therapists, however, appear to agree that it is indeed difficult to tell, and they also assert that recovered memories for abuse early in the process of treatment are likely to contain a mixture of real and distorted elements (Brown, 1995a,b; Grand, 1995b). Spiegel and Scheflin (1994) correctly remind us that it is illogical to assume that the appearance of erroneous details necessarily makes the entire memory for the abuse false. They also remind us that those accused of abuse, when they are genuine perpetrators, usually vehemently deny the allegations. Denial of an allegation of abuse is no more or less credible than disclosure based on recovered memories.

In general, resolving the veridicality of a memory is not the primary or necessary focus of treatment. Clinicians see their role as helping the patient make sense of distressing symptoms and construct a "narrative truth," which might not correspond to historical truth (Spence, 1982). Nash (1994) argues that helping the patient make sense out of the memories for abuse has a certain "clinical utility," even if the report is not entirely true. The real problem occurs when the patient takes legal action or publically discloses abuse, thereby forcing the issue regarding veridicality.

POSITIONS IN THE FALSE MEMORY DEBATE

Memory scientists, clinicians, forensic experts, and families have become polarized over the false memory controversy. Judith Herman aptly notes that sexual abuse is a volatile issue that encourages people to take sides (1994). A glance at Table 2.1 will allow the reader greater appreciation of the rep-

TABLE 2.1
Positions in the False Memory Debate

EXTREME TRAUMA ACCURACY POSITION
Bass & Davis, 1988
Frederickson, 1992

MODERATE TRAUMA ACCURACY POSITION
Gelinas, 1983
Courtois, 1988
Briere & Conte, 1993
Terr, 1994
Herman, 1994; Harvey & Herman, 1994
van der Kolk, McFarlane, & Weisaeth, 1996
van der Hart & Nijenhuis, in press

EXTREME FALSE MEMORY POSITION
Loftus, 1993; Loftus & Ketcham, 1994
Underwager & Wakefield, 1990; Wakefield & Underwager, 1994
Spanos, 1994
Ofshe & Watters, 1993, 1994

MODERATE FALSE MEMORY POSITION
Haaken & Schlaps, 1991
Gardner, 1991, 1992
Frankel, 1993
Yapko, 1994a
Kihlstrom, in press

BALANCED POSITIONS
Off-center toward the trauma accuracy position
Nash, 1994
Brown, 1995a,b
Koss et al., 1995
Whitfield, 1995
Chu et al., in press
Pope & Brown, 1996
Reviere, 1996
Waites, 1997
Hammond et al., 1995, 1996
Off-center toward the false memory position
Lindsay & Read, 1994
Schooler, 1994
Bruck & Ceci, 1995; Ceci & Bruck, 1995
Schacter, 1995

resentative positions in this debate. Those scientists and clinicians who have written about the false memory controversy can readily be classified into one of several positions in the debate. Generally speaking, some favor the accuracy of recovered memories for trauma (what we will call the *trauma accuracy* group) and others their inaccuracy (what we will call the *false memory* group). Each side of the argument is represented by a more extreme and more moderate position. Use of the term *extreme position* is not meant to imply disapproval about the merits of that argument. As defined here, those representing a more extreme position rarely include evidence for both sides of the debate in their work, and they reach very strong and global conclusions. Those representing a more *moderate position* consider the evidence of both sides, are reserved about their positions, yet draw a conclusion that, as Steve Ceci has said is "off center" (Ceci, 1994) toward one side of the debate, yet favoring neither the trauma nor false memory side strongly. More recently, a second generation of memory scientists and clinicians have written fairly balanced accounts of the false memory controversy, which, while also off center, are not especially representative of either a trauma accuracy or a false memory point of view.

Moderate Trauma Accuracy Position

The *moderate trauma accuracy position* largely consists of scientists who have written extensively on the assessment and treatment of trauma. Gelinas (1983) first wrote about a "disguised presentation" of adult incest survivors and was the first trauma expert to draw attention to the link between the sequelae of incest and the diagnosis of posttraumatic stress disorder. Others since then have attempted to delineate the range of symptoms associated with incest (Briere & Conte, 1993; Brown, 1990; Courtois, 1988; Kendall-Tackett et al., 1993), and some have offered models of memory failure associated with trauma, i.e., full or partial amnesia for abuse (Briere & Conte, 1993; Harvey & Herman, 1994; Herman & Schatzow, 1987; Williams, 1994a,b). Van der Kolk, Brown, and van der Hart (1989) have translated Pierre Janet's work on how trauma affects memory and how treatment of trauma must entail memory processing, and they have applied this model to the treatment of severe dissociative patients (van der Hart, Steele, Boon, & Brown, 1993). Courtois (1992a,b) and Sachs, Frischholz, and Wood (1988) have written specifically about memory processing in incest survivors and severely disturbed dissociative patients, respectively, and van der Kolk (1993) has presented a neurobiological model for trauma memory processing. The assumptions of most of these writings are that (1) at least narrative memory for early trauma is sometimes unavailable to consciousness, (2) psychotherapy and

hypnosis can facilitate memory processing and retrieval, and (3) under normal circumstances a generally accurate memory representation of at least the gist of the traumatic experience becomes available, but not necessarily an accurate representation in every respect.

One example of the moderate trauma position that speaks directly to the false memory controversy is Lenore Terr's book *Unchained Memories* (1994), in which she reviews a number of detailed clinical and forensic case studies. Drawing on her earlier work with children who survived the Chowchilla kidnapping and who never forgot it, she argues that memory for the gist of trauma is largely accurate, though some distortions or false details are common due to the operation of psychological defenses like repression, denial, displacement, and dissociation. She also says that signs of trauma are sometimes more readily observable in trauma-specific behaviors, like unconscious behavioral reenactments, than symptoms. These behaviors imply an implicit memory for the trauma even though the explicit verbal content of the traumatic memory may not be available to consciousness, or, if it is, is often partial or fragmented. After presenting a number of very detailed cases of allegations of recovered memories for trauma, some of which she believes are accurate, some mixed, and some of which are largely inaccurate, Terr concludes "each case stands by itself though some memories are false, many more are true with false components, and some are altogether true" (p. 247).

Another example of the moderate trauma position is found in Judith Herman's book *Trauma and Recovery* (1992) and in Harvey and Herman (1994). They describe the posttraumatic response to abuse in terms of symptoms of hyperarousal, intrusion, and constriction, as well as damage to self development and disconnection in relationships. According to Herman, amnesia for traumatic experiences is a common clinical observation. Herman describes a phase-oriented model of trauma recovery in three stages: (1) safety, (2) transformation of traumatic memory, and (3) reconnection with self and others. Because false memory advocates have attacked Herman's use of the term "repression" (Herman & Schatzow, 1987), Harvey and Herman (1994) have subsequently clarified their position on memory for traumatic experiences. They criticize the false memory position for failing to acknowledge that memory for trauma is rarely an all-or-nothing phenomenon. Along a continuum, the clinical manifestations of traumatic recollections include: continuous recall, partial amnesia, and full amnesia (and delayed recovery) for the trauma. Regarding the accuracy of traumatic memories, they challenge the extreme false memory position, which assumes "that most if indeed not all delayed memories of childhood trauma are confabulations" (p. 296). Herman and Harvey believe that false memory advocates "have overlook[ed] the evidence from documented cases in which the reports of adults who remembered childhood abuse after a period of amnesia have been independently confirmed by abundant evidence," as in the Father Porter case (p. 296). In other words, they accuse false memory advocates of a confirmation bias. Their own view of memory accuracy is respectful of both sides:

> Instead, the most apt characterization of the adult survivor is a person who arrives at adulthood with some, but not all, memories of the abuse intact, and who at some point in time begins to confront and rethink the past, blending new memories with earlier ones, new assessments with alternative ones, gradually reconstructing a meaningful and largely verifiable personal history: a history that is patently "true" though never complete and never wholly accurate in all detail. (p. 303)

This position is consistent with a partial reconstructive view of memory.

Extreme Trauma Accuracy Position

The *extreme trauma accuracy position* is largely represented in the self-help book, *The Courage to Heal* (Bass & Davis, 1988), and in *Repressed Memories* (Frederickson, 1992). Frederickson makes a distinction between two types of responses to childhood sexual abuse—posttraumatic stress disorder and repressed memory syndrome (p. 40). According to her, *repressed memory syndrome* is defined as "no memory for the abuse or remembers but significant amnesia" (p. 40). She believes that repressed memory syndrome is "more specific to the long-term response to childhood sexual abuse than PTSD" (p. 40). Moreover, *recovered memory syndrome*, for her, is pri-

marily the outcome of sexual abuse, not physical or emotional abuse (p. 23). Repressed memory syndrome is said to be identifiable by a cluster of symptoms: (1) attractions, fears, and avoidance unexplained by the patient's history; (2) indirect indications of emerging memories through dreams, images, flashbacks, and bodily sensations; (3) the operation of dissociative processes; and (4) evidence of memory blanks and time loss. Frederickson believes that a number of factors predict repressed memory syndrome, including age, hypnotizability, "a positive family history of memory repression," use of dissociation, and a need to deny the abuse and maintain normalization of family relationships after the abuse. While repressed memory sometimes emerges spontaneously after many years, Frederickson advocates the use of a number of memory retrieval techniques, e.g., guided imagery, hypnosis, journaling, body therapy, art therapy, and emotional work, so that bits and pieces of retrieved memories for the trauma can be recovered until a "critical mass" of traumatic memory is reached and the patient overcomes a "crippling disbelief" that he or she made up the abuse. According to Frederickson, disbelief is an "indication that the memories are real" (p. 171).

Moderate False Memory Position

The *moderate false memory position* is represented by clinicians and memory scientists who have been concerned about overzealous therapeutic methods used with adults and investigative methods used in child sexual abuse investigations. Yapko's (1994a) book, *Suggestions of Abuse*, is representative of this position. While Yapko has used hypnosis extensively in the treatment of trauma survivors, and believes that repressed memories do exist, he wrote the book to address therapeutic excesses, where therapists unwittingly suggest abuse to patients who have never been abused. He says, "But in our highest recognition that sexual abuse happens with shocking frequency, we have also created an environment that encourages a less that critical consideration of some of the most salient issues" (p. 26). In other words, a therapist's strong convictions that abuse had occurred in a client, in the absence of any memories for abuse, may substantially influence the unfolding therapeutic process and create false memory for sexual abuse. This occurs especially in the absence of any attempts to either disconfirm the therapist's own beliefs about the abuse or to seek independent corroboration. It especially occurs when such strong beliefs are combined with the use of memory recovery techniques. While Yapko acknowledges that psychotherapy and hypnotherapy may facilitate the retrieval of abuse memories, both in patients who know they were abused all along and in patients who were amnestic for the abuse for some period of time, he also makes it clear that in some instances therapists may suggest false memories of childhood sexual abuse, which may do harm to the patient and the family alike (p. 59).

Memory scientists like John Kihlstrom (1993) similarly believe that "exhumed memories" for childhood sexual abuse are often false—a product of the therapist's overenthusiastic use of memory recovery techniques that "promote confabulation" of memory, especially when the therapist strongly believes in the reality of the childhood sexual abuse and demands uncritical acceptance in the patient. Without "independent corroboration, there is no 'litmus test' that can reliably distinguish true from false memories" (Kihlstrom, 1994a, p. 337).

Frankel (1993) likewise asserts that "persistent encouragement to recall past events" (p. 954) in psychotherapy, combined with "unquestioning acceptance of the patient's report" (p. 957) in the absence of corroboratory evidence, leads to a remarkable increase in false memories in psychotherapy.

Haaken and Schlaps (1991), feminist psychoanalytic therapists, have specifically criticized so-called "incest resolution therapists" who focus too narrowly on recovery of sexual abuse memories at the expense of self and relational development. Such therapists are characterized by their "overconfidence in a limited set of clinical techniques and single-minded focus on sexual abuse in treatment" (p. 46).

A comparable moderate false memory position has been put forth by Richard Gardner, a noted child psychiatrist (1991, 1992). While he thinks that allegations of child sexual abuse within the family are often true, allegations of child sexual abuse that occur in the context of custody battles and in daycare and nursery settings are for the most part not credible. Gardner believes that false allegations of abuse in these latter settings are largely the result

of over-zealous child abuse investigations conducted by inadequately trained, and often incompetent, social service and law enforcement personnel, who use interpersonal pressure to obtain desired statements from frightened children.

The Extreme False Memory Position

The *extreme false memory position* is best reflected in the writings of Elizabeth Loftus, especially in her 1993 article in the *American Psychologist* and her book *The Myth of Repressed Memory* (Loftus & Ketcham, 1994). Based on two decades of laboratory research on eyewitness suggestibility (the misinformation effect), Loftus has attempted to demonstrate that misleading post-event information can significantly transform the original memory for an event. She has interpreted these research findings to mean that memories for nonexistent events can be "implanted" or "created" and that individuals can be made to accept and believe with a high degree of confidence false memories for events that never happened. While no research data on false memory creation in psychotherapy per se yet exist, Loftus has readily generalized her findings from eyewitness studies to psychotherapy.

Loftus's 1993 *American Psychologist* article is a clear position statement that false memories for childhood sexual abuse can be created in psychotherapy, and indeed are created with staggering frequency. The creation in psychotherapy of false memories of childhood sexual abuse, according to Loftus, is fueled by external sources of misinformation, including self-help books, survivor groups, and media statements, like the testimonials of Oprah Winfrey, Marilyn von Derber, and Roseanne Barr Arnold. In addition, false memories are fueled by *therapists' suggestive influences*, which include directly suggesting that abuse occurred based on vague symptoms, probing for abuse memories "relentlessly" with recovered memory techniques that blur the boundaries between fantasy and memory, use of hypnosis, and the uncritical acceptance of these manufactured false memories as fact. While Loftus is quick to assert that psychotherapy is useful for clients who always remember their abuse, she wrote her position paper to force the field, where recovered memories are in question, "to at least ponder whether some therapists might be suggesting illusory memories to their clients rather than unlocking authentic distant memories" (p. 530).

Underwager and Wakefield (1990) in *The Real World of Child Interrogations* and Wakefield and Underwager (1994) in *Return of the Furies: An Investigation into Recovered Memory Therapy* launch a twofold systematic attack on the "child abuse system," which they define in terms of child protective services that investigate allegations of abuse, and in terms of "recovered memory therapy" with adults. In both cases, they argue that child abuse investigations and recovered memory therapy in adults are not informed by logic or scientific research. According to Wakefield and Underwager (1994), the current child abuse system is exemplified by a "loss of freedom and reason" and thus a "return of the furies" of irrationality (p. 25).

Within the domain of child sexual abuse investigations, this irrationality is said to manifest itself in the remarkable proliferation of "false positive" claims. According to Wakefield and Underwager's Bayesian analysis, allegations of childhood sexual abuse must necessarily contain a high percentage of false claims. Thus, while the child protective services might have been originally designed to detect and reduce abuse, Wakefield and Underwager claim that the system itself has been abusive to many innocent parties who have become victims of false abuse allegations. Thus, a consistent focus of Underwager and Wakefield's (1990) work has been attacking the credibility of children's allegations of sexual abuse from both scientific and forensic points of view.

More recently, Wakefield and Underwager (1994) have described the irrationality of what they coin "recovered memory therapy." They never clearly define recovered memory therapy and loosely combine self-help and professional trauma treatment into the category of recovered memory therapy simply if memories of abuse are addressed in the overall treatment. They argue that recovered memory therapy "lacks scientific underpinnings." Moreover, they try to demonstrate that concepts such as repression, dissociation, PTSD, MPD, and trauma memory have not been modified or refuted by what they consider to be the "accumulation of disconfirming evidence" (p. 162). These unsupported concepts enable therapists to look for abuse where it does not necessarily exist and to implant false memories of abuse. According to surveys conducted by Wakefield and Underwager (1994), therapeutically suggested false memories of childhood sexual abuse fit a different profile from genuine memories of abuse. When the abuse memory is false, they claim, the reported abuse is said to occur at a younger age, to occur in the presence of witnesses, and to be characterized by unusual and deviant sexual abuse behaviors atypical of actual sex offenders.

The quality of the theories and writings of Underwager and Wakefield (1990) has been questioned by Salter (1991), who concluded that because Underwager and Wakefield repeatedly distort the data, misrepresent the findings of other studies, and examine the literature from a biased perspective, their conclusions are unreliable. In *Underwager v. Salter* (1994), Underwager and Wakefield sued Salter, claiming her criticisms of their work were defamatory. Judge Easterbrook examined the controversy and reached two important conclusions: first, Salter honestly believed her criticisms of Underwager and Wakefield to be true, and she had a mountain of evidence to support her conclusions. In fact, as the Court specifically points out:

> Psychologists Ralph Underwager and Hollida Wakefield have written two books: *Accusations of Child Sexual Abuse* (1988), and *The Real World of Child Interrogations* (1990). They conclude that most accusations of child sexual abuse stem from memories implanted by faulty clinical techniques rather than from sexual contact between children and adults. The books have not been well received in the medical and scientific press. A review of the first in the *Journal of the American Medical Association* concludes that the authors took a one-sided approach: "it may be that the adversarial system has so influenced this discussion [about child abuse] that objectivity no longer has value. The book contains almost 420 text pages and the authors cite over 700 references, but they do not really review this body of literature, they cross-examine it. When a given reference fails to support their viewpoint they simply misstate the conclusion. When they cannot use a quotation out of context from an article, they make unsupported statements, some of which are palpably untrue and others simply unprovable." David L. Chadwick, Book Review, in 261 *JAMA* 3035 (May 26, 1989).

* * *

. . . The monograph [by defendant Salter] is highly critical of the 1988 book and of Underwager's testimony. Like Dr. Chadwick's book review, the monograph states that the book misrepresents the studies, rips quotations from their context (and misleadingly redacts them), attributes to scholars positions they once held but have repudiated in light of more recent research, and ignores evidence contradicting its thesis. While Chadwick's indictment of the book advances conclusions but not the supporting evidence, Salter's is packed with details.

* * *

. . . Salter's view of the scholarly literature is congruent with Dr. Chadwick's, and all of the other reviews we could find take Salter's side rather than plaintiffs'. Sandra Shrimpton, Book Review (of *Accusations . . .*), 14 *Child Abuse & Neglect* 601–02 (1990); David L. Chadwick, Book Review (of *Real World . . .*), 15 *Child Abuse & Neglect* 602–03 (1991); Lenore Olson, Book Review (of *Real World . . .*), 37 *Social Work* 276 (1992); John E. B. Myers, The Child Sexual Abuse Literature: A Call for Greater Objectivity, 88 *Mich. L. Rev.* 1709, 1711–17 (1990) (discussing *Accusations . . .* and two books by other authors). Some judges have reached a similar conclusion. For example, the Supreme Court of Washington held that Underwager's analysis and conclusions are not accepted by the scientific community, making it appropriate for a trial judge to preclude him from testifying. *State v. Swan*, 114 Wash.2d 613, 655–56, 790 P.2d 610, 632 (1990). See also *Timmons v. Indiana*, 584 N.E.2d 1108 (Ind.1992) (sustaining a decision to limit Underwager's testimony severely). Cf. *Daubert v. Merrell Dow Pharmaceuticals, Inc.*, — U.S. ——, 113 S.Ct. 2786, 125 L.Ed.2d 469 (1993). It may be that Salter, the judges, and the book reviewers all err in evaluating the Underwager-Wakefield work. Scientific truth is elusive. Nothing in this record suggests, however, that Salter either knew that she was writing falsehoods or feared that she might be doing so but barged ahead without checking.

* * *

Underwager's approach has failed to carry the medical profession, but it has endeared him to defense lawyers. He has testified for the defendant in more than 200 child abuse prosecutions and consulted in many others. . . .

Second, the Seventh Circuit decided that the courtroom is no place to solve these scientific disputes. On this last point the Court said:

> Underwager and Wakefield cannot, simply by filing suit and crying "character assassination!", silence those who hold divergent views, no matter how adverse those views may be to plaintiffs' interests. Scientific controversies must be settled by the methods of science rather than by the methods of litigation. Cf. *Buckley v. Fitzsimmons*, 20 F.3d 789, 796–97 (7th Cir.1994). More papers, more discussion, better data, and more satisfactory models—not larger awards of damages—mark the path toward superior understanding of the world around us.

Nicholas Spanos (1994), a prolific researcher on hypnosis, advocates the position that recovered memories for childhood sexual abuse are the examples of the *social construction of reality*, produced through a combination of hypnotic procedures and social role-playing. He has argued that therapists teach patients to have memories for nonexistent abuse through a process of social learning, just as therapists teach patients to have multiple personality disorder, to believe and act as if they were hypnotized, to recount past lives, and to describe abductions by UFOs. Spanos, Burgess, and Burgess (1994) cite evidence of experimentally created past-life memories as examples of how social influence can result in the creation of "complex fantasy scenarios" in vulnerable people (p. 446).

In a similar sociological argument, Jeffrey Victor (1993) has written about the "psychotherapy hoax," in which therapists who are true believers about childhood sexual abuse and ritual abuse, along with the oral and written traditions of popular culture and mass communication, serve as the medium through which contemporary rumors and social propaganda about "consensually affirmed social anxieties" are disseminated throughout the culture.

A most outspoken advocate of the extreme false memory position has been Richard Ofshe, a sociologist who has conducted research on thought reform by governments and contemporary social groups (largely cults). Ofshe and Watters, in their article "Making Monsters" (1993), and a book by the same name (1994), see patients in therapy as "victims in training" (1993, p. 9)—victims primarily of therapists. Ofshe and Watters accuse therapists of misapplying their therapeutic influence through a combination of hypnotic and extreme social influence "to create grossly inaccurate memories." Ofshe and Watters say that they are addressing only "repressed memory therapists," and their citations on alleged recovered memory therapists include both self-help therapists and seasoned professional trauma experts (1994). "Repressed memory therapists" are defined as those therapists who concern themselves primarily with repressed trauma that is "entirely unknown and not even suspected when the client seeks treatment" (1993, p. 7), and who systematically persuade their patients, often by using memory recovery techniques and interpersonal influence techniques (Ofshe & Singer, 1994), that abuse occurred. Over the course of the treatment, patients come to reinforce and therefore maintain their false memories through rehearsal, elaboration, and positive feedback. According to Ofshe and Watters, memory recovery therapy is a kind of therapeutic "quackery," in which the innocent patient is transformed into a victim with an increasing conviction about false memories, and with increasing vengeance to painfully confront, or cut off relationships with, falsely accused family memories. In this sense, Ofshe and Watters liken the process of trauma treatment to a wide-scale process of thought reform or brainwashing, in which "tens of thousands of people" have become falsely "convinced that they have been harmed by abuse" (1993, p. 14).

This first generation of writings on the false memory issue have been very influential in shaping the current character of the false memory controversy. The emerging second generation of very recent or forthcoming articles represents a more sophisticated understanding of the complexity of the issues, in terms both of the memory research and of clinical practice.

The Second Generation

The second generation false memory position is best represented in the important recent articles by Lindsay and Read (1994) and Schooler (1994) on the adult false memory controversy, and by Steve Ceci on child research. Lindsay and Read's important paper in *Applied Cognitive Psychology* extends some of the criticisms of suggestive therapy found in Loftus's *American Psychologist* article, but is more cautious in its statements and conclusions. As memory scientists, Lindsay and Read carefully review research in the memory field pertaining to both the fallibility of memory and memory suggestibility. Like Loftus, they believe that psychotherapy can contribute to the "creat[ion of] compelling illusory memories [of abuse]." However, Lindsay and Read conclude that Loftus and some other advocates of the false memory position have overstated the problem and have "used an overly confrontational tone" in their attacks (p. 283), by implying that all or most memories of abuse recovered in therapy are not to be taken seriously because they are inherently a product of therapeutic suggestion.

Instead of a general polemic against psychotherapy characteristic of the first generation of false memory papers, Lindsay and Read are careful to limit their complaints primarily to poorly trained therapists and advocates of self-help manualized treatment of trauma victims, and not to seasoned and careful clinicians, because they believe that it is only the former, not the latter, therapists who excessively use memory recovery techniques. The authors' intention is not so much to attack the profession of psychotherapy as to inform therapists of what memory scientists know about suggestibility, so as to reduce the risks of two potential errors when working with patients with possible trauma histories: (1) missing actual abuse, and (2) creating memories of abuse that never happened. Lindsay and Read believe that "extensive use of memory recovery techniques" allows patients to confuse their own fantasies and accept therapeutic suggestions for actual events, especially under certain conditions, i.e., if the therapist (1) single-mindedly focuses on events that happened a long time ago, (2) has rigid beliefs about trauma, (3) is authoritative and has the patient consistently talk about possible abuse (memory rehearsal), and (4) uses extensive memory recovery techniques. The outcomes of this *constellation of suggestive influences* (p. 326) is likely to "lower decision criteria" so that fantasy and memory more easily become confused. They conclude:

> Our central argument is that extreme forms of memory recovery therapy constitute an extraordinary powerful suggestive influence that may lead some non-abuse clients to create illusory memories and beliefs of childhood sexual abuse. (p. 326)

The merit of the Lindsay and Read argument is its rejection of generalizations about suggestions in psychotherapy; instead they limit their discussion to a particular type of psychotherapy. They also provide a careful delineation of the complex conditions that must occur in therapy for that therapy to lead to false memories of abuse.

In a follow-up article, Lindsay (1994a) tries to "clarify [the] criticism of memory work in psychotherapy" (p. 426) in order to "reduce that polarization" (p. 427) that exists between memory scientists and trauma therapists around the false memory debate. Lindsay attempts to locate the debate within its wider historical and cultural context, noting that for centuries societies have ignored child physical and sexual abuse. He describes the 1970s and 1980s as a time of clinicians' "growing sensitivity" to childhood sexual abuse and concludes that:

> . . . it is not unreasonable to argue that some adult survivors of abuse would not remember the abuse and given that CSA [childhood sexual abuse] is associated with adulthood psychopathology, it is not unreasonable to argue that CSA might play a role in the psychological problems of clients who do not remember the abuse. . . . These reasonable and understandable ideas led to the development and promulgation of therapeutic approaches, techniques, and ancillary practices aimed at helping clients recover suspected repressed memories. . . . There is no reason to doubt that these techniques can enable people to recover accurate but long-forgotten memories of childhood traumas. Unfortunately, as explained below, there are many reasons to believe that these same techniques can also enable non-abused clients to develop compel-

ling but illusory memories and firmly held but false beliefs about CSA. (p. 429)

Lindsay goes on to carefully delineate the kind of therapeutic memory work that is at risk for creating illusory memories. He does not believe that a "few probing questions about CSA" will result in illusory memories, but he is suspicious of a "prolonged program oriented toward helping clients recover suggested repressed memories" (p. 430). While he agrees that laboratory studies on misinformation suggestibility are limited in their generalizability, he also believes that "approaches that include several [suggestive] factors . . . run a substantial risk of leading some non-abused clients to create illusory memories" (p. 432). A survey done by Poole, Lindsay, Memon, and Bull (1995) demonstrated that while the majority of professionally trained therapists do not conduct psychotherapy in an unduly suggestive manner, a "substantial minority" may (p. 433).

Schooler (1994), who has collaborated with Loftus on memory suggestibility research, acknowledges both sides of the repressed memory controversy. He begins by noting that some memories about abuse recovered in psychotherapy are probably real, while some are probably false. He does not think that there is a lot of scientific data in support of either side of the controversy. Therefore, he states that the controversy must be evaluated in terms of "*indirect evidence*" (p. 453), drawn largely from sources other than direct scientific study of suggestion in psychotherapy. Schooler believes that the sources of indirect evidence "converge" so as to offer some support to both positions. Genuinely traumatized individuals do sometimes forget the abuse and later recover their memory for it. Recovered memories for abuse sometimes can be corroborated. While not entirely accurate in all detail, these memories sometimes have "correspondence with actual abuse" (p. 452). On the other hand, patients are also quite capable of fabricating vivid fantasies in psychotherapy and then confusing them with actual memory. Once fabricated, these can easily be embellished. Schooler concludes that both positions have merit: "although the available evidence remains primarily indirect, there is nevertheless a reasonable foundation for the existence of both recovered and fabricated memories" (p. 465).

In a recent book, *Memory Distortion: History and Current Status* (1995), Schacter, an accomplished memory scientist, takes the balanced position that "memory is simultaneously fragile and powerful: memories are often ephemeral and distorted on the one hand, yet subjectively compelling and influential on the other" (p. 21). Unlike Loftus, however, who strongly emphasizes the "fallibility" of memory (1993), Schacter reminds us that "fortunately, memory operates with a high degree of accuracy across many conditions and circumstances" (p. 1). Yet, he believes that there is cause to take at least some of the false memory claims seriously because of extensive neurobiological, clinical, and experimental studies on memory distortion, including the studies on serious memory confabulation in some brain-damaged patients. While Schacter believes that false memories can be implanted in psychotherapy, he adds that "There is no hard scientific evidence that shows such a phenomenon unequivocally" (p. 28) and that "only a minority of healthy children and adults are prone to producing extensive false memories" (p. 29). Ultimately, Schacter hopes that future neurobiological research will clarify our understanding of serious memory distortion. He believes that currently available data implicate the role of the frontal lobes in memory distortion (Schacter, Kagan, & Leichtman, 1995).

A comparable balanced argument, informed by careful research, has been put forth by Ceci and his associates at Cornell University with respect to adults in psychotherapy, and to the suggestibility of children seen in psychotherapy and in child abuse investigations. In a paper co-authored with Loftus, "Memory Work: A Royal Road to False Memories" (1994) Ceci takes the central position that false memories of abuse are possible in psychotherapy:

> Specifically, we need to acknowledge the possibility that clients can be lead to co-construct vivid memories of events that never transpired; repeated suggestions, imagery instruction, journal writing, and trance inductions are potent psychological mechanisms that we are beginning to realize can lead to false memories. (p. 362)

As the title of the paper implies, the complaint about therapy is limited to "memory work," specifically to a set of so-called memory recovery techniques.

While the authors are careful to acknowledge that memories of childhood abuse recovered in therapy may be genuine, they believe that false memories of abuse in psychotherapy are "far from rare." They state that their argument is:

> not meant to claim that all accounts of incest that are recovered in psychotherapy are false, or that all suggestive techniques will inevitably lead to the creation of false memories . . . but that the creation of false memories is not just a cottage industry of memory researchers. (p. 353)

According to Ceci (1994; Ceci & Bruck, 1995), the problem comes down to numerators and denominators, i.e., the ratio of true to false memories recovered in psychotherapy. The dilemma for the psychotherapist is to increase disclosure about genuine abuse while decreasing false memory production, so as not to cause harm either way. While acknowledging that it is very difficult to obtain statistics on base rates about genuine and false abuse memories recovered in psychotherapy, Ceci (1994) believes that the "data are off-center" (p. 6), somewhat in favor of the false memory position. He bases his belief on extensive studies he and his associates have conducted on suggestibility in children. His work is especially known for discovering high base rates of children's suggestibility when expectations are experimentally manipulated and misleading suggestions are systematically repeated both within and across multiple interviews. The conclusion of his major APA address is balanced and fair to both sides:

> The majority of children are neither as hypersuggestible and coachable as some pro-defense advocates have alleged, nor are they resistant to suggestions about their own bodies as some pro-prosecutor advocates have claimed. Children can be led to incorporate false suggestions into their accounts of even intimate bodily touching, if those suggestions are made by powerful adult authority figures and delivered repeatedly over long periods. They also can be amazingly resistant to false suggestions and able to provide a highly detailed and accurate reports of events that transpired weeks or months ago. (p. 42)

As with other advocates of the balanced false

memory position, Ceci acknowledges the partial truths of both the trauma accuracy and the false memory positions and advances our understanding by refraining from a general polemic against therapy, and by limiting the argument to certain types of adult therapy and child abuse investigations conducted by certain interviewers who use a reasonably defined set of procedures in a systematic way.

Michael Nash, a practitioner and researcher on hypnosis, is representative of the balanced position (1994). With respect to suggestion in psychotherapy, he believes that clinicians and researchers alike need to give equal acknowledgment to two types of possible errors involving patients in psychotherapy—false positives and false negatives. False positives occur when a patient comes to believe that he or she was abused when it never happened. False negatives occur when a patient persists in the belief that he or she was not abused but abuse indeed had occurred. While the task of steering a therapy clear of both types of errors is indeed difficult, Nash, nevertheless, believes that there is a certain "clinical utility" to memory work with patients, in that the "construction of a compelling self narrative provides symptom relief whether derived from fantasy and/or memory" (p. 357). In other words, clinical goals and forensic goals may be somewhat incompatible. Memory work may be useful in the patient's clinical recovery, even if the memory is a mixture of fantasy and memory. The problem of memory accuracy becomes a problem only if the clinician and/or the patient fail to understand that all memory work in therapy is fallible, and especially if the patient pursues a course of action that may have legal consequences based on recovered memories alone.

Nash also correctly points out a logical error often made by advocates on both sides of the false memory controversy. Advocates of the trauma accuracy position are in error if they believe that recovering memories of actual abuse necessarily implies that therapy is not suggestive. Advocates of the false memory position are in error if they believe that emphasizing the suggestive nature of psychotherapy and the risks of false memory production necessarily negates the genuineness of all recovered memories for abuse.

Brown (1995a,b) critically evaluates the research on memory fallibility and memory suggestibility.

While acknowledging the partial truth of both the trauma accuracy and false memory positions, he argues that we must proceed with caution, especially with respect to memory suggestibility. He reminds us that there have been no direct empirical studies on suggestibility in psychotherapy per se, and that most of the research on suggestibility comes from other sources, especially the studies on post-event suggestibility with college students. While he believes the suggestion of false memories can occur in psychotherapy, whether or not it occurs depends on the type of suggestible influences in question and the context of suggestion. Suggestibility is the outcome of many interacting variables, which can be reduced to two main categories—trait variables and a variety of social influences. According to Brown, false memory production can occur in psychotherapy, but only under very specific conditions with a highly suggestible subject (trait) and/or a less suggestible subject who receives a particular type of interpersonal pressure, including techniques of interrogatory suggestion.

Brown criticizes the false memory position in that it oversimplifies the complex issues of suggestibility and overstates the case, as if all psychotherapy were unduly suggestive. Moreover, while bad therapy can cause false memories, Brown notes that such therapy should not serve as a justification for equally bad science. He observes that a lot of false memory arguments are highly speculative, not supported by data or by well designed research, and that premature, oversimplified, and overstated conclusions ultimately retard rather than advance our genuine understanding.

Koss, Tromp, and Tharan (1995) conducted an extensive and careful review of most of the available research on memory for negative emotional experiences, including the research on memory for shocking public events (flashbulb memories), the laboratory simulation studies on the effects of emotional arousal on memory performance, the laboratory studies on misinformation suggestion, and the field studies on victims' and eyewitnesses' memory. The value of the Koss et al. review is its succinct coverage of an entire field of memory research, along with its carefully considered conclusions. They make three general conclusions. First, with respect to Loftus's claims, they say, "Earlier characterizations of our most vivid memories as prone to error now appear unwarranted. . . . In fact, emotional memories have been characterized [in most research studies] as 'detailed, accurate, and persistent'" (p. 124). Second, with respect memory for traumatic experiences the research shows:

> . . . that memories for traumatic experiences contain more central than peripheral detail, are reasonably accurate and well-retained for very long periods, but are not completely indelible. (p. 111)

Third, with respect to memory suggestibility they say:

> This [Loftus's] conclusion appears to wildly overstate the strength of the evidence. Suggestiblity in emotional memories has consistently been lacking in studies of actual victims and witnesses of crime, who resist misinformation provided by the investigator and by the media. (p. 125) . . . The case for the suggestibility of real-life emotional memory to intrusions from postevent information is weak. (p. 127)

Chu et al. (1996) recently reviewed the available experimental studies on ordinary memory and on traumatic memory. They argue that the false memory position fails to take into consideration that "Traumatic memory is associated with psychobiologic features and cognitive characteristics that are quite different from ordinary memory." According to their understanding of the available scientific evidence, clinical and neurobiological studies strongly support the concept of "dissociative amnesia." They draw balanced conclusions, namely that trauma often results in "profound alterations of memory" in one or the other of two directions:

> . . . some studies suggest that brief or limited traumatization results in increased clarity or recall (hypermnesia), and a high level of accuracy concerning the central details of the experience. On the other hand, severe and chronic early traumatization may be correlated with denial, dissociation, and amnesia. Clinical studies have supported the existence of amnesia and recovered memories especially for severe and chronic childhood abuse. However, such memories also may be most vulnerable to distortion and errors in recall. (p. 2)

While it is clear that "horribly abused children do forget," it is less clear to what extent the memories they may later recover correspond to historical truth, especially since "the mechanisms and context of memory retrieval may have a profound effect in influencing the content of memory, particularly in susceptible individuals." Nevertheless, Chu et al. remind us that "despite the uncertainties concerning the processes of traumatic memory encoding and recall, recovered memories of severe childhood abuse cannot be dismissed out-of-hand." They, however, conclude that the false memory position on therapeutic suggestion is overstated. Their conclusion from the scientific studies on suggestion is that "There is little evidence that direct questioning about abuse per se, results in false memories of abuse" but that "certain kinds of interrogation" may, especially when combined with "regressive clinical practices."

In *Memory and Abuse: Remembering and Healing the Effects of Trauma* (1995), Charles Whitfield offers a comprehensive and fairly balanced rebuttal to "nine claims" of the false memory advocates (p. 228). While this book is essentially a clinician's response to false memory claims, he nevertheless has carefully and exhaustively reviewed the scientific literature on memory and suggestibility before framing his response. He asserts that advocates of the false memory position have failed to take into account that memory is "a complex, multilayered system" (p. 11). Generalizing from experimental data on normal autobiographical memory to traumatic memory fails to take into account that "traumatic memory differs greatly from ordinary memory." According to Whitfield, there are several important differences between ordinary memory and traumatic memory. First, with respect to encoding and storage, not all ordinary experiences are encoded and stored in memory, unless they are particularly meaningful. On the other hand, traumatic experiences "are nearly always encoded and stored" (p. 17). Second, although traumatic experiences are encoded and stored, "they are frequently forgotten" (p. 17). "Traumatic forgetting" occurs because the memory is "state-dependent" (p. 45). Whitfield reviews seven experimental studies, all of which demonstrate that "delayed memories are common among victims of childhood abuse" (p. 74). Third, traumatic memory, unlike ordinary memory, is usually accompanied by posttraumatic stress symptoms. Fourth, traumatic memory is not simply a verbal memory but is accompanied by behavioral, somatic, and visual dimensions.

Whitfield also reviews the evidence with respect to the suggestion of false memories in psychotherapy. He challenges Ofshe and Watters' claim that there are "thousands of documented cases of false memory syndrome," in that most of the supporting evidence is anecdotal. Many of these claims, according to Whitfield, represent "the most sophisticated guise of denial of abuse" (p. 66) in the form of "pseudoscientific" claims (p. 76). Nevertheless, Whitfield agrees that false memories can occur in therapy, although it is "rare" to encounter "completely untrue memories" (p. 11). He believes that the available evidence demonstrates that it is far easier to implant false ordinary memories than to implant false traumatic memories (p. 189). He says:

> Researchers are able to manipulate normal memory and implant false details into the minds of ordinary people under nontraumatic conditions of simple laboratory experiments, such as having them view pictures of traffic accidents or hear close relatives repeatedly falsify stories of their becoming separated from their parents in a shopping mall. However, it is hard to imagine that many thousands of therapists are implanting powerfully traumatic, state-dependent memories—with their accompanying painful symptoms—into hundreds of thousands of their patients or clients. Except under the circumstance of extremely abusive and inappropriate behavior by a helping professional, such as forceful seduction of a patient long term, or in other unusual circumstances, they cannot induce PTSD into them. (p. 49)

According to his reading of the available scientific data, he estimates that "92 to 99% of survivors are telling the truth and thus have real memories of having been abused" (p. 77), although some details may be "erroneous" due to the operation of psychological defenses (p. 217). However, mistaken details do not make the memory for trauma false.

He also questions the false memory claim that "there has been no independent corroboration of delayed memories" (p. 127). Available corroborative evidence that is sometimes available may include:

admission by the abuser; external corroboration (e.g., family members); witnesses; other victims; letters, diaries, and photographs; medical records; and internal corroboration (e.g., PTSD symptoms, traumatic reenactments, or certain characteristics of the memories).

Pope and Brown wrote *Recovered Memories of Abuse: Assessment, Therapy, Forensics* (1996) "to provide information and guidance helpful to clinicians, expert witnesses, and others when recovered memories are at issue" (p. 2). This book is written primarily for clinicians to help them "respond knowledgeably, competently, and effectively when they encounter clients who report recovering memories of child abuse" (p. 17). Rather than presenting a "fixed set of rote steps" for clinical practice (p. 17), Pope and Brown attempt to "identify significant concerns, suggest questions that might help . . . and present examples of research findings, hypotheses, and interventions relevant to the concerns" (p. 17). So that treatment of patients with recovered memories may be well informed by the available science, Pope and Brown briefly review the research on models and types of memory, memory retrieval, motivated forgetting, traumatic memory, and memory suggestibility (chapter 2). They also critically review the "evidence and logic" (p. 105) of scientific claims made about false memories. They warn against uncritically accepting false memory claims about a false memory syndrome until adequate validation studies have been conducted. In contrast, they argue that, while science offers a range of provocative findings, pseudoscientific and overgeneralized claims about false memories need to be replaced by an appreciation of the complexity of varying results, conflicting interpretations, and limits to the generalizability of the results. They add:

> However, these findings are not always in agreement, nor, in a sound science should they be. This requires careful reading and critical thinking by clinicians. (p. 64)

Ethical and competent clinicians, according to Pope and Brown, actively engage in a "process of scientific questioning" (p. 65).

Yet, while urging caution about false memory claims, they equally urge caution about the practice of trauma treatment. The book contains two chapters that address most relevant problems and concerns arising for the practitioner working with recovered memory patients, and an additional chapter on forensic issues arising with these patients. They discuss how the trauma therapist must avoid cognitive distortions or a premature cognitive commitment to abuse themes and must strive to develop critical thinking in order to conduct competent treatment. They advocate a well informed phase-oriented treatment protocol and discourage therapists from seeking external corroboration of abuse recollections, so as to avoid playing the dual role of therapist and clinical detective.

Several books have recently been written for clinicians that integrate the growing knowledge from the trauma/memory debate. Susan L. Reviere (1996), in *Memory of Childhood Trauma: A Clinician's Guide to the Literature*, shows an appreciation for the complexity of the human memory system. She views trauma as an event that disrupts memory networks and schema formation, resulting in "discrete, isolated pathways unintegrated and unconnected by a unified consciousness" (p. 79). Both repression and dissociation are processes that serve to fragment otherwise integrated memory processes. The goal of trauma treatment is integration. She advocates trauma treatment that represents "a balance of exploration and containment" (p. 126). Through her review of the literature on memory error and memory suggestion she concludes that treatment conducted around suspicions of trauma can best minimize false memories by avoiding "memory work" (p. 117) and "any form of repeated or coercive questioning" (p. 122) in favor of "nonleading exploration of the client's history, relationships, daily experiences, feelings, fears and the like" (p. 117). While any emerging memory may be the product of multiple distorting influences, she believes that "[t]hese constraints do not, however, preclude the truth of a client's essence" (pp. 107–108), and that memory research, except under conditions of suggestive interviewing, shows that the gist of trauma recollections generally are accurate even when the details are not.

In *Memory Quest: Trauma and the Search for Personal History* (1997), Elizabeth A. Waites writes about trauma treatment that is carefully informed by the currently available scientific research on memory. She warns about the misuse of data from

the memory sciences in "deliberate attempts to subvert memory" (p. 3). Agreeing that memory is fallible, she does not use this argument to debunk trauma memory. She says:

> It is also useful to keep in mind that reliability and usefulness of a memory do not require that either a memory or the person reporting it be perfect. (p. 15)

She believes that the "adversarial climate" created by the false memory debate places a special burden on trauma clinicians as well as on their patients:

> . . . most people who embark on the search for their personal past do not do so in an adversarial climate. The task before them is not proving the accuracy of their memories to the satisfaction of other people, but, rather, coming to terms with what they remember or what they don't. Autobiographical memory, like the self who bears witness to it, is a lifelong construction. When the search for the past becomes explicit or urgent, it may lead to troubling ambiguities and undecided questions. But can also lead to satisfying insights.
>
> The role of the therapist in such a search is not to function as an authoritarian arbiter or controlling decision maker. It is, rather, to supplement the skills and assets of the client with a specialized body of skills and training. The role of the therapist is not to tell the client what certainly happened in the past. It is, rather, to make it safe for the client to remember. (pp. 15–16)

Waites places herself strongly within the psychoanalytic tradition that emphasizes reconstruction of the past. But she avoids both extremes—that of dismissing all historical reconstruction in favor of a radically relativistic view of narrative truth, and that of naively accepting reconstruction as a reliable account of past trauma.

Waites demands that clinicians have a solid working knowledge of the complexity of memory that includes: the organization of autobiographical memory; the central role of self representation in memory; the nature of learned somatic responses; the role of fantasy, defense, and external social suggestive influences that distort memory; and the characteristic disturbances of memory subsequent to traumatization, in the form of dissociative disorders or implicit posttraumatic influences such as enacted behaviors, somatic reactions, and transference manifestations. While she agrees that it is very important for clinicians to gain knowledge of memory distortion and suggestive influences, she cautions against overgeneralization of the scientific data to construct the "myth of magical suggestion" (p. 218). Clinicians certainly need to be aware of the harm done by suggesting an abuse narrative to patients who were not abused. They need also to be aware of the operation of past and present social influences that have served to "subvert" the patients recollections about past abuse through the creation of either a false or distorted "cover story" that minimizes past abuse that really occurred.

The task of the clinician, according to Waites, is first and foremost "making it safe [for the patient] to remember" (p. 201), which has become difficult in this adversarial climate. Yet, she firmly believes that clinicians who shun exploration of the past may be doing their patients a disservice:

> An especially pernicious subversion is based on supposedly scientific arguments to the effect that clients should be discouraged from uninhibited explorations of their own minds, that therapists should dispute any reported memory that cannot be substantiated with objective, provable facts. This attitude misconstrues the basic premises of psychotherapy. In order to work effectively, psychotherapy must make the client more, not less, comfortable with exploring thoughts, even doubtful or troubling thoughts. (p. 214)

She believes that "[t]he difficulties in sorting out facts can be acknowledged without discouraging attempts to do so" (p. 158), especially where the patient's complaint involves a problem with memory. Rather, Waites believes that therapists have a duty to their clients to take on and tolerate the difficulties of this task:

> One effect of the sensationalized presentations has been to distract attention from the complexites of memory organization to simplistic evaluations about whether a particular memory is accurate or not.

Another is to replace reasoned debate about still unresolved questions with strident claims about what is or is not possible to remember. (p. 209)

With respect to the accuracy of the memory report Waites recommends that clinicians take the difficult road of tolerating the complexity of the memory report and carefully weighing the totality of the evidence:

> But therapists trained to understand the complexities of symbolic thinking are unlikely to accept just any idea that comes up at face value. Historical reconstruction always requires a careful matching of known facts with plausible hypotheses. In effective psychotherapy, any particular idea, whether labeled as a memory or a fabrication, must be considered in the context of everything else the client has talked about. (p. 276)

With respect to the therapeputic stance Waites sees the essential task to be enabling the patient to develop self-acceptance in a consistent narrative that provides continuity to personal history:

> The social reinforcement of any recollection affects how and how strongly it will compete in memory with previous versions. Affirmation validates the self as credible witness. Censure tends to create self-doubt and, sometimes, a revision of one's report. (p. 226)

As a therapist Waites helps the patient connect the memory and self representational fragments into a meaningful narrative. She reminds us that the false memory debate, by preoccupying itself with the issue of the veridicality of memory, gets derailed from the central therapeutic tasks of meaning-making and integration (p. 133).

Positions Adopted by Professional Associations

The American Medical Association

The American Medical Association Council on Scientific Affairs in 1994 prepared a "Report on

Memories of Childhood Abuse" in response to an earlier AMA Policy Resolution, which stated "the AMA considers the technique of 'memory enhancement' in the area of childhood sexual abuse to be fraught with problems of potential misapplication" (*AMA Policy Compendium*, Policy 515.978).

The Report was generated because of concerns "about the growing number of cases in which adults make accusations of having been abused as children based solely on memories developed in therapy. . . . Questions have been raised about the veracity of such reported memories, one's ability to recall such memories, the techniques used to recover these memories, and the role of the therapist in developing the memories." The Report acknowledges the sharp division in the therapeutic community concerning these volatile issues:

> At one extreme are those who argue that such repressed memories do not occur, that they are false memories, created memories, or implanted memories, while the other extreme strongly supports not only the concept of repressed memories but the possibility of recovering such memories in therapy. Other professionals believe that some memories may be false and others may be true.

The Report correctly accepts the false memory view that therapists, as trusted healers, can influence patients' memories of abuse, especially when therapists "advise patients that their symptoms are indicative—not merely suggestive—of having been abused. . . ." Repeated questioning may produce false reports of events that never occurred, but "the dynamics that underlie an individual's suggestibility are only beginning to be understood."

On the other hand, the Report also correctly notes that "research indicates that some survivors of abuse do not remember, at least temporarily, having been abused. . . . There are . . . instances in which recovered memories proved to be correct."

After recognizing that both sides have support for their positions, the Report states that, "While virtually all would agree that memories are malleable and not necessarily fully accurate, there is no consensus about the extent or sources of this malleability." Therapists are urged to use caution when working with memories and to adhere to the ethi-

cal standards contained in *The Principles of Medical Ethics*. When dealing with patients, they should be "empathic and supportive" and they should "address the therapeutic needs of patients who report childhood sexual abuse" because "these needs exist quite apart from the truth or falsity of any claims."

In a section on "Legal Concerns," the AMA blames court cases for the repressed memory problem by noting that numerous lawsuits have been filed against alleged perpetrators who will find it difficult to disprove the allegations, especially after the passage of time. The AMA, however, then notes that such confrontations by the victims against their perpetrators "might be deemed valuable in helping an abuse victim retake or reassert control of his or her life. Restoring control to the victim is a widely recognized part of therapy." The AMA concludes that "public policy may require standards of proof that must be met before allowing suits based on recovered memories to be filed or result in judgments against the accused."

The AMA Report reached two other conclusions. First, it amended Policy Statement 515.978 to read as follows: "The AMA considers recovered memories of childhood sexual abuse to be of uncertain authenticity, which should be subject to external verification. The use of recovered memories is fraught with problems of potential misapplication." Second, the AMA reaffirmed Policy 80.996, which dealt with the subject of "the refreshing of recollections by hypnosis."

Though the AMA Report is basically balanced, it has at least three serious flaws. First, the reaffirmation of Policy Statement 80.996, and the conclusion that it still "remains an accurate summary of the empirical literature," is mistaken. As will be demonstrated in chapter 10, the AMA's views about hypnosis and memory contained in that Policy Statement were not accurate when first published in 1985, and, based on the literature published since that time, are even less accurate today.

Second, the AMA Statement acknowledges its own severe limitations by noting that, "Neither the AMA nor the Council has studied other aspects of memory enhancement, such as amytal or age regression. . . . Rigorous scientific assessments of other methods of memory enhancement are not available." In short, the AMA issued its policy position without doing its homework, and by relying on its earlier inaccurate hypnosis conclusions. Failure to examine other methods of memory enhancement, which also flawed the 1985 hypnosis Statement, means that the AMA cannot with authority say that a false memory is an inevitable product of the inherent malleability of memory or involves the incorrect use of a memory enhancement technique.

Third, based on the failure to study memory and memory enhancement in wider contexts, the conclusion regarding legal cases is questionable. The AMA appears to have forgotten that a plaintiff in a civil suit or a prosecutor in a criminal proceeding has to meet the applicable burden of proof. While these cases are indeed hard to *disprove*, they may be even harder to *prove*. Thus, the legal system has already built into its procedures the protections mentioned by the AMA. Furthermore, by failing to have studied memory and memory enhancement in general, rather than specifically concerning repressed or recovered memories, the AMA's conclusion about extra-legal protections may have to be applied to *all* memory cases, and not just those involving repressed or recovered memory.

The American Psychiatric Association

One of the most balanced arguments put forth to date may be found in "The Statement on Memories of Sexual Abuse" by the American Psychiatric Association in 1993. The American Psychiatric Association Task Force wrote a statement for practitioners "in response to the growing concern regarding memories of sexual abuse." More particularly, the American Psychiatric Association was concerned "that the passionate debates about these issues have obscured the recognition of a body of scientific evidence that underlies widespread agreement among psychiatrists regarding psychiatric treatment in this area."

The Statement begins by validating the "severe negative consequences of childhood sexual abuse." It acknowledges, fairly, that it is very difficult to distinguish memories of genuine abuse from memories of suggested abuse. It also, correctly, acknowledges that some patients with corroborated abuse may include false and inconsistent elements in their memory, and that such distortions do not imply a false memory. Moreover, the report fairly acknowl-

edges that "memories can be significantly influenced by questioning" and that a psychiatrist must necessarily take a "neutral stance." Otherwise, a "strong prior belief, or disbelief can lead to suggestions of abuse, or invalidate actual abuse respectively."

The Statement rejects the false memory position that memories recovered in therapy should be disbelieved:

> Many individuals who have experienced child abuse have a history of not being believed by their parents, or others in whom they have put their trust. Expression of disbelief is likely to cause the patient further pain and decrease his/her willingness to seek needed psychiatric treatment.

On the other hand, the Statement acknowledges the false memory position that:

> . . . clinicians should not exert pressure on patients to believe in events that may not have occurred, or to prematurely disrupt important relationships or make other important decisions based on these speculations.

Moreover, a treatment plan "should address the full range of a patient's clinical needs," which implies a more broad-based treatment than memory recovery techniques per se.

On the issue of repressed memories, the Statement rejects the Ofshe and Loftus false memory position that repressed memories are a "myth." Instead, the Statement notes that:

> Children and adolescents who have been abused cope with the trauma by using a variety of psychological mechanisms. In some instances, these coping mechanisms result in a lack of conscious awareness of the abuse for varying periods of time. Conscious thoughts and feelings stemming from the abuse may emerge at a later date.

In an important concluding comment, the Statement makes reference to the binding ethical obligations contained in *The Principles of Medical Ethics with Annotations Especially Applicable to Psychiatry* and notes that "psychiatrists should refrain from making public statements about the veracity or other features of individual reports of sexual abuse."

The British Psychological Society

Another balanced position in the debate has recently been put forth by the working party of the British Psychological Society (1995). Its conclusions were based on "investigat[ing] the scientific evidence surrounding the phenomenon of recovered memories" (p. 6). The task force carefully reviewed and critically evaluated the available scientific evidence in a number of areas pertaining to recovered memories of childhood sexual abuse: the nature of memory, the accuracy of normal memory, the reliability of recall of early childhood experiences, the mechanisms of forgetting, the possibility of false beliefs, the effects of memory recovery techniques, the beliefs held by therapists about recovered memories, and the claims made by the British False Memory Society. The working group took the position that the videotape-recorder view of human memory based on naive realism is "greatly mistaken" (p. 7) and that the preponderance of the evidence suggests that memory is "reconstructive" (p. 9). Regarding memory accuracy, the Society concluded that memory for significant events is "broadly accurate" (p. 3). As the report notes, "Normal event memory is largely accurate but may contain distortions and elaborations" (p. 29).

The Society also concluded that central details for highly significant personal events are likely to be remembered better than peripheral details, although sometimes even central details may be "drastically misremembered" (p. 9). While the group acknowledged that "under most circumstances" people can successfully distinguish actual from imagined events, "extensive rehearsal of an imagined event" (p. 10), post-event misinformation, and other forms of suggestion can alter memories. However, the Society warns that much of the research on memory suggestibility has to do with "compliance with the researcher's expectations, rather than genuine alterations in memory" (p. 10).

The group's position on long-term recall of childhood experience is that the scientific evidence demonstrates that no verbal autobiographical recall is possible for events occurring before one year of age. A fragmentary verbal memory is possible for certain significant childhood experiences between two and four years. The group acknowledges that memory for significant childhood experiences occurring be-

fore age four may be "reflected in behavior but remain beyond awareness" (p. 12) so that when recovered in adulthood the memory is likely to be fragmentary until a "frame of reference" and verbal narrative are constructed, however accurate or inaccurate they may be.

Significantly, the Society considered the false memory position on repression to be an "extreme position" (p. 6) and preferred to discuss the available scientific evidence for traumatic amnesia. They concluded that "forgetting of certain kinds of trauma is often reported" (p. 14), ranging from war trauma to childhood sexual abuse. The available evidence suggests "between one-third and two-thirds of people having periods of time when they totally or partially forgot the abuse" (p. 13).

Regarding the evidence for false beliefs of childhood sexual abuse, the working group felt that a distinction needs to be made between incorrect memories (event actually happened but some details are incorrectly remembered), false memories (event never happened), and false confessions. They make it clear that "a great deal of evidence" is available about incorrectly remembering details, but that there is "much less evidence on the creation of false memories" (p. 29) and that scientific evidence for the common occurrence of misremembered details about actual experiences (memory fallibility) cannot be used to support claims about false memories.

With reference to memory suggestibility, the working group concluded that individuals who are highly suggestible, as well as less suggestible individuals in response to waking suggestions by "authority figures" or to hypnotic suggestions, may create false memories (p. 14). They caution, however, that there is little evidence that "a few suggestive questions in therapy" lead to false memories. They point out that the phenomenon of false memories is different from forensic data on false confessions, in that false memories are believed and retained over long intervals while false confessions extracted through interrogation are not believed and are unstable. They note that "there is no reliable evidence at present that this [false memory] is a widespread phenomenon" (p. 3).

Next, the working group addressed the claim that false memories are largely a product of a therapist's rigid beliefs about abuse in patients who do not present with abuse. The group conducted a survey about beliefs of 810 psychologists in the society. They discovered that, while the great majority believed that the gist of recovered memories about abuse was accurate, most were also well aware of the possibility of creating false memories. Only a "negligible number . . . believed that recovered memories were always accurate" (p. 19). The "nondoctrinaire" nature of these beliefs led the group to conclude that there was little scientific evidence to support the hypothesis that therapists' beliefs about abuse significantly created false memories.

The group concluded with recommendations that therapists should be "open to the emergence of memories of trauma which are not immediately available to the client's consciousness" (p. 25), but also alert to the possibility of therapeutic suggestion. When a patient reports a memory "it is important for the therapist not to form premature conclusions about the truth status of a recovered memory" (p. 24).

Hammond et al. (1995) took a balanced position in their national task force report on hypnosis and memory, published by the American Society of Clinical Hypnosis. They recognized that differences exist between emotional or traumatic memory and normal memory, and they supported the existence of traumatic amnesia. They acknowledged that "memory (particularly for details) is imperfect, whether or not formal hypnosis is used" (p. 11). They emphasized that it is how someone uses questions and suggestions that is problematic in psychotherapy or in hypnosis, and they questioned the false memory position that hypnosis per se is inherently contaminating. They produced the first detailed guidelines for clinicians on the use of hypnosis with memory and with potential victims of abuse and revised the guidelines for the use of forensic hypnosis. Some of their recommendations included: educate patients about the nature and imperfection of memory and obtain formal informed consent before exploring memories; objectively measure individual differences in suggestibility; seek to establish neutral expectations; discourage confrontation regarding or disclosure of memories without independent verification; avoid patient involvement in potentially contaminating experiences such as group therapy or 12-step groups; and avoid uncritically accepting the veracity of a patient's memories ("We can believe in patients without necessarily believing everything they produce" [p. 38])

The task force (which included three of the seven living members of the original AMA panel, and which afterwards received the support of a fourth member) criticized the 1985 AMA report as outdated and reached different conclusions based on current scientific research: (1) "Hypnosis is not magical in facilitating hypermnesia, but with emotion-laden memories for meaningful material, we believe it likely that hypnosis has the potential to clearly prove helpful with some individuals" for enhancing recall (p. 15). (2) Hypnotic techniques may mildly increase someone's confidence in what is recalled *if* the suggestions used to convey the expectancy that there will be highly accurate recall. (3) Pseudomemories associated with the use of hypnosis appear primarily to represent a response to demand characteristics of experiments and not genuine alterations in memory. This panel concludes that contaminating effects on memory are no more likely to occur from the use of hypnosis than from many nonhypnotic interviewing and interrogative procedures. Therefore, legal rules that single out hypnosis for restrictive treatment are unwarranted" (pp. 22–23).

The American Psychological Association Statement on Recovered Memories

The APA report is more tentative in its conclusions than the reports of the other professional societies, probably in part because of Recovered Memories Task Force consisted of three clinicians and three memory researchers, with each group representing very different—sometimes irreconcilably different—perspectives on some of the issues. For example, with respect to whether or not normal autobiographical memory and traumatic memory are seen as different memory systems, the committee says, "we cannot know." The committee felt that "the phenomenon of a recovered memory is rare" and that "most people who are sexually abused as children remember all or part of what happened to them." Nevertheless, the committee acknowledged that "Some clinicians theorize that dissociation is a likely explanation for a memory that was forgotten" and that dissociated memory "is for some time unavailable for retrieval." It adds, "Many researchers argue that there is little or no empirical support for such a theory."

With respect to the accuracy of recovered memory, the committee warned that "memory is not perfect" and a "variety of factors" contribute to the common inaccuracies of ordinary memory. Yet, they added that events "that are experienced directly" and/or "have strong emotional impact" are less likely than other events to be modified by suggestive influences. They add, however, that it is "impossible" to distinguish between true and false memories "without other corroborative evidence." Even though controversy exists about the accuracy of recovered memories, the committee felt that clients should still seek help from therapists when they believe that they have recovered memories of abuse. The committee felt that "The issue of repressed or suggested memories has been overreported and sensationalized" and that clients should not be discouraged from seeking treatment. The committee felt, however, that clients should seek treatment from licensed, well trained, and competent therapists who take an "unbiased position" with respect to the accuracy of abuse reports and who are "careful to let the information evolve" in treatment without suggestive influence.

Summary

What do the various statements of the professional associations have in common? first, all reject the extreme false memory position, which states that repressed memory does not exist. Second, all accept the false memory position that because therapists can have a substantial influence concerning the memories of their patients, therapists should be competent, cautious, and careful when working with memories, especially memories of childhood sexual abuse. Third, all urge therapists first and foremost to support their patients' mental needs without regard to the veracity of the claims of abuse. Fourth, all recognize that the political statements made by both sides in the debate have outrun, and often misrepresented, what the literature tells us. Finally, all urge continued study of the issues involved.

SATANIC RITUAL ABUSE

The false memory controversy is focused primarily on recovered memories of childhood sexual abuse,

but allegations of false memories implanted by therapeutic suggestion are not limited to childhood sexual abuse. While it is at least conceivable that false memories of childhood physical abuse or rape could be implanted, these types of memories for abuse have curiously escaped the false memory controversy. Other than childhood sexual abuse, the only other type of memory for abuse that has been a consistent focus of attention is that of ritual abuse. Ritual abuse (RA) is an extreme form of repeated abuse that combines intensely sadistic physical and sexual abuse with mind control techniques in the context of a tightly organized social, and sometimes familial, group structure. Ritualized abusive practices include multiple sadistic physical punishments, torture, mutilation, ritual sacrifice, and cannibalism—all organized around a shared religious or political belief system (Hill & Goodwin, 1989; Kahaner, 1988; Los Angeles County Commission for Women, 1989; Richardson, Best, & Bromley, 1991; Young, Sachs, Braun, & Watkins, 1991). Often these claims of RA add an additional element—the practice of devil worship, or Satanism. Satanic ritual abuse (SRA) claims appear to have been increasing in recent years.

Most of the case reports on ritual abuse come from two sources—adult patients with severe dissociative disorders who report memories for ritual abuse (Young et al., 1991), and children allegedly abused at home or in a daycare setting (Bybee & Mowbray, 1993; Faller, 1988b, 1990; Finkelhor, Williams, & Burns, 1988; Kelley, 1988, 1989, 1992, 1993; Snow & Sorenson, 1990; Waterman, Kelly, Oliveri, & McCord, 1993; cf. special issue on "Cult Abuse of Children" in the *Journal of Psychohistory*, 1994).

Reports of ritual abuse have become increasingly common since the middle 1980s. False memory advocates correctly point to two social trends that may partially account for this development. First, the publication of widely read books about sensational psychotherapy case reports may have fueled the imaginations of suggestible people. Books like *Michelle Remembers* (Smith & Pazder, 1980) and *When Rabbit Howls* (Chase, 1987), coupled with the presentation of these issues on talk radio and television, have undoubtedly created "copy cat" ritual abuse allegers.

The second factor influencing reports of ritual

abuse is the equally sensational forensic cases like the McMartin daycare case in California, the Country Walk daycare case in Miami, the "Cleveland crisis" in England, and similar cases in Scotland, North Wales, Belgium, Denmark, Germany, Ireland, and elsewhere (Pyck, 1994). One of the better known, and more controversial, occurrences was the Oude Pekala case in the Netherlands (Jonker & Jonker-Bakker, 1991).

Pyck (1994) describes the Oude Pekala case as beginning when two preschool-age boys told their parents that they had been sexually molested by strangers. Doctors found physical evidence for their allegations. Gradually, other children came forward describing additional instances of abuse. (Up to 50 children made allegations involving sexual games, pornography, sadomasochistic sexual practices, torture, and human sacrifice.) Critics soon gave media statements claiming that "mass hysteria" equivalent to the "witchhunts" was occurring, not sexual abuse. Myers, however, shows how the witchhunt analogy is misleading:

> Closer analysis reveals, however, that the analogy is flawed and misleading. In Salem, the women accused of witchcraft were, as a matter of objective fact, innocent. As far as we know, "real" witches do not exist. By contrast, many people accused of sexual abuse are, as a matter of objective fact, guilty. Unlike witchcraft, child sexual abuse exists. . . . The juxtaposition is misleading because it tempts readers to believe—incorrectly—that most accusations of sexual abuse are baseless. (Myers, 1994, p. 91)

Pyck's description of the unfolding events supports a very important observation—everyone close to the case, including the children, the parents, the police, the examining doctors, the psychiatrists, the outside expert brought in for a neutral evaluation, the district attorney, and even the Minister of Justice, believed the children were mostly telling the truth. Those who were not close to the investigation, such as media reporters, journalists, and outside mental health professionals, claimed that "mass hysteria" was the proper explanation.

The role played by the media was also studied by Pyck. He noted that the media adopted the "mass hysteria" view and excluded printing the evidence supporting the claims of the children. University experts on "mass hysteria" were quoted at great length. When the outside expert first entered the case, he was highly critical of the truth of what the children reported. The media quoted him and were favorably inclined toward him. As the investigation developed and evidence was accumulated, however, he became convinced that the children had not lied or spoken falsely. The media now treated him with derision. Factual accounts published by people inside the investigation were ignored by the media. Articles and books favoring the "mass hysteria" view were given high praise. As Pyck notes:

> Rossen's (1989) book is little more than an angry diatribe that is biased, poorly documented, and impossible to substantiate. Rossen indicates he spent more time in Minnesota discussing matters with Ralph Underwager than he spent on the spot in Oude Pekala. Nevertheless, the media is greatly interested in Rossen's book, and most journalists blindly accept Rossen's conclusion that Oude Pekala is a product of mass hysteria. The one-sided media coverage has its effect. . . . (p. 83)

The bizarre and extreme nature of reported abuses in these cases has made ritual abuse a prime target for false memory controversy (e.g., Ofshe & Watters, 1994, chapter 8).

As Putnam (1991) has said, "it is important to acknowledge that there is in fact a serious controversy within the child abuse community about the existence of satanic ritual abuse" (p. 178). On one side of the debate are those trauma accuracy advocates who find these ritual abuse reports for the most part credible, i.e., as reasonably genuine descriptions of extremely sadistic abuse (deMause, 1988, 1994; Feldman, 1993, 1995; Gould, 1987, 1995; Kelly, 1988; Mayer, 1991; Raschke, 1990). On the other side are those who find RA and SRA accounts to be entirely false, a product of therapeutic suggestion and/or social myth-making (Hicks, 1991; Lotto, 1994; Mulhern, 1994; Ofshe & Watters, 1994, Richardson, Best, & Bromley, 1991; Victor, 1993; Wright, 1994). Greaves (1992) has referred to these opposing views as the apologist and nihilist positions, respectively.

Those representing the *apologist position* take most ritual abuse reports at face value, as historically accurate, at least as examples of organized sadistic behaviors and sexual trafficking (Gould, 1987) and sometimes as examples of acts of organized Satanists or Satan himself (e.g., Smith & Pazder, 1980).

Ofshe and Watters (1994) have presented a clear example of the *nihilist position*, which is an extreme false memory position:

> The accounts of satanic-cult abuse are the Achilles' heel of the recovered memory movement. With no supported evidence, most reasonable people will eventually question the validity of satanic-abuse stories. . . . Repressed memory therapy promoters are boxed in another corner. If they admit that these stories of satanic abuse aren't true, they would have to admit that their therapy methods have produced false accounts that clients have mistaken for memory. (p. 194)

Note that Ofshe and Watters (1994) commit a logical error. Spiegel and Scheflin (1994) have criticized Ofshe's work based on its logical errors. Even if we assume that SRA does not exist, as Ofshe and Watters argue, the "recovered memory movement" would not be discredited. It does not follow that because patients can be led to believe one highly improbable thing, they must have been led to believe everything else, no matter how plausible. The fact that patient A has been led to believe falsely that she was a member of a Satanic cult that killed babies and drank their blood does not prove that patient B has been led to believe falsely that her long-buried memories of having been sexually abused by her father are accurate. Moreover, it does not logically follow that, if a patient falsely reports ritual abuse recollections, these were suggested in therapy.

Those who have addressed the history of demonic ritual practices are equally divided. Gould (1987), Hill and Goodwin (1989), Katchen (1992), Katchen and Sakheim (1992), and Nurcombe and Unutzer (1991) have tried to identify the basic elements and types of abuse characteristic of ritual abuse, and they have attempted to set ritual abuse within the wider historical context of Satanic rituals extending back to the fourth century A.D. These accounts typically emphasize the historical reality of Satanic ritual abuse.

On the other hand, Mulhern (1994), who has

also traced the history of demonic ritual practices, cites historical examples of SRA that were shown to be fabricated, i.e., "delusions" constructed by various social groups who imposed their political, theological, or psychiatric beliefs on highly suggestible individuals suffering from dissociative conditions.

A heated debate has occurred about the evidence supporting ritual abuse allegations. Those favoring the nihilist position do not believe that ritual abuse exists as an organized social practice, and they do not believe that any of the clinical reports of ritual abuse are valid. They emphasize the fact that physical corroborative evidence has not been obtained for most cases of alleged RA. Putnam (1991), a noted authority on multiple personality disorder, has stated that "there has never been a single documented case of satanic murder, sacrifice or cannibalism" (p. 175), although others have documented some cases (Feldman, 1995; Scammell, 1991).

Lanning (1991), the FBI official responsible for conducting ritual abuse investigations, agrees that the forensic evidence corroborating a "large-scale conspiracy" of ritual abuse by various organized social groups is largely lacking and that patients have described SRA events that may not have happened (p. 172). Lanning is skeptical of many of the SRA claims because of the "lack of physical evidence" (p. 172) and because if a large-scale conspiracy existed one would expect to find "mistakes" even if a cover-up were attempted. Lanning takes a "middle ground" by advocating "a continuum of possible activity" (p. 173). Because Lanning's work is often cited, sometimes incorrectly, we summarize his conclusions:

> I believe that there is a middle ground—a continuum of possible activity. Some of what the victims allege may be true and accurate, some may be misperceived or distorted, some may be screened or symbolic, and some may be "contaminated" or false. The problem and challenge, especially for law enforcement, is to determine which is which. This can only be done through active investigation. I believe that the majority of victims alleging "ritual" abuse are in fact victims of some forms of abuse or trauma. That abuse or trauma may or may not be criminal in nature. After a lengthy discussion about various alternative explanations and the con-

tinuum of possible activity, one mother told me that for the first time since the victimization of her young son she felt a little better. She had thought her only choices were either her son was a pathological liar or, on the other hand, she lived in a community controlled by satanists. (Lanning, 1992b, p. 39)

He acknowledges that whether or not evidence exists "depends on how you define the term" (1992a, p. 173). He reminds us that evidence for other organized practices of ritualized sex abuse, such as child pornography sex rings, is readily available. These multijurisdictional, and sometimes multinational, sex ring practices are characterized by multiple child victims and multiple offenders, the use of fear as a social control tactic, and bizarre or ritualistic elements (Lanning, 1992a,b).

Before continuing it is important to observe that most of the discussions on this subject have addressed the actual reality of RA and SRA. The evidence for and against has been hotly debated. There is another issue, however, that is equally as important, but which has been lost in the battles. That issue is whether it was reasonable for therapists in the late 1980s and early 1990s to believe that such practices existed. While the answer to the first issue might be negative, as false memory advocates claim, that does not automatically answer the second issue. We cannot definitively prove or disprove the first issue here, but we can address the reasonableness of therapists' believing that such practices have been occurring.

The accounts that stress the lack of evidence for either ritual murder or a conspiratorial social organization fail to cite important historical and contemporary evidence documenting instances of ritual murders. For example, the La Voisin scandal in France in 1680 documented numerous ritual murders of children by a mistress of King Louis XIV, Catherine DeShayes (Feldman, 1995; Raschke, 1990). Fifteen ritually sacrificed bodies were discovered in 1989 in Matamores, Mexico. They were part of a drug, pornography, and ritual human sacrifice group run by a known drug lord, Adolfo de Jesus Constanzo. The story is told in graphic detail by Pulitzer Prize winning journalist Edward Humes (1991) in his book Buried Secrets.

Other documented cases of ritual human sacri-

fice include the murders of Stephen Herd and Stanley Baker in Southern California in 1970, and that of Carl Drew in Massachusetts in 1979 (Feldman, 1995; Raschke, 1990; Scammell, 1991). Greaves (1992) has cited a police film of a human sacrifice in which participants devoured the liver of the victim. The story of a Satanic cult that engaged in ritualized murders, and the buried bones that were discovered, is told in Henry Scammell's (1991) book, Mortal Remains: A True Story of Ritual Murder. In Detroit two men were convicted of first-degree murder after police found the severed hand and finger of a woman in their refrigerator, and the rest of the mutilated body in their apartment (Hair, 1991). Cult murders were the subject of Colvin's (1992) Evil Harvest: The Shocking True Story of Cult Murder in the American Heartland, and Satanic killings are described in St. Clair's (1987) Say You Love Satan.

The McMartin daycare center case is paradigmatic of the polarization of positions around interpreting the available evidence. The Eberles' books debunk the evidence in the trial and see the McMartin case as a national witchhunt (Eberle & Eberle, 1986, 1993). On the other hand, Summit (1994) has pointed out that information contained in the children's reports may have been more accurate than could have been known at the time of the trial because a commissioned archeological excavation conducted after the trial discovered the tunnels and ritual abuse chamber that many of the children had reported.

False memory advocates have offered alternative explanations for ritual abuse allegations. Ganaway (1989) provides several possible explanations for these reports: (1) the reports are factual, (2) they are the result of dabbling in cult-like behaviors, but not the result of accounts of organized social group behavior, (3) they are screen memories, that is, symbolizations for intrapsychic conflict, and (4) they are the product of therapeutic suggestion. Ganaway believes that the therapeutic community should seek alternative explanations for these bizarre reports rather than to take them as statements of fact. He is strongly critical of therapists who believe their patients' ritual abuse reports, and thereby divert the treatment away from other, more appropriate clinical goals and toward a witchhunt. Lotto (1994) believes that ritual abuse allegations are the iatrogenic product of therapeutic suggestion with highly hypnotizable individuals.

Mulhern (1994), likewise, believes that ritual abuse stories are largely iatrogenic. She points to an informal network of self-help groups for trauma survivors, as well as workshops conducted by professionals on ritual abuse. These groups and meetings disseminate ritual abuse information to persons or patients who are highly vulnerable to suggestion.

The popular culture also supplies vulnerable people with suggestions for remembering ritual or Satanic abuses that never occurred. Apart from the unending grotesque displays on television talk shows, books like Smith and Pazder's *Michelle Remembers* (1980) and Chase's *When Rabbit Howls* (1987) also serve as sources for suggestions of victimization. Advocates of the iatrogenic hypothesis charge that therapists who readily believe RA allegations are enabling their patients to find external explanations for their distress instead of taking responsibility for their lives (Lotto, 1994). Coons (1994b) conducted a retrospective chart review of 29 patients in treatment for a dissociative disorder, which included their alleged Satanic ritual abuse. He noted that the frequency in Satanic ritual abuse allegations increased after a television show and a workshop on ritual abuse.

Jeffrey Victor (1993), who has conducted studies on how rumors spread, believes that the increased community panic about Satanism reflects wider social anxieties that inevitably accompany the disintegration of dominant cultural and familial values at a time of rapid social change. The spread of rumors about Satanism within a community reflect the process by which "urban legends" spread. Similarly, Hicks (1991) (cf. also Bromley, in Richardson et al., 1991) speaks of the spread of "subversion myths" when a community fears the "breakdown of social order" (p. 335).

The application of rumor theory to ritual abuse is part of a larger corpus of literature on the social construction of reality. In *The Satanism Scare*, Richardson et al. (1991) caution against viewing ritual abuse allegations as statements of objectively valid atrocities. They suggest that inquiry should focus on "Who makes the claims? Why are they making them? What do they say?" (p. 4). Their answer to these questions is that ritual abuse claims represent myths and legends constructed by contemporary social groups. In addition to alleged survivor accounts of ritual abuse, they identify four social movements that have contributed to the development of ritual abuse claims: anti-satanist television broadcasts by fundamentalist Christian groups, the anti-cult movement, the growth of satanist churches, and the abuse survivor movement. Elsewhere in the same volume: (a) Crouch and Damphousse describe how "cult cops" (i.e., police officers alleged to be overinvolved with cult investigations); (b) Victor how "moral crusaders"; (c) and Ellis how adolescent "legend trippers" (i.e., those who vandalize tombstones or churches and leave obscene graffiti) contribute to the spread of legends about contemporary Satanism.

Some advocates of the false memory position have extended the rumor hypothesis to the domain of psychotherapy. They accuse therapists who are true believers about Satanic ritual abuse of causing harm by "implanting" these bizarre and allegedly false memories of ritual abuse in a vulnerable patient population. This implantation may include not only the instilling of the therapist's beliefs about ritual abuse, but also the ratification of the preexisting beliefs the patient has acquired from books, television, or self-help groups.

Greaves (1992), however, identified the "post hoc, ergo propter hoc fallacy" of logic in the false memory position, i.e., "the erroneous assumption that that which appears earlier causes that which occurs later" (p. 45). This fallacy is replicated throughout the false memory literature, often hampering otherwise reasoned arguments. We will address the false logic of false memory in chapter 12.

On the other side of the debate, Bass and Davis (1994) see these reports of ritual abuse as largely genuine, but they admit that there may be some degree of distortion because the patient was often subjected to extreme pain or was drugged. Young et al. (1991) studied 37 adult RA patients over two clinical sites. They concluded that the descriptive features across all these cases were similar enough to constitute a distinct clinical syndrome, in which dissociation was a central feature. Young et al. question the reliability of the patients' reports, especially since many of the patients had read the same RA literature and many of the reports first appeared during or after hypnosis. However, they note that some corroborative evidence existed for some of the cases.

Faller (1994) reviewed the literature on ritual abuse. Most of the studies in Faller's review included a control group of children with histories of sexual abuse, but without allegations of ritual abuse. In all cases where comparisons were made, children alleging ritual abuse demonstrated more symptoms of trauma.

Van Benschoten (1990) asserts that patient reports of RA are often a mixture of genuine memories for abuse coupled with fantasies and distortions derived from the operation of defenses like dissociation and from post-event information derived from external sources. Van Benschoten warns of the dual dangers of not taking RA patients' accounts of abuse seriously or of taking them too seriously.

Kluft (1989a) concedes that "it is difficult indeed to know what to make of such accounts, because there is little hard data on which to rely," but warns that "forceful and ostensibly authoritative but grossly irresponsible statements on the basis of inadequate information" by either trauma advocates or false memory advocates serve only to retard our scientific understanding of the phenomenon. He advocates that we study the phenomenon more carefully before making premature statements in the media or in the courts. Greaves (1992), likewise, is critical of both the extreme apologistic and nihilistic positions in the debate. He argues:

> a better scientific methodology is needed to study the phenomenon, and until such a methodology is developed, there are still straightforward ways to assess the validity of the available clinical reports on alleged RA. (p. 47)

A consistent problem inherent in the Satanic ritual abuse debate has been the tendency to oversimplfy the issues and to assume that Satanic ritual abuse is a unitary, and drastic, phenomenon. Kinscherff and Barnum (1992) describe four different Satanic groups: (1) dabblers, (2) self-styled practitioners, (3) publicly acknowledged organized religions centered around Satanic worship and practices, and (4) esoteric Satanic cults, often associated with criminal activity. Greaves (1992) has identified at least five "diverse groups": (1) transgenerational Satanic cults, (2) neosatanic cults,

(3) groups organized around self styled charismatic cult leaders, (4) teen dabblers, and (5) solitary Satanists.

Hill and Goodwin (1989) have described a more detailed continuum of eight possible positions in the RA debate, from the most to the least skeptical about: (1) RA does not exist; (2) RA exists only as a projection of sexual and aggressive impulses; (3) RA exists only in the minds of those psychotic enough to believe it; (4) RA does not exist as an organized cult, but does exist as a contemporary remnant of ancient folk beliefs; (5) RA exists in isolated groups that engage in practices over generations that may be interpreted as RA; (6) RA exists as an organized secret witchcraft society which, in some form, has existed for centuries; (7) RA exists as part of a large conspiracy or secret cult; and (8) RA exists and Satan is a real entity. While the evidence for a large-scale conspiracy is very weak at best, they point out that organized secret societies that target vulnerable populations, such as the Mafia and the Ku Klux Klan, are neither unusual nor rare. According to Hill and Goodwin, most of the available evidence supports a position somewhere in the middle of the continuum.

Moreover, in more recent work, Goodwin (1993, 1994) has argued that the problem of credibility of reports of Satanic ritual abuse is largely the function of the term "Satanic ritual abuse." She correctly points out that many of the seemingly bizarre sadistic practices of so-called RA are not uncommon in sex rings, and that most of the extreme elements, like torture, mutilation, and even human sacrifice and cannibalism, are graphically described in Marquis de Sade's *The 120 Days of Sodom* (1789). She also notes that de Sade did not operate as an isolated deranged individual, but rather as a spokesperson for an extensive network of French aristocrats who engaged in sadistic sex ring behaviors. Therefore, she argues, when the term "Satanic ritual abuse" is replaced with the term "extreme sadistic abuse" these practices suddenly appear more credible.

Gould (1995), likewise, has pointed out that ritual abuse is often perpetrated by groups "deeply involved in organized crime" (p. 335), and that the motivation behind ritual abuse practices is often economic, i.e., to "create a group of people who function as unpaid slaves to the perpetrator group" (p.

335). Even informed skeptics, such as Ken Lanning of the FBI (1991), have advocated the use of the term "multidimensional sex ring." It is not so easy to dismiss the allegations of widespread ritual abuse organizations as totally fictitious in light of all that is known about child sex rings (Burgess & Clark, 1984) and the estimated one-half to one million children involved in child pornography including an estimated 100,000–300,000 boys under age 16 in the United States (Lloyd, 1976).

It is important to note that when some of the more extreme false memory advocates argue against the existence of Satanic cults, what they are really saying is that some of the *practices* alleged to occur in these cults do not exist. Baby killing, baby eating, blood drinking, and other ghoulish activities have been reported by patients. False memory advocates argue that these practices are inherently unbelievable. They then argue that because these practices are improbable, a belief in Satanic cults itself is naive.

Ross's (1995) *Satanic Ritual Abuse: Principles of Treatment* is an example of an integrative perspective on SRA reports. The books offers a complex multidimensional explanation for an equally complex phenomenon. He reviews historical evidence to show that secret societies have always existed. Human atrocity, unfortunately, also has a long history. Cults engage in human sacrifice in the name of religion. Ross reviews anthropological data on cannibalism and describes examples in Western history like the Spanish Inquisition, the Sect of Flagellants, the Cult of Assassins, the Illuminati, the Thule Society, and the Third Reich. He then reviews the contemporary literature on non-Satanic destructive cults in America. From this review he concludes, "Those who argue that there are no historical precedents for widespread Satanic ritual abuse and human sacrifice are mistaken" (p. 17). However, the real issue for Ross is whether Satanic atrocities are currently taking place.

According to Ross, there are five levels of SRA along a continuum: (1) isolated criminal deviants; (2) teenage dabblers; (3) noncriminal public Satanist churches; (4) Satanist practices associated with drug trafficking; and (5) multigenerational Satanic cults. With respect to multigenerational cults Ross concludes, "one must not forget that there is no objective public proof of the existence of such cults" (p.

70). Ross believes that the prevalence of SRA reports is best explained by understanding the logic of multiple personality disorder, since the great majority of SRA reports are made by patients with a DID diagnosis. Most DID patients have been abused and have learned to use extreme dissociative defenses against overwhelming experiences. The "central paradox" in understanding DID is:

> MPD is both real, in the sense that it is a serious illness, and not real, in the sense that there are not literally many different people living in the same body. . . . One has to empathize with the patient's inner world and work directly with the alter personalities as if they are separate people, while repeatedly defining explicitly for the patient that they are all parts of one person and need to be integrated. Concretely believing in everything as literally real will foster regression, dependency, evasion of adult responsibility, reinforcement of symptoms, and entrenchment in the sick role for secondary gain. Taking the opposite position of "skepticism" results in a flight into health, reinforcement of the patient's denial, or loss of the patient from therapy. These same principles should govern the therapeutic approach to Satanic ritual abuse memories. (pp. 79–80)

According to Ross, the therapist who uncritically accepts SRA reports confuses the structure and content of DID. Because of their extreme use of dissociative defenses DID patients:

> . . . have the most fragmented memories of anyone in our culture, and since they are highly hypnotizable, they are highly suggestible; this means that they must inevitably experience significant contamination of their memories from cultural sources, therapist expectations, and the media. Contamination of the MPD field with pseudomemories of ritual abuse is unavoidable. . . . The undeniable fact of false memories does not discredit either MPD or Satanic ritual abuse as a real phenomenon. . . . (p. 88)

Thus, the narrative memory of the person with DID is subject to a wide variety of contaminating influences, which might include therapeutic suggestion but certainly also includes the dissemination of abuse rumors through contemporary culture. Just as cultural forces determine the content of the delusions but not the structure of a schizophrenic illness, cultural trends determine the content of the recollections of the DID patient but not the structure of the illness.

According to Ross's four pathway model for SRA, these reports can reflect: (1) genuine historical accounts of atrocity; (2) distorted accounts of genuine abuse; (3) accounts that result from suggestive influences and cultural myths; and (4) accounts that are factitious. From his direct involvement in about 300 SRA cases Ross concludes:

> In none of these cases has the reality of the memories been objectively verified, and in several of them collateral history has proven that patient claims of Satanic ritual abuse were false. (p. vii) . . . My position is that 10 percent of the memories could be real. (p. 201)

Recently, Gail Goodman and her associates have described the first wide-scale attempt to scientifically evaluate the accumulating ritual abuse claims. Bottoms, Shaver, and Goodman (1993) found that of 2,292 alleged ritual abuse cases, 30% of the perpetrators in child cases and 15% of the perpetrators in adult cases confessed to abuse. In a more comprehensive survey for the National Center on Child Abuse and Neglect, Goodman et al. (1995) investigated the sources and characteristics of ritual abuse allegations in five separate studies.

The first study examined ritual abuse allegations in the context of psychotherapy. A total of 6,910 psychologists, psychiatrists, and social workers were surveyed and 31% reported that they had seen at least one or more cases of ritual abuse. Those respondents were given a detailed questionnaire about ritual abuse and about religion-related abuse (i.e., abuse in the context of fundamentalist and mainstream religious groups). Professionals across disciplines had generally seen on the average of three to four cases of ritual or religion-related abuse combined, although a small number of therapists had seen many more cases. The prototypical reported case included: devil symbols, excrement and blood, knives and candles, human and animal sacrifices, forced sex, and cult involvement accompanied by amnesia and a dissociative disorder. A very high pro-

portion of the cases had been diagnosed with a dissociative identity disorder. Allegations of ritual abuse by adults contained significantly more bizarre elements than child cases. Adult reports were of abuse that began earlier and ended later in childhood and that was more extreme than child cases. Ritual abuse cases generally involved a greater number of perpetrators (primarily male) than religion-related cases. Contrary to claims that ritual abuse allegations occur primarily in daycare settings, Goodman et al. Found that the most common setting for reported ritual abuse was parents' or relatives' homes, and secondarily, "cult locations" (p. 40).

Goodman and her associates also examined any corroborative evidence that was available. They classified the evidence into four categories: (a) testimony by eyewitnesses or other victims; (b) physical evidence such as ritual and Satanic paraphernalia; (c) admission by perpetrators; and (d) medical evidence such as scars or injury to sexual organs. Each category of evidence was assessed separately, as well as in a combined manner. They noted "the lack of evidence in many categories" (p. 44), so that the types of evidence needed to be combined to obtain statistically meaningful results. "The results indicated that, when the four categories of evidence were combined, child cases involved significantly more evidence than adult cases" (p. 44) and that these child cases "involved more physical evidence, more medical evidence, and more perpetrator confessions than adult cases" (p. 45). The type of evidence most frequently cited by respondents was bodily scars and Satanist paraphernalia like black clothing and devil symbols written on things. In an analysis of whether or not respondent clinicians tended to believe their patients' reports, Goodman et al. (1995) noted that clinicians' acceptance of their patients' stories as credible was "very high." They conclude:

> Thus, when the evidence involved in ritual abuse cases was examined in more detail, it tended to be ambiguous or to be reported by clinicians who were outliers on other variables. There was no hard evidence for intergenerational satanic cults that sexually abuse children. (p. 48)

A second study surveyed ritual and religion-related abuse allegations made to social service and law enforcement agencies, where the claims tended to be the subject of investigation. A total of 23% of 1,079 respondents from social service and law enforcement agencies reported that they had encountered one or more cases of ritual and/or religion-related abuse. The results of this survey in many respects were similar to the survey of clinicians and will not be repeated. With respect to corroborative evidence, the evidence for religion-related abuse was quite strong and often included medical evidence, other evidence of abuse or harm, and perpetrator confessions. Overall, the evidence for ritual abuse cases was weaker and was usually limited to bodily scars and ritual paraphernalia like Satanic symbols, books, costumes, etc. Only rarely were the ritual abuse cases accompanied by clear medical evidence of abuse (other than bodily scars), eyewitness reports, or admissions by perpetrators. Once again, regardless of the evidence, the respondents tended to believe the reports. Overall, Goodman et al. conclude:

> . . . the evidence for the child religion-related cases seemed particularly convincing. More of the religion-related perpetrators confessed their role in the abuse. . . . Evidence for the religious aspects of religion-related murders was often conclusive and publicly documented. This was not the case for alleged satanic cult-related murders. . . . Believers in ritual abuse assert that it has been occurring in the same fashion for generations. If the intergenerational view is valid, current reports by child and adult survivors should be quite similar because they are simply two views of the same phenomenon. Our data challenge that premise. (pp. 63–64)

The third study addressed the issue of "whether or not victims of childhood abuse can repress and later recover memories of early traumatic experiences" (p. 64). Goodman et al. wanted to know whether or not the characteristics of abuse and the corroborative evidence differed in self-reported repressed memory relative to nonrepressed memory cases. Of a total of 1,652 child and adult cases there were 44 repressed memory cases. There were only one child and 43 adult repressed memory cases. The evidence strongly suggests that children rarely forget abuse and later remember it (cf. Terr, 1988, 1994),

but that adults who are abused for significant periods of the childhood may later become amnestic for the abuse. A total of 4.5% of adults gave clear reports consistent with memory repression. Another 45% were "ambiguous" cases (p. 69). Overall, self-reported repressed memory cases involved significantly more severe abuse, more types of abuse, and more instances of multiple victims and perpetrators than non-repressed memory cases. The abuse was reported as occurring at a younger age and lasting for a longer duration of childhood in repressed vs. nonrepressed memory cases. Goodman et al. noted "the high proportion of MPD diagnoses in RM [repressed memory] cases . . . 68%" (p. 75). Moreover, the repressed memory cases were associated with significantly more overall corroborative evidence, specifically medical evidence, than the nonrepressed memory cases. However, "close examination of the evidence involved in RM cases indicated that the evidence clinicians reported was generally weak and ambiguous" (p. 77). Moreover, they note, "almost all of the physical evidence could be explained by factors other than satanic ritual abuse" (p. 81).

Goodman et al. conclude:

> Given the extreme claims associated with repressed memory cases (e.g., human sacrifice), one would expect that there would be more evidence of ritual or religious aspects of abuse in the repressed memory cases compared to the nonrepressed memory cases. Our findings indicated that repressed memory cases had more total evidence of abuse than nonrepressed memory cases. This finding is in line with the view that *although the ritual aspects of the abuse may not have been genuine, some kind of severe abuse may have occurred in a subset of repressed memory cases . . .* [italics added]. This means that the satanic ritual aspects of the alleged abuse were largely unsubstantiated. (p. 81)

The fourth study attempted to address where allegations of child ritual abuse might have come from—religious training, media, suggestion by authority figures, etc. The results demonstrated that "children have relatively little knowledge of satanic child abuse. . . . However, children's knowledge of satanic activities increased with age, as did their religious knowledge generally" (p. 95). Goodman et al. conclude:

The fact that children in this study lacked knowledge of satanic ritual abuse does not necessarily imply that children's reports of satanic ritual abuse are true. The findings do suggest, however, that children would be unlikely to make up such reports on their own. (p. 99)

Unfortunately, the study does not answer the central question as to how children develop allegations if they do not make them up. We are left wondering what portion of the overall variance of ritual abuse allegation is the result of genuine severe abuse experiences and what is the result of external suggestive influences.

The last study focused specifically on the religion-related abuse cases. Three types of cases were reported: (a) withholding medical treatment due to religious beliefs; (b) abuse associated with attempting to rid children of evil spirits; and (c) sexual misconduct by religious authorities. The great majority of the cases were sexual misconduct cases, and medical neglect and exorcism cases also often involved sexual abuse. The corroborative evidence for these cases was much stronger than for the ritual abuse cases.

Goodman and her associates drew a number of conclusions across all five studies. Their overall conclusion was:

Our results point to the possibility that some acts of child abuse which actually occur qualify as "ritualistic," but not that organized, intergenerational child-abusing satanic cults exist. Few people would deny the existence of pedophiles, sadistic killers, authoritarian religious cultists, or even practicing satanists. It would be surprising if these categories were *not* occasionally conjoined in a quasi-satanic mixture with serious consequences. A number of cases reported by our respondents contained realistic elements of brutality, some perhaps influenced by satanic themes, along with other seemingly unrealistic elements. (p. 116) . . . Concerning the difference in evidence between child and adult reports, it is possible that more adult than child claims are false. Alternatively, the lack of hard evidence may reflect the fact that adults are reporting abuse that allegedly occurred many years previously. . . . A large portion of clients in the ritual abuse cases, especially the repressed memory

cases, were diagnosed with MPD. Despite concerns in many circles of the high suggestibility of MPD patients clinicians who provided descriptions of these cases nevertheless believed in their clients' claims and were willing to accept ambiguous evidence as verification of the abuse. (p. 117) . . . We doubt that all of the allegations involved in the ritual cases were false. In fact, there may be some truth in the allegations. We are skeptical, however, that all of the allegations, especially those related to ritual features, were true. (p. 118)

The Goodman et al. (1995) study is important in that it is the first major scientific investigation of ritual abuse allegations. The results are mixed and in part favor both the credulous and skeptical positions in the debate about ritual abuse claims. On the one hand, the data strongly suggest that ritual and religion-related abuse reports are typically associated with very severe and often genuine abuse, albeit not always ritual abuse. On the other hand, the data also demonstrate that suggestion effects are clearly operative in some cases, especially those pertaining to highly suggestive individuals, namely, patients with major dissociative disorders. It is exactly in at least some of these cases that less corroborative evidence is available. Moreover, "a large portion of the evidence comes from a few clinicians" (p. 81).

It may be true that a few clinicians are overly zealous in looking for ritual abuse and are therefore overly suggestive in their treatment with such highly suggestible patients. Yet, we cannot readily conclude that these "outlier" clinicians have "caused" the ritual abuse allegations. An alternative explanation is that a few clinicians became "specialists" in ritual abuse simply because they were willing to see such patients when many clinicians were nervous about treating them. In other words, the beliefs of such specialists may be the *outcome* of their clinical observations of many ritual abuse patients, not the *cause* of the ritual abuse report itself.

Overall, the view taken in this book is that RA reports of patients may be mostly fictitious, a blending of internal and external sources, but sometimes mostly genuine (cf. also Van Benschoten, 1990). In most cases, these reports represent a mixture of fact and fantasy, derived perhaps from genuine and often extreme sadistic abuse by perpetrators, in more or less organized social groups or in loose family networks, but reported by a patient who is often prone to fragmentation and shifting states of consciousness, who easily confuses fantasy and reality, and who is highly suggestible. Thus, RA reports can neither be fully accepted at face value nor fully dismissed. These reports are rarely *entirely* a product of therapeutic or other external suggestive influences, nor are the reports devoid at times of significant suggestive distortions. Ritual abuse reports often begin with genuine and sometimes extreme abuse experiences that become embellished—internally due to the patient's need to develop an explanatory model for his/her extreme distress (Frank, 1961), and externally due to a variety of suggestive influences, of which psychotherapy represents only one source of suggestion. We refer to this as the *embellishment hypothesis,* although we acknowledge that with a highly suggestible population at least some of the allegations may be entirely false.

CONCLUSIONS

Unfortunately, the media and the courts have been the prime recipients of the overzealous amplification of a very young science. While the false memory advocates have argued that media coverage of recovered memories of childhood sexual abuse by public figures, such as Oprah Winfrey, Marilyn von Derber, and Roseanne Barr Arnold, may have been one source of influence that contributed to false memories in a large number of individuals (Loftus, 1993), it is also true that repeated public over-general statements about "scientific evidence" concerning memory fallibility and suggestibility is having

unpleasant consequences: it is causing real child abuse victims to hide their memories for fear of being disbelieved, it is making the arrest and conviction of child molesters and other sexual deviates more difficult, and it is making it more difficult for adult patients who recover memories of childhood abuse try to work these through in therapy.

The point is: no one wins if society conducts a media debate before the scientific evidence is accumulated. Likewise, no one wins by flooding the courts with allegations based on recovered memories of abuse or with allegations of malpractice against therapists who assist in processing these memories, when the evidence is *solely* recovered memories or scientific speculations about suggestive influences in psychotherapy, respectively.

So far, the media have given extensive coverage to three paradigmatic cases that depict both sides of the false memory controversy. The *Franklin* case in California is the first case of a murder conviction based mainly on recovered memory (MacLean, 1993; Spiegel & Scheflin, 1994). The *Joyce-Couch vs. deSilva* case in Washington and the *Ramona* case in California are the first claims for damages against therapists based on allegations of undue suggestive influences in psychotherapy where the plaintiff suing is not the patient.

A serious forensic problem in these suits is the fact that the result may turn on the testimony of expert witnesses who are more aligned with a political position than they are familiar with the evolving and complex scientific literature and clinical practice. The remaining chapters are designed to give the reader an in-depth understanding of the available scientific, clinical, and forensic evidence, as well as an appreciation of the complexity of the issues.

3

||||||||||||||||||

The Nature of Memory

In order to understand the nature of the false memory controversy, especially with respect to memory research on memory fallibility and memory suggestibility, the reader must have a working knowledge of the basic research questions and key concepts in the field of memory. This chapter is intended as a brief overview of the current understanding of human memory as it has evolved over the last century of scientific research.

A DEFINITION OF MEMORY

No single definition of memory could adequately represent the differing views of this complex human process. Suffice to say that, in general, memory represents the capacity to:

1. selectively represent (in one or more memory systems) information that uniquely characterizes a discrete experience,

2. retain that information in an organized way within existing memory structures, and

3. reproduce some or all aspects of that information at some future point in time under certain conditions.

THEORIES OF MEMORY REPRESENTATION

Trace Theory

An epistemological controversy has plagued at least a century of modern memory research. At the center of this controversy lies the question of whether or not a memory representation actually corresponds in any veridical way to the actual external stimulus event for which it has been created.

On one side of the controversy are advocates of some sort of *trace theory*. Trace theorists assume that the mental and/or biological representation of a given stimulus event is a more or less exact copy of a real event. Those on the other side of the controversy propose some sort of *constructivist theory* of how memory operates. Constructivists assume that the mental and/or biological representation of a given stimulus event is a more or less nonveridical representation of a real event. While the memory representation may preserve certain features of the stimulus event, it is by no means accurate. Often it contains some degree (perhaps a large measure) of erroneous information about the stimulus event.

The origins of the *trace theory* of memory are usually attributed to Richard Semon, although philosophers like Hobbes, Locke, Hume, and Moll all wrote about memory traces. In his book *Die Mneme* (1904) [*The Engram*, 1921], Semon defined the memory trace as an engram, and he saw it as "enduring through primary latent modification of the irritable substance produced by a stimulus" (p. 12). In other words, Semon believed that a given stimulus event acted upon the biological organism and produced a physiological transformation of some "irritable substance." The outcome of this biological change was the production of an engram, or a highly specific memory trace for a given stimulus event. According to Semon, each unique stimulus event results in the formation of a unique engram. Repeated stimulus events are stored as separate engrams, each time resulting in multiple traces for repeated events. An engram, once formed, becomes a kind of latent potential for excitation under certain conditions. During memory retrieval, or what Semon called ecphory, the engram becomes activated and becomes "manifested activity" in the form of remembering. The central assumption in *Die Mneme* is that a given stimulus event makes a highly specific and unique biological imprint, which is a veridical copy of the actual stimulus event, and that these imprints are stored as a permanent biological record of each and every stimulus event (Schacter, 1982).

From the turn of the century until the last two decades, trace theory was the predominant memory theory. Until the late 1960s, the tradition of laboratory research on human memory originating with Ebbinghaus in 1885 more or less assumed some sort of trace theory. Both Ebbinghaus's early meticulous experimental studies of memory for lists of nonsense syllables and the experiments by later memory scientists on interference tasks, serial learning, and the like (McGeoch, 1932) reflect the assumption that retention of learned materials in memory is generally accurate. In his review of the psychological significance of Semon's work in the field of memory science, Schacter (1982) argues that most laboratory studies on memory did not show much awareness of a possible discrepancy between a stimulus input and memory output until the 1970s. Then, in the context of the rise of modern information processing theory, memory scientists began to turn their attention squarely to the issue of memory fallibility.

Trace theory was given biological support in books like Donald Hebb's *The Organization of Behavior* (1949), and then later in the work of the famous British brain surgeon, Wilder Penfield (1958). Before removing certain parts of the brain in intractable epileptic patients, Penfield tried to determine the function of the area in question by electrically stimulating that brain area and asking the patient to give a report. Penfield discovered that free recall of what seemed highly specific and richly detailed memories for remote events, often minor events, were reported when certain areas of the brain were stimulated. As a result of his striking observations, Penfield made a compelling argument that the brain permanently and accurately stored *all* experiences. He assumed that if the greater portion of an individual's experience could not be remembered, it was simply a function of failure to establish the right retrieval conditions.

Within the domain of trace theory a controversy exists as to whether the memory trace is represented in the localized or distributed form (Schacter, 1982). Advocates of *localization theory* have tried to localize specific memory traces within a single neuron of the brain or within certain cellular substances like RNA. Gradually, this view received increasing competition from an alternate view, namely, that memory traces are represented in the associations established between networks of cells (Hebb, 1949). This latter view was made popular by Hebb and then later in Karl Lashley's critique of the classic trace theory "In Search of the Engram" (1950). In that paper Lashley critically reviewed the data around the question of localization of the engram. He concluded, in contrast to Penfield, that the data do not favor localization of the engram and that memory is a process of the interrelationships established across a large number of neurons.

While the "irritable substance" or presumed substrate of a memory trace remains a matter of controversy, trace theory was given further support in the pioneering tachistoscopic investigation of iconic memory conducted in the 1960s (Averbach & Coriell, 1961; Sperling, 1960). A tachistoscope is an instrument that allows the experimenter to present visual stimuli at very high speeds, in terms of thousandths of a second, i.e., faster than can be accounted for in terms of eye movements or even in terms of direct attention. Tachistoscopically presented visual stimuli, e.g., rows of letters, are a means to investigate preattentive factors in information processing (Neisser, 1967). The consistent and robust finding across many of these tachistoscopic experiments is that subjects continue to visually recognize the information for some period of time after the stimulus exposure has ended. This brief memory has been called *iconic memory*. And while conditions such as exposure and intensity of the visual stimulus affect recognition accuracy, it is nevertheless quite clear that stimuli presented above threshold are retained in the form of a brief iconic memory that rapidly decays after 100 to 200 milliseconds, unless reinforced by paying attention to it and thereby transferring it to short-term memory storage.

Neisser (1967), however, has characterized the epistemological assumptions operative in the tachistoscopic studies on iconic memory as a kind of *naive realism*. He says that these memory scientists believe:

> 1) that the subject's visual experience directly mirrors the stimulus pattern; 2) that his visual experience begins when the pattern is first exposed and terminates when it is turned off; 3) that his experience itself is a passive—if fractional—copy of the stimulus is in turn mirrored by his verbal report. All these assumptions are wrong. (p. 16)

Ironically, the same tachistoscopic experiments that sustained trace theory into the 1960s also helped to usher in a scientific revolution, the information processing revolution, and with the rise of contemporary cognitive sciences, trace theory began to give way to constructivist theory, which is now the dominant paradigm among memory scientists.

Constructivist Theory

The origins of constructivist memory theory are generally attributed to Sir Fredrick C. Bartlett in his seminal work, *Remembering: A Study in Experimental and Social Psychology* (1932). Breaking substantially both from the Ebbinghaus tradition of the study of memory through learning lists of nonsense syllables and from the dominant behavioral learning paradigms of his day, Bartlett set about to study the "normal processes of remembering" (p. 204) using a memory stimulus "closely resembling that commonly

dealt with in real life" (p.12). In other words, Bartlett pioneered research into memory for meaningful stimuli and was particularly interested in "social factors influencing remembering" (p. 95). Bartlett brought into the study of memory precisely those factors that Ebbinghaus tried to eliminate in the laboratory: meaning-making and socially shared remembering. He used as stimuli faces on postcards, simple symbols, and a story, "The War of the Ghosts," adapted from a Native American myth collected by anthropologist Franz Boas. Subjects were presented with the stimulus ("The War of the Ghosts") and told to remember it. They were asked to recall the story over successive intervals of increasing lengths. Bartlett found that the subjects rarely remembered the details accurately, although the general meaning of the story was retained reasonably well over repeated recall sessions. According to Bartlett, "accuracy of reproduction, in a literal sense, is the exception not the rule" (p. 93). Each version of the recalled story contained numerous omitted elements, imported elements and "unwitting transformations" (p. 61). Over repeated recall sessions subjects demonstrated "persistent transformation" of the story until some conventional or stereotyped general version remained.

In other experiments on serial remembering, Bartlett studied how stories and pictures were orally transmitted from one person to another. Again, the stories and pictures underwent numerous small changes as they passed from person to person, so that the final results bore little resemblance to the original material.

Bartlett's results stood in sharp contrast to the prevailing memory research of his time, in that his data explicitly addressed the *inaccuracy* of remembering. He criticized trace theory for its basic assumption that "The traces are generally supposed to be of individual and specific events" (p. 197). Instead, he interpreted the data as "a brilliant example of obviously constructed remembering" (p. 78). In contrast to the specificity of trace theory, Bartlett believed that most memory representations in individuals were rough approximations that capture the general meaning of the stimulus event at the expense of the accuracy of specific details:

> . . . an individual does not normally take such a situation detail by detail and meticulously build

up the whole. In all ordinary instances he has an overmastering tendency simply to get the general impression of the whole; and, on the basis of this, he constructs the probable detail. Very little of his construct is literally observed and often, as was easily demonstrated experimentally, a lot of it is distorted or wrong so far as the actual facts are concerned. (p. 206)

Arguing directly against trace theory, he says:

[r]emembering is not the re-excitation of innumerable fixed, lifeless and fragmentary traces. It is an imaginative reconstruction, or construction, built out of the relation of one attitude towards a whole active mass of organized past reactions. . . . it is hardly ever exact. (p. 213)

To explain the mechanism by which this general memory impression is formed, Bartlett draws upon Head's notion of a *schema* (1926) or "active organization of past reactions" (p. 201).

The essential disagreements between trace theory and constructivist theory can be summarized as follows: 1) relative accuracy versus relative inaccuracy in the memory representation as it corresponds to the original stimulus event; 2) highly specific versus general memory representation; and 3) subject as passive recipient who records an exact copy of the event versus subject as active constructor of memory representations.

Bartlett's pioneering research on the constructivist theory of remembering had little impact on mainstream memory research for the next 35 years, until Ulrich Neisser's modern classic, *Cognitive Psychology*, appeared in 1967. This book, along with J. J. Gibson's *The Senses Considered as Perceptual Systems* (1966), marked the beginning of the information processing revolution. Neisser (1967) begins his book with a flat rejection of trace theory:

The ancient theory of the eidola, which supposed that faint copies of objects can enter the mind directly, must be rejected. Whatever we know about reality has been mediated, not only by the organs of the senses but by the complex systems which interpret and reinterpret sensory information. (p. 3)

The key word here is *information*. Neisser does not believe that the memory representation is based upon reproduction of external perceptual features and attributes:

What is the information—the bone chips—on which reconstruction is based? The only possibility is that it consists of traces of prior processes of construction. There are no stored copies of finished mental events, like images of sentences, but only traces of earlier constructivist activity. . . . The present proposal is, therefore, that we store traces of earlier cognitive acts, not of the products of these acts. The traces are not simply "revived" or "reactivated" in recall; instead, the stored fragments are used as information to support a new construct. (pp. 285–286)

In a radical epistemological departure from naive realism, Neisser's neoconstructivist cognitive psychology replaces the engram with information as the basic element of the memory representation. The locus of the memory representation shifts from the external event to the actual process of reconstruction within the organism. Neisser is quite clear that the new cognitive psychology is a revival of Bartlett's theory of constructivism:

The present approach is more closely related to that of Bartlett (1932), than to any other contemporary psychologist . . . the central assertion is that seeing, hearing and remembering are all acts of construction, which may make more or less use of stimulus information depending on circumstances. The constructive processes are assumed to have two stages, of which the first is fast, crude, holistic and parallel, while the second is deliberate, attentive, detailed and sequential. (p. 10)

Neisser's *Cognitive Psychology* is essentially an application of this two-stage theory of information processing to visual perception, auditory perception, and the so-called "higher mental processes" of memory and thought. All of these processes follow the same two steps—a preattentive, global processing stage followed by a focal attentive, detailed analysis, and synthesis stage of information processing. While Neisser admits that the final chapter on memory was written primarily as an "epilogue" (p. 10) in a book that is largely devoted to perceptual processing, he nevertheless asserts that memory processing begins with a global construction of the gist of the stimulus event, followed by subsequent detailed elaboration of the memory.

In subsequent works, *Cognition and Reality* (1976) and *Memory Observed: Remembering in Natural Context* (1982), Neisser further develops his neo-constructivist theory specifically applied to memory. The implication of his biphasic theory of information processing for our understanding of memory is similar to the conclusion drawn by Bartlett decades earlier: namely, that remembered experiences are hardly copies of original stimulus events, and while the memory sometimes preserves the gist of the stimulus event in a more or less accurate manner, the total memory representation contains significant inaccuracies in detail simply because it was never an exact copy of the stimulus event in the first place.

Since the 1970s, neo-constructivist memory theory has become the dominant paradigm, at least within the circle of memory researchers (McClelland, 1995; Schacter, 1995), but not necessarily so in the wider field of professional psychology or broader popular culture. In a critical review, "On the Permanence of Stored Information in the Human Brain," Loftus and Loftus (1980) attempt to refute trace theory. As part of their argument they reanalyzed Penfield's data. Penfield electrically stimulated the brains of 520 patients, only 40 of whom recalled specific memories during the stimulation, and only 12 of whom recalled events that could be corroborated, although these remembered events seemed, a blend of reality and fantasy, more dreamlike than genuine memories (Loftus & Ketcham, 1994). Nevertheless, while the reanalyzed data were demonstrated not to offer strong support for trace theory, Loftus and Loftus wrote that the majority of psychologists persisted in their adherence to trace theory, even in the face of the advances in information processing theory.

The current false memory controversy is a more complex extension of the ongoing controversy between trace and neo-constructivist theories of memory. Yapko (1994a), in *Suggestions of Abuse,* used a Memory Attitude Survey to illustrate that therapists are ill-informed about the advances of memory research because a significant subgroup still believe that the mind actually stores events like a recorder. The implication of his survey, like the Loftus and Loftus review a decade and a half earlier, is that a

significant subpopulation of professional psychologists still favor trace theory over and against the constructivist paradigm dominant within the circle of memory researchers.

Our position is that neither trace theory nor constructivist theory is absolutely right or wrong, although certain types of data favor one theory over the other. It is perhaps no accident that trace theory exerted its dominance to the extent that simple stimulus events (like nonsense syllables, simple word lists, and brief tachistoscopic visual displays) were used as stimulus events. Constructivist theory exerted its dominance when meaningful everyday stimuli (like stories, personal experiences, and simulated or real eyewitnessed events) were used as stimulus events. There is ample evidence that the recall of normal, everyday personal experiences is largely reconstructed and is therefore subject to significant distortion of detail.

The critical question is whether or not memory for *traumatic* experience favors a trace or contructivist theory. And since there is little laboratory research data yet available on memory for trauma, it is simply premature to assume that memory for trauma favors a constructivist theory of memory, as is the case for normal personal memory. Trace theory persisted for nearly a century as the dominant model for simple stimulus information. Constructivist theory has more recently been in favor as memory sciences have turned to the more complex, meaningful stimulus material. It may turn out that neither theory adequately explains the nature of *traumatic memory.*

Some researchers have argued that trauma disrupts normal information processing. If traumatic material is processed differently from normal memory, it may not be subject to the same constructivist tendencies inherent in normal memory processing (van der Kolk, 1993). It may be equally true that at least verbal memory for trauma is quite prone to typical Bartlettian distortions as others have argued (Loftus, 1993).

Memory for trauma has not been sufficiently studied in the laboratory so that we can know exactly how it is processed. While the data accumulate, the reader needs to be informed of the context of a rather long and yet unresolved debate between two competing epistemological theories concerning memory representation. It is not yet clear whether a trace or constructivist theory best applies to trauma.

Brewer (1986) has argued that data on some types

of personal memory favor what he calls a *partially constructive theory* of memory. He believes the personal autobiographical memory (discussed in chapter 5) preserves the gist of the memory for important actions at the expense of less important details, which are reconstructed each time the memory is recalled. It is conceivable that a partially constructive theory might apply to trauma, where a traumatized individual preserves the gist of the traumatic experience but reconstructs, and thereby distorts, the details upon each recall.

A BRIEF HISTORY OF THE SCIENTIFIC STUDY OF MEMORY

Experimental Studies on Memory for Serial Learning

The first scientific studies on memory began with the work of Hermann Ebbinghaus in 1885 in his classic *Über das Gedächtnis* [*On Memory*]. Working within the context of association theory, Ebbinghaus designed a series of experiments to study memory for learned materials under controlled conditions. He decided to work on relatively simple stimulus material, the kind of materials that were not readily contaminated by meaningful associations based on previous experience. The nonsense syllables he used consisted of simple sequences of consonants-vowels-consonants. Ebbinghaus used primarily himself as a subject. He set about the task of memorizing list after list of nonsense syllables (over 833 hours) for a pool of 2,300 nonsense syllables, in order to understand how new associations developed in a nonsense list-learning task, relatively independent of the kind of meaningful associations that ordinarily develop when meaningful stimuli, like words and phrases, are used as stimuli. At designated points (retention intervals) after learning the list of syllables, Ebbinghaus tested his memory for the nonsense syllables. His concept of savings was defined either by the time saved when he relearned the previous list a second time, or by the savings in the number of repetitions required to relearn the previous test. Savings was a way to measure how much the memorized material was retained in memory.

These meticulous investigations resulted in the first major contributions to memory theory, mainly *theories of memory retention and forgetting*. Figure 3.1 reproduces the main results. Retention of the previously learned nonsense list in the form of savings is a function of retention interval, or the interval

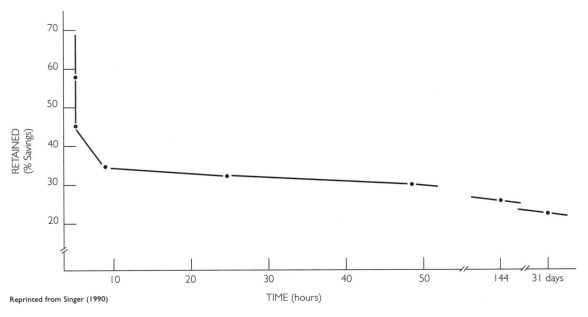

Reprinted from Singer (1990)

FIGURE 3.1
Ebbinghaus's Forgetting Curves

between originally learning the lists and the subsequent memory test. The now classic finding of these early serial learning experiments is the concept of "obliviscence" or *memory decay* and the graphic representation in the form of a forgetting curve as seen in figure 3.1. The striking discovery that Ebbinghaus made was that, at least for nonsense syllables, about 75% of the learned material was forgotten within 24 hours and that memory for the remaining material decayed rather slowly after that. Ebbinghaus saw these consistent and rather precise forgetting curves as representative of some general law of mental processes, specifically a law of decay for learned material. Ebbinghaus stressed that retention of list learning was a function of: the length of the list, the amount of practice, degree of forgetting, the time of day he learned the task, and the level of performance on the previous list. In other words, Ebbinghaus articulated some of the fundamental variables associated with encoding and learning.

Experiments in the early 1900s elaborated on Ebbinghaus's ideas. These experiments showed that the shape of the retention and forgetting curve is variable, depending on the nature of the stimulus material used and the mode of presentation. While Ebbinghaus presented the nonsense syllables to himself at a constant rate, subsequent research showed that the rate of presentation affected serial learning. When the nonsense syllables were presented slowly, they were better retained than when they were presented rapidly. This finding regarding rate stood up across a number of experimental studies using various stimuli from nonsense syllables, to digits, to words, to sentences, to poetry presented either visually or auditorially at varying rates.

Another important discovery was the "law of context." Robinson (1932) noted that learning serial lists was never entirely independent of contextual effects. He believed that the associations formed during learning the lists to some extent also included the context within which the testing occurred. Thus, some of the fluctuations in performance over time could be seen as the result of failing to reproduce the exact context of the original serial learning in subsequent learning trials. While the basic concept of memory retention and forgetting functions remained a robust finding across these experiments, the shape of the functions varied somewhat. The

new discoveries from these experiments concerned the great number of variables that affected retention and forgetting in serial learning experiments, and recognition that contextual effects also influence retention and forgetting.

The next major conceptual advance in memory theory was the development of the *interference theory*. Where Ebbinghaus and his followers dealt primarily with passive decay of memory, McGeoch (1932) began to investigate active interference with memory, as summarized in an important paper, "Forgetting and the Law of Disuse." Ebbinghaus, and shortly thereafter Thorndike (1931), had written that memory tended to fade away from disuse as time passed, unless the memory was remembered and rehearsed. In his paper McGeoch directly challenged that view. He used a paired-associate learning paradigm in which subjects learned randomly presented fixed pairs of stimulus items comprised, for example, of digits and words, like pen-4. He found that lists learned later interferred with what was initially learned. From these observations he developed the concept of *retroactive interference*. Forgetting was now reinterpreted as a function of active interference with learned associations made after the original learning.

In other words, interference is a function of learning new material between the time of the original learning and the subsequent memory test. McGeoch discovered that the degree of similarity between the original paired-associates and subsequently learned material significantly decreased retention and increased forgetting. Within this same tradition, one of McGeoch's students, Underwood (1948), popularized the concept of *proactive inhibition*, i.e., interference caused by prior competing learning. This began a series of detailed investigations into the exact mechanisms of memory interference. Thus, for nearly three decades, interference and the interference theory of forgetting became the dominant paradigm in memory research (Postman, 1961).

Following this experimental work on nonsense syllables and paired-associate learning, Murdock (1962) introduced a third experimental procedure, namely, free recall. Experimental subjects were given a list with a number of words on it to learn. Over a number of trials the order of words on the list was varied. The subject tried to recall as many of the words as possible in any order. Through such experiments Murdock demonstrated a *serial-position effect*. He discovered that the first of the words on the list (*primacy effect*) and the last few words on the list (*recency effect*) had a greater probability of being successfully recalled across trials than the middle words.

Naturally Occurring Memory

A fundamental assumption in nonsense learning, paired-associate learning, and free recall studies is that the stimulus materials necessary must be kept relatively simple under controlled laboratory conditions. Bartlett's classic book, *Remembering* (1932), broke sharply with the tradition of serial learning in that Bartlett sought to study "normal processes of remembering" (p. 204) by choosing complex, meaningful stimuli "commonly dealt with in real life" (p. 12), such as pictures and stories. As circumstances would have it, McGeoch's work on paired-associate learning and his interference theory were destined to become the primary focus of memory research for the next three decades. Bartlett's work on memory for everyday phenomena, largely overshadowed by those experimental paradigms, would remain in relative obscurity for the next half-century.

The cognitive psychology revolution in the 1960s and 1970s ushered in a radically different approach to memory research. Bartlett's work found a central place in Neisser's neo-constructivist theory of memory, first outlined as an epilogue to *Cognitive Psychology* in 1967, and then expanded into a general constructivist theory of memory in *Cognition and Reality* in 1976. Now that Neisser had rediscovered Bartlett's constructivist theory, it was simply a matter of time before Neisser and an entire generation of memory scientists rediscovered the value of studying the type of stimulus material that Bartlett originally used in his experiments. An evolving network of memory scientists turned away from laboratory learning paradigms involving simple stimulus materials and tackled straightforwardly the onerously complex task of studying memory for everyday experience.

The first manifestation of this revolution in memory research was a conference on "The Practical Aspects of Memory" (Gruneberg et al., 1978). Neisser's keynote address at the conference squarely attacked nearly a century of laboratory studies for their failure to address most of the areas of memory relevant to everyday experience. He concluded that the field of memory research needed to turn its attention directly to the study of everyday experience. Neisser noted that after almost a century of memory research, we knew almost nothing about memory for song and poems, memory for faces, names, and places, or memory for the personal experiences of our lives.

Neisser expanded these seminal ideas in his book, *Memory Observed: Remembering in Natural Context* (1982a), in which he argued in favor of taking the "low road" of "ecologically valid" memory research into the complex areas of everyday experience over and against taking the "high road" into simple laboratory investigations of learning functions for phenomena largely irrelevant to everyday experience.

By the second conference on "The Practical Aspects of Memory," held nearly a decade later in 1987, a variety of new experimental methods had been tested—those relying heavily on self-reports of experience, and those conducted in naturalistic settings or in simulated naturalistic settings. By then, an expanding number of memory scientists had mapped out the vast terrain of what Gillian Cohen came to call *Memory in the Real World* (1989). The new areas of memory research include such phenomena as:

1. keeping track of things versus absentmindedness in daily experiences;
2. memory for routine and novel actions;
3. memory for prospective future plans;
4. memory for places, objects, and events;
5. memory for people (names, faces, descriptions, characteristics);
6. memory for personal experience (autobiographical memory);
7. memory for significant public events;
8. memory for factual information;
9. memory for reading comprehension;
10. memory for conversation;
11. memory for world knowledge;
12. the development of memory in children;
13. the effects of stress, emotional arousal, and drug-induced states on memory performance;
14. the effects of suggestibility on memory; and
15. the effect of individual differences on memory performances.

In a relatively short span of about 15 years, the scientific study of memory had transformed itself from a laboratory science into an applied science and, as such, into a field in search of further applications—the newest area of application being psychotherapy. Whatever the outcome, memory scientists' recent fascination with recovered memories in therapy is quite clearly an extension of this trend toward becoming a valuable and significant applied science.

MODELS OF MEMORY ORGANIZATION AND PROCESSING

The research on serial learning inevitably led to concern with the amount of list information that could be memorized at any given time, i.e., memory capacity or *memory span*. The first important work on memory capacity appeared in the 1950s. Miller (1956), in his paper, "The Magical Number 7, Plus or Minus 2," presented data on retention as a function of the amount of information to be remembered. The greater the amount of information to be remembered, the less recalled. Miller's now classic interpretation of the results was that memory processing functions by organizing information into discrete "chunks" of information. He also argued that memory processing is limited in its capacity, and that humans can process roughly an upper limit of seven chunks of information at any given time. Improvement in memory performance is contingent on reorganizing the information so that more information is grouped into fewer chunks.

Miller's paper had two important consequences. First, it led to a productive line of research specifically on chunking (cf. Johnson, 1970). Second, it opened up a new conceptual dimension within the domain of memory research, namely interest in the organization of memory (Tulving, 1969; Tulving & Donaldson, 1972), although the conceptual foundations for memory organization had been laid some years earlier in the work of Gestalt psychologists on organizational principles in perception and thinking.

As experimental methods became increasingly refined and sophisticated within laboratory memory research, a method was developed to investigate the process by which forgetting a single item could be tracked over a short retention interval (Brown, 1958; Peterson & Peterson, 1959). This method is known as the *Brown-Peterson Method*. Subjects begin with some sort of preparatory signal, following which they are presented with the to-be-remembered material, usually a triad of consonants. The unique feature of the Brown-Peterson Method was the introduction of a distractor task for some defined interval after subjects were presented with the to-be-remembered material. The distractor task, e.g., counting numbers backwards, presumably prevented subjects from rehearsing the material. Following the distractor task, subjects were asked to recall some or all of the to-be-remembered material. Then, following some inter-stimulus interval, the procedure was repeated. In this manner, subjects could be presented with blocks of information to remember over many trials. The results demonstrated that, when prevented by a distraction task from rehearsing the learned material, subjects rapidly forgot the material.

The introduction of this new procedure stimulated an overwhelming amount of interest. Over 1,000 papers using some variation on this method appeared in the literature over the next two decades. Two key concepts emerged from the data: (1) memory is limited in capacity over short retention intervals, and (2) memory rapidly decays without rehearsal. The emerging interpretation of these data was the concept of a *limited-capacity, rapidly decaying short-term memory storage system*.

The seminal ideas—about organization of memory and about limited-capacity short-term memory storage—were destined to converge. What began to emerge by the late 1950s and 1960s was the now classic *structural model of memory*, i.e., the organization of a memory processing system into a number of independent storage systems. Broadbent presented the first major structural model of human memory (1958). He derived his model from his studies on dichotic or binaural listening. In a dichotic or binaural listening task, the subject is presented with different aural stimulus presentations in each ear at the same time, at a fixed rate of presentation, in order to measure memory performance while the subject is trying to attend to the information presented in both ears simultaneously (Cherry, 1953). Broadbent interpreted the results in terms of the subject's switching attention from one ear to the other during the task. Subjects learned to attend to one message while ignoring the other, much like attending to one conversation and not another at a cocktail party.

The central idea in Broadbent's work was the concept of a selective filter, in which attention acts likes a filter to select stimuli for further processing while ignoring other information. The concept of a limited-capacity, short-term memory processing system and a long-term storage system emerged from this work. Some of the information held temporarily in the short-term memory system is transferred to a long-term memory storage system. According to Broadbent, switching attention determines what is transferred and what is lost.

Treisman (1960) criticized Broadbent's model, in that it implies that information processing and transfer depends on switching attention on and off, as if attention were an all-or-nothing phenomenon. According to Treisman, attention control can be a gradual process. Information can be transferred to short-term memory (STM) or to long-term memory (LTM), according to the amount of attention given to it.

The other significant development in the early 1960s was the tachistoscopic investigation of high-speed visual display. Nearly the entire field of memory research prior to the 1960s had been devoted to the investigation of verbal memory following some sort of verbal learning paradigm. In sharp contrast to this tradition, researchers, notably Sperling (1960) and Averbach and Coriell (1961), began to focus on memory for visual stimuli. When subjects are tachistoscopically presented with an array of visual stimuli, like letters of the alphabet, at very high speeds (speeds faster than 200 milliseconds, which is the time required to direct attention to something), subjects typically recognize only a portion of the letters. However, if given a preparatory signal to attend to a particular subspan row of letters, subjects achieved almost 100% accuracy. Recognition of the targets decreases as the interval between the preparatory signal and the stimulus presentation increases.

Sperling (1960) and Averbach and Coriell (1961) used a similar procedure, except that subjects were asked to report a single letter after the preparatory stimulus. These studies were critical in the development of the concept of a transient sensory stor-

age system or *iconic memory system*. Incoming information is immediately stored in a transient sensory register in the form of an iconic (visual) or echoic (auditory) memory trace, which rapidly decays in 50 to 1000 milliseconds, depending on experimental conditions like the duration of the stimulus presentation, the luminance of the presentation, etc. (Neisser, 1967).

By the late 1960s a new model of human memory was emerging. This model was the synthesis of earlier concepts, like the organization of memory, the rapidly proliferating research on STM, and the work on the transient sensory register. Broadbent (1963) wrote an important paper on the flow of information within the organism. In 1967, Neisser published his now modern classic *Modern Cognitive Psychology*. Although this volume makes only brief mention of memory, it builds upon Broadbent's earlier work to present the outlines of a major theory, namely information processing theory. That same year, Murdock (1967) published an integrative review of the major research on STM, "Recent Developments in Short-Term Memory." After reviewing the main findings of nearly a decade of laboratory research on STM, he presented a "modal model" (p. 428), which synthesizes diverse findings. This model consists of: (1) an immediate sensory store; (2) a short-term primary memory store; and (3) a long-term secondary memory store. Attention to the information in the sensory register determines its transfer to its primary memory store. Rehearsal determines its transfer to the secondary memory store.

A year later Atkinson and Shiffrin (1968) published their seminal paper, "Human Memory: A Proposed System." This paper integrated all of the heretofore mentioned trends into a major theoretical formulation of an information processing of human memory. That model, known as *structural model of memory*, became widely accepted as the guiding theory of memory research, even though Atkinson and Shiffrin were quick to point out that their model does "not represent the general theory of the memory system" (p. 191), and that "the major contribution . . . lies in the organization of results and analysis of the data" (p. 191).

Like its predecessors, Atkinson and Shiffrin's is a multi-staged model, which integrates the previous work on the transient sensory register, the STM storage system, and the LTM system. Atkinson and

Shiffrin described three "permanent features of memory" or "memory structures" (p. 90):

1. the sensory register,
2. the short-term store, and
3. the long-term store.

Incoming information first enters the sensory register, which is not, however, unitary. There is also a sensory register for each modality of information, i.e., visual, auditory, etc. While most of this information rapidly decays, some may be transferred to the short-term store if attention is paid to it. The short-term store (STS) is limited in its capacity, in part because it receives information from both the sensory register and the long-term store (LTS). The STS is the working memory system. If information in the STS is rehearsed, it may be transferred to the LTS. Transfer is the process by which the selected information is copied into the LTS; while information is not necessarily removed from the STS in the process, whatever remains in the STS is likely to decay. Material transferred to the LTS is permanently stored. Central to Atkinson and Shiffrin's information processing theory of memory is the concept of bidirectional information flow from one memory structure to another (first described by Broadbent, 1963).

Another important feature of Atkinson and Shiffrin's model is their description of the various "central processes" that determine the flow of information from one memory structure to another. Central processes determine the "selection of particular portions of the information for transfer." Attention is a central process that determines the transfer of information from the sensory register to the short-term store. STS search processes and re-hearsal determine transfer to the LTS. LTS search processes determine how the sought for information is retrieved from the permanent store and transferred to the LTS, the conscious working memory system. Figure 3.2 summarizes the model.

While Atkinson and Shiffrin's structural model has remained the dominant information processing model of memory since its appearance up to the present time, alternate models have appeared. Craik and Lockhart (1972) developed their *levels of processing model* by reinterpreting the available data that supported the structural model. While they admit that the "box approach" characteristic of Atkinson and Shiffrin's multi-storage model has a certain intuitive appeal, they believe that the evidence accumulated since its appearance does not fully support it. More and more the data demonstrating the significant role played by central processes overshadow the data in support of independent and discrete memory structures. Craik and Lockhart review the three main sources of evidence used to support the existence of independent memory structures—limited capacity, distinct coding features, and forgetting characteristics. They argue that the evidence in favor of a limited-capacity STS system could be reinterpreted in terms of limited processing, not limited storage.

The structural model is based on the assumption that information is coded differently in the sensory register, STS, and LTS systems, respectively. Craik and Lockhart, however, argue that subsequent data have blurred this distinction. Moreover, the structural model presumes that each of the three structural systems is characterized by its own forgetting characteristics, e.g., decay in the sensory register and displacement in the STS, whereas Craik and Lockhart argue that the experimental data show

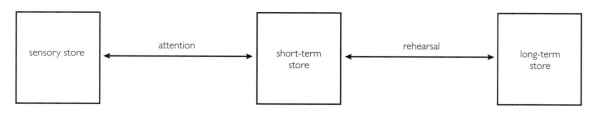

Reprinted from Atkinson & Shiffrin (1968)

FIGURE 3.2
The Structural Model of Memory Processing

such a wide variation according to differing experimental conditions that such clear-cut distinctions are not warranted.

In presenting their alternative information processing model, Craik and Lockhart assume that incoming information is rapidly analyzed at a number of different levels along a "continuum of analysis" from preliminary analysis to "deeper analysis" (p. 676). They describe three stages or levels of processing: *sensory analysis*, based on input processing; *primary memory*, based primarily on pattern recognition; and *secondary memory* based on stimulus elaboration. Persistence of the memory trace is a function of the depth of analysis, with deeper levels of analysis associated with more elaborate, longer-lasting memory traces (p. 675). While this model is similar to the structural model in many respects, in that both are information processing models, the levels of processing model does not necessitate the existence of multiple memory structures, nor does it require the transfer or flow of information between them. Moreover, the levels of processing model places a much greater emphasis than the structural model on the role of central processes like attention, rehearsal, and search in determining the nature and fate of the memory trace.

In their original paper, Atkinson and Shiffrin noted the virtual absence of experimental work on the search processes in the LTS system. To correct this deficit, a major focus of memory research in the 1970s, 1980s and 1990s has been on the LTS system. Various models have appeared depicting how information is stored and organized in the LTS. These models describe the architecture of the LTS system. The main controversy is whether or not verbal and visual information is coded separately in the LTS. Some theorists have presented data in favor of a dual coding model (Paivio, 1969), while others cite data in favor of a unitary coding model (Klatzky, 1975, p. 236). Many models for semantic encoding exist. In a review of these models, Klatzky (1975) demonstrates that they are similar in many respects:

1. The association model views the LTS in terms of networks of interconnected storage locations (Anderson & Bower, 1973; Brown & McNeill, 1966; McClelland, 1995; Quillian, 1969).
2. Set models view the LTS organization in terms

of sets of information (Meyer, 1970).
3. Semantic-feature models view the coding of information in terms of attributes or perceptual features.

While no single model explains all the functions of the complexity of the LTS, there is a consensus that the LTS is a highly organized permanent storage system. Synthetic models, which combine features of each of these models, have recently been described (McClelland, 1995).

MULTIPLE MEMORY SYSTEMS

An assumption made in many of the information processing theories of memory is that memory is a unitary phenomenon. With the plethora of LTS models appearing in the 1960s and 1970s, a new view emerged to challenge the unitary view of memory. Endel Tulving's (1972) classic chapter on episodic and semantic memory was the first significant challenge. Tulving argued from "the notion that memory takes different forms" (p. 385) and described two at least partially independent information processing systems, the episodic memory system and semantic memory system. According to his analysis these two systems differed along five dimensions:

1. the nature of the information stored;
2. the nature of the reference;
3. the way that retrieval affects the memory;
4. the degree of vulnerability to memory distortion; and
5. the relative dependence of each system on each other.

Episodic memory refers to memory that is temporally and spatially coded. Most episodic memory refers to unique personal experiences. Traditional laboratory studies on serial learning, paired-associate learning, or the Brown-Peterson Method, as well as contemporary studies on autobiographical memory, are examples of episodic memory, because all of these areas of memory presume temporal-spatial processing of information. Personal memories are always temporally dated. Serial learning tasks are always dependent on the relationships between lists and the time interval between presentation and recall. According to Tulving, these various examples of episodic memory always contain an autobiographical reference, in that they compare a single event to an existing memory database. Retrieval of memory from the episodic memory system changes the context of the memory. Episodic memories are very vulnerable to transformations and are readily prone to forgetting. Episodic memories are usually influenced by the semantic memory system, although sometimes they operate independently.

Semantic memory refers to memory stored in linguistic and symbolic form, each containing its own rules of operation. Examples of semantic memory include mathematics, chemical formulas, grammar and syntax of a given language, and facts that are not dependent on time or place. Semantic memories do not have an autobiographical reference; instead, they have cognitive reference, in that they refer to concepts, facts, interrelationships, or qualities. Semantic memory is always invented within some system of interrelationship. Semantic memories are not altered by retrieval and are much less vulnerable to transformation and forgetting than episodic memories. The semantic memory system functions relatively independently from the episodic memory system, but not vice versa. Tulving refers to the episodic memory system as the system of *remembering* personal experiences and the semantic system as the system of *knowing* and the transmission of meaning about concepts, words, and facts.

The second major challenge to the unitary view of long-term memory came from the work on implicit and explicit memory. Schacter (1992a, 1995) characterizes the 1980s as the period in the history of memory science that emphasized research on implicit memory. *Explicit memory* is defined in terms of conscious remembering of previous experience, typically measured by self-report, either by recall or recognition tests. The main feature of explicit memory is intentional retrieval accompanied by awareness. *Implicit memory* is defined as unintentional, non- conscious remembering, typically measured indirectly in terms of the influence of memory on task performance without awareness accompanying remembering (Schacter, 1992a,b, 1995). Jacoby and Witherspoon (1982), in their seminal paper on implicit memory, define it as "remembering without awareness."

The evidence for implicit memory comes from two sources: (1) task performance and (2) amnestic and normal individuals. Amnestics typically show a significant deficit on explicit memory performance, but no significant deficit on implicit memory tasks. Thus, while amnestics are unable to consciously report significant personal memories, they show an ability to learn new motor and perceptual skills, and sometimes even cognitive skills (Schacter, 1992a).

Normal individuals show the operation of implicit memory on indirect memory tasks. Typically, subjects are given some sort of task to learn, such as memorizing a list of target words or an array of visual stimuli. Sometime later they are given the same list or a similar list. These studies consistently demonstrate that prior exposure to the target stimulus results in enhanced subsequent accurate identification of the target, even if the subject shows no conscious awareness of having been exposed to the target previously. Many different types of experiments yield the same results—perceptual identification tasks, spelling tasks, sentence completion tasks, learning proper names, etc. Prior exposure is stored as an implicit memory that influences subsequent performance even if not accompanied by awareness.

While the evidence for implicit memory system is unequivocal, the interpretation of the findings is not. Some researchers (Tulving, 1972; Schacter 1992a,d) have argued in favor of a *dual memory system* or parallel memory systems (Squire, 1995). Others (Jacoby & Witherspoon, 1982) have interpreted the data in terms of differences in memory processing. According to Jacoby, postulating the existence of two structural systems is unnecessary. The difference between the explicit and implicit systems has to do with the level of abstraction at which information is processed. Explicit memory processes are experienced in terms of individual events, i.e., at a low level of abstraction. Implicit memory processes are experienced in terms of high levels of abstraction. Therefore, while discrete personal memory episodes are lost for amnestic patients, skills coded at a higher level of abstraction are not. In an attempt to integrate the two opposing views, Schacter (1992a) argues that the structure and process interpretations of implicit memory may be more complimentary than contradictory.

In an important paper, "The Evolution of Multiple Memory Systems," Sherry and Schacter (1987) integrate the work on episodic and semantic memory, and the work on implicit and explicit memory, into a general model of multiple memory systems. Proceeding from an evolutionary perspective, they present data from animal and human studies in support of the existence of two at least partially independent memory systems, roughly equivalent to Tulving's earlier distinction between episodic and semantic memory. Each memory system differs from the other in three significant ways:

1. the type of information it processes;
2. the rules of processing; and
3. possibly the brain systems that mediate it.

According to Sherry and Schacter, each memory system has a highly specialized function and each is "functionally incompatible with the other." The episodic system is designed for rapid single-trial learning, i.e., learning pertaining to specific situations. The semantic system is designed for gradual or incremental learning, i.e., the acquisition of habits or skills or "in variances across episodes" (p. 448). The differences between the implicit and explicit memory systems is essentially the result of dissociation between these two memory systems, seen most clearly in amnestic patients under the influence of certain amnesia-simulating drugs, and in normal individuals with certain types of task performance.

It should be noted that the implicit-explicit distinction is based primarily on performance of laboratory-based memory tasks and is not to be confused with the psychoanalytic notions of conscious and unconscious. Kihlstrom (1987) articulates the distinction between the cognitive unconscious and the psychoanalytic unconscious. Improved performance in the laboratory on memory tasks based on prior learning outside of awareness should not be confused with memory reports influenced by the vicissitudes of impulse life or previous traumatic experiences, as described by psychoanalysts. Likewise, behavioral memory for trauma, a concept to be developed later, should not readily be equated with the concept of implicit memory for laboratory memory tasks. In other words, the largely semantically predominant implicit memory system is not to be confounded with an episodic memory system, whether its contents be conscious or unconscious,

or whether they be manifest in narrative or behavioral form. Such confusion is exemplified in the "Statement on Memories of Sexual Abuse" of the American Psychiatric Association (1994), wherein the categories of explicit and implicit memory are used in reference to narrative, specifically traumatic, memory.

While memory research over the past two decades has focused extensively on the semantic-episodic and implicit-explicit memory distinctions, other classification systems for memory have been reported. While these have not received the same kind of research grouping to date, the concepts may prove important in the future.

Declarative memory is associated with the recollection of facts, details and events, is flexible, and can be applied to unique situations. Declarative memory has been found to be dependent on medial temporal lobe/diencephalic structures of the brain, operating in collaboration with the neocortex (Mishkin, 1982; Squire & Zola-Morgan, 1991). In contrast, *nondeclarative memory* is more contextually bound and inflexible, and is not as readily accessible. Although often encoded gradually, nondeclarative memories may be established in a single trial, as demonstrated in taste aversion conditioning experiments. Episodic memory is a term used to refer to specific autobiographical memories for events. The term semantic memory is used to refer to factual recall.

Nadel (1994) distinguished between a hippocampally based *locale* memory system and a nonhippocampally based *taxon* memory system. He explains:

> . . . taxon systems generalize over similarities and exhibit incremental acquisition and extinction, while the locale system focuses on the unique aspects of an episode and can learn from one trial. This distinction between systems focused on invariances and another system focused on variance was emphasized by Sherry and Schacter (1987). (p. 57)

William James made the distinction between primary and secondary memory system (Schacter, 1982, p. 146). Pillemer and White (1989), in an important review of child experimental data on memory development, make a case for the existence of two independent memory systems in children: a *behavioral memory system* that stores information in the form of actions, images, and sensations, and a *verbal memory* or *socially shared autobiographical memory system*. Terr (1981, 1988) has made a similar distinction between a behavioral memory for trauma and verbal narrative memory for trauma. She believes that trauma is stored as much in the form of behavioral reenactment and visual images as in verbal narrative form.

EVALUATION OF MEMORY

When a memory is retrieved and reported, how is that memory evaluated by memory scientists? Most modern memory researchers agree that some discrepancy exists between the stimulus input and the output memory report. Typically, memory scientists have measured this discrepancy along two dimensions: the *completeness* of the memory and the relative *accuracy* of the memory.

The *memory completeness* is a measure of the total amount of stimulus information that is reported at memory testing. With respect to relatively simple stimulus material, like nonsense syllables, Ebbinghaus measured memory completeness in terms of savings, i.e., how many of the learned nonsense syllables were retained at the time of the memory testing. In experiments using tachistoscopically presented arrays of letters, a typical measure is the percentage of letters that are recognized correctly. With respect to relatively complex stimuli events, like a slide or video presentation of a car accident, again the measure is typically the total amount of information remembered. In other words, a complex event, like a two-minute videotape of a car accident, is broken down into every possible perceivable detail, regardless of the salience of the detail. Memory completeness for a complex event is a function of the number of details actually remembered, as compared to the absolute number of details that could possible be remembered. For complex events, memory completeness is sometimes evaluated in terms of the so-called Deffenbacher (1983) criterion, namely, against a 70% baseline of recognition accuracy. That is, the normal subject viewing a complex event in a laboratory may remember approximately 70% of the details accurately.

Were a given subject to remember significantly less, we would say that his or her memory was incomplete. Were a subject to remember significantly more, we would say his or her memory was relatively complete.

The concept of memory completeness is closely related to the concepts of *amnesia* and *hypermnesia*. That is, relative to some assumed baseline for the amount of information normally remembered, amnesic patients (including some traumatized patients) remember much less than normal, at least for episodic (temporally-spatially coded) information. If the amnesic patient remembers none of the to-be-remembered information, he or she suffers from full amnesia; if the patient remembers some of the to-be-remembered information, but significantly less than the normal person, he or she suffers from partial amnesia. Under certain conditions, e.g., in the face of certain types of emotional arousal, a given individual may also become hypermnesic, i.e., remember a significantly greater amount of the to-be-remembered information than under normal conditions.

Another closely related concept to memory completeness/incompleteness is the concept of an *omission error* in memory testing. An omission error occurs when the subject fails to remember/report target information during memory testing. Memory failure can be measured in terms of an omission error for a single target item in a complex event, or in terms of the total number of omissions errors made, i.e., the total number of omitted target items relative to the absolute number of items in a complex event.

The problem with utilizing memory completeness measures in research on memory for complex events is that such measures often fail to address the complex interaction between memory for the total amount of information, the type of information to be remembered, the detail salience of that information, and other variables. In other words, memory may appear much more fallible than is actually the case *only* because memory for the *total* amount of information was used as the outcome measure, without any consideration for the *type* of information or salience of the detail. However, if the total amount of information for a complex event is categorized into various *types of information* and/or *detail salience* along some dimension of relevance to the subject, then a very different picture emerges.

For example, more sophisticated research designs might measure memory completeness along a number of discrete dimensions:

1. central versus peripheral detail,
2. action sequences relevant to emotional arousal versus neutral action sequences,
3. objects in the event relevant to the main action or plot versus objects irrelevant to the main action or plot.

In other words, memory completeness/incompleteness for a complex event depends to a large extent upon what aspect of the event we ask research subjects to remember. If we ask the subjects to remember everything about the event, as is often done in memory research, then, of course, the reported memory for the to-be-remembered complex event is less complete and human memory appears to be quite fallible. However, if we ask the subject to remember only selected details, then the memory is more complete or less complete, depending on the type of details and the salience of targeted details. If the main plot action sequences or highly salient details are asked for, human memory appears far less fallible.

The second major measure of memory is *memory accuracy*. Memory accuracy refers to whether or not remembered information (output) actually corresponds to the original stimulus event (input). With respect to simple stimulus material, like nonsense syllables, accuracy is an all-or-nothing phenomenon—the subject either remembers the letter list accurately or does not. With respect to more complex meaningful material, like Bartlett's "The War of the Ghosts" (1932), accuracy is sometimes assessed along different dimensions—accuracy for the gist of the story and accuracy for the minor details of the story. With respect to complex stimulus events, like viewing a videotape of a car accident, accuracy is measured in terms of the number of remembered items that are identical to the original stimulus items (hits). Inaccuracy is measured in terms of the number of remembered items that are different from the original stimulus items (misses).

Accuracy measures, of course, are relative, in terms of the proportion of total stimulus items accurately reported, or in terms of the ratio of accurately to inaccurately remembered items. Accuracy can also be assessed in one group of subjects relative to another. In some memory studies for complex events, a baseline of accuracy is established for control subjects, and accuracy for a group of experimental subjects is evaluated against this baseline, in a situation where the experimental condition may lead to a significant increase or decrease in accuracy.

The concept of memory accuracy is closely related to the concept of *commission errors*. Memory commission errors are remembered items that have no or only partial correspondence to the originally presented stimulus details. For simple stimulus information, commission errors typically mean no correspondence (total miss). For complex stimulus events, like Bartlett's "The War of the Ghosts" story, a commission error may also mean a partial distortion of the original stimulus material, while the report may retain some correspondence to the original stimulus. Bartlett (1932) attempted to classify these distortions: transformations, blending of memory items, substituting one detail for another, and inserting/deleting items. Many memory scientists since have developed a variety of systems by which to classify commission errors made by subjects in laboratory studies on memory performance.

The problem with accuracy measures of memory performance is that they are relative. Exactly how much memory distortion constitutes inaccuracy? If, for example, the memory report shows partial distortion, do we consider the memory report accurate or inaccurate? Many memories contain a mixture of accurate and inaccurate information, so that terms like "false memories" are, for the most part, misleading. Unfortunately, depending on the bias of the memory researcher, the same data on memory performance may be interpreted as evidence of memory inaccuracy or memory accuracy, as a partial hit or a partial miss. In the subsequent section on memory fallibility, largely drawn from investigations on the effects of emotions on memory, we will see that memory science itself is fallible, in that scientists repeatedly disagree on how much memory distortion constitutes memory inaccuracy or relative accuracy.

It is extremely important to understand that memory completeness and memory accuracy are not to be confused. Completeness and accuracy are *in-*

dependent measures of memory performance. A given memory may be quite incomplete, yet highly accurate, as is often the case in young children's memory reports. Or a given memory may be quite complete, yet highly inaccurate. It is extremely important that completeness and accuracy not be confounded when thinking about memory performance, especially as it pertains to the false memory controversy.

If a patient reports failing to have any memory of childhood sexual abuse for some significant duration of his/her life history, and then later recovers memories of childhood sexual abuse spontaneously or in psychotherapy, that patient had full or partial amnesia for the abuse recollections prior to recovery. Amnesia petains to *memory incompleteness*. Amnesia for memories of the childhood sexual abuse has absolutely nothing to do with the memories' accuracy or inaccuracy. A recovered memory may be quite accurate, quite inaccurate, or something in between. The relative accuracy of the memory needs to be assessed independently from the issues of memory completeness or incompleteness, full or partial amnesia, or from the methods of recovery of the memory.

Moreover, relative accuracy measures cannot be totally separated from their interaction with the type of information to be remembered and detail salience. A robust finding across memory studies is that under similar conditions relatively simple stimulus information is generally remembered more accurately than complex stimulus material. One need only consider the difference in memory accuracy for lists of nonsense syllables as compared to memory for complex stories, like Bartlett's "The War of the Ghosts," where subjects typically insert a number of inaccurate details and delete a number of accurate details. With respect to more complex events, like a videotape of a car accident, the subject may remember central action sequences accurately, yet remember peripheral details inaccurately. Therefore, *it is too simple, and sometimes outright misleading, to assess memory accuracy for the total amount of information in any complex event, without regard to the salience of selected information, and then draw global conclusions about that memory for the complex event as either accurate or inaccurate.*

While completeness and accuracy are the primary measures of memory performance addressed by memory scientists, there are a number of other dimensions along which to assess memory performance. Three of those additional dimensions are important in that they are often used by subjects themselves as subjective criteria by which to evaluate their own memory performance:

1. vividness of the memory,
2. emotionality associated with the memory, and
3. confidence in the memory.

Vividness in the memory refers to the richness and elaboration of detail of the memory. Vividness is not the same as accuracy. In fact, vividness and accuracy share a rather complex relationship. Research subjects and the ordinary person all too readily confuse vividness with accuracy. For example, the fact that a subject recalls a personal experience in rich detail and reports it as if he/she were picturing it clearly in mind does not mean the memory report is at all accurate.

Emotionality refers to the intensity and valence (pleasant/unpleasant/neutral) of the emotion accompanying the memory report. When subjects report their recall of personal memories, emotionality is often mistakenly taken as an indicator of the accuracy of the memory (Brewer, 1986). Once again, the relationship between memory accuracy and emotionality is quite complex, with emotionality predicting greater accuracy under certain conditions and less accuracy under other conditions. There may be no relationship between accuracy and emotionality under some conditions. Thus, it cannot be assumed that a recalled personal memory is accurate just because its recall is emotionally compelling.

Confidence means the degree to which the subject comes to believe that the memory report is accurate. Bowers and Hilgard (1988) have pointed out that the relationship between memory accuracy and memory confidence is quite complex. When accuracy and confidence are compared four possible interpretations exist: (1) high accuracy, high confidence; (2) high accuracy, low confidence; (3) low accuracy, high confidence; and (4) low accuracy, low confidence. Thus, it becomes clear from these categories that it cannot be readily assumed that confidence implies accuracy. Although a memory for which a subject is highly confident could be quite accurate, it could also be inaccurate.

The ordinary person in everyday life, and in the courts, often takes vividness, emotionality, and/or confidence as indices of memory accuracy. Although these factors *could* imply accuracy, they could also imply considerable inaccuracy. Likewise, both patients and therapists may mistake vividness, emotionality, and/or confidence as evidence that recovered trauma memories are accurate. Although these dimensions are sometimes associated with accurately recovered memories, they could also mislead the patient into falsely believing highly inaccurate memories were about historical events.

The literature on this subject has been well summarized by Spiegel and Scheflin (1994):

> Here is the paradoxical dilemma in the study of memory that has significant implications for researchers, therapists and jurists:
>
> On the one hand, as memory researchers universally agree, (1) the *amount of detail* in a memory is no guarantee of its accuracy, (2) the *richness of detail* in a memory is no guarantee of its accuracy, (3) the *clarity and vividness* in a memory is no guarantee of its accuracy, (4) the *emotional involvement* in a memory is no guarantee of its accuracy, (5) the *consistency over time* of a memory is no guarantee of its accuracy, (6) the *self-confidence* in a memory is no guarantee of its accuracy, (7) the fact that a person is known to be *honest* is no guarantee of the accuracy of a memory, and (8) the fact a person has a reputation for having a *good memory* is no guarantee of the accuracy of a memory.
>
> On the other hand, however, it is illogical to reason from the *fact* that a memory has *false details* to the conclusion that there is no *real incident* from which this false memory is an inaccurate depiction. Even if a memory is shown to be inaccurate, this does not prove that an event never happened. (p. 149)

Some researchers have chosen to focus on different aspects of the *phenomenology of the memory.* Historically, the earliest work in this area was on the *feeling-of-knowing* accompanying the memory report (Hart, 1965). Subjects often use their feeling-of-knowing previously learned material as a means to assess the accuracy of their memory report. Once again, feeling-of-knowing has a very complicated relationship to memory accuracy (e.g., Nelson, 1984).

More recent work in the context of the implicit/explicit memory research has focused on the *conscious experience of remembering* (Bowers & Hilgard, 1988). We generally assume that a memory report is accompanied by conscious recognition of the report as a memory. However, sometimes subjects give detailed and accurate memory reports that they fail to see as memory, when in fact their reports are accurate. They make this mistake because the memory report is not accompanied by the conscious experience that the mental event is indeed a memory. They misinterpret the event as an idea or fantasy.

A third phenomenological dimension of memory is the *phenomemological quality* of the memory. A few studies, for example, found that genuine and false memory reports for complex events could be distinguished statistically by certain phenomenological characteristics, such as the degree to which the memory report included reference to sensory-perceptual details (genuine) versus the extent to which it included references to cognitive processes instead of perceptual details ("I believe . . . I think . . .") (Johnson et al., 1988; Schooler, Gerhard, & Loftus, 1986). However, there has not been enough research in this area to draw definitive conclusions.

FACTORS AFFECTING MEMORY

According to current information processing models of memory, human memory processing is viewed as occurring in three distinct stages:

1. an encoding or acquisition stage,
2. a storage or retention stage, and
3. a retrieval stage (Loftus & Loftus, 1976).

Elizabeth Loftus (1979a) in particular, is known for her enumeration of the various factors that affect both the accuracy and/or completeness of memory processing in each of these stages.

Acquisition

During the *acquisition stage*, incoming information is encoded, first in terms of a highly transient iconic or echoic trace, and then, if processed further, in terms of a short-term memory trace and, perhaps, in terms of a long-term memory trace. A number of factors affect whether or not the information is actually encoded, and, if it is not encoded, whether the trace decays or persists. Not all types of information used as stimuli have the same likelihood of being encoded and subsequently remembered (Loftus, 1979a).

In memory research, a great range of stimulus events have been used—from single letters of the alphabet and arrays of letters in tachistoscopic experiments, to lists of letters in serial learning tasks, to meaningful stories in studies of memory for real-life situations. More recently, scientists have focused on memory for complex events, especially those events bearing some resemblance to real life. Typically, for purposes of experimental control, these events are presented in the form of a videotape, slide show, or a live stage action sequence. Memory for such complex events is divided into memory for the physical characteristics of the people (face recognition, body type, weight, height), the objects in the environment, and the nature of the action sequence (e.g., Reisberg et al., 1993). More or less information is encoded depending on how the information is organized by the subject at the encoding stage.

With respect to complex events, such as viewing a film of a bank robbery or a car accident, the subject's organization of information at encoding typically yields preferential processing of the action sequence over peripheral objects in the environment, and certain physical characteristics of people (height and body build, for example) may be given preferential processing over other characteristics (eye color, for example) (Christianson, 1992a,b). Generally speaking, a rough distinction is made in memory research on complex events between memory for the *central features* (like the action sequence) and *peripheral details* (like eye color).

In viewing complex events, *detail salience* is an important factor in what is remembered (Loftus, 1979a) because some aspects of the situation may capture the subject's attention and others will not. Salient details have a greater likelihood of being encoded and then persisting by being processed at higher levels, while seemingly minor or irrelevant details may never be encoded at all or, if they are encoded, their trace may not be processed at higher levels.

Exposure time and *frequency of exposure* also affect memory. In experiments using relatively simple stimuli, like tachistoscopic experiments using letters of the alphabet, the longer the duration (in milliseconds) that the subject views the target-letter, the greater the recognition accuracy. Moreover, the greater the luminance of the viewing field, the greater the recognition accuracy. With respect to complex events, exposure time is equally important. In eyewitness research, for example, the amount of time the witness actually is exposed to a face to a large extent determines whether or not it will be remembered accurately some time later (Loftus, 1979a).

In the laboratory-simulation studies on memory for complex, emotionally arousing events, subjects typically review the events at very brief exposures (for example, viewing a two-minute video or a series of slides in rapid succession), so that the research design is biased in favor of memory fallibility. Frequency of exposure refers to the number of times the subject perceives the stimulus information and has the opportunity to learn it before memory testing. Ebbinghaus learned and rehearsed the same lists of nonsense syllables a number of times and calculated memory savings in terms of a decreased number of repetitions required to relearn the material. In other words, savings is a measure of frequency of exposure. Curiously, most studies on memory for complex events, like viewing a videotape of a car accident, present the event only one time (sometimes twice). It is very rare to find a study on memory for a complex event that investigates memory performance on frequent exposures to that event.

Since the pioneering work of Robinson (1932) on how context affects serial learning, memory scientists have come to appreciate the extent to which contextual content impacts on memory performance in laboratory and naturalistic studies.

Information-processing theorists, like Atkinson and Shiffrin, Broadbent, and Neisser, have studied the extent to which control processes like *attention* and *rehearsal* affect memory processing. Incoming stimuli generally decay fairly rapidly unless attended to immediately. Attention enables the perseveration of the information, which is transferred to the short-term memory system. Subsequent rehearsal facilitates its transfer to the long-term memory system and its permanence. Conversely, failure to attend to certain aspects of the complex stimulus event greatly increases the likelihood of its decay, even if the material has been encoded at the level of the sensory register or the short-term memory system. Simply put, we may never retrieve the memory of what we never attended to in the first place.

Retention

Loftus (1979a) defines the retention stage as "the period of time that passes between the event and eventual recollection of a particular piece of information" (p. 122). She sees that this as a "crucial period," because once the stimulus event is encoded a number of factors may affect it.

Current thinking about forgetting is that there are two kinds of forgetting: (1) passive decay, which is operative at shorter intervals, and (2) active interference, which is operative at longer intervals. These mechanisms of forgetting may represent the short-term and long-term systems, respectively (Klatzky, 1975, p. 91). Passive decay occurs because the material was not acted upon by central processes like attention, as demonstrated by Ebbinghaus and many memory scientitsts in recent decades. Active interference occurs when information presented prior to or subsequent to the target information interferes with the target information, as shown by McGeoch (1932) and others.

Therefore, exactly what a given individual remembers about a target stimulus event is dependent on both the *retention interval* and also upon the *type of information* that precedes and/or follows the target material. The retention interval (RI) refers to the amount of time between encoding and retrieval. There have been numerous studies on the effect of the retention interval on memory performance in laboratories. General speaking, memory is better preserved over shorter RIs and less well retained over longer RIs. In actuality, the research findings are terribly complex. Certain types of emotionally salient as compared to less salient information, under certain conditions, are better retained over longer, rather than shorter, retention intervals. Therefore, *we cannot simply assume that a memory report is any less valid if the memory is recovered after long retention intervals.*

Most of the modern research on interference effects has addressed the impact of *post-event information* on memory performance, although very few

studies have also addressed *pre-event information*. Loftus (1979a,b) is known for her pioneering work on post-event interference on memory performance of subjects who view complex events. The typical experiment involves three stages. First, the subjects watch a slide presentation of a robbery, a car accident, or some other emotional and violent event. Second, sometime after watching the presentation, the subjects are given a post-event account of the events they witnessed. Usually, this post-event information is delivered orally or in a written narrative about the event. Control subjects are given an accurate description of the event; experimental subjects are given the same narrative, except that it contains two pieces of inaccurate or misleading information about the original event. Finally, the subjects are tested on their recall of the slides.

Numerous such experiments have been conducted by dozens of experimenters. These experiments are fully discussed in chapter 4. These experiments have repeatedly demonstrated that experimental subjects, relative to control subjects, significantly incorporate the misleading information into the memory report upon subsequent testing of their memory for the original event.

It is from these experiments that Loftus and others conclude that human memory is highly vulnerable to distortion. They argue that the longer the retention interval, and the greater the number of post-event interferences that could potentially influence the memory, the more likely the memory has been "reworked" or "reconstructed" by the time it is retrieved.

Retrieval

Retrieval is the process by which subjects access and remember stored information. Curiously, retrieval remained a neglected area of memory research for nearly a century (Schacter, 1982). Modern research on retrieval began with Tulving's classic work on retrieval cues (Tulving & Osler, 1968) in the late 1960s, on encoding specificity (Tulving & Thompson, 1973), and later on recall and recognition (Tulving, 1976).

According to the concept of encoding specificity, retrieval represents a complex interaction of three factors: (1) the specific way the stimulus information is encoded, (2) the specific information contained within the retrieval cue, and (3) the context of the retrieval. Thus, access and retrieval of a specific target stimulus are significantly enhanced if the information contained within the retrieval cue is sufficiently similar to the originally encoded information. The closer the match between the original information and the cues available upon memory testing, the greater the probability of retrieval. As Eich (1980) clearly states, "remembering [is a] joint product of information from two sources—the memory trace and the retrieval cue" (p. 159).

Memory retrieval is better or worse depending on the conditions at the time of the retrieval. A number of factors significantly affect retrieval: (1) the type of *retrieval strategy* utilized; (2) the *context* of retrieval; (3) the *state of consciousness* and/or state of emotional arousal; and (4) the nature of *social influences* operative at the time of the retrieval. Thus, even though material may be available within the long-term memory storage system, it is not necessarily accessible under certain conditions (Tulving & Pearlstone, 1966).

The type of retrieval strategy utilized greatly affects the accessibility of stored information within the memory system. Two types of retrieval strategies typically studied by memory scientists are *recognition* and *recall* (Tulving, 1976). *Recall* can be further classified as (1) *free recall*, which is also called free narrative recall, (2) *cued recall*, or recall cued by specific questions, and (3) recall cued by leading or misleading questions. In a *recognition task*, the subject is presented with cues, which are sometimes exact replicas of the original stimulus items (Tulving, 1976). The subject, for example, may view a slide presentation of a car accident. At the time of memory testing, the subject may be shown slide pairs; one slide in each pair previously appeared in the original slide presentation. The subject is asked to chose which slide of the pair was part of the original presentation.

In a *recall task*, the subject is not given specific information, and while remembering seemingly takes place without a specific cue, recall never occurs spontaneously. It is likely that the cues determining free recall are simply not apparent to the experimenter because they are not part of the experimental design. Free recall is derived from cues idiosyncratic to the subject (Eich, 1980). In free recall, for example, the subject is simply told, "remember everything that you can." These instructions initiate an internal search through the idiosyncratic associative network previously established by the individual (Klatzky, 1975).

The dividing line between recognition and recall is not especially clear-cut. As Klatzky (1975) notes, "recognition is essentially recall with the search processes removed" (p. 217). Thus, if the subject is given recognition cues that directly match the original stimulus material, an elaborate search process is unnecessary. The problem with *free recall* is that the information retrieved is quite often accurate but also incomplete, in adults and especially in young children.

In *cued recall* experiments, the subject at the time of memory testing is given specific questions to prompt recall, rather than a simple request to "remember everything that you can." Cued recall generally leads to a more complete memory, but one that is more or less accurate depending on the type of questions asked.

One danger of cued recall is that the questions asked may not be neutral; rather, they may either suggest the answer or contain contaminating information. *Leading recall* occurs when the specific question asked implies a desired answer. *Misleading recall* occurs when the specific question significantly mismatches the original stimulus information, so as to create an interference effect, the outcome of which is an alteration or distortion of the memory report.

In addition to the *technique* used for retrieval, *context* also affects retrieval. Generally speaking, retrieval is more likely when the context at the time of memory testing closely matches the context at the time the original information was encoded, and retrieval is less likely when the retrieval context is significantly different from that of encoding. Abernathy (1940) found that students' performance was significantly poorer on exams when the exam was given in a different room from their original classroom, and also if the exam was given in their familiar classroom by a different teacher from their usual teacher.

The discrepancy between context in memory encoding and memory retrieval significantly reduces memory performance. Godden and Baddeley (1975) taught experienced scuba divers word lists under water or on land. Subsequent memory testing included free recall and word recognition testing either in the same context (land-land/water-water) or in a discrepant context (land-water/water-land). Remembering was significantly better when memory testing reinstated the context of the original learning. Because of the strong effect of context on memory retrieval, context reinstatement, or returning to the scene of the crime, has become a primary strategy in fostering memory retrieval in forensic investigations (Fisher & Geiselman, 1992).

State dependent retrieval (SDR) refers to the similarity or discrepancy between the initial state of the individual at the time of memory encoding and subsequent memory testing. Gordon Bower (1981) defines SDR as follows: "events learned in one psychic state can be remembered better when one is put back into the same state one was in during the original experience" (p. 130). Conversely, memory for events is worse if the state of consciousness at the time of retrieval is significantly discrepant from the state of consciousness at the time of encoding.

The phenomenon of state dependent memory was first studied systematically by Overton (1964). Laboratory animals were taught to find their way through mazes while injected with a barbiturate. After the animal clearly had learned the maze pattern, it "forgot" how to negotiate the maze once the effects of the barbiturate wore off. However, if the same dosage of the drug were readministered, the animal would once again remember the maze pattern. In other words, retrieval of the maze learning was dependent on matching the drug-induced state at memory encoding to a similar drug-induced state at the time of memory testing. Overton conducted a series of later studies demonstrating comparable state dependent retrieval effects on animals for atrophine (1966), alcohol (1972), and opiates (1973). Over a decade of research on state dependent retrieval effects on animals is summarized in Ho, Richards, and Shute's (1978) book *Drug Discrimination and State Dependent Learning*.

The original masterpiece on state dependent retrieval effects on humans was Charlie Chaplin's 1931 movie, *City Lights*, in which Chaplin plays a poor man who saves a drunken millionaire from killing himself by jumping into a river. Chaplin and the man become friends and they spend the night carousing throughout the town. The next day the millionaire, once sober, fails to recognize Chaplin. Sometime later the man gets drunk. When Chaplin happens

to pass by, the millionaire immediately recognizes his new friend. Once again they spend time together and Chaplin spends the night in his mansion. The next morning the millionaire, sober, fails to recognize Chaplin and has him thrown out.

The experimental studies on state dependent retrieval in humans began to appear in the literature in the 1970s. Typically, subjects were given some target stimuli to learn (such as nonsense syllables, words, or symbols) under one of two conditions: (1) the normal waking state, or (2) a drug-induced state. A variety of psychoactive drugs was used, including alcohol, marijuana, barbiturates, and amphetamines. Subsequent memory testing was conducted either in the same condition (normal waking state-normal waking state/drug-drug), or in a discrepant condition (normal waking state-drug/drug-normal waking state). The experimenters believed that memory performance would be significantly reduced if the state of consciousness at the time of retrieval was discrepant from the state of consciousness at the time of encoding, as had been true in the animal studies. Unfortunately, the experimental findings across many studies sometimes appeared to support this conclusion and sometimes clearly did not, so that early reviewers failed to take the concept of human state dependent retrieval seriously. Hilgard and Bower (1975) concluded that the evidence on human state dependent retrieval "rests on precarious grounds" (p. 547). Eich (1977) emphasized the "apparent unpredictability" in the experimental findings.

In a subsequent review and reanalysis of the data across 27 studies and 57 experimental conditions, Eich (1980) considered the variables that might account for the inconsistent results:

1. the type of drug used,
2. the dosage of the drug administered,
3. the nature of the material to be remembered,
4. the level of information processing, and
5. the nature of the retrieval cues.

Eich discovered that most of the variance across the studies could be accounted for by differences in retrieval cues. Simply put, across all studies state dependent retrieval in humans occurred under *free recall conditions*, but did not occur under cued recall conditions or recognition conditions. In other words, it is not necessary to duplicate the state of consciousness when specific retrieval cues are used. In the absence of specific retrieval cues, the subject who is asked to freely recall whatever he or she can may be able to do so only to the extent to which he or she is in a similar state of consciousness to the state of consciousness at the time of the encoding. Thus, for example, a subject under the influence of alcohol at the time of encoding the memory for witnessing a staged-theft freely recalls significantly less information about the event when compared to a non-intoxicated subject watching the same event, if recall occurred for both in the waking state (Yuille & Tollestrup, 1990).

State dependent retrieval-like effects have been demonstrated for non-drug-induced altered states of consciousness, like hypnosis, and also for emotional states. A subpopulation of hypnotizable subjects, for example, produce spontaneous or suggested partial or complete posthypnotic amnesia (e.g., Kihlstrom, 1977).

The effects of emotional state on memory result in a similar state dependent phenomenon, at least for free recall. In an important paper, "Mood and Memory," Gordon Bower (1981) investigated the effects of emotional state at the time of memory encoding and at retrieval on memory performance. In one experiment, normal highly hypnotizable subjects were used, because it had previously been demonstrated that genuine and highly specific emotional states could be suggested in trance. Suggestions were given for one or another of two opposite emotional states—"a delightfully happy or a grievously sad mood." Subjects in each emotional state were given a list of words to memorize. Then they were given a second list of words to memorize in either the same or the opposite emotional state. At subsequent memory testing, hypnotic suggestions were given to reactivate the same or the opposite emotional state and subjects were asked to freely recall the word list. Subjects recalled significantly more words if the emotional state at the time of retrieval matched the emotional state of the original learning, and significantly less if it did not match.

Bower then demonstrated that the same mood-state-dependent effect applied to personal autobiographical memory. He asked subjects to report emotionally meaningful experiences in a diary, along with details such as the time of the event and the gist of the experience. He also asked subjects to rate each experience on a scale of emotional pleasantness or unpleasantness. After a one-week retention interval, subjects were hypnotized and given suggestions to activate a very pleasant or unpleasant emotional state. Then subjects were asked to freely recall the personal emotional memory recorded in their diary. Subjects recalled a significantly greater portion of pleasant experiences when in a pleasant emotional state and a greater portion of unpleasant experiences in an unpleasant emotional state. They recalled significantly less if the emotional state at the time of retrieval was opposite to that at the time of encoding.

In another experiment, subjects freely recalled significantly more pleasant childhood memories when in a hypnotically pleasant emotional state than when in an emotionally incongruent state at the time of retrieval. Bower discussed how emotional state can influence free associations, fantasy productions, the snap judgments people make, and individual interpretations of interpersonal situations. Bower interprets these data to mean that "people recall an event better if they somehow reinstate during recall the original emotion they experienced during the learning" (p. 147). Consistent with Eich's review (1980) on state dependent retrieval, Bower notes that "the state-dependent effects occur best with free recall" and are "greatly reduced when memory is tested with more adequate cues" (p. 136). He explains the state dependent effect in terms of an associative network theory of memory. According to that view, a specific emotion is associated with encoded specific memories. Activation of emotion at the time of retrieval aids retrieval by activating the memory network associated with it.

The main contribution of the psychoanalytic literature to memory is that *psychologically motivated defenses* can significantly interfere with memory processing and retrieval. Singer's *Repression and Dissociation* (1990) represents a summary of contemporary viewpoints and controversies regarding clinical and laboratory studies on ways in which individuals keep information from consciousness. That volume includes reviews of new studies on individual differences, namely the so-called repressive personality style. Individuals who measure high on social desirability (i.e., people who present an image of and think of themselves as well-adjusted and responsible and alter their responses in order to protect their esteem) and who measure very low on anxiety were thought to have a *repressive personality style*. Laboratory research has consistently shown that such individuals are more autonomically reactive (Schwartz, 1990), avoidant of negative affect, and have significantly lower recall of negative emotional memories (cf. review by Weinberger in Singer, 1990). Davis (1990) has demonstrated, however, that repressors have "limited accessibility," not necessarily "limited availability" to negative emotional memories, because at least some of the emotional memory material can be recollected under certain retrieval conditions (cited in Singer, p. 399). Thus, while the definition and validation of the concept of repression have a long history of heated controversy (Gleaves, 1996a; Holmes, 1990), Singer concludes that most experts are in agreement that "selective attention, selective rehearsal, and various cognitive filtering functions" (p. 485) are legitimate ways to explain the "general commonality of findings" (p. 486) that certain individuals have selective accessibility to negative emotional memories.

Another set of factors that can have an impact on retrieval is *social influence*. The effects of social influences on memory were first noted by Bartlett in 1932. Because exploring the effect that social influences have on memory constitutes the main theme of this book, discussion is deferred until the topic can be presented in greater length and detail in chapters 4, 5, and 6.

THE DEVELOPMENT OF MEMORY

As memory scientists began to focus their attention on naturally occurring memory in the 1970s, one important area of inquiry was the study of the development of memory in children. The 1980s was characterized by a marked proliferation of observational and experimental studies on memory performance in children. What emerged from this work was the broad outlines of the theory of memory development. Pillemer and White's monograph entitled *Childhood Events Recalled by Children and Adults* (1989) illustrates the kind of theoretical formulations that were emerging. Pillemer and White integrate an enormous amount of experimental data

across studies in children into a comprehensive theory. According to them, the data suggest a development of two parallel yet independent memory systems: (1) a *behavioral memory system* and (2) a *verbal or narrative autobiographical memory system*.

The behavioral memory system develops earlier. For young children, memory is expressed primarily in the form of behavioral reenactment and imagery. Evidence for a behavioral memory system comes primarily from studies on young children's memory for play. In experiments, children played with toys in a laboratory playroom. After a specified retention interval, each child returned and was asked to recreate the play sequence ("show me what you did with the teddy bear last time"). The child demonstrated his or her memory by behaviorally reenacting the play sequence. These studies consistently show that young children (ages two to three) retain a relatively complete and somewhat accurate behavioral memory of play events, even when they are not able to verbalize any memory for the event. Starting around two years of age, the child develops the capacity for organized speech phrases. Nelson's (1988) important analysis of the crib talk of a two-year-old, Emily, demonstrates that toddlers initially organize verbal memory around the gist of central and familiar activities—what are called *"general event schemas."* The toddler makes sense out of the world by developing schemas for familiar routines and assimilating new information to these existing memory structures. A cohesive self representation also emerges within the second year of life, so that the emerging memories are increasingly experienced as belonging to the self.

A new level of cognitive maturation is achieved in the third year. A cumulative outcome of these two changes is the emergence of a highly organized verbal memory system by the end of the third year. The three- or four-year-old child is clearly capable of talking about and remembering past experiences, and while these verbal accounts are relatively incomplete, they are reasonably accurate. According to Pillemer and White, this emerging verbal memory system has a much greater degree of internal organization than the earlier behavioral memory system.

According to Pillemer and White's analysis, additional developmental changes occur in the verbal memory system after the fourth year of life. During the fifth and sixth year of life, the verbal memory system becomes a "socially shared" autobiographical system for the increasingly socially conscious child. Personal experiences are observed, and elaborated, by sharing them with others—a process that memory scientists call *rehearsal*. Throughout latency years the child develops the capacity for memory for specific events, in addition to general event memory (Hudson & Nelson, 1986), roughly corresponding to the maturation of intelligence, namely, the development of concrete operation thinking by the eighth year of life (Piaget, 1962). By that time the older child is capable of verbalizing very *specific memories* for personal experiences, memories that are much more complete and elaborate than those of the younger child.

It is important to appreciate that, according Pillemer and White, the behavioral memory system and the verbal memory system develop independently from each other and yet coexist in the child. By the beginning of the fourth year of life, the verbal memory system becomes the dominant system, even though the behavioral memory system persists. According to Pillemer and White, childhood amnesia is primarily an outcome of a significant developmental shift, occurring around age four, in which the verbal memory system takes primacy over the behavioral memory system. The older child's or the adult's relative inability to access a verbal autobiographical memory for experiences occurring prior to the fourth year of life results from the fact that these earlier experiences are primarily retained in the behavioral memory system. While verbal memory for earlier experiences is certainly possible, insofar as the child has the capacity for organized speech phrases (typically around two years and sometimes as early as eighteen months), these verbal memories become less accessible because of a developmental shift. Even when accessible, these verbal memories are typically quite incomplete and are usually general event narratives.

As discussed in the next chapter, important exceptions to childhood amnesia do occur, especially for certain types of personally significant events that impact upon the child's life. Some older children and adults *do* retain a specific autobiographical memory for certain events occurring as young as one and a half years of age, although this may be more the exception than the rule. Certainly, an adult report of a specific and detailed memory for an event

occurring in the first year of life would have to be viewed with considerable skepticism; it would run totally against what is known about memory development. Yet, an adult's report of an incomplete verbal memory for the gist of an important experience occurring in the second or third year of life is certainly conceivable, even though such a memory would be the exception to the usual childhood amnesia. Persistent behavioral memories for these earlier experiences into later childhood and adulthood are quite likely.

Two significant questions need to be posed. First, are adult recollections from the behavioral memory system accurate? It is unfortunate that laboratory memory scientists have almost completely ignored the study of an adult's behavioral memory for early experiences. By contrast, behavioral memory for early emotionally salient experiences (including trauma) may be exactly what psychoanalytically oriented psychotherapists have been describing for years with terms like "repetition compulsion" and "posttraumatic reenactment."

Second, once the verbal memory system achieves prominence, is there one working model of normal memory, or are there separate memory systems for different types of stimuli? Is the behavioral memory system ever used after those first few precious years? More particularly, is memory for *traumatic* events encoded, stored, and retrieved in the same manner as for *nontraumatic* events?

TRAUMATIC MEMORY

Are Normal and Traumatic Memory the Same?

Memory scientists have virtually neglected the laboratory study of memory performance in traumatized individuals; also, a great deal of what has been learned about memory in the laboratory is based on presumably nonclinical subjects, mainly college students. The little that is known about memory performance in traumatized individuals is based on clinical observations and clinical research. Therefore, *scientists and clinicians can readily assume neither that the findings from the laboratory or clinical populations are cross-generalizable, nor that the basic concepts about normal human memory reviewed in this chapter automatically apply to memory in traumatized individuals.* Indeed, the concepts concerning traumatic memory derived from clinical studies suggest fundamental differences between clinical researchers' understanding of memory performance in traumatized patients and laboratory memory scientists' understanding of normal memory.

What Clinical Studies on Traumatic Memory Say

Freud's view of memory for trauma centered around two concepts, repression and screen memories. These two terms correspond roughly to memory omission and commission errors, respectively (Ross, 1991, p.47). Breuer and Freud in *Studies on Hysteria* (1895) and Freud in "The Aetiology of Hysteria" (1896) outline what later came to be known as the seduction theory. Initially, Freud saw neurotic symptoms as essentially arising from real-life traumatic events, notably childhood sexual seduction. Narrative memory for such traumatic experiences was often not consciously available to such patients, but was repressed, a form of unconsciously motivated forgetting. However, Freud believed that some form of memory representation persisted and was represented in consciousness in a disguised form, as a screen memory. Thus, the hysteric's fantasy productions and other thoughts indirectly alluded to childhood trauma. The free association technique offered a means to trace the disguised memories back to the original trauma. Once the hysteric patient brought the original trauma into consciousness, neurotic symptoms disappeared. Freud believed that trauma memory, while often disguised and distorted, persists and is not subject to the mechanisms of normal forgetting. Once recovered into consciousness, the memory for the infantile sexual trauma manifests a "freshness" and "undiminished vividness" (Ross, 1991, p. 65). An underlying assumption in Freud's seduction theory, which he later abandoned in favor of his oedipal fantasy theory of hysteria, is that memory for sexual trauma is processed differently from normal conscious memory due to the operation of psychological defenses.

Janet's theory of traumatic memory processing differed from Freud's in many respects, although both shared a view of motivated psychological defenses against conscious awareness of traumatic memories. Janet defines trauma in terms of failure to take adaptive action in the face of some overwhelming experience, the result of which was the intensification of affect—what Janet called "vehement emotions." This intensification of affect disrupts normal memory processing and causes a dissociation of the otherwise unitary nature of consciousness. The traumatic memory is split off, or dissociated, from ordinary consciousness (primary dissociation) and the memory, affects, physical sensations, and behaviors associated with the traumatic experience are dissociated from each other (secondary dissociation). Later, under certain conditions, dissociated aspects of traumatic memory may return in the form of automatisms, like conversion symptoms, dissociative symptoms, depersonalization, derealization, or personality fragmentation (van der Hart & Friedman, 1989; van der Hart & Horst, 1989; van der Hart & Nijenhuis, 1995; van der Kolk & van der Hart, 1989). The most important contribution in Janet's thinking to traumatic memory processing is the notion that *trauma disrupts normal information processing* through dissociation.

The modern clinical version of *disrupted processing theory* is Horowitz's information-processing theory of post-traumatic stress disorder (1976). The traumatic event is said to be overwhelming to the individual. The extreme fear arousal accompanying the traumatic experience will be encoded in sensory imagery along with associated emotions. The traumatized individual is unable to integrate these traumatic memories and associated affects and behaviors into consciousness. They persist in the form of intrusive experiences such as thoughts, images, dreams, flashbacks, and memory fragments associated with the original traumatic event. Clinical traumatic memory appears different from the relatively unstressed memory processes often studied in laboratories. Traumatic memories may be encoded differently due to both attentional and psychological variables, as well as physiological (stress-arousal) factors (Cahill, Prins, Weber, & McGaugh, 1994; Christianson, 1992a; Horowitz & Reidbord, 1992; LeDoux, 1992, 1994; McGaugh, 1992; Nilsson & Archer, 1992; Pitman, 1994; Saporta & van der Kolk, 1992; van der Kolk, 1984, 1987, 1988; van der Kolk & Saporta, 1993; van der Kolk & van der Hart, 1991; Weinberger, Gold, & Sternberg, 1984).

Modern clinical trauma theory, relying on Janet,

also views trauma memory in terms of *dissociated memory.* The memory for the overwhelming experience is dissociated from consciousness (primary dissociation) and is further dissociated into separate memory components, such as the memory content per se, the affects occurring at the time of the trauma, the physical sensations and degree of physiological arousal occurring during the traumatization, and the behaviors enacted at the time (secondary dissociation) (Marmar et al., 1994; van der Hart & Nijenhuis, 1995). Braun and Sachs' (1985) BASK model of traumatic memory describes four components of a memory believed to become dissociated in response to traumatization: the **B**ehavioral, **A**ffective, **S**omato-sensory, and **K**nowledge components associated with the traumatic memory. Zajonc (1980) has likewise argued that emotional memory is mediated by a special system that both is independent of systems that process more cognitive memory and operates in an unconscious way. Providing some degree of support for this possibility, there is considerable clinical and experimental literature documenting that a dissociation of affect and content (e.g., Christianson & Nilsson, 1989; Erickson & Rossi, 1979; Greenberg, Pearlman, Schwartz, & Grossman, 1983; Ohman, 1991).

Recent phenomenological studies of traumatic memories reported by clinic patients using the Traumatic Memory Inventory have lent empirical support to the concept of dissociated memory. Dissociation was found to be correlated with the lack of a contemporary verbal memory for a traumatic experience, as well as with affective, kinesthetic, and behavioral reexperiencing of the trauma (van der Kolk & fisler, 1995). Moreover, van der Kolk and fisler view the process of recovery from trauma in terms of the translation of the traumatic memory from its dissociated form into a verbal, narrative autobiographical form of memory, a process through which the dissociated BASK components of the memory become integrated. Studies of the process by which patients recover traumatic memories using the Traumatic Memory Inventory have shown that trauma patients initially report a somato-sensory–predominant memory, later an affect predominant memory, and finally a verbal autobiographical predominant memory for the traumatic event (van der Kolk & fisler, 1995).

Janet's notion of automatism, Breuer and Freud's

well-known comment that "hysterics suffer from reminiscences," Horowitz's concept of intrusive reexperiencing, and van der Hart's and van der Kolk's concept of dissociated memory share similar underlying assumptions, namely, an unusual persistence of a traumatic memory and perhaps also a type of encoding and/or storage in the form of other than, or in addition to, normal narrative autobiographical memory. Pillemer and White's (1989) landmark synthesis of the research on memory development in children demonstrates that humans develop two independent memory systems, a behavioral memory system and a verbal memory system. The numerous clinical observations on (1) conscious and/or unconscious behavioral reenactment of trauma, and (2) posttraumatic intrusive visual imagery, flashbacks, and accompanying affect storms imply that encoding/storage of traumatic experiences may occur primarily in the behavioral memory system rather than in the verbal memory system. Moreover, the data on the clinical phenomenology of trauma suggest that behavioral memory for trauma may be stored in the form of multiple, dissociated memory representations.

As an example, Terr (1988) studied 20 children an average of four and a half years after they suffered trauma (which occurred before age 5; average age 34 months; range between 6 months and 4 years, 10 months). Importantly, these were cases where there was documentation of the nature of the trauma. She discovered that between 28 and 36 months of age "appears to be about the time most children will be able to lay down, and later to retrieve, some sort of verbal memory of trauma" (p. 97), and girls appeared to be slightly more adept than boys at bringing up very early verbal memories. Single episodes of trauma (versus repeated events) and short (versus long) events were associated with better recall. Even though the children were on average less than three years of age at the time of abuse, a total of 50% of the verbal memories were accurate, and another 25% had inconsistencies in detail but "stayed true to outside documentations" (p. 97).

Terr (1988) believed that what was striking was how literal and accurate the "behavioral memory" of the children was, and how early it came into operation. Eighteen of 20 children she studied manifested behaviors (e.g., in their play) clearly demonstrating that they retained memories of their traumas, including a boy who was seven months old when he was a Satanic worship victim. "Verbal recollections require conscious awareness, but behavioral memories do not" (p. 103), she said in illustrating how there was a greater volume of information still unconsciously present. She concluded:

> From my review of these children I have concluded that traumatic events create lasting visual images. . . . Behavioral memory follows from visual memory, not from verbal memory. This accounts for the very early onset of behavioral memory. When a child reenacts, he recreates and reinforces already "burned-in" visual impressions. . . . Traumatic visions from early in life, it seems, stimulate more action than words.
>
> When a trauma or a series of extreme stresses strikes well before the age of 28 to 36 months, the child "burns-in" a visual memory of it, sometimes later becoming able as the years go on to affix a few words to the picture. These words, late in arriving, can only describe part of the preexisting imagery. Part tends to stand for the whole. (p. 103)

The Neurobiology of Traumatic Memory

There is a growing body of neurobiological evidence that lends support to the dissociated trauma memory theory. The administration of stress-related hormones and drugs can enhance or impair memory (McGaugh, 1992; McGaugh & Gold, 1989), and emotional events trigger a memory-modulating system associated with the release of noradrenaline in the brain and peripheral adrenergic (stress) hormones (McGaugh, 1983). Carefully controlled experimental research (Cahill et al., 1994) recently supported the hypothesis that emotional memory storage is clearly different from non-emotional memory, and is modulated by beta-adrenergic systems. They found that emotional arousal seems to activate beta-adrenergic receptors that are not necessary for the encoding of non-emotional memories. Specifically, Cahill's research examined recall of an emotionally neutral and an emotional story; one hour before being told the story subjects received either a placebo pill or propranolol (a drug

that lowers stress hormones). A week later, memory was evaluated. Subjects receiving a placebo demonstrated better memory of emotional aspects of the emotionally arousing story compared to the neutral story, while those whose stress hormones were blocked remembered significantly less about the emotional story than those receiving the placebo. However, the propranolol did not harm memory of the emotionally neutral story. Thus, the release of stress hormones associated with emotional experiences seems to strengthen memories for those experiences and may be associated with intrusive flashback phenomena in PTSD patients. McGaugh concluded, "Memory is fallible in the real world, but stronger emotional experiences make for stronger, more reliable memories" (Bower, 1994, p. 262). Relevant research concerning how emotionally charged events may be encoded differently in memory has been reviewed by McGaugh (1992), LeDoux (1992), Nilsson and Archer (1992), and Christianson (1992b).

Van der Kolk (van der Kolk, 1993; van der Kolk & Saporta, 1993) and Bremner (Bremner et al., 1996) have developed neurobiological models for the processing of traumatic memories. According to accumulating neurobiological data, normal verbal autobiographical memories are primarily processed in the hippocampus, using a semantic categorizing processing system. According to van der Kolk, traumatic memories are primarily processed in the limbic system, most likely in the amygdala. Van der Kolk and Saporta (1993) explained one of three trauma-related functions of the limbic system:

> The limbic system is also the primary area of the CNS where memories are processed, and is the most likely location to find an explanation for the memory disturbances which follow trauma. The hippocampus, which records in memory the spatial and temporal dimensions of experiences, does not fully mature until the third or fourth year of life. However, the system that subserves memories related to the quality (feel and sound) of things (which is mainly located in the amygdala) matures much earlier (O'Keefe & Nadel, 1978). Thus, in the first few years of life, only the quality of events, but not their context can be remembered. Even after that, the hippocampal localization system remains vulnerable to disruption: Severe or pro-

longed stress can suppress hippocampal functioning (Squire, 1987), creating context-free fearful
associations which are hard to locate in space and
time. This results in amnesia for the specifics of
traumatic experiences, but not the feelings associated with them (Sapolsky, Krey, & McEwen, 1984).
These experiences may then be encoded on a sensorimotor level without proper localization in space
and time. They therefore cannot be easily translated into symbolic language necessary for linguistic retrieval. (pp. 27–28)

LeDoux (1992, 1994) has described the amygdala
as an "emotional computer." It is centrally involved
in the processing of emotion, evaluating the importance of input from sensory processing areas of the
thalamus and cortex, and then conveying information to areas of the brainstem controlling behavioral
and autonomic responses. "These connections,"
LeDoux explains:

> allow the amygdala to transform sensory stimuli
> into emotional signals and to initiate and control
> emotional responses. . . . For emotional process-
> ing, the amygdala thus takes over at the point
> where sensory information exits the sensory sys-
> tem. . . . The amygdala thus evaluates the signifi-
> cance of complex information. . . . The activation
> of the amygdala by inputs from the neocortex is
> thus consistent with the classic notion that emo-
> tional processing is postcognitive, whereas the ac-
> tivation of the amygdala by thalamic inputs is
> consistent with the hypothesis, advanced by Zajonc
> (1980), that emotional processing can be precon-
> scious and precognitive. (1992, p. 275)

When the amygdala is electrically stimulated in
people, emotionally loaded experiences are evoked,
whereas lesions of the amygdala reduce affective and
aggressive responses and obstruct the development
of memories. Thus, LeDoux (1992) concluded:

> These findings suggest that emotional memories
> are indelible and normally maintained by subcor-
> tical circuits involving the amygdala. . . . The uni-
> versal, integrative processing that underlies
> conditioned emotional memory formation is thus
> likely to take place in the amygdala. Said differ-
> ently, the amygdala is likely to be the site of essen-

tial synaptic plasticity in the formation of emotional
memories. (pp. 280, 281)

The amygdala is not a component of the medial temporal lobe system involved with declarative memory
(Zola-Morgan, Squire, & Amaral, 1986), such as that
typically studied by false memory researchers. Squire
(1995) adds that amygdala processing of emotional
memories gives an emotional memory "strength,"
thereby making it less vulnerable to forgetting, as
well as to distorting influences (p. 265).

Interestingly, endogenous opioids, which are
found in abnormal levels in persons with PTSD (e.g.,
Bremner et al., 1996; McFall, Murburg, Roszell, &
Veith, 1989; Pitman, van der Kolk, Orr, &
Greenberg, 1990; Southwick, Krystal, Morgan,
Johnson, Nagy, Nicolaou, Heninger, & Charney,
1993; Yehuda, Giller, Southwick, Lowy, & Mason,
1991), have an inhibitory influence on the amygdala
and seem to impede the storage of early memory
through inhibiting projections from the amygdala
to the hippocampus (McGaugh, 1992).

McGaugh (1992) summarized research on the
involvement of stress hormones on the amygdala
and memory processes. He concluded that epinephrine, dipivalyl epinephrine, and clenbuterol influence long-term retention and influence the strength
of memory through activating the amygdala. He
concludes that there is strong evidence supporting
the belief that emotional experiences activate endogenous neuromodulatory systems that influence
memory storage:

> Emotionally exciting stimulation activates the re-
> lease of adrenal epinephrine (as well as other stress-
> related hormones) that, in turn, causes "sizzling
> circuits" (Lantos, 1990) in the amygdala and sites
> activated by the amygdala. Such effects serve to
> regulate the storage of long-term memory of the
> experience. The extensive evidence indicating that
> the memory modulating effects of hormones and
> drugs are dose-dependent suggests that the
> strength of memories depends on the degree of
> emotional activation induced by learning. (p. 262)

Summaries of research on the psychobiology of
PTSD (e.g., Bremner et al., 1996; Charney, Deutch,
Krystal, Southwick, & Davis, 1993; Krystal, Kosten,
Southwick, Mason, Perry, & Giller, 1989; Krystal,

Southwick, & Charney, 1995; Saporta & van der Kolk, 1992; van der Kolk, 1994; van der Kolk, McFarlane, & Weisaeth, 1996) reveal that patients suffering these PTSD symptoms have changes involving stress hormones, including catecholamines (adrenaline, noradrenaline, dopamine), hypothalamic-pituitary-adrenal axis hormones (CRF, ACTH, glucocorticoids), and endogenous opioids. In posttraumatic stress disorder, there is increased activity of midbrain dopaminergic neurons and an elevation in dopamine, especially in the prefrontal cortex (Charney et al., 1993). The dopaminergic system in the prefrontal cortex is associated with hypnotic response (Spiegel, 1995), and may be associated with focusing attention and the hypervigilant behavior seen in PTSD. Furthermore, this part of the brain, through connections to the hippocampus, may also mediate memory search and retrieval (Moscovitch, 1992).

Clinical experiences, as well as neurobiological evidence like that we have reviewed above, have led many people (e.g., Crabtree, 1992; Christianson, 1992a,b,c; Hammond et al., 1995; Kolb, 1987; Krystal et al., 1995; Squire, 1995; van der Kolk & Ducey, 1989; van der Kolk & van der Hart, 1991) to believe that traumatic memory is stored differently in the brain than conscious narrative memories. And, while normal narrative memory is more malleable and subject to constructivist distorting influences (Loftus, 1993), traumatic memories are more "indelible" (Krystal et al., 1995; LeDoux, 1992), "burned in" (LeDoux, 1992; Terr, 1988), visual and behavioral (Terr, 1988), and more likely to be associated with fear conditioning (Krystal et al., 1995; Weinberger, 1995; Weinberger et al., 1984) that produces flashbacks and emotional and autonomic responses "triggered" by stimuli reminiscent of the original trauma (e.g., Blanchard, Kolb, Gerardi, & Barlow, 1986; Dobbs & Wilson, 1960; Kolb & Multipassi, 1982; McFall, Mumburg, Grant et al., 1990; Pitman, Orr, Laforgue et al., 1987; Pitman, Orr, Laforgue et al., 1990). Moreover, traumatic memories are generally encoded relatively devoid of the usual contextual information accompanying the memory, because fear arousal enhances attention to salient emotional stimuli at the expense of contextual detail (Krystal et al., 1995). Weinberger (1995) has summarized evidence that fear conditioning produces highly specific retuning of receptive fields (e.g., in the auditory cortex) in the brain, so that responses to the conditioned stimulus are increased. "This receptive plasticity is associative and highly specific, is established rapidly, lasts indefinitely, and can be expressed under general anesthesia" (Weinberger, 1995, p. 1071). These neurobiological findings validate the clinical view that emotional and traumatic memory is undoubtedly very different from unstressed memory for nonmeaningful material.

A recent neurobiological study by van der Kolk and his associates (Rauch et al., 1996) using positron emission tomography (PET) has lent strong support to the hypothesis that traumatic memories are processed differently from normal memories. PET technology is a way to study relative areas of brain activity during a particular task. Eight patients with PTSD symptoms (including physiological reactivity to triggering stimuli) following traumas as diverse as childhood sexual abuse, domestic violence, rape, tragic accidents involving death, and war trauma were used in the study. Repeated measures were taken under three conditions—in response to a teeth-clenching control condition, in response to neutral stimuli, and in response to individualized trauma-related stimuli known to induce flashbacks and physiological reactivity in each patient. The experimental condition involved a stress interview to induce flashbacks while relative changes in cerebral blood flow were being measured, along with standard psychophysiological indices like heart rate, frontalis EMG activity, and skin conductance.

During the experimental but not the control condition, all eight PTSD patients, while reporting trauma-related intrusive reexperiencing symptoms, demonstrated increased cerebral blood flow, primarily in several regions of the brain—a right anterior temporal and insular cortex, the secondary visual cortex, and in the limbic and paralimbic areas (including the amygdala). While having reexperiencing symptoms, the subjects also showed significant decreased cerebral blood flow to the left cortical areas and in Broca's (speech) area. Rauch et al. interpret these data to mean that traumatic memories are:

> organized on a perceptual and affective level with limited semantic representation, and tend to intrude as emotional or sensory fragments related to

the original event, with stability over time. These observations have given rise to the notion that traumatic memories may be encoded differently than memories for ordinary events, possibly because of the high degree of emotional arousal at the time of consolidation. (p. 386)

These data strongly suggest that traumatic experiences are processed by the brain differently from normal experiences and support van der Kolk's hypothesis of an amygdala-based, rather than a hippocampally based, processing system for traumatic memories (van der Kolk, 1994). Brain imaging studies have lent additional support. Three independent studies have documented reduced hippocampal volume in PTSD patients (Brenmer et al., 1995b; Gurvitz, Shenton, & Pitman, 1995; Stein et al., 1994).

Teicher, Glod, Surrey, and Swett (1993) used a checklist of limbic symptoms (which was found to correlate .81 with the Dissociative Experiences Scale and .65 with somatization as measured on the SCL-90) to study somatic, sensory, behavioral, and memory symptoms suggestive of temporal lobe epilepsy. They discovered that a history of physical abuse was associated with a 38% increase in questionnaire scores, sexual abuse with a 49% increase, and combined physical and sexual abuse with a 113% increase (p<.0001) compared with non-abused subjects. Interestingly, physical or sexual abuse alone was associated with elevated scores only if the abuse occurred before age 18. Teicher and his colleagues (Ito et al., 1993) also conducted a retrospective study on 115 consecutive patients admitted to a child-adolescent psychiatric inpatient unit. They discovered that compared to non-abused patients, abused patients had increased electrophysiological (brain) abnormalities (54.4% vs. 26.9%, p = 0.021). These differences were predominantly on the left side, supporting the hypothesis that early abuse alters brain development, particularly impacting on limbic structures. Ito et al. (1993) cited unpublished data where they found that recall of a traumatic childhood memory shifted cortical activity from left hemisphere predominance to right hemisphere predominance and that the degree of the right shift was correlated with the severity of the early childhood abuse. They hypothesized from their findings that "left hemisphere dysfunction in

children may result in greater use of, or dependence on, the right hemisphere" (p. 407).

Schiffer, Teicher, and Papanicolaou (1995) studied auditory-probe-evoked potential attenuation as a measure of hemispheric activity in 10 subjects with a history of childhood trauma and 10 matched subjects with no history of abuse. Compared to normal subjects, the trauma subjects were found to have significant left hemisphere dominant asymmetry during neutral memories, which markedly shifted to the right hemisphere when recalling an unpleasant memory. Thus, they documented an asymmetry regardless of mental task. They concluded that they would have to agree with Muller's (1992) hypothesis:

> that early trauma may lead to a lack of integration of left-right hemisphere function, and we further speculate that traumatic memories may be preferentially stored in the right hemisphere. This hypothesis of deficient hemispheric integration and preferential right-sided storage of traumatic memories provides an interesting theoretical explanation for the fact that memory recollection following trauma can be both deficient (constricted or amnestic) and intrusive. (Schiffer et al., 1995, p. 174)

Research has suggested that the right hemisphere may be specialized for processing negative affect (Ahern & Schwartz, 1985; Ladavas, Nicoletti, Umilta et al., 1984; Schwartz, Davidson, & Maer, 1975). Like Schiffer et al. (1995) and Ito et al. (1993), Galin (1974) and Joseph (1988) have likewise hypothesized that painful memories from childhood may be preferentially stored in the right hemisphere, where these memories, as Wickramasekera et al. (1996) suggests, still continue to affect somatic processes so that even though they are out of mind, they are not out of body. The Teicher group's studies provide overall support that *early abuse is associated with left hemisphere abnormalities* (e.g., in limbic structures such as the amygdala and hippocampus) that may prevent greater hemispheric interconnectivity and foster specialization of the right hemisphere. The result may be that the two hemispheres of the brain do not work as cooperatively. They suggest that this lack of hemispheric interdependence may encourage inner conflict or affective instability if the right hemisphere floods the left hemisphere with affects that do not make sense. Furthermore, they have speculated that recall of abuse could lead to at least temporary worsening of adjustment if this activity exacerbated kindling or neuronal irritability.

The neurobiological findings also lend support to Pillemer and White's developmental theory of dual memory systems. Memories in the first three years of life may be difficult to remember because the immaturity of the hippocampus may inhibit the storage of consciously accessible memories. However, emotional memory that is associated with fear conditioning is not the kind of declarative (explicit, consciously accessible) memory that requires hippocampal involvement, but instead "it is mediated by a different system, which in all likelihood operates independently of our conscious awareness. . . . The emotional memory system, which may develop earlier, clearly forms and stores its unconscious memories of these events. And for this reason, the trauma may affect mental and behavioral functions in later life [e.g., sensory, "body memories" and flashbacks], albeit through processes that remain inaccessible to consciousness" (LeDoux, 1994, p. 57). However, in older children or adults, the hippocampus is a location of integration and initial processing of learned material and it has been noted (Phillips & LeDoux, 1992) that the hippocampus is involved in learning that is associated with aversive events in situations where the cues associated with the events are in a context with other cues so that some discrimination is needed, along with spatial and temporal processing. Thus, abusive or traumatic situations in which there is severe anxiety and where fear-provoking associations are learned appear to be complex enough to invoke hippocampal involvement in memory processing, particularly after the age of three.

When the literature clearly shows that emotional memories tend to be more "burned in" in laboratory studies, how can we explain the seeming contradiction that amnesia can be present? We believe that when emotional material reaches the point of being traumatic in intensity—something that cannot be replicated in artificial laboratories—in a certain subpopulation of individuals, material that is too intense may not be able to be consciously processed and so may become unconscious and amnesic. After reviewing the literature, we have also

concluded that this incomplete processing of emotional and cognitive material may quite possibly be associated with a dose-related effect of trauma (Briere & Conte, 1993; Feldman-Summers & Pope, 1994; Herman & Schatzow, 1987; Shore, Tatum, & Vollmer, 1986; van der Kolk, Vardi, Eisler, Herron, Hostettler, & Zakai, 1994). By this we mean that the more intense, violent, or life-threatening (or perceived as life-threatening by the child or individual) the trauma, or perhaps where the intensity is increased by the presence of more than one type of abuse (e.g., physical and sexual), this may increase the overall "input overload" for the individual and may be positively correlated with the use of dissociative or repressive defenses resulting in amnesia for the traumatic event. Thus, for example, Feldman-Summers and Pope (1994) discovered that 83% of psychologists who had been abused both physically and sexually reported periods of forgetting their abuse. In contrast, only 35% and 23% respectively of those who were either sexually abused or physically abused, but not both, reported a period where they forgot some or all of their abuse. It has also been hypothesized that traumatic or abusive events occurring at earlier ages may be more prone to incomplete processing and becoming amnestic, due to both the immaturity of certain brain structures and the cognitive inability of the young child to understand, handle, and integrate such material.

Retrieval of Traumatic Memories— State Dependent Effects

Studies on normal memory retrieval in the last quarter-century have helped us to understand something about the conditions that facilitate retrieval. Some of these principles may apply to *retrieval of traumatic memories*. For example, many traumatic patients describe that a traumatic memory is triggered by a stimulus that either directly or indirectly reminds them of the traumatic event. In the language of memory science, these patients are describing cued recall.

The issue of *free recall of traumatic memories* is perhaps more complex. The research on drug-induced state dependent memory (Eich, 1980) and mood dependent memory (Bower, 1981) is consistent in its view that state dependent retrieval ef-

→ material too intense may not be remembered

fects are operative in conditions of free recall but not in cued recall. These findings predict that trauma survivors would be significantly more likely to freely recall verbally encoded traumatic memories (exempting times being triggered) when the emotional state accompanying the trauma is reenacted, and conversely would be significantly less likely to recall the memory in a neutral or opposite emotional state. Therapy, in the best sense, may establish the emotional ambiance to gradually reinstate the emotional state and thereby establish the search conditions by which a traumatic memory can be freely recalled. It needs to be noted, however, that the findings from the great majority of laboratory studies on emotion and memory in normal subjects may not be readily generalizable to memory retrieval in traumatized patients, in part because they employ primarily recognition or cued recall strategies. Therapy in the best sense employs free recall. Moreover, state dependent effects do not necessarily apply to cued recall and recognition testing in the laboratory.

A FINAL NOTE

A final note is in order about the memory theory used to view traumatic memory. One very important implication of the disruptive processing and dissociated memory theories of trauma is that traumatic memories may not be subject to the same Bartlettian constructivist tendencies so characteristic of normal narrative memories, which are repeatedly reworked. Bartlettian construction and transformation of memories may apply only to normal verbal memories and not necessarily to traumatic memories nor to the persistence of dissociated memory components in the form of intrusive visual imagery, somato-sensory experiences, and behavioral reenactments characteristic of trauma, insofar as intrusive traumatic memories have not yet become integrated with the conscious verbal autobiographical memory system. Until a sufficient database is collected from studies measuring memory performance in traumatized as compared to nontraumatized individuals, we are not in a position to generalize the findings from laboratory studies on normal memory to memory for traumatic experiences.

4

I||||||||||||||||||||

Laboratory Simulation Studies on Memory for Negative Emotional Events

EMOTIONALLY AROUSING VISUAL STIMULI

Interest in memory performance under conditions of emotional arousal dates back over one hundred years to the pioneering work of Whipple (1909), who discovered that the degree of emotional arousal beyond a certain point results in a decrement in memory performance. Clinicians have also observed a relationship between emotionally significant events and failure to remember. Writing in 1936, Erickson noted that "the usefulness of the word-association test in detecting the presence of concealed or repressed memories is well recognized." The test was widely used as an uncovering technique to find repressed memories.

The earliest laboratory studies on emotional arousal and memory performance using the *word association procedure* were developed by Wilhelm Wundt (1903) and Carl G. Jung (Jung, 1906) and later modified by A. R. Luria (Rossi, 1980). Keet (1948) gave laboratory subjects a list of neutral and emotionally arousing words matched for frequency of usage. Sometime later, subjects were presented with the same list of words. Keet found that subjects failed to remember emotional arousing words significantly more often than neutral words. Levinger and Clark (1961) considerably improved the experimental design in a subsequent study us-

ing the word association procedure. Their subjects were presented with a list of half neutral and half emotionally disturbing words, and then were asked to say "the first word which comes to mind" (p. 100). Galvanic skin response (GSR) was measured as each successive word was spoken. Immediately after, and again four months later, subjects were retested. In contrast to the Keet (1948) procedure, which asked for any association to the stimulus word, in this study subjects were asked to remember their original association to each word ("remember the word you said last time," p. 100). Emotionally disturbing words, as compared to neutral words, were associated with significantly higher GSR response and significantly greater forgetting.

Kleinsmith and Kaplan (1963, 1964) measured galvanic skin response to neutral and emotionally arousing word-number pairs in a paired-associate learning task. They varied the retention interval between the original stimulus presentation and the memory test from two minutes (immediate) to one week. Emotional arousing words were remembered significantly less than neutral words at short retention intervals, but were remembered significantly more at longer retention intervals. A number of subsequent studies have replicated the Kleinsmith and Kaplan discovery that emotionally arousing words are *better* retained at longer than at shorter retention intervals (see Christianson,

99

1992b, pp. 130–134, 160–161 for a review).

Christianson and Nilsson (1984) used a combination of visual and verbal stimuli in their study. Laboratory subjects viewed either a neutral or emotionally arousing version of 18 color slides of human faces. Each slide contained a verbal description of various characteristics of the person in four categories—name, occupation, hobby, and personality trait. Half the subjects saw a neutral version of the slides showing faces of ordinary people. The other half (the experimental group) saw an identical sequence of faces, except that the middle six slides "showed a series of grotesque forensic pathology photographs of facial injuries" (p. 144). Skin conductance and heart rate were monitored immediately before, during, and after viewing the slides. After a 12-minute retention interval, during which subjects engaged in a filler activity to prevent memory rehearsal of the target information, all subjects were given a cued recall memory test. Subjects were presented with the slide of each face in the same sequence in which they originally viewed it and were then asked to recall the four verbal descriptors for the face.

The results of the physiological monitoring demonstrated that the experimental subjects were significantly more aroused during the presentation of the autopsy slides than during the earlier and subsequent presentation of the neutral slides. They were also significantly more aroused by the autopsy slides than control subjects were by the neutral slides. Cued recall memory performance was significantly poorer in the experimental than in the control condition. Subjects who viewed the autopsy slides recalled significantly fewer correct verbal descriptors of the autopsy slides relative to the neutral slides in the experimental group, and were significantly less correct in their report of verbal descriptors than the control group. The study clearly demonstrated that the memory deficit was "obtained for the items attached to the traumatic pictures" (p. 153). Christianson and Nilsson conclude that "amnesia was found for items associated with the traumatic events" (p. 142).

In another study, Christianson and Fallman (1990) examined the differential effects of emotional arousal on memory for visual and verbal stimuli. Subjects from two age groups (15–18 and 25–31 years old) viewed 25 slide pairs consisting of a picture and a word unrelated to the pictured scene first

at a very brief (50 milliseconds) and then at a brief (four seconds) exposure. The slide sequence contained five neutral, five positive, five very positive, five negative, and five very negative slides. The very negative slides were of accidents, war, and sickness. Heart rate was monitored during the slide presentation. Subjects recognized the very negative and negative slides (visual information) significantly more than the other slides. They recalled the words significantly more when paired with positive than with negative visual stimuli. No age differences were found.

In another experiment, Christianson (1987) looked more carefully at the nature of the autonomic arousal associated with viewing the autopsy slides. After improving the earlier design so that physiological monitoring occurred continuously during the viewing of the slide presentation, he found that skin conductance, but not heart rate, significantly increased when the subject saw the first autopsy slide embedded in the sequence of neutral slides. After the second or third autopsy slide, both skin conductance and heart rate significantly increased; the heightened physiological state persisted into the subsequent series of neutral slides. Subjects also reported the autopsy slides to be significantly more "distressing" than the neutral slides.

Kramer, Buckhout, Fox, Widman, and Tusche (1991) used the Christianson autopsy slide paradigm in a study of memory for visual stimuli. Subjects viewed a series of 19 color slides about neutral travel scenes. The tenth slide in the series was one of three critical slides: (1) a crime scene of a deceased man whose face had been disfigured by blows with a hammer, labeled "New York Police Department," (2) the same slide labeled "Courtesy of MGM Studios," or (3), a woman tourist posing for a photo. The subjects level of anxiety was assessed and then subjects were asked to recall as many slides as possible in any order they could. Memory performance was measured in terms of the mean number of slides correctly recalled and also in terms of recall accuracy based on a blind judge's rating of each recall report. Subjects were found to be significantly more anxious in the high stress (NYPD) condition relative to the other two conditions. After, but not before, exposure to the emotionally arousing slide (NYPD) condition, subjects in the experimental condition relative to the other two conditions recalled significantly fewer slides and recalled them with significantly less accuracy. The authors conclude that "traumatic stimuli result in poorer memory for stimuli which follow" (p. 487). This study essentially replicates the earlier Christianson findings.

The standard for modern laboratory study of the effects of emotional arousal on memory performance appeared in the 1970s. In this *Aussage method*, subjects observe primarily visual stimuli under controlled laboratory conditions (Dent & Stephenson, 1979). The typical laboratory experiment contains three parts.

First, experimental subjects, usually college students, observe a complex event in the laboratory. The event is presented either through the medium of a brief film or videotape or a sequence of slides. Some experiments have used live staged scenarios, in which confederates to the experiment role play the plot. The stimulus event is usually a complex event, in that it has a sequence of actions with one central and other less relevant action sequences and often involves a number of people. Two types of stimulus events are used: (1) In the experimental condition, subjects are presented with a complex event containing a central action that is presumed to be emotionally arousing. Christianson (1992a) defines *negative emotional events* as "events that are new, unexpected, and potentially threatening" (p. 284). These are "distinctive events or scenes that have unpleasant visual features (e.g., blood, injuries) and have the potential to evoke strong unpleasant feelings (emotional stress) in the viewer" (p. 285). The presumption is that such stimulus events evoke *emotional arousal*. Christianson defines emotional stress as "a consequence of a negative emotional event" (p. 285). However, it has not always been clearly established through experimental measurement that the stimulus event actually evokes emotional arousal; many studies simply presume that a given stimulus will emotionally arouse subjects. In the control condition, subjects are presented with the same complex event, except that the emotionally arousing stimulus has been left out. For example, subjects in both conditions might be presented with a brief film about a bank robbery or a car accident. The experimental group watches a film about a bank robbery that contains a shooting scene or a film about a car accident in which a pedestrian is in-

jured. The control group watches the same film about the bank robbery or the car accident without the shooting or injury scene, respectively.

Second, the experiment includes a defined *retention interval*. Subjects' memory performance may be measured immediately following viewing the stimulus event or after a designated period of time. Specifying a retention interval allows memory scientists to study differential forgetting rates under conditions of emotional arousal. Subjects typically engage in some filler activity during the retention interval.

Third, experimental and control subjects are given some sort of *memory test*, which may come in the form of free narrative recall, cued recall, and/or cued recognition. Most of the studies have emphasized cued recall as the dependent variable. Subjects answer a series of specific questions (usually in the form of a written questionnaire) about the original stimulus event. The questions may be worded in a yes/no or multiple choice format. Some experiments also include a photo identification task, in which subjects view a series of photographs of people and are asked to identify which one of the photographs represents a person in the original stimulus event. Memory performance on the cued recall task is sometimes calculated in terms of the *total amount* of correct information reported. The complex stimulus event is broken down into, say, 40 scorable items. One point is assigned for every reported detail that correctly matches a detail in the original film or slide sequence. *Accuracy* is calculated in terms of the percent of total details correctly reported. Memory performance is sometimes calculated in terms of correct or incorrect identification of one or a number of *specific target details* like whether the weapon used by the bank robbers was a gun or knife. In this case, accuracy is calculated in terms of the percent of subjects in the experimental versus control group that correctly identify the target detail. As we will see, these strategies for assessing memory performance are important, because they greatly affect the type of conclusions that can be made about memory performance for negative emotional events.

The measurement phase of the research may also include a variety of additional procedures. The better studies include some way of measuring the degree of emotional arousal evoked by the negative emotional event, although some studies simply presume that emotional arousal has occurred and do not include measurements of it. The measurements may be taken in the form of subjective measures, e.g., ratings on the degree of emotionality, or physiological measures, such as heart rate or galvanic skin response. Some studies also include confidence ratings, i.e., how confident the subject is that his or her report is accurate (see Deffenbacher, 1980, for a review of the studies on the relationship between confidence and accuracy).

In an early study using the Aussage method, Tichner and Poulton (1975) had subjects view a videotape of a complex street scene. Subjects were then asked to pick out the criminal actions and perpetrators from the rest of the activities occurring in the scene. They found that subjects were able to correctly identify the criminal actions significantly more often than they were able to identify the physical characteristics of the people involved.

In a series of experiments, Brian Clifford and his associates modified the Tichner and Poulton paradigm into a memory experiment. Clifford and Scott (1978) had 48 subjects (24 male and 24 female) view a videotape of an incident involving two policemen and an innocent bystander. In the neutral version of the videotape, the policemen are searching for a criminal and ask the bystander for help. The bystander is reluctant to get involved. A verbal exchange follows and one of the policemen weakly restrains the other officer and the bystander. The same videotape was used in the violent condition, except that a short critical sequence in which one policeman physically assaults the bystander has been spliced into the tape. Immediately after viewing one or the other version of the tape, subjects were either asked to give a free narrative report or were asked a series of 15 specific questions about the incident. Memory performance was then measured using a 44-item questionnaire. Each of the questions addressed either the *actions* in the original stimulus event or the *physical characteristics* of the people involved. Each subject in the experimental condition also rated the degree of violence associated with the critical sequence in the video. The overall accuracy of the report was measured by assigning one point for each of a maximum of 40 total video details (20 action details and 20 physical characteristics) that were correctly reported. The results indicated that the mean accuracy scores for all details were significantly lower in the experimental, violent condition than in the neutral, control condition. Women were significantly worse in their general recall accuracy than men in the violent condition, and they also rated the video as more violent. Women specifically recalled the actions significantly better and people descriptions significantly worse than men in both the violent and nonviolent conditions.

Clifford and Scott conclude that "recall of details from a violent incident was significantly worse than recall of a nonviolent incident" (p. 356). They believed that "a single emotional or arousing aspect of an event has a repressing effect that generalizes to the whole event" (p. 356), in that recall of both actions and people descriptions was significantly worse in the violent than in the neutral condition. Christianson (1992a), however, points out that "it is unclear whether the subjects were tested on identical portions of the critical emotional event (i.e., details associated with the bystander) or if the detrimental effects were found for all details in the violent condition" (p. 289).

Clifford and Hollin (1981) subsequently replicated the earlier study. A total of 60 subjects viewed either a violent or nonviolent version of a brief videotape. The nonviolent, control group watched a videotape about a woman walking alone on a street. A man approaches her and asks for directions. She points out the way and the man leaves. She continues walking alone. The violent, experimental group of subjects watched a similar videotape in which a woman is walking alone. In this version the man approaches the woman, grabs her arm, forces her into a wall, tears away her handbag, and runs off. The woman continues to walk along, sobbing. In each of the experimental and neutral conditions, groups of subjects saw videotapes with either one man, three men, or five men involved in the theft, making six conditions altogether. Memory performance consisted of a questionnaire about six descriptive characteristics of the main man (age, height, weight, sex, race, and clothing). All subjects rated the confidence of their memory report. Subjects also attempted to identify the man from a photo spread. No measure of emotional arousal was reported.

The results essentially confirmed the results of Clifford and Scott (1978). Subjects in the violent condition were significantly less accurate than those in the nonviolent control condition in their memory of the physical characteristics of the man involved—and even less accurate when asked about detail descriptions of other men who were present in the background. There was no significant relationship between memory accuracy and confidence in the violent condition. Photo identification of the man was quite poor (27%). The authors conclude that "testimony of witnesses to a violent incident was significantly poorer than given by witnesses to a nonviolent incident" (p. 367). Christianson (1992a), however, has questioned the conclusion:

> Can one conclude, as Clifford and Hollin (1978) do, that the presence of violence impairs accurate memory? Not uniformly. Apparently the witnesses have concentrated on the assaulted woman and the principal man. . . . Subjects in the violent condition performed less well in remembering detailed information as a function of increased number of perpetrators. (pp. 289–290)

The most widely cited study on emotional arousal and memory performance was conducted by Loftus and Burns (1982). They had their subjects view a brief film about a bank robbery. In the nonviolent, control version, a robber holds up a bank teller and leaves the bank. The teller shouts that she has been robbed and two bank employees chase the robber into the parking lot, where two young boys are playing. One boy is wearing a football jersey with the number 17 on it. Exposure time was two seconds for the number. Then, the film flashes back to the bank, where the teller is informing the people in the bank about the robbery. In the violent, experimental version of the film, subjects view the same sequence of events except for an additional parking lot scene. As the employees chase the robber to the getaway car, the robber turns and fires his gun. He misses the employees but hits one of the boys in the face. The boy then falls to the ground injured and bleeding.

Immediately after viewing the film, all subjects answered a series of 25 questions about the detail of the film or about filler items (recall task). The questions include one *critical item*. Among other details, subjects were asked to report the number on the boy's football jersey. Another group of subjects was asked to select the number on the football jersey

from one of four numbers (recognition task). All subjects were asked to rate their "interest level" in the film and "how upsetting" it was to them. They also rated their confidence in their memory report after each question about a stimulus detail. Subjects rated the violent version of the film to be significantly more interesting and more upsetting. The results demonstrated that the subjects in the recall experimental group, relative to the control group, were significantly less able to recall the number of the boy's football jersey (4% vs. 28%). In the recognition experimental group, likewise, the experimental subjects less accurately recognized the number as compared to the control subjects (28% vs. 55%). Of the remaining 16 stimulus details, 14 were also answered significantly less accurately in the violent condition relative to the nonviolent condition, even though many of these items were seen by the subjects more than once.

An additional experiment was conducted in which the same violent and nonviolent versions of the film were used in the experimental and control conditions, except this time the film ended with an unexpected event, namely switching to a scene of two people walking along a beach. The results essentially replicated the other recall and recognition experiments. No significant differences were observed in memory performance between subjects who saw the expected version and those who saw the unexpected version of the control film. Loftus and Burns interpret the results to mean that it must have been the emotional arousal, not the unexpectedness of the event, that contributed to the memory decrement. The authors conclude:

> exposure to mentally shocking events can cause retrograde amnesia for other events that occur. . . . Our results showed that impairment in memory occurred not only for an item seen immediately prior to the critical incident, but also for items occurring nearly 2 minutes earlier. (p. 321)

According to Loftus and Burns, these results "suggest that witnesses to emotionally traumatic events, such as crimes, accidents, or fires, may be less able to recall key events that occurred prior to the eruption of the trauma" (p. 322). However, Christianson (1992a) has questioned this interpretation of the data:

Can one conclude that all details about a highly emotional event will be less remembered than details about a neutral event? Not really. In the results of, for example, the E. F. Loftus and Burns (1982) study an interesting effect can be seen of impaired memory for detail information presented preceding the emotion-arousing event (cf. retrograde amnesia), that is, an impaired memory for the number on the football jersey; however, with respect to the details associated with the emotional or the neutral episode itself, there were small differences seen between the two conditions. (p. 290)

Following Christianson's reinterpretation of the Loftus and Burns (1982) findings, we have here recalculated the mean accuracy of the recall of all 17 stimulus items in the emotionally arousing condition (see Loftus & Burns, 1982, Table 1, p. 320). The mean accuracy for the recall of total information viewed by subjects in the emotionally arousing condition was 75.6%. Using the Deffenbacher 70% criterion as an indication of high accuracy, we come to a conclusion exactly opposite to that of Loftus and Burns: subjects in the emotionally arousing condition were indeed *very* accurate in their recall of the most of the information about the bank robbery, and were inaccurate only about a very minor detail. When all of the data are considered, there is little support for the memory fallibility interpretation.

Subsequent studies failed to find a significant decrease in memory accuracy in response to viewing presumedly emotionally arousing videotapes, films, or slides. Christianson (1984) showed his subjects either a neutral or emotionally arousing sequence of slides. The neutral version showed a mother and her seven-year-old son leaving their house, walking across a park, and then hailing a taxi to go to school. The emotionally arousing version showed a slide with "one of the boy's eye-globes hanging out from its proper place and bleeding heavily after being hit by a car" (p. 151) spliced into the neutral version at the point where the mother and boy hailed the taxi. The degree of emotional arousal was assessed by physiological measurements (skin conductance and heart rate) and by subjective ratings of discomfort. After a ten-minute filler activity, memory testing consisted of a recall task of both the objects and actions in the original com-

plex stimulus event. It also included a forced-choice recognition test in which subjects were given four slides (one correct and three new slides) to choose from for each of the 15 slides comprising the original stimulus event.

The physiological data demonstrated that subjects who viewed the emotionally arousing version of the slides were significantly more aroused than those viewing the neutral version. They also reported feeling greater discomfort. Subjects who watched the emotionally arousing version of the slides recalled significantly more correct total information about the stimulus event, especially after long retention intervals (two weeks). In the slide recognition task, experimental subjects recognized significantly fewer total accurate slides after short retention intervals (immediately after), but significantly more after long retention intervals. Christianson concludes:

> memory performance for those subjects presented with the traumatic version of the story performed less well at a short retention interval as compared to those subjects presented with a neutral version of the story, but performed better on a delayed test interval. (pp. 154–155)

He interprets the data to mean that "materials encoded under a state of heightened emotional arousal are less susceptible to forgetting than materials encoded under neutral conditions." (p. 157)

Scrivner and Safer (1988) demonstrated a similar enhancement in memory performance in response to an emotional arousing event. Their subjects viewed a police training tape about a burglary. In the tape, a neighbor views a burglar breaking into a house. The burglar enters the kitchen of the house and pulls out a gun. As he falls over a chair he wakes up the residents. When the wife enters the kitchen, the burglar shoots her twice; before making his escape, he shoots the neighbor and the husband. The videotape contains a total of 47 violent and nonviolent details. All subjects viewed the same videotape and no external comparison group was used. After viewing the film, subjects filled out an anxiety questionnaire and rated the extent to which they considered the film violent. Repeated memory performance was assessed against the subject's own baseline performance. Immediately after viewing the tape all subjects completed a baseline recall test and then they were randomly assigned to one of three conditions: emotion-cued recall, context-cued recall, or uninstructed recall. Upon each recall trial, subjects were told to "replay the videotape as though they had their own internal video screen" (p. 372).

In the emotion-cued recall condition, subjects were instructed to "use their feelings to help them remember the associated details" (p. 372), and in the context-cued recall condition they were instructed to "focus on the external surroundings as they mentally replayed the tape, and to use these context cues to help them recover details" (p. 372). Memory performance was measured in terms of the total number of the 47 details recalled on each of four successive recall trials over a 48-hour period—three successive recall trials in the first session and a fourth during the second session, 48 hours later. Because no significant differences were observed in performance across the emotion-cued, context-cued, and non-cued recall conditions, data were combined across retrieval strategies. Results demonstrated that subjects significantly improved their recall of the details over successive trials, with a total of 38% of the details remembered on the first trial, and 61% remembered by the fourth trial. This increase in the number of accurate details recalled over time was not accompanied by any increase in guessing. Scrivner and Safer conclude that "memory for significant details about a mentally shocking event improved with repeated testing" and that "these substantial gains in recall occurred without increased guessing" (p. 375).

Dunning and Stern (1992) attempted to replicate the Scrivner and Safer (1988) study. In their first experiment 17 subjects watched videotapes of robberies and shootings followed by immediate free recall of the event. Shortly thereafter subjects in the experimental group completed a second and third free recall of the event. As compared to control subjects who only recalled the event once, repeated free recall led to a significant increase in the total amount of information recalled (11%), but there was no significant increase in the amount of inaccurate or erroneous information recalled. Dunning and Stern conclude that repeated free recall can lead to "more accurate and complete accounts" (p. 648). In a second experiment, a similar hypermnesic improvement

was found even after a three-day or week delay before the initial free recall, presumably after subjects' memory had decayed somewhat. A third study was designed to investigate the effects of the memory retrieval strategies used. A multiple-choice questioning procedure (i.e., a recognition test) was used instead of a free recall procedure. This procedure did not lead to an increase in the amount of information recalled. Taken together these experiments demonstrate:

> that testimony does change over interrogations. Eyewitness reports become more accurate and complete over multiple interrogations when free-recall procedures are used. (p. 654)

A more recent study on memory enhancement replicated the Scrivner and Safer (1988) results. Turtle and Yuille (1994) had 93 subjects view a 4.5-minute videotape of a drug-related robbery that resulted in two people being shot. All groups recalled the videotape immediately after viewing it. Two experimental groups recalled the event at one-week intervals over the next three weeks for a total of four recalls, one group recalling it without further aid and the other recalling it after reviewing their previous statements. Two control groups recalled the event only one more time, three weeks later, one group without further aid and one group after reviewing their previous statements. The results indicated that repeated recall significantly increased the total of number of details recalled, irrespective of whether or not the subjects had reviewed their previous statements. While the number of errors was very low overall, there was an increase in the error rate over successive recalls. Turtle and Yuille conclude:

> Our reminiscence findings generally do support the notion that multiple eyewitness recalls can be beneficial in terms of overall recall without a severe increase in errors. (p. 268).

Geiselman and Padilla (1988) showed children ages seven and twelve a film about a robbery. After three days the children were given either a standard interview or a cognitive interview (Geiselman et al., 1985) adapted for children. The cognitive interview consisted of imagining the environmental context of the original event, recalling the feelings experienced, and then trying to freeing recall everything that happened. Compared to the standard interview, the cognitive interview resulted in a 21% increase in the total amount of information recalled without significantly increasing the amount of incorrect information recalled. Saywitz, Geiselman, and Bornstein (1992) replicated the former study in two additional experiments using a more refined cognitive interview method. Experiment #1 used a live stage event in which children ages seven to eight and ten to eleven years of age played games, including touch games, with a stranger. The children were each interviewed two days later with either a standard interview or the cognitive interview. Both types of interviews included instructions that it was acceptable to say "I don't know," to refuse to answer, or to ask for clarification. For both age groups children recalled 26% more information in the cognitive as compared to the standard interview. Although younger children produced more incorrect information, neither type of interview significantly increased the memory error rate. Saywitz et al. conclude:

> . . . the cognitive interview improved recall of correct information at both age levels studied and without an increase in errors. (p. 748)

Experiment #2 was intended as a replication with a larger sample. It also assessed the effect of prior experience with the cognitive interview. A total of 92 children of ages eight to nine or eleven to twelve years of age witnessed a staged argument. The children were interviewed with either the standard or cognitive interview. Those in the cognitive interview condition were divided into two subgroups, one that had a practice session with the cognitive interview and another that had a rapport session instead immediately after the staged event. After two days all children were given either the standard or cognitive interview. As compared to the standard interview, children in the cognitive interview group reported 18% more information, while children in the cognitive interview plus prior practice group reported 45% more information. There were no significant differences in the number of incorrect items reported across groups. The researchers conclude:

> . . . the recollections of children can be improved through cognitive interviewing and further through practice with cognitive interviewing. (p. 754)

STAGED CRIMES

In order to create laboratory research paradigms that approximate real-life crime situations better than viewing slides or videotapes, a number of researchers began to use live staged scenarios in which a crime was enacted in front of the research subjects. Buckhout, Apler, Chern, Silverberg, and Slomovits (1974) had research confederates enact a purse-snatching incident in front of two college classes. Subjects rated their degree of stress and filled out an anxiety inventory immediately following the incident. Then they were asked to recall some of the physical characteristics of the perpetrator and to estimate the duration of the incident. Three weeks later, subjects tried to identify the perpetrator in a line-up. Those subjects more stressed, at the time of the incident, as compared to those less stressed, were significantly better able to recall details when describing the perpetrator and were significantly less accurate in the photo identification task. While this study contains an innovative stimulus event, the results are difficult to interpret because non-equivalent memory measures were used in each of the two memory testing sessions.

Johnson and Scott (1976) had confederates enact a live scene while subjects sat in a room waiting for an experiment to begin. In the control group half the subjects overheard a conversation about laboratory equipment failure, following which a confederate appeared holding a pen. His hands were covered with grease. In the experimental condition, the other half of the subjects overhead a hostile verbal exchange. They could hear chairs crashing and bottles breaking in the background. Then a confederate entered the room holding a bloodied letter opener. Memory testing was conducted immediately after and one week after using free recall, cued recall, and also a photo recognition task. Recall memory was assessed for the details of the setting, the actions that occurred, and the physical characteristics of the confederate. In the emotionally arousing condition, relative to the control condition, males had significantly better recall and recognition on all measures, and females had significantly better recall on all measures except for the physical characteristics of the confederate.

Harmon Hosch and his associates have conducted a series of recognition memory experiments using a staged theft paradigm. These studies are designed to assess the differential memory performance of victims and bystanders to a crime. A group of laboratory subjects are present in a room with an experimenter. The experimenter asks the subjects to remove their watches and place them on a table to be used at a later point in the experiment. Then the experimenter leaves the room. In the neutral condition, a female confederate then enters the room posing as subject who has come late. She fills out the same information sheet as the other participants and then gets up and quickly leaves the room. The action in the bystander condition is similar to the neutral condition, except that the confederate discovers an expensive calculator on the table, says that she would like to have it, places it in her purse and quickly leaves. The action in the victim condition is similar to that of the control, except that the confederate takes the other subjects' watches. Then the experimenter enters the room, tells the subjects that it was a staged theft, and conducts a memory recognition test, namely a photospread identification.

In the first experiment, Hosch and Cooper (1982) found that recognition of the perpetrator from six photos was significantly better in both the victim and bystander conditions, relative to the control condition, but that victim and bystander recognition memory did not significantly differ from each other. Hosch and Cooper conclude "that the presence of a crime significantly increases identification accuracy" (p. 651).

In a subsequent experiment, Hosch, Leippe, Marchioni, and Cooper (1984) investigated the effects of personality and situational variables on recognition memory for the staged theft. Subjects were divided into those high or low in a personality trait called self-monitoring, i.e., the tendency to use either external social information (high) or internal attitudinal or emotional information (low) to guide behavior. The experiment used the same neutral, bystander, and victims conditions as in the previous experiment. The photo identification task was con-

ducted with or without biased instructions, i.e., strongly implying that the suspect was or was not in the line-up. The results replicated those of the previous study, with bystanders and victims performing better than control subjects. As predicted, those subjects in the biased line-up condition were significantly less accurate than other subjects, especially if they tended to rely on social information (high self-monitoring). Low self-monitorers were resistant to the biasing effect.

In a third study, Hosch and Bothwell (1990) measured physiological arousal (skin conductance) of subjects during the staged theft using the same three conditions. In addition to the memory recognition test, the study also included a measure of the accuracy of memory for the physical characteristics of the perpetrator. Victims and bystanders did not differ in the degree of their physiological arousal during the staged theft. Once again, victims and bystanders were significantly better than controls in the photo identification task. However, victims were significantly more accurate than bystanders in their description of the physical characteristics of the perpetrator.

Leippe and Wells conducted a series of experiments using a similar staged theft paradigm. Leippe, Wells, and Ostrom (1978) experimentally manipulated the seriousness of the crime. Their experiment had three conditions: (1) a no-theft control, (2) a less serious staged theft (stealing cigarettes), and (3) a more serious staged theft (stealing an expensive calculator). Subjects learned of the value of the stolen object either before or after the theft. The memory test consisted of a six-photo identification task given immediately after the staged theft had occurred. Recognition accuracy was significantly better for the more serious than less serious crime or no-crime control condition. Seriousness of the crime was determined by having the subjects know the value of the calculator beforehand so they perceived the staged crime to be serious.

Wells and Leippe (1981) used the same staged calculator theft in another experiment that assessed not only recognition memory for the perpetrator but also memory for peripheral details. The experimental procedure was similar to the previous experiment, but subjects were given an eleven-item memory test for trivial and peripheral details of the environment where the staged theft occurred. The results demonstrated that identification accuracy and memory for peripheral details were negatively correlated. Those witnesses who accurately identified the perpetrator in the photo spread remembered significantly fewer peripheral details than those who incorrectly identified an innocent victim as the perpetrator. This important study demonstrates that *judging the accuracy of an eyewitness's recognition memory for a perpetrator by the ability to remember other more peripheral details of the crime is simply wrong.*

Malpass and Devine (1981) used the staged scenario to investigate methods to improve recognition accuracy of witnesses. Laboratory subjects witnessed a staged act of vandalism in which a confederate changed some dials on electronic equipment. When told to leave them alone, he impulsively damaged the equipment and left. Subjects were tested with a photo line-up five months after the incident under one of two conditions: (1) a line-up with the vandal present in one of the photos, and (2) a line-up without the vandal present in any of the pictures. Half the subjects were given simple instructions to tell whether or not the perpetrator was present in the photospread. The other half were given guided memory instructions intended to enhance memory performance. The guided memory instruction consisted of a systematic visualization of the setting where the staged vandalism had taken place, visualization of the details of the room, the actions that took place, and the feelings that were evoked. The results demonstrated that subjects were significantly more accurate in their identification of the perpetrator in the vandal present, as compared to the vandal absent, line-up condition. Moreover, those subjects using the guided memory procedure were significantly more accurate (60%) than those receiving simple identification instructions (40%). Malpass and Devine conclude that the guided memory procedure enhances the accuracy of eyewitness identification.

RECONSIDERATION OF THE LOFTUS MEMORY FALLIBILITY HYPOTHESIS

What scientific conclusions can be drawn from these diverse laboratory simulation studies on emotion and memory? Interestingly, the first general interpretation, by Elizabeth Loftus, has received the most public attention, but it appears to be at best oversimplified and possibly in error. The Loftus memory fallibility hypothesis is instructive because it illustrates a fundamental law of logic: If you begin with an erroneous premise and do not correct that premise, it will lead you to even more extreme and incorrect conclusions.

In her book *Eyewitness Testimony* (1979a), Loftus argued that all eyewitness situations raise serious questions of reliability. Her premise was that the senses are fallible receivers and recorders of information, yet people generally believe that eyewitness identification is highly dependable. Many dramatic cases in the law attest to the fact that eyewitness identification can easily send an innocent person to prison. After the book was published, and ever since, Loftus has taken her position concerning the fallibility of the senses into hundreds of court cases to argue against the reliability of eyewitness testimony. The impact on the law has been profound and generally beneficial. Courts began addressing the deficiencies of sensory perceptions by allowing experts to explain eyewitness errors to juries. The result has been better informed jurors.

As Loftus studied what could go wrong in eyewitness identification, as Munsterberg (1908) had done decades earlier, three general factors emerged. The first concerned the deficiencies of the sensory organs. There are some events that people cannot see or hear from where they are situated. Yet, eyewitnesses would frequently identify a suspect under circumstances where accurate vision was physically impossible. Deficiencies in the working of sense organs provides a partial explanation for eyewitness misidentification. The second factor is memory. Even if witnesses have correctly perceived a situation, they might not accurately recall it for a variety of reasons. Memory is not a tape recorder; it can be interpretive and wrong. The third major problem with eyewitness identification is that it may be the product of suggestions that have influenced, altered, or implanted memories.

Thus, Loftus moved from the study of the deficits of eyewitness identification to the *fallibility of memory*. Because subjects viewing the violent version of the film were less able than control subjects to remember the number of the boy's football jersey, Loftus and Burns (1982) concluded that the "results showed that impairment in memory occurred" (p. 321). From the indisputable observation that memory may occasionally be impaired, especially for peripheral details, Loftus and Burns (1982) drew the more global conclusion that "witnesses to emotionally traumatic events . . . may be less able to recall key events that occurred prior to the eruption of the trauma" (p. 322).

In her basic textbook on *Memory* (1980), Loftus generalizes the notion of fallibility even further. She says, in essence, that all negative emotional stress makes memory fallible in all instances: "Generally speaking, strongly negative and stressful emotions hinder accurate perception and memory" (p. 78). More recently, Loftus has taken a further step and generalized the memory fallibility hypothesis to memories recovered in psychotherapy (1993).

The memory fallibility viewpoint has been widely disseminated among the authorities on eyewitness research. Kassin, Ellsworth, and Smith (1989) surveyed 63 experts. A total of 79% endorsed the view that "very high levels of stress impair the accuracy of eyewitness testimony." But is this what the scientific literature actually demonstrates? Our review of the research shows that emotional stress impairs memory accuracy under certain conditions but improves memory accuracy under other conditions. The simplistic conclusions reached by Loftus, which have now led her to testify against perception and against memory accuracy, does an injustice to the rich complexity of the data. As Christianson (1992a) aptly notes:

> Although there seems to be an expert consensus that stress impairs memory a body of studies have shown this relationship to be much more complex than the very general statement tested by Kassin et al. (1989). (p. 289)

In other words, Loftus and the others who adhere to the memory fallibility viewpoint have considerably oversimplified the findings across studies in a way that is misleading. When these erroneous views began influencing court decisions, great harm was caused to individual litigants and to legal theory.

MEMORY AND EMOTION: WHAT WE KNOW

There have been several attempts to provide a more accurate assessment of the scientific literature. Deffenbacher (1983) reviewed a total of 21 studies on the influence of arousal on eyewitness memory. He found that 11 of the studies demonstrated significantly decreased memory accuracy and 10 of the studies significantly increased accuracy under conditions of heightened arousal. He attempted to explain this seeming inconsistency in terms of the Yerkes-Dodson Law, wherein moderately high levels of arousal may increase memory accuracy while very high levels of arousal may decrease it. However, the application of the Yerkes-Dodson Law to emotion and memory studies is quite controversial (cf. Anderson, 1990; Neiss, 1988, 1990).

More recently, Christianson (1992a) thoroughly reviewed all of the studies on emotional arousal and eyewitness memory. Whereas earlier reviews failed to distinguish between general physiological arousal, emotional arousal, and emotional arousal specific to the to-be-remembered information, Christianson reviewed the effects specifically of negative emotional events on memory. Based upon his assessment of the literature, he challenges the conclusions drawn by Loftus and others that negative emotional stress makes memory fallible. This view, he notes, is largely based on three widely cited studies (Clifford & Hollin, 1981; Clifford & Scott, 1978; Loftus & Burns, 1982). He believes that the conclusions drawn from each of these studies are not warranted because they are dependent upon the way memory performance was measured. Memory accuracy seems impaired when the memory test addresses the *total information* or *peripheral details* in a complex event. However, when the *central information* is considered, memory impairment is rarely found. Christianson concludes:

> . . . they do not show memory impairment for the emotionally arousing event itself. Thus, it can be concluded that memory for some information, for example, details presented preceding and succeeding an emotional event, seem to be impaired, at least temporarily. But, one cannot conclude that memory for details about the emotional event per se is impaired. (p. 291)

Central information is defined as information related to the emotional arousal per se, such as the shooting in Loftus and Burns (1982) or the physical assault in either of the Clifford studies. In other words, these early studies fail to experimentally vary the *type of information* used in the memory test.

These early studies are useful in that they help us to identify a number of important interacting variables operative in the laboratory simulation studies on emotion and memory. These have been identified by Christianson (1992a, p. 291):

1. *Type of arousal* (general autonomic arousal vs. emotional arousal vs. arousal specific to the to-be-remembered event),
2. *Type of event* (emotional vs. neutral),
3. *Activity level* (victim vs. bystander),
4. *Retention interval* (immediate vs. delayed),
5. *Type of information* (central vs. peripheral), and
6. *Retrieval strategy.*

A pattern across these diverse studies suggests that decrements in memory accuracy appear in those studies that utilize general measures of arousal and measure memory for total information and/or peripheral details in passively witnessing subjects. Increments in memory accuracy appear in those studies that demonstrate arousal specific to the emotional event and measure memory for the central event itself (and associated details) in actively participating subjects. Unfortunately, most of the research designs in the eyewitness literature over the past few decades have not been sophisticated enough to address all of these variables and their interactions. Therefore, the data across studies appear more inconsistent than necessary. Considering the complex number and interaction of operative variables, oversimplified notions of memory fallibility distort the evidence and do not advance scientific understanding of the effects of emotional arousal on memory performance. We agree with Christianson that "there is no simple relationship between intense emotion and memory" (1992b, p. 316).

While no single study has experimentally manipulated all of the variables mentioned above, a number of studies have varied the *type of information* in the memory test. Kebeck and Lohaus (1986) had their subjects view a neutral or emotionally

arousing version of a film about an interaction between a student and teacher. The emotionally arousing situation was an argument between them. In contrast to the aforementioned studies, Kebeck and Lohaus had judges divide the 40 units of total information making up the complex event "into more central and more peripheral items" (p. 462). The results demonstrated no differences between experimental and control subjects in the recall of central (main plot) information, but a significant decrease in the recall of peripheral (subplot) information in the experimental group compared to the control group. The authors conclude:

> The results confirm the hypothesis that peripheral elements of a [complex stimulus] material are remembered less well when emotional arousal is high during acquisition. There seems to be a focussing effect on the central elements of a plot, but this focussing does not lead to better recall. (p. 462)

Christianson and Loftus (1987) conducted an important study that clearly differentiated memory performance for central and peripheral information. Experiment #1 used the same slide sequence used by Christianson (1984) about a mother and her son who hail a taxi. In the traumatic version, the boy gets hit by a car and his eye-globe is shown hanging out and bleeding. The instructions "forced subjects to focus upon some central aspects of the event they saw, and then rehearse those aspects" (p. 227). Specifically, subjects were told to "pay close attention to the slides, and for each one to write down the most distinguishing features" (p. 229). After viewing the slide sequence, subjects were given both a recall and a recognition memory test. The recall test consisted of having each subject write down all the details of the slides they had previously written down. The forced-choice recognition test consisted of having subjects choose between slide pairs, one of each pair being a slide from the original presentation. The retention interval was varied. Subjects were tested after 20 minutes and again after two weeks. Subjects viewing the traumatic version of the slides recalled significantly more central information than subjects viewing the neutral version of the slides. Recall accuracy was quite high after a 20-minute retention interval (78%) but dropped after two weeks (38%). Recognition of peripheral aspects of the slides was significantly worse in the trauma as compared to the neutral condition, and recognition accuracy also declined over the longer retention interval. Christianson and Loftus conclude:

> subjects who viewed a traumatic event and were induced to focus and rehearse the critical features of the event were better able to later recall those rehearsed features than were subjects who viewed a neutral event under the same instructions. But the act of focussing and rehearsing came with a significant cost. Those subjects who saw the traumatic event were less able to recognize the specific slides they had seen. (p. 233)

In another experiment reported in the same paper, Christianson and Loftus used the bank robbery film from the Loftus and Burns (1982) study. That experiment addressed memory performance over a longer retention interval. After six months, subjects who saw the traumatic version of the film relative to those who saw the neutral version had significantly greater recall of the central plot (e.g., the bank robbery and the boy's being shot in the face). Overall, Christianson and Loftus draw a different conclusion from the earlier studies:

> These results suggest that some information (the essence, the theme) of a traumatic event might be relatively well retained in memory, while memory is impaired for many of the specific, and especially peripheral details. (p. 225)

The results also suggest that "the occurrence of the event can be relatively well remembered over extended periods" (p. 238).

Heuer and Reisberg (1990) used neutral and emotionally arousing versions of a slide presentation about a mother and son visiting the father at his worksite. The neutral version was about a garage mechanic fixing his car. The emotionally arousing version was about a surgeon operating on an accident victim. A memorizing condition was added in which subjects were instructed to "memorize as much as possible of both the central storyline . . . as well as all of the circumstantial details" (p. 498). Heart rate was monitored during the slide presentation. Subjects were asked to rate the degree of emotionality associated with viewing the slides. Af-

ter a two-week retention interval, subjects were asked to recall as much as they were able of the slide presentation. Recall data were coded into central and peripheral details of the complex event. Recognition memory was measured using a series of four-alternative forced-choice questions about 78 peripheral and 42 central aspects of the 12 slides. The results were rather unusual. As predicted, subjects in the emotionally arousing as compared to the neutral condition correctly recalled significantly more central information. However, they also recalled significantly more peripheral and total information. Recognition memory was also superior in the emotional arousal condition relative to the neutral one, for both central and peripheral details after the point of emotional arousal.

Heuer and Reisberg also analyzed the type of errors made by subjects in their memory reports. While there were no significant differences in the number of errors across groups, subjects in the neutral group made significantly more errors about the plot, while subjects in the emotionally arousing group embellished the motives and emotions of the people in the slide presentation. This study may be limited because subjects viewed non-equivalent slide presentations, but it raises a number of interesting points: (1) It replicates the findings that central information is improved under conditions of emotional arousal. (2) In contrast to all other studies about a decrement in peripheral details as a result of emotional arousal, it raises the possibility that even peripheral information may improve under at least certain conditions of emotional arousal. (3) It suggests that the Christianson and Loftus (1987) study may have missed finding an improvement in peripheral information after emotional arousal because they instructed their subjects to rehearse only the central information. (4) It implies that the kinds of errors made about memory for emotionally arousing events have less to do with the event than with intentions and feelings associated with the event. (5) It suggests that "emotion may have had *multiple effect on memory*" (p. 504).

Burke, Heuer, and Reisberg (1992) used the same neutral and emotionally arousing slide presentations about visiting the father's worksite in a subsequent study designed to investigate the effects of retention interval on memory for central and peripheral aspects of an emotionally arousing event. Subjects were tested immediately after viewing the slides and again after one week. The research also included a much more sophisticated classification of types of memory information. Central information was further categorized into *gist* information (plot defining) and *basic level visual information* (e.g., an operating room). Peripheral information was subcategorized into *plot-irrelevant central details* (mother wearing a sweater) and *plot-irrelevant background details* (intravenous equipment in operating room). The results showed only a "small" contribution of the retention interval to the overall effect. However, the results regarding type of information were most interesting. The emotionally aroused group relative to the neutral group showed a significant increase in memory for both types of central information (gist of the plot and basic visual information) and for plot-irrelevant peripheral information that was centrally associated with event, but a significant decrease in memory for plot-irrelevant background information. Burke et al. point out that the existing studies fail to distinguish between "memory while emotional" and "memory for emotional materials" (p. 288). They interpret the data to mean that "emotion has different effects on different types of material" (p. 289).

CHILDREN AND MEMORY FOR EMOTIONAL EVENTS

A few studies have addressed memory for negative emotional events in children. Dent and Stephenson (1979) showed 10- and 11-year-old children a brief film about a man who steals a package from a car and who is then chased. The children were then asked about the film under three conditions—free recall, recall with general questions, and recall with specific questions. Five memory testing sessions were conducted over a span of two months. Memory performance was measured in terms of the total number of correct responses given out of 90 possible units of information about the event. Results demonstrated that children in the free recall condition gave significantly fewer correct and incorrect responses than children who were asked general or specific questions about the event. When memory performance was analyzed in terms of memory for their description of the people involved and for the ac-

tions that had occurred, the children reported significantly fewer people descriptive details than action details. The great majority of the errors were for people descriptions, not actions. Overall, the results demonstrated that 10- and 11-year-old children produced more accurate but less complete memory reports in free recall, and less accurate but more complete reports when asked questions about the event.

A second experiment addressed the consistency of memory retrieved by free recall over time. Children watched the same film and were asked to freely recall the film's details immediately, two weeks, and two months after viewing it. Repeated free recall sessions significantly increased the amount of accurate information reported, at least over the first few sessions, but did not affect the number of memory errors.

Peters (1991, Study #4) had 6–8-year-old children view a staged theft, in which a stranger entered a room where the child was sorting cards by him/herself, distracted the child, and then stole a money box. Immediately thereafter, the experimenter and the child's parent entered the room. The parent rated the child's anxiety level. Then the experimenter showed the child a photo line-up and asked the child if the perpetrator was in the line-up. The no-theft control condition was similar, except that the child was asked to play a memory game to identify the stranger who had entered the room. Results indicated that the children were significantly more anxious during the theft than during the no-theft condition. When the perpetrator was present in the line-up children in the theft condition made significantly fewer correct identifications (33%) than the children in the no-theft condition (83%).

List (1986) had subjects of three age groups— fifth graders, college students, and older adults (mean age 72 years old)—view a videotape of a staged shoplifting incident. A pilot study investigated subjects' expectation for a typical shoplifting scenario so that the experimental incident could incorporate details of either a high or low probability of occurrence. An equal number of such action and object details was included in the stimulus videotape. Memory was tested after a one-week retention interval using a free recall and recognition test. The recognition test consisted of 56 yes/no questions about the incident. The study assessed both memory completeness and memory accuracy. With respect to both recall completeness and accuracy, college students had significantly more complete memories than the children and elderly subjects. All subjects showed significantly more incompleteness in their memory with low probability of occurrence information and significantly more inaccuracy for high probability of occurrence information. In other words, memory commission errors were highest when the subject had fixed expectations about the event in question. List believes that these subjects tried to fit the memory for the event into an existing schema at the expense of accuracy.

Overall, the few early studies of memory for negative emotional events in children raise additional questions about age-related differences in memory performance for emotionally arousing events. The great majority of the adult studies address the issue of memory *accuracy*. Specifically, these child studies also demonstrate that children of younger ages give a relatively *incomplete* memory report in free recall, and while structured questioning may yield a more complete report, it may also yield a more inaccurate one. The List study also raises a further question about factors that might affect the accuracy of the report, not the least of which is prior expectations about the event. We will return to these questions in chapters 8 and 9. A number of additional studies have been conducted on children's memory for emotional events, but because they also addressed memory suggestibility, they will be reviewed in chapter 8 on post-event misinformation suggestibility.

CONCLUSION

What mechanisms can explain this differential pattern of memory for central and peripheral detail in response to a negative emotional event? The early theories attempted to explain memory performance in emotionally arousing situations according to the Yerkes-Dodson Law on arousal and performance (Yerkes & Dodson, 1908), i.e., an inverted U function (e.g., Deffenbacher, 1983). While this theory has a certain intuitive appeal, it is not supported by the data. Many studies show increased memory performance at high levels of arousal (Christianson, 1992a). Moreover, conceptualizing arousal along a single dimension has recently been called into question (Anderson, 1990; Christianson, 1992a; Neiss, 1988, 1990).

Another early theory is the *cue-utilization hypothesis*. Easterbrook (1959) hypothesized that increased emotional arousal leads to a progressive narrowing of attention and greater restriction in the cues used to process the emotional event. The well-known phenomenon of weapon focus supports the Easterbrook hypothesis. The victim of a violent crime may become so focused on the fact that the assailant has a gun that she or he simply does not attend to other details, such as the physical characteristics of the assailant.

Yet another early hypothesis is known as the *imaginal processing hypothesis* (Erdelyi & Becker, 1974; Payne, 1987). This view is based on the observation that hypermnesia for emotionally arousing stimuli is generally found with visual but not verbal stimuli. The emotional event may imprint the memory in the form of a vivid visual image and thereby increase the likelihood of its persistence.

Christianson (1992a,c) has developed a sophisticated multidimensional model, known as the *preferential processing hypothesis*, for the effects of a negative emotional event on memory performance. In his extensive review of the literature, he attempted to identify five "critical factors" that might explain the diverse results across studies:

1. A negative emotional event is accompanied by *arousal*. High arousal can mean general physiological arousal (along one or more dimensions of arousal), as well as emotional arousal. The important factor, according to Christianson, is that the "source of arousal is an inherent property of the to-be-remembered event" (p. 300). Measuring memory performance for information not directly associated with the source of emotional arousal simply confounds the issues.

2. Subjects pay *attention* to an emotional event differently than to neutral events. They may fixate on the central aspects of the event at the expense of other details.

3. Certain emotional events may be *unusual* and *distinct*. The event might capture subjects' attention more than a more neutral event.

4. Differential *preattentive processing* may account

for some of variability of what is remembered. Negative emotional events may result in an emotional priming effect, so that critical emotional details are given preferential processing over less relevant details of the complex stimulus event.

5. *Poststimulus elaboration,* such as rehearsal, may account for the unusual retention and sometimes detailed retention of memories for negative emotional events. The emotional significance of the event may compel the person to churn it over in his or her mind and to tell others about it. In this manner, the memory becomes more personalized and embellished over time.

Christianson's point is that "emotion may affect memory at early perceptual processing and at late conceptual processing" (1992c, p. 332). He concludes:

> Thus, the specific pattern of better central and poorer peripheral detail may result from the interaction between preattentive processes that alert people to orient to emotional information and more controlled processes (e.g. poststimulus elaboration) that cause them to preferentially process central versus peripheral details. (Christianson, 1992a, p. 302)

Based on the diversity of results across studies, we agree with Christianson's conclusion in *The Handbook of Emotion and Memory: Research and Theory* (1992b) when he says, "there is no simple, unidimensional relationship between intense emotion and memory" (p. 331). Many of the studies we have reviewed claim a deficit in memory accuracy for the experience of a negative emotional event; many of the studies claim the opposite—an improvement in memory accuracy for a negative emotional event relative to a neutral situation. While the earliest generation of studies, as well as the prevailing popular opinion, takes the position that emotional arousal makes memory more fallible because it "impairs" accuracy (e.g., Loftus, 1979a; Loftus, 1980; Loftus & Burns, 1982), this interpretation is both oversimplified and overstated.

We agree with Burke et al. (1992) that emotional arousal has *multiple effects* on memory and that the

effects are indeed quite complex. The great variability across studies is the outcome of a number of interacting variables: individual differences (e.g., age), type of arousal, type of event, activity level, retention interval, type of information, and type of retrieval strategy (cf. Christianson, 1992a). Among these variables, type of information is critically important. Whether emotional arousal is seen as improving or impairing memory depends to a large extent on the type of information measured. The results from the early generation of studies are misleading because they assessed memory performance in terms of the total units of information for the complex event, including rather minor details of that event. For such information, the conclusion that emotional arousal "impairs" memory accuracy is not surprising.

More recent studies, however, have employed experimental designs that more carefully distinguish between central and peripheral information (cf. Christianson, 1992a,c; Heuer & Reisberg, 1992, for reviews). These experiments, as exemplified by the Burke et. al. (1992) study, yield a very different conclusion, as summarized by Christianson (1992b):

> The literature indicates that negative emotional events are very well retained both with respect to the emotional event itself and critical, central detail information of the emotion-eliciting event, whereas peripheral, more irrelevant information, is less accurately retained. (p. 331)

In their review of the effect of emotion on detail memory, Heuer and Reisberg (1992) reach a similar yet more refined conclusion. According to their studies, emotional arousal enhances memory accuracy for the gist of the event (the main plot) and for the plot-relevant and plot-irrelevant information that is associated with the main event. Memory impairment is primarily limited to plot-irrelevant peripheral background details, i.e., "those aspects of the event that can be altered without changing the event's identity" (p. 154). Asking subjects to remember the number on the football jersey of a bystander who gets shot is a clear example of a minor background detail (Loftus & Burns, 1982).

Drawing general conclusions about memory performance when only minor details are measured biases the results in favor of the memory impairment hypothesis. As Christianson correctly reminds us, these studies rarely show any impairment of memory for the emotionally arousing event itself (1992a). How many subjects actually forget that the boy got shot in the face?

Retention interval is also important. Yet, there is no readily discernible pattern across the studies. There is a tendency to conclude that there is a decrease in memory accuracy at shorter retention intervals and an increase in memory accuracy at longer retention intervals (Heuer & Reisberg, 1992, p. 160), but there are notable exceptions to this pattern because the retention interval clearly interacts with the type of event, type of information assessed, and the nature of the retrieval strategies used. Repeated free recall has been consistently associated with a significant increase in the completeness of the memory without a significant decrease in accuracy in both adults (Dunning & Stern, 1992; Scrivner & Safer, 1988; Turtle & Yuille, 1994) and children (Dent & Stephenson, 1979; Malpass & Devine, 1981).

In general, the data do suggest that the gist of a negative emotional event may be preferentially processed and therefore be well retained over long retention periods with reasonable accuracy, although at the expense of the accuracy of at least some peripheral details.

5

||||||||||||||||||||

Personal Memories

A fundamental criticism of the laboratory simulation studies on emotion and memory pertains to the issue of *ecological validity* (Yuille & Cutshall, 1986). Conclusions drawn from studies of subjects viewing slides and films in the laboratory may not be equated with memory for real-life experiences. To address this concern some scientists began to investigate memory by exposing subjects to naturally occurring events in studies designed to test personal memories as an example of ecologically valid data (Bohannon, 1988).

Two important types of personal memories have become the focus of research on emotion and memory: (1) *flashbulb memory*, memory for reported events; and (2) *autobiographical memory*, memory for experienced events.

FLASHBULB MEMORIES

The first study on flashbulb memories was conducted nearly a century ago. Colegrove (1899) found that subjects were able to provide detailed descriptions of where they were, what they were doing, whom they were with, and when they heard the news about President Abraham Lincoln's assassination 33 years after hearing the news.

Modern investigation on flashbulb memories began with a pioneering paper by Brown and Kulik (1977). People retain strong memories surrounding shocking or catastrophic news events, such as the assassination of John F. Kennedy or the explosion of the space shuttle *Challenger*, which they usually have witnessed on television. According to Brown and Kulik, the event in question must be distinguished from ordinary news to produce a flashbulb memory. Upon hearing the reported event the viewer must be both surprised by its occurrence and shaken by its historical impact. Often the consequences will be experienced as major for both the individual and society.

What defines a flashbulb memory is not the memory for the reported news event itself, but rather the memory for the circumstances surrounding one's *first hearing* about the event— what has been called the *reception context* or *reception circumstances*. People who experience a flashbulb memory for the assassination of JFK seem to have unusually vivid memories of the exact spot they were in, who told them, what they were doing, what feelings rose up in them, how others around them reacted and what immediate consequences the news caused in their lives. Brown and Kulik defined these circumstances— place, informant, ongoing activity, own affect, affect in others, and aftermath—as *canonical categories* because these are the aspects of the flashbulb memory that are more likely to be recalled than any other information about the reported event or the context of its being heard. Over 50% of Brown and Kulik's subjects, for example, reported details on all six canonical categories. Sometimes highly specific and idiosyncratic details were included, such as the exact clothes being worn.

Brown and Kulik emphasized that what distinguishes a flashbulb memory is not a memory for the shocking event itself, but rather a memory for the otherwise incidental personal circumstances taking place in the individual's personal life at the time of hearing the shocking public news:

> Remember that it is not memory for the central newsworthy event that constitutes a flashbulb memory, but rather memory for the circumstances in which one first heard the news. (p. 96)

While the memory for the context of the major news event is culturally shared, the memory for the reception context is uniquely personal.

Brown and Kulik created the term "flashbulb memory" to highlight the remarkably vivid and precise visual images subjects offered. A flashbulb memory "suggests surprise, an indiscriminate illumination, and brevity" (p. 74). Because the reported news events were especially startling and altered the course of history, Brown and Kulik hypothesized that these rare historical moments have a unique "biological significance" to the human organism. According to the "now-print hypothesis," they reasoned that the registration of surprise and associated emotional arousal might cause the brain to make a special imprint or "strong initial representation" of everything that was going on at the time of the shock, like a photo snapshot, whereas such incidental details of the reception experience would otherwise normally be lost to memory. The implication of the flashbulb hypothesis is that flashbulb memories contain "exceptional detail and are unusually well retained." They are a permanent and enduring part of the memory (p. 85).

Brown and Kulik's original evidence for flashbulb memories seemed especially compelling. They interviewed 80 subjects—40 blacks and 40 whites—about news events that held major significance for each respective group. For the black subjects they focused on the assassinations of Martin Luther King, Jr., Malcolm X, and Medgar Evers, and the shooting of George Wallace. For the white subjects the assassinations of John F. Kennedy and Robert F. Kennedy, the attempted assassination of Gerald Ford, and the Chappaquiddick incident were used. Subjects were asked to recall the circumstances in which they first heard of important events like these. They also filled out a five-point consequentiality scale and were asked to report how many times they recalled telling the story to others, which was used as a measure of memory rehearsal.

Subjects showed remarkably little forgetting of the events surrounding their learning of these important events. After 13 years, 99% of the subjects recalled where they were and what they were doing upon hearing of the assassination of JFK. After eight years, 56% of the subjects recalled the circumstances surrounding first hearing the news of the RFK assassination. Even with the substantial passing of time, these flashbulb memories contained extensive detail. As predicted, blacks had significantly better flashbulb memories than whites for the assassinations of Martin Luther King and Malcolm X, and whites had significantly better flashbulb memories for the assassinations of JFK and RFK.

The greater the consequences associated with the event, the greater the number of times the subject was likely to tell the story of the reception circumstances to others. Because "informant" was a frequently endorsed canonical category, Brown and Kulik hypothesized that shocking news events of great significance created a need to tell the story. By including incidental personal details about the reception circumstances, the individual grants himself a role in unfolding history.

Early studies tended to support the view that flashbulb memories were unusually detailed and well retained in memory. At the same time that Brown and Kulik were completing their pioneering study, Yarmey and Bull (1978) conducted a larger study on American and Canadian subjects of four age groups. They found that 98% of their 23–27-year-old and 94% of their 28–65-year-old subjects remembered the circumstances of when they learned about the assassination of JFK 12 years after the assassination. However, younger subjects (23–27-year-olds) were relatively poor in their recollection of the reception circumstances, 66% in Canadian and 85% in American subjects. Yarmey and Bull also noted a significantly lower incidence of flashbulb memories in informants older than 66. While the 23–27-year-olds had the most complete and consistent memories for the reception circumstances of all age groups, they nevertheless believed that their memories were unclear. Yarmey and Bull hypothesized that an "amnesia-like" mechanism may be operative for some subjects, which might in part be offset by frequent rehearsal of a highly consequential big news story.

Winograd and Killinger (1983) further investigated whether or not age at the time of the JFK assassination affected adult recall. They noted that nearly a quarter of Brown and Kulik's (1977) sample of subjects were between the ages of 20 and 24 at the time they learned about the assassination. Sixteen years after the assassination, Winograd and Killinger interviewed a sample of subjects who were younger, between the ages of one and seven at the time of hearing the news of the JFK assassination. They also asked the subjects about six other public news events: the RFK and Martin Luther King assassinations, the first moon landing, President Nixon's resignation, the attack on Pearl Harbor, and the shooting of George Wallace. The questionnaire asked subjects about "recall of the circumstances in which you first heard of some public events . . . For example, where you were, what you were doing, and other canonical categories" (p. 415).

The results demonstrated the "developmental course of memory" for a historically significant public event like the JFK assassination. The proportion of subjects recalling the incident increased with age from one to seven. Subjects who were eight years old or older at the time of learning about the assassination were able to recall at least one or more (usually about four) of the canonical categories for the reception event. The likelihood of recall of specific categories of canonical information was: location > activity > source > aftermath > other information. About 90% of subjects who were eight years or older when JFK was assasinated recalled the location they were in at the time of the reception news, 77% recalled what they were doing, and 72% recalled who told them. Less than 50% of the subjects recalled the remainder of the information. Older subjects' recollections were more elaborate than younger subjects'. The overall level of recall was significant only for the JFK and RFK assassinations, but not for the other five public events, which suggest that flashbulb memories do not occur for all important public news events across subjects. The individual

meaning of the reported event plays some role in the occurrence of flashbulb memories.

Winograd and Killinger interpret the results according to a *disruption hypothesis*. It is well established that children organize memories around important daily routines (Nelson, 1986). Having someone burst into the classroom during an otherwise normal school day to announce that the President has just been shot greatly disrupts the normal routine and causes considerable anxiety in children. Older children are more likely than younger ones to comprehend the significance of the event and therefore form a more elaborate memory image for the reported event, a flashbulb memory that could be recalled 16 to 17 years after the event had occurred. However, the researchers point out that they had no way to assess the *accuracy* of these memories.

Other researchers have investigated flashbulb memories for different public news events. Pillemer (1984) studied adult subjects immediately after, shortly after, and again six and a half months after President Reagan had been shot in 1981. The research focused on the *consistency* of the flashbulb memory over repeated testing. The memory was "highly consistent" over time, with most subjects (98% shortly after; 91% six and a half months after) giving essentially the same report shortly after and six and a half months later, although often the later report was a considerably condensed version of the original recollection. Emotionality and surprise at the time of hearing the news, but not consequentiality and rehearsal, predicted greater flashbulb elaboration and consistency over time. In other words, many subjects did not find the failed assassination attempt highly consequential and did not rehearse it, yet the event generated a flashbulb memory.

McCloskey, Wible, and Cohen (1988) also asked subjects twice about memory for the reception circumstances of hearing about the assassination attempt on President Reagan: once five years after and again five years and nine months after the incident. The rates were considerably lower—56% and 48%, respectively, with 15% of the subjects giving inconsistent reports over the two testing intervals. Schmidt and Bohannon (1988) have pointed out that design flaws in the McCloskey et al. study limit the comparison of base rates across these two studies.

Christianson (1989) investigated flashbulb memories in a sample of Swedish subjects for their recollection of the reception circumstances when hearing about the assassination of Swedish Prime Minister Olaf Palme in 1986. Memory was tested six weeks after the assassination and then again one year later, in order to assess both the accuracy and the consistency of the memory over time. Subjects were asked to "recall the circumstances when they first heard about the assassination of Olaf Palme" (p. 436). They were asked about the canonical information, what clothes they were wearing, and what they first thought about the news. Subjects also rated how emotionally upset they became and how surprised they were upon hearing the news.

Christianson included questions about a control event to see how much subjects remembered about a vivid personal memory over the same one-year retention interval. Subjects were asked to think about a personal memory, "Describe in as much detail as possible your most vivid memory from last Saturday" (p. 437).

A very high portion of subjects recalled the canonical information about the assassination six weeks after it had occurred—over 90% across the five canonical questions asked. One year later their recollection was reassessed according to both more lenient and stricter criteria. A total of 86% recalled the information according to the lenient criteria and 61% according to the strict criteria. Recall was highest for how the person heard the news, where he/she was, and whom he/she was with. Recall of clothing worn dropped from 75% to 65% or 25%, according to the lenient and strict criteria, respectively. Recall of the first thought upon hearing the news dropped from 83% to 72% or 44%, according to the lenient and strict criteria. Over the same testing interval, 89% of the subjects initially recalled a vivid personal memory, but that recollection dropped to 22% or 11%, according to lenient and strict criteria. The results overall demonstrate "a performance level that is very high . . . the subjects were able to recall the essence of the circumstances over time . . . but . . . they exhibited a considerable loss of detailed information associated with these circumstances as revealed by the strict recall [scores]" (p. 439). Subjects who rated themselves as more emotional and/or surprised had a significantly higher level of recall at the end of the year than those rated

less emotional. Subjects were less confident about their recollections a year later. Overall, the results support the construct of flashbulb memories as being vivid memories for the reception circumstances of major news events that are well retained over time, much better retained than vivid personal memories. They also support the hypothesis that high emotional impact of the event is associated with a higher recall level in flashbulb memories. Christianson concludes:

> it seems that some core information was less vulnerable to memory loss, whereas the more specific, detailed information suffered somewhat more during 1 year (cf. the strict recall scores). A decreased accuracy with respect to specific details is further reflected in this study in the lower proportion of subjects able to recall the more specific circumstantial detail (cf. the two questions about clothing and first thoughts), as compared with the regular canonical detailed information. (p. 442)

These data contradict Brown and Kulik's view that flashbulb memories are permanent and accurate memory records of the reception circumstances. Rather, Christianson believes the data suggest that central information about the reception circumstances is well retained, but peripheral, more circumstantial information is not well retained over time. Bohannon (1988) concludes, however, that flashbulb memories are always about peripheral information, in that the information about the reception context considered canonical is quite peripheral to the memory for the big news event itself.

While these early flashbulb studies offer reasonable support for the persistence of a "gist" recollection for the reception circumstances of a major news event over long retention intervals, they do not guarantee the accuracy of these recollections. Brewer (1992) has correctly pointed out that Brown and Kulik's original paper on flashbulb memories had no explicit discussion of the accuracy of these recollections. The central problem with these early studies resides in the difficulty of obtaining accurate baseline measurements of the reception context information at the time of hearing about the big news event. Moreover, Larsen (1992) has pointed out that Christianson's inclusion of a control event by which to compare the rate of forgetting is invalid because subjects were not given the same types of retrieval cue for the respective flashbulb and personal memories at the one-year retention interval. Therefore, while these studies tell us a lot about the persistence of flashbulb memories they tell us little about the overall accuracy of the flashbulb memory or about the relative consistency and accuracy of the flashbulb memory as compared to vivid personal memories.

Critics like Loftus and Kaufman (1992), drawing on their extensive laboratory simulation data, believe that flashbulb memories, much like ordinary memories for emotionally arousing situations, are "dotted with error," despite their remarkable persistence (p. 213). Neisser (1982b), a strong critic regarding the presumed accuracy of flashbulb memories, cites a personal story of his own apparently erroneous flashbulb memory of hearing the news about the attacks on Pearl Harbor:

> For many years I have remembered how I heard the news of the Japanese attack on Pearl Harbor, which occurred on the day before my thirteenth birthday. I recall sitting in the living room of our house—we only lived in that house for one year, but I remember it well—listening to a baseball game on the radio. The game was interrupted by an announcement of the attack, and I rushed upstairs to tell my mother. This memory has been so clear for so long that I never confronted its inherent absurdity until last year: no one broadcasts baseball games in December!

Thompson and Cowan (1986), however, have pointed out that Neisser's conclusion about the inaccuracy of his flashbulb memory is itself inaccurate—Neisser's memory error was a rather minor reconstructive error: he was listening to a football game, not a baseball game, and the football team was called the Dodgers (easily confused with the Dodgers baseball team).

Wright (1993) studied flashbulb memories for the 1989 Hillsborough soccer disaster in England, in which 95 fans were crushed to death waiting to enter the soccer stadium. The cross-sectional design assessed memory in 247 students for the reception circumstances of hearing the news first two days, then one month, and finally five months after the event. Most subjects produced flashbulb memories

for this event. The study focused on the *stability* of the flashbulb memory over time. The degree of emotionality associated with the memory remained relatively constant over the three testing intervals. However, rated personal importance of the event significantly increased over the testing intervals. The authors interpret this finding to mean that "as time elapses the personal importance ratings were influenced by the more stable emotional reaction ratings" (p. 133). The major finding of the study was that memory for the reception circumstances significantly dropped off over time. Significantly more subjects at the five-month interval forgot what they were doing (17%), whom they were with (14%), and where they were (11%) at the time of the incident. As time passed people tended to report being with their families more than being with friends when hearing the news event. Wright interprets this drop in memory for reception circumstances in terms of "reconstructive memory processes" (p. 136). As the event takes on more personal meaning over time, subjects reinterpret the event in terms of individual meaning structures, which in turn cause some modification in the details of the memory. While these data do raise questions about the stability of flashbulb memories over time, caution is needed when drawing conclusions solely from cross-sectional data about the transformation of a memory over time.

The resolution of the debate over the accuracy of the flashbulb memory depends upon the collection of baseline data on the circumstances in which individuals learn about a major news event as it occurs. The next generation of flashbulb studies includes such data. The explosion of the space shuttle *Challenger* in 1986 72 seconds after take-off was an event that millions of Americans watched on television as it happened. This tragedy left a deep emotional impression on the millions who watched the astronauts die. Over the next few weeks a number of research teams collected baseline data on memory of the event and the reception circumstances (Bohannon, 1988; Bohannon & Symons, 1992; McCloskey, Wible, & Cohen, 1988; Neisser & Harsch, 1992; Warren & Swartwood, 1992), and later reassessed their subjects concerning the disaster.

Bohannon (1988) reported cross-sectional data first on a group of 272 subjects tested two weeks after the explosion; he then tested another group of

142 subjects eight months after the disaster. A unique feature of his research design was the inclusion of a *comparison memory*, namely a comparison of memory for the facts of the *Challenger* mission and the explosion available through the news on the day of the explosion, and memory for the personal reception circumstances upon hearing the news. Each sample was further subdivided into those subjects who first heard the news on the news media and those who heard about it directly from another person. All subjects were tested using free and cued recall.

Subjects gave estimates on their emotional reaction to the disaster, the number of times they told the story to someone else (rehearsal), and their confidence in the memory. There were no significant differences in the two-week vs. eight-month groups in the free recall narrative. On cued recall, subjects tested two weeks after the disaster were significantly better at remembering more canonical details than subjects tested eight months after the incident. These subjects were also significantly more confident about their memory than subjects tested later. Emotional reaction was not significant across groups. Subjects tested later told the story significantly more times than those tested earlier. Those subjects who were told the news by someone else reported significantly more canonical information than those who heard it on the news. Those who heard it on the news had more difficulty remembering when they heard the story and what they were doing at the time, which suggests that media presentation may cause some blurring of the memory. With respect to the subjects' memory for the facts of the *Challenger* mission, subjects tested at eight months had retained significantly less factual information than those tested at two weeks. Neither emotionality nor rehearsal significantly affected recall of the facts. Bohannon believes that the difference in the rate of forgetting factual vs. reception information:

> suggests the contention that the subjects' flashbulb memories of their discovery of the shuttle explosion are cognitive phenomena distinct from their memory of information about the shuttle itself even though the material-to-be-remembered was functionally related and the subjects may have initially been exposed to the material on the same day. (Bohannon, 1988, p. 191)

Larsen (1992), however, cautions against such an interpretation because memory for the facts of the *Challenger* mission is a type of semantic, not episodic, memory and is therefore inappropriate as a comparison control to the flashbulb memory. These data, overall, do not answer the question about accuracy and, being cross-sectional, do not lead to conclusions about the consistency of the flashbulb memory in the same subjects over time. The data do, however, shed some light on the mechanisms of flashbulb memories:

> It seems that, with short delays, either the factors of affect or rehearsal are sufficient to result in memories that resemble "flashbulbs," containing good amounts of details and confidence in these details. After a delay of 8 months, however, the pattern changes. Now the factors of affect and rehearsal are both required to maintain a significantly higher number of discovery details and confidence in those details (p. 194).

In other words, emotional arousal may contribute to creating a vivid impression of the reception circumstances associated with a major news event, but the memory for these details will be retained well over time only if the event was important enough that the person (1) kept telling the story to others and (2) personalized that story by including specific individual details.

A later report (Bohannon & Symons, 1992) includes additional cross-sectional data on the original groups plus a group tested after a 15-month and another after a 36-month delay. This latter study also included a longitudinal design, i.e., a sample of 116 subjects tested at two weeks and again at three years. In the longitudinal sample, neither affect, number of rehearsals, nor recall of shuttle facts changed significantly from two weeks to three years. The contribution of the subjects' emotional reaction to the flashbulb memory was more evident in this much larger study of over a thousand subjects. As with the earlier study, affect ratings did not significantly change across comparison groups, but number of rehearsals did significantly increase with a longer retention interval. Those subjects across groups who were more emotionally upset had more extensive memory reports in free recall and were more detailed in their recollections of the reception circumstances upon questioning. Bohannon and Symons note, however, that subjects sometimes made errors. From this rather large data base they conclude:

> Flashbulb memories are simply more extensive, more enduring, more consistent, and reported with more confidence than other memories. They are not perfect by any means. (pp. 86–87)

McCloskey, Wible, and Cohen (1988) also studied a population of subjects one week and nine months after the *Challenger* explosion with a combined cross-sectional and longitudinal research design. Memory was tested using cued but not free recall. Immediate and nine-month responses were compared according to the following categories: total information retained, generality of details, specific details, degree of forgetting, and inconsistency. The first four categories pertain to the completeness of the memory; the latter, to its accuracy.

While the gist of the overall memory for the reception circumstances was consistent across the nine-month retention interval, the memory report tended to become more general, less specific over time. There was "substantial evidence of forgetting and inaccuracy" (p. 174), a finding that runs counter to Brown and Kulik's claim that flashbulb memories are immune to forgetting (Conway, 1992). About a fourth of the subjects altered their memory report in some way when tested nine months later. Seven to eight percent significantly changed their report, although rarely were the errors "grossly incongruent" (p. 175) with the original report. McCloskey et al. conclude:

> Our data clearly indicate that flashbulb memories are neither uniformly accurate nor immune to forgetting. The results suggest that like other memories, memories for the circumstances of learning about a surprising, consequential event are subject to reconstructive errors, and to a decline over time in the amount of information that can be retrieved from memory. (p. 177)

McCloskey et al. believe that "strong claims" that a flashbulb memory is a detailed and accurate recollection of everything that the person was attending to at the time of hearing major news is "entirely without empirical support" (p. 177). However, as Conway (1992) has correctly pointed out, the McCloskey et al. data do not warrant the conclusion that a strong view of the flashbulb hypothesis is refuted, since forgetting rates in their study were remarkably low (5.6%), as was the general inaccuracy rate (7–8%). McCloskey et al.'s conclusion is actually misleading in that most of the "inaccuracy" is due to slightly different descriptions of the same reception information.

According to Conway (1992), no memory research would adhere to a perfect standard of 100% accuracy for a flashbulb or any other type of memory, and most memory scientists would agree that even very vivid memories can contain some inaccurate information. The essential point is "how inaccurate?" If we adhere to a 70% criterion (Deffenbacher, 1983), then Conway's reinterpretation of McCloskey et al.'s conclusion is well taken: he believes the data actually demonstrate the opposite, namely, "remarkable levels of retention" (p. 74).

Whereas the Bohannon and McCloskey et al. studies of the space shuttle disaster emphasize the *consistency* of the memory over time, a study by Neisser and Harsch (1992) addresses the issue of the overall *accuracy* of the memory report. They assessed their subjects' memory the morning after and again two and a half years after the space shuttle disaster, using free and cued recall. All of the subjects were given memory enhancement instructions during the later testing: half with a cognitive interview and half with a creative thinking approach.

Their results were strikingly different from the previously reviewed studies, in that subjects were remarkably inaccurate, yet highly confident, in their flashbulb memories some years after the event. Of the 44 subjects who were tested 32 months after the event, 11 subjects (25%) failed to remember any of the canonical information, 22 subjects (50%) remembered one or two of the canonical categories, and only three subjects (7%) remembered all of the original reception information. Neither the visual vividness of the flashbulb memory nor the number of rehearsals significantly correlated with accuracy. The original emotional reaction to the disaster did not predict later recall. Neisser and Harsch conclude:

Our data leave no doubt that vivid and confident flashbulb recollections can be mistaken. When this happens, the original memories seem to have disappeared entirely; none of our retrieval cues enabled the subjects to recover them. (p. 30)

These results are difficult to reconcile with the data from the other studies on space shuttle flashbulb memories. McCloskey (1992) has a more moderate interpretation of Neisser and Harsch's data:

. . . the results reported by Neisser and Harsch suggest that memory for the circumstances of learning about shocking news events is not as good as was initially assumed. (p. 233)

That is, the memory is vivid and consistent across long retention intervals, but contains both accurate and inaccurate information over time. It should be noted that 42% of Neisser and Harsch's subjects retained information on at least one canonical category after 32 months. This retention rate is not very different from the approximately 50% rate reported by Bohannon and Symons for the *Challenger* flashbulb memories after 37 months. Since these rates across the *Challenger* studies are generally lower than those for flashbulbs for the JFK assassination (note that the rate for the RFK assassination was 56% in Brown & Kulik, 1977), the Neisser and Harsch data do not necessarily refute the interpretation about the general accuracy of the gist of a flashbulb memory (Thompson & Cowan, 1986). Rather their data suggest that flashbulb memories for certain major news events (such as a presidential assassination) might make more of an impression than major news events that carry lesser weight (such as the space shuttle disaster or the RFK assassination).

Warren and Swartwood (1992) conducted a study on children's reactions to the space shuttle disaster. Because a teacher was on board the *Challenger*, many children had watched the launch and ensuing disaster on television. Both cross-sectional and longitudinal studies were conducted on over 800 children from kindergarten through eigth grade using free and cued recall two weeks, two months, and two years after the incident.

Age differences were apparent on almost all measures. Older children reported greater detail in their memory for the reception circumstances across canonical categories and gave more elaborate reports than younger children over the testing intervals. Those older children who had a stronger emotional reaction to hearing about the disaster told significantly longer and more detailed stories than those who reacted less strongly to the incident. Children, especially older children, who were tested more than once for their recall reported a greater number of canonical details and gave longer narratives than those tested only once. In other words, telling the story more than once (rehearsal) enhanced recall over time.

Across all ages the flashbulb memory was quite consistent over time for the gist of the reported event: 80% of the children who provided scorable reports at two weeks were highly consistent in their recall at two months and 70% of the children were highly consistent two years after the disaster. Only 15% of the children were inconsistent in their memory across testing intervals. Memory for the canonical categories was also quite consistent, with 90% of the older children retaining at least one and 75% retaining all of the canonical information over two months. A total of 70% retained the information over the two-year retention interval. Overall, while younger children are less complete in their recall of the big news event than older children, we can conclude that both younger and older children produce highly consistent flashbulb memories to important news events similar to those produced by adults.

One major drawback of studying flashbulb memories is the failure of most investigations to include in the research design a control condition for the reception circumstances of ordinary news. Larsen (1992) points out that Brown and Kulik's work on flashbulb memories assumes that the reception circumstances for ordinary news is normally forgotten and that shocking news must be better remembered.

Larsen (1988, 1992) used a diary methodology as a way to compare flashbulb memories and memories for ordinary news events. Almost every day over a six-month period Larsen recorded one ordinary public news event and one personally experienced event ("most remarkable event of that day") in a computer database. The testing period encompassed a number of major news events: the assassination of

Olaf Palme, the Chernobyl nuclear disaster, the *Challenger* space shuttle disaster, the U.S. bombing of Libya, and the overthrow of Marcos in the Phillipines. Each of the 320 events recorded over the six months included a description of the canonical information (what, who, where, and when), a critical event detail, a rating of its frequency of occurrence, the degree of personal involvement, and an evaluation of the event (good or bad).

Memory testing was conducted twice—at five weeks and at four months after the completion of the recordings. Each testing session involved a random sample of half news and half personal experiences. The results showed that ordinary news events had been rated by Larsen as being more neutral and less personally involving than remarkable personal experiences. It is not surprising, therefore, that memory for the reception circumstances of ordinary news events was significantly lower than memory for the news itself, and the memory for the news itself was significantly lower the memory for remarkable personal experiences. The more "central" news events and personal memories were significantly better remembered than the reception circumstances of the news. Larsen concludes that the reception circumstances of ordinary news "is not well remembered in ordinary cases" (p. 46), most being forgotten after one month. Results on memory for major news events that occurred, like the Olaf Palme assassination and the various disasters, over the six-month testing interval did not support the flashbulb viewpoint. Larsen summarizes the results:

> It is seen that my confidence in remembering the source and reception context of my first hearing of the big news was relatively high . . . but that accurate recall and recognition of the context [reception circumstances] was almost nil. In contrast, memory of the big news events themselves . . . was consistently good, far better than in the ordinary news items. . . . Altogether, the more intuitively impressive and emotionally involving those events are, the more memory of the event seemed to increase at the expense of the memory context; that is, they behaved exactly opposite to what is expected from flashbulbs. (p. 53)

Larsen did identify five news items in his database that unequivocally met the criteria for classic flashbulb memories. They, however, were not major news events on the same scale as presidential assassinations. Local news, certain sports events, and certain political news of personal significance produced these flashbulb memories. Confidence was extremely high, as was accuracy of the memory of the reception circumstances. These memories were extremely well retained over time. While none of these memories was for major news events, each event was remembered for quite personal and often idiosyncratic reasons.

Larsen concludes that memory for major news events and remarkable personal memories are best considered "central events" that follow a slower rate of forgetting than the more "peripheral" memory for the reception circumstances. Those were almost completely lost by a month for ordinary news and not much better retained for some major news events. Once again, Larsen's data suggest that the conclusions drawn about accuracy and consistency of flashbulb memories depend to a great extent on whether the major news event in question was personally significant enough to an individual to generate a flashbulb memory. His data do not lend strong support to the idea of a highly accurate and well retained flashbulb memory for a typical major news event like the Palme assassination or the space shuttle disaster. Yet, his data do lend strong support to the existence of flashbulb memories. These data suggest that those who study major news events need to be mindful of the personal and cultural meanings assigned to them. The space shuttle disaster, for example, may not have made the same impression on a Danish man, like Larsen, as it did on American subjects. Likewise, the assassination of the Swedish prime minister would not mean the same to Larsen as it did to Swedish subjects (Christianson, 1992a).

The weakness of all the flashbulb memory studies lies in their failure to assess the individual and cultural *meaning* of the news event as a variable distinct from the emotional reaction or personal involvement in the event or from its consequentiality. The meaning the news event comes to have for a given individual is not necessarily the same as the emotional reaction at the time of the event or the same as its consequentiality. Unfortunately, most of the flashbulb studies failed to measure meaning as a variable, even though these studies suggest that the individual and cultural meaning assigned to the event is a critical variable in whether or not the flashbulb memory is well retained.

A study by Rubin and Kozin (1984) on vivid autobiographical memories directly addressed the question as to whether or not flashbulb memories exist for events other than the major news events investigated in other studies. They hypothesized that flashbulb memories might not always have to be caused by surprising or consequential news events. Subjects were given a written description of classic flashbulb memories without any reference to surprise or consequentiality. Subjects were then asked to describe three of their "clearest, most vivid, most lifelike, autobiographical memories" (p. 82). The memories reported across subjects were rarely about public news events or events of national and/or historical importance. Yet all were described as very vivid and personally important, and the memory for the reception circumstances of these memories was well retained over long intervals (an average of six years' duration).

Rubin and Kozin found that the key element to the production of a vivid memory is its personal significance. These vivid memories were typically for personal injuries, relationships with the opposite sex, sports events, pets, deaths, the first week of college, and significant vacations. Rubin and Kozin conclude, much as did Larsen (1988), that the range of vivid memories that make flashbulb-like impressions is much wider than the major news events included in most flashbulb memory studies; from this wider perspective, flashbulb memories probably significantly overlap autobiographical memories.

Pillemer, Rinehart, and White (1986) conducted a study of "distinct memories" in college students. A total of 87% of the reported memories were discrete memories for unique events, such as taking an exam, interacting with someone, or engaging in some recreational activity. Eighty-four percent of the memories were associated with a specific emotional state, and emotionality predicted the vividness of the memory. In another study on vividness of personal memory, Conway (1988) found that emotionality and surprise predicted the rated vividness of the memory for novel experiences occurring during the first week of college four months later. Conway and Bekerian (1988) asked subjects to recall several memories that were highly personally signifi-

cant and several that were not. Only the personally significant memories were exceptionally vivid.

Most researchers agree that flashbulb memories exist as a type of personal memory, yet there has been very little agreement about the mechanisms that produce flashbulb memories. Brown and Kulik (1977) explained flashbulb memories in terms of the now-print hypothesis. This is essentially a copy theory of memory (Brewer, 1992), in which strong emotional arousal is believed to cause a vivid and accurate memory imprint that is a permanent memory record. Neisser (1982b) proposes a second theory—that flashbulb memories are best explained by a reconstructive script theory. While the subjects may initially construct an accurate representation for the gist of the news event and the reception circumstances, the subject is likely to alter details over time. Flashbulb memories are a special category of memory only in that they are memories that are frequently told to others. The canonical categories become integrated into a "narrative structure" (p. 47). The reception circumstances give a personal signature to the story as it is told to others, much like a journalist who tags a story by reporting who, what, where, when, and why (Conway, 1992):

> The flashbulb recalls an occasion when two narratives that we ordinarily keep separate—the course of history and the course of our own life—we momentarily put into alignment. (Neisser, 1982, p. 47)

Over time subjects reconstruct different versions of the story, each time filling in missing details to fit the schematic representation for the gist of the event and making the story their own.

A third hypothesis is that flashbulb memories are the result of the personal significance or meaningfulness of the reported news event. This functional interpretation of flashbulb memories (Pillemer, 1992) proposes that the personal details of the reception circumstances for a major news events are remembered and recounted because these memory details function in communicating the memory to others. These often minor personalized details play a crucial role in making the storyteller appear more truthful, accurate, and credible, and in that sense function as a kind of social persuasion.

Rubin (1992) has integrated elements of each of

these hypotheses into a multidimensional model of flashbulb memory:

> we would expect flashbulb memories to be in good narrative form, containing information that is new and potentially interesting to the listener, consistent with the teller's view of the self, and to contain concrete, imaginable details as well as emotional impact and reactions. Distortions for the original event should be in the direction of these constraints. (p. 269)

Others (Conway, 1992) argue that especially vivid memories are probably the result of "multiple causes" (p. 83):

> . . . events which directly engage a person's self-system are highly likely to lead to vivid or flashbulb memories. As a consequence, such events would provoke some type of emotional response and might involve frequent overt and covert rehearsals. In this way then we can agree with both Brown and Kulik and Neisser: emotions play an important role, as do rehearsal and the self. Presumably we could even (re)interpret Brown and Kulik's use of the phrase "biological meaning" to refer to events which engage a person's self-system in some direct way. (pp. 88–89)

Overall, what conclusions can we draw from the studies on flashbulb memories? First, there are serious design flaws in all the flashbulb studies that limit the scope of possible conclusions. In most studies it is difficult to get accurate baseline data on the memory for the reception circumstances, although the space shuttle studies and autobiographical studies attempt to address this problem. While some studies include control comparisons to either memory for the major news event itself (Bohannon, 1988; Bohannon & Symons, 1992), memory for ordinary news (Larsen, 1992), and memory for meaningful personal events (Christianson, 1989), no single study includes adequate control comparisons to all three.

Nevertheless, consistent patterns emerge across the extant studies. Flashbulb memories are characterized by a person's being able to recall the details of the reception context for a major news event and other personally significant news events. The flashbulb memory is generally described as a vivid, detailed visual memory. Great emotional intensity is often tied to the event, and subjects maintain great confidence about the accuracy of their recollections. In this sense, flashbulb memories probably do overlap autobiographical memories (Brewer, 1992). These memories are generally highly consistent and well retained over very long retention intervals. They are relatively resistant to normal forgetting.

The issue of accuracy is complex. In the Swedish studies, accuracy rates for memory of the reception circumstances of the news of the Olaf Palme assassination run comparably as high as in the American studies on flashbulb memories for the JFK assassination (over 90%). Accuracy rates can also be quite high for the reception circumstances of certain minor news events (Larsen, 1992) provided that these events strike a personal chord.

Overall, accuracy rates for the reception circumstances of the space shuttle disaster are much lower (around 50% after three years, Bohannon & Symons, 1992; around 42%, Neisser & Harsch, 1992), although rates for the gist of the event are considerably higher (McCloskey et al., 1988). Accuracy rates for the reception circumstances of ordinary news or for major news events that are not personally meaningful are very low (Larsen, 1992).

The pattern of findings across studies implies that the accuracy of flashbulb memories can be quite high for reported events that are especially personally and/or culturally meaningful (like the assassination of the leader of one's country or local and sport news that is personally meaningful), but that accuracy for the reception circumstances is generally much lower for reported events that are less personally or culturally meaningful. The problem, of course, is that it is not always easy to tell what news events convey the level of personal and cultural significance necessary to produce a flashbulb memory.

Memory for circumstantial (non-canonical) information at the time of learning about major news is neither accurate nor well retained over time. While the overall results suggest that accuracy for the reception circumstances of personally and culturally meaningful reported events is superior to memory for the reception circumstances of less meaningful events and for most ordinary experiences, it is also true that these flashbulbs contain errors. Brewer (1992) reminds us that "(s)ome portion of flashbulb memories are not veridical" (p.

291), although the general level of inaccuracy for personally and culturally meaningful reported events is probably not as low as the Neisser and Harsch data suggest.

Exactly how accurate a flashbulb memory is probably depends on whether the reception information is central or peripheral to the individual's meaning system (Larsen, 1992). Certain major news events, like the JFK assassination, alter the course of history and are no doubt central to individuals across varying cultures. It is also significant that the JFK assassination was the first "modern" American assassination and therefore has additional noteworthy value. Another factor involved in the JFK assassination was the charismatic leadership of JFK, especially to disenfranchised young people. Comparisons of his presidency to "Camelot" convey the sense of historical importance attributed to his expected political contribution. The destruction of that hope, as well as the taking of his life by violent means, made the JFK assassination unique.

Other major news events probably are significant to specific individuals or cultural groups, for instance, the assassination of RFK for Americans or the assassination of Olaf Palme for Swedes. Other events hold special meaning to certain religious or ethnic groups, such as the assassination of JFK to Catholics or Martin Luther King to Black Americans. The details of the reception circumstances for most ordinary news events are nearly always "peripheral or irrelevant" (Larsen, 1992, p. 57). With respect to certain personally or culturally meaningful news events, however, the reception circumstances may be central to the meaning of the event to the individual who hears the news.

Yet, while flashbulb memories for certain meaningful major news events are indeed quite accurate, at least for the gist of the reception information, it is rare to find a perfectly accurate flashbulb memory. We agree with Conway's (1992) conclusion about the flashbulb studies:

> it seems unlikely that any flashbulb memory will always lead to exactly the same memory description . . . what we can conclude from the research considered above is that flashbulb memories are remarkably consistent across many years. (p. 76)

Brown and Kulik (1977) originally hypothesized

that flashbulb memories were produced by the strong emotional impression made at the time of learning about the major news event. Brown and Kulik (1977) and Neisser (1982b) alternately hypothesized that rehearsal, i.e., the number of times one repeats the story to others, might account for flashbulb memories. The growing consensus is that no single mechanism adequately accounts for the production of flashbulb memories (Brewer, 1992). Flashbulb memories are probably produced by a complex interaction of a number of variables: (1) the degree of disruption of ongoing ordinary experience, (2) the degree of emotional intensity generated by hearing the news, (3) the degree of personal and/or cultural meaningfulness of the reported news event, and (4) the degree of rehearsal or the number of times the story is told to others (cf. Brewer, 1992).

Classifying flashbulb memories as an independent category of memory has not received consistent support. Most experts agree that flashbulb memories are a subtype of personal memory (Brewer, 1986, 1992). Brown and Kulik (1977) originally saw flashbulb memories as a unique type of memory produced by a special mechanism due to the emotionality and consequentiality of the major news event. McCloskey et al. (1988) found no empirical support for a special flashbulb mechanism and concluded that flashbulb memories are produced by ordinary memory mechanisms. Regardless of the outcome of the debate about mechanisms, many experts have noted, probably correctly, that flashbulb memories are not so easily separated from other types of personal memories, like autobiographical memories (Brewer, 1992; Rubin & Kozin, 1984). Probably the main difference lies in the fact that flashbulb memories pertain primarily to memory for reported events, while autobiographical memory pertains primarily to memory for experienced events. The next section will address the accuracy and consistency of memory for directly experienced events, or autobiographical memory per se.

AUTOBIOGRAPHICAL MEMORY

Autobiographical memory refers to memory for events that are directly experienced, not simply heard about as flashbulb memories are. Brewer

(1986) defines autobiographical memory as "memory for information related to the self" (p. 26). Autobiographical memory contains memory for unique and memorable events of one's life, repeated experiences that are integrated in "generic personal memories," the historical facts of one's unfolding life history, and the repeated experiences associated with the self or self-schemas (Brewer, 1986). Conway (1992) adds that autobiographical memories are "complex representations containing many different sorts of information about very complex events and information contained in these memories may be accessible in different ways" (p. 7). Autobiographical memories often contain "different levels of description" for the same event (p. 12):

> To begin with, autobiographical memories will typically be complex events . . . will contain high self reference, will usually feature sensory, perceptual and reflective information fairly equally and will be closely related to other memories. Any of these features taken on their own could apply to many different (non-autobiographical) classes of memory but the whole set of features would clearly apply to autobiographical memories only. (p. 8)

The study of autobiographical memory is one of the least developed areas of memory research. Serious research on autobiographical memory began in the context of a shift in the 1970s away from serial learning toward the study of memory in everyday life. The study of autobiographical memory nevertheless remains a relatively neglected area of research, in part because of the difficulty of developing a research methodology to adequately investigate autobiographical memory. Personal memories for the events of one's life are difficult to verify and are readily prone to distortion in the service of presenting the self in a favorable light. Just how much autobiographical memory represents an accurate retrieval of past experiences or a construction of the past is at the center of the false memory debate.

There are three approaches to the study of autobiographical memory. The first addresses the distribution of autobiographical recollections across the lifespan (the distribution approach). The second addresses the distribution of autobiographical memories within a certain specified time frame (the temporal referencing approach). The third approach addresses the completeness and accuracy of the autobiographical memory (the participant-observation methodology approach).

The Distribution Approach

The early study on the *distribution* of autobiographical memory began about a century ago. Galton (1883) investigated his own autobiographical memory using a *cue-word procedure*. He composed a list of 75 words, each of which served as a stimulus to probe autobiographical memory. He presented himself with each stimulus-word and recorded how long it took to bring to mind two separate spontaneous memories for each word within a short period of time. Subsequently, he repeated the procedure in different settings over several months. Galton found that he generated a memory for each stimulus-word at an average rate of one memory per 1.4 seconds. Only about half of the memories were for unique events; the rest were for repeated experiences.

A most interesting finding emerged when Galton attempted to date each of the memories. He discovered that the autobiographical recollections were not equally distributed across his life but roughly fell into three broad age-groups—very recent, adult, and childhood autobiographical memories.

Shortly thereafter, Colegrove (1899) conducted a massive questionnaire sampling of over 1,500 subjects, who were asked about earliest memories and autobiographical recollections from different periods of their lives. He found that both the frequency and the content of the memory varied according to the period of life sampled. Memories recalled from childhood were rather rare. In a variation on the original Galton methodology, Waldfogel (1948) had his subjects recall as many early autobiographical memories as they could within a fixed time interval (85 minutes). He plotted the number of memories recalled against the age at which the memory was estimated to have occurred, so as to develop a distribution curve. He found that the curve ascended gradually from the first two years of life, increased from two to three years, and accelerated rapidly through the sixth or seventh year before leveling off.

The consistent discovery across these pioneering studies was that autobiographical memories across the lifecourse are not equally distributed, but instead represent a complex function, with autobiographical memories for some epochs of life spontaneously recalled more frequently (recent events) and some less frequently (early childhood).

Modern laboratory investigation of the distribution of autobiographical memory began with the seminal work of Crovitz and Schiffman (1974). Using a modified version of the Galton cue-word procedure, they presented subjects with a list of 20 stimulus-words. Subjects were not asked for general associations. They were specifically asked for memories. Subjects were asked to "inspect a set of words one by one, and to note a word or two describing the memory associated to each word that first comes to mind" (p. 57). After completing the association task subjects were asked to "date each memory as accurately as they could" (p. 517). Crovitz and Schiffman plotted the frequency of distribution of the autobiographical memory according to their estimated date of occurrence as a logarithmic function. They found "the frequency of episodic memories markedly and regularly decreases as a function of their age" (p. 518). In other words, the more remote the memory, the less likely it would be recollected spontaneously in response to a simple stimulus-word.

Over the next decade this procedure was refined and the results were replicated in a number of studies using various types of stimulus-words and subjects of various ages. Rubin (1982) summarizes the findings of nearly a decade of work on the distribution of autobiographical memory by defining this distribution as a *retention function*. The frequency of autobiographical memories spontaneously recalled is a function of the age of the memory, "with the decrease in memory over time seen as a failure to retrieve" (p. 22). Using a procedure similar to Crovitz and Schiffman's, Rubin conducted several experiments. The results were plotted as histograms with the mean number of memories per hour reported as a function of the estimated age at which the memory occurred. These graphs essentially form a pictorial representation of the relative ease or difficulty of retrieving autobiographical memories at various points along the life span. He concludes "the distribution of memories obtained from autobiographical memory is quite stable over a wide variety of conditions" (p. 35). Moreover, this function is quite similar to curves obtained from memory studies using serial learning tasks.

In other words, these curves describe *forgetting curves* for autobiographical memory, roughly comparable to Ebbinghaus's forgetting curves for nonsense syllables. Conway (1992) summarizes the conclusions drawn from these studies:

> The studies of Crovitz and his colleagues and of Rubin quite clearly demonstrate that across the life-span most memories are recalled from recent time periods and least from remote time periods. This "retention" function is evident in individual subjects across groups of subjects, in response to single words, categories of words, heterogeneous lists of words, in recall from specific lifetime periods, and in free recall. The generality of the function . . . depends upon some general property of the memory system. (p. 34)

One major limitation of these early studies was their use of college students as subjects, i.e., subjects from roughly a homogeneous age-group. Subsequent studies have utilized essentially minor variations on the Crovitz-Schiffman procedure with a greater variety of age groups, ranging from the twenties through the seventies (Fitzgerald & Lawrence, 1984; Franklin & Holding, 1977; McCormak, 1979; Rubin, Wetzler, & Nebes, 1986). These studies fill out the distribution plot across the entire lifespan.

Rubin et al. (1986) summarize the data across studies using older subjects. They have identified three patterns:

1. Autobiographical memories for most adult subjects operate according to a *retention function*, with more recent memories more easily recalled and more remote memories recalled with more difficultly.
2. All studies consistently demonstrate a *childhood amnesia effect*, in that memories from early childhood are rarely recalled using the cue-word procedure.
3. Older subjects, but not younger ones, demonstrate a *reminiscence effect*, in which memories for the middle years of life (from 10 to 30 years of age) are reported with significantly greater frequency.

Rubin et al. postulate that a developmental transition occurs in mid-life, when a "life review" begins, thereby making adult memories more accessible than was the case in earlier years. Conway (1992) summarizes the findings:

> The life-span temporal reference system appears to be comprised of a number of components. Memories spanning a 20- to-30-year period are best characterized by a retention function in which memories of recent events are well retained and retention diminishes over time. Memories over 30 years in age may be subject to reminiscence and so become more available for recall, but memories relating to the very early years of life, even though these may be 30 years or older, are less available and therefore are less often recalled. (p. 41)

These studies essentially map the probability that memories of a particular age are likely to come to mind with minimal cuing. A major limitation of these cue-word studies is that they tell us nothing about how the *type of memory* affects the distribution. All these studies simply require the subject to generate a "memory" to a cue-word. We do not know if the distribution would differ substantially if the subject were asked specifically for a meaningful or significant memory. We cannot conclude from these studies that remote memory is relatively inaccessible relative to recent memory until it is established that the findings are generalizable across types of memories.

The Temporal Referencing Approach

A second major approach to the study of autobiographical memory is known as the *temporal referencing approach*. This methodology was pioneered by Robinson (1976) using a modified version of the Crovitz-Schiffman procedure. Subjects were given a list of 48 words and were asked to "think of an experience from your own life which the word reminds you of" (p. 581). So far the instructions are very similar to the Crovitz-Schiffman procedure.

However, Robinson specifically instructed subjects to bring to mind only experiences that they were directly involved in and that were unique. Another important modification in the procedure was to use three different categories of cue words:

affect, activity, and object cue words. After subjects generated their autobiographical memories they were asked to date each memory, much like in the Crovitz and Schiffman procedure.

While the distribution of autobiographical recollections by age in some respects replicated the Crovitz-Schiffman findings, in some respects it did not. Robinson found that analyzing the data according to type of cue-word led to different distribution patterns. Memories generated to affectively laden cue words were predominantly recent memories, while memories recalled to cue words pertaining to activities and objects were significantly more remote. Robinson interpreted the data to mean that "there is a functional separation of cognitive and affective data in long-term memory . . . perhaps autobiographical memory is organized in terms of categories or types of experience" (p. 591). In other words, the study raised the possibility that emotionally salient experiences may be organized differently from other more neutral experiences in the memory system.

Another study appearing almost at the same time also raised this possibility. Bahrick, Bahrick, and Wittlinger (1975) tested adult subjects for their memory of names and faces of high school classmates from two weeks to 57 years after their high school graduation. Memory reports were checked for accuracy against the high school yearbooks. The rate of forgetting was quite slow. Overall, subjects were 90% accurate 15 years after graduation but memory performance declined by 60% over 48 years since graduation. However, the nature of the relationship between the subject and the target classmate accounted for the major portion of the variance in free recall rates. Close friends and romantic partners were freely recalled with near 100% probability even after very long retention intervals. According to Bahrick et al. the emotional significance of the relationship was a "very important determinant of free recall performance" (p. 75).

What began to emerge from these studies is the reality that certain autobiographical memories are organized around key events in the subjects' life. While the earliest work in this area focused on the emotional salience of these events, later work began to focus on what became known as *temporally referenced events*. These latter studies show that temporal organization of experience within the personal memory system is at least as important as the affective salience of the experience.

Robinson (1986) reported several experiments on how autobiographical memories are temporally referenced. He focused on retrieval of autobiographical memories within fixed time intervals like a college semester or academic year. He hypothesized that within fixed time structures memory for experiences are organized in chronological order. In response to names of months as cue words, he asked college subjects to recall autobiographical memories of events occurring in the academic year either in the fall or winter semester. He found that autobiographical memories were not recalled with equal probability across the year interval. The autobiographical memories tended to cluster into three intervals corresponding to the three semesters of the college year—fall, winter, and summer. Moreover, there was a recency effect within each semester, i.e., the greatest number of memories were recalled for the ending of each of the three semesters and the least number of memories from the middle of each semester. He concluded that autobiographical memories are organized within independent structured time periods, like an academic calendar, and that the endings of each fixed time interval are characterized by a significantly greater number of memories recalled. The temporal structure of units of one's life history, like an academic year, the duration of a job, etc., can be used to guide retrieval of memories and also the dating of memories (Conway, 1992), but temporal referencing biases memory retrieval in favor of memories toward the end of the time period.

Other studies have used *landmark events* (e.g., birthdays, graduations, first day of class) as a means to guide retrieval. Landmarking generally reduces error in dating the memory and improves the accuracy of the memory (Baddeley, Lewis, & Nimmo-Smith, 1978; Conway, 1992). Thompson (1982) had college students keep diaries of two events per day four days per week for an entire semester (14 weeks). Subjects recorded "unique events that occurred in the course of the semester" (p. 325). These subjects also were asked to keep a record of events which they considered might be unique for their roommates. The roommates remained unaware that they were part of the study. The subjects rated each memory from "extremely memorable" to "not very

memorable" (p. 326). At the end of the semester memory testing consisted of randomly presented memories, which subjects attempted to date accurately. Each memory was rated from recalled "barely at all" to "perfectly." The mean memory ratings (recalled more perfectly) were significantly higher with shorter retention intervals, greater rehearsal, and greater memorability. Dating accuracy was a linear function, with each week elapsed being associated with a progressive increase in the magnitude of dating inaccuracy. Thompson concluded that "episodic memory is organized around landmark events" (p. 330).

Reiser, Black, and Abelson (1985) have developed a theory to account for the age-related distribution of autobiographical memories upon recall. They believe that life experiences are organized in memory according to "knowledge structures" which are schemas that "contain generalizations that have been abstracted from individual experiences." These knowledge structures may be temporally organized and contain within them the essential meaning of certain classes of experiences. Activities, and possibly affects, are central to the development of knowledge structures. Retrieval of an autobiographical memory occurs when the knowledge structure is first accessed, following which the specific content of the memory becomes accessible.

The Participant-Observation Methodology Approach

The third major approach to the study of autobiographical memory has focused not on the distribution of recalled memories, but on the completeness and accuracy of the recollected information. This approach utilizes what Conway (1992) has characterized as *participant-observation methodology* (p. 46).

Participant-observation study of autobiographical memory began in 1952 when a psychologist, Madorah Smith, then 63 years old, attempted to recall systematically the entirety of her earlier life. She used detailed dairies she had kept throughout her life as a baseline against which to test her autobiographical recollections. She classified her recollections into especially clear memories, ordinary memories, and forgotten memories. Forgotten memories were those events recorded in her dairies that she failed to recall. Despite the major methodological limitations of this pioneering study, it became quite clear from her study that an individual is capable of recalling a great deal about one's life, and that what is recalled can be verified. Smith found that novel experiences and those associated with intense emotions were the clearest of her autobiographical memories.

More systematic investigation of autobiographical memory began in the context of the cognitive sciences revolution in the 1970s. Marigold Linton (1975, 1978) recorded and later recalled the events of her own life systematically over a six-year period. She recorded two to five "most memorable experiences" each day on cards, in the form of short descriptions for each experience. The date of the experience was written on the back of each card. At the end of each month she randomized the cards for that month and then read the full description of any given experience. The memory test was to remember the date accurately once cued by the event description. One limitation of focusing exclusively on dating accuracy was that events were judged as "completely forgotten" if she couldn't remember the date. Nevertheless, the striking finding of this study was that autobiographical events were not forgotten quickly, even after long delays before recall. Linton's accuracy rate for the "most memorable experiences" of the day after one and a half years was 99%, and after two years was 89%. Moreover, unique and unexpected events had a much greater likelihood of being recalled.

White (1982) expanded on Linton's work by developing a more elaborate method for cuing the memory. He recorded one "memorable" experience per day for a period of one year, but failed to distinguish between "memorable" and "most memorable" experiences. Then he conducted all the memory testing over a one-week period at various retention intervals. Cuing was done first by using a short descriptive phrase for the event to see if the event in question could be recalled. A second and later cuing attempt used the same descriptive phrase to see if the date could be recalled. A third and later cuing attempt utilized the cue to determine the location of the event. White used a scale to assess the clarity of recall. Frequency of occurrence, vividness, and positive or negative emotionality significantly correlated with clarity of recall. White noted a slight tendency to suppress negative emotional experi-

ences. Approximately 60% of recorded memorable experiences could be remembered after one year and about 55% after two years using all three cuing strategies, but the rate of recollection was significantly lower (23%) when only the first cuing strategy was used. Clearly this study, when compared to the Linton study, demonstrates that most memorable, unique events are recalled at a significantly higher rate than less distinctive memories, and that accessibility of less memorable events may depend on the nature of the retrieval strategies used.

Wagenaar (1986) conducted a more rigorous study of his own autobiographical memory. Over 2,400 events were recorded daily for six years. Events recorded in the first and final years served as a baseline to insure that no significant qualitative change had occurred in memory recording over the duration of the study. The middle four years of daily recorded events served as the experimental condition. Wagenaar recorded the "most remarkable things that happened [to him each day]" (pp. 230–231). Events were scaled according to their frequency of occurrence, degree of emotional involvement in the event, and pleasantness/unpleasantness. All events were transcribed into recording booklets and randomized. Critical details were recorded for each event so that retrieval of the event more or less would guarantee the retrieval of the critical detail. In that manner Wagenaar could tell if an event was essentially forgotten, because the critical detail could not be retrieved even when a description of the event was used to cue recall. Four different cues were used: what, who, where, and when. At various retention intervals Wagenaar used one of these four cues to recall the other three aspects of the event. If the event was not recalled, a second and sometimes a third cue was used. Using one or a combination of the cues each event was recalled only one time in order to minimize rehearsal effects. The recall period lasted a full year. Wagenaar concluded:

> everyday life events were much more slowly forgotten [than suggested by earlier research]. The probability of recall depended on the number of retrieval cues, as well as on the nature and the particular combination of cues. No single instance of complete forgetting was found. . . . Retention was significantly related to the salience [frequency]

of the events, to their pleasantness, and to the degree of emotional involvement. The suppression of unpleasant memories was only significant for the shorter retention periods. (p. 249)

Recall rates of the "most remarkable events" of the day after one year using one cue was about 50%, but using three cues was 96%. According to this study, given the right retrieval context, nearly all significant events recorded over the span of the study were potentially retrievable.

One limitation of the Linton, White, and Wagenaar autobiographical studies is their exclusive focus on "most memorable," "memorable," and "most remarkable" daily experiences, respectively. As some critics have correctly pointed out, most days in an ordinary life are not filled with remarkable experiences. Brewer (1988) set out to compare autobiographical memories for memorable and mundane daily experiences. Like the previous studies, he asked subjects to record the "most memorable event that day." In addition, he utilized a beeper to randomly beep subjects during the day. At the time a subject was beeped he was asked to write down what he was doing and/or thinking about just before the beeper went off. The first experiment was a cued recognition study in which a description of an action or thought was presented at various retention intervals. The subject was required to make a memory judgment on a seven-point scale, ranging from having "no memory of the event" to being "certain to remember the event." Recognition accuracy (score greater than or equal to three) after 80 days was 87% for most memorable actions and 72% for most memorable thoughts, and 79% for random actions and 68% for random thoughts.

The second experiment was a cued-recall study in which either time, location, action, or thought was used as a cue. Recall accuracy after 60 days was greatest for location (92%), next for action (89%), then thought (84%), then time and emotions (75% each). While actions were recalled significantly more than thoughts, there was approximately a 50% error rate in recalling actions, primarily because details across different events were easily confused, although memory for nonexistent actions was very low (1.5%).

Repeated actions were associated with a significantly increased error rate because details of independent events sometimes became confused.

Infrequent actions and pleasant or exciting thoughts were especially well retained. Overall, it became clear that the actions taking place in a unique context and the thoughts subjects selected as "most memorable" were much better retained than the randomly selected mundane events and thoughts of ordinary daily life. This finding is consistent with Brewer's definition of autobiographical memory, in that self-selected "most memorable" experiences are precisely the kinds of daily experiences that become integrated into the self-schema.

Moreover, consistent with the previous autobiographical memory studies, these data suggest that most memorable events are remembered accurately and are well retained over time, but mundane events and thoughts are less well retained over time, unless the thoughts are particularly stimulating. The error rates are largely explainable in terms of the tendency to integrate repeated experiences into a generic personal memory across all such events.

An important limitation of these studies is their failure to include in the research design something to address the problem of potential false recognition of nonexistent experiences as part of the autobiographical memory. Whereas the ability to remember and retain memory for memorable life experiences appears quite remarkable across these studies, these findings can be misleading, in that they do not adequately address the fallibility of autobiographical memory.

One approach to this problem is to utilize a *foil strategy*. Barclay and his associates (Barclay & DeCooke, 1988; Barclay & Wellman, 1986) conducted two autobiographical studies in which subjects were presented with foil events along with accurate events in the recognition test. In the first study three subjects kept a daily record of "at least three memorable events a day, five days a week" (p. 96) over a period of four months. They were tested at various retention intervals up to two and a half years with a yes/no recognition test in which they were shown either their original description of the event or a similarly worded foil. Consistent with the previous studies, recognition accuracy for the original item was quite high across the various retention intervals, namely, 95% up to one year and 79% up to two and a half years.

However, the rate of false recognition of foils also increased with longer retention intervals, from 37%

to 52% over a three-month to twelve-month interval before memory testing. Subjects tended to accept the foils as their own memory. More disturbingly, their confidence ratings about their memory remained very high across retention interval events though memory performance declined, both in terms of a decrease in memory for the original items and a significant increase in false memory. Barclay and Wellman (1986) conclude, "recognition memory for autobiographical events is both strikingly accurate and inaccurate" (p. 99).

In a more recent study, Barclay and DeCooke (1988) improved upon the foil methodology by using two types of foils. In the first, the meaning of the original event remained the same, but the foil was written in a different style than the subject's description of the original event. In the second, the meaning of the original event was essentially altered, but was written in the same style as the subject's description of the original event. Once again the four subjects used in the experiment recorded the "most memorable" (p. 91) event of the day and were presented with making a choice between their original description or a foil description at some later retention interval. Consistent with the results of the previous study, recognition accuracy for the original events was very high, nearly 100% at 1–14 days or 32–45 days delay before memory testing.

With respect to the foils, only 14% of the foils in which the meaning of the event was altered, but 82% of the foils in which the style of the description but not the meaning was altered were falsely accepted by the subjects. These findings demonstrate that the memory for the gist of a memorable life experience is accurately and well retained, but that changes in minor details are easily incorporated into the autobiographical memory over time.

Neisser (1981) reported an interesting case study on the question of false autobiographical memory. During the Nixon impeachment proceedings in Congress, presidential attorney John Dean testified on national television for several days. The public perception was that his memory was extraordinarily accurate, even for minor details. So effective was the presentation of his recollection that it prompted the besieged President Nixon to release transcripts of White House tapes. Neisser compared John Dean's memory for the Watergate scandal as given in his Congressional testimony to the actual tape-recorded transcripts of the original White House conversations. While Dean was essentially accurate in his knowledge about what was going on in the White House, his memory was quite inaccurate. Not only was his testimony about details often inaccurate, but he was often inaccurate for the gist of specific events that transpired. Dean frequently gave testimony on the gist of a whole series of independent episodes as if they were a single event. Neisser concludes that "reconstruction played an exaggerated part in Dean's testimony" (p. 19).

Cohen and Java (1995) investigated memory for health-related events, e.g., illnesses, injuries, medication use, and visits to health providers. A total of 104 subjects kept health diaries for three months. The subjects were then asked to freely recall the health-related information. A recognition checklist and a cognitive interview were also used to assess memory. Memory testing was conducted immediately, one month, and three months after completing the diaries. A total of 47% of the health-related information was freely recalled immediately after, and 39% three months after the diary completion. The cognitive interview improved recall by only 6% and the recogniton checklist improved it by 29%. The "low level of recall of health events" (p. 284) in part may be due to the fact that the study failed to distinguish between minor and severe health problems. Just about a third of the subjects rated health events in the "very severe" range that might constitute events of impact. Cohen and Java note, "[h]ealth events that were rated as more severe were more likely to be recalled than those that were rated as less severe" (p. 284). The number of false positive reports, i.e., reporting health events at the interview that were never recorded in the diary and that probably never happened, was extremely low.

With respect to forgetting rates of autobiographical memory, the findings across these participant-observation studies show a pattern quite different from the cue-word studies of Crovitz and Schiffman (1974), Rubin (1982), and others. At least with respect to "most memorable" or remarkably unique life experiences, Rubin's retention function does not fit the data: more recent very memorable autobiographical memories are probably significantly more available than predicted by Rubin's discovery that older memories are less likely to be recalled than recent memories.

The fundamental difference in the respective experimental designs is that the cue word studies ask the subject to associate a "memory" (unspecified) to a cue word while the participant-observation studies ask subjects specifically to recall a memorable or very memorable life experience (specified). As Wagenaar says, "retention curves in Crovitz and Schiffman-type studies underestimate the accessibility of older autobiographical memories considerably" (in Conway, 1992, p. 48). Conway believes that asking a subject for an unspecified memory, as compared to asking a subject for a remarkable memory, probably evokes quite different retrieval strategies.

With respect to memory accuracy, the findings across these studies are most consistent with a "partial reconstructive" theory of autobiographical memory (Brewer, 1986, 1988). Brewer contrasts two theories of personal memory, Brown and Kulik's (1977) copy theory and Neisser's (1981) and Barclay et al.'s (Barclay & DeCooke, 1988; Barclay & Wellman, 1986) reconstructive theory. The former copy theory emphasizes the accuracy of remembering the original personal memory, while the latter reconstructive theory emphasizes the inaccuracy, in terms of misremembering details or the gist of an event or falsely remembering a nonexistent experience.

Brewer summarized his own data and data across studies to mean that autobiographical memories are generally quite accurate and well retained copies of original memorable experiences, but are also partially reconstructed, especially if associated with less memorable, more mundane experiences or memorable experiences that are recalled a number of times. The primary organization of autobiographical memory appears to be around important activities and events, not around thoughts and other internal experiences (Reiser, Black, & Abelson, 1985).

Overall, the data are strongly suggestive of a schema-based model of memory processing in which a memory schema is made for the gist of an important experience at the expense of peripheral details. While the gist is generally well preserved, each recall results in a partial reconstruction of details (Bartlett, 1932), and very frequent recall and/or motivated rehearsal, as evidenced by John Dean's testimony, can result in reconstruction of even the gist of an important event, and its integration into a general personal memory for a class of similar repeated experiences (Barsalou, 1992; Brewer, 1986).

Brewin, Andrews, and Gotlib (1993) reached a similar conclusion from their comprehensive review of retrospective self report specifically about the relationship between early childhood experience and adult psychopathology. They note that "Early childhood experiences have frequently been implicated as causal factors in the development of adult psychopathology, particularly anxiety and depression" (p. 82). They add, however, that the accuracy of retrospective self-reports have been challenged on several grounds:

> Given the theoretical agreement about the role of early experience in the development of psychopathology, it is striking to encounter the widespread assertion that, in practice, patients cannot give reliable and valid accounts of such experiences. (p. 84)

First, some critics have argued that autobiographical memory in general is inaccurate—that it is largely reconstructive. Brewin et al. review studies in which adult accounts of childhood experiences were compared either to parental or sibling accounts of these experiences or to available records. They also review many of the studies on autobiographical memory reviewed in this chapter. They conclude:

> . . . the evidence supports the view that adults asked to recall salient factual details of their own childhoods are generally accurate, especially concerning experinces that fulfill the criteria of having been unique, consequential, and unexpected. This does not mean that adults necessarily recall a wealth of peripheral details associated with these experiences, but rather that their recollections of the central features of the event are accurate and reasonably stable over time. (p. 87)

Second, they review a number of studies relevant to the criticism that psychopathology is typically associated with memory impairment, thereby making self-reports unreliable. While several studies consistent with this hypothesis have used "memory for impersonal stimuli," the data demonstrating memory deficits for meaningful material as a function of psychopathology are "inconsistent" (p. 88).

Third, it is true that numerous studies show that depressed patients show a mood-congruent bias, i.e., have slower recall of pleasant than unpleasant stimuli. Brewin et al. say, however, that these studies do not necessarily show a deficit in the recall of memorable autobiographical experiences. Brewin et al. conclude that the available data do not offer strong support for either a copy or reconstructive theory of personal memory but that "accuracy depends to a large extent on the characteristics of the event or events to be recalled" (p. 93). They believe that clinicians who operate with assumptions about a relationship between adult psychopathology and childhood experiences have made reasonable assumptions, in that the wealth of data on autobiographical memory illustrates the "basic integrity" of autobiographical memory, at least for quite memorable experiences (p. 94).

Psychologically Motivated Distortion of Autobiogaphical Memory

The problem with these essentially cognitive theories of autobiographical memory is their tendency to ignore *motivated forgetting* or the operation of psychological defenses in autobiographical recall and their contribution to the fallibility of autobiographical memory. Several empirical studies we have reviewed mentioned a tendency to suppress memory for negative emotional experiences (Wagenaar, 1986; White, 1982) or to modify the autobiographical memory to present a favorable view of the self (Erdelyi & Frame, 1995; Neisser, 1981). Psychoanalytic theory specifically emphasizes *motivated distortion of autobiographical memory* precisely where cognitive theories do not.

Ross (1991) succinctly summarizes Freud's memory theory and its relevance to research on memory. Freud's concept of childhood amnesia and repression pertains to omission errors and his concept of screen memory pertains to commission errors in memory. Thus, individuals sometimes fail to remember original personal memories due to repression (or other psychological defenses elaborated later by Anna Freud), or they erroneously remember personal information due to the operation of screen memories and secondary elaboration. Much like in dream work, memories for events unacceptable to

consciousness are transformed in the screen memory. Screen memories present essentially insignificant events as a cover-up for psychically charged experiences (cf. Davies & Frawley, 1994, pp. 220–225, and Pye, 1995, for additional psychoanalytic discussions of the interplay between memory and imagination in sexual abuse survivors).

Spence (1988) makes a similar case for memory commission errors in his discussion of unbidden memories and repetitious memories. Unbidden memories usually come into consciousness without the intention to remember. They typically represent some distortion introduced in a particular context, so that new information is substituted for the original event outside of the individual's awareness. As a result, the individual mistakes the unbidden memory for the real past experience. For Spence, repetitive memories are comparable to Freud's concept of screen memory. Such memories, which come into consciousness over and over again, are usually suggestive of defensive distortion and elaboration.

The major difference between Ross's and Spence's viewpoints on motivated distortion of autobiographical memory concerns the veridicality of the memory. Spence believes that reconstruction of historical facts from memory reports is impossible, whereas Ross contends that memories, even distorted ones, "are thought to convey important information" (p. 47).

In *Narrative Truth and Historical Truth*, Spence (1982) takes a radical constructionist position:

> Memory is more fallible than we realize, and it is vulnerable to a wide range of interfering stimuli. Substitute memories are perhaps much more frequent than Freud had assumed, and in fact, one might ask whether any kind of veridical memory exists. (p. 91)

Having been influenced by memory research on the fallibility of memory, Spence thoroughly criticizes Freud's attempt to reconstruct memory for the past as if he were an archeologist. Spence does not believe that an analyst is able to reconstruct what actually happened in the remote past, or that what is discovered about the past ever accurately corresponds with historical events. In the spirit of Bartlettian constructionism, Spence believes that recollection of the past is more akin to a creative act than to a process of historical discovery. Through interpretation, the patient and the analyst engage in a process of continuous construction of a narrative about the patient's life. Recent or remote memories can never be adequately verified as historical truth, but exist only as a constructed "narrative truth" arising out of the psychoanalytic dialogue. Interpretations are never historically accurate; they are "entirely suppositional" (pp. 140–141) and can never be disconfirmed. Interpretations, in short, are examples of the suggestive influence operative in psychoanalysis.

For Spence, psychoanalysis is essentially a process by which fictitious memories about the past are "created" in the service of providing the patient with a coherent explanatory model for his or her experience:

> . . . the analyst's construction of a childhood event can lead the patient to remember it differently if he remembered it at all; and if he had no access to the event, to form a new memory for the first time. Within his private domain, the newly remembered event acts and feels like any other memory; thus it becomes true. Once this kind of memory has been created, its roots in the patient's historical past become almost irrelevant, and even if it were objectively disconfirmed (by, for example, discovering an old letter or hearing from a long-lost neighbor), its subjective truth value would probably continue. (p. 167)

Spence makes a distinction between historical truth and narrative truth. The main theme of his book, reiterated and expanded in subsequent works (Spence, 1987, 1994a,b), is that psychoanalysis is more appropriately understood as the co-creation of narrative truth between patient and analyst than as the discovery of historical truth about real events in the past. The criterion for success in psychoanalysis is not that the memories for the past are *accurate*, in the historical sense, because they rarely are, according to Spence. Success means that the memories are *adequate*, in the sense that they provide the patient with a coherent, plausible, and compelling explanation in the place of uncertainty.

Spence is correct to criticize what he calls the "naive realism" of Freud (p. 25)—Freud's reacting as if (1) "recalling the past is a simple act of going back to an earlier time and place and reading off the contents of the scene that emerges" (p. 93), and as if (2) a patient were an unbiased reporter or an analyst were not at all suggestive. However, Spence has gone to the other extreme—the extreme of nihilism. The position taken in *Narrative Truth and Historical Truth* and his later writings is that historical truth about past experiences can *never* be known accurately, memory for the past is *never* veridical, and that unwitting and formal interpretations in psychoanalysis are *always unduly* suggestive. For Spence, there is no "kernel of [historical] truth in the patient's memory." Spence takes the position that we cannot really know *anything* about the past, especially the remote past. Nor does he think that it matters anyway, so long as the patient is able to create a plausible, self-coherent fiction. He says, "it no longer makes sense to speak of the historical validation of an interpretation" (p. 287). The idea that we can never know anything about the past is a position rendered meaningless by its very extremism.

Ross (1991), in *Remembering the Personal Past*, arrives at a more balanced conclusion about the psychoanalytic theory of memory, one that is comparable to Brewer's partial reconstructive theory within the domain of cognitive theory. Ross sees Spence's book as part of a "negative trend" (p. 129) within psychoanalysis in particular and psychology in general, which has emphasized the fallibility of memory to such an extreme that the entire enterprise of memory reconstruction is discredited. He says: "Almost all innovations in psychotherapy in the last half-century have in common a discounting of the importance of autobiographical memories" (p. 209). Ross believes that, although an autobiographical memory may be distorted, it still represents a memory for *something*, often something personally important.

Ross thoroughly reviews Freud's theory of memory, along with memory theories of other important psychoanalytic writers such as Fenichel, Kris, Greenacre, and Schafer, as well as the more recent advocates of narrative, hermeneutic theory, such as Spence and Ricoeur. Through this review he extracts what he believes to be useful psychoanalytic concepts:

1. *multiple memory registration* implies that the original and secondary distortion of the memory coexist;

2. *memory for fantasy does not equal memory for real events* implies that some distinction can be made, at least under certain conditions, between fantasy productions and genuine memory for past experience;

3. *deferred understanding* is relevant to the idea of delayed recovered memories, in that it suggests that memories that are forgotten and later recovered can be more painful upon recovery than at the time of the original event; and

4. *the role of association in memory* is not limited to verbal associations but may include symbolic, sensory, motoric, and symptom cues, thereby necessitating that retrieval strategies include a range of approaches besides verbal inquiry.

Ross believes that, coexistent with the "negative" trend, there has also been a "positive" trend emerging in psychoanalysis and in psychology, which represents a greater appreciation of the range of memory phenomena and an increasingly sophisticated understanding of the structure of memory, its processing, and the conditions of retrieval.

As part of this positive trend, Ross carefully reviews both developmental memory, as well as sociological theories of memory. He is critical of the narrow personal focus that memory scientists have taken to autobiographical memory, and he reminds us that in both the developmental and sociological theories autobiographical memory is always social memory, i.e., always significantly shaped by socialization processes. In this sense, autobiographical memory is always being constructed in the current social context. Such a view, nevertheless, does not lead Ross to a radical constructionist nihilism about the past.

He urges therapists to consider the methodology used by modern historians. Historians did not give up their search for historical truth, despite the fact that most historical evidence is based on reconstruction. Instead, the historians developed scientific methods to help separate fact from fiction in a reasonably informed way. Likewise, Ross remains open to the idea that the enterprise of psychotherapy might develop a comparable methodology. He states:

I argue, to the contrary, that to evaluate multiple versions of past happenings for truth content is a

necessary task. Memory cannot always be easily separated from fantasy [in every case], but approximate orderings can frequently be made. (p. viii)

Ross concludes that, whereas memory accuracy has been of little importance to psychoanalysis in the past, the very survival of reconstruction as a therapeutic endeavor may rest on establishing memory accuracy as the "central problem" (p. 209) and developing an appropriate set of procedures to distinguish distortions from facts. It is too easy to simply concede, as Spence does in his work on "narrative truth" (1982) or Nash has done in his concept of "clinical utility" (1994), that it makes no difference to the therapeutic task if fact and fantasy are confused.

CONCLUSIONS CONCERNING AUTOBIOGRAPHICAL MEMORY

Overall, the following conclusions can be drawn from the studies on autobiographical memory:

1. With respect to rates of forgetting and retrieval for autobiographical memories in general: recent memories are significantly more likely to be remembered and remote memories are significantly less likely to be remembered. For adults, early childhood experiences are generally not remembered (prior to age four). The major exception to these findings is that older adults (over 50 years old) are more likely to recall autobiographical memories for their middle years (10–30 years of age), probably because of a developmental shift in memory organization occurring in mid-life that biases memory retrieval in favor of increased reminiscences for recollections of the middle years. These conclusions are limited to autobiographical memories in general, irrespective of the personal meaningfulness of the memory.

2. Exact dates are not well retained in autobiographical memory, and dating remote memories may be highly inaccurate, unless the memory is tagged by a landmark event.

3. Autobiographical memories are organized within fixed time intervals or epochs of one's life history, and within these epochs retrieval is more likely

for memories marking the end of the epoch, for meaningful, affectively significant experiences, and for central activities within these time structures. In other words, specifically temporally referenced or landmarked events yield very different retention curves, in that temporally referenced or remarkable remote memories may be recalled more frequently than predicted by Rubin's retention function.

4. Remarkable autobiographical memories are extremely well retained over long retention intervals. If we compare retention rates across the studies, it becomes clear that the rates run 90–100% for most memorable experiences after several years (Brewer, 1988; Linton, 1975; Wagenaar, 1986), but drop to 60–80% for less remarkable to mundane experiences (Brewer, 1988; White, 1982).

5. The type of memory and the nature of the time interval interact. Thus, there is a bias to recall remarkable personally significant autobiographical memories; such recall is partially, but not completely, independent of the temporal organization of the memory. Remarkable autobiographical memories are more likely to be recalled than other autobiographical memories within fixed temporal units of the lifespan like an academic year, the years of a relationship, or the years of one's childhood.

6. With respect to the accuracy of the remarkable autobiographical memories, the gist is highly accurate while the details are not necessarily accurate and may be quite inaccurate. Conway (1992) summarizes our knowledge of autobiographical memory:

> In autobiographical memory, however, it is not usually the case that a memory is completely false but rather that a memory relates to an event which did occur but not exactly as remembered. It may be an important feature of autobiographical memories that they are never true in the sense that they are literal representations of events, and in this respect it makes little sense to ask whether an autobiographical memory is true or false. Nevertheless, autobiographical memories may be accurate without being literal and may represent the personal meaning of an event at the expense of [complete] accuracy. (p. 9)

Regarding the incorporation of false information into an autobiographical memory Conway adds:

> Yet it cannot be the case that, in general, most people's memories of events are complete fantasies (p.10). . . . Errors in autobiographical memories . . . are comparably minor if not trivial. They do not violate the meaning of the recalled episode; in fact, if anything, they seem to emphasize the meaning. (p. 11)

It is also clear that false memory for events or details that never happened can become confounded with the original memory. These commission error rates for salient events are low (about 14%), but are much higher for minor details. While the gist of the original memory is generally well retained, repeated recall of the same event leads to constructive distortion of details in each social context in which the memory is recalled.

7. Psychologically motivated forgetting interacts with the type of memory and the nature of the referencing time interval. Under certain conditions, the exact opposite may occur: some remarkable personally significant events sometimes, but not always, associated with conflict (including some traumatic experiences) within the temporal units of one's life history may be *less* likely to be recalled than other autobiographical memories due to the operation of psychological defenses. Whereas the experimental studies on autobiographical memory lend modest support to the notion that negative emotional experiences are suppressed, the psychoanalytic studies offer a range of theoretical constructs to explain motivated distortion of autobiographical memory.

We agree with Ross that the empirical and psychoanalytic evidence in favor of the fallibility and distortion of autobiographical memory does not justify a nihilistic conclusion. On a case-by-case basis, more often than not the gist of the original memory is potentially distinguishable from defensive distortions, provided that the right kind of therapeutic context is established and available procedures are used to help the patient distinguish fact from fiction in autobiographical memory.

6

|||||||||||||||||

Memory for Events of Impact

EVENTS OF IMPACT IN ADULTS

Generalizing from the results of laboratory simulation studies on emotion and memory to real-life memory performance has been criticized on the grounds of "ecological validity" (Yuille & Cutshall, 1986). Laboratory simulation research uses a homogeneous sample of subjects, often college students, who passively view slides or films that are assumed to be emotionally arousing. The selected visual stimuli of thefts, car accidents, or violent acts are neither unusual nor latent with lasting personal meaning for the subject. Indeed, often far more gruesome events are watched daily on television. Moreover, many of the laboratory simulation studies fail to establish that the target stimuli actually induce stress or evoke strong emotions.

In the spirit of developing research paradigms more relevant to real-life eyewitness experiences, Yuille and Tollestrup (1992) began a series of naturalistic investigations on what they defined as *events of impact*. Events of impact are "unique" and "salient" real life experiences (Yuille & Cutshall, 1986, p. 299), such as witnessing a shoot-out or robbery. Such experiences have immediate consequences for the individual, often carrying the threat of injury or death. The individual directly experiences and is

actively involved in the situation, unlike passively observing slides or films. Typically such events are associated with high levels of stress that may evoke intense emotions, although the specific emotional responses vary across individuals. Yuille and Tollestrup (1992) view events of impact along a continuum from low to high threat of injury or death. In this book, we make a clear distinction between low-level and high-level events of impact. As we view it, there is an important clinical difference between events of impact and traumatic events. Events of impact meet the criteria just described, as do traumatic events. In addition, *traumatic events* are characterized by the occurrence of posttraumatic stress symptoms. An event of impact does not necessarily result in such symptoms. We believe that this distinction is important to making sense of the consequences of events of impact and traumatic events on memory performance.

The notion of events of impact came from a review of police reports about violent crimes, including robbery, homicide, and sexual assault (Yuille, 1986), and a case study of an eyewitness to a crime (Yuille & Cutshall, 1986). Yuille found that eyewitnesses to crimes, even when they seem to be uninvolved bystanders, are actually victims in three out of four cases. Most eyewitnesses are deeply affected by the event (Yuille & Tollestrup, 1992). Many non-victim witnesses have a relationship with the victim of the crime. Even if no bodily harm occurred, non-victim witnesses typically report feeling very threatened by the weapon or potential for harm inherent in the situation. Thus, Yuille concludes that "the uninvolved bystander is a relatively rare type of witness" (Yuille & Tollestrup, 1992, p. 205).

John Yuille and his associates conducted a series of field studies on events of impact on witnesses of real crimes. The first study (Yuille & Cutshall, 1986) involved a shoot-out between a robber and an owner of a gun store. Both men were shot. The store owner was seriously injured and the robber was killed while 21 witnesses observed the incident from various vantage points on the street where it occurred. The police interviewed each witness within an hour after the incident. Five to six months later, the researchers interviewed 13 of the central and peripheral witnesses who consented to be involved in the study. A scale was used to assess the degree of stress each subject had experienced. The accuracy of each subject's memory for the incident five to six months later was compared to the report given to the police immediately after the crime. Each subject was asked to recall everything that had happened (free recall). Then, the interviewer asked specific questions (cued recall).

Memory reports were evaluated in terms of total information recalled and in terms of memory for: (1) action details, (2) descriptive details of the physical appearance of the people, and (3) object details involving the weapons, stolen property, and assailant's automobile. The results of the study showed no significant difference between memory performance using free-recall and cued-recall retrieval strategies. The total amount of information recalled, as well as memory for action details, was significantly greater after five to six months than in the initial police interview, probably because the researchers asked more questions about memory than the police did.

The results indicated that the five central witnesses, who had contact with the robber, store owner, or weapon, reported a high amount of stress and had some acute symptoms after the incident, e.g., sleep disturbance. The remaining, more peripheral eyewitnesses reported less or no stress and did not have any symptoms following the incident. The stress evaluation supported Yuille's hypothesis that eyewitnessing a crime is an event of impact, with greater involvement predicting greater psychological impact.

Accuracy was determined by comparing each subject's report to an account reconstructed from all the information available to the police and provided by the witnesses. The percentage of details remembered did not differ significantly between the original police interview and the delayed research interview. Accuracy rates were generally quite high, with object details remembered the best, action details next, and people descriptions the worst in both the police (89%, 82%, and 76%) and the delayed research interviews (85%, 82%, and 73%). Inaccurate details were "relatively rare" (p. 294), with the greatest proportion of inaccuracies occurring with respect to descriptions of the people's height, age, weight, hair color, etc. The least proportion of inaccuracies occurred with respect to objects, such as the weapon, car, or stolen property. Most (10 of 13) eyewitnesses were quite accurate in their memory for the actions, but three were not. All three were peripheral witnesses and two of them had a partially obstructed view of the crime. Most of the inaccurate memories occurred when these subjects were asked to recall a series of multiple actions, such as the pattern of shots fired by the perpetrator and victim. It should be noted that 60% of the information given in the delayed memory report was new information, not included in the police report, yet the accuracy of this report was nearly the same as that of the original police interview (81% v. 84%). The report of nonexistent actions was around 3% in both the original police and later research interviews. Most of the false memories were given by the same peripheral witnesses who had not fully seen the incident. Yuille and Cutshall (1986) conclude:

> . . . the relatively high accuracy rates found in this study may have been due, in part, to factors usually absent in experimental research [using laboratory simulation designs]: a particularly salient event with obvious life and death consequences, and the opportunity for active involvement by the same witnesses. . . . One of the more striking results was the lack of memory loss over time. Accuracy rates remained virtually unchanged five months after the incident. (p. 299)

In other words, *in contrast to the laboratory simulation studies*, the results of this study on memory for real-life events of impact run contrary to the expected decrease in memory accuracy associated with stressful events, at least for important actions and central objects, although the usual eyewitness inaccuracy for descriptions of the people involved did occur.

Since the 1986 report, Yuille and his associates have replicated the results with field studies on eyewitness memory for five additional crimes (Cutshall & Yuille, 1989). Cutshall and Yuille (1989) reported their results on field studies of two additional violent crimes. The first involved a restaurant shooting. After robbing a bank the robber was pursued by a pedestrian, both of whom entered the kitchen of a fast-food restaurant. A police officer arrived and the robber pointed his gun. The officer shot and killed the robber in front of eight witnesses. Cutshall and Yuille interviewed the witnesses two years later. The research interviews yielded seven times more information about the incident than the original police interviews. The accuracy of the witnesses memory for the event two years after it had occurred was "very high" (p. 112). "Overall accuracy was 92.3%, with person description accounting for most of the errors" (p. 112). The accuracy of the central action that occurred was 97%, while the accuracy of physical characteristics of the robber, the police officer, and the pedestrian was 79%. Cutshall and Yuille concluded, "A striking event of this sort leads to virtually no loss in the amount or accuracy of recall over a long retention interval" (p. 112).

The second field study involved a man who stabbed another man while both were standing in a food line. A police officer chased the attacker and was also stabbed. The assailant was shot and killed by a second police officer in front of 18 witnesses. Six of the witnesses were interviewed 13 to 18 months after the incident. As with the previous two field studies, the research interview yielded significantly more information than the original police interview (72% increase), and the overall accuracy of recall (85%) after a long retention interval was very high. Once again, the central action was recalled more accurately (92%) than the descriptive characteristics of the people involved (79%). Cutshall and Yuille summarize the results of these two and the 1986 field studies as follows:

> The previous three studies had a common focus on eyewitness recall for a violent event. The pattern of results across the three studies suggests that witness memory for such events may remain accurate and detailed over long periods of time. (p.114)

Another set of field studies addressed the related question of memory for non-violent crimes. Cutshall and Yuille (1989) pooled the interview data from witnesses to a series of bank robberies done by the same two robbers. Although in each robbery the robbers claimed to have guns, no weapons were actually used. The interviews occurred about two years after each robbery. As with the previous studies, the amount of information obtained in the research interview was significantly more than in the police interviews; however, the magnitude of the effect was significantly less (under 50%) than for eyewitnessing violent crimes. The overall accuracy after a two-year retention interval was again quite high (82%), with an accuracy rate of 83% for actions and 80% for details. Cutshall and Yuille (1989) conclude:

> The amount of information that witnesses retain about a crime appears to depend on the nature of the crime. The violent events were well remembered; the non-violent events, the robberies were not. It is not clear that violence per se is the basis for this difference, but it may have played a role. In the cases of robbery, the central witness recalled more than the peripheral witnesses (p. 117). . . . The results of our field research indicate that witnesses may have difficulty with some aspects of person descriptions but not with physical actions. The level of accuracy of real witnesses for striking events may be higher than the laboratory studies have generally suggested. (p. 119)

Tollestrup, Turtle, and Yuille (in press) report additional data that contrast memory performance for violent and non-violent crimes. The most recent work included a comparison of memory performance for victims of, and witnesses to, violent crimes and victims of fraud. The fraud primarily involved passing bad checks. As predicted, victims/witnesses of violent crimes reported significantly more information about the crime than fraud victims and were significantly more accurate in their memory.

These field studies of memory for actual crimes challenge the notion of memory fallibility for eyewitnessing crimes derived from laboratory-simulation studies (e.g., Loftus, 1979a,b). They demonstrate that memory for the actual events of the crime is accurately and well retained over long retention intervals. As Cutshall and Yuille (1989) definitively assert:

> . . . the assertion [is made] that memory declines dramatically over time (e.g., Penrod, Loftus, & Winkler, 1982). Our data demonstrate that this is simply not true for some events. For three of the four events we investigated [except the fraud studies], memory remained detailed and accurate over months and years. (p. 120)

The difference in the results across laboratory-simulation and field studies, according to Tollestrup et al., is that robberies, especially violent robberies, are events of impact, while fraud is not necessarily. Their results strongly suggest a differential memory performance for ordinary events and events of impact.

Yuille and his associates explain the difference in memory performance between their field studies and the laboratory-simulation studies in terms of the "distinctiveness of the events" (Yuille & Cutshall, 1989). Direct participation in an actual crime, often accompanied by violence, is quite different from passively viewing slides about a robbery in the laboratory. They believe that such distinctive events may lead to a very different kind of memory—what they have called a *remarkable memory*:

> . . . the accuracy of eyewitness testimony (i.e., the ability of the witness to provide accurate and detailed information) depends upon the event witnessed. For independent witnesses (those who have no motive to distort) who observe a distinctive event, it is likely that their memory will be detailed, accurate and persistent. We propose labelling these memories remarkable memories. We discuss some possible properties of remarkable memories below. Errors will be found in the memory of independent witnesses to distinctive events if they misperceive or misinterpret the event. Also, there are some errors which we expect to regularly occur: judgements of height, weight, age, distance and speed. . . .

For independent witnesses who observe a nondistinctive event their memory will be limited and will decrease with time, that is, they will not have a remarkable memory. This is the type of eyewitness memory which has been the focus of investigation for most laboratory studies of eyewitness memory. This raises the issue of the applicability of the laboratory research to actual forensic context. . . . It appears that the laboratory findings may be relevant to those cases in which the event of concern was not a distinctive one for the witnesses (i.e., if it did not lead to the formation of a remarkable memory). (Yuille & Cutshall, 1989, pp. 181–182).

According to Yuille and his associates, the difference between their data and those from laboratory-simulation studies may reflect a difference between memory processing for ordinary events and remarkable memory.

Fisher, Geiselman, and Amador (1989) reported similar results regarding eyewitness memory for crimes in the Miami area. In that field study, police detectives in one group were trained to use a cognitive interview procedure to enhance victims' and witnesses' recollection of crimes. The control group of detectives used standard police interviewing techniques. Most of the interviewees were "victims of either commercial robbery or purse snatching" (p. 724). The cognitive interview of eyewitnesses yielded on the average between 25–35% more total information about each crime and 94% of the reported information was corroborated by other witnesses. While Fisher et al. remind us that "one cannot determine exactly what transpired during the crime" (p. 725), so that the question of memory accuracy cannot be definitely answered, the data are nevertheless consistent with the Yuille et al. studies, all of which conclude that eyewitnessing a certain crime may constitute an event of impact, resulting in an accurately and well retained remarkable memory.

Christianson and Hubinette (1993) interviewed 58 witnesses of 22 bank robberies committed in Stockholm. Subjects were categorized into victims directly involved in the robbery (e.g., the bank teller held at gunpoint) and eyewitness bystanders who merely watched the robbery (fellow employees and customers). Between 4 and 15 months after the robberies had occurred, subjects were contacted and asked to fill out a memory questionnaire. Questions were categorized into action/event, people, and object descriptions. Victims who were directly involved were more accurate than bystanders in their memory for the robbery. Memories for the gist of the actions that had occurred, the weapons used, and the clothing worn were retained with "relatively high accuracy rates after an extended time interval" (p. 365). Descriptive details about the people (e.g., hair color, footwear) and the time and date of the incident were not well retained, and retention was directly related to the witness's viewpoint during the robbery. Whereas victims and bystanders all reported intense emotional arousal during the crime, emotionality did not significantly correlate with memory for the crime. Christianson and Hubinette conclude, "highly emotional events are relatively well retained after an extended time interval, and memory performance seemed to be not strongly related to self-rated emotional stress" (p. 375).

A second approach to the study of events of impact is known as *targeted recall* (Usher & Neisser, 1993). In contrast to the cue-word procedure used extensively in the study of autobiographical memory (e.g., Crovitz & Schiffman, 1974), the targeted recall procedure asks subjects specifically about an emotionally salient and temporally referenced target event from early childhood. Whereas John Yuille and his colleagues have investigated memory for eyewitness crimes using field studies, other researchers have used the targeted recall procedure to investigate a wider range of salient life experiences, such as the birth of a sibling, an early hospitalization, or the death of significant others.

Sheingold and Tenney (1982) pioneered the use of the targeted recall procedure. Their goal was to study "natural memory" for a "specific . . . salient childhood event" (p. 201), in this case memory for the birth of a younger brother or sister. They wanted to see how much a salient event like this would or would not be forgotten over time. The subjects involved a total of twelve children ages of three age groups, approximately four, eight, and twelve years old, and their mothers. A total of 42 college students served as a second group of subjects. All subjects were asked about the birth of a sibling that occurred at a specified age, namely, when they were four years old. Because subjects of various ages were

used, the researchers could study the memory over varying retention intervals, from one month to 16 years. All subjects were asked a series of 20 questions about the targeted event as a means to assess the relative amount of information they could recall about the circumstances associated with the birth. The results were striking. They found "virtually no forgetting" (p. 206) in child or adult subjects who were four years old at the time of the birth, regardless of the fact they were were asked to recall the event up to 16 years after it had occurred. A subsample of the college students (n=22) reported births of a sibling occurring when they were younger than age four. "Only three of the 22 births reported when college students were younger than three had scores above zero" (p. 209). In other words, childhood amnesia was demonstrated if the subject was three years old or younger when the sibling was born.

In an attempt to address the accuracy of the recollections, Sheingold and Tenney compared the children's memory to their mother's recollection. On average, nine of 13 of the children's recollections could be confirmed by the mother's report. Sheingold and Tenney conclude:

> First, how much can young children remember about a real-life event? Four-year-olds can remember an impressive amount about the birth of a sibling. They could answer a mean of 13 questions out of 20, nine of which were accurate. . . . Second, is information about a salient childhood event forgotten? Apparently it is not, for 16 years after the event occurred. (pp. 209–210)

These data suggest that, "salient childhood events" are an exception to Rubin's retention function for autobiographical memories in general, where remote experiences are less likely to be recalled than recent experiences. Events of impact, like the birth of a sibling, are accurately and well retained. They also are likely to be readily retrieved when the subject's recall is targeted with specific questions about the event.

There is one potential problem with the Sheingold and Tenney research design. It is possible that the high correlation between mother and child memories is not a product of the independent and accurate memory of each, but rather of the accurate or inaccurate memory of the mother repeated so often to the child that it has established itself as the child's memory. Nevertheless, the study reaches the same conclusion as other studies that do not contain this methodological problem.

Neisser (1982a, p. 201; Usher & Neisser, 1993) reported an "informal replication" of Sheingold and Tenney's study. While the results essentially replicated the earlier study, Neisser found one important difference between the studies. Subjects who were between the ages of two and three years, but not younger than two, at the time their sibling was born, could answer up to several questions about the birth of their sibling. Some people, then, can recall a salient childhood event like the birth of a sibling as far back as age two, i.e., quite a bit earlier than the Sheingold and Tenney data demonstrate. Neisser believes that the Sheingold and Tenney study failed to discover that even earlier salient experiences can be retrieved because their research design failed to control for other siblings born after age four, thereby decreasing the probability that the earlier memory would be retrieved (retroactive inhibition).

In order to collect additional data on adult memory for very early salient childhood experiences, Usher and Neisser (1993) conducted a more extensive study using the targeted recall procedure. They asked subjects (college students) about four different target childhood events: birth of a sibling, hospitalization, death of a family member, and a family move into a new home. Each subject was asked a series of structured questions about the target event. As with some earlier studies, the subjects' parents were contacted in order to verify the accuracy of the reports. The results are summarized as follows:

> Our results suggest that the offset of childhood amnesia—that is, the earliest age from which something can be remembered into adulthood—varies with what has been experienced; some events are more memorable than others. For hospitalization and the birth of a sibling, the critical age is appreciably earlier than previous estimates have suggested. (p. 155)

The subjects also reported "strong positive or negative emotional reactions to target events" (p. 160), but the affect was unrelated to the amount of information recalled. The subjects "reported seldom discussing or thinking about any of the events" (p. 161), so that rehearsal was not a factor related to the likelihood of recall. When the subjects' reports were compared to their parents' recollections for the same event, "most responses were judged to be accurate and . . . only a small fraction were definitely wrong" (p. 163). While the details for the most part were accurately recalled, most of the inaccuracy was misremembering the exact age at which the event occurred. For birth of a sibling and for hospitalization, but significantly less so for death of a relative or a family move, adult subjects could recall from one to three details about the event, even if they were as young as two years old, but not younger, at the time of the event. Thus, while people retain at least a partial verbal memory for certain emotional salient childhood experiences occurring when they were as young as two years old, most individuals retain a relatively complete memory for salient experience occurring when they were four years old or older. These data suggest that it is too simple to view four years of age as the cut-off for childhood amnesia. While adults generally do not remember most events before they were four years old, these data suggest that they will remember events of impact and will remember them accurately.

Barclay and DeCooke (1988) conducted a study of autobiographical memory for "memorable daily events" in four women. During the course of the data collection, one woman received a telephone call from her father telling her that her mother had had a serious accident, had been hospitalized, and had a 50% chance of surviving. The mother eventually died. The subject recorded in a diary the sequence of events as part of the autobiographical data. Barclay and DeCooke saw this as an opportunity to compare memory for typically experienced memorable daily events to memory for a tragic death. They note that most "memorable daily events" recorded in autobiographical studies do not have great personal significance. In contrast, the sudden death of a parent constituted something akin to what Yuille has defined as an event of impact. This unexpected event gave the researchers an opportunity to study directly memory for an event of impact by comparing the subject's personal memory of this tragic event to memory for other memorable daily events she had recorded. The researchers also used another subject's autobiography as a control.

Approximately three months after data had been collected for both subjects, each subject was given a cued-recall memory test, in which cues were taken from the previous diaries each had submitted to the researchers. Memory for memorable daily events did not differ significantly in the amount of information recalled prior to the accidental death. The experimental subject's ratings of the accidental death differed significantly from ratings for other personal memories and those of the control subject, in that the event was rated as significantly more memorable, personally meaningful, emotional, and infrequently occurring. The ratings supported the notion that the death constituted an event of impact.

Memory responses given on cued recall three months after the data collection revealed that the experimental subject's memory for the tragic death was significantly different from the memorable personal experiences of the control subject in the amount of gist information and the elaborateness of the detail retained about the experience after three months (as compared with the original diary recording of the event). Neither the experimental nor control subject differed in the amount of details recorded about either the death or about any other personal memorable event. Consistent with findings from other autobiographical studies, memory for peripheral details was not well retained over time. The authors conclude:

> Ordinary traumatic experiences do not necessarily interfere with recollections of daily events occurring before the upset. Memory for events surrounding the episode are enhanced compared with what was remembered about less significant events, even though memory for the exact wording of the original record was relatively poor (p. 121). . . . These experiences seemingly benchmark one's personal history. (p. 119)

Several studies have addressed the vividness and emotionality associated with memory for events of impact. Reisberg, Heuer, McLean, and O'Shaughnessy (1988) asked subjects about events such as the death of a close friend or relative and significant public events. Subjects were asked to rate the vividness of the memory (defined in terms of the completeness of detail), the quality and strength of the emotional response to the event, and the impact of the event on the person's life (consequentiality). Across three separate experiments, vividness of memory correlated significantly with the consequentiality and the emotional intensity, but not with the quality of emotion associated with the event.

Christianson and Loftus (1990) surveyed over 400 subjects in two experiments about "highly emotional events" (p. 195). Their research was designed to address Yuille and Cutshall's conclusion that events of impact lead to remarkable memories in which both central and peripheral details are well retained over long retention intervals. Subjects were asked to:

> If possible, think of the most traumatic event you have experienced in your life. By traumatic event, we mean an extremely sudden and disturbing event that overwhelmed you with shocking negative emotional feelings. (p. 196)

Events that subjects commonly reported were: the death of a relative, divorce of family members or friends, accidents, and injuries. (Note that while the questionnaire asked subjects about "traumatic events," only a small portion of subjects (6%) reported the type of events that are often associated with the development of posttraumatic stress symptoms, such as shootings or sexual assault.) Subjects were asked to rate the vividness (amount of detail), the number of central and peripheral details, and the strength of emotion associated with their recollections. Subjects rated their traumatic memories as "relatively vivid" (p. 196), although "there was a specific detail that they remembered much better than other details" (p. 197). Subjects also thought that they had remembered significantly more central than peripheral details. There was a significant correlation between the strength of emotion and the number of central details recalled.

While these two studies (Christianson & Loftus, 1990; Reisberg et al., 1988) are limited, in that there was no way to assess objectively the accuracy of the memory for emotionally significant events, the results lend further support to the claim that events of impact are events that have significant consequences to the person's life, evoke strong emotions, and result in unusually vivid recall over time, at least for the central action and other personally meaningful features of the experience.

A third approach to memory for events of impact involves the investigation of the 1989 San Francisco earthquake (Neisser, Winograd, & Weldon, 1991; Palmer, Schreiber, & Fox, 1991). In this study, three teams of researchers compared memory for the earthquake in subjects from three different geographic areas—Atlanta, Georgia, Berkeley, California, and Santa Cruz, California. The Atlanta group merely heard about the earthquake on the news. The latter two were located within the area of the earthquake, with the Santa Cruz group close to the epicenter. Subjects in both California groups had directly experienced the earthquake. By comparing memory recall across groups, the researchers were able to compare memory performance in subjects directly experiencing or just hearing about an emotionally significant event.

Unlike earlier flashbulb studies, these investigators were able to obtain baseline data on memory for the event. Subjects recorded their memory of the event itself within a few days after the earthquake; the place, activity, time of day, others present, and the informant of the news; what they did just as the earthquake began; what they did after the quake; and their emotional reaction to the event. One and a half years later, subjects were contacted and asked once again to recall the event, reception circumstances, and their emotional reaction at the time. Using a weighted scale of overall accuracy (0–7), subjects near the earthquake's epicenter (Santa Cruz) were extremely accurate, those elsewhere in California (Berkeley) were nearly as accurate, and those far away (Atlanta) were significantly less accurate in their recall of the earthquake itself (6.7., 6.0, and 3.8, respectively). Recall of the reception circumstances, e.g., time of day, place, activity, etc., for both California groups of subjects was near perfect.

In addition to their direct experience of the earthquake, the two California groups of subjects were also asked about an aspect of the earthquake that was not directly experienced. Most California subjects heard about the collapse of the San Francisco Bay Bridge on the news. While their recall of the reported event one and a half years later was significantly lower than recall of their direct experience of the earthquake over the same time interval, its was significantly better than that of the Atlanta group for the same event.

The results of this important study differ quite significantly from the earlier studies on flashbulb memories, i.e., delayed recall for reported significant news events. The results clearly demonstrate that delayed recall of a highly consequential big news event is significantly more accurate if the event is directly experienced than just heard about—both for the event itself as well as for the details of the circumstances surrounding the event. For the subjects who were residents in California and directly experienced the earthquake, in contrast to subjects in Atlanta who merely heard about it on the news, the earthquake clearly constituted an event of impact. Consistent with the other studies on events of impact, emotional reactions to the earthquake varied considerably within the sample of California subjects. Direct experience and consequentiality of the earthquake for the resident's lives were associated with high accuracy of the memory.

Overall, the conclusions drawn from studies of memory for events of impact in adults are limited due to the the paucity of studies. These studies, which essentially require "ambulance chasing," are very difficult to plan in advance. Consequently, these studies understandably suffer from various methodological limitations. The eyewitness studies lack an adequate baseline against which to compare accuracy of memory over time. As Christianson, Goodman, and Loftus (1992) have pointed out, "we don't know what actually happened" (p. 223) in the Yuille and Cutshall (1986) study. Because the event was reconstructed from a composite of all the police and eyewitness data, conclusions must be drawn with some caution.

The Barclay and DeCooke autobiographical study and the San Francisco earthquake studies are a clear improvement because they establish a baseline. Nevertheless, the studies do lend validation to the construct of an event of impact. In terms of memory processing direct experience of real-life stressful events that have immediate consequences for the individual's life does seem to represent a category of event separate from passively, observed laboratory-simulated events. *The data on memory accuracy are consistent across studies in support of the view that memory for events of impact show a very high accuracy rate over time in terms of total amount of information recalled and in terms of memory for central actions.* The accuracy rates generally range from 82 to 96% for the gist of the main action. Memory for peripheral details is more variable. Details central to the event, such as objects involved in the robbery (Yuille & Cutshall, 1986) or details about the reception circumstances of the San Francisco earthquake (Neisser et al., 1991; Palmer et al., 1991), are retained with remarkably high accuracy over time. Other details, such as descriptions of people present at the crime (Yuille & Cutshall, 1986), are not accurately retained.

Overall, the studies on events of impact in adults do not support the view that emotional arousal interferes with memory recall over time. No agreement exists as to why events of impact are so well retained over time. Because emotional response varies considerably across subjects for events of impact, emotional arousal does not appear to be an adequate explanation although rehearsal may play an important role (Cutshall & Yuille, 1989). Events of impact constitute a type of "remarkable memory" (Cutshall & Yuille, 1989, p. 212). Because of the uniqueness of the event and its impact on a person's life, eyewitnesses think about the event a great deal and talk about it to others, probably more often than they think or talk about less impactful daily experiences. Thinking about it and remarking upon it constitute a type of memory rehearsal that maintains the memory in storage.

Yuille and Tollestrup (1992) offer the intriguing hypothesis that events of impact may also be encoded differently from more mundane personal experiences. They believe that events of impact are "qualitatively different memories than the innocuous laboratory events" (Yuille & Cutshall, 1989, p. 178) used in simulation studies of memory.

EVENTS OF IMPACT
IN CHILDREN

In order to understand the types of events that might constitute events of impact in children, it is first necessary to understand something about memory development in children (Fivush & Hudson, 1990; Fivish & Shukat, 1995; Kail, 1990; Nelson, 1988). Early theories, like the childhood amnesia hypothesis (Freud, 1905/1953), and the encoding shift hypothesis (Underwood, 1969), advocated the view that memory organization in young children is es-

sentially different from that of older children and adults, and that some fundamental cognitive reorganization takes place at a critical point in childhood (Neisser, 1962; Piaget, 1962; Schachtel, 1947).

An increasingly accepted view is that the organization of memory in young children is in many ways similar to that of adults. Children as young as two years of age evidence semantic and temporal organization of experiences (Nelson, 1988), just as older children do, although the semantic categories of the younger children are not very elaborate. Children between the ages of three and six can accurately recall previous emotionally salient events in a consistent, coherently organized narrative after long retention intervals (Fivush & Shukat, 1995). Younger children also focus on different kinds of information from older children and adults (Ceci, Lea, & Howe, 1980). Preschool children organize memory around familiar recurrent experiences, especially stable daily routines. Such routines, like pre-sleep storytime, watching "Sesame Street," or familiar play sequences, constitute central events in the child's unfolding world. Studies of crib talk in two- to three-year-olds has shown that toddlers initially organize memory around the gist of some central and familiar activity, what are called *general event schemas* or *script knowledge* (Nelson, 1988). As the child attempts to make sense of the unfolding world, repeated experiences, including variations in or departures from daily routines, are assimilated into the event schemas. Thus, young children have clearly organized memory schema for the familiar and stereotyped experiences central to their worlds, but they do not have elaborate memory schemas for specific events, unless they are emotionally salient. Thus, free recall of familiar kindergarten play experiences are generally accurate but incomplete and highly stable five to nine years after the experiences (Fivush & Hudson, 1990; Gold & Neisser, 1980).

Younger children do not have much cognitive control over memory processes in the form of elaborate search and retrieval strategies and are therefore more dependent on external cues and the social context than older children when they retrieve memories (Kail, 1990). These familiar play sequences are significantly better recalled if the child actively participates in the play, or at least watches familiar peers play the game, rather than passively observes it (Baker-Ward, Hess, & Flannagan, 1990).

Older children evidence greater temporal organization of their memory for play sequences and therefore are able to incorporate a greater number and complexity of play sequences into their memory for repeated familiar play (Price & Goodman, 1990).

At a very young age, memories for specific events are blended into general event schemas, so that a memory for repeated experiences leads to a confusion of distinct experiences in preschoolers (Nelson, 1986). Recall of specific events, except for certain ones, may be difficult for the younger child. With later cognitive maturation, the child develops the capacity for more elaborate semantic processing of information and, therefore the capacity for *memory for specific events* (Hudson & Nelson, 1986) and also for interpersonal interactions. These latter developments mark the beginning of autobiographical memory (Nelson, 1988).

This emerging script theory of children's memory predicts that young children will retain specific episodes in memory less efficiently than familiar routines precisely because such experiences are less important than daily routines to the child's evolving memory organization. It is well documented that young children, relative to older children, freely recall significantly less total information about specific events. Yet, what they recall is quite accurate and stable over time. However, cuing the young child's memory with specific questions can result in a significant increase in the total amount of accurate information recalled. It is equally well documented that the amount of information given in free recall significantly increases with age. These findings do not necessarily mean that young children are especially fallible in their memory. The findings do suggest that a young preschool child's memory performance depends a great deal on what you ask the child and on the context in which you ask it. Young children's evolving schematic memory organization is highly dependent on context, whereas older children, in the concrete operational stage, have developed a more stable, decontextualized memory system, and a greater repertoire of semantic categories and cognitive retrieval strategies to recall specific events in more elaborate detail.

According to script theory, we would expect younger children to show better recall for familiar events and poorer recall for unfamiliar events that disrupt routines. Research on memory for *novel experiences* supports this view. Hammond and Fivush (1990) demonstrated that young children (two and a half years old) freely recalled significantly less total information than older children (four and a half years old) about a family trip to Disney World, although there were no differences in the accuracy of the memory for the novel event. Fivush, Hudson, and Nelson (1984) and Hudson and Fivush (1987) investigated kindergartners' recall for a class trip to an archeological museum immediately, six weeks, one year, and six years after the experience. Free recall of this unique event immediately after the event was complete and accurate for the main activities as well as for the less salient details of the trip. After six months, the total amount of information, as well as its accuracy, was well retained. After a year, the experience was quite poorly reported through free recall. Only 7% of the children remembered, even after they were specifically asked to tell what happened when they went to the museum. Yet, about 70% of the original material was recoverable with more elaborate verbal cuing or visual cuing in the form of photographs from the trip.

Fivush and Hammond (1990) studied recall memory for an airplane trip in two-and-a-half- to three-year-olds at six weeks and again at 14 months after the trip. At six weeks only 9% of the children freely recalled the trip, but recall was significantly greater when cued by specific questions about the experience. Each time a child was asked about the trip, s/he remembered a somewhat different version of the event. What was recalled at any given time depended on the social context of the interview. While memory for the event details was inconsistent across memory tests, the details of what was remembered each time were quite accurate. Memories for the gist of the trip were significantly better preserved over time than memories for specific details, such as when the trip took place, where they went, etc. Overall, the studies by Fivush and associates demonstrate that the memories of young children for novel experiences are not well retained over time, in contrast to memory for familiar routines. Such experiences are seldom spontaneously reported in free recall after longer retention intervals, but may be recoverable if the specific memory is stimulated by cued questioning or play reenactment. What is recovered is generally accurate yet highly inconsistent across repeated interviewing. Presumably, novel experiences are not as readily assimilated into general event schemas as are variations on familiar routines, so that the details of such experiences are generally not well retained over time.

Tessler and Nelson (1994) demonstrated that novel experiences are incorporated into the child's developing memory to the extent to which they become part of the ongoing discourse between the child and the caregiver. This study addresses how a memory for a novel experience is "jointly encoded" through the interaction and communication between mother and child. The ongoing discourse between mothers and their three-and-a-half-year-old children was tape-recorded during a visit to a natural history museum. One week later, the children's memory was assessed using open-ended questions without their mothers' being present. The first experiment demonstrated that children failed to recall any objects unless they were the focus of joint conversation during the actual visit to the museum. Information that either the child or the mother encoded alone was not freely recalled by the child at the time of memory testing, whereas information that was jointly encoded was readily recalled.

There were large individual differences in memory performance within the group of children, which Tessler and Nelson hypothesized were related to maternal style of discourse. Therefore, the tape-recorded discourses were coded in terms of maternal style emphasizing either a narrative or paradigmatic style (Bruner, 1986). Results indicated that the children's memories significantly correlated with the mothers' style of discourse. A second experiment involved taking pictures in a unfamiliar part of the city as the novel event, refined the coding procedure for assessing maternal style and essentially replicated the results of the first experiment. Tessler and Nelson conclude that young children's memories are "co-constructed . . . through social discourse" (p. 320). Although the target memory was a novel and non-traumatic experience, the authors discuss the implication of their findings for our understanding of traumatic memory. Because unfamiliar experiences are especially vulnerable to being shaped by adult communication, they may also be vulnerable to distortion:

> For example, a favorite uncle's sexual handling characterized by him as an important secret for the

two of them to keep, at an age when the child has no familiarity with that as a particular category of story into which she can fit the memory, may be easily distorted by the child in the direction of the adult's story. . . . How experiences are formulated in the child's accessible autobiographical memory system is then strongly dependent on how they are formulated by adults who share the experience. The possibility of distorting memories within this kind of system is obvious, and the possibility that the influence could be used in ways detrimental to the child's emotional and mental well-being cannot be discounted. (p. 322)

Thus, an adult who communicates to the preschool child during sexual abuse that the abuse is a kind of "special game" or otherwise isn't wrong, or who says that "this never happened," may significantly alter the child's recollection of the experience and/or the child's capacity to determine that the experience was harmful.

Fivush (1994) also investigated the extent to which children's memory for a novel experience is influenced by discourse with caregivers. A total of 24 children about 40 months old were allowed to discuss with their mothers salient, novel experiences, for example, past visits to the zoo or circus or a plane ride. Shortly after the discussion, and at three subsequent intervals over the next 30 months, the children's memory for the novel experiences were assessed with a free recall retrieval strategy. Memory performance was analyzed in terms of how much information each child incorporated from the initial discussion of the events with his/her mother, how much information was repeated over successive testing sessions, and how much new information was provided at each testing session. The results demonstrated that only 9% of the total information provided by mothers in the initial discussion was later incorporated into the child's memory. Yet, these children repeated only about 20% of the previous information in subsequent free recall sessions. In other words, most of the information in successive free recall sessions over time was new. Fivush concludes:

> . . . these results indicate little tendency to incorporate information provided by another into one's own recall of an event" (p. 363). . . . Young

children's memories are not simply a conglomeration of things they have been told. Young children's memories do not seem to be so fragile that they easily begin to "remember" aspects of events that others have recounted to them. (p. 367)

Because these data contradict the Tessler and Nelson data (1994), Fivush explains that the discrepancy:

. . . raises the interesting possibility that the way an event is discussed as it unfolds and the way it is discussed in retrospect may have different consequences for children's developing memories of the event. (p. 369)

The main difference in the Tessler and Nelson (1994) and Fivush (1994) experiments rests in the fact that social discourse between mother and child was assessed *during* the novel event in the former study and sometime *after* the novel event in the latter study. Thus, interaction with an adult primarily may affect the encoding of the event, i.e., how the mother helps the child to attend to and understand the experience, but does not greatly influence the memory for the event once it has been encoded, except in a small sample of children.

For children, an event of impact is defined in reference to familiar routines. Low-level events of impact are any emotionally salient, unfamiliar experiences that can be assimilated into stable routines. High-level events of impact are novel experiences that disrupt familiar routines and pose a threat to the child's sense of security.

Staged unfamiliar experiences with strangers have been used extensively as a means to investigate memory accuracy in children. A child is brought to an unfamiliar setting to interact with a male stranger, a confederate in the research. The child and the stranger play various games, like puppets, Simon Says, an imaginary tea party, or dressing up like clowns. The activities have been designed to capture a child's interest, be personally and emotionally meaningful, and yet be easily capable of assimilation into the child's familiar play routines. Sometime later, up to a week, memory testing is conducted in the child's home using free recall and cued recall, and occasionally a photo identification test for the stranger. While these experiments will

be discussed at greater length in chapter 8, a brief review of the results across many studies with children from three to six, but some studies with children up to ten or eleven years of age, have shown consistently that:

1. Younger children recall significantly less correct total information in free recall than older children.
2. Inaccurate recall is generally quite low across ages in children.
3. A significantly greater proportion of information is recalled when the child is cued with specific questions about the interaction, and such questioning is not associated with any remarkable increase in inaccuracy.
4. Actions are recalled significantly more completely and accurately than physical features of the stranger.

An interesting exception to these conclusions may involve children's memory for (nonsexual) touching that occurred between the child and the stranger during the interaction. In two independent studies, free recall rates of being touched were approximately 50–60%. In other words, children, especially school-age children, generally underreport being touched in free recall (Davies, Tarrant, & Flin, 1989; Peters, 1991). Overall, these studies demonstrate that even children as young as three years of age can give an accurate account of "personally significant" interactions. Although the younger child's free recall for such experiences is generally incomplete, a more complete and mostly accurate account is obtainable by cuing the child with questions. Accuracy is consistently quite high for central actions and significantly less so for more peripheral details such as the physical description of the stranger (Davies et al., 1989; Goodman & Aman, 1990; Goodman, Aman, & Hirschman, 1987; Goodman & Reed, 1986; Goodman, Rudy, Bottoms, & Aman, 1990; Peters, 1991).

A second group of studies focuses particularly on memory performance following emotionally stressful experiences for a child, such as visits to dentists or doctors or fire drills at school. In a pioneering study on children's memeory for real-life emotionally stressful situations, Peters (1987) studied recognition memory in children three to eight years of age one to two days and three to four weeks after a visit to the dentist. Older children were significantly more accurate than younger children in correctly identifying the target dentist or dental assistant in a line-up. Vandermaas (1990) also reported on memory performance of four- and eight-year-old-children after a trip to the dentist. Central and peripheral details were well retained and the stress did not significantly reduce the accuracy of recall.

Vandermaas, Hess, and Baker-Ward (1993) studied recall memory in children four to five and seven to eight years old immediately after a visit to the dentist for routine teeth-cleaning or a dental operation. A behavioral rating scale was used along with subjective ratings to assess the degree of anxiety for the dental procedures. Information for the event was classified into central ("directly involves the child, so that the child is touched in some way," p. 114) and peripheral information (child is not touched). Anxiety levels for the dental procedures were highly variable across subjects and age groups. Younger children were significantly more anxious than older children when anxiety was assessed behaviorally. Younger children freely recalled significantly less information about the event than older children. Children of both age groups produced an accurate memory for central information, but less so for peripheral information, in both the teeth-cleaning and dental operation conditions. Older children gave significantly more correct answers to specific questions about peripheral information than did younger children in both conditions. Memory commission errors were rare in both age groups. High levels of anxiety predicted decreased memory performance in older but not younger children. The authors conclude that the relationship between anxiety and memory is exceedingly complex and depends on a number of variables—age of the child, degree of familiarity with the experience, level of anxiety, retention interval, type of memory test (recognition vs. recall), and type of information to be retrieved (central vs. peripheral).

A number of recent investigations have used visits to medical facilities where inoculations, venipuncture, and genital examinations served as the emotional stressor. The results were highly consistent across studies:

1. No significant differences emerged across ages in the total amount of accurate information freely recalled about noxious medical procedures (except in the Peters, 1991, study, where older children recalled more information than younger children). Children of all ages were highly accurate in what they remembered about these procedures.

2. There were no significant differences in memory performance in the stress and non-stress control conditions. Children recalled the visit to the doctor regardless of whether or not they experienced a shot or venipuncture. An important exception is that older children reported significantly less total information about the genital exam than younger children, a finding consistent with the Peters (1991) and Davies et al. (1989) studies.

3. On cued recall, children across ages recalled significantly more information about the central event than about peripheral information, e.g., the descriptions of the people or the objects in the room (Goodman, Bottoms, Schwartz-Kenney, & Rudy, 1991; Goodman, Hirschman, Hepps, & Rudy, 1991; Goodman, Rudy, Bottoms, & Aman, 1990; Peters, 1991; Saywitz, Goodman, Nicholas, & Moan, 1991).

Pillemer (1992) investigated memory for a school evacuation due to a fire alarm. Two weeks later three-and-a-half- and four-and-a-half-year-olds were asked to give a free recall narrative and then were asked specific questions about the incident. There were no significant differences in the total amount of accurate information given by the three-and-a half- and four-and-a-half-year-olds. Children of both age groups remembered about twice as much accurate information in response to direct questions about the incident. A number of the three-and-a half-year-olds erroneously reported that they were outside when they heard the fire alarm, presumably because they had difficulty grasping the sequence for an event that disrupted their daily routine. The older children described a sense of urgency when evacuating the school and also correctly reported the cause of the fire.

Peters (1991) designed a simulated fire alarm study. Six- and nine-year-old children showed no significant differences in their free recall of the incident shortly after it occurred across the fire alarm and no fire alarm (control) conditions, although children who actually experienced the fire alarm scare gave more correct and fewer incorrect responses than control children. Accuracy rates were very high when specific questions were used to prompt memory in both the fire alarm (72%) and control (82%) groups. Both fire alarm studies suggest that the stress of the fire alarm does not negatively affect the accuracy of recall in children of different ages.

Overall, memory accuracy for events of impact in children is a complex interaction of differences in memory development, the nature of the event, and the context of testing. Developmental differences contribute to less complete free recall narratives in younger children and the need for external cues to stimulate recall.

With respect to accuracy, the data support the view that children, developmental constraints not withstanding, can accurately recall events of impact, especially when asked about the gist of the central activity in question. The children, however, are generally not very accurate about peripheral details like objects in the room or the physical characteristics of the people involved. When the situation is stressful, such as noxious medical procedures or fire alarms, the event is accurately remembered and well retained across age groups. In fact, these stressful events are more accurately remembered and well retained than memory for positive novel events like a special trip. Yet, the context of the stressful event and its meaning to the child is probably more important than the nature of the specific stressor per se.

7

|||||||||||||||||||||||

Trauma Memory

DSM-IV AND THE EFFECTS OF TRAUMA ON MEMORY

Traumatic memory can be distinguished from memory for events of impact by the occurrence of posttraumatic stress symptoms. Like events of impact, traumatizing events are very stressful, often emotionally arousing situations that an individual directly experiences and that have immediate consequences for the individual's unfolding life. Unlike events of impact, traumatic events entail "actual or threatened death or serious injury, or a threat to the physical integrity of self or others" and typically involve "intense fear, helplessness, or horror" (APA, 1994, pp. 427–428).

What distinguishes a traumatic event from an event of impact is not so much the nature of the event per se but its consequences. Some very stressful events produce temporary posttraumatic stress symptoms (PTSS), an acute posttraumatic stress disorder, or a more lasting chronic posttraumatic stress disorder (PTSD) in certain individuals. In this sense, a traumatic event is defined as an event of impact that results in PTSS or PTSD. However, L. Brown (1995a) has noted that *DSM* tends to define traumatic events as single-incident events. She says, "The *DSM-IV* revision has failed to provide us with a diagnosis to describe the effects of exposure to repetitive interpersonal violence and victimization"

(p. 111). This difference between an event of impact and a traumatizing event in terms of symptom occurrence is important, especially in terms of memory performance.

DSM-IV lists four defining criteria for PTSD: A) a traumatizing event, usually involving bodily injury or threat to life; B) intrusive reexperiencing of symptoms; C) generalized numbing of responsiveness; and D) physiological reactivity. This list was in part derived from the pioneering work of Mardi Horowitz in his classic *Stress Response Syndromes* (1976). According to Horowitz's information processing model, the extraordinary nature of a traumatically stressful event disrupts ordinary information processing. The usual posttraumatic adjustment progresses through a number of predictable stages: outcry, denial, intrusive reexperiencing, working through, and completion, as the traumatized individual attempts to process and integrate the emotions and memories associated with the traumatic event. Normal recovery from traumatic experiences typically involves episodes of denial (constriction of thought and numbing of emotions), intrusive reexperiencing (intrusion into consciousness of thoughts, images, nightmares, flashbacks, and intense emotions associated with the trauma), and persistent physiological reactivity, until the memories and feelings associated with the traumatic event are integrated into consciousness, at which point the symptoms disappear. Traumatic events, especially those that involve injury, loss, or threat to life, also destabilize the ordinary self representation and may activate latent pathological self representations (Brende & McCann, 1984; Brown & Fromm, 1986; Parson, 1984).

With respect to memory for traumatic events, the extreme emotional arousal accompanying the trauma affects memory processing, so that the memory impression is stored primarily as a vivid somato-sensory representation of the traumatic event (van der Kolk, 1993; van der Kolk & Fisler, 1995). Following a traumatic event, the traumatized individual may be either hypermnesic or amnesic for the incident, depending on the phase of recovery (Horowitz & Reidbord, 1992). Van der Kolk, McFarlane, and Weisaeth (1996) summarize, "trauma can lead to extremes of retention and forgetting" (p. 282). *DSM-IV* (APA, 1994) defines dissociative amnesia in terms of:

> . . . episodes of inability to recall important personal information, usually of a traumatic or stressful nature, that is too extensive to be explained by ordinary forgetfulness. (p. 481)

The clinical studies documenting PTSS and PTSD consequent to traumatic events as diverse as combat exposure, torture, rape, disaster exposure, and child abuse are too numerous to mention. The prevalence rate of PTSD in the general population, according to large-scale general surveys, is about 3.5%–9% and about 20% in Vietnam veterans who were wounded in combat (Breslau & Davis, 1992; Helzer, Robins, & McEvoy, 1987). A small portion of individuals exposed to trauma experience chronic persistent symptoms (e.g., Winje, 1996) and sometimes a deteriorating course (Wang, Wilson, & Mason, 1996).

More recently, it has become increasingly clear that the association between traumatic events and PTSD is too narrow, and that PTSD, dissociation, somatization, and various problems of affect dysregulation are closely associated (van der Kolk, Pelcovitz et al., 1996). We believe traumatization can result in any one of four broad categories of long-term sequelae or trauma damage: (1) posttraumatic symptoms, (2) dissociative symptoms, (3) pervasive developmental delays and personality disorder, and (4) pathological changes in attributions and beliefs about self and world.

EXPERIMENTAL STUDIES ON TRAUMA AND MEMORY

Unfortunately, until recently there have been very few well designed experimental studies on memory for traumatic events. Studies specifically comparing memory performance in traumatized and nontraumatized populations are just beginning to appear in the literature (e.g., Kuyken & Brewin, 1995; Lidz et al., 1996; McNally et al., 1990; McNally et al., 1993; Tromp et al., 1995; Yehuda et al., 1995; Zeitlin & McNally, 1991). Most of the studies, with a few notable exceptions, utilize clinical samples and suffer from the methodological limitations common in clinical research. The problem with many of these reports is the absence of baseline data against which to compare memory accuracy and consistency over time.

Disaster Studies

Memory impairments have been reported for victims of a number of disasters. Memory difficulties were found in 27% of the 102 victims of the Hyatt Regency skywalk collapse (Wilkinson, 1983). Unfortunately, the study failed to document the exact nature of the memory difficulty, i.e., whether a given victim suffered from intrusive memory, amnesia, or both. Memory impairment was also noted in survivors of the 1988 Armenian earthquake (Miller et al., 1993). "Recurrent intrusive memories" and "memory impairment" were among symptoms and manifestations of PTSD in the survivors. No data were reported on the distribution of traumatic memory impairments across survivors. A total of 59% of the survivors of a 1984 North Carolina tornado met the criteria for PTSD after the disaster (Madakasira & O'Brien, 1987) and the majority of those with PTSD had intrusive recollections (82%) and memory impairment (61%). Fifty-one percent suffered from a "mild to moderate" and 10% from a "severe" memory impairment.

Cardena and Spiegel (1993) found difficulties with everyday memory, intrusive recollections, and some evidence for partial amnesia in 8% and 3% of a sample of 100 students one week and four weeks after the 1989 San Francisco earthquake, respectively. They noted, however, that "Neither partial nor full amnesia for the traumatic event was frequently reported," except in a small group of "severely affected individuals" (p. 476).

Dollinger (1985) reported generalized anxiety symptoms, trauma-specific fears, depression, and somaticization in 33 children struck by lightning during a soccer game. One child had "no memory" for lightning-related injuries nine months following the incident.

McFarlane (1988) found that 3.6% of 469 firefighters who were survivors of a 1983 Australian bushfire disaster lost memory specifically for their injuries 11 months after the disaster even when they had reported the injuries four months after it had occurred. Contrary to expectation, the long-term failure to remember the injuries was observed in the subsample that did *not* suffer from acute or chronic PTSD.

Combat Studies

Clinical cases of traumatic amnesia and other forms of memory deficits have been consistently documented for war trauma, including World War I (Brown, 1918a,b, 1919, 1920–21; McDougall, 1920–21; Myers, 1915, 1916; Rivers, 1918; Southard, 1919; Thom & Fenton, 1920; Wingfield, 1920), World War II (Fisher, 1943, 1945; Grinker & Spiegel, 1945; Henderson & Moore, 1944; Kardiner, 1941; Kardiner & Spiegel, 1947; Kubie, 1943; Parfitt & Carlyle-Gall, 1944; Sargant & Slater, 1941; Torrie, 1944; Tureen & Stein, 1949; Watkins, 1949), the Middle East War (Kalman, 1977), and the Vietnam war (Cavenar & Nash, 1976; El-Rayes, 1982; Hendin et al., 1984; Kolb, 1985; Perry & Jacobs, 1982; Silver & Kelly, 1985; Sonnenberg, Blank, & Talbott, 1985; D. Spiegel, 1981; Yehuda et al., 1995). The most detailed prevalence data on traumatic amnesia for war experiences were reported by Sargant and Slater (1941). In 1,000 cases of war neurosis, 144 (14.4%) men had significant amnesia for war experiences, most of which related to the evacuation of Dunkirk in World War II. Torrie (1944), likewise, reported amnesia and/or fugue in 8.6% in 1,000 cases in soldiers from the North African campaign suffering from war neurosis during

World War II. Henderson and Moore (1944) reported amnesia in about 5% of soldiers in the South Pacific. A contemporary randomized survey of the general population documented that 16% of veterans reported a period of time where they completely forgot significant war experiences. Another 23% reported partial amnesia for war experiences (Elliott & Briere, 1994).

A number of experimental studies in Vietnam veterans (Lidz et al., 1996; McNally et al., 1990; McNally et al., 1993; Yehuda et al., 1995; Zeitlin & McNally, 1991) have demonstrated that traumatized veterans process trauma-related information differently from nontrauma information. Using a Modified Stroop Test to assess selective attention, many of these studies show that attention may be biased either toward or away from processing traumatic stimuli in traumatized Vietnam veterans.

Prisoner and Torture Studies

Goldfeld et al. (1988) reviewed the international literature on the medical and psychological effects of torture. Included in the review of four studies were data on memory disturbances subsequent to systematic torture. Memory disturbances were reported in all studies, with rates that varied from 29% to 45% across the studies. The authors noted, however, that it was difficult to distinguish between psychogenic and organic contributions to amnesia in torture victims because of the high incidence of head injury in this population (see Table 7.1).

Memory for the Nazi Holocaust

Amnesia for Nazi Holocaust camp experiences has also been reported (Krystal, 1968; Wagenaar & Groeneweg, 1990). Wagenaar and Groeneweg (1990) conducted a study specifically on the accuracy and consistency of memory for trauma over a very long retention interval. Like the Williams (1994a) and Widom and Morris (1997) studies, it is a *prospective study* on memory performance in a traumatized group that established a baseline of memory and then compared subsequent memory performance over a long retention interval. A total of 78 survivors of a Nazi concentration camp, Camp Erika in the Netherlands, were interviewed between 1943 and 1948. Most were young adults (mean of 27 years

TABLE 7.1
Incidence of Memory Disturbance Following Torture

SOURCE	DISTURBANCE	N	SAMPLE
Rasmussen & Lunde, 1980	45%	135	Danish
Allodi & Cowgill, 1982	29%	42	Canadian
Domovitch et al., 1984	38%	104	Canadian
Goldfeld et al., 1988	32%	19	American

GENERAL CONCLUSIONS:
- memory disturbance is common in subsample of torture victims
- samples address systematic (rarely single-incident) torture
- sexual abuse & rape are common in torture of women
- studies do not distinguish type of memory disturbance (hypermnesia/amnesia; full/partial amnesia)
- it is difficult to distinguish organic (head trauma) from psychogenic (torture trauma) contributions to memory disturbance

old). A subsample was interviewed 40 years later, between 1984 and 1988, during the investigation of a Nazi war criminal Marinus DeRijke, the cruel torturer of the camp. By comparing the testimony given by survivors 40 years later to their original interviews about Holocaust camp experiences, Wagenaar and Groeneweg were able to assess the accuracy of their survivors' current memories and the consistency of their memories over a very long retention interval. They found that even after 40 years the survivors' memories for the central experiences of the camp—the living conditions, the usual daily routines, malnutrition, etc.—were remarkably accurate and consistent, both within and across subjects. However, memory for more peripheral details of camp life, such as dates of arriving at or leaving the camp, names of the camp guards, photo recognition of DeRijke, or memory for the camp registration number were not well preserved. In this sense, Wagenaar and Groeneweg's data are consistent with what we know about autobiographical memory in general: the memories for the gist of the specific camp experiences are well retained and are quite accurate, as are memories for the gist of repeated experiences like daily camp routines labor routines, etc., which are stored as generic memories of camp routines. Yet unique, idiosyncratic details of prison camp life are often forgotten.

Wagenaar and Groeneweg found one important exception to what might be expected from the studies on normal autobiographical memory. A subpopulation of camp survivors failed after 40 years to recall memory for traumatic experiences. Consistent with other studies on PTSD (e.g., Dollinger, 1985; Kuehn, 1974; McFarlane, 1988), physical injury or threat of death was associated with the memory loss. Wagenaar and Groeneweg also found that this recall failure was reversed when the survivors were confronted with their previous testimony about atrocities experienced over 40 years earlier. These data provide additional evidence for the concept of trauma-specific amnesia, at least in a subsample of Holocaust survivors.

These data are also consistent with what is known both about normal autobiographical memory (gist accuracy at the expense of incidental details) and about traumatic experiences (amnesia predicted by injury or threat to life). The study also demonstrates once again that memory for trauma is generally accurate at least for the gist of the traumatic events that occurred even after many years, but is not necessarily readily accessible. Details like the physical characteristics of people are less accurately and consistently retained. In that sense, testimony of survivors based on witness memory for perpetrators' physical characteristics is not always reliable. Note, however, that *no* data are available in support of the claim that memory for the gist of traumatic events is grossly inaccurate. Wagenaar and Groeneweg conclude:

There is no doubt that almost all witnesses remember Camp Erika in great detail even after 40 years. The accounts of the conditions in the camp, the horrible treatment, the daily routine, the forced labor, the housing, the food, the main characteristics of the guards, are remarkably consistently. (p. 84)

In this sense, Neisser's (1981) account of John Dean's memory for the Watergate investigation helps us to understand the issue of accuracy of traumatic memory. His testimony some time after Watergate provides clear evidence that he got a lot of the factual details wrong, and yet his memory is testimony to the fact that he really *knew* exactly what was going on in Nixon's post-Watergate White House. Likewise, Holocaust survivors may not remember all of the details of their memory for traumatic incidents accurately, but they certainly *know* the gist of what happened to them, although for some that memory may not always be accessible or held with much confidence.

Mazor et al. (1990) studied the memory of survivors who were children during the Holocaust. A nonclinical group of 15 Holocaust survivors participated in a semistructured interview given 40 years after the war. They were asked about their recollections immediately after the war and their recollections 40 years later. The focus of the study was on how the survivors dealt with their memories over the decades since the war. Immediately after the war most of the survivors reported focusing on establishing a new life and "did not deal with war memories at all" (p. 6). Two of the fifteen subjects said that "they still try to forget and repress their memories" (p. 6). The 13 with continuous memories reported "affective anesthesias" and a general avoidance of memories about the war while they preoccupied themselves with rebuilding their lives. In recent years these 13 survivors reported no longer avoiding their war recollections. As part of a general life review occurring after age 50, "They made an effort to retain their [Holocaust] memories" (p. 6), yet the process of remembering was typically accompanied by intensely painful feelings and sometimes by increased dreaming about the war. They coped with the stress of remembering by crying, talking with other survivors about their experiences, and reading books. Most felt that remembering "creat[ed] a sense of sequence and cohesion in their personal history."

In *Holocaust Testimonies: The Ruins of Memory*,

Langer (1991) addresses the reasons why Holocaust camp survivors have difficulty reporting their recollections of camp experiences. Langer collected detailed oral testimonies from camp survivors. He noted the particular difficulty survivors had talking about camp experiences. According to his analysis, this difficulty comes from the extraordinary nature of the camp conditions and the atrocities witnessed and experienced. Such experiences are so discrepant from everyday experience that the camp survivor is left with a "dual existence" (p. 23)—everyday life versus the "co-temporal" recollections of life in the camps. These extremely traumatic memories are "discontinuous" from everyday autobiographical memory. They do not fit in everyday schemas. They are what Langer calls "deep memory." In addition, such memories are "anguished memories," in that they will never make any sense in terms of everyday autobiographical memory.

Furthermore, Langer correctly points out that survivors, under the extremes of camp conditions, often found themselves behaving in ways quite contrary to everyday behavior in their pre- or post-camp "normal" lives. Survivors under such conditions were confronted with their own sense of deep impotence to affect camp conditions, their own conduct which at times conflicted with everyday moral standards, and their own failure to behave in the camps in ways that matched heroic ideals. Thus, the Holocaust recollections constitute a kind of "humiliated" or "tainted" memory; such recollections are extremely painful to put into words or share as part of everyday autobiographical memory. Langer also points out not only that failure to report extreme trauma is a function of failure to retrieve the traumatic memory, but also that, even if retrieved, the memory has no place in autobiographical memory and one's normal, everyday self representation. Since such extreme traumatic memory is discontinuous with everyday memory, significant periods of the Holocaust survivor's life remain inaccessible.

Memory for Violent Crime

An early empirical study on memory performance in a traumatized population was conducted by Kuehn (1974). The study focused on the completeness of memory for the physical characteristics of assailants in victims of violent crimes. Kuehn randomly sampled police reports on violent crimes, e.g., homicides, forcible rapes, and aggravated assaults, in a metropolitan area, to assess whether victims' memory for the physical characteristics of their assailants (race, sex, age, height, weight, build, complexion, hair color, and eye color) was more or less complete. Across these nine categories, 85% of the sampled victims could describe six or more of these physical characteristics of their assailants, with a high of 93% describing the sex and a low of 23% of the subjects describing the eye color of the assailant. Kuehn concluded that "victims have a general impression of their assailants but cannot recall discrete features of the suspect" (p. 1161). However, he noted that several factors significantly predicted memory completeness, notably the type of crime and the degree of injury. Victims of robberies were more complete in their description than victims of rape or assault. Uninjured victims' descriptions were more complete than injured victims'. Short-term memory for the assailant's physical characteristics is significantly less complete when the victim is injured in the crime. Consistent with this study, the disrupted processing model of memory for trauma supports a biphasic model of posttraumatic memory performance, with a relatively complete memory for the gist of the event in a larger subgroup of noninjured victims, but a relatively incomplete memory in a smaller subgroup of presumably more traumatized injured victims.

A number of studies have documented some sort of *limited amnestic syndrome* in a large subsample of perpetrators of violent crimes. Presumably, commission of a violent crime, notably homicide, is accompanied by arousal, which in turn can affect memory processing (Kopelman, 1987; Schacter, 1986). What is unusual about amnesia following commission of a murder is that it is frequently limited to memory for the crime itself, and hence has been called limited amnesia (Schacter, 1986) or situation-specific amnesia (Gudjonsson, 1992). The more typical functional retrograde amnesia, in which the individual loses large amounts of autobiographical memory for his personal past and may also lose his sense of personal identity (fugue) is extremely rare following the commission of murder. If classical retrograde amnesia is reported for significant portions of a life history, it may signify that the amnesia is being simulated (Schacter, 1986).

Amnesia limited to the violent crime itself and the circumstances surrounding the crime is not uncommon. Harris (1969) discusses the well-known case of Sirhan Sirhan, who could not recall assassinating Robert F. Kennedy except under hypnosis. In the available studies on subjects charged with or convicted of murder, the prevalence rate of limited amnesia for the crime ranges from 22–65%, while the prevalence rate for general retrograde amnesia is less than 10% (see Table 7.2). Two early studies reported prevalence rates of around 30% in 36

TABLE 7.2
Amnesia for Homicide

Source	% Amnesia	N	Sample
Hopwood & Snell, 1933		100	inmates who attempted/completed homicide and who alleged amnesia
Leitch, 1948	31%	51	convicted murderers
Guttmacher, 1955	33%	36	convicted murderers
O'Connell, 1960	40%	50	homicide cases
Bradford & Smith, 1979	65%	30	consecutive homicide
Taylor & Kopelman, 1984	26%	34	convicted homicide
Parwatikar et al., 1985	22%	105	men accused of first degree murder
Gudjonsson et al., 1989	56%	16	homicide cases

Summary:
• limited (or trauma-specific) amnesia is a relatively common occurrence in homicide offenders (ranging from 22–65%)
• general retrograde amnesia is rare in homicide offenders (< 10%)

(Guttmacher, 1955) and 51 (Leitch, 1948) convicted murderers. Another early study investigated predictors of psychogenic amnesia for serious crimes. Hopwood and Snell (1933) looked at factors commonly associated with amnesia in a sample of 100 prison hospital inmates who had claimed amnesia for their crimes, about 90% of whom had completed or attempted homicide. Among the variables predicting functional amnesia for the crime were: (1) psychopathic predisposition, (2) depression, (3) seriousness of the crime, (4) close relationship to the victim, (5) strong emotional reaction at the time of the crime, and (6) previous history of amnestic episodes.

Subsequent studies compared reports of amnestic and non-amnestic convicted or charged murderers in order to identify variables that predicted limited amnesia for the homicide. O'Connell (1960) found that 40% of the 50 homicide cases had amnesia and that low intelligence, personality variables (hysteria), and alcohol intoxication at the time of the crime predicted amnesia. In a similar study of 30 cases of homicide, Bradford and Smith (1979) found that alcohol intoxication, extreme emotional arousal at the time of the crime, and more severe personality disorder distinguished the amnestic cases (65%) from the non-amnestic ones (35%). They noted that it was rare for a murderer to report complete memory loss for the crime; rather, the memory was fragmentary ("patchy") and/or unclear ("hazy"). Power (1977) has added that extreme life stressors, depression, and the impulsiveness of the homicide also predict amnesia for the crime.

Taylor and Kopelman (1984) investigated the predictors of amnesia for many types of crime, not just homicide. They found that 26% of 34 men convicted of homicide reported limited amnesia, but less than 10% of the 212 criminals in the overall sample were amnestic for their crimes. Amnesia for the crime was significantly related to a rating of the degree of violence for the crime, actually violent behavior (personal attack of the victim), depression, impulsiveness (lack of premeditation), personal relationship with the victim (close friend, lover, relative), and alcohol/drug consumption at the time of the crime.

Parwatikar, Holcomb, and Menninger (1985) studied 105 men charged with first-degree murder, 50 of whom had confessed, 31 of whom denied the crime, and 24 of whom were unsure about committing the crime. They used an interview, along with psychological testing, to identify variables predicting limited amnesia for the crime. Amnesia, seen in 22%, was associated with elevated levels of depression, hysteria, and hypochondriasis on the MMPI and with the use of alcohol and drugs at the time of the murder. Gudjonsson, et al. (1989) found that 56% of 16 murderers were amnestic; all nine were intoxicated at the time of the crime.

While prevalence rates vary considerably across these studies (22–65%), the studies are remarkably consistent in identifying both intoxication and emotional state at the time of the crime as predictors of limited amnesia for the crime. It is also not surprising that limited amnesia is more common in subjects committing homicide than in subjects committing other crimes, if one assumes greater emotional arousal accompanying homicide.

A major limitation of these studies is the failure to design research paradigms that are able to identify which portion of the overall amnesia variance is attributable to alcohol/drug intoxication, which is attributable to the level of emotional arousal, and which to simulation. Since alcohol and drug intoxication is frequently reported at the time of committing a homicide, the prevalence of genuinely functional amnesia for the crime is likely to be lower than the reported rates of 22–65%. Parwatikar et al. (1985) have pointed out that alcohol/drug intoxication and psychological factors probably interact in producing amnesia for the crime, and it may be that intoxication aids the dissociative process (p. 102).

More recent studies have suggested some ways to distinguish between genuine and simulated amnesia for homicide based on qualitative features of the murderer's report (Hopwood & Snell, 1933; Power, 1977; Schacter, 1986). Yet, if alcohol/drug intoxication and simulation were statistically factored out of the variance, it is reasonable to assume that a subsample of murderers would remain with genuine limited functional amnesia for the crime, not associated with organicity. Such amnesia is rarely complete, but includes either a general clouding of memory (Bradford & Smith, 1979) or amnesia with some "islets" or fragments of memory (Kopelman, 1987).

Extreme emotional arousal at the time of the

crime and the degree of violence are associated with the development of limited amnesia (Schacter, 1986; Taylor & Kopelman, 1984). Kopelman (1987) has proposed that functional amnesia for murder can occur when the degree of emotional arousal interferes with memory encoding and/or accessibility to the stored memory for the murder, due either to repression of the unacceptable information from consciousness or to state-dependent memory retrieval failure, i.e., failure to retrieve the memory because the person is no longer in the extreme emotional state.

Whatever the mechanism, at least some murderers are probably genuinely amnestic for the murder, even though this finding may become obscured and exploited in the service of providing a legal defense for murderers who never were amnestic for their crimes. When these data on murderers are compared to Kuehn's (1974) data on victims of violent crimes, we can conclude that extreme violence resulting in injury or death is associated with a decrease in the completeness of the memory for the violent act in a significant subpopulation of both perpetrators and victims. The memory is relatively complete for the crime in a larger sample of perpetrators and victims who are not injured. However, the factors contributing to genuine trauma-specific amnesia for a crime are complex. Table 7.3 summarizes the predictors across studies.

Adult Memory for Childhood Physical Abuse

The data available on memory performance of victims and perpetrators of violent crimes largely pertain to memory for single-incident traumatic episodes occurring in adulthood. What about an adult's remote memory for traumatic events that occurred in childhood? There are a few notable studies on adult memories for physical abuse. The first important documentation on later recall of childhood physical abuse was part of a 30-year prospective study on deviant children (Robins, 1966). Robins and her associates collected detailed demographic and clinical data on 524 children referred to a child guidance clinic for assessment and treatment, as well as 100 normal school children matched for demographic characteristics. The majority of the clinic referred children were evaluated for deviant behavior, primarily antisocial behavior, e.g., theft, sexual deviance, and running away, and other behavioral problems. About half were referred from the courts. Many were from disrupted families characterized by divorce, non-support or neglect of the children, arrests, gambling, alcoholism, and physical abuse. About a third of the children had spent some time in a foster home. The primary objective was to contact and interview as many of the children as possible after they had grown up in order to identify predictors of sociopathy and to understand

TABLE 7.3
Predictors of Amnesia for Homicide

Source	B	I	Dp	Dx	Hx	St	EI	V	Imp	Rel
Hopwood & Snell, 1933			X	X	X		X	X		X
O'Connell, 1960	X	X		X						
Bradford & Smith, 1979	X			X			X			
Taylor & Kopelman, 1984	X		X				X	X		X
Kopelman, 1987	X		X				X			X
Power, 1977			X			X		X		
Parwatikar et al., 1985	X		X	X						

B = biological factors, e.g., drug or alcohol intoxication
I = intelligence
Dp = depression at time of incident
Dx = diagnosis, e.g., hysteria, personality disorder
Hx = previous history of amnestic episodes

St = other life stressors
EI = emotional intensity at time of incident
V = degree of violence/seriousness of crime
Imp = impulsiveness of the attack
Rel = close relationship to victim

the long-term course and adult adjustment of the adult sociopathic personality.

The database contained a subsample of 71 subjects assessed in the original child guidance clinic interviews as being physically abused. Thirty years later, 78% of these subjects failed to report their father's documented "cruel or abusive" behavior in the follow-up clinical interview (p. 279), even though the interviewer specifically focused on parental treatment of the subject as a child and asked about abuse. It must be pointed out, however, that the subjects failed to report a number of other documented parental problems, such as the father's sociopathy (68%), abandonment of the family (77%), lack of limit setting (87%), mother's sociopathy (88%), and parental inadequacy (89%). It appears that the majority of these subjects failed to report most of serious parental failings, of which physical abuse was just one aspect of a larger profile of severe parental dysfunction. While the failure to report physical abuse 30 years later may be suggestive of amnesia for physical abuse in at least some of these subjects, the study unfortunately did not lend itself to conclusions about memory for previously documented abuse per se. It remains unclear whether subjects failed to report the previous abuse because of a memory failure or because they simply did not want to talk about it.

In a similar prospective study on long-term recall of childhood physical abuse, Femina, Yeager, and Lewis (1990) conducted follow-up interviews on 69 subjects who had been incarcerated in adolescence for delinquency. All of the subjects had a detailed clinical or court record on file. They were all interviewed nine years after their release from incarceration. Regarding follow-up data on physical abuse, 26 (38% of the subjects) gave a follow-up report discrepant with their original clinical record—18 denied ever having been physically abused and eight reported having been physically abused, even though it had not been originally documented.

Eleven of the 26 subjects agreed to participate in a "clarification interview," during which the researchers confronted the subject with the discrepancy between the original and follow-up report on physical abuse. Femina et al. (1990) state, "all 11 subjects with discrepant data who were reinterviewed had, as far as could be ascertained, been abused" (p. 229). The eight subjects who had

clear documentation of the abuse in the original record gave various explanations for their failure to report the abuse in the follow-up interview, but each subject admitted it when confronted. The three subjects who had reported abuse in the follow-up but not in the original interview also gave reasons why they concealed their history of physical abuse during adolescence. As the researchers correctly point out, these data merely demonstrate "a tendency in adulthood to minimize or totally deny having experienced serious physical abuse in childhood" (p. 229). While the value of these data lies the fact that they come from a prospective study, the data do not directly address whether any of these subjects failed to remember the childhood physical abuse for any period of time. The utilization of a "clarification interview" is not without difficulties—there is no way to rule out that subjects' responses to the clarification interview were not unduly influenced by demand characteristics or suggestive interviewing.

In nonrandom survey of 484 college students, Elliott and Fox (1994) reported that, of the 100 respondents who reported a history of physical abuse, 17% were fully amnestic and another 10% partially amnestic for the physical abuse for some significant period of time. Recovery of the memory for the physical abuse was typically accompanied by a significant increase in posttraumatic stress symptoms and other types of reported psychiatric distress. In another nonrandom sampling of 613 college undergraduates, Golding, Sanchez, and Sego (1996) found that of the 13% who claimed to have recovered a repressed memory for a traumatic experience, at least 21% reported that the repressed memory had been about a nonsexual assault or a violent incident.

Elliott and Briere's (1995) randomized survey of the general population documented that 10% of respondents who had a history of childhood physical abuse had completely forgotten the abuse for a significant period of time. Another 15% had periods of partial forgetting. Melchert (1996) randomly surveyed 553 adults at a university and found that 21% reported periods of time when they had no memory for the physical abuse. Of these respondents, 54% claimed they "had repressed it" and 33% said they were "merely just avoiding the memory" (p. 442). Fish and Scott (in press) randomly sampled 423 counselors and found that, of the 58 who reported familial physical abuse, 21% reported forgetting the abuse for some period of time. Of these subjects 10% reported forgetting all of the abuse by one person, but no one had forgotten all the physical abuse across all perpetrators. Another 15% said that they had forgotten a lot of the abuse for a period of time.

In a recent 20–year prospective study about 40% of 110 people with court-substantiated childhood physical abuse failed to report the abuse in an extensive structured interview 20 years later, and there was a significant relationship between the childhood physical abuse and adult violent behavior (Widom & Shepard, 1996). These studies demonstrate that about one-fifth of adults with childhood physical abuse histories report a period of time when they had fully or partially forgotten the physical abuse and later recovered the memory, although a portion of these individuals report avoiding consciously thinking about the past physical abuse and another, probably smaller portion report not having the physical abuse memories available at all for some period of time.

Adult Rape

There is a surprising paucity of data concerning amnesia for rape. The Elliott and Briere (1995) randomized survey of the general population found that a total of 3% were fully amnestic and another 10% partially amnestic for the rape experience for some period of time. Several richly detailed clinical case studies have described traumatic amnesia following rape. Christianson and Nilsson (1989) discuss the dramatic loss of memory and identity in a 23-year-old female following rape. Kaszniak et al. (1988) also report retrograde amnesia in a 27-year-old male following a rape experience. In both cases memory for the traumatic rape returned after a period of amnesia.

Table 7.4 summarizes the available data on the prevalence of full and partial amnesia for disasters, combat experience, prisoner and torture experiences, physical abuse, and rape. Despite the sampling method, *all* studies document full amnesia in a subsample (ranging from 3–17%) and partial amnesia in another subsample (ranging from 4–51%) of the overall sample of respondents. Rates for no amnesia consistently run much higher than rates for amnesia across each type of traumatization.

Adult Memories for Childhood Sexual Abuse

Survey Studies

The existence of functional amnesia for a subpopulation of survivors of childhood sexual abuse (CSA) has also been the subject of recent investigation. These studies typically draw primarily on clinical and nonclinical samples, in which adult subjects are asked (1) whether or not they had always remembered incidents of CSA, or (2) whether or not there was ever a period of time in their lives when they could not remember the sexual abuse and then later recovered their memory for it. Reports of periods of amnesia limited to sexual abuse incidents have become the center of the recovered memory controversy.

CLINICAL SAMPLES Herman and Schatzow (1987), in the first study directed expressly at traumatic amnesia for childhood sexual abuse, studied 53 white, primarily single, working women who were being treated in 12-week psychotherapy groups for incest survivors in an outpatient clinic. All of the women were in individual psychotherapy. They were diagnosed as having depression, anxiety symptoms, chemical dependency, and/or personality disorder, in addition to being incest survivors. Most of the women who reported or "strongly suspected" incest identified their fathers or stepfathers as the abuser (75%), but brothers (26%), uncles (11%), and grandfathers (6%) were also identified. All patients were asked if they had always remembered the sexual abuse. A total of 36% of the women "had always remembered the abuse in detail" (p. 4). The other 64% had at least some degree of amnesia for the sexual abuse for some period of their lives. Of this group, 36% of the women had mild to moderate amnesia—they claimed that they always remembered the sexual abuse, but had recently recovered additional memories in or outside of therapy. The other 28% of the total sample of women had "severe memory deficits," in that they reported a period of time when they had no memory for the sexual abuse, which later intruded into consciousness. Some of these severely amnestic women suffered from amnesia limited to the sexual abuse and some had a more general retrograde amnesia for significant periods of their childhood, although the study

TABLE 7.4

Traumatic Amnesia—Physical Abuse, Rape, Combat, POW, Accident, & Natural Disaster

SOURCE	N	No A	F + P	P	F	SAMPLE
PHYSICAL ABUSE						
Elliott & Briere, 1995	485	75	25	15	10	general census
Elliott & Fox, 1994	484	73	27	10	17	undergraduates
Golding et al., 1996	613		21			undergraduates
Melchert, 1996	553		21		11	college students
Fish & Scott, in press	423		21		10	counseling psychologists
Femina et al., 1990	69	26/8*				9-year prospective
Robins, 1966	524/71	78*				prospective study on delinquency
Widom & Shepard, 1996	110		40			prospective study
RAPE						
Elliott & Briere, 1995	485	77	23	10	13	general census
COMBAT						
Sargant & Slater, 1941	1000	85.6	14.4			WW II consecutive cases
Elliott & Briere, 1995	485	61	39	23	16	combat
POW						
Wagenaar & Groeneweg, 1990	78	gist	injury; death threat			Camp Erika
CAR ACCIDENT						
Elliott & Briere, 1995	485	92	8	4	4	general census
DISASTER						
Dollinger, 1985	33		3			child lightning victims
McFarlane, 1988	469	100	57%**			Australian bushfire
Wilkinson, 1983	102.	27***				Hyatt skywalk collapse

N = sample size; No A = no amnesia; F+P = full & partial amnesia; P = partial amnesia; F = full amnesia

* denial
** failed to report injury at 11 months
*** memory disturbance (intrusive memory or amnesia)

does not give the prevalence rates of either of these subgroups of severe amnestic incest survivors.

Subsequent remembering of the incest was often associated with posttraumatic stress symptoms. The experience of being in an incest survivors' group and individual therapy provided the context for memory recovery. The Herman and Schatzow study includes data on predictors of amnesia: age of onset of the incest, duration of abuse, and degree of violence associated with the incest (overt violence or sadism). One notable consequence of being in the psychotherapy group was that most of the women sought to corroborate the incest stories that they reported or uncovered. The majority of women (74%) were able to collect corroborating evidence from some source other than their own recollection, with 40% getting confirmation from the perpetrators themselves, from other family members, or from physical evidence, and 34% from siblings or other children who also claimed to have been abused by the same perpetrator. Another 9% indicated a "strong likelihood" of abuse in other family members. Herman and Schatzow conclude that recovered memories of sexual abuse cannot be attributed solely to fantasy and that a significant subpopulation of adult survivors of incest are fully or partially amnestic for the incest for some period of time, mainly due to "massive repression," along with the operation of other psychological defenses (p. 11). When these women at some later point in their lives recovered the memory for the incest, they typically developed PTSD symptoms.

In a landmark national survey on the prevalence of intrafamilial sexual abuse of women in the Netherlands, Draijer (1990) found that 164 of 1,054 women reported a history of sexual abuse. A total of 82% reported denying the abuse at some time or another and 57% reported partial or full amnesia for the sexual abuse for some period of their lives.

Ensink (1992) conducted a study on 100 women in the Netherlands. "The central question of [the] study concerns the connection between a history of child (sexual abuse) and psychological problems in adult life" (p. 14) in four broad symptom areas: (1) dissociative disturbances in consciousness, (2) hallucinations, (3) self-injury, and (4) suicidality. These four areas of psychiatric symptoms were chosen because their association with childhood sexual abuse is "well-established" (p. 8), although Ensink makes it clear that the correlation between these symptoms and CSA does not necessarily imply that CSA is the cause of the symptoms. Ensink decided not to use a random sample because, "In a randomly selected sample of women with a history of childhood sexual abuse, one will find women who hardly remember child abuse incidents. Women who hardly remember anything about child abuse can not be expected to function as adequate informants [about psychological symptoms]" (p. 16). Thus, Ensink selected "women who already had some kind of psychological support" (p. 18) in that the subjects recruited were primarily women in incest survivor groups (72%), individual therapy (13%), and other sources (14%). (A total of 24% had a previous history of hospitalization.) These women reported long-term cumulative and often severe sexual abuse in childhood. Less than 5% of the women in this sample had been abused only a few times or for less than a year and over a fourth of the sample had been abused for over ten years. Most of the women were abused by a father or stepfather. Severe psychological or physical coercion by the perpetrator was commonly reported in this sample. Multiple perpetrators were reported in 41% of the sample.

Amnesia for the sexual abuse was reported by a significant subsample of the women. Ensink says:

> Of the women who participated in our study 28% reported to have had intervals in which they hardly gave any thought to their history of sexual abuse, and 29% have had intervals in which they had completely forgotten it. (p. 133) . . . 57% have had intervals during which they never thought about, or had completely forgotten, child sexual abuse. (p. 137)

Women who were amnestic for the narrative memory of the CSA were more likely than women who had continuous memories for the CSA to experience time loss and flashbacks, and were more likely to report the recovered abuse memory initially in the form of "unbidden images" (p. 137), devoid of emotions and devoid of self reference ("this is not happening to me").

Dissociative symptoms, assessed by responses to the Dissociative Experiences Scale and by means of a structured interview, were frequently reported by the women in this severely abused sample. A total of 64% of the women had a score of 30 or higher on the DES, which meant that they had a high probability of having a major dissociative disorder. Approximately 38% of the sample met the criteria for multiple personality disorder. Severity of dissociative symptoms significantly correlated with severity of coercion by the perpetrator, the presence of multiple perpetrators, and cumulative, long-duration abuse, if accompanied by force. Severe dissociation was also more likely if the abuse occurred between ten and twelve years of age than if it occurred earlier. A total of 64% of the women also reported hallucinatory symptoms, such as experiencing flashbacks or visual hallucinations and hearing voices. Self-injurious behavior and suicide attempts were common in about half of the women.

In a related Dutch study, Albach, Moormann, and Bermond (in press) compared responses of 97 women with a history of childhood sexual abuse to a matched control group of 65 non-abused women. The sexually abused women "were at the severe end of the abuse spectrum" (p. 7), in that most of the abuse involved penetration and most lasted longer than one year. The control group had experienced "incidental unpleasant ordinary childhood events" but not sexual abuse. Participants were asked series of interview questions about their recollections:

1. Some individuals who have experienced an unpleasant event as a child (or sexual abuse), have forgotten this for a long time. It may happen that, after years, they start to remember this, because they read about it, because they see a movie, or because of other causes. Did you experience that, too?
2. If so, how long had you forgotten it?
3. Did you really forget it or did you just not think about it?
4. Some women still rather tend to avoid thinking of their unpleasant childhood events. Is that the case with you, too?
5. Do you still have the idea that you don't remember certain details of this event?
6. Did you recover more details of the event during the last few years?
7. For some individuals who recover their memories, this can happen very suddenly and it can be very dramatic to the person. Was this the case with you?
8. Was there a cause for your memory recovery, and if so, which was this cause? (p. 8)

A total of 35% of the women in the sexually abused group reported amnesia for sexual abuse during some period of their lives, as compared to 1% in the control group who reported amnesia for nontraumatic unpleasant childhood experiences (e.g., being teased). In addition to amnesia for the sexual abuse, 85% of the sexually abused women, as compared to 5% of the control women, reported intentionally avoiding thinking about the target event when they were able to recollect it. Recovery of the abuse memory typically occurred spontaneously and suddenly, and was significantly more likely to be accompanied by anger, guilt, and/or fear than recovery of other unpleasant memories. The majority of the sexually abused women also reported dissociative phenomena at the time of the abuse, such as "freezing" or "a feeling of detachment or estrangement from one's self."

Age, duration, frequency, nature of the sexual acts, degree of force, secrecy, and degree of disso-

ciation at the time of the abuse failed to predict amnesia for the sexual abuse. However, women who reported consenting to the abuse to get attention, compared to those who did not, were significantly more likely to be amnestic. Memory for the sexual abuse was typically triggered by a variety of stimuli that specifically reminded the women of the sexual abuse, such as becoming emotional, getting raped, discovering that a child had been abused, or encountering a specific situation that served as a reminder of the abuse. Psychotherapy was not typically reported to be a cause of recovering the abuse memory. Albach et al. add, "no empirical evidence has been found for the notion that most patients recover memories of childhood sexual abuse because during psychotherapy the therapist suggested to them that they were abused as a child" (p. 13). Albach et al. conclude:

Regarding the question "How common is robust repression [in the general population]?" the answer is "very rare." Only 1% of the Control Group reported to have suffered from an episode of inability to recall the traumatic event. . . . However, when we look at the Traumatized Group a completely different picture emerges: about one third of the abused women (35%) had known at least one episode in which they were unable to recall the event. Our results are in agreement with the notion of Loftus, Polonsky and Fullilove (1994) that remembering abuse is more common than forgetting it, but our data also imply, contrary to the suggestion of Lindsay and Read (1994), that temporary complete amnesia is not so rare among people who had been repeatedly abused over a lengthy period of their childhoods. (p. 14)

Cameron (1994, 1996) studied 60 women over a nine-year period. All of the women were in psychotherapy and all had a history of CSA. Data collection consisted of questionnaires given four times over nine years. While the primary focus of the study was on women survivors confronting their abusers, the sample also contained data on amnesia for CSA. A total of 35% of the women had always remembered the abuse, another 23% had partially forgotten and 42% had completely forgotten the abuse for somewhere between 15 and 50 years. A total of 73% recovered their memories for the CSA prior to therapy and 27% after beginning therapy. In fact, the great majority had entered therapy not to recover memories but to stabilize after the crisis of recovering the memories in some other way prior to treatment. A total of 46% of those who had always remembered the abuse and 63% of those who had been amnestic but later recovered the memory "felt a desire to confront their abuser." The confrontation rate was higher in the formerly amnestic group mainly because their wish to confront the abuser arose "largely out of a need to have him validate and help them understand their returning memories" (1994, p. 13). The therapists in this sample "did not advise or encourage early confrontation" (1994, p. 13).

Significant predictors for the memory loss included young age of onset, severity, not duration), multiple perpetrators, multiple acts, sexual violence, and having the perpetrator be a natural parent. Some external validation was found for the alleged abuse in 65% of the cases. The sample was subdivided into an amnestic and a non-amnestic group in order to test several predictions. With respect to events that triggered the recovery of the abuse memory there were significant differences between the amnestic and nonamnestic groups:

> Amnestics were nearly 3 times as likely as nonamnestics (68% vs. 24%) to believe that they had remembered their sexual abuse at a "safe" time in their lives. Half as many amnestics as nonamnestics (21% vs. 42%) sought help because they were feeling overwhelmed. Feeling safer or feeling overwhelmed formed a general life context of the two groups and played a significant role in the readiness of amnestics and nonamnestics to confront the past (1996, p. 54). . . . What was meant by a "safer time"? Apparently, it was whatever had strengthened them—distance from the family of origin, death of the abuser, a supportive work and marriage environment, good friends, or earlier therapy (e.g. For addictions) that had expanded their repertoire of coping. (1996, p. 61)

Recall of the abuse evoked a "crisis" for many of the respondents in both the amnestic and non-amnestic groups. Non-amnestic respondents typically reported never discussing the abuse, denying certain aspects of it, or having a distorted understand-

ing of the meaning of the abusive events. For some of them, dealing with the abuse evoked strong reactions. For amnestic respondents, recovering the memory was typically a crisis. They were significantly more likely than non-amnestic respondents to report strong emotional reactions (horror, disillusionment), manifest avoidance behaviors or suicidal ideation, have disturbed sexual feelings, and require greater help from therapists and other social supports. Cameron concludes, "amnesia for psychic trauma is not a recent, rare, or unverified phenomenon" (1996, p. 66).

Despite Loftus's skepticism about amnesia for CSA—what she calls "the myth of repressed memories" (Loftus & Ketcham, 1994)— data from her own recent survey are consistent with the previous studies. Loftus, Polonsky, and Fullilove (1994) surveyed 105 women in outpatient treatment for chemical dependency. Of the 54% who reported a positive history of childhood sexual abuse, 69% always remembered the abuse, another 12% partially remembered the abuse but not all of it, and 19% had completely forgotten the abuse for a period of time and then later remembered it. Loftus et al. claim that the lower base rates had to do with conducting intensive interviews (one and a half hours) with subjects as compared to mailing questionnaires to subjects (e.g., Briere & Conte, 1993). There is a more obvious explanation for the lower rates, however. This study is seriously contaminated, in that the vast majority of the participants were in an early stage of detoxification from substance dependence at the time of the survey. As Loftus et al. note, "85% had been so [drug free] for at least a week" (p. 74). Curiously, the researchers fail to mention the impact of early detoxification on the reliability of the verbal report.

Nevertheless, while the prevalence rate of abuse-specific amnesia is generally lower in this study than in all of the other comparable studies, Loftus and her associates did indeed identify a subsample of subjects who failed to remember the abuse for some period of their lives. She interpreted the memory failure as normal forgetting, not repression or dissociation. Pope and Hudson (1995b) dismiss the 19% result in the Loftus, Gary & et al. (1994) study on the grounds that corroboration was not available and that "forgetfulness" was not carefully defined or investigated.

Violence failed to predict the memory failure, although Loftus points out that she defined violence differently from other studies. She defined it in terms of vaginal, oral, or anal sex and not by the standard clinical definition of physical injury or threat to life, as it was defined in the other surveys. What she defines as "violence" is more correctly defined as genital penetration.

An important feature of the Loftus, Polansky & et al. (1994) survey is its inclusion of subjective ratings on the quality of memory, such as the clarity, pictorial vividness, sensory quality, emotionality, and degree of rehearsal. Loftus et al. Found that the memories of subjects who had partially or completely forgotten the sexual abuse and later remembered it had a significantly different quality from those of subjects who had always remembered the abuse. Their memories were less clear, less vivid, and contained less intense emotionality about the abuse.

Roe and Schwartz (1996) also recently reported survey data on adult memory for childhood sexual abuse in an inpatient population of 52 women who had been hospitalized for sexual trauma. The questions about memory for abuse were included as part of a follow-up study on the effectiveness of hospital treatment. A total of 88% of the former inpatient sample reported a history of childhood sexual abuse. A total of 77% of these woman responded that they "had not remembered having been sexually abused" for some significant period of their lives, ranging from 3.5 to 45 years (mean 23 years). In this survey, the patients were asked about the circumstances under which they recovered their first memories of CSA. A total of 44% of the amnestic women said their first suspicion of being sexually abused involved an actual memory. A total of 68% of the amnestic women said that the suspicion first occurred at a time when they were in therapy, but only 32% said that the first suspicion actually occurred during a therapy session. In order to assess whether or not the abuse might have been suggested by a therapist, respondents were asked if their therapist told them that they might have been sexually abused. Twenty-three perecent reported being told this by a therapist. Only 7% of the subjects first began to suspect CSA during hypnotherapy sessions per se.

The focus of Roe and Schwartz's study was on the phenomenological characteristics of the respondents' recovered memories of abuse. When asked about the quality of the first memory of CSA, 60% said that the memory initially came in the form of a flashback. While the great majority of the sample recalled the identity of the perpetrator, the location, and specific abusive actions performed as part of the initial memory, only about half of the respondents could recall how they felt emotionally as part of the initial memory for the abuse. Memory for the details of the abuse situation were also less likely to be recalled as part of the initial memory. A total of 63% said that the memory became more vivid over time, and 96% said that additional memories for abuse were recovered after the first memory. Most respondents (96%) said that over time (typically about two years) they became "sure" that they had been abused, especially if new memories came forth. Overall, the findings that the rate of amnesia for CSA is higher in this study than all previously reported studies is probably due to the fact that this is a highly select sample, namely, those women whose current symptoms were significant enough to require hospitalization. In other words, we suspect these women were on the more severe end of a continuum of variable long-term sequelae to CSA.

Pomerantz (in progress) gave a Memory for Childhood Sexual Abuse Inventory to 26 adult women in psychotherapy for childhood sexual abuse with therapists in Denver, CO. The majority of respondents (50%) reported no memory and 42.5% a partial memory for some period of their lives (typically between ages 18 and 28) and later recovering the memory after age 28. The most frequent trigger for the abuse memory was an encounter with stimuli that reminded them of sexual acts or sexual abuse. Significant predictors for forgetting the abuse included early age of onset, longer duration of abuse, multiple perpetrators, multiple acts including forceful acts, and abuse by a natural parent. A unique feature of this study was the inclusion of an assessment of various categories of possible implicit memories for the abuse, such as visual imagery, auditory recollections, bodily experiences, and emotions. Reports of visual imagery, e.g., flashbacks, were significantly correlated with losing the memory for the CSA.

One criticism of most of these clinical surveys is that they do not consistently make a distinction between full, partial, and no amnesia for childhood sexual abuse. As the science becomes more refined, we have learned that such a distinction is necessary in order to meaningfully interpret the data. Harvey and Herman (1994) developed a classification system for the recovered memories of adult survivors of CSA. They note that recovery of a traumatic memory is seldom an all-or-nothing phenomenon and that dichotomous distinctions like repressed vs. remembered all along, or true vs. False memory, fail to capture the complexity of the phenomenon. Their clinical observations yield three categories of post-traumatic memory along a continuum: (1) continuous recall (no amnesia) but delayed understanding, (2) partial amnesia and delayed recall, and (3) total or "profound" amnesia along with delayed recovery. They point out that a variety of "life cycle changes" are associated with recovery of memories in the amnestic groups, not the least of which is a significant change in relationships. Psychotherapy is sometimes associated with memory recovery, but the majority of patients who enter therapy do so because they have recently recovered the memory by some other means and are distressed by the emerging memory. They enter therapy primarily to stabilize and only sometimes enter therapy specifically to recover memories per se.

The Herman and Schatzow (1987) study, along with the more recent clinical studies just discussed, have been criticized on the grounds that the samples were limited to individuals who were in psychotherapy. As Pope and Hudson (1995a,b) have observed, however, the Herman and Schatzow study does not explain how subjects were selected, nor does it clearly identify individual subjects, a substantial weakness that makes it impossible to tell whether the women who obtained corroboration were the same women who had severe amnesia. In addition to the claim of sample selection bias in these clinical surveys, Loftus (1993) and Lindsay and Read (1994) have argued that the alleged childhood sexual abuse in these clinical studies could have been suggested iatrogenically by the therapists. Elliott and Briere (1995) assert that the alleged abuse reports could have resulted from demand characteristics inherent in using the therapists as experimenters in collecting the data.

In order to address such criticisms, and correct for them, Gold, Hughes, and Hohnecker (1994) conducted a survey attempting to answer Loftus's criticism that recovered memories of CSA are a product of therapeutic influence. They conducted a structured sexual abuse interview with 105 subjects (87% women) as part of an initial intake at an outpatient mental health center. Because the sexual abuse data were collected in an *initial interview*, before the onset of treatment, the researchers reasoned that therapeutic influences upon the memory report were minimal or nonexistent. All subjects were asked, "Was there ever a period of time when for at least a full year you were unable to remember any or all of the abuse?" (p. 441). Responses were categorized along a continuum of remembering: 30% had no memory for the abuse; 10% had a vague sense or suspicion but no definite memory for the abuse; 16% remembered at least one abuse episode, but had not remembered all episodes; 14% had a partial memory, i.e., remembered some aspects of the abuse; and 30% always remembered most of the episodes of abuse in a relatively complete manner. Pooling the data across categories of partial memory, 30% had no memory whatsoever, 40% had some sort of partial memory, and 30% had always remembered. The combined full and partial amnesia data yield a prevalence rate (70%) quite close to the 64% reported by Herman and Schatzow. The authors note that these responses represent patients' initial beliefs about memory for sexual abuse and that these beliefs typically changed over the course of treatment. Many patients initially held the belief that they had always remembered the sexual abuse, only to discover in treatment that their memory was more fragmentary or partial than initially realized, since new memories often emerged. Whether or not these new memories are the false product of therapeutic suggestion or recovered memories of genuine abuse cannot be determined. Nevertheless, the Gold et al. data add further support to the claim that reported amnesia for childhood sexual abuse cannot readily be dismissed as simply false memory produced in treatment.

While these clinical surveys contain obvious sample selection biases, the hypothesis that the amnesia for the childhood sexual abuse is an iatrogenic product of therapeutic influence is not supported by the available data. It is significant that (1) the evidence for amnesia for childhood sexual abuse is a robust finding across all the clinical surveys, and (2) the rates of amnesia for CSA are reasonably consistent across these studies, with two exceptions—the Loftus, Polonsky et al. (1994) low rate, which can be explained by the effects of chemical dependency detoxification on memory reporting, and the Roe and Schwartz (1996) high rate, which can be explained by the severity of abuse-related symptoms in this inpatient sample.

NONCLINICAL SAMPLES   One answer to the selection bias criticism has been to conduct comparable surveys on nonclinical populations. Several surveys have been conducted on college student samples. Bernet, Deutscher, Ingram, and Litrownik (1993) reported on a survey of 624 undergraduates (536 women and 86 men). This study is significant in that it represents a *nonclinical* and therefore presumably less pathological sample. Subjects were given the Finkelhor Family Experiences Questionnaire to assess the occurrence and prevalence rate of CSA prior to age 15. The researchers inserted four questions about amnesia for the CSA: "Did you always have a memory of this abuse experience? If no, when did you recover the memory of it? What event triggered the memory to return? and What is that memory like to you now?" (p. 1). A total of 21% of the normal undergraduates reported at least one experience of sexual abuse prior to age 15. Of those subjects reporting CSA, 36% reported "having had no memory for at least one experience of abuse" (p. 1). In response to critics who try to dismiss these surveys as a product of suggestion in psychotherapy, the researchers noted that only 30% of their respondents had ever been in psychotherapy and "It seems unlikely, therefore, that these subjects remembered their abuse as a consequence of psychotherapy" (p. 4). Positive predictors of amnesia for CSA were: severity of abuse, the use of physical force, and emotional pressure, although some of these factors interacted with age of onset of the CSA. The authors conclude, "It appears that childhood sexual abuse experienced before age 12 is likely to be 'forgotten' for some period of time by a large number of victims—36% in this study, up to 64% in others" (p. 3). They note that the base rate of full amnesia in this nonclinical sample is quite similar to the base rate found in the clinical surveys.

In a Canadian study at Brock University, Belicki et al. (1994) conducted a study on the frequency and content of nightmares of sexually abused, physically abused, and non-abused college students. The sample consisted of 170 students—64 non-abused students, 41 reporting a history of childhood sexual abuse, 9 reporting physical abuse, and 24 reporting both sexual and physical abuse in childhood. One innovative feature of this study was the inclusion of a control group of 32 "simulators" of childhood sexual abuse. Simulators were subjects who reported no history of abuse but who "were asked to complete all questionnaires as if they had been sexually abused." The questionnaires asked a series of questions about sexual abuse, defined from four different perspectives; whether the abuse had been forgotten or had always been remembered; whether and what kinds of corroborative evidence existed; and the frequency and content of nightmares. A total of 55.4% of their sample of abused students reported they had forgotten the abuse for some period of time (disrupted memory).

Subjects reporting no abuse responded significantly differently from the other three groups with respect to definitions of sexual abuse, psychiatric symptoms, and sleep and dream behavior. There were no significant differences in response to the questions between those subjects who reported and who did not report corroboration of the abuse. There were also no significant differences in response to the questions between those with disrupted and continuous memory for the childhood sexual abuse. Those who had recovered memories for the childhood sexual abuse were just as likely as those who had a continuous memory to have corroborative evidence for the abuse, and were also no more or less likely to seek psychotherapy for the abuse. The only significant differences between the disrupted and continuous memory groups were that those with disrupted memories were significantly more likely to have (1) experienced repeated episodes of sexual abuse, (2) have experienced a combination of both sexual and physical abuse, and (3) been abused by a family member. Simulators responded significantly differently from those who reported being sexually abused across all measures, but some showed no significant differences between the simulator, disrupted memory, and continuous memory groups. Thus, it appears that instructing subjects who were not abused to respond as if they were abused—that is, to intentionally fake it—results in responses that are both similar to and in some respects different from the responses of subjects claiming sexual abuse.

In another Canadian study, Kristiansen, Felton, Hovdestad, and Allard (1995) reported their preliminary findings on an ongoing Carlton University "Ottawa Survivors Study" of women who reported a history of childhood sexual abuse. Subjects were recruited through E-mail, media, and posted advertisements asking for women survivors to participate in a survey. A total of 113 women ages 18–57 participated. Most of the women were white women, currently employed, and with at least a high school degree. The reported sexual abuse typically occurred within the family, with over half of the abuse allegedly by the father. In this sample, however, the women reported multiple abusers, on the average 3.7 perpetrators. The abuse typically began between the ages of five and six and continued for five years. Some sort of corroborative evidence was available for 62% of the reported cases. Most of the women (93%) had been in psychotherapy at some time in their lives, and the women estimated that less than half of the total time of therapy (42%) was devoted directly to abused-related themes.

Loftus, Polonsky et al. (1994) had criticized the earlier self-report studies on childhood sexual abuse because they hypothesized that differences in the wording of questions about forgetting sexual abuse might account for vast differences in reporting rates of forgotten and later recovered memories for abuse. Therefore, Kristiansen et al. asked the questions about forgetting abuse a number of different ways. The findings failed to support Loftus's hypothesis. No matter what way the question about forgetting abuse was asked, the results were "highly consistent." The recovered memory group consisted of those women (n=51) who had answered all of the memory questions affirmatively and the continuous memory group consisted of those who answered all the memory questions negatively (n=49). Thirteen women in the total sample could not be classified in a clear-cut way.

A total of 51% of the women had either partially or fully forgotten the abuse for a significant period of time before they had subsequently recovered the abuse memories—25% reported being exclusively amnestic for the childhood sexual abuse prior to recovering the memory and another 26% were partially amnestic. The other 49% always remembered the childhood sexual abuse. Women with continuous memories were significantly more likely (72%) to have corroborative evidence for the abuse than those with recovered memories (45%). Yet, it should be noted that some sort of corroborative evidence existed for almost half of the subjects with recovered memories. Significant predictors of forgetting the abuse included sexualized photos, physical or ritual abuse associated with the sexual abuse, use of threats, perpetration by a family member, and younger age. Kristiansen et al. conclude that "the findings were entirely consistent with those reported in other studies."

Elliott and Fox (1994) sampled 484 students from a Christian college. The majority of the subjects were single white women. A total of 30% (36% women and 15% men) reported sexual abuse and a total of 21% (18% women and 28% men) reported physical abuse. Respondents answered a questionnaire about a possible history of childhood physical and sexual abuse and also about self-reported amnesia for the abuse. Sexual abuse was defined as sexual contact before age 17. Physical abuse was defined as the use of physical force by a caretaker that resulted in tissue damage. Amnesia was defined as a "yes" response to the question, "Was there ever a period of time when you had less [or no] memory of this event than you do now?" Respondents also answered questions about a variety of potential triggering stimuli for the return of the abuse memories. Subjects were also given the Trauma Symptom Inventory to assess presence of posttraumatic stress and other psychiatric symptoms.

Elliott and Fox (1994) found that 30% of the respondent students with a history of childhood sexual abuse reported that there was a significant period of time where they had "no memory" for the CSA. Another 14% reported "less memory" at some period of time. Consistent with Elliott's other random sample study (Elliott & Briere, 1995), the college sample yielded a 44% rate of combined full or partial amnesia for the CSA. The most commonly reported triggers were "experiencing something similar to the original incident" (47%), "experiencing something sexual" (31%), and having "a dream or nightmare" (30%). The least commonly reported triggers were "conversation with a nonfamily member" (5%), "experiencing something violent" (9%), "conversation with a family member" (10%), and "psychotherapy" (19%). Results from the Traumatic Stress Inventory revealed that subjects who reported amnesia and later recovery of childhood sexual or physical abuse were significantly more likely to report a variety of posttraumatic, dissociative, anxious, or depression symptoms and/or sexual dysfunction upon recovery of the abuse memory than subjects with no abuse history or those with a continuous memory of sexual or physical abuse. Recovery of previously forgotten memories was associated with significantly "higher levels of distress" than always remembering the abuse.

Golding, Sanchez, and Sego (1996) investigated the beliefs of the general public regarding repressed memories. The surveyed 613 college undergraduates. Respondents were sent a cover letter with a definition of repressed memories taken from Loftus (1993, p. 518):

> . . . a repressed memory occurs when something happens that is so shocking that the mind grabs hold of the memory and pushes it underground, into some inaccessible corner of the unconscious. There it sleeps for years, or even decades, or even forever—isolated from the rest of mental life. Then, one day, it may rise up and emerge into consciousness. (p. 431)

Respondents were asked a series of 30 questions about repressed memories defined accordingly. A total of 89% of the respondents were aware of circumstances wherein someone had recovered a repressed memory. Respondents, especially women, generally found repressed memories to be believable. The vast majority felt that psychotherapy helped in the recovery of accurate repressed memories but that therapy sometimes contributed to implanting false memories. While the survey mainly focused on beliefs about repressed memories, it also included questions about personal experiences with repressed memories. A total of 13% of the respondents reported personal experiences of recovering repressed memories of the kind described in the survey. Interestingly, not all of the reported repressed/recovered memories were trauma-related—about 70% were. Recovery of the repressed memory typically occurred after encounter with an event that was similar to the original trauma; it was not typically associated with psychotherapy:

> It is also interesting that the circumstances surrounding the recovery of repressed memories run counter to suggestions in the literature and the media. Do individuals always recover repressed memories in therapy? On the basis of the present study's results, the answer is a resounding "No." In fact, only 11% of the participants reported the recovery of their own or someone else's repressed memory in such a context. (p. 435)

The authors interpret the low rate of fully repressed memories (13%) in terms of the younger age of their sampled respondents. Memories of CSA are often recovered in at later ages, twenties and thirties (Roesler & Wind, 1994). Another likely explanation may be the idiosyncratic definition of dissociated amnesia used in the survey, which restricted the definition only to cases of full amnesia and only to cases where recovery of the memory occurred all at once. Later in this chapter we will review a number of studies which consistently show that recovered narrative memory for trauma rarely occurs all at once. Rather, fragments are progressively recovered and become increasingly organized.

Another strategy used by researchers to overcome the objection of clinical bias has been to use advertisements asking for volunteer abuse survivors to participate in the survey. Van der Kolk and Fisler (1995) recruited people "haunted by memories of terrible life experiences" (p. 514) to participate in a two-hour structured clinical interview regarding the experience of previous trauma, the occurrence of PTSD and dissociative symptoms, and the nature of traumatic memories. The interview included a 60-item Traumatic Memory Inventory. A total of 46 adults were interviewed, 36 of whom experienced significant childhood traumas and 10 of whom experienced trauma in adulthood. The great majority of subjects suffering childhood traumas had experienced sexual abuse (29 of 36). Of the 36 people with childhood trauma, "42% had suffered significant or total amnesia for their trauma at some time in their lives" (p. 516). Corroborative evidence was available for 75% of the subjects who had experienced childhood trauma. This study focused primarily on the way participants remembered the trauma when the memory was recovered. "All these subjects, regardless of the age at which the trauma occurred, claimed that they initially 'remembered' the trauma in the form of somato-sensory flashback experiences [not as a narrative memory for the trauma]" (p. 519).

Using a similar sampling strategy, Roesler and Wind (1994) studied women who called a toll-free number regarding research on child abuse following former Miss America Marilyn van Derbur Atler's disclosure of her incest history on national television. Those who identified themselves as having a childhood sexual abuse history were sent a questionnaire about the abuse and about the circumstances under which they disclosed the abuse. It included questions about who they first told and what that person's reaction was. A "reaction to disclosure scale" was used "to measure the reaction the person got to their (*sic*) telling about the abuse" (p. 329). The great majority of the 228 women who answered the questionnaire experienced cumulative sexual abuse starting in their latency years and lasting on average 7.6 years. A little over a third of the women disclosed the abuse prior to age 18, mainly telling a parent (42%) or a friend (23%). They found that "parents reacted to disclosure significantly less favorably than did other people" (p. 330), especially if the child was younger. In over half the cases (52%), the sexual abuse continued for at least another year after disclosure. Disclosure was made significantly more to a parent during adolescence, to a friend or another family member during early adulthood (on the average around 26 years of age), and more to a therapist in adulthood (on the average 38 years of age). While the survey primarily addressed disclosure experiences, some data were collected on memory for the sexual abuse. A total of 28.5% of the sampled women reported that they had repressed their memories for the childhood sexual abuse for a significant period of their lives. Those who reported repressing the memories were significantly more likely to have disclosed the abuse later in life and to have disclosed it for the first time in psychotherapy rather than earlier in life to a parent. Those suffering from repressed memories who later retrieved the memories had a significantly higher educational background than those who had always remembered the CSA.

The second public event to trigger sexual abuse memories was the exposure of Father Porter, a Catholic priest. One day, without therapy or other allegedly suggestive influences, Frank Fitzpatrick recovered memories of being sexually abused decades earlier by Father Porter. Eventually, Father Porter was brought to trial. After confessing that he had molested more than 100 young boys and girls, he was convicted and is now serving a term in prison. Because of the national media attention given to this case 99 individuals identified themselves as victims of Father Porter. Grassian and Holtzen (1996) sent the self-identified alleged victims a questionnaire about their experiences. They note that no independent corroborative evidence was available for the allegations made by each of the 99 respondents, but that Father Porter did admit to multiple pedophilic acts during the relevant time period. According to the demographic data collected these respondents represented a "unique sample," in that they generally came from "relatively stable childhood homes." Family disruption by death, divorce, psychiatric illness, or alcoholism was relatively low. Moreover, the alleged victims generally reported "high levels of premorbid functioning," such as good grades in school, outside interests, good peer relationships, and a low incidence of medical or psychological problems prior to the abuse. All respondents were abused by the same alleged perpetrator. Unlike other studies on CSA, these alleged victims were mostly males (77 of 99 respondents) who did not experience long-term cumulative sexual abuse (68% reported fewer than five episodes of abuse). The average age at the time of the abuse was 11 years.

A total of 42 subjects responded to questions about their memory for the alleged abuse by Father Porter. Grassian and Holtzen were sensitive to the way in which respondents were asked about possible amnesia for the CSA (cf. Ceci & Bruck, 1995, p. 203). They say:

> A decision was made in our study to avoid entirely questions which inquired in some fashion about a negative event—not remembering. Instead, our respondents were questioned simply as to whether they "had thoughts" of the abuse. (p. 4)

A total of 19% reported that prior to the media exposure of Father Porter in 1992 they had "no thoughts, even brief ones, about the abuse" (p. 6). Another 28% reported having "some" thoughts about the abuse at specific periods in their life course but not others. Another 31% reported "frequent (daily or weekly) lengthy thoughts about their abuse" (p. 6). Both the recovered and continuous memory groups had more thoughts about the abuse in adulthood as compared to adolescence. Grassian and Holzen point out that those who lacked continuous vivid thoughts about the abuse for a period of time prior to the media exposure were either characterized by a "relative paucity of such thoughts, and that the thoughts they *did* have were strikingly lacking in detail" or by a "compete absence of thoughts" (p. 7). Those who had a period of "no thoughts" about the sexual abuse, generally had thoughts that were "vague, affectless, and lacking in detail" when they did have thoughts about it.

The commonly reported triggers for thinking about the abuse were attending church, engaging in sexual activity, seeing someone from the period of time when the abuse occurred, and seeing a child reaching the same age as the victim was when the abuse occurred. Other, less common triggers included a spouse's affair, a sexual assault, or a specific smell (e.g., the smell of cigarettes). For the respondents the media exposure had the following effect:

> [It] had a fairly dramatic effect, resulting in a flood of vivid, lengthy—often intrusive—thoughts about the abuse, and often also in a significant initial worsening of symptoms of psychological distress. (p. 8)

The psychiatric distress typically occurring upon triggering the memory included flashbacks, nightmares, depression, and anger. Those respondents who had no thoughts about the abuse were significantly less likely than those who continuously thought about it to have significant psychiatric distress, like anxiety, depression, and nightmares, upon focusing attention on the abuse because of media exposure or some other trigger. More women than men were likely to have no thoughts about the sexual abuse prior to the media exposure. Those who had continuous memories of the alleged abuse throughout adolescence were significantly more likely to manifest conduct and behavioral problems and alcoholism during adolescence that were likely to continue into adulthood.

Thus, the data revealed two distinct groups—internalizers who had few thoughts about the abuse over significant life periods but had symptoms such as anxiety, depression, and nightmares throughout their lives and showed an intensification of symp-

toms when they recovered the memory, and externalizers who retained a continuous memory for the abuse but showed consistently lower adjustment in the form of conduct and addictive behaviors throughout significant life periods. With respect to the former group, Grassian and Holtzen conclude:

> Many victims present, not with a complete absence of memories, but rather with a paucity of memories, memories which tend to have a dissociative feel—lacking detail or affect—until some event (the news media, a life event, a moment of readiness in psychotherapy) opens the floodgates of traumatic memory and emotion. And when these floodgates are opened, we are able to view both the adaptive function of the failure to remember—the avoidance of overwhelming, disorganizing affect—and also the heavy price the individual pays for such a defensive adaptation—emotional constriction, numbing, and compulsivity. (p. 13)

However, Grassian and Holtzen qualify their findings by saying, "this data does not prove the existence of a causal relationship between memory for the abuse and subsequent life course" (p. 12).

The research also addressed predictors of continuously thinking about or failing to think about the abuse. Those respondents with higher grades at the time of the abuse were significantly less likely to think about the abuse during adolescence. Experiencing a greater number of episodes of abuse predicted a continuous memory for the abuse and poorer adjustment following the abuse. Women victims were significantly less likely to think about the abuse than men, and were significantly more likely to develop symptoms after the abuse than were men.

RANDOM SAMPLES   The only genuine way to eliminate sample selection bias in survey studies is through the use of random sampling strategies (Dawes, 1994). A large sampling of both men and women was conducted by Briere and Conte (1993). Using a national network of therapists treating abuse survivors, they randomly sampled 450 (420 female and 30 male) subjects in treatment for sexual abuse. Subjects were given a questionnaire about sexual abuse and a general symptom checklist. In particular, subjects were asked, "During the period of time between when the first forced sexual experience happened and your 18th birthday was there ever a time when you could not remember the forced sexual experience?" (p. 24). A total of 59% of the subjects reported "not having remembered their abuse at some point after it occurred but before their 18th birthday" (p. 24).

As in the Herman and Schatzow (1987) survey, Briere and Conte investigated factors that predicted either amnesia or no amnesia for the sexual abuse. Significant predictors were age of onset, duration of the abuse, degree of violence (extent of injury or fear of death), number of abusers, and severity of current symptoms. No corroborative data was reported. Briere and Conte conclude that "amnesia for abuse (partial or otherwise) appears to be a common phenomenon among clinical sexual abuse survivors" (p. 26).

While these findings more or less replicate Herman and Schatzow's results regarding prevalence rates for abuse-specific amnesia with a larger clinical sample of both men and women (64% in Herman and Schatzow; 59% in Briere and Conte) and for the predictors of amnesia (age of onset, duration, and degree of violence), they add two predictors to the list—number of perpetrators and severity of current symptoms. Briere and Conte have a different interpretation for the mechanisms of amnesia in sexual abuse survivors. Whereas Herman and Schatzow understand amnesia to be a function of "massive repression," Briere and Conte see the amnesia as resulting from dissociation.

Methodological objections have been raised to the Briere and Conte (1993) study by Pope and Hudson (1995a,b) on the grounds that (1) there is no confirmation of the abuse, (2) there is no clear explanation of how subjects were included or excluded, and (3) a "yes" answer to the single question could mean that the subject did not think about the trauma for an extended period—not that the subject repressed a traumatic memory. Pope and Hudson (1995b) also raise the concern that the subjects may have been influenced by suggestion and expectation, because all were in treatment with therapists who were part of an "informal sexual abuse treatment referral network" espousing belief in repressed memories. If the therapists pick the subjects, and all hold similar beliefs, there is the possibility of ideological contagion, which raises questions about the reliability of the "yes" answers.

Another recent large national survey on "forgetting" childhood sexual abuse was conducted by Feldman-Summers and Pope (1994). A total of 500 (250 men and 250 women) psychologists were randomly selected and sent a questionnaire about whether or not they "had experienced sexual or nonsexual physical abuse before their 11th birthday" (p. 636), and if so, whether or not there was a "period of time when they could not remember some or all of the abuse" (p. 636). The 330 participants who returned the questionnaire were also asked about the events that led to their recall of the forgotten abuse. Physical abuse was reported in 24% and sexual abuse in 22% of the population. Of all the respondents who reported abuse (sexual or nonsexual), 40% reported a period of time when they could not remember some or all of the abuse. Contrary to the previous surveys, age and duration did not significantly predict amnesia, but experience of more than one type of abuse did. Nearly half (47%) of the respondents reported that they had obtained some sort of corroboration for the abuse. Slightly over half (56%) said that psychotherapy, or psychotherapy along with other events, such as working with abused families or having abuse survivors as friends, was associated with recall of the forgotten abuse.

The data of the Feldman-Summers and Pope survey appear to contradict Loftus's claim that therapy bias is "creating" false reports of recovered memories of CSA, since Feldman-Summers and Pope found that the differences between those amnestic subjects who first recalled abuse in therapy and those who first recalled it under a variety of other circumstances was not significant. Feldman-Summers and Pope conclude that their study "lends support to the observation that many people forget, for various periods of time, some or all of the trauma they have experienced" (p. 638) and that "reported forgetting and recall of past trauma are common phenomena" (p. 639).

Westerhof, Woertman, and van der Hart (in press) essentially replicated the Feldman-Summers and Pope (1994) study by conducting a random survey of psychologist members of the Netherlands Institute of Psychologists, who were asked about abuse histories and whether or not they had ever forgotten the abuse. Childhood sexual and/or physical abuse was reported by 18% of female and 9% of the male respondents. The 9% reporting rate for childhood sexual abuse in the Dutch sample was much lower than in the American sample. Westerhof et al. Found that 39% of the surveyed psychologists reported forgetting and later recovering the memory for the abuse; this is comparable to the 40% forgetting rate in the original Feldman-Summers and Pope study. One improvement over the original Feldman-Summers and Pope design was the inclusion of questions to distinguish between full and partial amnesia. Full amnesia was reported by 22% of the sample. A total of 68% claimed that psychotherapy was associated with recovery of the abuse memory but only 19% said that the memory had been triggered by therapy. A total of 70% of those who recovered memories reported corroborative evidence. Age (young age of abuse onset), but not type or duration of abuse, predicted the likelihood of reported forgetting of the sexual abuse. Westerhof et al. conclude that ". . . the current Dutch study converges with the U.S. survey it replicates and extends to lend support to the hypothesis that people can forget and later recall both sexual and nonsexual abuse" and that delayed recall is "not a North American culture-bound phenomenon."

Fish and Scott (in press) randomly sampled 1,500 members of the American Counseling Association. The 423 respondents completed two measures of dissociation, the Dissociative Experiences Scale-II and the Tellegan Absorption Scale, as well as a survey about childhood physical and sexual abuse. A total of 14% reported being physically and 25% being sexually abused. A total of 52% of the abused respondents reported that they had forgotten all or part of the abuse for some period of time. Of the 104 respondents who reported that they had forgotten childhood sexual abuse, 17% indicated that they had forgotten their sexual abuse completely for some period and another 38% reported some degree of forgetting. Respondents' perceptions that their abuse had been secret, or that there had been pressure to keep the abuse secret, were associated with reported forgetting of the abuse. Scores of dissociation on both the Dissociative Experiences Scale and the Tellegan Absorption Scale were significantly higher in the group that had forgotten the abuse, as compared to those who had not forgotten. Age at abuse onset was not a predictor of forgetting, but there was a statistically nonsignificant trend for

abuse of longer duration to be associated with forgetting the abuse. A total of 44% reported that recovery of the memory was associated with psychotherapy. The authors conclude that these data "add to the evidence that the experience of forgetting some or all childhood abuse is a common phenomenon among adults reporting childhood abuse."

An innovative feature of this study is its careful breakdown of various types of forgetting such as trying not to think about the abuse, blocking it out, could have remembered if I thought about it, not having any memory, and part of the mind having the memory and another part not having it. While respondents often endorsed more than one type of forgetting, those physically abused were more likely to report that they could have remembered it if they thought about it, while those sexually abused were more likely to report that the memory was inaccessible. These data suggest that "there may be different mechanisms at work in forgetting physical as opposed to sexual abuse."

These random samples are not without methodological flaws, in that all the samples entail recruitment by or of therapists (Pope & Hudson, 1995a,b). A more recent survey by Elliott and Briere (1995) corrects for this problem. They surveyed a general adult population using random telephone numbers stratified according to geographic location. They mailed questionnaires randomly to 800 subjects. A total of 505 individuals responded and were given a Traumatic Events Survey, three measures of PTSD symptoms, and a general symptom checklist. A total of 70% of the 466 subjects sampled responded. A total of 30% of the women and 14% of the men reported being sexually abused (n=107 combined men and women). These 107 subjects were asked, "Was there ever a period of time when you had less or no memory of this event than you do now?" (p. 635). A total of 20% indicated that they had no memory for the CSA and another 22% indicated that they had "less memory" at some time prior to the time of the survey. That is, a total of 42% reported either full or partial amnesia for the CSA. Only 7% of the subjects were in therapy at the time of the survey and only 13% said that the recovery of the memory was specifically triggered by therapy. In fact, therapy was the least endorsed trigger of the recovered memory. Recent recall was associated with elevated PTSD symptoms (intrusive reexperiencing, avoidance, and hyperarousal), dissociative symptoms, and impaired functioning. Threat of harm by the perpetrator predicted amnesia for the childhood sexual abuse, but not age of onset, abuse frequency, or use of physical force.

Polusny and Follette (1996) randomly surveyed 1,000 clinical and counseling psychologists about their beliefs and practices regarding treatment of patients who had remembered childhood sexual abuse. A total of 223 respondents filled out a 97-item questionnaire. As part of this practice-related survey, the psychologists were also asked about their own personal experiences remembering abuse. Of the 32% who reported a history of CSA:

> One third of female therapists and one quarter of male therapists reported having partial memories of CSA that existed before participating in any therapy. Only 3% of the women and 5% of the men reported that they had no memories of CSA before entering therapy and subsequently recalled such memories during therapy. (p. 44)

Golding (1996) and his associates conducted a state-wide random telephone survey of adults. The 663 respondents were given a written definition of repressed memories:

> . . . a repressed memory happens when something extremely traumatic or troubling happens to a person and their (*sic*) mind simply cannot deal with remembering the event. Sometimes the memory comes back to the person long after the event happened. (cited in Golding et al., 1996, p. 435)

Participants were asked if they ever heard about or were familiar with media events concerning repressed memories. A total of 61% had become aware of repressed memories. A total of 14% "responded that a friend or family member had informed them of the recovery of a repressed memory" (p. 436) and 77% of the reported repressed memories were memories for traumatic events.

Melchert (1996) surveyed 553 college students randomly selected from a large subject pool. They were given a Family Background Questionnaire that included questions about different types of abuse and about memory for abuse. A unique feature of the study was the inclusion of questions on physical abuse (PA), emotional abuse (EA), and sexual abuse (SA) in childhood, so that the variable features of memory for each type of abuse could be investigated. A total of 27% of the subjects reported experiencing one form of abuse or another. Significantly more women than men reported sexual, physical, and emotional abuse. More women than men also reported more severe sexual abuse. Respondents who had experienced one form of abuse or another did not have a poorer general childhood memory than those who did not report any abuse. Melchert says, "the study findings are in direct contrast to hypotheses suggesting that a history of child abuse is associated with poor (or enhanced) memory for early childhood" (p. 443). A total of 21% of those alleging physical abuse, and 18% of those reporting either emotional abuse or sexual abuse, reported "a time when they had no memories of the abuse but the memories later returned to them" (p. 441). There were no significant differences in the clarity of the abuse memories or in beliefs about the relative accuracy of the abuse memories across all three types of abuse. Age of onset and severity of the abuse failed to predict memory loss.

Another innovative feature of this study was its attempt to inquire about different reasons for the reported memory loss. Respondents were asked to chose between unconsciously blocking out the memory and avoidance of the memory:

> Which of the following is true for you?
> 1. I would not have been able to remember the abuse even if someone had told me about it because I simply did not have any memories of it at the time.
> 2. I could have remembered it during that time if I had wanted to think about it or someone reminded me of it—I was mainly just avoiding the memories at that time. (p. 442)

Moreover, the respondents who were not able to remember were asked to make even finer discriminations between reasons for the memory loss. These included repression, avoidance, normal forgetting, and intentionally not thinking about it. Although the respondents endorsed all of the reasons for memory loss across all types of trauma, except for intentionally not thinking about sexual or emotional abuse, "the largest group for all three abuse types indicated that they had repressed the abuse (i.e., 'unconsciously blocked out the memories')" (pp. 441–442). Nevertheless, of those who reported not being able to remember the abuse by repressing it, just about half said that the memory might have been available had they not been avoiding it. Other respondents (31%, 23%, and 8% of the SA, PA, and EA groups, respectively) also reported that, while always remembering the event, they had not appraised it as abuse until they were much older. These findings suggest that the total group of individuals reporting amnesia for childhood sexual abuse, as well as for other forms of abuse, may be composed of several subgroups, which may include a subgroup for whom the memory is unavailable and another subgroup for whom the memory is available but may or may not be accessible under certain conditions:

> It appears, however, that several of the study participants did not necessarily lack conscious access to their abuse memories before these memories were reported as having been recovered. In fact, nearly one half of those who indicated that they thought they had unconsciously repressed their memories also indicated that they "could have remembered it." (p. 443)

Only 8% of the respondents in each of the PA, SA, and EA groups reported that normal forgetting accounted for the memory loss. Like all of the other studies Melchert's data supports amnesia for childhood sexual abuse, as well as for other forms of childhood abuse, in a subsample of respondents. Because of the comparable base rates across different types, Melchert concludes that "no unique effects on childhood memory were found for any form of abuse" and that "SA may have no unique effects on memory as compared with other types of abuse" (p. 444). Yet, the data show that a variety of mechanisms account for the memory loss for each type of abuse.

While the consistency of the results across these clinical-based and random surveys clearly suggests that a subpopulation of sexual abuse survivors endure a significant period of amnesia for the abuse, some skeptics have cautioned about the kinds of conclusions that can be drawn from surveys such as these, based as they are largely on retrospective self-report data. Rich (1990) believes that these surveys

like Herman and Schatzow (1987) merely tap *reported* abuse, not actual abuse. Because it is very difficult to get independent corroboration for such abuse reports, some of the abuse reports may be false, thereby inflating the base rates. Likewise, Loftus (1993) and Loftus, Polonsky, and Fullilove (1994) have commented that participants may have reported memories for CSA that never happened.

On the other hand, Sandfort (1982) has critically reviewed the literature on retrospective self-report data and concluded that, despite the limitations of this methodology, no study has found it to be completely unreliable. Sandfort argues that the confidence placed in self-report data is greatly increased when different interview techniques are used across a number of studies. Brewin, Andrews, and Gotlib (1993) argued that retrospective reports about the relationship between childhood abuse and adult psychopathology are likely to reflect what is known about autobiographical memory in general, namely, that the gist of memorable experiences is generally accurate while the details may not be, especially for personally meaningful childhood experiences. In a recent prospective study, Widom and Morris (1997) have demonstrated that even after 20 years self-report data for recollections of childhood sexual abuse can be quite accurate.

We believe that the truth lies somewhere between the positions set forth by Rich and Sandfort. We cannot summarily dismiss the consistent observation across all these self-report studies that a significant minority of sexually abused individuals are fully or partially amnestic for the abuse for a period of time and later recover the memory for the abuse. Nor can we readily accept all such self-report data as completely valid, even if current research shows that these reports are more likely than not to be valid for at least the gist of the abuse (Widom & Morris, 1997).

Prospective Studies

Some of the methodological limitations in these surveys have contributed to a heated debate about the interpretation of the data on amnesia for CSA. Many of these limitations were addressed by Williams (1992, 1993, 1994a) in a *prospective study* on memory for childhood sexual abuse. Williams studied 129 women, mostly African-American, who had originally been part of a research study on the immediate consequences of sexual abuse, as their abuse had caused them to be evaluated clinically and forensically in an outpatient department of a city hospital. Detailed medical records were available documenting the abuse and its effects. Medical evidence on physical injury accompanying the abuse was available on 34% of the women. Having the baseline data corrects two lacks in the previous surveys, which are: (1) independent medical corroboration existed for the abuse, and (2) actual abuse then forgetting was established in many cases. As Loftus, Polonsky et al. (1994) have correctly stated about the existing surveys, we are in the "odd position of asking people about a memory for forgetting a memory" (p. 71). The Williams prospective study (1994a) provides a way objectively to document abuse and later forgetting. And since it was a nonclinical survey, there was no question of respondents' reporting abuse as a function of being in psychotherapy.

Seventeen years after the original study, Williams contacted the CSA survivors and conducted a detailed free recall and cued recall interview about their childhood experiences with sex. The interview included questions about reports of sexual abuse and other kinds of abuse, but respondents were not asked explicitly about the target CSA. A total of 38% of the women either failed to report or were amnestic for the CSA, even though it was clearly documented in the medical record 17 years earlier, and 32% said they had *never* been abused. An additional 16% reported that they experienced some period in the past when they did not remember the abuse, although they had recovered the memory some time prior to the interview. Over half of these women who failed to report the target abuse reported other abuse incidents and/or talked openly about other very personal and often embarrassing things. While it remains unclear how many of the women were genuinely amnestic for the abuse and how many remembered it and failed to report it, Williams (1994a) concludes that "having no memory of child sexual abuse is a common occurrence" (p. 1173). Over one-third of the women failed to report victimization, which occurred 17 years earlier, and most who did not report "appear to not recall the abuse" (p. 1173).

Williams (1993, 1994a) addresses some of the objections that Loftus and others have raised about the survey studies, including her own work. One very important objection raised by Loftus is that the reported abuse-specific amnesia might have been the product of therapeutic influence, since the subjects in other surveys were either in therapy or referred by therapists (Briere & Conte, 1993; Feldman-Summers & Pope, 1994; Herman & Schatzow, 1987). The Feldman-Summers and Pope survey addressed this criticism by showing that those who recovered the memories of their abuse in therapy were not significantly more likely to report amnesia than those who recovered them by other means. The Williams work addresses this criticism by identifying a nonclinical sample of women with abuse-specific amnesia, many of whom had not been in therapy.

Loftus, Polonsky et al. (1994) argue that the prevalence rates for amnesia are higher in the other surveys than in their survey because many of the other surveys used questionnaires instead of live interviews. Williams, however, conducted interviews with her subjects that were about twice as long as those reported by Loftus, Polonsky et al. (1994) (three hours vs. one and a half hours).

A very important objection raised by Loftus, Polonsky et al. (1994) is that the reported abuse may never have occurred in some of the subjects in these survey studies. Even in Williams' prospective study, where independent corroboration of abuse existed, a small number of subjects (2%) contradicted this evidence and said that they had been referred to the hospital based on a fabricated allegation of abuse. To address this objection Williams reasoned that the 38% forgetting rate could have been inflated by false positives. This was not the case. The base rates for those women for whom unequivocal physical evidence of sexual abuse existed and the rates for the overall sample did not significantly differ, which demonstrates that the 38% of forgetting was not inflated due to false reporting; in fact, there was a tendency for women with the clearest evidence of abuse to be *more* amnestic.

An objection raised by Pope and Hudson (1995b) concerns the young age of some of the women, thus reflecting normal childhood amnesia rather than repression of traumatic memories. Furthermore, the 38% figure reported by Williams must be further discounted, they argue, because of (1) normal forgetting and (2) the established fact that approximately one out of every three people fail to report to interviewers brief hospital visits, doctor visits, or noninjury car accidents. Ceci and Bruck (1995) dismiss the studies because in "most instances of memory failure can be accounted for by ordinary forgetting processes" (p. 208). Pope and Hudson's (1995b) point that the reported amnesia had less to do with the operation of psychological defenses than with the young age at the time of the abuse (childhood amnesia) suggests that the younger women in Williams' sample would be expected to have a higher prevalence rate of amnesia than the older women. When women three years of age or younger at abuse onset were compared to women who were four to six years of age, no significant differences were found in the rate of amnesia for the target CSA. Thus, the abuse-specific amnesia could not be explained solely as a function of childhood amnesia.

Another objection was that the women may have been embarrassed to talk about the sexual abuse or otherwise preferred not to think about it. Williams found no significant differences in the likelihood of recalling the target sexual abuse as compared to recalling other personal or embarrassing topics, like abortion, prostitution, or sexually transmitted diseases. If the women were not embarrassed to talk about these other topics, there is no reason to assume they would be especially embarrassed to talk about the target sexual abuse.

Pope and Hudson (1995b) have objected to the Williams study because of her failure to include a "clarification interview," as was done in the Femina et al. (1990) prospective study on physical abuse. They say, "[subjects] were not then presented with the fact of their documented visit to the hospital to see whether they acknowledge remembering it" (p. 9). They point out that "Femina and colleagues yielded no cases of amnesia under comparable conditions" (p. 11). The logic of using the Femina et al. data to question Williams's claim may not be entirely merited, since the Fish and Scott data imply that the mechanisms underlying memory loss for physical and sexual abuse may be different for a number of individuals.

We agree that the design of the Williams study makes it difficult to discriminate between those subjects who actually forgot the abuse and those who remembered the abuse and did not report it. However, we do not agree that a "clarification interview"

is best way to make this determination. False memory advocates like Pope and Hudson cannot have it both ways: they can not claim, on the one hand, that therapy interviews are unduly suggestive to the point of implanting false memories, and then claim, on the other hand, that research interviews are "clarifying," with the implication that research interviews are somehow free from suggestive effects while therapy interviews are not. Following false memory reasoning, a follow-up interview could not have been included in the Williams study if the intention was to minimize suggestive effects in the research interviews.

A free recall interview, as was exemplified in the Williams study (cf. also Widom & Morris, 1997), is the only way to minimize the memory commission error rate, while a "clarifying" interview, with its leading questions, would increase this error rate and not necessarily lead to what it purports.

Moreover, the data from the more recent survey studies, which included specific questions on the reasons for reported loss of the memory for abuse, imply that groups reporting memory loss may be composed of several subgroups, some of whom do not have the memory consciously available and some of whom may consciously access the memory under certain conditions were they not to avoid thinking about it (Melchert, 1996). The Fish and Scott (in press) data suggest that those reporting memory loss for sexual abuse are more likely to be repressing it, while for physical abuse are more likely to be avoiding it.

These data suggest that even if Williams's figure of 38% failing to report the target sexual abuse contains a portion of women who were avoiding the sexual abuse memory rather than being amnestic for it, it is unlikely that avoidance could serve as the sole explanation for the entire subgroup.

Williams (1993, 1994a) also reported on predictors of amnesia. In addition to previously reported predictors, a significantly greater number of subjects who were molested by family members, as compared to strangers, and a significantly greater number of women who had a close relationship to the perpetrator, as compared to having been abused by a stranger, were amnestic for the abuse, when age of onset of the abuse was statistically controlled. Unlike other researchers (Briere & Conte, 1993; Herman & Schatzow, 1987), Williams did not find that the use of physical force was significantly related to amnesia for CSA. Williams's data demonstrate that the "relationship to the offender" is a significant predictor of amnesia. In addition, young age at the time of abuse predicted amnesia for the CSA.

Williams (1994a) concludes that "having no memory of child sexual abuse is a common occurrence not only among adult survivors in therapy for abuse . . . but among community samples of women" (p. 1173). She adds, "If as these findings suggest, having no recall of sexual abuse is a fairly common event, we should not be surprised by later recovery of memories of CSA by some women" (p. 1174). These data go a long way toward answering skepticism about reported abuse-specific amnesia. Unfortunately, the data do not address the accuracy or consistency of the memory over time, although Williams has recently published her analysis of the data, as will be discussed below.

In response to the Williams study, Loftus, Garry, and Feldman (1994) state that "having no memory" does not necessarily imply repression, but may be an instance of "normal forgetting." Loftus et al. do, however, concede that the Williams study does "provide evidence of genuine memory failure" (p. 1180). By contrast, other false memory advocates, such as Pope and Hudson (1995a), have specifically observed that in studies where the traumatic abuse is known to have occurred, and where the trauma is so severe that "no one would be reasonably expected to forget it, the postulated mechanism of the amnesia—whether it be called 'repression,' 'dissociation,' or 'traumatic amnesia'—is unimportant" (p. 122).

Pope and Hudson (1995a) acknowledge that designing a definitive study is not easy, and that the Williams study provides "a useful starting point" (p. 125). The study that should prove persuasive of the claim that traumatic memories may be repressed would have the following structure: (1) it would begin with subjects whose experience with a trauma is "unequivocally documented," (2) all subjects must be above the age of five at the time they endured abuse "too traumatic to be normally forgettable," (3) all subjects would be interviewed "with suitable ethical and therapeutic precautions" about "any past history of trauma," (4) subjects who still denied abuse would be given a "clarification interview," which would directly focus on the known abuse occurrence. According to Pope and Hudson (1995a),

"if some subjects still reported amnesia even in response to the direct questions, this finding would suggest repression" (p. 125). Indeed, they go even further by stating that even a modest number of subjects meeting their criteria would be useful in suggesting the validity of repression, and "even a series of several case reports" might be persuasive evidence of the existence of repression.

An important large-scale (n=1,196) prospective study has recently been reported that meets all of Pope and Hudson's criteria, except for the "clarification interview," which would not accomplish what they claim it would. Widom and Morris (1997) report data on a long-term follow-up study of children with a documented history of physical abuse, sexual abuse, and neglect, as compared to a demographically matched control group of non-abused children. The abused group consisted of cases "serious enough to come to the attention of the authorities. Only court substantiated cases of child abuse and neglect were included" (p. 36). The overall intent of the study was the "disentangle the effects of childhood victimization from other potential confounding effects" (p. 36).

Both groups were followed over a 20-year period. After 20 years a two-hour interview was conducted. Both interviewees and interviewers were blind to the reason for study, so as not to be "leading" in interviews. The study included four independent measures of abuse: (1) responses to questions about a list of explicitly sexual behaviors that might have occurred in childhood; (2) a cognitive appraisal of the abuse behaviors ("Do you consider any of these experiences to have been sexual [physical] abuse?"); (3) measures of the age of the perpetrator (ten years or older than the victim); and (4) an assessment of the degree of force used. To determine the accuracy of the reports, responses to interview questions about abuse were compared with the official court records of the abuse 20 years earlier. While significantly more sexually abused individuals than control subjects reported sexual abuse 20 years later, sexually abused individuals significantly underreported the documented abuse. A total of 63% of the sexually abused subjects reported some sexual abuse incident in the follow-up interview, while 37% failed to report the documented CSA in the interview. Males were significantly less likely than females to interpret the CSA as sexual abuse, and when they reported it as sexual abuse they were more likely than women to report that force was used.

Unlike the Williams study (1994a) where younger age predicted amnesia for the CSA during adulthood, age was not a significant predictor of the underreporting in the Widom and Morris prospective study. The research also attempted to assess the construct validity of the sexual abuse reports. Widom and Morris studied the likelihood that symptoms commonly associated with CSA in adults, like depression, PTSD, chemical dependency, and self-destructive behaviors, would be more representative of the abused relative to the control group. Both the official record and self-report data significantly predicted alcoholism and self-destructive behavior, but only the self-report predicted depression 20 years after the documented sexual abuse. Widom and Morris conclude:

> Overall we found substantial underreporting of sexual abuse among known victims of childhood sexual abuse. This is particularly impressive because these are court–substantiated documented cases of childhood sexual abuse. (p. 43) . . . The combined results indicate that the relationship between childhood sexual abuse and subsequent alcohol problems and suicide attempts in females is robust, demonstrated empirically with prospective as well as retrospective data. (p. 44)

Further examples exist demonstrating the validity of amnesia for childhood sexual abuse. Each is consistent with the scientific data just reviewed. Kluft (1997) reported that corroborative data could be found to confirm the abuse reports of 19 of a sample of 34 patients who met the diagnostic criteria for dissociative identity disorder. Of these 19 patients with confirmed abuse, 13 (68%) reported that they had not known about the abuse prior to their treatment for DID.

Predictors of Amnesia for CSA

Table 7.5 combines the data on positive predictors of amnesia across sexual abuse studies. Braun and Sachs' (1985) categories of predisposing, precipitating, and perpetuating factors provide a useful way to conceptualize the material. *Predisposing factors* for functional amnesia for trauma might include:

TABLE 7.5
Predictors of Amnesia for Childhood Sexual Abuse

PREDISPOSING FACTORS
  Biological factors
    intoxication
    head injury
    personality factors
    memory-vulnerable diagnosis (hysteria, dissociation, depression)
    level of intelligence
    use of dissociation at time of trauma (peritraumatic dissociation)
    previous history of amnesia
    previous history of trauma
  Developmental factors—age of onset of trauma
  Closeness of relationship between victim and offender

PRECIPITATING FACTORS—THE TRAUMATIC EVENT
  Intensity of emotional arousal
  Degree of violence
  Physical injury
  Coping ability during event (e.g., dissociation)

PERPETUATING FACTORS
  Duration, repeated traumatization
  Number of perpetrators
  Conspiracy to silence (threats and rewards)
  Victim's cognitive appraisal of the abuse
  Accommodation and consent

(1) a "memory vulnerable" diagnosis such as hysteria, dissociation, or depression where memory distortion is one among a number of other diagnostic criteria; (2) a propensity to use dissociative defenses at the time of the trauma; (3) a previous history of amnestic episodes; (4) high intelligence; (5) a close attachment between victim and perpetrator that necessitates amnesia for the abuse as a means to protect the relationship and its continuation; and (6) substance or alcohol use that introduces state-dependent memory effects; and (7) young age at onset of traumatization. The state-dependent vulnerability to memory loss can become activated at the time of traumatization because of such *precipitating factors* as: (1) emotional arousal; (2) physical force, violence, threat; and (3) sustaining physical injury.

Perpetuating factors include: (1) repeated traumatization, especially of extended duration and involving multiple perpetrators—this can condition the propensity for memory loss, especially if there is a survival need to preserve the relationship with the perpetrator(s) (in fantasy or reality); (2) the conspiracy of silence, either explicit threats by the perpetrator about disclosure, emotional pressure, or familial or societal denial; (3) the victim's appraisal of the abuse, which plays an important role in certain long-term effects, like degree of depression (Widom & Morris, 1997); and (4) accommodation to the abuse by consent in order to get attention (Ensink, 1992). The large number of factors contributing to amnesia necessitates thinking in more complex ways about the mechanisms of amnesia than is captured in the grossly oversimplified false memory controversy about repression vs. simple forgetting.

The available data on predictors of amnesia for CSA summarized in Table 7.6 contain many contradictions. Early age of onset of the abuse is sometimes a predictor (Bernet et al., 1993; Briere & Conte, 1993; Cameron, 1996; Golding et al., 1996; Herman & Schatzow, 1987; Kristiansen et al., 1995; Pomerantz, in progress; Westerhof et al., in press; Williams, 1994a) and sometimes not (Albach et al., in press; Elliott & Briere, 1995; Ensink, 1992; Feldman-Summers & Pope, Fish & Scott, in press; Melchert, 1996; Polusny & Follette, 1996; Widom & Morris, 1997). Actual force, penetration, or violence causing injury is sometimes a predictor (Bernet et al., 1993; Briere & Conte, 1993; Cameron, 1996; Herman & Schatzow, 1987; Pomerantz, in progress) and sometimes not (Albach et al., in press; Elliott & Briere, 1995; Grassian & Holtzen, 1996; Williams, 1994a). Severity (type and number of abusive acts) sometimes predicts amnesia for abuse (Bernet et al., 1993; Cameron, 1996; Ensink, 1992; Feldman-Summers & Pope, 1994; Fish & Scott, in press; Kristiansen et al,. 1995), and sometimes does not (Albach et al., in press; Melchert, 1996; Westerhof et al., in press), and sometimes predicts continuous memory for the abuse (Grassian & Holtzen, 1996). Repeated sexual abuse sometimes predicts amnesia (Belicki et al., 1994; Cameron, 1996). Abuse by a family member predicts amnesia (Belicki et al., 1994; Cameron, 1996; Kristiansen et al., 1995; Pomeranz, in progress; Williams, 1994a). Level of intelligence and/or academic achievement also predicts amnesia (Grassian & Holtzen, 1996; Roesler & Wind, 1994). Dissociation at the time of the abuse sometimes predicts amnesia (Ensink, 1992) and sometimes it does not (Albach et al., in press).

How are we to make sense out of these contradictory findings? Obviously, no simple conclusions can be drawn, though some trauma experts have attempted to draw them. Van der Kolk, for example, summarizes that "Amnesias . . . seem to be age- and dose-related" (van der Kolk; McFarlane; & Weisaeth; 1996; p. 285). While it is true that age of onset, degree of violence, more severe types of abuse, and multiple perpetrators do appear as significant predictors of amnesia in more studies than not, there are exceptions. Terr (1996) says that the operation of psychological defenses "is the most likely explanation" for amnesia for CSA (p. 75). Cohen (1996) believes that amnesia for CSA can be explained in terms of our general understanding of functional retrograde amnesia outside of the domain amnesia for CSA, both of which entail a "functional separation or encapsulation of some subset of memories that would prevent those memories from being accessed through the usual associative linkages" (p. 92). Bowers and Woody (1996) remind us that the extensive laboratory investigation of hypnotic amnesia offers a ready explanation for amnesia for CSA. We believe the problem of making sense out of the prediction data lies in searching for single predictors of amnesia of CSA, rather than in appreciating the complex *interaction* that probably exists across multiple variables depending on the context of the abuse.

Second, the assumptions underlying the choice of predictors studied reveal a cognitive bias (e.g., early age of onset) and a severity of trauma bias (severity, multiple perpetrators, multiple acts, degree of force, etc.) and reveal an under emphasis on social factors. A similar bias is reflected in the general trauma field, as exemplified in the PTSD section of *DSM-IV*, which defines a traumatic event as one causing physical injury or a threat to life (derived from the disaster literature), while it is abundantly clear in the clinical literature that relation-based trauma, especially if it involves fiduciary violation (e.g., incest, spousal rape, or sexual misconduct) is perhaps much more damaging than physical injury per se.

A recent reappraisal of the central contribution of "betrayal trauma" to overall trauma damage can be found in J. Freyd's *Betrayal Trauma* (1996). Freyd (1994, 1996) has argued that victims of sexual abuse typically fail to remember the abuse because of their deep sense of betrayal, arising from violation of a trusted dependency relationship, like that of a par-

TABLE 7.6
Inconsistencies in the Evidence on Predictors of Amnesia for Childhood Sexual Abuse

Predictors	1	2	3	4	5	6	7	8	9	10	11	12	13	14	15	16	17	18	19	20	21
gender									x	-	-	-				-					
age of onset	x	-	-	x		x			x	-	-	x	-	x	x	-	x	x	-	-	-
frequency	x		-		-					-		-									
duration	x	-	-						x	-	-					-		x	-		
repeat abuse			-		-		x		-*										x		
number of abusers		x		x	-	x			x		-							x	x		
types and number of abusive acts		-	-	x		x	x				x					-	x		x		-
intelligence							x	x													
close relationship to abuser		-		x	-		x						x					x	x		
penetration										-			-	-				x	x		
actual force		-				x							-	-				x			
violence, injury	x				-				x										x		
emotional pressure			x		x				-		x										
appraisal of abuse											x										
resistance		-																			
consent		x																			
secrecy; disclosure fear		-							x								x				
current life symptoms; functioning							x	x													
current life therapy						-															
dissociation at time of abuse		x	-																		

KEY:

X = predictor of CSA
- = not a predictor of CSA
-* = predicted opposite of what was expected

1 = Herman & Schatzow, 1987	10 = Briere & Conte, 1993
2 = Ensink, 1992	11 = Feldman-Summers & Pope, 1994
3 = Albach et al., in press	12 = Elliott & Briere, 1995
4 = Kristiansen et al., 1995	13 = Williams, 1994a
5 = Loftus, Polansky et al., 1994	14 = Widom & Morris, 1997
6 = Bernet et al., 1993	15 = Golding et al., 1996
7 = Belicki et al., 1994	16 = Westerhof et al., in press
8 = Roesler & Wind, 1994	17 = Fish & Scott, in press
9 = Grassian & Holtzen, 1996	18 = Pomerantz, in progress
	19 = Camron, 1996
	20 = Melchert, 1996
	21 = Polusny & Follette, 1996

ent and child. Consequently, severity of trauma may not be the primary predictor of amnesia. Because of the primary importance of the attachment relationship, failing to remember the abuse, i.e., "information blockage," has a "survival advantage" or "social utility," in that it ensures continuity of a primary attachment relationship and protects the relationship from dissolution subsequent to the abuse. She says:

Profound amnesia (as opposed to other symptoms

of PTSD) is likely to result in cases involving betrayal of trust that produces conflict between external reality and social dependency. (1996, p. 75)

According to Freyd's hypothesis, "There are reasons to suggest that incestuous abuse is forgotten at a higher rate than other sexual abuse" (1996, p. 47), although she adds that war trauma and date rape are often examples of betrayal trauma. To test this hypothesis Freyd reanalyzed the data on prediction of CSA in available studies (those by Cameron, 1993; Feldman-Summers and Pope, 1994; Loftus, Polansky et al., 1994; and Williams, 1994a). The data were recategorized in terms of abuse by a relative. She found that "incest is forgotten and recovered at a much higher rate than other forms of abuse" (pp. 145–146) and adds that, "I have not found any studies in which it is claimed that incest is negatively predictive of amnesia" (p. 156).

A number of recent studies appear consistent with Freyd's model. Liem, O'Toole, and James (1996) compared stories written by women with and without a history of childhood sexual abuse. The stories of women with a history of CSA contained significantly more material reflecting a preoccupation with themes of powerlessness, a need for and fear of power, and a sense of betrayal by others. Relationships were seen as deceptive and exploitative rather than collaborative and reciprocal significantly more in women with than without CSA histories. Waites (1997) emphasizes that all memory is recollected (and revised) in a social context:

> Modern controversy about "repressed memories" should be evaluated in the light of how reported memory may be distorted by external pressures and intimiating threats as well as by internal dynamics. The erosion of veridical memory is seldom simply a matter of banishing the past. It is more commonly a matter of reconstructing the past to make it more acceptable to others as well as to the self. (p. 157)

Feiring, Taska, and Lewis (1996) have emphasized the central role of shame and stigmatization in the child's adaptation to sexual abuse. Shame is defined as "a desire to hide, disappear, or die" (p. 770). They note that shame is "highly characteristic of victims" (p. 771) and see shame as central to the long-term

maladjustment of sexual abuse survivor.

Taken together these studies suggest that abuses of power in significant relationships and the associated betrayal, especially if it evokes fundamental conflicts in attachment, may be important in understanding the long term maladjustment following relation-based trauma, including long-term amnesia for the trauma. In the *DSM-IV* field trials for PTSD, van der Kolk, Pelcovitz et al. (1996) found that individuals who developed PTSD after interpersonal trauma had significantly more PTSD symptoms than those who developed PTSD symptoms after experiencing a natural disaster; among those who experienced an interpersonal trauma, those who experienced it in childhood had significantly more PTSD symptoms than those who experienced the interpersonal trauma in adulthood. Consistent with betrayal trauma theory, the emerging trend in trauma research suggests that violations in interpersonal relationships may be more damaging than physical injury or threat to life in contributing to the overall posttraumatic effects.

The Process of Recovery of the Narrative Memory for Trauma

The Roesler and Wind (1994) study is unique in that it contains valuable data on the point in the overall life cycle that forgotten memories of childhood sexual abuse are likely to be disclosed. Essentially, they found that memory recovery clustered around three points in the lifecycle. One group of victims of CSA was likely to disclose the abuse to a non-abusing parent or other family member in adolescence. Typically, disclosure was not favorably received by other family members, nor did disclosure necessarily result in cessation of the ongoing sexual abuse. A second group of victims was likely to disclose the abuse in their mid-twenties, typically to friends. A third group of victims was likely to disclose the memories for the first time later in life, usually in their mid- to late thirties, typically to a therapist. Consistent with these data, Roe and Schwartz (1996) found that adult woman on an inpatient unit for childhood sexual abuse generally recovered their memories for the CSA in their thirties. These data suggest, that if abuse is not disclosed in adolescence or early adulthood, it may be subsequently associated with a relatively incomplete narrative memory for the abuse, which when recovered in more detail, either spontaneously or in treatment, may result in psychiatric symptoms that serve as the basis for treatment.

Recently, a number of studies have appeared documenting the progressive changes in the narrative memory for trauma once it has been recovered. Roe and Schwartz (1996), for example, found that their subjects reported the recovered memory initially occurring as a flashback and not as a narrative memory. Brett and Ostroff (1985) emphasize the central role of posttraumatic imagery. This study is consistent with the frequent observation that memory for trauma is often manifested in the form of an implicit, behavioral memory and not in an explicit, narrative memory (American Psychiatric Association, 1994; Terr, 1994; Waites, 1997), and that narrative memory for trauma returns progressively over time. When flashbacks or other intrusive reexperiencing symptoms occur, "reliving of trauma is experienced as a real and contemporary event" because of the "distorted time sense" that accompanies traumatic reenactment (Reis, 1995, p. 216).

With respect to clinical studies, Davies and Frawley (1994) observed that their analytic patients initially manifested dissociated memories of CSA in the form of transference reenactments. These memories were "remembered first in unsymbolized ways" (p. 98) and only later in treatment did the narrative content of the abuse memory become clear. Davies and Frawley describe the stages typically observed when a narrative memory for CSA is progressively recovered in treatment: (1) These "memories" first occur in the form of "unsymbolized" memories of abuse, i.e., as reenactments in the transference. (2) Next, the memories "are expressed through somatic experiences that symbolically represent some aspect of the original trauma" (p. 99). (3) The memory next occurs in the form of "hallucinatory-like experience during which she relives some aspect of the sexual trauma" (p. 99). These events typically occur in the transition between waking and sleeping or sleeping and waking. (4) Dreams and nightmares appear "that are virtually undisguised depictions of their abuse" (p. 100). (5) Next come memories that are triggered directly by internal or external stimuli. "During a flashback, the patient suddenly reexperiences some aspect of her

victimizations." "Partial dissociation" is common during the flashback (p. 101). (6) As the patient begins to integrate the abuse memory into a narrative form, persistent "obsessive thoughts about the abuse plague the patient" (p. 101). (7) The patient integrates the dissociated aspects of the memory, namely, the affects and somatic experiences, with the narrative memory for the CSA. By "working through" the dissociation, the patient gains "mastery over traumatic past events" and "gradually gains control over their disorganizing impact" (pp. 101–102).

Van der Kolk and Fisler's (1995) study contained data on the process by which traumatic memories were retrieved. Their Traumatic Memory Inventory was designed to distinguish between sensory, affective, and narrative elements of traumatic memories. They noted that of their 46 subjects "No subject reported having a narrative for the traumatic event as their initial mode of awareness (they claimed not having been able to tell a story about what had happened), regardless of whether they had continuous awareness of what had happened, or whether there had been a period of amnesia" (p. 517). All subjects who had retrieved recollections of previous trauma:

> reported that they initially "remembered" the trauma in the form of somato-sensory or emotional flashback experiences. At the peak of their intrusive recollections all sensory modalities were enhanced, and a narrative memory started to emerge. (p. 517)

As time passed, most of the subjects recovered a more complete narrative memory, and the narrative memory became relatively integrated with the affective and sensorimotor aspects of the traumatic memory. However, 11% of the subjects who had experienced childhood trauma (mostly sexual abuse) "continued to be unable to tell a coherent narrative, with a beginning, middle, and end, even though each of them reported outside confirmation of the reality of their trauma" (p. 517). These subjects retained "fragmentary [narrative] memories" (p. 518). Van der Kolk interprets these data in terms of his neurobiological theory of traumatic memory processing, i.e., that the trauma is originally processed as a sensorimotor and affective event and not primarily as an ordinary narrative memory. He says, "trauma is organized in memory on a perceptual level . . . traumatic experiences were not initially organized in a narrative form, and they seem to serve no communicative function" (1996, pp. 287, 289). Memory retrieval entails reprocessing or "transcribing" the memory into an explicit, narrative form.

The Kristiansen et al. (1995) study also contained data on the process of recovering the memory of childhood sexual abuse. Their subjects reported that the memory most frequently returned in the form of body memories, flashbacks, fragments, sudden intense feelings, avoidant behaviors, images, sensory processes, and dreams. They conclude:

> the women in this study did indeed state that their memories returned implicitly, as fragments of emotions, bodily feelings, and sensory experiences such as flashbacks, rather than explicitly as complete stories. . . . [This] provide[s] support for the suggestion that it is dissociation, that is, the disconnection of the explicit and implicit information processing systems, that underlies the nature of traumatic memory.

Likewise, Cameron's longitudinal study (1996) contained data on the process of recovering abuse memories over time. She found that amnestics as compared to non-amnestics were significantly more likely to report "sensory memories." Initially these memories returned in "bits and pieces" and over time became more detailed and organized. Cameron interprets this progression in terms of "the transfer of information from implicit to explicit memory" (p. 64). She adds:

> The recovery of early childhood "memories for abuse" for both groups generally involved sensory and emotional experiences dissociated from other elements found in complete memories. (1996, p. 64)

This longitudinal study also became an opportunity to track what happens to individuals over the years after recovering abuse memories. Substantial changes were noted in four areas: (1) positive changes in self-concept and related beliefs about the world and the world of relationships; (2) a shift to healthier coping strategies; (3) a decrease in PTSD symptoms; and (4) a decrease in somatic symptoms and maladaptive health-related behaviors. The dif-

ferences in improvement between amnestic and non-amnestic groups was not significant.

Like the Cameron (1996) study, a number of other studies have documented that recovery of memory for trauma is typically accompanied by a marked increase in psychiatric symptoms in the form of intrusive reexperiencing symptoms (Elliott & Fox, 1994; Grassian & Holtzen, 1996; Harvey & Herman, 1994; Herman & Schatzow, 1987; Roesler & Wind, 1994), psychophysiological reactivity (Wickramasekera,1994), dissociative symptoms (Elliott & Fox, 1994; Ensink, 1992; van der Kolk & Fisler, 1995), strong emotions (Albach et al., in press), and trauma-related behavioral reenactments in relationships (Davies & Frawley, 1994). Some trauma researchers have implied that recovery of narrative memory for trauma is necessarily accompanied by psychiatric symptoms (e.g., Cameron, 1996; van der Kolk & Fisler, 1995). However, other studies do not fully support this view. Grassian and Holtzen's data on the Father Porter victims suggest that victims could be classified into "two relatively distinct groups"—those using internalizing and those using extrnalizing psychological defenses. The internalizers showed higher premorbid functioning (e.g., good grades in school, outside interests, stable peer relationshps). They were much more likely to have dissociated amnesia for the childhood sexual abuse, especially during adolescence, and they were much more likely to manifest overt psychiatric symptoms upon recovery of the memory. The externalizers showed lower premorbid functioning. While they were more likely to have a continuous memory for the abuse, they were more likely to develop conduct problems and alcoholism in adolescence, but were less likely to develop trauma-related symptoms. Thus, dissociation of the memory seems to be both an asset and liability: it helps the victim attain a higher level of functioning throughout development at the cost of retaining a clear narrative memory for the abuse. Once the dissociation breaks down, the victim is likely to become symptomatic.

Integrating Cameron's (1996) data with Grassian and Holtzen's (in press) data, we might speculate on the differences between those with continuous and recovered memories. Cameron found that amnestics were more likely to recall CSA when they felt safe, whereas non-amnestics didn't like to think about the abuse or didn't fully comprehend its meaning. Non-amnestics recalled the abuse when they were "overwhelmed." Presumably, those with continuous memories for abuse and who have lower premorbid functioning, behavioral problems, or addictions begin to process such memories when the issue is forced. Those who internalize, mainly through dissociative defenses, maintain a higher level of functioning by means of their amnesia until some external event triggers the recovery of the abuse memory or until they find a safe time in their lives to begin to process such experiences. In either case, recovery of the abuse memory evokes a psychological crisis, following which the individual needs to establish a context of safety, typically in therapy, first to restabilize and then to recover a more complete and organized narrative recollection of the abuse over time.

The available studies, like those conducted by van der Kolk and Fisler and Grassian and Holtzen, are quite consistent in their observation that at least a significant subpopulation of trauma victims who recover memories initially have little or no narrative recollection of the traumatic event. None of van der Kolk and Fisler's (1995) subjects initially reported a trauma memory in narrative form. Grassian and Holtzen (1996) reported that many of their subjects "had, not a complete absence of thoughts . . . but rather a relative paucity of such thought, and that the thoughts they *did* have were strikingly lacking in detail—vague, fleeting, and affectless" (p. 7). Loftus, Polonsky et al. (1994) found recovered memories to be "less clear" than continuous memories.

Tromp et al. (1995) conducted a large-scale study of the characteristics of narrative memories for rape as compared to other unpleasant and pleasant memories in a population of 1,037 women medical center employees and another population of 2,142 women university employees. About 8% had experienced an attempted rape and about 30% had experienced a completed rape in each group. Respondents were given a Memory Characteristics Questionnaire. The memories of the rape victims could be significantly distinguished on the basis of their characteristics:

> Rape memories are not differentiated from other unpleasant memories simply by their level of unpleasantness. Rape memories are also differenti-

ated by the extent to which they are less well-remembered, are less clear and vivid, involve less visual detail, have been talked and thought about less, and are less likely to occur in a meaningful order. (p. 618)

In other words, the data demonstrate significantly less clarity of the narrative content of the rape memory as compared to other unpleasant memories. Not only was the narrative content relatively incomplete and, therefore, not well remembered, but the content was reported in disorganized fragments rather than in the form of a coherent narrative.

Koss et al. (1996) replicated the Tromp et al. (1995) study on a second sample of 2,142 women university employees. The second study was also designed to identify the relative contribution of different variables to the overall effects of rape on memory. The researchers attempted to determine whether the effects of rape on memory arose from the trauma of forced, nonconsensual, and often violent sex per se, from the cognitive appraisal of being a victim, or from both. Respondents were given a survey that objectively assessed their rape experience. They were also asked to subjectively rate the degree to which they felt victimized by the experience. The results showed that the rape experience per se had a direct effect on all four dimensions of memory tapped by the Memory Characteristics Questionnaire. The greatest magnitude was on the affect associated with the memory and its clarity. Compared to other unpleasant memories, rape memories were experienced with greater emotional intensity and were significantly less clear, less coherently organized, and less often talked or thought about. The degree to which the rape survivor appraised herself to be a victim, independent from the objective severity of the rape trauma, also had a mild but significant indirect effect on the clarity, emotional intensity, and sensory quality of the rape memory, as well as on the propensity toward intrusive reexperiencing of the memory. While these changes in memory "were better predicted by the event itself as opposed to the cognitive appraisal of victimization" (p. 430), the overall effect on memory was:

> . . . the rape memories . . . compared to memories for unpleasant experiences, were rated as less clear and vivid, less visually detailed, less likely to occur

in a meaningful order, less well-remembered, less talked about, and less frequently recalled either voluntarily and involuntary; with less sensory components including sound, smell, touch, and taste; and containing slightly less reexperiencing of the physical sensations, emotions, and thoughts than were present in the original incident. Thus, memories of events that were unexpected and highly negative both in their emotional valence and in their consequences were differentiated from memories of pleasant life events. (p. 430)

In a similar type of comparative study of traumatic and other memories, Kuyken and Brewin (1995) investigated narrative memory in a sample of clinically depressed women patients with and without a history of childhood sexual and/or physical abuse. All subjects were also given the Impact of Events Scale and the Beck Depression Inventory. With the Autobiographical Memory Test subjects were given one minute to retrieve a specific personal memory in response to five positive (happy, surprised, interested, successful, and safe) and five negative (clumsy, angry, sorry, hurt, and lonely) cue words. If a subject failed to produce a memory after the minute s/he was prompted, "Can you think of one particular event?" and another minute was given to produce the memory. The groups did not differ significantly in the latency of retrieval of specific positive or negative memories. However, the patients with a history of childhood sexual abuse, but not the patients with a history of physical abuse or the non-abused patients, produced significantly overgeneral memories in response to both positive and negative cue words. The total score on the Impact of Events, an inventory of PTSD symptoms, was significantly correlated with the tendency to retrieve overgeneral memories in response to negative, but not in response to positive, emotional cue words. The Avoidance subscale of the Impact of Events scale significantly correlated with the tendency to retrieve overgeneral memories to both positive and negative cues.

In other words, the Kuyken and Brewin (1995) study demonstrates that at least some patients reporting a history of childhood sexual abuse who also report suffering from PTSD symptoms in their current life, especially phobic avoidance of stimuli reminding them of the abuse, tend to retrieve vague,

overgeneral memories that lack specific detail in response to emotional cue words. The Tromp et al. (1995) study reports similar findings for rape victims. Taken together, these comparative studies of narrative memory in traumatized versus nontraumatized individuals suggest that narrative recollections in traumatized individuals can be both over- and undergeneral, i.e., vague and nonspecific, on the one hand, and fragmented and disorganized, on the other, relative to the episodically organized gist and specific detail of narrative memory in nontraumatized individuals.

In another comparative study Klein and Janoff-Bulman (1996) compared the narrative features of life stories of a group of normal individuals with a demographically matched group reporting histories of physical, sexual, or emotional abuse. The research addressed "the storyteller's focus on the past versus the present and future, and his or her focus on the self versus others" (p. 46) through comparative analysis of the reports. Both groups were given a general symptom checklist as well as a coping inventory. While the groups did not differ in coping ability, the abuse group reported significantly greater psychological distress in the symptom checklist. With respect to narrative reports of life histories, the abuse group, relative to the control group, made significantly fewer references to the self, devoted a greater percentage of their stories to the past, and wrote longer narratives. A second study comparing normal control subjects to those with traumatic parental divorce in their backgrounds found a similar pattern of results. Klein and Janoff-Bulman conclude that the abuse-related dwelling on the past and having a "clearer sense of their abuser(s) than of themselves" (p. 52) were associated with poorer coping and the persistence of symptoms.

Other researchers have investigated changes in the characteristics of the narrative memory for trauma over time, once it has been retrieved. Foa et al. (1995) addressed the "cohesiveness of narratives" in rape victims (p. 678). They hypothesized that because rape victims have difficulty processing the information about the rape due to the extreme distress they experienced, the narrative recollection of the rape often remains disorganized and fragmented. Foa et al. further predicted that prolonged exposure treatment would result in greater organization of the narrative memory for the rape experience.

They say, "The natural process of recovery from trauma . . . involves the organizing and streamlining of the memories" (p. 675) with a concomitant decrease in PTSD symptoms. Conversely, those who fail to recover from rape would be expected to remain symptomatic and retain a "disjointed" memory for the rape.

To test these hypotheses Foa et al. studied 14 rape victims, all of whom had documented chronic PTSD symptoms. The rape victims participated in nine biweekly, 90-minute treatment sessions of prolonged exposure training. The sessions emphasized "repeated reliving" of the rape:

> I'm going to ask you to recall the memories of the assault as vividly as possible. I don't want you to tell a story about the assault in the past tense. Rather, I would like you to describe the assault in the present tense, as if it were happening now, right here. I'd like you to close your eyes and tell me what happened during the assault in as much detail as you remember. This includes details about the surroundings, your activities, the perpetrator's activities, how you felt and what your thoughts were during the assault. (p. 679)

The majority of clients showed a significant decrease in PTSD and depressive symptoms from the onset to the end of treatment. Those who improved the least from treatment "expressed more negative feelings, particularly helplessness" throughout the treatment (p. 688). "Degree of cohesiveness" of the narrative rape recollection was the primary focus of the study (p. 681). The narrative accounts of the rape memories at the first and last treatment sessions were compared using a number of coding categories. They found three main results: (1) The post-therapy rape narratives contained a significantly higher portion of organized thoughts than the initial narratives. (2) However, the percentage of utterances associated with fragmented narrative recall (e.g., unfinished thoughts and speech fillers) did not significantly decrease over the course of the treatment. (3) The post-therapy rape narratives contained significantly more references to thoughts and feelings than the initial narratives.

The authors conclude that "narratives of traumatic memories recounted by rape victims change over the course of repeated imaginal reliving of the trauma"

(p. 686). The treatment was said to cause "a shift in emphasis toward greater processing of emotions and meanings associated with the trauma and reduced attention to the details of the assault itself" (p. 687). Reduction in the fragmentation of the rape recollection over the course of treatment was significantly correlated with improvement in trauma-related symptoms, but not with depression. As the fragmentary dissociated memory decreased, PTSD symptoms decreased. An increase in the organization of the memory was significantly correlated with a decrease in depression, but not with a decrease in PTSD symptoms. Thus, the treatment seemed to address two independent issues—reducing dissociated memory and making meaning of the rape—and each of these was associated with a different area of improvement, reduction of PTSD and depressive symptoms, respectively. However, brief treatment did not necessarily result in a substantial decrease in the degree of fragmentation of the memory. Fragmentary recollection persisted throughout treatment, even when PTSD symptoms decreased. Consistent with this Foa et al. study, Tromp et al. (1995) found that their subjects' rape memories were still "less ordered" even two years after the rape experience.

While the Foa et al. study addressed the *organization of narrative memory for trauma* over time, Gold, Hughes, and Hohnecker (1994) addressed the *beliefs* that trauma victims hold about their trauma recollections. They found that:

> Many clients who enter treatment believing that they have full memory of the sexual abuse they experienced as children come to realize that their recollections are much more fragmentary than they originally thought. (p. 441)

As the patients recovered more details or new memories they modified their beliefs about their abuse recollections in the direction of seeing their previously held beliefs about their abuse as based on partial information. Roe and Schwartz (1996) noted that many women in their inpatient sample of incest survivors became more "sure" about their childhood sexual abuse as they recovered more narrative detail over time. Please note, however, that beliefs about recovered memories do not necessarily imply accuracy of the recovered memory.

The Accuracy of Recovered Trauma Memories

False memory proponents have generally assumed that recovered memories of childhood trauma are necessarily inaccurate, although they cite no research data directly in support of this hypothesis. D. Spiegel (1995) reminds us, "Memories in dissociative amnesia are not so much distorted as they are segregated one from another" (p. 134). Recent data-based research specifically designed to investigate the accuracy of recovered memories fails to support the false memory assumption that recovered memories are necessarily inaccurate.

As part of her 17-year prospective study, Williams (1995) specifically addressed the question of the accuracy of the sexual abuse memory after many years. A total of 75 of the 129 women recalled the details of the target sexual abuse during the follow-up interview 17 years after the abuse had occurred. Of these 75 women, 12 (16%, or 10% of the overall sample) reported a significant period of time when they had forgotten the abuse incident and then later recovered the memory. The study compared the characteristics and accuracy of sexual abuse memories in the continuous and recovered memory subsamples. Those in the recovered memory group, as compared to those with continuous memories, were younger at the time of the abuse and were less likely to have been subjected to physical force. Contrary to false memory claims of memory suggestion in therapy, "the women with recovered memories were somewhat *less* likely to have received any counseling" (p. 659). To evaluate the accuracy of the sexual abuse recollections, the 17-year follow-up interview was compared to the original medical record. Williams found:

> In general, the women with recovered memories had no more inconsistencies in their accounts than did the women who had always remembered (p. 660) . . . their retrospective reports were remarkably consistent with what had been reported in the 1970s (p. 662) . . . the stories were in large part true to the basic elements. (p. 670)

The only remarkable memory errors were minor detail errors and common memory dating errors. Many of the women could not accurately remem-ber the age at which the abuse occurred, nor could they report the age at which they had forgotten the abuse. Thus, Williams concludes:

> . . . this study does suggest that recovered memories of child sexual abuse reported by adults can be quite consistent with contemporaneous documentation of the abuse and should not be summarily dismissed by therapists, family members, judges or the women themselves. (p. 670)

The Williams (1995) study is important as the first data collected to test the false memory hypothesis that recovered memories of childhood sexual abuse are necessarily inaccurate.

While the Williams (1995) addresses the accuracy of recovered memory in general, Dalenberg (1995, 1996) has reported findings on the accuracy of trauma memories specifically recovered in psychotherapy. This study is important in that it is the only study to date to directly study memories for physical and sexual abuse specifically recovered in psychotherapy. The sample consisted of 17 women who had been in psychotherapy and who had completed their treatment. Patients were used as their own baseline. The sample of patients were selected only if they met strict criteria: (1) had always remembered some abuse incident from childhood (either physical or sexual abuse); (2) had recovered a "substantial percentage" of new abuse memories in the course of their treatment; (3) were not involved in the self-help abuse movement; and (4) did not have family members involved in the False Memory Syndrome Foundation. These latter two criteria were included to rule out contaminating influences. Memories of all patients were divided into two categories: (1) continuous memories for abuse, which may or may not have included the recovery of additional details over the course of treatment; and (2) recovered memories, which were defined in terms of the recovery of completely new episodes of abuse of which the patient had no prior awareness and which often entailed information about new events or new perpetrators. A unique feature of this study is its intra-subject design, wherein the accuracy of continuous and recovered memory units were compared within the same subject(s). Dalenberg argues that such a design is well suited to the false memory debate, in that recovered memories are compared to the general childhood autobiographical memory of the same individual to assess their accuracy.

The accuracy of both the recovered memories (RM) and continuous memories (CM) were assessed by two methods. First, the incest survivors who had recovered memories and the alleged perpetrators participated in a collaborative evidence gathering procedure. Physical evidence of the abuse was collected and family members were interviewed. Evidence was divided into two categories: (1) primary evidence pertaining to the alleged abusive acts per se; and (2) contextual evidence, such as where and when the event in question took place. All memory units were viewed as "potentially verifiable facts." They were rated according to their perceived truth value along a five-point scale, from very convincing facts that speak for themselves, to reasonable certainty about the evidence, etc.

Second, a team of six independent raters evaluated the overall evidence for each memory unit, much as a jury decides about the totality of the evidence at hand. About 60% of the abuse memories could be confirmed across the sample of therapy patients and about 75% of the RM and CM were judged by the raters as either very convincing or reasonably certain. In other words, the gist of both continuous and recovered memories of abuse in this study was generally accurate. More importantly, there were no significant differences in the accuracy ratings between continuous and recovered memories of abuse. Dalenberg (1996) says, "false memories in the absolute sense, and inaccurate memories in the absolute sense, were almost non-existent."

Contrary to false memory claims, *memories of abuse recovered in psychotherapy were no more or less accurate than memories of abuse that had always been remembered and at least the gist of abuse memories recovered in psychotherapy in many instances was highly accurate.* The false memory hypothesis that abuse memories recovered in psychotherapy must necessarily be inaccurate and must be the product of therapeutic suggestion was not supported by the study. The overall accuracy rate of both continuous and recovered memories of abuse was quite high (over 70%). This high accuracy rate is consistent with accuracy rates of events of impact, as we learned in chapter 6. Moreover, contrary to false memory claims, just about half of the patient sample

significantly *improved their accuracy* for their abuse memories in the course of psychotherapy. Source misattribution errors, however, were common. That is, after completing therapy some patients confused which abuse memories were continuous and which were recovered in the treatment.

The Dalenberg (1996) study also investigated predictors of accurate and inaccurate abuse memories in psychotherapy. Accuracy of memory for what occurred in previous psychotherapy sessions (irrespective of abuse) proved to be a strong predictor of accuracy of recovered memories for abuse. In other words, those patients who have more accurate recall of what transpired in recent therapy sessions are more likely to recover more accurate abuse memories than those who are less certain about what happens in treatment sessions. Memories recovered in the last six months of therapy were significantly more accurate than memories recovered early in treatment. Moreover, memories that were recovered following transference interpretations of therapeutic ruptures and alliance repairs were significantly more accurate than memories recovered under any other conditions during treatment. This study is consistent with good psychodynamic technique, namely, that free recall over the course of treatment and careful attention to the transference, in the absence of suggestive interviewing, leads to reasonably accurate recovered memories at least for the gist of abuse episodes for the majority of the patients sampled, even though both continuous and recovered memories contained inaccurate details and even though certain abuse memories in certain patients were quite inaccurate. For example, patients with memory-vulnerable diagnoses, like borderline personality disorder, represented the low accurate subsample of the overall group studied.

A number of clinical studies have also appeared that have attempted to externally corroborate child abuse reports of adult patients with dissociative identity disorder. Responding to Frankel's (1993) criticism that many reports of abuse in patients with multiple personality disorder lack independent corroboration, Coons and Milstein (1986; Coons, 1994a) reported an attempt to seek external corroborative evidence through a retrospective chart review of 31 child and adolescent patients, 19 of whom met the diagnosis of multiple personality disorder (MPD) or dissociative disorder not otherwise specified (DDNOS). Abuse reports had been confirmed in 18 of the 19 cases diagnosed with a major dissociative identity disorder, either by means child abuse investigations or witnesses to the abuse. Martinez-Taboas (1991, 1996) reported 18 DID cases in Puerto Rico for which some sort of corroboration could be found for the recovered memories of abuse. Corroboration was obtained from family members or from forensic or medical records.

Kluft (1997) conducted a "naturalistic pilot study" on 34 patients (32 females, 2 males) all of whom met the *DSM-IV* diagnostic criteria for dissociative identity disorder. They had been in treatment an average of 5.5 years. He reviewed the charts for evidence that might corroborate the patients' abuse reports. Kluft noted that the longer the patient remained in treatment, the greater the likelihood that the patient would give evidence that would confirm the abuse report. He found:

> Most of the patients made many allegations that could neither be proven nor disproven with the available data, and some made allegations that were not very likely to be accurate. (p. 33)

However, the abuse reports could be confirmed for 56% of the patients, i.e., 19 of the 34 patients. Of these 19 who had confirmed memories, 10 (53%) retained a continuous memory for the abuse, as compared to 9 (47%) who had not recalled the abuse prior to the treatment. Another 9% made reports that had been disproven by corroborative evidence. Recanting was not included in the disconfirmation category, nor was denial by the alleged abuser. It is noteworthy that several of the genuinely disconfirmed abuse reports were made by patients who also had confirmed instances of abuse. In other words, the abuse reports of at least some DID patients contain a mixture of accurate and inaccurate recollections. It was also notable that "in all cases but two the first discovery of all these incidents in therapy occurred in connection with the use of hypnosis" (p. 35). The hypnosis was "used gently without the exertion of undue influence" (p. 41) and memory recovery was based on the "principle of informed uncertainty." Kluft concludes:

> These findings seem to indicate, in contradistinction to the position taken by numerous extreme

proponents of the false memory perspective, that memory of genuine trauma can be absent from awareness for protracted periods of time, and then recovered, and that genuine trauma can be documented in the childhoods and adulthoods of many adults with DID. Furthermore, they cast doubt on the argument that materials emerging from hypnotic exploration should be discounted in a peremptory manner. (p. 35)

Kluft qualifies the findings by adding that "The memories that were either confirmed or disconfirmed represent a fraction of all of the memories reported and recovered in these patients' treatments" (p. 35). Moreover, even where specific instances of reported abuse could be corroborated, most of the abuse recollections of these DID patients contained both accurate and inaccurate information. The study, however, "demonstrates that the phenomenon of recovered memory is a clinical reality" (p. 38).

A Summary of the Studies on Amnesia for CSA

There are now 30 studies specifically on amnesia for CSA, if we include in the Goodman et al. (1995) survey on repression of ritual abuse memories reported in chapter 2 and the Burgess et al. prospective study on amnesia for childhood abuse to be reviewed later in this chapter. In a recent critical review of the evidence on amnesia for CSA, Pope and Hudson (1995a,b), advocates of the false memory position, have taken a skeptical view of the available evidence. Because of methodological weaknesses in many of these studies, Pope and Hudson (1995a) say, "present evidence is insufficient to permit the conclusion that individuals can 'repress' memories of childhood sexual abuse" (p. 14). Kihlstrom (1995), likewise, says, "With respect to the question of amnesia for childhood trauma, the evidence is even more scanty, and even more ambiguous" (p. 64). Their conclusions, we believe, are unwarranted. First, it should be noted that Pope and Hudson's review failed to cite a sizeable number of these 30 studies. Second, they have attempted to apply unusually stringent methodological criteria to these studies. Their criteria are: (1) adequate documentation that the abuse actually occurred; (2) exclusion of cases where the victim failed to report for reasons other than amnesia, e.g., remembering but not wanting to talk about the abuse; and (3) exclusion of biological reasons for the amnesia.

We interpret these data differently. Granted that most scientific studies can be criticized for methodological weaknesses, such design limitations should not obscure the fact that the data reported in *every* one of the 30 studies demonstrate that either partial or full abuse specific amnesia, either for single incidents of childhood sexual abuse or across multiple incidents of CSA, is a robust finding. The consistent finding across all 30 studies simply cannot be dismissed. Not a single study, including three important prospective studies, failed to find amnesia for CSA in at least a portion of the sampled individuals. Partial or full amnesia for CSA was found across studies regardless of whether the sample was a clinical or nonclinical sample, a nonrandom or random sample, or a prospective study.

In our opinion, these studies meet the true test of science, namely that the finding holds up across quite a number of independent experiments, each with different samples, each assessing the target variables in a variety of different ways, and each arriving at a similar conclusion (Dawes, 1994). When multiple samples and multiple sampling methods are used, the error rate across studies is reduced. Even where a small portion of these cases of reported amnesia may be associated with abuse that may not have occurred or at least could not be substantiated, the great preponderance of the evidence strongly suggests that at least some subpopulation of sexually abused survivors experience a period of full or partial amnesia for the abuse. Moreover, for a good portion of these amnestic subjects some sort of corroboration of the abuse was available. The percent of subjects for whom corroborative evidence existed ranged from 34% (physical corroboration in Williams, 1994a), 47% (Feldman-Summers & Pope, 1994), and 74% (Herman & Schatzow, 1987) to 100% (Widom & Morris, 1997). Dawes (1994) argues, however, that the type of corroborative evidence sought in at least some of these studies does not constitute an adequate determination of accuracy (pp. 172, 177).

These 30 studies illustrate how scientific inquiry evolves, in the best sense. The earliest clinical surveys were appropriately criticized on the grounds of possible sample and experimenter bias. Perhaps those reporting amnesia for CSA represented a highly select group of patients. Perhaps their report of recovered memories was influenced, even "implanted," by the therapist-experimenters. Then nonclinical samples began to appear in the literature as a way to address the sample bias problem. A number of the subsequent studies clearly demonstrated that psychotherapy was *not* frequently endorsed as the reason for recovery of the CSA memory. Then the nonclinical samples were criticized on the grounds of possible selection bias. However, a number of random sample studies began to appear in the literature that appropriately addressed this objection. Finally, all of the self-report studies were criticized because they lacked objective verification of the reported childhood sexual abuse. In response to this criticism well designed prospective studies began to appear in the literature. These studies (Widom & Morris, 1997; Williams, 1994a, 1995) document an inability to recall a critical childhood sexual abuse incident up to one or two decades after the event in a subpopulation of sexually abused individuals. These prospective studies were criticized for the failure to include a follow-up interview to distinguish between memory failure and denial. However, these criticisms failed to take into consideration that such an interview could not easily be conducted without introducing response bias and other possible expectation and suggestive effects. Both the Williams and Widom and Morris studies specifically attempted to reduce interviewing bias and approximate the conditions of free recall in the research design.

Overall, we believe that the 30 studies represent effective scientific inquiry. Whenever objections have been raised to certain of the available studies, others have appeared that have addressed these problems, and yet amnesia for CSA has been repeatedly demonstrated. At what point do we say that amnesia for CSA has met the test of science? It depends on what level of evidence the reader finds acceptable. Our own opinion is that the Pope and Hudson conclusion that the "present evidence is insufficient" is overly cautious and ultimately nihilistic. A more reasonable position is that the great preponderance of the evidence across all 30 studies demonstrates that amnesia for CSA is a robust finding. Given the intensity of the debate about "repressed memories," the absence of even a single study among the available 30 studies documenting no amnesia for CSA in a sampled group is remarkable finding in science.

Table 7.7 summarizes the data across studies on the base rate of amnesia. Full amnesia was reported to range from 4.5% to 68%. The average rate of full amnesia was 29.6% and most studies cluster within 10% of this figure (except the studies specifically on dissociative identity disorder or ritual abuse). The studies report partial amnesia ranging from 12% to 40%, and combined full or partial

TABLE 7.7
Amnesia for Childhood Sexual Abuse

SOURCE	N=	FA	PA	C	NA	IC	Rx	C/NC	R/NR	SAMPLE:
CLINICAL STUDIES:										
Herman & Schatzow, 1987	53	28	36	64	36	74	100	c	nr	outpatient rx
Draijer, 1990	1,054			57						national survey
Ensink, 1992	100	29	28	57	43		100	c	nr	incest & Rx groups (high DID)
Albach et al., in press	97e			35	65		100	c	nr	women with hx of CSA
	65c			1	99					normal controls
Cameron, 1994	60	42	23	65	35		100	c	nr	women in rx with hx of CSA
Loftus, Polansky et al., 1994	105	19	12	31	69			c	nr	women in drug tx
Roe & Schwartz, 1996	52			77	23	44	68	c	nr	women in inpatient tx
							32			
Pomerantz, in progress	26	50	425	97.5	7.5			c	nr	women in outpatient tx
Gold et al., 1994	105	30	40	70	30			c	nr	intake interview in rx
NONCLINICAL SAMPLES:										
Bernet et al., 1993	624	36			64		30	nc	nr	college undergraduates
Belicki et al., 1994	68			55	45			nc	nr	college undergraduates
Kristiansen et al., 1995	113	25	26	51	49	61	93	nc	nr	community sample, women
Elliott & Fox, 1994	484	30	14	44	56		19	nc	nr	college undergraduates
van der Kolk & Fisler, 1995	36			42	58	75		nc	nr	volunteers, terrible life experiences
Roesler & Wind, 1994	228	28			72					triggered by M. von Durber disclosure
Grassian & Holtzen, 1996	42	19	28	47	53			nc	nr	triggered by Fa. Porter disclosure
Golding et al., 1996	613	13						nc	nr	college undergraduates
RANDOM SAMPLES:										
Briere & Conte, 1993	450			59	41			c	r	in tx for CSA
Feldman-Summers & Pope, 1994	330			40	60	47	56	nc	r	psychologists
Westerhof et al., in press	500	22	17	39	61	69	68	nc	r	psychologists
Fish & Scott, in press	423	17	38	55	45		44	nc	r	counselors

TABLE 7.7 (CONTINUED)
Amnesia for Childhood Sexual Abuse

SOURCE	N=	FA	PA	C	NA	IC	RX	C/NC	R/NR	SAMPLE:
Elliott & Briere, 1995	505	20	22	42	58		7 13	nc	r	general population
Polusny & Follette, 1996	223	5m 3f		30 39	70 61			nc	r	psychologists
Melchert, 1996	553	18			82			nc	r	college undergraduates
Golding, 1995	663	14						nc	r	telephone survey
PROSPECTIVE STUDIES:										
Williams, 1994a	129	38			62	100	0	nc	nr	women with clinic documentation of CSA
Widom & Morris, 1997	1,114	37			63	100		nc	nr	court substantiated CSA
Burgess et al. 1995	22	14	27	41	59	100	0	c	nr	daycare CSA
OTHER STUDIES:										
Kluft, 1997	19	68			32	100	100	c	nr	DID pts in tx; confirmed abuse
Goodman et al., 1995	1,652	4.5	45	50	50			c	nr	ritual abuse allegations

KEY:

N = sample size
FA = full amnesia/no memory for a significant period of time
PA = partial amnesia
C = combined percentage of full and partial amnesia
NA = no amnesia; continuous memory
IC = percentage of sample for which some sort of independent corroboration existed
Rx = percentage of sample where memory recovery

was associated with (but not necessarily caused by) therapy; percentage of sample where memory initally recovered in therapy
c/nc = clinical vs. nonclinical sample
r/nr = random vs. nonrandom sampling
Rx = therapy;
tx = treatment;
e = experimental group,
c = control group
csa = childhood sexual abuse
DID = dissociative identity disorder

amnesia ranging from 31% to 77%. The average rate combining full and partial amnesia was 51% across studies. Generally speaking, approximately a third of sexually abused victims report some period of their lives where they did not remember anything about the abuse and later recovered the memory of the abuse. While Loftus and her associates remain skeptical (Loftus, Gary et al. 1994), their own survey data are consistent with all other evidence for full amnesia for CSA, although their base rate (19%) is generally lower than the base rates of other surveys.

Data on predictors of amnesia for CSA are less clear-cut. Table 7.6 summarizes the data on predic-

tors of CSA across studies. Although there are exceptions, age of onset, types of abuse, duration/repetition of the abuse, closeness of the relationship between victim and perpetrator, and degree of violence have emerged in a number of these surveys as predictors of amnesia under at least certain situations. Certain personality factors, such as level of intelligence and dissociative capacity, also appear to play a role in amnesia for CSA under certain, but not all, circumstances. More work needs to be done around peritraumatic amnesia and childhood sexual abuse, since peritraumatic amnesia has consistently turned out to be a strong predictor of chronic PTSD for other types of trauma.

To summarize the findings about predictors of amnesia for CSA across studies, it appears that the development of amnesia following sexual abuse in childhood is probably due to a complex interaction of a number of variables: age of onset (greater amnesia if younger); duration, severity, and type of sexual abuse; the nature of the attachment relationship to the perpetrator(s); the degree of dissociation; and the nature of the cognitive appraisal of the abusive event(s). Whereas the findings on violence as a predictor per se seem somewhat inconsistent, violence may interact with duration of abuse. Early in the abuse cycle violence may be associated with amnesia. However, it is well documented that ongoing and repeated abuse results in adaptation to the abuse in the form of active coping and sometimes direct participation in the abuse, which may mitigate the effects of violence (Summit, 1983). Later in the abuse cycle, consent, however conflictual it may be experienced as, may be a stronger predictor of amnesia than violence or force per se (e.g., Albach et al., in press).

These data suggest that a significant subpopulation of childhood sexual abuse survivors are partially or fully amnestic for the abuse, at least for some period of their lives. Yet we should not forget the other subpopulation who always and completely remembers the abuse. The base rate of the *continuous memory subsample* ranges from 23% to 72% and averages 50% across studies. Overall, these data are consistent with the *biphasic stress response model* (Horowitz & Reidbord, 1992), which predicts two forms of posttraumatic adjustment to traumatization with respect to narrative memory—amnesia and hypermnesia, respectively. We should note, however, that both amnesia and hypermnesia refer to the *relative incompleteness or completeness* of the memory, not to its *accuracy or inaccuracy*. One reasonable hypothesis based on the available data is that memory for genuinely traumatic experiences (those that produce PTSS or PTSD) is bimodally distributed across subjects, with about half the sample retaining a relatively complete, continuous memory for the incident, and the other half of the sample being partially or fully amnestic for the incident(s) for at least some period of their lives. The average rate of full amnesia runs lower, generally under a third of the sample across studies.

Unfortunately, with the exception of the available corroborative data in some of these studies, and several very recent studies of the accuracy of recovered memories, we still do not have a lot of data about the accuracy or inaccuracy of the memories in either the amnestic or hypermnesic group. Yet the available data do not support the false memory claim that recovered memories of sexual abuse are necessarily inaccurate. When research has been conducted specifically on the issue of accuracy of recovered memories, the findings have consistently supported the view that the gist of recovered memories is generally accurate.

Furthermore, it is premature to make general statements about the mechanisms involved in amnesia—e.g., repression, dissociation, denial, or normal forgetting. We can say with some degree of certainty that amnesia for trauma is a robust finding in at least a significant subsample of traumatized individuals. While the base rates vary considerably across studies, a great deal of this variation is attributable to the failure to distinguish either between full and partial amnesia or between severity levels of the current symptoms, with less severity associated with lower rates (Loftus, Polonsky et al., 1994) and greater severity associated with higher rates (Elliott & Fox, 1994; Ensink, 1992; Roe & Schwartz, 1996).

These data on amnesia for CSA are consistent with the data on amnesia for victims and perpetrators of violent crimes in that both delineate amnesia largely limited to the specific traumatic incident(s). A more general functional amnesia for autobiographical memory has sometimes been reported in CSA victims (Ensink, 1992; Vardi, 1994), much like the general impairment of autobiographical memory that has been reported in patients with dissociative disorders, who sometimes have a "profound deficit" in memory for childhood events (Kihlstrom & Schacter, 1995). However, the current data from these CSA surveys implies that a general impairment of autobiographical memory may be more the exception than the rule in CSA victims, except in those suffering from a major dissociative disorder. It should be noted, however, that survey questionnaires may not be adequate instruments to measure general amnestic effects and may bias the data toward finding limited rather than general retrograde amnesia. Moreover, irrespective of whether the amnesia is limited to the sexual abuse or extends to other areas of childhood, amnesia for CSA pertains primarily to explicit, not implicit, memory. In other words, dissociated memory still exerts an implicit influence on the person (Kihlstrom & Schacter, 1995; Loewenstein, 1997).

These studies often focus the inquiry very narrowly on a single incident of crime or sexual abuse, so we do not have extensive data available on memory for abuse repeated over major developmental phases. Are memories for repeated abuse stored like memories for single incidents of abuse? Is each specific abuse episode stored independently or in the form of a generic or episodic memory? We simply do not know.

Additional data derived from studies of patients with organic as well as functional amnesia are consistent with documentation of one of two kinds of memory deficits subsequent to traumatization—either general retrograde or trauma-specific amnesia. Baddeley and Wilson (1979) have shown that some organic retrograde amnestic patients typically have well preserved autobiographical memory (e.g., Korsakoff patients), while others show marked deficits in memory for autobiographical events and public knowledge (frontal lobe patients). Treadway, McCloskey, Gordon, and Cohen (1992) discussed two cases in detail, one patient with significant deficits in autobiographical memory and one with additional deficits in memory for world knowledge. They believe that deficits in memory for public and personal information illustrate the nature of memory organization. They hypothesize that personal memory is organized around landmark life events. There may be a number of independent constellations of memories, each organized around and tagged by separate and salient landmark life events or sequences of events closely related in time. They point out that functional amnesia nearly always follows a landmark life event, i.e., an event (s) that significantly alters the quality and course of the individual's subsequent life. Presumably, sexual abuse by a trusted family member is the kind of event that drastically alters the course of one's life history and therefore constitutes a landmark life event. Thus, autobiographical information and knowledge for public events concurrent with the abuse are organized as part of the same constellation. Consequently, it is not surprising to find deficits in general

autobiographical memory and/or memory for public events accompanying amnesia for sexual abuse. The weakness in this theory, however, is that it fails to explain why impulsively killing someone close, which is presumably a landmark event, is not typically accompanied by general amnesia but simply by amnesia largely limited to the crime itself.

CONCLUSIONS DRAWN FROM STUDIES OF TRAUMATIC MEMORY IN ADULTS

While the research data on memory performance in traumatized populations are too sparse to warrant definitive conclusions, consistent patterns emerge across the extant studies:

1. Traumatizing events differ from events of impact by the *occurrence of posttraumatic stress symptoms*. Recovery of a traumatic memory is typically accompanied by posttraumatic, dissociative, and/or depressive symptoms.

2. The data on *completeness* of memory for trauma suggest a bimodal distribution, with a larger sample who always remember the trauma, often vividly and accompanied by intrusive reexperiencing symptoms, and a smaller sample who are amnestic for the trauma for some period of their lives and may or may not later recover the memory. The data on full or partial amnesia for trauma are robust across all of the studies on different types of trauma, and false memory claims that repression of trauma is a "myth" (Loftus & Ketcham, 1994) are an oversimplification and distortion of the scientific data on amnesia for trauma. Traumatic amnesia is a common occurrence in a subsample of traumatized individuals for most types of trauma, including childhood sexual abuse. If *DSM-IV* is taken as an example of the general acceptance of traumatic amnesia within the mental health community, then the section in *DSM-IV* on dissociative amnesia is a good summary of our current understanding:

> A. The predominant disturbance is one or more episodes of inability to recall important personal information, usually of a traumatic or stressful nature, that is too extensive to be explained by ordinary forgetfulness. (APA, 1994, p. 481)

3. The subsample of traumatized individuals who are amnestic for the trauma can be differentiated into those who are *fully or partially amnestic* for specific traumatizing event(s) versus those whose amnesia also encompasses personal autobiographical memory or memory for socially shared events. The difference between *trauma-specific amnesia* and *general functional retrograde amnesia* subsequent to traumatization may in part be determined by the type of traumatization, with limited amnesia being more characteristic of single-incident trauma and general amnesia more common of multiple or cumulative trauma. We could also speak of *injury-specific amnesia* in that several studies suggest selective amnesia for significant bodily injuries (Dollinger, 1985; Kuehn, 1974; McFarlane, 1988; Wagenaar & Groeneweg, 1990).

4. There are few data available on whether traumatic memories are stored in the form of *specific or generic memories* for cumulative abuse experiences. Studies on the development of memory in normal children would suggest that cumulative traumatic experiences may be stored more often in the form of generic memories across traumatic experiences, rather than in the form of memories for single traumatic experiences.

5. Functional, psychogenic, and organic amnesia sometimes overlap, especially where the traumatization involved injury or intoxication.

6. When failure to remember a traumatic event and later remembering is reported, it is difficult to distinguish genuine traumatic *amnesia* from *denial* (i.e., remembering the event and not wanting to think about or talk about it).

7. The *predictors* of amnesia subsequent to traumatization represent a complex interaction of a number of variables, some of which have been identified: biological (intoxication, injury), cognitive (age of onset, level of understanding of the event, intelligence), affective (coping ability and degree of mastery), duration, number of perpetrators, injury and threat to life, and relationship to the perpetrator. Predictors of traumatic amnesia represent a complex interaction of multiple factors. No data are available on predictors of continuous memory for a traumatic experience.

8. There is no consensus on the *mechanisms* by which trauma-specific amnesia occurs. The hypotheses include: repression, dissociation, betrayal of attachment, state-dependent retrieval failure, and normal forgetting. The most frequently endorsed mechanism, however, appears to be dissociative amnesia. This is the term that is endorsed by *DSM-IV*.

9. *Recovery of memories* for trauma in those who are amnestic occurs through expectable retrieval strategies such as free recall, context reinstatement (Fisher & Geiselman, 1992), or reinstatement of emotional arousal (Schacter, 1986). Recovery of trauma memories occurs much more frequently spontaneously, when the individual encounters stimuli that remind the individual of the trauma and trigger the memory, and when the individual finds a safe context. Recovery of CSA memories occurs much less frequently inside, as compared to outside, psychotherapy.

10. Hypermnesia and amnesia for the trauma pertain to the relative completeness or incompleteness of the memory and have little to do with its *accuracy*. Accuracy and completeness are independent constructs. Terms like memory fallibility simply confuse the distinction and falsely imply that incompleteness means inaccuracy. There are few data available to support the view that individuals who are amnestic for the trauma and later recover their memories are any less accurate in their memory, at least for the gist of the traumatizing event, than those who have a continuous memory for the trauma. The available data imply that, irrespective of completeness/incompleteness, memory for traumatic experience is generally quite accurate for the gist of the traumatic experience, but that accuracy for less salient details is highly variable over time, as is also true for flashbulb memory, autobiographical memory, and memory for events of impact. The recent studies that specifically address the accuracy of recovered memories both outside of (Williams, 1995) and within (Dalenberg, 1996; Kluft, 1997) psychotherapy suggest that *memory recovery per se is not necessarily associated with inaccuracy of the traumatic memory.* This conclusion is generally consistent with Brewin et al.'s findings (1993) regarding the accuracy of retrospective self-reports of childhood experiences.

11. Nearly all of the available data on the completeness and accuracy of memory for trauma is limited to one category of memory, namely, verbal autobiographical memory. Clinical, developmental,

and neurobiological studies document the existence of a *behavioral or implicit memory for trauma*, which may be the primary memory system in which traumatic experiences are encoded and stored (van der Kolk, 1989).

12. A significant subpopulation of traumatized individuals retain no or little narrative memory for the trauma. When the trauma recollection is recovered, it is often initially recovered in a somato-sensory, imagistic, and affective form. *The initial narrative memory is often fragmented, incomplete, and overly general.* Over time a more organized form of the narrative memory is likely to be reported, although fragmented or dissociated aspects of the trauma memory may persist.

13. There has been little research on how "different traumas may impact on memory differently" (Alpert, 1995c, p. 126).

TRAUMATIC MEMORY IN CHILDREN

The Development of Memory in Children

In order to understand memory for trauma in children, it is necessary to understand it in the context of the development of memory in children. In a landmark monograph, *Childhood Events Recalled by Children and Adults*, Pillemer and White (1989) review all of the available research data on the development of personal autobiographical memory in children and adults and synthesize the data into a general model of memory development. They make a convincing case for the existence of two parallel and "functionally separate" memory systems (p. 326). The first system to develop organizes memory for salient naturally occurring events of early childhood in terms of images, emotions, and behaviors. This *behavioral memory system* is predominant up to about three years of age.

Empirical support for a behavioral memory system comes from extensive studies conducted by Fivush and others on event memory in preschoolers (Fivush & Hammond, 1989; Gray & Fivush, 1987; Smith, Ratner, & Hobart, 1987). In these studies, young children, typically two to three years of age, play with toys in the laboratory. After some reten-

tion interval (e.g., one to three months), the children return to the laboratory playroom for a memory testing session. They are given the same toys and are then told to do the same thing they did with the toys last time. In other words, the children reenact their memory for the sequence of play events in their behavior. The consistent finding across these studies is that two- to three-year-old children preserve a relatively stable behavioral memory for salient and novel play sequences. This behavioral memory has its own internal organization and, while errors occur, the behavioral memory generally preserves a high level of accuracy.

A second narrative personal memory system develops in later childhood. A "developmental shift" occurs starting roughly around three years of age, following the acquisition of language. As cognitive development matures, a new memory organization develops—what Pillemer and White call a logical filing system. Concurrent with cognitive maturation there is increased organization of the self system. The outcome of the changes between the ages of three and five is the development of an autonomous personal memory system. Between the ages of five and six a further reorganization takes place within the personal memory system concurrent with socialization. As the child gains skill in social communication, s/he learns that the personal memory system becomes the medium of social exchange. According to Pillemer and White (1989) such "socially shared remembering" of the past becomes the foundation of autobiographical memory. They call this personal memory system the "socially accessible memory system."

Pillemer and White contend that childhood amnesia is not so much a function of repression as it is the natural outcome of developmental trends, specifically increased reliance on the narrative autobiographical memory. Both the behavioral memory and the socially accessible autobiographical system remain active into adulthood; however, since each system is functionally autonomous, the private, idiosyncratic content of the behavioral memory system is not voluntarily available to the adult in the form of a narrative memory. The implication of this theory is that most experiences of early childhood, as well as some experiences of later childhood and adulthood, are stored both as behavioral memory and as narrative autobiographical memory. It is at least conceivable that all memory is stored in both the behavioral memory and the verbal memory systems.

The Behavioral Memory System and Memory for Trauma in Children

The behavioral memory system may play a critical role in memory for traumatic events in both children and adults. Within the clinical field and completely independent of the research supporting the concept of behavioral memory in normal children, Lenore Terr developed a similar idea about behavioral memory for traumatic experiences. Most of the early work derived from a prospective study of 23 school-aged children on a school bus in Chowchilla, California, who were kidnapped and buried alive for 16 hours. They were studied immediately after the incident (Terr, 1979), in a follow-up study five to thirteen months later (Terr, 1981) and then again four to five years later (Terr, 1983a), while being compared to a control group of normal children matched for developmental age (Terr, 1983b).

Many of the initial symptoms associated with the traumatic event could be observed in the children's narrative about the incident. Most of the children reported an intense fear of future traumas and were hypervigilant for signs or "omens" of future bad things happening. While all of the children were old enough to report the trauma in narrative terms, Terr observed that the traumatic effects of the incident were much more apparent in their play sequences, or "*posttraumatic play*." Even older children preserved their memory for the extreme trauma in the form of readily observable behavioral reenactments, as well as in their narrative reports. With respect to the accuracy of their narrative memory for the trauma, Terr noted that about two-thirds of the children remembered the event completely accurately, including the kidnapping of the bus, being buried inside of a mountain, and having to dig themselves out. However, about one-third of the children, while remembering the gist of the event accurately, reported details of the event in the wrong sequence and misidentified the physical characteristics of the perpetrators. In this sense, Terr's findings about narrative memory for trauma in her sample of children is consistent with the findings of the laboratory research on memory for emotional events, in that the

gist of the action is accurately retained but peripheral details and descriptive details of people are less accurately retained.

Terr's main finding (1981, 1983a, 1988, 1994), however, was that over time the lasting effects of the trauma were observable more as a behavioral memory than as a narrative memory. As a behavioral memory, the effects were observable in the forms of reenacted behaviors, in imagery, and in affective states. In their spontaneous posttraumatic play the children monotonously repeated the same play sequences about the kidnapping and being buried, without resolution and without symptom relief. In their spontaneous behavior they reenacted themes of being kidnapped. These same trauma-related themes were apparent in their fantasy productions and dreams for months and years after the incident. The children also reported trauma-related fears, e.g., an inability to feel safe in the world. Terr noted that *none* of her sample of children reported amnesia for the incident, although some of the memories were mere fragments of the entire incident. None of the children experienced flashbacks.

In subsequent works Terr refined her theory of traumatic memories in children (1988, 1996) and adults (1994). In an important clinical paper, "What Happens to Early Memories of Trauma?", Terr (1988) conducted a chart review of 20 children who had suffered some major psychological trauma before age five. The type of trauma included sexual abuse, kidnapping, and serious accidents. From careful clinical observation she was able to identify two types of memory for trauma, depending on age of traumatization. First, children who were traumatized prior to 28–36 months of age subsequently manifested their memory for the trauma primarily as a behavioral memory. Nine of the eleven children in this age group, and 18 of 20 of all the children overall, manifested a clear behavioral memory for the trauma, in the form of posttraumatic play, personality change characterized by frequent reenactments, and trauma-specific fears. Second, while some children who were traumatized after 28–36 months of age also manifested a behavioral memory for the trauma, they were able to report some sort of verbal memory for the trauma. A small number of younger children (two of 20) gave a full verbal recall of the incident, but this was more the exception than the rule. More information about the trauma was recalled for single-incident when compared to recurrent trauma, but type of trauma made no difference on what was or was not remembered.

To assess the accuracy of their memories, Terr compared the children's report to external documents about the trauma. Accuracy did not correlate with age, sex, or type of trauma. Fifteen of the children had sufficient verbal memory to assess accuracy. Ten (two-thirds) were quite accurate. The other five (one-third) retained accuracy for the gist of the trauma but were inaccurate for significant details of the event—memory was fragmented, omitted painful emotional details from consciousness, or the meaning of the event was reworked as the child got older. Terr concluded that there is a "general accuracy of early verbal memories of trauma despite individual tendencies to add or to delete from these memories over time" (1988, p. 103; cf. 1994).

Overall, Terr's work demonstrated that young children preserve memory for significant trauma primarily in terms of a behavioral memory and that even older children preserve their memory for trauma primarily as a behavioral memory event, though older children also show increasing development of a narrative autobiographical memory for the trauma. The prerequisite to verbal memory for trauma, according to Terr, is the development of organized speech phrases by the third year of life. Generally speaking, a child's memory for trauma is accurate, at least for the gist of the trauma. However, for some children, especially those who experience cumulative trauma or continuous trauma, the narrative memory "becomes less complete" over time (1994, p. 74).

In *Unchained Memories* (1994), written in response to the false memory controversy, Terr extends these same conclusions to adults. She presents a number of richly detailed case studies which demonstrate that adults also store trauma primarily in terms of a behavioral memory. Unlike her traumatized Chowchilla children, who "never forgot" or "never repressed" trauma (p. 11), adults sometimes are amnestic for trauma for a significant portion of their lives. Such amnesia for trauma is due to the nature of the trauma, as well as to the operation of psychological defenses like repression, dissociation, splitting, and displacement.

Nevertheless, adults, like children, preserve a

reasonably accurate imprint of traumatic experience in the form of a behavioral memory of trauma. She says, "Memory does not go bad or vague just because it is repressed. And traumatic memories, in particular, do not deteriorate much at all" (p. 40). As examples of the persistence of a behavioral memory for trauma, Terr discusses the Eileen Franklin case about an adult who recovers a repressed memory of witnessing her father murder her childhood girlfriend and also molest her. Terr describes how the memory for the alleged murder and incest persisted over the years in the form of "trauma-specific behaviors" (p. 56), like the compulsion to take a child home if she found the child playing in the park alone, or in the form of promiscuity in adolescence. She describes another case of a man whose mother physically abused him and threw him in an irrigation ditch as a young child. A behavioral memory for the abuse persisted in the form of about 300 recurrent water dreams and fear of the water, even though the man was a scuba diver. According to Terr, a behavioral memory for trauma "established in childhood remains an important influence into adulthood" (p. 109) (cf. also van der Kolk, 1989).

Terr believes, however, that traumatic events can also manifest themselves in adulthood in the form of a verbal memory. Sometimes they persist in a disguised form. Terr discusses the case of a murder mystery novelist, James Ellroy. She sees the recurrent themes in his murder stories as disguised ways to work through his own mother's murder when he was a child. She discusses another case of an adult man whose brother was killed by a drunken driver when he was six years old. Bits and pieces of the memory started returning when the man had a boy of his own. Verbal autobiographical memory, according to Terr, is a way for an adult to transform a behavioral memory for trauma by telling the story.

In 1984 a sniper opened fire repeatedly on children playing in an elementary school playground in Los Angeles. A child and a passerby were killed and 13 other children were shot. Many additional rounds were fired onto the playground and through the windows and doors of the school. Children on the playground were pinned down and those in the school were trapped in the classroom. They hid under desks and in closets and feared that intruders would enter the school and shoot them. Some time later, armed police entered the school to counter the sniper fire. Several hours after the gunfire ceased the police found that the sniper, who had lost eight family members in the Jonestown Massacre, had killed himself.

Data on the children's response to the shooting were collected by an interdisciplinary crisis team. The children ranged in age from five to thirteen. The incidence of acute PTSD was assessed one month after the incident using the children's version of the PTSD Reaction Index (Pynoos et al., 1987). A total of 38% of the children had moderate or severe, 22% had mild, and 40% had no acute PTSD symptoms after the incident. Level of exposure was directly related to the severity of the acute PTSD symptoms. Those children on the playground and directly in the line of fire were significantly more likely to have severe, acute PTSD symptoms, those in the school building moderate PTSD symptoms, and those absent from school on that day no PTSD symptoms, respectively. While individual PTSD symptoms varied markedly across children, reexperiencing and numbing symptoms accounted for the greatest portion of the variance of the PTSD symptoms. Children who knew the child who was shot and killed had significantly more severe PTSD symptoms.

A follow-up study was done approximately one year after the incident, using the same Reaction Index, in order to assess predictors of chronic PTSD reactions in the children. While there was some drop-off in PTSD symptoms in all groups of children—those on the playground, in the school, and absent from school—74% of the children who were most exposed to the violence and witnessed a death (on the playground) continued to have significantly more severe persistent PTSD symptoms than the other groups of children (Nader et al., 1990).

A subsequent study specifically addressed children's memory for the sniper attack (Pynoos & Nader, 1989). About 10% of all the children were interviewed somewhere between six and 16 weeks after the incident. The children interviewed were representative of the three groups along a continuum of proximity to the violence—on the playground and in the direct line of fire, in the school building, or absent from school. Each child was asked to freely recall the incident; following that they were asked specific questions about the shooting. To account

for the fact that children store memory in a behavioral as well as a verbal form, children were also encouraged to draw and dramatize the sequence of events that occurred. The main finding was that children's memory reports varied with proximity to the violence. Pynoos and Nader write:

> In their initial recall, children directly exposed to the violence, as well as those who were less exposed, tended to alter their degree of life threat. The most endangered group reduced their life threat by (1) not mentioning their own injury, (2) increasing their distance from the deceased or injured persons, (3) not mentioning moments of direct danger, or (4) situating themselves in a safe location. The least threatened group, on the other hand, tended to increase their life threat by (1) bringing themselves closer to the danger, or (2) imagining the danger moving closer to them. (pp. 239–240)

In other words, memory distortions were a function of the operation of psychologically motivated defenses. Children directly exposed to injury or threat to life (those with the most severe PTSD symptoms) after the incident tended to minimize the danger to themselves, intensified their worry about the safety of siblings who attended the school, and exaggerated their own sense of efficacy in recollecting the incident (e.g., pride about finding a place to hide). Common memory errors included misestimating the proximity to the danger, failing to report injury to oneself or to another child, or misremembering the duration of time being pinned down. In other words, the memory distortions were largely a consequence of psychological needs, wishes, and fears.

Generally speaking, however, while memory distortion was found in all groups, the degree and type of distortion varied as a function of proximity to danger. More significant memory distortions were found in children who were in the school building than on the playground, and the most blatant memory errors were made by children who were absent from school during the incident. Absent children were susceptible to incorporating rumors (postevent information) into their recollection. One child, for example, was on vacation at the time but misremembered being on the way to school and hearing shots.

While memory distortions were found across groups, most children directly involved in the incident were quite accurate in their recall of central information about the incident, although not necessarily about peripheral details. Children on the playground correctly recalled crying for help. They vividly recalled the sight of other injured children, including the fatally injured child, with "all that blood coming out" (Pynoos & Nader, 1989, p. 239). Children in the school building during the shooting accurately recalled central details, like being in a safer place than the playground, hearing repeated gunfire, or seeing armed police. Misremembering central details was primarily seen in children who were absent from school and sometimes by children in the building. Accurate recall of central details was a function of the degree of participation in the event.

Memory for Trauma in Preschool Children and Infants

While Terr makes a compelling case that young children and even older children and adults retain memory for trauma primarily in the form of a behavioral memory for trauma, her findings can easily obscure the fact that some very young children, and certainly older children and adults, sometimes retain a detailed and accurate verbal memory for trauma. Terr's data (1988) largely support her hypothesis that children between the ages of 28 and 36 months retain primarily a behavioral memory for trauma, because they have not yet developed a highly organized verbal memory system. However, it should be noted that two of Terr's young children between 24 and 36 months of age retained a full and detailed verbal memory for their trauma.

Sugar (1992) criticizes Terr's work for its implication that toddlers are not able to verbalize their memory for traumatic events and primarily express the memory in some behavioral form. Sugar presents two case histories in which children were able to provide detailed and accurate verbal descriptions of serious accidents occurring prior to the age of 28 months some months after the trauma. He also presents a third case of an adult in psychoanalysis who was able to accurately recall the details of her mother's miscarriage when she was 18 months old. Sugar concludes that "children [toddlers] may have

some difficulty providing a smooth, coherent sequential narrative, but their recall of facts is considered accurate" (p. 248). While it is generally true that "the earlier the age of traumatization, the less likely the child will organize the memory into a narrative about the traumatic event," it is also true that there are important individual differences in time of onset of the organization of speech phrases and the cognitive development associated with autobiographical memory, so that it is conceivable that verbal memory for trauma occurring as early as 18 months is sometimes retained in an accurate narrative form and is accessible under certain conditions as a verbal autobiographical memory for the trauma.

Gisalson and Call (1982) studied three children between 20 and 36 months of age who had been traumatized by being severely bitten by dogs. Memory for the traumatic event was assessed when each of the children was around three years of age. All three children retained a behavioral memory for the dog bite incident and two of the children retained a clear, detailed, and accurate verbal memory for the incident months after it had occurred.

Howe, Courage, and Peterson (1994) report their findings on 25 children ranging from ages 18 to 66 months who were treated in the emergency room for broken bones or lacerations requiring stitches. Each child's memory was assessed later the same day of the injury in the child's home using free recall following by cued-recall memory inquiry. Each child's memory was reassessed at about six months after the injury. The results demonstrated that very young children (18 months) were unable to give a verbal memory for the injury, although most of these very young children manifested a behavioral memory for the traumatic event. Age was associated with recall in that older children recalled significantly more correct information than younger children. However, children as young as two and a half years of age and older children retained an accurate verbal memory for the gist of the traumatic event over a six-month retention interval, although the verbal memory was sometimes fragmentary, especially in the younger children. Memory for peripheral but not central details significantly declined over the six-month retention interval. Recall was extremely accurate for the gist of the event in both free and cued recall, but contained errors for peripheral details, especially in cued recall. There was no evidence of amnesia for the trauma in any of the children who were old enough to produce a verbal memory for the event. Howe et al. summarize the results as follows:

> these observations substantiate the general position that although peripheral details tend to diminish with time from the memories of abuse victims, the central information about what happened to them remains available. (p. 348)

The authors interpret these results in terms of the development of autobiographical memory, which is, according to their view, the outcome of two previous developments—language acquisition and the development of a sense of self, both of which occur within the 18–30-month range. Thus, younger children may retain a memory for a traumatic event in a behavioral memory form or fragmented verbal form, but are unable to manifest an organized verbal autobiographical memory for the event, whereas older children (24–30 months) are able to manifest both a behavioral and verbal autobiographical memory, at least for events of impact and traumatic events.

In *If Someone Speaks It Gets Lighter*, Share (1994) synthesizes data from a wide variety of sources to make the case that infants encode and can later recollect very early trauma from the first years and months of life, even birth trauma, although not typically in narrative form. She says:

> The contention of this book is that there now exists sufficient clinical case material, some of it previously reported and some of it reported for the first time here, to warrant the assumption that birth and infant experiences, and the emotional meaning of these experiences, are stored in the unconscious from the beginning of life. (pp. 7–8)

The weakness of the false memory position, according to Share, is that it is based on an erroneous assumption that memory is a "single entity" (p. 117). Share concedes Spence's position (1982) that verbal, narrative memory is largely constructed and that reconstruction of historically accurate truth about childhood experience in adults in psychoanalysis may be difficult. However, Share is unwilling to throw out the entire enterprise of historical reconstruction in psychoanalysis. She believes that the available scientific evidence (cf. Chamberlain, 1987) strongly favors the existence of a second memory system, a perceptual/behavioral memory system, which operates mainly at an unconscious level in infants:

> Those who feel that reconstruction from earliest life is possible are referring to reconstruction from a different type of memory experience than those who say reconstruction is impossible. Both types of memories exist in the mind. In fact, the narrative approach in psychoanalysis is particularly conducive to "memory image" or "verbal memory" data, whereas veridical reconstruction is more likely with "perceptual image" or "behavioral memory" data. The difficulties centered on "verbal memory" or "memory image" reconstruction would not, then, negate the possibility of "behavioral memory" or "perceptual image" reconstruction. (p. 143)

Infant memory is encoded and stored as an unconscious representation in both perceptual and behavioral memory systems. Memory for infant trauma is encoded accurately and indelibly:

> The research and clinical evidence presented here support two related findings in regard to memory of infant trauma: (1) memory for infant trauma can be stored veridically and can be indelible; and (2) infant trauma forms memory schemas . . . or "templates" through which future development is filtered. (p. 226)

She reviews three sources of data: (1) studies on REM sleep in utero; (2) work demonstrating the maturation of the amygdala circuits in the neonate; and (3) studies on learning and behavioral memory in infants as young as six months of age. From these data she concludes that neonates and very young infants have a variety of mental structures that allow for "the possibility of a mental recognition or registration and storage of early experience and therefore the capacity for its reconstruction in adult analysis" (p. 106). According to her model, infant trauma can be registered in very early infancy, even in utero. The infant memory schemas for trauma persist in the form of a "perceptual image" in dreams, and in the form of a "behavioral memory" in somatic symptoms, nonverbal behavior, and behavioral reenacments, which can become the focus of historical reconstruction in psychoanalysis decades later. In support of her argument, Share reviews a number of published case studies within the psychoanalytic literature, in which "very specific reconstructions of earliest trauma" (p. 144) were reported. The examples of early infant trauma include birth trauma, accidental weaning, medical trauma, and sexual molestation. In each case, a perceptual or behavioral memory for the trauma persisted implicitly and had a profound influence on later development, even when no narrative memory was available.

Amnesia for Trauma in Children

False memory advocates have based their criticism of claims of amnesia for CSA in adults in part on the failure to document amnesia for trauma in children. If claims of amnesia for CSA in adults are credible, then we ought to find data of the development of amnesia in children who were previously traumatized. The Terr and Howe et al. studies on single-incident trauma failed to find evidence in support of amnesia for trauma in childhood. However, the Chowchilla school bus kidnapping was a highly sensational event. The children were closely studied for years after the incident. Presumably, consistent focus on the event would mean repeated memory rehearsal that might offset forgetting the trauma or the development of amnesia in some of the traumatized children. The retention interval in the Howe et al. study was too short (six months) to draw conclusions about amnesia for the injuries over time. Some of the children in the Pynoos and Nader (1989) sniper study subsequently selectively "forgot" that they had been injured, but no child became amnestic for the sniper incident itself within the retention interval of the study.

A recent prospective study provides some of the missing data demonstrating the development of amnesia for trauma in children. Burgess, Hartman, and Baker (1995) studied three groups of sexually abused children over a five- to ten-year interval. The purpose of the study was "to follow the natural presentation over time of childhood traumatic memories in a sample of children" (p. 10). A total

of 34 "physically, psychologically, and sexually abused children" (p. 10) were studied. The children came from three groups. One group of ten children, all under age five, seven of whom had been under age two at the time of the abuse, had been ritually abused in a daycare center. Another group consisted of 11 children, all under age five and most under age three when they were abused by several offenders working at another daycare center. These first two groups of children were followed for ten years. The third group consisted of 13 children, mostly under five years of age at the time of the abuse. Abuse consisted by multiple incidents of sexual abuse by a mother, father, and adolescent son who ran a daycare center. This group of children was followed for about five years. In each group, "The abuse was validated through criminal proceedings in one case and civil settlements in all three cases" (p. 10). Moreover, forensic abuse criteria (see chapter 15) were used to validate the abuse allegations. These data are important in that they include victims from a documented and substantiated case of severe daycare ritual abuse (the "Presidio case"; cf. Ehrensaft, 1992).

A follow-up interview was conducted on 22 children and their parents either five or ten years after the abuse had occurred. A total of 13 of the children (59%) retained a relatively complete verbal memory for the abuse years after it had occurred. Three of the children (14%) had become fully amnestic for the abuse years later, even though their report (often detailed) of the abuse had been previously recorded through investigative interviews some years earlier, and even though it had been witnessed by others. Another six children (27%) had become partially amnestic for the previous abuse some years later.

Burgess et al. also studied other dimensions of memory than the verbal, narrative memory for the abuse. These included somatic, behavioral, and visual representations. Somatic complaints related to the abuse included persistent genital and anal pain, vaginal discharge, and bowel complaints that persisted years after the abuse. Parents reported that the great majority of the abused children engaged in behaviors that were clearly related to the abuse, such as posttraumatic play and other behavioral reenactments, years after it had occurred. Years after the abuse, the memory was retained in the form of vivid drawings transparently depicting abuse scenes. These somatic, behavioral, and visual memories persisted irrespective of whether or not the child retained a verbal, narrative memory for the abuse. Burgess et al. conclude that:

> much of the learning that strong experiences force on an individual fall into the area of procedural memory which is not available for retrieval via language, but may manifest itself in behavioral, nonverbal patterns (p. 14) . . . [while a] fragmented verbal memory of childhood sexual abuse [may persist] (p. 14). . . . It appears that different types of memory are split off at various times and, possibly, under various contextual conditions. . . . The dissociative states may represent a failure of the integration of these various levels of biological memory systems. (p. 15)

What is most striking about these prospective data on severe sexual abuse is that while the great majority of these children retained a behavioral memory for the trauma over a five- or ten-year period, a subsample became unable to fully or partially recollect a verbal, narrative memory for the abuse over the same interval, even though these children had been able to do so shortly after the abuse. This study, considered along with the Grassian and Holtzen (1996) study of alleged victims of Father Porter, suggests that amnesia following childhood trauma is delayed and probably does not occur until later childhood or early adolescence. These data imply that, while the narrative memory may become unavailable at least for some traumatized children by late adolescence, an implicit memory for the trauma clearly persists throughout childhood and beyond, as manifest in play and relational behavior.

Comparative Studies of Memory in Traumatized and Nontraumatized Children

The problem with the clinical research on behavioral memory for trauma in children is that most of this research lacks a comparison group against which to compare memory performance. Terr (1983b) attempted to correct for this problem by studying a sample of normal children in comparison with the survivors of the Chowchilla kidnapping. A few studies have been conducted on the use of sexually anatomically correct (SAC) dolls as a medium to study behavioral memory for trauma in abused and nonabused children. Unfortunately, the considerable controversy that surrounds the use of these dolls can easily obscure the importance of these studies: these are the *only* studies on comparative behavioral memory performance in abused and nonabused children that exist to date.

White, Strom, Santilli, and Halpin (1986) conducted a comparative study on 50 children, 25 of whom had been referred for suspected sexual abuse to the hospital. Another 25 normal control children were recruited. The children ranged from two to six years old. Parents and hospital staff independently rated each of the children suspected of abuse for the likelihood that sexual abuse had occurred. All children were interviewed, first with a 10-minute free play period and then with an interview that used the SCA dolls. Children in the suspected abuse group had significantly more sexualized doll play than the normal children, although some of the children with a high likelihood of abuse did not spontaneously provide a verbal account of the abuse in the structured doll interview. The normal children showed no unusual behaviors during the SAC interviews. While this study has been criticized because there is no way of knowing for sure whether the children in the group suspected of having been sexually abused had actually been abused (Yates & Terr, 1988), the study does demonstrate a clear differential response in the play reenactments of those suspected of sexual abuse and those not.

Shortly thereafter Jampole and Weber (1987) reported a similar study using 10 sexually abused and 10 control, non-abused children matched for age, sex, and race. The 10 children in the sexually abused group were chosen based on the outcome of a child sexual abuse investigation and the report of a parent that sufficient evidence was available to consider that sexual abuse had occurred. After a 10-minute free play period the children were given a structured interview with the SAC dolls. An observer blind to the children's abuse status observed the interview behind a one-way mirror. Ninety percent of the sexually abused children demonstrated highly sexualized behaviors with the SAC dolls, while only 20% of the control children did. Jampole and Weber conclude, "significantly more children who had been sexually abused demonstrated sexual behavior with the anatomically correct dolls than did the non-sexually abused group" (p. 192).

August and Forman (1989) reported their findings comparing the behaviors with SAC dolls in 16 girls referred for an evaluation and treatment of sexual abuse to 16 non-abused girls matched for age and race. All children interacted with an interviewer in a 15-minute free play period. Then the children were given the SAC dolls and the interviewer left the room for five minutes (alone condition). Following that, the interviewer returned and asked the child to tell a story about the dolls for three minutes (story-telling condition). All interviews were videotaped and shown to raters blind to which children were in the abused and non-abused groups. The children's play and stories were rated for the degree of aggression, avoidant behavior, and reference to private, sexual parts of the body. During the alone condition the children in the suspected abuse group demonstrated significantly more aggression and reference to private parts than the non-abused children. During the story-telling condition, the children in the suspected abuse group showed significantly more avoidant behavior relative to the non-abused children, while the non-abused children showed significantly more play that was free from sexual and aggressive overtones than those children suspected of abuse. Overall, the authors conclude that the results:

> . . . support the contention that there are differences in how sexually abused and non-sexually abused children respond behaviorally to anatomically correct dolls while playing alone with the dolls and when asked to tell a story about the dolls. (p. 43)

Moreover, the authors noted two sets of responses: the behavioral memory for the suspected sexual abuse was readily apparent when the children were playing alone, and the child was more avoidant about the suspected sexual abuse when the interviewer was present and interacting with the child. These findings imply that it is better to minimize interaction with the child and simply observe the child's free play, so as not to inhibit spontaneous expression of suspected abuse in play themes.

More recently, Ceci and Bruck (1995) have up-

dated the research on anatomically correct dolls. They cite three comparative studies that failed to show significant differences between doll play in abused and non-abused groups (Cohn, 1991; Kenyon-Jump, Burnette, & Robertson, 1991; McIver, Wakefield, & Underwager, 1989) and two additional studies wherein trained professionals could not discriminate abused from non-abused children based on doll play (Realmuto, Jensen, & Wescoe, 1990; Realmuto & Wescoe, 1992). Because of the lack of normative data on the behavior of normal children with anatomically correct dolls, Ceci and Bruck caution against overgeneralizing from the available data:

> Although the data, taken together, do not present persuasive evidence for the value of dolls in forensic and therapeutic settings, there are small pockets of data that would appear to provide some support for the validity of doll-centered interviews. . . . However, we feel that these types of studies are not very relevant . . . because those interviewing procedures bear little relationship to the procedures used in actual interviews with children suspected of sexual abuse. In the later situation, children are rarely observed for over an hour in a free play situation, nor are these children merely asked to undress a doll and name its body parts. Rather, children are asked direct, leading, and misleading questions about abuse with the dolls, and they are often asked to reenact alleged abusive experiences. (p. 174)

The problem with these comparative studies is the failure to establish norms for the behavior of non-abused children's interactions with the SAC dolls at various stages of development (for an exception see Boat & Everson, 1993). While it is certainly true that significantly more sexually abused children than normal children interact with the dolls in sexually explicit ways, it is also true that the majority of normal preschool children explore the dolls' genitals and breasts and a minority of non-abused children exhibit sexually explicit behavior with the dolls (Kuehnle, 1996).

The issue of using SAC dolls as the principal means of investigating behavioral memory for abuse in children has been surrounded by controversy. The 1988 issue of the *Journal of the Academy of Child and*

Adolescent Psychiatry presents both sides of the debate. Based on the consistent research findings, Yates (Yates & Terr, 1988) argues in favor of the use of SAC dolls in child abuse investigations because it helps focus the interview and gives the child permission to explore sexual topics that might otherwise be avoided. He notes, however, that sexualized play does not constitute "proof" that sexual abuse occurred. Terr (Yates & Terr, 1988), a pioneer in the concept of behavioral memory for abuse, argues against the use of SAC dolls. She feels that the dolls carry an explicit demand to "play sex" and are therefore inherently suggestive. While the dolls might be useful in many situations in eliciting behavioral and verbal reports of sexual abuse, she warns of the danger of producing false positives with the SAC dolls. She advocates that investigators use more open-ended free play as a means to get the same information; although open-ended free play may take more time, it is less suggestive than play with SAC dolls.

More recently critics have argued that interviewing with SAC dolls has no predictive validity (Wolfner et al., 1993) and runs the risk of suggestive contamination of the abuse report (Ceci & Bruck, 1995). In response, Everson and Boat (1994) have argued that, provided the dolls are used to gather information and not misused as a "diagnostic test" of the veracity of the report, they indeed have a useful place in a comprehensive assessment of abuse allegations. As we see it, the controversy about the dolls represents a problem of misplaced emphasis: the use of SAC dolls per se is not the problem. The problem is how the interview is conducted with the dolls—whether or not the interview is suggestive. Thus, the use of SAC dolls may significantly reduce the rate of false negatives while modestly increasing the rate of false positives. Provided that the dolls are introduced in a manner that minimizes suggestive influences, this may be a useful trade-off in many respects, but the risk of false positives is never eliminated.

Genuine vs. False Memory for Abuse in Children

The problem with the available literature on behavioral memory for trauma is that demonstrating the existence of a behavioral memory for trauma does not necessarily imply *accuracy* of the behavioral memory. We simply do not always know if a behavioral memory for a given trauma is accurate or not. Terr argues that the behaviors evident in a behavioral memory are highly specific and have a clear relationship to the traumatic event. The studies on comparative play with SAC dolls also imply that the sexualized and aggressive play of children suspected of abuse is somehow directly related to the abuse. However, to date there are no empirical studies on the accuracy of behavioral memory for trauma per se, if we mean by that studies which directly compare the behavioral memory to the original traumatic event.

With respect to *verbal memory for trauma in children*, Terr and others agree that verbal memory for trauma is not always accurate in its detail. Terr, however, believes that most, but not all, traumatized children preserve an accurate memory for the gist of the traumatic event. What her work does not emphasize as strongly is under what conditions a child preserves a completely inaccurate memory for trauma. In *Unchained Memories*, Terr presents one case of a false verbal memory in which a child and mother sued two therapists for abuse. She shows how the child's verbal memory for the alleged abuse was quite unlike that of the Chowchilla children in that it was inconsistent about central events and was not accompanied by a behavioral memory for trauma. She concluded that the false information about abuse was deliberately implanted by the child's mother.

The question of accuracy or inaccuracy of the verbal memory for trauma in a child has been looked at indirectly in studies of memory for events of impact in children. Goodman, Quas et al.'s (1994) study of memory for a painful urethral catheterization contained some data pertinent to the question of memory and posttraumatic symptoms. Of the 46 children who experienced one or more catheterizations four had nightmares, five had a trauma-specific fear (e.g., fear of genital touch), and four manifested posttraumatic behavioral reenactments of the medical procedure in their play (p. 285). While the sample size is small, these data are consistent with the view that some children are more traumatized than others by the same event, and that age, level of understanding, coping resources, and degree of social support may predict the presence or absence of a posttraumatic stress response to an event of impact. These data support the concept of a behavioral memory for a traumatic event, at least in a subgroup of children. Regarding amnesia for the event, Goodman, Quas et al. Found little evidence for total amnesia for previous catheterization experiences, although omission errors about the current medical procedure were common and "not all children were able to recount in detail what had occurred. Some children failed to provide any relevant information in free recall" (p. 288). Regarding accuracy, children who manifested posttraumatic symptoms following the medical procedure produced a greater number of incorrect responses and made significantly more commission errors about the event than children who were symptom-free. Thus, this important study suggests that children who lack adequate understanding and coping ability for a traumatic event that is not offset by the quality of social support during or immediately after the event are more likely to manifest posttraumatic stress symptoms, to have a relatively incomplete memory for the event, and to be more suggestible to postevent misleading information.

Direct studies on accuracy of verbal memory for abuse in children are rare. One interesting example of thinking along this line is Gardner's *True and False Allegations of Child Sexual Abuse* (1992). As a result of extensive experience interviewing children alleging that they were abused, Gardner developed a list of "indicators" or criteria useful in differentiating true and false sexual abuse allegations. These include 30 indicators by which to evaluate the child's report. A child's report is more likely to be genuine if it includes a number of the following indicators: (1) hesitancy regarding disclosure, (2) fear of retaliation, (3) guilt over consequences to accused, (4) guilt over participation in the sexual act, (5) specificity of detail, (6) credibility of report, (7) stability of report over time, (8) advanced sexual knowledge for age, (9) sexual excitation and preoccupation, (10) attitude toward genitals, (11) posttraumatic play, (12) threats and bribes by accused, (13) invisible loyalty to accused, (14) spontaneous, nonrehearsed report, (15) lack of "borrowed" elements to story, (16) depression, (17) withdrawal, (18) pathological compliance, (19) psychosomatic disorders, (20) regressive behavior, (21) sense of betrayal, (22) sleep disturbance, (23) chronicity of symptoms, (24) seductive behavior, (25) pseudomaturity, (26) acting-out behavior, (27) poor

school attendance or performance, (28) anxiety and fears, (29) history of running away, and (30) evidence of severe psychopathology. Gardner also developed 30 indicators by which to evaluate the inaccuracy of a parent's report of abuse. These are essentially the opposite of the previously mentioned criteria. They were developed to scrutinize claims made in custody disputes or in the context of abuse allegations arising in a day care center.

According to Gardner, these criteria are not to be used as a checklist. Presence of a larger number of these indicators results in greater likelihood of false allegations of abuse (pp. 181, 229), but there is no absolute number or cut-off point by which one can say with certainty that abuse did or did not genuinely occur. Until more formal research is conducted on the accuracy of verbal memory in traumatized children per se, by comparing their memory to baseline documentation of the original trauma, such clinical guidelines will have to suffice. We do not yet have scientific studies by which to distinguish between true and false verbal memories for abuse in children. At present, these guidelines are at least suggestive of the fact that the clinical presentation of genuine and false reports of sexual abuse by children are, at least in some instances, discernibly different.

CONCLUSIONS FROM THE STUDIES ON MEMORY FOR TRAUMA IN CHILDREN

1. We have seen the convergence of a large body of evidence from empirical studies on the development of children's memory and from clinical studies consistent with the theory describing two independent memory systems, a behavioral memory and a narrative, autobiographical memory system. The *behavioral or implicit memory system* is the primary medium for storage of memory for trauma in younger children. In infants trauma may also be stored in a perceptual and somatic memory system (Share, 1994). Although memory for trauma is also encoded as a verbal memory system, a behavioral memory for trauma evidently persists in older children and adults, and may represent the primary mode of memory for traumatic experiences. Behavioral memory for trauma may manifest in the form of be-

havioral reenactments in relationships, posttraumatic play, trauma-specific fears, or somatic symptoms. *Behavioral or implicit memory for trauma* is a robust finding across all available studies. Whether or not this behavioral memory is observable depends on the context. For example, a behavioral memory for trauma is more readily observable in the free play of children when uninterrupted by an adult (August & Forman, 1989; Terr, 1988); yet, even when a behavioral memory for trauma is readily observable its meaning is not always decipherable.

2. Nevertheless, children as young as 36 months, and sometimes as young as 18 months, manifest a *verbal memory for trauma*, as do older children and adults. This verbal memory, however, is likely to be *fragmented* and incomplete, especially in younger children, but often in older children and adults, too.

3. As of yet, there are virtually no data on what *predicts* whether a traumatic experience in childhood is stored and manifested primarily as a behavioral memory, a narrative memory, or both. Developmental factors contribute to the primacy of a behavioral memory for trauma over verbal memory in young children. It remains unclear why an implicit, behavioral memory for a childhood trauma may predominate over a verbal memory in an older child or an adult. Some clinicians have argued that trauma disrupts normal information-processing (Horowitz & Reidbord, 1992) and that such disruption of ordinary cognitive processing may favor the more archaic behavioral memory over higher cognitive verbal memory processing of a trauma.

4. In contrast to the adult studies on memory for trauma, some child studies on single-incident trauma fail to find evidence for *amnesia for trauma* (Goodman, Quas et al., 1994; Howe et al., 1994; Terr, 1988), at least up to several years after traumatization. However, *selective amnesia for bodily injury* does occur in some traumatized children exposed to single-incident trauma over relatively short retention intervals (Pynoos & Nader, 1989). Moreover, full or partial amnesia for multiple, repeated sexual abuse does occur in some children over longer retention intervals and into adolescence (Burgess et al., 1995; cf. also Chu et al., 1996). Com-

bining the child and adult data, there is some indication that amnesia for trauma in childhood does not typically manifest itself shortly after the event and may not manifest itself until later childhood or adolescence (Burgess et al., 1995; Grassian & Holtzen, in press).

5. The specificity of a behavioral reenactment of a trauma is not necessarily an indicator of *accuracy*. With the exception of Terr's work and the Goodman, Quas et al. (1994) study of urethral catheterization, very few data exist about the accuracy of a behavioral memory for traumatic experience per se in children. Children's narrative memories for trauma vary in their degree of completeness and accuracy. Although there are exceptions, most studies demonstrate that the gist of the child's verbal memory for a real traumatic experience is generally accurate, although the details may be distorted. The Goodman, Quas et al. (1994) study also demonstrates that children who manifest a behavioral memory and posttraumatic symptoms may be more suggestible to post-event information than children who do not manifest posttraumatic symptoms. It is also clear that a subpopulation of children, at least in particular settings like in custody disputes, can report elaborate false memories for abuse that never happened, although some research suggests that these narratives may differ from genuine reports in important respects and are often not accompanied by clinical symptoms and/or a behavioral memory more characteristic of genuine abuse (Gardner, 1992).

6. The child studies demonstrate very specific *psychologically motivated distortion* of memory for trauma (Pynoos & Nader, 1989; Terr, 1988), especially when traumatization involves injury or threat to life, and possibly betrayal trauma (Freyd, 1996).

7. Some of the *predictors* of completeness and accuracy of memory for traumatic events in children are similar to those in adulthood, except that age, quality of interaction with caregivers and other forms of social support, level of understanding, and coping ability are significant predictors of at least the child's verbal memory for the trauma (Goodman, Quas et al., 1994).

8

IIIIIIIIIIIIIIIIIIIII

Misinformation Suggestibility

THE MISINFORMATION EFFECT IN ADULTS

The Original Paradigm

Cognitive scientists have come to an understanding of suggestibility primarily in terms of the distorting effects of post-event misinformation on memory performance. This phenomenon, known as the "post-event information contamination effect" (Frischholz, 1990), or simply the "misinformation effect" (Loftus, 1975, 1979a,b), is central to understanding how some memory researchers describe the conditions under which false memory production is said to occur in psychotherapy.

The original idea that post-event information can significantly alter memory for the original event is attributed to Munsterberg (1908). In his brilliant book, *On the Witness Stand*, he reports how asking eyewitnesses questions about an event in certain ways sometimes leads to distorted reports. If, for example, a witness describing a room were asked a very specific and leading question like, "Did you see a stove in the room?", Munsterberg found that some witnesses included a stove in their narrative about the room, even when there was no stove in the room. The leading question served as a type of suggestion to the witness. While Munsterberg's original observations, namely, that inaccurate or leading questions

contaminate testimony, became common wisdom in the courts over the years, it was not until the 1970s, during the era when cognitive science was becoming an applied science and naturalistic studies of memory first appeared (Neisser, 1982), that this phenomenon was studied extensively in the laboratory.

The great majority of these early studies were pioneered by Elizabeth Loftus and her associates (Garry & Loftus, 1994; Loftus, 1975, 1979a,b; Loftus, Miller, & Burns, 1978; Loftus & Palmer, 1974; Loftus & Zanni, 1975). The Loftus et al. (1978) study has been widely cited as an example of the original experimental design used to investigate the misinformation effect. The original research design consists of three phases.

In phase 1, the subjects are exposed to some sort of stimulus event, usually an audiovisual presentation—either a brief slide show, video, or film about some complex, fast-moving, and often emotionally arousing event (such as a moving vehicle accident, robbery, mugging, or classroom disruption). The stimulus event contains a total number of items, say, up to 50, that could be perceived, encoded, and stored in memory. The stimulus event also contains one or several *critical items* or target items, which are subsequently targeted for possible post-event contamination effects. It is generally assumed that the subjects who view the stimulus event encode it, encode it correctly, and are capable of later remembering it.

Phase 2 is the *post-event misinformation manipulation*. All subjects fill out a questionnaire or read a narrative about the slide sequence or video. The experimental group is exposed to accurate information about most of the events and inaccurate or misleading information about the critical item(s) in the slide or video presentation. The control group is exposed to accurate information about all items, including the critical items.

Phase 3 consists primarily of the *memory test*. After some period of time (*retention interval*)—either immediately after or some time after filling out the questionnaire or reading the narrative—the subject is given a *forced-choice recognition test*. Typically the subject is shown two slide pairs, one of which is an original stimulus item, the other is not. For each slide pair, the subject must choose which slide was part of the original stimulus event. The magnitude of the misinformation effect is usually measured in terms of the percent of subjects responding "yes" to the misinformation critical item in the experimental group relative to the percent of subjects responding "yes" in the control group. Table 8.1 summarizes the experimental design.

The Loftus et al. (1978) study contained five experiments with a combined subject pool of 1,242 subjects, all of whom were volunteer college students. In phase 1, the subjects viewed a slide sequence of 30 color slides about a red Datsun approaching an intersection, making a right turn, and then hitting a pedestrian. The slide series contained a stop sign at the intersection. The original stimulus event used a stop sign for half of the subjects and a yield sign for the other half. Immediately after viewing the slides the subjects filled out a questionnaire, in which the post-event misinformation was presented to subjects in the experimental group. The critical question was, "Did another car pass the red Datsun while it was stopped at the *stop sign?*" Half the subjects were asked the question about a *stop sign*, and half the experimental subjects were asked the same question about a *yield sign*. Thus, relative to the original information in the slide presentation (either a stop or yield sign), the post-event manipulation contained accurate information for half the subjects and inaccurate information for the other half.

After 20 minutes of some filler activity, namely, reading an unrelated short story, all the subjects took a *forced-choice recognition test* consisting of paired slides. One slide of each pair contained a slide from the original slide sequence. Results were scored in terms of the percentage of subjects correctly or incorrectly responding to the critical item on the forced-choice recognition test. Typically, subjects given correct post-event information responded better than chance (50% chance of guessing in a forced-choice format) and subjects given misleading post-event information responded significantly worse than chance. Subjects consistently showed "less than accurate responding" (p. 19) in the misinformation condition relative to controls across all five experiments. Loftus et al. concluded that a subject's recollection of a complex event like a traffic accident can be significantly modified by information introduced after the event.

Extrapolating from this basic experimental paradigm, Loftus and her associates have conducted a series of studies over the past two decades to determine the exact nature of post-event suggestion. For example, she has convincingly demonstrated that subtle changes in the wording of post-event questions have a significant impact on subsequent recollections. In one study (Loftus & Zanni, 1975), subjects were asked a misleading post-event question about an item not originally seen in a film about a multiple car accident, "Did you see *a* broken head-

---

TABLE 8.1

The Original Loftus Research Design to Demonstrate the Misinformation Suggestion Effect

---

PHASE I. VIEWING SLIDES OR A VIDEO OF A COMPLEX EVENT

> e.g., car stops at a *stop sign*, makes a turn, then has an accident
>
> Emotionally arousing (experimental) or neutral (control) version of the stimulus event

PHASE II. READING A POST-EVENT NARRATIVE OR RESPONDING TO QUESTIONS ABOUT THE ORIGINAL STIMULUS EVENT

> Inclusion of one or two critical *misinformation items*
>
> e.g., *yield sign* (not in the original stimulus event)

RETENTION INTERVAL

PHASE III. FORCED CHOICE RECOGNITION TEST

> e.g., *stop sign* or *yield sign?*

---

light?" If the question were changed to include a definite article, "Did you see *the* broken headlight?", nearly twice as many subjects (15% vs. 7%) reported "seeing" the nonexistent headlight. Likewise, asking subjects questions about the car accident, such as "About how fast were the cars going when they *smashed into* each other?" instead of "About how fast . . . *hit* each other?" also increased the misinformation effect (Loftus & Palmer, 1974).

From observations such as these over a number of experiments, Loftus and her associates became impressed with how easy it seemed to get subjects to incorporate *nonexistent items* into their recollections by the simple manipulations of the language of post-event questions. Nonexistent items are items that are not present in the original stimulus series but are included in the post-event critical questions and are subsequently falsely incorporated into the subject's report during the recognition test as being part of the original stimulus event. As it became clear that subjects were incorporating false information into their subsequent recollections, Loftus and her associates conducted a number of experiments to see what kinds of nonexistent objects could be incorporated into people's recollections. After viewing a presentation about a car accident, a subject, for example, might be asked about a nonexistent barn ("How fast was the white sports car going when it passed the barn?" [experiment #3, Loftus, 1975]), a nonexistent school bus in the background ("Did you see the school bus in the film?" [experiment #4, Loftus, 1975]) or broken glass (Loftus & Palmer, 1974). After viewing slides about a bank robbery, subjects were misled to think they saw a nonexistent alarm button by the bank teller (Lesgold & Petrush, 1977).

However, subjects could not be led to incorporate just any kind of false information into their report about the stimulus event. If the post-event information was blatantly different from the stimulus event, and if the subject clearly perceived/encoded the original event, then the subject was likely to resist the false information. For example, subjects viewed a wallet-snatching incident in which a very noticeable, bright red wallet was taken. Subjects subsequently read a narrative of the slide sequence allegedly written by a professor. The professor described that a dark brown wallet was taken. The misinformation effect under such conditions was

significantly less than expected. Loftus concluded that misinformation is typically incorporated into subjects reports only when it is *plausible* (Loftus, 1979a). However, it is possible systematically to introduce misinformation in such a way that an implausible situation seems quite plausible.

There is little doubt from two decades of research on the manipulation of post-event information that some sort of misinformation effect is a consistently demonstrable, robust, and replicable finding across many studies with adult subjects. Loftus, building on the original insights of Munsterberg and following in the footsteps of generations of effective trial lawyers, has identified an important type of *suggestion effect*, one characterized by the manipulation of the wording of post-event information (cf. Garry & Loftus, 1994, for overview). In this sense, the misinformation effect constitutes a verbal suggestion effect. While few would debate the existence of the misinformation effect, Loftus's interpretation of this phenomenon has generated considerable controversy.

First, Loftus believes the misinformation effect is *easy to create*, and therefore is an example of the "malleability" of human memory (Loftus, 1979b). If the difference between the percent of subjects in the experimental vs. control group incorrectly choosing the critical item is taken as a measure of the *magnitude of the misinformation effect*, then the rate of the misinformation effect generally ranges from 4% to 25% across experiments, when one or a small number of critical misinformation items are used. When the experiment follows the original paradigm, the *effect size* generally runs around 20% (Frischholz, 1990; Loftus et al., 1978; McCloskey & Zaragoza, 1985).

Second, Loftus believes that the misinformation effect is an example of a *memory commission error,* in which subjects come to believe events never perceived or experienced, like the yield sign or barn, to be part of memory. Loftus generally assumes, however, that the subjects correctly perceived the original information, which in eyewitness research is not always the case.

Third, Loftus has interpreted the misinformation effect as an example of actual *memory alteration*. She believes that the post-event misinformation is incorporated into the original memory, thereby permanently altering that memory. In this sense, Loftus believes that the misinformation effect is an example of *false memory creation* (Loftus, 1979b). As we will see, many types of memory errors, in addition to memory alterations, could account for the misinformation effect. Bartlett (1932), for example, spoke of insertions and deletions in addition to transformations of memory.

Weingardt, Toland, and Loftus (1994) conducted a study to find out whether or not subjects believed in their suggested memories. "True belief" was assessed by means of whether or not subjects would bet money on their memory reports. The experiments compared willingness to bet money on genuine vs. suggested memories under lax and strict response criteria. Under more lax criteria "subjects who reported misleading suggestions were willing to bet as much, on the average, as they did on real memories. . . . With a stricter criterion . . . it appears that subjects believe their suggested memories, on the average, less than their real memories" (p. 24). While Weingardt et al. conclude, "Witnesses can exhibit strong belief in their memories, even when those memories are verifiably false" (p. 25), such a conclusion merits qualification. The data show that, while witnesses *can* hold strong beliefs about suggested memories under certain conditions, they do not necessarily become true believers.

While Loftus continues to adhere to her earlier interpretation of the misinformation effect, especially in her expert court testimony, and more recently in her writings about false memory production in therapy (Loftus, 1993), there is an ever-growing corpus of recent experimental studies with increasingly sophisticated experimental designs on the misinformation effect, the results of which warrant greater caution about the kind of conclusions that can be drawn about misinformation suggestion. This is especially true with respect to how easily the misinformation effect can be created, and with respect to whether or not the misinformation effect has anything to do with memory processes per se.

It has recently become clear that the ease with which the misinformation effect can be produced has a great deal to do with the *type of information* studied, i.e., both the *nature of the target information* embedded in the sequence of original stimulus events and also the *type of post-event misinformation suggested*. Scientists have become interested in "defining the functional boundaries of the false-memory phenomena" (Reisberg, Scully, & Karbo, 1993, p. 2). In the great majority of misinformation studies, the misinformation effect was demonstrated on stimulus details rather peripheral to the central action in the film or slide sequence. For example, the misinformation questions typically addressed a stop sign, a barn, the color of a passing car, or the number of people, rather than the central action, namely, the accident per se. Therefore, it remained to be seen whether or not subjects would make commission errors for central events or whether the misinformation effect was limited to rather minor details.

Christiaansen and Ochalek (1983) demonstrated that the misinformation effect could be generalized to descriptions for people. After subjects viewed a staged incident, they were given post-event information pertaining to the weight and age of the confederate performing the action. Subjects were significantly misled in their descriptions of the people they saw. Miller and Loftus (1976) showed subjects a series of 20 slides about various activities performed by research confederates, e.g., blowing up a balloon, reading a book, or working on a jigsaw puzzle. Then subjects were asked a series of questions about the slides. Four of the questions were about actions performed by a different confederate than the one performing the action in the original slide. Subjects were then given a forced-choice recognition test about the slide sequence. A significant misinformation effect was demonstrated. In this case, the post-event misinformation "was to increase the likelihood that a person was recalled having committed some act that he did not commit" (p. 10). Therefore, the misinformation effect is generalizable to descriptions of the people involved in the activities viewed by the subjects. Under certain conditions, the subject may totally misidentify the person in question.

Dritsas and Hamilton (1977) designed an experiment to test the degree to which memory of central and peripheral details could be affected by misleading post-event information. Subjects were shown three videotapes about industrial accidents—an employee getting hit by a metal chip in the eye, another getting hit by a spinning metal rod, and a third getting her hand caught in a punch press. The stimuli on each videotape were independently categorized into central and peripheral details. After viewing the sequence of tapes, subjects were asked a series of three questions about the tapes. The questions contained three misleading questions about peripheral details and three misleading questions about central details. While the misinformation effect was demonstrated for both central and peripheral details, subjects made significantly greater commission errors for peripheral details than for central events.

Reisberg et al. (1993, experiment #2) also designed a study to directly compare misinformation for objects and actions. Subjects viewed a slide sequence about a robbery in a university bookstore. Then they were asked a series of questions about what had taken place. The questions contained misleading questions both about the objects ("Did he have sneakers?") and about the actions ("She slipped an arm around his waist") matched for baseline memorability. After a 24-hour delay subjects were given a memory recognition test. They were told that some of the items they were questioned about did not appear in the original slide viewing. Subjects were asked to discriminate the source of the information—which items they saw and which they read about in the post-event narrative. A significant misinformation effect was demonstrated for the objects, but not for the actions. Subjects reported "seeing" objects they only read about later, but failed to report "seeing" the action that did not really occur. Interestingly, the subjects also failed to identify reading about the action misinformation. In other words, subjects seemed not to notice the misinformation about the action enough to recall it, presumably because it was too discrepant with what they actually saw.

Nearly all of the misinformation studies have utilized films, slides, or staged events as the original stimulus event. Crombag, Wagenaar, and Van Koppen (1996) recently opened up a new area of inquiry into the misinformation suggestion effect. In an innovative attempt to make misinformation research more ecologically sound, they used a real-life situation as the original stimulus event. The event was an airplane crash in 1992 in the suburbs of Amsterdam shortly after the airplane took off from the airport. The clean-up from the disaster was covered extensively in the news media, but the crash itself was not filmed, nor had anyone seen the crash on television. The story about what presumably happened during the crash, however, was circulated

widely. Ten months after the incident 193 subjects were given a questionnaire about the event, which included three factual questions and a misinformation question presented as a fact. The misinformation question was:

> Did you see the television film of the moment the plane hit the apartment building? (p. 99)

Memory testing consisted of yes/no answers to each of the questions. Those who answered yes to the critical item were then asked an additional question:

> After the plane hit the building, there was a fire. How long did it take for the fire to start? (p. 99)

A total of 55% of the subjects accepted the misinformation suggestion and responded that they had actually seen a television film of the crash itself. Crombag et al. summarize the findings as follows:

> So more than half of our subjects erroneously reported having witnessed something they had only heard about, and of those 82% did not choose the prudent and readily available alternative "I don't remember," but felt confident enough to report on a detail. (p. 99)

In a second replication experiment 93 subjects were presented with much more detailed misinformation about the plane crash. In that study 66% of the subjects accepted the misinformation that they had seen the film of the plane crash, where no film existed. The researchers interpret the high rates of misinformation suggestibility in these experiments in terms of the relative ease to produce memory source monitoring errors. Moreover, Crombag et al. believe that these experiments raise the question that real-life disasters may be more prone to memory distortion than witnessing films in the laboratory:

> . . . dramatic events may be more vulnerable to post-event information, because they are usually highly publicized and by their very nature may more readily evoke visualization, thus interfering with "source monitoring" required of legal witnesses. (p. 103)

These important experiments challenge the hypothesis of some proponents of the trauma accuracy position that traumatic events relative to normal events are less vulnerable to suggestive distortion.

In summary, subjects can be led to alter their memory report for various types of information, but not necessarily to the same degree. The greatest magnitude of the misinformation effect can be demonstrated for information that is *peripheral* to the central event in question, like the color of a passing car quite irrelevant to the car involved in an accident. Subjects will also incorporate misinformation into their memory report for *descriptive details of people*, and sometimes, but considerably less so, for central *actions*, unless those actions represent information derived from sources other than the original stimulus event so as to evoke source-monitoring confusion.

The issue of whether adult subjects will create false memory reports for actions needs further study before conclusions can be drawn. The few existing studies suggest that subjects will not incorporate false beliefs about fictitious actions, so long as they have a memory for the real action in question (Reisberg et al., 1993), but may incorporate beliefs about fictitious actions if there is no baseline memory for action against which to compare the misinformation. Because actions are easier to remember than peripheral details, it is not surprising that central actions are less prone to distortion than peripheral details by post-event misinformation. Smith and Ellsworth (1987) reach a similar conclusion:

> Memories for some facts are relatively immune to alteration by the presentation of misleading information . . . it appears that only memories that are somewhat indefinite are subject to distortion on the basis of subsequent information. (p. 199)

When the memory is indefinite it is also open to reinterpretation. While actions are generally easier to remember than other details, it is at least conceivable that under certain conditions of social influence the subject could be influenced to reinterpret the meaning of the action and thereby create a distorted memory for the action.

The Mechanisms of the Misinformation Effect

While the misinformation effect has been consistently demonstrated across many experiments, the mechanisms by which it occurs are not well understood and the various interpretations of the misinformation experiments have been the subject of ongoing controversy. While few scientists doubt the existence of a misinformation effect, the 1980s have been characterized by a debate between five or six competing hypotheses to explain its occurrence. Table 8.2 summarizes these hypotheses.

Memory Interference

Loftus's original interpretation of the misinformation effect is known as the *memory impairment*, memory alteration or destructive updating hypothesis. Her interpretation traces its roots to philosopher Immanuel Kant, who described the tendency to merge different experiences into new ideas (Loftus, 1979b). This notion about blended experiences has had a profound impact on psychology: in the psychology of perception, in the form of summation effects; and in the psychology of memory, where it serves as the basis for Bartlett's (1932) constructionist theory of memory for gist experiences at the expense of details. In keeping with that tradi-

---

TABLE 8.2
Proposed Explanations for the Misinformation Effect

I. MEMORY INTERFERENCE (BELLI, 1989; McGEOCH, 1932)
    A. Memory impairment/alteration (Loftus, 1975, 1979a&b; Loftus & Hoffman, 1989)
    B. Source misattribution (Johnson & Lindsay, 1986; Lindsay & Johnson, 1987;)

II. MEMORY ACCEPTANCE (BELLI, 1989)
    A. Accessibility or coexistence (Christiaansen & Ochalek, 1983; McCloskey & Zaragoza, 1985; Morton et. al., 1985; Pirolli & Mitterer, 1984; Wright, Varley, & Belton, 1996).
    B. Response bias (McCloskey & Zaragoza, 1985)

III. NONRETENTION (FRISCHHOLZ, 1990; McCLOSKEY & ZARAGOZA, 1985; PEZDEK & ROE, 1995)

IV. SOCIAL PERSUASION

tion, Loftus interprets the data from misinformation experiments as an illustration of how post-event information permanently transforms the memory for the original information. These are called "synthetic recollections" or "blended memories" (Loftus, 1979b), the outcome of the integration of the original and post-event information into a new memory product. As a result, Loftus assumes (and it is an assumption) that the original information is, therefore, "irreversibly distorted" (Wells & Turtle, 1987, p. 372). This position is known as the *impairment view* (Garry & Loftus, 1994; Loftus & Hoffman, 1989). It is one type of "storage-based memory impairment" (Loftus, Feldman, & Dashiell, 1995). As Loftus states, "sometimes new information about the event comes to his attention and becomes incorporated into his memory, supplementing or altering the original memory" (Loftus, 1979b, p. 312). From this perspective, Loftus feels justified to interpret the misinformation effect as an example of the creation of new memories" (Loftus & Hoffman, 1989). The underlying assumption is an interference with or transformation of the original memory by the post-event information. Bartlett (1932), however, initially described a number of memory errors besides transformations, such as deletions and insertions, which do not imply impairment of the original trace.

Another type of interference theory is known as the *source misattribution* hypothesis (Lindsay & Johnson, 1987, 1989), which assumes that both the original and post-event information are accessible at the time of retrieval, but that the subject confuses the source of the information. As a result, misled subjects genuinely believe that they "saw" the suggested detail in the original stimulus event, even though in reality the misled information came from a different source, namely, the verbal or written post-event questionnaire about the stimulus event. In other words, the subject has confused the respective sources of original and post-event information, and reports the post-event suggested detail as if it were part of the original stimulus event. Because source misattribution, like memory impairment, assumes that the misinformation may have some influence on the original memory, Belli (1989) classifies source misattribution as a type of *memory interference* hypothesis. However, Lindsay and Johnson (1989) are careful to state that, while the source misattribution hypothesis assumes that post-

event misinformation *may* affect the original memory, it need not have such an effect; further, source misattribution can occur whether the memory for the original detail is intact or impaired.

To test this hypothesis, Lindsay and Johnson (1989) introduced a modified version of the original Loftus paradigm. In phase 1, subjects viewed a slide of a complex office scene. In phase 2 they read a detailed narrative about the event. Half of the subjects were given misinformation about eight objects not actually present in the original slides. The modification occurred in phase 3 of the experiment regarding the recognition test. Lindsay and Johnson (1989) argued that the forced-choice recognition test typically used by Loftus and her colleagues may induce subjects to make source-monitoring errors on critical items. Because subjects are presented with paired slides—some aspect of the original event plus a distractor item—they are likely to make decisions based on *familiarity* and ignore the source of the item's familiarity. Instead of Loftus's forced-choice recognition test, Lindsay and Johnson tested their subjects with either a yes/no recognition test or a source-monitoring test. Both tests included items present in the slides only, the misleading text only, the slide and text, or neither slide nor text. In the yes/no recognition test, subjects were required to answer "yes" or "no" as to whether the item was part of the original slide sequence. In the source-monitoring test, subjects were required to discriminate whether the presented item was present only in the slides, only in the text, both in the slides and text, or in neither. This latter test was designed "to orient subjects to attend to information about the sources of their memories." Subjects given misleading information were significantly more likely than controls to report they had "seen" the suggested items in response to the yes/no recognition test. However, subjects given misleading information performed no worse than controls in response to the source-monitoring test. In other words, the predicted misinformation effect could be demonstrated only when the recognition test was used, but was entirely eliminated by using a source-monitoring test that helped subjects to discern the sources of their memories. The results were replicated in a second experiment.

Lindsay and Johnson interpret the results in terms of source confusion. They explain the misinformation effect as an example of confusing post-event misleading suggestions for original stimulus items. However, when specifically instructed to discriminate the source of their memories, the misinformation effect is greatly attenuated, as if subjects were able to "edit out" (p. 355) the memory for the misleading post-event information by adopting more stringent criteria in evaluating memory performance.

Memory Acceptance

A second type of explanation is known as the *memory accessibility* or *memory coexistence* hypothesis. Unlike the memory impairment hypothesis, the coexistence hypothesis does not assume that the original memory trace is altered by post-event information. Rather, it is assumed that the original memory trace and the memory for the post-event information coexist. The problem is not so much one of the destruction of the original memory but more a *problem of retrieval* or *accessibility*. According to this "retrieval-based" view (Loftus, Feldman, & Dashiell, 1995, in press), the memory for the post-event information is more likely to be retrieved than the original memory for a variety of reasons, not the least of which is that the post-event memory is more *recent* than the memory for the original stimulus event. Furthermore, the *context* of the experiment can easily introduce a bias toward retrieval of the post-event over the original memory. Yet, it may be that the original memory remains undisturbed (Wells & Turtle, 1987) and readily accessible if an appropriate retrieval method were used (Christiaansen & Ochalek, 1983). The reader is reminded of the distinction between availability and accessibility (Tulving & Pearlstone, 1966). Loftus assumes that the original information has been altered and is no longer available. Others have assumed that the original information is available, yet may not be accessible.

Some early evidence for the coexistence hypothesis was presented by Pirolli and Mitterer (1984). They used a text in the form of stories containing central and peripheral passages during phase 1 of the experiment, followed by a series of questions (phase 2) containing consistent, misleading, or neutral questions about each target sentence. Then subjects were given a recognition test, which included either the target sentence or foils. One innovation

in the research design was the inclusion of a recall test after phase 1 to determine the extent to which subjects actually remembered the target passage. Another innovation was the inclusion of neutral, as well as consistent and misleading, information during phase 2. Consistent questions resulted in a significant improvement in recognition relative to the neutral or misleading information, while misleading questions resulted in a significant increase in commission errors. The inclusion of a neutral control allowed the researchers to demonstrate both the classic misinformation effect and also the fact that accurate post-event information significantly improved recognition accuracy. In other words, the memory for the target information was certainly *not* altered by misleading questions and actually could be enhanced by asking accurate questions. The researchers interpret the results as "showing that misleading information can coexist in memory along with the original information" (p. 139). Moreover, the inclusion of the recall test of memory for target passages demonstrated that the misinformation effect was more likely when the original information was not accessible in memory.

Other early evidence in favor of the coexistence hypothesis came from a series of experiments conducted by Bekerian and Bowers (1983; Bowers & Bekerian, 1984). They noted that the original Loftus research paradigm presented items in *random* order for the forced-choice recognition test in phase 3. Presenting items randomly was a marked departure from the original order of presentation, which may have made the original information less accessible than the post-event misinformation. This same point forms the basis for the cross-examination tactic of skipping from one item to another in random fashion, thereby forcing the witness to remember matters in nonsequential order. The result is often memory confusion or error.

Bekerian and Bowers repeated the Loftus experiment with one important modification. They used a sequential retrieval test in which the items presented in phase 3, the recognition test, exactly matched the sequence of the originally viewed series of slides. Under these sequential retrieval conditions, the misinformation effect was virtually eliminated. The results demonstrated that the original information was not lost. Using the Loftus research paradigm, the original information became less accessible, but it became more accessible with a more appropriate retrieval procedure. Bekerian and Bowers interpret the data as evidence for memory coexistence, although two subsequent studies using sequential procedures failed to replicate the findings (McCloskey & Zaragoza, 1985; Wagenaar & Boer, 1987).

The basic strategy used in support of the coexistence hypothesis is to somehow demonstrate that the original memory still exists and can be retrieved at the time of the recognition test. Whereas the Bekerian and Bowers sequential retrieval strategy has failed to receive support in more recent research, other *context-reinstatement strategies* have lent support to the coexistence hypothesis. Kroll and Timourian (1986) repeated the Loftus research paradigm with two important alterations. Following the original three phases of the Loftus design, using a staged purse-snatching as the original stimulus event, they added two additional phases. Subjects were "returned to the scene of the crime," in that they were shown a series of slides about scenes in the same town in which the purse-snatching took place minus the characters in the purse-snatching. Moreover, subjects were explicitly warned that the post-event questions (phase 2) had included information that may have caused them to make errors. Then subjects were given a second recognition test. While the misinformation effect could be demonstrated in phase 3, subjects were significantly more likely to choose the original information correctly on the second retrieval test after the context had been reinstated. Kroll and Timourian interpret the results to mean that the original information is not destroyed but is more difficult to retrieve, unless aided by special retrieval procedures. They conclude that "misleading questions do not really affect memory—only the guessing biases" (p. 167).

A similar retrieval strategy was employed by Gibling and Davies (1988) in an experiment using a videotape of a shoplifting as the stimulus event, following which subjects were given either correct or misleading information about the appearance of the shoplifter. As predicted, a misinformation effect was demonstrated. The experimental modification entailed giving half the subjects a guided memory interview designed to reinstate the context. It included comments on what the room looked like, where the people were sitting, what they were doing, etc. There was a significant reduction in the misinformation effect in both recognition and recall memory testing following reinstatement of the context by means of the guided memory interview.

While context-reinstatement strategies are one approach to demonstrating that under certain conditions the original memory is retrievable, another approach is to *warn* subjects that the post-event information may contain inaccurate information. Warning sometimes enables subjects to dismiss inaccurate post-event information and recover the memory of the original stimulus event. Kroll and Timourian (1986) included a warning in their experiment along with a context-reinstatement strategy, so it is difficult to know from that experiment what the effect of warning the subject per se had on the magnitude of the misinformation effect. The issue of warning subjects was explicitly addressed by Loftus and her associates. In one study (Greene, Flynn, & Loftus, 1982), subjects were explicitly told that some of the post-event information may have been inaccurate. In another study, subjects were given post-event information in phase 2 that blatantly contradicted the original information. Loftus and her associates found that the warning reduced the misinformation effect when it preceded the post-event information, but not if it was introduced after the post-event information, at the time of the recognition test. Loftus interpreted these results to mean that the original information could not be retrieved, and that the warning was ineffective once the post-event information had been encoded in memory and had therefore altered the original memory trace. However, whether or not the warning reduces the misinformation effect may depend on how subjects are warned, and if a warning does significantly reduce the misinformation effect under certain conditions, it may imply that the unaltered original memory is retrievable.

Christiaansen and Ochalek (1983) repeated the Greene et al. (1982) study using a more explicit warning than in the earlier study. They also included a test to determine whether or not the original event was actually encoded in memory. The original event was a slide sequence about a shoplifting incident in a department store, followed by a memory accuracy test to ensure that the stimulus events were encoded in memory. Following that procedure, subjects were given post-event information, which in the experimental group included misinformation about four critical details. Subjects were informed either immediately after reading the post-event information or just before the final recognition test that "a few of the details in the description are inaccurate—some of the details are correct and a few are incorrect" (p. 469). While a misinformation effect did occur in subjects who were not warned, subjects who were warned that some of the information they read may have been inaccurate did not produce a significant misinformation effect. Warning subjects just before the final recognition test was more effective than warning them immediately after the post-event information in reducing the magnitude of the misinformation effect. The authors conclude, "The fact that warned subjects responded as accurately as subjects who had never been exposed to the biasing information implies that the original and narrative versions of the event must coexist in memory, and that subjects can retrieve these two representations and determine the source of each" (p. 473). The results are supportive of the coexistence hypothesis.

A third strategy for testing the coexistence hypothesis entails explicitly instructing subjects to discriminate their memory for the original stimuli from their memory for the post-event information. Hammersley and Read (1986) presented their subjects with a tape-recorded story about an escaped convict (phase 1). Following the story, the subjects listened to a "summary" of it. The summary contained a mixture of true statements and misinformation about the original story (phase 2). The subjects were then asked to rate the degree of congruence between the original story and the summary. "In each sentence in the summary, we want you to decide how much your memory of the story agrees with the summary" (p. 332). Then (phase 3) all subjects were asked to recall in writing the original story or the summary. While a misinformation effect did occur, subjects mentioned true and misleading statements equally often and recalled the misinformation more frequently as part of the summary than as part of the original story. When the experiment was repeated with a one-week delay before the subjects read the summary, misleading statements were mentioned less often than the true statements. The researchers interpret the data as support for the coexistence of the original and misleading information, as if the subject uses "two separate records, one of the original

story and one of the summary—in reconstruction of the story" (p. 329).

A fourth strategy entails letting the subjects have a "second guess" after phase 3, the memory testing. Loftus (1979a) initially developed this approach. She found that second guesses by misled subjects were not above chance guessing. Wright, Varley, and Belton (1996) recently repeated the *second guess strategy* with a more sophisticated research design. The outcome was quite different. Across four experiments subjects watched a slide presentation, either of a woman shopping or of a woman's handbag being stolen. Each experimental condition included from one to four critical items of misinformation. During phase 3 subjects first had to choose among four choices: the original item, the misled item, and two foil items. Following this, subjects had an opportunity to make a second guess. In comparing the response of control and experimental subjects, a misinformation effect was demonstrated across all four experiments, although the magnitude of the misinformation effect varied considerably depending on the type of misinformation presented. With respect to second guessing, the responses of subjects across all four experiments were significantly above chance guessing for most of the questions. Wright et al. interpret the results as "strong support for some form of coexistence explanation," since above-chance responding implied that the original memory trace still had an implicit influence on the response given. However, since the retention interval in the experiments was relatively short (15 minutes), the researchers speculate that the original and misleading information initially coexist as separate memory traces but may blend over longer time periods.

Morton, Hammersley, and Bekerian (1985) have put forth a model to explain the results of the experiments favoring the memory coexistence hypothesis. They propose that memory for each experience is composed of discrete units of information. Each and every experience is contained within a separate, unconnected memory unit or record. Memory across experiences is therefore fragmentary. According to their theory, each independent memory record has its own unique access key or heading, much like a file name in a computer storage system. The model assumes that retrieval of a memory record depends upon correct identification of the access key or memory heading, much as access to a particular computer file depends upon identifying the file name and its path description. Like the computer, the authors assume that access to a memory record is an all-or-nothing process, and that only one file can be called up at any given time.

The misinformation effect, viewed in terms of this model of memory, is an example of the problem of accessibility or "discriminability of the headings" (p. 17). The model assumes that both the original information and the post-event information coexist as separate, unconnected records. Because only one memory record can be accessed during any given retrieval attempt, the post-event memory record is more likely to be retrieved than the original memory record for several reasons: (1) it is more recent, (2) the random order of presentation of the forced-choice memory recognition items favors the post-event information over the sequence of original stimulus slides, and (3) the recognition test fails to reestablish the state of emotional arousal that accompanied the original stimulus event (in the experimental group). Thus, recency effect, contextual factors, and state dependent memory effects are likely to favor retrieval of the post-event information over the original information.

A third hypothesis is known as the *response bias* hypothesis (McCloskey & Zaragoza, 1985). Zaragoza and her associates conducted what has become known as the "modified version" of the original Loftus research design (Zaragoza, 1991). Like the Lindsay and Johnson study, the main modification occurs in phase 3 of the research design. McCloskey and Zaragoza (1985) criticize Loftus's use of a forced-choice recognition test, in which the subject is forced to make a choice between the original information and the misleading information. They assert that this type of forced choice introduces a response bias, or social pressure to agree with the experimenter's misleading suggestions over the original information.

To correct for this bias, McCloskey and Zaragoza eliminated the misleading information as an option in the forced-choice recognition test. Instead, subjects were forced to choose between either the original information or some novel item of comparable perceptual similarity to the original and post-event information. According to McCloskey and Zaragoza, this modification "eliminates the social pressure to agree with the experimenter's suggestion . . . [and] eliminates the bias toward the misleading response"

(Zaragoza, 1991, p. 30). Moreover, under those conditions, misled subjects were hypothesized to perform worse than control subjects only if their ability to remember the original stimulus event had been impaired.

Across six independent experiments, the magnitude of the difference between the misled and control conditions never reached significance. In other words, the magnitude of the misinformation effect was drastically reduced by using the modified recognition test, which implies that a great deal of the variance of the misinformation effect pertains to the social influence inherent in the way the questions are asked and responded to, and not to the transformation of the memory representation per se. McCloskey and Zaragoza interpret their data to mean that "available evidence does not imply that misleading post-event information impairs memory for the original event, because the procedure used in the previous study is inappropriate for assessing effects of misleading information on memory" (p. 1).

In another study Zaragoza, McCloskey, and Jamis (1987) replicated their refutation of the memory impairment hypothesis using a cued-recall procedure. They note that all previous studies on the misinformation effect used some sort of recognition test. Their procedure involved subjects' viewing a slide sequence wherein a maintenance man stole a $20 calculator. The two critical items were the brand of soft drink and the name of the magazine in the room. The post-event narrative contained either accurate or misleading information about the critical item. The recall test consisted of a series of questions about the event, including questions about the critical items. In two experiments, there were no differences between the experimental and control groups on the recall test. Again, Zaragoza et al. conclude that the misinformation effect is largely due to response bias. Bowman and Zaragoza (1989) also used the theft paradigm in an additional study, but with an interesting modification in phase 2. They used slides, not a narrative text, to introduce the control and misleading post-event information.

In a second experiment, Bowman and Zaragoza used a narrative text for both the original stimulus and the post-event information. In each experiment, when the original and post-event information were presented in the same medium, both slides or both text, no significant misinformation effect occurred.

Bowman and Zaragoza interpret the results as further evidence for the response bias hypothesis. The implication is that the misinformation effect occurs primarily because subjects in the original Loftus experiments were presented post-event information in a very different form from the original stimulus event, and may have used this shift in context to favor the misleading post-event information over the other information available to them.

Further support for the response bias hypothesis is given in a more recent study. Zaragoza and Koshmider (1989) note that with respect to the misinformation effect, subjects may report the misinformation whether or not they actually believe they remember seeing it as part of the original stimulus event. It cannot be readily established from the misinformation experiments that the *report* of misinformation means an actual *transformation* of the memory representation, because subjects in the experiment were never encouraged to discriminate between what they actually remember seeing in the original stimulus event and the misinformation they later came to believe to be part of the original event. Therefore, Zaragoza and Koshmider designed an additional modification of the original Loftus research paradigm in which subjects were instructed to try to distinguish between the original items they saw and the suggested post-event information. The original stimulus event was once again about the theft of the calculator. Four critical items were used: a brand of soft drink, a brand of coffee, the name of a magazine, and a type of tool taken from a tool box. In phase 2, subjects were presented with accurate or misleading information. In phase 3, the recognition test consisted of eight slides, four of which were the critical items and four of which were filler slides. Instead of the original forced-choice recognition test, subjects in this experiment were asked to indicate for each slide which alternative best described their memory for the item originally presented in the slide: (a) select *saw* if the subject was sure he or she recalled seeing that item in the original slide sequence, (b) select *read* if the subject did not remember seeing the item but did remember reading about it in the post-event narrative, (c) select *consistent* if the item was consistent with what the subject remembered about the event, but did not know where it came from, and (d) select *inconsistent* if the item contradicted what they remem-

bered about the event. The lack of significant difference between the experimental and control groups with respect to what subjects reported seeing implies that exposure to the misinformation "did not impair the subjects' ability to remember seeing the original item" (p. 250). Moreover, subjects were able to identify accurately the source of the originally seen information.

Because no source misattribution occurred, Zaragoza and Koshmider's results do not support the misattribution hypothesis (Lindsay & Johnson, 1987). Their experiment mainly shows that "many subjects who reported the misinformation did so in spite of the fact that they remembered reading about it" (p. 250). They conclude:

> "The consistent finding, at least in research with adults, has been that misleading post-event information does not impair subjects' ability to retrieve originally seen details. . . . Rather, it appears that misinformation effects are largely due to those subjects who fail to remember the original critical details and accept the misinformation because it fills in a gap in their memory" (pp. 252–253).

In other words, explicitly cautioning subjects to not report what they do not actually remember seeing, or asking subjects to discern whether they later read about something, greatly reduces the magnitude of the misinformation effect (cf. also Frischholz, 1990). From the perspective of all of the Zaragoza experiments, the misinformation effect appears to be primarily a function of response bias, a bias introduced in a social context that invites subjects to report inaccurately, especially about complex events regarding which they are uncertain.

While the series of Zaragoza experiments with their consistent findings call into question the memory impairment hypothesis, Loftus and Hoffman (1989) and Belli (1989) are correct in pointing out that Zaragoza's modified test does not fully rule out memory impairment. Because the modified recognition test fails to include the post-event information as an option, the test may have been insensitive to detecting any memory impairment caused by the misleading information. Later we will review research with more sophisticated designs that attempt to distinguish between response bias and memory impairment.

Nonretention

Still another hypothesis is known as the *nonretention* or *no-conflict* hypothesis (McEwan & Yuille, 1981; Wagenaar & Boer, 1987; Zaragoza & Koshmider, 1989). There is a serious flaw in the original Loftus research paradigm. It assumes that the details for the original stimulus event were encoded and stored in memory. The *nonretention hypothesis* challenges this assumption by suggesting that a certain number of subjects probably fail to encode all of the original details of a complex stimulus event and that, even when the details are encoded, some details are forgotten over time. McEwan and Yuille (1981) noted that, when subjects were given a free recall test of their memory for the original information prior to exposure to post-event information, subjects who clearly remembered the critical items were far less likely to be misled than those who had forgotten them. Therefore, the basic position of the nonretention hypothesis is that the misinformation effect is primarily a function of failure to remember the original stimulus details. Subjects who fail to encode, or whose memory has decayed for the original stimulus details, are more prone to the misinformation effect, because they depend on the post-event information to fill in the gaps of their imperfect memory. Thus, there is really no conflict between the original post-event information for those subjects because the original stimulus event was not part of their memory.

Advocates of the nonretention hypothesis have inserted an *initial recognition test* between viewing the original stimulus event (phase 1) and exposure to the post-event information (phase 2) (Frischholz, 1990; Pirolli & Mitterer, 1984; Wagenaar & Boer, 1987). As predicted, a good portion of the variance of the misinformation effect is found in those subjects who score low on the initial recognition test. In this sense, the misinformation effect could be interpreted as a kind of *uncertainty effect*: subjects are susceptible to post-event suggestion when they are uncertain about their original memory.

Social Persuasion

Yet another important hypothesis needs to be considered. The *social persuasion hypothesis* states that a *highly credible* communication can *persuade* a recipient to change an attitude about a particular message. An attitude, strictly defined, pertains to the desirability (like or dislike) of something. While the social persuasion hypothesis is primarily about *attitude change* and not about memory alteration, research on attitude change has also shown how under certain conditions a changed attitude may become transformed into a stable belief. To the extent to which the misinformation effect pertains to subjects' beliefs about what they experienced/remembered, the social persuasion hypothesis may be quite relevant to our understanding of at least certain aspects of the misinformation effect. It is quite remarkable that nearly three decades of social psychology research on social persuasion is rarely acknowledged by the memory scientists who have studied the misinformation effect. A brief review of the main findings from social persuasion research is warranted in order to identify important variables contributing to the misinformation effect that are not obvious in the memory literature. More extensive reviews may be found in Cohen (1964), Insko (1967), and Ronis, Baumgardner, Leippe, Cacioppo, and Greenwald (1977).

In contrast to memory research on the misinformation effect, which emphasizes the wording of the message (e.g., Loftus, 1975), the earliest research on *persuasion effects* focused primarily on the characteristics of the individual communicating the message. This research is known as *source credibility* research, in which various characteristics of the communicator were manipulated in experiments in order to discover what led to the greatest attitude change. Research on attitude change consistently demonstrated that subjects were more persuaded to change their attitude when the message was delivered by someone who was a well-known *expert* on the topic, especially when the message demonstrated the expert's degree of knowledge about the topic in question (Hovland, Janis, & Kelly, 1953; Hovland & Weiss, 1951; Kelman & Hovland, 1953). A smoker is more likely to change his or her attitude about smoking when the Surgeon General, not a less credible source, communicates the health warning.

The perceived motives of the communicator are also quite important. Communications are more effective in producing attitude change when the communicator is *trustworthy* (Kelman & Hovland, 1953), *fair* (Weiss & Fine, 1956), and not motivated to push a particular point, i.e., *unbiased* (Allyn & Festinger,

1961), in contrast to communicators who are perceived as untrustworthy and having some ulterior motive to their communication. American subjects, for example, were more likely to develop a favorable attitude to building nuclear submarines when a nuclear physicist like Oppenheimer communicated the message than when it was communicated through a Soviet newspaper (Hovland & Weiss, 1951).

One of the findings from early social persuasion research is that it was very difficult to separate source credibility from other variables affecting attitude change. *Source credibility* and the *type of message* were often confounded. An enormous amount of research was conducted on the type of message leading to more or less attitude change. The reader is referred to an excellent review of the extensive message variables (Cohen, 1964), since only some of the relevant variables have been selected for comment here: (1) one-sided communication, (2) message discrepancy, (3) message complexity, (4) message threat, and (5) message incentive.

Research comparing one-sided and two-sided messages has shown that *one-sided messages*, i.e., those which fail to present opposing views, were a more effective means of persuasion than two-sided messages for recipients who initially favored the advocated message, while two-sided messages were more effective for recipients who initially opposed the advocated message (Cohen, 1964; Hovland, Lumsdaine, & Sheffield, 1949). Moreover, messages that were more discrepant from the recipient's initial view led to greater attitude change than similar messages, as long as the communicated message did not surpass the subject's latitude of acceptance (Hovland & Pritzker, 1957). Simple, plausible messages worked better than complex messages (Cohen, 1964). Messages resulted in greater attitude change when they led to a moderate degree of fear-arousal, especially if the threat was something that the recipient was familiar with and found relevant (Higbee, 1969; Janis & Feshbach, 1954). No fear, or intense fear, reduced the effectiveness of the message (Higbee, 1969; Leventhal, 1965).

Just as perceived threat can affect attitude change, so too can *incentives and rewards* (Cohen, 1964). The point of all this research on the type of message is that not all messages persuade the recipient to the same degree, and that social psycholo-gists have contributed far more to our appreciation of the complexity of the message structure than the more recent work by memory scientists on how the wording of post-event information affects the misinformation effect (e.g., Loftus & Zanni, 1975). From the tradition of social persuasion research, it can be predicted that simple, one-sided, post-event messages that are discrepant from, but not blatantly discrepant from, the original stimulus event, and that are about a stress-arousing situation, would have the greatest influence on the recipient, especially if communicated by a source who is perceived as highly credible—expert and trustworthy, like the experimenter. While source credibility and type of message typically interact, and thereby magnify the effect (Insko, 1967), each variable has been shown to make an independent contribution to the overall *persuasion effect* (Aronson & Golden, 1962).

Source credibility and the *personality of the recipient* also interact (Abelson & Lesser, 1959). Maximum persuasion occurs between a highly credible source and a highly persuasible subject. Hovland, Janis, and Kelly (1953) conducted extensive research on what they called the *trait of persuasibility*, which they defined as the degree to which subjects could be made to alter their attitude first in one direction and then in another. Later, the definition of persuasibility was defined in terms of the number of different attitudes that could be influenced within the same subject (King & Janis, 1956). While early research clearly demonstrated that some subjects were more persuasible than others under similar conditions, later research focused on identifying the characteristics of highly persuasible individuals. While no consistent profile of the highly persuasible subject emerged, some personality variables that correlated with persuasibility included: low self-esteem (Janis & Field, 1959); cognitive style, like field dependence, i.e., the degree to which the response depends on environmental cues (Cohen, 1964); and response involvement, i.e., the degree to which the recipient becomes actively involved with, not just passively listens to, the message because of concern for the social consequences of his or her response (Zimbardo, 1960).

Thus, the literature of social psychology predicts significant *individual differences* in persuasibility. When the misinformation effect is considered in light of this social psychology research, it becomes readily apparent that individual differences in misinformation suggestibility are greatly under-emphasized in the memory research (for one exception cf. Loftus, Levidow, & Duensing, 1992). Yet it should be immediately obvious in examining the data in the misinformation studies that some subjects are more persuasible than others in response to post-event information. Thus, social psychological research has shown with respect to attitude change that source credibility, type of message, and individual persuasibility that each contributes independently to the overall persuasion effect, and that they interact in complex ways. Seen from the perspective of social psychology, the memory research on the misinformation effect, with its narrow emphasis on the wording of post-event (mis)information, presents a much too simplistic viewpoint to explain the complex variables likely to operate in the overall misinformation effect.

While the early research on attitude change concerned itself with demonstrating the existence of a persuasion effect and on identifying the variables that maximized attitude change, later research focused more on how attitude change might lead to behavioral change and to the development of stable beliefs. The consensus of early researchers on attitude change was that attitude change through persuasive communication is quite *unstable* (e.g., Hovland, Janis & Kelly, 1953). A number of studies clearly demonstrated that attitudes adopted through social persuasion decayed in the weeks after the experiment, especially if persuaded by a highly credible source. Adopted attitudes rarely became part of the subject's stable belief system. Moreover, attitude change seldom led automatically to behavioral change.

One exception to the general instability of attitude change came to be known as the *"sleeper effect"* (Hovland, Janis, & Kelly, 1953). Subjects presented with an attitude counter to their original attitude did not change their attitude if tested immediately afterward. However, when tested a week later they were found to have changed their original attitude appreciably. Moreover, Hovland et al. noted that the attitude had become dissociated from its source; subjects claimed that they had always held the experimentally presented attitude.

In light of these transient responses, researchers began to focus on the conditions under which adopted attitudes were transformed into stable beliefs and could affect behavior in consistent ways. While experimentally manipulated attitudes typically decay over time, there is one notable exception—namely, when attitude change is mediated by direct, persistent contact with the communicator (Fazio & Zanna, 1978; Wicker & Pomizal, 1971). Hovland believed that the instability of attitude change across most early persuasion experiments was due to the fact that subjects typically were shown slides or films and had little or no direct contact with the communicator (Hovland, Janis, & Kelly, 1953). Later research stressed the importance of the direct *presence* of the communicator in conveying the message and also the *behavior* of the communicator while giving the message. The later research came to be known as research on the "attitude-object" and the "specificity" of his or her communication behavior (Fishbein, 1967; Wicker & Pomazil, 1971). This later research marked a distinct shift away from the communicated message and toward the specific behavior of the communicator.

This later research demonstrated that recipients were more likely to develop stable attitude change, as well as associated behavioral change, when they directly witnessed very specific verbal and nonverbal behaviors of the communicator. Consistent with these conclusions, Bandura (1977a) published his findings on vicarious learning, i.e., learning by direct observation of others.

The well-known research on cognitive dissonance is also about the relationship between attitude change and behavioral change. Festinger (1957) noted that the stability of attitude change depends upon social acceptance and sensitivity to social criticism. According to dissonance theory, when experimental subjects are asked to behave in ways contrary to their original attitude, they are more likely to change their original attitude and adopt an attitude more in line with their current behavior.

Thus, social psychology research has shown that altered attitudes become more stable when the communicator is directly present and behaves in specific ways that can be observed and learned by the recipient and/or when the recipient directly adopts a behavior consistent with the suggested message. Viewed from the perspective of social psychology, memory research on the misinformation effect needs to address a variety of issues: the presence or absence of the experimenter, the specific behaviors of the experimenter during the experiment, and the possible dissonance-producing consequences of getting the subject to report a misremembered experience in response to the recognition test.

Some persuasion research has specifically addressed the conditions under which changed yet unstable attitudes become transformed to stable beliefs and incorporated into one's belief system. This research is known as *cognitive consistency theory* (Brock, 1962; McGuire, 1960). These researchers focus on the organizational elements of an attitude in order to identify consistent and inconsistent elements within the overall cognitive structure of the attitude. Using a counterattitudinal paradigm in which subjects were asked to defend a position contrary to their own religious beliefs, Brock (1962) found that subjects sometimes reduced the cognitive dissonance through "cognitive restructuring," i.e., changing the organization of the elements within the overall structure of the attitude in the direction of greater internal consistency.

Cognitive consistency theory has some relevance to our understanding of the misinformation effect. The theory predicts that some misled subjects, when told that some of the information was inaccurate, would revert to their original report and yet others would persist with even more stable erroneous beliefs. Some subjects who originally saw a traffic light and were misled to believe they saw a stop sign may report a traffic light after being told it was a traffic light. Some subjects might persist even more in their misbelief that it was a stop sign. Unfortunately, neither the research on cognitive consistency theory nor that on the misinformation effect has yet identified the conditions under which cognitive restructuring is likely.

There have been surprisingly few studies on the relevance of the persuasion hypothesis to the misinformation effect. It is remarkable that most of the studies on misinformation suggestion fail to cite nearly three earlier decades of careful research on social persuasion. In reviewing the literature on the misinformation effect in adults, it becomes clear that most studies locate the effect primarily within the type of post-event information communicated and not within the social context of the communication. Research on the misinformation effect in adults

contains a number of important blind spots: (1) Few studies address the subjects' confidence in the memory. (2) There are no studies measuring individual differences in misinformation suggestibility. (3) No studies directly address how misinformation becomes transformed into a stable misbelief. (4) We could find only four studies that directly addressed the issue of source credibility.

With respect to source credibility, Loftus (1979a) cites an early study by Marshall (1966) on the contribution of communicator expertise. Subjects, either law students or police trainees, viewed a film about a boy, a baby carriage, and an angry woman. Then they filled out a questionnaire about the film. In the experimental condition, they filled out the questionnaire in the presence of either a law professor or a police captain who said, "It is extremely important that each of you gives us as much of his recollection as he possibly can, both as to what he heard and saw" (Loftus, 1979a, p. 97). Control subjects filled out significantly longer reports when in the presence of the status figure, but there were no significant differences in the accuracy of the report across conditions.

In a better designed study, Smith and Ellsworth (1987) had subjects view a video of a bank robbery. Then they were questioned about the video, either by someone represented as being highly knowledgeable about the crime in question or by someone completely naive about it. The questioner included both neutral and misleading questions in the inquiry. A significant misinformation effect was found when the questioner was highly knowledgeable, but when the questioner was reported as naive, no significant misinformation effect occurred. Smith and Ellsworth conclude, "the power of a misleading question to distort a listener's memory is not simply a matter of semantics or sentence construction, but involves the listener's perception of the social context" (p. 299). The misinformation effect occurs primarily when the questioner is assumed to have expertise.

Dodd and Bradshaw (1980) addressed another dimension of source credibility, namely, the *intention* of the communicator. Recall that social psychologists found that trustworthiness was a significant factor in attitude change. Subjects viewed a slide sequence about a staged car accident and then answered a series of questions including some misleading questions about the incident. In the experimental condition, the sheet of paper upon which the questions were written indicated that the questions were prepared by a lawyer representing the case. In the control condition, no source was indicated. Subjects then filled in a questionnaire about the incident. A significant misinformation effect was found when no source was mentioned, but the misinformation effect did not occur when the suggested misinformation was attributed to the lawyer. The authors interpret the results as meaning the misinformation effect depends in part upon the perceived intention of the communicator. The lawyer was perceived as having an ulterior motive to influence the subject's perception of the accident, thereby making it less likely that the subject would accept the misinformation. A second experiment used a neutral eyewitness to the accident and the driver of the car causing the accident as sources of post-event information. The significant misinformation effect found in the neutral condition was not found when the source was the driver of the car. The authors state that the misinformation effect is canceled out when the subjects see the source as biased.

Ceci, Ross, and Toglia (1987) compared memory performance across four experiments with children. The experimental conditions varied source credibility (authority figure, i.e., the experimenter, vs. a peer) and response bias (original vs. modified procedure). A significant misinformation effect was demonstrated when the original Loftus procedure was used. A significant reduction in the misinformation effect occurred when a peer introduced the misinformation instead of the experimenter, and also when the Zaragoza modified procedure was used. However, Ceci et al. noted that memory performance in the modified group was less than in the control group even when a peer presented the misinformation. In other words, when source credibility and response bias are separated out from the overall variance of the misinformation effect, a portion of the variance remains. They interpret the data in terms of "individual differences" in post-event suggestibility (p. 90), which implies that at least some subjects are vulnerable to making memory commission errors regardless of the nature of the social interaction.

Even though very few studies exist comparing the *interaction of misinformation suggestion and social persuasion*, it is clear that persuasion, at least in the form of source credibility, is an important variable contributing to the overall misinformation effect. The persuasion hypothesis offers a viable perspective on the misinformation effect, even if studies in support of this hypothesis are yet to be done. These studies are valuable for several reasons.

First, the research on *source credibility* alerts us to an important variable that has been under-emphasized in the memory research. The fact that subjects are likely to perceive the experimenter as a highly credible source certainly needs to be considered as a variable operative in the misinformation effect. Just how much of the misinformation effect is a function of persuasion? Cipriani (1988) experimentally manipulated interviewer status. Interviewers of higher status and credibility produced a greater misinformation effect on subjects than interviewers whose credibility had been discounted. She found, however, that if the interviewer's status was left undefined, subjects generally assumed that the interviewer had high credibility. The subjects showed a magnitude of persuasion comparable to those exposed to a highly credible source. Such findings demonstrate a strong "silent" source credibility contribution to most misinformation studies precisely because most researchers fail to address it.

Second, at least some social psychology research exists on the conditions under which a changed attitude can become transformed into a stable belief. There needs to be more scrutiny on how misled subjects handle the cognitive dissonance produced once they are led to give an inaccurate report about the original stimulus event, because under certain conditions they may edit out the misinformation, and under certain conditions they may restructure their beliefs about the original stimulus event in the direction of a stable false belief. It should be noted, however, that a false belief is not necessarily a false memory. Zaragoza and Koshmider (1989) remind us that Loftus and other researchers on the misinformation effect too loosely confound *memory representation* with *memory reports* or *beliefs* about the original stimulus event. They urge greater caution in our use of terms like false memory, especially because very few experiments exist that lend strong support to the memory alteration hypothesis. Using terms like "memory report" or "memory belief" more accurately convey that some of the variance of the misinformation effect is a function of social persuasion, especially source credibility.

Third, the social psychology research offers us a way to understand that the misinformation effect is not simply a matter of subtly manipulating the wording of suggested information. That research helps us to appreciate that a number of interacting variables no doubt contribute to the overall misinformation effect. To summarize, these include:

- source credibility
  - expertise
  - trustworthiness
  - motive
- presence and specific behavior of communicator
- type of message
  - one-sided
  - plausible
  - moderate degree of fear-arousal
- persuasibility
  - self-esteem
  - response-involvement
- dissonance-reducing behavior of recipient once misled
  - attitude change
  - cognitive restructuring; stable belief development

The misinformation effect is neither a simple phenomenon nor a unitary phenomenon. In order to ascertain the degree to which each of these variables contributes to the overall variance of the misinformation effect, more sophisticated research designs are needed to unpack the phenomenon.

Unpacking the Misinformation Effect

Increasingly sophisticated research designs have been used more recently to apportion how much of the overall variance of the misinformation effect is due to actual interference with the original memory (memory interference) and how much is due to a change in the subject's report in response to questions about the original stimulus event (memory acceptance). Belli (1989) correctly pointed out a flaw in Zaragoza's modified test. Not offering the post-event information as an option in the memory recognition test (phase 3) makes it impossible to

adequately detect memory impairment. Therefore, Belli included two additional modifications in the recognition test. First, he used a *yes/no retrieval test* instead of a forced choice retrieval test to measure recognition memory for the items in the original slide sequence—"Did 'x' appear in the slide sequence, yes or no?" The yes/no format pertains to the critical target items. In contrast to the Zaragoza forced-choice design, a yes/no format does not exclude responses based on remembering the post-event information. Belli reasoned that if control performance for the critical target item were greater than performance for the misled subjects, then some degree of memory interference had taken place. Second, Belli introduced *novel items* on the memory recognition test, i.e., items that were not part of the original target information or of the post-event information. Belli argued that if control performance were worse than misled performance for the novel items, then some degree of response bias would be operative. If misled subjects had indeed accepted the post-event misinformation, they would be more likely to say "no" to any novel items because of their bias toward the post-event information. The experiment used the same slide series used by McCloskey and Zaragoza (1985) about a man stealing a calculator.

In the first experiment, memory performance for the control relative to the misled subjects for the recognition of the original items was not significantly different, but for the novel items memory was significantly worse for the controls relative to the misled subjects. The finding is consistent with a response bias effect, but not with the memory interference hypothesis. Belli believed that the lack of a memory interference effect might have been due to poor memory for the target items. Therefore, he repeated the experiment with some minor modifications. He shortened the time of the interval between viewing the slides and answering questions about the slides, and also between the slides and the recognition test, so that subjects would be more likely to remember the original stimulus event. He reasoned that subjects needed to first remember the target stimulus before post-event memory interference could be demonstrated.

The results of the second experiment confirmed both hypotheses. With respect to memory for the original target items, control performance was significantly more accurate than the performance of misled subjects. With respect to the novel items, control performance was significantly worse than that of misled subjects. Belli interpreted the results to mean that, at least under certain conditions, "both memory interference and acceptance influence the response in the misled condition in comparison with those in the control condition" (p. 77). The misinformation effect nearly always contains some element of a response bias because of the way the questions are asked about a memory for a previous event; it may also contain some degree of actual memory interference, but only under certain conditions. The magnitude of the memory interference effect is relatively small. While it makes no sense to talk about memory interference for an event for which the individual has no memory, memory interference can occur, especially for events that the individual remembers, but about which he or she is quite uncertain. Moreover, when the subject is questioned in a plausible way, the subject may shift his or her decision criteria and report greater certainty about misinformation contained in the post-event inquiry, while not distorting the original memory.

Tversky and Tuchin (1989) repeated the original McCloskey and Zaragoza experiment (1985) with an important modification. They used a yes/no recognition test in which the original, misleading, and novel items were each tested separately. In contrast to the numerous Zaragoza experiments in which no significant misinformation occurred with the modified design, Tversky and Tuchin's design modifications resulted in a significant misinformation effect. Furthermore, misled subjects rejected the novel items significantly more than they rejected the misleading information. These data imply that some misled subjects were significantly more inclined to incorrectly recognize the misled over novel information than to correctly reject it. Tversky and Tuchin interpret the data as "substantial support for the claim that misleading information affects memory for the original information" (p. 88) and say that the "data argue against the claim that nothing happens to the memory for the original event as a consequence of the misleading information" (p. 89). Nevertheless, they also say that some of the data demonstrate that certain subjects remembered both the original and the misleading information—a finding consistent with the coexistence hypothesis.

Chandler (1991) found support for the memory impairment hypothesis using the modified test with a mixed list recognition test to reduce response bias. In her study, subjects were presented with slides of nature scenes in phase 1 and then with very similar, distractor (experimental) or dissimilar (control) slides as post-event information in phase 2. During the recognition test (phase 3), subjects chose between the target slide and a novel, related slide. A significant misinformation effect occurred after a 15-minute retention interval, but was not observed after a 48-hour retention interval. In one experiment Chandler tested the coexistence hypothesis by presenting the distractors before (pre-event misinformation) the target slides. She predicted that a misinformation effect occurring under these conditions would favor the coexistence hypothesis. No significant misinformation occurred under these conditions. Chandler's data pose some problems for the memory impairment hypothesis, in that the misinformation effect occurred with a shorter but not with a longer retention interval. Chandler believes that the memory impairment hypothesis could be "revised" to account for the data by assuming that the post-event information causes "temporary suppression" (p. 123) of the original memory trace under certain conditions, but not necessarily its destruction.

Belli, Windschitl, McCarthy, and Winfrey (1992) designed an experiment to better detect the exact conditions under which memory impairment does and does not occur. They used the McCloskey and Zaragoza (1985) modified test procedure with two additional modifications. First, the retention interval between the post-event information and a forced-choice recognition test was varied from 15 minutes to five to seven days across four experiments to see if greater forgetting was a necessary condition of memory impairment. Second, Belli et al. attempted to use more centrally viewed target items, i.e., critical items that were related to the central action in the slide sequence about a mother and a child arguing about a jar of spilled pennies. Central targets were used to more or less guarantee that the subject encoded the target in memory. With the short retention interval no significant misinformation occurred with the modified test. The near perfect performance demonstrated that subjects clearly encoded the central information in memory. With a longer retention interval, a significant misinformation effect occurred. Belli et al. conclude that "substantial memory impairment will occur under limited conditions" (p. 366). Memory impairment can occur with the modified test, but it depends upon two conditions: (1) good initial encoding, and (2) a long retention interval so that "substantive forgetting of the event items" occurs (p. 362).

Wagenaar and Boer (1987) made a very innovative modification in the original test in order to ascertain whether or not the misinformation effect is due to actual interference with memory. They used essentially the same research design that the original used (Loftus et al., 1978). Subjects were shown a slide sequence in which a car leaves a gas station, pulls up at an intersection, makes a right turn, and then is involved in an accident with a pedestrian. The original stimulus is a traffic light (phase 1). For any given subject the color of the traffic light may have been red, green, or yellow. Next (phase 2), all subjects are asked a series of 20 questions about the slide sequence. The set of questions contained one or two critical items. Subjects were tested in three conditions: (1) a consistent condition (traffic light), (2) an inconsistent or misleading condition (stop sign), or (3) a neutral condition (intersection). For example, subjects in each respective condition were asked, "Did a pedestrian cross the street when the car, after leaving the gas station, arrived at the . . . [(1) traffic light, (2) stop sign, or (3) intersection]?" After 20 minutes of filler activity, subjects were given a forced-choice recognition test (phase 3), in which each subject was shown a pair of black and white slides and asked which slide was part of the original stimulus event. So far, the research paradigm follows the original Loftus paradigm very closely. But Wagenaar and Boer add a fourth phase. All subjects were given an additional questionnaire, in which they were told that they had actually seen a traffic light in the original slide sequence. They were given the correct feedback regardless of whether or not they had correctly or incorrectly responded to the questions about the critical item in the forced-choice recognition test (phase 3). However, they were not given information about the color of the traffic light in the original slide sequence, and were asked to indicate which color they had originally seen. The research paradigm is designed first to demonstrate the misinformation effect (phases 1–3), and

then to see if some of the original information (presumed to be altered or lost by the post-event information) could be retrieved through subsequent questioning. If so, it would cast doubt on the memory interference hypothesis; if not, the memory interference hypothesis would be supported.

The results replicated previous work on the misinformation effect in that subjects in the misleading condition relative to other conditions were significantly misled by the critical question about the stop sign. However, in phase 4, after they were told that the original stimulus item was a traffic light, the recall of the color of the traffic light was about the same across all three conditions. The results are at odds with the memory interference hypothesis, which would predict a significant decrement in recall for misled subjects relative to the consistent or neutral subjects in phase 4. Moreover, Loftus has asserted that the introduction of misleading information results in a "blended memory" combining the original and misleading information. Wagenaar and Boer reason that if such "blended" memories occur, then misled subjects relative to control subjects would have been more likely to have been biased toward reporting a red traffic light in phase 4, because of their being previously questioned about a red stop sign (phase 2). There were no differences across groups in the color reported. Wagenaar and Boer interpret these data as meaning "subjects are only misled when they fail to encode the traffic light" (p. 298), and the data are strongly supportive of the nonretention hypothesis. They state unequivocally, "Hence a drastic version of the theory, stating that the original information will always be destroyed by misleading post-event information, can be rejected" (p. 305).

Lindsay (1990) conducted an experiment using a source-monitoring design. In order to rule out demand characteristics, subjects were told immediately before the recognition test that information in the post-event narrative was wrong and should not be reported. The experiment varied two conditions— high and low discriminability. In the high discriminable condition, the post-event narrative was read in a different voice from the narrative accompanying the original slide sequence, and the recognition test was given some time later in a well-lit room. In the low discriminable condition, the post-event narrative was read in the same voice, and the original narrative and the recognition test were given immediately after the original slide presentation in a darkened room. As predicted, experimental subjects in the low, but not the high, discriminable condition reported significantly more often that they had "seen" the post-event misleading detail than the controls. They made significant source misattributions. Furthermore, subjects in both the high and low discriminable conditions recalled significantly fewer details on misled items than on control items. These results demonstrate that *both* source misattribution and memory impairment occurred, although the magnitude of the memory impairment was generally quite small. Lindsay concludes that the data:

> provides strong support for the hypothesis that misled subjects sometimes forget the source of the misleading information . . . indicate that misleading suggestions impair subject's ability to remember event details. (p. 1082)

Both of these mechanisms occur and are not reducible to demand characteristics or response bias.

While the Belli, Chandler, Lindsay, and Wagenaar and Boer research modifications represent an advance over the original Loftus paradigm, they nevertheless are limited to study of the following variables: (1) memory encoding for the target item, (2) type of misleading information, and (3) type of recognition test as independent main effects. Frischholz (1990) hypothesized that the misinformation effect probably represents an *interaction* of a number of variables. He designed a study complex enough to test this assertion. Subjects were shown a film of a robbery of a liquor store, in which a shoot-out occurs. One police officer and one robber are shot (phase 1). Immediately after viewing the film, subjects were given an initial recognition test. To minimize response bias, subjects were explicitly told not to guess. A multiple choice, not a forced-choice recognition test, was used. "Don't know" was included as an option. After a week delay, subjects were tested with one of four types of post-event information: correct, misleading, neutral, or no post-event information. Two critical items were included, one about a peripheral detail (name of store owner) and another one about the action (outcome of the gun battle). All subjects were shown a narrative

about the post-event information designed to make it appear credible but fallible. Subjects were told that it was not possible for any subject to remember all of the details of a complex event like this. Subjects were then given a "discrepancy detection test" in which they were asked to carefully evaluate a written testimony about the film against their own memory for the film in order to identify memory omission and commission errors. Then they were given a final multiple choice recognition test and a stimulus reinstatement procedure "in which subjects were shown either the same or a modified version of the original film and asked to determine if the it was same as the one they originally saw."

The results again demonstrated the existence of a misinformation effect. The results were inconsistent with the response bias hypothesis and were "partially consistent with the memory alteration hypothesis" (p. 107), in that the misinformation effect still occurred even when subjects were given a strong demand not to guess in the instructions and were explicitly told that they did not have to guess in the multiple choice test. More important, the results suggest an *interaction* between the initial encoding status and the type of post-event information (p. 109), in that subjects who failed to encode the original target detail in memory, as compared to those who remembered it well, were significantly more likely to be influenced by the post-event information—both the inaccurate and the accurate post-event information. For example, those subjects who responded "don't know" in the original recognition test were more likely to change their recollection to an inaccurate response when given inaccurate post-event information or to a correct response if given accurate post-event information. Significantly fewer subjects made memory commission errors if they had encoded the original information.

The studies described so far all utilize explicit memory tests in which the subject is explicitly asked to remember the original items. An alternate strategy is to utilize *implicit memory tests* in which subjects are not explicitly told to remember the original items but the memory for these items is measured through its indirect influence on task performance. Loftus, Feldman et al. (1995) report on several experiments using an implicit memory test. The first experiment utilized the original

Loftus paradigm. The target information was a hammer and the critical misinformation item was a screwdriver. The experiment included an implicit memory test, in which subjects were "not told to remember particular events, but rather are to perform some other task" [seemingly part of a separate experiment] (p. 51). The test required that subjects "Name the first five tools that come to mind" (p. 52). Since the subjects had previously seen the hammer as the original stimulus item, it was expected that the hammer would have a priming effect on the implicit task performance, i.e., subjects would be more likely include a hammer in their memory of types of tools. It was also hypothesized that exposure to misinformation would reduce the expected priming effect. If exposure to misinformation impaired the original memory trace of the hammer, no priming effect would be observed in those subjects exposed to misinformation. The results were mixed. Exposure to misinformation did not reduce the priming effect across all subjects exposed to it, but it did reduce the priming effect in a subsample of subjects who "bought the misinformation." Loftus et al. conclude:

> While this result is consistent with the notion that the event memory was impaired, the particular implicit test used makes the results open to other interpretations. (p. 52)

Therefore, Loftus, Falman & Dashiell, 1995 designed another experiment using a degraded picture task as the implicit memory test. Subjects viewed a slide show about a shoplifting incident and then read a narrative that included critical misinformation items. The implicit test, presented to subjects as a separate experiment, had subjects try to identify common objects when presented only with fragmentary stimuli of the objects (along a continuum from highly fragmented to not at all fragmented). Subjects in implicit degraded picture tasks typically require less information to identify the object if they have been previously exposed to it. Loftus et al. hypothesized that exposure to misinformation would reduce the expected implicit memory savings if such exposure had impaired the original memory trace. Subjects exposed to misinformation produced the predicted misinformation effect on an explicit memory recognition test. They also produced the

expected savings or priming effect on the implicit degraded picture task. However, exposure to misinformation resulted in only:

> a very small reduction in priming of the event item after exposure to misinformation . . . critical items that were primed by having been seen earlier in the slides remain almost equally primed despite the presence of misinformation. (pp. 53–55)

Thus, the experiment failed to support the memory impairment hypothesis.

Conclusions Drawn from the Adult Misinformation Studies

Two decades of research on the misinformation effect have shown it to be a robust and replicable phenomenon. While the existence of the misinformation effect is irrefutable (Loftus et al., 1995), its interpretation is more controversial. Based on the research of the past decade, a strong interpretation of the Loftus memory impairment hypothesis has been given very little support. At least partial support for some sort of memory impairment is given by some of the studies, although the magnitude of the effect is generally quite small and occurs only under certain conditions (Belli, 1989, experiment #2; Belli et al., 1992; Ceci, Ross et al., 1987; Chandler, 1991; Frischholz, 1990; Howe, 1991; Lindsay, 1990; Loftus, Feldman et al., 1995; Tversky & Tuchin, 1989). The memory impairment thesis failed to receive support in other experiments (Belli, 1989, experiment #1; Loftus et al., 1996; Wagenaar & Boer, 1987). Thus, at this point it seems safe to say that it is no longer acceptable to view the misinformation effect as a simple overwriting of the memory for the original event.

It is perhaps safer to assume that the misinformation effect is not a unitary phenomenon, but rather represents a number of variables and a complex interaction among these variables. The search for a single underlying mechanism to explain the misinformation effect has proven fruitless. The misinformation effect is a *multidimensional* phenomenon. Strong support for the *interactive view* is given by the fact that the magnitude of the misinformation effect greatly differs across experiments with minor modifications in the research design. When a research design varies any of the following variables, the magnitude of the misinformation effect changes: response bias (Ceci, Ross et al., 1987; McCloskey & Zaragoza, 1985), demand characteristics (Lindsay, 1990), source attribution (Lindsay, 1990; Lindsay & Read, 1994), source credibility (Ceci et al., 1987; Smith & Ellsworth, 1987), or retention interval (Belli et al., 1992; Chandler, 1991). In this chapter we have at least identified a number of important variables, each of which contributes to the overall misinformation effect:

- encoding status
- retention interval
- type of post-event information
  - -central/peripheral
  - -one-sided vs. two-sided
  - -degree of discrepancy with original information
  - -simple vs. complex message
  - -degree of emotional arousal
- retrieval conditions
  - -social persuasion
  - -source credibility
  - -response bias
- persuasability
- dissonance reducing behavior once misled

Reducing this list of variables to those that are the most important, we might say that the misinformation effect is largely a function of *uncertainty*, either because the subject failed to encode or incorrectly encoded the original memory, or because the subject was asked about peripheral details less likely to be clear in his/her memory. The magnitude of this uncertainty effect is greatly increased in a *social context* in which the misinformation is suggested by a highly credible source (like the experimenter or a police interrogator) who asked questions in a particular way (response bias) so as to permit the subject to shift his or her decision criteria, especially for uncertain experiences, in the direction of making memory commission errors.

Based on a more sophisticated appreciation of the complexity of the variables contributing to the overall misinformation effect, it becomes understandable how the original Loftus research design magnifies the misinformation effect. Subjects are asked post-event questions largely about peripheral details about which they are uncertain. They are

never tested to see if they remember the original stimulus event. The post-event information is given by a highly credible source (the experimenter) who the subject presumes knows more about the stimulus event in question than he or she does. Subjects are given a forced-choice recognition test that introduces a bias to respond to the post-event information over the original information. The original design pulls for an interaction between the uncertainty of the subject's memory, high source credibility, and response bias, which greatly increases the magnitude of the misinformation effect.

Precisely because of the complexity of the variables involved, it is a serious overstatement for Loftus to refer in her current work to the entire misinformation effect as an example of "the creation of new memories" (Loftus, 1993; Loftus & Hoffman, 1989). The Loftus and Hoffman paper (1989) is her attempt to respond to the emerging research that fails to lend strong support to her original memory impairment hypothesis. She concedes that a strong memory impairment position is not supported by the data, though she cites the Belli (1989) and Tversky and Tuchin (1989) experiments to conclude that "memory impairment plays some role" in the misinformation effect. Loftus replaces her memory integration or overwriting hypothesis with a *memory weakening* hypothesis: "memory impairment could refer to a weakening of the memory trace, or a clouding of memory, or an intrinsic impoverishment of memory" (p. 101). She also concedes that "memory acceptance plays a major role" (p. 100) in the phenomenon, and in this sense concedes that social influence factors, like response bias and source credibility, make a significant contribution to the overall variance of the misinformation effect compared to memory alteration per se. She reframes memory acceptance as a "worthy" phenomenon (p. 102) ripe for further investigation. She reasons that if memory commission errors occur in subjects who failed to encode the original information, this could be evidence for the "creation" of new memories. Overall, the intent of the Loftus and Hoffman argument is to downplay social influence factors and to locate the misinformation effect squarely back within the memory domain, even though the preponderance of evidence suggests otherwise.

Our own opinion is that very little compelling evidence exists to justify a general interpretation of the misinformation effect in terms of the *overwriting or creation* of memories, except in "a fraction of the subjects" (Loftus, Feldman et al., 1995, p. 62). We agree with Zaragoza and Koshmider (1989) that memory performance does not equal memory representation, and that most of the data from the misinformation experiments pertains to memory performance, not necessarily to the memory representation per se. The continued use of terms like "memory impairment" or "creation" confounds these issues and does not lead to the refinement of scientific understanding that a complex phenomenon like the misinformation effect merits.

CHILD EXPERIMENTAL STUDIES ON THE MISINFORMATION EFFECT

Because the misinformation effect is quite robust for adults, the question arises of whether children are more vulnerable to post-event suggestion than adults. While there is a paucity of studies with adults on post-event suggestions for central actions as compared to peripheral details, the bulk of the studies on the misinformation effect in children directly focuses on post-event suggestibility for central actions, including abuse-related actions. Because of the great number of allegations of childhood sexual abuse that require investigation, the researchers on post-event suggestibility in children have evolved rather sophisticated research designs to address this question. The results are quite consistent across studies.

The earliest studies on the misinformation effect in children simply applied the research paradigms developed for adults with little modification. Like the Loftus original test, these studies primarily utilized a laboratory simulation strategy, in which children viewed slides, films, or a staged incident. Dale, Loftus, and Rathbun (1978) conducted a study in which four- and five-year-old children viewed four short films. Following the viewing, each child was asked a series of questions, some of which were about events that actually occurred in the films and some of which were about plausible events that were not part of the original stimulus event, i.e., were misleading. The questions were presented in a variety of forms, e.g., "Did you see a . . . ? Didn't you see the

. . . ? Didn't you see a . . . ?", etc. Then the children were asked to tell the experimenter everything they remembered (free recall). The results indicated that children sometimes made memory commission errors. As predicted, the form of the post-event question significantly affected the children's answers, but only to misleading questions about events not actually in the original films. The form of the question did not affect the answers to questions about events that were part of the original stimulus event. The authors conclude that young children are vulnerable to post-event suggestions and that "the form of the [misleading] question actually modifies the memory" (p. 276). Despite limitations in the research design, the value of this study lies in its early demonstration of the misinformation effect in children.

Other studies followed. Cohen and Harnick (1980) had subjects in three age groups (grades 3, 6, and college) view a film about a purse-snatching. Then the subjects were asked 11 accurate and 11 inaccurate, misleading questions about the events in the film in a counterbalanced design. Subjects were tested for their recall of the event, and then a week later were given 22 multiple choice questions about their recognition memory for the film. Relative to the sixth graders and college students, the third graders performed worse in terms of the amount they remembered in response to nonsuggestive questions, and they showed a significantly greater tendency to be misled by false information, although all three groups showed some tendency to be misled. Cohen and Harnick conclude that younger children were more susceptible to misleading questions because they did not remember the film as well as the older children, and therefore tended to utilize the misleading questions when the correct information was not available.

Duncan, Whitney, and Kunen (1982) showed subjects of various age groups from six years to adulthood slides about a cartoon story, following which subjects were questioned with three types of information—no information, correct information, or misleading information. Subjects in one experiment were later asked follow-up questions to cue their recall of the slides, and in another experiment were given a yes/no recognition test. Both recall and recognition accuracy for the original events increased with age. To correct for the fact that a portion of the younger children may have responded to the misleading information because they had not remembered the original event, the data on post-event information were analyzed only for instances where subjects had an accurate recall or recognition memory for the original details. The misinformation effect increased with age, i.e., was lowest in younger children and highest in college students. The researchers interpreted the data in terms of developmental differences. Younger children tend to process information in sensory ways, while older children and adults process information semantically because of cognitive maturation. Thus, younger children were presumed to be less vulnerable to semantic post-event misinformation.

Zaragoza (1987) replicated Loftus's original test with preschoolers. However, when she modified the recognition test to minimize response bias, no significant misinformation effect could be demonstrated for young children across a series of experiments. Zaragoza (1987) showed preschoolers between three and six years of age slides of a young girl riding a yellow toy giraffe and having various adventures in a park. After viewing the slides the children were given a synopsis of the story, which included both accurate and misleading information. Then they were shown slides in a forced-choice recognition test, much like in the original Loftus paradigm with adults. The difference was that the misleading item was not offered as a possible choice. Subjects made a choice between slide pairs containing an original stimulus item and a nearly identical but novel item. By not offering the post-event information as part of the final recognition test, Zaragoza hoped to avoid biasing the children to respond to the misleading information. No significant differences were found between the misled and control conditions. No significant misinformation effect occurred. Zaragoza replicated the findings in a second experiment using the same design except that the children were exposed to the misleading information twice. Still, no significant misinformation effect could be found.

Zaragoza (1991) reported four additional, more recent experiments in which she tested preschoolers with the Loftus original and then with the Zaragoza modified design, and also with a modified version of a cued-recall test. Across all experiments and age groups, with 260 subjects viewing the same slide event, a significant misinformation effect occurred when the original test was used and no significant misinformation effect occurred when the modified test was used. Zaragoza concludes that preschool children's original memory is not impaired by exposure to post-event misinformation, and that the misinformation effect occurs only when children are uncertain about their memory for the original event and are therefore more susceptible to the social influence inherent in the testing situation, such as the perceived authority of the interviewer and the pressure to fill in the gaps of memory.

Marin et al. (1979) had subjects of five age groups (kindergarten, first grade, third to fourth grade, seventh to eighth grade, and college years) serve as "eyewitnesses" to a staged incident in which an angry argument broke out between two confederates about a double booking of a room for the experiment. The innovative strategy of using a live staged incident presumably was more engaging for children than watching slides or a film. Subjects' memory for the staged event was tested using free recall, specific questions (including one misleading question about a nonexistent object), and a photo identification. The misleading question about the peripheral detail was either, "Was the package the man carried small?" or "Did the man close the door as he left?" After two weeks, the subjects' memory was retested with the same retrieval strategies, but this time with a nonleading question for the critical item. Consistent with many other studies, the youngest children recalled significantly less than the older children and adults in the free recall condition. A significant misinformation effect occurred for either misleading question. No significant age differences were observed; children and adults were similarly misled.

Ochsner and Zaragoza (1988) had first graders experience a staged purse-snatching by a man who entered a room while they were working on a puzzle. In comparison to a control group in which the man entered the room but did not steal the purse, children in the theft group produced significantly more accurate statements about the event free recall, and were significantly less likely to select misleading alternatives on a forced-choice recognition test about the event.

Another innovative strategy involves the use of *story recall tasks* instead of viewing slides, films, or staged events. Drawing on Nelson and Gruendel's (1986) concept of scripts as fundamental to how children organize experience, investigators began to move away from adult-biased research strategies, like viewing slides, toward research strategies clearly adapted to the child's world, like listening to stories about events common to the child's world. Children's memory is organized around routines. The repeated, personally meaningful events of a child's daily life are given an internal cognitive organization in the form of memory scripts. The structure of stories is well matched to the child's evolving cognitive organization.

Saywitz (1987) had third, sixth and ninth graders listen to an audiotaped story about a crime. Children were instructed to watch the story happening in their minds as they listened to the story. Then they were asked for free recall of the story, following which they were asked specific questions that served as recognition cues for the story's details. The questions included three misleading questions. Five days later, the free recall and recognition strategies were given again. In free recall, the third graders, relative to the older children, made significantly more omission errors. They also added many more details that were not in the original story and embellished many of the details of the story. Overall, children of all age groups tended to resist post-event misinformation. Only 14 of 72 subjects made some sort of commission error. No significant age differences in commission errors were found.

Ceci, Ross, and Toglia (1987) reported four experiments using the story recall procedure. The first two experiments were about a girl who had eaten her eggs too quickly and got a stomachache (phase 1). A day later, half of the children ages three and twelve years old were presented with either accurate or plausible but misleading details about the story (phase 2). Three days later, all the children were given a recognition test. In both experiments, the procedure was the same except that an adult experimenter told the story and gave the post-event information in experiment #1 whereas a seven-year-old child told the story and gave the post-event information in experiment #2. In both experiments, older children were significantly more accurate than younger children in their memory for the story. A significant misinformation effect was found for the three year olds, but the twelve year olds were fairly resistant to misleading post-event

information. Nevertheless, some older children were also vulnerable to misleading post-event suggestions. The main finding was that the misinformation effect was significantly reduced when the story and post-event information were presented by a child than by an adult. Ceci et al. interpret the results to mean that part of the misinformation effect is due to source credibility, i.e., how young children modify their memory report in response to an adult authority figure.

The third and fourth experiments essentially adapt the original Loftus research paradigm and the Zaragoza modified research paradigm to the story recall procedure with children and compare memory performance across both experimental procedures. In both experiments, a seven-year-old boy read the story and provided the post-event information and misinformation a day later. As predicted across these experiments, the misinformation effect was greater when the original Loftus design was used, and was significantly reduced when the modified Zaragoza design was used. However, Ceci et al. note that the memory performance of the children was somewhat less than control performance even when the modified design was used, implying that these children are still somewhat vulnerable to misinformation suggestions. In experiment #4, the percent of accuracy in the original, modified, and control conditions was 46%, 72%, and 88%, respectively. Ceci et al. note that, even when the variance due to social influence is factored out of the overall misinformation effect by using children to present the post-event information to minimize source credibility effects and by using the modified design to minimize response bias, a portion of the variance of the misinformation effect still remains. Ceci et al. correctly note that individual differences in post-event suggestibility remain. At least some children are susceptible to misinformation suggestions even when social influences are controlled.

In an even further departure from slides and films, other researchers have sought to design experiments more around *personally significant events*, such as concern for physical safety, bodily injury, or abandonment (Goodman, Rudy, Bottoms, & Aman, 1990). King and Yuille (1987) report a series of experiments in which the original event was constructed around what was presumed to be a central concern of the child. Children of different ages were used as subjects. In one experiment, for example, a child is left alone in a room. A stranger enters the room to attend to some plants. In another experiment a staged bicycle theft occurs. Following each event, the post-event interview included one or several misleading questions about the incident, concerning either salient or peripheral details. While younger children were more easily misled than older children, at least for peripheral details, younger as well as older children were generally resistant to post-event suggestions "about matters that are salient and memorable" (p. 27).

A perhaps better experiment about children's emotional concerns, such as concern for security, was conducted by Peters (1991), who constructed a misinformation experiment about children's fear of fire. Children ranging from ages six through nine were asked to perform a series of tasks in a psychology building. Included in the tasks was a baseline measurement of blood pressure and pulse rate. Then, as a female confederate entered the room, a smoke detector went off. While the children's blood pressure and pulse rate were being measured again, the woman expressed concern that there may be a fire in the building. No fire alarm was used nor was the possibility of a fire mentioned in the control group, but the woman acted otherwise similarly. Following the incident, the children were questioned about it with both accurate and misleading questions. "Did the girl wearing a yellow sweater have brown hair?" (no yellow sweater). The results demonstrated that the children in the fire alarm condition relative to the control condition were indeed significantly more physiologically aroused. A significant misinformation effect was found in the no fire alarm group when the effect of accurate vs. misleading information was compared. A much greater misinformation effect occurred in the fire alarm group relative to the control group. Peters interprets the results to mean that the misinformation effect is compounded by events that are central to the child's concerns: "the experience of high stress in the fire alarm condition coupled with a series of misleading questions greatly reduced their eyewitness accuracy" (p. 73).

The difference between the King and Yuille (1987) and Peters (1991) data may have to do with just how significant an event is to a child. While personally memorable experiences may be more resistant to post-event contamination, memorable but overly stressful experiences may make the child more

vulnerable to post-event suggestion, precisely because in these situations the child is worried and apt to look to a parental authority figure for reassurance.

These early studies show that younger children recall significantly less than older children, but what they recall is nevertheless accurate. Like adults, younger children may be vulnerable to post-event suggestive effects, but only under certain conditions. However, the findings regarding the misinformation effect are highly inconsistent in these early studies, and the question of whether younger children are more susceptible than older children to post-event suggestion remains largely unresolved across these studies. The inconsistencies are: a greater misinformation effect in younger children (Cohen & Harnick, 1980), lesser misinformation effect in younger children (Duncan et al., 1982), no misinformation effect in young children (Zaragoza, 1987, 1991), and a misinformation effect equivalent across all ages (Marin et al., 1979; Saywitz, 1987). However, if those subjects who failed to remember the original stimulus details are factored out, the remaining young children do not appear significantly more vulnerable to misinformation than adults. Yet, some individual children are still more vulnerable (Ceci, Ross et al., 1987).

Cole and Loftus (1987) attempted to make sense out of these findings by stating that whether a misinformation effect occurs in younger children depends upon the clarity of memory for the original event and upon the time interval between the original event and the final memory test. In other words, if the child does not encode the original stimulus detail, or if the memory decays over time, then a greater misinformation effect is likely. Zaragoza (1987) adds that, in addition to uncertainty about the memory for the original event, certain social factors, like response bias, also greatly influence the misinformation effect. Ceci et al. (1987) demonstrate how source credibility is an important contribution to the misinformation effect in younger children (cf. also McGough's (1994) review of the studies on social conformity in children (pp. 71–76).

Thus, it may be misleading to believe that young children are more vulnerable to misleading questions than adults, unless we mean that young children certainly have poor total memory for the original events, and are therefore more susceptible to social influences about memory performance. Nevertheless, even when social influences and the status of the memory for the original stimulus details are statistically controlled, some children, although not most children, are quite vulnerable to memory commission errors when asked about their memory for a past experience. Ceci et al. remind us that individual differences in post-event suggestibility no doubt do occur and that a small subgroup of children probably exist who will make memory commission errors under most circumstances.

The evolving standard of research on post-event misinformation suggestibility in children was introduced by Gail Goodman and her associates (Goodman & Reed, 1986). Because children have been increasingly called upon to give testimony regarding allegations of child abuse, Goodman wanted to know whether children's reports were accurate or vulnerable to suggestive influences. Therefore, she designed events that were likely to have personal significance to children. Such events must (1) capture the child's interest (being relatively unique or novel), (2) be personally meaningful, (3) actively involve the child, and (4) evoke strong emotions about a social interaction (Goodman, Aman, & Hirschman, 1987). The purpose was to select meaningful events closely resembling the context of child sexual victimization and to see whether children were suggestible in that context. As Goodman states, "Our primary focus is on whether false reports of abuse can be created through suggestive questioning" (Goodman, Rudy, Bottoms, & Aman, 1990, p. 257). These studies came to be known as the *Simon Says studies.*

Goodman and Reed (1986) had children, ages three and six years old, and adults interact with an unfamiliar male stranger in an unfamiliar setting. The children directly interacted with the stranger, playing a game similar to Simon Says that involved various arm movements. Four or five days later the subjects were asked 18 accurate and four misleading post-event questions. Memory performance was measured by free recall narrative and a photo line-up identification. The three year olds performed poorly on the total amount of information recalled and in the photo identification, but the six year olds responded nearly as well as adults. A clear age difference emerged with respect to the suggestive questions. The three year olds were the most vulnerable

to the misleading suggestions, then the six year olds, and the adults were the least suggestive. However, suggestive questions for central actions, like the arm movements, were resisted by children of both age groups as well as by the adults. More importantly, even when children answered the suggestive questions inaccurately, the misinformation rarely became incorporated into their free recall narrative. Goodman and Reed conclude,

> if 5-to-6-year-old children are questioned in a nonsuggestive manner and are provided with a nonsuggestive target present line-up, their eyewitness accuracy can equal or even exceed adults . . . both 6- and 3-year-old children were more suggestible than adults. . . . For central information about which all age groups had an accurate memory . . . even the 3-year-olds were not significantly more suggestible than adults. (p. 328)

Over the next five years, Goodman and her associates made a number of important modifications in the Simon Says procedure. Each child was alone with the male confederate, sometimes in an unfamiliar laboratory room (Goodman & Aman, 1990), and sometimes in an unfamiliar trailer (Goodman et al., 1990; Rudy & Goodman, 1991). The confederate asked the child to play games like playing with puppets or having an imaginary tea party. The Simon Says game was modified to include *nonsexual touch,* such as having the confederate and the child touch each other on the knees or tickle each other. Other games included having the confederate dress the child in a clown costume placed over the child's clothing and lifting the child onto a table and taking photographs of him or her in several poses. The activities were selected based on a review of child sexual abuse cases. The idea was to include "related (but non-abusive) actions" (Goodman et al., 1990, p. 260) that bore some affinity to actual sexual abuse, like sexual touching, having clothes removed, or having pictures taken while posing naked.

A second important modification pertained to the post-event misleading questions. Goodman and her associates developed an elaborate classification of misleading questions into time, room, person, and action categories (e.g., Rudy & Goodman, 1991) in order to distinguish more carefully between the relative suggestive influence of different types of post-event information, from peripheral to more central information. A very important innovation was the inclusion of "*abuse questions*." These suggestive questions were specifically created to address "actions that might lead to an accusation of child abuse, such as 'He took your clothes off, didn't he?' . . . [or] 'Did he kiss you?'" (Goodman et al., 1990, p. 260). They also included correct leading questions as a control, e.g., "He didn't touch you, did he?" (Rudy & Goodman, 1991, p. 529). The questions were derived from ratings by professionals as to the kind of questions likely to be asked in an abuse investigation.

A third important modification concerned the degree of participation by the child. Goodman correctly criticizes the adult misinformation studies on the grounds of ecological validity. Data drawn from college students viewing slides in the laboratory are not readily generalizable to real-life eyewitness situations. Therefore, Goodman wanted to investigate whether post-event suggestive influences in children were different under the conditions of passive witnessing and active participation (Goodman et al., 1990; Rudy & Goodman, 1991). They predicted that children who actively participated in the Simon Says game would remember the incident better and be more resistant to post-event suggestions than those children who merely observed the game. Pairs of children were used in each experimental trial. As part of the beginning of the game, each child was asked to draw a marble from a box. The strange man then said to one child, "OK, since you get the red [yellow] marble, you get to be the one who watches today. Your job is to sit very quietly in this chair and pay attention to what happens" (Rudy & Goodman, 1991, p. 529). The other child was told that she or he would actively participate in the Simon Says and other remaining games. Post-event information was given to, and memory testing was conducted for, children in both the bystanding and participating conditions (Goodman et al., 1990; Rudy & Goodman, 1991).

A fourth innovation was the use of regular and anatomically correct dolls as part of the memory test phase (phase 3) (Goodman & Aman, 1990; Saywitz, Goodman, Nicholas, & Moan, 1991). Because it is well documented that young children rarely give detailed memory reports of abuse, anatomically correct dolls have been used as interview props to stimu-

late memory retrieval (Boat & Everson, 1993; Friedemann & Morgan, 1985). While the use of these dolls as part of child sexual abuse investigations has become widespread, their use has also become highly controversial. Some experts believe that the dolls themselves are unduly suggestive and can elicit false reports of abuse (Yates & Terr, 1988). Therefore, Goodman and her associates used the dolls, along with the other recall and recognition memory tests, in subgroups of child subjects to see if children in the anatomically correct doll condition were indeed more vulnerable to post-event suggestions than children not given the dolls. Four experimental conditions were used: (1) anatomically correct dolls as part of a play session to stimulate memory, (2) regular (non-anatomical) dolls in a play session, (3) anatomically correct dolls in view but out of reach and not used for play, and (4) no dolls.

The children were interviewed about 10 to 12 days after the session with the stranger. First they were asked to tell the interviewer everything that happened in the trailer (free recall). Then they were asked a series of specific post-event questions (cued recall) to cue their memory, including a series of misleading questions (post-event suggestion) about the room, the timing of the event, the physical description of the man, and the games and other activities that took place. These misleading questions included the "abuse questions." Children were also given a line-up in which they were asked to identify the stranger. A second session with the parents was used to see if the children had talked with their parents about the trailer incident and if the parents might have influenced the children's report in any way (Goodman & Aman, 1990; Goodman et al., 1990; Rudy & Goodman, 1991).

The results of each of the Simon Says studies are summarized as a group, because the findings were highly consistent across experiments. First, in free recall, older children recall significantly more correct information than younger children, especially information about descriptions of people and the actions that took place. No significant differences were found across ages when incorrect and ambiguous information was evaluated. In other words, younger children remembered less about the complex event, but what they remembered was as accurate as that of older children. Children who participated in or passively observed the Simon Says event did not differ in the total amount of information correctly recalled about the event.

Second, in response to the cued-recall condition, older children answered a greater portion of specific questions about the incident correctly than did younger children, especially questions about the description of the man and the activities that took place. Both participating and bystanding children remembered the actions very well.

Third, memory errors of omission were far more likely than errors of commission in each age group.

Fourth, in response to the various categories of post-event misleading questions, younger children were more suggestible and older children were significantly more resistant than younger children to misleading post-event suggestions. Overall, neither older nor younger children made a great number of commission errors. Children who directly participated in the Simon Says play, both younger and older, made significantly fewer commission errors regarding their memory for their own actions than children in the bystanding condition. The older bystanding children made significantly fewer commission errors in their memory for the action than the younger children.

Fifth, with respect to memory for actions, Goodman and her associates conclude, "On misleading action questions, participants were less suggestible than bystanders" (Rudy & Goodman, 1991, p. 534). Moreover, the children were generally more influenced by suggestive questions about their descriptions of the unfamiliar man than for the activities they participated in. Older children were significantly more accurate in their descriptions about the stranger than the younger children. Younger participating children were significantly more accurate in their description of the man than younger bystanding children. Children were quite poor in their ability to identify the stranger in a line-up, especially the older children.

Sixth, regarding the misleading abuse questions, older children were significantly more resistant to misleading questions about abuse-like actions than younger children. Only one seven-year-old child made a commission error in 252 opportunities. However, younger children were also quite resistant to making commission errors about post-event abuse-like suggestions, especially if they directly participated in the activity rather than passively observing

it. The commission errors rates for younger children—three year olds in one study and four year olds in another study—were consistently around 5%, and this figure is no doubt inflated because the researchers noted that a very small subgroup of children made most of the total number of commission errors in the group. Thus, while Goodman and her associates correctly conclude that even young children are "highly resistant" to suggestive questions about actions that might be confused with abuse (Goodman et al., 1990, p. 265; Rudy & Goodman, 1991, p. 1869), Ceci, Ross et al. (1987) are also correct in reminding us that there are important individual differences in post-event suggestibility, so that even a small subgroup of highly suggestible children (about 3–5%) is problematic in terms of false allegations of abuse.

Seventh, with respect to the anatomically correct dolls, no significant differences emerged across the four doll conditions. These dolls "do not in and of themselves lead 'non-abused' children to make false reports of sexual abuse" (Goodman & Aman, 1990, p. 1867).

Eighth, Goodman and her associates conclude that direct participation generally heightened resistance to post-event suggestions.

Ninth, Goodman and her associates (1990) summarize the results, and the relevance of the results to child abuse investigations, as follows:

> In conclusion, the data indicate that even very young children can give accurate, unsuggested testimony about actions that are significant to them. (p. 266)

Another innovation made by Goodman and her associates was to expand the research paradigm on "children's concerns" to include *real-life stressful events*, because much of the emotion and memory research has demonstrated that highly emotional events are better remembered than less stressful events. Yet, there are few data on the impact of highly emotional events on vulnerability or resistance to post-event suggestions. Building on earlier research involving a visit to the dentist and the fire alarm stress (Peters, 1987, 1991), the Goodman group developed a series of studies on the effects of stressful medical procedures on children's memory. While the Simon Says research paradigm in part addresses the problem of the ecological validity of post-event suggestion studies, there are limitations in how close the Simon Says paradigm approximates real-life abuse. While the more recent Simon Says studies incorporate nonsexual touch into the play sequence, the game does not involve undressing the child or genital touch. To overcome these limitations, Goodman and her associates investigated memory suggestibility in the context of a real-life medical examination, which did or did not include a vaginal and anal examination. Thus, the procedure included common elements of child sexual abuse, namely undressing the child followed by genital touch (Saywitz et al., 1991).

Other medical procedures, namely, inoculations and venipuncture, were used, presumably because such procedures are typically quite emotionally upsetting to a child, constituting an attack on the child's body (Goodman, Bottoms, Schwartz-Kenney, & Rudy, 1991; Goodman, Hirschman, Hepps, & Rudy, 1991; Goodman, Rudy, Bottoms, & Aman, 1990). Therefore, children were assessed for their memory performance and responsiveness to post-event suggestion in the context of a routine visit to the doctor, as part of their ongoing health care.

These stress studies also include other variables believed to affect post-event suggestibility, such as (1) the use of anatomically correct dolls as part of the memory test for the pediatric genital examination (Saywitz et al., 1991), (2) the use of long delays before the memory testing (Goodman et al., 1990), (3) the influence of social factors such as the status of the examiner and the degree of social support given (Goodman, Bottoms, Schwartz-Kenney, & Rudy, 1991), (4) assessment of the child's understanding of the stressful event as well as the emotional reaction to it (Goodman, Quas, Batterman-Faunce, Riddlesberger, & Kuhn, 1994), (5) assessment of the quality of the mother-child interaction (Goodman et al., 1994), (6) the use of multiple suggestive interviews (Goodman, Hirschman et al., 1991), and (7) the inclusion of "competence questions" similar to those asked by forensic child abuse investigators, e.g., "Is everything you said today the truth?" (Goodman, Aman, & Hirschman, 1987; Goodman, Hirschman, Hepps, & Rudy, 1991).

The experimental design used in these studies was similar to that used in the Simon Says studies. Children of ages three or four and five or six were used as subjects in the inoculation and venipuncture studies, and of ages five and seven in the genital examination study. Children were tested at the medical clinic. Parental ratings and/or videotaped and experimenter-rated measures of the children's level of stress were included as objective measures of the degree to which children experienced emotional stress as a consequence of the procedure. Three to four days after the medical visit, memory testing was done. This included (1) free recall of everything that happened in the medical office, (2) specific questions about the room, description of the people, and the actions that took place, (3) misleading questions about the room, people, and actions, including misleading abuse questions (e.g., "Did that doctor touch you there?" or "Did the person hit you?"), and (4) a photo identification line-up. Anatomically correct dolls were used in one study (Saywitz et al., 1991), and a long delay of one year for a second memory test in another study (Goodman et al., 1990). Support to the emotionally stressed child was provided by a parent in one of the studies (Goodman, Bottoms et al., 1991), and the effects of multiple suggestive interviews were studied in another (Goodman & Clarke-Stewart, 1991).

The results were consistent across the experiments, so they are discussed as pooled data. First, the stressful medical procedures generally had an enhancing effect on children's memory. In their free recall narratives, no significant differences emerged across ages with respect to the total amount of accurate information recalled about the inoculation and venipuncture. Children were extremely accurate in what they remembered about the examination. Moreover, there were no significant differences in the stress vs. control conditions, indicating that children generally recall those events accurately regardless of whether or not they experienced a noxious procedure.

Second, the one exception was that older children gave significantly less total information about the genital exam. The researchers took this to mean that older children were socialized into being more self-conscious and embarrassed about sexuality and suppressed their report. However, in response to specific questions about genital touch and/or in response to their memory being stimulated by anatomically correct dolls, the older children significantly increased the amount of information recalled specifically about the genital touch. There was a modest but significant rise in inaccuracies when the dolls were used, but none of the errors was about sexual behavior.

Third, on cued recall, both the control and stressed children recalled significantly more central than peripheral information across all ages. Memory for activities was significantly better than memory for descriptions of the medical examiner or the objects in the room.

Fourth, emotionally stressed children were significantly less vulnerable to post-event suggestions than nonstressed or control children. Being emotionally upset did not make the children any more suggestible than would otherwise be expected in normal situations. Actually, the children were more resistant to take in false information about an experience that had a strong emotional impact on them. Generally speaking, younger children were more vulnerable to post-event suggestions than older children. The children tended to be significantly more suggestible for misleading suggestions about peripheral objects in the room, somewhat more suggestible for descriptions of the people, and quite resistant to misleading suggestions for actions. Children of all ages were highly resistant to misleading questions.

Fifth, children of all ages were also highly resistant to misleading abuse questions. Absolutely no memory commission errors occurred regarding confusions about touch in their recollection of the genital exam. The rate of commission errors on abuse questions for three to four year olds was about 2%.

Sixth, competency questions turned out to be a rather poor predictor of children's memory performance.

Seventh, parental social support provided to the child during the stressful medical procedures significantly increased the accuracy of the memory in free recall and also significantly increased resistance to misleading post-event suggestions (cf. also Greenstock and Pipe, 1996, where peer support failed to affect response to misleading information for both younger and older children).

Eighth, interviewing the children twice instead of once generally led to greater accuracy in response to specific questions about the action, but did not significantly increase the children's vulnerability to post-event suggestions for actions, person descriptions, or objects in the room.

Ninth, retesting the children after a long delay of one year significantly decreased the total amount of correct information freely recalled, but did not increase incorrect information recalled about the medical procedure. The *delayed memory testing* also significantly increased omission errors in response to specific questions about the incident, as well as significantly decreased performance in the photo identification task. More importantly, the delayed memory testing was associated with a significant increase in vulnerability to post-event suggestions of all types, including misleading suggestions about actions. However, with respect to the misleading abuse questions per se, there was no significant increase in suggestibility even after a one-year delay in memory testing. Thus, Saywitz et al. (1991) conclude:

> resistance to suggestion lessened over time. As memory fades, children may become more vulnerable to accepting information implied in suggestive questions, a phenomenon true of adults, at least in laboratory settings . . . effects . . . were primarily a function of incompleteness, not confabulation. Commission errors were relatively infrequent. (p. 690)

Tenth, the researchers make the overall conclusion:

> The results of this study do not support the notion that stress interferes with a victim's memory. . . . Their [children's] suggestibility is greater for characteristics of the room in which the event occurred than for actions that took place or the physical characteristics of the "culprit." Interestingly, across the studies children never made up false stories of abuse even when asked questions that might foster such reports. (Goodman, Aman, & Hirschman, 1987)

The latest improvement in the research design by Goodman and her associates has been to utilize *real-life stressful procedures* that might be construed as traumatic by a child, such as urethral catheterization (Goodman et al., 1994):

> [the urethral catheterization] is in some ways like a sexual assault, even like a rape—it involves genital contact and physical penetration, it is commit-

ted against children's will, it is embarrassing for many children, and it hurts. (p. 290)

The purpose of the experiment was to study children's memory for a genitally invasive, painful medical procedure. Memory for a urethral catheterization was assessed in 46 children, ages three to four, five to six, and seven to ten years old between one and three weeks after the procedure. Various behavioral and subjective ratings of the children's stress level, emotional reaction, and understanding of the procedure were included. Ratings of the quality of the interaction between mother and child were also included. The memory assessment included an initial free recall period followed by direct questions, some of which were accurate, some misleading, and some open-ended.

The results are summarized as follows: (1) As with the previous studies, age predicted memory performance, with younger children answering fewer questions and making significantly more omission and commission errors than older children. (2) The child's emotional reaction to the catheterization also predicted performance. Children who felt a sense of mastery and pride for having successfully undergone the painful procedure had significantly more accurate recollections for the event. Children who were sad gave more correct information in free recall of the event but also made significantly more memory commission errors than children who were not sad. (3) The child's level of understanding of the medical procedure also significantly affected memory performance. Children who had a greater understanding were significantly more resistant to making commission errors in response to misleading questions. As Goodman et al. (1994) summarize, "Our results suggest that children who lack adequate understanding of a stressful experience may have less accurate memories of it" (p. 287). (4) The quality of the interaction between mother and child also significantly affected memory performance. Lack of a supportive mother-child interaction—in the form of not having time to attend to the child, failing to explain the procedure, failing to talk empathetically to the child, or failing to physically comfort the child—resulted in significantly more incorrect information and commission errors about the event than was the case for children who were

given support by their mothers. Goodman et al. state:

> Taken together, the results of these studies implicate parental communication and emotional support as important influences on accurate memory for stressful events experienced in childhood. (p. 289)

(5) Multiple, as compared to single, catheterizations were associated with greater negative emotional consequences. Younger children who experienced multiple catheterizations made significantly more memory commission errors than older children who had repeated catheterizations. (6) A small number of children demonstrated posttraumatic stress symptoms following the medical procedure. These PTSD symptoms did not significantly correlate with the behavioral or subjective stress measures obtained during the procedure. These findings imply that level of stress per se may not be a strong predictor of posttraumatic reactions. Children who experienced nightmares, trauma-specific fears (e.g., fear of genital touch), and/or posttraumatic reenactments in play gave significantly more incorrect responses to specific questions and made significantly more memory errors than children without PTSD symptoms. (7) Overall, the results suggest that memory performance for those types of events of impact that might lead to posttraumatic reactions is the outcome of an interaction of a number of complex variables: age, degree of understanding of the event, emotional reaction to the event (especially, coping and mastery), quality of social support during and after the stressful event, and the presence or absence of posttraumatic reactions (p. 290).

More recently, a number of additional studies have appeared by independent research groups that also focus on the impact of stressful medical procedures on memory performance in children. Mertin (1989) reported two experiments in Australia, one with four- to five-year-old children, and a second with young children, as compared with adolescents and adults, on the effect of immunizations on memory assessed by free recall, cued questioning, and misleading questioning. The results essentially replicated Goodman's findings with American children. Young children made more omission errors yet were generally accurate in free recall. Fewer omission errors occurred with cued recall. The children were generally resistant to misleading questions. Mertin noted, however, a great "variability" in the memory performance within their sample—an observation also made by Ceci, Ross et al. (1987)—that more attention needs to be paid to individual differences in post-event suggestibility in children.

Leippe, Romanczyk, and Manion (1991) conducted a "skin sensitivity test," a participatory event that involved touching five- to six- and nine- to ten-year-old children and adults. The study specifically addressed "memory for touching" (p. 369). Memory testing was done using free recall, specific questions, suggestive questions, and a line-up recognition. The results were consistent with the Goodman experiments, namely, greater omission errors in younger than older children or adults in free recall, especially about where they were touched; poor recognition memory for an "intruder" during the touch experiment; and more commission errors in younger than older children, but very rarely commission errors regarding the location of the touch across all ages (i.e., children rarely reported being touched in their private parts when they had not been).

Ornstein, Gordon, and Larus (1992) replicated the Goodman findings on a sample of three and six year olds who experienced a pediatric exam that involved both a genital exam and inoculations. An interesting innovation in the research procedure was the inclusion of an unexpected activity, not part of a routine medical exam, namely, taking a Polaroid photograph of the child. The researchers wanted to assess memory performance in response to an unexpected event, as well as for the stress of the medical exam. The predicted age differences in total information freely recalled and vulnerability to commission errors was confirmed, and there was a further increase in both omission and commission errors when the children were retested after a three-week delay. No child forgot the unexpected event.

Oates and Shrimpton (1991) attempted to replicate the Goodman research on two Australian samples of children from four to six and seven to twelve years of age using the venipuncture procedure and a variation on the Simon Says paradigm (meeting a friendly stranger in the school library). Generally, the same conclusions were drawn: greater omission errors in free recall in younger than older

children, less accuracy in response to specific questions in younger vs. older children, low rates of commission errors about the action that took place across all ages, greater commission errors in younger vs. older children, and a decline in memory accuracy in response to delayed recall. The notable finding was a lack of significant difference in memory performance between the stressed experimental and nonstressed control group. Goodman, Rudy et al. (1987) found no significant difference between stressed and nonstressed children in an earlier study, but later found a significant stress effect, in that stress was found to improve memory performance (Goodman et al., 1990). Peters (1991) found that the fire alarm stress significantly impaired memory in the form of an increase in both omission and commission errors. Thus, the effects of stress on memory performance across studies shows the same pattern reported by Deffenbacher for adults: sometimes stress enhances memory performance; sometimes it impairs it.

Mulder and Vrij (1996) conducted a misinformation experiment on children ages four to eleven. The children watched a staged event in which a man tries to snatch the book away from a woman who has come to their classroom to read them a story. Following the incident the children are asked one accurate and three misleading questions about the story. The main hypothesis tested was that explaining conversational rules at the onset of the interview would reduce misinformation suggestibility. Children in the experimental groups were given one or the other of two types of explanations: (1) expectation of help (i.e., that the interviewer did not necessarily know the answers and could not assist the child to answer correctly); and (2) I don't know (i.e., that "I don't know" was an acceptable answer when the child was unsure of the answer). The results showed that children of both age groups made significantly fewer incorrect answers and gave more correct information when provided with either type of pre-interview instructions than when not provided any information.

Overall Conclusions Drawn from the Child Misinformation Studies

There are a number of robust findings across many studies (cf. a review by Baxter, 1990). Younger children generally recall significantly less total information about personally significant events than older children in free recall, yet what they recall is quite accurate. Younger children generally make more commission errors in response to misleading post-event questions than older children, but the children in general are quite resistant to misleading post-event information, at least under the conditions of the experiments described in this chapter. The rates of commission errors ranges from 2–5% in these studies. Omission errors are much more common than commission errors in children of all ages.

In contrast to the adult laboratory simulation studies, these child studies on events of impact offer considerably more data on the effects of *type of information* on post-event suggestibility. Children are more vulnerable to post-event misinformation about peripheral details, such as objects in the room, when some central activity is taking place. They are somewhat vulnerable to misinformation about descriptions of unfamiliar people involved in these activities. They are generally resistant to post-event misinformation about the activities, especially if they are directly participating in the activities and the actions are personally meaningful and relevant to their concerns. When a long duration of time elapses between the original event and the assessment of memory, significantly more omission errors and commission errors are made.

Second, the child studies offer a clear demonstration that the magnitude of the misinformation effect depends on *memory trace strength*. Pezdek and Roe (1995) conducted a convincing test of the nonretention hypothesis using a signal detection paradigm as a test of the strength of the memory trace. They hypothesized that misinformation suggestion is a function of memory trace strength and that "weak memories might be more vulnerable to suggestibility" (p. 117). A total of 60 four year olds and 60 ten year olds saw one or another of two slide presentations about either a woman working in a kitchen or a man building a house, presented either one or two times. The post-event narratives included two misinformation items. Recognition memory testing consisted of choices between the original item, the misled item, or a foil item. The foil item was included to see whether or not the subjects forgot the original item. Signal detection analysis compared

the difference in the hit rate for the control items to the false alarm rate to misinformation items in a way that separated response bias from memory response. As predicted, stronger memory traces (original items viewed twice) led to significantly lower misinformation suggestion rates than weaker memory traces (items viewed once). Pezdek and Roe conclude:

> Specifically, strong memories are more resistant to suggestibility than are weak memories. Thus, if a child is recalling an event that occurred several times to him or her, he or she would be expected to have more accurate memory for the event and be less vulnerable to suggestive influences such as biased interviewing procedures, compared to an event that occurred only a single time. Of course it would also be important to evaluate the relative strength of the suggested information in memory. If a suggestive interview had been repeated numerous times, then the strength of the suggested item may exceed that of the original item. (p. 126)

Using a somewhat different approach, Marche and Howe (1995) had half of their 216 preschool subjects view a slide presentation about a little girl anticipating attending a costume party and the other half review the slides consecutively until they learned the material well. Three weeks after the presentation, subgroups of children either did or did not receive post-event information in a narrative or questionnaire form and those that did were either given misleading or correct information. This study contained a higher proportion of misleading information (10 of 20 items) than in most previous studies (two to four items). Four weeks after the original presentation the children were given four recall trials. As predicted, the misinformation effect was significantly higher in subjects who saw the slide presentation once than in those who saw the slides continuously until they learned the items. Thus, the results support the conclusion that the misinformation effect occurs primarily "when initial encoding was weaker" (p. 563). Those children exposed to misinformation three weeks after the event did report significantly more misinformation at the time of testing but did not report other kinds of erroneous information. The results suggest an "absence of widespread memory impairment" and that "the memory-impairing effects of misinformation were rare" (pp. 563–564). Both the Pezdek and Roe and the Marche and Howe studies, using quite sophisticated research designs, clearly demonstrate that the magnitude of the misinformation effect is a function of memory trace strength and that weaker or no memory trace significantly increases vulnerability to misinformation suggestion.

Third, these child studies offer considerably more data on the effects of *situational factors* affecting misinformation suggestion. Baxter (1990) concludes:

> If it is true that people accept misleading suggestions about what they have seen because they are "suggestible" it also seems true that this kind of suggestibility is highly modifiable by situational factors . . . there is no unequivocal support for the idea that there is anything inevitable about the suggestibility of child witnesses (p. 403). . . . It may be that if social pressures are absent, mild, or undermined . . . then 5-year-olds, and possibly even younger children, will often be no more susceptible to misleading information than much older children and adults. (p. 404)

Interviewing a child in a supportive context generally increases resistance to misleading post-event suggestions. The effects of emotional stress on memory performance are inconsistent across studies. Emotional stress tended to enhance memory performance in the Goodman studies, but other studies exist wherein stress was found to decrease memory performance (Davies, 1991; Peters, 1991).

Overall, these data across studies do not support the view of some advocates of the extreme false memory position who assert that false memories (including those related to abuse issues) are easy to create (e.g., Loftus, 1993; Loftus & Hoffman, 1989). As the conclusions of Goodman's research team point out:

> In summary, children evidenced considerable accuracy in answering specific questions and even in resisting strongly worded suggestions about actions associated with abuse; they often responded to these questions with embarrassment or amazement. These findings counter the view held by many that children are highly suggestible when asked ques-

tions about abusive actions. (Goodman & Clarke-Stewart, 1991, p. 95)

Nevertheless, these same studies also point to conditions under which children are vulnerable to post-event suggestion:

> . . . children are especially likely to accept an interviewer's suggestions when they are younger, when they are interrogated after a long delay, when they feel intimidated by the interviewer, when the interviewer's suggestions are strongly stated and frequently repeated, and when more than one interviewer makes the same strong suggestions. (Goodman & Clarke-Stewart, 1991, p. 103)

Thus, *under certain conditions*, children, especially young children, may be vulnerable to misleading suggestions about abuse, but this vulnerability is primarily a function of the way the interview is conducted. More will be said about this point in the next chapter on interrogatory suggestibility.

The Ceci research team, whose data on suggestibility in children are most at odds with those of the Goodman team, draws a similar conclusion, but with a different spin:

> Our own data indicate that very young children's memories *can* be distorted through post-event suggestions, not that they inevitably *will be* (Ceci, Ross, & Toglia, 1987, p. 47)

According to Ceci et al. (1987), one variable underemphasized in the Goodman data is the issue of *individual differences in post-event suggestibility* in children. Davies (1991), for example, has pointed out that the question of whether post-event suggestibility is a *state* or *trait* is not raised in the literature on post-event suggestibility. The assumption is all too readily made by the memory scientists that post-event suggestibility is a state induced by the experimental situation. Yet, Goodman and her associates did find a very small number of children in their sample who made a disturbingly high number of commission errors. Thus, more research is needed on *trait differences in post-event suggestibility*.

Another limitation of the Goodman research is that the conclusions are *context-dependent*. As McGough (1991) has remarked:

Two possible conclusions can be drawn from the Goodman data. The first is that children are amazingly nonsuggestible in a relatively benign interviewing environment. The second is that children can be resistant to suggestibility if and only if a benign interviewing environment is created and maintained until their account is recorded. (p. 116)

Likewise, Ceci and Bruck (1995) have pointed out:

The misleading questions in these studies were embedded in an unemotional, neutral interview that contained a host of other types of questions, so that the interview was not tilted toward having the child respond in only one way. . . . However, the Goodman and Ornstein studies are not informative about the accuracy of children's statements when the latter are obtained by more aggressive interview methods such as those that are sometimes used with actual child witnesses. (pp. 73–74)

What about a less benign interviewing environment? As learned from the decades of research on social persuasion, social influences can greatly affect vulnerability to post-event suggestion. The Ceci research team has addressed these types of social influence factors more thoroughly and has reached a different conclusion:

The research also shows, however, that with more powerful and persistent methods of suggestion, such as those described in this brief, a substantial percentage of children can be led to make false reports of events that never occurred, including events that involve their own bodies and that would have been quite traumatic had they occurred. (Bruck & Ceci, 1995, p. 308)

Interviewers conducting child abuse investigations vary considerably in their level of skill. There are, no doubt, what Helen Dent (1991) has called different "levels of prompting" (p. 141) possible in any interview situation, so that an unskilled interviewer may mislead more than is being realized.

Furthermore, none of the Goodman et al. research addresses the very real question of *motivation to misrepresent*, either by a child who has been threatened to lie about abuse or by an interviewer who intentionally and systematically coaches the child to tell a lie:

Although some researchers and professionals concerned with sexual abuse believe that the studies by Goodman and her colleagues demonstrate that children are invariably resistant to suggestions of sexual abuse, their results tell us nothing about the suggestibility of children regarding statements of sexual abuse in the real world. Unlike the situation in the physician's examining room, with which almost all children have relevant experience and no motive to misrepresent, sexual abuse is generally unfamiliar to children. The alleged sexual abuse situation may include motives to misrepresent, persistent attempts by one or more powerful and significant adults to influence the child, and suggestive interview techniques that lead the child to make statements that the child believes the interviewer wants to hear and will also believe. (Raskin & Esplin, 1991, p.159)

The next chapter will address intentional and systematic misleading suggestive influences—what is known as interrogatory suggestibility—where a much higher rate of memory commission errors and false beliefs have been found to occur in both children and adults than the relatively low 2–5% rates reported by Goodman and her associates.

The conclusions drawn from the child data reviewed here parallel those drawn from the adult studies on post-event misleading suggestion, namely, that a number of variables contribute significantly to the overall misinformation effect and that the relative contribution of each of these variables determines the magnitude of the misinformation effect. These are:

- Trait difference in suggestibility
- Memory strength
  - encoding status
  - age/developmental level
  - retention interval
  - source misattribution
- Type of post-event information
  - objects in the environment
  - people descriptions
  - central actions

- Social influence
  - -response bias
  - -source credibility
  - -support/intimidation

This list is similar to that summarizing the adult data, except that age/developmental level is an important dimension of memory strength, especially in younger children. Children are probably more susceptible to social influences, like the presence of an authority figure or parent. Certainly, the desire to please an adult, as well as the fear of intimidation by an adult, is more prominent in child than in adult interviews. Thus, the younger child who is uncertain about a past event because of the high rate of omission errors characteristic of early development may be more vulnerable to persuasive influences. The exact nature of the persuasive influences that can lead to a significant increase in the magnitude of the misinformation effect will be the subject of the next chapter.

GENERALIZATION OF THE MISINFORMATION EFFECT TO THERAPEUTICALLY SUGGESTED FALSE MEMORIES

Loftus (1993) and Lindsay and Read (1994) readily generalize the findings of these misinformation studies to the development of false memories for childhood sexual abuse in psychotherapy. But how generalizable are these results to the domain of psychotherapy? While Loftus and Lindsay and Read offer no scientific data to justify the generalization of these misinformation results to psychotherapy, a recent study suggests that *"constraints"* may need to be placed on the generalization of misinformation suggestibility. Pezdek and Roe (1994) correctly point out that most reports of recovered memories of childhood sexual abuse are not about single-incident abuse but about frequently occurring, cumulative abuse. All of the laboratory studies on misinformation suggestibility are limited to an original stimulus event presented only one time to the subjects. Therefore, in order to generalize misinformation data to recovered memories of abuse, research needs to be conducted comparing post-event

misinformation suggestibility for events originally occurring once to events occurring more than once.

In Pezdek and Roe's study, 120 children in two age groups (four and ten years of age) viewed two slide presentations about a woman returning home after shopping for groceries and a man building a house. The slide presentations contained four target slides, two presented one time and two presented twice. Following the presentation, they were read a post-event narrative that contained either accurate or misleading information about the two events. Memory testing involved presenting the children with three versions of each of the target items—the original item, the item contained in the post-event misinformation narrative, and a foil item (not contained in either). The results, analyzed using a signal detection model, demonstrated that children were significantly more vulnerable to post-event misinformation if the original target slides were presented only one time than if they were presented twice. They conclude:

> Together, the results of this study support the trace strength hypothesis that stronger memories are more likely to resist suggestibility than weaker memories. These results are important because they articulate conditions under which children are likely to be reliable or unreliable eyewitnesses. For example, if a child is recalling an event that occurred several times to them [sic], they would be expected to have more accurate memory for the event and be less vulnerable to suggestive influences such as biased interviewing procedures, compared to an event that occurred only a single time. This is especially important in child abuse cases because it is common for perpetrators to frequently abuse the same child. (p. 380)

Pezdek and Roe (1994) have identified a critical difference between the laboratory misinformation experiments and the situation of therapeutically suggested false memories:

> Most of the suggestibility studies are structured such that event A is observed, event B is suggested, and memory is tested for A versus B. In the generalization claims, A is never observed, A is suggested, and memory is tested for A versus not A.

There are significant differences between the structure of these two situations. (pp. 380–381)

Using a more sophisticated design than was used in the earlier misinformation studies, Pezdek and Roe experimentally manipulated each of the following conditions:

(1) A is observed, B is suggested (classic misinformation effect),
(2) A is not observed, A is suggested (therapeutic false memory), and
(3) A is observed, it is suggested that A was not observed

The control conditions of the experiment were:

(4) A is observed, nothing is suggested
(5) A is not observed, nothing is suggested (p. 381)

In the experiment, 80 ten-year-old girls viewed a slide of a rose. The target information selected was about touching, since it has direct relevance to abuse allegations. Then the experimenter either put her hand on the child's hand (event A) or on the child's shoulder (event B). After a 15-minute filler activity in which the children watched a slide sequence of a story, each child heard a narrative that "reviewed" the original event. Each child was told either that she had been touched in a different way (condition 1), that she had been touched when she had not been (condition 2), that she had not been touched when she had been (condition 3), or nothing (control conditions 4 and 5). During the subsequent memory recognition test, each child was asked about all three possibilities—"did I touch you? . . . did I put my hand on your hand? . . . did I put my hand on your shoulder?" (p. 381). Using a signal detection method to analyze the data, Pezdek and Roe discovered a significant suggestion effect only for condition 1—the classic misinformation effect—but failed to find a significant suggestion effect for either conditions 2 or 3. This pattern was replicated in a second experiment using a different type of touch. Pezdek and Roe conclude:

these results confirm that it is relatively easy to suggestively influence someone to believe that a different event occurred other than the event that was experienced. However, we were not reliably able to suggest that nothing occurred when it had, and although there was some qualified support for the ability to plant a memory for an event that had not occurred, the large majority of the participants were correct in rejecting a suggested plant. These results raise doubts about the claim that a significant number of children who had never been sexually abused, could, by the suggestion of a police officer, social worker, or therapist, come to believe that they had been abused, often repeatedly and often by a parent or teacher. (p. 383)

Second, although it is relatively easy to suggest that one event happened when a different but similar event really occurred, it is more difficult to suggest that an event happened when it really had not. . . . At this point, however, there is no empirical support for the view that childhood memories for frequently occurring events are generally unreliable or that it is easy to plant illusory memories for sexual abuse. (pp. 384–385)

The Pezdek and Roe experiment is the *only* experiment designed directly to compare classic misinformation suggestion and alleged false memory suggestion. It does not support the generalizations made by extreme false memory advocates that the findings from the misinformation experiments are directly applicable to the psychotherapy setting.

FUTURE DIRECTIONS

The misinformation effect has been well established in both a number of adult and child studies. Considerable effort has been directed toward establishing the mechanisms by which it occurs. If memory scientists like Loftus wish to generalize an exceedingly complex phenomenon like the misinformation suggestion effect to possible suggestive effects in psychotherapy, then more research like that conducted by Pezdek and Roe (1994) is needed. Until such data-based research has been conducted, we caution against generalizing the misinformation effect to "implanting" false memories in psychotherapy. Schacter (1995) makes a similar point:

A further question concerns whether people can falsely create an entire history of traumatic abuse when none occurred. There is no hard scientific evidence that shows such a phenomenon unequivocally (p. 28) . . . only a minority of healthy children and adults are prone to producing extensive false memories. (p. 29)

We recommend a new direction. It is time to move beyond demonstrations of the misinformation effect per se. Rather than accusing therapists and child abuse investigators of being suggestive based on findings from misinformation research, two additional research directions would actually be helpful to therapists and child abuse investigators: (1) additional research on ways to minimize memory error (e.g., Hoorwitz, 1992; Saywitz & Moan-Hardie, 1994; Zaragoza & Kosmider, 1989); and (2) research specifically on ways to facilitate accuracy as well as completeness of recollections (Frischholz, 1995).

9

||||||||||||||||||||||

Interrogatory Suggestion and
Coercive Persuasion

Misinformation suggestibility is a rather robust find-ing across many studies. Yet, as we have seen, the magnitude of the misinformation effect reported across studies is rather small when encoding factors (e.g., Frischholz, 1990) and social influence factors (e.g., Zaragoza, 1991) are statistically segregated from the variance of the misinformation effect. Under these conditions, usually less than 3% of all subjects tested are vulnerable to misleading sugges-tions. Moreover, we have seen that results from stud-ies using more sophisticated research designs have helped us appreciate that a number of very differ-ent factors contribute to the overall misinformation effect through complicated interactions, so that it is somewhat misleading to reduce this complexity to a simplistic interpretation about the creation of false memories.

Nevertheless, some researchers continue to over-state the findings from these misinformation stud-ies when speculating about psychotherapy, intending to imply that (1) the magnitude of false memory production in psychotherapy might be very large, (2) therapy can result in the actual creation of a false memory about abuse, and (3) such false memo-ries persist so that the patient's subsequent behav-ior is potentially damaging to others, usually to family members who are allegedly falsely accused (Loftus, 1993).

While few would quarrel with the fact that com-mission errors about childhood abuse can occur in therapy under certain conditions, the data on the misinformation effect do not offer strong support for this claim. The weakness of the misinformation data as applied to therapy lies in the fact that the studies on misinformation suggestibility emphasize primarily cognitive factors while deemphasizing so-cial influence factors in suggestibility (Gudjonsson & Clark, 1986).

There is much stronger research support avail-able regarding memory commission errors, but those data are not typically cited by most of the memory scientists who have focused narrowly on misinformation suggestibility. Strong support for high rates of false belief development in normal subjects comes from two sources. First, data from studies on interrogatory suggestibility (IS) have accumulated in two areas: (1) extensive forensic studies on extracting false confessions during in-tensive police interrogation with criminal suspects and (2) child empirical studies on potential areas of suggestibility associated with child abuse inves-tigations. Both these sources of data on IS lend strong support to the hypothesis that normal indi-viduals, when questioned about their memory for past events, *can* show very high rates of memory commission errors under very specific conditions of social influence—from 42–76% in the forensic studies and from 37–72% in the child experimental studies. The reader need only compare these figures to the 3–5% rate in most misinformation suggestibility studies (when social influence is controlled for) to appreciate that a proper understanding of potential commission errors about abuse in therapy necessitates looking beyond misinformation suggestibility per se to consider the important data on interrogatory suggestibility.

Second, detailed studies on coercive persuasion (so-called "brainwashing" or "thought reform") collected in the 1950s, along with later studies on ideological conversion as part of religious cult social behavior, offer a wealth of data specifically about the conditions under which normal individuals radically transform their beliefs. Because the false memory controversy about trauma therapy is essentially about the formation of misbeliefs about abuse, it is important to consider the data on coercive persuasion. It is this body of research that has carefully documented how stable belief systems can be intentionally destabilized and new beliefs "implanted."

THE STUDY OF INTERROGATORY SUGGESTION

Police Interrogations

The law has always recognized confessions as a most trustworthy form of evidence. It has also been suspicious when the circumstances surrounding the confession suggest that the confession was not voluntarily given (Kamisar, 1980). The earliest recognition of interference with the voluntariness of a confession involved police use of what have been called "third-degree" tactics, by which is usually meant physical torture and/or sensory deprivation. The classic statement on the value of such methods was penned by Sir James Stephen (1883): "It is far pleasanter to sit comfortably in the shade rubbing red peppers into a poor devil's eyes than to go about in the sun hunting up evidence" (p. 442).

Physical beatings and torture leave visible marks. When courts began excluding confessions from evidence if they were based on physical coercion, police turned to psychological methods, what came to be known as "the fourth degree," because these techniques leave no telltale traces (Kamisar, 1961; Zimbardo, 1967).

The Scientific Study of Interrogatory Suggestion

A Model for Interrogatory Suggestion

Most of the modern pioneering work on interrogatory suggestibility has been conducted by Gisli Gudjonsson and his associates. The concept of interrogatory suggestibility was derived from detailed studies of police interrogations and from interrogation manuals written since the 1950s to guide police in the conduct of interviews (e.g., Aubry & Caputo, 1972; Inbau, Reid, & Buckley, 1986; Irving, 1980; Kassin & McNall, 1991; Softley, 1980; Zulawski & Wicklander, 1993). O'Connor, writing a chapter in the Gerber and Schroeder (1972) edited text, *Criminal Investigation and Interrogation*, provides a link between coercive persuasion and police interrogation when he notes that "brainwashing" is "a very handy device" (p. 361).

Gudjonsson has argued that IS is a "special type" of suggestibility (1992, p. 105). He believes that IS "bears little resemblance to traditional types of suggestibility," like hypnotic suggestibility or misinformation suggestibility (Gudjonsson & Clark, 1986, p. 83), and he and Loftus have debated this claim in a special edition of *Social Behavior* (Schooler & Loftus, 1986).

Essentially, the differences between misinformation suggestibility and IS are largely due to the "operation of a variety of social influences" in IS, as compared to the largely cognitive factors operative in misinformation suggestibility. However, IS, as the broader concept, is inclusive of misinformation suggestibility. IS is misinformation suggestibility plus social influence factors such as response bias, source credibility, and especially some sort of "interpersonal pressure" in a closed social interaction (Gudjonsson & Clark, 1986, p. 84).

In a special edition of *Social Behavior*, Gudjonsson and Clark (1986) set forth their model of IS as follows:

> IS can be defined as the extent to which, within a closed social interaction, people come to accept messages communicated during formal questioning, as the result of which their subsequent behavioral response is affected. (p. 84)

This definition has essentially three components:

(1) misinformation suggestibility ("people come to accept messages"), (2) social influence ("within a closed social interaction . . . communicated during formal questioning"), and (3) the demand for a behavioral response ("subsequent behavioral response is affected"). In this sense, Gudjonsson and Clark's definition of IS is inclusive of misinformation suggestibility, but extends beyond it into the realm of a variety of social influences and into the suggestive implications of requiring a behavioral response to these social demands (much like the effects of counter-attitudinal behavior in cognitive dissonance research). Simply put, IS is *misinformation suggestibility plus*—misinformation suggestibility plus a variety of social influences. These may include response bias (Zaragoza, 1991) and source credibility (Smith & Ellsworth, 1987), as do some of the studies on misinformation suggestibility, as well as other types of suggestive social influences, most notably "interpersonal pressure" like explicit and implicit positive and negative emotional feedback.

In line with Gudjonsson's definition of IS derived from police interviews, Stephen Ceci, in his review of children's suggestibility, has asserted that both *cognitive* and *social* factors contribute to the overall suggestibility (Ceci & Bruck, 1993). Thus, while the issue of whether IS is a type of suggestibility distinct from misinformation suggestibility may not yet be resolved, it is fair to say that (1) the studies on misinformation suggestibility generally downplay social suggestibility factors in favor of cognitive factors (such as encoding status, type of post-event misinformation) and the nature of the retrieval strategies, and (2) the studies on IS generally pay much more attention to the complexity of social suggestibility factors that contribute to overall suggestibility.

Because therapy is essentially a social interaction, these studies on IS are perhaps more directly relevant to the questions of false memory for abuse in therapy than the misinformation studies per se. Gudjonsson and Clark's (1986) criticism of Loftus's studies on misinformation suggestibility is that her studies emphasize cognitive factors and overlook the complexity of social influence factors that are often brought to bear on developing false reports about past events.

According to Gudjonsson and Clark's classic paper (1986), IS has six interrelated elements. These are worth describing in some detail.

First, IS involves a *closed social interaction*. By closed social interaction Gudjonsson and Clark mean that the social exchange is not reciprocal. The flow of information goes in one direction. In a police interrogation, for example, the interviewer carefully controls the setting, the rules of discourse, the information provided, and the type of response that is allowed. The interviewer typically implies that he has some knowledge about the crime in question and perhaps even "proof" that the suspect did it. The suspect is *given little opportunity to learn alternative hypotheses* about the event in question. Moreover, the social exchange is based upon a clear *power differential* between the interviewer and interviewee, in which the interviewee is not allowed to challenge the authority of the interviewer.

Second, IS involves a *questioning procedure*. Gudjonsson and Clark correctly emphasize that this questioning procedure *specifically focuses on memory for some past experience*. During this questioning procedure, the interviewee's *general cognitive set* and *coping resources* interact with the interviewer's strategies, the outcome of which is that the interviewee becomes either more suggestible or more resistant than before the interrogation. Typically, the interviewer poses a question to the suspect about the events associated with a crime and the suspect in turn begins to process the information. According to Gudjonsson and Clark, the three factors involved in this *cognitive processing* that are associated with an increase in suggestibility are: (1) the degree to which the suspect is *uncertain* about the past event in question (an interviewee is intentionally not told very much), (2) the degree to which the interrogator manipulates the *expectation* that the event in question can definitely be known (and that the interrogator may have a definite bias or rigid hypothesis about what happened and how the suspect was involved), and (3) the degree to which *interpersonal trust* develops between the interrogator and suspect. With this trust, the suspect does not question whether or not the interrogator is acting in his/her best interests. The interrogator conveys the message that s/he can understand the suspect's reasons for committing the crime and can help the suspect get a more lenient sentence if the suspect cooperates by telling the "truth" about what happened. Moreover, the questioning procedure may involve *systematic rewards and punishments*—what Gudjonsson and Clark have called "interpersonal pressure" or "feedback," such as the strategic and exploitative use of kindness, the use of various bribes and threats, and sometimes the use of outright coaching.

An increase in suggestibility is also a consequence of the type of *coping strategy* that the suspect uses to deal with the pressure of the interrogatory interview. Those suspects who primarily resort to a passive avoidant coping style, i.e., who wish to avoid confrontation with the interrogator, are likely to become more suggestible than those suspects who use active coping strategies.

Third, IS also involves a *suggestive stimulus question*. The interrogator usually has very clear prior assumptions about the suspect's involvement in the crime (called an "event-model") and communicates these assumptions in the form of some *plausible premises* about the suspect's involvement in the event. These premises are often *leading and misleading questions*, in that the questions imply the desired answer (and sometimes false answer). In this respect, the suggestive stimulus question is comparable to the concept of post-event information and misinformation. Both concepts imply the communication of a plausible leading/misleading premise.

Fourth, Gudjonsson and Clark state that IS involves some form of *acceptance* of the stimulus message (cf. Kassin & Wrightsman, 1985). The term "acceptance," as Gudjonsson and Clark use it, should not be confused with the term "acceptance" used in the research on the misinformation effect (Belli, 1989) because it means the opposite. By "acceptance," Gudjonsson and Clark mean that the suggestive stimulus actually permanently alters the memory of the suspect ("memory interference" in Belli's terminology), and is not merely a compliant verbal response to the social demand of the interrogatory situation.

However, Gudjonsson has acknowledged that coerced confessions extracted by police interrogation methods may be of two types: those that are situationally bound and largely compliant, and those that are more internalized and persist as a stable memory alteration (Gudjonsson, 1992; Gudjonsson & MacKeith, 1988).

Fifth, IS also entails a *behavioral response*, either increased suggestion or resistance to suggestion. It should be noted that the recognition or recall memory test (phase 3) in the misinformation research requires a kind of behavioral response from the subject. The behavioral response required of the suspect of a police interrogation is typically much more elaborate. In a police interview this behavioral response is often concretized in the form of an oral or written confession about involvement in the crime. The elaborateness of the behavioral response required is important, because the very behavioral response itself can serve to increase subsequent suggestibility. While the studies on misinformation suggestibility generally ignore this aspect, a long tradition of research on cognitive dissonance has convincingly shown that requiring subjects to behave in a manner contrary to their original attitude significantly contributes to attitude change (Festinger, 1957). Therefore, the ritual of making a confession in a police interview (or behaving in a therapy group or toward a family as if one has been abused) may reinforce the individual's suggestibility to the suggested event.

Sixth is feedback. In the case of a police interrogation this usually means negative emotional feedback. The feedback element is different from the other elements of interrogatory suggestibility in that feedback is typically used only *after* a suspect has responded to the interrogator's premises. Feedback is "intended to strengthen or modify subsequent responses of the witness" (Gudjonsson & Clark, 1986, pp. 93–94). The entire interrogative interview can be seen as a dynamic interaction, in which the interrogator skillfully controls the information, suggests the intended premises about the crime and then manipulates the emotional tone of the interchange so as to get the suspect to accept the premises and elaborate upon them in the form of a confession of an actual memory.

Gudjonsson and Clark developed their model of IS to help scientists understand how and under what conditions significant commission errors in memory for past criminal events can occur. It is no accident that their model is derived from studies of police interrogation, since a study of such interrogatory strategies helps us appreciate the relative contribution of interpersonal pressure to the overall suggestibility of the individual. The list of pressuring tactics that significantly increase the likelihood of getting the suspect to confess is extensive. Tactics include manipulative maneuvers such as confrontation with damaging evidence, utilizing information-bluff tactics, minimizing the seriousness of the offense, befriending or being tough on the suspect, or cajoling the suspect into believing it in his or her best interest to confess (Gudjonsson & MacKeith, 1982); asserting authority, making promises (Irving, 1980); and using outright pressuring tactics, such as confining and isolating the suspect, carrying on a very lengthy interview, reminding the suspect that s/he has memory problems, stating with great confidence a belief that the suspect is guilty and claiming to have "proof" of this, demanding that the suspect accept the interrogator's premises about the crime, and attempting to induce fear in the suspect (Ofshe, 1989). Gudjonsson (1992) believes that these interpersonal pressuring tactics are specifically intended to make the suspect lose confidence in his/her memory so that s/he will uncritically accept the interrogator's premises about the event in question and make a confession based on those premises.

While the list of interpersonal pressuring tactics used by police interrogators could be greatly elaborated, the main point is that they are effective. The closed social interaction, questioning procedures, interpersonal pressure, and demand for a behavioral response in the form of a confession that characterize police interrogations go far beyond the more cognitively based misinformation suggestions characteristic of laboratory research, both in the *range* of social influences brought to bear on the suspect and also in the *outcome*. Gudjonsson (1992) reviewed eight empirical studies on the effectiveness of police interviewing methods. The confession rates across these studies ranged from 42% to 76%. If data on partial confessions are included (i.e., when some damaging self-incriminating statement is made that falls short of a full confession), the confession rates jump to 61–85% across these studies. These figures are staggering: just about half to three- quarters of suspects interviewed in the "right way" confess to the crime.

Keep in mind that confession does *not* mean that the suspect actually committed the crime. As Gudjonsson and MacKeith (1988) point out, "It is at present impossible to estimate the frequency with which individuals confess to crimes they have not committed (p. 189). However, it is reasonable to assume (as we have learned about hypnosis), that the introduction of interrogatory tactics probably

significantly increases both the frequency of true confession and the frequency of false confession. With overall confession rates as high as they are across these studies, the significant increase in false confession rates that likely occurs when such tactics are used constitutes a major problem in the forensic field. Even where the absolute number of false confessions is not known, it is clear that the interrogatory suggestion tactics typically get individuals to make significant admissions about past events that they are otherwise unwilling or unable to make. In this sense, interrogatory methods make an individual far more vulnerable to suggestion than would be the case under less pressured circumstances.

It is important to understand that the concept of interrogatory suggestibility is actually composed of two very different elements. First is the *trait* of suggestibility. Gudjonsson (1992) correctly emphasizes that there are considerable individual differences in suggestibility. Personality factors, such as the general cognitive set and nature of coping resources of the suspect, account for these differences in suggestibility. Some individuals are very vulnerable to commission errors in memory even with very little interpersonal pressure. Others are highly resistant to suggestion even when strong pressuring tactics are used.

Second is the *nature of the interpersonal influence*. In a closed social interaction where the flow of information is highly controlled, where leading and misleading questions are repeatedly introduced, and where various forms of interpersonal pressure are used, even the less suggestible individual may come to incorporate the interrogator's suggestions into his/her belief about the event in question. Interrogatory suggestibility is an interaction between the individual's degree of suggestibility and the nature of the interpersonal pressure applied.

Individual Differences in Interrogatory Suggestibility

Gudjonsson and his associates have conducted a large number of empirical studies in an attempt to validate the concept of interrogatory suggestibility as a distinct form of suggestibility. An inventory of interrogatory suggestibility was constructed—the Gudjonsson Suggestibility Scale (GSS) (Gudjonsson, 1984a). Taking this scale, which draws from the tradition of the Wechsler Memory Scale, the subject is read a story about a woman who goes on vacation in a foreign country and has her handbag stolen. She is interviewed by the police and gives them the details. Shortly thereafter, the police charge three men with the robbery. The subject is asked to listen carefully to the story and tell the experimenter everything s/he remembers (immediate free recall). The content of the story is divided into 40 scorable units so that a total memory score can be obtained. The experimenter also has the option of introducing a delayed memory test. For example, the subject may be asked to freely recall the story again 50 minutes after hearing it. After either the immediate or delayed recall, the subject is asked a series of 20 questions about the story. Five of the questions are accurate and 15 of the questions are misleading, i.e., suggested details that were not in the original story. After the subject responds to these questions, the experimenter reviews the subject's answers and then in an authoritative and disapproving manner, tells the subject that s/he has made a number of errors, must try to be more accurate, and must answer the 20 questions again.

The scale is designed to measure two important features of memory: (1) memory recall; and (2) memory suggestibility. *Memory recall* is a measure of the total number of details the subject remembers of the original story immediately and/or after some delay. *Memory suggestibility* is a measure of how much the subject can be made to alter his/her memory for story details based on two kinds of interrogatory influence: (a) how many of the 15 misleading questions the subject incorporates into the report about story details (called the "Yield" score); and (b) how much the subject changes his/her answers after negative emotional feedback (called the "Shift" score). Thus, the Gudjonsson Suggestibility Scale is constructed to measure *both* misinformation suggestibility (Yield score) and vulnerability to clear interpersonal pressure (Shift score). The Yield score is a measure of vulnerability to systematic misleading (15 misleading of 20 post-event questions). The Shift score is a measure of the extent to which negative emotional feedback affects misinformation suggestibility, i.e., can the subject be made to change his/her memory report in response to direct interpersonal pressure? An additional score, the Total Suggestibility score, is the sum of the Yield and Shift scores.

While the Yield and Shift subscales were constructed based on a theoretical model of interrogatory suggestibility, empirical studies have been done to validate them. Factor analytic studies on the GSS have shown that two factors exist. These factors, called Yield and Shift, each correspond reasonably closely with yielding to misinformation suggestions and vulnerability to shifting one's report in the face of negative emotional feedback, respectively.

One important difference between the Yield score on the GSS and Loftus's original paradigm is the number of misleading questions used. Whereas studies on misinformation suggestibility typically employ one or two misleading questions, and sometimes up to four misleading questions (but rarely over 25% of the total information), the GSS uses 15 misleading questions out of 20 (75% of the total information). Where many normal individuals may be vulnerable to accept post-event misinformation for minor details, the Loftus original test fails to identify the subgroup of very highly suggestible individuals through this method. By utilizing a very large ratio of misleading to nonleading questions, the GSS is able to identify those very highly suggestible individuals more readily than the Loftus original test.

Normative data accumulated from the various subscales on the GSS generally support the view that interrogatory suggestibility is a *stable trait* composed of two elements—*misinformation* plus vulnerability to *interpersonal pressure* (in this case, negative emotional feedback by an authority figure). In the general population, the mean Yield and Shift scores are skewed toward the low range (X=about 4 out of 15 possible points on both scales). These data support the view that the normal individual is less, not more, suggestible, at least to systematic misleading. However, the use of the GSS also supports the view that there exists a subpopulation of individuals who are highly vulnerable to interrogatory suggestion (total score X=7 SD 5 for normal subjects, > 12 for highly suggestible subjects).

In a later study, Gudjonsson (1987a) described the development of a parallel form of the GSS— the GSS-2. The construction and scoring of the scale are identical to the original GSS-1. The only difference is that the subject is read a different story. The story is about a couple running after their small boy, who is going down a steep hill on his bicycle. The scale was developed in part so that one version, e.g.,

GSS-1, could be given during the first testing session and an alternate form, e.g., GSS-2, could be given after some delay, say, 50 minutes later or eight months later. That way delayed memory could be investigated without having to give the same scale twice. The test-retest reliability between these two versions of the GSS is quite high and thus giving one version or the other was shown in research to be equivalent. Using both forms of the test, Gudjonsson was able to demonstrate that a *trait of suggestibility* is highly consistent, even after long retention intervals.

Further research on the GSS has contributed greatly to our understanding of the relationship between memory and suggestibility. A robust finding has been that *suggestibility and memory capacity are negatively correlated* (Gudjonsson, 1987a)—the lower the free narrative recall (i.e., the greater the uncertainty about the story), the greater the suggestibility. This finding lends support to the relative contribution of *uncertainty* for past events to overall suggestibility (Gheorghiu et al., 1989). Another important finding is that the *rate of memory decay* is also significantly correlated with suggestibility, regardless of the total amount of information recalled. Subjects whose memory decayed more rapidly over a 50-minute interval between immediate and delayed testing (difference between the total memory score on the first and subsequent testing) were significantly more suggestible (Gudjonsson, 1983; Gudjonsson, 1992, p. 134).

Another very important measure derived from the GSS is the *Confabulation score*, which is a measure of the number of units of information reported as part of the immediate recall that are different from the original content of the story. For a normal subject, the mean number of confabulations is quite low (about 0.5; Smith & Gudjonsson, 1986). Over time, however, the number of confabulations generally increases as memory decays for normal subjects. However, negative emotional feedback significantly increases the degree of confabulation. Extreme negative feedback increases the number of confabulations even more (Tata & Gudjonsson, 1990). Repeated questioning without negative feedback also increases the number of confabulations (Gudjonsson, 1992; Register & Kihlstrom, 1988).

The value of instruments like the GSS to the study of memory suggestibility cannot be underesti-

mated. This scale is very easy to administer and does not require much time. It has many advantages:

1. The GSS is a way to measure individual differences in memory suggestibility so as to quickly identify those individuals most vulnerable to interrogatory suggestibility.
2. The GSS identifies which subjects are quite resistant to interrogatory suggestion.
3. The GSS allows us to identify that subgroup of subjects most vulnerable to confabulate their memory for a past event.
4. The GSS allows us to distinguish the relative contributions of misinformation and interpersonal pressure to the overall suggestibility of the individual.
5. The GSS helps us to understand the relationship between memory forgetting (uncertainty and/or rate of decay) and subsequent suggestibility.
6. The GSS allows us to understand suggestibility specifically for delayed memory.

All six of these points are directly relevant to the false memory controversy.

It is important to keep in mind that the GSS total score is essentially a measure of a given subject's potential for interrogatory suggestibility; it is not a measure of the subject's accuracy or inaccuracy of memory in any given situation. Gudjonsson is careful to point out that subjects measuring in the high range on the GSS may nevertheless have an accurate memory for certain past events, and that subjects measuring in the low range may under certain conditions show a significant degree of memory distortion (Gudjonsson & MacKeith, 1988). It is crucial that the reader appreciate that the GSS merely measures the overall *probability* that a given subject may accept misleading information, especially in an interrogatory context. Failure to observe this point results in universal judgments about high- and low-suggestible people that are unfair and unjust. For example, it would be an error to say that high-suggestible people should never be believed or that low-suggestible people should always be believed.

Research using the GSS to predict the *accuracy* of memory is needed. Unfortunately, only one such study has been reported. Tully and Cahill (1984) gave the GSS-1 to a group of mentally retarded witnesses, along with a battery of other psychological tests. Then the subjects watched a staged scenario about taking some plants. After one week the subjects were given an interrogatory interview by the police. Because the staged scenario constituted baseline data on memory for the original event, Tully and Cahill were able to score subjects' responses in terms of the number of accurate and erroneous memories for each detail in the scenario. Gudjonsson (1992) reanalyzed the data to determine the relationship between accuracy/inaccuracy and suggestibility. As predicted, there was a highly significant negative correlation between suggestibility and accuracy, and a significant positive correlation between suggestibility and the number of memory errors. In other words, more suggestible subjects gave less accurate information and more erroneous information about the staged event.

Comparable research on the relationship between accuracy and interrogatory suggestibility is needed on normal subjects, as well as on psychotherapy patients, before firm conclusions can be drawn, but these initial findings lend some support to the view that subjects high in interrogatory suggestibility have a greater likelihood of making an inaccurate memory report about past events, while those low in interrogatory suggestibility have a greater likelihood of making an accurate report, even though exceptions to this rule sometimes exist.

In a recent study Gudjonnson and Sigurdsson (1996) further developed another dimension of the GSS, namely use of the GSS as a measure of *confabulation potential*. Confabulation potential was defined as "problems in memory processing where people replace gaps in their memory with imaginary experiences which they believe to be true" (p. 85). People who confabulate are especially "vulnerable to giving fabricated accounts of events" (p. 86). A sample of 255 prison inmates were given the GSS along with a variety of assessment instruments to measure intelligence, personality, social compliance, social desirability, and self-deception. Coding systems were developed to measure two types of confabulations—distortion of the story content, and fabrication, i.e., introduction of new material. Distortions and fabrications were not highly correlated, nor was either correlated highly with personality measures. A total confabulation score correlated significantly with the GSS Shift score (which mea-

sures vulnerability to negative emotional feedback) and negatively with intelligence. These data imply that negative emotional feedback, not suggesting systematic misinformation per se, is mildly associated with the potential to confabulate, especially in less intelligent people. The researchers add, however, that "both correlations were very low and accounted for less than 3% of the variance" (p. 89).

In another series of studies, Gudjonsson and his associates have attempted to discriminate more carefully between the construct of interrogatory suggestibility and related constructs like compliance and acquiescence. According to Gudjonsson, *compliance* is defined in terms of the "eagerness to please" and "the avoidance of conflict and confrontation and fear of people in authority" (Gudjonsson, 1989a, p. 536). While Gudjonsson acknowledges that some criminal suspects may make a confession in a compliant manner after interrogation, many suspects actually "accept" the premises of the interviewer as part of their memory. The distinction between *compliance* and *memory acceptance* in the forensic field (cf. Gudjonsson & Clark, 1986; Irving, 1986) is comparable to the debate between memory acceptance and memory interference among memory scientists (Belli, 1989), in that an attempt is being made to distinguish between those subjects who simply make a false report about a past event in response to social pressure and those who actually undergo an alteration in their memory representation.

Gudjonsson (1989a) constructed a scale specifically to measure compliance, the Gudjonsson Compliance Scale (GCS). Factor analytic studies on the scale have revealed that it measures *reaction to pressure by someone in authority*. The GCS significantly correlates with the GSS, especially with the Shift scale, which implies a "certain overlap between the two constructs" (p. 539), in that both tap the potential to change a response in the face of interpersonal pressure by an authority figure.

Acquiescence is "the tendency of an individual to answer questions in the affirmative irrespective of control" (Gudjonsson, 1992, p. 140). Gudjonsson developed an Acquiescence Scale (AS) consisting of opposite statements like "I'm happy most of the time. . . . I'm sad most of the time." Gudjonsson hypothesized that highly acquiescent individuals relative to normal subjects would endorse both questions affirmatively, despite the contradiction in doing so. He found a weak but significant correlation between the Acquiescence Scale and the Total Suggestibility Scale on the GSS (Gudjonsson, 1986), but failed to replicate the findings in a subsequent study (Gudjonsson, 1990b). The implication of these studies is that interrogatory suggestibility is essentially different from simple response bias phenomena.

Gudjonsson's research using the GSS is largely restricted to the forensic field. In that context, the GSS has proven itself as a valid instrument to identify individuals most vulnerable to the development of false memory. It is generally accepted that the type of interpersonal pressure used as part of a police interrogation results in a high rate of confessions, some of which are genuine and some of which are false. Gudjonsson used the GSS to test the hypothesis that those suspected of false confessions were significantly more vulnerable to interrogatory suggestions than those who resisted making a confession under any circumstances. Gudjonsson (1984b) identified two groups of subjects. One group consisted of "alleged false confessors," i.e., suspects who made confessions about a crime under the pressure of a police interrogation but who later retracted their confessions. Gudjonsson acknowledges that the group of alleged false confessors probably consists of both genuine false confessors and retracted but true confessors. The other group consisted of "deniers," i.e., suspects who persistently denied any involvement in the crime throughout all interrogatory pressure, often despite substantial circumstantial evidence that caused them to be charged with the crime. The GSS-1 was given to both groups with the interrogatory questions and negative feedback given after a 40–50-minute delay. As predicted, the alleged false confessors as a group were significantly more suggestible (higher Total Suggestibility score), both in terms of misinformation suggestibility (higher Yield score) and vulnerability to interpersonal pressure (higher Shift and Yield-2 scores) than the deniers. Gudjonsson noted, however, that there were remarkable individual differences: some of the subjects who confessed and later retracted did not score especially high on the GSS, even though as a total group they were significantly more suggestible. Also, as predicted, the deniers were significantly less suggestible. Their total scores on the GSS were extremely low, often falling on the low end of the normal distribution of scores.

More recently, Gudjonsson (1989b, 1991) replicated these findings with a larger sample of alleged false confessors and deniers matched for age, sex, level of intelligence, and memory capacity (total score on immediate recall of the GSS). The study also included another forensic group that served as a control. All three groups were given the GSS and the GCS. As predicted, the alleged false confessors had significantly higher scores on both the GSS and on the GCS relative to other forensic subjects, while the deniers had significantly lower scores on both the GSS and the GCS. An important finding was that *these differences in suggestibility were evident even when memory capacity and intelligence were statistically controlled.* Analysis of the relative contribution of each of the scores to the group differences revealed that the greater portion of the overall variance was contributed by the difference of the Shift and Yield-2 scores between alleged false confessors and deniers. In other words, *vulnerability to interpersonal pressure* (negative feedback and repeated questioning after negative feedback) contributed much more to the differences between alleged false confessors and deniers than other aspects of suggestibility like misinformation suggestibility, memory capacity, or level of intelligence. This finding is very important because it clearly implies that *genuine false memory is more a function of interrogatory suggestion than misinformation suggestion per se*, i.e., it is mainly a function of interpersonal pressure and not the more cognitively based misinformation effect (Gudjonsson, 1992, p. 157). As individuals, then, those subjects who are highly prone to develop false memories "are markedly more suggestible and compliant" (Gudjonsson, 1989b, p. 106), and if such high-risk individuals are subjected to an interrogatory interview they will produce a high rate of false memories about past events.

In another series of studies Gudjonsson and his associates have attempted to distinguish between which subjects in the alleged false confession group genuinely alter their memory for the past event in question and which do not actually alter their memory but comply with the demand of the social situation and report false information. We have discussed this thorny problem previously in chapter 8 on misinformation suggestibility, a field of study in which increasingly sophisticated research designs have been used to distinguish memory interference from memory acceptance. A comparable debate exists within the forensic field.

Wrightsman and Kassin (1993) and Gudjonsson and MacKeith (1982, 1988) describe three types of false confessors:

1. Voluntary false confessors who offer a confession without any interrogatory pressure. These individuals make the confession for a variety of reasons—notoriety, unconscious guilt, inability to distinguish fantasy from memory for actual events, or an attempt to protect the actual perpetrator of the crime.

2. Coerced-compliant false confessors who bend under intense police interrogation pressure. As the term "coerced-compliant" implies, these confessors are merely overly complying with the demands of the situation and do not actually undergo an alteration in their memory. They believe that by "confessing" they will be relieved of interrogatory pressure, allowed to go home, and somehow be able to retract the confession and tell the truth at some later point in time.

3. Coerced-internalized false confessors are also an outcome of police interrogation, but these confessors actually come to believe that they committed the crime. Often this type of false confession occurs when the suspect is uncertain about the alleged crime and comes to accept the suggestive premises supplied during systematic interrogation.

   Gudjonsson and MacKeith (1982) consider this third type of confession an example of a "memory distrust syndrome," because the suspect is typically very unclear about the events in question and is more vulnerable to accept external information to fill the gaps in actual memory. The outcome is a type of "pseudo-memory" (Gudjonsson, 1989b).

A coerced-internalized false confession differs from a coerced-compliant false confession in that the memory of the former but not the latter type of confession is "permanently distorted," making the original content of the memory "irretrievable" (Gudjonsson & MacKeith, 1988, p. 191; Kassin & Wrightsman, 1985, p. 78). Retractions are very uncommon among internalized false confessors. As

Gudjonsson and MacKeith (1988) have noted, coerced-compliant confessions are more likely the product of intense pressure, while coerced-internalized confessions are more likely the product of subtle and enduring persuasion.

Idiosyncratic personality factors and the type of interrogatory pressure interact to determine the type of false confession an individual makes. According to Kassin and Wrightsman's and Gudjonsson and MacKeith's observations, the strongest predictor of a coerced-compliant false confession is a highly manipulative and often very aggressive police interview. This type of confession is situationally-bound and quite unstable. There is a high rate of retraction among coerced-compliant false confessors.

The strongest predictors of a coerced-internalized false confessor are: uncertainty of memory for the event in question and certain personality factors like high hypnotizability, low self-confidence, and strong trust in authority; and a certain interview style characterized by "more subtle less coercive methods" (Kassin & Wrightsman, 1985, p. 77). During this type of interrogation, the suspect is systematically, subtly, and repeatedly persuaded to accept the interrogator's premises. The suspect is reminded of his/her own inability to remember, and the social environment is controlled to prevent other sources of information to contradict the interrogator's premises about the suspect's guilt. Eventually, the suspect comes to genuinely believe that s/he actually committed the crime (Wrightsman & Kassin, 1993).

The genuine value of the coerced-compliant vs. coerced-internalized distinction, we believe, does not lie in whether or not the memory representation is altered by the interrogation. Distinguishing between memory interference and memory acceptance, as we have seen, is very, very difficult. The real value of the coerced-compliant/coerced-internalized distinction is in the identification of a number of *personality* and *interactional* variables, the interaction of which *substantially increases the rate of false reports* about memory for past events, especially when those false memories are held with great conviction even though the consequences are known to be damaging. In this sense, forensic research on false confession merits careful scrutiny by both memory scientists and clinicians, because these data have more direct applicability to the heart of the false memory controversy than do the studies of misinformation suggestibility. Therefore, a more detailed look at which personality factors contribute to false confession is warranted. To this end, Gudjonsson and his associates have conducted a number of personality studies. Gudjonsson (1990b) studied the psychological characteristics of 100 alleged false confessors, as compared to general forensic referrals. These individuals were of lower intelligence and were significantly more suggestible on the GSS and significantly more compliant on the GCS than other forensic subjects.

In other research Gudjonsson and his associates investigated the personality factors associated with high interrogatory suggestibility. While this research does not utilize alleged false confessors as subjects, it does, nevertheless, have some bearing on the issue of personality traits that may be predictive of vulnerability to interrogatory suggestion and the production of false memories. Gudjonsson (1983) administered the GSS along with the WAIS and Eysenck Personality Questionnaire (EPQ) to a group of normal subjects. Replicating previous work, suggestibility was significantly negatively correlated with both immediate and delayed memory on the GSS. All of the suggestibility scales on the GSS, but particularly the Total Suggestibility score, were significantly correlated with intelligence (especially the full scale IQ on the WAIS) and with neuroticism and social desirability on the EPQ, although intelligence and poor memory accounted for most of the variance of the traits correlated with interrogatory suggestibility. In another study (Gudjonsson, 1988), interrogatory suggestibility correlated with low assertiveness on the Rathus Assertive Schedule (Rathus, 1973) and with fear of negative social evaluation on the Fear of Negative Evaluation Inventory (Watson & Friend, 1969). State but not trait anxiety on the Speilberger State-Trait Anxiety Inventory also significantly correlated with interrogatory suggestibility.

Our understanding of how poor memory makes subjects more vulnerable to interrogatory suggestibility was enhanced by a subsequent study in which subjects were given the GSS twice, with a one-week retention interval in between. As predicted, subjects were significantly more suggestible during the second interview, presumably because their memories for the story had decayed over the retention interval. That study (Singh & Gudjonsson, 1984) also included the semantic differential method (Osgood, Soci, & Tannebaum, 1957), which measures a variety of dimensions of self-concept. Interrogatory suggestibility was significantly negatively correlated with those attributes of self-concept most closely associated with self-esteem (e.g., competence, intelligence, strength, forcefulness), especially after the first but not the second interview. Singh and Gudjonsson (1984) conclude that "the impact of self-esteem upon suggestibility is particularly likely to occur when subjects are unfamiliar with interrogative tasks and procedures" (p. 208).

Curiously, subjects in that study had significantly higher Yield scores and significantly lower Shift scores on the second test than on the first. Singh and Gudjonsson interpret these data to mean that the Shift score is a relatively unstable factor that is highly susceptible to situational demands. The data imply that vulnerability to negative emotional pressure may work less effectively in repeated interviews to the extent that the suspect learns to cope better with the interrogation over time. The data also imply that false premises systematically introduced and repeated over time in the context of established interpersonal trust could lead to an increase in memory suggestibility (significant increase in the Yield scores over the two testing sessions).

The Gudjonsson Suggestibility Scale recently has been used to investigate the suggestibility of individuals who have recovered memories of childhood sexual abuse (Leavitt, 1997). Some false memory proponents have assumed that recovered memories of abuse are the result of suggestive effects operative in psychotherapy (Loftus, 1993; Ofshe & Watters, 1993). To test this hypothesis, Leavitt administered the GSS to 75 psychiatric inpatient women—44 women who had recovered memories of childhood sexual abuse and 31 who had not. Both groups also were given the Dissociative Experiences Scale (DES) and the Minnesota Multiphasic Personality Inventory-2 (MMPI-2). Contrary to the false memory claim, Leavitt found, "Patients in the Recovered Memory group had significantly lower suggestibility scores than patients in the Psychiatric comparison group" (p. 268). When compared with Gudjonsson's norms for the GSS, Leavitt found:

Recovered Memory patients are not more suggestible than psychiatric patients, they are not even as suggestible. They are less suggestible than psychiatric patients without a history of sexual trauma, and even at the low end of the suggestibility spectrum in terms of norms reported for populations in other studies. (p. 296)

He also found that "suggestibility was negatively correlated with the Pd scale (distrust of authority measure) . . . [and that] . . . high Gudjonsson scores are associated with low Pd scores" (p. 268). Leavitt interprets the low suggestibility of recovered memory patients in terms of an abuse-related mistrust of authority.

The Interaction of Interrogatory Suggestibility and Suggestion

These personality data support the view that interrogatory suggestibility represents a complex interaction between a *trait of suggestibility* and the *type of interpersonal pressure exerted*. While it is no doubt true that certain types of individuals (those with low intelligence, low self-esteem, low assertiveness, high neuroticism, high need to be seen in a socially desirable way) are more vulnerable to interrogatory suggestion than others, it is equally true that a certain style of interrogatory interview can also greatly increase vulnerability to interrogatory suggestions and false memory production (by systematic, repeated presentation of plausible but false premises in the context of a closed social interaction and in combination with rewards and threats).

Ofshe (1989) conducted a detailed case study of personality factors and types of interrogatory pressure that contributed to the development of coerced-internalized false confessions in four persons. Individuals more likely to produce false confessions lack self-confidence, tend to trust people in authority, and are highly suggestible. These personality factors make such individuals highly vulnerable to pressuring interrogatory tactics. Ofshe identified seven interrogatory strategies that contributed to false confession:

1. The suspect is isolated from people so that the flow of information is controlled.
2. The interrogator repeatedly says that he has

"proof" of the suspect's involvement in the crime.
3. The interrogator repeatedly communicates great confidence about this belief regarding the suspect's guilt.
4. The suspect is repeatedly reminded of his/her memory problems.
5. The interrogator demands that the suspect accept his premises and theory about the crime.
6. The interrogator induces fear.
7. The interrogation is lengthy.

Ofshe's list of interrogation factors mirrors Gudjonsson and Clark's (1986) concept of interrogatory suggestibility. In the context of a relationship where the subject trusts the interrogator's authority, and in which a suggestible suspect is uncertain about the past events in question and is in a state of emotional arousal, the interrogation tactics listed above have a high likelihood of producing a substantial false confession. Systematically and repeatedly presenting the suspect with false premises about the past events in question, coupled with a demand that the subject demonstrate acceptance of these premises in his/her behavior, forces the suspect to rely only on himself with his admitted uncertainties of memory and insecurities regarding self-worth. In such an environment, isolation of the individual prevents the suspect from exposure to alternate premises that might allow him to doubt the information presented by the interrogator.

While Gudjonsson and Clark's and Ofshe's works bear some important similarities, there is also an important difference in emphasis. Gudjonsson and Clark, in their model of interrogatory suggestibility and in the subsequent research using the GSS, have consistently emphasized individual differences in interrogatory suggestibility. Ofshe, while recognizing personality differences in suggestibility, has consistently emphasized the nature of the interrogatory tactics. While both Gudjonsson and Ofshe acknowledge that personality factors and interpersonal pressure combine to greatly increase the likelihood of false confession, each tends to emphasize one factor over the other.

The value of Ofshe's work lies in its implication that extreme forms of interrogatory pressure may yield false confessions even in individuals who are not on the high end of the interrogatory suggestibility continuum. In other words, if the interpersonal pressure is intense enough, even normal, not especially suggestible individuals can be made to produce false beliefs. If we follow this line of reasoning to its logical conclusion, then, in addition to a subpopulation of highly interrogatory suggestible individuals who are vulnerable to make memory commission errors under many circumstances, a much larger population of less suggestible individuals are vulnerable to make memory commission errors if the right type of interpersonal pressure is applied. Perhaps this is why the confession rates (including an increase in both true and false confessions) are so high in police interrogations, where interpersonal pressure is intentionally part of the interview procedure.

Unfortunately, despite the promise that the GSS holds as a measure of memory suggestibility, there are very few reports of scientific studies using the GSS to identify those patients in psychotherapy or hypnotherapy who are most vulnerable to interrogatory suggestibility. One of the authors (DB) is currently collecting data using the GSS as a measure of suggestibility and vulnerability to memory distortion in psychotherapy patients. It is hoped that the results of the study will provide useful information translating the GSS into the therapy setting.

COERCIVE PERSUASION

To appreciate the extent to which extreme forms of interrogatory pressure override trait differences in interrogatory suggestibility (unless the individual measures extremely low in interrogatory suggestibility, like Gudjonsson's "deniers"), we need only to consider the research on so-called "brainwashing," also technically known as thought reform (Hinkle & Wolff, 1956; Lifton, 1956; Scheflin & Opton, 1978) or coercive persuasion (Ofshe, 1991; Schein, Schneier, & Barker, 1961), where programs of false belief development were carried out on a large social scale, presumably with many normal and not necessarily highly suggestible individuals.

Interest in social influences that could be manipulated to control minds developed in earnest beginning with the rise of totalitarian governments in the early part of this century (Cohen, 1953). The clarion call for research on extreme social influence was sounded in the Soviet Union with the infamous Moscow Show Trials in the 1930s (Conquest, 1990; Koestler, 1940; Vaksberg, 1990). Staunch revolutionaries were reduced to marionettes when put on trial for alleged crimes against the state. Torture did not provide the explanation; something more sinister was afoot.

Ofshe and Singer (1986) have noted "two generations of interest" in extreme social influence and programs of social control. The first generation consisted of studies on Soviet and Chinese thought reform in the 1950s (Beck & Godin, 1951; Hinkle & Wolff, 1956; Lifton, 1956, 1961; Meerloo, 1956; Sargeant, 1957; Schein, 1956; Schein et al., 1961). Interest in these social influence programs coincided with research describing the effects of isolation or sensory deprivation (Barabasz & Barabasz, 1993; Brownfield, 1972; Schultz, 1965; Solomon, Kubzansky, Leiderman, Mendelson, Trumbull, & Wexler, 1965; Vernon, 1963; Zubek, 1969), and also of motivational research (Dichter, 1960, 1964, 1971; Packard, 1957) and subliminal advertising.

The second generation of interest consisted of studies of religious, political, and therapeutic cults from the early 1970s to the present time (Conway & Siegelman, 1978; Evans, 1973; Galanter, 1989a, b; Halperin, 1983; Hassan, 1988; Keiser & Keiser, 1987; Langone, 1993; Marks, 1988; Richardson, 1980; Sargant, 1973; Singer & Lalich, 1995; Streiker, 1984). These studies coincided with related reports of an evolving science of mind and behavior control (Brown, 1963; Lausch, 1974; London, 1969; Pear, 1961; Schrag, 1978; Winn, 1983; Zimbardo & Leippe, 1991).

A third generation of interest, not mentioned or discussed by Ofshe and Singer, (1986) has focused on often secret government mind control programs (Biderman & Zimmer, 1961; Bowart, 1978; Marks, 1988; Scheflin & Opton, 1978; Stover & Nightingale, 1985; Watson, 1978). The crucial event triggering intense government interest in secret mind control programs was the trial of Cardinal Mindszenty and others in Eastern Europe in the late 1940s (Scheflin, 1982; Scheflin & Opton, 1978). By the 1950s, when American POWs in Korean prison camps began "confessing" to germ warfare, the concept of "brainwashing," a term coined by Office of Special Services propaganda specialist

Edward Hunter in 1949 (Hunter, 1951; Smith, 1972), spawned an international human rights crisis. Western political leaders feared that communist scientists had developed the ability to manipulate minds. Faced with the possibility that the Soviets could control innocent minds, it was decided that countermeasures would have to be taken.

The blueprint for one of these countermeasures was explained by CIA Director Allen Dulles in a public speech in 1953 (Dulles, 1953; *U.S. News & World Report*, 1953). The United States and the Soviet Union, he told his audience, were locked in what he called a "battle for men's minds." The Soviets possessed the power to "wash the brain clean of the thoughts and mental processes of the past and . . . create new brain processes and new thoughts which the victim, parrotlike, repeats. In effect," Dulles continued, "the brain under these circumstances becomes a phonograph playing a disc put on its spindle by an outside genius over which it has no control." Subversion of the personality and the creation of human automatons had now become the finish line in a most dangerous race run by Eastern and Western governments. The goal, as described in a secret 1952 CIA document, was succinctly stated: "Can we get control of an individual to the point where he will do our bidding against his will and even against such fundamental laws of nature . . . as self-preservation?" (Scheflin & Opton, 1978).

If there were to be any hope that the United States would win the "brain warfare" struggle, Dulles opined, at least one serious obstacle must be overcome: "we have no human guinea pigs . . . on which to try out these extraordinary techniques." That problem was quickly solved. A CIA document from 1963 noted, in reference to certain mind control techniques, that "the effectiveness . . . on individuals at all social levels, high and low, native American and foreign, is of great significance and testing has been performed on a variety of individuals within these categories" (Scheflin & Opton, 1978). The document concluded that the testing phase of the mind control experiments "places the rights and interests of U.S. citizens in jeopardy."

Immediately after his speech, Dulles authorized what was called MKULTRA, a massive program that included 149 subprojects specifically directed to provide information for the purpose of conquering the mind and controlling behavior (Biomedical and Behavioral Research, 1975; Human Drug Testing by the CIA, 1977; Individual Rights and the Federal Role in Behavior Modification, 1974; Project MKULTRA, 1977). Many of these experiments were unethical and illegal. Federal law now forbids such experimentation (Executive Order, 1982).

Each generation of interest in coercive persuasion has published research findings about the conditions under which normal individuals can be made to behave with extreme conformity toward, or be converted to, the ideology of the controlling social group. *Behavioral control* and/or *ideological conversion* are typically the complementary goals of coercive persuasion/thought reform.

Journalist accounts of so-called brainwashing in China (Hunter, 1951) and the Soviet Union (Beck & Godin, 1951) began to appear in the late 1940s. These accounts captured the public interest because of the frequency with which seemingly normal individuals mysteriously confessed to blatantly false criminal charges and, worse still, came to espouse the ideology of their communist interrogators. By the mid 1950s, scientific studies on the mechanisms of thought reform began to appear in the literature.

Hinkle and Wolff (1956) offer the most extensive analysis of the methods of interrogation utilized in the communist police state. Their significant study reached a chilling conclusion:

> The Communists are skilled in the extraction of information from prisoners and in making prisoners do their bidding. It has appeared that they can force men to confess to crimes which they have not committed, and then, apparently, to believe in the truth of their confessions and express sympathy and gratitude toward those who have imprisoned them. (p. 116)

Hinkle and Wolff point out that most of these interrogation methods trace their roots to police practices utilized by the Czar as part of a secret police system far before the Russian Revolution. A central characteristic of Czarist police practice was indefinite detention. The prisoner was isolated from everyone except the interrogators, and was held for an uncertain amount of time, usually under very severe conditions without adequate food or sanitation. Another central characteristic was subjecting the prisoner to relatively continuous interrogation. While the Czarist secret police system was dismantled shortly after the Russian Revolution, it was reinstated shortly thereafter as a means to suppress counter-revolutionary activities. The leaders of the communist state utilized this new police system toward a new and quite idealistic goal, namely, to eradicate the old social order in favor of the new communist state. Nevertheless, they often rehired the original Czarist prison guards and interrogators, and therefore inherited the main features so characteristic of Russian thought reform, namely, total isolation of the prisoner combined with "continuous repetitive interrogation" (p. 134). The goal of these new KGB interrogation tactics was to attack the established political beliefs and social status of the prisoner to get the prisoner to undergo an ideological conversion. Not only was the prisoner required to adopt communist political beliefs, but s/he was required to make a written and sometimes public confession of his/her crimes against the people.

Hinkle and Wolff observe that the period of detention and isolation creates a very strong urge to talk. By controlling the prison environment (the temperature of the cell, eating schedule) and the nature of the daily routines (the hours required to stay awake without sleeping; the schedule of bowel and bladder elimination; requiring the prisoner to stand for many hours), the interrogator could create a state of bewilderment and behavioral dyscontrol. The objective of these practices was to prepare the prisoner for the interrogation tactics. The prisoner was often required to stand or adopt a painful posture throughout very lengthy interrogation sessions. The goal of the interrogation tactics was to get the prisoner to accept the interrogator's statement about the prisoner's "crimes against the state" in the form of a written confession.

Hinkle and Wolff note that the preparatory isolation contributes to the development of a strong interpersonal relationship between the prisoner and the interrogator. The interrogator manipulates the patient's emotional state through "a period of pressure" (p. 135), i.e., the expression of displeasure or verbal and sometimes physical aggression alternating with a "friendly approach" (p. 136). The interrogator continues until the prisoner accepts the interrogator's premise about fictitious crimes and makes a written statement about his/her new beliefs. Confession typically is accompanied by a "feeling of relief" (p. 142). Hinkle and Wolff conclude that all these police methods constitute a form of coercive persuasion.

In the latter section of their classic document, Hinkle and Wolff analyze the Chinese communist interrogatory practices. They make the point that these practices derived from the earlier Soviet practices and are therefore essentially similar to the Soviet methods, but with some notable differences. First, whereas the Soviets were primarily concerned with past "crimes," the Chinese were mainly concerned with future behavior and beliefs. The goal of Chinese thought reform was to develop stable and lasting behavioral conformity and ideological conversion in large numbers of individuals, so that they would not pose a threat to the power of the communist state. The Chinese, like the Soviets, also utilized detention practices, but the periods of detention were typically much longer and extreme physical brutality was commonly used during detention. The fundamental difference between Soviet and Chinese thought reform, however, is in the use of peer groups. Along with private interrogation sessions, Chinese prisoners were typically detained in cells with about eight other prisoners, at least some of whom were successful candidates of thought reform and who served as informants to the interrogators. Thus, the prisoner, when not in isolation or being interrogated, faced constant peer group pressure to convert. Since there was never any privacy in the prison cell, very intimate relationships developed among the prisoners.

Upon initial confession the prisoner began an intensive training program of indoctrination in communist ideology. All information in the study group was carefully controlled so that only communist-oriented materials were provided. Information to be learned had to be repeated by rote many times and discussed with peers. Prisoners were required to demonstrate their mastery of communist ideology in front of peers as well as interrogators. Peers competed among themselves for advance in their studies. Group behavior included sessions of extensive self-criticism. Thus, while the Chinese utilized one-on-one interrogation tactics similar to those of the Soviets, they also developed an elaborate system of peer group contact to reinforce the process of ideological and behavioral conversion. Moreover, they required their prisoners to make a more elaborate behavioral demonstration of their conversion to peers and interrogators alike.

Those who have investigated thought reform have attempted to identify the basic principles operative in the development of ideological conversion and behavioral conformity. Lifton (1956) interprets thought reform as an "agonizing drama of death and rebirth" of the prisoner (p. 188), beginning with a systematic "emotional assault" on the prisoner's identity. The primary means to accomplish this assault was through *total milieu control.* For example, Lifton points out that the Chinese communist prison is probably the most tightly controlled and manipulated group environment ever to exist. Its system of communication—from officials to cell mates to the prisoner—is virtually airtight (p. 191). By cutting the prisoner off from all previous social contacts and personal relationships and providing the prisoner with a new system of totally regulated social interactions, the interrogators sought to have complete control of the information provided. By eventually appearing "lenient" to the prisoners, the interrogators offer the prisoner a way out via confession, i.e., rebirth to a new world view.

Schein (1956) describes three basic principles of thought reform: (1) disruption of existing social organization and personal relationships and manipulation of the prison social setting, (2) direct and indirect attack on existing values and beliefs, and (3) systematic use of often extreme rewards and punishments. Schein et al. (1961) also describe three stages of ideological conversion: *unfreezing,* destabilization of the person's identity and beliefs; *change,* the adoption of the new ideology as a means to escape the destablization procedures; and *refreezing,* the reinforcement of belief conformity and ideological conversion. Farber, Harlow, and West (1957) describe the *three Ds* of brainwashing: debility, dependency, and dread, i.e., the use of harsh detention conditions to foster physical debility and emotional fear arousal so that the prisoner becomes dependent upon his interrogator(s). West and Martin (1994) have recently suggested that victims of intense "prolonged environmental stress" may dissociate "by generating an altered persona, or pseudo-identity" that is "superimposed" on the original personality, which, "while not completely forgotten,

[is] enveloped within the shell of the pseudo-identity." They note that:

> Through the exercise of psychosocial forces . . ., people can be deliberately manipulated, influenced, and controlled to a considerable degree, and induced to express beliefs and exhibit behaviors far different from what their lives up to then would have logically or reasonably predicted. (p. 271)

Ofshe and Singer (1986), in their extensive research on the basic mechanisms of both first and second generation thought reform programs (including religious, political, and therapeutic communities and cults), note one crucial difference between these programs: first generation thought reform programs, namely, the communist thought reform methods, focus primarily on attacking what Ofshe and Singer consider to be "peripheral elements of self" (p. 14), i.e., political and social beliefs, social status, social roles, and conformity with social norms, while the second generation thought reform programs focus on central elements of the self, such as personal identity, self-esteem, and social identity with intimates, family, and peers. Ofshe and Singer emphasize that these newer and more sophisticated programs of thought reform are not able to rely on government control and so rarely utilize detention or physical punishment. Instead, leaders of second generation thought reform social groups exploit the enormous power of the social group so that the peer group itself functions as the primary mechanism of behavioral control and ideological conversion. Prospective cult members are initially recruited by leading them to believe that the cult can provide them with a useful service and is committed to the values they espouse. The objective of cult initiation strategies is progressive group involvement and systematic isolation of the initiate from previous social contacts (unless they are also initiated) and from his/her former lifestyle. Gradually, the initiate comes to accept the authority of the cult and shift the basis of his/her social attachments and livelihood to the cult. This is done by exploiting the recruitant's vulnerability, e.g., dependency needs, fragile self esteem, or previous drug or trauma history. Cult members make it appear to the recruitant that cult membership offers a solution to whatever problems the person has had in his/her life. Eventually, the recruitant's outside contacts dwindle and the individual becomes highly dependent on the cult for all social contacts, means of employment, and avocational interests. At that point, threat of expulsion means nothing less than loss of one's entire world.

Peer group pressure to conform to the ideology of the cult is used extensively in second generation thought reform programs. Public and even private disagreement with the group ideology is strictly prohibited and cult members are expected to make frequent public expressions of their agreement with the cult's beliefs. Another central feature of second generation thought reform is the use of sophisticated psychological techniques to attack central aspects of the self. These include the manipulation of *altered states of consciousness* using hypnosis, meditation, and drugs, the use of group confrontation to destabilize the recruitant's primary coping and defense mechanisms, and the use of progressive involvement in a hierarchical social status system to manipulate the recruitant's self-esteem. The only way for the recruitant to enhance self-esteem is through further involvement with the group. Members are rewarded by taking more responsibility and achieving social status within the social organization as they succeed in their ideological conversion.

According to Ofshe and Singer (1986), there are three fundamental differences between first and second generation programs of thought reform. First, the nature of *milieu control* differs. First generation programs utilize temporary special detention environments like a prison or reeducation camp before releasing the prisoner back into mainstream society. Second generation programs extend the milieu control to establish permanent residential communities "within which family, occupational, educational, spiritual, and social life is conducted" (p. 14). This allows for ongoing peer monitoring of all activities to ensure behavioral conformity and maintain ideological conversion. Second, the programs utilize *altered states of consciousness*, like hypnosis and meditation, and *group therapy methods*, especially confrontational and reenactment strategies. Third, the first and second generation programs differ in the selection of coercive persuasive tactics. While physical affliction, a system of rewards and punish-

ments, and fear arousal characterize first generation programs, *sophisticated psychological tactics*, like the manipulation of guilt, personal failure, and esteem vulnerability, are used in the second generation programs to break down the recruitant's established coping and defense mechanisms.

No absolute statistics are available on the effectiveness of first and second generation thought reform programs. There is some consensus among the experts that even with all the massive human resources the Soviets and Chinese communists brought to bear toward the goal of ideological conversion, these programs were never as successful as was feared by the public. In their extensive review, Hinkle and Wolff (1956) conclude that the Soviet and Chinese communist thought reform was "never more than partly effective, but it always had some effect" (p. 164). Thought reform seldom impaired an individual's capacity to think and did not lead to a deficiency in memory, but it did result in belief conversion. For most victims, however, this belief conversion was quite temporary, generally disappearing "within a few weeks after the convert is removed from his Communist environment." But a very small portion of converts appear to experience long-lasting, even permanent, changes in their attitudes and behavior, especially if they are among the "most susceptible group" (p. 172).

Schein (1956), likewise, concluded that considering the amount of systematic effort devoted to controlling every aspect of the prisoner's life as a means of inducing thought reform, these programs largely failed, in that "only a small number of men decided to refuse repatriation" (p. 169). Schein observed that the thought reform programs often led to overt behavioral compliance, but were less successful in changing beliefs. Schein later suggested that these techniques be used by federal prison wardens on difficult prisoners (Schein, 1962). Lifton (1956) described three possible outcomes: (1) no or only minimal effects upon the prisoner's existing beliefs or ideology, (2) unstable compliance with the demand behavior and ideology that is reversible upon release from prison, and (3) stable internalized beliefs that last a long time after release.

It should be noted that the findings of Lifton and Schein parallel Wrightsman and Kassin's (1993) and Gudjonsson's (1992) forensic data on deniers, coerced-compliant false confessors, and coerced-internalized false confessors. While all the experts agree that some subgroup of prisoners will undergo stable ideological conversion, the consensus is that thought reform for most prisoners results in merely temporary compliance. Ofshe (1991) aptly coined the term "situationally adaptive belief change" (p. 213) to emphasize that ideological conversion for most victims is highly dependent on keeping the prisoner in the controlled environment, sustaining interpersonal pressure, and conducting a central assault on the self representation of the victim in order to maintain the ideological change. The most striking finding of the first generation thought reform studies is how ineffective the programs were in producing stable false political beliefs, except in the case of a relatively small number of highly suggestible individuals.

Ofshe and Singer (1986), while not reporting statistics, state that second generation programs use a more sophisticated technology of coercive persuasive methods, thereby implying that these programs may be more effective in producing not just limited change in political beliefs, but also stable false beliefs central to one's self-image.

Ofshe (1991) defines *coercive persuasion* in terms of "programs of social influence capable of producing substantive behavior and attitude change through the use of coercive tactics, persuasion, and/or interpersonal and group-based influence manipulations" (pp. 212–213). According to this view, social and psychological forces may be manipulated to induce changes in belief.

Scheflin and Opton (1978) have noted that there is no one accepted definition or explanation of brainwashing or coercive persuasion in the expert community:

> When people look at Herman Rorschach's famous inkblots, they tend to project their explanations into those unfamiliar, murky and ambiguous splotches. So also with brainwashing adherents of each major psychological theory [who] have discovered that brainwashing exemplifies the mental events which they believe are the most important. Drs. Sargant and Meerloo are convinced that Pavlovian conditioning is the explanation. Drs. Hinkle and Wolff see physical collapse as a producer of mental collapse; for them stress, fatigue, pain, isolation, humiliation, malnutrition and other stresses crack the body first, then the psyche. Drs. Farber, Harlow and West concluded that debility, dependency, and dread were the keys to forced conformity. Drs. Moloney and Lifton color the picture of brainwashing with the pigments of psycho-analytic theory, guilt, ego and superego, "working through," catharsis, and so on. Others have emphasized the breaking down of identity, the influence of the group, cognitive theory, dissonance reduction, and more. Eclectics like Dr. Schein suspect that all explanations are partially right, and that no one theory is sufficient. (p. 93)

Modern brainwashing theory centers around a debate as to whether the belief-altering techniques used by the Soviets, the Chinese, and the Koreans are possible in the absence of force, coercion, and deprivation (Anthony, 1990; Anthony & Robbins, 1992; Singer & Lalich, 1995). This debate has surfaced in courts and has led to the disqualification of Ofshe and Singer on the grounds that their views have not met with approval in the relevant scientific community (*United States v. Fishman*, 1990). Ofshe and Singer filed suits first in New York and then in California against the American Psychological Association and the American Sociological Association. Both suits were dismissed (*Singer v. American Psychological Association*, 1993).

A COMPARISON OF INTERROGATORY SUGGESTION AND COERCIVE PERSUASION

To what extent are interrogatory suggestion and coercive persuasion similar or different? Ofshe (1991) has identified four factors that distinguish coercive persuasion from other forms of socialization. These are: (1) an intense psychological and interpersonal attack designed to destabilize the victim's sense of self, (2) the application of interpersonal pressure to promote conformity, (3) the use of organized peer pressure, and (4) the manipulation of the total environment to stabilize the desired behavioral and ideological conversion. While these factors may serve to distinguish coercive persuasion from other forms of persuasion, they do not clearly distinguish between interrogatory suggestion and coercive persuasion.

It is our position that interrogatory suggestion and coercive persuasion can be seen along a continuum. Figure 9.1 lists each distinct element that has been identified as a defining feature of interrogatory suggestion and coercive persuasion. Interrogatory suggestion involves the following elements:

TABLE 9.1
A Continuum of Interrogatory Suggestion and Coercive Persuasion

INTERROGATORY SUGGESTION
  1. Interrogatory bias
  2. Power differential (source credibility persuasion)
  3. Closed social interaction (extreme dependency)
  4. Systematic misleading within and across interview sessions
  5. Emotional pressure (threats and rewards or coaching)

COERCIVE PERSUASION
  1. Environmental control and total information control
  2. Social control (detention or group pressure)
  3. Psychophysiological destabilization

1. Interrogatory bias in either the interviewer, interviewee, or both. Typically, the interviewer has a fixed idea about the crime in question and communicates that bias to the suspect in the form of premises about the past event(s). Moreover, the interrogator may also try intentionally to manipulate the suspect's expectations about the interview, especially in the form of cuing the subject about what type of response is desirable.
2. Interrogatory suggestion nearly always involves a clear difference in power between the subject and interviewer. Studies on source credibility within the domain of attitude change research have convincingly shown that authoritative sources wield more influence. This phenomenon is often intentionally exploited in interrogatory police interviews.
3. Interrogatory suggestion presumes a closed social interaction that involves some degree of dependency, and often some degree of trust. Gudjonsson has argued that suggestion in-

creases as a function of trust. Lifton (1956), too, speaks of the use of leniency at a strategic point in the thought reform process to facilitate ideological conversion. However, studies on the Stockholm Syndrome (Strentz, 1982) have made it clear that the key operative factor may be the extreme dependency on the interrogator/captor and not degree of trust, since the captor may be quite untrustworthy and abusive.

4. Interrogatory suggestion presumes systematic leading and misleading. Interrogatory suggestion differs from misinformation suggestion in the total number of leading and misleading suggestions introduced in any given session and repeatedly across sessions. Systematic misleading refers to the relative quantity of misleading information suggested to the subject within and across sessions. In legal terms, we might say that the interrogation was unduly suggestive by the systematic repetition of misleading questions within and across sessions. Except for very highly suggestible people, occasional leading or misleading typically falls short of what is necessary to produce stable false beliefs.

5. Interpersonal pressure refers to the intentional manipulation of the subject's emotional state, by using either positive and/or negative emotional feedback or a system of rewards and punishments.

The basic ingredients of coercive persuasion are, in addition to the five above:

1. Behavioral control. The objective of coercive persuasion is for the prisoner to make a confession, often a written false confession. Most second generation programs demand public expression of acceptance of the social group's core beliefs and enactment of those beliefs through behaviors, such as solicitation and recruitment of new members, earning a livelihood for the cult, etc. It is well documented in the attitude change literature that requiring a person to behave in a way that runs contrary to his or her original beliefs facilitates attitude change in the direction of the contrary behavior (Festinger, 1957).

2. Milieu control can be seen along a continuum from environmental control, e.g., kidnapping or arrest and detention, to information control. The key factor in information control is to monitor all aspects, so that the individual is given only information pertinent to the interrogator's belief system and is denied access to alternative or contradictory ideas. Isolation and indoctrination are generally used to accomplish information control. Control of the social milieu traces its odyssey from the use of detention by the Soviets, to the use of peer reeducation groups by the Chinese, to the use of psychologically oriented peer groups by second generation thought reform programs. The goal of milieu control is, on the one hand, to disrupt completely the subject's relationship to his or her usual physical and social environment and sources of information and, on the other hand, to provide the subject access to only an artificial physical and social environment and sources of information that will shape the individual's beliefs in the desired direction.

3. Psychophysiological destabilization refers to the use of strategies to disrupt normal physiological processes through disruption of sleep and waking, temperature control, control of eating and elimination, and other normal routines, and also to the use of physical violence and other ordeals to induce physical affliction. It also refers to the use of strategies to destabilize the psychological sense of self and self-esteem, as well as the typical pattern of coping and defense mechanisms. The use of altered states of consciousness accomplishes destabilization of both the physical and psychological sets at once.

Clearly, interrogatory suggestion and coercive persuasion are both similar and different. Coercive persuasion usually involves the five elements of interrogatory suggestion *plus* milieu control and psychophysiological destabilization. When a given influence procedure is being evaluated, elements that fall more to the top of continuum represent interrogatory suggestion and those on the bottom of the continuum fall more within the domain of coercive persuasion. Police interviews typically involve interrogatory suggestion but may shade off into coercive persuasion if there is an excessive demand for compliant behavior and if more extreme forms of milieu control are used. However, according to this continuum, we would not consider a program to be a thought reform program unless it involved both milieu control and psychophysiological manipulation. Most police interviews fall short of "brainwashing." These distinctions between interrogatory suggestion and coercive persuasion will become important in chapter 12, when we return to the false memory debate and specifically consider the applicability of the concepts of interrogatory suggestion and coercive persuasion to the hypothesized suggestive influences in psychotherapy.

LABORATORY MEMORY RESEARCH AND INTERROGATORY SUGGESTION

The Child Studies

Most of the research on interrogatory suggestion comes from the forensic field. In this section we will examine research on interrogatory suggestion and memory in both normal children and adults. This research is especially important because commission error rates are generally much higher when interrogatory methods are used, as compared to misinformation suggestions per se. Recall that misinformation suggestion and interrogatory suggestion differ, in that the former emphasizes primarily cognitive factors and the latter encompasses cognitive and interpersonal pressure operative in suggestion (Gheorghiu, Netter, Eysenck, & Rosenthal, 1989).

Outside of the forensic field, no studies exist that reproduce all of the conditions of interrogatory suggestion. However, a number of studies exist in which subjects' suggestibility and the interviewer's expertise have been experimentally manipulated and in which post-event suggestions have been given systematically, i.e., a relatively large number of misleading suggestions have been given within a single interview and/or across interviews. Most of the misinformation studies reviewed in chapter 8 use one to four misleading post-event questions in the experiments. The interrogatory suggestion studies generally use a larger number of misleading questions and often use multiple suggestive interviews. These studies were designed to parallel an unfortunately common practice in child abuse investigations—inexperienced or poorly trained protective service interviewers systematically asking a large number of misleading questions and conducting multiple suggestive interviews. During the investigation of an abuse allegation, the average child is interviewed between four and eleven times (Ceci & Bruck, 1993); in this sense, some allegedly abused children are subjected to interview tactics that constitute a kind of interrogation (Gardner, 1992) approximating at least some of the elements of interrogatory suggestibility. Many of the experiments discussed below were designed to study the effects of *systematic* suggestion on memory (Ceci, 1995).

The most important work on interrogatory suggestion has been done by memory scientists Stephen J. Ceci and his associates at Cornell University. Ceci (1994) believes that memory scientists need to take a "broader view of suggestibility" than is typically represented in the studies on misinformation suggestibility. The narrower view of misinformation suggestibility is succinctly summarized by Gudjonsson and Clark (1986): "suggestibility is defined as the extent to which individuals come to accept and subsequently incorporate post-event information into their memory recollections" (p. 195). Ceci believes that suggestibility must necessarily include both *cognitive* and *social* factors. He says that "suggestibility concerns the degree to which children's encoding, storage, retrieval, and/or reporting of events can be influenced by a range of internal and external factors" (Ceci & Bruck, 1993, p. 404). External, primarily social, factors may include manipulation of expectations, explicit threats, other forms of internal pressure, and repeated misleading questions within and across multiple interviews.

In one of the first studies to experimentally manipulate expectations, Lepore and Sesco (1994) had children play a series of games in the laboratory with a man named Dale. As part of the game sequence Dale asked each child to help him take off his sweater. When subsequently interviewing the children, the interviewer adopted either a neutral or accusatory stance. With respect to the sweater incident, the accusatory interviewer said, "He wasn't supposed to do or say that. That was bad. What else did he do?" At the end of the interview, children in either the neutral or accusatory group were asked several misleading questions, including abuse-like questions ("Did he take some of your clothes off?"). Children in the accusatory as compared with the neutral condition committed significantly more memory errors, including errors in response to abuse-like questions. Moreover, they were much more likely to embellish their false reports.

In an important study known as the "Sam Stone Study," Leichtman and Ceci (1995; Bruck & Ceci, 1995; Ceci, 1995) experimentally manipulated children's *expectations* about a protagonist in an upcoming staged event to see if they would alter their suggestibility for the event. A large sample of children, ages three to four and five to six years of age were randomly assigned to one of four conditions: control, stereotype, suggestion, and stereotype plus suggestion. A research assistant met with all of the children four times at their day care center. During each meeting in the stereotype, suggestion, and combination groups, but not the control group, the children were read three separate stories about a man named Sam Stone. The children were asked to engage their imaginations and form a mental picture of Sam Stone after each story. All 12 stories presented to the children contained a common theme about Sam Stone's clumsiness, in which he gets into an accident or breaks something. For example, one story described Sam Stone spilling a glass of soda over someone; another described him playing with a doll and breaking it. The experimenter systematically introduced *pre-event* misleading information to intentionally manipulate the children's expectations about Sam Stone.

At the end of the four weeks, Sam Stone visited the classroom while the experimenter was reading a story to the class. He entered the room and said, "Hello." As the experimenter continued with the story, Sam Stone walked around the perimeter of the classroom. At one point he said, "This is one of my favorite stories." Other than making that one statement, Sam Stone did nothing.

Following the staged event, the children were subjected to multiple suggestive interviews, sometimes with misleading questions and sometimes with a separate interviewer. In the suggestion condition, the children were asked two misleading questions about non-events, one about Sam Stone ripping a book and the other about his soiling a Teddy Bear while visiting the classroom. These children were asked the same misleading questions during each of four interviews with the same interviewer and then again in a fifth interview ten weeks later by a second interviewer. During each post-event interview the children were given the opportunity to give a free narrative recall of the event. They were asked specific questions about Sam Stone's visit (including the two misleading questions). They were also specifically asked if they actually *saw* Sam Stone rip the book or soil the Teddy Bear, as opposed to just hearing about it. Finally, each child was challenged, "You didn't really see him do anything to the book [or bear], did you?"

The results of the experiment were very revealing. In the control condition, when neither pre-event or post-event misleading information was supplied, *no* child made any commission errors when free recall was used as the interview strategy. About 10% of the children made commission errors in the control condition when asked specific questions about Sam Stone's visit. About 5% persisted in making commission errors when asked if they *saw* him do these things, and 2.5% persisted in their erroneous recall even after being explicitly challenged. Leichtman and Ceci conclude that the control children's reports were "largely, although not wholly, void of errors" (p. 571), which implies that the control group contained a minority of highly suggestible children, at least younger children. Once again, pre-event stereotyping had little effect on free recall of Sam Stone's visit, even after long retention intervals. Yet, an impressive 37% of the children reported actually *seeing* Sam Stone rip the book or soil the bear when asked specific leading, but not necessarily misleading, questions after the visit. A total of 53% of the young children and 38% of the older children recalled Sam Stone ripping the book or soiling the bear when asked misleading post-event questions repeatedly over multiple interviews (suggestive condition). A total of 72% of the preschoolers recalled actually *seeing* Sam Stone rip the book or soil the bear when hearing the 12 scripted pre-event stories about Sam Stone's clumsiness and also hearing the two post-event misleading questions about his actions during the visit repeatedly over multiple interviews (stereotype and suggestion condition). About 10–12% of the children in the stereotype condition, and 21% in the combined condition, persisted in their erroneous beliefs about Sam Stone's actions, even after being explicitly challenged. Moreover, Leichtman and Ceci noted that the children who made commission errors in their memory for the event often gave richly detailed narratives about Sam Stone's actions that never happened. Leichtman and Ceci conclude:

> . . . stereotypes resulted in a modest number of false reports, and suggestions resulted in a substantial number of false reports. Children in the stereotype-plus-suggestion group made high levels of false reports. (1995, p. 568)

Because the commission error rates are so much higher in the Leichtman and Ceci study than in any of the misinformation studies previously reviewed, it becomes clear that *at least under certain conditions*, namely, those conditions that intentionally manipulate the subjects' expectations and systematically and repeatedly introduce misleading suggestions, normal children can be substantially misled in their recollections of past events. By "under certain conditions" we mean conditions that reproduce some or all of the basic elements of interrogatory suggestibility. As Leichtman and Ceci remind us, "children's suggestibility is best viewed as heavily reliant on the entire *context* in which the event reported takes place" (p. 576). When the context is heavily weighted in the direction of interpersonal pressure to accept a fixed set of erroneous beliefs, then a large portion of normal, not necessarily highly suggestible children (assuming that very high suggestibility accounts for 2.5–10% of the variance as in the misinformation condition alone) can be made to produce substantial memory commission errors for a past event. It should also be emphasized that *the rate of commission errors was quite low during free recall across conditions and ages*, which implies that commission errors are significantly reduced when children are not at all pressured in their recollection of an event.

According to Ceci and Bruck (1995), *interviewer bias* has a strong relationship to false reporting in children. They cite an unpublished study by Pettit, Fegan, and Howie (1990), in which two experimenters acting as park rangers visit a preschool classroom and ask the children to help them find a bird's nest. One of the rangers knocks over and smashes a cake. After a two-week retention interval, a group of interviewers is provided with either accurate, inaccurate, or no information about the original cake incident. All interviewers were instructed to interview the children until they found out what happened. Interviewers in all groups asked leading and sometimes misleading questions. Interviewers given inaccurate information asked four to five times more misleading questions than the other interviewers.

In another study, Ceci (1994, 1995; Bruck & Ceci, 1995; Ceci & Bruck, 1995) experimentally manipulated the *beliefs of the interviewer*. The experiment was designed to investigate the effect of the interviewer's hypothesis on children's memory for an event. The interviewers, trained social workers, were given a one-page report containing information that "might" have occurred in a staged event that preschool children witnessed. The report contained accurate information in the control condition and erroneous information in the biased, experimental condition. The children were interviewed by the first social worker shortly after the event. After a one-month retention interval they were re-interviewed by a second social worker, who saw the same one-page report (either accurate or erroneous) seen by the first social worker. During each interview the social worker was instructed to obtain a free narration of the child's memory for the event and was specifically instructed to avoid all forms of suggestion and leading questions. Relative to the control condition, 34% of the preschool children, ages three to four years old, and 18% of the school-age children, ages five to six years old made commission errors in their recall of the event. That is, a significant subgroup of the children, especially the younger children, made a false report when the interviewer was biased through the experimental manipulation. These commission errors occurred even in the absence of misleading post-event suggestions, and even when a free recall style of interview was used. However, when the interviewer had no confirmatory bias and was accurately informed, the children accurately recalled nearly 100% of the details of the event. The combination of biased interviewer beliefs and systematic misleading questions was not investigated, but a reasonable hypothesis is that the commission error rates would be substantially higher with a combination of elements of interrogatory suggestion, as was the case in the previous Leichtman and Ceci study. Ceci and Bruck conclude:

> . . . that interviewer's biases and beliefs about an event can influence the conduct of their interviews and influence the accuracy of the children's testimony. (p. 92)

One of the most important studies from Ceci's laboratory is known as the "Mousetrap Study" (Bruck & Ceci, 1995; Ceci, 1994). The purpose of the experiment was to examine the effects of *repeated rehearsal of false information* on memory. Preschool children were randomly assigned to one of two conditions, an actual memory and a fictitious memory condition. In the actual, control condition children were asked to repeatedly think about an actual known event from their distant past, e.g., an accident that resulted in stitches. In the fictitious condition children thought about a fictitious event that they never experienced, e.g., getting a hand caught in a mousetrap. For each of 10 consecutive weeks each child selected a card about some fictitious event. If, for example, they selected the "mousetrap card," they then read a brief description about someone getting his or her finger caught in a mousetrap and having to go to the hospital. In each of the 10 interview sessions, both experimental and control subjects were asked to "think real hard" about the event in question and "tell me if this ever happened to you" (p. 28). Each child was encouraged to make a mental image of the event in question and to rehearse it by thinking real hard about it. After 10 repeated interviews, each child was interviewed by another interviewer. The interviewer asked both open-ended questions and leading questions, such as, "Did you ever get your finger caught in a mousetrap and have to go to the hospital to get the trap off?" (p. 29).

An impressive total of 58% of the preschool children produced a false belief to one or more of the fictitious events, and about 25% produced false beliefs about the majority of the 10 fictitious events. Furthermore, the children's answers went far beyond simply stating that they had experienced the fictitious event. The experimental children who made commission errors typically gave highly detailed, embellished, and internally coherent yet completely fictitious accounts. Ceci's assumption, although not formally part of the experimental design, was that many of these children came to believe that they actually experienced that fictitious event, and some of these children refused to accept that the event never happened when debriefed about the research. Furthermore, video segments of actual and fictitious reports were shown to child psychologists. They were not able to distinguish the real from the false memory reports.

In a follow-up study, Ceci, Loftus, Leichtman, and Bruck (1994) repeated the Mousetrap Study with one important modification. In the original study children were asked to think about a fictitious event. In the more recent study children were told that the fictitious event "actually did happen" (p. 307), and children were asked to create a mental image of the event to see if they could remember it. The experiment included positive (going on a hot air balloon ride with classmates), negative (falling off a tricycle and having to get stitches), and neutral (waiting for a bus) events. Three-to-four and five-to-six year olds were interviewed weekly for 12 weeks using fictitious or real events (supplied by parents). Each child was presented with four real and four fictitious events and was then instructed to "play a 'picture-in-the-head' game" (p. 309), following which they attempted to recall the events. During the last session, conducted by a separate interviewer, children were warned that not all of the things presented in the earlier interviews actually happened and were then asked to freely recall the events that actually happened.

There were no significant differences in the recall of actual events over the 12-week period. Accuracy rates were generally high for real events across interviews. Recall rates for the fictitious events were moderately high in the first interview in both younger (34%) and older (25%) children, and significantly increased with repeated interviews over the 12-week interval (45% and 40%, respectively). However, when the data were analyzed according to the *type of event* presented, it became clear that both younger and older children significantly reported many more positive and neutral than negative fictitious events. The rate of reporting fictitious negative events as memories of real events was around 20% after 12 weeks of repeated false suggestions that the event actually had occurred combined with visualization of the event as a memory. Ceci et al. conclude:

These findings suggest that it is possible to mislead preschoolers into believing that they experienced fictional events, and to do so with increasing conviction and vividness over time. . . . Certain types of events were much more easily incorporated into children's false beliefs than others. Specifically, neutral events and, to a lesser extent, positive events, were easier to bias than were negative events. . . . Yet, even negative events did reveal some degree of false assenting, increasing over sessions. (pp. 315–316)

It should be noted, however, that the 20% rate of false reports of negative events is particularly unimpressive considering the combination of interrogatory techniques used—source credibility manipulations, being told the event actually happened, systematic repetition of misleading suggestions within and across sessions, and visualizations designed to confuse memory source attributions.

In a second follow-up study, Ceci, Crotteau-Huffman, Smith, and Loftus (1994) repeated the Mousetrap Study in an experiment in which children were given two actual and two fictitious events to visualize in the same session and between seven and ten sessions over ten weeks. The children were able to recall the actual events accurately across the sessions. Overall, children did not significantly increase their report of fictitious events over repeated sessions. However, when the children were separated into younger (three to four year olds) and older (five to six year olds) children, a significant effect was found. Twice as many younger (44%) as older (25%) children reported remembering a fictitious event during the initial session, but the effects were not significant during the final session. While this study showed that asking children to visualize a fictitious event may lead to a source confusion between an actual and imagined experience, it failed to demonstrate that repeated misleading suggestions for a fictitious event across interviews significantly increased false remembering. One explanation for the failure to find a repeated suggestion effect is that children were told "not all the things that I am going to read to you really happened" (p. 394). Thus, when the children were not told that the event had actually happened and were given appropriate warnings, the repeated misinformation suggestion effect did not occur.

Another of Ceci's studies focuses particularly on the effects of *systematically repeating misleading suggestions* given over multiple interviews (Bruck & Ceci, 1995; Ceci, 1994). In this study, however, the research question addressed whether or not systematic misleading could affect memory for an event of impact pertaining to the child's body, namely, an inoculation. Five year olds went to the pediatrician's office for an annual check-up that included an inoculation. Immediately after the exam the pediatrician left the room and the researcher gave the child either accurate or inaccurate feedback about how he or she had acted when getting the shot. Some children were told that the shot hurt (hurt condition), some that it had not hurt and that they had acted brave (non-hurt condition), and some were told simply that the shot was over (neutral condition). After a one-week retention interval, children were asked to rate how much the shot hurt. The results were significantly variable across all three conditions. Ceci concluded that the "children's reports about the stressful, personally significant and physically invasive check-up procedures were not rendered less accurate by our suggestive questions" (p. 37). In this sense, the conclusions were consistent with the majority of studies on suggestion and events of impact.

However, the children were *repeatedly* interviewed three times over the next year, and each time the children in the experimental group were given different types of misleading information about the inoculation experience, such as being read a story or being given a treat by the pediatrician. After a one-year retention interval the children were reinterviewed. A total of 45% of the misled and 22% of the control subjects produced substantial commission errors, both about the central event, the inoculation, and about other suggested events that never really occurred. Ceci and Bruck (1995) conclude, "Multiple suggestive interviews may have deleterious effects on reporting . . ." (p. 110).

Each of Ceci's studies addresses one or several of the basic elements of interrogatory suggestibility. Taken as a unit, these studies demonstrate that the more elements of interrogatory suggestion that are introduced into an interview about a past event, the greater the rate of memory commission errors. Bruck and Ceci conclude:

The research also shows, however, that with more powerful and persistent methods of suggestion . . . a substantial percentage of children can be led to make false reports of events that never occurred, including events that involve their own bodies and that would have been quite traumatic had they occurred. (p. 308)

The commission error rates vary between 20% and 72% in preschoolers. An interview that incorporates most of the identified elements of interrogatory suggestion is capable of producing memory commission error rates in well over 50% of at least very young subjects.

Overall, the commission rates in Loftus's misinformation studies tend to run low when response bias is controlled for (less than 10%) (Lindsay, 1994b; Loftus, 1979b). These rates are similar to the rates in control subjects in Ceci's studies. Ceci's studies convincingly show that when various elements of interrogatory suggestibility are added, like the intentional biasing of the subject's expectations or the interviewer's beliefs, or the systematic and repeated introduction of misleading information within and across interviews, the commission error rate increases substantially. These data strongly imply that the overall suggestive effect is a function of the *interaction* between a *trait* of suggestibility and the nature of the *interpersonal pressure* applied.

In other words, a reasonably small subgroup of individuals measures high on a trait of interrogatory suggestibility and would be suggestible under many (but not all) conditions. Less suggestible subjects (but probably not very low-suggestible subjects) will also make significant commission errors about past events, but only under very specific conditions, namely, those conditions that reproduce the basic elements of interrogatory suggestibility. Ceci's data also suggest that, even when commission error rates run very high, the risk is substantially lowered (but not eliminated) in a free recall interview and in an interview in which the subject is asked to examine critically the source of his/her memory, is challenged about the truth of his/her recollections, or is warned not to answer unless s/he is sure that the event actually occurred. These findings, derived primarily from studies of preschoolers, need to be viewed with some caution. Whether generalizations can be made to adults has not yet been established.

Just as interrogatory pressure can be used to significantly increase suggestibility in children, Saywitz and Moan-Hardie (1994) have raised the question as to whether interrogatory methods can be used to reduce memory errors in children. Seven-year-old children participated in a craft activity that was interrupted by a staged argument by the teachers. Two weeks after the incident half the children were assigned to an experimental group and the other half to a control group. Children in the experimental group were warned that some of the questions asked might be misleading. Children were taught the distinction between saying "I don't know," "I don't remember," and "I remember." Then they were educated about the negative consequences of misremembering (the wrong person would be punished). They were instructed to stop and think before answering, to mentally replay the event, and they were encouraged to answer "I don't know" when applicable. Children in the control group were not given the instructions designed to increase resistance to suggestions. Both groups were interviewed the next day. The interview contained correct and misleading questions (e.g., "The man . . . pushed the history teacher," p. 416). Results indicated that a significant portion of children were misled by the misinformation supplied, but also that there was a significant decrease (26%) in the memory error rate in the experimental group that was trained to resist misremembering in contrast to the control group that was not. This innovative study demonstrates that, just as a constellation of interrogatory methods can be used to significantly increase suggestibility, a constellation of interrogatory methods might also be used to significantly decrease memory commission errors.

A number of child experimental studies relevant to various aspects of interrogatory suggestibility have appeared in the literature. Warren, Hulse-Trotter, and Tubbs (1991) gave the Gudjonsson Suggestibility Scale to adults and children seven and twelve years of age. Half the subjects were warned that the questions might be tricky or difficult and were told to answer the questions that they "really remembered" about the story (p. 278). The other half were not warned. Younger children (seven year olds) had significantly poorer total recall of the story and yielded significantly more to misleading questions as well as shifted their answers significantly more in response to negative feedback than the older children and adults. Both seven and twelve year olds were significantly more vulnerable when the misleading questions were repeated a second time after the negative feedback. Recall of the story details was inversely related to suggestibility: the fewer story details remembered, the greater the vulnerability to misleading information. Warning subjects significantly decreased their vulnerability to misleading information (decreased Yield score) across all age groups. This study adds further confirmatory data to the view that interpersonal factors greatly affect suggestibility, in that negative emotional feedback and repeated questioning significantly increased suggestibility, while warning subjects significantly decreased suggestibility.

Several other studies have focused on the effects of repeated misleading questions on memory. Moston (1987) looked at the effects of repeated questions within the same interview session. Children ages six, eight, and ten years old viewed a staged event in which a confederate told the school children at morning assembly that some people from the university would come to ask them some questions. Each child was asked to recall the event freely and was also asked 16 questions about the event, half of which were true and half of which were misleading. One group of children was explicitly told to say "don't know" if they were unsure of the answer; the other group did not receive the "don't know" instructions. Data were analyzed in such a way that initial responses to questions could be compared to responses to repeated questions—either the same questions or two similar questions about the same event detail. The total number of correct responses to the staged event was significantly lower after *repeated questioning* when compared to the initial questioning, especially for younger children. Instructing children to say "don't know" failed to produce any significant effect on the number of accurate or inaccurate details. Moston concluded that "repeated questioning, within a single interview session, does weaken response accuracy" (p. 76) and "is a factor that may partially explain why children can appear to be so suggestible" (p. 77).

Poole and White (1995) also investigated *repeated questioning within the same session*. In various age groups of children they found that repeated open-ended questions and yes/no questions helped in the recall of information. Repeated questioning per se did not contribute to memory inaccuracy in children unless the repeated questions were suggestive, i.e., contained misinformation. Warren and Lane (1995) found that repeated questioning is especially helpful in preserving the memory and increasing the likelihood that more information will be recalled and accurately recalled if interviewing begins shortly after the event rather than long after the event. Thus, the *timing of interviews* is another important variable in memory recall.

Memom and Vartoukian (1996) studied the effects of repeated questioning in five and seven year olds who witnessed a staged event about an argument. Immediately after the event the children were interviewed either with free recall or with open-ended or closed questions about central and peripheral details of the event. Ten of the 30 questions asked in the brief interview were repeated within the same interview. Half of the children received a warning that some questions would be repeated. Repetition of questions combined with free recall did not significantly affect accuracy, nor did repeated open or closed questions. The warnings also had no significant effects. Memon and Vartoukian conclude:

> Repetition of open questions appears to have no harmful effects; children increased the total correct information they provided without decreasing the accuracy of responses. There was a non-significant trend for an increase in accuracy of responses to open questions that were repeated. . . . In contrast, children tended to be less accurate in response to closed questions that were repeated. (p. 410)

Tucker et al. (1990) studied the *effects of multiple interviews* in five and six year olds' memory for an inoculation immediately after and one week after the event. Each of the two interviews included a free narrative period followed by asking 28 questions (including seven "mildly suggestive" questions) (p. 120). There were no significant differences in memory performance across both interviews, although the total amount of information declined over the one-week retention interval. Under 20% of the suggestive questions were answered incorrectly.

Poole and White (1991) interviewed four-, six-, and eight-year-old children and adults about a staged

fight over a writing pen. Following the event subjects were interviewed with a free recall format followed by seven specific questions, six open-ended questions, and one speculative question about the man's occupation. The speculative question could not be answered with the information provided in the staged event. The questions were asked three times, either within the same interview session or one week later. Consistent with many other studies, the amount of information given in response to free recall instruction significantly increased with age. Repeated open-ended questions did not significantly affect memory accuracy, either within or across interview sessions, in any age group. Adults speculated significantly more than the children during each interview and speculated significantly more about something for which they originally had no information in the second interview as compared to the first, although "they generally did not give grossly misleading answers" and "indicated some uncertainty about the accuracy of their responses" (p. 981).

Poole and Lindsay (1995) compared the effects of both nonsuggestive and suggestive interviewing techniques on preschoolers. A total of 39 children in groups ages three to four and 68 children ages five to seven who either witnessed or directly participated in a live staged event with Mr. Science. Immediately after they were interviewed using a free recall strategy. Error reducing strategies were introduced, such as instructing the children not to guess and instructing them that the interviewer did not know the answers. Free recall was followed by five open-ended questions: tell me everything you can; tell me more; tell me how everything looked in the room; tell me about all the things you heard; and think about what you told me and let me know if there is more (pp. 135–136). Data were analyzed in terms of units of accurate and inaccurate responses. Younger children reported significantly fewer units of accurate information than older children in the free recall interview. The average amount of inaccurate information reported was 7% under nonsuggestive interview conditions. Having the child use a sensory-imagery prompt ("looked" or "heard") resulted in significantly more accurate information than free recall alone:

> These two prompts increased the number of accurate SUs reported by 56% for the younger group

and 68% for the older group. Importantly, the proportion of this new information that was inaccurate (2%) was not higher than the proportion inaccurate on initial free recall (9%). (p. 139)

Three months after the encounter with Mr. Science, the parents of 21 of the children read a story to each of them about the encounter with Mr. Science. Parents read this story over three consecutive days in an attempt to "coach" the children about the parents' narrative version of what occurred with Mr. Science. The story did or did not contain a description of an event that the child actually experienced in the original encounter with Mr. Science. In the misled groups the children heard about science demonstrations that were never part of the original encounter with Mr. Science. The story also contained misinformation about touch (Mr. Science wiped the child's face with a wipe that tasted "yucky"). Immediately following the three days in which the children were read the story, they were interviewed. The interview began with a free recall period. Then the interviewer asked nine leading questions about the science demonstrations that were or were not experienced and about the yucky touch. Each leading question was followed by a prompt. Children were also asked source-monitoring questions:

> Some of the games in the story were games that you played. But some were games that you didn't play. Now I am going to ask you about which games you really played with Mr. Science. (p. 141)

The results showed that the children produced "high error rates" (24%) (p. 142). A total of 96% of the children responded "yes" to at least one leading question about the fictitious science demonstrations, and their response to leading questions was significantly greater for information heard in the story than about control information. Parental coaching significantly increased response to leading questions about the fictitious events. "Across all leading questions, the children averaged 50% inaccurate information . . . with individual performances ranging from 24 to 76% inaccurate" (p. 144). Poole and Lindsay emphasize the important contribution of source-monitoring errors to the high memory error rates in this study. They conclude:

> . . . preschoolers' testimonies about a set of experiences were both highly accurate and grossly inaccurate, depending upon the timing of the interview, the nature of the questions, and the children's exposure to misinformation. (p. 147)

This study identifies the important contribution that parental definition of a child's reality makes to the accuracy or inaccuracy of children's reports.

Overall, whether or not repeated questioning significantly increases memory commission errors seems to depend on the *type of questions* that are repeatedly asked. While systematically repeating clearly misleading questions substantially increases commission errors (Ceci studies), systematically repeating *open-ended* questions does not necessarily lead to a substantial increase in commission errors (Memon & Vartoukian, 1996; Poole & White, 1991, 1995), nor does systematically repeating "mildly suggestive" questions (Tucker et al., 1990).

Unfortunately, there is very little research on the effects of more blatant interrogatory tactics and coercive tactics on children's memory. One notable exception is a study by Clarke-Stewart, Thompson, and Lepore (1989). Groups of five- and six-year-old children witnessed a staged event in which a janitor named Chester cleaned the experiment room. In the control condition he simply cleaned the room and rearranged the toys. In one of the experimental conditions he loafed and played aggressively with the toys. Another experimental group saw the same scene except that the children were bribed with candy not to tell on Chester. The children then were interviewed by Chester's "boss" in one of two ways: he either asked neutral, open-ended questions about the event or emotionally pressured the child to admit that Chester hadn't done his job cleaning the room. Subsequently each child was interviewed twice by the experimenters and once by the parents about the event. After an initial attempt to influence the child's report, about a quarter of the children assented to the boss's interpretation of Chester's behavior. With greater pressure about half the children falsely assented. By the end of the second interview nearly all of the pressured children falsely reported the boss's interpretation of the event. Most of the children failed to change their false report when interviewed by their parents (cited in McGough, 1994, pp. 68–69).

Haugaard, Reppucci, Laird, and Nauful (1991) report another study on preschool and kindergarten children and college undergraduates who viewed a videotape about a girl playing at a neighbor's pond after she had been told not to go there. The neighbor discovers her, tells her that he is going to call the police, and sends her home. The neighbor never touches the girl. She goes home and waits in her room for the police to come. During the interview she falsely tells the police that the neighbor hit her twice. There are two versions of the video. In one version the girl outright lies. In another version her mother coaches the girl to lie to the police. All subjects saw the same version of the video twice, following which each subject was interviewed with both open-ended and specific questions, including a misleading question about whether the man hit the girl. While none of the adult subjects made any commission error, 29% of the children told the interviewer that the man hit the child. While commission errors occurred after viewing both versions of the video, significantly more commission errors occurred when the girl lied than when her mother coached her to lie. Haugaard et al. conclude that "a relatively high percentage of young children in this investigation had inaccurate memory concerning a central aspect of the videotape that they saw, even though they saw the videotape two times" (p. 270).

These data suggest that coercive persuasion by an authoritative source or social modeling of lying by a peer can lead to significant distortion about central past events, especially when the target behavior is repeatedly presented (the subjects saw the video twice in a single session). Much more research is needed on the effects of coercive persuasion because of the belief that coaching children sometimes occurs in child abuse investigations and in custody disputes (cf. McGough, 1994, pp. 77–95, for a review of the experimental studies on deception in children).

The conclusions from studies on interrogatory suggestion in children must suffer the same constraints as conclusions from adult misinformation studies, as we learned in the last chapter. We cannot readily assume that children's reports of errors in recollections, even under conditions of interrogatory suggestibility, constitute substantial changes in the original memory representations. Cassel and Bjorklund (in press) found in their research, for ex-

ample, that children reported more inaccurate information than adults in interviews in response to cued recall questions. However, they also found that the memory errors were *not* incorporated into subsequent free recall narratives. In other words, the apparent negative effect of interviewing on the children's memory reports were a function of the social context of the interview and did not necessarily result in stable changes in the children's memory representations overtime.

Adult Memory Research and Interrogatory Suggestibility

While there is a growing body of memory research on children relevant to the basic elements of interrogatory suggestibility, represented in the work of Ceci and others, there is little comparable research on adults. Nearly *all* of the research on memory and suggestibility in adults is limited to misinformation suggestion for minor details in a complex event. A number of scientists and clinicians have criticized the applicability of misinformation suggestion studies to psychotherapy on the grounds of ecological validity. In other words, it has not yet been adequately demonstrated that the studies on misinformation suggestibility are directly relevant to our understanding of suggestion in psychotherapy, even though Loftus (1993) has hypothesized that therapists can suggest false memories for past childhood sexual abuse.

To answer this criticism Loftus and Coan (in press) recently attempted to develop a research paradigm to "implant" a specific childhood memory for an event that never really happened. In what has come to be known as the Shopping Mall study, Loftus and Coan had an older, trusted family member intersperse in conversation with another family member a specific suggestion for an event in the subject's childhood that never really happened. This strategy worked for five subjects. For example, an eight-year-old girl was persuaded by her father that she had been lost at a shopping mall when she was younger. Another eight-year-old girl was convinced by her mother that she had been lost in a condominium complex with her best friend. A 14-year-old boy was convinced that he had been lost in a shopping mall by his older brother. A 22-year-old young man was convinced by his aunt that he had been lost as a child in a sporting goods store. A 42-year-old man had been convinced by his sister that he had been lost in a department store as a child. Loftus and Coan (in press) conclude that "it is indeed possible to suggest to adults complete childhood memories for events that never happened" and this original Shopping Mall study was widely cited by Loftus and by Lindsay and Read (1994, p. 294) as a "demonstration" that false childhood memories can be implanted.

Caution is needed, however, before such conclusions can be drawn. This study is seriously flawed. The study includes five subjects and no control group, and in that sense does not constitute an experimental manipulation. More serious, Loftus and Coan state that the five subjects were "all friends and relatives of our research group," and in that sense, experimenter bias and demand characteristics cannot be ruled out as a main effect. A later description of the study (Loftus & Ketcham, 1994) reveals more of its flaws. The research design failed to control for consistency of either the experimenter or the context. The first "implanted memory" came from a discussion between Loftus and a friend at a party, following which the friend tried to implant a memory in her daughter, who was also at the party. The next two subjects came from a "term project" in which graduate students were asked to implant memories. We are not told how many graduate students failed to implant memories, only that two did it. The last two subjects came when the Loftus group "tried out our ideas" (p. 99) with two other subjects. We are hard-pressed to see how this type of informality meets even the lowest standards of an experimental design, or how it constitutes "proof" of the "creat[ion of] false memories" (p. 99). Loftus herself is aware that the Shopping Mall study is different from all previous misinformation studies, in that it addresses suggestion of autobiographical memory (Garry & Loftus, 1994, p. 365). It also differs in that social persuasion factors probably account for more of the report variance than post-event misinformation suggestions per se.

Loftus and Pickrell (1995) conducted a follow-up study to the original Shopping Mall study. The 24 adult subjects in this study were led to believe that they "were participating in a study on childhood memories, and that we were interested in how and why people remembered some things and not others" (p. 722). The researches presented each of the subjects with four short stories describing events that allegedly happened to them during their childhood between the ages of four and six. Three of the stories were true and a fourth was false. The three true stories were previously obtained by interviewing the subject's family members. The false story was about a plausible trip to a department store or mall. It contained information about a specific department store or mall that the family would have frequented with the subject in his or her childhood. After reading the stories each subject was told to:

> . . . writ[e] what they remembered about each event. If they did not remember the event, they were told to write, "I do not remember this." (p. 722)

Each subject was interviewed one to two weeks after reading the stories and again one to two weeks after that. Subjects were given fragments of each story as retrieval cues and were then asked to remember each story in detail. Confidence and clarity ratings were also estimated for each of the recollections.

Results showed that the subjects remembered 68% of the true events. A total of seven of the 24 subjects (29%) fully or partially remembered the false events. Partial memory for the false event "included remembering parts of the event and speculations about how and when it might have happened" (p. 722). No data were reported on the percentage of partial and full false reports, so the reader must note that the data do not show that full false memories were implanted in 29% of the subjects but only in a portion of them. The 71% of subjects who resisted the misinformation suggestion continued to do so during the first and second interview. Clarity and confidence ratings for the genuine memories were significantly higher than for the false recollections, although some subjects who falsely reported gave increasingly clear memories for events that never happened after two interviews. Loftus and Pickrell interpret these data to mean:

> . . . that people can be led to believe that entire events happened to them after suggestions to that effect. (p. 723)

Hyman, Husband, and Billings (1995) also designed a study to "create" false memories of childhood events in adults. In the first experiment, parents of college undergraduates were sent questionnaires about specific childhood events occurring between the ages of two and ten, such as getting lost, going to the hospital, having a memorable birthday, losing a pet, or going on a family vacation. Parents were asked to date the memory and give the details of the activities that took place. The 20 subjects were interviewed twice, one week apart. They were asked to remember about five specific target childhood events after being cued with the title of the event and the age. The target events included four events established as factual according to the parental reports. The fifth event was a false event. Two types of false events were used in the experiment—a positive false event (a birthday party where pizza was served and a clown visited) or a negative event (going to the hospital with a high fever). Recall of factual events was quite high—84% in the first interview and 89% in the second interview. No subjects incorporated the false information during the first interview but four of the subjects (20%) incorporated the false information on the second interview, but only in reference to their knowledge of similar events. The authors conclude that "wholesale adoption of an event . . . may be rare" (p. 11), but that false events can be suggested.

A second experiment was designed to see if "less likely events" (p. 17) could be incorporated over repeated interviews. While the design was similar, the false events included spilling the punch bowl at a wedding reception, evacuating a grocery store because of a malfunction in the sprinkler system, and having a car roll down a hill because the parking brake released. The latter experiment used a larger sample size (n=51). Three interview sessions were used. Again, recall of factual events was high—54% in the first interview, 82% in the second, and 92% in the third. While no subjects incorporated the false information during the first interview, 25% did by the third interview. The authors conclude that there are "instances in which people will create false recalls of childhood experiences" but do not rule out "experimental demands," "source confusion," and "social demands" as possible explanations for the results.

Like the child studies, this study demonstrates

that isolated suggestions are not effective but suggestions repeated over several interview sessions are effective in creating beliefs about fictitious events. To their credit, Hyman et al. admit that the design fails to control for social/contextual influences that probably inflate the base rates for those accepting false information about entire events.

Pezdek, Finger, and Hodge (in press) also designed a shopping mall type study to investigate "conditions under which memories are likely to be suggestively implanted or not" (p.2). Pezdek and her associates reasoned that the suggested event:

> must first be evaluated as true before it can be incorporated into autobiographical memory, and if one has neither specific episodic memory for the event nor generic script relevant knowledge about the event, the asserted event is not likely to be evaluated as true. (p. 6)

They designed two experiments to study the relative ease or difficulty implanting familiar and unfamiliar events, respectively. In the first experiment 32 Jewish and 29 Catholic high school students read descriptions of true and false events (derived from questionnaires sent to subjects' mothers) alleged to have happened when they were eight years old. They were then asked to recall the events. Using a counterbalanced design, both Jewish and Catholic subjects read descriptions of several true and false events and were told that their mothers had remembered these events. For the Catholic subjects receiving communion constituted a true event and returning to the wrong seat after communion was the plausible false event, and dropping bread at Shabbot dinner was the implausible false event. For the Jewish subjects Shabbot dinner was the true event and dropping the bread during the prayer was the plausible false event, and returning to the wrong seat after communion was the implausible false event. They were asked to think about the events during the week and were retested a week later. As predicted, some (seven of 29) Catholic subjects accepted the false suggestion for becoming disoriented after communion but only one accepted the false suggestion regarding Shabbot dinner. Similarly, three of 32 Jewish subjects accepted the false suggestion about dropping the bread during Shabbot but none accepted the false suggestion about disorientation at communion. Suggested familiar false events, e.g., communion disorientation for Catholics and dropping the bread for Jews, were significantly more likely to be accepted than unfamiliar false events. With respect to the phenomenological characteristics of the memory, true events were recalled with significantly more words than false events. False events about familiar but not unfamiliar scenarios were reported with greater clarity and greater confidence.

A second experiment was designed "to specifically test the generalizability of the results" (p. 14). Pezdek et al. used being lost in a shopping mall as the "familiar" false event and receiving a rectal enema as the unfamiliar false event. In this experiment 20 graduate student confederates read descriptions of one true and two false events to subjects and told subjects that they remembered the target event. The subjects were younger siblings or close relatives of the confederates. Subjects were told to "search your own memory and recall everything that you can about it" (p. 18). Subjects's memories were tested three to five days later. A total of three of the 20 subjects accepted the familiar false suggestion (lost in the mall), but no subject accepted the unfamiliar suggestion (rectal enema).

Pezdek and her associates interpret the results of both experiments to mean:

> . . . the familiar event was significantly more likely to be planted in memory than the unfamiliar event (p. 21). . . . Thus, if the described activity is one that a person has neither specific episodic memory for nor generic script relevant knowledge of, then it is less likely to be verified as true [or accepted as a suggestion]. (p. 23)

Pezdek et al. caution about overgeneralizing from the Shopping Mall studies to the situation of suggestion in therapy:

> The results of the present study suggest that it should be far more difficult to plant false memories of childhood sexual abuse than false memories of being lost in a mall as a child. Further, it should be easier to plant false memories of childhood sexual abuse with people for whom childhood sexual contact with an adult was more familiar than with people for whom childhood sexual contact with an adult was less familiar. (p. 25)

The trouble with all the Shopping Mall studies is their failure to control for social/contextual variables, such as demand characteristics and source credibility effects. While Loftus has used the Shopping Mall paradigm to demonstrate that false memories for complex events can be "implanted" in some subjects, and has readily generalized these findings to psychotherapy, her studies, as well as the related studies using the Shopping Mall paradigm, show a remarkable failure to address suggestive influences inherent in the research itself. This failure is especially curious since the influence of response bias, as one type of suggestive effect, is well documented in the literature on misinformation suggestibility (e.g., McCloskey & Zaragoza, 1985).

Moreover, many of the studies using the Shopping Mall paradigm make the assumption that uncorroborated parental memory can serve as an accurate baseline and that if a subject's report differs from the parental memory it is necessarily inaccurate. No study controls for the possibility of a parent misremembering the target event. Brewin, Andrews, and Gotlib (1993) critically review a large number of studies on the relationship between adult psychopathology and retrospective reports of childhood experiences. This review contains a detailed discussion of studies in which adult reports of childhood experiences were compared to parental and sibling reports as well as to records of the target childhood experiences. A robust finding across these studies is that parental reports were generally invalid except for highly memorable events like the birth of a sibling. Sibling reports and other records consistently served as a better baseline. Brewin et al. conclude, "recall by parents of their children may not be a good guide to the accuracy of recall in general" (p. 85). In light of these clearly established data, it is remarkable that all the so-called Shopping Mall studies are based on clearly invalid baseline data and reflect a bias regarding parental authority as a baseline for retrospective memory reports.

At best, these studies raise some interesting questions about suggestibility to be followed up with an appropriate design to control for demand characteristics and the other variables that need to be addressed before generalizations can be made. However, in our opinion, the questions raised may have less to do with misinformation suggestion than with interrogatory suggestion, in the sense that the *social/contextual factors* operative in these experiments are at least if not more important than cognitive factors. The social factors include source credibility (message given by a trusted family member) and some of the elements of interrogatory suggestion (systematically repeating a false premise in the context of a closed social interaction).

From what is known about interrogatory suggestion, it is not at all surprising that subjects could be persuaded to *report* their belief about a fictitious childhood event. Whether such reports tell us anything about a change in the memory representation remains to be seen. It is quite premature and misleading to call the effect an example of an "implanted" or "created" memory. We cannot tell whether the report is a coerced-compliant false report or an coerced-internalized false report. Until an acceptable standard of research is reported, we are left with no convincing evidence to support the view that specific memory representations for fictitious childhood events can be "implanted" in adults (except in hypnosis). However, according to what is known about interrogatory suggestion, it is conceivable that selected subjects might be persuaded to report such a belief in a closed social interaction, especially if they were uncertain about the event in question and if the trusted source systematically presented a plausible but false story about the past.

INTERROGATORY SUGGESTION AND SUGGESTION IN PSYCHOTHERAPY

In our opinion the forensic research on interrogatory suggestion, as well as the comparable research on memory and systematic suggestion in children, has much greater direct relevance to the question of whether false memory for abuse can arise from a psychotherapeutic interaction than the research on misinformation suggestibility per se. One important reason is that psychotherapy is a social interaction. The construct of interrogatory suggestion emphasizes social influences on memory suggestion, while the misinformation suggestion studies often minimize social influence in favor of a study primarily of cognitive factors operative in memory suggestibility. Another important reason is that the *base rates* of extracted confessions and false reports in both

the Gudjonsson and Ceci studies, respectively, are remarkably higher, and consistently so, than in the misinformation studies. Although there are no studies on suggestion in psychotherapy per se, the construct of interrogatory suggestibility has implications for our understanding of how suggestion might occur in psychotherapy. We hypothesize that *false beliefs about past events have a high likelihood of developing in psychotherapy when most or all of the basic elements of interrogatory suggestion are recreated in the therapeutic interaction*. This happens when:

1. The therapy is a *closed social interaction*
   (a) with a *one-way exchange* of information from therapist to patient and with little opportunity given to explore alternative hypotheses about the experiences in question,
   (b) where there is a marked *power differential* in the therapy relationship, so that the risk is greatest with an authoritative therapist, and
   (c) when the therapist fosters a progressive *sense of dependency* in the patient.
2. The therapist utilizes a *questioning procedure* that
   (a) *narrowly focuses on the past*, e.g., strictly memory recovery,
   (b) specifically focuses on events for which the patient has a high degree of *uncertainty*,
   (c) introduces a clear *interrogatory bias* in which the therapist intentionally manipulates the patient's *expectations* about the past event in question and/or the therapist has a rigidly narrow and fixed belief about the past abuse that is held with great conviction and certitude, and
   (d) exerts *interpersonal pressure* in the form of positive and negative emotional feedback or rewards and punishments for the patient's responses that do or do not confirm the therapist's beliefs about the abuse.
   (e) These interrogatory strategies are likely to be more effective in patients who do not have adequate *coping resources* to resist the therapist's unduly suggestive influences.

3. The therapist *systematically leads and misleads* the patient instead of allowing the patient an open-ended opportunity to freely recall his or her experience. The therapist persistently introduces plausible misleading suggestions repeatedly, both within and across therapy sessions.

4. The therapist overtly or subtly demands that the patient *accept* the premises about the abuse as his or her own memory.

5. The therapist encourages a *behavioral response* in the form of a written abuse narrative, a testimonial in a survivor group, or a confrontation with the perpetrator or other party associated with the alleged abuse.

Moreover, we learn from the studies on thought reform that the more extreme the information control, and especially social control, the greater the effect of the coercive persuasive tactics. These are seen in certain self-help and therapeutic groups that put the emphasis on traumatic memory recovery, especially those groups characterized by a closed social interaction in which peer confrontational techniques that attack the patient's sense of self and associated psychological defenses are used. Do these kind of practices occur in psychotherapy? No doubt. Do they occur frequently or infrequently in trauma treatment? The answer to that question is at the heart of the false memory debate. Our discussion may be found in chapter 11.

10

||||||||||||||||||||||

Hypnosis and Memory:
Analysis and Critique of Research

INTRODUCTION

Before discussing the nature of hypnosis and memory it is important to distinguish between two important types of hypnotic applications—suggestive hypnosis and insight-oriented or exploratory hypnosis. In the context of the current trauma and memory debate it is useful to keep in mind that a significant portion of hypnotic techniques have nothing at all to do with the exploration of memories. Criticizing the entire field of clinical hypnosis because of one area of focus where hypnosis is sometimes applied is rather like attacking the entire field of psychotherapy because one questions the value of a particular psychotherapeutic method such as systematic desensitization. While this chapter will address the hypnosis and memory research in great detail and will not address the broader domain of clinical hypnosis, it is nevertheless important for the reader to understand the difference between techniques focused on symptom amelioration as contrasted with insight-oriented hypnotic methods.

Suggestive hypnosis refers to the fact that frequently when hypnosis is integrated into medical or psychotherapeutic treatment, the focus is on offering suggestions for symptom relief or management and teaching the patient self-hypnosis for self-management of problems (Hammond, 1990b). A short-term suggestive approach to hypnosis is typically the

initial treatment of choice when we are treating less complex clinical conditions, such as habit disorders, medical conditions, and monosymptomatic or situational problems. Thus, for instance, brief, suggestive hypnosis and training in self-hypnosis have often proven invaluable (Hammond, 1994) in working with gastrointestinal disorders, chronic and acute pain, burns, smoking, weight control, anxiety, phobic disorders, dermatologic and allergic disorders, asthma, fibromyalgia, low self-esteem, many sexual dysfunctions, sleep and eating disorders, and in working with applications in obstetrics and gynecology (e.g., hyperemesis gravidarum, premature labor, labor and delivery), and dentistry (e.g., hyperactive gag reflex, bruxism, dental anxiety and phobias, oral habit control, and in promoting compliance for oral hygiene).

In contrast, *insight-oriented hypnotic techniques* may be used in psychotherapy to explore intrapersonal dynamics, adaptive functions or purposes of symptoms, or the relation of past events to current symptoms or perceptions. It must be emphasized that the potential relationship of events in one's past with current problems represents only one of many areas of focus in fostering insight. Thus, for example, when using hypnotic ideomotor signaling techniques for exploration (Hammond & Cheek, 1988), the role of past events in fostering insight is only one of seven suggested areas for inquiry and investigation.

Insight-oriented hypnotic techniques (Brown & Fromm, 1986; Rossi & Cheek, 1988; Watkins, 1992) are most appropriate when resistance is encountered in treatment or when insight is deemed important because a patient's problems are more complex and long-standing, have generalized to a larger number of life areas and are not circumscribed, where initial evaluation suggests that adaptive functions and conflicts may be associated with presenting problems, and where the current life stressors and relationships do not seem to adequately account for symptomatic complaints. When such conditions exist, and when the patient seems to possess adequate impulse control and the capacity to tolerate affect that may be involved in an exploration process, is psychologically minded, holds the expectation that insight will be curative, and desires increased self-awareness, insight-oriented hypnotic techniques may also be appropriate.

We believe, however, that some therapists may err and overuse hypnotic exploration techniques beyond what is reasonably indicated. Let's provide an example. Suppose we have a patient who presents with the symptom of hyperemesis gravidarum (serious nausea and vomiting associated with pregnancy) or with an exaggerated gag reflex that impairs dental work. Might either of these problems conceivably be associated with the influence of some past event, such as abuse? Possibly, but the probabilities of this seem relatively small. And when research (Fuchs, Paldi, Abramovici, & Peretz, 1980) has found that a straightforward, suggestive approach to hypnotic treatment produces good or excellent results with 80% of hyperemesis gravidarum patients, why would we want to use more time consuming, insight-oriented hypnotic techniques as the initial level of intervention? In working with many such conditions, suggestive hypnosis focused in the present proves effective, without looking to the past or to insight. However, when a patient is quite responsive to hypnosis and two to four sessions of suggestive hypnosis do not produce symptomatic improvement, then it is reasonable to use more insight-oriented hypnotic techniques to explore the source of the resistance, and whether it may be related to underlying dynamics or functions, or related in some manner to events in the past.

Thus, insight-oriented hypnotic techniques have their place in a *balanced and comprehensive approach* to psychotherapy with a variety of problems, including with victims of abuse. This position is congruent with the American Psychiatric Association (1994) statement on memories of sexual abuse, wherein they affirm the existence of repressed or delayed memories:

> Children and adolescents who have been abused cope with the trauma by using a variety of psychological mechanisms. In some instances, these coping mechanisms result in a lack of conscious awareness of the abuse for varying periods of time. Conscious thoughts and feelings stemming from the abuse may emerge at a later date. (p. 26)

We likewise agree with their conclusion that special knowledge and experience are needed by therapists working with patient memories through hypnosis.

After a brief consideration of the nature of hypnosis, this chapter will review the professional literature on hypnosis and memory. Critics of hypnosis commonly cite the American Medical Association (1985) scientific report authored by a committee chaired by Martin Orne. However, many criticisms about the validity of the AMA report conclusions have appeared (Beahrs, 1988; Frischholz, 1996; Hammond et al., 1995; Reiser, 1986; *Rock v. Arkansas*, 1987; Scheflin & Shapiro, 1989; Spiegel, 1987; Spiegel & Spiegel, 1987; Watkins, 1989). These criticisms have focused on (1) the definition of hypnosis adopted by the AMA, (2) the committee's limited focus on laboratory research for nonmeaningful details of unstressed memories, (3) the paucity of good studies conducted on hypnosis and memory before 1985, and thus the acceptance of conclusions without data to support them, (4) the creation of incomplete and inaccurate guidelines intended for forensic hypnotic settings, and (5) the fundamental misunderstanding that the errors in memory were artifacts of memory itself and not hypnosis used with memory. As we shall see, most of the sophisticated research on hypnosis and memory has been published since the 1985 report. This research draws different conclusions from the scanty research upon which the 1985 AMA report was based.

Unfortunately, the more recent American Medical Association Council on Scientific Affairs (1994) report on memories of childhood abuse reiterated their outdated 1985 conclusion about hypnosis, namely that "hypnosis-induced recollections actually appear to be less reliable than nonhypnotic recall" (p. 2). This conclusion was based on a review mainly of the earlier generation of laboratory research on normal memory, typically for nonmeaningful material. Furthermore, no additional research was reviewed to update the 1985 report, and generalizations from semi-relevant laboratory research to clinical work with patients is very questionable in light of scientific standards that emphasize that one should not draw conclusions from one population (e.g., normal memory in college students for nonmeaningful material) to an entirely different population (traumatic memory in survivors of abuse). However, certain aspects of the recent AMA report with respect to traumatic memory are congruent with our conclusions seen in other chapters of this book. The AMA report noted that although memory may be flawed, repressed or delayed memory exists.

It should be noted that recently the American Society of Clinical Hypnosis, the largest professional scientific society and certifying body in North America of health care and mental health professionals, reviewed the literature on hypnosis and memory. This committee, chaired by Richard B. Garver, Ed.D., and Charles B. Mutter, M.D., included three members of the original AMA panel. Their recent report (Hammond et al., 1995) reached somewhat different conclusions from the old AMA report:

> Based on the scientific evidence from numerous studies, this panel concludes that contaminating effects on memory are no more likely to occur from the use of hypnosis than from many nonhypnotic interviewing and interrogative procedures. Therefore, legal rules that single out hypnosis for restrictive treatment are unwarranted.... The committee wishes to emphasize that we believe there is reason to question whether hypnosis itself is innately distorting. We believe that for the most part it is the manner in which hypnosis is sometimes used in eliciting recall of memories and the nature of the subject being hypnotized that contributes to distortion.... (pp. 22–23)

The ASCH panel, consisting of 11 members and involving about 40 consultants, then created two sets of guidelines, one for licensed therapists using clinical hypnosis, and updated guidelines and recommendations for the conduct of forensic hypnosis interviews. In the remainder of this chapter we seek to provide an even more comprehensive literature review than space permitted in the ASCH report, followed by recommendations for clinicians in chapter 14 that in many cases build on the ASCH recommendations.

WHAT IS HYPNOSIS?

Since the term was first used in the 1820s, there have evolved numerous definitions and theoretical orientations seeking to conceptualize what hypnosis is (Lynn & Rhue, 1991). However, most of the so-called "theories" of hypnosis are descriptive rather than explanatory. It is not the purpose of this chapter to summarize the complex theoretical and research issues in the entire field of hypnosis. However, a brief discussion of the nature of hypnosis seems in order before we turn to reviewing research on hypnosis and memory.

One of the more popular definitions of hypnosis is that hypnosis is a phenomenon that is characterized by a *state of attentive, receptive concentration* containing three concurrent features: *dissociation, absorption, and suggestibility*, all three of which need to be present in varying degrees (Spiegel & Greenleaf, 1992). Some of the leadership of the Psychological Hypnosis Division of American Psychological Association, in an effort to remain theoretically neutral, have suggested that we define hypnosis as a procedure during which changes are suggested in sensations, perceptions, thoughts, feelings, or behavior. A *hypnotic context or state* is usually established through the use of an induction procedure, but may also occur spontaneously. People experience hypnosis differently, some describing it as an altered state of consciousness, others as a relaxed state of focused attention. People also differ in their responsiveness to hypnosis, with some individuals being highly responsive and others less so. In that sense, hypnosis is a *trait* or ability, with some people being more or less talented in hypnosis (Hilgard, 1965).

Different theories of hypnosis have emphasized such variables as: the involvement of conditioned reflexes (Pavlov, 1923); alterations in brain processes (e.g., Crasilneck, McCranie, & Jenkins, 1956; Crawford & Gruzelier, 1992; DeBenedittis & Sironi, 1986, 1988; DePascalis & Penna, 1990; Rossi, 1993); hypersuggestibility, fading of generalized reality orientation, and suspension of critical judgment (Hull, 1933; Kline, 1958; Meares, 1961; Orne, 1977; Shor, 1959); social-psychological processes such as compliance (Wagstaff, 1991), goal-directed role-playing, or believed-in imagining (Coe & Sarbin, 1991; Spanos & Chaves, 1989), and expectancy (Kirsch, 1991); cognitive strategies (Sheehan, 1991; Sheehan & McConkey, 1982); a special interpersonal relationship experience (Ferenczi, 1916); a regression in the service of the ego, psychological regression, or loss of ego boundaries (Gill & Brenman, 1959; Kubie & Margolin, 1944; Nash, 1991); and hypnosis as a kind of altered state of consciousness or dissociative phenomenon (e.g., Bowers & Davidson, 1991; Fromm, 1992; Hilgard, 1977/1986; Watkins & Watkins, 1979–80, 1981; Weitzenhoffer, 1989). Processes like absorption (Tellegen, 1979e), imaginative involvement (Hilgard, 1970), focused concentration (Spiegel & Spiegel, 1978/1987), and imagery vividness (Spanos, Brett, Menary, & Cross, 1987) have also been stressed.

We personally believe that hypnotic response is a *multidimensional phenomenon* wherein the equation varies from person to person. It may consist of physiological and state variables (e.g., dissociative capacity), cognitive variables (e.g., expectations, motivation, cognitive strategies, role-taking), imaginative variables (e.g., imaginative strategies, absorption, fading of reality orientation), and contextual-interpersonal variables (e.g., relationship factors, reinforcement, transference, cultural role conceptions, history of abuse). Thus, hypnotic response is likely multicausal, representing a dynamic interaction with a reciprocal influence process between these variables. We believe it may be of more value to view the competing theories as complementary, rather than as exclusive and competing dimensions. It seems to us that no single theoretical model of hypnosis is entirely adequate (Hammond, in preparation). Several multidimensional theories of hypnosis currently exist (e.g., Banyai, 1991). Brown and Fromm (1986), for example, define hypnosis as composed of three primary dimensions—the *trance state*, the *hypnotic relationship* and the *hypnotic con-*

text. Differences in the capacity to enter trance reflect trait differences in *hypnotizability*.

Apart from theoretical definitions of hypnosis, one must also be aware that courts have also pragmatically defined hypnosis (Scheflin, 1994a; Scheflin & Shapiro, 1989), often in part based on whether or not a *hypnotic induction ceremony* was performed, although measured hypnotizability has also been taken into account in ascertaining whether someone was hypnotized for legal purposes (e.g., *People v. Caro*, 1988).

No matter how one defines hypnosis, many authorities in the field acknowledge that hypnotic response may also occur spontaneously (Beahrs, 1988; Dumas, 1964; Frankel, 1975; Spiegel & Spiegel, 1978/1987) and through informal encouragement and suggestions delivered conversationally. In fact, what has become clear in hypnosis research, and what is vitally important to our discussions, is that processes that may be facilitated through hypnosis are rarely entirely unique to a "hypnotic state," but rather may occur without the formal use of hypnosis (Spanos & Chaves, 1989). Suggestions that are administered without a formal hypnotic induction ritual, for example, often still bring about the same effects (Barber, 1969, 1978), though perhaps to a somewhat lesser degree.

However one defines hypnosis, there is certainly evidence that hypnosis is often effective in facilitating therapy with patients (Brown, 1992; Hammond, 1994). Hypnosis often allows us to affect autonomic and physiologic processes, promote healing, and influence behavior, attitudes, cognitions, perceptions, and emotions. It may be effective for symptom amelioration and rapid unconscious exploration of dynamics and causes of symptoms. When a hypnotic procedure is used with someone who is responsive to it, there may also sometimes be an increased awareness of factors beyond conscious recognition.

THE HISTORY AND NATURE OF HYPNOTIC AGE REGRESSION AND MEMORY ENHANCEMENT

Historically, there have been a variety of reports of the use of hypnosis to enhance recall. Cases were reported over 100 years ago (Benedikt, 1894; Felkin, 1890) where hypnotized subjects were able to speak in foreign languages known in childhood, but long since forgotten by the adult. By the 1880s, Janet (1901/1977; 1925/1976) was using hypnosis with patients for memory processing. Shortly thereafter, Breuer and Freud began using hypnotic age regression and abreactive treatment techniques. They jointly published *Studies in Hysteria* in 1895 on the use of cathartic hypnotic techniques with hysterical patients, making the famous statement that "hysterics suffer mainly from reminiscences." Freud relied on hypnosis from 1887 to 1892, then began using it more selectively, and abandoned hypnosis in 1896 for free association—a method with distinct similarities to Janet's technique of automatic talking.

As in earlier historical periods, hypnosis was not accepted in some quarters and Freud had been criticized as "only a hypnotist." But there were several other reasons for Freud's rejecting hypnosis (Gravitz & Gerton, 1984). He found that hypnosis did not work equally well with all patients and varied with the quality of the therapeutic relationship. In fact, he stated, "When I found that, in spite of all my efforts, I could not succeed in bringing more than a fraction of my patients into a hypnotic state, I determined to give up hypnosis" (Freud, 1910, p. 22). This is not surprising given that Freud's hypnotic technique seems to a considerable degree to have been simplistic and authoritarian (e.g., sternly commanding "Sleep," as he grasped the patient's head).

Freud was also concerned with possible symptom substitution (something found to be overrated), that the techniques seemed like a lab experiment, and with the possibility of hypnosis interfering with the eliciting of psychodynamics. Freud was also probably uncomfortable with hypnosis because he was uncomfortable with patients looking at him—thus, his famous use of the couch, which was symptomatic of this problem, became standard operating procedure in psychoanalysis. Freud was also uncomfortable with hypnosis because he believed (or perhaps projected) that it may have sexual meaning or stimulation for the patient; this belief probably stemmed in part from a patient's suddenly embracing him and from his own countertransferential reactions. This event, which occurred in about 1891–92, also led to Freud's discovery of

and emphasis on the concept of transference (Chertok & de Saussure, 1979).

There is also one other factor that may have encouraged Freud to abandon hypnosis. In the 1800s sexual abuse appears to have been as widespread as it is today. For instance, Ambroise Tardieu (Masson, 1984) recorded 11,576 cases of accused rape in France between 1858 and 1869 (almost 80% involving child victims). But Tardieu was one of the few professionals of the time who was willing to believe in sexual abuse, and by 1880, shortly after his death, others vociferously attacked beliefs in incest and molestation as based on imagination, hysteria, and the unreliability and suggestibility of children— charges strikingly parallel to those made by persons associated with the false memory movement today.

Early in his career, Freud spoke out in his original seduction theory as an advocate of children, expressing his belief in childhood victimization and sexual assault, and that such trauma was at the root of considerable adult psychopathology. Immediately after expressing this view in 1896, he became scorned and alienated from the professional community for taking such a stance. "I am as isolated as you could wish me to be: the word has been given out to abandon me, and a void is forming around me," he stated (Masson, 1984, p. 10). In order to regain professional acceptability, and to ever hope to rise above obscurity and become influential, Freud may have felt consciously or unconsciously that he had to recant his seduction theory (Goodwin, 1985; Herman, 1981; Masson, 1984; Rush, 1980). Therefore, soon the new psychoanalytic theory of oedipal conflicts was born, accepting the popular view of the time that children are not really traumatized, but simply have sexual fantasies reflecting their own underlying desires. This is undoubtedly a prominent reason that Freud rose in professional acceptance while Pierre Janet did not become recognized for his enormous contribution for another hundred years. This may have been one more reason that Freud finally completely abandoned hypnosis, to avoid exploration of possible background experiences of patients. With Freud's exceptional influence subsequently on psychotherapy, interest in hypnosis declined for a time. However, the one very close friend of Freud who later refused to renounce childhood abuse and trauma theory was Ferenczi, and he was therefore banished from the inner circle

(Summit, 1988). Ferenczi discovered that abuse could be dissociated from consciousness, but could be recalled in trance-like states wherein the patient seemed to relive the experiences again. He was even insightful enough to have discovered what have been more recent developments in the diagnosis of dissociative disorders and dissociative identity disorder. He stated:

> When the child recovers from such an attack, he feels enormously confused, in fact, split—innocent and culpable at the same time—and his confidence in the testimony of his own senses is broken. (Ferenczi, 1932/1984, p. 162).

> If the shocks increase in number during the development of the child, the number and the various kinds of splits in the personality increase too, and soon it becomes extremely difficult to maintain contact without confusion with all the fragments, each of which behave as a separate personality yet does not know of even the existence of the others (p. 165).

Moll (1902) described the occurrence of hypermnesia in hypnosis, as well as "the possibility of inducing errors of memory" (p. 146). Loewenfeld (1901) experimented with hypnotic age regression and memory recall in four subjects. The memories were taken down in stenography, and reportedly, were later verified. One of the memories from the age of four was associated by the patient with a chronic symptom.

Hypnosis received renewed attention as mental health personnel struggled to treat posttraumatic effects they encountered in soldiers during World Wars I and II. Soldiers experiencing intense battle and war situations sometimes responded by becoming amnestic, as reviewed in chapter 7. These hundreds of cases of amnesia associated with war trauma certainly refute the claim of Ofshe and Singer (1994) that "neither amnesia nor robust repression was implicated in posttraumatic stress disorder" (p. 398) literature until recently. Hypnotically facilitated recall, abreaction, reassociation, and reintegration of amnestic memories was found to be tremendously valuable and was frequently used in treating trauma ("shell shock") victims in World War I (Brown, 1918a,b, 1919, 1920–21; McDougall, 1920–21;

Myers, 1915, 1916; Rivers, 1918; Southard, 1919; Thom & Fenton, 1920; Wingfield, 1920), "war neurosis" in World War II (Fisher, 1943, 1945; Grinker & Spiegel, 1943, 1945; Henderson & Moore, 1944; Kardiner, 1941; Kardiner & Spiegel, 1947; Kubie, 1943; Parfitt & Carlyle-Gall, 1944; Sargant & Slater, 1941; Simmel, 1944; Torrie, 1944; Tureen & Stein, 1949; Watkins, 1949), and with what we now call posttraumatic stress disorder in subsequent wars (Archibald & Tuddenham, 1965; Cavenar & Nash, 1976; El-Rayes, 1982; Hendin, Haas, Singer et al., 1984; Kalman, 1977; Kolb, 1985; Perry & Jacobs, 1982; Silver & Kelley, 1985; Sonnenberg, Blank, & Talbott, 1985; D. Spiegel, 1981).

When we delve into the literature from these wars—a literature about what occurs in intense and traumatic situations which one cannot duplicate in an experimental laboratory—we find reports like Brown (1918) describing the successful treatment of 100% of 121 cases of loss of speech (hysterical mutism) through hypnotically facilitated recall, abreaction, and suggestion. Kartchner and Korner (1947) believed that hypnosis was particularly indicated as part of psychotherapy "in most cases in which there existed amnesia or 'black-out' for a part or total of the combat experience" (p. 630). They also felt that therapeutic hypnosis was indicated when patients were in a state of confusion that made communication difficult or impossible, to assist in minimizing the effects of severe symptoms to allow patients to participate more effectively in therapy (ego-strengthening and symptom management), to facilitate insight concerning the correlation of emotional conflicts and somatic or psychological symptoms, to assist in the diagnostic differentiation between acute combat reactions and long-standing psychopathology, and as a way of calming patients. They found that "very frequently symptoms such as stuttering, headache and paralyses are immediately relieved when the factors producing them are remembered and accepted by the patient" (p. 634), even though presumably there was generally no opportunity for independent verification of the traumatic material that was emerging during the treatment of these soldiers.

Shortly after World War I, Morton Prince (1924) began doing controlled experiments where subjects were asked under hypnosis to recall letters they had written in the past, letters still available to compare with their recall. Two of his talented hypnotic subjects were able to achieve virtually verbatim recall of fairly lengthy letters which they could not do in a nonhypnotic state—a report with distinct similarities to research that will be reviewed shortly (Hofling, Heyl, & Wright, 1971).

There was also debate in the last century concerning what occurred in hypnotic age regression. Some persons were reported to believe that hypnotic age regression consisted simply of role enactment (Loewenfeld, 1901) and represented hallucinations and illusions (Vincent, 1897). Others (Kohler, 1897) believed that age regressed subjects were not role-playing, but may be using a combination of earlier life memories along with adult understandings and imagination in creating age-regressed scenarios from childhood. Kohler (1887) described experiences like those cited by more contemporary hypnosis workers (Orne, 1951; Spiegel, Shor, & Fischman, 1945), in which a hypnotically age-regressed individual may possess information far beyond the age to which s/he were reoriented.

Krafft-Ebing (1889), Kline (1951), Weitzenhoffer (1953), and Erickson and Kubie (1941) believed that a full age regression (revivification) consisted of a mixture of role-playing an earlier age and some psychophysiological return to an earlier age, with a reinstatement of some childhood cognitive patterns and an ablation of adult memories. Reiff and Scheerer (1959) did not believe that a genuine biological reinstatement occurred, but concluded that early memories were reactivated and became more available to consciousness. Rubenstein and Newman (1954) were among the earliest authors to challenge the validity of age regression studies, and they readily acknowledged that they believed hypnotic regression involved simulated behavior and confabulations. They indicated, however, that their doubts did not apply to reenactment of traumatic past experiences. They particularly believed that there was a "great difference" between an experimental subject discussing his/her regression to a relatively uneventful day, versus a patient spontaneously dissociating and reexperiencing a traumatic experience from childhood, which today would sometimes be referred to as a flashback.

During this century, there has accumulated a tremendous amount of evidence concerning the degree of genuine regression that occurs in cognitive and perceptual processes during revivification experiences; this research was summarized by Nash (1987). Such research has examined tests of memory, cognitive and intelligence tests, projective test performance, EEG records, Bender-Gestalt test performance, Piagetian-based tests of cognitive developmental level, and illusion tests to which children respond in predictable ways.

Most of the research on cognitive-perceptual functioning of age-regressed individuals demonstrates that an actual psychophysiological reinstatement of childhood mental processes does not appear to occur. For instance, subjects who are regressed to a certain age are found to have higher IQ scores than when they were that age (Sarbin, 1950). The cognitive performance of age-regressed subjects is generally found to exceed norms for the regressed age and, thus, is not a reinstatement of childhood mental processes. However, the performance of age-regressed subjects on developmental tasks has been found to produce a greater number of childlike responses than a simulation condition (Greenleaf, 1969), perhaps suggesting that age regression may represent a *mixture of role playing an earlier age and an elicitation of some actual childhood perceptions and memories*, not too different from what was proposed by Kohler (1897).

Methodological designs have been criticized as flawed in many of the studies of cognitive-perceptual processes and age regression (Erickson & Kubie, 1941; Fellows & Creamer, 1978; Foenander & Burrows, 1980; Greenleaf, 1969; Pattie, 1956; Reiff & Sheerer, 1959). But, despite the fact that early memories and perceptions may be recalled during age regression, overall there is a strong body of evidence suggesting that age regression is certainly not a return to the childhood experience any more than hypnotically suggested amnesia, blindness, or deafness is the functional equivalent of its physiological counterpart (Nash, 1988; O'Connell, Shor, & Orne, 1970). Age regression does not allow subjects to return to previous modes of mental functioning with an inaccessibility to adult stores of information, although it may to varying degrees access early memories and perceptions.

But, although research has severely challenged the degree to which regression reinstitutes cognitive, perceptual, or physiological states from the past, it is interesting that some experimental evidence suggests that during an age regression experience there may be a *reinstitution of affects and self and object representations* associated with the earlier target age (Nash, 1987, 1988; Nash et al., 1979). And, in fact, the most effective age regressions in experimental work appear to be those associated with affect-laden events (Nash et al., 1979; Sheehan & McConkey, 1982; Watkins, 1971). This research suggests that under conditions of emotional arousal, such as those encountered in clinical work, memory and associated self representations might be more effectively revived. Nash (Nash, 1987, 1988; Nash et al., 1979; Nash, Lynn, Stanley, Frauman, & Rhue, 1985) further found that, unlike persons simulating hypnotic age regression, when hypnotized persons are age regressed to the age of three and a frightening situation is suggested, they behave age appropriately and begin searching for transitional objects (e.g., teddy bears). However, a later study found that such transitional objects were recalled less accurately by hypnotized subjects than by simulators (Nash, Drake, Wiley, Khalsa, & Lynn, 1986).

However, as the reader will learn shortly, there is abundant evidence that age-regressed subjects may at least in some cases retrieve memories and information that was not originally available to them consciously, perhaps especially under circumstances where emotional trauma has created a block to memory (Hammond et al., 1995; Nash, Johnson, & Tipton, 1979; Sheehan & McConkey, 1982; Smith, 1983). On the other hand, this chapter will make clear that people are at the same time clearly capable of filling in gaps of memory with confabulated information, of distorting information, and of being influenced in what is "remembered" by leading questions or suggestions.

THE CURRENT STATE OF SCIENTIFIC RESEARCH ON HYPNOSIS AND MEMORY

Now that we have created a historical perspective, we will examine the scientific research in the past eighty years on the influence of hypnosis in enhancing memory. Specifically, we will first evaluate the literature on the degree of accuracy and involvement of confabulation in hypnotic recall versus ordinary recollection. As you will discover, very se-

rious methodologic flaws have characterized, and in many cases continue to exemplify, this research.

Hypnotically Enhanced Memory: Hypermnesia

Studying Memory for the Unmemorable: The Questionable Relevance of Stimuli Used in Hypnosis and Memory Studies

The scientific literature clearly indicates that memory in general, and especially for details about non-emotional events, is imperfect. Likewise, memory recall facilitated through hypnosis is also imperfect. About this there should be no debate. Therefore, let us emphasize from the outset that one may not know the veridicality of any memory, whether recalled while sitting at home or through the use of hypnosis, without independent corroboration. Whether someone is in or out of an hypnotic state, s/he is capable of distorting memory or confabulating details in response to leading questions or because of gaps in memory.

One major domain of hypnosis and memory research has addressed the question of *hypnotic hypermnesia* effects. Hypermnesia may be defined as increased memory accessibility that results in a significant increase in the total amount of information recollected about a target event. Hypermnesia refers to the relative amount of information recalled, not necessarily to its accuracy. Research on hypnotic hypermnesia addresses whether or not the hypnotic condition does or does not significantly increase the relative amount of information recollected about a target event. As you will see, many laboratory studies of hypnosis and memory have found that hypnosis does not generally seem to improve *memory recall for nonpersonally relevant details*, associated with unemotional events, that have been briefly observed, in normally functioning persons (Erdelyi, 1988). We believe that the interpretation of these outcome data is probably reasonably sound; that is, hypnosis probably does not usually facilitate hypermnesia for these kinds of stimuli. This is the kind of information most of us quickly forget—it is unremarkable and not particularly memorable in the first place.

A major problem with many of these studies failing to find *hypermnesia* associated with hypnosis is that they have often used questionable stimuli (e.g., nonsense syllables, paired-associate words, faces, slides of objects, numbers, word lists, and line drawings). Such stimuli are not likely to be associated with negative emotion or so affect-laden that they would be blocked from memory, and their lack of personal relevance would not be anticipated to cause the information to be favored in storage.

The findings for research on hypnotic hypermnesia using nonmeaningful stimuli cannot be readily generalizable to traumatic life experiences. Common sense tells us that people do not normally develop lasting recall for nonsense syllables and are not memorably impressed with nondescript line drawings, slides of common objects, or nonmeaningful faces associated with irrelevant situations. We consider it questionable scientific practice to overgeneralize in this manner, using these findings to question the use of hypnosis with abuse or crime victims. The laboratory memory and hypnosis research that has been done, as reviewed up until a dozen years ago by the AMA Council on Scientific Affairs (1985) report, does not provide us with decisive conclusions about clinical uses of hypnosis with abuse or crime victims where memories are affect-laden or may be blocked by trauma. In fact, the AMA report itself endorsed this principle in stating that, "Generalization from the laboratory to the real world depends on the degree to which the laboratory situation accurately represents the field situation" (p. 1920). As we review these studies, you will find that there is often very little resemblance between laboratory memory stimuli and clinical-forensic field situations.

The serious deficiencies and shortcomings in the existing research (Hammond et al., 1995; Spiegel, 1980; Spiegel & Spiegel, 1987; Watkins, 1989, 1993) warrant caution in generalizing beyond the population on whom the existing research was performed—normal individuals, with normal memory for nonpersonally meaningful and nontraumatic material to which they were briefly exposed. For example, samples in studies of hypnosis and memory are not the random samples of victims of abuse or trauma, or of witnesses to actual crimes, whose memories have been blocked by emotional factors. The relevance of personally experienced trauma, and even largely of emotion, has been ignored in laboratory studies of hypnosis and memory.

A variety of laboratory studies of memory enhancement through hypnosis have studied *recall for nonsense syllables* and comparable stimuli. Should it surprise us that nonsense syllable research (e.g., Baker, Haynes, & Patrick, 1983; Barber & Calverley, 1966; Huse, 1930; Mitchell, 1932; Young, 1925, 1926) has failed to find enhanced memory when using hypnosis compared to a waking state? But when one of these researchers (Young, 1926) age regressed two subjects to the age of five, one of them:

recovered facts which he could not touch in waking, and of which he could not recognize the truth when told afterward that he had given them in hypnosis, but which were verified in detail by an older sister, who had been with him almost constantly while he was a child. (pp. 349–350)

The other subject remembered more limited new information:

However, in the manner of saying the alphabet, of counting, and of saying the name "Connecticut," he fell into childhood habits which he could not reproduce in waking, however hard he tried to recall them. (p. 350)

A skeptical experimenter would undoubtedly immediately identify such behavior as the product of role-playing and imagination. However, Young (1926) noted:

These mannerisms were verified by his mother, who, without being told what the S [subject] had done in this respect in hypnosis, wrote detailed descriptions of his early habits, writing directly to E [the experimenter]. (p. 350)

In the Barber and Calverley (1966) study, the nonsense syllable stimuli were so meaningless that at the time of testing (two months after they were learned), many subjects could not remember any of them, in or out of hypnosis. In fact, the mean recall was less than 1 in 12 items, and in some groups the recall average was as little as 0.1 item. When virtually no subjects remember *anything*, how can one expect to find a meaningful difference between experimental groups?

By at least 1932, researchers like Stalnaker and Riddle were distinguishing between memory for nonsense material, meaningful material that has been learned, and "lost memories" that are "associated with traumas of a somatic, or emotional, nature." By 1940, White, Fox, and Harris emphasized that the *type of stimulus* used by a hypnosis researcher would determine the nature of recall. Following White, Fox, and Harris (1940), Rosenthal (1944) documented that hypnosis hypermnesia suggestions, compared to a nonhypnotic state, produced enhanced recall of poetry that had been learned and of experiences of an emotionally disturbing nature, but not for nonsense syllables or words. Similar results have also been found more recently (Dhanens & Lundy, 1975). In light of these findings, already emerging in the 1940s, we find it startling that laboratory researchers have continued in many cases to use personally meaningless stimuli in hypnosis research and have at times used this kind of research as the basis for their generalizations to clinical work regarding hypnosis and memory enhancement.

True (1949) sought to use more relevant memories, but used as his experimental variable a single, small detail. He used hypnotic age regression with 50 subjects to their birthdays and Christmas at ages ten, seven, and four, and then asked them to tell him what day of the week these events fell on. Following hypnotic age regression, subjects were asked in succession, "Was it Monday? Was it Tuesday? Was it Wednesday?" and so forth. True (1949) discovered that 81% of the time subjects correctly identified the day. It was learned later, however, that he had available to him (during the experimental sessions) a table that revealed what the accurate days of the week would be. Thus, the experimenter was not "blinded," and could have nonverbally or in voice tone conveyed reinforcing cues. Subsequent research studies (Barber, 1961; Best & Michaels, 1954; Fisher, 1962; Leonard, 1963; Mesel & Ledford, 1959; O'Connell, Shor, & Orne, 1970; Reiff & Sheerer, 1959) were not able to confirm True's (1949) findings, thus validating the likelihood of such contamination. But should this surprise us? After all, how many of us find the day of the week on which our birthday fell to be personally meaningful or relevant? In fact, how many of us can even

remember what day of the week our birthday fell on last year? This is the kind of detail about which we would expect relatively poor baseline memory recall, with or without hypnosis. Nonetheless, this research is informative about the kind of information with which hypnotic techniques are unlikely to enhance recall. It also importantly demonstrates that with a technique where a therapist is asking a hypnotized subject question after question, obtaining either verbal or nonverbal replies, and where the therapist has definite ideas about what the correct answer is, he or she may subtly influence the patient's responses.

By 1932, Stalnaker and Riddle had shifted from using nonsense material to using somewhat more *meaningful information* that was previously learned. They studied the effects of hypnotic hypermnesia (requests to recall information under hypnosis, not hypnotic age regression to a past event) on the memory for previously memorized prose or verse. Highly hypnotizable subjects were asked to recall the selections they learned in the past, to then open their eyes in trance, and write what they had previously learned. They discovered that the average gain in correct units of recall varied between 66.8% and 53.7%, depending on what was being measured. The difference between total waking recall and total recall in hypnosis was highly significant, beyond the .001 level of probability, although Orne's review referred to this as only "a modest increase in accurate recall" (Orne et al., 1984, p. 186).

Stalnaker and Riddle (1932), however, did note a qualitative difference in response between hypnotic and waking recall. In hypnosis, when subjects were blocked in their recall, they "improvised more freely" and "wrote more of both correct and incorrect words" (p. 439). However, this tendency for subjects to confabulate under hypnosis was not quantified, thus not permitting the kind of conclusion made by some false memory proponents that increases in memory through hypnosis are "accompanied by an equivalent or greater increase in confabulations and false recollections." In spite of the increased willingness to "improvise" incorrectly, the authors concluded that "hypermnesia in the trance for sense material learned a year or more before has been clearly established" (p. 439).

ANALYSIS OF STUDIES CONCERNING ACCURACY VERSUS CONFABULATION UNDER HYPNOSIS

Confabulation has been defined as the "filling in or fantasizing of information that seems plausible" (Orne, Soskis, Dinges, & Orne, 1984, p. 177). It has been claimed that research shows that any increase in memory associated with hypnosis "may be accompanied by an equivalent or greater increment in confabulations and false recollections" (Kihlstrom & Barnhardt, 1993, p. 107), and that "agreeing to be hypnotized is accepting an invitation to engage in fantasy" (Karlin, 1997). In this section, we will evaluate the research on this issue, along with its serious flaws.

Orne (1951) examined hypnotic age regression from a theoretical perspective of role enactment. He discovered that when a hypnotic subject was age regressed to the age of six, and was then asked a question in English—a language he did not speak at the age of six—the subject would still understand the question. Likewise, when such a subject was asked what time it was, he looked at his wristwatch. On another occasion, an age-regressed subject was still able to define the word "hypochondriac." These kinds of data have been taken by Orne (1959) and his associates (e.g., Kihlstrom & Barnhardt, 1993) as evidence that a hypnotized subject freely mixes illusion and reality. Such responses from subjects might be just as easily interpreted as subjects responding to demand characteristics by an experimenter—something verified as usually occurring in experiments attempting to produce false memories, which will be discussed later. And, in fact, Reiff and Scheerer (1959) suggested that if a hypnotized and age-regressed subject is asked such a question or prompted to respond in a way incompatible with the historic situation, that *the investigator is contaminating the regressed situation* with suggestions that give permission to deviate from the regressed condition.

Orne (1951) further noted how a subject who was age regressed to his sixth birthday may *confabulate* a response. For instance, when one subject was asked if he was attending school that day, he replied, "No," and explained that it was a Saturday. It was found, afterward, that his birthday fell on a

Sunday that year. Although the response was incorrect, it was overlooked that the important recall in the subject's mind may have been that he simply wasn't in school that day, and, therefore, it may have seemed like a Saturday (a non-school day). In another case, a regressed subject was unable to remember the name of his first grade teacher. Perhaps feeling demand pressure, he later called her "Miss Curtis," but in a waking state, he later could not recall the names of any elementary school teachers, but remembered that a middle school teacher was named "Miss Curtis." This response was taken as a confabulation without independently verifying either the waking or hypnotic memory, perhaps thus revealing a bias of the experimenter.

Another regressed subject, who did not begin speaking English until his teens, described a childhood birthday party in English. In a partial age regression with an English-speaking hypnotist, this is a situation any clinician would expect. But, rather than allowing free recall, Orne contaminated the situation and directly engaged in leading the subject. Orne said, "You see your mother, she is speaking to you. What does she say?" The subject replied, "Do you like your present?" Orne then suggests that "this statement is obviously not one of historical validity, since at the suggested time the S [subject] did not understand English, and it is clear that his mother would not have used this language in addressing him" (p. 222). However, to our knowledge, Orne did not ask the subject, following hypnosis, what precisely he heard, seeking to ascertain if the subject heard his mother in German and translated it for his English-speaking hypnotist. Orne also did not present his questions to the regressed subject in the German language. Nor did he acknowledge the manner in which he may have contaminated the situation and the influence of his own demand characteristics, as noted by Reiff and Scheerer (1959).

Despite Orne's (1951) belief that "random memories from a long period of life are combined and further supplemented by appropriate confabulations" (p. 223), he nonetheless did not question the therapeutic value of age regression:

> The experiments undertaken in this study have no bearing upon the therapeutic efficacy of the hypnotic regression technique. The process of catharsis is aided by the momentary reality of the

hypnotically structured situation, and it may well be that a reconstruction of the patient's life history on the basis of hypnotically obtained data has sufficient subjective validity to be a significant aid in the therapy. (p. 224)

In a similar fashion, after reporting experimental findings, O'Connell, Shor, and Orne (1970) noted the limited validity of laboratory investigations: "Age regression, as studied in the laboratory, is rarely accompanied by profound emotional experiences or overt evidence of extreme affect, but revivification in a therapeutic context recaptures experiences that evoke extreme feeling states, almost invariably frightening and extremely unpleasant for the patient" (p. 29). Despite their findings that hypnotic age-regressed behavior did not involve a complete reinstitution of childlike mental processes, they further concluded, "Neither the therapeutic importance nor the genuineness of revivification is challenged by our present findings" (p. 29). Thirty-seven years after Orne's initial report (Orne et al., 1988), he similarly indicated that, "the task of the therapist is not to establish the accuracy of historical events recounted by the patient, but to help the patient to work through his or her own version of history . . ." (p. 52). We agree.

However, we also believe that the situation with hypnosis and memory is not quite as straightforward as Orne and his colleagues suggest. Persons in hypnosis may certainly confabulate information, just as people may confabulate when they are trying to remember something in a nonhypnotic situation. However, we believe that an objective evaluation of the scientific data does not necessarily indicate that this occurs more often when hypnosis is used. Rather, certain *styles of questioning or demand characteristics*, whether they are used with a hypnotized or non-hypnotized person, may provide pressure and increase the amount of confabulated information.

Other more recent studies have also found what Orne (1951) originally claimed—that persons in hypnosis, who are highly hypnotizable, will sometimes tend to confabulate information. Dywan's (1988; Dywan & Bowers, 1983) findings and those of Nogrady, McConkey, and Perry (1985) are usually cited to indicate that confabulatory, false recollections occur more often with more highly hypnotizable subjects who are hypnotized and given

suggestions for enhanced memory. As these studies are methodologically flawed, their conclusions should not be accepted at face value without qualification.

The Dywan studies asked college students to recall black and white slides of line drawings to which they had been exposed for only 3.5 seconds. These are stimuli not anticipated to be personally meaningful or to make much of an impression, nor are these stimuli associated with emotional arousal—and yet they continue to be used 56 years after the findings of Stalnaker and Riddle (1932) and 48 years after White, Fox, and Harris (1940). Subjects had been given extensive repeated recall trials before the use of hypnosis, during which they were told that when they ran out of recollections, they must make "educated guesses" and fill in all the remaining spaces. Thus, subjects were accustomed to guessing in trying to recall as much information as possible. Furthermore, subjects knew that the information recalled would not have important implications in a criminal case or their own lives.

In Dywan's experiments, significantly more correct information was produced in a hypnotic recall condition, but there were three times as many errors (in newly recalled information that was not correct). What do we actually know from Dywan's studies? All that we know is that with stimuli of no significance or personal relevance, at tremendous variance from situations encountered clinically or in forensic investigations, which were not associated with emotional arousal, and which were seen only momentarily, and with subjects accustomed to trying hard to recall more and more information (and, in fact, required to guess), suggestions for hypnotic recall somewhat enhance recall but produce more memory errors. Under these circumstances, this should not be surprising and is hardly what we would refer to as "a substantial and highly reliable effect" (Dywan, 1988, p. 324) that can be used as a basis for the generalization that "hypnotized subjects are more likely to confuse imagination with perception" (Kihlstrom & Barnhardt, 1993, p. 107), when referring to clinical and forensic efforts to recall real life events.

Dinges, Whitehouse, Orne, Powell, Orne, and Erdelyi (1992) produced another laboratory study alleging no superiority for hypnotic memory enhancement efforts and an increase in confident recall of incorrect items. However, we must comment on a defect in the research design of this and many of the other reports (Dywan, 1988; Dywan & Bowers, 1983; Orne et al., 1996; Putnam, 1979; Wagstaff & Maguire, 1983; Wagstaff, Traverse, & Milner, 1982; Whitehouse et al., 1988, 1991; Zelig & Beidleman, 1981) finding that greater confabulation occurred with hypnotic recall efforts. There was theoretical concern that hypnotized subjects may be motivated to disclose memories that otherwise may not be reported and that this might account for hypermnesia effects. Therefore, these researchers used a forced-choice procedure that *required* everyone to answer all questions, in many cases explicitly (and in others simply implicitly) conveying that subjects must guess when they were unable to remember something. Thus they were under the constraint that they could not say, "I don't remember," and they were often placed under considerable additional pressure to continue guessing in an effort to remember more and more. This procedure, it was reasoned, would provide more rigorous experimental control and response criterion shifts would be prevented. However, theoretical considerations aside, *if someone is going to generalize from this research to clinical situations, we must ask, is this representative of acceptable clinical and forensic practices?*

Despite any advantages this procedure may have for ascertaining what might account for hypnotic hypermnesia effects, this method includes an *inherent bias* that characterizes and has colored all of these studies. Dinges et al. (1992) admitted that this procedure "has the effect of causing subjects to offer a certain number of subcriterion responses (i.e., low-confidence responses that, in the context of free recall, would likely not have been reported) to achieve the required output" (p. 1140). They even acknowledged that there is evidence (Erdelyi, Finks, & Feigin-Pfau, 1989) that this procedure produces a response bias wherein subjects who are instructed to guess if necessary exert less retrieval effort than free recall subjects during at least part of the recall efforts.

Likewise, Gudjonsson (1987b) documented that a forced-choice response can encourage arbitrary responses when a subject does not clearly remember something. Timm (1985) also found that when the demand characteristics of experimental proce-

dures compelled subjects to guess instead of remaining with their initial responses of "I don't know," *there were more incorrect (confabulated) responses.* Over the course of three procedures pressuring subjects to respond, there was a 41% greater increase in incorrect responses (over improvement in correct information) in high-hypnotizables, and among low-hypnotizable subjects there was a 63% increase in inaccurate information over improvement in correct answers.

What if such a procedure—not allowing patients the option of indicating "I don't remember" and requiring them to guess when they couldn't recall—were adopted by therapists? Loftus and Ketcham (1991) responded strongly to such a procedure:

> Guessing can be extremely dangerous, because when a witness is uncertain, guessing may actually fill the gaps in the initial skeletal representation of the event, causing an actual change in the underlying memory. Later, when searching her memory, the witness may incorrectly recall something that had earlier been merely a guess as an entrenched part of memory. (p. 250, emphasis added)

Although we and others (Zaragoza & Koshmidir, 1989) disagree that actual changes in memory are as easy to produce as Loftus suggests, we do agree that guessing is not a desirable technique. If someone in a laboratory is conducting theoretically oriented research to ascertain reasons that hypnotic hypermnesia may occur, forced-choice procedures and requiring someone to guess may be acceptable. But when almost everyone would agree that this response format would be an unacceptable, "extremely dangerous" clinical technique, then it seems hard to justify its use in research from which someone would make inferences about the value of hypnosis in psychotherapeutic or forensic settings.

Eisen (1996) recently confirmed that when subjects have to guess and answer every question concerning material that they do not remember well, they often respond in an arbitrary manner. However, *allowing subjects the option of saying that they did not remember was found to significantly decrease their endorsement of misleading information.* Furthermore, forced-choice testing requires the subject to behaviorally commit to an item, which cognitive dissonance research indicates carries a social demand to conform to the experimenter's expectations. Thus, once again we see that the experiments using this kind of forced-choice format (Dinges et al., 1992; Dywan, 1988; Dywan & Bowers, 1983; Orne et al., 1996; Putnam, 1979; Wagstaff & Maguire, 1983; Wagstaff, Traverse, & Milner, 1982; Whitehouse et al., 1988, 1991; Zelig & Beidleman, 1981) are not only very different from applied contexts, but have such serious defects in design that they are predisposed to produce biased, unreliable data. It has not been established that nonhypnotic misinformation studies (summarized in chapter 8) or the hypnosis studies we have reviewed that used forced-choice recognition testing are generalizable to situations using free recall, such as hypnotically assisted psychotherapy or forensic hypnosis.

If this experimental hypnosis procedure of requiring and pressuring subjects to guess (without being able to say "I don't know") were used by clinicians, experimentalist generalizations (e.g., Karlin & Orne, 1996; Kihlstrom, 1994a; Orne et al., 1984; Orne, Whitehouse et al., 1988) that are based on the studies cited in the paragraph above (and the conclusions reached by an AMA [1985] committee which was chaired by Orne) would be justified. If such techniques characterized accepted therapeutic practice, then we would agree that the memories that patients recalled through them could quite possibly be biased and would be likely to include excessive confabulations—*not because hypnosis itself is inherently contaminating, as critics allege, but because of the nature of the prejudicial hypnotic technique that was used.*

However, requiring patients to guess and not allowing them to indicate that they cannot recall are not acceptable or recommended clinical hypnosis practices (Brown & Fromm, 1986; Hammond & Elkins, 1994; Hammond et al., 1995; Rhue, Lynn, & Kirsch, 1993; Spiegel & Spiegel, 1978; Udolf, 1987; Weitzenhoffer, 1989; Yapko, 1990), nor are they recommended forensic or investigative hypnosis practices (Hammond et al., 1995; McConkey & Sheehan, 1995; Orne, 1979; Orne et al., 1984, 1988; Scheflin & Shapiro, 1989). Generalizations to clinical work should not be made from the kind of flawed studies we are reviewing, in which the laboratory techniques deviate dramatically from clinical techniques. *Indeed, the assertions that hypnotically assisted recall represents an invitation to enter fantasy land and is inherently distorting are substantially a result of drawing conclusions from certain studies that by their very design have required subjects to fantasize and guess when they did not recall an answer.*

Returning to the Dinges et al. (1992) study, their memory stimuli consisted of 40 slides of black and white line drawings of common objects, to which subjects were exposed for five seconds. Again, we see the use of the same kind of questionable stimuli used in several other studies finding confabulation (Dywan, 1988; Dywan & Bowers, 1983; Nogrady et al., 1985; Orne et al., 1996; Wagstaff et al., 1982) Then, during hypnosis, subjects were given "a number of direct suggestions" to the effect that "hypnosis would bring additional memories from their subconscious minds, and all their recollections would be vivid and clear" (p. 1142), suggestions that by their very nature should be anticipated to increase confidence. Introducing yet another major confound, subjects (who were in the top third of hypnotizability in one experiment, and ranged from low to high in the other) were required to open their eyes numerous times *during* hypnosis to write down their recollections—a technique at variance with clinical-forensic applications and that in any but exceptionally high-hypnotizable subjects would be anticipated to substantially interfere with and significantly lighten the hypnotic process.

Another study commonly cited as supporting the view that hypnosis encourages the production of confabulated, inaccurate memories is Nogrady et al. (1985). They asked students to recall the same questionable "memory" stimuli (slides of black and white line drawings of common objects) that were used in Dywan's two experiments. Given the nature of the unmemorable stimuli, it is not surprising that the results showed that neither the use of hypnosis nor an imagination condition increased memory beyond what was obtained in a waking condition. Nevertheless, high-hypnotizable persons in hypnosis recalled more incorrect items than low-hypnotizable persons. To their credit, however, Nogrady et al. (1985) acknowledged the limited validity of the study and that their techniques "*did not follow procedures associated with the applied use of hypnosis to enhance memory*" (p. 202, emphasis added), and that their stimulus materials were not emotionally arousing and carried no affective meaning or personal relevance. Furthermore, the student subjects knew that there were no consequences for recalling information incorrectly, unlike individuals in more naturalistic settings.

Putting these deficient studies aside, persons who denigrate the value of hypnotic exploration and favor the exclusion of hypnotically refreshed testimony from the courtroom (e.g., Orne, Soskis, Dinges, & Orne, 1984; Orne et al., 1988; Perry, Laurence, D'Eon, & Tallant, 1988) have often failed to cite some very important studies. One of the most powerful and exceptionally well done studies examining hypnotic age regression and memory was conducted by Hofling, Heyl, and Wright (1971). High-hypnotizable subjects were asked for 15 consecutive days to spend half an hour each night writing a diary account of the events of their day. Exactly three weeks after five of these particular nights, control subjects were asked to visualize, without the formal use of hypnosis, that they were in their room on the evening three weeks prior, thinking over the events of the day. They were then to reconstruct their diary account as accurately as possible, and were given half an hour to do so. Following a 10-minute break, which they spent alone, subjects were asked to make a second recall effort (without access to their previously recalled and written materials), being motivated by being told that it was often possible to do better on a second recall attempt. Subjects were asked again to do their very best at reconstructing the original account and given half an hour to do so.

Three weeks after the original days on which they made diary entries, the hypnotic subjects in the Hofling et al. (1971) study were also provided with a motivated attempt to remember everything possible. Thus, the repeated retrieval effort that Erdelyi (1994) believes is the only factor responsible for hypnotic hypermnesia effects was employed and controlled for in the experiment with both control subjects and hypnotic subjects. Following their 10-minute break, the subjects in the hypnotic condition were hypnotized. Depth of trance was verified through the successful induction of anesthesia to a pin-prick. Then the hypnotized subjects were *age regressed* in time to the original nights with instructions that, after thinking over the events of the day, they were to write them down.

Hofling et al. (1971) then used a very rigorous analysis procedure. After dividing each diary account into semantic units, three psycholinguists independently scored each account. This analysis included categories of "additional units" that represented "added material" (possible confabulatory material) and "contradictory units," representing information contradicting original diary accounts, which may be regarded as inaccurate confabulations or "false memories." The investigators corrected for "the naturally occurring, although slight improvement" that subjects made in their second recall effort when hypnosis was not used, which represented a ratio of only 1.1:1 for control subjects. This figure represents the degree of improvement (11%) one could expect to obtain from a first repeated recall effort, as stressed by Erdelyi (1994), with this type of material.

When the correction for a repeated recall effort was included in the analysis by Hofling et al. (1971), they found the ratio of memories obtained by hypnotic age regression versus waking memories was 4.25:1. "This ratio, 4.25:1, represents the superiority of the hypnotically regressed recall over what would presumably have been the amount of recall of the subjects in the hypnotic group if their second attempts had been made in the ordinary waking state" (p. 378). This study provides compelling data to challenge Erdelyi's (1994) contention that hypnotic hypermnesia produces only the kind of enhancement that any repeated recall effort would produce. Instead of the 11% for repeated recall efforts, hypnotic enhancement efforts produced an improvement of 46.9%, and after correcting for the inclusion of a repeated recall effort, there was a 42.5% improvement in memory. Furthermore, expressing their observations at the end of the research, the investigators said, "It was striking to observe that, under hypnotic regression, subjects used the precise phrasing of their original accounts more than they did in their waking attempts and more than did the control group" (p. 377).

Although they unfortunately did not provide a full report of data concerning confabulation, in summary data Hofling et al. (1971) at least provided examples of the contradictions (false information) produced by control and hypnotic subjects. There were only 1.07% contradictions obtained in a hypnotic condition for a daily memory account, compared to .53% in a control condition. The "additional units," representing possible or likely confabulation (where there was material added in the recall efforts that was not in an original diary account), averaged 8.4% per recall day for the hypnotic condition, versus 20.3% per recall day for the control condition.

It seems significant that the Hofling et al. (1971) study did not simply give suggestions for enhanced recall (hypermnesia). They age regressed subjects to the original situation, seeking to revivify it in much the same way that clinicians usually apply hypnosis with their patients. Furthermore, the situation to be recalled may not have been an emotional or traumatic event, but the incident had been lived through and personally experienced, rather than being superficial memories stemming from three-second exposures to drawings of nonmeaningful objects. We can feel far more confidence in generalizing from studies of this nature than from the previously mentioned laboratory investigations, where someone tries to remember unmemorable stimuli of questionable relevance, using techniques that most experienced hypnosis professionals would never consider using in clinical practice. The Hofling et al. study has far more *ecological validity*—that is, it resembles the real-life, clinical applications of hypnosis.

This kind of study is much more difficult and time consuming to produce than a memory study using a slide show, and regrettably, in an environment of pressure to be professionally productive, it may not be as enticing to conduct as the more rapid, easily done study. However, if academic research is to be taken seriously by clinicians, the public, and the courts, it must have ecological validity. Researchers must learn how hypnosis is used clinically and conduct experiments using clinically oriented hypnosis, rather than doing "experimental hypnosis" (Erickson, 1967; Thompson, 1970).

Another study has also strongly contradicted the hypothesis that hypnotic recall encourages unusual degrees of confabulation. It is a study, interestingly, that studied recall of somewhat more contextually relevant information—details from a 15-minute movie. Stager and Lundy (1985) found that highly hypnotizable persons produced greater recall in a hypnotic condition than did high- or low-hypnotizable subjects in a nonhypnotic state, without a concomitant increase in inaccurate information. Part of the reason for this positive outcome may have been that subjects were asked specific open-ended questions, as contrasted with a forced-recall format used in much experimental research. Such cued recall with open-ended questions may have provided cues for retrieval, but this procedure resembles investigative or clinical settings more closely than a forced-recall format forcing subjects to guess. But, despite the availability of these cues to *all* the subjects, only those who were highly responsive to hypnosis and who had undergone a hypnotic induction manifested the enhanced memory.

Lytle and Lundy (1988) found that hypnosis did not significantly increase confabulation, but failed to replicate Stager and Lundy's findings of enhanced recall through hypnosis. Their hypnotic procedures, however, were very different from ones used clinically. For instance, they did not use hypnotic age regression or revivification suggestions. They merely suggested to subjects that they would find that their answers to questions would be "coming more easily" than before. These suggestions were also given to high-hypnotizable subjects who served as control subjects, as well as those who were hypnotized. Thus, although they found that only the high hypnotizables showed an improvement in memory (regardless of whether they were hypnotized or not), this may demonstrate a general response to suggestion effect. Whitehouse et al. (1988) used the same procedures at Lytle and Lundy (1988), simply telling subjects their answers would come more easily (and that they would remember the film very clearly now). Again, their procedures were different from clinical-forensic settings in that they did not use age regression suggestions, used a forced-choice format (as opposed to free recall), and even *required* subjects to guess if necessary. They found no difference in recall between a hypnotic and waking condition.

In contrast, Shields and Knox (1986) produced results similar to Stager and Lundy's (1985) findings of a memory enhancement effect from the use of hypnosis, without an increase in inaccuracy. Furthermore, Shields and Knox suggested that when hypnotic recall studies find an increase in incorrect material, this may be due to a flaw in experimental design. More specifically, they suggested that there is likely to be an increase in confabulated or inaccurate material when the experiment has included a waking memory test prior to a memory test associated with hypnosis because subjects under these conditions will naturally endeavor to generate more responses than they did during the testing in a waking condition. Nogrady et al. (1985) and Register and Kihlstrom (1987) have likewise observed no significant effect of hypnotic techniques on incorrect recall.

The Shields and Knox (1986) study is particularly interesting because it suggested that the *level of processing* of memory information (shallowly or deeply processed) may be a relevant variable in why hypnotic hypermnesia may occur (in contrast to the meaningfulness of the material). They discovered that the use of hypnotic techniques with hypnotically responsive individuals increased the recall and recognition of material processed at a deep level, even though their stimuli were simply word lists rather than meaningful material. Their outcome is particularly interesting in relation to the review of literature we will shortly provide on the hypnotic retrieval of amnestic information encoded under chemical anesthesia, although this issue is far from settled in research.

Critics will note that three studies have not replicated the Shields and Knox (1986) findings concerning level of processing. This is correct, but these investigations included experimental designs with problems and with significant differences from Shields and Knox that do not allow ready comparison.

For instance, Pitts and Heaps (1996) examined shallow versus deep processing of memory material, comparing a hypnosis group and a "dummy" induction group (which resembled an active-alert hypnosis condition, where subjects were told to remain relaxed and comfortable, with their eyes closed, but oriented to the immediate situation). Unlike Shields and Knox (1986), they did not find a difference between the hypnosis and control groups. However, their control condition was defined to subjects as being hypnosis, thus creating influential expectancies that they were also being hypnotized. And, it appears in fact that the control subjects accepted the subsequent suggestions (which were for hypermnesia and were identical for both groups) as if a hypnotic induction had been performed. Thus, predictions that the hypnosis group would experience time distortion, greater relaxation ratings, and would rate themselves as less aware of the real world were not found. The control subjects were, in fact, not

serving as a nonhypnotic control condition, but were found to be experiencing hypnotic effects as much as the hypnosis group—thus explaining the lack of different findings between the groups. The researchers then performed a subsequent analysis, on the assumption from Shields and Knox (1986) that "awareness of reality" in hypnosis may be related to superior memory for deeply processed words. And, supporting Shields and Knox, they found that a greater inner focus of awareness (as determined from ratings by subjects) did promote the retrieval of deeply processed over shallowly processed material. Pitts and Heap (1996), for convenience, also used auditory rather than visual stimuli—another potential experimental confound, since hypnosis seems especially linked to visual-imagery processes.

Wagstaff and Mercer (1993a) did not reproduce the findings of Shields and Knox (1986), but they also did not faithfully duplicate their experiment. Their groups were not constructed based on their level of hypnotic responsivity (and the depth of processing of material might only occur for highly hypnotically responsive subjects), and they did not tell subjects that this was a study of hypnosis. Thus, the context measured was quite different. Considerable research has demonstrated that some measures (e.g., absorption) will correlate very differently in studies where the experimental procedure is defined to subjects as "hypnosis," versus being told that something else is being studied. The differences in experimental design used by Wagstaff and Mercer (1993) were designed to examine whether differences found in the Shields and Knox (1986) study were due to demand characteristics. But, as Gregg (1993) pointed out, "unless their success at doing so [eliminating a possible artifact] is followed by, for example, a successful, controlled reinstatement of the effect, they are left exposed to criticisms such as that they introduced new artifacts by failing to distinguish levels of hypnotic suggestibility adequately, or that their tests of memory are not sufficiently sensitive, i.e. that they too are likely to commit a type II error" (p. 68). Gregg (1993) went on to explain what a true challenge to the Shields and Knox (1986) findings of an effect of hypnosis on deeply processed words would need to include:

If this finding is to be accounted for by demand characteristics, the challenge becomes to identify how the experimenter might communicate demands for hypermnesia not generally, but differentially, for deep and shallow processed words. Likewise, it could be asked how many simulating subjects would anticipate an experimental outcome of that kind and adjust their behavior accordingly. (p. 68)

Responding to Gregg, Wagstaff and Mercer (1993b) responded, "we feel that, if nothing else, we have questioned the robustness of an unlikely finding, and although our explanation for Shields and Knox's finding may not be very convincing to some, at least we have proposed an explanation" (p. 71).

More recently, Gosschalk and Gregg (1996) examined this issue, but their research was not about hypnosis, but about the effects of progressive relaxation. Thus, this preliminary study cannot strictly be considered as providing confirmation of the Wagstaff and Mercer (1993a) conclusion that demand characteristics might account for the Shields and Knox (1986) findings concerning depth of processing, although the Gosschalk and Gregg study does support Wagstaff and Mercer. Hypnosis and progressive relaxation exercises, it is widely conceded, are not the same. Thus, the issue of whether the mechanism underlying hypnotic hypermnesia might involve greater depth of processing has not been definitively determined.

There have been some attempts, such as the Stager and Lundy (1985) study, to examine *more relevant stimuli* in laboratory studies through using videotapes. However, even when videotapes of staged robberies are used, this type of stimulus material may not always authentically generate the same kind of emotionally mediated impact on research subject "witnesses" as it does upon real witnesses (Christianson & Hubinette, 1993; Cutshall & Yuille, 1989; Fisher, Geiselman, & Amador, 1989; Yuille & Cutshall, 1986; Yuille & Kim, 1987). Still, these stimuli certainly have more face validity and are a closer approximation of life than line drawings of objects.

Putnam (1979) is widely cited in the literature as a study demonstrating that hypnotic recall (of a videotape recording of a car-bicycle accident) produced no better recollection than that obtained from waking subjects and produced more errors in response to leading questions. And yet, as you will see, the results of this study have been highly overinterpreted, given some of its serious limitations. In addition, more recently, the results have been disconfirmed by much sounder research (Sheehan et al., 1993; Spanos, Gwynn, & Terrade, 1989; Yuille & McEwan, 1985). Spanos, Gwynn, & Terrade, (1989), for example, found in an elegantly designed study that hypnotic procedures that used leading questions were no more likely to create incorrect recall or identification than leading questions used with nonhypnotized persons. Persons with high hypnotic capacity were more likely to respond to leading questions, but this was just as likely to occur when they were asked leading questions without hypnosis as when they were hypnotized.

Let's examine some of the typical problems and limitations of the earlier research that is so often cited by those critical of hypnosis, beginning with the Putnam study. Putnam's (1979) sample size consisted of only four student subjects per condition. This is all the more interesting because, in their review of hypnosis and memory studies, Geiselman and Machlovitz (1987) found that 80% of the studies that reported memory facilitation through hypnosis, without an accompanying increase in errors, used large sample sizes.

Putnam's (1979) results were also confounded by the fact that the leading questions that were used *all* had a correct answer of "no." Expectancies were likely created that hypnosis would enhance memory through being told, prehypnotically, that under hypnosis it would be possible for them to see the entire sequence "just as clearly as they had seen it the first time, only this time they would be able to slow it down or zoom in on details if they chose" (p. 442). Furthermore, on questions that subjects had difficulty answering, *inappropriate pressure and experimental demands were exerted* through instructing them to watch the videotape again in their mind, to form a clear image of the scene, and then to determine the correct response. "I don't know" was not an acceptable answer. Such pressure and forced-answer responses, as contrasted with free recall, would be unacceptable in investigative hypnotic work (Hammond et al., 1995; Orne et al., 1988) and would be fully expected to cause confabulation in response to experimental demands. In addition, subjects in the no-hypnosis condition were asked to use imagery, which is another experimental confound in working with highly hypnotizable subjects. Ultimately, the experiment produced exactly the results one would expect from the design.

Yet, despite all these limitations and the very small sample size in Putnam's (1979) study, the results were overinterpreted to argue "*strongly* that *great* caution" be used in employing hypnosis with eyewitnesses. It was claimed that subjects could not distinguish between what actually occurred and what was subsequently suggested to them. Such a claim should not be made by an experimenter whose small sample research lacked the experimental rigor of having subjects debriefed away from the experimental context by other experimenters and motivating them to give honest responses. One review article (Steblay & Bothwell, 1994) found that, of 17 studies that they examined, Putnam's (1979) study reported the greatest negative effect outcomes.

More recent and exacting research has contradicted conclusions that hypnosis causes a person to be unable to distinguish between what occurred and what was suggested (e.g., Barnier & McConkey, 1992; Labelle et al., 1990; Lynn et al., 1994; McConkey et al., 1990; Murrey et al., 1992; Sheehan, Garnett, & Robertson, 1993; Sheehan et al., 1991a,b; Sheehan & McConkey, 1982; Spanos & Bures, 1993–94). Curiously, however, those who typically cite Putnam (1979) do not quote the place where he affirms a very important limitation of the experiment:

> The data indicate that hypnosis may not aid recall when there is little emotional involvement on the part of the witness; they do not indicate that hypnosis will never aid recall. It may be that hypnosis aids recall by reducing retrieval difficulties caused specifically by emotionally upsetting events. (pp. 445–446)

This position has been proposed for a long time by many highly respected persons in the field of hypnosis (Dorcus, 1960; Schafer & Rubio, 1978) and by persons in criminal investigation (Stratton, 1977).

In an attempt to extend Putnam's (1979) findings to a situation involving stress and emotional response in subjects, Zelig and Beidleman (1981) did an almost identical study with the stimulus being a black and white film showing shop accidents

(e.g., a finger being cut off). Once again, however, serious experimental confounds were present. Just as in the Putnam (1979) study, the leading questions *always* required a "no" response, thus making it impossible to ascertain whether the format of the questions or the condition of their being leading or nonleading accounted for the experimental outcomes. Accuracy of recall was not determined in the waking state, and thus it was also actually impossible to know whether the same results would have carried over into a nonhypnotic condition following realerting. As you will see in data reviewed later, more recent evidence clearly demonstrates that most of the time pseudomemory reports that are made in hypnosis to an experimenter are able to be readily distinguished by the subject (from what actually occurred) when the subject is motivated to give honest answers to a different experimenter, in an alert state, away from the original experimental context.

Furthermore, in Zelig and Beidleman's study, unlike personal victimization or eyewitness crime situations, subjects were forewarned that they would see a film of something stressful, thus eliminating the element of surprise. Seeing a black and white film of accidents, with such forewarning, was assumed by the experimenters to have "evoked stress somewhat similar to witnessing an actual crime"— a questionable assumption. Most of us are desensitized enough and sufficiently detached intellectually that if we watch an old black and white video where someone gets stabbed or shot, knowing from the description provided on the video rental box that something like that will occur, it simply does not arouse much emotion. But, if we see such a situation in person, "up close and personal," you can bet that the adrenalin would be pumping, our hearts would be racing, and afterward, most of us would find our hands trembling.

Once again, Zelig and Beidleman (1981) used a relatively small sample, with only nine subjects per condition. Furthermore, *subjects were not able to engage in free recall* in hypnosis—the condition shown to produce the most accurate information. Instead, *a forced-choice format was used*, requiring them to answer only "yes" or "no"—hardly a situation comparable to forensic hypnosis or questioning in a criminal investigations in the real world. Once again, "I don't know" was not an acceptable response. Subjects also gave their responses with finger signals, but their description of the procedure suggests to us that these may have been voluntary finger signals and not the involuntary ideomotor signals typically used in clinical or forensic settings.

Sanders and Simmons (1983), like previous studies that have been cited by those critical of the use of hypnosis with memory (e.g., Dinges et al., 1992; Dywan, 1988; Dywan & Bowers, 1983; Lytle & Lundy, 1988; Nogrady et al., 1985; Putnam, 1979; Zelig & Beidleman, 1981), found that hypnotized subjects were less accurate than nonhypnotized persons in recalling a brief videotape clip of a pickpocket at work. But, what was particularly interesting in this study was that there was a negative relationship between hypnotic susceptibility and susceptibility to leading questions. Average suggestibility was 6.2 out of 10 in response to suggestions from the Harvard Group Scale of Hypnotic Susceptibility, and the more hypnotically responsive the subject, the fewer leading questions to which s/he responded.

However, a major flaw was present. Subjects viewed a suggestive lineup rather than only a fair lineup. In one condition, the thief was present, but he was dressed differently. But, in the suggestive lineup, the thief was not present, but someone in the lineup was wearing his distinctive coat. No chance was provided for subjects to try to distinguish the two. Persons more responsive to hypnosis tended to more often misidentify the person wearing the coat in a lineup (who was not the pickpocket) as the thief. But what does this mean? In this study, "the subjects did not get a long or careful look at his face," which was of "reasonably normal appearance." *Yet, admittedly, "the most salient thing about him was his jacket"* (p. 74). Thus, those most responsive to hypnosis more often seemed to be remembering the jacket ("the most salient thing about him"), as opposed to a nondescript face that they hardly saw. This represents a very ambiguous outcome that is open to more than one interpretation.

A similar result was obtained by Ready, Bothwell, and Brigham (1997) when an identified person was absent from a lineup of persons similar in appearance, but with only one person wearing a blue T-shirt and mustache like the original person wore ("a decoy"). However, Ready et al. (1997) did find some evidence of improved recall attributable to the use of hypnosis. When viewing a lineup in which the target person was present, even though another person in the lineup was wearing the previous clothes worn by him (a condition not present in the Sanders and Simons, 1983 experiment), significantly more (75%) persons who were hypnotized correctly identified the target person than did persons given only motivational instructions (30%). Only 30% of a no-expectations control group and 55% of subjects in a context reinstatement condition (modeled after the guided memory procedure of Malpass and Devine, 1981) correctly identified this target person. Thus, this study provided support that hypnotic memory enhancement does not occur merely because of the inclusion of contextual reinstatement, or because of relaxation, or motivational suggestions. This study also challenged the findings of Wagstaff and Maguire (1983) who found no difference between no-treatment control subjects, subjects with whom Malpass and Devine's (1981) guided memory procedures were used, or hypnotized subjects receiving the Malpass and Devine guided memory procedures. Further, these researchers found the persons higher in hypnotic responsivity showed better factual memory, and hypnotized persons were not more susceptible to the influence of leading questions.

Returning to other problems in the Sanders and Simmons (1983) study, hypnosis was not simply used to refresh recollection before being exposed to the lineup. In the hypnosis condition, in the middle of the hypnosis experience, subjects were told to open their eyes to view the videotaped lineup. This is tremendously at variance with the kind of procedures used clinically (and was also required by Dinges et al., 1992, Wagstaff and Maguire, 1983, and Wagstaff, Traverse, and Milner, 1982) and is not at all comparable to techniques used in investigative hypnosis. Thus, the findings of this study about hypnotic recollection being less accurate are seriously called into question by methodological problems. Results were further compromised by the fact that the hypnotic technique used was one of having the subject imagine a TV screen, with the capacity to slow it down, speed it up, stop-action, or zoom in—features believed to introduce extra possibilities for confabulation and that are not recommended for clinical or forensic use (Hammond et al., 1995; Orne et al., 1984).

Another study (Spanos, Quigley, Gwynn, Glatt, & Perlini, 1991) that failed to find greater eyewitness recognition for hypnotized than nonhypnotized individuals also had serious defects in procedure. Following only a brief, five-minute induction technique, the experimenters simply gave a posthypnotic suggestion that subjects would much more vividly than before recall events from a videotape of a crime that they had seen. *Age regression and revivification were not done with subjects.* Thus, this study has virtually no resemblance to the use of hypnosis in real world contexts, where such a procedure is simply not used. It illustrates the problem of some academic experimentalists, isolated from the actual techniques and procedures used in clinical hypnosis work, attempting to conduct research on clinical applications. And, in fact, what Spanos et al. (1991) found was that the majority of hypnotic *and* nonhypnotic subjects misidentified a mugshot—a finding consistent with the actuality that subjects seeking to make eyewitness identifications are often inaccurate (Cutler, Penrod, & Martens, 1987; Lindsay & Wells, 1980).

Thus, when general reviews of literature (e.g., Orne et al., 1984; Perry, Laurence, D'Eon, & Tallant, 1988) or meta-analysis reviews of hypnosis and memory studies (e.g., Steblay & Bothwell, 1994) do not screen out or appropriately qualify seriously flawed investigations such as Putnam (1979), Zelig and Beidleman (1981), Dywan (1988), and Dywan and Bowers (1983)—and then do not include articles like Stager and Lundy (1985) or Hofling et al. (1971)—statistical summaries and conclusions that "hypnotized subjects show only a minimal, unreliable edge over control subjects" (Steblay & Bothwell, 1994, p. 648) cannot be considered trustworthy or scientific because of the obvious sampling bias. In such a situation, both the data and any conclusions that are reached will inevitably be biased and skewed because of the inclusion of deficient studies and the exclusion of other investigations with positive outcomes.

Other inadequacies in studies such as those of Putnam (1979) and Zelig and Beidleman (1981) include questioning subjects after a *very brief retention interval* (e.g., 15–20 minutes or 24 hours) following exposure to the material to be recalled. Once again, we have a situation tremendously at variance with clinical and investigative settings where a much longer time period has elapsed, potentially allowing for psychologically motivated or defensive forget-

ting to occur when strong emotions were involved. Bennett (1988) found such a time interval to be a highly relevant factor in studies of recall of chemically dissociated information heard while under anesthesia. Subjects questioned shortly (e.g., 12–24 hours) after exposure to the stimulus that was presented to them under anesthesia were much more likely to have difficulty recalling what was said than subjects who were questioned under hypnosis later (e.g., one week later). It is interesting in this regard that Hull (1933) hypothesized that hypnosis could impact memory recall for remote events but not for relatively recent incidents.

Quite possibly one of the reasons that Stalnaker and Riddle (1932) and Hofling et al. (1971) found that hypnosis enhanced recall was because of the *longer retention intervals* between events and hypnotic attempts to remember them. Stalnaker and Riddle had a delay of one year or more, and Hofling had a delay of three weeks. Similarly, Stager and Lundy (1985) found significantly better recall of correct material, without an increase in memory errors, among high-hypnotizable subjects one week after immediate recall efforts.

Griffin (1980) found that when subjects were tested between two and 13 days after viewing a film of simulated crimes, and after 18–28 days, significantly more accurate information was recalled (and this study controlled for false, confabulated, or misleading information) by subjects who had been hypnotized versus those who had not. Further evidence for the relevance of the *retention interval* used in experimental designs comes from McConkey and Kinoshita (1988). They found that the use of hypnosis among high-hypnotizables increased correct recall, and that the increase in recall from one day after exposure to a stimulus to one week later was greatest for high-hypnotizable subjects who underwent hypnosis. In regard to the relevance of the time interval used in hypnotic recall experiments, it is interesting that Putnam's (1979) data showed a strong but nonsignificant trend (remember, a very small sample size was involved) for hypnotic responses to nonleading questions to be much greater when there was a longer time interval rather than a short one.

In their review of hypnosis and memory studies, Geiselman and Machlovitz (1987) supported the position taken in this chapter. They concluded that, *"hypnosis tends to be more successful with retention intervals of days to weeks"* (pp. 41–42) compared with memory tests delivered immediately or after a matter of minutes. And, in fact, all the studies they reviewed that found hypnotic memory facilitation without an accompanying increase in errors, used longer intervals between the original memory stimulus and the hypnotic interview. Logistically, of course, it is much easier for experimenters to test memory on the same day in the laboratory. But the problem with such a procedure is that it is completely different from clinical and forensic conditions under which hypnosis is actually used and thus cannot be expected to be comparable or permit generalization.

In comparison to the small number of subjects in the Putnam (1979) and Zelig and Beidelman (1981) studies, Sturm (1982) used 101 subjects to examine hypnotic memory enhancement compared to waking recall and guided memory for a two-minute color film of an accident. She discovered no differences between the groups in the amount of material remembered in a free recall condition using Reiser's (1980) television technique. Similar to Putnam (1979) and Zelig and Beidleman (1981), she found that highly susceptible persons tended to be more easily misled by leading questions. When hypnosis or guided memory were used with highly hypnotizable individuals, they were found to have more memory errors (12.3% and 12.7%, respectively) in free recall, compared to when they engaged in waking recall (5.7%). Unfortunately, just as in the other studies, her leading questions always required a "no" response, thus making it impossible to ascertain whether it was the format of the questions or their being leading or nonleading that accounted for this outcome.

Very importantly, Sturm's (1982) study also examined *moderately hypnotizable* individuals—the sample most resembling the bulk of the general population, who are most likely to be clinical patients or subjects in investigative inquiries, and yet who are most often not examined in hypnosis research. Moderately hypnotizable persons performed better in hypnotic conditions (6.9% error rate) than they did in guided memory (9% error rate) or waking recall (11.5% error rate) conditions. Moderately hypnotizable persons additionally tended to have more correct answers. In contrast, those low in hyp-

notic responsivity did not differ in the accuracy of their recall across conditions. Moderately hypnotizable individuals also made significantly fewer errors than either low- or high-hypnotizables on multiple choice questions across all conditions.

Unfortunately, Orne et al.'s (1984) widely read review of hypnosis and memory literature included the Sturm study but failed to mention the enhanced memory effects (with fewer errors) that occurred in moderately hypnotizable subjects. Instead, they only noted that the overall effect of hypnosis (on the entire sample of high, moderate, and low susceptibility subjects) was that "there was no increase in accurate information with hypnosis" (p. 191)—the position to which they subscribe. The review failed to mention that when examining the *entire* sample, subjects in hypnosis were *not* more prone to making memory errors in response to leading questions—a finding contrary to their opinion. This is important because critics of the use of hypnosis with memory take the position that hypnosis not only does not increase accurate recall, but that it also produces substantially greater production of confabulated, inaccurate information.

Shaul (1978) compared hypnosis with imagery versus imagery alone or a control procedure in examining eyewitness recall to either low- or high-stress films depicting a crime (but the research found that the high-stress film was not very stress-provoking). *Both the hypnosis and imagery conditions produced greater recall, and greater correct recall with fewer incorrect items, as well as the recall of more salient information, than the control condition.* Hypnosis was found to have increased effects over imagery alone in producing greater recall accuracy, and the use of hypnosis interacted with recall conditions, susceptibility, and stress levels in generating greater recall and the recall of more salient information. Additive effects of hypnotic induction particularly occurred among high-hypnotizable subjects. All groups were found to produce *less incorrect recall under narrative reporting in comparison with direct questioning*, although direct questioning produced more salient items.

More recently, Dasgupta, Juza, White, and Maloney (1995) compared the relative efficacy of four methods of memory retrieval: hypnosis, "cognitive interview," spontaneous free recall, and "guided imagery." Tested in an academic setting, these methods were paired with retrieval efforts for four different kinds of memory stimuli: an audio-tape of a lecture on an anthropological view of personality; a muted video of a CBS documentary on police brutality; an audiovisual tape on learning from the Discovery of Psychology series; and written material consisting of a psychology journal article on the savant syndrome.

No significant differences were found in the recall percentage scores, although the cognitive interview and hypnosis produced very similar and higher percentages than free recall and guided memory (16% compared with 13%–13.5%). There was no significant difference found in the amount of confabulation between groups, and it was believed that the relatively minimal amount of confabulation occurred because free recall was used in all four retrieval conditions. The authors offered the opinion that hypnosis as an intervention with trauma still seems more effective clinically than the other available alternatives for working through emotional memory material. Although the study did not find hypnotically facilitated recall to be superior, hypnosis was *not* found to result in greater confabulation and was equivalent to other memory retrieval methods.

As with many of the academic studies we have reviewed, however, the Dasgupta et al. (1995) study contained some important deficiencies limiting the generalizability of the findings that hypnosis did not enhance memory. The memory stimuli were not personally relevant and were unemotional in nature. An adequate measure of hypnotizability was not included in the study, thus not permitting a differential evaluation of medium- or high-hypnotizable individuals. Further, while the level of expertise of the persons doing hypnosis was not stated, from the descriptions of the researchers' rehearsals we would judge that the level of practical experience with hypnosis may not have been very high. One of the most serious limitations of this study (along with the nature of the memory stimuli) is that there was only "a short period of time" between exposing subjects to the stimuli and the retrieval efforts. As we have just reviewed, research finds that the longer the interval between exposure and recall efforts, the greater the recall with hypnosis.

Somewhat similar to Dasgupta et al. (1995), Timm (1981) compared waking recall with hypnotic recall and with an imagery condition identical to the hypnotic condition except that it did not include a hypnotic induction. The imagery and hypnotic conditions had very similar outcomes and produced more correct recall than the control group, but this did not reach statistical significance. Hypnosis and imagery conditions also did not produce more incorrect recollections, perhaps because subjects were able to respond, "I do not recall." The author noted that his very small number of subjects limited his study and may have resulted in the finding that there were no recall differences between groups. The experimenter was also not blinded to the correct answers or the groups assignments of subjects, and the study failed to control for hypnotic susceptibility. Although this study has been cited as demonstrating no advantage for hypnosis, the author indicated that "any conclusions drawn from this study should be made with extreme caution" (p. 192) and that readers should "avoid generalizing these results to cases involving anterograde and retrograde amnesia" (p. 193).

DOES HYPNOSIS INCREASE CONFIDENCE IN WHAT IS REMEMBERED?

Apart from the issue of whether accurate memories may be elicited through hypnosis, Orne (1979) and Diamond (1980) contend that hypnotized subjects may incorporate false information into their memories, be unable to distinguish false from genuine memories, and then have such greatly enhanced confidence that upon cross-examination in a courtroom they will be unshakable. Apart from the issue of accuracy of memory, research has in fact shown that a mild increase in false feelings of confidence may and often does occur *in the laboratory* when hypnosis is used to elicit memories in highly hypnotizable persons (e.g., Dinges et al., 1992; Dywan & Bowers, 1983; Laurence, 1982; Laurence & Perry, 1983; Nogrady et al., 1985; Rainer, 1983; Sheehan & Grigg, 1985; Sheehan, Grigg, & McCann, 1984; Sheehan & Tilden, 1983, 1984, 1986; Spanos, Quigley, Gwynn, Glatt, & Perlini, 1991; Wagstaff, 1981; Wagstaff, Traverse, & Milner, 1982; Whitehouse et al., 1988, 1991; Zelig & Beidleman, 1981).

Recently, Orne, Whitehouse, Dinges, and Orne (1996) did a retrospective reanalysis of data from two previous studies (Dinges et al., 1992; Whitehouse et al., 1991)—studies with serious methodological weaknesses limiting generalization to clinical settings. In the Dinges et al. (1992) study, hypnosis failed to enhance correct recall in high- or low-hypnotizables, and the level of confidence in what was recalled was higher with the use of hypnosis, particularly in high-hypnotizable subjects. As you may recall, this study used a forced-recall format that compelled subjects to give an answer to every question, even if they had to guess—likely causing subjects to offer responses in which in free recall would most likely not have been reported, and quite possibly producing a response bias or arbitrary responding, with subjects exerting less retrieval effort than they would in free recall. The memory stimuli were the five-second exposures to slides of black and white line drawings of common objects. In addition, biasing suggestions were provided that would, by their very nature, be anticipated to increase subject confidence. There was the further confound that the hypnotic techniques used were extremely at variance from the manner in which hypnosis is used in clinical and investigative settings (e.g., opening their eyes many times to write down their recollections).

In their recent report and reanalysis, Orne et al. (1996) sought to expand their traditional position (that hypnosis contaminates memories and introduces false confidence) by implying that a "vulnerability to distortions of memory induced by hypnotic techniques" is not unique to highly hypnotizable individuals, and that virtually anyone exposed to hypnosis for purposes of memory enhancement may experience "considerable" memory distortion. In the reanalysis, low-hypnotizable subjects (under pressure to guess) produced a significant increase of 144% in cumulative confidence errors, while low-hypnotizables in a waking condition produced only 55% more (p<.05)—but this represented a trial-by-trial increase of only $1/2$ item out of 40 items, which, considering the confounding variables cited above, is surprisingly small. High-hypnotizable subjects also experienced more cumulative confidence errors than low-hypnotizables. Rather than demonstrating the inherent danger of clinical hypnosis, the reanalysis of a study such as this merely suggests that when laboratory procedures drastically at variance with clinical techniques are used, which include po-

tentially confidence-enhancing suggestions (that subjects would have "enhanced accurate recall" and that "hypnosis would bring additional memories from their subconscious minds, and all their recollections would be more vivid and clear" [p. 1142]), while forcing subjects to fantasize and guess about the recall of nonrelevant stimuli to which they were only very briefly exposed (thus encouraging more arbitrary responding), such results can occur. When someone pressures subjects to fantasize and guess, then provides them with confident, expectancy-enhancing suggestions that a procedure (there were no nonhypnotic comparison procedures which included these suggestions) will cause them to recall more information accurately and vividly, should anyone be surprised that persons in this group create more answers and feel more confident?

However, increased confidence in memories has not been found in all studies (e.g., Ready, Bothwell, & Brigham, 1997; Gregg & Mingay, 1987; Mingay, 1986; Putnam, 1979; Sanders & Simmons, 1983; Spanos, Gwynn, Comer, et al., 1989; Spanos, Quigley, et al., 1991; Sturm, 1982; Timm, 1985; Yuille & McEwan, 1985). McConkey and Kinoshita (1988), for example, discovered a more complex pattern of confidence errors in their study. In memory testing after an interval of one day, they found increased confidence for high-hypnotizable subjects undergoing hypnosis. However, after one week (a period when, as reviewed earlier, we would anticipate hypnosis to be more likely to enhance memory), the use of hypnosis only increased confidence in low-hypnotizable subjects, but not among high-hypnotizables. They concluded that "the difference suggests that processes other than the experience of hypnosis may be the basis of confidence errors," and that this pattern with low-hypnotizables "points to the role that social demands associated with hypnotic procedures may play" (p. 52). This finding may very well explain Orne et al.'s (1996) very mild confidence increase found in low- hypnotizables. However, Orne et al. (1996) did not discuss the possible role of demand characteristics, nor did they cite any of the references listed earlier in this paragraph or referred to in our discussion of confidence in the remainder of this section.

In relation to the issue of confidence, Spanos et al. (1989, 1991) conducted the only two studies to directly evaluate whether the use of hypnosis "immunized" eyewitness testimony against being broken down during cross-examination. Spanos, Gwynn, Comer, et al. (1989) found that hypnotic and nonhypnotic subjects were equally likely to misidentify mugshots, and just as likely to incorporate misleading information into their eyewitness descriptions. Their results directly contradicted Diamond (1980) and Orne (1979). Furthermore, the United States Supreme Court has also disavowed the Orne and Diamond position, where in *Rock v. Arkansas* (1987) they concluded that it "has not been shown that hypnotically enhanced testimony is always so untrustworthy and so immune to the traditional means of evaluating credibility that it should disable a defendant from presenting her version of the events for which she is on trial."

Spanos, Quigley, et al. (1991) found a decrease in the certainty of identifications during cross-examinations, *and that hypnosis did not interact with cross-examination confidence.* Hypnotic subjects and subjects who were not hypnotized had their confidence broken down under cross-examination to a comparable degree. *In fact, the usual pretrial preparation and rehearsal of a witness were found to have substantially more influence on confidence level and in immunizing subjects against breaking down during cross-examination than did hypnotic suggestions directly aimed at increasing confidence!* Concerning the area of false memories, which will be discussed shortly, Sheehan, Statham, and Jamieson (1991a,b) have also found that higher confidence was not found to be associated with the presence of responses to suggested false recollections.

In this regard, the reader must be aware that, entirely apart from hypnosis, the lack of simple relationship between confidence and accuracy is a common finding in eyewitness research (e.g., Deffenbacher, 1980; Sanders & Warnick, 1980). Such a finding is not unique to hypnosis. We find it interesting that in their research (which found no relationship between hypnosis and the confidence that was held concerning memories), Sanders and Simmons (1983) did not simply ask for the usual experimental confidence rating on a scale of 0–10. Instead, they asked whether subjects would feel confident enough to offer their testimony in a courtroom trial—a situation comparable to forensic settings, with the result that they did not find increased confidence associated with the use of hypnosis.

We must also keep in mind the difference between a statistically significant finding in a laboratory and a genuine, meaningful difference in life situations. For instance, Whitehouse et al. (1988) evaluated high-hypnotizable subjects who were hypnotized and simply told that they would remember a movie very clearly and that answers to questions would now come more easily to them. High-hypnotizable subjects who were hypnotized were found statistically to not have more confidence in their correct answers, but they were more confident in their incorrect answers. However, this increase in confidence represented an increase of only 10.6%—and this was in a situation where subjects were forced to respond to fixed choices (not a free recall format) and were required to guess when they were uncertain. *Thus, in a memory situation tremendously at variance with what occurs in clinical and forensic hypnosis, there was a 10.6% increase in confidence. It seems unlikely that this represents a concretizing effect.* If such subjects were not asked to guess, and were required to use Sanders and Simmons' (1983) criterion of indicating whether they would feel confident enough to offer their testimony in a courtroom trial, we suspect that the 10.6% figure would disappear. Similarly, Sheehan and Tilden's (1983) significant increase in confidence of high- over low-hypnotizable subjects for hypnotically enhanced memory for misleading information amounted to a difference between 2.58 and 2.25 on a scale of 1–3.

From examining *the nature of suggestions used in studies* with findings of increased confidence (when they were included in reports), we believe that, when enhanced confidence does occur, in many cases it is due to the nature of the specific suggestions given and the influence of social psychological variables, such as those to which McConkey and Kinoshita (1988) refer, rather than to hypnosis itself. For example, Sheehan et al. (1991) "emphasized to subjects that everything that had happened in the video had been recorded in their minds" and "that they may remember events and details that their conscious mind had forgotten but that their subconscious mind would remember" (p. 132). Similar suggestions were given repeatedly by Dinges et al. (1992). Spanos et al. (1991), who did not even use age regression suggestions, simply suggested that subjects would be able, when asked, to recall the events of the film "much more vividly and clearly than they had in the last session" (p. 643) and would have an enhanced ability to identify the offender if his picture appeared in a mugshot display. Isn't it likely that directly telling someone that s/he will recall things much more vividly and clearly will increase his/her confidence? We believe so, and even then, the net confidence increase between hypnotized subjects given this suggestion and nonhypnotized subjects was only one point on a seven-point scale—not a particularly dramatic difference. In addition, Spanos, Quigley, et al. (1991) did not give such suggestions to their nonhypnotic subjects, thereby reinforcing the likelihood that such a small, though statistically significant ($p < .05$), outcome may have resulted simply from the content of the suggestions.

There is still another uncontrolled contaminant in these studies. Several studies suggest that it may well be that the level of hypnotic susceptibility, and not whether someone was hypnotized or not, may be the actual variable associated with increased confidence ratings (Dinges et al., 1992; Putnam, 1979; Ready, Bothwell, & Brigham, 1997; Spanos, Gwynn, Comer, et al., 1989; Timm, 1985; Zelig & Beidleman, 1981). Thus, hypnotizability combined with the content and nature of inappropriate suggestions may combine to account for this effect.

It may well be that the interaction of a specific hypnotic technique, the nature of the suggestions, and prehypnotic expectations concerning the nature of hypnosis results in mildly increased confidence, rather than simply the use of hypnosis itself. Subject beliefs prior to hypnosis have been shown to impact on the nature of hypnotic experiences (e.g., Baker, 1982; Council et al., 1983; Council et al., 1986; Johnston et al., 1989; Kirsch, 1991; Kirsch et al., 1987; Spanos et al., 1991; Wickless & Kirsch, 1989). Despite our view that hypnotic response is influenced by more than just the subject's expectations, it is clear that subject beliefs and expectations have a definite impact on subject productions that should be considered and that these beliefs may be influenced by waking suggestions from therapists.

Concerning a subject or patient's expectations, previous studies have shown that hypnosis has been publicly misperceived by many people as facilitating vivid reinstatement of memories (McConkey & Jupp, 1985; McConkey, Roche, & Sheehan, 1989; Wilson, Greene, & Loftus, 1986). This might cause a jury to give added weight to recollections obtained through hypnosis (Diamond, 1980; Odgers, 1988). Juries (and patients) need to be educated to create more neutral expectations about hypnosis outcomes. Furthermore, given the recent publicity about false memories of child abuse (which have often presented hypnosis in a strongly negative light), there is a need to repeat earlier studies about public conceptions of hypnosis, particularly among people who have been exposed to such material. Patient expectations about hypnosis may be evaluated prehypnotically, and efforts made to create realistic and neutral expectations (Hammond et al., 1995).

In the series of studies by Sheehan (Sheehan, Garnett, & Robertson, 1993; Sheehan, Statham, & Jamieson, 1991a,b; Sheehan & Tilden, 1983), increased confidence was found to be associated with persons who were highly hypnotizable and with the use of hypnosis. However, most importantly in light of research findings by Spanos et al. (1989, 1991), simulating subjects portrayed just as much confidence as real subjects. In harmony with our view, Sheehan (1988) concluded that *expectancies of subjects* (e.g., about hypnosis), some of which may have been conveyed by the nature of the suggestions used by the researcher, and the context of hypnosis, may be variables associated with increasing confidence. He concluded:

> Just how likely context is to play a role, is indicated by the fact that simulating Ss [subjects] reported higher confidence levels than real Ss when results were analyzed for the hypnotic setting . . . , simulating Ss were not distinct from hypnotic Ss under waking conditions of testing. It seems that the hypnotic setting itself, or expectations about it, obviously communicated that an expression of strong conviction was required. Collectively, results demonstrated that simulating Ss believed that a hypnotized person would be more confident, and they therefore reported greater confidence levels during their act of pretense. (pp. 305–306)

In summary, there are significant limitations in the studies demonstrating increased confidence stemming from the use of hypnosis to enhance memory. Conclusions from such research that hypnosis falsely increases confidence in hypnotically refreshed recollections are overstated. The research certainly shows that although modest increases in confidence often occur in the laboratory under certain conditions, they do not always occur, and when they do, expectancies (e.g., conveyed through explicit suggestions and expectations about the nature of hypnosis that are held by subjects) may account for much of this effect. Findings by Spanos and Sheehan strongly point to such factors. In relation to this, we believe that when new clinical and forensic guidelines (Hammond et al., 1995) are followed, wherein therapists seek through vigorous education prior to hypnosis and by the nature of their suggestions to create neutral expectations, the modest increases that have been seen in many research studies may well be eliminated. Research with ecological validity that incorporates such efforts is needed. In addition, hypnotic susceptibility, and not whether hypnosis was used, may also be a variable accounting for some of these small increases in confidence.

But, despite the fact that mild increases in confidence may occur, the more recent and most sophisticated experimental evidence seems compelling in disputing the position of Orne (1979) and Diamond (1980) that hypnosis immunizes witnesses to cross-examination. As Spanos et al. (1991) concluded:

> These findings provide no support for the notion that the influence of hypnotic procedures on memory is so powerful that witnesses cannot be effectively cross-examined, or for the related notion that testimony from witnesses who underwent a hypnotic interrogation should be inadmissible in court because such witnesses are particularly resistant to cross-examination. (pp. 651–652, emphasis added)

The literature on hypnosis and confidence in what is recalled importantly informs us that it is definitely possible for modest increases in confidence to occur, including confidence in inaccurate or distorted memories. Thus, in order to minimize this documented possibility, it is incumbent on clinicians to work cautiously and to be careful in their phrasing of suggestions associated with memory retrieval. Likewise, we must seek to structure neutral and appropriate expectations about the nature of hypnosis. This should be included as part of our routine education of patients about myths and misconceptions about hypnosis before hypnosis is ever used (Hammond et al., 1995). Efforts to establish neutral expectations about whether any further

information will be forthcoming, and concerning the fact that, if any further information is produced, it may be accurate, partially accurate, or inaccurate, should also be made immediately prior to using hypnosis for insight-oriented exploration.

Source Amnesia and Its Relevance to Cases of "Retractors"

Evans and Thorn (1966) noted a distinctive type of amnesia, *source amnesia*, which may be associated with hypnosis but may also be associated with nonhypnotic recall. They had highly hypnotizable subjects learn idiosyncratic, rather esoteric facts; for instance, that the color of the gemstone amethyst, when heated, is yellow. After suggestions were given for posthypnotic amnesia, it was found that in an alert state subjects possessed this knowledge. However, when queried about how they knew these facts, the amnestic subjects were either amnestic for the source or context where this information was acquired or rationalized and provided confabulated responses. This phenomenon was found in about one-third to one-half of high-hypnotizables (Evans, 1979; Laurence et al., 1986).

This seems to be a variable that may be associated with some cases of reported past life age regressions and investigations of claims of reincarnation. For example, there is the famous Bridey Murphy case (Bernstein, 1956), which initiated much of the interest in that area. In this case, a lay hypnotist hypnotized a woman who subsequently imagined herself to be the reincarnation of an Irish woman. Credible hypnosis experts of the time immediately debunked this idea (Kline, 1956), and in fact investigative reporters discovered background experiences of the woman (during her childhood an Irish woman lived across the street, whose maiden name was Bridie Murphy) that accounted for her seemingly inexplicable knowledge about Ireland (Gardner, 1957). Source amnesia seems adequate to account for this and the many similar cases (Barker, 1979; Edwards, 1987a, 1987b; Harris, 1986; Hilgard, 1977/1986; Wilson, 1982) where investigations have both revealed flaws in the accounts of the subjects and also identified that they had been exposed to historical information related to their presumed past lives.

What we see in this phenomenon is a *dissociation*

of content and context. Thus, a memory or information may exist in someone's mind for which the person lacks knowledge of the context where the memory occurred or the knowledge was gained. This seems to be what occurs when someone unconsciously plagiarizes something, or when subjects in memory experiments make source attribution errors. It is simply another illustration of the imperfection of memory that may occur *with or without hypnosis,* as we summarized in chapter 8 regarding research on source misattribution errors. Clinicians must be aware that errors of memory may occur. The fact that this can happen has been a reason for recommending that in forensic hypnosis one memorialize the prehypnotic recollections of the subject on videotape by having him or her fully discuss everything s/he remembers before hypnosis commences. There is almost no research on hypnotic source amnesia, but what little recent research exists does suggest that, without such preparation, witnesses may not always be able to reliably distinguish between memories that they had before being exposed to hypnosis and those that occurred through hypnosis (Whitehouse, Orne, Orne, & Dinges, 1991). However, Whitehouse et al. (1991) used a forced-choice recognition test that has been found in nonhypnotic experiments (Lindsay & Johnson, 1989) to produce biased results, whereas if a source-monitoring test had been used, such source confusion would likely have been greatly diminished. Nonetheless, even given this almost nonexistent and flawed research base, we still continue to recommend establishing a videotape record of the prehypnotic recollections of a potential witness in a legal case.

Although the Whitehouse et al. (1991) research has not been replicated and possesses some of the previously discussed problems in research design, it nonetheless has implications for therapists who are subjected to lawsuits alleging the induction of false memories. Because their data suggest "that most subjects are incapable of differentiating the temporal origin of prior recall productions" (p. 57), their findings draw into question the validity of the memories of "retractors" concerning the timing and source of their allegedly false and iatrogenically created memories. When the reliability of personal retrospective judgments about the context where one's memory productions originated has been called into question, how can such fallible attributions be relied upon in courtroom testimony, without incurring reasonable doubt? The "memories" of retractors may have originated in their prior expectations, or from influences such as peers, the media, or reading outside the therapy context. They may then subsequently have recalled such "memories" in working with a therapist, but the source of contamination was extratherapeutic.

Whitehouse et al. (1991) reported "a consistent tendency" for subjects to misidentify the source of their memory productions. Therefore, referring to the adoption by several states of the *State v. Hurd* guidelines of eliciting videotaped and detailed recollections prior to hypnotizing a witness, they concluded: "If such a 'hard' record is not available, however, it will need to be recognized that the testimony of the witness about what he or she had known prior to hypnosis is not a suitable alternative" (p. 58). Thus, there is no more reason to place faith in a retractor's current source attributions (that a therapist was a contaminating influence) than to believe the reports of the same individual when he or she was previously a patient and alleging to have recovered memories.

Generalizability of Research Findings: Discrepancies between the Laboratory and the Use of Hypnosis in the Real World

It is probably impossible to create a condition similar to trauma or abuse for a laboratory study of memory. Research (e.g., Christianson, 1992c; Saporta & van der Kolk, 1992; van der Kolk, 1994) reviewed in other chapters of the book strongly suggests that trauma may both enhance the encoding of memories and at the same time block retrieval in a subpopulation of individuals. It is vitally important for everyone to remember that subjects in memory and hypnosis studies are generally college undergraduates. Thus the research subjects from which memory scientists are generalizing are not representative of a population suffering with traumatic blocks to memory. There are no hypnosis laboratory studies on this population. Stimuli used in studies of hypnosis and memory have in many cases been ridiculously unmemorable, usually irrelevant to the subject, and have, in many cases, been presented out of logical sequence. Recognizing the profound limitations and the entirely disparate population and stimuli that have been studied, a recent law review article (Kanovitz, 1992) on hypnosis, memory, and the law concluded:

> Because the research community has not studied the impact of childhood sexual abuse or any other major traumas on memory or the impact of hypnosis on subjects who have been traumatized, experimentalist testimony about the unreliability of memory may bear little relevance to the trustworthiness of memories restored in psychotherapy. (p. 1226)

An admirable attempt to create a "traumatic arousal" condition by DePiano and Salzberg (1981) failed to find that it produced differential effects on memory recall. Although a hypnotic induction condition with task-motivating instructions yielded greater recall than task-motivating instructions alone, the effect appeared to be independent of the subject's level of induced arousal. However, one must realize that the stimuli used in this study were incidental and peripheral material. Unfortunately, this is the very kind of stimulus material shown to be least likely to be attended to in emotionally arousing circumstances (Christianson, 1992b; Christianson & Hubinette, 1993; Read, Yuille, & Tollestrup, 1992). Thus, the outcomes should not be surprising. Furthermore, the "traumatic" situation consisted of watching a movie of a transorbital lobotomy, which was documented to arouse emotion, but concerning which the authors readily acknowledged that "the range of arousal found might have been considerably smaller than would be found in individuals truly involved in life threatening situations" (p. 397).

But, overall, it has been discovered that *the closer the research design is to real-life uses of hypnosis, the more likely hypnosis facilitates memory without an increase in errors or confabulation* (Geiselman & Machlovitz, 1987). In fact, Geiselman and Machlovitz found that all of the studies that reported memory facilitation with hypnosis, without any increase in errors, used either live events or films as memory stimuli. They further discovered that the greatest probability of success occurred when interactive hypnotic interviews were used, much as happens in clinical and investigative situations. When

memory scientists use procedures (e.g., suggestions for hypermnesia instead of age regression or revivification, forced recall instead of free recall, and interactive interviewing in hypnosis) far removed from the type of clinical and forensic techniques used with actual patients, victims, and witnesses, and with nonpersonally meaningful and unemotional stimuli, they typically find no facilitative effects from the use of hypnosis to enhance memory.

Geiselman, Fisher, MacKinnon, and Holland (1985) used police training films in an effort to provide true-to-life stimuli. They discovered that hypnosis interviews by experienced persons produced 35% more correct facts than standard police interviews (and a "cognitive interview" using imagery and various cognitive strategies also produced results comparable to hypnosis). While it is conceivable that a hypnotist could be ineffective or cause confabulation, Geiselman and Machlovitz's (1987) analysis of 38 experiments did not support this claim; in fact, *it was the differences in experimental methodology that predicted the success or failure of hypnosis-aided recall*. A similar conclusion was recently reached by McConkey (1992). Geiselman's analysis found that the more natural and ecologically valid the conditions of the experiment, the more likely hypnosis was to successfully promote enhanced recall.

Thus, studies like Stalnaker and Riddle (1932) and Hofling et al. (1971) found that hypnosis enhanced recall. Similarly, Griffin (1980), using a film of simulated crimes (and where subjects could also answer, "I don't remember"), found that "memory was significantly enhanced by using hypnosis," and "that the hypnotized witness did not confabulate any more than the nonhypnotized witness and that with the use of proper question design, false or misleading information was at a minimum" (p. 389). Griffin (1980) concluded:

> From this, one could conclude that hypnosis will not have an adverse effect upon a witness giving false or misleading answers to the investigators, nor will it result in confabulation if the questions are not leading and are prepared properly. (p. 389)

Researchers who have vigorously emphasized that hypnotically retrieved memories cannot be trusted and are likely to be distorted, and who, therefore, insist that all forensic interviews must be fully videotaped to evaluate potential contamination, do not apply these same rigorous standards to their own hypnotic and pre- and posthypnotic work with research subjects. Thus, *they have failed to control for the potential contamination that their own skeptical viewpoints have on experimental outcomes* (Watkins, 1993). In our review, we were distressed to find that in many cases the specific, detailed suggestions offered to research subjects were not even provided in the report, thus preventing further scientific scrutiny for potential bias on the part of the experimenters.

Erdelyi (1988) reviewed hypermnesia research and stated, "There is no doubt that concentration [which is what occurs in hypnosis] produces reliable and powerful recall hypermnesia for pictures and imagistic/high-sense materials, but not, apparently for low-sense materials" (p. 90). His review of *laboratory research* found, however, that the specific use of hypnosis increases correct and also false recall for high-sense materials. He reached the conclusion, "It remains an open question whether hypnosis contributes to the hypermnesia effects observed under hypnosis" (p. 90). Clearly, hypnosis was found to have a hypermnesia effect, but the technical question was whether a hypnotic mode of concentration contributed more recall than simple nonhypnotic concentration, and if it caused more confabulation.

More recently, Erdelyi (1994) indicated his conviction that hypermnesia or enhanced memory exists and "occurs with or without hypnosis," but he believes that "hypnosis does not uniquely add to (*or subtract from*) hypermnesia" (p. 386, emphasis added) with nontraumatic memory. He believes that *repeated retrieval efforts* (whether in hypnosis or not) are responsible for increased recall. Thus, for example, Geiselman et al. (1985) found a nonhypnotic guided memory interview (which took longer and used many more questions than hypnosis) increased correct recall as much as a hypnotic procedure (and both yielded more than a police interview).

A memory researcher may find it theoretically interesting to ascertain which aspect of a technique enhances the recall of non-traumatic memory. But even if Erdelyi's conclusion, or more accurately, hypothesis of equivalency were found to hold for normal and traumatic memory, one person could still use a hypnotic procedure while another person may prefer to make a repeated retrieval effort through the medium of a nonhypnotic interview. It seems of questionable relevance whether this variable is embedded within a "cognitive interview" or within a hypnotic procedure, provided that it produces a hypermnesia effect, without detracting, negative effects. Furthermore, we do not believe that this issue has been adequately laid to rest by research. We found it interesting that Erdelyi's (1988, 1994) reviews of hypnotic hypermnesia literature did not include Hofling et al.'s (1971) study, where hypnotic recall for personal life material was found to dramatically exceed simple repeated recall efforts. The Hofling study possesses much more ecological validity than most of the studies reviewed by Erdelyi. Relatedly, we have already noted Ready et al.'s (1997) study, which suggested that hypnotic memory enhancement exceeds and does not occur merely because the hypnotic procedure implicitly includes contextual reinstatement, relaxation, or motivational suggestions.

Furthermore, when we actually leave the laboratory and look at evidence from bona fide police investigations using hypnosis versus standard police interviews, the picture is somewhat different than Erdelyi's conclusions from reviewing laboratory research. Yuille and Kim (1987) examined actual cases from police files where there was sufficient evidence to evaluate the accuracy of the accounts of witnesses to crimes. *Hypnosis was found to almost triple the amount of total information provided in regular interviews.* Critics of the use of hypnotic recall would theorize, based on laboratory research, that this increase is because a less strict criterion (Klatzky & Erdelyi, 1985) is used by hypnotized subjects to report data. This enables them to produce more information, including some accurate details, but more confabulated or imaginary information.

However, Yuille and Kim's (1987) results did not confirm what some of the laboratory researchers have reported. They examined "descriptive details" that could be compared to available forensic evidence for corroboration. An average of 84.4% of such details that were reported in a regular interview were found to be accurate, compared to 82% of the details produced in a hypnotic interview. They concluded, "Thus, the accuracy of the information provided by the present witnesses appears to be high, *and hypnosis had no appreciable [negative] effects on the accuracy rate*" (p. 424, emphasis added). They further discovered that 67.9% of the facts from the hypnosis interview were new, and 94.1% of the details were consistent across the nonhypnotic and hypnotic interviews. In a real-world setting where accuracy of recall was compared with or without hypnosis, the inaccuracy and confabulation often reported in laboratory research using hypnosis with memory for relatively irrelevant stimuli observed shortly before were not found.

Yuille and Kim's (1987) crime victim data directly challenge Erdelyi's (1994) conclusions that hypermnesia resulting from hypnosis may simply be the result of repeated retrieval efforts. Two witnesses had experienced two standard interrogative interviews before having a hypnotic interview. Thus, this provided some information about the effects of repeated interviews in a naturalistic setting, independent of hypnosis. These witnesses produced an increase in facts of 28.4% in a second retrieval effort (interview). But, with hypnosis they provided an increase in facts of 401.7% over the first prehypnosis interview, and 292.2% over the second prehypnosis interview!

> These data suggest that it is not simply a second interview that is the basis of the improvement in recall found with the hypnosis interview, since only a marginal increase in information occurred with the second pre-hypnosis interview while a very large increase was found with the hypnosis interview. (Yuille & Kim, 1987, p. 423, emphasis added).

Yuille and Kim (1987) pointed out that it was possible that certain aspects of the hypnotic techniques being used could be used without a hypnotic induction and that they might produce the same results, which is of academic and theoretical interest. But the fact remains that hypnotic techniques were judged by the hypnotist, police officers, and the researchers who examined the data later to be uniformly beneficial. They further found that leading questions were not used in either hypnotic or nonhypnotic interviews. And, once again, the hypnotically elicited information did not contain more inaccuracies or confabulations.

The Geiselman and Yuille studies have critically important implications. In leaving the laboratory and working with bona fide witnesses, exposed to actual crimes, who were being interviewed by professionals—as contrasted with watching videotapes or role-play scenarios and being questioned by graduate students or their professors—*we find a three-fold increase in information (over a second nonhypnotic retrieval effort) without a decrease in the accuracy of the information produced.* And, in fact, we find remarkable consistency of information between hypnotic and nonhypnotic interviews. These results also concur with Hofling et al.'s (1971) findings of age regression to personal life circumstances, where the available information did not suggest that confabulation was increased, and even after correcting for the inclusion of a repeated recall effort, there was a 42.5% improvement in memory. These results are also congruent with Geiselman and Machlovitz's (1987) findings that *the closer the laboratory approximates real life, the more likely hypnotic interventions have proven effective without an increase in errors.* Just as foreign facsimiles of Rolex watches are usually extraordinarily disappointing, so laboratory efforts to reproduce real-world circumstances sometimes represent very poor imitations of life.

In this regard, several reviews of literature on memory and hypnosis (Hammond et al., 1995; Kanovitz, 1992; Relinger, 1984; Scheflin & Shapiro, 1989; Smith, 1983; Weitzenhoffer, 1953) reached the conclusion that, *although hypnosis does not aid in the recall of meaningless stimuli, it may facilitate recall of personally meaningful information or material associated with emotional situations or aid recall where strong or traumatic emotion impedes memory retrieval.*

It is interesting that DePiano and Salzberg's (1981) study, which found enhanced recall of accurate information in a hypnotic condition compared to waking recall reached the following conclusion:

> A key difference in the present study, however, was the nature of the material used for testing recall. This information had been learned incidentally, was meaningful, and was presented as part of a logical sequence. This is in contrast to most of the laboratory studies where material was intentionally learned, was of little relevance to S [subjects], and was not part of a logical (contextual) sequence. (pp. 395–396)

Referring to the dearth of clinically relevant research, Frankel (1988), who supports a false memory viewpoint, indicated that perhaps:

a subject that must be addressed before discussing concerns about the factual accuracy of hypnotic recall is the factual accuracy of any material recalled in analysis or therapy *without* the aid of hypnosis. (p. 250)

Referring specifically to the problems with laboratory memory research, he stated:

So, for example, while it is clear that nonsense syllables are not remembered more easily in hypnosis and that recognition of previously learned material is not enhanced (Council on Scientific Affairs, American Medical Association, 1985), the recall of meaningful, potentially emotion-laden, personal memories remains a clinical exercise that is not easily duplicated in a laboratory setting. (p. 250)

He wisely concluded:

We are forcefully reminded here that theories and the data from experimental studies, relevant as they are to the growth of the field, might best be regarded as beacons, not barriers. Part of their purpose is to illuminate, not to dictate, the paths that we follow clinically. Because of rather than despite the data accumulated thus far, hypnosis will probably continue to lay claim to its use as an aid to recall in therapy, because not infrequently it seems to do just that. (p. 263)

Another major review of research on hypnosis and memory continued this same theme and tone. McConkey (1992) reached the determination that:

The varying findings [about hypnosis and memory] that have been reported in the literature appear to have as much to do with the experimental methods used as they do with the phenomena being investigated. This is an important point to underscore. (p. 411)

These were precisely the findings of Geiselman and Machlovitz (1987).

Nash et al. (1985) observed an important difference between experimental and clinical hypnosis:

It is the clinical efficacy of hypnotherapy in its capacity to produce ego regressed states that sparks much laboratory interest in hypnotic age regression. These features of the therapeutic context, however, are typically not incorporated into, or measured by experimental procedures. If hypnotized-simulating differences are rarely obtained in the laboratory, then E [experimenter] failure to focus on the important interpersonal and emotional features of the therapeutic context may be a factor. The authors posit that the magnitude of the hypnotic age regression effect in the present study, and certainly in clinical situations, is due to the extent to which emotive experiences are elicited and sensitively measured during the hypnotic procedure. . . . Given the important status of emotion in clinical work, the affective dimension deserves more attention than it has received in the experimental literature. (pp. 232–233)

Clearly, as we have shown, experimental hypnosis and laboratory situations often differ dramatically from clinical and forensic situations. For instance, Kihlstrom and Hoyt (1990) explained: "In our laboratory, for example, we go to great lengths to defuse the hypnotist-subject relationship" (p. 183). Many theories of hypnosis, however, emphasize the crucial importance of a trusting and caring relationship between subject and hypnotist. Furthermore, some evidence exists (Shubat, 1968) that in the recall of material after a short time interval (e.g., 24 hours) like that often used by some experimentalists, the quality of the relationship between the experimenter and the subject may be the most influential factor influencing the recall of material. This is an uncontrolled variable in virtually all the experimental research, but is a factor always deemed centrally important in clinical contexts (Hammond et al., 1977). Interestingly, these broad conclusions about the discrepancies between the laboratory and real life even received support from Orne, Whitehouse, Dinges, and Orne (1988), some of the experimenters most critical of using hypnosis to retrieve memories:

However, it must be kept in mind that the laboratory rarely if ever reproduces the intensity of emotion associated with some autobiographical memories, and certainly does not approximate the guilt-related, highly personal, traumatic experiences that are often involved in treatment. (p. 52)

Pettinati (1988) concluded that "none of the contributors [to her book on hypnosis and memory] appear to object to employing hypnosis to provide leads that can then be corroborated by independent sources" (p. 284). In pointing out the gross limitations of existing research, Pettinati (1988) powerfully stated: "Clinical research on hypnotic hypermnesia in the therapeutic setting has not simply been overlooked by the contributors; it is completely lacking," and once again echoed that the condition of highly emotionally charged, traumatic memories "are not easily duplicated in the laboratory setting" (p. 288).

Problems like these have afflicted eyewitness memory research in general, even independent from hypnosis (e.g., Zaragoza & Koshmidir, 1989). There was such a parallel pattern of reliable incongruities between laboratory research concerning memory with uninvolved bystander witnesses and witnessing actual emotional events that Fisher et al. (1989) concluded:

> If this difference between laboratory and field studies continues to appear, one may question the validity of describing in court the accuracy rates found in the laboratory as evidence of the general unreliability of eyewitness testimony in field cases. (p. 725)

Recently, studies have improved in their ecological validity. Christianson (1992d) noted that more current real-life studies and simulation studies of memory for emotional events have been consistent in finding that centrally important information is better retained and less prone to be forgotten. Christianson and Hubinette (1993) also observed that the discrepancy in research reports in many instances seems dependent upon what certain researchers concentrate on in their experiments, with the incongruence often related to variations in the type of memory test, the timing of test, and type of details evaluated. Thus, we find that certain researchers examine accuracy and persistence of memory (e.g., Christianson, 1984; Heuer & Reisberg, 1990; Reisberg, Heuer, McLean, & O'Shaughnessy, 1988; Yuille & Cutshall, 1986), while other investigators focus on errors in memory and deterioration of memory over time (e.g., Clifford & Hollin, 1981; Clifford & Scott, 1978; Loftus & Burns, 1982; Neisser & Harsch, 1992; Wagenaar &

Groeneweg, 1990), and still others focus more on memory in non-laboratory settings for actual events involving emotion (e.g., Christianson & Hubinette, 1993; Read, Yuille, & Tollestrup, 1992; Yuille & Cutshall, 1986; Yuille & Kim, 1987).

The literature on hypnosis and memory is further characterized by another very substantive delimitation: it does not differentiate between the global concept of hypnosis and the numerous methods, kinds of suggestions, and strategies that may be used within a hypnotic context. This is analogous to the deficiencies in the unimaginative psychotherapy research that for many years only vaguely evaluated the effectiveness of "psychotherapy," without specifying what particular psychotherapeutic methods (out of the dozens available) were used. To ambiguously discuss the use of "hypnosis" or "hypnotic treatments," without thoroughly explicating the specific techniques, exact wording of suggestions, and the expectations created and waking suggestions given prior to and following hypnosis, is pseudoscientific. It may have the appearance of scientific rigor, but outcomes from such research are relatively meaningless and do not advance work with actual patients or crime victims.

Because many investigations and real-world cases suggest that hypnotic attempts often do enhance recall under some conditions for some people (e.g., Block, 1976; Brown, 1918a; Hammond, in press, a; Kaszniak et al., 1988; Kroger & Douce, 1979; Raginsky, 1969; Smith, 1937; Tayloe, 1995; Yuille & Kim, 1987), studies with better ecological validity should examine why and under what circumstances memory may be enhanced. Moreover, rather than simply pursuing a one-sided experimental orientation of primarily measuring the fallibility of memory for details, balanced research is needed that also evaluates the relative overall veracity of recall with very emotion-laden, personal memories. Hypnosis is believed by many professionals to be significantly involve a controlled dissociation (e.g., Hilgard, 1977/1986; Spiegel, 1993; Spiegel & Greenleaf, 1992), and because of the indications that many persons experiencing trauma and abuse enter trance-like, dissociative states during and after trauma (e.g., Bremner et al. 1992, 1993, 1996; Eth & Pynoos, 1985; Holon, 1993; Krystal, 1993; Marmar et al. 1994; Terr, 1991), the recreation of an emotional and dissociative context through the use of hypnosis integrated within psychotherapy may facilitate both the recovery and working through of traumatic memories (Spiegel, 1993).

Clinicians must recognize that evidence from both academic and therapeutic settings validates that people, with and without hypnosis, sometimes distort or produce false information. However, an informed middle-ground position on this subject also requires that researchers and clinicians alike acknowledge that through the use of hypnosis, startlingly accurate memories may at times be retrieved.

For example, one of several cases cited by Kroger and Douce (1979) was a kidnaping and rape. In this case, a teenaged crime victim was hypnotized, and during this process she recalled significantly more details. She remembered unique rust spots on the car, various items inside the car (for instance, the specific brand names and color of a box of tissues and cookies), a gear shift knob held in place with a piece of tissue, a noise made when a window was rolled up, the location of a service station, a red, white, and blue credit card that was used, and that the gas station repairman said, "You need Freon," even though she did not know what this word meant. These additional, hypnotically elicited details were all independently confirmed, and the suspect (a minister) was located. Subsequently, other young girls that the man had sexually abused came forward after they recognized his photograph, and he was convicted.

Kroger and Douce (1979) also cited the valuable use of hypnosis in the Chowchilla kidnaping case in 1976. Twenty-six school children and their bus driver were kidnaped and sealed in a tomb-like structure in a rock quarry. After the bus driver escaped, his recall was sketchy, despite his effort to memorize the numbers on two license plates. Under hypnosis, he recalled two license plates; one was incorrect, but the other, with the exception of one digit, matched the license plate of a van driven by the kidnappers, hastening the rescue of the children. Although the hypnotically recovered information was not necessary or admitted at trial, this case nicely illustrates the fact that relatively accurate information, as well as confabulated material (Orne, 1979), may be obtained through hypnosis. In fact, this case is often cited by one of us (DCH) in educating patients about the imperfect nature of memory and of hypnotic recall—indicating that through hypnosis

both accurate but previously forgotten, and confabulated material may be elicited, and that only through independent corroboration may one know with certainty the degree of accuracy of hypnotically elicited historical material.

Despite finding hypnosis extremely valuable in criminal investigations, Kroger and Douce (1979) were also very realistic about hypnosis. They did not present it as magically or unerringly effective. On the one hand, they stated that hypnotic hypermnesia seemed to work better for affect-laden material, as contrasted with the nonpersonally meaningful details seen in university hypnosis experiments. On the other hand, they discussed the imperfection of memory and the possibility of pseudomemories—four years before Laurence and Perry's (1983) case report. They explained, "Nevertheless, any type of revivification and age-regression may involve some degree of role playing with resultant production of pseudo-memories" (p. 363), and "even deeply hypnotized subjects may be capable of purposively lying; they may also inadvertently distort versions of actual fact, can confabulate, have screen memories, or fantasize" (p. 366). They acknowledged the possible influence of demand characteristics, expectancies, cues, and prior information. Kroger and Douce (1979) also described efforts to create the kind of neutral expectations advocated by Hammond et al. (1995): "For instance, our subjects were often told *not to expect greatly increased recall*, thus decreasing the feeling of pressure to remember additional material" (p. 366). They likewise stressed the importance of independent corroboration.

The reality of traumatic amnesia and its relation to psychiatric symptoms (e.g., derealization) and somatic sensations is illustrated in a nonhypnotic case report by Rosen (1955). This is relevant to hypnosis due to the numerous clinical reports of hypnotic exploration of somatic symptoms that later appeared to be associated with the dissociation of the somatic sensations associated with a repressed memory (popularly referred to as "body memories"). He recounted the case of a 27-year-old depressed and suicidal patient. The patient experienced somatic sensations of "choking" and "twisting," and at one point a "wry neck" that "felt as if my head were being twisted from my body," as well as obsessional rumination that women he picked up would be found strangled. In treatment, the patient recovered a memory from the age of three of his mother attempting suicide by hanging herself. After an abreaction of this memory, there was an alleviation of symptoms—the kind of scenario that clinicians using hypnosis often encounter. Some credulous individuals associated with the false memory movement might well suggest that such a recollection simply represents a "screen memory" or fantasy, because there is no such thing as repressed memories. They would undoubtedly simply prescribe medication for "biological" depression and obsessive-compulsive disorder. They would likely also suggest that a patient might receive relief following the recovery of such a "memory" only because it was a "believed-in imagining" or cathartic fantasy. However, Rosen was able to obtain corroboration for the validity of the event from the patient's father.

In a number of cases reported anecdotally in the literature, hypnotic enhancement of memory was found to be useful. Hammond (in press, a) described the successful treatment and ten-year follow-up of a case of a woman with psychogenic dyspareunia and Crohn's disease. Hypnotic exploration uncovered a memory of paternal incest at the age of three (her father had since died), the age at which her parents divorced. The patient's older sister confirmed the incest. Block (1976) and Clifford and Bull (1978) have described comparable experiences of extensively and successfully using hypnosis in numerous major criminal cases and in cases reported by the Israeli National Police Force.

Smith (1937) described the successful treatment of a 19-year-old man's phobia for the dark through hypnotic age regression to traumatic memories from the age of three, which were then verified. Brown (1918a), in treating a case of speech disorder in a military officer, hypnotically age regressed him back to a near drowning incident at age three. The patient produced "a wealth of detail," and these memories, rather than representing confabulated details, were confirmed by the patient's mother "in every particular" (p. 199). Raginsky (1969) used hypnosis to restore a repressed memory of an airline pilot for the events surrounding a major airline crash. This real-life case was all the more unique because the pilot had previously (over a two-year period) undergone psychoanalytic interviews, directive interviews, intravenous Pentothal, and psychological interviews, all with well qualified professionals (in-

cluding a past president of the American Psychiatric Association, a past president of the American Psychoanalytic Association, and a world-famous psychologist), as well as interviews with leading airline safety investigators, all of which were aimed at the goal of memory recovery, and all of which were unsuccessful in restoring details of memory.

Recently, Tayloe (1995) described new evidence that was externally verified when hypnosis was used with a murder suspect who was amnestic for the violent scene, one in which he was also shot. Based on the corroboration of the hypnotically recovered memory (the details of which were unknown to the investigators and attorneys), the court found that the death was accidental and first-degree murder charges were dropped and the defendant pled guilty to manslaughter. Some academics might question the genuineness of the amnesia in this case. However, emotional and physical trauma were involved, the death occurred without premeditation or financial profit, and there was no evidence to call into question the amnesia. "Most importantly, he held the key to his own defense, since only he knew the placement of all the shots and would, therefore, have every reason to remember and no reason to fake amnesia" (Tayloe, 1995, p. 30). Innumerable cases such as these, where independent corroboration was obtained for hypnotically elicited memories, could be solicited from therapists utilizing hypnosis and from experts in forensic hypnosis.

Kluft (1996) reported on a pilot study of confirmations and disconfirmations of memories of 34 patients diagnosed with dissociative identity disorder. He found that during the course of long-term psychotherapy, *56% of the patients were able to confirm abuse memories*. The nature of confirmations included siblings who witnessed abuse, confirmation by a parent, confession by a parent, and confirmation by police or court records. This naturalistic study is all the more enlightening because 85% of the memories of abuse had been uncovered through the use of hypnotic techniques.

In the forensic arena, the Los Angeles Police Department (Reiser, 1980; Ross, 1977) discovered that, in 348 investigative hypnosis interviews, 79.3% yielded additional information (not necessarily accurate information), and 66.4% was considered to be valuable to the case investigator. In 295 cases where corroboration was sought, 48.8% could neither be verified nor disconfirmed. But in the 151 cases where follow-up information was obtained, information hypnotically obtained was verified in 90.1%. Of 113 cases that had been solved using hypnosis, the case investigators felt that hypnotically retrieved information was valuable to them 65.5% of the time. Schafer and Rubio (1978) similarly summarized 14 criminal cases where victims of crimes or witnesses were questioned under hypnosis. In 10 of the 14 cases, information recalled under hypnosis was considered to have "substantially" assisted the case.

Researchers who prefer the laboratory to the real world are sometimes prone to dismiss such reports as merely uncontrolled anecdotal cases. This is a mistake. As we have said, *it is very important for therapists to be open to being informed by evidence from the laboratory that possesses relevance for clinical practice, realizing, for instance, that memory can sometimes be influenced and modified and confabulated material produced.* Therapists can learn from experimentalists. But life is not always like an artificial lab. One cannot always prove in a laboratory that a certain kind of surgery saves lives; we must turn to real-life results. Neither clinicians nor experimentalists should mistakenly believe that the laboratory is the same as the real world when it comes to such complexities as traumatic memory. Since it is so difficult to approximate the real world of repressed memory and traumatic amnesia, *it is crucial for researchers to realize that they can learn from the corroborated real-world cases found in therapy offices and the legal community.*

Fromm (1970) provided another dramatic case report that demonstrated how a Japanese-American man, unable to speak or understand Japanese, was able to speak Japanese fluently, accurately, and in an age-appropriate manner when regressed to early childhood (when he had lived in a relocation center during World War II). This could not have been due to therapist bias, since the therapist believed the man did not speak Japanese, and "had these experiences been subjectively real but *confabulated* experiences in Orne's sense . . . his means of expression would have been the language he used in his adult years, English. He would not have spoken Japanese below the 4-year level without the hypnotist's structuring the situation for him so that he would use Japanese and would use it only below

age 4, just as Orne's (1951, p. 222) German-born student spoke English when regressed to age 6 until the hallucinated environment was restructured by addressing him in German" (pp. 85–86). Moreover, subsequent linguistic analysis of his speech demonstrated that he was using a young child's form of Japanese language when age repressed.

A similar case involving the recovery of a forgotten childhood language (Finnish-Swedish) was documented by As (1962). Fascinatingly, a century ago such cases were also described in which a hypnotic subject began to speak in Welsh, a language used only in childhood (Benedikt, 1894; Felkin, 1890). Although Kihlstrom (1978, cited in Kihlstrom & Barnhardt, 1993) reported a failure to revive Mandarin in a college undergraduate student who had not spoken the language since kindergarten, he admitted that the subject was "completely refractory to hypnosis."

Hadfield (1920, 1940) described the value of using hypnotic age regression and abreaction to treat 600–700 cases in World War I of what we would today call posttraumatic stress disorder. Brown (1918b, 1938) similarly found great value in the use of hypnotic age regression for working with trauma victims in World War I. He documented successful treatment of a series of 121 cases of hysterical mutism in soldiers with "shell shock." Taylor (1923) and Ross (1918) likewise attested to the great value of hypnosis in working with victims of trauma in World War I.

Schilder (1927/1956) described successfully treating some cases of retrograde amnesia of persons who had been revived after hanging and the benefits of hypnosis in overcoming amnesias. At the same time, however, almost a lifetime ago, Schilder displayed magnificent clinical wisdom. He demonstrated the balance of finding hypnosis invaluable in overcoming amnesia, while at the same time he acknowledged that "in clearing up of amnestic episodes, there is never any assurance that distorted material will not inject itself. . . . There can be no assurance against deceptions which may originate in the patient's 'unconscious' or represent straight simulation" (p. 125). Therefore, Schilder (1927/1956) concluded that "it must always be taken into account that testimony given in hypnosis cannot be considered absolutely truthful and that it must be verified by other methods, if truth is the issue"

(p. 109). He also made essentially the same point as Frankel (1994) in concluding:

> Here again, we must always ask ourselves whether the information the patient gives us is memory or fantasy. It is frequently quite difficult to make this distinction, which is actually irrelevant as far as the therapeutic result is concerned since it is not the purpose of cathartic hypnosis to establish historic actuality. Such invented fantasies may conceal important psychic realities. . . . (p. 161)

We do not consider ourselves to be "recovered memory therapists," in the sense that we believe that focusing on exploration of the past is only one of many strategies in therapy (Hammond, 1990b; Hammond & Cheek, 1988) and trauma therapy (Brown & Fromm, 1986), and one that is in many cases not necessary to produce positive therapeutic results (e.g., Hammond, 1994). We concur with Wolberg (1964), who has stated, "The expectation that recovery of traumatic experiences will invariably produce an amelioration or cure of the patient's neurosis is founded on a faulty theoretic premise" (p. 321). On the other hand, there are times when elaboration and working through of traumatic memories are extremely valuable and necessary for therapeutic progress.

From our review of the scientific literature, we believe that hypnosis is especially more likely to assist someone in recalling personally meaningful, affect-laden events, than nonmeaningful information about which the person is indifferent. For instance, hypnotically enhanced recall is more likely to occur in someone where emotional trauma has created a block to his/her ability to recall a memory (due to the state-dependent nature of some memories and the manner in which a trained professional may reinstate the encoding context and mood through hypnosis). Likewise, it appears that hypnosis may also facilitate enhanced recall in situations where early traumatic memories were encoded in visual images more than in verbal form (Terr, 1988). The reason is that hypnosis enhances the vividness of imagery and imagery has been found to be greater in hypnotically responsive individuals (e.g., Bowers, 1976; Crawford & Allen, 1983; Sanders, 1969; Sheehan, 1979; Spanos, Brett, Menary, & Cross,

1987). However, hypnosis techniques may play an important role apart from potential memory enhancement when treating patients where past trauma or abuse appears to be present. Thus, in phase-oriented trauma treatment, hypnotic ego-strengthening techniques and suggestions for managing symptoms (Hammond, 1990a) are important preparatory steps that are often needed before any exploration of the past. Likewise, during a memory integration phase of treatment, hypnotic reframing and reinterpretation of cognitive errors may accelerate the working through of traumatic events.

Finally, it should be stressed that hypnotic age regression is not simply something that is done to uncover trauma. There is also positive age regression, where a therapist uses hypnosis with "memories" that may be accurate, partially accurate and partially confabulatory, or even simply imagined and possibly lacking in literal historic accuracy, as a method for ego-strengthening, therapeutically altering perceptions, and increasing feelings of self-efficacy (Hammond, in press, c).

Hypnosis is not a truth serum for facilitating the pristine recovery of memories. However, when working with emotion-laden, meaningful, personally experienced memories, hypnosis definitely proves helpful with some persons. Memory is not fully accurate no matter what method someone uses to examine the past, and it may be influenced by suggestions offered in a waking or hypnotic state. However, a recent law review article reached these conclusions: "Psychodynamic psychotherapies use techniques to uncover the past that are slower than hypnosis and provide no superior guarantee that memories recovered are accurate," "'talking' psychotherapies are as capable of implanting false memories of childhood sexual abuse as hypnotic ones," and "there is as much opportunity for memory alteration to occur in nonhypnotic psychotherapies as in hypnotic ones" (Kanovitz, 1992, pp. 1243, 1246, & 1251, emphasis added). The art in using hypnosis to enhance recall in clinical and forensic settings involves maximizing hypnotic memory enhancement (hypermnesia) while minimizing the memory error rate. The genuine value of laboratory research on hypnosis and memory is its delineation of specific conditions that do or do not help achieve these dual objectives.

PSEUDOMEMORY REPORTS VERSUS GENUINE DISTORTIONS OF MEMORY

Over a century ago, Bernheim (1888/1973) age regressed a highly hypnotizable patient to a night sometime earlier and gave her the suggestion that she had awakened several times that evening to go to the bathroom and on one occasion had fallen and bumped her nose. Although the incident never happened, the patient subsequently reported feeling the pain of her hypnotically hallucinated injury. This phenomenon of accepting suggestions about memory details that never happened has come to be known as *hypnotic pseudomemory suggestion*. While the phenomenon has been the focus of considerable research, contrary to what was previously thought, it now seems questionable that pseudomemory production is a product of hypnosis per se. Considerable evidence demonstrates that memories may be contaminated and pseudomemories (or verbal reports of pseudomemories) constructed as a result of uncontrolled social psychological variables and situational demands (Lynn, Rhue, Myers, & Weekes, 1994; McCloskey & Zaragoza, 1985; Murrey, Cross, & Whipple, 1992; Zaragoza & Koshmidir, 1989).

In previous chapters, we reviewed the scientific literature on nonhypnotic memory contamination and pseudomemory production. Broad consensus exists that there are a variety of nonhypnotic factors that may substantively affect the accuracy of a person's recollection for past events. However, as we have indicated, there are some hypnosis researchers who impugn the value of hypnotic exploration of memories in a psychotherapeutic or even investigative setting. As the reader will see, while some caution is merited, these conclusions are overstated. Before examining research on hypnosis and pseudomemory, we begin our discussion with a brief historical overview.

Orne (1959, 1979) and some of his colleagues seem to have relied on his *theory* about what he considers to be the "essence of hypnosis" as a basis for condemning the use of hypnosis for memory enhancement. Orne believed that once "artifacts" were controlled, you could find the true essence of hypnosis—which he considered to be trance logic, involuntariness, changes in subjective experience that are different from the waking state, and the ability to experience distortions in perception, feeling, and memory that contrast with reality, but feel subjectively real. It has basically been Orne's theoretical conception that hypnosis is a transient delusional state where distortions are accepted as real.

In Orne's terms, "trance logic" refers to the alleged ability of hypnotized subjects to accept and tolerate logical incongruities that defy reality. Although this sounds reasonable in an essay, subsequent scientific research has failed to support Orne's theory that trance logic is a defining characteristic of hypnosis (reviewed in Kihlstrom, 1984; Spanos, 1986; Spanos, deGroot, & Gwynn, 1987). The hypnotized person's mind is not simply putty in the hands of a hypnotist. The data show that only a small percentage of hypnotic subjects are capable of the profound distortions said to usually typify hypnotic response, and the literature is clear that using hypnosis is not a unique contaminant. Nonetheless, there are persons who continue to rely on and espouse this unsupported, outdated theoretical position. Thus, when hypnosis and memory are discussed, one sees references to "the hypnotized subject's tendency to freely mix illusion and reality," "suspend critical judgment," "temporarily relinquish reality orientation," and to the "inherently unreliable" nature and "malleability of memory" in hypnosis. Of course, Orne (Orne & Bates, 1993) also talks about patients' self-report memories of their childhood experiences as "inherently unreliable" (p. 257).

As we examine the literature, there are *three generations of reports* concerning the pseudomemory phenomenon. The *first generation* consisted of historical reports, for example, by Bernheim in the 1880s, and by twentieth-century experimenters, including Luria, Erickson, Kubie and Reyher, who were going beyond the implantation of false memories. These researchers, hoping to study psychopathology and design treatments, used hypnosis to implant false memories of significant matters that would induce emotional conflicts.

This first generation also includes Herbert Spiegel's film "Fact or Fiction," which was produced at the NBC-TV studios after the assassination of Robert

Kennedy (*Time*, 1968), and it includes Martin Orne's replication, on a BBC documentary film, of Bernheim's classic hypnosis experiment (Barnes, 1982). These seeming demonstrations for the media of the ability of a hypnotic subject to distort memory were anecdotal and uncontrolled, but they now enjoy a wide audience. They are particularly impressive to the nonscientific observer who is not acquainted with the rigorous controls necessary for the experimental documentation of pseudomemory production.

We may think of this first generation as representing a pre-controlled experimental period culminating with Orne's (1979) recommendations and his demonstration of the ease by which he claimed pseudomemories could be created and believed (Barnes, 1982). It was this early anecdotal and pre-experimental, uncontrolled literature that formed the basis for the arguments that hypnotically refreshed testimony should always be excluded from testimony because it was unreliable and contaminated. We have shown earlier that another significant claim made by Orne and others, that hypnosis immunizes subjects to resist cross-examination, now has been experimentally refuted.

The *second generation* of reports on the production of hypnotic pseudomemories consisted of elementary experiments that did not control for the influence of hypnotizability level in and out of hypnosis. This literature basically began with the report by Laurence and Perry (1983), reporting Laurence's (1982) dissertation results, and the later report by Laurence, Nadon, Nogrady, and Perry (1986). In this literature, various levels of hypnotizability and the influence of suggestions given in a nonhypnotic state to individuals of varying levels of hypnotizability were not included. Nevertheless, Lawrence and Perry claimed, as Orne had previously, that hypnotic pseudomemories were easy to implant and were readily and sincerely believed by the subjects.

McCann and Sheehan (1988), in their review of the literature at that time, concluded that "only three studies to date . . . bear directly on the experimental creation of false memories in hypnotically responsive subjects" (p. 339). Analysis of these studies, coupled with their own experimental work, brought McCann and Sheehan to the following significant conclusion:

Pseudomemory response, like other hypnotic re-

sponses, is clearly shaped and determined by psychological factors of influence. *It appears also that pseudomemory response should not be viewed as a standard posthypnotic reaction.* (p. 345, emphasis added)

McCann and Sheehan (1987, 1988) also concluded that (1) "pseudomemory in recall was significantly reduced when subjects were exposed to recognition testing prior to the test of recall," (2) "hypnotic pseudomemory can be breached by exposure to incontrovertible evidence relating to original events," and (3) "pseudomemory components are not irreversibly integrated with original memories."

Thus, while the courts and the American Medical Association (1985) relied heavily on the conclusions claimed from the first few uncontrolled studies, McCann and Sheehan's (1988) demonstration that those conclusions were unwarranted has gone unheeded by judges and also by the American Medical Association (1994) in their reaffirmation of the position taken in the original 1985 report. Several members (Hammond et al., 1995) of the AMA (1985) panel have publicly indicated that they no longer support its conclusions.

Finally, the *third generation* of scholarly literature represents the most recent and sophisticated studies. These studies have controlled for (1) *hypnotizability level*, (2) whether or not a *hypnotic state* was induced using a formal induction ceremony, and (3) *the nature of the social/contextual demands*. Such research has been reported by investigators such as Spanos, McConkey, Lynn, and Murrey.

We will now examine each of the three generations of research in more detail.

The First Generation of Hypnotic Pseudomemory Research

The first generation begins over a century ago with experiments by Bernheim and Moll on implanting false memories. As noted by Scheflin and Shapiro (1989):

Albert Moll (1889/1958) put the point succinctly:

Retroactive hallucinations are of great importance in law. They can be used to falsify testimony. People can be made to believe that they have witnessed certain scenes, or even crimes. . . . (pp. 345–346)

Moll's observations mirror those of Bernheim (1891/1980):

> I have shown how a false memory can cause *false testimony given in good faith*, and how examining magistrates can unwittingly cause false testimony by suggestion. (p. 92, emphasis in original)

By the early part of the twentieth century, researchers had designed a more provocative procedure.

In the 1920s, Soviet psychologists experimented with the potential uses of hypnosis to implant false memories. The experiments appeared to work. Psychologist A. R. Luria and his associates concluded that (1) the false memories were fully accepted by the subject, and (2) the subject would "confabulate"—add fuller descriptive detail—thereby imaginatively embellishing the original false memory (Luria, 1932, 1979).

After replicating the successes of the French and German hypnotists 30 years earlier, Luria and his colleagues began new experiments designed to explore the emotional consequences of the suggested false memories. The experiments, which were conducted at State Institute of Experimental Psychology in Moscow, successfully demonstrated that hypnosis could be used to induce an innocent person to experience and develop intense guilt feelings concerning a shameful or reproachable act, incident, or event that never happened, but which was suggested to the person by the hypnotist.

Luria reported these studies and then went one step further. Once a subject was in a deep trance, an emotionally negative and significant false memory was suggested, and the subject was then given amnesia for its source (paramnesia). Also, the subject was instructed that, although there would be no memory for these false experiences, there would be an emotionally disturbing consequence posthypnotically. Guilt and motivational conflicts could then be artificially induced because the awakened subject would be "loaded" with affective complexes, the source of which would be hidden from awareness. In short, the experiments appeared successful in hypnotically implanting altered emotional states and neurotic conditions.

Kihlstrom and Hoyt (1990) note that, "according to Luria's reasoning, the subjects' posthypnotic

behaviors should be influenced by these conflictual, threatening (but not consciously accessible) memories" (p. 186). Of greater significance, however, was the fact that these hypnotically created neuroses could then be the stimulus for controlled posthypnotic behaviors, such as public confessions of illegal or immoral conduct that never happened. Indeed, it is no historical accident that Luria's laboratory work in the 1920s found practical application in the "confessions" elicited at the infamous Moscow Show Trials of the 1930s.

The concept of repression was central to these experiments on induced conflicts. Writing in 1936, Erickson noted that "the usefulness of the word-association test in detecting the presence of concealed or repressed memories is well recognized." Erickson's reference is to the word-association test developed by Wilhelm Wundt and Carl G. Jung, later modified by A. R. Luria (Rossi, 1980). The test was used as an uncovering technique to find repressed memories.

In the 1930s, American experimenters Paul E. Huston, David Shakow, and Milton H. Erickson replicated, and extended, Luria's work to the creation and cure of induced neurotic conflicts (Erickson, 1935, 1944; Huston, Shakow, & Erickson, 1934).

Huston et al. (1934) examined the effects of *hypnotically suggesting conflictual pseudomemories*, for which the subjects were made hypnotically amnestic. Studies such as these essentially attempt to provide an experimental analogue of repressed or amnestic memories of a negative or conflictual nature. Fascinatingly, one of the common findings of Huston et al., as well as others, has been that such amnestic memories or conflicts in fact do produce psychosomatic, psychophysiologic symptoms until verbalized or brought into consciousness. This finding provides an important experimental analogue of what clinicians report that they generally find in patients prior to the emergence of negative memories for which they were amnestic; that is, the patients described nonverbal and somatic symptoms, sometimes described as symbolic "body memories" or sensations that are related to sensations originally experienced in a traumatic situation (e.g., as cited earlier in the corroborated findings of Rosen, 1955).

Huston et al. found that it seemed to be important for the subject to be able to verbally express and discharge the affect associated with the induced conflict—not unlike what occurs with verbalization and working through of memories in therapy—in order to reduce the nonverbal and somatic disturbances associated with the conflictual "memory." Unlike these experiments where amnesia was induced, recent public cases of alleged false memory induction by therapists are cases where the patient is supposedly fully aware and does not have amnesia. For ethical reasons, experimental hypnotic studies have not sought to create memories of traumatic events. Thus, overall, the literature on hypnotic pseudomemory production is generally limited to attempts to induce innocuous memories or, to go one step further, to induce emotionally significant material to trigger neurotic symptoms or posthypnotic behaviors.

In the 1960s, researchers returned to these more intrusive type of experiments on induced conflicts, motivations, and desires. These studies provided some support for the phenomenon of repression and the effects of amnestic material of a conflictual nature on later behavior (Sommerschield & Reyher, 1973). The research also showed that the use of hypnotic suggestions and imagery can produce conflict, emotional reactions, and somatic symptoms. In fact, Reyher and Smyth (1971) even found that a hysterical paralysis occurred.

Reyher's (1958) writing about hypnotically induced conflicts began in the late 1950s; by the mid 1960s he noted that there were three identifiable strands of research on hypnotically induced psychopathology (Reyher, 1967): "(1) direct suggestion, (2) the induction of artificial conflicts, and (3) the activation of natural conflicts" (p. 115).

Work with direct suggestion proved little more than that psychopathology can sometimes be suggested in select subjects. According to Reyher (1962), "direct suggestion tests nothing but itself" (p. 346). Most research concentrated on the second strand, hypnotically inducing artificial conflicts, and the third, activation of natural conflicts. Reyher (1962) believed that a convincing experiment had to meet four points. First, the subject must not receive clues about how the experimenter wants or expects the subject to respond. This elimination of demand characteristics was essential because it was a flaw in prior research by Luria, Huston and associates, and others. In these flawed experiments, the subjects were told that they would feel disturbed by the induced conflict. Second, the induced process must produce a responsive behavior that has not been suggested. Third, part of the induced response must be psychopathological. Fourth, adequate control groups must be used. As one of his goals, Reyher included studying the relationship between repression and psychopathology. His work suggests that the relationship is proportional, that is, the type and frequency of psychopathology are related to the degree of repression.

However, these psychoanalytically oriented studies of the pseudomemory phenomenon did not control for demand characteristics by using a waking suggestion group of high hypnotizables, blind the hypnotist to the group assignment, or utilize someone other than the experimenter in an entirely different context to evaluate the ability of subjects to distinguish suggested pseudomemories from reality when they were motivated to respond honestly. Thus, Sheehan (1969) concluded that the demand characteristics of the research were responsible for the psychopathology seen in Reyher's studies. And, in fact, Smyth (1982), who participated in studies with Reyher, expressed the belief that high-hypnotizable subjects "probably become *temporarily* absorbed in the conflictual paramnesias to the point where the suggested fantasies take on an air of reality" (p. 556, emphasis added), and that the resulting emotion, combined with desire to fulfill the role of a good hypnotic subject, produced the behavior seen in the experiment. Note that in cases where there was a quality of reality to the memory, it seems to have been because there was amnesia for the source of the suggested memory—very unlike current lawsuits involving clinical cases where it is alleged that pseudomemories were produced by a therapist.

Matthews, Kirsch, and Allen (1984), unlike earlier researchers, used a sample of moderate- and high-hypnotizables to seek experimentally to induce psychopathology. This is important because it tests more closely the population likely to be seen by clinicians using hypnosis. This more recent, more sophisticated research used Sommerschield and Reyher's (1973) paramnesia verbatim, but included control conditions. They found that symptoms occurred equally in all four experimental conditions.

Thus, they demonstrated that in fact the suggestions could have a symptom-eliciting effect, but it was not due to the nature of the oedipal conflict suggested, and the mean scores for subjects where an oedipal conflict was suggested and where no paramnesia was suggested were virtually identical. The authors concluded, "If the posthypnotic suggestion is capable of eliciting symptoms without the implantation of a paramnesia in moderately hypnotizable Ss [subjects], then it is at least plausible that it would have a similar effect in highly hypnotizable subjects as well" (p. 365).

It was Matthew et al.'s belief that simply giving suggestions (e.g., about a situation capable of inducing anger) elicits discomfort in subjects that can cause symptoms. Their research found that subjects simply simulating hypnosis were as symptomatic (actually somewhat more symptomatic) than those who were hypnotized and given suggestions for the induction of an experimental conflict.

The first generation of research on pseudomemory production also includes two visual presentations that might lead the viewer to conclude that implanting memories with hypnosis is simple and effective. The earliest visual demonstration is Herbert Spiegel's riveting film "Fact or Fiction," in which a high-hypnotizable subject is told in trance that he is aware of a communist plot to take over the media in America. The subject was directly instructed that he would recall specific information about this plan. Immediately after the hypnosis, the subject discussed the plot, confabulating and elaborating details as he had been told to do, as well as responding to waking (nonhypnotic) suggestions. After removing the suggestions, and the amnesia for the hypnotically implanted beliefs, the subject, upon viewing the film of his conduct, expressed amazement at his behavior and at the sincerity with which he expressed political viewpoints that were diametrically opposed to the viewpoints he actually held.

Spiegel (1980) labeled this the "Honest Liar Syndrome," and appropriately so, because, although someone can purposely or consciously lie in hypnosis, sophisticated research evidence (Kinnunen, Zamanski, & Block, 1994; Kirsch, Silva, Carone, Johnston, & Simon, 1989) suggests that highly hypnotized subjects do not generally consciously give deceptive reports of their experiences to suggestions and do not tend to simply fake their responses. They may, nonetheless, not be fully aware of a powerful motivation to accede to the demand characteristics of the experimenter and provide him or her with the responses desired.

But, as will soon be shown, the average person on the street would be incapable of responding in the manner that Spiegel's subject or Orne's subject (in the next example) responded to suggestions. Furthermore, research that will be reviewed shortly (e.g., Lynn et al., 1989; Murrey et al., 1992; Spanos, Gwynn, Comer, et al., 1989) suggests that a large proportion of those subjects talented enough to respond in a similar manner to Spiegel's subject, would, if they were interviewed away from the context of the experiment by persons other than the experimenter, be found capable of distinguishing hypnotic suggestion from reality. Furthermore, the subject in the Spiegel film was a high-hypnotizable who had worked extensively with Spiegel and had come to trust and respect him. Also, there was no demonstration that "memories," as opposed to "beliefs," were altered, or that these reports were not explainable by the demand characteristics of the situation.

Another visual attempt to demonstrate a hypnotically altered memory may be found in Martin T. Orne's presentation filmed by the BBC (Barnes, 1982). A nurse reported that she had slept through the night. While in trance, she is told that she awakened in the middle of the night after hearing loud noises, like gunshots or a car backfiring. After the trance, she reported being awakened at night. When Orne played her the audiotape of her prehypnotic statement that she had slept through the night, she expressed surprise but stuck to the hypnotically implanted false story rather than her previously expressed true memory.

Orne's demonstration, which lasts about seven or eight minutes on film, has been introduced into courtrooms as *documented* proof of the ease of implanting memories and obtaining confabulation. The Orne demonstration may, as with the Spiegel film, have involved a high-hypnotizable who trusted Orne, but this point is not clear from the film. A careful viewing of the film makes it clear that (1) the subject resists Orne's suggestions until it is clear that he wants a certain report from her, (2) the report is a product of her hypnotizability and social influence (repeated insistence on a correct answer and demand characteristics) rather than hypnosis, and (3) the report may be merely a *report* and not necessarily a false *memory*. As McCann and Sheehan (1988) note:

> The Orne demonstration particularly raises the question as to whether the effect produced is really a memory effect or is a response to an implied posthypnotic suggestion. Orne's (1979; Barnes, 1982) procedure specifically instructs the subject to confuse and confound the events of the evening to be remembered and the events of the hypnosis session, thereby providing specific directions for posthypnotic recounting of the confounded memory. (p. 340)

Unless experts are prepared to neutralize the persuasive impact of the film by showing that it does not prove what it appears to prove, juries will undoubtedly be influenced by it. In *Slavik v. Routt* (1995), two women diagnosed as having multiple personality disorder sued their psychiatrist for sexual abuse. The psychiatrist had committed suicide, so his testimony was unavailable. The defense offered a traditional false memory argument, namely, that memory is fallible, especially in cases where the plaintiffs are highly hypnotizable and dissociative. The Orne film was played to the jury. The plaintiff's expert, however, was able to explain the defects in the film and the jurors apparently were not persuaded by it. They awarded the plaintiffs 4.5 million dollars.

Spanos and McLean (1986) have commented that in their experiments they were able to obtain high levels of pseudomemory reports using the Orne procedure, but these reports disappear when "hidden observer" instructions are given. In other words, even though there are initial reports of the pseudomemory, with proper instructions the highly hypnotizable subjects were later able to discriminate between their suggested "pseudomemory imaginings" and "actual memories." When initially asked for pseudomemories, some high-hypnotizables readily comply, but when asked for the truth, they disown the pseudomemories.

Tapes such as Orne's BBC demonstration (Barnes, 1982) and Spiegel's "Fact or Fiction" (1968) are easily interpreted by someone without sophisti-

cation in research methodology as proving that any person who has been hypnotized will easily come to believe a false memory suggested through hypnosis. However, this would be a grossly oversimplified view of hypnotically suggested false memory. As we review the overall research, we believe, with McCann and Sheehan (1988), that such a dramatic and essentially involuntary effect cannot be caused by hypnotic suggestion with the vast majority of people—that is, except in the small percent of persons who are "hypnotic virtuosos." Spiegel's subject was what he refers to as a "Grade 5" hypnotic subject. This means he was in *at least* the top 15% of people in hypnotic responsivity. An additional, vitally important, fact that we shall discuss shortly is that in hypnotic virtuosos, hypnotic induction is not a necessary condition for responding to suggestions (Orne, 1980) and distorted memories probably occur as easily with such persons from waking suggestion as from hypnotic suggestion.

It is interesting that some of this same debate took place in the late 1800s. For instance, Binet (1896) noted that two subjects who responded similarly to a suggestion for altering their identity or personality might do so for very different reasons. There were two theoretical camps at that time in Europe. Some professionals studying hypnosis (e.g., Delboeuf, 1889, 1893–94) believed that the subject enacted the role assigned (e.g., acting as if he were a peasant or a soldier) in order to please the hypnotist—a position very similar to contemporary social psychologically-oriented theories of hypnosis emphasizing role enactment (Coe & Sarbin, 1991; White, 1941). Others (e.g., Bernheim, 1888/1973) believed that the subject genuinely accepted the suggested state of affairs. Binet (1896) wisely concluded:

> It does not seem necessary to pass judgment upon these two diametrically opposed opinions, because they appear to me to be equally correct, only they apply to different cases. There are persons who are by no means the dupes of the suggestions given to them, but who will still carry them out because they are unable to resist the influence of the operator. This class of patients never forget who they are—their identity. If they are told to represent a priest, a general, or a nun, they will be capable of doing it as any of us might do it when requested,

but they know that they are playing a part. They try to assume the characters desired, but they always retain the memory of their proper personality. Others, on the contrary, are completely the victims of the suggested illusion, because the memory of their former ego is for the moment entirely obliterated. (p. 259)

It seems to have been Binet's (1896) position that some persons respond due to the social psychological aspects of the situation, seeking to please and meet hypnotist expectations and demand characteristics. Such persons, when given suggestions for a pseudomemory, may thus verbalize the suggested memory. It would represent, however, a response bias or hypnotically suggested false *report*, not a genuine distortion or creation of a new memory representation. On the other hand, some persons who are exceptionally high in hypnotic capacity, may, in fact, be capable of at least temporarily accepting a pseudomemory suggestion. For these persons, the suggested state of affairs may, temporarily at least, seem real.

The Second Generation of Hypnotic Pseudomemory Research

By the second generation of research, which began in the late 1970s in response to the emerging forensic questions about the admissibility of hypnotically refreshed recollection (McConkey & Sheehan, 1995; Pettinati, 1988; Scheflin & Shapiro, 1989), the emphasis shifted away from the Luria, Erickson, and Reyher experimental model, and back to the basic implanted memory studies conducted by Bernheim and Moll at the end of the last century.

The report by Laurence and Perry (1983) typifies reports during the early and mid 1980s. Using only subjects who scored in the top 9% or higher of hypnotic responsivity, they age regressed subjects to a night in the previous week. Following the Bernheim paradigm, they then suggested being awakened by a loud noise (suggesting a pseudomemory and a hypnotically suggested auditory hallucination), a suggestion to which 17 of 27 (63%) subjects responded. In interviews afterwards, 48% of subjects (13) were defined as accepting the suggestion that the event had taken place, while other subjects indicated that the event had been

suggested. This might be extrapolated to represent about 4.3% of a general population (48% of the top 9% of the population in hypnotic responsivity). Six of the 13 subjects who reported the suggested memory as "real" (22% of the sample of very high-hypnotizables, or what may amount to perhaps 1.9% of the general population) reportedly "were unequivocal in their certainty" (p. 524) that the event had occurred. Allegedly, even when told that the event was suggested in hypnosis, they continued to maintain that the event occurred.

Most of the earlier experimental studies (Labelle, Laurence, Nadon, & Perry, 1990; Laurence & Perry, 1983; Lynn, Milano, & Weekes, 1991; McCann & Sheehan, 1988) of hypnotically facilitated pseudomemory simply had hypnosis groups; they were not sophisticated enough to include nonhypnotic and simulating control groups. Thus, a severe limitation of earlier studies was that they did not allow conclusions to be drawn about whether the use of hypnosis itself was a variable of importance in pseudomemory production.

Just as we have seen in the hypnosis and memory research in general, we find that the earlier scientific publications about hypnotically produced pseudomemories are in many instances very limited by the lack of sophisticated design and methodology. There are several things that limit our ability to generalize, especially from the less recent studies, to real-life situations. For instance, some studies have used astonishingly *liberal criteria for what constitutes a pseudomemory*, such as merely the expression of uncertainty or confusion (e.g., Labelle et al., 1990; Laurence & Perry, 1983). It was the belief of Barnier and McConkey (1992) that using such liberal criteria may spuriously inflate pseudomemory reports, when in actuality such criteria "hardly [represent] a major change in memory," and are something that could just as easily be interpreted as evidence for the nonexistence of pseudomemories.

Generalization from existing pseudomemory research to real life is also made difficult because the memories suggested in research are usually irrelevant and commonplace, not possessing even a passing resemblance to traumatic memories reported in therapy. When, for example, such everyday occurrences as a telephone ringing, a pencil dropping, or hearing a noise while asleep are suggested as false memories, these seem hardly comparable to patient reports of physical or sexual abuse.

Some of the earlier pseudomemory research is further flawed by the fact that subjects were tested for having a hypnotically created memory *during* hypnosis, instead of following hypnosis, in a nonhypnotic condition. When a subject has reported that a distorted memory was recalled during hypnosis, he or she could feel considerable pressure to continue to provide the same consistent response and to maintain a consistent role when questioned after hypnosis (Leippe, 1980; McCann & Sheehan, 1989; Spanos & McLean, 1986). In addition, available data indicate that original memories are not lost irretrievably when a false memory is hypnotically suggested, and that such suggested distortions do not become irreversibly integrated with original memories (McCann & Sheehan, 1987, 1988; Murrey et al., 1992).

During this phase, there was also research conducted on the manner in which overall accuracy of hypnotically retrieved memories *for details* may be influenced or distorted through suggestion and the deliberate inclusion of misinformation. Many of these *hypnotic misinformation studies* were conducted in Sheehan's laboratory (e.g., Sheehan, 1988; Sheehan & Grigg, 1985; Sheehan, Grigg, & McCann, 1984; Sheehan & Tilden, 1983, 1984, 1986) using Loftus's methods for introducing false information either prior to or following hypnotic induction. Just as Loftus and her colleagues have shown that it is possible to influence people so that they incorporate misleading information into their waking memory reports, this research has similarly shown that this may be done in hypnosis as well. This should represent no surprise to anyone. However, such findings remain subject to the criticisms that have been made of the Loftus research, for instance, that such memory reports do not necessarily overwrite genuine memories and may represent reporting biases to meet experimenter demand characteristics (McCloskey & Zaragoza, 1985; Murrey et al., 1992; Zaragoza & Koshmidir, 1989).

In his research, Sheehan examined: high- versus low-hypnotizable subjects in hypnosis and waking conditions where false information was given prior to hypnotic induction (Sheehan & Tilden, 1983); real versus simulating subjects where misinformation was presented before hypnotic induction

(Sheehan & Tilden, 1984); memory reports of high- versus low-hypnotizable subjects who were hypnotized when the misinformation was likewise presented prior to induction; the effects of the same misinformation being introduced after hypnosis had been induced (Sheehan & Grigg, 1985; Sheehan, et al., 1984); and the effects of misinformation given after hypnosis on high- and low-hypnotizable subjects in and out of hypnosis (Sheehan, 1988). In all Sheehan's studies, the stimulus was a series of slides of a robbery, and subjects were regressed back to the time that they saw the slides. The misinformation and distortions that were introduced had to do with: (1) misperceiving the slogan Nixon instead of Yukon on a jacket, (2) suggesting a man has money in his hand instead of an object, and (3) describing that the man and woman waved goodbye to each other instead of just the woman waving goodbye. Force-choice recognition and free recall testing were incorporated in all the studies.

Thus, Sheehan's series of studies is a parallel to Loftus's work, only applied to hypnosis. This means that the focus of these studies was basically on demonstrating the imperfection of memory, showing that it is possible to distort memory reports through the incorporation of misleading detail information prior to or after hypnosis. Thus, it is important for readers to realize that the systematic research bias or interest in these studies is one of examining how one may create errors in details of memory, rather than examining the overall relative accuracy and persistence of memory over time. This is a worthy topic, but represents only one side of the coin. Naturally, memory may be influenced, and memories for peripheral details in particular may be flawed. But it is an entirely different question when we seek to examine the relative overall accuracy of personally relevant emotional or traumatic memories. Sheehan's experiments are limited in their focus and therefore their generalizability. Furthermore, Sheehan's studies are limited by having used hypnosis almost immediately, without a delay of days, weeks, or months. Bear in mind Geiselman and Machlovitz's (1987) finding that all the studies that they reviewed that found hypnotic memory facilitation without an accompanying increase in errors used longer retention intervals between the original memory stimulus and the hypnotic interview.

As one might expect, Sheehan's series of studies

found no difference between accuracy of memory for hypnotized versus nonhypnotized subjects. Four of his six experiments that followed the Loftus model found that, when distortion was present, greater errors were apparent in high-hypnotizable persons who were hypnotized than among low-suggestible individuals. Hypnotized subjects also demonstrated more distortion than simulating subjects. Of relevance to findings in third generation studies, the *social context itself* and *high hypnotizability* were found to be associated with facilitating distortion. In this regard, Sheehan (McConkey & Sheehan, 1995) recently concluded from these studies that *"there is no support for the position that hypnosis is appreciably more distorting than the waking state"* (p. 190).

The Third Generation of Hypnotic Pseudomemory Research

As later investigations improved earlier designs, several third generation studies (Eisen, 1996; Malinoski, Lynn, Martin, Aronoff, Neufeld, & Gedeon, 1995; McConkey, Labelle, Bibb, & Bryant, 1990; Spanos, Gwynn, Comer, Baltruweit, & de Groh, 1989) found comparable numbers of subjects in hypnotic and nonhypnotic conditions reporting suggested pseudomemories, while others found more of the hypnotized subjects (compared to waking subjects) reporting false memories (Sheehan, Statham, & Jamieson, 1991a,b). However, once studies began evaluating the differential impact of high, medium, and low hypnotizability, the experimental results became clearer and more consistent.

The more recent data supporting the idea that hypnosis may create false memories have been derived mostly from laboratory studies of student samples scoring high or moderately high in hypnotic responsivity (e.g., Barnier & McConkey, 1992; Labelle, Laurence, Nadon, & Perry, 1990; McConkey, Labelle, Bibb, & Bryant, 1990; Sheehan, Statham, & Jamieson, 1991a,b). In general, this literature suggests that *the lower one scores in hypnotic susceptibility, the less vulnerable one is to accept a suggestion for a false memory detail.* Also, highly and moderately hypnotizable individuals appear more vulnerable to comply with or respond to a suggestion for a pseudomemory than low-hypnotizable persons.

Some earlier literature (Labelle & Perry, 1986)

showed that highly hypnotizable subjects were more prone (45%) than moderately hypnotizable subjects (30%) to respond to pseudomemory suggestions by reporting such events. Similar differences were found in a later unpublished study by Labelle, Bibb, Bryant, and McConkey (1989, as reported in Sheehan, Statham, & Jamieson, 1991a,b), but when a telephone survey evaluated the persistence of reported pseudomemories, there was no evidence for hypnotizability effects. The later study also found no evidence for any distinctive hypnotic outcomes.

But in this third generation research, as in the uncontrolled case reports published by Lawrence and Perry (1983), commonly only a minority of subjects produce what on the surface appear to be false memories. However, these reports are typically for *peripheral details* imbedded in events that could conceivably happen to someone. Such "memories" are not for events that would contradict one's life perceptions of another person or be of a traumatic nature. These results simply indicate that in a selected portion of the population it may sometimes be possible to create a false memory *report* for plausible details. As Binet (1896) concluded a century ago, however, false memory reports in experiments do not necessarily represent genuinely believed false memories. The more sophisticated third generation research reaches the same conclusion.

The use of hypnotic procedures alone does not appear to introduce a significant biasing factor in the creation of pseudomemories; in fact, hypnotic procedures contribute relatively little to the overall variance of pseudomemory production. Thus, McConkey et al. (1990) determined that "the administration of an *hypnotic induction procedure* did not appreciably influence the incidence of reporting a suggested pseudomemory" (p. 202), and after reviewing the pseudomemory research, McConkey (1992) concluded: *"There may not be anything particularly hypnotic about hypnotic pseudomemory"* (p. 423). He further stressed in these experiments that "it is wrong to assume that variation in memory is necessarily a function of hypnotic procedures" (p. 424). And, in fact, research demonstrates that reports of pseudomemories may be created through suggestion without hypnosis (Garry & Loftus, 1994; Loftus & Coan, in press; Malinoski, Lynn, Martin, Aronoff, Neufeld, & Gedeon, 1995), as well as in hypnosis.

Clearly, *the primary factor contributing to the production of pseudomemories or pseudomemory reports appears to be social influence* (Brown, 1995a,b; Eisen, 1996; Malinoski et al., 1995), which interacts with hypnotizability in certain selected individuals. The research literature suggests that there are several *primary risk factors* which may interact with each other, that may allow a false belief to develop: (1) social and interrogative suggestive influence, which may stem from extratherapeutic experiences (peers, family members, group experiences, media) or from a therapist; (2) the personality trait of high hypnotizability; (3) uncertainty about past events (which, as noted in chapter 8, also makes nonhypnotized persons more vulnerable to accepting misinformation); and (4) an individual's personal beliefs and expectations. We will discuss each of these variables.

Eisen (1996) studied the relationship between suggestibility and hypnotic susceptibility, and their relationship with memory for personally experienced events that had occurred in a hypnotic and in a waking state—more salient stimuli than studies employing minor details of slides or videos. The 85 subjects were administered the Harvard Group Scale of Hypnotic Susceptibility, but three false items were added to the response booklet, asking subjects to indicate if they responded to suggestions that had never been given to them. They were also given misleading questions about events that occurred before the hypnotic induction. Subjects who had the best recall for the hypnotic procedures and for prehypnotic events were found to show the greatest resistance to misleading information. But, fascinatingly, 57% of the subjects responded to at least one of the three confederate items. This pattern was not related to hypnotizability; that is, the intrapersonal quality of hypnotizability was not related to the endorsement of events that never occurred in hypnosis. There was, however, a significant correlation between the endorsement of confederate items during hypnosis and memory errors for events outside of hypnosis (.25). Social-interpersonal influence appeared to operate independent of hypnotic suggestibility, highlighting the importance of clearly defining constructs when using the term suggestibility.

Recently Malinoski et al. (1995) studied 133 subjects who had been administered a hypnotizability

scale, measures of dissociation and fantasy proneness, a social desirability scale, the Gudjonsson Scale of Interrogative Suggestibility, and personality measures. In another session, billed to participants as a different experiment, subjects were asked to recall their earliest memory. The average "earliest memory" recalled was at 3.7 years of age. The experimenters continued to ask if there was anything earlier that they could recall, continuing this line of questioning until subjects had twice denied having had any earlier memory. The mean age of their first memory was now 3.2 years. Using social influence and waking suggestions, they subsequently told subjects that most young adults could recall very early events, including their second birthday. They were then asked to close their eyes and to try very hard to visualize, concentrate, and focus. After a minute, they were asked to report a memory. Fifty-nine percent of the subjects now produced a memory of their second birthday. This correlated .33 with scores on the Gudjonsson scale and from .24 to .26 with hypnotizability scores. Even when a birthday memory was not forthcoming, they were asked to visualize and focus on earlier and earlier memories, with standardized probes and compliments for newly reported memories. This continued until the subject denied any further memories for two consecutive probes.

With this kind of *systematic interrogatory social influence*, 78.2% of the sample ended up reporting a memory at age 24 months or less. This mildly correlated (.25) with the Yield score (how often one yields to leading questions) on the Gudjonsson scale. Furthermore, *one-third* of the sample reported a memory at age 12 months or less, and 18% gave a memory in the first six months of life. Furthermore, *confidence* in the memories was relatively high: for instance, an average of 3.59 (on a 5-point scale) for the very earliest memory, with 94% indicating that they believed their memories to be accurate to at least a moderate degree. And, on a 5-point scale, the average participant only felt a relatively moderate level of pressure (2.87). Clearly, *social influence* was the most influential factor, with the quality of hypnotizability correlating weakly and demonstrating a less significant but mild influence. Correlations with fantasy proneness were only .21.

In chapter 8 we learned that there are a number of variables related to social influence, including such things as perceived competence, trustworthiness, attractiveness, prestige, perceived personal similarity and similarity of values, and rapport (e.g., level of empathy, warmth, genuineness). One hypnosis study (Sheehan, Green, & Truesdale, 1992) evaluated the influence of *rapport* on the production of pseudomemory reports. It demonstrated that in cued recall (as opposed to free recall), a more positive interpersonal relationship between the experimenter and the subject produced more pseudomemory reports. In contrast, inhibition of rapport lowered the strength of pseudomemory reports. Thus, at least for some subjects, positive rapport may motivate pseudomemory *reports*, either through increased desire on the part of the subject to please the experimenter (or therapist) by reporting what was suggested, or perhaps through actually increasing the believability of suggestions. Rapport is likely to be operative independent of whether or not hypnosis is used.

To reiterate again, *social influence, uncertainty* about past events, and sometimes the quality of higher *hypnotizability* within a patient (not the use of hypnotic procedures) are three of the variables most strongly implicated in creating *reports* of hypnotic pseudomemories (Barnier & McConkey, 1992; Labelle et al., 1990; McConkey et al., 1990; Sheehan, Garnett, & Robertson, 1993; Sheehan et al., 1991a,b). Thus, for example, Sheehan et al. (1993) found that highly hypnotizable persons *in hypnosis* were *not* more vulnerable to the effects of leading questions.

When we talk about social influence, we are talking about suggestive influences that may be part of therapeutic or extratherapeutic interactions (e.g., with relatives, friends, an attorney) and that may be part of conversations or associated with interaction in hypnosis. There are several empirical studies demonstrating that the use of leading questions in nonhypnotic situations may significantly influence how someone describes his or her recollections of events in the past (Loftus, 1979). As reviewed earlier in the book, a question may be said to be "leading" when its form or content suggests the desired answer. Thus, Loftus and Palmer (1974) found that when student subjects who had viewed a film of an car accident were asked, "How fast were the cars going when they *smashed* each other?" as opposed to "How fast were the cars going when they *contacted* each other?" the estimates were higher

(40.8 mph vs. 30.8 mph). This study shows how an indirect form of suggestion, known in hypnosis as implication (Hammond, 1990a), may influence perceptions. This has important ramifications for therapists concerning the language that they use. Fortunately, clinicians who study hypnosis are generally very attuned to the implications of their words, and they both study and pay attention to this far more than the majority of psychotherapists.

But, concerning the Loftus and Palmer (1974) study, we must also note that the single attempt to replicate this study in a real-world context found that all the subjects resisted this kind of suggestion (Yuille & Cutshall, 1986). Yuille (1994) interpreted this discrepancy by suggesting that the context (e.g., real-life versus experimental) may influence the degree to which a person is susceptible to leading questions. He did not suggest that leading questions were not a problem—they are—but simply that the context may affect the extent to which a person is susceptible to certain leading questions.

It is important to note the limitations of our knowledge. The literature on leading questions has not been scientifically studied with enough emphasis on varying contexts. Thus, while virtually all of us would agree that leading and misleading questions may sometimes influence perception and memory, the available experimental literature on leading questions does not yet permit a full contextual analysis. Nonetheless, we recommend that clinicians be cautious and minimize the use of such questions when working with recollections of the past in either hypnotic or nonhypnotic therapeutic interactions.

Now, let's return to a discussion of the other risk factors that may increase one's vulnerability to creating an hypnotic pseudomemory or to making a pseudomemory report. It appears that if an event has a *high perceived likelihood of occurrence* (Weekes, Lynn, & Myers, 1993), it is more prone to be "remembered" by someone. *Thus, if an individual believes from reading various literature, or viewing television documentaries, or attending incest survivors twelve-step groups, that abuse may have occurred, this expectation may increase the likelihood that the person may "recall" such an event.* While this is a tentative finding, which needs further replication, it has important implications for clinicians. Consider the situation where a patient reports a verbally and emotionally abusive parent, who was emotionally absent throughout childhood. Is it possible that such a person, in hypnotically facilitated psychotherapy or any other kind of therapy (or peer-guided group), may come to believe that s/he was physically or sexually abused by the parent? Certainly it is possible because it is congruent with and mirrors his/her fundamental perceptions of the atmosphere in which s/he was raised and of the basic nature of the other person.

Such speculation is congruent with a case reported by Kluft (1996). One of his patients described a Satanic abuse experience that could later be disproven. However, three sibling witnesses confirmed her memories (which she had always recalled) of incest by her father, which was also confirmed by her mother, and to which her father confessed and apologized during the course of therapy. In addition, through hypnosis this patient recovered a memory of being raped by an older brother. Three years later, while dying of cancer, this brother spontaneously confessed this abuse to her and apologized, thus confirming the hypnotically retrieved memory of abuse. In light of the research findings, one could anticipate that this particular patient may have responded to some kind of socially suggestive influence and produced the Satanic abuse report because it was relatively congruent perceptually with her cognitive schemas from childhood about the nature of the world—perceptions shaped by the abuse by her father and brother.

Relatedly, from currently available research evidence, it appears that if a research subject or patient, prior to the introduction of hypnotic procedures, holds distinct personal beliefs that are congruent with what is later "remembered" in hypnosis, and s/he holds the expectation that s/he will find something through hypnotic exploration that is compatible with this belief (Baker, 1982; Spanos et al., 1991a), and this belief is about something that cannot be very well verified (Lynn, Milano, & Weekes, 1992; Lynn, Weekes, & Milano, 1989; McCann & Sheehan, 1987, 1988), s/he possesses a greater probability of creating a hypnotic fantasy that s/he may come to believe occurred in his/her past.

Let's take an example. Suppose that a patient subscribes to a personal belief in reincarnation. S/he has read literature about reincarnation and likes New Age literature and seminars. This has led to a belief that the source of his/her current problems reside not only in the past, but in a "past life." If s/he is quite responsive to hypnosis and requests hypnotic exploration, fully expecting, based on what s/he has read and heard from others, that s/he will be able to remember what occurred in the past, s/he may report a "past life regression." This personally created hypnotic fantasy may be metaphoric and may symbolize fundamental perceptions of self, other people, and the world, but have no basis in reality. In this sense, it is personally and therapeutically meaningful, but not veridical. It may also meet a variety of unconscious needs, for example, to avoid accepting responsibility for one's own role in problems or to carry out an unconscious wish to punish and obtain retribution.

We suspect that a large proportion of patients who do not currently recall abuse would probably not consider abuse as something that would have a high likelihood of having occurred unless they came from a generally abusive background, like Kluft's (1996) patient. To provide objectivity, during routine patient evaluations, clinicians may want to ask patients who do not recall abuse to rate their belief in the likelihood that they might have been abused but have repressed the memory and do not recall it. One of us (DCH) did that with 41 consecutive female patients, with a variety of psychotherapeutic complaints, who did not remember any incest or molestation in childhood. They rated on a percentage scale their degree of belief that sexual abuse could have occurred in their background but that they could remain amnestic for it. The mean degree of perceived probability was only 7.2%. However, this figure was inflated by a fairly small number of patients. For instance, one patient rated the percent as 90% because her sisters were all molested by an older brother and she recalled him once trying to tempt her to become engaged in sexual activity by offering her candy. Another patient rated the probability as 50% because she could recall very few memories of her childhood, and another patient rated the probability at 20% because her sister had been sexually abused by her grandfather. But, interestingly, 66% of the sample rated the probability as either being 0% or 1%.

However, even though the majority of our patients may consider it extremely unlikely that they have amnestic memories of abuse, it must be considered possible that this expectation could be altered by a therapist's confident expression of a hypothesis that sexual abuse likely accounted for the patient's symptoms and could have been repressed. Thus, therapists should be cautious about sharing such hypotheses that could potentially alter a patient's expectancies. To avoid errors of overconfidence, therapists should also avoid creating an expectancy that everything is recorded in the patient's mind and that hypnosis will uncover whatever is there.

How Genuine Are Research Reports of Pseudomemory Production?

When a research subject in hypnosis experiments does report a pseudomemory, what does this mean? One of the most important outcomes found in the more sophisticated recent research is that the *context* in which suggested pseudomemories are evaluated is a critical variable in whether a subject says that he or she experiences a pseudomemory. McCann and Sheehan (1987, 1988) were the first of the third generation researchers to begin noting contextual effects and finding that the incidence of pseudomemory reports may be dramatically less than the early reports by Perry and his colleagues (Labelle & Perry, 1986; Laurence & Perry, 1983).

As more of this type of research has accumulated, it actually appears that in many cases, rather than representing a genuine distortion or change of memory, pseudomemory effects represent something more akin to a *response bias* resulting from uncontrolled social psychological variables and situational demands (Lynn et al., 1994; McCloskey & Zaragoza, 1985; Murrey et al., 1992; Zaragoza & Koshmidir, 1989). Thus, it appears that false memory reports produced by subjects given hypnotic suggestions to attempt to create distortions of memory are probably most often not genuine distortions of the memory representation at all, but constitute conscious or unconscious compliance on the part of a subject who is trying to conform to the perceived desires and expectations of the experimenter.

This should not surprise anyone thoroughly familiar with hypnosis research. As early as 1954, Fisher gave posthypnotic suggestions to 13 subjects, instructing them that they would be compelled to scratch their ear whenever they heard the word "psy-

chology." Immediately upon awakening, all 13 subjects scratched their ears when the cue was given. Later, behaving as if the experiment were now over, only 4 of 13 subjects responded to the cue, but after being reminded that the experiment was still ongoing, 11 of 13 now responded to the word "psychology." St. Jean (1978) likewise found that the majority of experimental hypnosis subjects quit responding to a posthypnotic cue when the experimenter feigned having to leave the laboratory due to an emergency. Most recently, Spanos, Menary, Brett, Cross, and Ahmed (1987) produced comparable findings to those of Fisher (1954). Student subjects responded posthypnotically in a manner compatible with suggestions they had been given when they were formally tested by the person who hypnotized them within the laboratory context. But, when informally tested outside the experimental laboratory by someone else, none of the highly hypnotizable subjects responded as instructed.

The responding of experimental hypnosis subjects may thus be seen to be responsive to their perceptions concerning what the experimenter wants and desires. Very few subjects in the St. Jean and Fisher experiments continued to respond as suggested after the experiment was over, and none of the Spanos et al. (1987) subjects continued to respond as suggested once they were outside the experimental situation.

We see the parallel to these findings in recent hypnotic pseudomemory studies where subjects were interviewed after the experiment ended, away from the experimental context, by someone other than the experimenter, and when subjects were motivated to respond honestly. As you review the results of these more carefully designed studies, you will see the validity of Watkins' (1993) critique of much of the hypnosis and memory research, in which he emphasized that these experimenters commonly failed to control for the contaminating influence on their experimental outcomes of their own cynical views.

Thus, McConkey et al. (1990) documented that the rate of pseudomemories reported went down when subjects were in a different physical context, separated by the passage of a greater length of time. Thus, when immediately tested, 50% of subjects gave a report of a pseudomemory, but when contacted 4–24 hours later by a person not involved in the experiment, and while they were at home, only 2.5% of high-hypnotizable subjects continued to report a suggested memory. Barnier and McConkey (1992) found an initial rate of pseudomemory reports of 60% among high-hypnotizable subjects, which declined to 10% when it appeared that the experiment had ended, and the rate at which another suggestion was reported declined from 27% to just 6%. We would add that these small percentages are being found in a sample of highly hypnotizable individuals, where one would anticipate finding the most elevated false memory rates, and not from a sample of the general population where these figures would probably be substantially lower.

Murrey et al. (1992) studied the effects of pseudomemory suggestions one week after they were received by high-hypnotizable subjects and by a group not screened for suggestibility who either received the suggestions in a waking state or became control subjects. They discovered that when the subjects were motivated to provide honest reports, high-hypnotizable subjects who were hypnotized, those in a waking suggestion group, and those in a control group demonstrated no differences in the frequency of reported pseudomemories. In contrast, a group of high-hypnotizable subjects who were hypnotized and who had not been motivated to give unbiased reports, claimed to have significantly more pseudomemories (80%). The authors concluded that "response bias may be a confound in pseudomemory research, and *thus researchers need to be cautious when making inferences to specific situations from data obtained in an experimental setting*" (p. 77, emphasis added). They continue: "This suggests that if response bias is controlled for, there may not be significant differences in manifestations of pseudomemories between highly hypnotizable subjects [who are hypnotized] and subjects representative of the general population" (p. 77). Even a hypnosis researcher strongly favorable to the false memory position, like Kihlstrom, says, "it remains unclear whether the pseudomemories reflect actual changes in stored memory traces or biases in memory reporting" (Kihlstrom & Barnhardt, 1993, p. 109). Sheehan, Green, and Truesdale (1992) likewise indicated that "*pseudomemory does not necessarily involve genuine memory distortion; indeed, often it may not*" (p. 698).

Although he has not seemed to use it in his memory studies in recent years, Orne (1959, 1962) originated the real-simulator experimental design as a method for controlling for artifacts and experimenter demand characteristics (cues conveying the experimenter's expectations). Early anecdotal reports (videos of Orne and Spiegel) and studies by Perry (Labelle et al., 1990; Laurence & Perry, 1983) of hypnotically suggested pseudomemory did not control for compliance with perceived experimenter expectations by using simulator comparison groups. When pseudomemory research incorporated simulator controls, considerably greater clarity was obtained about what usually occurs when someone reports a pseudomemory.

Lynn et al. (1992) used strong suggestions in an effort to produce a false memory of a telephone ringing and a brief conversation occurring in a previous hypnotic session. A telephone was prominently displayed in the front of the room, making the innocuous suggestion even more plausible. However, in open-ended reports, they found no difference between high-hypnotizable subjects *who were hypnotized* and low-hypnotizable subjects who were asked to simulate being in hypnosis. And, in fact, none (0%) of the real or simulating subjects indicated that a real phone actually rang, and in response to a forced-choice measure, there was *no difference* in the response rate of real versus simulating subjects. This 0% response rate was similar to and revalidated previous research where Lynn et al. (1991) found 0% of hypnotized subjects (responding to open-ended, free recall questions) reported a pseudomemory, and to a still earlier study (Lynn et al., 1989) where the rate was 12.5% for high-hypnotizable and 10% for subjects simulating hypnosis. Lynn et al. (1989) not only confirmed no difference in responding to pseudomemory suggestions by real and simulating subjects, but also found that when the small number of subjects who did respond with a pseudomemory report were presented with forced-choice options, no subjects showed evidence of a pseudomemory.

These kinds of reports have led to the conclusion that *contextual factors* (such as the mode of testing, timing of the post-experimental inquiry, who does the post-experimental inquiry, whether the questioning after hypnosis takes place in a different physical setting) are major factors determining the extent to which false memory reports are made.

Thus, in an experimental setting, free recall tends to yield higher rates of reporting pseudomemories than recognition testing, which produces lower rates.

Some of the earlier studies also tested memory immediately after the suggestion was given (e.g., Labelle et al., 1990; Lynn et al., 1989; McCann & Sheehan, 1988), while other researchers evaluated pseudomemory production at longer retention intervals following the hypnotic experience. As we just indicated, McConkey et al. (1990) found that *the longer after the hypnotic suggestions that a memory test was given, the lower the rate of reports.* Similarly, Spanos, Gywnn, Comer, et al. (1989) found fewer false memory reports were made at a 14-day cross-examination than in an interrogation after seven days. One report (McCann & Sheehan, 1988) did not find a temporal deterioration.

Spanos and Bures (1993–94) examined this issue carefully using 44 hypnotic, 30 simulating, and 33 task-motivated subjects. The subjects were given a suggestion for a false memory of hearing noises while reliving events of an earlier night. The simulating subjects reported the suggested noises more often than hypnotic subjects, and subjects in the three conditions did not differ in endorsing the noises as real following termination of the reliving procedure. In the three conditions, subjects were also equally prone to reverse their pseudomemory reports after receiving hidden observer instructions, and only 6.8% of the high-hypnotizable subjects who were hypnotized maintained a pseudomemory response through the entire experiment. In a hidden observer procedure, it is suggested that some part of the mind knows what occurred in the original situation, and that this part of the mind can provide this information. The results of this study are consistent with a view that *hypnotic pseudomemory production seems to generally represent a response bias* resulting from uncontrolled social psychological variables, *thus consisting of a pseudomemory report, rather than a genuine memory distortion.* This study provides still further confirmation for previous research results (Lynn et al., 1994; McCloskey & Zaragoza, 1985; Murrey et al., 1992; Zaragoza & Koshmidir, 1989).

Similarly, Spanos and McLean (1986) used careful research to examine the question posed by Orne (1979) and Laurence and Perry's (1983) early reports concerning whether hypnosis can create firmly held delusions that will persist. They found that *among high hypnotizable subjects,* one-third (11/33) claimed to have heard a suggested noise—again, hardly an improbable memory. During a posthypnotic interview, two of these subjects equivocated and indicated that the noises may have been imagined. However, under a hidden observer manipulation, *only 6% of the highly hypnotizable subjects* (two of the total 33 highly hypnotizable subjects, and only two of the 11 who reported the "pseudomemory") continued to maintain that they had heard the noises. The remainder were able to distinguish suggestion from reality. These highly respected researchers concluded, "*Although subjects reports were distorted, their memories clearly were not*" (p. 158, emphasis added), and that "*there is certainly little empirical evidence to support the hypothesis that hypnotic interviews are more likely than nonhypnotic ones to produce such distortion*" (p. 159, emphasis added).

However, in conspicuous contrast to such findings, critics of the use of hypnosis with memory seek to portray the hypnotized person as someone who becomes so suggestible and delusional in the hands of a clinician that he or she becomes like the malleable clay in the hands of a sculptor. Such characterizations are nothing new to hypnosis. Historically, hypnosis has been characterized by numerous myths and fictional fears, usually associated with Svengali images of the all-powerful hypnotist. Thus, there have been widespread myths about surrendering one's will, that only gullible persons may be hypnotized, or that someone can be forced to betray secrets. *The latest contemporary myth about hypnosis is that one's mind is so vulnerable to its powers that destructive false memories may often be created.* As with all the other myths, the implication is that one must beware of hypnosis, and certainly not trust its use for memory enhancement. Therefore, in this view, because of the prejudicial nature of hypnosis and its "inherent problems" in distorting memory, "agreeing to be hypnotized is accepting an invitation to engage in fantasy" (Karlin, 1997, p. 32).

Significant perceptual alterations in fact *can* occur in a small minority of highly hypnotizable persons. One of the figures just cited (Spanos & McLean, 1985–86) for the possible creation of a noncomplex, elementary memory—about a potentially commonplace occurrence, with no personal significance or meaning—was about 6% of the mi-

nority of subjects who scored in the high hypnotizability range. Other research has also elucidated how infrequently someone can actually facilitate profound perceptual distortions through hypnosis.

For instance, the capacity to experience visual hallucinations with one's eyes open, as well as auditory hallucinations, have been seen in 3% and 13%–17% respectively of an adult research sample (Hilgard, 1965). There is, however, tremendous individual variability in how real such "hallucinations" seem and in the degree of reality awareness that is maintained, even among this small minority of individuals who report such distortions (Hilgard, 1965; Sheehan & McConkey, 1982). Our review of the literature suggests that, overall, probably less than 5% of those experiencing such phenomena find that the experience seems very real and lifelike (that is, only 5% *of the 3% reporting visual hallucinations in hypnosis*—perhaps three-twentieths of one percent of the general population). For instance, Hilgard (1965) found that about one-fourth of those who in a laboratory meet *experimental* criteria to pass a suggestion for experiencing a kinesthetic hallucination (e.g., moving one's hand to brush away an imaginary mosquito or fly) rate it as "not real at all," while only 2%–5% of lower- and higher-hypnotizables (who passed the criteria for the kinesthetic hallucination) respectively, perceived it to be "very lifelike and real."

Thus, overall, hypnotic perceptual alterations so profound that they would appear almost true-to-life and would seem to have potential of being difficult to distinguish from reality *can only be experienced by an extraordinarily small percentage of people.* In the field of hypnosis, a fairly small percent of the general population (usually identified as about 6%) are referred to as "hypnotic virtuosos" (Green, Lynn, & Carlson, 1992; Register & Kihlstrom, 1986), with the capacity to possibly experience a transient delusion stemming from a hypnotic suggestion.

Noble and McConkey (1995) studied the effects of suggestions for an improbable event, namely that a person's sex had changed (e.g., "You are not a man, you are a woman") that were given to hypnotic virtuosos, to low-hypnotizable subjects simulating being hypnotized, and to high-hypnotizable subjects. Hypnotic virtuosos rated the suggested delusion as significantly more real than did high-hypnotizables or simulators, and were more likely to maintain this

response when confronted with contradictory information *while they were still in hypnosis.* This suggested that their self- reports of experiences while in a hypnotic state (not necessarily after a period of time out of hypnosis) "cannot be accounted for solely by the demand characteristics of the setting" (p. 73). So we do find that among some persons in a very limited subgroup of the population ("hypnotic virtuosos"), hypnotic suggestions can be experienced with a quality of reality that may be convincing. However, it must be noted that Noble and McConkey (1995) did not use the Experiential Analysis Technique (Sheehan & McConkey, 1982) for a detailed dissection of the subjective experience of subjects, nor was there any attempt to have subjects experience these suggested effects for periods of time after hypnosis had been concluded, or to have them debriefed later in a separate context by someone other than the hypnotist. Only this kind of experimental rigor would allow evaluation of the degree to which subjects were responding to demand characteristics, having transient experiences that felt somewhat genuine but were still distinguishable as suggested experiences, or experiencing something that felt compellingly real and persisted beyond the brief hypnotic experience.

The Noble and McConkey (1995) results thus do not mean that all high-hypnotizable individuals, or even all "hypnotic virtuosos," will verbalize *and believe* a suggestion for profound perceptual alteration. As Spanos and McLean (1986) concluded, although the *reports* of some hypnotic subjects to their experimenters may be altered, their actual memories clearly are not usually distorted, except in rare instances.

Sheehan and McConkey (1982) did use their Experiential Analysis Technique (EAT) to examine the internal cognitive and imagery responses of subjects experiencing various hypnotic phenomena. Their highly respected work clearly demonstrates that even highly hypnotizable subjects do not simply become mindless, mentally pliable automatons without adequate "reality orientation." Rather, *overall, even highly hypnotizable persons are found to retain the ability to monitor external events as they process suggestions.* Further, Sheehan and McConkey's (1982) research documented that hypnotized persons remain responsive to the demand characteristics of experimenters, and they often still actively try to please experimenters (Lynn et al., 1989; McCann & Sheehan, 1987, 1988, 1989)—thus producing pseudomemory reports for experimenters. Hypnotizability, even high hypnotizability, is not synonymous with gullibility or acquiescence (Bowers, 1976).

Thus, we find that laboratory research confirms that *the great majority of hypnotized people, including persons who are highly hypnotizable, do not seem to generally mistake hypnotically suggested fantasies for real events*, as alleged by those perpetuating the most recent in the long line of myths about hypnosis. Instead, available studies substantiate that when subjects are encouraged to provide honest and candid descriptions, pseudomemory reports appear to be minimized (e.g., Lynn et al., 1989; Murrey et al., 1992; Spanos & Bures, 1993–94; Spanos et al., 1989a), just as they are when the person is questioned away from the compliance pressure of the experimental testing context (e.g., McConkey et al., 1990).

As Spanos and Bures (1993–94) discovered, hypnosis can be used to produce *reports* of pseudomemories, but the highest probability is that the vast majority of these productions simply represent biased reporting to comply with expectations of the experimenter, rather than genuine false memories of enduring quality. In addition, and very important for clinicians, research has documented that *giving hypnotic suggestions for age regression and reexperiencing a past event, like those used by therapists in psychotherapeutic work, is not a variable associated with the creation of pseudomemories* (Lynn, Milano, & Weekes, 1991).

These findings provide further support for the research on hypnosis and accuracy of memory reviewed earlier in this chapter. With the use of hypnosis, when leading questions were not used, Griffin's (1980) experimental results caused him to conclude that "hypnosis will not have an adverse effect upon a witness giving false or misleading answers to the investigators, nor will it result in confabulation if the questions are not leading and are prepared properly" (p. 389). As noted elsewhere in our book, such findings in the field of hypnosis also receive vigorous support from the experimental literature on imagery—a procedure that strongly overlaps hypnosis. When imagery has been combined with free recall, it has consistently produced enhanced recall,

without an increase in error rate. We find that there is abundant support for the conclusion that it is not hypnosis or imagery that is problematic, but suggestive interviewing (social influence).

Perhaps the outcomes of the third generation studies on hypnosis and pseudomemory should not surprise us. Once again, turning to authorities in hypnosis more than a century ago, the current findings correspond with what the famous hypnosis pioneer and astute observer Bernheim (1888/1973) concluded from his uncontrolled experiments: "The memory of the suggested event does not appear to be as persistent as the memory of the real event" (p. 177). Bernheim sensed that suggested pseudomemories did not irrevocably destroy or replace other memories and could be distinguished from actual memories. He further concluded that "there is nothing in induced sleep which may not occur in the waking condition" (p. 179), once again supporting what the finest of our modern experimentalists are finding.

Recent research has also produced evidence that hypnotically produced reports of pseudomemories can be breached by exposure to evidence associated with the original events (e.g., McCann & Sheehan, 1987, 1989), and that pseudomemory reports are low when the object of the pseudomemory suggestion is more verifiable (Lynn, Milano, & Weekes, 1992; McCann & Sheehan, 1987, 1988). McCann and Sheehan (1988), for instance, found the *reported* pseudomemories for nighttime noises that would be difficult to verify and not unlikely to occur (like those used by Laurence and Perry, 1983) were at 50% among high-hypnotizables. But, when they changed to a more objective and verifiable stimulus (a videotape of a bank robbery), distortions that were suggested dropped to 23% in free recall reporting and to only 6% when recognition testing was used.

Given all these factors, perhaps it should not surprise us that the baseline frequency rate for the production of pseudomemory reports in a highly hypnotizable population varies from a spectacular 80% to 0%, depending on the nature of the testing circumstances, of the pseudomemory suggested, and the demand characteristics of the experiment. Such incredible variability provides further confirmation of the flimsiness of existing evidence that hypnotic suggestion contributes anything unique to the production of genuine false memories. And, when experimental controls are introduced into research, the number of high-hypnotizable subjects who continue to maintain a belief in a simple and not implausible memory ranges in the literature between 0% (Lynn et al., 1991, 1992), 2.5% (McConkey et al., 1990), 6%–6.8% (Spanos & Bures, 1993–94; Spanos & McLean, 1986), and 12.5% (Lynn et al., 1989). However, in well controlled research, these rates appear to be no different for subjects who are not hypnotized but who receive waking suggestions (Murrey et al., 1992) or are merely simulating that they are hypnotized (Lynn et al., 1989, 1992; Spanos & Bures, 1993–94).

Given the strong and consistent nature of laboratory research evidence, in contrast to the claims made on the basis of uncontrolled anecdotal case reports (e.g., Orne's or Spiegel's videotaped case presentations; Laurence & Perry, 1983; Ofshe & Watters, 1993), *a scientifically minded person faced with making a probability statement about the likelihood that an actual false memory was produced by hypnotic suggestion would have to state that by far the greatest probability is that this did not occur, except in a minority of select subjects (hypnotic virtuosos) under very interview-specific conditions.* What is much more likely to have occurred is that a subject may have sought to please a hypnotist and may have *reported* something corresponding with his or her perception of what the hypnotist wanted him/her to experience based on the nature of the suggestions, but that the subject is very likely capable of distinguishing reality from suggested fantasy. We are not suggesting that it is impossible for someone to develop a pseudomemory or false belief about his/her past, either from social influence outside of a hypnotic context or through hypnosis, and especially when the "memory" is about a period which the person does not recall and if the "memory" is congruent with his/her perceptions. *But the research seems compelling that hypnotic techniques do not appear to contribute anything unique to producing pseudomemory reports. Furthermore, hypnotic suggestion appears insufficiently potent to produce a genuine alteration in memory (as contrasted with a pseudomemory report) in the great majority of cases, although it may be possible to do so in a very small percentage (e.g., less than 6%) of the highly hypnotizable population of people.*

Why is it that high-hypnotizable individuals, compared to low-hypnotizable persons, are just as prone to *report* pseudomemories out of hypnosis as in hypnosis? We don't know, but it may be interesting to speculate. Perhaps further research will demonstrate that the trait or intrapersonal quality of high hypnotizability is only a mildly influential variable, and that the primary variable, social influence, also impacts nonhypnotized high-hypnotizable individuals and can often create such reports in them in a waking state. Recent research by Eisen and by Lynn compels us to consider this possibility.

Another hypothesis that may explain why many studies find an association between higher hypnotizability and reporting of pseudomemories *either in or out of hypnosis* is that high-hypnotizable individuals may be physiologically "hard wired" differently from persons low in responsiveness to hypnosis. It appears that persons high in hypnotic responsiveness more easily experience altered states of consciousness spontaneously (Beahrs, 1988; Conn, 1958; Dumas, 1964; Frankel, 1975; Spiegel & Spiegel, 1978/1987), and may, in fact, be in a different state of consciousness most of the time compared to low-hypnotizables. Fascinatingly, evidence for this has been documented by Kumar and Pekala (1989), who found that, while simply sitting with their eyes open and without any hypnotic induction procedure, high-hypnotizables reported significantly greater altered state of consciousness experiences than low-hypnotizables.

Research on brainwave activity associated with hypnotic responsivity also supports such a hypothesis. There is considerable evidence that greater theta brain wave activity is found in high-hypnotizable individuals (Apkiner, Ulett, & Itil, 1971; Crawford, 1990; Galbraith, London, Leibovitz, Cooper, & Hart, 1970; Graffin, Ray, & Lundy, 1995; Sabourin, 1982; Sabourin et al., 1990; Tebecis, Provins, Farnbach, & Pentony, 1975). For example, Tebecis et al. (1975) found subjects experienced in self-hypnosis produced more theta activity *both while waking and in hypnosis* compared with low-hypnotizables who had never been hypnotized. Crawford (1990), in a sophisticated study, reported that high-hypnotizable persons exhibited significantly greater power than persons low in hypnotic responsivity in the high theta range (5.5–7.5 Hz). When cold pressor pain was induced, and during pain along with hypnotic anesthesia suggestions, there were no differences between hemispheres in low subjects. Highs, however, demonstrated significantly more left hemisphere dominance when they experienced pain, and a dramatic left shift during hypnotic anesthesia and dissociation from a painful stimulus, with a significant increase in right hemisphere theta power and a significant decrease in left hemisphere theta power. She hypothesized that this reflects hippocampal generated theta.

In an exceptionally well designed study, Sabourin et al. (1990) documented that high-hypnotizables generated substantially more mean theta power than lows *during both waking and hypnotic conditions* in occipital, central, and frontal locations, confirming earlier studies. Both high- and low-hypnotizables demonstrated increased mean theta power in hypnosis and a uniform decrease in theta when coming out of hypnosis. Still another recent study (Graffin et al., 1995) confirmed that high-hypnotizables had greater frontal and temporal theta *even in a baseline condition* than low-hypnotizables. In this study, theta increased in all subjects in posterior areas (parietal and occipital) during hypnotic induction. But, *during a prehypnotic baseline, high-hypnotizable individuals had more theta brainwave activity* in the frontal areas (frontal and temporal cortex) than low-hypnotizables, suggesting a greater state of attentional readiness or continuous concentration of attention in high-hypnotizables compared to persons low in responsivity. These findings, which are consistent with previous research (Sabourin & Cutcomb, 1980; Sabourin et al., 1990; Tebecis et al., 1975), suggest that hypnotic susceptibility possesses a stable trait-like nature.

All of these findings may relate to Barber's (Barber et al., 1974) conclusion, reaffirming opinions expressed by Bernheim in the 1800s, that hypnotic effects (i.e., the elicitation of phenomena associated with hypnosis) may occur without a hypnotic induction procedure. It was Bernheim's (1888/1973) clinical observation that "many somnambulists are susceptible to suggestion in the waking condition" and that "there is, then, reason for thinking that the somnambulist often goes spontaneously into the somnambulistic condition of consciousness" (p. 155). Bernheim further believed that "hypnotism does not really create a new condition: there is nothing in induced sleep which may not occur in the waking condition, in a rudimentary degree in many cases, but in some to an equal extent. Some people

are naturally susceptible to suggestion" (p. 179). Many contemporary authorities also believe that hypnotic response occurs spontaneously (Beahrs, 1988; Dumas, 1964; Frankel, 1975; Spiegel & Spiegel, 1978/1987) and through informal encouragement and suggestions delivered conversationally (Erickson, 1980).

Findings by Pekala also suggest that behavioral progressive relaxation may produce greater hypnoidal effects than hypnosis among low hypnotizables, and phenomenological effects that are roughly comparable to those produced with hypnosis among high hypnotizables (Pekala & Forbes, 1988; Pekala, Forbes, & Contrisciani, 1988–89), despite the fact that "progressive muscle relaxation" is commonly thought of as a behavioral technique rather than hypnosis. The implications of this finding with regard to memory have not been explored in research.

RELATED AREAS OF RESEARCH: DISSOCIATIVE PHENOMENA

Fantasy-Prone Patients and Dissociative Patients

Some researchers have suggested that highly hypnotizable individuals are simply fantasy-prone. Such arguments refer to the fact that hypnotic responsiveness and imaginativeness were found to be associated by Wilson and Barber (1981, 1983) in their research on the fantasy-prone individual. They suggested that persons who have a high frequency of fantasy experiences in everyday life tend to be very responsive hypnotic subjects. However, subsequent studies (Council & Huff, 1990; Green, Lynn, Rhue, Williams, & Mare, 1989; Lynn & Rhue, 1988; Rhue & Lynn, 1987; Siuta, 1990) have found that fantasizers were more hypnotizable than nonfantasizers, but that hypnotizability and fantasyproneness were only mildly correlated (e.g., about .25).

Barrett's (1991, 1992) work has identified two distinct subgroups of high-hypnotizable subjects who appear to differ in highly significant ways: *fantasizers* and *dissociaters*. Interestingly, waking (nonhypnotic) imagery of 16 out of 19 fantasizers was found to be "entirely realistic" (compared to none of 15 dissociaters), 14 of 19 could experience orgasm strictly through absorption in fantasy without any physical stimulation (compared to none of the 15 dissociaters), and the earliest memories of fantasizers were all identified as before the age of three, and before the age of two in 11 of 19 subjects. In contrast, none of the dissociaters had a memory before age three, and six dissociaters reported their earliest memory as between ages six and eight. Although all subjects in both groups were highly hypnotizable, fantasizers experienced hypnotic amnesia only when it was suggested (and there was no spontaneous amnesia reported), six fantasizers were unable to experience amnesia even when it was suggested, and only five of 19 experienced total suggested amnesia. In comparison, all 15 dissociaters experienced total suggested amnesia, nine of 15 reported spontaneous amnesia, and some dissociaters experienced persistence of amnesia even after suggestions were given for recall of hypnotic events. Furthermore, only three of 19 fantasizers experienced amnesia for their (waking) daydreams, while 14 of 15 dissociaters experienced this phenomenon.

While all dissociaters needed time to reach what they perceived as a deep trance, all fantasizers felt that they rapidly entered deep trances and that it was very similar to what they experienced when fantasizing in daily life. While no fantasizers reported recurring nightmares, six dissociaters reported them. Trauma also appeared to be much more common in the background of dissociaters compared with fantasizers, and no fantasizers came close to meeting criteria for diagnosis of having a dissociative disorder or PTSD, while five dissociaters met criteria for a dissociative disorder diagnosis. While both fantasizers and dissociaters could become absorbed in external stimuli (e.g., a movie), this absorption was more often combined with experiencing amnesia (e.g., after a horror movie for the content of the movie) by dissociaters. Additionally, psychophysiological reactivity seemed more extreme among dissociaters, with half of them experiencing symptoms of false pregnancy previously.

Barrett's work offers meaningful leads for future researchers. Her data fit with the conception that a subpopulation is prone to demonstrating amnesia for life circumstances that are distressing, and that these are persons who often have demonstrable background experiences of abuse and trauma. In contrast, there does seem to be a fantasy-prone group predisposed to live in a compelling self-hypnotic-like fantasy world wherein it is difficult for them to distinguish fantasy from reality. Barrett's research tentatively suggests that these individuals readily become absorbed in deep trance because they live much of their life in a similar state. Such persons seem to believe they can recall things from exceptionally early ages, so early that memories are much less likely to be reliable and valid.

In this regard, there have been studies finding a relationship between fantasy-proneness and reports of childhood abuse (Bryant, 1995; Lynn & Rhue, 1988; Nash et al., 1984; Wilson & Barber, 1983). Supporting Barrett's work, Bryant (1995) found that the earlier someone claimed to have been abused, the higher s/he tended to score on a measure of absorption and imaginative involvement, as well as on measures of adult recollections of imaginative activities and fantasies during childhood and of how much fantasy is involved in current adult functioning. This supports a hypothesis that fantasy-proneness may influence reported memories of abuse. On the other hand, Rhue, Lynn, and Sandberg (1995), evaluating children who had actually been sexually abused (usually not severely, violently, or repetitively), did not find support for the hypothesis that they would score higher in fantasy-proneness.

Relevant to these findings, Labelle, Laurence, Nadon, and Perry (1990) found that subjects who were both highly hypnotizable and who had a strong preference for an imagic cognitive style were more likely to engage in pseudomemory reporting than subjects who scored high on only one of these factors. Thus, it is possible that the trait of high hypnotizability (but, again, not the use of hypnosis) and fantasy-proneness may interact to encourage some pseudomemory reports. Whether persons with these combined qualities, when offered suggestions for pseudomemories, actually tend to believe them more often (creating actual memory distortions), is not known. But we might hypothesize for purposes of future research that individuals who are both highly hypnotizable and fantasy-prone may be more likely to report accepting a suggestion for a pseudomemory. Whether they might also have more difficulty distinguishing a suggested memory from reality should also be clarified. Future research should address these hypotheses.

It must be emphasized that Bryant's (1995) correlational data cannot establish causation. It must also be recognized that it is possible that traumatic events that occur in early childhood, before adequate intellectual skills have developed that may allow one to cope somewhat better with abuse, may encourage a developing child to turn to fantasy as a means of distancing from aversive or traumatic situations (Powers, 1991). Because fantasy-prone thinking often occurs in young children anyway (LeBaron, Zeltzer, & Fanurik, 1988), it may be only natural for them to turn to fantasy as a way of dissociating from overwhelming situations. Rhue et al. (1995) did find that in children physical punishment was more reliably associated with measures of fantasy, dissociation, and imagination than were milder forms of sexual abuse. The most recent literature on fantasy-proneness (Rauschenberger & Lynn, 1995) does suggest that, no matter what the etiology or direction of influence, twice as many of the most fantasy-prone college students as of the medium fantasy-prone students have an Axis I psychiatric diagnosis. Furthermore, highly fantasy-prone young adults had more frequently been diagnosed with depression in the past and reported more dissociative experiences and symptoms.

Newman and Baumeister (1996) recently theorized about the variables accounting for reports of UFO abductions. They suggested an etiology rooted in a desire to escape from self-awareness and masochistic fantasies in persons high in fantasy proneness. Alleged abductees, they speculate, then elaborate on hypnogogic hallucinations through the use of hypnosis, used with them by a UFO devotee who shares their beliefs and expectations.

A discussion commentary by Orne, Whitehouse, Orne, and Dinges (1996) and another recent publication (Orne et al., 1996) reinforces Orne's (1979) long-held position that "hypnosis provides a license for fantasy" (Orne et al., 1996, p. 172), but then introduces a new wrinkle to false memory arguments. Orne now takes the position, based on retrospective analyses of the methodologically compromised research we already thoroughly reviewed (e.g., Dinges et al., 1992; Whitehouse et al., 1991) that even low-hypnotizables are vulnerable to contamination from the inherently corrupting influence of hypnosis—a position that we believe cannot be supported by the bulk of research.

On the other hand, Lynn and Kirsch (1996) debunk Newman and Baumeister's (1996) theorizing:

> However, they present an unnecessary and exaggerated account of the role of hypnosis and fantasy proneness. False memories can be created with or without hypnosis, and the role of hypnosis in their creation is likely to be quite small. Similarly, the available data suggest that the trait of fantasy proneness is not likely to be of great importance. . . . Hypnosis does not reliably produce more false memories than are produced in a variety of nonhypnotic situations in which misleading information is conveyed to participants. (p. 151)

Lynn and Kirsch (1996) further note that "the role of hypnosis in enhancing confidence in false memories is also exaggerated" (p. 152), and they criticized the "outdated view" of hypnosis taken by Newman and Baumeister (1996). Lynn and Kirsch (1996) presented recent research evidence (Lynn & Pezzo, 1994) supporting the important role of preexisting, culturally derived beliefs in the formation of UFO scenarios.

The hypotheses of Newman and Baumeister (1996) were also challenged by McLeod, Corbisier, and Mack (1996). They noted that, although hypnosis is often used by UFO "investigators," it cannot account for the origin of these accounts because 30% of them are obtained without hypnosis, and 60%–70% of the information gathered by persons where hypnosis is used is obtained before hypnosis was used—a fact reinforcing the possible etiologic role of preexisting beliefs held by subjects. But even more damning of the conjecture that hypnosis creates such "memories" is the fact that studies have documented that persons alleging alien abduction are not highly hypnotizable (Rodeghier, Goodpaster, & Blatterbauer, 1991), including when they have been compared to control subjects (Spanos et al., 1993). Furthermore, when abduction reports which were elaborated through hypnosis were compared with material elicited in a nonhypnotic state, the material was found to not differ in basic structure from that of persons alleging a clear waking memory for the events, where hypnosis was not used. Thus, the premise that hypnosis creates false memories of alien abductions remains unsupportable by science.

In the field of hypnosis, we differentiate three

types of memory recall: hypermnesia, revivification, and partial age regression. *Hypermnesia* pertains to hypnotic suggestions for enhanced recollection. In a *revivification*, the hypnotized person has a sense of actually being the regressed age. A person experiencing a *partial age regression* to the age of five finds that part of her feels five years old, and part of her retains a sense of adult perspective. Perry and Walsh (1978) discovered that about half of highly hypnotizable persons report this kind of "duality." The other highly hypnotizable subjects tend to experience a revivification—actually feeling as if they are the regressed age and even temporarily losing a sense of their adult sense of perspective or identity while in hypnosis. Subjects who are able to respond to a dissociative suggestion for having a hidden observer have also been found to be more likely to report experiencing duality in age regression (Laurence & Perry, 1981; Nadon, D'Eon, McConkey, Laurence, & Perry, 1988; Nogrady et al., 1983) and to express belief in the accuracy of a hypnotically suggested pseudomemory (Laurence et al., 1986; Laurence & Perry, 1983). These are other variables worthy of investigation as we seek to further understand the phenomenon of pseudomemory reports.

The Influence and Recall of Chemically Dissociated Memory

Hypnosis and Implicit Memories for Hearing Under Anesthesia

One final body of research literature has relevance concerning the reliability of hypnosis in accessing memories, particularly memories for events where there is amnesia. This is the area of *chemically dissociated memory* and the use of hypnosis to explore implicit memories for events heard under chemical anesthesia.

Can events that we have experienced but for which we have no conscious recall influence our behavior and feelings? The answer is "yes," and cases from the hearing under anesthesia literature certainly illustrate this. In examining and understanding the whole issue of amnesia for memories and implicit memory, it is vitally important to become familiar with the literature on hearing and awareness under chemical anesthesia. Here, instead of looking at retrograde amnesia, we are examining

chemically produced anterograde amnesia. Just as clinical and forensic situations have demonstrated that memory enhancement for personal and emotional/traumatic memories may occur with hypnosis, clinically oriented research has found that what is heard under an adequate plane of chemical anesthesia (wherein the patient is left with a conscious amnesia for what was said during surgery) may sometimes be recalled accurately through the use of hypnosis or be spontaneously remembered.

Of further relevance to the recovered memory debate is the fact that there are verified cases of memories returning for events that had been experienced and mentally recorded, but for which the patient had been amnestic because the event occurred under anesthesia—a relevant parallel to repressed memory cases seen in therapy. These cases further illustrate, as with the forensic hypnosis cases, that there is implicit perception—that is, much more information may be recorded in someone's mind than can be consciously recalled or verbalized. Although the mind does not work like a tape recorder, indelibly encoding information that is not open to further influence, there is such a thing as preconscious processing, which may leave implicit (unconscious or preconscious) memories. We develop *implicit memories* for information that we have not focused on or have not attended to, such as we sometimes find in clinical settings where investigative hypnosis elicits further details. As experimentalists (Zacks, Hasher, & Sanft, 1982) have found, we seem to have automatic memory processes hard-wired to operate, even in the absence of attention to the data, so that unattended information is still recorded.

Munglani and Jones (1994) recently reviewed studies on information processing in anesthesia. They concluded that information processing and implicit memory during general anesthesia are real phenomena, and may occur even during "adequate" anesthesia. Anesthetic agents tend not to inhibit processes in the hippocampus that are associated with learning; further, some anesthetic agents spare metabolically the auditory pathway. Thus, when Levinson (1993) gave anesthesia to a cat "until it seemed that the cat had died," he found that "right up to that moment [when it died] the cat responded with an alarm reaction in all the [EEG] leads, to the sound of a dog barking" (p. 499).

Munglani and Jones (1994) further determined

in their research review, as did Goldmann (1990), that salient and repetitive stimuli increase the chances of recall of material heard under anesthesia. They additionally proposed that there may be subgroups of patients, such as highly hypnotizable individuals, who may be more prone to process information under anesthesia. Their scrutiny of the literature further led to the conclusion that amnestic memories of conversations and sounds heard under chemical anesthesia can be retrieved, but because general anesthesia dissociates explicit and implicit memory, tests of the latter must be used along with both verbal and nonverbal methods of retrieval. They further recognized that information presented intraoperatively (an implicit, amnestic memory) has the capacity to alter performance in psychological tasks postoperatively.

Although noting that events that occur under surgical anesthesia are not always reliably stored in implicit memory, Kihlstrom and Schacter (1990) wrote:

> Just as the failure of conscious recollection does not necessarily imply a prior failure of conscious perception, neither does it imply a complete failure of memory. It is entirely possible that surgical events are perceptually processed, at least to some degree, that residual traces of this perceptual activity are encoded and remain available in memory storage, and that these memories can influence the patient's post-surgical experience, thought, and action—all outside of conscious awareness. (p. 26)

When it is believed that this may occur with memories for events that occurred under chemical anesthesia, why can not this likewise occur with memories for childhood events that transpired at such a young age that verbal, narrative encoding may be impaired? Thus, applying Kihlstrom and Schacter's (1990) statement to childhood memory, we might suggest that a failure of *conscious recollection* of a childhood memory does not necessarily imply a failure of perception or memory; traces of such memories can be encoded, remain available, and influence behavior outside conscious awareness.

Milton Erickson (1963) described an experiment performed in 1932. He wished to ascertain if a man could recall further childhood memories, which had not previously been explored in extensive therapy,

through stimulation from questions given under a deep plane of anesthesia. Under ether anesthesia, 20–25 questions were asked in various order and with a number of repetitions. Erickson indicated:

> In general summary, it was learned that he could spontaneously, that is, without any leading question except, "Were you asked something else?" or, "What did you remember?" or, "What comes to your mind now?" recall questions asked him in deep surgical anaesthesia; that he recalled "forgotten" memories that had not come forth in his analysis; that he could remember 70 to 80% of the questions from his [the man's questions] list; 50 to 60% of the questions from my list [Dr. Erickson's questions had never been seen by the patient]; feelings of resentment when I mixed questions from both lists, and when I changed (deliberately) the wording of questions he had prepared. He also expressed irritation that I had "willfully" alternated questions from the lists, and had asked them in an order different from the actual order of his lists. (p. 32)

Although we have no way of determining if Erickson obtained independent corroboration of the "forgotten memories" that were evoked, what was significant is that Erickson successfully ascertained that someone could remember a chemically dissociated memory—that is, that amnestic material can be consciously recalled.

Cheek (1959, 1964, 1966) reported successful cases of patients accurately remembering events and conversations that transpired during surgery through the use of hypnosis, sometimes reproducing the exact words that were verified to have been expressed during surgery. Since research has suggested that usually less than 1% of patients in a general population undergoing surgical anesthesia have conscious recall of any of the events transpiring during the surgery (Bennett, 1988; Jordening & Pedersen, 1991; Liu, Thorp, Graham, & Aitkenhead, 1991; Wilson, Vaughan, & Stephen, 1975), such real world reports, although anecdotal rather than experimentally controlled, should be regarded as vitally informative.

Levinson (1969, 1990) described controlled research in which four of ten patients who experienced an unusually deep plane of anesthesia later correctly recalled "everything the anaesthetist had said" during a staged "crisis" during surgery. This recall was facilitated through the assistance of hypnotic ideo-motor signaling techniques (Cheek & LeCron, 1968; Hammond & Cheek, 1988; Rossi & Cheek, 1988). In this mock crisis, the anesthetist read a script with realism, suggesting the patient was "too blue," and that he was not satisfied with the patient's condition. Then, after a few moments of oxygenating the patient, he expressed satisfaction with the patient's condition and allowed the operation to continue. The four patients, in hypnotic age regression, "could describe other incidents that had taken place during the operation" (Levinson, 1969, p. 74). "They knew who had been talking, where he had been standing, and described the urgency of the moment. They understood the crisis and described a feeling of relief when the operation continued" (Levinson, 1990, p. 14). Four other patients, despite continuing amnesia, demonstrated an "alarm reaction" when the events were explored under hypnosis and demonstrated partial recall. "They knew who had been talking. They could recall a snatch of a word. They became extremely anxious. Some burst out of the trance and were reluctant to be re-hypnotized" (Levinson, 1990, p. 14). One of these four patients correctly remembered that the surgeon had said that the inferior dental artery was cut, because the surgeon said this to an assistant. This actual event, accurately remembered, seemed to block out complete recall of the staged crisis. Perhaps it is important, given the research reviewed earlier that implies that hypnosis may be more effective in facilitating recall for events occurring days or weeks later (e.g., Geiselman & Machlovitz, 1987) and Bennett's (1988) findings concerning successful recall in relation to longer times following surgery, that Levinson hypnotized the patients and used an ideomotor review of the surgery one month after discharge from the hospital, as contrasted with soon after surgery.

Psychosomatic Disorders Following Anesthesia

"Beached whale" and "fat lady" comments that were made by derogatory surgeons have also been accurately recalled through hypnosis (Bennett, 1988). In one case noted by Bennett, this was the only one of 55 patients to have been insulted directly and the only one who experienced unexplained complications following surgery! In another case, a woman who postoperatively suffered many autonomic and vegetative symptoms for several days suddenly recalled her surgeon making this kind of belittling remark and was able to confirm through an operating room nurse that the disparaging remark had, in fact, been made.

Furthermore, there are numerous clinical reports (e.g., Ewin, 1990; Goldmann, Shah, & Hebden, 1987; Levinson, 1965) indicating that after negative suggestions that were apparently made to patients while under a plane of anesthesia (but that in some cases have not been independently confirmed, much like we see with cases involving alleged memories of abuse) were recognized during hypnosis, negative psychosomatic symptoms that seemed to be traumatic sequelae ceased. Thus, for instance, Howard (1987) described a woman who suffered chronic insomnia for three years. In age regression, she remembered hearing an anesthesiologist remark, "She will sleep the sleep of death." Once the patient "uncovered" this remark, she overcame her insomnia and remained symptom-free on three-year follow-up.

Levinson (1965) recounted the case of a woman with facial injuries and scars from a car accident that required reconstruction. While inspecting her lip in surgery, her surgeon remarked, "Good gracious! It may not be a cyst at all; it may be a cancer!" Following surgery, the patient had no conscious memory of this remark or of anything transpiring during surgery. She complained, nonetheless, of depression. In hypnotic ideomotor exploration, the woman initially reported an innocuous surgical experience, but during the ideomotor review became agitated and spontaneously realerted from hypnosis, afterward becoming steadily more depressed. Three weeks later under hypnosis, she remembered the surgeon's remark, "Good gracious!" She then said, "He's saying this 'may be malignant,'" substituting the word "malignant" for "cancer." Despite conscious, waking reassurance by her surgeon following the surgery that her cyst was benign, and the fact that she had seen the laboratory report saying the cyst was nonmalignant, the woman had become increasingly depressed and fearful, seemingly because of the unconscious, implicit memory. Once the amnesia was pierced and the dissociated memory restored, reassurance proved effective and her symptoms resolved.

Similarly, following a taped hypnotic induction

and suggestions to remember being back in the operating room, Rath (1982) discovered a patient who recalled an anxiety-provoking, unexpected actual event that occurred during surgery. When asked during hypnosis if he recalled anything from surgery, he indicated, "Yeah, that they operated on the wrong side." Review of the surgery found that midway through a nurse came in with a form and asked the surgeon, "Doctor, what side are you operating on?" The surgeon said, "Left." A different nurse said, "You'd better not or you're on the wrong side" (p. 53). Everyone laughed because the surgeon had spoken incorrectly, and he then corrected his verbal error.

Nonverbal Exploration of Implicit Memory

In addition to validated case reports (e.g., Cheek, 1959, 1966; Ewin, 1990; Levinson, 1965, 1969, 1990; Rath, 1982; Rossi & Cheek, 1988), several experimental studies of chemically dissociated memory (two by Bennett, 1988; Levinson, 1969; and Rath, 1982) have shown that hypnotic ideomotor signaling may have merit as a means to explore implicit memory (cf. also, Rossi & Cheek, 1988). Rath (1982) evaluated memory for suggestions he personally administered during surgeries, under chemical anesthesia, and for which patients had amnesia postsurgically. Afterwards, patients listened to experimental and control messages presented randomly, providing ideomotor finger signals concerning whether they had heard or not heard the intraoperative messages. Ideomotor responses were found to accurately discriminate between messages they received versus those they did not receive with statistically significant results. Although hypnotic recognition testing through ideomotor signaling was certainly imperfect, this study seems significant for two additional reasons. First, Rath used a random sample (N=44) which we must assume likely included medium- and low-hypnotizable patients. Supporting this probability is the fact that the experiment produced a bimodal distribution of memory scores like we see in a hypnotizability distribution (Hilgard, 1965). Second, memory was generally evaluated later on the same day as the surgery, and as we will review shortly, greater memory for events occurring under anesthesia occurs with recall efforts that occur at longer time intervals fol-

lowing the surgery. And, as reviewed earlier in the chapter, hypnosis itself also appears to be most effective in enhancing recall after a longer time interval. In this study, memory testing occurred at a time when patients were maximally uncomfortable and under maximal levels of narcotic use. Despite Rath's using a random sample rather than higher hypnotizable subjects, and notwithstanding the almost immediate effort at hypnotic recognition of what occurred, 12 subjects recalled at chance level or below, while 32 subjects recalled above the level expected by chance.

In two other studies, Bennett (1988) tested Cheek's findings about the utility of ideomotor finger signaling. He obtained partial verbatim recall for material for which there was conscious amnesia, validating to Bennett "the existence of memory systems that are highly resistant to verbal systems but accessible through nonverbal means" (p. 226). Bennett's studies included the use of hypnotic-like suggestions given under anesthesia, for which there was amnesia, but which many subjects nonetheless responded to behaviorally when cues were given in a postsurgical context. Clearly, it was Bennett's (1987, 1988) opinion that implicit memory information concerning surgical events, for which there is conscious amnesia, is more likely to be accessed through nonverbal (e.g., ideomotor) methods than through verbalizations. And some of the finest proof for information processing occurring during stage one sleep—a state resembling that seen with highly hypnotizable individuals where there is a great deal of theta brainwave activity—comes from response to ideomotor suggestions (Evans, 1990).

When Bennett (1993) more recently analyzed 12 studies of auditory perception under anesthesia, nonverbal measures were the only variable that was statistically significant—that is, positive memories were significantly more often revealed when nonverbal measures were used that did not require the patient to access conscious processes and make verbalized responses. Implicit (amnestic) memories seem to be more successfully accessed through nonverbal behavior than through conscious verbal recall. We must remember that the fact that there is no conscious (verbal) recall, does not mean memory has not been recorded (Squire, 1982). Is it only a coincidence that amnestic patients with Korsakoff's syndrome were found to perform poorly on tests using verbal recall that required explicit, effortful recall, but that when a free association word completion task known to elicit implicit memory was used, their memory increased to the level of normal control subjects (Graf, Squire, & Mandler, 1984)? In a similar fashion, Erickson (1936), noted that "the usefulness of the word-association test in detecting the presence of concealed or repressed memories is well recognized."

Where we have a patient under chemical anesthesia, information that is encoded is part of implicit memory rather than explicit, declarative memory. Thus, when amnesia-producing drugs like scopolamine have been used, studies found that information is encoded, but retrieval is impaired and dependent on the type of memory task used (Caine, Weingartner, Ludlow, Cudahy, & Wehry, 1981). Bennett (1988) explained:

> What scopolamine appears to do is to disrupt efficient encoding processes, leading not to an absence of retention but to a deficiency in effective retrieval. Intentional processes are disrupted by the amnestics, but the automatic processes of pattern recognition are not. (pp. 201–202)

Methodology and Outcomes in Implicit Memory for Surgery Studies

The methodological shortcomings of the research on recognition or memory for implicit memories of things heard under surgical anesthesia parallel the design deficiencies that have plagued traditional laboratory studies of memory and hypnosis. Many, for example, have used paired-associate letter-word associations or memory for words (e.g., Cork, Kihlstrom & Schacter, 1993; Dubovsky & Trustman, 1976; Kihlstrom, Schacter, Cork, Hurt, & Behr, 1990; Millar & Watkinson, 1983), memory for nonsense syllables or nonsense words (e.g., Block, Ghoneim, Sum Ping, & Ali, 1991; Eich, Reeves, & Katz, 1985; Loftus, Schooler, Loftus, & Glauber, 1985), familiarity judgments (Stoltzy, Couture, & Edmonds, 1986, 1987), a poem (Lewis, Jenkinson, & Wilson, 1973), lists of exemplars of semantic categories (e.g., colors, fruit) (Block et al., 1991; Bonebakker, Bonke, Klein, Wolters, & Hop, 1993; Villemur, Plourde, Lussier, & Normandin, 1993; Westmoreland, Sebel, Winograd, & Goldman,

1992), postoperative spelling of homophones (e.g., Eich, Reeves, & Katz, 1985; Westmoreland et al., 1992), or preference judgments (e.g., for a color mentioned under anesthesia) (Block et al., 1991; Bonke, Van Dam, Van Kleef, & Slijper, 1993; Winograd, Sebel, Goldman, Clifton, & Lowden, 1991). Results on various recognition or recall measures for such information is very mixed—an outcome that is not surprising to us given the irrelevant, impersonal, and nonmeaningful nature of the stimuli to a surgical patient.

It is not surprising that Eich (1984) did not find evidence of surgical memories when he used a test of homophones presented only once to anesthetized patients. But later, 12.5% (6 of 48) of the patients remembered something personal about their surgeries, and the memories of two patients were corroborated. A confirmed memory by one of these patients was for a personally meaningful, negative comment about her obesity making it difficult to access her veins. Relatedly, Goldmann and Levy (1986) found that patients undergoing surgery showed very little galvanic skin response to their own name or that of the anesthetist or surgeon. But coal miner patients who were out on strike did respond to the name of their union leader. *The memory stimulus that is used is a crucial determinant in the outcome of studies.*

Laboratory memory tests simply do not appear highly relevant in a non-laboratory setting that is emotion-laden. Surgical patients are concerned with life and death. It seems only logical that a person concerned with his or her very survival will be much more alert and attuned to (and, therefore, likely to remember) personally relevant information, instead of lists of nonmeaningful words.

Cheek (1981) has emphasized his belief that recall and memory of information heard under anesthesia will be most likely when it is in a voice known to the patient, preferably given "live" instead of on a tape, about something meaningful to the anesthetized subject, and at a relevant time in the surgical process. Goldmann (1990) similarly expressed that, "An event must be salient in order for it to be attended. Events that are highly salient are more likely to be recollected, providing that they are not so highly charged as to be repressed in some manner" (p. 48). In explaining some of the failure to replicate studies in this area, he further said:

The study by Weinberger et al. (1984) of conditioned responses in rats under general anesthesia suggests that the injection of epinephrine is an essential ingredient. It is a chemical tap on the shoulder, and says "Pay attention!" Calling a patient's name during the operation may perform the same function. (p. 47)

Even in this specialized area of memory research, scientists have begun to recognize the difference between memory for mundane, nonmeaningful material, versus emotional, anxiety-laden, and meaningful material. Recently, scholars in this specialty area of memory research (e.g., Bennett, 1993; Munglani & Jones, 1994) have acknowledged the likely influence of adrenergic activity on memory. When catecholamines (stress hormones) are elevated in lengthy and life-threatening surgeries (Bennett, Sullivan, & Savelle, 1990), memory encoding may be different. Thus, when pentobarbital anesthesia is used, learning is found to occur only when epenephrine is involved (Weinberger et al., 1984). Goldmann (1990) further stressed the importance of the motivation of the patient, the design of the memory task and form of the questions asked, demand characteristics, and the relationship with the patient as other variables differing between studies.

Bennett (1988) has also criticized the methodology of these types of studies that used hypnosis to facilitate recall, finding in his analysis that the time interval between hearing information under anesthesia and the attempt to obtain a recall or recognition measure of the chemically dissociated information is a highly relevant and neglected factor. For instance, subjects questioned shortly (e.g., 12–24 hours) after exposure to the stimulus under anesthesia (which is also a time they are least comfortable and still most likely to be using strong analgesics) were much more likely to have difficulty recalling what was said than subjects who were questioned under hypnosis later (e.g., one week later). Adams (1979) has likewise documented that recovery of memories for occurrences under anesthesia continues to increase for at least two weeks after surgery.

Bennett (1990) has noted the importance of the phrasing of suggestions. Thus, he pointed out, Evans and Richardson (1988) obtained good outcomes from the use of positive suggestions ("You will want to get up and out of bed very soon after surgery"), but not for negative suggestions ("You will not feel sick; you will not have any pain"). Clinicians treating patients through hypnosis (Hammond, 1990) have long recognized the critical importance of using positive rather than negative suggestions.

In contrast to these important elements, however, let's examine a not atypical study in this area. Loftus et al. (1985) provided a case report. Taking her usual position on the fallibility of memory and of being a witness in defense of persons accused of perpetrating abuse, Loftus had been a consultant for a hospital chain being sued over allegations from 169 female patients for sexual abuse by an anesthesiologist. Some of the claims were lodged after the story appeared in newspapers, and following the use of hypnosis to facilitate recall. Loftus needed to undergo surgery personally, so she arranged for the anesthesiologist to read her 100 *nonrelated words* under anesthesia at a pace of a word *every 2 seconds*. Recognition was then tested at 28, 53, and 82 hours after surgery. She scored at chance levels—but so did a medical resident who heard the word list given during the surgery (while she was alert and awake) when she was tested 82 hours later! Memory for irrelevant, impersonal, nonmeaningful information—especially in association with an anxiety-provoking and possibly life-threatening event like surgery—would not be anticipated (at least by anyone outside of the laboratory) to be mentally recorded as something memorable.

In comparison to the kinds of studies reported above, Caseley-Rondi, Merikle, and Bowers (1994) have carefully studied the capacity of surgical patients to hear at some level under chemical anesthesia, to unconsciously process the information heard, and, despite having conscious amnesia for the information, to still be influenced by it. In a double-blind experiment that was in most respects as exceptionally designed and well controlled as any research in this area to date, they evaluated a total of 96 adult patients who were undergoing elective surgery. These patients were assigned randomly to four tape-recorded conditions: music only, suggestion only, suggestion plus music, and blank tapes. An important feature of the suggestions given was that patients were called by name and told at the beginning: "Mary, I am now going to put the headphones on you. Listen carefully. It is important that you listen, Mary" (p. 181).

As we would expect, only the relevant therapeutic suggestions showed a significant effect, and there was no evidence for the recall of melodies, except to some degree when they were interspersed with relevant suggestions of a therapeutic nature. However, patients who received therapeutic suggestions (regardless of hypnotic capacity) while they were under an adequate plane of chemical anesthesia required less morphine after surgery (when measured by a very sensitive measure—amount of self-administered morphine). This demonstrates that anesthetized patients can hear at some level under anesthesia, can process information, and, despite the memories being implicit and having conscious amnesia for what occurred, patients can still be influenced by what they experienced. This finding is all the more impressive because the investigators seemed to have had a pre-experiment belief that intraoperative suggestions did not influence patients. Their outcome, however, clearly supports the proposition that unconscious, implicit memories and information can influence autonomic and involuntary body processes (e.g., level of pain). This parallels what researchers like van der Kolk and innumerable clinicians discover with phenomena like somatic sensations ("body memories") and their association with experiences that were encoded as implicit (amnestic) memories.

Furthermore, and very importantly, it was ascertained by Caseley-Rondi et al. (1994) that *patients with high hypnotic capacity were able to accurately discriminate whether they had received therapeutic suggestions, rather than hearing only music or a blank tape. In fact, patients with high hypnotic ability were 100% accurate in their guesses.* Thus, in a forced-choice recognition situation, somewhat like that involved in the use of hypnotic ideomotor signaling (except in ideomotor signaling, patients can respond, "I don't know"), and when patients in the top third of hypnotic responsivity were asked to guess, thereby perhaps lowering their response criteria (maybe somewhat like some persons believe may occur when hypnosis is used), *"their guesses were unconsciously informed"* (p. 188) and were 100% correct. This finding is all the more fascinating because when Evans and Richardson (1988) used a forced-choice question format, asking patients postoperatively to guess

what kind of tape was played to them, 18 of 19 patients (95%) were able to accurately discriminate whether they had been played therapeutic suggestions, while only 11 of 20 patients who did not receive therapeutic suggestions were able to accurately indicate whether they heard suggestions. Attempts were not made by Caseley-Rondi et al. (1994) to have subjects recall details of what was suggested through the use of age regression techniques. These findings are also interesting because Evans (1990) discovered a moderate correlation between hypnotizability and the ability to recall words spoken during sleep. In contrast to Caseley-Rondi et al. (1994) and Evans and Richardson (1988), we note that Bethune, Ghosh, Walker et al. (1993) did not find general surgical patients capable of distinguishing whether suggestions were used; those researchers did not assess hypnotizability.

Thus, when "high hypnotic ability seems to be associated with responsivity to information that is not available to conscious awareness" (Caseley-Rondi et al., 1994, p. 177), should it be surprising that persons who are very responsive to hypnosis are able under hypnosis to sometimes retrieve memories for amnestic past events in their lives? Given the Caseley-Rondi finding, it is also not surprising that nonverbal (e.g., ideomotor signaling) techniques that call for effortless, involuntary responses appear more capable of accessing implicit (unconscious) memories than effortful, verbal responding.

There are a variety of other studies reporting findings similar to those of Caseley-Rondi et al. (1994). McLintock, Aitken, Downie, and Kenny (1990) studied 63 women undergoing elective abdominal hysterectomy. They were randomly assigned to a tape of positive suggestions or a blank tape during the operation. Anesthesia was standardized for all of the women. Postoperative analgesia was provided through a patient-controlled analgesia system for the first 24 hours. An outcome measure, morphine consumption in the first 24 hours, was 51.0 mg in women played positive suggestions and 65.7 mg in those played a blank tape (p=0.028). They concluded that intraoperative suggestions seem to be registered at some level below conscious awareness and had a positive effect in reducing patients' morphine requirements in the early postoperative period. Although some might argue that these results may have occurred because some patients were inadequately anesthetized for the entire operation, they were nonetheless consciously amnestic for the suggestions. Thus, it was the effects of implicit or amnestic memories that created the positive response.

Recently, Couture, Kihlstrom, Cork, Behr, and Hughes (1993) verified a significant difference in a measure of well-being between patients who received specific therapeutic suggestions under anesthesia versus controls, with strong trends (p<0.10) for patients receiving suggestions to report less discomfort and less total pain. Specific suggestions were more effective than general suggestions. Congruent with findings noted earlier, patients did not have memories for low-frequency, irrelevant words that were said under anesthesia, but nonetheless, their therapeutic improvements demonstrated implicit memory and influence from relevant, meaningful suggestions. Korunka, Guttman, Schleinitz, Hilpert, Haas, and Fitzal (1993) likewise documented positive effects of suggestions on patients in reducing the consumption of postoperative analgesics compared to control patients, despite having conscious amnesia for the suggestions. Steinberg, Hord, Reed, and Sebel (1993) also found positive suggestion effects in reducing pain medication requirements soon after surgery compared to control patients, as did Furlong (1990) and Hutchings (1961). Bethune et al. (1993) likewise found that patients who received suggestions under anesthesia required fewer days in the hospital, as did Pearson (1961) and Bonke et al. (1986).

Although there are also studies failing to replicate positive outcomes from intraoperative suggestions (Block et al., 1991; Boeke et al., 1988; Liu et al., 1992; Woo et al., 1987), Bennett (1993) concluded in his overview: "learning certainly occurs in some, if not most, surgical operations during at least some portion of the anesthetized period" (p. 464). Munglani and Jones' (1994) review also affirmed that suggestions given under anesthesia may create implicit memories having postoperative effects.

In addition to memory for events under anesthesia and evidence of postoperative recovery and improvement, there are also studies of behavioral responses to what amount to posthypnotic suggestions delivered under anesthesia. Bennett, Davis, and Giannini (1985) gave suggestions that during a

postsurgical interview patients would touch one of their ears. Although all patients had conscious amnesia for the suggestions following surgery, 10 of 13 patients (77%) in one study and 9 of 11 (82%) in another study responded to the cues—a much higher rate than found in a control group who only heard conversations during surgery. Goldmann et al. (1987) more recently replicated the study, as did Bennett, DeMorris, and Willis (1988) and Block, Ghoneim, Sum Ping, and Ali (1991), although two other studies have not been able to provide replication (Bethune, Ghosh, Gray, Kerr, Walker, Doolan, Harwood, & Sharples, 1993; Jansen, Bonke, Klein, van Dasselaar, & Hop, 1991). Fascinatingly, none of the patients in the Bennett et al. (1985) or Goldmann et al. (1987) studies recalled the intraoperative suggestions (e.g., to touch their ears or chins), even under hypnosis, and yet they still tended to respond to them.

CONCLUSIONS ABOUT HYPNOSIS AND MEMORY

In concluding this chapter, what can we say we know about hypnosis and memory? First, it must be acknowledged that there are many limitations to our knowledge about hypnosis and memory, in part because of the deficiencies in laboratory memory research. Although some of this research literature may appear scientific, there is a danger in its becoming a kind of pseudoscience when an attempt is made prematurely to generalize findings beyond the limited population and stimuli investigated. Close examination of this literature finds that a moderate amount of the research on hypnosis and memory lacks sufficient validity and bears very little resemblance to the uses of clinical and forensic hypnosis in the real world. Careful scientists must, therefore, be extremely cautious about making generalizations from such research to anything except memory by normal individuals for unremarkable, personally unmeaningful, unemotional details that are relatively unmemorable for most people.

Extreme positions concerning the value of hypnosis and memory must be rejected. Hypnosis is not a spectacular medium through which memories may be recovered with pristine accuracy. Memory may sometimes be influenced and is imperfect, whether recall occurs spontaneously or through assistance from any method. On the other hand, a critical review of the research clearly suggests that the extreme position of most false memory advocates must also be rejected. Hypnosis does not inevitably contaminate memory and produce more fantasy than factual recall. Such a conclusion is both overstated and too simple. We conclude that *hypnotic procedures, when used appropriately, are not any more likely to contaminate memory than techniques such as routine interviewing or questioning, the results of which are admissible in courts.*

Historic, naturalistic, and case report literature from real world (as opposed to laboratory) settings demonstrates that hypnosis may facilitate the recall of earlier life memories, at least some of which can be corroborated as accurate. However, despite the fact that hypnotic age regression may elicit some childhood perceptions and memories, it does not create a psychophysiologic reinstatement of childhood processes. Confabulation and fantasy may be included in hypnotic productions, just as they may be part of a person's ordinary recall of childhood memories. Nonetheless, in clinical situations, hypnotically elicited "memories" that are neither fully accurate nor inaccurate may still provide useful grist for the mill when they are viewed metaphorically, as reflecting cognitive-perceptual overgeneralizations about oneself, other people, and the world. *Without independent corroboration, however, they should not be considered as necessarily being historically accurate, and probably contain a mixture of accurate and inaccurate information.*

Research suggests that hypnosis will at best produce minimal improvement over ordinary memory processes in enhancing recall for personally nonmeaningful, unemotional, or trivial and basically unmemorable details. But, when investigations without serious methodological flaws are examined, investigations that possess ecological validity, one must reject the conclusion of false memory proponents that hypnotic recall is inherently unreliable. Such a conclusion is based on seriously flawed research. In fact, such a difference exists between methodologically weak laboratory studies that use hypnosis in an effort to recall personally irrelevant details and field or laboratory studies possessing ecological validity, that *one must vigorously challenge the validity of drawing conclusions in a courtroom based on a review*

of such studies. It is our belief that to generalize from this kind of laboratory research to entirely different circumstances, memory stimuli, techniques, and populations is questionable scientific practice.

Our review finds that the closer the laboratory approximates real life, the more likely it is that the research will document that hypnotic interventions are generally but not always effective, without an increase in confabulation or memory errors, except where the interviewing methods are unduly suggestive. Thus, we conclude that when the information to be remembered is personally relevant and emotional, hypnotic techniques appear to possess definite potential to enhance recall to a mild or moderate degree in some individuals, without necessarily including an increase in inaccuracies or false recollections. David Spiegel (1995) reached a similar conclusion about using hypnosis with dissociated traumatic experience:

> Hypnosis is one useful technique for bridging amnesia, especially resulting from traumatic experience. It may also be used to produce amnesia, and it may influence both the content and assessment of the accuracy of memory retrieval. Hypnosis is neither simply a solution nor a contaminant of memory processes, but rather an interesting if complicating factor in understanding memory, especially in relation to traumatic events. (pp. 142–143) . . . Ironically, hypnosis may involve selectively tapping the implicit memory domain. (p. 141)

However, memory in general is imperfect and may be influenced at times through social influence. Thus, research documents that what is recalled in hypnosis may be influenced by the prehypnotic expectations of a subject or through expectations created by waking suggestions and the social influence of other people. Therefore, we must emphasize again that, no matter how a memory returns to an individual, it cannot be regarded as veridical unless it can be independently corroborated. There is currently no scientifically validated method for distinguishing between accurate, partially accurate, and inaccurate memories, although we will review a number of innovations in this area in chapter 15.

A critical review of the available research on hypnosis and memory leads to a number of conclusions, which are worth summarizing:

1. (a) Hypnotic *hypermnestic effects* are unremarkable when the information recollected consists of nonpersonally relevant details. (b) Significant hypnotic hypermnestic effects do occur in selected subjects under certain interview conditions, especially when personally relevant information is recollected using hypnotic age regression procedures (and to a lesser extent also with direct hypermnesia suggestions), under repeated free recall interview conditions. While repeated free recall amplifies hypnotic hypermnesia, hypnosis also makes a unique contribution to the overall effect. (c) The error rate may or may not increase during hypnotic hypermnesia, depending on how the hypnotic interview is conducted (cf. also Hammond et al., 1995; McConkey & Sheehan, 1995, p. 187).

2. *Distortions in memory accuracy* and confabulation during hypnotic memory enhancement are: (a) significantly increased under conditions of interviewer bias, suggestive interviewing, forced-choice memory response (and requiring subjects to guess), and short retention intervals, especially in certain moderately and highly hypnotizable subjects; and (b) significantly decreased under conditions of neutral interviewer expectations and revivification combined with free recall interviewing at longer retention intervals. Confabulation may be included in hypnotic productions, just as it may be part of a person's ordinary recall of childhood or other memories. However, the closer the laboratory research approximates clinical uses of hypnosis, the more likely it is that the research documents that hypnotic interventions are generally but not always effective, without an increase in confabulation or memory error.

3. (a) A *mild* increase in confidence *might* occur in some cases of hypnotic memory enhancement, but this increase in confidence is most likely attributable to the social demands of the situation and the specific nature of the suggestions given, and to a lesser extent to the level of hypnotizability, rather than to the use of hypnotic procedures per se. (b) *Hypnosis does not increase resistance to cross-examination* and is generally less effective than usual pretrial preparation in immunization to cross-examination. The currently available standard of research fails to support Orne's (1979) hypothesis that hypnosis creates artificial confidence in a witness that may immunize him or her against cross-examination in a courtroom. We do not find support for the belief that hypnosis influences memory in such a unique manner that it should cause hypnotically refreshed testimony, particularly when it has followed careful forensic guidelines (e.g., Hammond et al., 1995), to be inadmissible in a court of law. However, existing research should inform us that if hypnotic techniques are not used carefully, they do possess the potential to increase confidence to some degree, including confidence in inaccurate recollections. We suspect that social influence and waking suggestions in nonhypnotic interviews may likewise falsely increase a person's confidence.

4. *Source attribution errors* can occur with or without hypnosis. Insufficient research exists to know if the use of hypnotic procedures may contribute anything unique to such errors. Forensic guidelines for videotaping detailed recollections prior to hypnotizing witnesses provide a safeguard concerning such errors in judicial settings.

5. The current generation of the most sophisticated research demonstrates that *hypnotic pseudomemories reports* do occur through suggested misinformation, in a manner similar to waking misinformation suggestion, with the exception that hypnotic pseudomemory suggestions are often more "directly misleading than indirect waking misinformation suggestions (McConkey & Sheehan, 1995, p. 190). However, *the use of hypnotic procedures does not appear to constitute a unique risk factor in the development of pseudomemories.*

(a) Reports of pseudomemories associated with the use of hypnosis are primarily a function of the social/contextual demands of the situation and occur in certain highly and moderately hypnotizable subjects, especially those who are uncertain about targeted past events. *Induction and other specific hypnotic procedures do not significantly contribute to hypnotic pseudomemory production.* And, in fact, research has found that offering hypnotic suggestions for age regression and reexperiencing of a past event, as is sometimes done in psychotherapeutic work, does not seem to be a variable associated with the creation of hypnotic pseudomemories. In a recent review of this same literature, McConkey & Sheehan (1995) likewise conclude that "contextual variables appeared to play a major role" (p. 191) and where "those memories . . . are retrieved under pressure, or as constraints vary, are not likely to reflect genuine memory impairment" (p. 206).

(b) Reports of pseudomemories associated with hypnosis are more likely to occur in a certain social context characterized by biased interviewer expectations, interviewer rapport and source credibility, and systematic suggestion (e.g., a high ratio of suggested misinformation-to-accurate information and emotional manipulation), primarily pertaining to peripheral nonpersonally relevant details, especially in certain high-hypnotizable subjects and especially when cued or forced choice recollection is demanded.

(c) Hypnotic pseudomemory reports are less likely to occur in a social context characterized by neutral interviewer expectations, an egalitarian interview relationship, and free recall, primarily pertaining to personally meaningful information.

(d) Although we believe that it is possible to foster genuine pseudomemories in a small percentage of subjects, much of the research reporting pseudomemory production through hypnosis has not adequately controlled for experimenter demand characteristics. Most hypnotic pseudomemories studied in the laboratory constitute altered memory reports that are a function of response to social context demands. *They are relatively unstable and in the vast majority of cases do not appear to constitute a change in the memory representation per se.* A minority of persons (tentatively estimated at under 6%) are at risk for actually altering their memory representation in response to hypnotic pseudo-memory suggestions, and an even smaller minority of subjects have the capacity to hallucinate the false memory in a way that they cannot distinguish from reality. *We conclude that the great majority of hypnotized persons, including high-hypnotizable subjects, do not usually mistake hypnotically suggested fantasy scenarios for real events.*

(e) It was further suggested that when persons retract previous allegations of having been abused (a not unusual event that may be associated with alternating phases of posttraumatic stress disorder and with high memory suggestibility), they may have many of the same vulnerabilities as persons more prone to developing a false memory. Thus, these may be the very persons most vulnerable to modifying their beliefs in response to the social influence and group pressure effects of family members and false

memory movement representatives. *There is no greater reason to believe that retractors are telling the truth than to believe that abuse victims are telling the truth,* especially when they are exposed to potentially contaminating social influence from family members, lawyers, and other persons alleging that false memories were created and where there is the potential of lucrative secondary gains.

(f) Hypnotically suggested neurotic conflicts can occur temporarily in certain moderately and highly hypnotizable subjects, but these effects are largely attributable to the demand characteristics of the situation and not necessarily to hypnosis per se.

6. With the exception of hypnotic hypermnesia, any distorting effects of hypnosis on memory accuracy, source amnesia, confidence, and pseudomemory production are largely a function of social/contextual demands, and modestly a function of hypnotizability, but *are not a function of induction or other specific hypnotic procedures.*

7. Studies and the literature on chemically dissociated memories for events occurring under surgical anesthesia provide still further evidence that *amnestic, implicit memories* may influence feelings and behavior, may create psychophysiologic symptoms, and sometimes may be relatively accurately recovered through the use of hypnotic techniques. In addition to experimental studies, cases with independent verification of the memories were reviewed. Because research suggests that usually less than 1% of patients undergoing surgical anesthesia have conscious memory for events transpiring during surgery, these corroborated real world reports should be considered as vitally informative N=1 research. Furthermore, four experimental studies of such dissociated, non-laboratory memories have provided support for the likely clinical utility of the ideomotor signaling technique. Some of the latest research also suggests that patients with high hypnotic capacity have a receptivity and capacity to accurately access or discriminate amnestic information that is consciously unavailable, perhaps to a startling degree. Thus, nonverbal (e.g., ideomotor) techniques that call for effortless, involuntary responses may literally be capable of identifying implicit memories. Once again, as with hypnosis in general, memory error rates may or may not significantly increase with ideomotor techniques, depending on how they are used.

Importantly, the literature on memory for events heard under anesthesia demonstrates the same delimiting inadequacies found in many of the hypnosis and memory studies. When memory is tested for stimuli that are irrelevant, impersonal, and nonmeaningful to a surgical patient who is concerned with life and death, it often fails to find that such information has been attended to and encoded. These studies emphasize again that the memory stimulus used in studies powerfully influences what the outcome will be. Researchers in this area are beginning to recognize the influence of adrenergic activity on memory, just as other sophisticated researchers are likewise beginning to recognize that very different attentional, biochemical, and brain processes appear to be involved with traumatic and emotional memories in contrast to the unstressed memories so typically studied in academic laboratories.

Despite its limitations, the existing research literature does have important implications for clinicians. For instance, research demonstrating that a modest degree of increased confidence *may* occur, even in inaccurate memories, and that subject reports or, in some cases, memories may be distorted through suggestion, should alert clinicians to be very careful in the phrasing of suggestions associated with memory retrieval. Such findings further underline the importance of structuring *neutral expectations* and using relatively *nonsuggestive, free recall interviewing methods* as part of hypnotic efforts at enhancing recall (Hammond et al., 1995). We consider it vitally important for clinicians to educate patients about misconceptions about hypnosis, as well as about memory and confabulation, and to engage in a formal informed consent process before using hypnotic exploration techniques. More detailed recommendations for clinicians will be elaborated in chapter 17.

We conclude that exploratory hypnotic techniques may be of value and play a beneficial role when insight-oriented psychotherapy is indicated as part of a comprehensive treatment approach for a patient's problem. At the same time, however, there are many problems where a more behavioral and symptom-focused approach to treatment is indicated, and where insight-oriented hypnotic techniques should not be an initial form of intervention. The law of parsimony should be taken into account in planning therapeutic interventions, and hypotheses concerning the possible involvement of past events or experiences must be held with great tentativeness and only shared with patients very carefully. When exploratory hypnotic techniques are used with memory in clinical situations, therapists are advised to follow the careful guidelines that have been recommended by a national task force in this area (Hammond et al., 1995).

11

||||||||||||||||

A Critical Evaluation of the Memory
Scientific Experiments

A CRITICAL EVALUATION OF
RESEARCH ON EMOTION AND
MEMORY

In this chapter we will critically review the scientific studies on memory and emotion, memory suggestibility, and alleged false memory implantation in psychotherapy. The first section will address the problems inherent in the available scientific studies in the following areas: subject selection, research design, and interpretation of or generalization from the data. Of course, it would be impossible to methodologically critique every study. The purpose of this critical review is to highlight certain recurrent weaknesses in the designs across many of the available studies.

The second section is a reflection on what the scientific studies actually tell us, despite limitations in research design. We hope to present the reader with a concise summary of what we really know about human memory, memory for trauma, and the processes which might influence memory in psychotherapy. The purpose of this chapter is to urge caution, in that overly zealous beliefs on either side of the debate run the risk of compromising an acceptable standard of science. To put it bluntly: false memory allegations about bad therapy do not justify bad science.

Ecological Validity

A very important question is: how applicable are the results from these laboratory simulation studies to memory for trauma? The position of the false memory advocates, like Loftus, of course, has been that these research findings are *very* applicable. Others have challenged this view on the grounds of the *ecological validity* of the laboratory simulation studies. Neisser (1978) leveled the first significant criticism against laboratory memory science on the grounds of ecological validity at the first conference on the Practical Aspects of Memory. His concern was that laboratory memory science up to that time seldom addressed memory functioning in real-life situations.

Loftus and many other memory scientists developed the laboratory simulation paradigms in an attempt to apply memory science more directly to real-life situations, namely, memory for eyewitnessing a crime. Ironically, other memory scientists, notably John Yuille, have since leveled the same criticism against Loftus's work. In the original laboratory simulation paradigm subjects watch a brief videotape or slide presentation of either a neutral (control) or emotionally arousing (experimental) event, and subsequently are given a memory test for that event. Yuille believes that the laboratory subject is in a position much like that of an uninvolved bystander at a crime. Laboratory subjects, like the uninvolved bystander, do not directly participate in the emotionally arousing event, do not experience a personal threat, and may not even experience any relevant degree of emotional arousal. Moreover, the laboratory subject does not experience the film or slides as having any lasting impact on his/her life, and certainly does not manifest posttraumatic stress symptoms after watching the stimulus presentation (Yuille & Tollestrup, 1992). A very real question, then, is whether or not the findings from these laboratory simulation studies are at all applicable to memory performance in real-life witnessing of actual crimes, especially for those subjects who directly and personally experience the impact of the crime.

Yuille's criticism focuses on two aspects of the laboratory simulation research: (1) the nature of the stimulus event and (2) the nature of the experimental subjects selected. He asks, "how comparable is a filmed or staged event to an actual criminal event?" and how comparable is "the typical laboratory eyewitness to a witness of an actual crime?" (Cutshall & Yuille, 1989, p. 100). Yuille's solution to the problem, as we saw in chapter 6, was to conduct field studies on memory performance of actual witnesses and victims of crime.

Yuille's concept of ecological validity could be equally applied as a criticism of Loftus's more recent attempt to generalize her laboratory simulation findings to patients who have recovered memories of abuse. Loftus's position in the false memory debate has been to persuade other memory scientists, therapists, legal authorities, and the public that her laboratory simulation data demonstrate that a patient's recovered memories are indeed fallible memories. But just how generalizable are memory data derived from college students watching videos and slide presentations about car accidents and robberies to patients recovering memories of traumatic experiences? The college students used as subjects in laboratory memory research are, so far as we know, normal and do not suffer from posttraumatic stress symptoms, unlike patients who recover memories. The laboratory subjects, unlike trauma patients, simply watch a slide presentation and do not directly participate in a traumatic event, do not experience the threat of bodily harm of possible death, and may not even experience relevant

emotional arousal while watching the stimulus presentation. Unlike trauma patients, normal laboratory subjects do not experience the stimulus presentation as having a significant impact on their lives, nor do they manifest posttraumatic stress symptoms following the stimulus presentation.

The findings derived from the laboratory simulation studies on memory performance *may* be generalizable to therapeutically recovered memories, but we cannot simply *assume* that these data apply nor present this as if it were an established scientific fact, as is so often done in the false memory literature (e.g., Loftus, 1993). The point is this: memory fallibility in patients who recover abuse memories is a legitimate *hypothesis*, but it is only a hypothesis. Any reasonable standard of science necessitates testing this hypothesis directly, especially on the population in question, namely, testing memory performance in traumatized patients in general and with recovered memory patients in particular.

Advocates of the false memory position have failed to design experiments to test their hypothesis about therapeutic suggestion. They justify this failure by stating that it is impossible to study traumatic memory in the laboratory because subjecting trauma patients to negative emotionally arousing stimuli or suggesting misleading information to them would be unethical (Loftus & Ketcham, 1994). This argument is simply not credible. There are many creative ways to design experiments that might address this very issue in a nonharmful way. For example, we could study *comparative memory performance* in normal, acutely traumatized, and chronically traumatized individuals (e.g., Kuyken & Brewin, 1995; Tromp et al., 1995). It is also possible to *study the trauma memories of patients* in psychotherapy directly. For example, Dalenberg (1996) has recently reported on her study of the accuracy of trauma memories recovered in psychotherapy as compared to recollections of abuse that were never forgotten. As this study presents the only data presently available on the accuracy of memories recovered in psychotherapy, it is noteworthy that, contrary to the false memory hypothesis, she found that recovered memories of abuse were no more or less accurate than recollections of abuse that had always been remembered. Furthermore, the reader is reminded of an entire tradition of research within social psychology, namely, *laboratory simulation of counseling sessions* (Corrigan et al., 1980). These simulation studies specifically address suggestion and persuasive influence in psychotherapy. The point is that none of these research strategies is *ever* mentioned by false memory advocates who argue in favor of the fallibility and suggestibility of memory in psychotherapy. Typically, science develops by designing research strategies to test hypotheses and accumulating data about these hypotheses; it does not advance by retooling a similar set of largely untested false memory hypotheses in numerous professional articles and as expert testimony in numerous court proceedings.

Emotion and Memory: Research Design and Generalizations

It is not our intent to review the methodological flaws in the laboratory simulation research on emotion and memory in any great detail. We can only highlight some of the design problems that merit caution in interpreting the evidence. First, with respect to the nature of the *stimulus materials* used or the *type of event to be remembered*, subjects typically are shown either a neutral or an emotionally arousing version of a brief videotape or slide presentation. The stimulus event is *complex*, in that it contains a central theme, like a robbery or car accident, a series of actions, a number of people, and a number of background details. The very choice of stimulus materials in itself can be a problem. Are these the right type of stimulus events by which to learn about recovered memories of CSA? Unlike most of those conducting adult studies on memory for laboratory simulated eyewitnessed events, at least the researchers conducting comparable child studies have attempted to address the choice and relevance of stimulus materials more directly. They have studied children's memory for encounters with male strangers, unfamiliar play situations involving nonsexual touch, play with sexually anatomically correct dolls, and real-life situations involving emotional arousal, like getting an inoculation or blood drawn or getting a genital examination at the doctor's office.

Another closely related problem pertains to the *stimulus equivalence* of the neutral and emotionally arousing stimulus presentations. An attempt is made to keep all aspects of the video or slide presentation

identical in each version, except for the critical emotionally arousing scene. For example, in the experimental version the bank robbers fire guns at and hit an innocent bystander in the face. In the neutral version subjects are shown a conversation in the bank (Loftus & Burns, 1982). The problem is that these two stimulus presentations simply are not at all equivalent, in terms of perceptual features. This phenomenon is known as the *von Restorff effect* (Wallace, 1965). Christianson (1992b) explains, "isolating an item by making it more vivid than surrounding items positively influences memory for the isolated item" (p. 225).

The problem is that memory performance depends on what is selected as the target item. Loftus and Burns selected a minor background detail—the number of the bystander's football jersey—as the target stimulus for the memory test. They conclude that memory is fallible when comparing memory recognition for that target item in the experimental versus control conditions because subjects in the emotionally arousing condition showed significantly less recognition of the target item than controls. Christianson points out the quite obvious fact that presenting a salient stimulus item, like the shooting, in the experimental but not the control condition is likely to bias the subjects in the experimental condition to focus on the salient event at the expense of minor background details. Christianson (1992b) also points out that "there were no differences seen between the two conditions with respect to the details associated with the critical emotional or the neutral episode itself" (p. 312). In other words, selecting a minor detail as the only target stimulus introduces a *confirmatory bias* to produce results favorable to the memory fallibility hypothesis. Recognition memory for more salient details in that experiment was actually quite remarkable, even though Loftus and Burns drew conclusions about memory fallibility based only on the minor target detail.

This problem of target selection is, from the subject's perspective, a problem of detail salience. Even if a complex, meaningful stimulus event is presented for only two minutes, the subject has many possible details to focus upon out of the total amount of information presented. It stands to reason that a subject would focus more on central actions and less on other things. Memory appears especially fallible in some of these studies only to the extent to which minor background details are used as target stimuli. As Christianson correctly points out, few subjects in either the experimental or control condition forget the central actions, and experimental subjects typically do not show a memory deficit for the central emotionally arousing event itself, namely, the shooting or injury caused by the car accident.

Another problem with the laboratory simulation studies on emotion and memory is the assumption, often untested, that the stimulus event is indeed emotionally arousing. It is disturbing to see studies in print where conclusions are made about the effect of emotional arousal on memory where no or inadequate measures of emotional arousal were included in the research design. Even those studies that include arousal measures fail to demonstrate much appreciation for the complexity of the issues surrounding the construction of arousal and its measurement. Revelle and D. Loftus (1992) critically review the research on arousal and memory performance. They point out that a long-standing scientific controversy exists regarding whether arousal is a unitary or a multidimensional phenomenon. Arousal can be viewed as *nonspecific* or general, although the experimental evidence only weakly supports this view. Arousal is better supported as *specific*, i.e., arousal along specific physiological indices in response to a particular stimulus situation. To make it more complex, various physiological indices of arousal may be dissociated or change in different directions in response to the same event.

Revelle and D. Loftus also review the complex relationship between physiological arousal and emotional arousal. Depending on the type of emotion in question, an emotionally arousing event may be accompanied by an increase or sometimes a decrease in specific and/or general physiological indices of arousal. The problem is that memory scientists have grossly oversimplified their understanding and measurement of emotional arousal in the laboratory simulation studies on emotion and memory. Revelle and D. Loftus argue that much more sophisticated research designs are needed before we can drawn conclusions about the effects of presumed emotional arousal on memory performance in these studies. Such designs need to include independent measures of both specific dimensions of physiological arousal and emotional arousal:

It is our suspicion that both arousal and affect have substantive and some qualitatively different effects on information processing. As such, the importance of considering both dimensions of emotion in experiments that seek to change arousal or affective state should not be minimized. As the earlier summary of the arousal literature suggested, arousal tends to enhance information transfer, decrease short-term retrieval capacity, and increase long-term retention; most likely, it also has some kind of inverted-U relationship with retrieval processes in general. Affect, on the other hand, appears to have a significant tendency to bias the encoding and retrieval of hedonically laden materials and, to some degree, affect the retrieval of neutral information also. Given the interrelatedness of affect and arousal, it would seem that the most reasonable tack would lie in experimental paradigms that overtly cross both dimensions or, at least, study one dimension while trying to hold the other constant. (pp. 141–142)

The relationship between emotional arousal and memory is even more complicated, in that the research data merit very different conclusions depending on whether the presumed arousal is related to the target memory stimulus. Bower (1992) developed the "*causal belongingness hypothesis*" from his studies on mood-dependent retrieval to explain the fact that autobiographical memories are better retrieved if the emotion associated with the original memory is reinstated at the time of retrieval. These memories are more easily retrieved because the emotion in question causally belongs with the memory of the original stimulus event. Christianson has applied the causal belongingness hypothesis to the laboratory simulation studies on emotion and memory. He says:

[A] general increase in emotional arousal is significant as an intervening variable only when the source of the emotional arousal is directly associated with the TBR [to be remembered] event—that is, when the emotional reaction is an inherent property of the TBR event. (p. 319)

In the Loftus and Burns (1982) bank robbery study, for example, the presumed emotional arousal has no causal relationship to the target stimulus item (number of football jersey). If the experimental design were to account for the causal belongingness of the emotionally arousing event and the critical stimulus item, one or the other of these would have been changed. The researchers could leave the shooting as the arousing event and select, say, the gun as the target stimulus, or they could have kept the number on the football jersey as the target stimulus and changed the emotionally arousing event to a touchdown pass.

We have discussed the complex issues surrounding the measurement of physiological arousal and emotional arousal so that the reader can appreciate that drawing conclusions about memory fallibility from these laboratory simulation studies on emotion and memory is premature. E. Loftus's interpretation of these data in favor of the memory fallibility hypothesis is oversimplified and overstated. Christianson, who has collaborated with Loftus on some of these very studies, has drawn a different conclusion (1992b):

> In sum, there are several findings in the emotion and memory literature that challenge the view that intensity of affect, or a general increase in arousal, promotes memory for a broad spectrum of detail. At the same time there is no case for the view that memory is generally impaired during states of high affect. (p. 319)

The literature indicates that negative emotional events are very well retained with respect to both the emotional event itself and critical, central details; peripheral background information is less accurately retained. This pattern indicates that there is no simple unidimensional relationship between intense emotion and memory. Highly emotional events are neither necessarily poorly retained nor necessarily accurately retained. In fact, current research in this field, independent of the approach used, shows that the way emotion and memory interact is a very complex matter. The existing research designs have generally failed to address this complexity with sophisticated enough experimental designs.

Another problem with the research pertains to the conditions associated with and the strategies for *memory testing*. These studies typically employ one or a number of *retrieval strategies*: free recall, cued recall, and/or forced choice recognition. It is important that the reader recall Eich's (1980) and Bower's (1981) conclusions regarding the interaction between type of retrieval strategy and state/mood-dependent retrieval. Free recall is associated with state/mood-dependent effects, while cued recall or recognition is not. To our knowledge, no studies on the misinformation effect have attempted to reinstate the presumed original emotional arousal at the time of memory testing. Insofar as recognition tests are used, state/mood reinstatement may not be necessary, but the findings drawn primarily from recognition studies may not be readily generalizable to phenomena occurring in psychotherapy, which are largely based on free recall retrieval. Before attempts are made to generalize the findings drawn from emotion and memory research to psychotherapy, we would prefer to see more sophisticated research designs that cross over recognition and free recall retrieval strategies under state/mood similar and discrepant conditions.

The measures used in these studies also bias the results. Studies that assess memory performance in terms of the *total information* remembered fail to distinguish between central and peripheral information. Loftus and Burns (1982) select a very specific minor background detail as the target detail. Under these conditions it is misleading to conclude that less total information or fewer target details are reported in the emotionally arousing group relative to the control group. Those studies that incorporate into the research design some way to distinguish between central and peripheral information yield very different conclusions, namely, that memory for central actions is *not* impaired (and is sometimes improved) under conditions of emotional arousal, whereas memory for minor background details is consistently impaired across studies.

The research on hypnosis and memory has contributed a vast number of studies on the complex interaction between hypnotic and contextual factors in memory performance. Since Robinson's (1932) pioneering work on contextual effects in serial learning tasks, memory scientists have been acutely aware of how contextual factors confound memory performance in laboratory studies. Therefore, it is quite surprising to see how rarely contextual variables, like the relationship to the experimenter, the nature of the filler tasks, and the environment of the memory testing, are mentioned as possible confounds in these reports.

While major limitations in the research designs merit caution in the kind of conclusions drawn about the effects of negative emotional arousal on memory, Loftus has overstated her conclusions. She has used these data as an illustration of memory fallibility (1979a,b, 1993), even though an important review of studies conducted mostly before 1980 illustrated that emotional arousal can either increase or decrease memory accuracy (Deffenbacher, 1983). More sophisticated research designs that experimentally manipulated type of information have consistently demonstrated that emotional arousal has multiple effects on memory and that emotional arousal generally enhances memory for central events while making memory more fallible only for peripheral background details. As Christianson says, "there is little evidence to support the view that emotional stress is bad for memory" (1992a, p. 303). Loftus's conclusions about memory fallibility are justified only insofar as they fail to take into account the type of information assessed; therefore, as general conclusions about negative emotional arousal and memory, they are misleading.

Memory Suggestibility: Research Design and Generalizations

Many of the same methodological criticisms of the laboratory studies on negative emotional arousal and memory apply to the laboratory studies on misinformation suggestion, in that the same Aussage procedure is used in both types of experiments. There are additional problems with the misinformation studies. Most of the misinformation suggestion experiments conducted throughout the 1970s and 1980s followed the original Loftus three-phase paradigm. It is incredible how many experiments were conducted and continued to be conducted using the original paradigm, even after it had been pointed out that the original paradigm failed to control for encoding of the original stimulus event. Loftus simply assumed that the subject encoded all the information in the briefly presented audiovisual stimulus event. A number of studies appearing throughout the 1980s that included a control for encoding consistently demonstrated that the magnitude of the misinformation as originally reported by Loftus and

her associates was significantly reduced when encoding failure was controlled (Christiaansen & Ochelek, 1983; Frischholz, 1990; McEwan & Yuille, 1981; Pirolli & Mitterer, 1984; Wagenaar & Boer, 1987).

An equally persistent problem with the original procedure was the failure to control for type of target post-event misinformation. The great majority of the studies used peripheral details as targets for post-event suggestion; therefore, it is not surprising that subjects appeared more suggestible than might otherwise be the case (Dritsas & Hamilton, 1977). Subsequent research with both adults (Burke et al., 1992; Christianson, 1992a,b; Reisberg et al., 1993) and children (Goodman et al., 1990, Goodman, Hirshman, et al.,1991) varied the type of target information. Not surprisingly, the data from these later experiments constrained the type of conclusions that could be made about misinformation suggestibility. While it seemed relatively easy to demonstrate vulnerability to misinformation suggestions for peripheral background details, subjects generally (with some exceptions) were much more resistant to suggestions involving central actions.

A repeated blind spot in the misinformation studies is the failure to adequately control for the context of the memory testing. The original Loftus paradigm fails to control for possible social influence by the experimenter giving the post-event information and/or the memory test. The McCloskey and Zaragoza (1985) study was the first experiment to raise the question that some type of social influence, in that case response bias, might be operative in misinformation suggestion. Only a few studies since have experimentally manipulated source credibility (e.g., Ceci, Ross, & Toglia, 1987; Dodd & Bradshaw, 1980; Smith & Ellsworth, 1987). Such studies, however, remain more the exception than the rule. To a large extent the existing studies on misinformation suggestion are representative of primarily cognitive suggestive factors (Ceci & Bruck, 1993) and mostly have failed to manipulate experimentally and measure the effects of social influence factors in any systematic manner. While Loftus has been outspoken about possible suggestion effects in psychotherapy, most of her own research on misinformation suggestibility fails to control adequately for possible suggestion effects inherent in the research situation itself, like response bias.

Overall, the existing research designs on misinformation suggestibility are not complex enough to handle the number of variables operative in misinformation suggestibility. While it is true that the misinformation effect is a robust finding across many studies (Lindsay, 1994b; Loftus & Hoffman, 1989), most of the available research designs are not sophisticated enough to apportion the variance of each of the variables contributing to the overall misinformation effect. The variables identified in the research include: (1) memory strength (encoding status, age, retention interval, source attribution); (2) type of post-event information; (3) context of the memory test (random vs. sequential presentation; state/mood reinstatement; recall vs. recognition test); (4) social influence (response bias, source credibility, social support or pressure). No single experimental design has approximated accounting for all of these conditions and their interaction (with the exception of the Frischholz, 1990, study); therefore, it is not surprising that the magnitude of the misinformation effect varies considerably across studies, depending on which of these factors are addressed or ignored.

The complexity of the misinformation effect merits some "constraint" on the kinds of conclusions that can be drawn from the experimental studies (Pezdek & Roe, 1994). Loftus's interpretations of the misinformation effect have been consistently overstated. While alteration of the original memory trace (Loftus, 1979a,b) may be operative in misinformation suggestion at least under certain conditions, more recent experiments using more sophisticated designs than the original procedure have clearly demonstrated that memory alteration explains only a small portion of the overall variance of the misinformation effect (Belli, 1989; Belli et al., 1992; Chandler, 1991; Frischholz, 1990; Lindsay, 1990, 1994b; Tversky & Tuchin, 1989; Wagenaar & Boer, 1987). Moreover, the magnitude of memory alteration is consistently small (Lindsay, 1994b). Thus, Loftus's descriptions of misinformation suggestion that imply a change in the memory representation overstate the data.

The problem of overstating the data is magnified when Loftus (Loftus, 1993; Loftus & Ketcham, 1994) attempts to generalize the research on misinformation suggestion to delayed recovered memories and alleged false memory creation in psychotherapy. There are a number of problems with making this generalization. First, psychotherapy is case-focused. Loftus's failure to develop a standardized assessment tool to measure individual differences in misinformation suggestibility limits the application of her findings in an individual case in anything but a hypothetical way. Second, most of the studies on misinformation suggestion experimentally vary relatively short retention intervals as compared to the long delays typically associated with recovered memories in therapy. Some available research has demonstrated that the magnitude of the misinformation effect may be reduced with longer retention intervals (e.g., Chandler, 1991). Third, most of the target items in misinformation experiments are peripheral stimulus details. It has not been established that results from these studies are generalizable to complex, emotionally significant autobiographical events. The work of Hyman et al. (1995) and Pezdek et al. (in press) using the Shopping Mall paradigm has demonstrated that *type of information* may be an important variable in this research, in that false suggestions are significantly more likely to be accepted for familiar than for unfamiliar false events. Fourth, the most frequently used memory test in the misinformation experiments is a recognition test. It has not been established that misinformation findings are generalizable to free recall situations like psychotherapy, especially since state-dependent effects operate under recall but not recognition conditions (Eich, 1980). Fifth, most of the misinformation studies pertain to suggestively altering the recollection of a perceived stimulus event. The Pezdek and Roe (1994) experiment failed to demonstrate a misinformation suggestion effect for the condition of suggesting a non-event, but did find the expected misinformation effect for the condition of suggesting an alteration in an originally perceived stimulus event. The hypothesis about creation of false memories for a non-event was not supported by the experiment. The results imply that Loftus (1993) cannot so readily generalize misinformation research to suggestively creating false events in therapy. Sixth, most of the studies using the Shopping Mall paradigm fail to address social/contextual factors, such as response bias, demand characteristics, source credibility, and other suggestive influences inherent in the research itself. Seventh, the Shopping Mall studies fail to establish an adequate baseline for true and false target events. True and false events are typically generated from questionnaires sent to parents and other relatives of the research subjects. No corroboration is sought. Thus, determination of "true" and "false" events is based on the shaky assumption that the parental memory is accurate, an assumption that has not been supported by the available data (cf. Brewin et al., 1993, for a review). If the subject gives a report that deviates from the parental memory, it is assumed to be false. These design flaws are quite significant. Until they are remedied with better studies, we urge caution in generalizing from either the misinformation or Shopping Mall studies to suggestive influences hypothesized to take place in psychotherapy.

The experimental studies on interrogatory suggestion set a better standard of science than is found in many of the adult misinformation suggestion studies. First Gudjonsson has consistently addressed the question of individual differences in suggestibility by developing a standardized assessment instrument, the Gudjonsson Suggestibility Scale (1984a). The test specifically measures suggestibility for memory for a complex negatively arousing event, and has the flexibility to be useful at both short and long retention intervals. Gudjonsson has developed norms for the instrument and has used it specifically in research to understand how interpersonal pressure might lead to false reports. Moreover, the research specifically addresses personality factors associated with interrogatory suggestibility, both factors that increase and decrease (e.g., coping resources) vulnerability to interrogatory suggestions.

One strength of the research on interrogatory suggestibility is the systematic attempt to identify the basic elements of interrogatory suggestion. This model addresses both individual differences in suggestibility and factors contributing to suggestion in an interpersonal situation. Gudjonsson and Clark's (1986) model for interrogatory suggestion enumerates a number of complex variables hypothesized to be operative in the overall suggestive effect. Following this conceptual analysis based on a detailed study of police interrogations, Gudjonsson and his associates developed an instrument to directly test the model. Factor analytic studies done on the GSS have identified two main elements—systematic misleading and interpersonal pressure (Gudjonsson, 1992), although Register and Kihlstrom (1988) believe that

the scale is composed of three elements—misinformation suggestion, repetition of misinformation, and interpersonal pressure.

The work of Ceci and his associates, likewise, has been more broad-based than the adult misinformation studies. Ceci has identified both cognitive and social factors operative in suggestibility (Ceci & Bruck, 1993) and has designed experiments to assess the effects of various combinations of cognitive and social suggestive factors, such as interviewee's beliefs, interviewer's beliefs, repetition of suggestions within and across interview sessions, and mental rehearsal of misinformation. The strength of these studies lies in their experimental manipulation of a variety of suggestion variables. However, short of constructing multifactorial designs, this research so far has not systematically varied the various factors operative in suggestion so as to ascertain the relative strength that each contributes to the overall suggestive effect. All that we can say is that *combinations* of suggestive variables increase the overall suggestive effect, at least for some individuals. Moreover, the research by Ceci and his associates, at least so far, has not addressed the suggestive contribution of negative emotional pressure, as measured by the GSS. It would be useful to understand how much emotional pressure to create a false recollection contributes to the overall effect. Furthermore, the reader is cautioned about the kind of conclusions that can be drawn about the contribution of repeated suggestions of misinformation over multiple interviews. The Ceci studies clearly demonstrate a marked increase in memory commission errors after misleading suggestions are given repeatedly over a number of interviews. Another set of studies clearly demonstrates a hypermnestic effect (increase in the total information remembered without a substantial increase in memory inaccuracy) after multiple interviews, provided that free recall is emphasized (e.g., Dent & Stephenson, 1979; Dunning & Stern, 1992; Scrivner & Safer, 1988; Turtle & Yuille, 1994). Thus, multiple interviews focused on a particular theme per se are not unduly suggestive provided that free recall is emphasized and the systematic introduction of misleading suggestions is avoided.

One merit of the GSS is that it has been used to distinguish between deniers and retractors, i.e., those who resist and those who readily accept information suggestions to make a confession, respectively.

A major strength—but also a limitation—of the GSS is that it predicts the *probability* of accepting information during an interrogative interview. While it can identify a group of individuals most at risk to suggestion, it does not tell us in an absolute sense that these individuals will accept misinformation suggestions. High scores on the GSS do not guarantee that the individual will produce a false confession, nor do low scores guarantee that the individual is entirely resistant to post-event misinformation. Moreover, scores on the GSS tell us nothing about the relative accuracy of memory for events other than the story in the GSS. Only one study exists on the relationship between GSS scores and memory accuracy (Tully & Cahill, 1984). A very high score on the GSS may cause us to question the accuracy of a reported recollection, but it does not necessarily mean that the memory is false. Conversely, a very low score on the GSS may cause us to have confidence in the reported recollection, but it does not necessarily guarantee that the recollection is free from all suggestive influences.

While studies with the GSS have demonstrated that alleged false confessors are significantly more suggestible than other individuals, a major limitation of the GSS is that it cannot help us to distinguish between coerced-compliant and coerced-internalized false confessors. The two main differences between compliant and internalized confessors are the *stability* of the accepted suggestion and the degree of *alteration of the memory representation*. Studies of interrogatory pressure have shown that with the "right" kind of pressure a significant number of people can be made to say just about anything. But do they actually change their memory? Probably not. A much smaller group of people probably change their memory representation during interrogation. These are the internalized false confessors, whose false recollection is stable and well retained over time. A much larger group of people probably change their memory report, but do not actually change their memory, in response to interrogatory pressure. These people usually revert to their original beliefs once out of the interrogation. Since the current research on interrogatory suggestion does not distinguish coerced-compliant from coerced-internalized false confession, the working group of the British Psychological Society (1995) is correct to caution us that "There are a number of significant differences between false confessions and false (recovered) memories which preclude generalizing from one to the other" (p. 29).

The central issue in the research on interrogatory suggestion is that of *response criteria*, i.e., criteria used to evaluate the subject's report in response to the memory test. A strict response criterion would require that the research design demonstrate an alteration in the memory representation prior to drawing conclusions about false memories. A loose criterion would consider all reports to be a product of memory. A major limitation in the existing research is that rather loose response criteria have been adopted, as if all reports pertain to memory changes. The data suggest otherwise. With the exception of highly suggestible individuals, *the greater the interrogatory pressure applied, the more likely that the coerced false report is a function of social compliance and not an internalized change in the memory representation*. Thus, while Gudjonsson's forensic studies and Ceci's child suggestibility studies have clearly demonstrated a significant increase in the rate of false reports about past events when a constellation of interrogatory suggestive factors are systematically used, the increase is just that—false *reporting*, not necessarily false *remembering*. In fact, the greater the interrogatory pressure, the less likely that the false report is a change in the memory representation. Thus, while Loftus may be partially correct in referring to the classic misinformation effect as memory impairment, she is incorrect in referring to the Shopping Mall study as a demonstration of false *memory* creation, in that the social influences tapped in the Shopping Mall study are very different from the cognitive influences tapped in the classic misinformation effect. Once a constellation of social suggestive influences is used, the resultant suggestive effect is much more likely to be an instance of compliant reporting than an internalized change in the memory representation. *The problem with the discussions of alleged false memory creation in psychotherapy is that a very loose response criterion is used in the discussion.* It would be technically more accurate to speak of alleged false *reports* or false *beliefs* about abuse than about false or illusory *memories* per se. We agree that compliant false beliefs can be produced through interrogatory pressure, but the available evidence suggests that few of these beliefs would be stable, internalized memory changes, except in very highly suggestible individuals.

The standard of science for hypnotic suggestibility is also good. As we learned in chapter 10, a number of standardized assessment instruments are available to measure hypnotizability in both clinical and laboratory settings. The earlier studies on hypnotic hypermnesia that utilized nonmeaningful stimuli are being upgraded with studies using meaningful stimuli. With respect to hypnotic pseudomemories, a number of sophisticated research designs have appeared that enable us to apportion the relative contribution of hypnotizability, hypnotic procedures, and the hypnotic context to the overall suggestive effect. Recent research designs illustrate an appreciation for the complexity of variables that contribute to hypnotic pseudomemory production. However, a careful reading of these experiments makes it clear that the greater portion of the variance of memory distortion in hypnotic pseudomemory experiments has more to do with social/contextual factors than with hypnotic procedures per se, and while hypnotizability plays some role as a risk factor, hypnotic procedures per se do not contribute much to pseudomemory production in hypnosis. In other words, the issue of pseudomemory production in hypnosis has less to do with whether or not hypnosis was used than with how it was used (Hammond et al., 1995; Mutter, 1990). The main limitation inherent in these current hypnosis studies is the inability to establish procedures or identify conditions that distinguish between hypnotically suggested peripheral details and hypnotically suggested complex events. Most of the available data on hypnotic pseudomemory production is limited to suggested minor details, although a few anecdotal reports make it clear that entire fictitious events can be suggested in at least a small number of hypnotic subjects.

WHAT DO WE KNOW ABOUT MEMORY FALLIBILITY?

Loftus's claim that human memory in general is fallible (1979a,b) and that therefore memories recovered in psychotherapy are equally fallible (1993) is both overstated and oversimplified (Koss et al., 1995). Conclusions in a textbook that negative emotional arousal "hinders accurate . . . memory" (Loftus, 1980, p. 78) is misleading in that the statement fails to specify the conditions under which arousal hinders or enhances memory. Her conclusion correctly applies only to laboratory simulation studies of memory for complex visual presentations and only when a particular type of information is assessed. These simulation studies rarely show memory fallibility with respect to the emotional arousing event itself. Moreover, it is misleading to generalize findings on memory fallibility for certain types of visual information presented in the laboratory to *autobiographical memory* of patients in psychotherapy.

What do the laboratory simulation studies actually demonstrate? Heuer and Reisberg (1990) have correctly pointed out that negative emotional arousal has *multiple effects* on memory, depending on the type of memory information assessed. Claims about memory fallibility are only valid when considered in terms of the *type of memory information* assessed. Negative emotional arousal has different effects on different types of memory information. As we have seen, memory for visual information is different from memory for verbal information about a negative emotionally arousing event (Christianson & Fallman, 1990; Christianson & Nilsson, 1984). The early studies on emotional arousal and memory performance led to a distorted view of memory fallibility because they were biased toward assessing memory performance in terms of the total information contained within a complex visual stimulus presentation (Clifford & Hollin, 1981; Clifford & Scott, 1978) or because they assessed memory for peripheral background details like the number on the football jersey of an innocent eyewitness to a crime (Loftus & Burns, 1982). More sophisticated studies that clearly distinguished between plot-relevant central information, basic level visual information, and plot-irrelevant central and background details (Burke et al., 1992) have clearly demonstrated that memory is well and accurately retained for the gist of a central action (plot-relevant action) or a negative emotional event even over long retention intervals, while only the peripheral background details are poorly retained. These findings are consistent with Bartlett's (1932) original studies on memory for the War of the Ghosts, in which gist memory was well preserved while memory for minor details was highly inaccurate.

General, overstated claims about memory fallibility fail to take into consideration the complex interaction of variables that affect memory performance. As we have seen, these include the type of arousal (physiological, emotional, arousal specific to the TBR information); type of event (emotional vs. neutral); activity level of the subject (passive witnessing vs. actively affected); retention interval (immediate vs. delayed testing); type of information (central plot-relevant actions, basic visual information, plot-irrelevant details, and peripheral background details); and the type of retrieval conditions (internal and external context reinstatement); retrieval strategy (free recall, cued recall, or recognition); and number of retrieval trials (one vs. repeated retrieval trails). The outcome of any given experimental study may favor the memory fallibility hypothesis or the memory hypermnesia hypothesis (high accuracy and completeness) depending on how the experiment is constructed. The general pattern emerging across these studies is that memory for the gist of a negative emotionally arousing event is accurately and well retained even over long retention intervals, while memory for peripheral background details is inaccurately and poorly retained over long retention intervals. However, since these laboratory simulation studies are limited to memory for primarily visual and sometimes verbal information, we do not know if these conclusions can be generalized to autobiographical memory.

Studies on personal memory, like flashbulb memory and autobiographical memory, demonstrate that an equally complex number of variables affect the experimental outcomes. The flashbulb studies demonstrate that individuals may retain highly consistent memories of the reception circumstances of a significant public news event over very long retention intervals, depending on the personal and cultural significance of the event, the number of canonical categories evaluated, the criteria used to evaluate the response, the number of retrieval cues given and the nature of the retrieval conditions, and the length of the retention interval. Retention rates for highly significant events that alter the course of history, like the JFK assassination for Americans or the Olaf Palme assassination for Swedes, generally run around 90% one or more years after the assassination (Brown & Kulik, 1977; Christianson, 1989, 1992d; Yarmey & Bull, 1978). Retention rates for memorable public events that are less personally and historically significant, like the space shuttle explo-

sion, generally run around 50% for one or several canonical categories and significantly less for all categories (Bohannon & Symons, 1992; Neisser & Harsch, 1992). The problem with these studies is that retenion rates are not the same as accuracy rates and there is no way to know if the highly personal remembered reception circumstances are accurate.

Participant-observer studies on autobiographical memory also demonstrate highly variable retention depending on the memorableness of the information assessed, the criteria used to judge accuracy, the nature of the retrieval cues, the conditions of retrieval, and the length of the retention interval. However, a clear pattern emerges. Those studies that explicitly ask for "most memorable experiences" show retention rates above 90% (Linton, 1975, 1978; Wagenaar, 1986), while those that ask for "memorable experiences" show retention rates around 50–60% (White, 1982). Random sampling of mundane daily experiences also shows low retention rates (Brewer, 1988).

Studies on memory for events of impact generally yield high retention rates. Yuille and his associates have reported three field studies on violent crimes and another on a nonviolent bank robbery (Cutshall & Yuille, 1989; Yuille & Cutshall, 1986). The overall accuracy rates in each of these studies across one- to-two-year retention intervals were: gun store shooting, 81%; restaurant shooting, 92%; breadline shooting, 85%; and the nonviolent bank robbery, 82%. Memory for the central actions of each eyewitnessed crime was consistently high across all of the studies: 82%, 97%, 92%, and 83%, respectively. Memory for the descriptions of the people involved was not as high: 73%, 79%, 79%, and 80%, respectively.

Targeted recall studies, such as Usher and Neisser's study (1993) of important childhood events like the birth of a sibling or a hospitalization, also yield high retention rates. Over 80% of college students who were three or four years old and 100% of those who were five years old or older at the time a sibling was born accurately answered at least one of the critical questions about the event. All of the college subjects remembered at least one critical item about a hospitalization that had occurred when they were three or older.

The studies on flashbulb memories for the San Francisco earthquake also yield very high retention rates. The percentages of accuracy on a weighted scale of accuracy were 96%, 86%, and 54% for subjects living at the epicenter, subjects living in the earthquake area but not in the epicenter, and subjects living outside of the epicenter, respectively. Thus, the gist of "remarkable memories" (Yuille & Cutshall, 1989), but not necessarily minor details, is extremely well and accurately retained over very long retention intervals.

MEMORY FOR NEGATIVE EMOTIONAL EVENTS AND TRAUMA MEMORY

Figure 11.1 depicts what we currently know about memory for negative emotional events. The X axis describes a continuum of involvement in the to-be-remembered (TBR) experience. Subjects are the least involved in the laboratory simulation studies of an emotionally arousing event. Subjects in the flashbulb memory studies reported the personal re-

ception circumstances of a big news event. These subjects are more personally involved, in that the TBR event is defined as a news event that is believed to have direct consequences for the individual's life, even though the person did not directly experience the new event in question (Brown & Kulik, 1977). In contrast to memory for laboratory simulated and big news events, autobiographical memories are memories for direct personal experiences. Memories for events of impact are in a special class of autobiographical memory. Like flashbulb and autobiographical memories, they are characterized by consequentiality. Like autobiographical memories, they are about real-life events that are directly experienced. But unlike flashbulb and most autobiographical memories, memories for events of impact are unique and deeply affect the individual's life. Traumatic events are a special class of events of impact defined in terms of the occurrence of post-traumatic stress symptoms. Traumatic events deeply affect not only the person's life but also his/her mental status. Thus, these categories of events can be

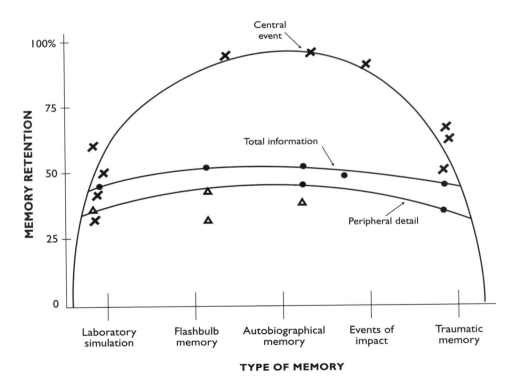

FIGURE 11.1
Memory Retention for Types of Negative Emotional Events

arranged along a continuum from least to most personally involving: laboratory simulated experience, flashbulb big news events, memorable personal (autobiographical) experiences, events of impact, and traumatic events.

The retention rates across all studies are defined along the Y axis. Retention rate is defined in terms of the percentage of information remembered after some retention interval, as compared to the information remembered immediately after the event. Retention rate is not the same as accuracy rate, except in the laboratory simulation studies where retention is measured in terms of the percentage of accurate details remembered over time. There is no way to measure accuracy for the reception circumstances of a big news event. Therefore, many of the flashbulb memory studies assess the percentage of reception details remembered over time against the details remembered at some earlier point, often immediately after the event. Likewise, there is no way to know exactly what happened in a real-life crime. Therefore, memory for events of impact are assessed against a composite reconstruction of the crime based on all the information available. Having noted these limitations, it is nevertheless possible to plot the data across many of the studies on emotion and memory in terms of a retention rate.

The pattern across these studies becomes clear only when the data are segregated into different *types of information*, namely, central versus peripheral information. As can be seen from the figure, measurement of retention of *total information* is misleading, in that the retention rate is deflated and memory appears more fallible than it is. So let's look at what happens when the data are divided into memory for central actions and peripheral details. Measurement of retention of *central actions* is consistently high across most studies, as the top line of Figure 11.1 depicts. Deffenbacher (1980) defined 70% accuracy as the lower limit of "high optimal conditions" for the encoding, retention, and retrieval of a given memory for an emotionally arousing event. In his review of 25 studies on memory and emotional arousal, he found that most of the laboratory simulation studies on negative emotional arousal and memory yield accuracy rates of 70–75%. However, if the data are divided in terms of high versus low optimal conditions for information processing, the rates differ substantially: around 80–90% in high optimal and 25–62%

in low optimal conditions. Thus, retention rates vary considerably depending on the conditions of the experiment. In particular, the type of information measured greatly affects the outcome. Central actions typically meet the criteria for high optimal information processing in the laboratory simulation studies. Thus, passive witnessing of visual stimulus presentations generally yields a retention rate above 70% for central actions and as high as 90% in the laboratory simulation studies. If one considers memory for the reception circumstances of a personally meaningful big news event to be memory for central details, then these retention rates generally run above 90%. In the participant-observation autobiographical memory studies, if one factors out those studies that ask for "most memorable" experiences of the day, the retention rates run above 95% after one year. The retention rate for central actions of the crime across Yuille's field studies on memory for events of impact averages around 89%. The retention rates for verbal memory of traumatic events are complicated by the fact that a subpopulation of traumatized individuals are fully or partially amnestic for the traumatic event, i.e., they have no memory or a very incomplete verbal memory for the trauma. Thus, overall retention rates even for the gist of a traumatic event are generally lower than retention rates for events of impact.

Thus, across all studies, a robust finding is that narrative memory for the gist or central action of a negative emotionally arousing event is extremely well retained. The more involved the person is, the more likely the memory will be retained. Traumatic events are a significant exception to this general rule. A significant portion of traumatized individuals suffer from traumatic amnesia; even if their narrative memory for the traumatic event is retained, it may not be readily accessible.

Measurement of retention for *peripheral background details* is very misleading. For example, only 4.3% of subjects correctly identified the number on the football jersey of the eyewitness who got shot in the Loftus and Burns study (1982). This critical item was a very peripheral background detail. However, the mean percent of correct items across 17 total items was 76%, and for four action details 88% in that same study. Memory for peripheral detail across the laboratory simulation studies ranges from 4% to 62%, with an average rate of around 40%. Memory for less personally meaningful (low consequentiality) flashbulb events, like the space shuttle disaster, runs around 50–60% for one or more canonical category (Bohannon & Symons, 1992; Neisser & Harsch, 1992). Memory for "memorable" but not "most memorable" autobiographical experiences generally runs around 50–60% (White, 1982). Memory for the descriptive characteristics of people involved in events of impact runs around 78% in the Yuille field studies (Cutshall & Yuille, 1989; Yuille & Cutshall, 1986, 1989). Retention rates of narrative memory for peripheral details of traumatic events cannot be determined from the available data.

Overall, memory for less important details associated with a negative emotional event are significantly less well retained than memory for central actions. Retention rates generally fall below the Deffenbacher 70% criterion, with the exception of the studies on events of impact. Retention rates for peripheral details are especially low in the laboratory simulation studies but increase along the continuum of involvement from flashbulb, to autobiographical, to events of impact. The few data that exist on verbal memory for peripheral details associated with traumatic events suggest that these details are well retained by some traumatized individuals and very poorly retained by others.

Overall, Figure 11.1 illustrates quite clearly that simplistic statements about the fallibility of memory for negative emotionally arousing events are very misleading. A robust finding across most studies is that the *gist* of the emotionally arousing event is extremely well retained (over the 70% criterion), but peripheral details are not well retained unless the event makes a significant impact on the individual's life (below the 70% criterion, except for events of impact).

Since we have reviewed a great number of studies on emotion and memory it might be useful to highlight some of the main points:

- Autobiographical memory access is greatly influenced by retrieval conditions. Retrieval conditions that reinstate the emotional state and context of the original target event significantly increase recall.
- Nonspecific free recall is biased toward more recent over more remote experiences (Rubin, 1982).
- More remote autobiographical memories are

accessible if they are temporally referenced, landmarked, or tagged as emotionally significant or very memorable (Baddeley et al., 1978; Bahrick et al., 1975; Conway, 1992; Linton, 1975; Robinson, 1986; Wagenaar, 1986).
- Older people have greater access to autobiographical memories especially for the middle years of their lives—reminiscence function (Rubin et al., 1986).
- Nonspecific free recall of autobiographical memories generally hits a lower limit of four years of age—childhood amnesia (Rubin et al., 1986).
- Certain events of impact (and possibly some traumatic events) are an exception to childhood amnesia. A partial or full narrative autobiographical memory may be accessible under certain conditions for accidents, hospitalizations, or the birth of a sibling, occurring when the child was as young as 18 months. There is no evidence that specific emotional events can be remembered by adults in the form a verbal autobiographical memory for events occurring prior to 18 months of age (Sheingold & Tenney, 1982; Sugar, 1992; Terr, 1988; Usher & Neisser, 1993).
- Narrative memory for traumatic events is bimodally distributed, with a group always remembering the trauma and another group having partial or full amnesia for the trauma for some significant period of their lives. Amnesia for trauma is a robust finding across all types of trauma, including amnesia for childhood sexual abuse in a significant minority of victims. While narrative autobiographical memory for trauma may be relatively incomplete and fragmented for some traumatized individuals, accuracy for the gist of the traumatic experience is generally high, although peripheral details are less well preserved.
- Traumatic experiences may be processed differently from ordinary experiences and memory for traumatic experiences may be processed predominately within an implicit, behavioral memory system rather than within an explicit, narrative autobiographical memory system in both children and adults (Pillemer & White, 1989; Terr, 1979, 1988, 1994). Behavioral memory for trauma is possible by the end of the second year of life. It is unclear how neo-

nates and infants encode and store trauma memory, since the behavioral memory system is not yet developed. There is some suggestion, however, that REM dreaming and an amygdala-based affective memory system are available to neonates and infants, which could serve as the basis for a prebehavioral memory system for emotionally salient and traumatic experiences (Share, 1994).

- Memory for negative emotional events may be influenced by the distorting effects of psychologically motivated forgetting (Ross, 1991; Spence, 1988).

- The most common memory errors are: (1) memory dating errors; (2) mistaken descriptions of the physical characteristics of people; (3) omission, insertion, or transformation of peripheral details; and (4) source misattribution errors. Memory errors for the gist of an experience are relatively uncommon, especially for emotionally significant experiences. Thus, misdating a memory or remembering it with some mistaken details does not necessarily invalidate the gist memory.

WHAT DO WE KNOW ABOUT MEMORY SUGGESTIBILITY?

The claim of therapeutically suggested false memories for abuse is both overstated and oversimplified in terms of our current scientific understanding of human suggestion (cf. also Koss et al., 1995). The overly general claim of therapeutic suggestion fails to distinguish between what Hilgard (1965) has called *suggestibility* and *suggestion*. This is not to say the suggestive influences are not operative in psychotherapy. The point is that we need to be much more precise about suggestive effects if we are to understand how these may or may not operate in psychotherapy. After nearly a century of scientific study on human suggestive effects, we do know a great deal about this rather complex phenomenon. Generally speaking, there are two broad categories of suggestive effects that must be considered: (1) individual differences in the *trait of suggestibility*, and (2) a variety of contextual and social *suggestive influences*. Each of these broad domains can be broken down into a number of distinct variables, any

combination of which contributes to the overall suggestive effect.

What do the scientific studies reviewed in chapters 8 through 10 inform us about individual differences in a trait of suggestibility? More specifically, how do individual trait differences and/or contextual/social influences contribute to a vulnerability to make *memory commission errors*?

First, the extensive studies on the misinformation effect have demonstrated that a subsample of individuals are vulnerable to confounding post-event misinformation with their memory for an event. The misinformation effect is a robust and replicable finding over numerous experiments. If we separate source monitoring errors and response bias from the overall variance of the misinformation effect, we are left with an estimate of 3–5% of laboratory subjects who are vulnerable to post-event misinformation suggestions under experimental conditions relative to control subjects. It is important to note, however, that a small subsample of control subjects also commit memory errors. These data reflect individual differences in response to waking post-event misinformation suggestions. We can say that an estimated 3–5% of the general population are especially vulnerable to misinformation suggestion when other memory suggestive influences are controlled. We might consider this phenomenon a trait of *waking post-event misinformation suggestibility*. Unfortunately, memory scientists have failed to develop a standardized instrument to measure trait differences in misinformation suggestibility per se, nor have they published norms on misinformation suggestibility. Conceivably, the original Loftus paradigm could be used for this purpose. Moreover, we do not know whether or not a trait of misinformation suggestibility is stable over time or variable according to contextual influences.

Vulnerability to commit memory *source monitoring errors* is another robust finding within the memory suggestibility literature (Lindsay, 1990, 1994b). Subjects who make a source monitoring error misidentify the post-event narrative information as if it were a memory for the original slide presentation. According to Lindsay and Johnson (1987), individuals differ widely in the criteria they use to monitor and identify the sources of their memories under different conditions. Under certain conditions some subjects use "lax source monitoring criteria" (Lindsay, 1994a,

p. 34). While the source monitoring literature emphasizes within-subject situational variability in the use of source monitoring criteria, it could equally emphasize the across-subject variability in vulnerability to source monitoring errors. Lindsay (1990), for example, found that 27% of his experimental subjects (relative to 9% of control subjects) made source-monitoring errors under conditions in which the sources of information might easily be confused, but this dropped to 13% under conditions that made it easier to discriminate between the original stimulus presentation and the post-event narrative. Lindsay's findings imply that 13–27% of subjects are highly vulnerable to these kinds of errors "when a memory derived from one source is misattributed to another source" (Lindsay, 1990, p. 1078). In other words, some people are significantly more vulnerable than others to shifting their criteria in evaluating the sources of their memories.

Hypnotizability, as a personality trait, is also a robust and replicable finding over a large number of studies. About 5–8% of the general population is in the high-hypnotizable range. However, within the overall domain of hypnotizability there is a variety of distinct subtalents, such as the capacity to respond to ideomotor suggestions, to manifest posthypnotic effects, or to alter memory in certain ways (Hilgard, 1965). Therefore, in addition to individual differences in hypnotizability, it is especially important to consider individual differences in *hypnotic pseudomemory suggestibility*. According to the existing studies, approximately 25% of high-hypnotizable subjects are vulnerable to pseudomemory suggestions for peripheral details, when other factors are controlled (and this figure can go up to as high as 80% when pseudomemory suggestibility is combined with a constellation of social influence variables). The 25% of high-hypnotizables means about 4–6% of the general population is at risk to produce pseudomemories at least for peripheral details based on their hypnotizability. We can say with considerable confidence that a certain subgroup of people within the general population is highly hypnotizable, and within that group, a subsample of individuals is vulnerable to report pseudomemories under certain conditions. It is true that most of the evidence for hypnotic pseudomemories is produced by high-hypnotizable subjects and that high and moderate hynotizability is a risk factor for pseudomemory pro-

duction (Laurence & Perry, 1983). However, as we learned in chapter 10, it is also true that social influence variables contribute much more to the risk for hypnotic pseudomemory production than hypnotizability per se, and therefore, whether or not a high-hypnotizable individual is at risk for pseudomemory production is perhaps more a function of how interviews are conducted than a function of hypnotizability per se.

The Gudjonsson Suggestibility Scale (GSS) (Gudjonsson, 1984a) measures individual differences in the *trait of interrogatory suggestibility*. This scale specifically measures memory suggestibility. While the scale is designed to give a Total Suggestibility Score, or overall measure of interrogatory suggestibility, it also has three other subscales— Shift, Yield 1, and Yield 2. Register and Kihlstrom (1988) believe that "there are three possibly independent components to interrogatory suggestibility: response to negative feedback, response to leading questions, and response to repeated interrogation" (p. 556), assessed by the Shift, Yield 1, and Yield 2 scores, respectively. Factor analytic studies have shown that the GSS is composed of two independent factors roughly equivalent to misinformation suggestibility and vulnerability to negative emotional feedback. The GSS measures individual differences in response to a combination of cognitive (misinformation suggestion) and social (negative emotional feedback and repeated misleading) suggestion variables, the combination of which is defined as vulnerability to interrogatory suggestion.

While each of these three types of suggestibility is supported by an established scientific tradition of research, little research has been conducted on the interrelationship between these three types of suggestibility. Whether there is a variety of independent types of suggestibility or whether there is an underlying unitary factor of suggestibility represents an ongoing controversy. The prevailing consensus favors the *multidimensional view of suggestibility* (e.g., Eysenck, 1991), although some empirical research implies that there might be more overlap between different types of suggestibility that was seen in earlier studies (Linton & Sheehan, 1994).

The interrelationship between these three types of suggestibility is yet unclear. Since *none* of the studies on misinformation suggestibility ever assessed hypnotizability, we do not know the degree to which misinformation suggestibility overlaps with hypnotizability. There is a possibility, of course, that hypnotizability might account for a significant portion of the variance of misinformation suggestibility.

There are some data on the relationship between hypnotizability and interrogatory suggestibility. Register and Kihlstrom (1988) investigated the effects of hypnosis on interrogatory suggestibility. Subjects were prescreened for hypnotizability using standardized instruments to measure hypnotizability and then classified into high- and low-hypnotizable groups. Then subjects were given the GSS and asked to immediately recall the story. Four days later subjects were given three successive recall trials—an initial free recall session, recall following an hypnotic induction and suggestions for memory enhancement, and recall after hypnosis. During the hypnotic session subjects were given the 20 interrogatory questions from the GSS. The negative emotional feedback instructions were not given. Subjects showed a progressive increase in their recall of the GSS story with each successive recall trial, but also increased the number of confabulations with each recall trial. Hypnotizability had no effect on recall or on the number of memory commission errors made. Register and Kihlstrom conclude, "These results support Gudjonsson's (1987b) hypothesis that interrogative suggestibility is independent of suggestibility as measured in a hypnotic context" (p. 556). Unfortunately, the research design did not allow for a comparison of the relative contribution of hypnotizability, hypnotic procedures, and the hypnotic context to the overall effect.

In a better designed study Linton and Sheehan (1994) randomly assigned subjects to the following conditions: hypnotizability (high vs. low); state (waking vs. hypnotic induction); and feedback on the GSS (negative vs. neutral). High hypnotizability correlated significantly with the Total Suggestibility Score, the Yield 1, and the Yield 2 scores on the GSS. The induction of trance did not differ appreciably from the waking condition. Therefore, *hypnotic procedures designed to induce a state of trance did not significantly increase subjects' vulnerability to interrogatory suggestions.* Linton and Sheehan conclude that "subjects who are highly responsive to hypnosis are more likely than those who are not to yield to leading questions in an interrogatory context . . . high susceptible subjects responded significantly

more affirmatively to leading questions than did low susceptible subjects" (pp. 62–63).

While both studies yield contradictory results about the relationship between hypnotizability and yielding to systematic misleading suggestions (Yield 1 on the GSS), no relationship has been established between hypnotizability and negative emotional feedback (Shift) on the GSS. Thus, it appears that hypnotic suggestibility and interrogatory suggestibility are at least partially independent.

Identifying a trait (or traits) of suggestibility may not be entirely separable from the question: suggestibility for what type of information? Or in what social context? Most of the adult studies on misinformation suggestibility address primarily a small number of suggestions for plot-irrelevant peripheral details. Most of the studies on hypnotic pseudomemory likewise investigate suggestions for a few minor details. The studies on interrogatory suggestibility using the GSS, by way of contrast, consistently emphasize a larger number of misleading suggestions (systematic misleading) for both plot-relevant actions as well and background details. Therefore, instruments like the GSS that measure suggestibility for complex events are especially relevant to the false memory debate.

Until the possible interrelationship among misinformation suggestibility, interrogatory suggestibility, and hypnotizability is established through more carefully designed experimental studies, we are left with the conclusion that *there are at least three partially independent types of suggestibility.* About 3–5% of people are highly vulnerable to misinformation suggestions for peripheral details (*high misinformation suggestibility*), although a larger group of people (moderate misinformation suggestibility) may make commission errors to post-event misinformation in a context where the original and post-event information are easily confused (source monitoring error) and/or in a social interaction that encourages a response bias or a more lax decision criterion (up to 27%). About 25% of *high hypnotizables* (25% of the 8% of the overall population that are high hypnotizables) are vulnerable to hypnotic pseudomemory suggestion, at least for peripheral detail information. Some but not all of these high-hypnotizables may have a more difficult time than low-hypnotizables distinguishing memory content from fantasy productions in the stream of consciousness. *High interrogatory suggestibility* specifically pertains to those subjects who are highly vulnerable to making memory commission errors for both central actions and peripheral details when subjected to *systematic* misleading information (within and across sessions) and interpersonal pressure.

How are these data on individual differences in suggestibility pertinent to the false memory debate? First, they demonstrate that a subgroup of individuals is vulnerable to suggested memory commission errors. Second, they suggest that there may be several distinct subgroups of individuals who are vulnerable to memory suggestion effects. The subgroups of individuals most at risk of making substantial memory commission errors in response to suggestions are: (1) certain high-hypnotizable people and (2) high interrogatory suggestible people. Third, these data make it very clear that clinicians need to assess memory suggestibility in a standardized way, at least when trauma is suspected by the patient or therapist but the patient has no memories of trauma.

In addition to a trait (or traits) of suggestibility, a variety of *situational variables* contributes significantly to vulnerability to memory commission errors. Because of the number of variables and the complex interaction among variables that affect memory suggestibility, these variables have been organized along a continuum from less to more suggestive—what we will call the *situational suggestive continuum*. This continuum is further divided into cognitive factors and social factors, each of which makes an independent contribution to memory suggestibility (Ceci & Bruck, 1993). Thus, the *overall suggestive effect* is the result of a *complex interaction of a trait of suggestibility as well as a number of cognitive and social situational influences.*

One important cognitive factor contributing to memory suggestibility is the *strength of the memory* (Loftus & Hoffman, 1989). The misinformation studies have clearly demonstrated that memory suggestibility is directly related to *uncertainty* about the target event. The weaker the memory strength, the greater the vulnerability to external suggestion. *Encoding status* is strongly related to suggestion. Studies on the misinformation effect have demonstrated that subjects who fail to encode the original stimulus details, or who encode it but suffer from a decay in the memory, are especially vulnerable to misinformation suggestion. Encoding status is in part

a function of attention. If the subject failed to attend to the original stimulus information, it is not encoded in memory.

Retention interval is another aspect of memory strength. A tradition of memory research going back as far as Ebbinghaus has shown that memory decays more and more over time, although the rate of decay is in part dependent on the type of information to be remembered. Generally speaking, memory strength is weaker at longer as compared to shorter retention intervals, although, as we have seen, memory for certain types of emotionally arousing events may be the exception to this rule. Longer retention intervals are also associated with hypermnesia under certain conditions.

Age also is related to the strength of the memory. It is clearly established that younger children give a less complete verbal memory report than older children in most situations, presumably because the cognitive organization of memory is less mature than that of older children.

Gheorghiu and Kruse (1991) summarize that, in addition to individual differences in suggestibility, suggestion is largely a function of "*ambiguous situations*" (p. 63). "Ambiguity is defined as the possibility of multiple interpretations" (p. 67). Suggestion makes the situation less ambiguous through "fill[ing in] the gap[s]" or "putting a special interpretation" on the situation. Gheorghiu and Kruse define suggestion as a process of "disambiguation" (p. 60) by which experience is made more certain (though not necessarily more accurate). *Source misattributions* are in part a function of the ambiguity of the situation, since the rate of source monitoring errors is about twice as high in situations where the original and post-event information are easily confused, as compared to situations where they are easy to tell apart (Lindsay, 1990).

Overall, both the internal status of the individual's memory (encoding status, retention interval, and age) and the nature of the external situation (degree of ambiguity) contribute in complex ways to determining the overall strength or weakness of the memory for a target event. The weaker the memory strength, the greater the vulnerability to suggestion; the stronger the memory strength, the greater the resistance to suggestion. Thus, younger children and adults who suspect abuse after a long interval has elapsed, who are quite uncertain about the past event(s) in question, *are* more vulnerable to social suggestive influences in and outside of therapy, independent of their memory suggestibility.

Another cognitive factor contributing to suggestion is the *type of post-event information* suggested. We have seen that it is relatively easy to demonstrate suggestion for plot-irrelevant peripheral background details in adult and child subjects. With the exception of highly suggestible people, most people are generally resistant to plot-relevant misinformation for central actions and especially for actions directly related to the source of emotional arousal, at least in a situation free of systematic suggestion and/or interpersonal pressure. Studies on the misinformation effect in children have shown that children rarely accept misleading suggestions about abuse-like actions that never actually happened. The adult misinformation studies also demonstrate that suggested *plausible* more than improbable information contributes significantly to memory commission errors. Thus, the available data demonstrate that most adults in psychotherapy would *not* readily accept a therapist's suggestions for central abuse actions, although they might accept suggestions that result in distortion of peripheral background and person descriptive details, the exceptions occurring when the person is very highly suggestible and/or is subjected to systematic interrogatory pressure.

Both the interviewee's and interviewer's *expectations* can contribute to suggestion. From a theoretical perspective, Gudjonsson and Clark's (1986) model of interrogatory suggestibility illustrates how the "general cognitive set" of the suspect can be manipulated in a police interview to increase the likelihood of confession. Leichtman and Ceci's Sam Stone study (1995) is a good example of how *subjects' pre-event expectations* can be experimentally manipulated so as to significantly increase their vulnerability to memory commission errors. Gudjonsson and Clark's model also emphasizes that *interrogatory bias* on the part of the interviewer is an important contributing factor to suggestibility. Those police interrogators who have a fixed belief or a priori rigid idea about a suspect's involvement in the crime in question are more likely than others to extract a false confession. We have also seen that an interviewer's beliefs can be experimentally manipulated in the laboratory in a way that significantly increases memory commission errors (Ceci, 1994). Moreover,

what questions are asked, and the way they are asked by the interviewer, can introduce a response bias that increases the likelihood that the subject will give a distorted memory report (Loftus & Zanni, 1975; McCloskey & Zaragoza, 1985).

Overall, these studies demonstrate that memory commission errors are likely to increase when a subject enters an interview having already been influenced by biased pre-event information and is matched with an interviewer who has such a rigid belief about some uncertain past event(s) that s/he frames the interview questions in a biased way. Thus, a patient who enters therapy having been biased by a thorough immersion in the self-help popular literature on abuse or who has attended many survivor groups who is matched with a trauma-identified therapist is at risk to develop false beliefs about abuse that never occurred. Likewise, the patient who has recovered memories and who is only exposed to FMSF propaganda in consultation with accused family members, FMSF members, and lawyers, all of whom strongly believe that recovered memories of abuse are false, is at risk of creating a fictional belief that the recovered memories were falsely implanted by the therapist.

Source credibility is a powerful factor in changing a subject's report, although it is not clearly established that source credibility effects alter the memory representation per se. A long tradition on research on attitude change has made it clear that subjects are influenced by an interviewer who is seen as highly credible, expert, and trustworthy (e.g., Cohen, 1964; Insko, 1967). Research on interrogatory suggestibility has demonstrated that confessions are more easily extracted in the context of a closed social interaction, wherein there is a clear *power differential* between an authoritarian interrogator and the dependent subject. Thus, vulnerability to suggestion is increased when an interviewer is perceived as credible and expert, but more so when the interviewer acts in an authoritarian manner and exploits the power imbalance in the relationship. Thus, memory suggestibility is increased in the context of an hierarchical as compared to an egalitarian therapeutic relationship, especially when the therapist presents himself as an authoritative source about the patient's past. Likewise, patients who recover accurate memories of abuse in therapy may come to doubt these memories when notable memory scientists say that such recovered memories cannot be trusted. Prestigious memory scientists who make public statements about memory fallibility and memory suggestibility may serve as a good example of source credibility persuasion.

Systematic misleading greatly contributes to suggested memory commission errors. Most of the adult studies on the misinformation effect utilize a relatively small number of post-event misleading suggestions (one or two, sometimes up to four, critical items) relative to the total information provided. These are presented in a single session (phase II of the experimental design). The Gudjonsson Suggestibility Scale utilizes a much larger number of misleading questions (15 of 20 post-event questions). The subject is asked these same questions twice. The work of Ceci (1994) and his associates utilizes misleading suggestions repeated both within and across multiple interviews (up to 10 sessions). In a police interrogation, it is not uncommon for an interview to last for many hours, sometimes days. It is clear from the Ceci studies that the *amount* and *duration* of exposure to misinformation suggestions, both *within and across multiple interviews*, significantly increase memory commission errors. However, we need also to remember that a number of experimental studies on hypermnesia have found the opposite, namely, a significant increase in the amount of accurate information recalled without a substantial increase in memory errors as a result of repeated interviews where free recall strategies were used (Dent & Stephenson, 1979; Dunning & Stern, 1992; Malpass & Devine, 1981; Scrivner & Safer, 1988; Turtle & Yuille, 1994). Thus, the crucial issue may not be one of repeated interviews per se, but how the interviews are conducted.

It is very clear that free recall minimizes memory commission errors over repeated interviews. Increasing the amount and duration of exposure to misinformation within and across interviews, along with a demand to respond to misleading questions, is defined as *systematic misleading*. Any given interview is likely to contain some misleading information. Generally speaking, occasional misleading comments are far from being unduly suggestive. Serious memory commission errors, like relatively stable false memories about past events, are rarely a function of occasional misleading suggestions. With the exception of very highly suggestive individuals, the research data demonstrate that false memories for complex events are usually a function of systematic misleading. While most therapeutic interactions probably contain occasional misleading statements, systematic leading is *not* characteristic of professional trauma treatment. We suppose that some very bad therapy, and certainly bad child abuse investigations, are characterized by systematic misleading, especially when the duration of interview sessions is extended and misleading suggestions about abuse are systematically repeated both within and across multiple interview sessions. Unlike the forensic context in which Gudjonsson observed high memory error rates, most professional therapy, however, does not resemble a police interrogation.

Emotional manipulation makes an independent contribution to memory suggestibility (Gudjosson, 1984a; Linton & Sheehan, 1994). Threats and rewards are an integral part police interrogations (Gudjonsson & Clark, 1986). Disapproval for giving the "wrong" answer or threat of longer detention alternate with approval and leniency when the "right" answer is given. Research on the GSS has shown that negative emotional feedback (Shift score) can directly influence a subject's memory about a complex event (Gudjonsson, 1984a). More systematic attack on self-esteem (Gudjonsson, 1992) or the core self representation (Ofshe & Singer, 1986) can substantially increase vulnerability to memory commission errors. Directly encouraging someone to lie (Haugaard et al., 1991) or otherwise coaching a subject to give a certain answer (Gardner, 1992) also significantly increases vulnerability to memory commission errors. Thus, therapists and child abuse investigators who praise or otherwise demonstrate approval of patients who recover abuse memories, or who become critical or rejecting when patients fail to produce such memories, are increasing the risk to producing false beliefs about past abuse in their patients. Likewise, accused family members who offer a patient loving acceptance for retracting recovered abuse memories or those who hold out the possibility of lucrative financial gain through suing the former therapist are equally at risk of unduly influencing the patient's beliefs.

Requiring a *behavioral response* from a subject also increases the suggestion effect. A long tradition of cognitive dissonance research has clearly demonstrated that subjects change their attitudes more when they are asked to behave in a way contrary to their original attitude, for example, writing an essay in favor of a religious or political belief contrary to their own (Festinger, 1957). Most studies on the misinformation effect utilize a forced multiple choice recognition test without understanding that requiring the subject to make a behavioral response in the form of choosing one item over another is in itself suggestive. Most standardized instruments used to measure hypnotizability are also constructed around requiring a demonstrable behavioral response to each hypnotic suggestion given (Hilgard, 1965). Requiring a behavioral response is clearly exploited in many police interrogations in the form of demanding an oral or written confession.

Thus, a pattern emerges from very diverse sources: introducing a social demand that a behavioral response to a suggestion is expected greatly increases the likelihood the subject will change his/her behavior or report in the direction of the expected behavior. Thus, the therapist who requires a written statement of the trauma story and/or encourages a patient to take action against an accused family (cut off relationships or sue) is increasing the potential for memory distortion. Likewise, accused family members who encourage a retractor to give talks on the dangers of recovered memory therapy or sue the former therapist are increasing the patient's distortion about recovered memories.

Studies on coercive persuasion have demonstrated that *milieu control* contributes to belief change. Total control of the environment through detention, isolation, and control of daily routines was characteristic of early communist thought reform programs. The main element, however, is total *information control*. Prisoners receive only propaganda provided by their interrogators; they are not exposed to alternative sources of information (Hinkle & Wolff, 1956; Lifton, 1956; Schein, 1956). The importance of information control is also found in Gudjonsson and Clark's (1986) model of interrogatory suggestibility. Vulnerability to suggestion is significantly enhanced in the context of a closed social interaction characterized by a one-way flow of information. Control of the social milieu is also critical. Studies on Chinese communist thought reform document the powerful effect of the peer social group on thought reform (Hinkle & Wolff, 1956). Later studies on cults have also demonstrated the powerful effect of peer group

influences on belief change (Ofshe & Singer, 1986).

Overall, these studies demonstrate that a subject is significantly more likely to alter his/her beliefs if s/he is severely restricted in his/her social contacts, in such a manner that the information provided is limited solely to what an individual interviewer and/or peer group systematically presents, than if s/he is exposed to alternative or competing viewpoints. Thus, a patient with a very restricted lifestyle, whose primary contacts are a trauma-identified therapist with rigid beliefs and one or more self-help peer survivor groups, who reads only popular survivor literature and who is not exposed to alternative viewpoints, is more vulnerable to develop false beliefs about abuse. Likewise, a patient who has recovered memories of sexual abuse who has returned to live with the accused family but otherwise has few other social contacts, and is exposed only to the information distributed by the FMSF, who repeatedly attends local FMSF meetings, and is coached by FMSF associated lawyers to sue the former therapist, is more vulnerable to retract and falsely report that the recovered memory was made up. The key here is the severity of information control and indoctrination by either the therapist (and peer survivor group) or the accused family (and false memory advocacy group).

Psychophysiological destabilization is another important ingredient of thought reform, in the form of disruption of sleep routines, eating and elimination habits, physical ordeals and beatings. Whereas these techniques of physical affliction are not relevant to the therapy situation, the techniques of psychological destablization sometimes are. Ofshe and Singer (1986) have shown that a combination of altered states of consciousness and peer group influences contributes to radical belief changes in cult members, especially if these methods destabilize the individual's coping and defense structures and core self representation. Therapies that foster undue regression by breaking down a patient's defenses while failing to enhance coping ability and/or undermining self-esteem may contribute to the development of false beliefs.

Figure 11.2 summarizes all of the factors known to affect memory suggestibility. A number of conclusions can be drawn from this figure:

1. There are two main contributing factors to memory suggestibility: (a) a trait (or traits) of

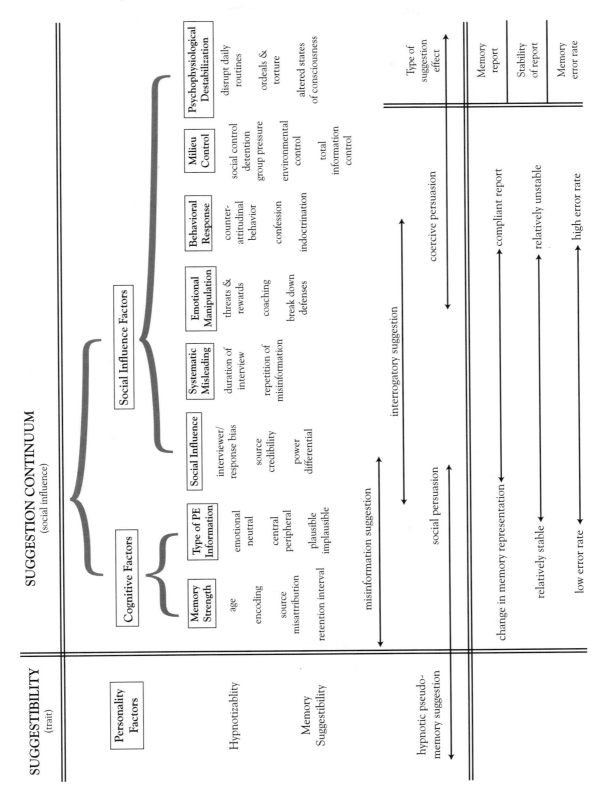

SUGGESTION CONTINUUM
(social influence)

SUGGESTIBILITY
(trait)

memory suggestibility and (b) a specific suggestive situation.

2. Memory suggestion is significantly increased when a combination of situational suggestive factors is operative. The greater the number of situational suggestive factors operative, and the more factors drawn from the social rather than the cognitive domain (those factors more representative of the right end of the continuum), the greater the memory commission errors.

3. The combination of a high-suggestible subject (high interrogatory suggestibility and/or hypnotizability) and a specific constellation of a number of cognitive and social suggestive influences significantly increases memory suggestibility.

4. However, the more the situational suggestive factors are representative of the right end of the continuum (predominance of social over cognitive factors), the less likely that the distorted report constitutes a change in the memory representation per se. A trade-off occurs. It is quite possible to increase substantially the incidence of false reporting about past events by applying a pattern of interpersonal pressure in an interview, yet the report that results is more likely to be a function of social compliance and less likely to be a function of memory alteration.

5. The more the situational suggestive factors are representative of the right end of the continuum (predominance of social over cognitive factors), the more unstable they are. Belief change produced primarily through interpersonal pressure and milieu control is context-dependent; once the person is removed from the context the unstable belief is subject to decay unless otherwise reinforced. On the other hand, memory suggestion that is the outcome of suggestive factors representative of the left end of the chart (a trait of memory suggestibility, weak memory strength, biased expectations, and source credibility) can lead to stable, relatively context-resistant changes in beliefs about past events, at least some of which constitute newly "created" memories.

An examination of Figure 11.2 should make it clear why the false memory argument is oversimplified. Loftus (1993) and Lindsay and Read (1994) argue that false memories for childhood sexual abuse are the consequence of therapeutic suggestion. As evidence, these researchers draw upon several decades of laboratory research on the misinformation effect. This is not the strongest source of evidence on suggestibility to make a case for therapeutically suggested false memories. This research merely shows that some subjects, whose memory strength for the original item is poor when given post-event misinformation primarily about minor details, give false reports about their recollections of the original information. This research rarely assesses trait differences in suggestibility. With the exception of response bias, and occasionally source credibility, the research designs rarely include measurement of the various social influence variables that affect suggestibility. Misinformation research falls on the left side of the situational suggestion continuum, where suggestive effects are the weakest, though more stable, and where the memory commission error base rates are generally low, except for minor details about which the person is uncertain. The primary value of the research on the misinformation effect is its clear demonstration that people accept suggestions when they are uncertain about the event in question.

Richard Ofshe, another outspoken advocate of the false memory position, bases his argument on years of research on thought reform. His research falls more on the extreme right side of the situational suggestion continuum. Therefore, his argument about therapy is too extreme, unless we are to accept that what he calls "memory recovery therapy" is a form of brainwashing. Most psychotherapy does not use milieu control procedures. Psychotherapy is rarely an example of extreme information control, in that even where a therapist may have a strong bias about suspected abuse, a patient is exposed to alternate sources of information outside of psychotherapy. The value of Ofshe and Singer's work (1986) is that it reminds us that total immersion in a peer cultural group can be a very powerful source of indoctrination. When research on coercive persuasion is used to understand suggestion in psychotherapy, it becomes clear that peer group influences, such as immersion in a number of peer self-help groups for abuse survivors, probably serve as a much more powerful source of suggestion of illusory reports about abuse, than individual therapy. Moreover, individual or group therapies that break down the patient's coping ability, defenses, or self representation—what we consider regressive therapies—can also contribute to the development of false beliefs about abuse.

The trouble with the sources of evidence used by Loftus and Ofshe is that they miss the main effects. We are not going to understand the conditions under which false memories develop in psychotherapy from research on misinformation suggestion and coercive persuasion alone. The data we have reviewed clearly demonstrate that hypnotizability (and more specifically pseudomemory suggestibility in high-hypnotizable subjects) and interrogatory suggestibility make substantial contributions to our understanding of suggested memory commission errors for complex events. Some very high-hypnotizables process information in a way that makes it difficult to distinguish between an actual memory and a fantasy. Those high on the GSS are vulnerable to systematic and repeated misinformation and/or manipulation of negative emotional feedback. Some individuals are at risk to make memory commission errors in any therapeutic situation, as well as elsewhere in their lives. Those in the moderate range of suggestibility are relatively resistant to memory commission errors about central events, except for peripheral details. However, their memory suggestibility can be substantially increased in a therapeutic relationship that introduces a number of cognitive and social influence factors characteristic of situational suggestion, especially if the therapeutic interaction recreates many or all of the components of interrogatory suggestion.

Based on the available evidence, we disagree with the argument false memory advocates have put forth about therapeutic suggestion of false memories of childhood sexual abuse because it is overstated and oversimplified. A therapist's beliefs about suspected abuse, as a sole factor of suggestion, in and of itself is an inadequate explanation of illusory memories of childhood sexual abuse unless the therapist's beliefs translate into a specific pattern of interview behavior, namely, systematically supplying misinformation to the patient about suspected abuse. Occasional unwitting misleading suggestions (Yapko, 1994a), even the suggestion of a diagnosis of abuse,

cannot adequately explain illusory memories of CSA. Occasional suggestions about complex emotional interactions like abuse are not generally effective except in highly suggestible subjects.

Stable false recollections for entire, complex events like CSA that never happened are not so easy to demonstrate in the great majority of people within the moderate range of memory suggestibility, unless a very specific constellation of interrogatory tactics is used systematically over time, like systematic rewards and punishments, the manipulation of expectations, and the systematic repetition of misleading information over many interview sessions. In order to "create" false beliefs about abuse that never happened, the therapeutic situation must meet a number of the following criteria:

- memory suggestibility (patient must demonstrate trait of high suggestibility, specifically memory suggestibility). If the patient is low to moderately suggestible, then the therapeutic situation must contain a number of the following suggestion factors:
- weak memory strength (patient is preschool age or, if adult, is quite uncertain about the past event in question);
- type of information (patient will more readily accept misleading suggestions for peripheral background and person description details than for central actions like abuse);
- source credibility (therapist acts like authoritative expert);
- patient bias (patient has been exposed to pretherapy information that has caused suspicion of abuse);
- therapist bias (therapist has fixed belief that patient was abused; and this belief must directly influence how the interview is conducted, in that the therapist must systematically supply misinformation);
- systematic misleading (therapist introduces a large number of misleading statements about abuse both within and across multiple interview sessions, rather than encouraging free recall by patient);
- emotional manipulation (therapist threatens to blame or reject patient for failing to produce desired memories and/or praises or rewards patient for producing such memories);

- behavioral response (therapist expects behavioral response in form of a written trauma narrative, presentation of trauma story to others, or taking action against alleged perpetrator);
- milieu control (therapist absolutely controls information flow and patient is denied alternative perspectives both within and outside of therapeutic context);
- psychophysiological manipulation (therapist breaks down patient's defenses, fails to enhance coping, assaults patient's esteem or core self representation, or otherwise fosters a seriously regressive therapy).

This is a *very specific* set of conditions, which most professional psychotherapy, unless it is very bad, fails to approximate. Most professional psychotherapy is not at all conducted like a police interrogation, although lay psychotherapy within the self-help movement may approximate these conditions in certain cases. Some child abuse investigations may also approximate these conditions. Retractors who have been influenced by their accused families, have internalized the systematic information disseminated by the FMSF, and have been coached by FMSF associated lawyers certainly meet many of these criteria.

The lesson learned from the false memory debate is that therapists should consider assessing suggestibility in some standardized way, especially when

abuse is suspected, so as to identify those genuinely at risk for making significant memory commission errors. Therapists should also assess their own therapeutic conduct so as to refrain from obvious interrogatory excesses like rewards and punishments, systematic repetition of misleading information about abuse, etc.

To illustrate what we currently know about memory suggestibility, let's return to the question of *base rates* for memory commission errors. The false memory advocates wish the reader to believe that the rates are quite high. Our view is that they are quite low, at least in professional trauma treatment, although they may be higher in self-help peer group therapy. There are no available data drawn from psychotherapy per se to support either speculation. What do the data from the various research sources we have reviewed actually tell us about base rates? Table 11.1 summarizes the base rate data across the different sources of suggestion. A clear pattern emerges. (1) The base rates in the adult misinformation studies are highly variable, ranging from 0–27%. When response bias and source misattribution are controlled, the rate drops to 0–5%. The base rate in Goodman's child misinformation studies consistently runs around 3–5%. Combining the adult and child data, it appears that somewhere between 3 and 5% of individuals within the general population are vulnerable to suggestive distortion of their memory for past events. (2) Perhaps 4–6% of high

TABLE 11.1
Base Rates of Memory Commission Errors across Different Sources of Memory Suggestion

AREA OF MEMORY RESEARCH	MISINFORMATION SUGGESTION	HYPNOTIZABILITY AND PSEUDOMEMORY	HYPNOTIZABILITY PLUS SOCIAL INFLUENCE	INTERROGATORY SUGGESTION
adult studies	0–5%*	4–6% [25%]**	25–80%	42–76%
child studies	3–5%			37–72%
Rates of False Allegations in Child Abuse Investigations	general population 4–8%			custody disputes 28–36%
Suggestion Variable Involved	trait	trait	trait plus social influence	trait plus social influence

* when social influence like response bias and source credibility is factored out of the overall variance
** 25% of high hypnotizables, or 4–6% of the general population

hypnotizable subjects produce hypnotic pseudo-memories for peripheral details in response to suggestions either in a waking or hypnotic conditions when situational influence is controlled for (Lynn et al., 1989, 1991, 1992; Murrey et al., 1992; Spanos & Bures, 1993–94; Spanos & McLean, 1986). However, the rate of such *reports* may increase up to 80% under certain conditions of social influence. High-hypnotizables constitute about 7–10% of the general population, depending on how hypnotizability is measured; about 4–6% of this select group may be genuinely vulnerable to hypnotic pseudomemory suggestions. The base rates of reports of hypnotic pseudomemory production are remarkably close to those of the nonhypnotic misinformation studies. (3) The base rates in the adult forensic studies on interrogatory suggestibility are much higher—from 42–76%. Ceci's child studies, where a combination of social influence factors are manipulated, are also high—from 37–72%. Again, these are within the same range. (4) The base rates on false allegations occurring in the context of child abuse investigations show a similar pattern. A total of 4–8% of all allegations of CSA made within the general population are false. However, if reports made specifically within the context of custody disputes are considered as a separate sample, the false allegation rate rises to 28–36%, presumably because of coaching or other interrogatory pressure by a parent (Benedek & Schetky, 1987a,b; Green, 1986; Jones & McGraw, 1987; Schuman, 1986).

These figures across studies suggest a *bimodal distribution* of rates for memory commission errors. First,

about 3–6% of the overall population possess a trait of high memory suggestibility, either related or unrelated to hypnotizability. These people are highly vulnerable to make memory commission errors, at least for peripheral information, although they may make errors for central information under certain conditions of social influence. Second, one- to two-thirds of all other people could conceivably make memory commission errors in an interrogatory social interaction characterized by a combination of source credibility manipulation, manipulation of expectations, systematic misleading, emotional manipulation, information control, and/or psychophysiological destabilization. Third, about one-third of all individuals appear to be resistant to memory commission errors in all but very extreme conditions.

If we apply these figures to the false memory debate, our hypothesis is that about 3–6% of individuals entering psychotherapy have a trait of high memory suggestibility, and although they are certainly at risk for making memory commission errors, they may not necessarily make these errors in a particular therapy. Our second hypothesis is that any psychotherapy that recreates many or most of the components of interrogatory suggestion will substantially increase the risk of memory commission errors about abuse that never happened. An upper limit of about two-thirds of patients seeing an extremely interrogatory therapist may develop false beliefs about abuse. However, we do not know how many therapists fulfill the extreme condition of conducting therapy with most of the elements of interrogation suggestion.

12

∥∥∥∥∥∥∥∥∥∥∥∥∥∥∥∥∥∥∥

The False Logic of the False Memory
Controversy and the Irrational Element in
Scientific Research on Memory

THE FALSE LOGIC OF THE
MEMORY DEBATE

The Nature of Memory

It has been a common practice in the history of memory science to explain memory processing in terms of the prevailing technology of the day. Freud used a metaphor derived from quantum mechanics, Broadbent (1958) used an image of the brain as a telecommunications switchboard, and Morton et al. (1985) have explained memory storage in terms of a computer filing system. Today, false memory advocates have criticized therapists for adhering to a so-called tape- or video-recorder view of memory processing (Lindsay & Read, 1994; Yapko, 1994a). The tape-recorder view of memory essentially is a recasting of a strong trace theory in a metaphor of contemporary technology.

While there is nothing wrong with the metaphor per se, the question is whether or not trauma therapists actually adhere to such a view. As Braude (1995) points out, "it is simply false that so-called memory recovery therapy is committed to any such view" (p. 256). While he admits that therapists hold a range of views on the nature of memory, he correctly points out that few therapists actually adhere to an extreme trace view, namely, that memory is completely and accurately recorded for all events,

and that such memory can be completely and accurately recovered, without distortions, if the correct memory recovery techniques are carefully used.

The view that many therapists hold is that any given verbal memory for a past event is more or less complete and is a mixture of accurate and inaccurate information depending on the situation. There has been a tendency of some more vocal false memory advocates to take an extreme, almost caricaturized, view concerning memory, and then state that this view is representative of the entire clinical field. Between the extremes on either side— that memory is completely accurate or very fallible— is a position that most clinicians probably adopt—what Brewer has called a "partial constructive view" (1986), i.e., the gist of significant personal experiences is reasonably accurately recalled, while the details may be less accurately recalled. As Braude (1995) says:

> the mere attempt to uncover or search for hidden traumatic memories rests on two relatively modest assumptions: a) that it is possible for memories to be hidden by some form of traumatic amnesia, and b) that it is possible to reverse traumatic amnesia by means of memory recovery techniques. . . . [R]emembering . . . does not presuppose that memory recovery techniques elicit infallible or totally accurate memory reports. (pp. 256–257)

We do not need an extreme tape-recorder view of memory to justify the use of memory recovery techniques, nor must recovered memory reports be absolutely accurate. In this regard, clinicians generally maintain the same view of memory as do courts of law. Memory may be challenged by attorneys because of the possibility of errors in acquisition, storage, and retrieval. The law handles memory issues as it handles all issues, by asking whether the entire evidence meets the requisite burden of proof.

Those contending that clinicians hold the extreme tape-recorder view of memory have cited as primary evidence the misuse of otherwise helpful anecdotal studies. For example, Yapko (1994b) surveyed primarily master's level clinicians with a Memory Attitude Questionnaire and found that 30% adhered to the tape-recorder view. But Yapko's survey, as he readily acknowledges, is not intended to be scientific. Because he surveyed mostly master's level clinicians, there is a sampling bias. Sampling clinicians less trained and presumably less knowledgeable about memory may have contributed an inflation in the base rate of clinicians seeming to adhere to the tape-recorder view. More importantly, however, from a scientific perspective, there is a serious flaw in the questionnaire he used, namely, respondents were not given a range of less extreme alternate choices about their model of memory. Either they endorsed the extreme tape-recorder view or they did not. The question was posed in a way that stacked the deck toward confirming the extreme tape-recorder view. The value in Yapko's data, however, when they are not taken beyond their limits, is the evidence they provide that accurate information about memory and about the use of hypnosis with memory is not fully shared by clinicians. Despite its methodological flaws, Yapko's informal study makes its essential points: (1) there is much misinformation about memory, (2) clinicians need to be informed about laboratory data, and (3) researchers need to be familiar with clinical findings.

Some therapists clearly do adhere to the extreme tape-recorder view, especially when childhood sexual abuse is at issue. With the great diversity within the clinical field, it is not surprising that some therapists are ill-informed. Most clinicians are trained to understand the operation of psychological defenses. Because they would readily concede

that memory is subject to psychologically motivated distortion, they also accept, or already believe, what memory scientists claim about the fallibility of memory. Yet, credit must go to the false memory advocates who have made it clear that some small percentage of therapists hold an entirely erroneous view of memory, while others hold a variety of incorrect views concerning memory and hypnosis. Further education on these crucial topics is clearly the solution. Nevertheless, some extreme false memory advocates, in their zeal to expose therapeutic excesses, have engaged in a form of reverse scientific lapse in logic. This has resulted in the formulation of a view of memory that is itself in error. In particular, the following positions asserted by extreme false memory proponents are mistaken:

1. All or most therapists working with childhood sexual abuse believe in the tape-recorder theory of memory.
2. Repressed memory does not exist, or, as Ofshe has stated, "repressed memory is the scientific quackery of the twentieth century." (Ofshe, cited in Loftus & Ketcham, 1994, p. 206)
3. There is only one "normal" model for memory, whether traumatic or nontraumatic.
4. Memories of events are stored the way books are stored on library shelves—as an entire unit.

Many trauma advocates and almost all memory researchers (Schacter & Tulving, 1994) adhere to a *multidimensional view* of memory systems, and they correctly point out that false memory advocates who apply research findings on normal autobiographical memory to the domain of trauma have incorrectly assumed a unitary model of memory (Share, 1994; Whitfield, 1995b).

Explicit, Narrative vs. Implicit, Behavioral Memory for Trauma

Some false memory advocates have assumed that a recovered memory for a traumatic experience is limited to a verbal, narrative memory report. They have repeatedly ignored the scientific evidence on other memory systems. Berliner and Williams (1994) make an important statement on this point:

Cognitive psychologists seem to be arguing that current theories and principles of memory can fully account for all of the ways that memory might work. (p. 383)

Pillemer and White's (1989) landmark review on the development of a behavioral memory system is rarely cited by memory scientists like Loftus (1993) and Lindsay and Read (1994), or by expert witnesses who appear frequently in court, such as Ofshe, Ganaway, and Underwager. Terr's (1994) work on behavioral reenactment of trauma is seldom cited or addressed by clinicians like Frankel (1993) and McHugh (1993) who favor the false memory position.

There is a growing corpus of scientific and clinical data in support of the view that traumatic experiences are encoded and stored both as behavioral memory and verbal memory, and that in certain instances the implicit, behavioral memory for the trauma may take primacy over the verbal memory in the form of behavioral reenactment and intrusive reexperiencing. While false memory advocates almost never mention the behavioral memory system, they do mention and criticize the more limited case of body memories, which they use as an example of a dangerous memory recovery technique (Lindsay & Read, 1994; Loftus, 1993). They argue that there is no scientific evidence in support of body memories. It is true that body memories in particular have not been the subject of extensive scientific inquiry, although some evidence exists (Lipin, 1955; Rosen, 1955; Share, 1994; van der Kolk, 1994). However, normal behavioral memory in children and behavioral memory for trauma in children and adults have been the subjects of numerous scientific investigations.

Some false memory advocates consistently ignore these data. To ignore the entire corpus of scientific data on implicit, behavioral memory because it might lend some credence to clinicians' description of unconscious behavioral reenactments of trauma, which in turn might even justify memory recovery techniques, is poor science. To debunk a poorly understood subset of the phenomenon (body memory) as a way of dismissing the more substantive evidence on the general phenomenon (implicit, behavioral memory) is also poor logic. Dismissing the validity of recovered memories of abuse on the grounds that

the memory is accompanied by somatic distress (or a body memory) is neither logical nor scientific.

Kihlstrom (1994b) makes a very significant point about the implicit influences of memory:

The role of consciousness in the dissociative disorders is further indicated by the fact that the temporarily inaccessible memories nevertheless exert an impact on the patient's experience, thought, and action outside of awareness. In other words, psychogenic amnesia, fugue, and multiple personality entail a dissociation between two forms of memory, explicit and implicit. (p. 379)

Implicit memories, which are not currently available to consciousness, nevertheless exert influence on thoughts and behaviors (Graf & Masson, 1993). Kihlstrom cites several case illustrations:

For example, Madame D., a patient studied by Janet (1904), lapsed into an amnesic state after being victimized by a practical joke. During her waking hours she had no recollection of the joke, or of anything that happened during the 6 weeks prior to the event. Nevertheless, she froze in terror whenever she passed the location where the joke had been played, and her nocturnal dreams contained a clear but unrecognized representation of the event itself. Similarly, a rape victim studied by Christianson and Nilsson (1989) became upset whenever she returned to the scene of the assault, a footpath constructed from crumbled bricks; she also reported the frequent intrusion of the words "bricks and the path" into her thoughts. Another patient, Jane Doe, was unable to identify herself or provide any information about her family or place of residence; but when asked on a number of occasions to randomly dial a telephone, she consistently produced a number that proved to belong to her mother. (Lyon, 1985, pp. 379–380)

Kihlstrom's work with implicit memories is consistent with the possibility that traumatic memories may exist and exert influence outside conscious awareness; it is also consistent with the evolving biochemical data on an alternative memory storage system (behavioral memory) for traumatic events. Further, the concept of implicit memory lends support to the idea that some somatic memories may be real, though not in the sense that some extreme trauma advocates have maintained. More precisely, body memories may be the influences generated by implicit memory for events encoded under conditions of high fear arousal (van der Kolk, 1994).

Extreme trauma theorists argue that (1) the body retains memories as though it were a tape recorder, and (2) there are certain bodily responses that unerringly prove the presence of prior sexual abuse. They assume that *every* maladaptive behavioral pattern, like specific avoidance behaviors (Fredrickson, 1992), necessarily means that the patient has been abused, or that every somatic complaint is a body memory for abuse. This extreme position is vastly different from the implicit memory hypothesis and has no support in the scientific literature.

Our position is somewhere between the two extremes: unconscious behavioral reenactments, intrusive visual images in the form of dream-like recollections or flashbacks, and specific somatic discomfort are *sometimes* indicative of a behavioral memory for trauma and are sometimes indicative of other things. The clinician who ignores these signs is in danger of a false negative error; the clinician who overzealously sees all behavioral signs as examples of memory for trauma is in danger of a false positive error.

Memory vs. Belief about the Past: Variable Response Criteria

Memory scientists advocating the false memory position have consistently used phrases like "false memory" (Loftus, 1993; Loftus & Ketcham, 1994), "illusory memory" (Lindsay & Read, 1994), and "created memory" or "implanted memory" (Loftus & Coan, in press). The problem is with the use of the word "memory." As reviewed in chapter 8, the greater portion of the variance of the misinformation effect has little to do with a change in the memory representation per se. In fact, a number of experiments have been conducted since 1989 specifically to determine the extent to which post-event information actually interferes with the memory representation. These studies have consistently shown that the magnitude of the memory interference effect is quite small. Proponents of the false memory position who persist in the use of terms like "false memory" and "illusory memory" do a disser-

vice to the data. Lindsay and Read, however, are not unaware of the potential distortion, and to their credit they have modified their position in light of the accumulated data. They speak in some cases of *false beliefs* instead of *illusory memories*:

> Thus some cases of inaccurate delayed accusations might be better characterized as involving false beliefs rather than illusory memories. The reason this is important is that it is probably much easier to induce false beliefs than it is to induce full blown illusory memories. People do sometimes experience compelling and detailed illusory recollections . . . but false reports may not always be accompanied by such false memories. (Read & Lindsay, 1994, p. 429)

Ceci, Loftus, et al. (1994) likewise talk about "false assents" to misleading questions and not about false memories.

Some advocates of the false memory position use *variable response criteria* depending on the context: they use more cautious response criteria speaking in the context of memory research ("beliefs," "reports," "assents") and more liberal response criteria when referring to the creation of false "memories" in psychotherapy. Yet, in showing their skepticism about the studies on traumatic amnesia for childhood sexual abuse, they evaluate these studies by strict response criteria (the studies are said not to be about "amnesia," but merely about "forgetting" [Loftus, Garry, et al., 1994e]. This double standard may be persuasive in some contexts, but it is harmful in the scientific arena. Waites (1997) echoes the conclusions we have arrived at in this book when she says, "many effects attributed to suggestibility may not be a function of memory at all, but merely a result of compliance" (pp. 79–80).

The Unitary vs. Multidimensional Views of Memory

Advocates of the false memory position speak about memory as though it were a unitary phenomenon. When Loftus argues that memory is fallible and suggestible (1979a,b) or speaks about false memory (1993), she is describing memory along a single dimension. At a remarkable meeting between Loftus and *Courage to Heal* co-author Ellen Bass, Bass asked if Loftus could ever believe in the possibility of re-pressed memory as a defense mechanism. Loftus noted that she could not accept Ofshe's extremist position that repressed memories and memory work are one of this "century's most intriguing quacker-ies," which "no human society since the dawn of time has ever recorded except a bunch of wacked-out psychologists in America" (Loftus & Ketcham, 1994, p. 206). On the other hand, Loftus said:

> If you define repression as a process in which the mind selectively picks and chooses certain memo-ries to hide away in a separate, hidden compart-ment of the mind and decades later return in pristine form, then I would have to say "No, noth-ing I have seen or witnessed would allow me to believe in that interpretation." But if you define repression as a theoretical possibility, a rare and unusual quirk of the mind that occurs in response to terrible trauma, I could not dismiss the theory out of hand. I would say "Yes, that is possible, but I would have to see some proof before I'd call my-self a believer." (Loftus & Ketcham, 1994, p. 219)

What type of proof would satisfy Loftus? She an-swered, "I would like to see proof for the claim that traumatic memories are engraved or encoded in abnormal ways and then stored in a separate sec-tion of the mind. I would like to see cogent cor-roboration for individual accusations based on supposedly derepressed memories" (Loftus & Ketcham, 1994, p. 218).

This articulation of a proof requirement makes sense. Loftus could have found it in the only places such proof would be available—the neurobiologi-cal literature on traumatic memory and the litera-ture on children's behavioral memory (although Hembrooke and Ceci [1995] doubt that traumatic memories are different from normal memories even in the face of this evidence). Kandel and Kandel (1994) describe how the biochemistry of memory might work:

> Let's suppose that a memory is stored weakly in the explicit system because endogenous opiates interfered with its consolidation—so weakly that the person has no conscious memory of the origi-nal wrenching event. That same event, though, might also be captured by the implicit system

through a characteristic physical sensation or ges-ture. Perhaps later the implicit system may pro-vide clues—such as physical sensations—that help stir the recall of weak explicit memories.

> In fact, people who say they were abused as children often do describe their memories return-ing first as bodily sensations. . . . (pp. 37–38)

Conclusions drawn by false memory advocates from studies of verbal memory may not necessarily be generalizable to behavioral memory. Furthermore, it is misleading to speak about "memory" in general as being inherently fallible *in every respect*. The great preponderance of the scientific evidence strongly demonstrates that *specific aspects of memory*, rather than memory as a whole, must be addressed. If our understanding of memory in psychotherapy is to advance, we need to go beyond general concepts about memory fallibility and suggestibility to specify which aspects of memory, in what context, and un-der what conditions, are hypothesized to be affected. A similar point is made by Schacter (1995):

> Under what conditions is memory largely accurate, and under what conditions is distortion most likely to occur? . . . the key issue is not whether memory is "mostly accurate" or "mostly distorted"; rather, the challenge is to specify the conditions under which accuracy and distortion are most likely to be observed. (p. 25)

Even when dealing with "normal" memory for nontraumatic events, some false memory advocates have a tendency to adopt the worst case conclu-sion, even though the data support less extreme claims. For example, it makes a great deal of differ-ence in misinformation effect studies whether the memory is for central or peripheral details. Failure to remember minor details is not the same as failure to remember the gist of a central event. Similarly, suggestibility for peripheral details is not the same as suggestibility for central actions. Even Bartlett (1932) noted that the transformation of memory for the "War of the Ghosts" was largely limited to de-tails, while the gist of the story was well preserved.

Trauma advocates sometimes err in the opposite direction and make the memory system more diverse than is supported by available evidence. Ofshe and Watters (1994, p. 84) correctly criticize Fredrickson

(1992) for expanding the definition of memory to include too much, such as "imagistic memory, body memory, acting-out memory," and what she labels "feeling memory." They also correctly criticize the "willingness to label anything a memory" (p. 85), though they themselves frequently confuse memories with beliefs.

The middle ground between these extremes is the view of at least a *dual memory system*—an explicit, verbal autobiographical system and an implicit, behavioral memory system. Some false memory advocates incorrectly assume that these processes are never associated with memory, and some trauma advocates incorrectly assume that imagery, affect, somatic sensations, and behavior are always associated with traumatic memory. The behavioral memory system may not yet be developed in neonates and infants, who may rely on REM dreaming and the amygdala circuits for encoding and storage (Share, 1994). By the second year of life, however, these functionally separate systems may become integrated into the behavioral memory system that includes visual, affective, somato-sensory, and behavioral dimensions—what in the adult trauma literature has been called the BASK model of memory (Braun, 1988).

Memory in Children

Many years ago Whipple (1909) described children as being unfit to give testimony in the courts because they could not easily distinguish between fantasy and reality. This view persisted over the years in the courts and popular media. More recently, this extreme view has emerged again in support of the false memory position. Underwager has argued as an expert witness in over 200 cases, entirely for the defense, that children's allegations of abuse cannot be relied upon because they were the victims of suggestive interviews (Salter, 1991).

Some supporters of the trauma advocacy position likewise adopt the equally extreme position that children always tell the truth. They fail to consider the fact that children are vulnerable to the suggestive influences of parents and other authority figures, including child sexual abuse investigators, law enforcement agents, and lawyers.

Neither of these extreme views is informed by the major advances during the last decade in research on children's suggestibility. A robust finding across numerous experiments conducted by Goodman and her associates is that at least older children are "highly resistant" to suggestions, although McGough has added that these conclusions may be limited to "benign interview conditions" (1991, p. 116). Ceci's research, in contrast, shows that children are quite vulnerable to suggestions under certain conditions, when a variety of social influences are manipulated and when misleading suggestions are systematically repeated within and across multiple interviews.

In an important interview on television, Ceci (1996) has recently noted that his research is often misused by false memory advocates to persuade juries that children are easily led by suggestion and that their memories are not to be trusted. Ceci himself noted that to obtain his results, the pressure on children must be extensive and intensive. Ceci's own position is that children are generally believable and resistant to suggestion, except under the very specific, extreme interviewing that was the focus of his research.

The view that emerges from a careful reading of the literature and an evaluation of the clinical data is that children's memory for significant events is generally accurate, though not necessarily complete, especially at younger ages, but that it is vulnerable to suggestive influence under very specific conditions. Both false memory advocates who persist in seeing children's memory as nothing but unreliable and trauma advocates who see it as always reliable are expressing political, not scientific, opinions. The wealth of scientific data fails to support either of these extreme positions.

Memory Fallibility

We have seen that in speaking against the specific instance of body memory, Loftus further attacks the general concept of behavioral memory. With respect to her argument about memory fallibility (1979a,b), however, she uses the reverse logic, namely, trying to debunk the specific instance by arguing from the position of generality. The term *memory fallibility* is overly general. The problem with using such a term is that it confounds two very different memory constructs—memory completeness and memory accuracy. The relationship between memory completeness and memory accuracy is very complex. Under many conditions, the relative completeness or incompleteness of a memory has very little to do with its accuracy. For example, a preschool-aged child's narrative memory for an event of impact is often quite incomplete, yet is quite accurate. The problem with using the overly general term "memory fallibility" is that it suggests to the reader inaccuracy along with incompleteness. The reader is then left with an instilled belief that memory is more malleable or mistaken than it actually may be.

A related problem with some of the false memory literature is the tendency to exaggerate the inaccuracy of memory and minimize the research data on memory accuracy. Berliner and Williams (1994) have pointed out how the false memory advocates selectively misuse the data to overstate the inaccuracy of memory:

> One of the most curious aspects of the scientific literature on the memories of events from childhood is the recurring tendency for cognitive psychologists to rely on interesting, but strictly anecdotal accounts of supposed wrongly recalled events from childhood. Stories about Piaget, Mark Twain, or a friend or relative abound. Lindsay and Read engage in this practice as well. At the same time that these critics employ anecdotes in support of their argument for the fallibility of memories of early childhood events, they seem to ignore or downplay some important findings based on larger samples and more sophisticated research designs. For example, Usher and Neisser (1993), in their research on childhood amnesia, report on 222 college students' memories. They found that the subjects' mothers judged most of their children's memories as accurate. The study provides evidence for accurate memories from substantially earlier ages than has been reported and suggests that certain significant events of early childhood, such as the birth of a sibling, are more likely to be remembered. There is a certain selective use of research to support the following illogical argument: If abuse really happened, it would be remembered all along, and as many of the reported memories are for experiences from very young ages, this proves the memories are false, because people cannot ordinarily recall early events. (pp. 380–381)

Arguing from the specific to the general case in a given case is also used as a strategy. Some false memory advocates incorrectly argue that the existence of inaccurate or distorted details means that the entire memory is false (Spiegel & Scheflin, 1994). If certain details of a memory are erroneous, that does not mean that the entire memory is therefore erroneous. If, for example, a patient recovers a memory of being sexually abused in the bathtub and includes an erroneous detail about pink wallpaper, it does not necessarily follow that the abuse memory is a false memory, or that the abuse never occurred, simply because of the inclusion of a false detail about it. Braude (1995) has exposed this aspect of Loftus's (1993) faulty logic by observing that she first takes issue with the idea that "traumatic events leave some sort of indelible fixation in the mind" (Loftus, p. 530), but then she argues that since memory is malleable and details change, therefore, the entire memory is non-veridical (p. 258).

Actually, this problem has been largely avoided in the older history of memory research. Bartlett's classic book *Remembering* (1932) included a detailed analysis of the type of errors his subjects made in their memory of the "War of the Ghosts." Bartlett was careful to point out that most of his subjects accurately recalled the gist of the story, yet made predictable errors in minor details. Brewer (1986) also included a detailed analysis of types of errors in his study of autobiographical memory. Like Bartlett, Brewer found that his subjects accurately remembered the gist of memorable personal events but made a number of predictable errors like misestimating the time, adding erroneous details, etc. Memory scientists like Bartlett and Brewer do not make the logical mistake of assuming that if a memory contains an erroneous detail then it necessarily means that the memory for the gist of the event is inaccurate. In fact, their research suggests the opposite.

False memory advocates who argue that the existence of erroneous details necessarily negates the memory for the gist of an autobiographical memory, like an abuse memory, make a significant departure from the tradition of memory research. For example, it is very common to assign the wrong time to an otherwise accurate memory. A patient who recovers a memory for childhood sexual abuse might easily assign the wrong time to the memory. If the abuse happened at age four, the patient may mistakenly say that it happened at age two. False memory logic would have it that the entire memory for the childhood sexual abuse must be dismissed, as though the memory for the gist of the event were refuted by the mistaken time assignment.

A related error is to assume that if a patient's recovered memory contains inconsistent or erroneous details, then these errors therefore prove that the memory has been suggested in therapy. To assume that most or all of the variance of memory suggestion is due to therapy is not good science. Patients come in contact with a number of potentially suggestive influences in their lives, most of which have nothing to do with psychotherapy. To assume that, if a memory is questionable, then it must have been suggested in therapy is illogical. As we have seen in chapter 7, some of the recent surveys, using the general population instead of former therapy patients, have documented amnesia for childhood sexual abuse and later recovered memories, and have shown that, contrary to the claim of false memory advocates that the recovered memories were suggested in therapy, only a small portion of the subjects were ever actually in therapy. Harvey and Herman (1994) have remarked that patients who recover memories usually arrive at them in a number of ways, and often initiate therapy immediately after, not before, recovering memories. They see "lifecycle changes," notably changes in relationships, as a very important precipitant of memory recovery.

It is well documented in eyewitness studies that different witnesses often have different memories for the same crime. These differences are in part due to the fact that the witnesses view the same event from different vantage points and therefore see it differently. This phenomenon is often called the "Rashomon" effect in honor of the brilliant 1950 Kurosawa film by that name. They may also construe the same event differently depending on the meaning the event had to the individual. The fact that two people have differing versions in their memory for the same event does not necessarily mean that their memories are inaccurate. At least some erroneous details may be due to differences in perspective.

Even if it were conceded that memory is fallible under certain conditions, it does not necessarily follow that memory is therefore always fallible. The false memory advocates have adopted a *nihilistic*

position reflected in the Loftus and Ketcham (1994) statement that "memory is a form of fiction" (p. 268). This position also appears in Loftus's appearances as an expert witness. She has argued that memory is fallible in over 150 cases, mostly for the defense and mostly against eyewitness identification or an alleged victim's allegations of recovered memories of trauma.

This emphasis on fallibility fails to account for the fact that everyday memory works more than it does not work (Schacter, 1995). Gruneberg et al.'s *Practical Aspects of Memory* (1978) and Cohen's *Memory in the Real World* (1989) describe a trend in memory research that focuses on how memory works in everyday life. Loftus's position is certainly not representative of modern applied memory research.

Another fallacy of the false memory argument is the one-sided nature of the logic. Even if we concede anihilistic position, that memory is fallible in general and inaccurate in particular, there is still no logical reason why memory problems should apply so selectively to patients who recover memories of childhood sexual abuse. *We find it curious that the memories of alleged perpetrators and other family members are rarely considered fallible in the same way that the memories of recovered memory patients are.*

We find it even more curious that the memory of recanters is used as "evidence" that their former memories of childhood sexual abuse must be fictitious or that allegations of therapeutic malpractice of implanting false memories must be factual. Reason would have it that recanters probably have a more fallible/malleable memory than most people. Gudjonsson's forensic data on alleged false confessors, those who later retract their confessions, have demonstrated that *recanters are on the high end of the suggestibility continuum.* Over and against these data, false memory advocates continue to assume that post-therapy recanter memories are true, whereas the memories of abuse recovered in therapy are false.

Logical fallacies regarding memory accuracy are not limited to the false memory advocates. Some trauma advocates make a similar error in the opposite direction. Trauma advocates who adopt a *naive realism* position fail to consider that recovered memories can have erroneous details and sometimes might be entirely fictitious. One common mistake is to confound the emotionality, vividness, and/or confidence in a memory with the accuracy of the memory. Or, as Loftus and Ketcham (1994) phrase the assumptions sometimes made by trauma therapists, "I find it difficult to escape the conclusion that if something feels real, it is real, and hang the fact that you don't have any memories" (p. 54). Research on flashbulb memories (Winograd & Neisser, 1992) and hypnotic pseudomemories (Pettinati, 1988) has convincingly shown that the relationship between emotionality, vividness, and confidence is exceedingly complex, and that under many conditions these factors have very little to do with accuracy. Over and against this research, some trauma advocates erroneously assume that, if a patient reports a memory with considerable emotional intensity, reports very vivid detail, and/or is highly confident about the memory, then it must be accurate.

Between the extremes of nihilism and naive realism is what Braude (1995) calls the "prevailing view" among clinicians, namely, that any given memory may contain accurate and inaccurate information, but is neither extremely inaccurate nor completely accurate. He criticizes Loftus for attacking a memory position that most clinicians do not actually take:

> The first thing to notice about Loftus' position is that it is irrelevant to at least a sensible interpretation of the view she is challenging. The claim that traumatic events leave indelible impressions on the mind does not have to be understood as meaning that traumatic events get recalled perfectly in all details or that traumatic memories are unchanging. But it is only that absurdly strong claim that Loftus can undermine by observing that genuine traumatic memories might be wrong in certain details. (p. 258)

The key issue is whether the *memory for the gist* of the past experience, like an abusive act, is accurate, not whether all of the details are accurately recalled. Moreover, where a genuine memory of past abuse is recovered, it is likely to be accompanied by PTSD symptoms (Whitfield, 1995b), behavioral reenactment or somatic distress (Davies & Frawley, 1994; Share, 1994), and/or physiological reactivity (Wickramasekera, 1994).

Repression, Dissociation, and Forgetting Trauma

One of the most serious infractions of logic has to do with the concept of repression. Bowers and Farvolden (1996a) criticize false memory proponents for linking repression with memory suggestibility. They say, "Whereas we agree that the risk of suggesting memories of abuse is considerable, we do not think it is necessary to abandon the notion of repression to make this point" (p. 355). The "logic" of linking repression with suggestion is part of an overall false memory strategy to promulgate the view that memory is fallible. However, this strategy confounds memory omission with memory commission errors.

Loftus (1993) speaks of the "myth of repression"; Ofshe and Watters (1993) claim there is no such thing as "robust repression" for childhood sexual abuse; and Lindsay and Read (1994) speak of "total repression" for childhood sexual abuse.

False memory advocates have been relentless in their claim that there is very little evidence that repression exists. Although Loftus currently sees repression as a "myth," Pope (1996) points out that Loftus previously discussed a case of a college professor, R. J., documenting his inability to remember trauma. Banks and Pezdek (1994) identify one error in logic of the false memory advocates:

> Recovered memory is sometimes said to be impossible because there is no support for the concept of repression. This argument is flawed: it assumes that repression is the only mechanism by which psychogenic forgetting can happen and, further, that recovery can happen only when this repression is lifted. (p. 267)

In chapter 7, we reviewed 30 studies, all of which document a period of memory failure for childhood sexual abuse. With the exception of Herman and Schatzow (1987), who speak of "massive repression," and Roesler and Wind (1994), the researchers in most of the remaining studies describe these memory failures with traditional memory concepts like "period of forgetting," "dissociation," or "traumatic amnesia." There has been a curious reversal in the use of terminology: the false memory advocates, many of whom are memory scientists, persistently use a clinical term, repression, while the researchers on memory deficits in victims of childhood sexual abuse, many of whom are clinicians, use laboratory memory concepts, like forgetting or amnesia.

Why is the term repression used? The concept of repression can be made more controversial than traditional ideas like forgetting or amnesia. The "logic" is as follows: in order to debunk a general construct A, equate A with a small subset of A, namely, B, because it is easier to refute B. Loftus (1993) tries to debunk the increasing evidence for amnesia for childhood sexual abuse by calling it something other than it is. Ofshe and Watters (1993) make an even more transparent leap in logic with their use of the term robust repression—a term that does not exist anywhere in the clinical or memory literature. Ofshe and Watters made up this extreme term to derail the legitimacy of the idea that severe abuse can be dissociated over a long period of time and later recalled with some accuracy.

The main point, however, is that 30 studies have appeared in the last eight years, each documenting amnesia for childhood sexual abuse in a subpopulation of individuals. These studies are consistent with studies for amnesia for many other kinds of trauma. Loftus, Garry, et al. (1994) are quick to point out that the rates of forgetting across these studies are "highly variable" and then use this point to negate the finding of the existence of trauma-related amnesia. We have shown in chapter 7 that the variability decreases considerably if the data are considered in terms of full versus partial amnesia versus no amnesia, as well as in terms of the severity of current symptoms. By persistently pigeonholing these data into the category of repression, rather than amnesia for childhood sexual abuse, Loftus and Ofshe attempt to draw attention away from the rather robust findings for amnesia for childhood sexual abuse across all studies.

Loftus is correct that the studies on amnesia for childhood sexual abuse have certain limitations and methodological flaws. However, it does not necessarily follow that the conclusions they reach about traumatic amnesia are wrong, and it certainly does not follow that the opposite conclusion, that robust repression does not exist, is true. The studies on the misinformation effect all have methodological limitations (Loftus & Hoffman, 1989), yet scientists generally believe the substantial evidence on the misinformation effect should not be called into question.

Lindsay and Read (1994) are more conservative, and they appear to have modified their position based on the available data. While they speak of "total repression" in the body of their text, the title of the section of their paper is called "total amnesia." In other words, their new position concedes that amnesia for childhood sexual abuse exists, based on available data, but they argue that "such forgetting is probably less common" (p. 315). Their concession is more clearly stated in their follow-up paper:

> We also acknowledge that some adult survivors of childhood abuse may not remember the abuse. (Read & Lindsay, 1994, p. 430)

Loftus and Ketcham (1994, p. 215) discuss the difference between repression and several other mental mechanisms. First, forgetting, even motivated forgetting, involves conscious recognition that unpleasant thoughts are being pushed out of awareness. Thus, if successful, the person will remember that s/he forgot. Not so with repression, according to Loftus and Ketcham. With repression, there will be no memory of having suppressed or forgotten traumatic events.

Ellen Bass asked Loftus two most sensible questions: "Isn't it possible to be so severely traumatized that the memory traces are deeply and permanently imprinted in the unconscious mind? Then, years later, something triggers the memory and it returns to consciousness?" (Loftus & Ketcham, 1994, p. 215). Loftus responded that repression was different from anterograde amnesia, which requires a reduced ability to remember events after a physical injury to the brain has prevented the storing of biochemical impressions. Repression is also different from retrograde amnesia, which is the reduced ability to remember events that occurred before an injury or insult to the brain. Instead, repression, as defined by its advocates, involves "a process of selective amnesia in which the brain snips out certain traumatic events and stores the edited pieces in a special, inaccessible memory drawer" (p. 215). Repression also differs from traumatic (or psychogenic) amnesia. Loftus and Ketcham acknowledge that traumatic amnesia has been "documented" in the scientific literature, but they claim that it is "rare." According to Loftus and Ketcham, who cite some of Schacter's work, traumatic amnesia "involves a relatively large assemblage of memories and associated affects, not just single memories . . . [and] is typically reversible, and the memories soon return" (p. 216). Presumably, repression, as they use the term, involves single memories and memories that return only after considerable delay. In addition, traumatic amnesia, in the Loftus and Ketcham view, involves an emotionally disturbing event that disrupts "the normal biological processes underlying the storage of information in memory; consequently, the memory of the event is improperly encoded or imprinted in disconnected, unassimilated fragments" (p. 215). This discussion ignores Schacter's important review (1986) and other works on traumatic amnesia for homicide, which show traumatic memory is both selective and not always immediately reversible. Thus, Loftus and Ketcham make a false distinction between repression and traumatic amnesia. This distinction can be made only by failing to cite the wider literature on amnesia and traumatic dissociation across types of trauma (Calof, 1994; Gleaves, 1996a).

As noted above, Loftus and Ketcham themselves say, "It all hinges on evidence" (p. 218), and then add, "I would like to see some kind of evidence that the brain responds to trauma in this way" (p. 218). They may find it in van der Kolk's (1993) review of the neurobiological evidence in favor of amygdala memory processing for trauma versus hippocampal memory processing of normal memory. Although his theory has been received with skepticism by false memory advocates (Hembrooke & Ceci, 1995), recent positron emission topography (PET) scanning of eight trauma patients during flashbacks supported the theory that the brain does indeed process trauma differently from normal memory (Rauch et al., 1996). They might also find evidence in the numerous laboratory studies on hypnotic amnesia, which indicate that complete or partial non-volitional amnesia can easily be demonstrated in certain subjects (e.g., Bowers & Woody, 1996).

None of the researchers who have conducted the surveys on amnesia for childhood sexual abuse, with the exception of the original Herman and Schatzow (1987) report, provides a discussion of the mechanisms by which the amnesia for childhood sexual abuse occurs. Most clinicians, even so-called memory recovery therapists, would say that amnesia for childhood sexual abuse can be caused by a variety of mechanisms, repression being only one; others are repression, dissociation, denial, splitting, disavowal, embarrassment, and even normal forgetting (Cohler, 1994; Hembrooke & Ceci, 1995; Terr, 1994). In an important critical review, Gleaves (1996a) points out a fundamental error in the logic of criticizing repression as a means to debunk the existence of amnesia for trauma:

> An analogy with another clinical phenomenon illustrates the nature of the current problem. There are numerous proposed underlying mechanisms for depression including learned helplessness . . . , low response-contingent positive reinforcement . . . , and negativistic cognitive schema . . . , etc. Examination of the laboratory evidence for any one of these possible underlying mechanisms would not allow one to draw conclusions about the existence of depression. (p. 10)

False memory advocates prematurely discuss the mechanisms before accumulating the data for or against the existence of amnesia for childhood sexual abuse. Since the debate is about the *existence* of amnesia for trauma, it is hard to see how the discussion of the mechanism of repression is directly relevant (Gleaves, 1996a).

But what about the evidence for repression? False memory advocates have repeatedly cited the Holmes (1990) review to debunk the concept of repression. What false memory advocates seldom say is that the Holmes paper is found in a volume (Singer, 1990) that contains 17 other chapters, each of which presents evidence in favor of repression or dissociation. Moreover, Gleaves (1994, 1996a) and Braude (1995) both have noted that the false memory advocates, like Loftus and Ofshe, "apparently ignore Holmes's explicit caveat that other processes might generate selective memories and perceptions" (Braude, 1995, p. 262) and that "he focuses only on 'after expulsion' repression rather than 'primary repression'" (Braude, 1995, p. 263). The false memory advocates, according to Braude, "set up a straw man" (p. 262) by the "illegitimate conflation of repression with traumatic amnesia" (p. 262) and then selectively use (or misuse) the available data to refute the straw man.

Holmes himself acknowledges in his paper that his view is a distinct minority position. When Loftus and Ofshe cite the Holmes paper, they fail to note that it is not a mainstream viewpoint. Gleaves (1996a) adds:

> In summary, Holmes' (1990) conclusion, which generally differed from the original investigators of much of the research, was that the memory-related phenomena that were observed in the laboratory studies could be best explained by mechanisms other than repression. Thus, although his conclusions have been cited as being that there is no scientific support for the concept of repression, a more accurate description of his conclusions would be that, although many data are consistent with repression theory, Holmes found no evidence for repression that could not (in his opinion) be explained by a mechanism other than repression. (p. 9)

Some false memory proponents have improperly cited Holmes as *proof* that there is no laboratory evidence for, and no scientific support for, the existence of repression.

Our conclusion is similar to that recently drawn by Gleaves (1996a) in his critical review of the repression debate:

> A wealth of clinical and experimental data do support the concept of extensive traumatic amnesia and the subsequent recovery of accurate memories. This is not to imply that such recovered memories are always accurate or that more research on this challenging topic is not needed. However, the frequently repeated statement that there is no scientific support for the reality of "repressed" memories should be understood as being based on one review article out of context while at the same time ignoring decades of relevant data. (p. 16)

A very important logical error is to confound repression with memory recovery. Loftus and Ketcham (1994) say, without citing adequate proof, that "Repressed memories are typically recovered in therapy" (p. 141). They erroneously assume that if a memory is repressed and later recovered, it necessarily must have been the result of suggestive influences, notably of therapeutic suggestion. As Harvey and Herman (1994) have countered, most memories are spontaneously recovered due to changes in one's life course, especially as a result of changes in relationships. Memories are only sometimes recovered in psychotherapy. Most patients go to therapy not to recover memories, but as a consequence of having recovered memories and being in distress about them. Loftus, and others, are guilty of the logical fallacy known as *post hoc ergo propter hoc* (after this, therefore because of this). The fact that an event precedes another does not mean that it has caused the other. The fact that memories are sometimes recovered in therapy does not mean that therapy has caused or created those memories.

Some trauma advocates make a comparable logical error when they assure us that if an abuse memory had been forgotten for a period of time and then later remembered, it must necessarily be accurate, or, if patients claim to have no memories, they must be in denial (Loftus & Ketcham, 1994, p. 149). As we have seen, there is no simple relationship between memory incompleteness (or amnesia) and memory accuracy, and, furthermore, retrieving a more complete memory (reversal of full or partial amnesia) does not necessarily mean that the memory is accurate:

> To invoke the concept of repression as a mechanism that seals memories intact to be recovered in full, accurate detail in adulthood goes beyond the available evidence. There is at present no reason to believe that memories that were unavailable for some time and then were "recovered" are any more accurate than memories that were available all along for the same period of time. (Banks & Pezdek, 1994, p. 267)

Early in the retrieval phase of treatment, the content of traumatic memories that come into consciousness is likely to be disguised, and therefore distorted, due to the operation of psychological defenses (Brown & Fromm, 1986). However, as we learned in chapter 7, Dalenberg's (1996) study, the only currently existing study on the accuracy of memories recovered in psychotherapy, demonstrated that recovered memories of abuse indeed *are* as accurate as memories for abuse that were never forgotten in most circumstances and memories recovered later in treatment are significantly more accurate than those recovered early in treatment.

A logical error occurs when a therapist strongly believes in suspected abuse and conducts treatment with a consistent focus on recovering the presumed traumatic memories. Once the patient reports the memory, the therapist assumes that the memory must be real. Kihlstrom (1993) refers to this aberration of logic as the "tally theory." Once a patient gives a report about a recovered memory consistent with the therapist's beliefs, i.e., once the emerging clinical evidence "tallies" with the therapist's expectations, the therapist is convinced that his or her beliefs were correct, and that the patient's recovered memory represents an historical truth about abuse.

Some trauma advocates make a similar logical error when they infer repression from certain signs and symptoms. Fredrickson (1992), for example, gives a list of symptoms as confirmatory of a "repressed memory syndrome." While these signs *might* be indicative of repression in some cases, it does not follow that these particular signs and symptoms necessarily mean that a repressed memory syndrome exists in every case, nor is the use of memory recovery techniques justified every time such signs and symptoms occur.

Overall, the scientific data are rapidly accumulating strongly in favor of *amnesia for childhood sexual abuse*, at least in a subsample of the overall population in general, and particularly in the overall clinical population. These data on amnesia for childhood sexual abuse are robust across *all* the available studies. While scientists may legitimately debate the base rates, the evidence for amnesia for childhood sexual abuse should be beyond dispute. Few clinicians and scientists would argue that repression is the *only* mechanism by which amnesia for childhood sexual abuse is produced. We agree with Braude that to persist in recasting traumatic amnesia as repression and then attempting to debunk repression in light of the available data is "intellectually dishonest."

As we will see in chapter 17, the reason the debate continues is probably less for scientific reasons than for political and, especially, legal reasons. A forensic goal of some false memory proponents has been to reverse the increasing application of the delayed discovery rule to cases of repression for childhood sexual abuse. Because most of the delayed discovery rulings require complete repression for

childhood sexual abuse, the expert witnesses associated with the false memory position *must* keep the argument focused on repression if they wish to change the laws.

The Accuracy of Recovered Memories Within and Outside of Therapy

Terms like "false memory syndrome" reflect the assumption that recovered memories are necessarily inaccurate and that memories of childhood abuse specifically recovered in therapy are necessarily false. While the issue of accuracy of recovered memories lies at the heart of the memory debate, it is indeed surprising how far the debate has gone on the mere assumption that recovered memories are inaccurate. But is this assumption valid? In chapter 7 we learned that recovered memories for childhood sexual abuse contained no more inaccuracies than continuous memories for the abuse (Williams, 1995), and that new abuse memories specifically recovered in psychotherapy were no more or less accurate than continuous abuse memories in incest survivors (Dalenberg, 1996). The assumption that memory recovery in therapy necessarily implies memory inaccuracy is not supported by the available scientific data.

A logical error made by some trauma advocates is that recovered memories must necessarily be accurate because of the vividness or emotionally compelling nature of the recovered memory. Bryant (1996), however, discusses several cases of closed head injury patients demonstrating that posttraumatic intrusive imagery "need not reflect historical truth" (p. 626) and that traumatized patients can develop pseudomemories. Another logical fallacy made by some trauma advocates is to assume that clinical improvement somehow implies that a recovered memory is accurate. Banks and Pezdek (1994) have identified this logical error:

> we have heard and read implications and direct assertions to the effect that because a patient improved after coming up with a memory of childhood sexual abuse, the recovered memory must reflect something that actually happened. We call the principle behind this reasoning the aspirin deficiency fallacy because it leads to absurd conclusions such as since aspirin cures headaches, then

headaches are caused by aspirin deficiency. There are many reasons why the apparent recovery of memories could lead to a remission of presenting clinical symptoms, even when the memories are completely imaginary. (pp. 265–266)

Apart from both extremes, the available data suggest that most recovered memories contain a mixture of accurate and inaccurate information, and that in many circumstances the gist of the traumatic event is accurately retained but the details are not. However, there are many factors that affect the application of this general principle, including personality variables associated with inaccurate recall and systematically suggestive interviewing. Thus, the relative accuracy of recovered memories must be determined on a case-by-case basis by evaluating the totality of the evidence and assigning confidence ratings to each type of evidence evaluated.

Memory Suggestibility

The fact that memory may be fallible does not necessarily mean that memory has been manipulated by suggestion in a given case. Consider the following passage from Loftus and Ketcham (1994):

From these and many other experiments, psychologists specializing in memory distortion conclude that memories are reconstructed using bits of fact and fiction and that false recollections can be induced by expectation and suggestion. (p. 79)

Note how memory distortion and memory suggestion are linked. As Banks and Pezdek say, "Assumed in this [false memory] debate is the presumption that if the recovered memory is not real, then it was suggested by, for example, a therapist or a self-help book" (1994, p. 268). The other related assumption is that allegedly false memories are typically "implanted" in psychotherapy. Yet, as Grand says, "most adults who recover memories of incest do not do so while in therapy" (1995b, p. 258), and the 30 studies on amnesia for childhood sexual abuse that we reviewed in chapter 7 do not support the hypothesis that recovered memories typically occur in psychotherapy.

Gudjonsson (1987) demonstrated that memory fallibility and memory suggestibility are related. His research shows that memory that is more fallible is more suggestible. However, as with any statistical relationship, the relationship does not hold up in every case, so a high degree of memory fallibility does not necessarily guarantee high suggestibility. The other important aspect of Gudjonsson's work is that it deals with individual differences in suggestibility. We find it disturbing how little of the research on misinformation suggestibility, in contrast to that on interrogatory and hypnotic suggestibility, has addressed the question of individual differences. Baars and McGovern (1995), for example, argue that high suggestibility may explain *both* the vulnerability to suggested false memories, on the one hand, and the vulnerability to amnesia for abuse, on the other.

There is no standardized instrument to assess individual differences in misinformation suggestibility comparable to the GSS for interrogatory suggestibility or the hypnotizability scales for hypnotic suggestibility. We have no problem with the hypothesis that some therapy is suggestive, even unduly suggestive. The problem occurs when Loftus (1993) and others apply very general ideas about memory and therapeutic suggestibility to individual cases involving both recovered memory patients and their accused families without ever formally assessing the suggestibility of the parties involved. According to Loftus, we should accept at face value that her general arguments about memory fallibility and suggestibility apply to the recovered memories of Eileen Franklin, Marilyn von Derber, Holly Ramona, and hundreds of other individuals in court cases involving recovered memories, even though individual differences in suggestibility were never measured in most of these cases. Thus, Loftus repeatedly commits the logical fallacy of applying the hypothetical general argument to the individual case. We also wonder why there are seldom references to evidence that undercuts false memory generalizations, such as the evidence for repressed memories found in the Father Porter cases. As victim Frank Fitzpatrick (1994) has stated, "I totally repressed all memory of Father James R. Porter's sexual assaults on me at age 12, until I was 39." These memories were recovered without hypnosis, without therapy, and without suggestive techniques. Fitzpatrick found and identified Father Porter, who is now in prison after confessing to having molested between 50 and 100 young girls and boys, many of whom retained memories of the abuse.

A related problem is to assume that if therapists talk about abuse with patients, then such discussions are automatically suggestive (Loftus & Ketcham, 1994, p. 151). The assumption is that any mention of abuse, no matter how tentative, is uncritically accepted by the patient, becomes the object of confabulation, and leads to a false memory.

Another difficulty found in the false memory arguments is the tendency to confound very different types of suggestibility, such as misinformation suggestibility, social persuasion, interrogatory suggestibility, coercive persuasion, and hypnotic suggestibility. The use of general terms, like misinformation suggestibility, do little to advance our scientific understanding of suggestibility effects in psychotherapy. As a good example of how different types of suggestibility get confounded, compare Loftus's research on misinformation suggestibility (e.g., Loftus, 1979a) with her more recent Shopping Mall study (Loftus & Coan, in press). Her former research hardly ever addresses and rarely manipulates or measures social persuasion variables like source credibility. The more recent Shopping Mall study represents a radical departure from the original misinformation research design and is essentially a rather classic manipulation of source credibility. The problem arises when Loftus presents the Shopping Mall study as an extension of her earlier work, as though it were simply an example of post-event suggestion for a central action instead of a peripheral detail.

Our main concern pertains to how some scientists generalize from their laboratory memory research to psychotherapy. First, the misinformation studies are about post-event information, not about autobiographical memory. Second, a well documented criticism of studies on misinformation suggestibility is that they are limited to misleading post-event suggestion for relatively peripheral details in a complex stimulus event, details that have very little causal relationship to the action of the central event (Christianson, 1992a,b). It cannot be readily assumed that these results are generalizable to "implanting" entirely fictitious events like abuse (Berliner & Williams, 1994).

Lindsay and Read (1994) apparently are aware of this criticism and try to address it by saying that "the

same sorts of memory errors have also been demonstrated with relatively rich, complex, naturalistic events, such as the detailed memory of child sexual abuse" (p. 294). A close look at the evidence that "demonstrated" this result, however, reveals that Lindsay and Read cite three questionable sources: (1) Loftus and Coan's Shopping Mall study, (2) Ofshe's (1992) study of the Ingram case in which Ofshe attempted hypnotically to suggest a false memory for abuse. His field experiment was disallowed as evidence in court, and (3) the Ceci studies, which do indeed demonstrate suggestion of certain kinds of entire fictitious events in at least some children, but these effects are created by a combination of powerful social-influence variables very different from the primarily cognitive variables operative in misinformation suggestion. Moreover, the magnitude of acceptance of fictitious events in Ceci's studies was significantly reduced in replications that added appropriate warnings to not report events unless they really had happened. Thus, Berliner and Williams (1994) remind us, "it has not been proven that full-blown memories for traumatic childhood experiences can be created from nothing" (p. 385).

False memory advocates fail to cite the Pezdek and Roe (1994) study, which is the *only* experimental study designed specifically to address the issue of generalizability of misinformation studies to psychotherapy. We might assume that it is not cited because the results suggest "constraint" in generalizing from classic misinformation research to false memory creation in psychotherapy (cf. Pezdek & Rue, 1997).

Kathy Pezdek (1994) has succinctly identified the logical fallacy in Loftus's attempt to generalize from misinformation experiments to the psychotherapy situation, namely, none of the misinformation studies concerns suggestions for an action that never really happened:

> The large majority of the studies on the suggestibility of memory involve a procedure in which: 1) something is observed (e.g. a stop sign); 2) a different thing is later suggested (e.g. a yield sign); and then 3) the test probes what the participants remember having seen. However, suggestively planting memories involves the situation in which: 1) an event never occurred; 2) it is later suggested that the event did occur; and then 3) memory is

tested for whether the event occurred or not. There are significant differences between the structure of these two situations that would restrict the generalization of the results regarding suggestibility obtained from the first situation (i.e. something happened and it is suggested that a different thing happened) to the second situation (i.e. nothing happened and it is suggested that something did happen). (p. 347)

In order to demonstrate that the two conditions are not equivalent, Pezdek and Roe (1994, 1997) conducted an experiment on suggestions for physical touch under each of the two conditions. The results clearly demonstrated a classic misinformation effect (condition 1), but failed to demonstrate suggestibility for something that never really happened. Implanting a suggestion for an event that never occurred is very different from suggesting an alteration in details for a complex event. They conclude, "it appears erroneous to generalize conclusions from the classic suggestibility paradigm to the situation in which a memory is planted for an event that never occurred" (p. 348). Loftus's generalization of her misinformation results to recovered memories in therapy is supported neither by logic nor by the recent scientific evidence.

Berliner and Williams (1994) have identified the motivation driving this research:

> The cognitive psychologists who have become involved with the issue appear to be primarily interested in further confirming the fallibility of memory and the possibility that false memories of abuse can be created. Trauma therapists and researchers are more concerned with understanding the mechanisms which produce memory loss and impairment. (p. 385)

The reader is given the impression by Loftus that it is relatively easy to mislead subjects in the laboratory and also in psychotherapy. Ofshe and Watters (1994) likewise create the impression that the creation of false abuse memories is very easy:

> Convincing a client that she has a memory of abuse can be a simple two-step process. First, the therapist assures her that a symptom is a reliable indicator of abuse. Then he or she proceeds to change

the client's definition of memory so that the indicator can be defined as a memory. (p. 83)

Other, more careful researchers have argued that these effects are not so easy to produce. Pezdek (1994) has pointed out that the magnitude of the misinformation effect is highly variable across studies. More recent studies have consistently reported the magnitude of the misinformation effect to be much less than claimed in the original Loftus studies of the 1970s and '80s (Lindsay, 1994b). Berliner and Williams (1994) have pointed out that it took a year of repeated false suggestions "to convince some very young children that it was the doctor, not the assistant, who gave them an injection and to persuade some children when they had been upset at the time that they really were not" (p. 380). Pezdek et al. (in press) found that some subjects did indeed accept suggestions for plausible false events but that no subject accepted misinformation for implausible events. However, none of the so-called Shopping Mall studies adequately controlled for social/contextual factors that probably inflate the magnitude of the effect. Thus, except for a small subgroup of highly suggestible individuals, it may not be so easy to implant suggestions for entire complex events (Grand, 1995b).

If individuals in the general population were so readily suggestible, the clinician's job would be significantly easier. Why is it that patients seem to accept suggestions for horrible experiences like childhood sexual abuse or Satanic ritual abuse so readily, yet seem so resistant to reasonable clinical efforts to stop smoking or to enhance self-esteem? Are we to believe that patients are only highly suggestible to specific suggestions for childhood sexual or ritual abuse and not for other types of more beneficial suggestions?

There is another problem with the logic here. Let's assume that at least *some* individuals are highly suggestible and will accept post-event suggestions easily. *Should we not also assume that the suggestions go both ways?* If a suggestible patient reports recovering memories in psychotherapy of childhood sexual abuse, then Loftus (1993) might assume that the memory is a false memory. Ofshe and Watters (1994), likewise, assume that retraction invalidates the diagnosis of multiple personality disorder and invalidates recovered abuse memories (p. 209). False memory advocates have used *retractors* as evidence for therapeutic suggestion of false memories (Lief & Fetkewicz, 1995). But what about *post-therapeutic suggestive influences?* False memory proponents readily assume that therapy is unduly suggestive, but that once the patient terminates therapy all suggestive influences cease. They fail to mention often significant post-therapeutic suggestive influences, not the least of which may involve strong familial and cultural influences to deny genuine abuse (Grand, 1995b):

> Is therapy the only locus of powerful, authoritative suggestion? The culture and the family system are rife with daily suggestion. (p. 268)

As expert witnesses we have encountered malpractice cases against therapists for allegedly implanting false memories of abuse in which it was apparent that the plaintiff/retractor had had significant involvement with other retractors, all of whom had made malpractice claims. Sometimes several plaintiff retractors had prepared their malpractice cases together, all of whom had become well versed in the false memory literature, some of whom had been persuaded by therapists with explicit false memory biases that their previous abuse recollections were false, and some of whom may have been coached by attorneys in preparing their malpractice claims. Should we not assume these forces to be significant post-therapeutic suggestions, probably unduly suggestive influences? Or should we accept the assumption of the false memory argument that vulnerability to suggestion stops at the point the patient leaves therapy? A more reasonable assumption is that potential suggestive influences operate both within therapy and after therapy, and where false memory arguments are used by retractors as the basis of malpractice claims, significant post-therapeutic suggestive influences are likely to be operative. We are to asked to believe defendant therapists who recommend *The Courage to Heal* to their patients are committing malpractice because such books implant false memories of abuse, but that plaintiff attorneys who recommend *The Myth of Repressed Memory* are helping the retractor set the truth straight.

While there is no logical connection between retraction and memory accuracy, there is a clear connection between retraction and suggestibility,

as we learned from Gudjonsson's studies on alleged false confessors (1992). But such individuals are vulnerable to *multiple suggestive influences,* not just suggestive influences in therapy. For example, let's assume that a hypothetical patient who has recovered abuse memories in therapy confronts her family. Sometime later she terminates therapy. Meanwhile, her family becomes involved with false memory advocates, other accused families, and experts. The family members eventually have contact with the patient and over time she retracts her story of abuse. Subsequently, the patient and family attempt to sue the therapist for implanting false memories of childhood sexual abuse and iatrogenically causing harm to the patient. They are further encouraged by a network of false memory advocates and in the process are exposed to extensive false memory literature. In the process of preparing a malpractice claim they may actually be coached by attorneys. Why is it that the more recent retracted report is considered valid by false memory advocates, while the recovered memory report from psychotherapy is considered invalid? If false memory advocates argue that the patient is vulnerable to post-event misinformation specifically in psychotherapy that might lead to false memories, they must also accept that the patient might have become subsequently vulnerable to post-event false memory misinformation, namely, false suggestions from the family and FMS consultants that real abuse never happened. In fact, one could argue that the suggestive effects of multiple family members, combined with the considerable propaganda disseminated by false memory advocates, and sometimes with the actual coaching by lawyers, constitute a constellation of *very* powerful suggestive influences, strong social influences that make therapeutic suggestion pale in comparison. Accused family members sometimes have a strong investment in actively seeking to alter the beliefs of individuals recovering memories of abuse and may bring social pressure to bear to get the individual to retract the abuse allegation. False logic becomes tragedy when judges are told to disbelieve therapy patients and to believe recanters. Ironically, the very type of person most vulnerable to pseudomemory creation in therapy is also the very person most vulnerable to changing his or her beliefs when the winds of social influence blow in a different direction. We even know of a case of a retractor who retracted her retraction.

Erickson's (1938) detailed case examples of retraction of corroborated abuse make it clear that the phenomenon of retracting has a long history in forensic psychiatry. Contrary to claims made by false memory advocates, recanting tells us nothing about the truth or falsity of the original report. Reports of genuine abuse recovered in psychotherapy might later be vehemently denied through retraction for a variety of reasons, due to either the internal operation of psychological defenses or external post-therapeutic systematic suggestive pressure. Thus, when Lief and Fetkewicz (1995) give a survey to retractors to scientifically demonstrate that they were victims of "bad therapy" (p. 432), the only thing they demonstrate is failure to consider the research on the suggestibility of retractors as well as their own confirmatory bias in assuming that a retractor's self-report has validity.

An American Psychiatric Association report on memory clearly states that retraction cannot be taken as a means to negate the genuineness of the abuse allegation:

> . . . hesitancy in making a report, and recanting following the report can occur in victims of documented abuse. Therefore, these seemingly contradictory findings do not exclude the possibility that the report is based on a true event. (1993, p. 24)

Retraction tells us nothing about the truth or falsity of an abuse allegation. It may tell us a lot about the phenomena of suggestibility and suggestive influences.

Loftus and Ketcham assume that retraction means that the memories were created in therapy (1994, pp. 209–210). While this may sometimes occur, it is not the most plausible explanation for retraction. Retraction probably means that the person is highly suggestible. It does not necessarily mean that the abuse report is invalid.

False memory proponents imply a double standard. They argue that abuse memories recovered in psychotherapy are not credible unless independent corroboration exists. However, they assume that retraction reports are historically accurate and do not require independent corroboration. As Ken Pope says of false memory syndrome, "How did the researchers, clinicians, or others who validated this [false memory] syndrome determine in each case that the memory was 'objectively false'?" (1996, p. 959). Since the available research implies that retractors are generally at the high end of the memory suggestibility range, it is a gross error in logic to give unquestioned credibility to retractor reports. This error of logic is typically illustrated in false memory proponents' discussion of cases. McElroy and Keck (1995), for example, discuss a case in which "recovered memory therapy" caused a false memory syndrome in a patient. Because the patient presented at a later point in treatment without evidence of PTSD symptoms or memory difficulties, and denied a history of abuse, McElroy and Keck readily assume that the abuse recollections had been implanted in the previous therapy. They fail to consider alternate hypotheses, such as that the previous treatment was effective for the PTSD and memory symptoms and that the subsequent retraction may have been the result of post-therapeutic suggestive influences. Moreover, they take the retraction story at face value without seeking independent corroboration. Rubin (1996) points out that it may very well be the case that alleged perpetrators can have a "false" memory of their innocence due to alcoholic blackouts, unconscious reenactment of abuse in a dissociated state, denial, or outright lying.

Pope (1996; Pope & Brown, 1996) has pointed out that the very name "false memory syndrome" seems to imply that objective evidence exists to prove that the abuse allegation is indeed false (p. 959). Yet, the FMSF has not produced such data, and when the British Psychological Society task force on memory analyzed the FMSF records they found little support for the claim that abuse allegations made against FMSF members were typically false (1995). "About half" the records examined "were very brief and sketchy . . . revealing very little of the actual circumstances" of the allegations (p. 20). These documents gave "no information" about the abuse or "the nature of recovery [of memories]" (p. 21). They conclude:

> . . . in only just under half was there explicit mention of memory recovery from total amnesia. If all the records we examined are considered this proportion is reduced to a quarter. (p. 21)

In other words, the FMSF records fail to substantiate their own claims, in that the data demonstrate that only a quarter of the accusations were based on recovered memories of alleged abuse. We do not know how many of these recovered memory cases involved memories actually recovered in therapy and how many cases considered false reports had corroborative evidence to suggest that the report was indeed false.

To their credit, Read and Lindsay (1994) have understood the fallacy of assuming recovered memories to be false:

> Therefore, the fact that a person reports false memories does not prove that the person was not sexually abused as a child. . . . attempting to prove that a person was not abused as a child amounts to attempting to prove the null hypothesis (i.e., it is in principle impossible). (p. 414)

Alpert (1995b) adds that if we accept the false memory hypothesis as applying to suggestions of abuse that never occurred, then we must equally accept the hypothesis that abused individuals can come to believe they were never abused through suggestion:

> The literature offers little support for either these stories of false memory of nonabuse or the earlier story of false memory of abuse. However, if the memory literature is used to support one of the positions, it could be applied to the other as well. (p. 13)

Her view is that the debate is largely about the use of science for political ends—what she calls a "false issue syndrome" (p. 14).

Some advocates of the trauma accuracy position commit a similar lapse in logic in believing that memory for trauma is hardly ever fallible and therefore is not subject to suggestive influences. They also fail to appreciate the relationship between memory fallibility and memory suggestibility, as well as the fact that this relationship predicts, at least in general but not with respect to individual cases, that those patients who are especially uncertain about past events have a significantly greater likelihood of being vulnerable to suggestions about those past events. Such therapists may unwittingly suggest

abuse details to certain patients without being aware of the extent to which their therapy has become a suggestive process. However, the fact that a given patient is uncertain about a specific past event does not necessarily mean that she or he will accept suggestions about it. Moreover, the fact that a given patient is shown to be highly suggestive on the GSS and/or hypnotizability scales does not necessarily mean that she or he will accept suggestions of a particular type, by a particular therapist, in a particular setting, at a particular time in the ongoing therapy.

Overall, with fallacies of logic regarding suggestive effects in therapy on both sides of the false memory debate, we note that both sides have (1) failed to address individual differences in suggestibility, (2) failed to appreciate the variety and complexity of suggestive influences, and (3) failed to address the important contribution of social influences, like source credibility and interrogatory pressure, to suggestion. We agree with Bowers and Farvolden's (1996a) critical review of suggestive influences in psychotherapy:

> Recognizing the inevitability of suggestive influences in psychotherapy helps minimize their untoward effects, whereas minimizing or denying the ubiquitous role of suggestion renders the therapist—and the patient—especially vulnerable to its unintended, unrecognized, and potentially damaging influence. (pp. 368–369)

FALSE MEMORY SYNDROME

In a data-based study, Hovdestad and Kristiansen (1996) applied criteria (similar to those used by Pope and Hudson [1995a,b] to evaluate repressed memories) to the concept of false memory syndrome. The importance of this study is that it is the only data-based study to date to directly test the validity of the widely used concept of false memory syndrome. Hovdestad and Kristiansen used their community sample of 113 women survivors of CSA—the Ottawa Survivors Study. The women who identified themselves as survivors of CSA were subdivided into recovered memory and continuous memory subgroups. The researchers reasoned that women in the recovered memory group could potentially have false memories. Drawing upon false memory publications, Hovdestad and Kristiansen identified four primary criteria and 13 subcriteria for false memory syndrome. The primary criteria include: (1) a strong belief in the historical reality of a memory that may be a pseudomemory, often accompanied by the adoption of a survivor identity and the absence of confession by the alleged perpetrator; (2) evidence of disrupted family relationships; (3) an increase in emotional distress and PTSD symptoms progressively over the course of treatment wherein false memories are recovered; and (4) evidence that the individual sought therapy for reasons other than abuse but was persuaded by a trauma-focused therapist to recover memories through the use of memory recovery techniques. A discriminant function analysis was conducted in order to assess whether or not the criteria significantly discriminated between the recovered and continuous memory groups. Hovdestad and Kristiansen reasoned that there should be significant differences between respondents with continuous and recovered memories. The results showed than the primary false memory criteria failed to discriminate between continuous and recovered memory subjects. Only five of the 13 subcriteria for false memory syndrome were confirmed. Correlational analysis further demonstrated only "weak evidence for the construct validity" (p. 330) of the various subcriteria making up the construct of false memory syndrome. Using relative and absolute estimates of the incidence of potential false memory syndrome, Hovdestad and Kristiansen found that between 3.9% and 13.6% of the women with recovered memories met a few of the false memory criteria, but rarely did they meet the full list. With respect to the main criteria they found:

> The relative estimates indicated that, at most, 3.9% of women with recovered memories could be diagnosed with FMS, and the absolute estimate gave an upper limit of 13.6%, a rate equivalent to that among women with continuous memories. (p. 329)

Hovdestad and Kristiansen conclude:

> In sum, the weak evidence for the construct validity of the phenomenon referred to as FMS, together with the finding that few women with recovered

memories satisfied the criteria and that women with continuous memories were equally likely to do so, lends little support to FMS theory. (p. 330)

We question why the public and legal community has so readily adopted the idea of a false memory syndrome when the only available data-based study failed to support its existence in all but a small minority of cases.

Pope (1996) warned that premature, uncritical acceptance of the concept of false memory syndrome has a "chilling effect on the professional services provided by therapists who disagree with these claims" (p. 966). In another study on the Ottawa sample of women, Allard et al. (in press) found that exposure to false memory rhetoric also had a negative impact on survivors. They assessed symptoms in women having recovered and continuous memories and also asked both groups to rate various ways they may or may not have been affected by the public false memory debate. With respect to symptoms they found a "mild but significant negative effect" in the form of a reported increase in anxiety, depression, sleep disturbances, dissociative symptoms, posttraumatic symptoms, and sexual problems. With respect to various areas of subjective distress they found "increased self-doubt about their memories, and an overall slowing of the progress of therapy." Just about half of the women who had recovered memories reported that they had been accused by someone of having false memories. Women who had recovered memories as compared to those who had continuous memories for their abuse reported significantly greater distress, especially if they were not far along in their treatment.

Assessment

Symptom Checklists

The false memory advocates have criticized certain trauma therapists for diagnosing abuse or recovered memories from certain lists of signs and symptoms (Lindsay & Read, 1994; Loftus, 1993; Ofshe & Watters, 1994). They raise three issues. First, the existence of *signs and symptoms* does not necessarily mean that abuse had occurred. As Ofshe and Watters have pointed out, the assumption is that such signs and symptoms have "a causal relationship with childhood sexual abuse" (p. 70) (cf. also Pope & Hudson, 1995a,b). We agree that the logic here is problematic:

> You cannot say that because many people with brain tumors have headaches, most, or even many, people with headaches have brain tumors, for the equally obvious reason that headaches are a result of any number of different causes. (Ofshe & Watters, 1994, p. 76)

Likewise, current signs and symptoms may have numerous causes other than childhood sexual abuse per se, not the least of which is the wider context of family-of-origin psychopathology (e.g., Alexander, 1993; Gartner & Gartner, 1988; Nash et al., 1993). Although moderate false memory advocates agree that the signs and symptoms associated with childhood sexual abuse are highly variable, some false memory advocates believe that such signs and symptoms are never associated with recovered memories of childhood sexual abuse.

Second, some false memory advocates have argued that the lists of signs and symptoms are so "all-inclusive" (p. 79) that they are meaningless (Ofshe & Watters, 1994):

> Who, after all, does not have headaches, nightmares, "relationship problems," or can't sometimes deeply identify with the feeling of being "different from other people"? (p. 69)

Third, the false memory advocates accuse therapists of essentially suggesting abuse by offering a diagnosis of abuse based on signs and symptoms (Ofshe & Watters, 1993, 1994; Yapko, 1994a). Conceivably, this does happen, but it depends on how the therapist communicates his or her beliefs about memories and abuse.

A reasonable position is that some portion of the variance of current life symptoms may be explained by past abuse, while another portion may be explained by other factors. Gartner and Gartner (1988) have argued, for example, that some portion of current life symptoms in adult survivors of sexual abuse is best explained by the wider context of preexisting family pathology than by the sexual abuse acts per se. Similarly, Alexander (1993) has demonstrated that a significant portion of current life relational

disturbance in survivors of childhood sexual abuse is attributable to preexisting insecure attachment patterns within the parent-child system and not to the subsequent sexual abuse. In that study current life relational disturbance was attributable to preexisting family pathology and current life PTSD symptoms were attributable to the sexual abuse per se. Likewise, Lee et al. (1995), in a 50-year prospective study of long-term sequelae to combat exposure in World War II, found that combat exposure per se predicted PTSD symptoms a half-century later but that premorbid vulnerability predicted other forms of adult psychopathology.

The current trend in the research is to assess the differential effects of neglect, physical abuse, and sexual abuse, as well as non-abuse variables, on current life functioning and psychopathology (e.g., Briere & Runtz, 1988; Gauthier et al., 1996; Melchert, 1996). The emerging view is that neglect predicts some forms of adult psychopathology, e.g., cyclical dependent and avoidance attachment patterns (Alexander, 1993; Gauthier et al., 1996), while physical and/or sexual abuse predicts posttraumatic and dissociative symptoms and sometimes predicts traumatic bonding in relationships and addictive behaviors.

The Causal Relationship between Child Abuse and Adult Psychopathology

While some proponents of the false memory position have argued that there is no causal relationship between adult psychopathology and child abuse (e.g., Dawes, 1994), this extremely nihilistic position has not been supported by the evolving research. Some trauma advocates agree that "it is usually simplistic and misleading to view adult problems as a simple consequence of a few childhood experiences" (Waites, 1997, p. 219). The answer to the relationship between childhood abuse and adult symptoms will be decided by well designed prospective studies in which matched abused and non-abused children are followed for several decades. Fortunately, the data from such studies are beginning to appear in the literature. In a 20-year prospective study with demographically matched normal and court-substantiated physically and sexually abused children, Widom and Morris (1997) found a clear causal relationship between childhood sexual abuse and adult psychopathology, especially with respect to suicidality and alcoholism. In another 17-year longitudinal study of abused and non-abused children and adolescents, Silverman, Reinherz, and Giaconia (1996) found that abuse was causally related to and predicted poorer functioning in adulthood; it also predicted depressive and anxiety symptoms and certain psychiatric disorders. These recent prospective studies utilizing matched abused and non-abused children clearly establish a causal relationship between childhood abuse and neglect and adult psychopathology and fail to support the extreme false memory position that there is *no* relationship between childhood abuse and adult psychopathology. On the other hand, establishing a clear causal relationship between child abuse and certain forms of adult psychopathology does not mean that all current life problems arise from abuse.

The lesson learned from these increasingly sophisticated prospective studies is that not all current life psychopathology is attributable to earlier trauma but some definitely is. The emerging pattern is that PTSD and dissociative symptoms, and probably addictive behaviors, are consistently associated with earlier trauma but that other forms of psychopathology may or may not be.

Risk Factor Analysis

The middle ground between the extremes of arguing that clusters of signs and symptoms are *never* indicators of abuse or that they are *always* indicators of abuse is the view that certain signs and symptoms raise the *index of suspicion* about abuse but do not necessarily imply certainty about abuse. This approach is known as *risk factor analysis*. Since the Framingham Heart Study, physicians have assessed the probability that a given individual would develop heart disease in the next decade or two based on the occurrence of a number of positive risk factors, e.g., high diastolic blood pressure, high cholesterol level, weight problems, etc. The physician determines the presence or absence of a number of empirically derived risk factors and calculates the increase in probability that a heart condition will occur in the future within a designated period of time. Finkelhor (1980) applied this kind of risk factor assessment to incest. He identified a number of risk factors for incest based on family history. Ac-

cording to his research, a patient who presents with five of these risk factors has a 66% chance that incest occurred, even in the absence of any memories for childhood sexual abuse. Each additional risk factor raises the probability by 10%. Risk factor assessment is one example of an evolving empirical approach to the problem of evaluating signs and symptoms when the patient does not remember being sexually abused. Its value is that it does not rely on the therapist's prior beliefs. If the therapist, for example, determines that the patient has an 80% chance of having been sexually abused as a child, it does not necessarily follow that the patient has definitely been abused.

The critical question is how the therapist uses the information. We do not think it inappropriate or unduly suggestive for the therapist to communicate an index of suspicion of abuse, based on scientific principles, so long as the communication avoids absolutes and is not phrased in ways that are likely to unduly influence the patient. Some false memory advocates might still consider this approach to be unduly suggestive and complain that the therapist is implanting a false memory for abuse. But if we follow this logic to its conclusion, then it means that every physician who tells a patient that she or he *might* develop a heart condition unless she or he reduces weight and the cholesterol level is at risk of being sued for malpractice for therapeutically suggesting a heart attack to every patient who subsequently develops a heart condition.

The Problem with the PTSD Diagnosis When Trauma Is Inferred

The main problem with the false memory argument against using lists of signs and symptoms to diagnose recovered memories of abuse is that this kind of practice is not generally what *most* professional therapists do, although some self-help manuals describe how certain signs and symptoms are taken in an absolute sense to mean that abuse occurred even in the absence of memories. Here again, much like the debate about repression, the false memory strategy appears to be to call the phenomenon something other than what it is for the purpose of debunking it. Most clinicians, however, except as represented by the extreme (e.g., Fredrickson, 1992), do not make a diagnosis of recovered memories or, for that matter, a diagnosis of abuse, for a very simple reason—recovered memories and abuse are not diagnostic categories represented in *DSM-IV*. A common diagnosis might be posttraumatic stress disorder. Still, we agree with the false memory advocates that making a diagnosis of PTSD in the absence of memories for abuse is problematic. PTSD is unique among the diagnostic categories of *DSM-IV* in its requirement that a specifiable stressor exist before the diagnosis may be made.

The technically correct diagnosis, when signs and symptoms include intrusive reexperiencing, generalized numbing, and physiological reactivity, but when no memory for abuse exists, is PTSS (posttraumatic stress symptoms) and/or dissociated amnesia. We believe that making the diagnosis of PTSD in the absence of memory for abuse is a frequent mistake among clinicians, perhaps because the technically correct category of PTSS is a relatively recent development and is not yet used by many clinicians. We do not believe that a diagnosis of recovered memories is a common practice among professionals, because most professionals are required to use *DSM-IV* and recovered memories and abuse are not *DSM-IV* diagnoses. The false memory advocates who speak about making a diagnosis of recovered memories (Lindsay & Read, 1994; Loftus, 1993) do not take into account professional diagnostic practices, or they are indicting the entire diagnostic enterprise for the excesses in a handful of books like *Repressed Memories* (Fredrickson, 1992).

The Argument of DID and Iatrogenisis

A vocal minority of clinicians have argued that dissociative identity disorder (DID) is an iatrogenic artifact of suggestive therapeutic practices (McHugh, 1993; Merskey, 1992; Piper, 1994). This claim stands in stark contrast to the generally accepted position that DID is a legitimate diagnostic entity as represented in *DSM-IV* (American Psychiatric Association, 1994; Spiegel & Cardena, 1991). These critics have argued that the diagnostic criteria represented in *DSM-IV* were developed by clinicians and researchers who failed to appreciate the suggestive and self-confirming practices that helped create the mistaken view about the existence of DID (Frankel, 1996; Piper, 1994). To support their position the critics of DID have drawn upon laboratory

simulation studies in which multiple role enactments resembling the behavior of alter personalities in DID patients have been demonstrated in normal laboratory subjects (Spanos, 1994; Spanos, Weekes, & Bertrand, 1985).

The main criticisms represented by the DID iatrogenesis hypothesis are: (1) There is no clearly defined set of diagnostic categories that validly and reliably distinguishes DID from other diagnostic conditions. The diagnosis is said to considerably overlap other diagnoses. (2) The diagnosis has no stability over time. (3) There is no relationship between DID and childhood trauma. (4) The recent increase in the incidence and prevalence of DID is an artifact of misdiagnosis and therapeutic suggestion, typically by a minority of clinicians, primarily in North America, who see large number of these patients. The evolving literature on DID is said to encourage overdiagnosis. (5) Alter behavior is a result of suggestive interviewing behavior, notably the use of hypnosis or interviewing that creates and reinforces alter behavior. Alter behavior is said to be shaped by the therapist. (6) Reinforcing alter behavior disempowers the patient and results in harmful, regressive treatments (Frankel, 1996; McHugh, 1993; Merseky, 1992; Piper, 1994). (7) Falsely diagnosing DID in a patient who does not have it and treating the patient for this condition mean running the risk of psychiatric malpractice. Clinicians critical of DID recommend keeping the treatment focus on here-and-now issues and discouraging any alter behavior or any focus on presumed childhood trauma and memory recovery.

In a definitive review, Gleaves (1996b) systematically identifies the logical errors and selective misuse of scientific evidence by proponents of the DID iatrogenesis hypothesis. He says that the diagnostic category, DID, was empirically derived from numerous studies, which yielded a "relatively clear set of clinical DID features" (p. 43). Using a variety of empirically sound self-report instruments, like the Dissociative Experiences Scale and the Structured Clinical Interview for *DSM-IV* Dissociative Disorders (SCID-D), he demonstrates that a set of stable clinical features has been identified, which validly and reliably discriminates DID patients from patients with other disorders and from normal individuals. In addition, he cites an abundance of cross-cultural studies that demonstrate that DID is not culture-bound but is diagnosed around the world. Gleaves points out that proponents of the DID iatrogenesis hypothesis rarely cite any of this increasingly sophisticated diagnostic research, nor do they show much awareness of the list of clinical features that define DID. Instead they make the logical error of assuming that "multiple identity enactment" is the core and only relevant feature of DID:

> Given that recent research has demonstrated the complex psychopathology of DID, equating the disorder with one specific but broadly defined behavior (multiple identity enactment) is clearly unwarranted. The latter should be conceptualized as one observable behavior that may or may not be related to a feature of the disorder (identity alteration). As an analogy, equating major depressive disorder with "acting sad" would be similarly unwarranted because the former is a complex depressive disorder characterized by a clear group of depressive symptoms, whereas the latter is one specific behavior that may or may not be related to one of the symptoms of the disorder (sad affect).
> . . . Conclusions based solely on data relevant to the concept of multiple identity enactment cannot be generalized to the complex dissociative psychopathology of DID. (p. 44)

With respect to iatrogenically creating DID, it may be true that the multiple identity enactments created in the laboratory demonstrate how alter-like behavior can be shaped in certain social interactions, including therapy, but whereas "some of the phenomena of DID can be created iatrogenically, there is no evidence to suggest that the disorder per se can be created" (Gleaves, 1996b, p. 42; cf. Ross, 1989; Ross, Norton, & Fraser, 1989; Spiegel & Cardena, 1991).

While proponents of the iatrogenesis hypothesis have argued that patients simulate DID in order to seek attention, Gleaves cites a number of empirical studies that have shown no significant relationship between DID and histrionic personality and other attention-seeking traits. In response to the hypothesis that DID is a by-product of using hypnosis, Gleaves cites a study by Ross, Norton, and Wozney (1989) demonstrating that only 27% of the DID patients had been hypnotized prior to establishing the DID diagnosis. Moreover, the iatrogenesis ar-

gument fails to take into account that many of these patients had a long history of dissociative symptoms long before the DID was made. It is illogical to argue that a treatment created the disorder when evidence shows in many cases that the condition preceded treatment. Another study (Putnam et al., 1986) revealed no significant differences in the clinical features between those DID patients with whom hypnosis was or was not used in the treatment.

While proponents of the iatrogenesis hypothesis see no relationship between DID and a history of childhood abuse, Gleaves says, "Researchers of recent studies have consistently found a strong association between DID and forms of childhood trauma" (p. 52). Gleaves points out that proponents of the iatrogenesis hypothesis fail to understand the DID treatment literature. According to their view, "MPD patients come to believe that their alter identities are real personalities rather than self-generated fantasies" (Spanos, 1994, p. 144, cited in Gleaves, p. 47). Gleaves says that Spanos's view is:

> at odds with what is recommended in the clinical literature on DID . . . according to this treatment literature, one of the goals of treatment for DID is to help the individual understand that the alters are in fact self-generated, not to convince the patient that alters are real people or personalities. (p. 47)

Gleaves believes that the treatment strategy recommended by proponents of the DID iatrogenesis hypothesis, namely, to discourage alter behavior and recollections of abuse, may be harmful:

> . . . proponents recommend that alters should be ignored (e.g., McHugh, 1993). The argument is based on the logic that to speak of alters as real would reify them in the mind of a confused and suggestible patient, thus worsening his or her condition. . . . What is critical to understand is that acknowledging a patient with DID to have genuine experience of alters as real people or entities is not the same as stating that alters are actually real people or entities. An analogy with another mental disorder may help clarify the distinction. Many individuals with anorexia nervosa state that they experience themselves as obese, even though they are emaciated. To tell such a patient that one un-

derstands and believes that he or she experiences the self in that fashion is not the same as understanding that he or she is truly obese. . . . Most mental health professionals would probably agree that it would be inappropriate to tell a patient with anorexia nervosa that one simply does not believe his or her perceptions. (p. 48)

Gleaves argues that not addressing the DID condition with a specific treatment may result in interminable treatment. He calls this phenomenon "iatrogenesis by neglect" (p. 54).

Based on a careful review of a large body of scientific data, Gleaves concludes:

> . . . the data do not support the hypothesis that assessment or treatment procedures are responsible for the creation of DID. State-of-the-art assessment of dissociative disorders is consistent in format with that of other mental disorders and recent prevalence studies and large-scale investigations on the clinical features of the disorder have been based on the use of such assessment procedures. Furthermore, available data do not support the commonly stated hypothesis that hypnosis can create or significantly alter the clinical presentation of DID. Although some of the features of DID can be role-played, these data do not meaningfully address the etiology of any mental disorder. Criticisms of the treatment of dissociative disorders appear to be based on many misconceptions regarding how treatment is actually conducted. Patients with DID also appear to have experienced their symptoms most of their lives, well before they were ever in treatment for a dissociative disorder (p. 49). . . . [The] model . . . is fundamentally flawed and lacking in support. (p. 54)

Our own conclusions regarding the DID iatrogenesis hypothesis match those drawn by David Gleaves in his critical review. In addition, as experts in hypnosis, we wish to remind the reader that a similar debate occurred in the hypnosis field several decades ago. The debate was about the reality of trance phenomena. Barber and Spanos argued that trance behavior occurred in response to a particular set of social demands, so the hypnotic subject could be motivated to respond to the particular hypnotic task without a formal trance induction ceremony. According to what became known as the task motivational perspective, hypnotic behavior was interpreted as simulated or role-taking behavior in response to the social demands of the hypnotic context, and the condition of trance did not exist.

Subsequent research using more sophisticated designs demonstrated that hypnotic behavior is a *mixture* of both a trance condition and a task-motivated response to the social demands of the hypnotic situation. Thus, while particular behaviors manifested during trance occur clearly in response to the social context, the underlying capacity for trance and its specific manifestations as part of the overall response are clearly not functions of social role-playing. Role-playing theory accounts for part but not the primary part of overall trance behavior (cf. Brown and Fromm, 1986, for a review). Likewise, role-playing theory may account for part of DID alter behavior but not the primary features of the condition. Proponents of the DID iatrogenesis argument have made the same mistake previously made about hypnosis, namely, reducing all the variance of the overall effect of a complex phenomenon to a single dimension while ignoring the primary condition in question.

In our opinion, the analogy drawn from hypnosis research informs us about a more balanced view of DID: DID represents an underlying psychiatric condition wherein some but not all alter behaviors and some but not all descriptions of experience occur in response to the demands of the social context. Piper (1994) sees "mutual shaping" as an illustration of iatrogenesis of the condition. We see mutual shaping as an example of capitalizing on the creativity of both patient and therapist in response to the overall goals of treatment, namely, memory and representational integration. The clinical objective is to shape alter behavior in an informed way toward these goals and to avoid the creation of therapeutically harmful alter effects (Fine, 1989b). To argue that the DID condition does not exist or that alter behavior is never a response to social influence completely ignores how similar questions have been raised and sufficiently answered in other domains of science.

The Satanic Ritual Abuse Controversy

It is also curious that so-called recovered memories apply primarily to childhood sexual abuse and sometimes to Satanic ritual abuse. Why is it that the false memory advocates never speak about recovered memories of physical abuse, of narrowly escaping death, or of war traumatization? In chapter 7 we reviewed the evidence in support of amnesia for a wide variety of traumatic events, including childhood sexual abuse, physical abuse, rape, homicide, and war trauma. The false memory advocates are curiously selective when they address the issue of recovered memories, or, more accurately, traumatic amnesia.

Some false memory advocates, when speaking about Satanic ritual abuse, create semantic difficulties. Jean Goodwin (1993, 1994) correctly notes that the name, "Satanic ritual abuse" should be dropped in favor of "extreme sadistic abuse." She reminds us that all of the extreme and bizarre practices attributed to Satanic ritual abuse are graphically described in *The One Hundred and Twenty Days of Sodom* (de Sade, 1789/1987), and that these practices are not uncommon among international and national sex rings, whose existence is not denied. Recasting Satanic ritual abuse in terms of the kind of extreme sadism often accompanying sex ring practices gives the phenomenon a completely different spin. The existence of extreme sadistic abuse is all too credible.

Moreover, the term "extreme sadistic abuse" does not require a belief system like Satanism on order to be understood. The only requirement is an abuse of power. According to Goodwin, pigeonholing the range of extreme sadistic practices into the very narrow category of an international conspiracy of Satanic ritual abuse distorts our understanding of the phenomenon and falsely creates a crisis of credibility.

Goodman and her associates (1995), in their massive examination of ritualistic childhood abuses, noted that "religious" abuses were far more prevalent than had been recognized. When we evaluate the rate of "religious" or "occult" abuses, which include "beating the devil out of a child" (p. 6), we find overwhelming evidence to support the existence of such practices:

> For instance, there was no hard evidence for intergenerational Satanic cults that sexually abuse children. There was, however, evidence in a few "borderline" cases, typically involving a lone individual or two people whose abuse of children involved Satanic themes. In contrast, convincing evidence of religion-related abuse was often found. (p. 5)

Goodman and her associates (1995) also note that "nearly all abuse perpetrated by religious professionals (94%) was sexual in nature" (p. 12). Their study found that "religion-related abuse is actually more common than Satanic abuse" (p. 14), which led them to conclude that "there are more children being abused in the name of God than in the name of Satan" (p. 12).

Some false memory advocates pigeonhole Satanic ritual abuse very narrowly, as though ritual abuse practices exist *only* as part of an international conspiracy. The available research demonstrates that extreme sadistic practices occur along a continuum from the poorly organized practices of individuals, to loosely organized practices within families and extended families, to organized cults, to larger social networks, only a portion of which may be associated with Satanism, and more commonly are associated with provable national or international sex ring trafficking. The prevailing view is that extreme sadistic practices are not uncommon if understood in the context of sexual trafficking. Some Satanic ritual abuse may occur in families, extended families, and local community networks, but it is not likely to be found in the form of larger organized social groups, especially groups with international components. While an international Satanic conspiracy may strain credibility, the role of internationally organized crime in promoting sexual trafficking does not.

The reductionistic strategy, reducing the complexity of the entire domain of extreme sadistic sexual practices to a very narrow category like organized Satanic ritual abuse, is employed so that the entire phenomenon can be refuted, but only by ignoring the available data on sex rings and familial practices. Note the structural similarity between two common false memory arguments: (1) Classify traumatic abuse by a narrow subset, repression. Ignore the wider evidence on traumatic amnesia for other types of trauma, and then emphasize the lack of evidence on repression in order to debunk it. (2) Classify extreme sadistic sexual practices by a narrow subset, international Satanic ritual abuse. Ignore the wider evidence on extreme sadistic sexual practices and emphasize the lack of evidence proving international Satanic ritual abuse, as though extreme sadistic sexual practices did not exist.

Loftus and Ketcham (1994) and Ofshe and Watters (1994) have argued that the seemingly bizarre accounts of Satanic ritual abuse reported by patients in psychotherapy are necessarily a product of therapeutic suggestion. Satanic ritual abuse recollections are given as examples of iatrogenically implanted memories. Loftus and Ketcham cite the misinformation suggestion studies including their Shopping Mall study to demonstrate how such seemingly bizarre recollections of ritual abuse can be implanted in therapy. Since all of these studies except the Shopping Mall study are largely restricted to suggestively altering memory reports for minor details of a complex event, fail to support the iatrogenesis hypothesis specifically as it applies to ritual abuse recollections.

Since the original Loftus and Pickrell Shopping Mall study (1995), two studies (Hyman et al., 1995; Pezdek et al,, in press) have varied the type of information, and while 15–20% of subjects accepted or partially accepted post-event misinformation for plausible events, like being lost in a Shopping Mall as a child, considerably fewer subjects accepted misinformation for implausible events (12–14% of subjects in Hyman et al., 1995, and none in Pezdek et al, in press). In Pezdek et al.'s study (in press) no subject accepted misinformation for an implausible event (see Table 12.1). These data do not support the hypothesis that bizarre events can be easily implanted, if at all, through post-event suggestion. False memory proponents cannot cite the Shopping Mall data as a demonstration that complex events can be implanted in subjects and then ignore some of these same data that demonstrate that it is very difficult to implant bizarre events. Clearly, some al-

ternative hypothesis, other than iatrogenic suggestion, must be put forth to explain the incidence of most ritual abuse recollections in patients.

Recovered Memory Therapy

This section will address the logical errors inherent in the argument that therapy, specifically "recovered memory therapy," can result in false memories for childhood sexual abuse. Advocates of the false memory position (e.g., Ceci & Loftus, 1994; Lindsay & Read, 1994; Loftus, 1993) seem to agree that suggested false memories of abuse occur in what they have called "recovered memory therapy." Ofshe and Watters (1993) consider recovered memory therapy to be a type of "new miracle cure," the latest in a series of therapeutic fads, all of which are forms of "quackery." The obvious problem with this argument is that the term "recovered memory therapy" is essentially an invented term—invented by false memory advocates as a strategy to debunk psychotherapy. As Alpert (1995b) notes:

> This search for buried memories is not promoted by professional programs in psychology or mainstream professional literature on treatment of adult survivors. . . . There is no training program or mainstream literature that presents memory retrieval to the exclusion of other therapeutic tasks as the treatment goal or that promulgates the utilization of techniques that are suggestive. (p. 7)

Grand (1995b) adds:

> The very term recovery therapy itself derives solely from the linguistic frame of the false-memory movement, rather than from the terminology of

TABLE 12.1

The Shopping Mall Studies: Acceptance of Plausible and Implausible Misinformation

Study	Sample Size	Factual Information	Plausible False Information	Implausible False Information
Loftus & Pickrell, 1995	24	68%	29% full or partial	
Hyman et al., 1995 Exp. #1	20	84%	20% by 2nd interview	
Hyman et al., 1995 Exp. #2	51	82%		12% full, 14% partial by 3rd interview
Pezdek et al., in press	20		15%	0%

responsible clinicians; it bears a subtle and unmistakable connotation of lack of training. (p. 266)

It should be obvious that *all* memories are "recovered" memories—that is what it means to be a memory. It is also true that many therapies are based on the principle that the past has shaped the present.

Among the false memory position papers it is difficult to find a clear definition of recovered memory therapy, except for vague generalizations that recovered memory therapists espouse the tenets of popular self-help books like *The Courage to Heal* or *Repressed Memories*, persistently focus on childhood sexual abuse, and use memory recovery techniques. False memory proponents have not yet offered any scientific evidence to demonstrate the existence of so-called recovered memory therapy as a type of psychotherapy. Recovered memory therapy is not listed among the schools of therapy in textbooks on psychotherapy. Pezdek (1994) points out that clinicians do not take courses on recovered memory therapy in graduate-level clinical training programs. Olio (1994) criticizes the false memory advocates on the grounds that very few professionally trained therapists use the kind of memory recovery techniques that they have been accused of abusing.

To counter critics, Poole and his associates (1995; cf. also Lindsay & Poole, 1995) randomly surveyed licensed American doctoral therapists listed in the *National Register of Health Care Providers* (Lindsay & Poole, 1995) and then surveyed British psychologists listed in the *Register of Chartered Clinical Psychologists* (Poole et al., 1995). The combined data (Poole et al., 1995) provided weak support for the false memory position. Poole et al. found that, "across samples, 25% of the respondents reported a constellation of beliefs and practices suggestive of a focus on memory recovery, and these psychologists reported relatively high rates of memory recovery in their clients" (p. 426). About 90% of the respondents were clearly aware of the possibility that suggestions could influence memory in therapy. According to their criteria, Lindsay and Poole (1995) classified these therapists as "memory focused clinicians" (p. 434). Poole et al. correctly qualify their conclusions, namely, that identifying a subsample of therapists who use memory recovery techniques does not necessarily imply that these therapists were using such techniques "in single-minded and highly suggestive ways" (p. 435). We agree with Pezdek's (1994) conclusion that some false memory advocates have fabricated the term "memory recovery therapy" essentially as a straw man in order to "reprimand the whole field of psychotherapy" (p. 342).

Of course, a good part of the problem is that laboratory memory scientists, like Loftus and Lindsay, and sociologists, like Ofshe, are not practicing psychotherapists. They rarely cite any of the authoritative literature by trauma experts on phase-oriented treatment of trauma. Instead of citing professional practice sources, these and other false memory advocates have chosen to cite the popular self-help books, like *The Courage to Heal*, as though to imply that the self-help and professional practice literatures are one and the same, and as though the self-help books were more representative of the standard of care of abused patients than professional phase-oriented treatment. As Pezdek (1994) succinctly states:

> I also generally take issue with the strategy of these authors of spotlighting some extreme, popular-press books on the topic, e.g. *The Courage to Heal* (Bass & Davis, 1988) and then criticizing the whole field for the views in these books. A comparable application of this strategy a little closer to home would be, for example, to criticize the field of cognitive psychology for the views expressed in such books as *Drawing on the Right Side of the Brain* (Edwards, 1988). (p. 341)

The assumption made by false memory advocates is that professional trauma therapists have read the self-help books and actually assigned them to patients as homework. While there is no doubt that some poorly trained therapists actually have done and continue to do this, we suspect that this is a very small percentage. And, of course, the number is not relevant to the legal standard of care, which is at a higher level than these works suggest.

Some false memory advocates really have used informants as a source of knowledge about the practice of psychotherapy through discussions with a small number of therapists. Loftus and Ketcham (1994), for example, thank a mixed list of self-help and professional therapists "for illuminating discussions about psychotherapy" (acknowledgment section, p. ix). The field of anthropology has a long tradition of established methodologies to deal with the methodological pitfalls inherent in using informants to make generalizations about culture. When some false memory proponents use a small group of therapists as informants to understand the culture of psychotherapy, their approach fails to address the limitations inherent in using informants as a strategy to understand psychotherapy.

An even more serious problem pertains to the scientific explanation offered by false memory advocates, namely, that recovered memory therapy leads to suggestions of false memories of childhood sexual abuse. "While suggestibility effects could theoretically occur in therapy, it does not follow that they indeed do" (Alpert, 1995b, p. 7). False memory advocates have assumed that a particular form of therapy is unduly suggestive without ever designing a single experiment to demonstrate suggestive effects in psychotherapy in general or the implanting of false memories of abuse in particular. Lacking research data to back up their claim, false memory advocates must make the argument on the basis of logic, scientific explanation, and "indirect evidence" (Schooler, 1994) derived from other areas of research on suggestibility. However, generalization is more difficult across than within samples. The generalization of memory suggestibility to psychotherapy has been criticized on the grounds of ecological validity (Yuille & Cutshall, 1986). The generalization also seriously overstates the data (Brown, 1995b; Koss et al., 1995). Pezdek (1994) points out that it is unusual to offer a scientific explanation prior to data collection and that it is a logical error to confound the existence of a scientific explanation with an empirical demonstration of the phenomenon in question:

> A phenomenon must be demonstrated before consideration of an explanation for it is justified. The central thesis of Lindsay and Read's paper is that "memory recovery therapies" may "inadvertently lead some adult clients to create illusory memories of childhood sexual abuse." The bulk of the paper is devoted to elaborating an explanation for this phenomenon and then suggesting ways to overcome the problem. Although an elaborate explanation for this phenomenon was proposed, the phenomenon was never demonstrated! The

existence of the phenomenon was thus inferred from the fact that there might be an explanation for it. Just because illusory memories can occur does not mean that they do, and just because some "recovered memories" are unlikely, does not mean that most recovered memories are therefore false.

> In the field of aeronautical engineering there is a formal explanation for why it is impossible for bumblebees to fly, given the relatively large size of their bodies and the small size of their wings (Wingfield & Stine, 1992). Despite this explanation, bumblebees do fly, and flying does not appear to be difficult for them. The point is that it is a logical fallacy to infer the existence of a phenomenon from the possibility of explaining it. (p. 340)

Another closely related problem is the assumption that therapy contributes significantly more to the variance of false memory suggestion than other sources of suggestibility. Loftus (1993) cites two types of suggestive sources—therapeutic suggestion and popular writings. Ofshe and Watters (1993) and Lindsay and Read (1994) speak of both recovered memory therapy and victim support groups as sources of suggestion. The shared assumption across these works is that individual and/or group therapy leads to false memories of childhood sexual abuse. If false memory advocates were to use the same logic here that they employ when calling into question the association between childhood sexual abuse and adult symptomatology, we would expect them to argue that the amount of the overall variance of false memory suggestion accounted for by therapy would be quite small because other variables probably account for a significant portion of this association. Here, however, they imply exactly the opposite, namely, that the greater portion, if not all, of the variance is contributed by psychotherapy.

Most of the false memory position papers fail to mention other nontherapy variables that might contribute to suggestions of false memories of childhood sexual abuse (Grand, 1995b). In fact, a *multifactorial explanation* of memory suggestive influences is the only explanation warranted by the available data. Single-factor explanations are both oversimplified and unsupported by the evidence. As an expert witness, Loftus has committed the same logical error: she assumes that if a patient recovers a memory of childhood sexual abuse and happens to be in therapy at the time, then therapy caused the memory to be recovered, and therefore the memory is not credible. The logical error is: if a memory appears in therapy, then it must be a product of therapeutic suggestion. As we noted earlier, it does not necessarily follow that a memory recovered in therapy was caused by therapeutic suggestion. Other explanations need to be ruled out. In Table 12.2 we have tried to summarize all of the multifactorial suggestive influences currently known, so that the reader can appreciate the complexity of therapeutic and extratherapeutic variables that potentially contribute to memory distortion. The correct question is: what portion of the variance of recovered memories is accounted for by therapeutic (or other variables) in a particular case?

Moreover, Loftus's single-factor theory has not been supported by available evidence. Loftus (1993) has argued that reported forgetting and later remembering of childhood sexual abuse are the product of therapeutic suggestion. She cites as evidence the fact that early surveys (Briere & Conte, 1993;

TABLE 12.2
Multidimensional Sources of Misinformation Suggestion

Misinformation about abuse that never happened, or about retracted alleged false memories of abuse that historically occurred, potentially could arise from many sources:

- Sociocultural belief systems, e.g., exposure to religious and political advocacy groups
- Media exposure: films, books, news articles
- Social influences
  - Parents
  - Siblings
  - Spouse and children
  - Peer influences
  - Significant others
  - Friends
  - Peer groups
- Therapeutic influences
  - Previous therapies
  - Current therapy
  - Participation in self-help groups
- Legal influences
  - Exposure to attorneys

Herman & Schatzow, 1987) documenting forgetting of childhood sexual abuse were conducted on therapy samples. However, more recent surveys conducted on nonclinical samples have generally supported the view that a significant subpopulation of adults with a history of childhood sexual abuse are amnestic for the experience. In several of these surveys, only a very small portion of the subjects who recovered memories reported doing so in therapy (Bernet et al., 1993; Elliott & Briere, 1995; Roe & Schwartz, 1996). In other words, the false memory advocates are not yet able to explain the fact that a significant number of people report recovering memories without the influence of therapy, e.g., through watching television, being triggered in an intimate relationship, or interacting with family members or one's own children.

Another logical error made by the false memory advocates is: if a memory is recovered after being in therapy—whether (1) within the session, or (2) outside of the therapy hour, or (3) during therapy, or (4) after its termination—then it must be false (Loftus, 1993). A related logical error is: if a memory is recovered after an hypnotic intervention, then it must be false (Ofshe, 1992). These arguments have been used by expert witnesses to persuade the courts to dismiss claims of recovered memories of childhood sexual abuse (e.g., Ofshe, 1992). Berliner and Williams (1994) have identified the logical fallacy of this frequently used argument:

> There is a certain selective use of research to support the following illogical argument: If abuse really happened, it would be remembered all along, and as many of the reported memories are for experiences from very young ages, this proves the memories are false, because people ordinarily cannot recall early events. (p. 381)

If we follow this argument to its conclusion, false memory advocates would have us consider only pretherapy memories as possibly valid phenomenon. The underlying logical error is that recovered memories are necessarily false. Recent data on the accuracy of memories recovered in therapy contradicts the false memory hypothesis (Dalenberg, 1996). We find it ironic that memory scientists need to be reminded not to confound memory incompleteness/completeness with memory accuracy/inaccuracy.

On the other hand, some trauma advocates make the logical error of assuming that recovered trauma memories must necessarily be accurate, or that the longer the process of memory recovery the more accurate the memory must be. Ofshe and Watters (1994) say:

> While recovered memory therapists believe that the more hours they spend with a patient focusing on memories, the more truth about the client's past they will uncover, the exact opposite is true. . . . Considering the pressures and distortions inherent in the long-term-memory-retrieval process of recovered memory therapy, it seems likely that the patient's true recollection of the past will be better in the first set of sessions than at the end of treatment. (p. 62)

Our view is that there is probably no clear relationship between duration of treatment and memory accuracy, and that among the critical variables the nature of the therapeutic interaction plays an important role in the degree of accuracy or inaccuracy of the resultant recollections. Dalenberg (1996), however, found that memories recovered later were significantly more accurate than those recovered earlier in therapy.

We turn now to the specific ways in which psychotherapy are said to result in suggestions of false memories of childhood sexual abuse. A therapist's a priori beliefs about the existence of childhood sexual abuse in a patient who does not remember any abuse are said to contribute to false memories of childhood sexual abuse (Loftus, 1993; Yapko, 1994a). The problem with this argument is that none of the false memory advocates ever offer a detailed explanation of how a therapist's beliefs actually become internalized by the patient. This position represents something akin to an infectious model of belief transmission: the innocent patient is a passive recipient who becomes infected by the therapist's abuse beliefs. However, the theory fails to explain why some patients might be more vulnerable to, and some less vulnerable to, a therapist's beliefs, and under what conditions.

False memory advocates generally fail to mention individual differences in patient suggestibility, and they place the emphasis solely on the therapist's beliefs. There are, of course, numerous instances in which a therapist believed a patient was abused and the patient never recovered memories of abuse in therapy—a phenomenon rarely mentioned by false memory advocates. The infectious model of belief transmission fails to explain why the patient seems so vulnerable to the therapist's beliefs about childhood sexual abuse, and not to other beliefs a therapist might hold. While it is true that patients selectively identify with certain qualities in, and sometimes beliefs of, their therapists, patients rarely finish therapy having adopted their therapists' political or religious beliefs. Few therapists have ever been accused of making a patient a Democrat or Republican.

Another argument put forth by false memory advocates is that the activity of psychotherapists is inherently suggestive. Therapists are said to suggest false memories for childhood sexual abuse by: (1) "persistent encouragement to recall past events" (Frankel, 1993, p. 954; cf. also Yapko, 1994a, p. 18); (2) "suggestive therapeutic procedures" (Yapko, 1994a, p. 41), which sometimes may entail interpersonal "pressure" (Haaken & Schlaps, 1991; Ofshe & Watters, 1993; Yapko, 1994a); and (3) the use of specific "memory recovery techniques" (Lindsay & Read, 1994; Loftus, 1993; Ofshe & Watters, 1993; Yapko, 1994a). A century of research on human suggestibility leads us to the conclusion that many forms of human interactions are indeed suggestive. There is nothing innovative about the claim made by false memory advocates that the psychotherapy process can be suggestive.

Frank (1961) and others believe that effective psychotherapy operates as a form of social persuasion, in which the therapist provides the patient with an organized, coherent belief system for his/her symptoms of distress. Strong (1968) explicitly labeled counseling as purposeful social-influence processes. His landmark paper initiated a decade of laboratory studies on suggestive influences in laboratory simulated psychotherapy sessions (for a review cf. Corrigan, Dell, Lewis, & Schmidt, 1980). Most of these studies focused on source credibility effects, i.e., the therapist's ability to influence clients was associated with his or her perceived expertness, attractiveness, and trustworthiness.

We agree with Frankel and others that a consistent focus on past experiences for which the patient is uncertain can result in a shift in the criteria by which the patient distinguishes fantasy from memory. These conditions can encourage guessing and increase the likelihood that fantasy and memory productions are confused. However, a consistent focus on past experience in and of itself does not automatically result in confusing fantasy and memory. Many therapists would argue that the critical factor is not focus on the past per se, but, rather, how it is focused upon by patient and therapist alike. Patients and therapists who approach the reconstructed fragments of the past as a series of working hypotheses, from the perspective of a "scientific attitude" (French & Fromm, 1964), may actually increase their ability to discriminate fantasy from memory.

The logical error made here is to assume, prior to designing research to test the hypothesis, that focus on the past per se is the variable causing the failure to distinguish fact from fiction, without considering other variables that might account for this effect, such as the way, to what degree, and under what conditions the past is focused upon.

We also agree with Yapko (1994b) that "suggestive therapeutic procedures" are sometimes used by therapists, and that under certain conditions false memories occur in therapy. The problem with the false memory argument, however, is that it is too general. None of the false memory advocates clearly delineates the factors involved in the production of false memories for childhood sexual abuse in psychotherapy. Here and there in his book, Yapko (1994a) makes casual references to therapeutic suggestion ("process suggestions," p. 105; "indirect suggestions," p. 119). Ofshe and Watters (1993) present a more detailed model. The suggestive process begins with persuading the patient about the diagnosis of abuse (direct suggestion), followed by memory recovery techniques that encourage guessing, through which the false memories are generated, followed by repetitive retelling and reshaping the story (rehearsal), then followed by elaboration of the false story.

These explanations fail to distinguish between suggestive influences, which probably always operate in psychotherapy, and unduly suggestive influences, which operate primarily in substandard treatment. Moreover, these explanations fail to specify the exact suggestive conditions that significantly increase the likelihood of false memory pro-

duction in psychotherapy. The erroneous implication of this argument is that the very nature of psychotherapy as a social-influence process necessarily leads to false memory production. In the last chapter we saw that a complex interaction between a great number of cognitive and social variables contributes to the overall suggestive effect under certain conditions. We also saw that the likelihood of producing false memories is significantly increased under very specific conditions. Simply put, the interviewer has to systematically supply a good amount of the content of the interview, content that is false. The false memory position papers oversimplify the argument, and therefore are unable to explain why suggestions are accepted under certain conditions and not others, or why certain types of suggestions are accepted and others are not.

False memory advocates make the argument about therapeutic suggestion so general that one is left with the impression that the very nature of suggestive influences inherent in psychotherapy makes psychotherapy an impossibly problematic enterprise in the treatment of trauma. Clinicians with extensive experience using hypnosis are puzzled by the false memory argument: why would patients so readily accept even the subtlest suggestive hint of childhood sexual abuse and then build it into an elaborate false belief, and yet all too often resist quite explicit and sometimes doggedly persistent healthy suggestions that they stop smoking or begin to feel good about themselves?

The main false memory argument is that extensive use of memory recovery techniques significantly contributes to false memory production (even though recent surveys have shown that most memories are recovered *prior to* therapy [Andrews et al., 1995]). It is hard to find a clear definition of a memory recovery technique in the false memory position papers. It is also hard to find a section on memory recovery techniques in any textbook on psychotherapy, since it is a term fabricated by false memory advocates. Instead, the false memory advocates give us a laundry list of procedures, including: hypnosis, guided imagery, dream-work, journaling, and body work (Lindsay & Read, 1994; Loftus, 1993; Ofshe & Watters, 1993; Yapko, 1994a). It remains unclear whether there is any scientific basis (e.g., construct validity) for classifying these quite diverse methods under the generic category of memory recovery techniques. The presumed common factor seems to be that any or all of these methods can encourage guessing, thereby increasing the likelihood of confounding fantasy and memory. While the argument sounds logical, it ignores the scientific evidence to the contrary. We have seen that hypnotizability, not any specific hypnotic technique, contributes significantly to hypnotic pseudomemory production. Yet, Loftus (1993) and Lindsay and Read (1994) still speak of "hypnosis" as a memory recovery technique, as though it were the procedure instead of hypnotizability that leads to memory distortion, even though elsewhere Loftus seems aware that hypnotizability is the main contributor to memory distortion (Loftus & Ketcham, 1994, p. 255).

Under certain conditions, hypnotic procedures significantly increase recall of *both* accurate and inaccurate information (Pettinati, 1988). Certain hypnotic procedures increase accurate information without increasing inaccurate information provided that social/contextual influences are minimized. The conclusion we drew in chapter 10, very similar to the conclusion drawn by the task force members who drafted the American Society of Clinical Hypnosis Memory Guidelines (Hammond et al., 1995), is that specific hypnotic techniques per se do not make a substantial contribution to memory distortion; rather, significant memory error will or will not occur depending on how the interview is conducted—either in trance or in the waking state.

The scientific data demonstrate that guided imagery techniques per se do not contribute to substantial memory distortion. Table 12.3 summarizes data from 21 laboratory studies. Two of these studies use repeated open-ended questions without imagery as the primary memory strategy (Memon et al., 1992; Memon & Vartoukian, 1996). The other 19 studies use imagery techniques or making mental pictures of one sort or another to refresh memory about a target event. In the two studies in which no imagery was used to refresh memory for the target event, there was no increase (Memon et al., 1992) or only a slight increase in the total amount of information. In 15 of the studies, where imagery techniques (loosely defined in terms of making mental pictures) were combined with free recall and repeated questions over one or more sessions, the procedure led to a significant increase in the total amount of accurate infor-

mation obtained about the target event (from 11% to 96%). There was no significant increase in the memory error rate in 13 of these 16 studies. Only two studies reported a significant increase in the error rate, and in both studies interviewing techniques were used that were a departure from free recall, namely, a review of previous recollections (Turtle & Yuille, 1994) and asking specific questions (Dent & Stephenson, 1979). However, in the last four of the 21 studies subjects were instructed to repeatedly visualize misinformation supplied to them by the interviewer or a parent. Using this procedure there was a remarkable increase in the error rate (Ceci, 1994; Poole & Lindsay, 1995), especially when subjects were told that the fictitious information was true (Ceci, Loftus et al., 1994). Yet, in an attempted replication of that study where the subjects were given warnings not to report events unless they were really sure that it actually had occurred, the error rate dropped to an insignificant level (Ceci, Crotteau-Huffman et al., 1994).

The most reasonable conclusions across all 21 studies where imagery of some sort was used to refresh memory are: (1) Guided imagery per se as a technique to recover memories does not lead to significant increases in the memory error rate, when combined with free recall strategies and appropriate warnings to reduce error. (2) Guided imagery per se combined with free recall and appropriate warnings may actually be helpful as a memory recovery technique, in that it typically leads to a significant increase in additional information about the target event. (3) *Memory distortion is a function of how the interviewing is conducted and is not a function of the use of guided imagery per se.* When guided imagery is used in conjunction with suggestive interviewing, wherein misinformation is systematically supplied by the interviewer, guided imagery leads to substantial increases in the memory error rate. (4) Even in the context of systematically suggestive interviewing, the expected significant increase in the memory error rate can be partially offset by the use of appropriate warnings.

Pennebaker and Memon (1996) have made a similar argument with respect to journaling. They argue that "nondirective writing . . . [about traumatic experiences] may be helpful in reducing suggestive influences in recall" (p. 381). Schoutrop et al. (1995) have shown that nondirective journaling

TABLE 12.3

Imagery and Memory Enhancement: Completeness and Accuracy Data

Study	Target	Times	TI	ER	Strategy
Memon et al., 1992			ns	ns	repeated open-ended questions without imagery
Memon & Vartoukian, 1996 (c)	staged argument	1	1–6%	ns	FR + repeated open- ended questions without imagery + warning
Scrivner & Safer, 1988	burglary	4	23%	ns	FR replay of videotape
Dunning & Stern, 1992	robberies shootings	3	11%	ns	repeated FR
Malpass & Devine, 1981	staged vandalism	1	20%	ns	photo line-up vs. guided memory re: setting, actions, feelings
Turtle & Yuille, 1994	robbery	4	11%	*	repeated FR + review of previous statements
Fisher et al., 1989	field study of witnessed crimes	5–7	47%	ns	cognitive interview
Fisher et al., 1987	video of bank robbery	1	96%	ns	revised cognitive interview emphasizing mental imagery
George, 1991	staged argument	1	35%	ns	revised cognitive interview
Fisher & McCauley, 1995	video of car accident	1	65%	ns	revised cognitive interview
Dasgupta et al., 1995	police brutality film	1	13.5% 13%	ns	guided imagery or cognitive interview
Dent & Stephenson, 1979 (c)	robbery	5	20%	**	FR + specific questions
Geiselman & Padilla, 1988 (c)	film of robbery	1	21%	ns	cognitive interview + warnings
McCauley & Fisher, 1992	Simon Says game	1	65%	ns	cognitive interview
Saywitz et al., 1992 (c) Exp. #1	staged event	1	26%	ns	cognitive interview + warnings
Saywitz et al., 1992 (c) Exp. #2	staged argument	1	18% 45% with practice	ns	cognitive interview + practice with cognitive interview
Poole & Lindsay, 1995	staged event with Mr. Science	1	56–68%	2% ns	5 open-ended questions including how everything "looked" and what "heard" in classroom
Poole & Lindsay, 1995	staged event with Mr. Science	1 time after 3 months		24% **	FR + 9 leading questions + parental coaching + source monitoring questions
Ceci, 1994 (c)	mousetrap study	10		37–72%	rehearsed images
Ceci, Loftus, Leichtman, et al., 1994 (c)	mousetrap study	10	20%		told event happened + rehearsed images + warning
Ceci, Crotteau-Huffman, et al., 1994 (c)	mousetrap study	10		ns	warning

KEY:

Times = number of interview sessions used to enhance memory	ns = not statistically significant
TI = Total percentage of new information retrieved in the interview	FR = free recall interview
	C = child study
	* p< 0.5
ER = Increase in the memory error rate	** p<0.1

can also lead to substantial new information about the traumatic experience.

False memory proponents who mischaracterize guided imagery, hypnosis, and journaling as danger-ous memory recovery techniques (Loftus, 1993; Lindsay & Read, 1994) fail to cite the greater body of thirdgeneration hypnotic pseudomemory studies reviewed in chapter 10 or guided imagery studies tabulated in Table 12.3 (except the Ceci studies). Considering the totality of the scientific data currently available on both hypnosis and guided imagery for refreshing memory, characterizing these techniques as substantial contributors to iatrogenically implanting false memories of abuse is both inaccurate and oversimplified.

The focus on hypnosis and/or guided imagery illustrates a problem of misplaced emphasis: *hypnotic and guided imagery techniques per se for refreshing memory are not the problem; systematically suggestive interviewing is the problem.* Hypnotic and imagery techniques are useful when combined with free recall and appropriate warnings. Hypnotic and imagery techniques are very risky when combined with suggestive interviewing. So is suggestive interviewing without hypnosis or imagery. Of course, it is much easier to identify certain techniques as being presumably risky, and much harder to identify those therapists who systematically supply a good portion of the content of the patient's emerging narrative rather than letting the report come from the patient through free recall. Attacking memory recovery techniques does nothing to solve the problem of bad interviewing. As Kluft says, "there is virtually no way to avoid the risk of instigating inaccurate recall simply by declining to use one technique or another" (1996, p. 107).

Braude (1995) says that the use of memory recovery techniques "does not presuppose that memory recovery techniques elicit infallible or totally accurate memory reports" (p. 257). The false memory advocates claim therapists hold the naive belief that all aspects of recovered memories are accurate. A balanced position would be: memories recovered through the use of memory recovery techniques associated with free recall contain accurate information not otherwise available to ordinary consciousness, and also contain some inaccurate information. Depending on the conditions of interviewing and the type of information targeted, the ratio of accurate to inaccurate information can be skewed substantially in one direction or the other. We agree with Braude that what are called "memory recovery techniques" are perhaps better called "memory enhancement techniques," because the therapist intends not so much to recover the memory as to establish the conditions under which the patient can freely recall memories not ordinarily available to consciousness. Another way of saying this is that such therapeutic strategies are designed to reduce the problem of state-dependent memory retrieval (Braude, 1995 , p. 261). Even with such techniques, Braude adds, it is illogical to assume that all memories will be recalled. Braude concludes:

> such techniques can sometimes improve the accuracy or completeness of recollections of past experiences. Put this way, the more modest view apparently presupposed or held by reasonable clinicians is analogous to the view that the taste of food can be enhanced by the judicious application of spices—that is, flavor enhancement techniques. In fact, in both cases the techniques have their pitfalls. Memory enhancement techniques can produce various artifacts, and flavor enhancement techniques can likewise produce anomalies or undesired results. (p. 261)

Once again, the effects of using memory enhancement procedures is neither as one-sided nor as simple as the false memory advocates would have us believe. If the overall objective of both false memory proponents and trauma therapists alike is to increase the total amount of accurately recollected information about a target event while minimizing the error rate, then this controversy would be better served by careful focus on suggestive interviewing, not on the use of hypnosis or imagery per se.

Base Rates for Recovered Memories of Abuse

False memory advocates have assumed that the incidence of therapeutically suggested false memories for abuse is rapidly growing. This "growing momentum" (Frankel, 1993), according to Yapko (1994a, p. 19), is reaching "epidemic" proportions. Ceci and Loftus (1994), however, have correctly reminded us that research has not yet established any known base rate for falsely recovered memories. Because it is virtually impossible to collect data on base rates for false recovered memories, all arguments about base rates are necessarily speculative. How, then, do false memory advocates justify their claims about high base rates? Essentially, two strategies have been used. First, the growing membership in the FMSF is taken as evidence of the "growing momentum" of false allegations. Because the great majority of members of the FMSF are accused perpetrators, this group is not representative of a neutral or unbiased sampling, nor has any independent corroborative evidence been offered by the FMSF to show that the allegations are objectively false.

Lindsay and Read (1994) have constructed a mathematical probabilistic model to illustrate how base rates of therapeutically suggested false memories may be high. They weigh the hypothetical diagnostic accuracy of any assessment tool (say, 90% accurate) against the known base rate or incidence of the condition (say, 33% of the population of women have been sexually abused) and against the fact that a portion of these women have amnesia for the childhood sexual abuse (say, 50%). They argue that, given these figures, "almost one-third of the diagnoses of repressed memories would be false" (p. 317). Pezdek (1994), however, has identified an erroneous assumption made by Lindsay and Read. Their probabilistic model presumes incidence rates based on random sampling. She says:

> But this is not how it happens. The people who walk into a clinic . . . are not a random sample of the population at large, but rather, are more likely than the population at large to be members of a high-risk group. (p. 342)

She adds:

> Again, these calculations reflect the expected outcome from the population at large, that is, if "people off the street" were sampled randomly and diagnoses of sexual abuse were made for each. But again this is not how it happens. The only people who are clinically diagnosed regarding sexual abuse are those who select to see a therapist. I think it is safe to assume that the base rate of sexual abuse among people who see a therapist is very much higher than the base rate of sexual abuse among people in the population at large. . . . Then, the probability of a false-positive diagnosis of sexual abuse is reduced from the 31 per cent figure calculated by Lindsay and Read to 18 per cent. (p. 343)

The heated controversy as to whether we are facing an "epidemic" of false allegations is nothing more than speculation. Currently, at least, there is no evidentiary, logical, or probabilistic basis to the claim about a growing epidemic, nor is there evidence that innocent people are being convicted as molesters.

Fish (in press) has applied traditional epidemiological analysis to the controversy regarding base rates. He reminds us that the clinician faces a dual diagnostic responsibility to correctly identify true positive cases of childhood abuse and to correctly rule out true negative cases in adults being evaluated for treatment. He criticizes Lindsay and Read (1994) for their one-sided emphasis on minimizing the problem of false positives (implanted false memories). Fish asserts that the techniques false memory proponents recommend to minimize false positives might actually be harmful from an epidemiological standpoint. These techniques include discouraging clinicians from asking intake questions about an abuse history, disbelieving patients' recollections about abuse without corroborative evidence, and eradicating the use of memory recovery techniques or any techniques that persistently focus on the past. Such recommendations fail to consider the possibility that accurate information about the past may be obtained. Fish demonstrates that traditional epidemiological probability models used to estimate the rates of false positives and false negatives

> yielded values for true false positives and negatives in which the absolute number of false negatives always exceeded false positives . . . we must conclude that the more pressing epidemiological problem, in terms of prevalence and incidence, is under-assessment of CSA history. (in press, p. 44)

Thus, Fish believes that while the potential for false positives may be legitimate but relatively infrequent, the methods some false memory proponents advocate to minimize therapeutic suggestion of false memories may actually iatrogenically create a higher incidence of false negative diagnoses of CSA and thus impede clinicians' attempts to effectively identify and treat survivors of CSA.

Conclusion

The first position papers on the false memory viewpoint (Loftus, 1993; Ofshe & Watters, 1993) and the popular books that followed (Loftus & Ketcham, 1994; Ofshe & Watters, 1994) outlined the main false memory hypotheses. In this book we have critically reviewed all of the scientific studies relevant to this set of false memory hypotheses. Based on the scientific evidence currently available, we draw the following conclusions:

1. The extreme memory fallibility hypothesis (Loftus, 1979b, 1993) seriously overstates and is not supported by the available data (Christianson, 1992a,b). Autobiographical memory in general favors a partial constructive view (Brewer, 1986; Conway, 1992), as does memory for adverse childhood experience and its relationship to adult psychopathology (Brewin et al., 1993). Most narrative autobiographical memory contains a mixture of accurate and inaccurate information. For emotionally meaningful personal experiences, the gist memory is generally accurate and well retained, while the details are not.

2. The evidence strongly favors a multidimensional view of memory systems in both children and adults, with an explicit, narrative system and an implicit, behavioral memory system especially relevant to the memory debate. Neurobiological and phenomenological studies support the view that under certain condtions traumatic memory is processed differently from normal personal memory. The dissociated aspects of traumatic memory exert an implicit influence, although little is known about the relative accuracy or inaccuracy of the implicit, behavioral memory for trauma. The available data do not support the position that traumatic memory can be explained solely in terms of research on normal autobiographical memory.

3. Evidence on amnesia for trauma in a subsample of traumatized individuals is a robust finding across all types of trauma. Thirty studies currently favor the hypothesis that a subgroup of childhood sexual abuse victims forget the abuse and later recover the memory of it. No available studies failed to find periods of forgetting CSA in some subjects. The false memory position that repressed memories are a myth (Loftus & Ketcham, 1994) is given no support by the available data. While the mechanisms of forgetting remain controversial, the existence of amnesia for childhood sexual abuse is well established by the available data. The evidence further suggests that the sample of individuals who forget childhood

sexual abuse is probably heterogeneous, with one subgroup having the CSA memory potentially accessible at least under certain conditions and another subgroup having no available CSA memory.

4. The few data-based studies on accuracy of recovered memories of abuse demonstrate that recovered memories of abuse are no more or less accurate than continuous memories of abuse. The false memory hypothesis that recovered memories are necessarily inaccurate is given no support by the available studies.

5. The hypothesis that false memories can easily be implanted in psychotherapy (Lindsay & Read, 1994; Loftus, 1993; Loftus & Ketcham, 1994; Ofshe & Watters, 1993, 1994; Yapko, 1994a) seriously overstates the available data. Since no studies have been conducted on suggestion effects in psychotherapy per se, the idea of iatrogenic suggestion of false memories remains an untested hypothesis. Three so-called Shopping Mall studies, none of which controlled for social/contextual variables affecting the memory report and none of which provided for an adequate baseline for distinguishing real from fictitious childhood events, do not constitute an adequate test of the hypothesis that entire fictitious events can be implanted through suggestion. When false reports are given, the evidence suggests that these are primarily a function of compliance and only rarely a function of changing the memory representation per se. A large body of available indirect evidence drawn largely from laboratory based studies on various types of suggestive influences implies that suggestion effects operate in psychotherapy. However, these data imply that substantial suggestive distortion of memory in psychotherapy probably occurs only under very specific conditions, namely, with individuals who are high on the continuum of the trait of memory suggestibility and/or who are subjected to the extremes of interviewing, in which the interviewer systematically supplies a high proportion of misinformation and fails to warn the interviewee about memory distortion.

6. There is no evidence that retractors are capable of giving reliable reports about their former psychotherapy experience. False memory proponents who cite research on memory suggestibility to encourage retractors to sue therapists for allegedly implanting false memories through therapeuti-

cally suggestive influences remain blind to how this same research applies to post-therapeutic suggestive influences, not the least of which include significant familial coaching and/or systematic post-therapeutic misinformation supplied by false memory advocacy groups and the media.

7. The hypothesis that bizarre recollections like Satanic ritual abuse memories must be the result of therapeutic suggestion is given little support in the so-called Shopping Mall studies, which demonstrate that suggestions for implausible events that never occurred are not readily accepted by most subjects.

8. The DID iatrogenesis hypothesis is seriously overstated and is given little support by the available data (Gleaves, 1996). While there is no evidence that the psychiatric disorder itself can be suggested, there is evidence that specific alter behavior (one dimension of a larger set of core clinical features) is influenced by social/contextual demands.

9. The idea of a false memory syndrome has little construct or discriminant validity (Hovdestad & Kristiansen, 1996) and there is no adequate evidence that the majority of families associated with false memory advocacy groups were accused by individuals fitting the profile of a false memory syndrome (British Psychological Society, 1995).

10. The long-term effects of childhood sexual abuse are highly variable; no single set of defining features currently exists. However, the false memory view that there is no causal relationship between adult psychopathology and childhood maltreatment (e.g., Dawes, 1994) is refuted by the available prospective studies (e.g., Silverman et al., 1996; Widom & Morris, in press). A reasonable conclusion is that a portion of the variance of adult psychopathology (e.g., posttraumatic and dissociative symptoms, trauma-based pathological schema change, certain forms of relational pathology like traumatic bonding, and sometimes addictive behaviors and depression) is causally related to childhood abuse, while another, perhaps greater, portion of the variance is unrelated to childhood abuse. Adult narrative reconstruction of childhood experiences, including traumatic experiences, is neither completely accurate nor completely inaccurate and is generally representative of what is known about autobiographical memory, namely, that the gist of memorable experiences is generally accurate while the details are not

(Brewin et al., 1993). Yet, psychologically motivated defenses and certain psychiatric diagnoses can contribute to substantial memory distortion, at least in certain individuals with a history of childhood trauma (e.g., Dalenberg, 1996).

11. The false memory view that professional trauma treatment is a form of "memory recovery therapy" (Lindsay & Read, 1994; Loftus, 1993; Ofshe & Watters, 1994) seriously mischaracterizes the growing corpus of clinical literature on phase-oriented trauma treatment. Phase-oriented trauma treatment does include an emphasis on memory integration among its broad-based treatment goals; memory recovery plays a limited role with select patients who suffer from dissociated amnesia.

12. Reconstruction of a narrative memory for trauma is a legitimate goal within the context of phase-oriented trauma treatment. Reconstructed recollections typically contain a mixture of accurate and inaccurate information, and the gist of what is reconstructed in treatment is generally accurate (Brewin et al., 1993), except for a select minority of patients who would give distorted memory reports under most circumstances, and except under the extremes of systematically suggestive interviewing. The skilled clinician remains neutral with respect to the relative accuracy or inaccuracy of these recollections and helps the patient to develop his or her capacity to test the reality of these recollections critically.

13. The false memory hypothesis that certain memory recovery techniques, such as guided imagery, hypnosis, and journaling, are dangerous and contribute to significant pseudomemory production when used in therapy represents a problem of misplaced emphasis. The available data consistently demonstrate that imagery and hypnotic procedures combined with free recall and appropriate warnings result in a significant increase in the total amount of information recollected about a meaningful target event without a corresponding significant increase in the memory error rate. However, guided imagery or hypnotic procedures combined with suggestive interviewing, in which a high proportion of misinformation is supplied by the interviewer within and across sessions, along with other interrogatory techniques not accompanied by warning about memory distortion, result in a highly significant memory distortion rate, at least in certain individu-

als. The false memory view that imagery and/or hypnotic techniques per se significantly increase the memory error rate is not supported by a large number of studies with sophisticated research designs adequate to apportion the variance of what variables do and do not contribute to pseudomemory production.

14. The assessment and treatment techniques recommended by false memory proponents, such as never asking about childhood abuse, maintaining a consistent focus on current life problems, never focusing on past recollections, and never inquiring about dissociative states or alter behaviors and experiences, may be harmful. While these methods may indeed reduce false positives of abuse, they are likely to substantially increase false negatives of abuse (Fish, in press) and do little to solve the clinician's dilemma of reducing both false positives and false negatives.

While we certainly agree that pseudomemories even for complex events that never occurred can and do occur in psychotherapy, at least under very specific conditions (systematically suggestive interviewing) and/or with certain very select individuals (who have the trait of high memory suggestibility and/or whose psychological defenses contribute substantially to memory distortion), we also have critically reviewed a large body of research over these chapters leading to the conclusion that most of the false memory hypotheses are seriously overstated or oversimplified and for the most part are not supported by the available research data. Ken Pope (1996) says:

> An open, fair, and independent analysis must also allow for the possibility that the evidence and logic [of false memory syndrome] do not convincingly establish the validity of some or perhaps any such claims.... What if, for example, tens of thousands of individuals have been wrongly diagnosed with a label [false memory syndrome] lacking adequate scientific validation? (p. 971)

Given the fact that these false memory hypotheses, most of which are overstated and unsubstantiated by the evolving scientific data, have been rapidly and widely disseminated, we are left wondering how to explain the remarkable success false memory proponents have had reshaping the beliefs of clinical

and popular cultures in just a few years. The answer lies not so much in the transmission of an established corpus of scientific knowledge as in the behavior of scientific interest groups.

THE FALSE MEMORY CONTROVERSY VIEWED FROM THE PERSPECTIVE OF THE PHILOSOPHY AND SOCIOLOGY OF SCIENCE

Science as a Rational Enterprise

How are we to evaluate the scientific truth of claims made about traumatic memory processing, memory recovery in psychotherapy, and memory fallibility or suggestibility by advocates of each side of the false memory controversy? The question is quite difficult to answer without raising a more central question: by what perspective on science are we evaluating the scientific claims? Within the modern literature on the philosophy of science, two very different views have emerged. One view emphasizes *scientific method* as a rational endeavor. The other view emphasizes the *practice of science* as a manifestation of social behavior. Scientists function as representatives of social groups within the wider scientific community. This distinction is important because scientific group behavior, like any group behavior, is not always rational.

Scheffler's classic, *Science and Subjectivity* (1967), has served as a reference work on what has been called the "standard view of science" (Mulkay, 1979). While some philosophers of science have argued that there is no standard view of science, but rather a variety of classifiable perspectives on the scientific method (e.g. Lakatos, 1970), Scheffler's work is useful in that it articulates a popularly held stereotype about the nature of scientific inquiry. According to this perspective, science is grounded in realism and empiricism. The external world is seen as real. Scientific empiricism is viewed as a rational procedure through which the scientist is able to observe, measure, discover, and accurately describe natural processes. The scientist who makes these observations is seen as a detached observer who operates relatively free of biases and who follows a more or less fixed set of rules—the so-called "scientific method." Knowledge is acquired in a methodical manner and a body of seemingly neutral "facts" progressively accumulates. The theories that evolve are taken to be actual descriptions of regularities within the natural world (Mulkay, 1979).

According to this view, the scientific experiment is the primary means by which scientific truth claims are evaluated. The eminently rational scientist develops a hypothesis or set of hypotheses within a relevant research area and designs an experiment or series of experiments to test that hypothesis. Truth claims are evaluated primarily in terms of how well the scientist designs the experiments, what sort of evidence is generated by the experiments, and what sort of interpretations are made based on the data. Certain standards for experimental design and statistical analysis have evolved in the social sciences. These include a priority given to experimental over quasi-experimental designs, the value of randomization, and the value of replication in multiple contexts with varying subject samples.

Karl Popper's *The Logic of Scientific Discovery* (1959) was one of the first major modern statements on the rationality of the scientific method—what Popper has called his "theory of scientific method." According to Popper, scientific procedure is a set of "rules as will ensure the testability of scientific statements; which is to say, their falsifiability" (p. 49). Methodological rules are the "conventions" that scientists use in order to test their hypotheses. Truth claims are viewed as "scientific" if they are able to withstand falsification or potential falsification. A scientific truth claim is proven only insofar as it has not been falsified. Popper says, "We shall take it as falsified only if we discover a reproducible effect which refutes the theory" (p. 86). In this view of science, the "game" of science is to design crucial experiments in an attempt to falsify existing scientific truth claims. Those claims that withstand falsification are taken to be scientifically sound. Lakatos (1970) has classified this view of science as a type of "justificationism" in which scientific method is viewed as a rational procedure for eliminating false theories; what survives, and is thereby accepted as scientific fact, is considered science's "proven propositions."

Early work on the sociology of science was faithful to the view of science as a rational enterprise.

Merton's *The Sociology of Science* (1973) traces modern science's historical roots to Puritan values. The "normative structure of science," as well as the scientific institutions that promulgate science, are based upon a very specific social value system—what Merton calls the "moral imperatives" of science. These include four basic values: (1) the scientist manifests *disinterestedness* and does not become personally involved in the problems being addressed; (2) the scientist makes truth claims in the spirit of *universalism* and refrains from scientific explanation that reflects personal or social interest group values; (3) the scientist acts with *communalism* and does not withhold knowledge from the public, from specific interest groups, or from other scientists; and (4) the scientist participates in a wider scientific community characterized by *organized skepticism*, in which testability and falsifiability represent the highest standard of scientific practice shared by members of the scientific community. For Merton, these four moral imperatives function as ideals that scientists strive to maintain. The social reward system functions to reward those scientists who manifest these ideals.

Merton's version of the sociology of science shares with the aforementioned work on the scientific method the assumption that science is essentially a form of rational behavior. These works virtually ignore the important influence of group behavior on knowledge acquisition and portray science as "the disembodied application of a set of rules" (Longino, 1990, p. 13). They fail to take into account irrational elements inherent in either the psychological make-up of the individual scientist or the group behavior of scientists within the scientific community.

Scientific Practice and the Irrationality of Scientific Group Behavior

Other works within the wider domain of the sociology of science have deemphasized *scientific reasoning* in favor of a more careful investigation of *scientific practice*, more specifically, scientific practice by individuals as part of a *social group*. One of the first major statements on scientific practice was Stephen Toulmin's *Human Understanding* (1972). Toulmin defines science in terms of group behavior. Within any scientific discipline a subgroup of scientists defines a particular research area. The members of that group determine the "basic questions" or problems to be addressed. The group devises a set of methods to answer these basic questions. As scientific methodology is refined in a given research area, scientists within the group reach greater consensus on the explanations given to the basic research questions. They develop progressively refined and technically precise language to describe their answers to research questions. The greater the agreement on the basic questions to be addressed within a research area, and the more precise the methodology, the tighter the scientific discipline. The greater the disagreement and the greater the variability in methodology, the looser the scientific discipline. The evolution of a scientific discipline is essentially the evolution of its technical language. From this perspective, science essentially is defined by what a group of scientists comes to agree upon—in terms of basic research questions, the set of procedures, and the technical language used to explain the data. In other words, science is defined more by consensual social behavior and less by an abstract set of rules about scientific method or normative values.

Michael Mulkay's *Science and the Sociology of Knowledge* (1979) addresses how specialized areas of scientific practice are influenced by sociocultural context. In a sharp criticism of Scheffler's standard view of science, Mulkay says:

> Gone is the simple notion that science is built upon a growing corpus of neutral facts. Gone also is the idea that well-established facts are unrevisable and that, consequently, scientific knowledge accumulates in a relatively straightforward fashion. (p. 41)

In his view, scientific practice is never entirely rational and scientific method is "never unbiased" (p. 43). *Irrationality* in science comes from two sources: (1) *individual biases*, e.g., distorted observation, emotional involvement, intellectual prejudice, and erroneous scientific reasoning; and (2) *group irrationality*. Mulkay doubts that scientific truth claims are ever fully evaluated by rational criteria, such as on the basis of the nature of the experimental design, the replicability of the results, and/or the potential testability of the hypotheses. He correctly points out that evaluation of different scientific truth claims is seldom made against some universal standard or set of rules, but all to often is "*flexible.*" Mulkay defines a flexible standard as a standard that changes according to the respective social reference groups that have conducted the research and that are evaluating its truth claims:

> The rules of evidence, criteria of consistency, and so on, in science are not rigid. They are certainly flexible enough to allow scientists considerable leeway in interpreting evidence so as to support well-entrenched assumptions. (p. 59)

The implication of Mulkay's concept of flexible standards is far-reaching. A great diversity of research subgroups makes up the wider scientific community. It is inherent within the nature of group behavior for a particular subgroup to use a more flexible standard in evaluating experimental designs, evidence, and interpretations consistent with its own values and views and to adopt a more rigorous standard in evaluating experimental designs, evidence, and interpretations inconsistent with its own values and views. It is simply a myth to believe that all scientific experiments are evaluated by the same standards. Scientific ideas that are received with skepticism by one scientific subgroup are subjected to a much more rigorous standard of evidence by that group, while relatively unproven or easily falsifiable truth claims made by members of that same group are subjected to a much looser standard of evidence, at least by members within that same group. Scientists know all too well that a submitted paper receiving a scathing rejection by peer reviewers of one journal may find ready acceptance in another. We cannot explain this phenomenon in terms of evaluating scientific truth claims by a universal standard.

Evidentiary standards vary as a function of subgroup behavior within the wider scientific community. According to Longino (1990), when a particular scientific reference group uses a more rigorous evidentiary standard to evaluate the scientific claims of a scientific group other than its own, then such behavior often tells us more about the "background assumptions" (p. 60) of that particular group than it does about scientific truth claims in question. Each scientific reference group's behavior is directed toward advancing its beliefs. When those beliefs come in conflict with the beliefs of another group, each group attempts to assert its dominance by applying a more rigorous standard of evidence to the "science" of the opposition. This perspective on the group behavior of scientists helps us to understand how it often comes to pass that two opposing groups of researchers can use the same set of data to justify conflicting hypotheses.

Just as Polanyi (1958) said that individual scientists tend to "dwell within" their own theories, groups of scientists also tend to dwell within the basic questions, methodologies, and theories that are defined by that group. Insofar as science is a reflection of the group behavior of its scientists, some degree of irrationality is inherent in any scientific enterprise.

In an important book, *Little Science, Big Science*, Price (1963) defines scientific practice on two levels. First, the social structure of science could be viewed in terms of the larger *formal networks* of science, as represented by academic institutions and departments, specialized professional societies and academies. This is the "big science" perspective. Second, the day-by-day practice of science is more accurately described in terms of small group behavior—both within a particular research laboratory or within an informal network of scientists across institutions who communicate regularly about their active work in a particular research area. This is the "little science" perspective.

The larger formal networks of science define research priorities and current controversies. These formal networks serve as the forums for presenting and evaluating research claims and for transmitting scientific knowledge within the wider scientific community (Collins, 1985).

The informal networks reflect how new areas of scientific inquiry develop. These networks typically are established across academic institutions and thereby have come to be known as "invisible colleges" (Crane, 1972; Price, 1963). According to Crane (1972), an invisible college starts with an important scientific innovation. An innovation is typically a recent publication or group of publications concerning a particular question that captures the interest of a diverse group of scientists across institutions and sometimes across disciplines. Innovation simply means that a number of scientists value the ideas addressed so that an informal research group begins to coalesce around the idea— what Crane calls a "social circle." The social circle

can be characterized by direct social contact, for example, Freud's Vienna circle at the onset of psychoanalysis (Grosskurth, 1991), or by an invisible network of researchers who communicate their ongoing ideas by telephone, mail, FAX, or e-mail.

The most successful invisible networks, according to Crane, are linked by "highly influential members" who are "productive" both as scientists and as leaders, and who exhibit "aggressive leadership." Essentially, Crane is describing what amounts to a charismatic model of informal research network development. As the informal network establishes regular lines of communication, it more clearly delineates the basic research questions that drive the group behavior. As methods and scientific evidence accumulate around the basic research questions, the relationships among network members may become more formalized. New specialized journals and sometimes new professional societies develop.

According to this view, success in science is more a matter of network building and leadership within the network than it is about the accumulation of scientific knowledge per se. Crane makes it clear that the publication and rapid social acceptance by a group of scientists of an innovative contribution bear no relationship to the quality of the work. Scientifically sound (or scientifically unsound) works are taken to be innovative and are valued only insofar as they reflect a growing area of concern among some scientists. As Mulkay (1979) says:

> each experimenter (or research group) uses the available technical culture and his own expertise in a flexible manner to reveal the inadequacies of the other's findings and to support his own claims. (p. 59)

In the best sense, invisible networks serve as the means by which entirely new and important areas of scientific inquiry are advanced. Historically, psychoanalysis developed this way. More recently, psychotherapy outcome research developed out of an informal network. In the worst sense, invisible networks arise out of the sociopolitical trends of the day and become essential political movements under the guise of science, such as the network of "scientists" (1) in Nazi Germany who developed a methodology to "prove" the superiority of the Aryan race (Annas & Grodin, 1992; Caplan, 1992; Kater,

1989; Lifton, 1986), with the subsequent approval of courts of law (Muller, 1991), (2) in the Soviet Union, whose views were crafted to conform with Stalin's political ideology (Bloch & Reddaway, 1977), and (3) in the United States, who claimed that there is scientific proof of the inferiority of certain races (Chase, 1977; Larson, 1995), even arguing that slaves who try to run away to obtain their freedom are mentally disordered (Cartwright, 1851).

The essential point is that, when we view science as group behavior, especially in terms of informal group behavior as opposed to large formal social structures, then scientific behavior is revealed as containing a significant element of irrationality. Merton's characterization of the scientific community as "organized skepticism" is a nice ideal for the aspiring scientist. In actuality, that is not how scientists in social reference groups behave. If, for example, a scientist upheld the values of "organized skepticism," we would expect the scientist to behave by designing experiments with the explicit goal of trying to falsify or disconfirm his or her own hypotheses or those within his or her informal research circle. All too often the opposite occurs—the scientist designs experiments solely to confirm preexisting beliefs. In a rather polemic style, Dawes (1994), a member of the FMSF scientific advisors, has illustrated how such a *confirmatory bias* operates in the minds of clinicians when they take unfolding clinical material that is consistent with preexisting and still unproven beliefs as confirmation of these beliefs. We agree. Clinicians, however, are not alone in falling victim to confirmatory bias. Scientists, too, are so motivated.

A closely related concept is the notion of a *false consensus bias* (Marks & Miller, 1987; Ross, Greene, & House, 1977). A false consensus bias is based on the social psychology observation that "people tend to perceive a false consensus for their own beliefs, attributes, and behaviors" (Marks & Miller, 1987, p. 72). While social psychologists have mainly focused on false consensus perception by individuals, the same is true of social groups, including groups of scientists. One danger inherent in scientific group behavior is that the members of a scientific group, based on its interest in and strong positive valuation of a particular research question, might use an especially lax standard to evaluate its evidentiary claims. Consensual acceptance among group members then becomes *the* standard of scientific proof, as though the claim were established. The evaluation of scientific truth claims is accurate only insofar as the irrational biases within the scientific reference group and its members can be identified and minimized. As Longino (1990) reminds us, "evidential reasoning is—both everyday and scientific—context-dependent" (p. 13). By context, we mean group context. If members of an informal research network believe in something, they use a more flexible evidentiary standard; if they disbelieve something, they use a more rigorous standard.

Essentially what may develop out of the informal network's investigations is more a body of consensually shared beliefs than a reflection of established scientific facts. From the perspective of the sociology of knowledge (Mannheim, 1946), some sociologists of science have argued that scientific truth claims are socially constructed beliefs (Knorr-Cetina & Mulkay, 1983; Latour, 1987) and that the seeming "facts" of science are nearly always value-laden (Longino, 1990). The idea that psychotherapy is a socially constructed belief system, not a science, has many recent adherents (Cushman, 1995; Fancher, 1995; Hale, 1995).

The *transmission of knowledge* within the scientific community is through its *peer review* system. The question of acceptance of ideas for publication within scientific journals also can reflect the irrational element of science. In the ideal sense, peer review would be disinterested, universal, communal, and skeptical (Merton, 1973). In actuality, peer review can be quite biased, in that it is a reflection of the social group(s) through which the peer reviewer references himself or herself. Mulkay (1979) correctly points out that the standards for journal peer review acceptance vary remarkably both within and across journals. Hypothesis acceptance is always social in nature (Longino, 1990). Thus, whether or not a given hypothesis is accepted within a scientific reference group is a function of what the group members do with it. If a particular scientific reference group is favorable to a given hypothesis, the ideas may gain acceptance, sometimes irrespective of their scientific merit. What can develop is a scientific microculture that disseminates scientifically unsound information under the name of "science" that is endorsed by respected members of the scientific reference group.

The transmission of false information is compounded by *selective citation* and *miscitation* in scientific journals. Selective citation is defined in terms of selectively citing primarily those other works that agree with the author's viewpoint and failing to cite those that conflict with it. A related problem is miscitation. There is some built-in safeguard against miscitation in scientific journals in that other scientists can write a challenge. Selective citation and miscitation are more problematic in the courts, where an expert may pull together various scientific sources of data into an "expert opinion" that is seldom checked against the original sources.

The False Memory Debate and the Irrationality of Scientific Group Behavior

As we have learned throughout this book, many of the false memory hypotheses are not supported by or have been refuted by actual scientific experimentation. A unique feature of the false memory debate has been the extent to which unsupported hypotheses have been repeatedly promulgated in the media and the courts without designing adequate data-based experiments to test these hypothesis. Where experimental data have been collected, they do not support a number of the claims made by false memory advocates. The specific hypotheses that have generally not been supported by available data-based research include: the alleged myth of traumatic amnesia; the assumed inaccuracy of recovered memories; the assumption that false memories are easily implanted in therapy, other than when false misinformation is systematically supplied by the interviewer under certain conditions with select individuals; the concept of false memory syndrome; the view that there is no relationship between childhood abuse and adult psychopathology; and the argument that DID is iatrogenically created. Since this set of hypotheses constitutes the majority of the important false memory arguments a reasonable conclusion is that the rapidly emerging data-based studies demonstrate that the false memory argument is largely unsupported by the available data. The scientific discourse used by false memory proponents is grossly overgeneralized and oversimplified in, for example, the areas of memory and emotion and of hypnosis and memory.

How do we explain the widespread dissemination of seriously overgeneralized and often unsupported false memory information on the part of well established scientists and clinicians—information spread often in the absence of the emerging scientific data that refutes it? The sociological studies on the irrational element of scientific group behavior help us to understand both the development and persistence of a debate that has seriously strayed from the available scientific data. In our opinion, much of the current rhetoric of the false memory debate is the outcome of the dissemination of a seeming *false consensus bias*, not strongly supported by the existing scientific data. Yet, we agree with the intent of the false memory advocates, who wish to warn clinicians and the public about bad therapy practices that may be unduly suggestive. We disagree, however, with disseminating information that significantly departs from the practice of science as the rational accumulation and interpretation of evidence. Pope (1996) says:

> Claims grounded most firmly in the scientific tradition are those emerging from hypotheses that are falsifiable. Scientists bear an essential responsibility to examine primary data, research methodology, assumptions, and inferences. Science works best when claims and hypotheses can be continually questioned. (p. 971)

It is highly unusual that the false memory debate has gone so far in the media and courts without the appropriate accumulation of data to support many of the claims about therapeutic suggestion or implantation of false abuse memories. In fact, false memory advocates have presented no data on suggestion in psychotherapy per se and no data in support of a false memory syndrome as a valid scientific construct. Pope has pointed out that the FMSF claims to have 12,000 documented cases of allegedly falsely accused family members where false memories were implanted mainly in therapy. From a scientific perspective that is a large sample. However, the FMSF has yet to provide information on what sort of "documentation" constitutes their scientific proof. In fact, an independent investigation of these data by the British Psychological Society found them to be largely incomplete, poorly documented, and more often than not failing to support the claim that allegations were the result of thera-peutic suggestion. Many of the family members were accused of abuse by alleged victims who had remem-bered the abuse all along and who never recovered memories in or out of therapy. The only data-based study to test the false memory syndrome hypothesis found that only 3.9–13.6% of the women sampled potentially met any criteria for false memory syn-drome and none of the women met all of the pri-mary criteria (Hovdestad & Kristiansen, 1996). Yet, accomplished scientists who serve on the advisory board of the FMSF repeatedly publish professional papers, give expert testimony, and make public state-ments as though undue therapeutic suggestion and false memory syndrome were firmly established sci-entific facts. From the standpoint of the sociology of science, all that has been established is a rich case study in the development of a false consensus bias by false memory advocates, although this is not to deny that some of their hypotheses may eventually be supported by the accumulation of an appropri-ate data base.

The false memory controversy is an excellent case study in the irrational aspects inherent in the be-havior of scientific reference groups. This is not to say that the debate lacks scientific merit. It is only to say that it is crucial that the reader learn to dis-tinguish between those aspects of the debate that advance scientific knowledge and those aspects that are pseudoscientific, yet put forth under the guise of science. Both the trauma advocacy and false memory positions within the debate contain their share of irrational elements. Robyn Dawes's *House of Cards* (1994) is essentially an exposé of the irra-tional element within psychotherapy. We are un-aware of any existing comparable work that addresses the irrational element within the false memory position. Recently, a few papers have ap-peared that address this issue (Harris, 1996; Pope, 1996). This section will focus primarily on the irra-tionality manifest in the group behavior of those scientists who make up the informal network that have defined the false memory position.

As a rapidly developing and expanding informal network, this group of false memory advocates is rather different from the informal networks de-scribed by Price (1963) and Crane (1972): most sci-entific informal networks develop internally, around an innovative idea originally put forth by one or

several scientists that eventually captures the inter-est of a larger group. The network of scientists cur-rently representing the false memory position developed externally. A number of these scientists were actively solicited and recruited to be members of the scientific Board of Advisors of the False Memory Syndrome Foundation. Others joined the network around the ideas, although not all became associated with the FMSF. Some time thereafter, the first position papers of this network appeared in the professional journals (Lindsay & Read, 1994; Loftus, 1993; Ofshe & Watters, 1993). *What we will call the false memory network of scientists is unique among in-formal scientific groups because its original formation was at least associated with, if not organized around, an external political group, namely, the FMSF.* Our concern is that when an informal scientific network organizes around an explicit political agenda, the irrational element found in scientific social refer-ence group behavior greatly increases.

Recall Crane's analysis of how a new area devel-ops within science largely from the publication of one or several innovative papers around a particu-lar theme. One of the early innovative and highly influential papers stating the false memory position is Loftus's paper in the *American Psychologist* (1993). Other early papers include those by Ofshe and Watters (1993) and Lindsay and Read (1994).

Loftus, Kihlstrom, and some other prestigious scientists associated with the FMSF meet Crane's criterion as "productive" and "highly influential" scientists. Loftus's (1992) formal address to the American Psychological Association, her active participation as a scientific advisor to the False Memory Syndrome Foundation, her numerous public and forensic statements about memory fal-libility and memory suggestibility, and her recent nomination for the presidency of the American Psy-chological Association are examples of the type of "aggressive leadership" that help make an infor-mal scientific network successful, at least in the sociological sense. In fact, one need only consider how rapidly and large this informal network has grown in the relatively short span of several years since the False Memory Syndrome Foundation was chartered to appreciate the power of informal so-cial organization. Loftus is just one among a small group of scientists associated with the FMSF who have currently come to exert a significant minority influence within the overall domain of clinical science.

Adrienne Harris (1996) has written one of the first socio-historical accounts of the irrationality of the false memory syndrome movement. She situates Loftus, and to some extent Kihlstrom, squarely in the center the dissemination of information about a so-called false memory syndrome. According to her analysis, "The term itself, 'false memory,' may have been too easily assimilated into our discourse, its status as syndrome too accommodatingly taken on" (p. 156). She defines her objective as:

> This legal scene pervades the discussions and presentations of the False Memory Syndrome Movement, leaving science privileged and unassailable and obscuring the discursive practices of science with its particular modes of inquiry and argument. It is this rather specialized, and I would argue, distorted picture of science and scientific evidence in regard to memory that I want to analyze. (p. 161)

Harris examines the "discursive practices" of Loftus and Kihlstrom as "central figures" (p. 157) in the false memory movement, who have helped shape a now culturally accepted view that false memories of abuse that never occurred are easy to implant in psychotherapy, as though the tenets of false memory beliefs are "a secure and unassailable set of [scientific] facts" (p. 171). Harris, however, sees their false memory position as "reductionistic and skewed." Analyzing Loftus's use of language, Harris demonstrates how Loftus, particularly in her popular writings, creates a view of memory, abuse, and psychotherapy that is remarkably oversimplified, and then legitimizes this view as something "unassailable" through discourse about laboratory memory experiments.

What the dissemination of knowledge about alleged therapeutically implanted false memories lacks, according to Harris, is an "active critical argument" about the empirical memory research, its design, its limitations, and the interpretation of results derived from it. Harris cites several examples of how Loftus has used discourse to create a "normalizing veil of science" (p. 161) around the false memory syndrome concept. She shows how eyewitness research on cases of mistaken identity are

largely irrelevant to the phenomenon of recovered memories of abuse. She points out that Loftus's research design and interpretation of results from her studies on misinformation suggestibility have drawn justifiable criticism from memory scientists (e.g., Bekerian & Bowers, 1983; McCloskey & Zaragoza, 1985). She also points out how Kihlstrom's attacks on basic psychoanalytic constructs like repression and the unconscious are written in a discourse that obscures his own extensive research on hypnotic amnesia and implicit memory (1994b, 1995, Kihlstrom & Schacter; in press). The overall effect of such seemingly scientific discourse is that is reduces all complexity out of abuse memory and its recovery. An appreciation of complexity is at the heart of rational scientific discourse:

> The experimental tradition in cognitive science helps us to build an extremely complex picture of memory and abuse. An original event or original experience may never have been or be accessible as a coherent remembered event but nonetheless affects behavior. Its "recovery" will inevitably be a construction. Events may be encoded but remain unavailable. The emotional salience of forgotten inaccessible material may factor into its fate. Rehearsal, ongoing reorganization, and belief about an event may affect its memorability. Remembering will always meld stored representation with narrative elaboration and construction, and the arrangements of power in the social and narrative process of remembering will always be significant. (Harris, 1996, p. 176)

In contradistinction to the irrational element inherent in the false memory debate, Harris advocates a return of what the rational element of cognitive sciences can genuinely provide. To do so both researcher and clinician alike must appreciate the real complexity of what is being studied.

It is hard to see how some scientists associated with the FMSF in their social behavior represent any of Merton's four "moral imperatives" of science. Some scientists passionately attempt to defend parents allegedly falsely accused of childhood sexual abuse (e. g., Loftus & Ketcham, 1994) or others who file defamation suits against other scientists with opposing views (Pope, 1996) are hardly behaviors that exhibit the "disinterestedness" of Merton-type scientists. The truth claims made about memory fallibility, while seeming to espouse universalism, are more accurately representative, as we have seen in this book, of research on one type of memory, namely, normal everyday verbal memory, but not necessarily of behavioral or traumatic memory. The scientific claims made about memory suggestibility are both overstated and oversimplified and do not accurately represent the complexity of our current scientific understanding of various types of human suggestibility (Brown, 1995b; Koss et al., 1995).

Scientists associated with the FMSF held a major scientific conference at Johns Hopkins Medical School over several days (False Memory Syndrome Foundation, 1994). Only a few of several dozen presenters were invited to give a view other than the false memory position. Such behavior hardly represents the principle of communalism.

There is very little behavior representative of the false memory advisory scientists that we might consider in terms of Merton's "organized skepticism." What is noticeably lacking in the behavior of some false memory scientists is any systematic attempt to design experiments to disconfirm or falsify their *own* hypothesis.

If we lived within a Mertonian scientific world, we would expect the publication of Loftus's position paper on the false memory controversy (1993) to be followed by a flurry of research papers by scientists within the same informal network attempting to falsify or disconfirm her hypotheses about memory fallibility, memory suggestibility, repressed memories, and therapeutic suggestion. Instead what do we see? A subsequent series of articles which essentially embellish the same untested hypotheses and thereby give the impression that these are accepted scientific facts (e.g., Kihlstrom, 1993; Lindsay & Read, 1994). Instead of increasingly sophisticated research designs to put these hypotheses to test, we see increasingly poorly designed studies, notably Loftus and Coan's (in press) original Shopping Mall study consisting of five subjects and no controls, all of whom had a relationship with the experimenters (cf. Pope, 1996, and the discussion in chapter 8 of this volume for critical reviews), and anecdotal surveys (e.g., Yapko, 1994b) designed to scientifically illustrate the researcher's preexisting beliefs. Even the misinformation studies using Loftus's original paradigm consistently fail to address

suggestive influences inherent in the research itself, like response bias, demand characteristics, and source credibility.

The amazing fact about the current false memory controversy is how far the debate has gone in the absence of adequate experiments and data. As a case in point, nearly every paper advocating the false memory position addresses suggestibility in psychotherapy. Yet, the scientists within the false memory network have not yet reported a single study on suggestibility in psychotherapy per se or in laboratory simulation of therapy interviews. One excuse is that it is unethical to study suggestion in psychotherapy. These same scientists, however, have conducted countless studies using a laboratory simulation approach to the study of memory suggestibility. The false memory advocates have failed to design laboratory simulation paradigms to test memory suggestibility in psychotherapy. These scientists seem unaware of a rather long tradition within counseling psychology that utilized laboratory simulated psychotherapy paradigms as a means to investigate suggestive influences in psychotherapy (for review see Corrigan, Dell, Lewis, and Schmidt [1980]). They also rarely cite recent research directly comparing memory performance in abused and nonabused populations (e.g., Kuyken & Brewin, 1995; Tromp et al., 1995) and on the accuracy of memories recovered directly in psychotherapy (Dalenberg, 1996). In a rational scientific approach to the memory controversy, additional data-based studies like these must be developed.

Dawes (1994), a member of the FMSF Board of Scientific Advisors, has accused therapists of operating with a confirmatory bias, in that they often select clinical evidence to confirm their beliefs about the patient. As noted earlier, we believe that confirmatory biases do operate all too frequently within clinical practice. However, confirmatory biases operate all too frequently within the practice of science as well. Within the informal network of false memory scientists, a very clear example of a confirmatory bias can be found in the Loftus and Coan (in press) Shopping Mall study. The study contains no control group. Subjects are hardly selected randomly—they are friends and family members of the research team. The study does not control for demand characteristics and other social/contextual influences. In other words, to qualify as an acceptable experimental design, the study would have to meet these criteria. The study would be fine if it were presented as pilot data. But when the data are offered as "scientific evidence" for the hypothesis that false memories for complex events can be implanted, they go beyond any acceptable standard of science.

The problem gets worse when such data are subsequently cited by others as examples of scientific proof. Note, for example, how Lindsay and Read (1994) treat the original Loftus and Coan (in press) Shopping Mall study. They describe it as one of "several more formal studies" that "demonstrated" how illusory memories can be implanted. The language here is revealing. What does the study actually "demonstrate" in terms of scientific truth claims? Very little about changing memory representation. It does, however, replicate some rather well founded principles of social persuasion, and it does demonstrate the confirmatory bias of the researchers. To use Dawes's own metaphor, a great deal of false memory science is likewise a "house of cards." The Shopping Mall study is further cited in a number of professional journals as proof of the false memory position, and then is cited frequently in the media and courts. In fact, Pope (1996) likens the first subject of the Shopping Mall study, Chris, to Anna O., because of the wide publicity that this unfortunate experiment has received.

The dissemination of the false memory position is a good example of a *false consensus bias*. Extreme false memory advocates have used the very same false consensus argument against trauma advocates who take Satanic ritual abuse stories seriously:

> The reasoning used to propagate and bolster the Satanic-cult scare is the same sort of reasoning that is currently used by the so-called Holocaust "revisionists," who have, with growing efficiency, propagated the belief that it was a hoax. According to Deborah Lipstadt, who recently published *Denying the Holocaust: The Growing Assault on Truth and Memory*, those who deny that the Holocaust took place have achieved a veneer of academic respectability and have created a belief that relies not on evidence but on the constant quoting and referencing of others who hold the same beliefs. "They have academic conferences, and even a journal that looks respectable," she says during a recent interview. "Their evidence is a merry-

go-round of cross-fertilization. One expert quotes another expert, who quotes another expert, who quotes another. The arguments go in circles. But they portray themselves as people who are exploring the truth. It's a cloak of respectability that fools people." (Ofshe & Watters, 1994, pp. 202–203)

It is precisely this "veneer of respectability" and evolution of a false consensus bias that characterizes the false memory scientific position. The essential false memory position, presented in chapter 2, includes a few essential themes such as: (1) memory in general, and recovered memory in psychotherapy in particular, are fallible; (2) memory in general is subject to suggestive influences, and memory in psychotherapy in particular is prone to suggestive distortion; and (3) therapists make suggestions or bias the inquiry toward uncovering the past in ways that lead to memory commission errors about past events, especially about falsely believed-in past traumatic events.

The arguments presented by Loftus, Ofshe, Lindsay and Read, Ceci, Kihlstrom, etc., show surprisingly little variation despite the fact that these scientists represent very diverse disciplines and areas of scientific competence. What is noticeably absent is written disagreement with any aspects of these essential positions or, more appropriately, attempts to design research to falsify the hypotheses within the false memory network itself, although they certainly have been challenged by researchers within the trauma network. False memory scientists have not designed a single experiment directly addressing suggestion effects in psychotherapy or in laboratory-simulated psychotherapy.

What has developed is mainly a body of consensually shared *beliefs* within the false memory network, which are then disseminated as examples of "proven" scientific knowledge. The trouble with beliefs is that they are relatively difficult to change and they are not necessarily corrected by disconfirming evidence. The history of science is replete with examples of how scientific reference groups tenaciously adhered to erroneous beliefs until a virtual scientific revolution occurred (Kuhn, 1962).

The fundamental contribution of Michael Mulkay's work is his notion of the *variable evidentiary standards* used by differing scientific social reference groups to evaluate the truth claims of science. The behavior of the false memory scientists with respect to the concepts of repression—or, better, traumatic amnesia—illustrate the point. No less than 30 studies currently exist regarding the question of whether childhood sexual abuse can be forgotten for a significant period of time and later remembered. Every one of these studies reports a subsample of individuals who could not remember the trauma for some time and later remembered it. While the rates for full amnesia vary from 4.5%–82% across the studies, the majority of the studies suggest that about one-third of adult survivors of childhood sexual abuse are fully amnestic for the abuse for some period of time. At least three of these surveys are rather well designed prospective studies (Burgess et al., 1995; Widom & Morris, 1997; Williams, 1994a). These data meet Dawes's (1994) standard for scientific evidence, in that multiple studies in different contexts using different sampling methods all show the same pattern of results:

> the generality of my conclusions is dependent on multiple studies conducted on multiple problems in multiple contexts. (p. 71)

In a rational scientific world, these data would meet an acceptable standard of science. Yet, in the face of the increasingly accumulating information in favor of the concept of traumatic amnesia for childhood sexual abuse, false memory scientists persist in their claim that "present evidence is insufficient" (Pope & Hudson, 1995a, p. 125) to support the concept of repression. False memory scientists have repeatedly held these amnesia studies up to a more rigorous standard of evidence than they have applied to the literature they cite in support of their own claims (Pope & Hudson, 1995a,b). Kihlstrom (1994b) and Loftus, Garry & Feldman, (1994) have both attacked the Williams study on the grounds that it does not prove that failure to report the abuse was actually a memory failure. Using a similar set of standards, the misinformation studies would not prove that misinformation suggestion is actually a memory failure and thereby negate the concept of implanting false memories.

As Pope (1996) has correctly pointed out, the primary strategies used by some scientists associated with the FMSF to handle disagreement has been intimidation and ridicule. Yet, Loftus repeatedly uses

terms like "false memory," and Lindsay and Read likewise use the term "illusory memory" in their writings, even in the face of an accumulating body of scientific evidence that demonstrates that the magnitude of the misinformation effect pertaining to a change in the original memory representation is indeed quite small (under 5%, as shown in chapter 11).

Here we see a rather blatant double standard. It is acceptable for false memory scientists to speak about suggesting false *memories instead of false reports*, but challenge trauma scientists who speak of recovered *memories* or amnesia.

Moreover, Loftus and others have assumed that any memory that is recovered must be the product of psychotherapy, even though the available surveys have demonstrated that a much larger subgroup of people who have never been in therapy report failure to remember and later recovery of the memory than those in therapy. In other words, the false memory scientists have used lax standards to evaluate their own truth claims and rigorous standards to evaluate the scientific evidence about traumatic memory.

The selective use of citations presents a distorted view of the science and fails to alert the reader that other viewpoints are available. Pope (1996) illustrates how Loftus and Ketcham (1994) selectively cite certain sources and label all other sources with which they disagree as the "True Believers." As a good example of selective citation, Loftus and Ketcham (1994) cite the Neisser and Harsch (1992) study on flashbulb memories to show that "not one of the memories was entirely accurate" (p. 91). Because this is the *only* flashbulb study they selected out of all the flashbulb studies reviewed in chapter 5, and, of course, because it is the study that most favors the memory inaccuracy position, Loftus and Ketcham have biased their selection in favor of the conclusions about memory inaccuracy they wish to draw.

Both Loftus and Ketcham (1994) and Ofshe and Watters (1994) cite the Pynoos and Nader (1989) study of children's memory for a traumatic sniper attack. They cite the same two examples of children who misremember the event. What they fail to tell the reader, however, is that the central theme of the Pynoos and Nader article was that memory for the event was directly related to proximity to the attack. Children on the playground and directly under fire minimized the threat, but otherwise accurately remembered the central actions taking place, like the shootings or the blood spewing from a dying child. Children who were in the school (outside the line of fire) or away on vacation were more likely to misremember the central events. The Loftus and Ketcham (p. 77) and Ofshe and Watters (pp. 41–42) discussions of this article fail to inform the reader that neither of their two selected examples of memory distortion was drawn from children in the line of fire. One child was on vacation at the time of the incident and the other was not on the playground where the direct threat occurred. Once again, the data taken out of context imply that children's memory for trauma is more distorted than the study actually demonstrated. Instead of the balanced view of accuracy and inaccuracy and a sophisticated discussion of factors which affect accuracy, as in the original article, we get simple, reductionistic conclusions that the evidence illustrates "incorrectly remembering" (Ofshe & Watters, 1994, p. 42).

Loftus and Ketcham's handling of body, imagistic, and acting-out memories is similar. They say:

> Furthermore, the massive body of scientific literature on the working of memory contains no evidence that different kinds of memories exist in the unconscious mind, Thus, "imagistic," "feeling," "acting-out," and "body" memories must be viewed as interesting but improvable theories. . . . (p. 162)

Loftus and Ketcham seem to ignore the "massive body of scientific literature" on observations of normal children reviewed by Pillemer and White (1989) in support of a behavioral memory system, as well as the numerous clinical studies reviewed by Share (1994) on posttraumatic reenactment and physiological memories (cf. also American Psychiatric Association, 1993; Terr, 1994).

Another blatant example of selective citation has to do with psychotherapy sources. Loftus (1993) and Lindsay and Read (1994) primarily address the self-help recovery literature. Ofshe and Watters (1993) and others speak of recovered memory therapists, a term that they essentially made up. What is noticeably absent in any of the papers representing the false memory position is a review of the growing body of literature on phase-oriented trauma treatment.

It is also notable that with the great proliferation of papers on misinformation suggestibility in the past two decades, we could find only four papers that made any reference to earlier decades of research on social persuasion and attitude change.

In addition to selective citation is the failure to report controversies within the research. The position papers on the false memory argument (Lindsay & Read, 1994; Loftus, 1993; Ofshe & Watters, 1993) make no mention of the extended controversy regarding memory interference and memory acceptance within memory science. Because both Loftus (Loftus & Hoffman, 1989) and Lindsay (1994b) have written seminal papers about this very controversy in memory journals, it is noteworthy that they fail to inform their professional readers and the general public of this controversy when they write about false memories in psychotherapy.

A related problem pertains to the dissemination of the technical language of science. We agree with Toulmin (1972) that the evolution of a scientific discipline is measured by the precision and consistency of its technical language. Physics, for example, utilizes a very precise formal mathematical language to convey many of its theories. Within the realm of clinical psychopathology, by contrast, there are no less than a dozen different definitions of the word "borderline." Toulmin's work on the refinement of a technical language within a circumscribed research area does not adequately address the irrational element of language use by scientific reference groups. Members of different scientific reference groups use, and sometimes misuse, scientific language to bolster their socially constructed beliefs. There is nothing more legitimate-sounding than a new scientific term or the misapplication of a traditionally accepted technical term. Terms like "implanting false memories" suggest something much more scientifically established than the actual data merit.

While we agree with Toulmin that the evolution of a scientific area is largely the evolution of its technical language, at least from a rational perspective, we also believe that *technical language can be used or misused* to promulgate the beliefs of a scientific reference group. In this sense language is more political than scientific. For example, researchers who have conducted laboratory simulation research in the area of emotional arousal and memory performance have repeatedly misused the language of trauma. Loftus and Burns (1982) continually refer to viewing their film about a boy who is shot in the face as though it produced "mental shock" (p. 318). Christianson and Loftus (1987) refer to viewing a video about a boy who is hit by a car in terms of "memory for traumatic events." Christianson (1987) and Christianson and Nilsson (1984) describe viewing autopsy slides as "traumatic stimuli."

In the clinical field, the word "trauma" is used in a very precise way. Trauma is defined by the presence of posttraumatic stress symptoms and a traumatic event in terms of "an event that is outside the range of usual human experience and that would be markedly distressing to almost anyone" (APA, 1987, p. 250). Laboratory subjects who have watched slides and films with violent consequences rarely develop posttraumatic stress symptoms. By misusing terms that imply traumatization when no traumatic symptoms exist, the laboratory scientists make it appear that their data are perhaps more readily generalizable to our understanding of clinical trauma than is indeed the case.

Memory scientists have also misused terms that imply more pervasive memory deficits than the data warrant. Strategic phrases like "impaired memory" (e.g., Loftus & Burns, 1982) imply a general failure of memory and fail to make a distinction between impairment for central and peripheral details. Terms like "memory fallibility" (Lindsay & Read, 1994; Loftus, 1993) confound the issues of memory completeness and memory accuracy and erroneously suggest that memory incompleteness implies memory inaccuracy. Loftus (1993) and Loftus and Ketcham (1994) have used the term "repression" when referring to reports of an initial failure to remember and then a later remembering of childhood sexual abuse. Ofshe and Watters (1993) go one step further and invent their own term, "robust repression." It is curious that these scientists use clinical terms like "repression" instead of traditional terms within the domain of memory science, like "incompleteness" or "amnesia," no doubt because it is considerably harder to dismiss the scientific evidence on amnesia for trauma in general and childhood sexual abuse in particular.

With respect to psychotherapy, false memory advocates have likewise used language in a distorted way. Loftus (1993) and Lindsay and Read (1994)

persist in their use of the word "hypnosis" as an example of a memory recovery technique that they say contributes to suggested false memories for childhood sexual abuse. They ignore an entire tradition of research over decades that has carefully delineated the relative contribution of hypnotizability, hypnotic procedures, and nonhypnotic contextual effects to the overall variance of hypnotic suggestion. As we have seen in chapter 10, the robust finding across these studies is that hypnotizability (a trait), not a specific hypnotic procedure, contributes modestly to hypnotic pseudomemory production, and suggestive interviewing significantly contributes to pseudomemory production. Using a general term like "hypnosis" only confounds these distinctions and leads the reader into the erroneous conclusion that the use of hypnotic procedures contributes significantly to pseudomemory production. The potential for misunderstanding gets worse when hypnosis is classified as a memory recovery technique—a category that emphasizes therapeutic procedures, not a personality trait that places some individuals at a disadvantage in distinguishing fantasy and memory.

It has been claimed that abuse memories are "created" (e.g., Loftus & Ketcham, 1994, pp. 69, 71) or "implanted" in psychotherapy. Roediger and McDermott (1995) recently claimed "dramatic evidence of false memories" (p. 812) based on a list learning experiment. They readily generalize findings from list learning to the very different situation of implanting false memories in psychotherapy. Freyd and Gleaves (1996) correctly criticize Roediger and McDermott for going "far beyond reporting laboratory science, however, when they set the context of this work in terms of the current controversy surrounding recovered memories of child abuse" (p. 811). They point out that laboratory experiments on memory for word lists are very different from studies on memory for stressful events and that such "bold speculations" about the applicability of word list experiments to the false memory controversy, while sounding scientific, fail to respect "the limits of appropriate generalization" (p. 813; cf. also Pope and Brown, 1996, p. 11, for a similar criticism). As we have seen, data documenting suggestion of complex scenarios that overwrite the original memory trace are extremely rare. This strategic misuse of language makes it appear as though the phenomenon of implanting memories in therapy is well established in science.

Perhaps the most blatant misuse of terms pertains to the enterprise of diagnosis. Advocates of the false memory position use the phrase "false memory syndrome" even though there is little scientific basis to the term (British Psychological Society, 1995; Hovdestad & Kristiansen, 1996). Yet they deny the biphasic model of posttraumatic stress response (Horowitz, 1976) and the generally accepted view of dissociated amnesia, which have become the backbone of the *DSM-IV* sections on PTSD and dissociation, respectively. These *DSM* chapters define the acceptable standard within the clinical field.

Another language game has to do with the misuse of terms related to the evidentiary evaluation of science. When false memory advocates say there is "insufficient evidence" for hypotheses they do not agree with, like repression of childhood sexual abuse, they must ignore the data of no less than 30 independent studies, including three prospective studies (see Table 7.7). This is no trivial matter when the phrase *"no scientific evidence"* is used as a strategy in the courts to force a pre-trial hearing in an attempt to block plaintiffs from claiming damages of childhood sexual abuse or as a strategy to lobby for Mental Health Consumer Protection legislation, the effect of which would be to abolish trauma treatment.

The opposite occurs, too, namely, using the *language of proof* when referring to their own untested hypotheses. We have already discussed, for example, the strategic use of the word "demonstrated" by Lindsay and Read (1994, p. 294) when drawing upon flawed studies like the original Loftus and Coan (in press) Shopping Mall study and upon the Ingram case (Ofshe, 1992) as evidence for suggestion of illusory memories for complex events. Loftus, in referring to her seriously flawed Shopping Mall study, says, "Through careful experimental design and controlled studies . . . it is possible to create an entire memory for a traumatic event that never happened" (p. 90).

Loftus and Ketcham (1994) say there is "no formal study to support" Terr's distinction between Type I and Type II trauma (p. 59). Yet, regarding Loftus's own version of the misinformation suggestion she says, "Hundreds of experiments involving tens of thousands of individuals have shown that post-event

information can become incorporated into memory . . ." (Loftus & Ketcham, 1994, p. 62).

In each of these examples, and there are many more, language is strategically used to create an impression—either to refute opposing views or to create the image of scientific respectability and validity for relatively untested false memory beliefs. Another type of language misuse pertains to the strategic use of "telling stories" as scientific evidence. Pope (1996) shows how Loftus and Ketcham (1994) illustrate the alleged suggestive nature of psychotherapy not by conducting research on psychotherapy but by telling a story of a therapist, Barbara. The problem is that Loftus's portrayal of Barbara, while having "the persuasive power of narrative," is significantly different from Barbara's own version of the same transaction as conveyed to us. Such misuse of language falls far short of Toulmin's description of the rational evolution of language in science, in which scientists as a group participate to obtain greater and greater refinement and precision of their technical terms.

Actually, the rise of the false memory controversy has less to do with the accumulation of scientific knowledge and more to do with scientific group behavior as represented in the evolving informal network of false memory scientists. It is necessary that the reader understand this perspective on the sociology of science so that advocated truth claims are not confused with scientific knowledge. This is certainly not to say that false memory scientists are unable to be good scientists, which on other occasions they clearly have been, but to do so in the context of the current debate they have to behave like scientists, in the sense of designing experiments to test and attempt to falsify their own claims instead of announcing beliefs in the guise of scientific knowledge.

Scientific Communication as Social Persuasion

Finally, when we consider the transmission of scientific knowledge beyond the more limited scope of scientific journals into the public domain through the media or the courts, the standard of evidence typically drops. Ideally, scientists are bound by codes of ethics to be conservative in making public statements, and they are not supposed to make statements that go beyond what is scientifically known. They are supposed to inform the public about controversies that exist within the scientific community. In the actual practice of science, this ideal is not always achieved. Public and forensic misstatements often serve more as vehicles of *social persuasion* than of established scientific fact.

It is well documented that a message communicated by a scientist who is perceived as highly credible and as an expert carries more *persuasive influence* than a less credible or expert source (Bostrom, 1983; Petty & Cacioppo, 1986; Stiff, 1994). The public, and sometimes the courts, may not realize that these statements may have less to do with the transmission of scientifically established facts than with the power of skillful social persuasion. We find it ironic that some false memory advocates, who have so vehemently accused therapists of implanting suggestions in their innocent patients, have been so sophisticated in their use of social persuasion and suggestion in the name of science, especially when communicating to the media and the courts.

Our concern here is that the evolution of scientific knowledge, especially in the forensic context when human lives are in the balance, not become superseded by *social influence or persuasion* (Bettinghaus & Cody, 1994; Cialdini, 1984; Perloff, 1993). Some false memory advocates have repeatedly made public and/or forensic statements that grossly oversimplify and overstate the evidence. Note, for example, that Loftus says "I've conducted more than twenty of these studies, most of which support the theory that stressful experiences eat away at memory" (Loftus & Ketcham, 1994, p. 57). Her appeal to the authority of her research experience represents a kind of source credibility manipulation to an unsuspecting reader. But is the statement accurate? Chapter 4 in this volume, and Christianson's (1992a,b) reviews of the emotion and memory literature, suggest a very different conclusion. What Loftus is demonstrating in her popular books, and also in the courts, has less to do with scientific method and more to do with scientific discourse as a form of social influence. We find it ironic that some memory scientists have been so vehement in their accusations about undue suggestion in psychotherapy, and yet are seemingly so oblivious to the blatant social suggestion effects inherent in the very way they communicate their false memory beliefs

to the courts and the public. It may be that some of the more prestigious outspoken scientists associated with the extreme false memory position are systematically suggesting or implanting false beliefs about false memories in the professional and lay community and in former psychotherapy patients? (See Pope, 1996, p. 961, for a discussion of how such suggestive influences have led to the widespread belief that false memory syndrome has been scientifically validated.) *Are we to remain blind to suggestive influences inherent in laboratory research or inherent in public or forensic communication about false memory beliefs, and only focus on suggestive influence in psychotherapy?*

Our main concern is about extremism in science. On the one extreme is scientific incompetence. On the other extreme is scientific fundamentalism in which the beliefs of a particular interest group are promulgated in the name of science and with the intention of obliterating opposing views. Studies like the Shopping Mall study have been cited in journals as "demonstrations" of false memory suggestion. When some false memory advocates sue, or threaten to sue, respected professional organizations or publishers, or encourage parents to sue therapists based on untested ideas about suggestibility in psychotherapy (Pope, 1996)—these are the seeds of scientific fundamentalism. Bekerian and Goodrich (1995) say that in offering expert opinion based on a set of what are largely unproven hypotheses about implanting false memories false memory "psychologists are attempting to address questions for which they simply may not have answers" (p. 120). This is not to say that all scientists within the false memory informal network are extreme; it is only to say that scientific group behavior always has its irrational elements, and the wider scientific community bears some responsibility to balance these elements with the rational evolution of technical knowledge within an area of scientific inquiry.

We strongly believe that the scientific study of suggestibility in therapy is an important area of inquiry. We also believe that a failure to understand the role of suggestion, coupled with a preexisting agenda of therapists working with highly suggestible patients, has produced some of the tragedies reported by the FMSF. But scientific knowledge will advance only when scientists return to the more rational position within the sociology of science, which includes greater neutrality, a more comprehensive view of the problem (universalism), a willingness to develop an informal network that includes opposing views (communalism), and, above all, a willingness to design experiments creatively to test hypotheses and to replicate these tests *prior to* the dissemination of public knowledge.

Short of such behavior, the false memory controversy needs to be seen for what it is—more political than scientific, more the dissemination of propaganda than the distribution of scientific knowledge, and more the strategic use of pseudoscientific arguments as social persuasion to influence public policy and sway juries than the articulation of lasting truths about the human condition. Pope (1996) warns us that we must "examine the process by which these claims are evaluated and institutionalized, including the tactics used to promote them" so that the scientific process not be "subverted" (p. 971). This kind of polarization of the debate and the extreme and overstated positions taken, in his view, does "the field an injustice." In our view, science advances slowly and conservatively. We have no disagreement with the claim that bad therapy is sometimes conducted. A central theme of our book, however, is that bad therapy does not justify equally bad science.

13

||||||||||||||||

Phase-Oriented Trauma Treatment

INTRODUCTION

Advocates of the false memory position have pitted their criticism against what they have called "memory recovery therapy" (Lindsay & Read, 1994; Loftus, 1993; Loftus & Ketcham, 1994; Ofshe & Watters, 1993, 1994). As we learned in chapters 1 and 12, the term "memory recovery therapy" was coined by individuals outside of the trauma field—in fact, outside of clinical practice whatsoever. The term cannot be found in any textbook on systems of therapy or in the curriculum of any graduate or postgraduate clinical training program. As we learned in chapter 12, this unfortunate stereotype of trauma treatment was invented by individuals who have little direct knowledge of the practice of psychotherapy and who are therefore describing a phenomenon largely outside of their area of competency.

The term memory recovery therapy grossly oversimplifies the complexity of contemporary trauma treatment and readily leads to the misunderstanding that *all* forms of abuse and trauma treatment are forms of memory recovery therapy. Outside of a few exceptions (e.g., Claridge, 1992; Frederickson, 1992) "ongoing memory reconstruction" (Claridge, 1992, p. 245) is rarely the primary focus of most trauma treatment. Moreover, some false memory advocates who use the term memory recovery therapy readily confound lay, self-help abuse treat-

ment with trauma treatment practiced by licensed, competent mental health professionals. With respect to the complexity of trauma treatment itself, terms like memory recovery therapy lead to the oversimplification that whenever memory becomes a focus of treatment the treatment is considered to be a type of memory recovery therapy, even when it is only one of a number of important treatment foci or even when memory recovery plays a minor role in the overall treatment. This type of erroneous thinking easily leads to confounding *memory integration*, an important goal of all trauma treatment, with *memory recovery*, which plays a more limited role in the overall trauma treatment (Waites, 1997). Courtois (1995b) has commented on the overgeneralizing tendency of some false memory advocates, who consider all treatment of patients who have alleged abuse backgrounds to be memory recovery therapy.

As we learned in chapter 12, the use of the term "memory recovery therapy" represents a straw man strategy, in which the term is invented for the purpose of refuting it. Outside of serving the arguments of the false memory position, the term does little to advance our understanding of trauma treatment. With the exception of Lindsay and Read (1994), few of the main position papers of the false memory advocates contain any review of the available professional literature on trauma treatment. Thus, promulgation of terms like memory recovery therapy only serves to maintain a distorted view of most trauma treatment.

A book on the trauma memory debate would be incomplete without a detailed review of the professional trauma treatment literature. This chapter will review the available expert literature of professional trauma treatment. We will show the reader that there is a remarkable consensus among the experts on the treatment of posttraumatic stress and dissociative identity disorders about the nature and scope of the treatment of the short- and long-term effects of all types of trauma. The type of treatment generally accepted by trauma experts is known as *phase-oriented treatment*. Phase-oriented treatment divides the overall trauma treatment into discrete phases or stages of treatment, each with its own treatment objectives or goals. As we will learn, while trauma experts have divided the overall treament into different stages and have used different names at times for each of these stages, there is reasonable agreement across the literature that there are three major stages to the overall treatment. We will refer to these stages as: (1) stabilization, (2) integration, and (3) post-integrative self and relational development.

Each phase is defined by a unique set of treatment problems and symptoms that become the focus of treatment at that stage only. Each phase of treatment is characterized by a specific set of treatment procedures. Each phase of treatment requires a certain type of treatment alliance. Transference manifestations also differ at each stage. Each stage is characterized by its own unique benchmarks of progress and also by certain treatment challenges and special problems typical to that stage. As we will see, while there has been a number of important technical refinements within phase-oriented treatment in the past few decades, as well as differences in perspective among trauma experts on what treatment objectives are to be emphasized at each phase in the overall treatment, most trauma experts clearly agree on the basic phase-oriented model, as well as on the main goals of each phase in the overall treatment.

Memory recovery per se is only one limited goal, which pertains only to certain patients, among a variety of treatment goals in only one phase of the three-phase treatment. Thus, to define professional trauma treatment narrowly as memory recovery only serves to maintain a distorted view of most therapy completely misses the point of what professional trauma treatment is all about.

THE NATURE OF TRAUMATIC MEMORY

As we learned in chapter 3, a fundamental assumption made by many trauma experts is that traumatic memory—encoding, storage, and/or retrieval—is somehow different from the usual types of ordinary memory, namely, verbal autobiographical memory, semantic memory, and procedural memory. We saw that numerous clinical and neurobiological studies support this perspective. Before addressing phase-oriented treatment, we will attempt to define the *clinical theory of traumatic memory* that has guided most professional trauma treatment. We will also outline the fundamental assumptions about traumatic memory made and generally accepted by most clinicians whose area of competence is trauma treatment. The first contemporary position paper on the clinical theory of traumatic memory was van der Kolk and van der Hart's (1991) article, "The Intrusive Past: The Flexibility of Memory and the Engraving of Trauma." Drawing on the seminal work of Pierre Janet (1928), they argue for the existence of multiple memory systems and for "the differences between narrative memory and traumatic memory" (p. 428). They argue that traumatic memory is dissociated from ordinary narrative memory:

> . . . familiar and expectable experiences are automatically assimilated without much conscious awareness of details of the particulars while frightening or novel experiences may not easily fit into existing cognitive schemas and be remembered with particular vividness, or totally resist integration. Under extreme conditions, existing meaning schemas may be entirely unable to accommodate frightening experiences, which causes the "memory" of these experiences to be stored differently. (p. 427)

Horowitz (1976), likewise, argued that information about a traumatic experience is processed differently from information about ordinary events. Van der Kolk and van der Hart (1991) state that what makes traumatic memory unique is that traumatic memories *resist integration* into or are *dissociated* from ordinary verbal autobiographical memory. They state:

> Lack of proper integration of intensely emotionally arousing experiences into the memory system results in dissociation and the formation of traumatic memories. (pp. 431–432)

We will refer to this theory as the *theory of dissociated traumatic memory.*

Traumatic experiences typically are outside of the range of ordinary daily experience (American Psychiatric Association, 1987). In ordinary memory preexisting cognitive schemas determine what information is and is not processed and integrated into the explicit verbal memory storage (Bartlett, 1932). Since traumatic experiences, by definition, do not fit these preexisting schemas, memory for traumatic experiences is generally not easily integrated into narrative autobiographical memory networks (van der Kolk & van der Hart, 1991, p. 439) and, at least for some traumatized individuals, the memory for the traumatic experience remains dissociated from ordinary memory.

One important implication of the *theory of dissociated traumatic memory* is that traumatic memory, being at least in part dissociated from ordinary memory, may not be subject to the same constructive operations characteristic of ordinary memory processing, i.e., the kind of transformations, deletions, and insertions that make ordinary memory malleable over time (Bartlett, 1932; Loftus, 1979b). Trauma experts have asserted that traumatic memory, unlike ordinary memory, may not be altered by the passage of time and therefore may not be so malleable as ordinary memory (van der Kolk & van der Hart, 1991). Grove and Panzer (1989) have argued that traumatic memory is frozen in time. The result is that traumatic memory is "inflexible" and "invariable" (van der Kolk & van der Hart, 1991, p. 431), "timeless" and "immutable" (van der Hart & Nijenhuis, in press a, p. 22).

Yet another consequence of the dissociation of traumatic memory, especially for patients with complex PTSD and DID, is that the various components of the memory are dissociated from one another. The verbal aspect of the memory for the traumatic experience is dissociated into a number of verbal memory fragments. These verbal memory fragments,

in turn, are dissociated from the affects, beliefs, somato-sensory dimensions, and behaviors associated with the traumatic experience, and each of these dimensions in turn is dissociated from each other (Braun, 1988). As we learned in chapters 3 and 7, it is parsimonious to refer to all of these nonverbal dimensions of the traumatic memory as the *behavioral memory for the trauma* (a generic term for the affective, somato-sensory, and behavioral aspects of the memory). Terr (1994) discusses a series of clinical vignettes to illustrate how this behavioral memory for trauma exerts a powerful but implicit influence on ordinary consciousness and behavior.

Still another consequence of the dissociation of traumatic memory is that the memory is not integrated into the conscious self representation. In a recent paper, van der Hart and Nijenhuis (in press, a) reconsider the *alternate consciousness paradigm* for traumatic memory, popular a century ago, first in the work of Janet (1889, 1928) and later in the work of McDougall (1926; cf. Crabtree, 1993; Price, 1995). These trauma theorists illustrated how each traumatic memory is associated with its own personality state, or what we might call in contemporary language its own unique self representation, associated beliefs, and unique state of consciousness. Overwhelming traumatic events can result in the creation of a separate state of consciousness or group of states of consciousness and associated self representations and beliefs (van der Hart & Nijenhuis, in press, a).

Trauma experts have asserted that traumatic memory storage is *state-dependent* (van der Kolk & van der Hart, 1991). Dissociated memory fragments of the experience are stored in the form of independent states of consciousness, each with its own self representation, trauma-specific beliefs, and associated affects (Steele & Colrain, 1990; van der Hart & Nijenhuis, in press, a). Each of these state-specific memory fragments is in part dissociated from the conscious self representation with its explicit narrative autobiographical memory system, and in part from other discrete states (cf. Tart, 1975, for a detailed discussion of state-specific consciousness).

Many trauma experts assume that *retrieval* of traumatic memory is state and/or context dependent. It is common to refer to the specific cues that retrieve traumatic recollections as *"triggers"* (Courtois, 1992; van der Hart & Friedman, 1992; Whitfield, 1995b).

Following the generally accepted view, *DSM-IV* states that direct or indirect exposure to situations reminiscent of the original traumatic event can trigger verbal and/or behavioral memories of the trauma. *DSM-IV* favors a context-dependent reinstatement view of trauma triggers, or what van der Hart and Nijenhuis (in press, a) have called "stimulus-driven reactivation" (p. 16). However, state changes can also trigger traumatic recollections (van der Kolk & van der Hart, 1991). These state changes can include: (1) nonspecific physiological arousal (Southwick et al., 1993); (2) emotional arousal unrelated to the original trauma; (3) emotional arousal associated with the original trauma; (4) exposure to subsequent traumatic events/arousal; and (5) normal, phase-specific developmental changes; (6) being in a safe relationship; (7) sensory information associated with the original traumatic event; and (8) stress in daily life and/or in therapy (cf. Courtois, 1992; van der Hart & Friedman, 1992; Whitfield, 1995b, for classification systems of trauma triggers). Because of the great variety of context- and state-specific cues that could potentially trigger a traumatic memory over time, identifying specific traumatic triggers is sometimes exceedingly difficult. Courtois says "virtually anything can be a trigger for anyone at any time" (1992, p. 21).

Moreover, the activation of aspects of traumatic memory is subject to complex learning processes. It is well understood that drinking behavior is subject to complex conditioning forces, the long-term result of which is the conditioning of alcohol dependence. At some point in the learning curve drinking behavior takes on a life of its own (Johnson, 1980). Janet (1889, 1907) and van der Hart and Nijenhuis (in press, a) have described a similar process of *"emancipation"* of dissociated traumatic memories. Through conditioning, traumatic memories can take on a life of their own in a manner comparable to the conditioning of drinking behavior and its transformation into alcoholism (Johnson, 1980). The overlearned use of dissociated states is central to the etiology of dissociative identity disorder. Dissociated states take on a life of their own in the form of alter personalities (Braun & Sachs, 1985; Kluft, 1985a). Once these complex learning processes have occurred, it becomes exceedingly difficult to identify specific triggers and switching states becomes relatively automatic. At that point the patient is

likely to say, "I used to know what stirred me up, but now the intrusive recollection or shift in state just seems to come on by itself."

Traumatic memories can *implicitly influence* consciousness and behavior even where little or no explicit narrative memory for the trauma exists (American Psychiatric Association, 1993). Janet's concept of "automatism" is an early example of attempts to convey the implicit influence of traumatic memory on ordinary everyday experience and behavior. According to Price (1995), use of dissociation results in the paradox of both "knowing and not knowing" about the abuse—knowing in the sense of an implicit memory and not knowing in the sense of "being disconnected from the actual concrete facts" (p. 297) or the coherent narrative memory for the trauma.

Trauma authorities have described several unique characteristics of retrieved traumatic memories as they come into consciousness. First, the retrieved traumatic memory, at least as it first makes its way into consciousness, is typically accompanied by intense physiological arousal (van der Hart & Nijenhuis, 1995; Wickramasekera, 1994). Second, reactivation of traumatic memories often has negative consequences, such as the intense affective distress accompanying the intrusive recollection or the tendency to reenact aspects of the trauma in current life when the traumatic memories implicitly "exert their harmful influences" (van der Hart & Nijenhuis, in press, a, p. 22). Third, the activation of one dimension of a traumatic memory generally activates all other dimensions, although not all other dimensions may come into explicit memory at the same time. This principle is known as *restituto ad integrum* (Janet, 1928). Van der Kolk and van der Hart (1991) define it as follows:

> When one element of a traumatic experience is evoked, all other elements follow automatically. Ordinary memory is not characterized by restitutio ad integrum. (p. 431)

Fourth, activation of one element of a traumatic memory and the concurrent activation of others does not mean that all elements come into consciousness at the same time. Integration of traumatic memory elements over time entails a transformation in the phenomenology of the memory over time.

The earliest aspects of the traumatic memory that come into consciousness are predominantly somatosensory in nature. Later, at the peak of intrusive distress, the affective component of the memory predominates in consciousness. Over time fragments of the narrative components of the traumatic memory come into consciousness, so that late in the integration process narrative, autobiographical components of the traumatic memory are predominant in consciousness (van der Kolk & Fisler, 1995).

Van der Kolk and van der Hart succinctly summarize their theory of dissociated traumatic memory:

> . . . psychiatry is beginning to rediscover the reality of trauma in people's lives, and the fact that actual experiences can be so overwhelming that they cannot be integrated into existing mental frameworks, and instead, are dissociated, later to return intrusively as fragmented sensory or motoric experiences. We are rediscovering that some experiences are encoded in memory but not in such a way that people can acknowledge and accept what happened to them. . . . Traumatic memories are the unassimilated scraps of overwhelming experiences, which need to be integrated with existing mental schemes, and be transformed into narrative language. It appears that, in order for this to occur successfully, the traumatized person has to return to the memory often in order to complete it. (1991, p. 447)

This concept of returning to a memory in order to complete it is, of course, part of what occurs when a therapist uses procedures for accessing and processing a traumatic memory experience. The fundamental concepts are: *dissociation* and *integration*. To the extent that traumatic memory remains dissociated, the basic assumption guiding treatment is the *integration* of the dissociated memory components.

Kafka (1995) reminds us that "Debate on whether early memories of survivors of incest be false or true . . . misses the point" (p. 136). She adds, "Repressed memories are but a symptom of pervasive memory dysfunction" (p. 136). Memory plays a critical "organizing function" in the normal development of the self. Trauma not only disrupts memory but guarantees a "discontinuous self" (p. 140). According to Kafka, a narrow focus on recovered memories may "skew" the treatment away from the

wider issues of "analysis of the damaged self" (p. 143) in the forms of, for example, dissociated self representations and the failure of self-soothing.

Pye (1995) further elaborates that what abuse survivors lack is a sense of self agency. In her view, the goal of treatment is less "the slippery slope of deciding the status of those images [as historic truth] (p. 164) of recovered memories, but more to restore the "capacity for reverie" (p. 156). She emphasizes:

> . . . the primary goal is not to ascertain the truth of memory as such, but rather to help the patient to move out of a rigidly persecutory, victimizing structure of mind into states that include the agentic and the imaginal. (p. 156)

Pye correctly points out that discerning the veracity of memory cannot take place unless the therapist has helped the patient restore a sense of agency:

> Before it is possible to decipher the psychological truth of images that have arisen in this assaultive way, it is necessary to find one's way to more agentic structure of mind. . . . (p. 178)

> The pressure may be for the therapist to make reconstructive interpretations. However, for the patient to use reconstructions he must be able to take them as hypotheses and as a possible framework to try on, modify, and/or reject. When an individual is caught in a persecutory paradigm such a metaphoric entertaining of possibilities and ambiguities is impossible. (p. 180)

Thus, distinguishing between true and false recollections takes as a prerequisite substantial repair of self and self agency structures. Assuming that the therapist should expect the abuse patient to possess a priori this capacity to distinguish between true and false recollections is clinically naive.

THE NATURE OF DISSOCIATION: PRIMARY AND SECONDARY DISSOCIATION

Asserting that professional trauma treatment centers around the integration of dissociated memory components makes sense only to the extent to which a clear, working definition of dissociation is available. Two papers have appeared in the trauma literature that accomplish this task. Spiegel and Cardena's (1991) seminal paper, "Disintegrated Experience: The Dissociative Disorders Revisited," summarizes thinking about dissociative disorders that was instrumental in formulating the revisions for the dissociative disorders section of *DSM-IV*. Spiegel and Cardena comment on the recent "rediscovery of dissociation" since the publication of *DSM-III-R* in 1987. In response to Frankel's (1990) criticism that the concept of dissociation lacks conceptual clarity, they offer a precise definition of dissociation:

> Dissociation can be thought of as a structured separation of mental processes (e.g., thoughts, emotions, conation, memory, and identity) that are ordinarily integrated. . . . At the center of the problem, then, is not merely the apparent automaticity of behavior but the intentionality of dissociative processes and the concurrent inability to integrate compartmentalized aspects of experience. (p. 367)

Spiegel and Cardena's definition contains three important elements: (1) separation or *compartmentalization* of mental processes; (2) *integration failure*; and (3) *intentionality*, which they define as how "material out of conscious awareness can nonetheless exert a tangible [yet implicit] effect [on consciousness]" (p. 367). The remainder of the paper goes on to describe each of the forms of "pathological dissociation" found in *DSM-IV* and presents evidence in favor of the association between traumatic experience and dissociative symptoms. In a subsequent paper, Spiegel and his associates (Butler et al., 1996) explain how normal hypnotizability in children or adults interacts with trauma. The development of pathological dissociation is seen as the outcome of autohypnotic attempts to cope with traumatic experiences.

In a very recent paper, van der Hart and Nijenhuis (in press, a) make an important conceptual distinction between primary and secondary dissociation. They define *primary dissociation* as follows:

> Relative to the evasiveness of the effect, traumatic experiences will remain separated from the habitual personality state. We tend to address this

basic dividedness into a normal state and a traumatic state with its (fixed) ideas and disturbances of functions as primary dissociation. (p. 6)

In an earlier paper they write:

> This traumatic disintegration is expressed in a dissociation of the personality: accompanied by their own sense of self, systems of ideas and functions such as traumatic memory states start to lead a kind of life of their own, outside the control and, in the more extreme cases, the consciousness of the habitual personality. (van der Hart & Nijenhuis, 1995, pp. 80–81)

Primary dissociation refers to the structured separation of the traumatic memories (and associated affects, sensations, cognitions, behaviors, and self representations) from ordinary consciousness, the ordinary sense of self, and normal narrative autobiographical memory. Primary dissociation is typically defined along two independent dimensions: (1) *lack of conscious awareness*, and/or (2) *involuntarism*. These dissociated aspects of the traumatic experience intrude into consciousness in the form of posttraumatic and/or dissociated symptoms, such as intrusive recollections, thoughts, images, flashbacks, and anxiety-related affects, or they implicitly influence unfolding conscious experience and behavior.

Secondary dissociation is defined in terms of further dissociation *within* the traumatic memory system itself. The term was developed by van der Hart & Nijenhuis (in press, a). Similarly, Marmar et al. (1994) observed that combat veterans frequently reported distancing themselves from a traumatic experience while it was happening by dissociating the observing and experiencing parts of the ego (Fromm, 1965), by "leaving their body" or "disappearing." Van der Hart and Nijenhuis (in press, a) identify several types of secondary dissociation:

> (1) dissociation of the observing and experiencing parts of the ego *during* a traumatic experience and thereafter during its reactivation. (Noyes & Kletti, 1977)
>
> (2) dissociation of the components of the traumatic memory itself, such as the narrative, affective, somato-sensory, and behavioral aspects of the trau-

matic memory (separation of the BASK components of the traumatic memory); or dissociation of the subcomponents within each of these components of traumatic memory, such as dissociation of the narrative component of the traumatic memory into numerous narrative fragments for the trauma, or compartmentalization of all of the affects associated with the traumatic experience into separate affect constellations, such as fear, rage, despair, etc.

Secondary dissociation is said to occur once the traumatized individual is already in a dissociated state, and van der Hart and Nijenhuis (in press, a) suggest that "the degree of dissociation at the moment of trauma is the greatest predictor of chronicity . . . and severity of PTSD" (p. 12). According to van der Hart and Nijenhuis, the main function of secondary dissociation is to separate the awareness of the traumatic event from the experienced emotions about that event (p. 6). The distress and other affects about the experience are, nevertheless, registered in memory and continue to exert an influence on conscious experience and behavior at least implicitly. Moreover, to the extent to which these dissociated states become conditioned, they may take on a life of their own and manifest in the form of intrusive reexperiencing of PTSD symptoms, dissociative switching of states of consciousness, or full-blown reenactments of the traumatic experience (sometimes referred to as spontaneous abreaction).

There is a growing body of empirical research to support the critical role of dissociation as a predictor of chronicity of PTSD. In a early report, Noyes and Kletti (1977) used structured interviews to assess "accounts of subjective experiences during moments of life threatening danger" (p. 375). While a great variety of dissociative experiences were reported in their subjects, Noyes and Kletti observed that "a dissociation between and observing and participating self" (p. 384) during the traumatic event was the underlying factor that explained the variety of subjective experiences. More recent empirical studies have consistently demonstrated that the degree of dissociation *during* traumatic experiences as diverse as war trauma (Bremner et al., 1992; Marmar et al., 1994; Tichenor et al., 1996) and natural disasters (Cardena & Spiegel, 1993; Holon, 1993) is a significant predictor of chronic PTSD

years later. This phenomenon is known as *peritraumatic dissociation* (Marmar et al., 1994).

Likewise, the degree of dissociation *immediately following* a trauma predicts long-term PTSD. Those individuals who are prone to dissociate *during* a trauma are significantly more likely than others who do not dissociate to become "high distress responders" (p. 81) shortly after the traumatic event and are also significantly more likely to develop chronic PTSD (Marmar et al., 1996). In a prospective study, Shalev et al. (1996) found that in civilian and military accident victims seen in an Israeli emergency room, the degree of peritraumatic dissociation one week after injury predicted 30% of the variance of PTSD symptoms six months later, when all other variables were controlled. Thus, dissociation appears to be both an asset and a liability. Individuals prone to dissociate have a coping strategy that they can readily draw upon to cope with potentially overwhelming traumatic experiences. While dissociation at the time of or immediately after a trauma may enable them to get through the experience, dissociation also disrupts information processing of the traumatic experience, thereby making it difficult to assimilate dissociated traumatic recollections and associated affects over time (van der Kolk, 1996). Moreover, some data suggest an interaction between severity of trauma and dissociative capacity. Subjects who experienced more severe child abuse measure higher in dissociation (e.g., Chu & Dill, 1990). Thus, individuals high on a continuum of dissociative capacity are likely to dissociate during traumatic experiences irrespective of the severity of the trauma and are therefore more prone to develop chronic PTSD. Individuals with more moderate dissociative capacity may also dissociate during a traumatic experience provided the traumatic experience is severe enough, and likewise become more prone to develop chronic PTSD.

Tertiary dissociation is defined as dissociation between the traumatic memory and the self representational system (van der Hart, cited in van der Kolk, van der Hart, & Marmar, 1996). Van der Hart defines the function of tertiary dissociation as follows:

> [Tertiary] dissociation allows people to maintain their existing schemata, while separate states of mind process the traumatic event. As a result, trau-

matic memory structures may contain trauma-related cognitions and self-schemata that differ from one another and from the habitual state, since they rely on divergent life experiences. (van der Hart, cited in van der Kolk et al., 1996, p. 317)

"Complex forms" such as the dissociation of internalized pathological self representations (the perpetrator and/or failed protector self representations) from the rest of the trauma-related self system, or the compartmentalization of the trauma-related self representation into a number of alter personalities, each with its associated memory content and affects, are commonly observed in patients with dissociated identity disorder.

Reenactments of traumatic experiences are often accompanied by a reinstatement of the state of consciousness that accompanied the traumatization. When conducting research on people who were merely writing about past traumas, Pennebaker (1987) noted that, "subjectively, most people who talk or write about traumas appear to enter a different level of consciousness during the study" (p. 220). As subjects talked into a tape recorder about their traumas, their voice qualities changed as a function of the topic. Pennebaker says:

> Often, as subjects began to disclose the most intimate aspects of their traumas, they began to whisper and to accelerate their speech dramatically. In many cases, their voice characteristics were so different (e.g., tone, volume, even accent) from their normal ways of speaking that they sounded as though they were different people. In our writing studies, we frequently find that people change their handwriting style when writing about different topics even within the same essay. It is not uncommon for subjects to switch from cursive writing to block lettering for a given topic and then return to the original writing style after completing a particularly significant topic. (p. 220)

THE SPECIAL CASE OF TRAUMATIC AMNESIA

As we learned in chapter 7, there is abundant clinical and research data supporting the concept of trau-

matic amnesia across all types of traumatization. These data suggested a bimodal distribution of long-term memory for trauma: a large sample of individuals who remain hypermnesic, and a smaller sample of individuals who remain amnestic for trauma over long retention intervals. Several important clinical papers have appeared that have attempted to lend greater conceptual clarity to the notion of traumatic amnesia (Courtois, 1992b; Harvey & Herman, 1994; van der Hart & Nijenhuis, 1995, a). The evolving consensus is that a clear distinction needs to be made between hypermnesia, partial amnesia, and full amnesia for trauma because each instance requires, at least in part, a different treatment strategy.

Courtois (1995a) and Harvey and Herman (1994) both state what most clinicians observe in their intake evaluations, namely, the majority of patients with alleged trauma/abuse backgrounds do not enter treatment to recover memories. Many of these patients have a *"relatively continuous memory"* (Courtois, 1995a, p. 8). They enter treatment with a wide range of problems, which may also include a wish to manage intrusive reexperiencing, generalized numbing, or physiological PTSD symptoms, dissociative shifts in state, and/or what they understand to be the impact of the alleged trauma on current functioning, including possible behavioral reenactments of the aspects of the trauma, often in significant relationships. Their "relatively continuous memory" does not imply a complete memory: further recollections and associated affects, etc., are likely to become clear within or outside of therapy, once the patient begins to focus attention on the traumatic experience.

A second group of patients who enter treatment, typically for reasons other than memory recovery per se, are those who have a partial memory for the alleged trauma/abuse. We believe that Courtois (1995a) and Harvey and Herman (1994) do not go far enough in their categorization of partial amnesia for trauma. This term needs to be subdivided into a number of specific manifestations of *partial amnesia for trauma* commonly observed by clinicians:

1. memory for the gist but not the details of the trauma, with or without intrusive/numbing PTSD symptoms;
2. memory for the peripheral details but not for

the gist of the central information about the trauma, with or without intrusive/numbing PTSD symptoms;

3. patchy memory for the trauma, i.e., some episodes/details are clear, but not others. The patient expresses a desire to know more about what happened;

4. memory for at least the gist of the trauma is somewhat clear (although not necessarily the details), but the patient evidences secondary dissociation, e.g., the patient is dissociated from the affects associated with the trauma;

5. memory for at least the gist of the trauma (although for neither the details nor affects) is clear and the patient has no clear understanding of its meaning, the impact of the trauma on current life, or any possible causal relationship to current symptoms;

6. very partial memory, i.e., simply a general sense of previous trauma background, without memory of specific incidents or memory for the gist or details of such incidents. The patient evidences a pattern of symptoms consistent with trauma, believes that trauma caused these symptoms, and expresses a desire to know the details about what happened.

A third group of patients who enter treatment have had a *relatively complete amnesia* for trauma. The great majority of these patients enter treatment because some situation has recently triggered a partial memory for the alleged trauma and the intrusion of that recollection into consciousness has been accompanied by serious emotional distress and/or intrusive reexperiencing and physiological PTSD symptoms. A smaller portion of these patients enter treatment for problems not consciously associated with previous trauma. Patients rarely enter treatment with amnesia as their chief complaint. They rarely ask to recover memories as the sole treatment focus, although in this climate some do. Those patients with full amnesia for previous alleged trauma are at the center of the recovered memory debate.

Courtois (1995a) describes a fourth group. In the current climate some patients specifically enter treatment to uncover "repressed memories." Courtois reports that such an illogical chief complaint is sometimes reported in intake evaluations,

although it is rare. How does the patient suspect abuse if the memories are genuinely repressed? Courtois believes that such complaints are "the least likely . . . to be a true case of sexual abuse" (p. 10) and that such complaints are transparently the result of external suggestive influences. Cases in this category that we have reviewed are often the result of experiences in self-help groups that mix abuse survivors who remember abuse with patients who may or may not be abuse survivors, who enter the group with no memory for any abuse and are influenced by the group.

While the distinctons between no amnesia, partial amnesia, and full amnesia refer specifically to the verbal, narrative memory for trauma, Laub and Auerhahn (1993) have developed a much more elaborate continuum that includes behavioral as well and verbal manifestations of knowledge about previous traumatic experiences:

1. The patient has no knowledge of the trauma. Memory for the trauma is defended against and coexists with normal autobiographical memory without integration.

2. The trauma is reeactivated in flashbacks, fugues, and other intrusive experiences.

3. Fragments of the verbal memory occur but are decontextualized and thereby remain devoid of meaning.

4. The trauma is reenacted in transference phenomena.

5. The patient has a narrative memory, but in telling the story loses perspective on current reality and spills forth an "overpowering narrative" of the trauma.

6. The patient has partially sublimated the trauma but reenacts it in life themes.

7. The patient has integrated the trauma and can describe it objectively as a "witnessed narrative."

8. The patient has moved beyond the trauma to complete developmental tasks and refers to the trauma primarily in metaphor.

According to their model, this "continuum" describes traumatic experiences from least to most integrated, and patients from least to most capacity to observe and "own" the traumatic experience.

MEMORY INTEGRATION VS. MEMORY RECOVERY AS TRAUMA TREATMENT GOALS

While the treatment objectives differ in some respects for each of groups described above, treatment of all three groups (not including those complaining of "repressed memory") shares one thing in common: *integration of dissociated aspects of memory is the primary treatment goal, but only after the patient demonstrates an ability to stabilize symptoms.* Patients with partial or full amnesia, and even those patients with a relatively continuous memory for the trauma, suffer from dissociated memory and a lack of integration. As Courtois says, the goal is "to reassociate whatever is dissociated" (1991, p. 56; cf. Phillips & Frederick, 1995). Similarly, van der Hart and Nijenhuis (in press, a) describe the goal in terms of gaining "relief from trauma-induced dissociation" so that the patient achieves "wholeness" (p. 34). The result of integration, according to van der Hart and Nijenhuis, is *"realization."* Realization occurs when the patient has grasped the full emotional impact of the trauma, has worked through the "existential crisis" induced by the traumatic event, and has given satisfactory meaning to the event in the context of his or her life course.

First, patients need to integrate the narrative memory for trauma, however complete or incomplete it may be, into existing cognitive schemas and the ordinary conscious self representation (Horowitz, 1976; Waites, 1997) and must also transform existing cognitive schemas and the self representation through this integration (van der Kolk & van der Hart, 1991, p. 447). Always having remembered the trauma does not necessarily mean that the available narrative memory for the trauma has been integrated with the conscious self representation and its associated belief system. In that sense, even continuous memory for trauma, and more so, partial or full amnesia for trauma, may necessitate a treatment focus on integration of the narrative trauma memory with the conscious self representation and its associated beliefs, through which the trauma narrative is given new meaning in the context of the patient's life. Thus, *reversal of primary dissociation is nearly always an important treatment goal*

of professional trauma treatment at the appropriate phase of treatment.

Second, patients need to integrate the dissociated affective, somato-sensory, behavioral, and self representational components of the trauma memory with the narrative trauma content, regardless of how complete or incomplete the narrative memory for the trauma has been. Van der Hart and Nijenhuis add:

> A traumatic memory cannot be adequately processed if the affective and sensory-motor states remain isolated from the rest of the traumatic memory.... For adequate processing to take place, *all* dissociated aspects must be integrated. (in press a, p. 30)

In other words, *reversing the lasting effects of secondary dissociation is always a main goal* of professional trauma treatment across all three groups.

What are the consequences if there has been no integration of primary or secondary dissociated memory aspects? Professional trauma clinicians have generally assumed since Janet (1889) that:

> Healthy psychological functioning depends on the proper operation of the memory system which consists of a unified memory of all psychological facets related to a particular experience: sensation, emotions, thoughts and actions. (van der Kolk & van der Hart, 1991, p. 426)

Horowitz (1976), likewise, proposed that the completion of the task of processing information about the traumatic event was necessary for the resolution of PTSD symptoms. Thus, most professional trauma clinicians have assumed that individuals who have so far failed to integrate the dissociated memory components of the trauma or complete its processing are likely to manifest any of a variety of trauma-related problems: (1) sustained chronic hyperarousal; (2) vulnerability to intrusive reexperiencing symptoms, e.g., intrusive imagery, nightmares, and flashbacks; (3) generalized numbing or responsiveness; (4) vulnerability to dissociative symptoms; (5) a sustained propensity to reenact elements of the traumatic experience in everyday relationships and/or in the transference in therapy; (6) an increased vulnerability to subsequent retraumatization; (7) an arrest in self and self-esteem development; and/or (8) a failure to transform everyday beliefs that have been shattered by the trauma and/or internalized trauma-related pathological beliefs. A number of ancillary symptoms like depression and anxiety-related symptoms or characterological problems may also persist over long periods in patients who have not integrated dissociated memory components of previous trauma, although false memory advocates are correct in asserting that the mere presence of such ancillary symptoms does not necessarily imply a history of trauma.

Our detailed discussion of *integration* as a necessary treatment goal at the appropriate stage of treatment is in part designed to emphasize to the reader, and especially to advocates of the false memory position, that *memory recovery per se is **not** the primary focus of professional trauma treatment*. This is not to say that memory recovery is *never* important as a treatment focus in professional trauma treatment. Certainly, helping the patient develop a more complete narrative memory for a traumatic experience is an appropriate *subsidiary goal* of professional trauma treatment, among a range of other treatment goals at the appropriate phase of treatment, to the extent to which partial or complete amnesia for trauma is a problem. Under such conditions we prefer to call this subsidiary treatment objective *memory enhancement* rather than memory recovery, since such a focus presumes the manifestation of either a partial narrative and/or behavioral memory for the trauma that has affected the patient's current functioning. In patients who are fully or partially amnestic for the trauma, memory enhancement may be necessary before integration of the trauma can occur, although memory enhancement is rarely an end in and of itself.

The trauma memory debate in the best sense is appropriately limited to those patients where memory recovery is a focus, although the debate has unfortunately been at times overly general. Some advocates of the false memory position, many of whom do not practice trauma treatment, have confused memory integration and memory recovery. Some advocates of the trauma accuracy position have used overly general terms like *memory processing*, which fail to distinguish between memory integration and memory recovery. We dis-

agree with the false memory claim that memory recovery should never be a focus of treatment. Yet, we believe that memory enhancement is always a subsidiary goal when compared to memory integration and that memory enhancement should always be limited to those patients for whom reasonable clinical evidence of full or partial amnesia (i.e., incomplete narrative memory for the trauma) exists and for whom such amnesia has been shown in the intake assessment to be associated with PTSD and dissociative symptoms. It is likely, however, that advocates of the false memory and trauma accuracy positions of the debate are not going to agree regarding the issue of memory enhancement, specifically for those patients wherein little or no narrative memory for the trauma exists and where the primary memory manifestation is a behavioral or implicit memory for the trauma.

Professional trauma clinicians find the concept of an *implicit or behavioral memory for trauma* generally acceptable (American Psychiatric Association, 1993; Davies & Frawley, 1994; Share, 1994; Spiegel & Cardena, 1991; Terr, 1994). Memory scientists who have researched memory development in children also find ample support for a behavioral memory system (Pillemer & White, 1989). To our knowledge, no advocates of the false memory position have acknowledged a behavioral memory system. As we saw in chapter 12, they try to reduce the behavioral memory system to a less credible concept—the concept of body memory. The heart of the debate centers on whether or not memory recovery is *ever* justifiable for those patients for whom there is reasonable clinical evidence of a behavioral memory for alleged or suspected trauma but who have little or no narrative memory for the trauma. Until memory scientists expand the scope of their research beyond nontraumatic narrative memory and accumulate data on the operation of the behavioral memory system in both normal and traumatized adults, and also on the interaction between the behavioral and narrative memory systems, the debate is likely to continue. Meanwhile, clinicians are likely to continue to focus on helping patients translate the behavioral memory into a narrative memory for the trauma (Terr, 1994; van der Kolk & van der Hart, 1991) and false memory advocates are likely to accuse them of malpractice.

ABREACTION VS. INTEGRATION

We have asserted that memory integration is an essential goal of professional trauma treatment at the appropriate phase of the overall treatment. When reversal of secondary dissociation is a treatment focus, the clinician helps the patient integrate the narrative memory for trauma with dissociated affects and other BASK components of the memory. Linking dissociated affect and memory content is inevitably a focus of all trauma treatment at the right stage of treatment. In the history of the trauma field, however, there has been a long-standing controversy about the best clinical procedure to facilitate the integration of the trauma memory and the affects associated with it. This controversy has centered around the often misunderstood concept of *abreaction*.

Breuer and Freud (1893–1895) saw abreaction as being essential to the treatment of hysteria to facilitate the discharge of excess emotional excitation, although van der Hart and Brown (1992) have correctly pointed out that Breuer and Freud also adhered to integration as the goal of treatment for hysterics. The classical abreactive model is based on the assumption that the *release or discharge of pent-up emotion* is essential to the resolution of trauma-related symptoms. This model has persisted throughout the history of twentieth-century psychiatry. Watkins (1949), for example, likened abreaction to lancing a boil through encouragement to give full and often dramatic expression to intense emotions. The American Psychiatric Association has essentially preserved the *emotional discharge* model in its definition of abreaction:

> An emotional release or discharge after recalling a painful experience that has been repressed because it was consciously intolerable. A therapeutic effect sometimes occurs through partial discharge or desensitization of the painful emotions and increased insight. (1980, p. 1)

While contemporary phase-oriented trauma treatment has shifted considerably from its historical emphasis on abreaction toward a *dissociation-integration model* of treatment (Phillips & Frederick, 1995; van der Hart & Brown, 1992), an important minority of experts in the field of dissociative disorders still define their treatment in terms of abreaction (Peterson, 1991; Sachs, Braun, & Shepp, 1988; Sachs, Frischholz, & Wood, 1988; Steele, 1989; Steele & Colrain, 1990), van der Hart and Brown (1992) have recommended that the experts representing this minority view drop the term abreaction, because their work resides more within the domain of the integration model than within the classical abreaction model of trauma treatment.

Clinical research has demonstrated the usefulness of emotional discharge for a wide variety of clinical problems other than trauma. A review of the large literature on emotional expression (Greenberg & Safran, 1987) has shown that by far the largest proportion of studies support the value of cathartic, emotionally expressive methods of intervention, while very few studies have not supported the effectiveness of such methods. For example, laboratory analogue studies (Bohart, 1977; Bohart & Haskell, 1978) have documented that emotionally expressive techniques, such as the gestalt therapy "two-chair technique," produce greater reduction in anger and hostile behavior than intellectual analysis or control conditions. Furthermore, Bohart documented that emotional expression combined with cognitive restructuring seems to produce the most effective outcomes—a finding also supported in group therapy research (e.g., Hammond, 1974; Lieberman, Yalom, & Miles, 1973). The experimental findings of other studies (e.g., Bohart, 1980) have also led to the conclusion that emotional expression of specific feelings such as anger is primarily effective when it includes perceptual change.

Frank (1961/1973) observed that the arousal of strong affect is an excellent precondition for facilitating attitude change, provided that the arousal is not too excessive, and Hoehn-Saric et al. (1968, 1972, 1974) experimentally documented that optimal affective arousal increases responsiveness to subsequent suggestions. One may profitably think of suggestibility as increasing in two situations: very low autonomic arousal (e.g., in a hypnotic state) or very high autonomic arousal (e.g., associated with an abreaction or with a traumatic situation, in which comments made by an abuser may function much like hypnotic suggestions). However, research also definitely suggests that when there is *only* cathartic release (e.g., verbally or by pounding a pillow), this will generally provide merely transitory relief, rather than a corrective emotional experience with long-lasting benefits (Bohart, 1977; Bohart & Haskell, 1978; Hammond, 1974; Lieberman, Yalom, & Miles, 1973; Pierce et al., 1983; Yalom, 1970).

It appears that what makes an emotionally charged experience integrative and most therapeutic is the accompanying cognitive-perceptual change that evolves after the catharsis. Many times this cognitive reorganization may occur spontaneously from recalling previously dissociated memories or from insightful patients reaching conclusions or changing perceptions to give meaning to abreacted experiences. However, this perceptual change may occur most reliably when the therapist obtains unconscious commitments (Hammond, 1990a) and provides suggestions during and after the abreaction. The process referred to as reframing or reinterpretation is one of the most central in bringing about therapeutic change. When we can help a patient with distorted perceptions that are causing symptomatic problems, or with negative memories from the past, to perceive some things differently, this may be healing and promote symptomatic relief.

Grinker and Spiegel (1943, 1945), working with cases of PTSD in World War II, hypothesized that, when strong emotions could not be consciously experienced and processed, they manifested themselves in physiological or perceptual motor symptoms, such as gastrointestinal, cardiac, dermatologic, joint, and muscle difficulties, urological problems, headaches, and vertigo. They believed that the most potent method of treatment consisted of abreaction followed by "working through" and conscious integration of the memories that were uncovered. The concept that internalized affect may play a significant role in psychosomatic disorders has been emphasized by many persons (Bastiaans, 1969; Brown, 1918a,b; Gerbert, 1980; Gitelson, 1959; Groen, 1957; Lipowsky, 1968; Sifneos, 1973; Sifneos, Apfel-Savitz, & Frankel, 1977).

Emotional discharge as an end in itself without accompanying cognitive and perceptual change has limited usefulness in most contemporary phase-oriented trauma treatment. In fact, with the majority victims of interpersonal violence and other relational-based abuse, classical abreactive treatment

holds some potential for harm to the patient (Jung, 1921/22; McDougall, 1920–21; Myers, 1920–21; van der Hart & Brown, 1992). First, a therapist who pressures the patient to give full expression to pent-up emotions may *destabilize* the patient. Signs of such destabilization may include an increase in intrusive posttraumatic symptoms, an increased use of dissociative and somatic symptoms, or pathological regression. Furthermore, release of painful emotional states might be perceived by the patient as a *form of reenactment of a traumatic, abusive relationship within the transference.* Clinicians who frequently rely upon cathartic release as an *end in itself* in treatment sessions run the *risk of maladaptively conditioning* violent and other forms of acting-out behaviors in their patients. Moreover, practitioners who have a very narrow focus on emotional discharge techniques are likely to *miss the broad range of treatment objectives* characteristic of contemporary phase-oriented treatment, such as symptom reduction, coping enhancement, correcting cognitive distortions, enhancing affect regulatory skills, and fostering self and relational development (cf. Davies & Frawley, 1994, p. 201). Because of these risks with patients with chronic relational-based traumatization, classic abreaction alone is contraindicated. Classic abreaction, nevertheless, retains some limited usefulness, namely for patients with a history of adult-onset single-incident traumatization characterized by extreme affective numbing, and also with a history of ego strength and good adjustment prior to the traumatic incident (Watkins, 1971). Yet, we believe that even if classical abreaction is still used, the main goal of treatment should be integration.

In an important paper, van der Hart and Brown (1992) describe the history and transformation of classical abreaction into the modern, generally accepted dissociation-integration model of trauma treatment (we will refer to it as the "integration model" for short, i.e., the middle of the three-phase, phase-oriented trauma treatment model). They point out how "technical advances in treatment" (p. 127) have made concepts such as "abreaction" and "repression" unnecessary in understanding how trauma treatment works. According to their review of the history of abreaction since Breuer and Freud (1893–1895), two competing models for understanding trauma treatment have existed—the classical abreaction model attributable to Breuer and

Freud, and the dissociation-integration model attributable to Charcot (1887) and Janet (1889), but also described by Breuer and Freud. Gradually, the trauma field has shifted away from an emphasis on emotional discharge as a focus of trauma treatment in favor of the integration model. Integration is defined in terms of: (1) "re-integration of previously dissociated aspects of the personality" (van der Hart & Brown, 1992, p. 137) or reversal of primary dissociation; and (2) "the gradual processing of all relevant aspects of the personality" (p. 137), or reversal of secondary dissociation.

Thus, the concept of integration includes within it, but is not limited to, the integration of the BASK components of dissociated traumatic memory (Braun, 1988), i.e., the behavioral, affective, somato-sensory, and narrative knowledge aspects of the memory. In other words, *emotional discharge alone has been replaced by the integration of affect and memory content as one of a number of dimensions of integration work.*

Thus, the majority of current experts on the treatment of posttraumatic stress and major dissociative disorders agree that the integration of affects and memories associated with trauma is an important goal in phase-oriented trauma treatment (Courtois, 1992; Sgroi, 1989). An important minority of trauma experts have continued to utilize the term abreaction in the literature (Peterson, 1991; Sachs, Braun, & Shepp, 1988; Sachs, Frischholz, & Wood, 1988; Steele, 1989; Steele & Colrain, 1990). However, some of these experts have subsequently dropped their use of the term abreaction because they agree that its use is misleading, since the primary goal of trauma treatment is integration (e.g., Peterson, 1993; cf. also Putnam's [1989] discussion of integration while discussing "abreactive episodes" in treatment, pp. 246–47). In fact, trauma treatment has undergone such a radical transformation in the direction of integration that it bears little resemblance to classic abreaction in a number of respects:

1. While some contemporary experts still retain the assumption that abreaction involves emotional release (Peterson, 1992) or the discharge of energy (Steele, 1989; Steele & Colrain, 1990), such emotional release has been transformed from an "irreversible" (Alpert, Carbone & Brooks, 1946) "pouring out" (Shorvon & Sargant, 1947) of emo-

tion into a "*controlled*" (Peterson, 1991, p. 2) or "*fractionated*" (Kluft, 1982) abreaction. The modern procedure of fractionated abreaction places the emphasis squarely on "mastery" (Peterson, 1991) of affect, instead of on its release. Hypnotic suggestions are used to highly structure the abreaction so that intensification of affect is presented to the patient in a titrated manner, in a way that is tolerable and leads to mastery.

2. Contemporary abreaction does *not* emphasize memory recovery. The minority of trauma experts who use the term abreaction usually refer to abreaction as "*planned abreaction.*" The patient may be *gradually exposed* to affect of greater and greater intensity. The planned abreaction procedure is based on the assumption that one is working with a patient who already has a continuous memory for at least the gist of the traumatic event, either because s/he always remembered the event, a dissociative alter has revealed content of the memory, or because s/he has previously retrieved the memory by some other means. Peterson makes it very clear that abreaction is not to be confused with memory recovery:

> Furthermore, hypnotic techniques should not be used for simply exploring or finding "proof" that a patient has been sexually abused. "Digging" causes symptom escalation. This work revolves around symptom alleviation. Patients need to be well grounded in hypnotic techniques and learn how to pace themselves as they explore their symptoms. (1991, p. 4)

The purpose of the planned abreaction, then, is to integrate the memory and its associated affect after the memory has already been recovered, not primarily to elaborate the memory content.

3. Most adherents to contemporary abreaction place a strong emphasis on cognitive therapy. Fine (1989a) and Ross (1988a, 1989) have strongly emphasized that one important goal of abreaction is to identify and correct significant cognitive distortions and pathological beliefs arising as part of the original traumatic experience. Steele (1989) says, ". . . in order for abreactive work to be effective, catharsis must be linked with cognitive restructur-

ing" (p. 154). Contemporary abreaction rarely emphasizes affect release per se apart from the equally important goal of cognitive restructuring.

4. The primary goal of contemporary abreaction is integration, not emotional release, i.e., integration of the BASK components of affect (reversal of secondary dissociation) and integration of memory content into the consciousness personality (reversal of primary dissociation). Sometimes this latter treatment objective also entails integration of heretofore fragmented recollections into a more comprehensive picture of the traumatic incident (Peterson, 1992).

Whatever aspect of integration is emphasized at a given point in the overall treatment, even the minority of contemporary trauma experts who still use the term abreaction are in agreement with the majority of trauma experts that integration per se is the main goal of trauma treatment following stabilization. We agree with van der Hart and Brown (1992) that use of the term abreaction confounds the issues and should be discontinued, since even those trauma experts who currently use the term provide a treatment that is very much within the domain of phase-oriented treatment with its emphasis on integration.

POSITIVE OUTCOMES ASSOCIATED WITH ACKNOWLEDGING TRAUMA AND EXPRESSION OF ASSOCIATED FEELINGS

Contemporary research on the disclosure of trauma to another person and the expression of the feelings associated with the traumatic events has confirmed positive outcomes emanating from such expressiveness and sharing. Not only have positive outcomes been seen in experiencing emotional relief and in improvements in psychiatric symptomatology (Foa, Rothbaum et al., 1995), but recent research confirms that very positive benefits also occur with regard to health and physiological functioning (Harber & Pennebaker, 1992).

Trauma has been found to be associated with negative physiological effects in animals and humans (Figley & McCubbin, 1984; Selye, 1976; Sowder, 1985; VandenBos & Bryant, 1987). However, expressing and talking through feelings about traumatic events assist in integrating such experiences, even when there is no amnesia associated with the negative memories. Thus, for instance, Pennebaker and O'Heeron (1984) discovered that the more individuals whose spouses had died unexpectedly by suicide or car accident talked with others about the death, the healthier they were and the less they engaged in rumination about the spouse one year later.

Researchers have discovered (Harber & Pennebaker, 1992; Pennebaker, Colder, & Sharp, 1990; Pennebaker & Hoover, 1985; Pennebaker & Susman, 1988) that when traumas experienced in childhood are not discussed with anyone, the individuals tend to have more currently diagnosed health problems (e.g., cancer, diarrhea, hypertension, influenza). Independent of social support, disclosing traumatic events is significantly associated with greater health.

Some contemporary therapists, particularly those associated with a false memory persuasion or managed care environment, suggest that it is unnecessary to deal with events of the past. They suggest that one need only focus on the present and future. While we see great value in spending substantive parts of therapy focused on the present and future (Hammond, 1990a), we also believe that, when someone has been traumatized in the past, it is vitally important to process and integrate such experiences. Research in the past decade now provides further support to bolster the experience of clinicians concerning the value of emotional expression *and* trauma integration.

It has been documented (Pennebaker & Beall, 1986), for instance, that when volunteers write about *both* their feelings and the facts about earlier traumas in their lives, they are found to visit physicians significantly less often during the next six months when compared with persons writing about either the facts alone or the feelings alone associated with traumatic events in their lives. It was also verified that those persons who simply expressed their feelings about trauma were healthier, reported fewer illnesses, and had less time restricted because of illness. Pennebaker and Bell found that expressing feelings, and not just the facts surrounding a traumatic experience, was associated with long-term health benefits.

Pennebaker, Kielcolt-Glaser, and Glaser (1988) studied the effects of disclosing facts and feelings about the most upsetting events in one's life versus writing about superficial topics. Persons who expressed feelings about traumas experienced enhanced functioning of their immune systems, with a significant drop in subsequent visits to physicians for illnesses—a finding since replicated (Murray, Lamnin, & Carver, 1988). *Furthermore, those persons who disclosed traumas that they had not previously told others demonstrated significantly greater immune enhancement.* In other studies these first-time disclosers were compared to persons expressing intellectual ideas about superficial topics and to persons disclosing feelings about traumas discussed previously with others; in both cases they experienced greater brainwave symmetry, lower skin conductance level (usually found to be associated with not being deceptive and letting go or integrating past experiences), and improved immune function (Pennebaker, 1987).

Such findings have caused Pennebaker (1987) to conclude that "failing to confront traumas can be physically harmful, whereas talking or writing about them can be helpful" (p. 229). Pennebaker believes that these benefits accrue from persons' becoming aware of and expressing *both* their deepest emotions and the facts or thoughts associated with them. According to Harber and Pennebaker (1992), "translating traumatic memories into language" (p. 360) is critical to the assimilation of traumatic memories. Whereas writing about unexpressed facts and feelings is found to produce such benefits, the process of disclosing and expressing feelings about traumas to a therapist is found to produce similar benefits, but without feelings of sadness or depression afterwards.

It is our belief that such findings will also eventually be replicated with patients working through amnestic or partially amnestic traumatic memories. We are encouraged in this belief because of recent findings like those of Putnam and Teicher (1994), who studied 402 children and adults, many of whom had been sexually or physically abused. This research revealed that abuse was associated with high levels of an antibody that weakens the human immune system. Interestingly, they also found that abuse

seemed to arrest the growth of the left hemisphere, which may hamper the development of language and logic, and was linked to an increase in the right hemisphere at an abnormally early age.

A HISTORY OF PHASE-ORIENTED TREATMENT

The Origins: Pierre Janet

Phase-oriented trauma treatment traces its origins back a century to the pioneering work of Pierre Janet (1889, 1925/1976). Janet described three phases in the overall treatment: (1) stabilization, containment, and symptom reduction; (2) modification of traumatic memories; and (3) personality reintegration and rehabilitation (van der Hart, Brown, & van der Kolk, 1989; van der Hart & Nijenhuis, in press, a; van der Hart et al., 1993).

The treatment objectives of the first phase, called *stabilization* for short, are: reducing the general level of stress, including the level of trauma-related hyperarousal and reactivity to intrusive reexperiencing of PTSD symptoms; helping the patient to feel safe within and outside of the treatment relationship; and aiding the patient in learning to contain spontaneous reenactments of the trauma and unwanted intrusion of traumatic memories into consciousness. The focus of the stabilization phase is not the recovery of memories but the opposite, namely, their containment. Janet used hypnotic procedures during the stabilization phase to enhance coping and mastery over trauma-related symptoms.

The treatment objectives of the second phase, the *modification of traumatic memories*, does include a focus on memory. However, Janet believed that memory recovery was rarely useful as an end in itself (van der Hart et al., 1989). He felt that traumatic memories needed to be modified and transformed. The primary treatment objective of this middle phase was to help the patient overcome dissociation both of the trauma memory from the conscious personality and within the components of the trauma memory itself. In order to accomplish this goal, hypnosis was used both to help reinstate the state of consciousness in which the original trauma was encoded and to modulate the degree to which and pace at which the patient faced the full realization of the trauma. The overall goal of this phase of treatment was to help the patient integrate the heretofore dissociated trauma memory into the conscious personality, so that the trauma narrative became a part of the patient's ongoing personal history (van der Hart & Nijenhuis, in press, a).

The treatment objectives of the third phase entailed helping the patient *develop a unified sense of self* as well as full participation in ongoing daily life. During this final phase of the overall treatment, Janet helped the patient to define and engage in meaningful daily activities.

Recently, Nijenhuis and van der Hart 1994 described Janet's phase-oriented treatment model in terms of helping the patient successively to overcome three phobias: (1) the phobia of PTSD symptoms and/or dissociated identities; (2) the phobia of traumatic memories; and (3) the phobia of participating in normal daily life (van der Hart et al., 1989). In this sense, exposure can be seen as an important mechanism of treatment success (Foa et al., 1989), i.e., exposure to the PTSD symptoms as well as to the situations that trigger them, exposure to aspects of the traumatic memory that have been avoided, and exposure to dimensions of everyday living that have been avoided, respectively, over the three phases of the overall treatment.

It is a tribute to Janet's genius that his three-phase model of treatment has survived for a century and has become the backbone of contemporary trauma treatment, with no major modifications being made in the overall view of each stage. Janet's extended three-phase model became somewhat obscured by the essentially short-term abreactive treatment of combat trauma during World Wars I and II, as well as by the short-term grief reduction and meaning-making approach to natural disasters starting with the famous Coconut Grove fire 50 years ago (Lindemann, 1944).

The Modern Rediscovery of Phase-Oriented Treatment: Mardi Horowitz's Information-Processing Model

Contemporary trauma treatment began in the 1970s with the appearance of Mardi Horowitz's now classic articles, "Phase-Oriented Treatment of Stress Response Syndromes" (1973) and "Stress Response Syndromes" (1974) and the elaboration of these

articles into an important book, *Stress Response Syndromes* (1976). Horowitz's work, more than any other, was responsible for shaping the modern definition of posttraumatic stress that now appears in *DSM-IV*. Horowitz (1973) lamented that the first two editions of the *DSM* did not contain any section on response to trauma. He presented data from a variety of field studies on trauma—as diverse as combat stress reactions, the experiences of concentration camp and nuclear holocaust survivors, rape reactions, and bereavement—to illustrate that there was a sufficiently definable group of signs and symptoms to merit the existence of a "general stress response syndrome" in response to traumatization. In contrast to earlier studies on war neurosis, which emphasized premorbid personality vulnerability to traumatic stress reactions, Horowitz said that certain types of stressful events—those that are sudden and unanticipated and those that threaten injury or death—are highly likely to cause predictable symptoms in almost anyone, "no matter what the pre-stress personality" (1973, p. 509). Such events leave the individual at a loss to process the emotional reactions to and ideas about the traumatic event.

According to Horowitz, there is a "natural course" (1974, p. 768) or "stress response curve" following exposure to a traumatic situation, much analogous to the stages of bereavement and recovery from loss. These stages are: (1) the initial emotional outcry or cognitive realization that a trauma has occurred; (2) subsequent emotional numbing and denial of the impact of the event; (3) oscillation between numbness/denial and intrusive repetition of the thoughts and affects activated by the traumatic experience; (4) a subsequent phase of working through; and (5) disappearance of the intrusive and denial symptoms.

One of the fundamental assumptions in Horowitz's model, like those of clinicians who preceded him (Janet, 1904; Kardiner, 1941; Myers, 1940) is the *phasic repetition* of posttraumatic response. Horowitz wrote, "After a traumatic event there is a compulsive tendency toward repetition of some aspect of the experience" (1976, p. 20). Another fundamental idea is that posttraumatic adjustment is contingent upon processing the information about the trauma. In Horowitz's *information-processing model*, the experience of a traumatic event must be processed on two levels—the emotional level and the cognitive level. However, other forces interfere with processing the trauma. Extreme stress causes an "information overload" (1974, p. 769) in most individuals, making traumatized individuals vulnerable to characteristic over- and under-controlled reactions to the traumatic event. Moreover, a particular traumatic event can activate dynamic conflicts specific to a given individual, so that idiosyncratic psychological defenses also function to thwart processing of the traumatic event.

Thus, posttraumatic adjustment typically is characterized by a *failure to process either the emotional or cognitive information of the traumatic event*, and thus interruption of the natural course of posttraumatic recovery. As a result, the individual remains fixated at some point along the recovery curve and will manifest one or the other of two types of posttraumatic symptoms: denial or intrusive symptoms. During the denial phase, the traumatized individual is numb to any feelings about the traumatic event, fails to understand its meaning, and may have an incomplete memory for the trauma. During the intrusive reexperiencing phase, the traumatized individual is flooded with intense affects associated with the original traumatic event and manifests intrusions into consciousness of thoughts, images, dreams, and flashbacks associated with the original traumatic experience. Posttraumatic stress syndromes can be denial-predominant or intrusion-predominant at any given point along the recovery curve over time. The basic idea is that dynamic tension exists between the individual's struggle to control and defend against the impact of the trauma and his or her fundamental need to complete the cognitive and emotional processing of the traumatic event.

Horowitz's treatment model is solidly built upon his information-processing model of posttraumatic adjustment. In his original 1973 article he argues that it is time to reconsider the classical abreaction model of trauma treatment and replace it with a *phase-oriented* treatment model. Since the natural course of trauma recovery occurs in stages, it stands to reason that any trauma treatment plan should attempt to match these stages. In the 1973 paper, Horowitz describes five phases of treatment: (1) help to release the patient from the continuing influence of the traumatic event; (2) reduce the amplitude or intensity of oscillations between denial and intrusive reexperiencing symptoms; (3) expose the patient to "doses" of trauma-related information so that he or she can continue processing of the event; (4) help the patient work through the impact of the traumatic event on emotions, cognitions, and self-image; (5) terminate treatment (1973, see Table III, p. 513).

In contrast to classic abreaction, which emphasizes emotional processing, Horowitz stresses the importance of "cognitive completion." He writes:

> . . . the task is to bring stress-related information to a point of completion. This "completion" can be defined, at a theoretical level, as a reduction of the discrepancy between current concepts and enduring schemata. The critical feature is not discharge of pent-up excitation, as suggested by the terms "abreaction" and "catharsis," but processing of ideas. To complete the response cycle, either new information must be reappraised or previous concepts must be modified to fit an altered life. (1974, pp. 771–772)

Having been influenced by the disaster literature, Horowitz sees *meaning-making* or making sense out of a trauma, not emotional discharge, as essential to recovery. Until processing is complete there will be a "strong impulsive tendency toward repetition" (1973, p. 512). Once information processing is complete, but not until, intrusion and denial symptoms are said to disappear.

Of particular relevance to the current trauma memory debate, Horowitz saw the tendency to repeat to trauma through intrusive reexperiencing symptoms as an example of *active memory*, which he defined as follows:

> . . . memory storage has an intrinsic tendency towards repetition of representation of contents until the contents held in active memory are actively terminated. A second key assumption is that this tendency towards repetition of representation is part of a general tendency toward completion of cognitive processing, and hence that completion of cognitive processing is what actively terminates a given content in active memory storage. (1976, p. 93)

Thus, the traumatized individual has a psychologically motivated need to keep the trauma memory active until processing is complete. This need is in dynamic tension with the need to control the intensity of the experience and to defend against conscious recognition of whatever dynamic conflicts may have been activated by the original trauma. Making an active trauma memory inactive occurs only when emotional and cognitive processing of that memory is complete.

In addition to proposing a stage-by-stage treatment plan, Horowitz stressed that clinicians must be sensitive to adapt the "nuances of technique" (1976, p. 354) to the personality and defensive style of the given traumatized patient. In each treatment-oriented paper, as well as in his book, he illustrates how treatment at each phase in the overall course of recovery differs for the patient with hysterical, obsessive, or narcissistic defenses, respectively. Moreover, the transference manifestations and specific dynamic themes activated differ for each of these patients. A sensitive clinician always strives to make the interventions "patient-specific," though the basic phase-oriented model is to be followed with all patients.

In subsequent works (e.g., 1979), Horowitz and Kaltreider tighten up their conception of treatment stages and package it into a brief dynamic psychotherapy approach to trauma treatment. Still, the fundamental assumptions remain:

> After a serious life event, persons usually consider the meanings and plans for response to that event in a manner that is systematic, step-by-step, and dosed. When emotional responses become excessive, or threaten flooding, the person initiates control operations. The recollection of the unfinished processing of sets of meanings will tend to counteract these controls. (p. 374)

In this article, however, a clearer definition of each stage appears: (1) establishing a good treatment alliance and a safe relationship; (2) modification of the patient's control processes; (3) helping the patient to reappraise the traumatic event. Horowitz describes a 12-session treatment plan but also states that it may take a "year or more" before completion is reached (p. 375).

An Integrated Foundation for Contemporary Treatment: Parson's Developmental Model

Horowitz's phase-oriented treatment model was limited, because it was derived largely from studies of acute trauma. The first comprehensive statement of contemporary trauma treatment derived from more complex traumatization appeared in 1984, a little over a decade after Horowitz's pioneering work.

Erwin Parson's (1984) seminal paper, "The Reparation of the Self: Clinical and Theoretical Dimensions in the Treatment of Vietnam Combat Veterans," while written specifically about treatment of Vietnam combat veterans, describes a general model of treatment that carried contemporary trauma treatment to a new level of sophistication. Parson describes the unusual nature of the Vietnam war relative to other wars. Such an unusual guerrilla war, in which the combat soldier faced an "environment of danger and uncertainty" (p. 7) in the battlefield and "massive denial" back home resulted in difficulty adapting both to the conditions in the battlefield and to those encountered upon return from the war. Parson characterizes the failures in adaptation characteristic of many Vietnam veterans in terms of "sustained hypervigilance" and a "psychic split" that interfered with the otherwise normal integrative processes for stressful life experiences. In a significant departure from Horowitz's thinking about posttraumatic adjustment primarily in terms of PTSD symptoms, Parson speaks of the "dual pathology" resulting from some forms of severe traumatization:

> My own observations led me to the following conclusions: Combat stress pathology forms an "autonomous" split-off mental organization of its own that, at primitive psychic levels participates in the general personality of the individual, but in a noninterated, non-ego coordinated fashion (hence, the split-off, dissociated phenomena of flashbacks and other incursive automatic ideas and feelings). (p. 15)

While Parson fails to cite Janet's work, his conception of traumatization as failure of adaptation and of its consequences as dissociation of an autonomous mental organization is quite similar to

Janet's concept of trauma as adaptive failure and its consequences in terms of dissociation and the development of automatisms. Parson's unique contribution is his idea that severe trauma can manifest in either Axis I (PTSD and/or dissociative symptoms) or Axis II personality disorder. Thus, severe traumatization was conceptualized as having a wide range of possible posttraumatic outcomes, of which PTSD symptoms were only one type. These Axis II manifestations, according to Parson, are often misdiagnosed as schizophrenia instead of personality disorder. They are more correctly seen as evidence of dissociative fragmentation and interference with normal lines of development. Parson coins the term *"fluid character pathology"* (p. 19) to illustrate that these seemingly characterological manifestations are the *consequence* of exposure to extreme crises, not the inevitable outcome of premorbid traits. Thus, extreme combat exposure could make otherwise normal individuals appear personality disordered after the war. Using psychoanalytic/developmental theory, Parson illustrates how much of the Axis II pathology seen after extreme combat exposure is the outcome of interference with the normal lines of self and object representational development. The result of this interference is severe self and attachment pathology.

Parson describes a very detailed, phase-oriented treatment model, which consists of four major phases and a variety of subphases within each phase. Again, the broad outlines of his phase-oriented model are quite similar to those Janet described a century earlier, but we see its return within the context of a sophisticated developmental theory of psychopathology. The four stages are: (1) stabilization-maintenance; (2) consolidation-stabilization; (3) in vivo affective revivification; and (4) reintegration-cohesion.

Parson sees the combat veteran's initial internal psychic state as highly chaotic and fragmented. Thus, the early focus of the stabilization phase is to reduce the "inner state of mental chaos" (p. 35). Treatment objectives include: restoration of inner calm, enhancing a sense of control over emotional life, reducing flooding of intrusive symptoms, enhancing self-esteem and social competency, dampening hypervigilance, and helping the patient adapt to the problems of daily life. The therapist flexibly draws upon a variety of methods, including cognitive restructuring, behavioral self-regulation, and relaxation training. The second part of stabilization begins when the patient demonstrates some control over intrusive reexperiencing and other trauma-related symptoms. Now the patient is gently introduced to his or her internal world and, along with the therapist's interested and empathic stance, learns to become a keen observer of his or her internal state.

In the third phase, called "in vivo affective revival," the patient begins the "process of reliving intense emotions" and to:

> re-experience and recollect previous traumatic "ego-disengaged," dissociated events in the present—alive—with much of the attendant immediacy of recapitulated emotions as is realistically and clinically permissible given the degree of the combatant's stability of ego functions. (p. 43)

Parson considers this phase of treatment to be a "controlled regression . . . to the original traumatic experience," through which fragmentation is overcome and through which the patient is able to "restructure the traumatic memory" (p. 43). He describes a process parallel to what therapists using hypnosis seek to accomplish through controlled age regression. Note that, while Parson uses the term abreaction, he qualifies its use, in that cognitive restructuring is seen as the main objective with respect to traumatic memories. In the fourth and final phase, called "reintegration-cohesion," the therapist helps the patient integrate dissociated self and object representations toward the goal of "cohesion of the self" (p. 46).

Parson's paper marks the beginning of contemporary phase-oriented treatment. It stands as a wonderful synthesis. While not citing Janet, Parson describes a similar phase-oriented sequence of stabilization, memory integration, and post-integrative consolidation. Moreover, he subsumes Horowitz's treatment of intrusion and numbing symptoms in his stabilization work (cf. Parson, 1984, p. 50), yet goes on to show that subsequent treatment must address developmental pathology, at least in those patients who suffer from more severe posttraumatic effects. Furthermore, Parson sets these earlier phase-oriented treatment models firmly within the context of contemporary psychoanalytic/developmental theory. He also raises the standard of care for trauma treatment to a new level: trauma therapists must be informed by a wide range of treatment orientations as diverse as cognitive/behavioral methods during stabilization, to classic psychodynamic theory during the affective revival phase, and then to self and object relations theory during the cohesion phase of the overall treatment. In this sense, his paper stands as the watershed of contemporary phase-oriented treatment. Subsequent works build upon and refine the basic treatment model.

CONTEMPORARY PHASE-ORIENTED TREATMENT

General Models of Phase-Oriented Treatment

Shortly after Parson's work a number of general models for phase-oriented treatment began to appear in the literature. Scurfield (1985) made a distinction between short-term crisis intervention treatment for acute PTSD (e.g., Burgess & Holstrom, 1974; Caplan, 1964) and longer-term phase-oriented treatment for chronic or delayed PTSD. These more complicated interventions are indicated when the PTSD symptoms persist, the patient has less control over symptoms, the patient is preoccupied with intrusive reexperiencing of symptoms, and/or the trauma has severely impacted upon a number of areas of daily functioning. Scurfield describes "five principles of PTSD intervention" for more complicated cases (p. 241). These are: (1) establishing a trusting therapeutic relationship; (2) psychoeducational interventions regarding traumatic stress; (3) stress management and stress reduction; (4) regression back to the experience of the trauma; and (5) integration of the traumatic experience. The first three treatment principles pertain to stabilization strategies. Emphasis is on helping the patient develop better coping strategies and self-control over symptoms. The fourth and fifth treatment principles pertain to trauma integration. Much like the work of therapists who utilize hypnosis in trauma treatment,

Scurfield (1985) sees reexperiencing the trauma as essential to effective trauma treatment:

> Perhaps the central purpose to be achieved in the treatment of stress disorder is to facilitate the (eventual) fullest possible reexperiencing and recollecting of the trauma in the here and now. . . . It is essential, however, that the survivor be guided through "tolerable doses of awareness," preventing the extremes of denial on the one hand and intrusive-repetitiousness on the other. (p. 245)

"Multimethod approaches to treatment," such as hypnosis and exposure-based interventions, are used to accomplish systematic reexperiencing of the trauma (p. 250). Once the trauma can be reexperienced, it must be integrated with the patient's conscious self representation:

> The "final step" in the stress recovery process is the integration of all aspects of the trauma experience, both positive and negative, with the survivor's notion of who he or she was before, during, and after the trauma experience. (p. 246)

Such integration also includes an understanding of the impact of the trauma on the patient's familial and peer social support system. Scurfield's model, while derived mainly from his experience with Vietnam veterans, is generalizable to most trauma populations. Scurfield has essentially taken Horowitz's treatment model and extended it for application to more severe forms of PTSD, and while it lacks the developmental sophistication of Parson's treatment approach, it nevertheless preserves the broad outlines of successive treatment stages wherein stabilization is a necessary prerequisite to trauma processing.

Brown and Fromm (1986) reported a similar phase-oriented treatment model specifically designed for hypnotherapeutic intervention applicable to a wide range of trauma populations. Like Parson (1984), Brown and Fromm see the necessity of assessing both PTSD symptoms and developmental pathology subsequent to traumatization. They make a distinction between "simple PTSD and complicated PTSD" (p. 269). Simple PTSD patients have failed to complete information processing about the traumatic experience. The underlying assumption in Horowitz's treatment model is that, if the patient is given the right kind of recovery environment, then he or she will be able to complete processing the trauma and his or her symptoms will disappear.

Brown and Fromm (1986) describe cases of "complicated PTSD," where enduring psychobiological disregulation and/or enduring developmental pathology persists even when information about the traumatic experience has been processed, at least in a relative sense. They argue that such cases of complicated PTSD, which include most kinds of cumulative relational-based trauma and abuse, require a more comprehensive phase-oriented treatment plan. Treatment is undertaken in five successive stages: (1) stabilization of symptoms; (2) systematic integration of (a) dissociated memories and affects, and then (b) self and object representations ("introjects"); (3) self development; (4) drive integration; and (5) reducing physiological reactivity. Different hypnotic procedures are recommended for each stage of the overall phase-oriented treatment. In the first phase, hypnotic methods are used to help the patient establish safety and self-soothing capacity, as well as to enhance the ability to cope with trauma-related symptoms. In the second stage, waking and hypnotically facilitated "indirect . . . guided imagery not directly associated with the traumatic event" (p. 280) is used to encourage "spontaneous return of memories and affects associated with the traumatic event" (p. 279). Following integration of affects and memories, treatment focuses on the active integration of split-off "introjects," such as the perpetrator self and failed protector introjects (p. 282). The subsequent post-integrative stages of treatment emphasize enhancement of self and self-esteem development, affect development, and reversal of the trauma-induced, enduring psychobiological sensitivity using a wide variety of hypnotic interventions.

The overall phase-oriented model requires that the clinician flexibly shift between different treatment orientations in each stage of the overall treatment. Cognitive-behavioral and ego-psychological methods are particularly relevant during the stabilization phase. Classical psychodynamically based interventions and hypnotic techniques serve as the basis of the early memory integrative work, while object relations theory may guide the methods fostering the integration of introjects. Self psychology and affect development theory may also profitably serve as theoretical foundations for the post-integrative self development and drive integration phases of treatment. Psychobiological self-regulation theory derived from behavioral medicine may guide the work addressing the enduring biological sensitivity.

McCann and Pearlman's *Psychological Trauma and the Adult Survivor: Theory, Therapy, and Transformation* (1990) was one of the first books to appear that was entirely devoted to describing a general model of phase-oriented treatment. Their work is an integration of developmental theory (e.g., Parson, 1984), especially self psychology, constructivist cognitive theory (e.g., Epstein, 1973, 1991), and ego psychologically based hypnotherapy (Brende & Benedict, 1980; Brende & McCann, 1984; Brown & Fromm, 1986). They refer to the theory guiding their work as "constructivist self development theory." They define constructivist theory in terms of how an individual defines his or her sense of self and reality. The construction of the self, in turn, is defined by four aspects: (1) self capacities, like affect regulatory skills or self-soothing ability; (2) ego resources, like intelligence, initiative, awareness of needs, or the capacity for attachment; (3) psychological needs, such as safety, trust, autonomy, and esteem; and (4) cognitive schemas, especially with reference to beliefs about self and world. Trauma is defined as an event that disrupts the aspects and functions of the self and also disrupts memory. McCann and Pearlman adhere to a "dual encoding" theory of traumatic memory, in that they see trauma as being encoded both in the form of imagery and affect and in the form of verbal narrative memory (pp. 28–29). Trauma memory is both fragmented and state-dependent.

McCann and Pearlman (1990) wish to present a "coherent theory-based treatment plan" (p. 89). For chronic PTSD the treatment occurs in two major stages: (1) self work, followed by (2) memory work. The initial goal of treatment is not to explore traumatic memories but to foster self development. A detailed assessment is recommended to identify the specific self capacities, psychological needs, and cognitive schemas about self and world that have been disrupted or damaged by traumatization. The initial stabilization phase of treatment utilizes primarily supportive psychotherapy procedures to develop affect regulatory skills and strengthen other self capacities, mobilize the patient's ego resources, help the patient find appropriate ways to satisfy critical psychological needs, and modify cognitive schemas through the correction of cognitive distortions and the restoration of positive beliefs about self and world. In other words, the proper foundation of trauma treatment is enhanced self development.

Memory work begins during the initial intake with a detailed inquiry about "to what extent the memories are repressed or accessible, whole memories or fragments, tolerable or distressing, and intrusive or avoided" (p. 204). Both the verbal and imagery (behavioral memory) systems of memory are evaluated. McCann and Pearlman assert that it is equally important to evaluate the patient's readiness to explore and capacity to tolerate memory integration. If intrusive reexperiencing symptoms predominate, coping enhancement is indicated over exploratory methods. Exploration and integration of trauma memories and affects are made easier when the treatment plan emphasizes enhancement of the patient's self capacities and is sensitive to the "dosing" and "pacing" of memory work:

> Memory work consists of gradually encouraging the client to talk about what happened, in detail, including what s/he felt or thought at the time and what s/he feels and thinks now about the images s/he recovers. (p. 97)

Such "gradual encouraging" of the recall of state-dependent trauma memories via the enhancement of self capacities is what in this book we have called a free recall retrieval strategy. Specific uncovering procedures like hypnotic methods and guided imagery are used when "the self capacities are strong enough to allow the person to approach traumatic memory fragments gradually in a way that allows the person to master them emotionally and cognitively" and only when the traumatic memories "are to some degree fragmented and/or out of conscious awareness" (p. 92).

While the approach clearly emphasizes self developmental themes over relational developmental themes, nevertheless, McCann and Pearlman believe that "resolving transference reactions" is a necessary focus at all stages of both the self work and the memory work (p. 235). The overall goals of treatment are to: (1) explore the meanings of the

traumatic event; (2) repair the damage to self development; (3) help to patient find balanced ways to gratify psychological needs and repair the damage to the schemas and beliefs about self and world (p. 99).

Meichenbaum's *A Clinical Handbook/Practical Therapist Manual for Assessing and Treating Adults with Post-traumatic Stress Disorder (PTSD)* (1994) is a massive synthesis of current works on the assessment and treatment of PTSD. Meichenbaum presents his own "integrative cognitive-behavioral treatment approach," which consists of five phases, each with its own treatment goals:

(1) The introductory phase of treatment includes a detailed assessment using state-of-the-art assessment inventories, establishing a therapeutic alliance and collaboratively establishing treatment goals, and psychoeducation about PTSD and the nature of memory.

(2) In the next phase, current symptoms and signs of comorbidity become the main focus of treatment. Stabilization addresses flashbacks, hyperarousal, avoidance behaviors, alter personalities, anger, and addictive behaviors. The wide variety of clinical techniques drawn upon to accomplish these goals includes behavioral contracting, education, reframing symptoms, enhancing self-efficacy, enhancing coping skills, direct-exposure-based methods, guided imagery, cognitive processing of beliefs, stress inoculation, skills development, cognitive restructuring, therapeutic metaphors, and relapse prevention training.

(3) In the third phase, the therapist helps the patient to restructure his/her story and transform traumatic memory, and shift from "victim" role to "survivor" role and "thriver" role (p. 332). Meichenbaum takes a "constructive narrative perspective" on traumatic memory (p. 330). While he believes that the available scientific evidence justifies taking traumatic amnesia seriously (p. 264), he is cognizant that it is very difficult for clinicians to make a determination of the historical accuracy of alleged trauma memories. Nevertheless, Meichenbaum argues that most patients will improve through constructing a coherent narrative memory for traumatic experiences, regardless of whether its historical accuracy can or cannot be known. He argues that clinicians should neither try to challenge the patient's belief in the authenticity of his/her account nor engage in sugges-

tive memory recovery procedures. Instead, clinicians should educate patients about the nature of autobiographical memory, especially about its reconstructive nature, the possibility that retrieval procedures can contaminate the memory, and that illusory memories are possible to create. Exposure-based methods are recommended when "a fear of the memory of the trauma" exists (p. 302). Once the patient can recollect the trauma, helping him/her construct a narrative account of the trauma "leads to 'integration' and a 'sense of mastery,' as well as provide[s] an opportunity to 'find' meaning" (p. 332). Emphasis is given to helping the patient develop a healthy belief system through review of the trauma that will guide the patient's current lifestyle.

(4) In the next phase the focus of treatment shifts from the past to the present and future. The clinician helps the patient establish better connections with others and ability to work.

(5) The final phase is devoted to relapse prevention skills training and termination.

Application of Phase-Oriented Treatment to Specific Clinical Populations

Adult Women Survivors of Childhood Sexual Abuse

Despite the tremendous proliferation of articles on the effects of childhood sexual abuse in the 1970s and 1980s, professional literature detailing phase-oriented treatment of sexual abuse in adult women survivors did not begin to appear until the late 1980s and early 1990s.

One of the first books to describe stages of treatment in adult women survivors of childhood sexual abuse was Christine Courtois's *Healing the Incest Wound: Adult Survivors in Therapy* (1988). While describing the characteristics and effects of incest in considerable detail, she also makes an initial attempt to present at least some of the techniques and goals of "incest therapy." The book, however, is largely dedicated to enumerating the various "multimodal techniques" used by therapists in working with incest survivors (p. 184). These include stress reduction and coping enhancement methods, experiential and expressive methods, exploratory techniques, and cognitive-behavioral strategies. Nevertheless, the book also contains the basic ele-

ments of a phase-oriented approach to incest treatment. Treatment needs to include: (1) building an adult treatment relationship; (2) acknowledgment of the incest; (3) recounting the incest; (4) overcoming social isolation and acknowledging feelings; (5) resolution of responsibility for the abuse, and grieving; and (6) breaking old patterns of behavior and reclaiming lost aspects of the self.

In a subsequent series of articles Courtois presents a more detailed and refined phase-oriented treatment model (1991, 1992a,b). In her more refined treatment model there are three main stages to incest treatment: (1) the preliminary phase; (2) the incest resolution phase; and (3) the post-resolution or reconnection phase (1991, 1992a,b). Treatment begins with a careful assessment of the long-term effects of incest. According to Courtois, these effects fall into three major categories: (1) PTSD symptoms; (2) dissociative symptoms; and/ or (3) Axis II or characterological problems. The goals of the preliminary phase are to establish a consistent and reliable working treatment alliance, address current life problems, reduce self-destructive behaviors, enhance the ability to cope with symptoms, and enhance the sense of self. Courtois(1991) agrees with McCann and Pearlman that self development precedes memory work and, like most trauma experts, believes that memory exploration too early in treatment is contraindicated. The cumulative effects of the preliminary stage of treatment reside in "creating a therapeutic environment conducive to remembering" (1992, p. 23).

Memory work begins in the "incest resolution phase" of treatment. Drawing upon Horowitz's notion of a biphasic response to trauma (cf. also earlier work on the biphasic response by Kardiner, 1941 and Myers, 1940), Courtois describes the alternation between intrusive reexperiencing and numbing symptoms in incest survivors. For those survivors in whom intrusive reexperiencing symptoms predominate "containment strategies" are indicated, and for those in whom numbing symptoms predominate "evocative strategies" are called for (1991, 1992a). Courtois makes it absolutely clear that the primary goal of the resolution stage is memory integration. Memory recovery per se is a prerequisite in those patients who are in the numbing phase of post-traumatic adjustment and have partial or full amnesia for the abuse:

As a general rule, uncovering of traumatic memories ought to proceed slowly and carefully with respect for the client's defenses. In this phase, the survivor strives to remember specifics about the trauma and to "reassociate" whatever has been dissociated or disconnected.... The goal is to help the client to recollect and recount specific abuse incidents and eventually to connect affect with the memory. (1991, p. 56)

Elsewhere she writes:

The resolution of sexual abuse trauma requires the retrieval of memory and the working through of associated affect.... Therapy is geared not only to the retrieval of autobiographical memory, but towards the integration of affect with recall to achieve resolution of the trauma. (1992a, pp. 15, 16)

Retrieval of memories is necessary only to the extent that it serves the wider purpose of memory integration:

While it is not necessary for survivors to recover every incident of abuse in absolute detail, representative abuse memories must be captured with enough associated affect to process the trauma in some detail and to work it through. (p. 16)

Integrating the fragments of memory with the affect associated with the abuse entails a "gradual reconstruction of the [abuse] story along with its associated affect" (1992b, p. 48). As a result the patient is able to "assimilate" the information about the abuse and find new meaning in it in the context of his or her current life. As the incest is recounted it becomes "normalized and legitimized" (1988, p. 206). Resolution also leads to "alleviation of the negative effects of incest" (1988, p. 176).

In the final "post-resolution phase" the incest survivor is able to resolve ongoing characterological problems, self-destructive and addictive behaviors, and sexual difficulties, and to restructure trauma-related pathological beliefs. The main treatment focus is on helping the patient reconnect in relationships and to develop fulfilling intimate relationships. Working with transference and countertransference issues as a consistent focus at each stage

of the treatment establishes the foundation for reconnection. Overall, Courtois's phase-oriented model for the treatment of sexual abuse is quite consistent with the available general models of phase-oriented trauma treatment.

Sgroi (1989) also presented one of the early models on the "stages of recovery" from childhood sexual abuse. She believes that it is "possible to identify predictable stages of recovery for adult survivors" (p. 111). Her five stages are: (1) acknowledging the reality of the abuse; (2) overcoming secondary responses to acknowledging the abuse; (3) ending self punishment; (4) adopting positive coping behaviors; and (5) relinquishing survivor identity. The treatment foci of the first stage are on addressing the "protective denial" and "dissociative coping mechanisms" characteristic of long-term post-abuse adjustment. Because "significant memory gaps" sometimes occur, memory retrieval is sometimes indicated. However, Sgroi strongly believes that, whereas free recall and context-reinstatement methods may be indicated for some abuse survivors, memory recovery techniques are contraindicated. Memory retrieval is "not to be viewed as an end in itself" (p. 115) but serves the larger purpose of moving beyond a victim-self identification and functioning better in one's current life. Sgroi believes "peer group therapy" to be the "most effective type of clinical intervention" (p. 111) to help survivors overcome the denial, shame, and guilt associated with sexual abuse. However, she warns that such groups should not be offered to patients who have "no memory" for abuse.

Another phase-oriented approach to the treatment of incest is Briere's "abuse-focused psychotherapy" (1992). Briere sees the treatment of abuse in two stages. The first phase addresses the "therapeutic structure" (p. 89). He warns against focusing prematurely on abuse memories prior to the firm establishment of a therapeutic relationship based on safety and enhancement of the the patient's self-control and self-determination. The initial phase of treatment is characterized by a wide range of treatment goals: alleviating PTSD symptoms (e.g., flashbacks) and other symptoms like anxiety and depression; establishing a sense of safety in the treatment relationship; correcting abuse-related cognitive distortions; building affect regulatory skills; and dealing with relational impairments, in particular boundary confusion and dependency conflicts.

The second phase of the treatment entails "trauma-based interventions" (p. 130). Briere believes that partial and sometimes full amnesia is indeed a legitimate treatment problem for incest survivors (cf. Briere and Conte's 1993 research documenting amnesia for childhood sexual abuse). The survivor's "incomplete" (p. 100) and "state-dependent" memory (p. 134) must sometimes be addressed using guided imagery techniques, the purpose of which is to reinstate the affective conditions of the original abuse situation:

> . . . techniques that allow the survivor to "return" to the original abuse event (e.g. through guided imagery) may replicate enough of the survivor's original affective experience to allow recovery of state-dependent material. (p. 134)

More generally, however, Briere asserts that the quality of the therapeutic relationship itself often "creates the requisite conditions for eventual memory recovery" (p. 151). While memory recovery is a circumscribed treatment focus in those patients who are amnestic for the abuse, the main treatment foci of the trauma-based phase for all patients are: (1) the exploration of available abuse recollections and (2) desensitization of painful affects. Briere recognizes that:

> Although trauma specialists often stress the importance of working with repressed or incomplete memories, abuse-focused psychotherapy even more commonly addresses memories that are already present at the time of treatment. . . . Even though conscious memories of childhood trauma are technically available to the abuse survivor, she or he may attempt to suppress or withhold them during treatment.

In other words, Briere's conception of trauma-based treatment resides very much within the domain of *memory integration*:

> The goal is the integration of split-off cognitions, affects, and memories into conscious awareness, so that there is less need for dissociation or tension-reducing behaviors to control abuse-related distress. (p. 131)

Through careful attention to the therapeutic relationship, the pacing of the treatment, and the affects that have been avoided, the abuse survivor "gradually" explores abuse recollections in greater detail (p. 134), is able to integrate appropriate affects with these recollections, normalizes his or her understanding of the abuse, and relinquishes avoidant and dissociative defenses, the outcome of which is that PTSD, dissociative, anxiety, and depressive symptoms subside.

The main textbook on phase-oriented treatment of childhood sexual abuse and other types of trauma to appear in the professional literature to date is Herman's *Trauma and Recovery* (1992). Her earlier book, *Father-Daughter Incest* (1981), outlined the sociocultural conditions, familial patterns, and after-effects of incest. The follow-up volume adds further clarity to the after-effects of incest but also is specifically about treatment. Herman describes two main categories of effects of traumatization: (1) simple posttraumatic symptoms (hyperarousal, intrusion, and numbing) and the sense of "terror" associated with these symptoms; and (2) complex posttraumatic symptoms and the sense of fragmentation and disconnection associated with these effects. Complex PTSD is the result of prolonged and repeated traumatization that typically involves enforced pathological dependency (p. 83) or "traumatic bonding" (p. 92) with perpetrators. While political captivity and torture is a classic example of the kind of traumatization that commonly results in complex PTSD, Herman argues that "domestic captivity," with or without battering, and child abuse situations often fulfill the conditions that cause complex PTSD. Complex PTSD is characterized by personality fragmentation in the form of chronic affect regulatory problems, self pathology, relational disturbance, and significant disturbances in meaning and belief systems, in addition to Axis I PTSD symptoms.

Herman believes that the recovery process for all types of traumatization "follows a common pathway" (p. 3). In her model recovery from the effects of sexual abuse occurs in three stages: (1) establishing safety; (2) reconstructing the trauma story; and (3) restoring the sense of connection with others. Since more severe and complex PTSD is typically the result of chronic and repeated violation in a relationship, Herman sees healing relationships as the key to recovery, namely, relationships "based upon empowerment of the survivor and the creation of new connections" (p. 133) both within therapy and within the wider community. The first objective of therapy is to provide a relationship firmly based on a sense of "safety" (p. 156) and "to restore power and control to the survivor" (p. 159) before any other therapy work can be accomplished (such as remembering the abuse). According to Herman, "Establishing safety begins by focusing on control of the body and gradually moves outward toward control of the environment" (p. 160). Establishing bodily control begins with attention to daily care like sleeping or eating but also includes addressing chronic hyperarousal and other PTSD symptoms through medication. Establishing a safe environment means addressing "destructive attachments" to abusers and social alienation through the use of shelters and other safe living quarters and through establishing a social support network, including supportive groups.

The second stage of recovery, "remembrance and mourning," begins only after internal and external safety has been firmly established. Herman warns against "premature or precipitate engagement in exploratory work, without sufficient attention to the tasks of establishing safety and securing a therapeutic alliance" (p. 172). The objective of this phase of treatment is:

> . . . the survivor tells the story of the trauma. She tells it completely, in depth and in detail. This work of reconstruction actually transforms the traumatic memory. (p. 175)

The problem with telling the story, according to Herman, is that traumatic memory is not encoded primarily in a verbal, narrative form but more often in the form of "imagery and bodily sensation" (p. 38) and in a fragmented narrative form. The therapist helps the patient to:

> reconstruct the traumatic event. . . . Out of the fragmented components of frozen imagery and sensation, patient and therapist slowly reassemble an organized, detailed, verbal account, oriented in time and historical context. (p. 177)

Herman believes that a "complete memory" for the abuse is one that has necessarily integrated the bodily sensations and images about the abuse into the narrative memory—what elsewhere we have referred to as BASK integration. In another work she writes, "the purpose of the work is not primarily catharsis but rather integration of the traumatic experiences" (Lebowitz, Harvey, & Herman, 1993, p. 381). In this, she describes the overall goal of treatment similarly to how we have described integration in this chapter.

While many abuse survivors always remember the abuse, at least in part, some survivors, especially those with "prolonged, repeated abuse" in primary relationships may be partially or fully amnestic for the abuse (p. 184). In these special cases Herman (1992) believes that the therapist should begin with "the careful exploration of memories the patient already has" (p. 184). Exploration of available memories often leads to becoming aware of the "full emotional impact" of the trauma, which in turn leads to the recovery of additional recollections about the trauma. In those cases where narrative recall of the abuse fails to reverse the amnesia Herman recommends "the judicious use of powerful techniques such as hypnotherapy" (p. 185). Whenever memory reconstruction is attempted, Herman cautions the therapist against "zealous conviction" and reminds us that the "an open, inquiring attitude" (p. 180) wherein the therapist "make[s] no assumptions about either the facts or the meaning of the trauma to the patient" (p. 179) is likely to lead to fewer memory reconstruction errors. As the trauma story becomes clear the patient and therapist conduct a "systematic review of the meaning of the event" (p. 178). Once a relatively complete recollection of the event is available in therapy, "telling the story to others" is seen as a necessary part of recovery. In chapter 5 we learned that narrative memory is always social memory, and in this same spirit Herman believes that giving testimony of the abuse transforms the memory. As a consequence, simple and complex PTSD symptoms disappear.

The third and final stage of treatment begins when the patient "reclaims her own history and feels renewed hope and energy for engagement with life" (p. 195). The treatment focus shifts from the past to current and future life. The objectives of this phase of treatment are (1) reconnecting with oneself and (2) reconnecting with others. The patient is encouraged to become "more adventurous in the world" (p. 203). Treatment in part addresses repairing the damaged self and establishing a coherent meaning system. With respect to reconnecting with others, the treatment addresses intimacy and sexual intimacy as well as peer involvements.

In more recent work Herman and her associates have attempted to identify "clear criteria for successful recovery" from sexual abuse (Lebowitz et al., 1993, p. 382). The seven criteria are:

1. *Memory.* The patient develops control over recall of his or her traumatic memory so that it can be recalled at will. The patient is not amnestic and has a coherent narrative memory for the abuse.
2. *Affect.* The patient experiences a range of affects free from the extremes of numbing and intrusive reexperiencing.
3. *Memory integration.* The patient has integrated memories and affects associated with traumatic experiences.
4. *Symptom mastery.* The patient has developed effective coping strategies for acute and chronic PTSD symptoms.
5. *Self-esteem.* The patient has worked through self-hatred and has developed a positive and realistic self-image.
6. *Attachment.* The patient has worked through his or her social isolation and has developed stable attachments.
7. *Meaning.* The patient develops a sense of meaning for the abuse in the context of his or her ongoing life and no longer evidences distorted beliefs about self and world.

According to Lebowitz et al.'s "stage-by-dimension" model of recovery, progress through each of the respective stages of the overall recovery is benchmarked by clear signs of change across each of the seven criteria. For example, memory changes at each stage. In the first stage memory is experienced as a symptom. The patient has no context for the memory. Through the first, stabilization stage the patient develops a context for the memory. In the second stage of remembrance the patient's progress is marked by the development of a relatively complete narrative memory for the abuse. In the third, reconnecting stage the patient applies his or her understanding of the meaning of the abuse

to "seeking meaningful reparative experiences" (p. 385). While Lebowitz et al. see the process of recovery as having "great variability" (p. 387), they make it clear that our understanding of treatment is reaching enough precision that clear benchmarks of progress within each stage are now identifiable.

Male Survivors of Childhood Sexual Abuse

In addition to the treatment of female survivors of childhood sexual abuse the phase-oriented treatment model has been applied to the treatment of a number of other special populations. Crowder (1995) described a "four-phase model" (p. 49) for the treatment of male survivors of sexual abuse, based on her review of the available professional and self-help published literature on treatment of male survivors. While many of the treatment issues parallel those with female abuse survivors, Crowder believes that "there are some significant differences between the sexual victimization of boys and girls" (p. 34) that justify writing specifically about male survivors. The preliminary stage of treatment begins with "breaking the silence," i.e., when the sexual abuse is both remembered and acknowledged. During the subsequent initial stage of treatment, the "victim" stage, the patient and therapist work to establish a sense of safety and containment in the therapy. After learning stress management and self-care skills, the survivor organizes his memory for the abuse into a "sexual abuse autobiography" (p. 52), which includes:

> Remembering how he was groomed for the abuse, who offended against him, how often the abuse occurred, what explicitly happened, what his reactions were at the time, whether or not he told anyone and what, if anything, he liked about the experience. . . . (p. 52)

This task of organizing the recollection is "cognitively focused" (p. 51) and the abuse is remembered without associated affect. During the middle phase of treatment, the "survivor" phase, the survivor "reclaims dissociated parts of the self (behavior, cognition, and/or affect)" (p. 81). Although Crowder recommends "abreactive and regressive work" (p. 81), and techniques that are more suggestive than they need be, her conception of the goals of this stage is consistent with most of the other works reviewed in this chapter, namely, memory integration, specifically BASK integration and also representational integration—what she refers to as working with "revenge fantasies, perpetration, and deviant sexual fantasies" (pp. 82–83). The final stage, the "thriver" phase, begins when "abuse-created patterns have been replaced by healthier ones" (p. 95). Focus turns to current everyday life concerns, such as relational difficulties, sexual behavior, and termination of therapy. The goal of the third stage is to "transcend survivorship" (p. 4).

Sex Offenders and Victims

Salter (1988, 1995) has developed a phase-oriented approach to the treatment of sexual offenders. Her first book (1988) integrates the trauma and addictions treatment literature into a comprehensive model of offender treatment. She argues that "a pedophile is addicted to his behavior, as surely and as entirely as an alcoholic" (p. 51). Like the requirement of abstinence for treating the alcoholic, Salter demands an "absolute ban on child molestation" (p. 88) and a waiver of therapeutic confidentiality so that preventive steps can be taken should the pedophile show signs during treatment of increased risk of committing a sexual offense. The primary goal of treatment is for the offender to "learn to control his deviant arousal patterns," as well as to help the offender develop effective ways to handle nonsexual problems. A related goal is for the offender to "take responsibility" for the abuse (pp. 66–67). Salter recommends group treatment. Between sessions offenders are required to complete a variety of behavioral assignments designed to change their deviant sexual arousal patterns, restructure the serious cognitive distortions accompanying deviant sexual addictions, and monitor relapse risk. She recommends a "sequence of treatment" (p. 128), in which the first step is to introduce methods that will effectively control the deviant sexual behavior, followed by techniques to correct cognitive distortions and prevent relapse. Detailed recommendations are given to measure treatment progress using a variety of assessment instruments.

In her more recent book, Salter (1995) applies her understanding of sexual perpetration to the treatment of victims. She correctly reminds us that treatment of victims per se will remain limited as long as trauma experts fail to master the treatment of offenders because victim specialists often do not recognize the "internalized offender" (p. 3) in most victims. As in her previous work she sees sexual perpetration as "a highly compulsive and repetitive behavior" (p. 13) centering around a "deviant arousal pattern" (p. 25). She presents convincing evidence to show that sexual perpetration is rarely impulsive but rather "is frequently carefully thought out and well-planned" (p. 39). The cycle begins with emotional arousal that leads to deviant sexual arousal. The sexual arousal is supported by frequent masturbatory behavior fueled by deviant sexual fantasies. Then the offender engages in a variety of "seemingly unimportant decisions," the underlying intent of which is to increase access to potential child victims. A high-risk situation is marked by the offender's clear access to a targeted child victim. Once a victim is identified the offender increases his masturbatory fantasizing and behavior and begins carefully planning strategies to get the victim, either by direct force or by "grooming." Following the offense the offender must manipulate the victim into maintaining secrecy. A variety of "thinking errors" are used to protect the offender from appreciating the full impact of harm to the victim. While the deviant cycle is typically repeated with a number of victims, it is also clear that sexual perpetration is a "progressive disorder" (p. 83), in that the frequency, type, and severity of sexual offense increase over time in at least a significant subgroup of sex offenders.

Salter believes that therapists working with victims need to understand this complex cycle of abuse in order to appreciate the degree to which victims internalize the pattern of abuse. In other words, offender psychology has very important implications for victim treatment. For example, Salter explains how nonsadistic and sadistic offenders differ:

> The nonsadistic offender who projects his sexual arousal onto the child wants to believe that the child desires him sexually. He reduces physical discomfort rather than increases it, and he pretends emotional suffering does not exist . . . he leaves behind victims who are more frightened of not being known emotionally than of being known, more fearful of emotional invisibility than visibil-

ity. . . . The sadistic offender, by contrast, listens very carefully. He attends to the child's pain and suffering because he finds it sexually arousing, and he uses the child's reactions as a guide for increasing the suffering and therefore his own pleasure. He leaves behind victims who do not want their thoughts and feelings known for fear that others will use those thoughts and feelings against them. (p. 251)

Victims of nonsadistic and sadistic offenders reenact these basic patterns in the transference. While the former victims need to be emotionally "seen" in treatment, the latter victims may misperceive the genuinely empathic therapist as knowing them emotionally in order to gain power over them. Treatment of both types of victims begins with a "here and now" emphasis on internal safety and self-soothing skills, positive affirmations, and the identification of traumatic overreactions to stimuli and trauma-related defenses. Then, the treatment proceeds to the "then and there," in which the patient attempts to "tell the tale" of the abuse. Telling the story is often accompanied by "affective flashbacks" (p. 262). The therapist's task is to listen for the "live affect" so as to grasp empathically the emotional impact of the abuse on the victim. The final task of this stage of treatment is "meaning-making" (p. 264). During this middle phase of treatment the therapist also helps the patient identify the "punitive, sadistic parent," the "sadistic attacker," the "perpetrator-based critic," the "guardian," and other "differentiated parts" of the self. The goal is to help the patient recognize the internal conflict between internalized abuser and protective parts of the self and then to foster an "internal confrontation," the outcome of which is to transform the fundamental cognitive distortions that perpetuate the self-abuse cycle in the victim and to facilitate integration of these parts of the self. In the last phase of treatment the focus returns to the here and now and to current life problems.

Traumatized Children

James (1989) and Rice-Smith (1993) have applied the phase-oriented trauma treatment model to the treatment of abused children. One unique feature of James's treatment program is the requirement that primary caregivers become involved with the child's treatment. Another interesting feature is that her work constitutes a "developmentally sequenced treatment" (pp. 5–6) with children. Because trauma and abuse often cause an arrest along one or more developmental lines, James asserts that treatment must include assessment of each step in the child's development. At each major stage of child development, it may be necessary for the child to return to treatment to readdress how the abuse specifically impacts on that stage of development. Sequenced treatment is rarely continuous. Typically, after a longer initial trauma-based treatment successive follow-up treatments tend to be brief. The initial phase of treatment is "multidimensional" and addresses a wide variety of treatment issues: identifying "hidden trauma-reactive behaviors" (p. 15) such as dissociative conditions and sexualized posttraumatic play; dealing with feelings of powerlessness, self-blame, loss, and betrayal; managing destructive or abusive behaviors; establishing bodily integrity; and repairing attachment disturbances. The second phase of the initial treatment addresses "integration of traumatizing events" (p. 157). This is said to occur through four steps: (1) "slowly and carefully examin[ing] what happened to them" (p. 157) through "non-directive techniques" (p. 11) such as free play and storytelling; (2) recreating the traumatic elements in fantasy where the child experiences mastery over the situation(s); (3) acknowledging and integrating ideas, feelings, and behaviors associated with the trauma; and (4) "accepting the realities of their experiences without minimizing or exaggerating the significance of what happened" (p. 157). The steps that James describes closely follow a process that leads to the goals of memory integration and realization that we previously described. Note that James emphasizes integration of and mastery over traumatic experiences, not memory recovery per se. These two main phases of the initial treatment are followed by an "open-door termination" (p. 177), in which reactivation of trauma-related themes at future points in development is addressed as indicated.

Rice-Smith (1993) describes a phase-oriented treatment model for use in group psychotherapy with sexually abused children. The main focus of the group is to "learn new coping approaches to difficult and overwhelming situations" (p. 531). Group treatment proceeds through six stages. (1) During the "acknowledgment phase" children are prepared for and begin group treatment. In initial group sessions children acknowledge that they have "had an experience of touch and sexualized interaction that was unfair and unsafe" (p. 543). (2) During the "stabilization phase" the children make the group a "safe and trusting environment" (p. 543) through learning relaxation, safety, self-soothing, and other coping skills. (3) In the "mastery phase" the children learn to identify in themselves and other group members self-affirmations, skills, and competencies, including mastery over individual problems and symptoms. (4) During the "uncovering phase" children speak of their experiences of disclosing the abuse, share their abuse recollections, and explore feelings and body sensations associated with the abuse. Such exploration also includes conflictual feelings about the perpetrator. (5) During the "integration phase" the various components of the recollection are "pieced together" and acknowledged as "part of oneself," the result of which is a new "sense of continuity of self" (p. 544). (6) During the final "transformation phase" the abuse is "reworked . . . from the points of view of the perpetrator, the victim, the investigator, the nonoffending parent and siblings, and imagined protectors and helpers with different resolutions from actual occurrences" (p. 544). In addition to such cognitive restructuring of the abuse, the children are encouraged to take on new challenges in their daily lives and to discover their strengths. The overall goal is to help the children overcome the interruption of development caused by traumatization and restore normal developmental progression.

Dissociative Identity Disorder

The rapidly evolving field of research on dissociative disorders firmly grounds treatment of dissociative identity disorder (DID) within a phase-oriented model. Ross (1989) considers the year 1980 to be "a major landmark in the history of multiple personality disorder" (p. 44) because of the resurgence of interest in the phenomenon of multiplicity. Around this time a number of important clinical papers appeared documenting the relationship between trauma and MPD (Coons, 1980; Coons & Milstein, 1986; Greaves, 1980; Spiegel,

1984) or hypnosis and MPD (Bliss, 1980) and beginning to outline treatment (Allison, 1974; Schreiber, 1973; Wilbur, 1984). None of this early modern work presented a detailed phase-oriented treatment model. However, the beginnings of conceptualizing treatment of MPD in terms of stages is implied in Wilbur's work (1984). Wilbur, made famous for her treatment of Sybil (Schreiber, 1973), over time began to think about the steps in her analytically based treatment. These include establishing trust in the therapy relationship, dealing with the repetition of abuse in the patient's current life, exploring the circumstances under which each alter became separate and abreacting trauma-related affects, facilitating fusion of alter personalities, and facilitating further integration of the self system after fusion has been achieved. Although Wilbur does not explicitly say that these observations about treatment imply stages in the unfolding treatment process, they do nevertheless imply a clear progression within the overall course of treatment.

Kluft's pioneering work contributed much to the repertoire of clinical techniques specifically designed for use with MPD patients. These include a variety of "carefully applied hypnotic procedures" to facilitate inner dialogues between alters and to achieve eventual fusion of alters (Kluft, 1982); manage crises created by alters, e.g., self-mutilation, suicidality, and alter-induced forced premature emergence of painful traumatic memories and/or affects into consciousness (Kluft, 1983); pharmacologically manage symptoms in MPD patients (Kluft, 1984a,b); monitor the alter system and treatment progress (Kluft, 1985b); foster tolerance and integration of trauma-related affects through hypnotic methods like the "slow-leak" and "fractionated-abreaction" methods (Kluft, 1988a); foster the integration of trauma-related memories and affects (Kluft, 1989b); facilitate integration and post-integration treatment goals (Kluft, 1988b, 1993b); and process traumatic memories (Kluft, 1996). While none of these papers explicitly addresses treatment stages in any detail, the progression of Kluft's treatment-oriented papers from 1982 through 1996 follows a successive focus on elaborating techniques for stabilization, trauma processing, and post-integrative treatment. In more recent works (1993a, 1996) Kluft has explicitly stated that his work on the treatment of DID, along with that of most other experts, follows a three-stage model: (1) stabilization; (2) working through trauma and the necessity to use dissociative defenses; and (3) facilitating post-integrative development (Horevitz & Loewenstein, 1994). The primary goal of treatment is integration of alters into a relatively stable unitary personality (Kluft, 1982, 1988b, 1993b; cf. also Greaves, 1989).

Braun, like Kluft, wrote some of the early treatment-oriented papers on MPD. "Issues in the Treatment of Multiple Personality Disorder" (1986) outlines 13 issues that need to be addressed in the overall treatment. While these 13 issues do not constitute a stage model, Ross (1989) has pointed out that Braun's description of them actually is sequential. The issues include: (1) developing trust; (2) making and sharing the diagnosis; (3) communicating with each personality state; (4) contracting with the alters around safety; (5) gathering a history from each alter; (6) working with the problems each alter presents, especially with reference to traumatic experiences; (7) utilizing special procedures for abreaction such as mapping, sand tray therapy, use of restraints, and hypnotic structuring of the abreaction; (8) fostering interpersonality communication, especially with respect to having alter personalities share the respective knowledge each has about traumatic events; (9) achieving resolution of conflicts between alters and integration of the personality system; (10) acquiring new behaviors and coping skills; (11) developing a social network; (12) solidifying the treatment gains; and (13) following up the treatment. The first four issues pertain to what elsewhere we have called the stabilization phase, issues five through nine pertain to what elsewhere is the trauma integration stage, and issues 11 through 13 pertain to the post-integration stage of treatment.

Ross's book, *Multiple Personality Disorder: Diagnosis, Clinical Features, and Treatment* (1989), was one of the first clinical manuals available to clinicians for understanding and treating MPD. Like Kluft, Ross saw the main goal of treatment in terms of integration (p. 42) and the achievement of "continuity of consciousness" (p. 43). Similarly, his earlier treatment-oriented papers (e.g., Ross, 1988b) describe a variety of techniques designed specifically for MPD patients, like system mapping, teaching alters negotiating skills, and reframing the activity of persecutory alters. In his book these techniques are integrated into a three-stage treatment model.

The initial stage of treatment includes assessment, sharing the diagnosis, educating the patient about abuse and dissociation, establishing the treatment frame and goals, establishing a treatment alliance based on trust, beginning to map the personality system, and establishing cross-communication among alters—what Ross calls "interpersonality communication" (p. 242). The middle stage pertains to "dismantling amnestic barriers" and "controlled recovery of abuse memories" (p. 250). Ross uses abreaction extensively during this stage of treatment, primarily to integrate painful affects with the patient's previous recollection of "memories at an informational level" (p. 247). Abreaction begins with helping the patient organize at least an intellectual understanding of the traumatic event, proceeds to a structured abreactive intensification of the affects associated with that event, and ends with a "debriefing," in which a variety of cognitive errors associated with the trauma are worked on (p. 251). During the "late preintegration stage" conflicts among alters that might prevent fusion and integration are resolved through facilitated negotiations, up to the point that fusion across alters and integration into a unitary personality are achieved. During the post-integrative work the patient learns to handle daily life problems as a unitary personality, i.e., without resorting to dissociation.

Putnam's book, *Diagnosis and Treatment of Multiple Personality Disorder* (1989), was one of the first clinical, research-based books to appear that outlined the stages of treatment and techniques recommended for each stage in the overall treatment of MPD. Putnam presents "a developmental model of multiple personality" (p. 50), in which he demonstrates that "consolidating self and identity across behavioral states" is a normal developmental achievement of childhood (p. 53), unless that process is disrupted by severe trauma or other developmental contingencies, the outcome of which is a chronic vulnerability to shifting states of consciousness and personality states, which under certain conditions become organized into multiple personality disorder. Putnam describes eight stages of treatment—five "early stages," two trauma integration stages, and a final, post-integration stage. The five early stages (what others have called stabilization) include (1) making the diagnosis; (2) initial interventions designed to gather a history, identify alters, and develop a working relationship with the personality system; (3) initial stabilizations, notably the use of behavioral contracting to reduce self-mutilation and suicidality; (4) helping the patient and personality system accept the MPD diagnosis; and (5) fostering cross-communication between and cooperation among the alters through methods like therapist-as-go-between and suggested internal dialogues. The two trauma integration stages include (6) metabolism of the trauma and (7) resolution and interaction. These stages are roughly equivalent to what elsewhere we have described as memory integration and representational integration, respectively. The former stage pertains to "hypnosis-facilitated abreactions" (p. 239), although Putnam's abreactive techniques do not show careful discrimination between BASK integration and memory recovery per se. Abreaction is seen as a method of memory recovery (p. 243) as much as it is a method of memory integration in which split-off affects and sensations associated with traumatic experiences are integrated (p. 248). Hypnotic abreactions, however, are highly structured and followed by waking processing of the experience to facilitate integration. In the latter stage the various alter personalities resolve their conflicts and fuse, the outcome of which is a unitary personality system. Focus then shifts to everyday concerns and helping the patient to achieve a variety of post-integrative skills.

Sachs and Peterson (Peterson, 1991; Sachs, Frischholz, & Wood, 1988; Sachs & Peterson, 1994) have described a phase-oriented approach that emphasizes hypnotic abreaction as a central method in the overall treatment. The earliest stage of the treatment draws upon multilevel positive hypnotic imagery to help the patient and the respective alter personalities develop safety, containment, and grounding skills to master intrusive reexperiencing symptoms and spontaneous abreactions and develop the capacity to modulate and regulate affective states. Alters are taught to use ideomotor signals to rapidly communicate their needs as preparation for trauma-related work. Careful attention is given to establishing a treatment alliance with all alter personalities, especially perpetrator and malevolent alters, prior to working with the trauma. The second stage of the treatment is called memory processing. The critical treatment strategy is planned abreaction. Planned

abreaction begins by having the patient write a detailed narrative of a traumatic experience. If the traumatic memory is dissociated across a number of alters, so that each alter holds a different part of the overall memory, ideomotor signaling is used so that respective alters will share with other alters only what they are ready to remember at any given time, so that over time the details of the entire traumatic memory are known at least to some subsystem of alters within the overall personality system. A detailed narrative account of at least the gist of any given traumatic event is necessary prior to a planned abreaction. The purpose of the planned abreaction is to facilitate an integration of dissociated affects and other BASK components of the trauma memory with the narrative memory for the traumatic event. A planned abreaction entails the "controlled release of affect" (Peterson, 1991, p. 2) in the context of a hypnotically structured "memory processing" session. For example, the alters participating in the processing session respond to the hypnotic suggestion that they will experience the fear associated with the traumatic event more and more intensely as the hypnotherapist counts from one to ten, until the counting is reversed and the alters return to their respective safe places. The process is repeated until the alters are able to fully experience whatever fear was associated with the original traumatic event. The procedure is repeated for each affect until the personality system is able to recover the full range and intensity of feelings associated with the traumatic event. Ideomotor signaling and cue-released containment imagery ensure that the respective alters can tolerate the process. While additional memory details are often recalled during abreactive sessions, the primary objective of the abreaction is integration of the BASK components of the memory, not memory recovery per se. Abreactive sessions end with attention to correcting cognitive distortions, notably the pathological trauma-related beliefs held by various alter personalities. Successful or complete memory processing is said to result in alleviation of PTSD and dissociative symptoms.

A much more elaborately detailed phase-oriented model drawing on these same planned abreactive techniques was developed by Steele (1989; Steele & Colrain, 1990). She writes:

Planned abreaction can provide a step-by-step framework in which memory work can be done safely, giving the client mastery over what he or she could not control as a child. (Steele & Colrain, 1990, p. 1)

Treatment is built upon a detailed assessment of which BASK components "are missing from the client's experience" (p. 5). Steele's underlying assumption is that dissociated memory processing protects the traumatized patient from experiencing the *existential crisis* (p. 11), i.e., the "worst subjective moment" (p. 11) or "critical period in which one confronts death, meaninglessness, isolation and/or issues of freedom and responsibility" (p. 12). As the patient learns to integrate the various components of the traumatic memory through planned abreaction sessions, he or she is able to come face to face with the existential crisis evoked by the trauma and resolve it. Steele and Colrain say:

> The therapeutic goal of abreaction is to unfreeze this moment of ontological insecurity and bring it into conscious awareness so that it can be reexperienced in a different way within the context of therapy. The existential crisis must be alleviated during abreaction by recreating the trauma as a contiguous experience on a continuum of space and time with the four dimensions of BASK reconnected in the client's experience. As the BASK components are linked, they will add clarity and new perspectives to the memories. The existential crisis will become manifest during this process. Cognitive frames that have been formed during preabreactive work can then be added to create new perspectives from which the client can discover the resolution of the crisis. (p. 13)

Steele and Colrain describe three major stages of treatment: initial containment, planned abreaction, and application. One of the first goals of treatment is to help the patient contain spontaneous abreactions, which typically retraumatize the patient and rarely lead to mastery.

Beyond the initial containment work Steele and Colrain describe five subphases to the planned abreactive work: preparation, eliciting dissociated aspects, alleviating the existential crisis, creating a new gestalt, and ending the abreaction (described

by the acronym, PEACE). (1) During the "preparation phase" every effort is made to establish the context of safety within the treatment relationship, and also within the patient, through teaching the patient to find "internal safe places" and to modulate the intensity of affects. (2) When "eliciting dissociated aspects," the therapist and patient "gather as much knowledge as possible about the particular memory" (p. 30). If the patient is largely amnestic for the trauma, Steele and Colrain recommend contextual reinstatement (exploration of "the general historical context of their childhood," p. 30) followed by state reinstatement ("explore more affectively loaded areas related to the abuse issues," p. 30). "Gradually, as more informaton is gained" (p. 30) the patient is able to reconstruct a "cognitive frame" for the trauma experience(s). In addition, the other BASK components must be identified. Steele and Colrain make it clear that the content of at least the gist of a particular traumatic experience, along with the affective, somato-sensory, and behavoral components of the memory, must be clear before a planned abreaction can be undertaken. The therapist and the personality system of the patient also agree to a clear written contract to conduct the planned abreaction on any particular traumatic experience. Moreover, planned abreaction takes place only once internal safeguards have been established and all the respective alters in the personality system consent to its occurrence. (3) The planned abreaction takes place in the next phase called "alleviating the existential crisis" (p. 35). The therapist helps the patient establish a "time line" for the traumatic experience. Hypnotic techniques are used to "titrate" the intensity of the affects during the abreaction (p. 35). The objective is to progressively expose the patient to the complete affective intensity of the experience in order to evoke the existential crisis inherent in the traumatic experience along with its associated cognitive distortions. Once the patient "has discharged the affect, the intensity of the experience will begin to decline naturally" (p. 36). (4) The past traumatic experience is assimilated into the patient's current life in the next phase called "creating a gestalt" (p. 36). The therapist helps the patient identify and modify the "dysfunctional beliefs" associated with the traumatic experience and thereby resolve the existential crisis. (5) "Ending the abreaction" entails reorienting the patient to the current context, helping the patient work through any residual effects, and continuing the cognitive restructuring of the experience (p. 40).

The goal of the final "application phase" is to help the client move from "the identity of victim to that of survivor" (p. 41). The patient is encouraged to experience both positive and negative feelings in his or her everyday life and to function relatively free from the previous cognitive distortions. Emphasis is on "empowering" the patient "to make healthy life choices" (p. 43).

In response to the appearance in the literature of increasingly detailed phase-oriented treatment models for DID based on planned abreaction, van der Hart, Steele, Boon, and Brown (1993) wrote an important paper entitled, "The Treatment of Traumatic Memories: Synthesis, Realization, and Integration." The paper was written to "clarify concepts" so that planned abreaction would not be confused with classical abreaction (p. 162). Van der Hart et al. recast Steele and Colrain's planned abreaction phase of treatment in terms of the Pierre Janet's concepts of dissociation. MPD is defined as a "disorder of non-realization," in that the trauma cannot be put into words or consciously accepted by the personality system (p. 162). A main objective of treatment is to help the patient move beyond avoidance of the traumatic memories, process them, and thereby reduce the need for dissociation.

The overall treatment is viewed in terms of Janet's three phases—stabilization, modification of traumatic memories, and personality integration. This paper is devoted to describing the middle phase, the modification of traumatic memories, in considerable detail. The purpose is to get the respective alter personalities to share with each other and the host personality the dissociated aspects of traumatic memories that each holds. This process is called *synthesis* of the traumatic memory, not *abreaction*:

> Synthesis of a traumatic memory involves its controlled reactivation in a collaborative effort by the therapist and the patient (p. 168). . . . The purpose of synthesis is to alleviate the dissociation, by helping alters to share their respective traumatic experiences of the trauma both with each other, and with the therapist. This orientation is, at the very least, semantically diffent from those ap-

proaches which encourage abreaction and catharsis of emotions (p. 165). . . . When synthesis of a trauma occurs, the memory ceases to be re-experienced in a traumatic way. The trauma becomes a "neutral" historical fact. (p. 166)

The subphases of memory processing include: (1) preparation, (2) synthesis, and (3) realization and integration. (1) The preparation phase includes helping respective alters and the host feel safe; establishing control over reactivated traumatic memories; constructing the narrative account of the trauma and identifying the role of each alter in this account; correcting cognitive distortions; and planning the synthesis sessions. (2) Hypnotic interventions are typically used to structure the synthesis sessions. Van der Hart et al. describe two strategies to achieve synthesis—serial and parallel synthesis. Serial synthesis occurs over a number of treatment sessions wherein respective alters bring forth the aspects of the traumatic experience each holds at whatever pace and in whatever order can be tolerated by the personality system. Parallel synthesis is a highly structured method in which synthesis occurs in a single session (p. 168). During the process each alter that holds some aspect of the memory for the trauma (both narrative content as well as other BASK components) comes forth and synthesizes its knowledge with the other alters in a highly structured session until memory integration has occurred. (3) During the "realization and integration" phase "the traumatic memory has now become transformed from an intrusive re-experiencing, to a trauma-related narrative within the overall stream of consciousness" (p. 171). Realization entails developing coherent undistorted beliefs about the traumatic event(s) and "owning" the trauma as "an experience of one's history as one's own" (p. 171). During this subphase the existential crisis is resolved and the use of dissociative defenses diminishes.

Another paper, "The Rational Treatment of Multiple Personality Disorder" (Horevitz & Loewenstein, 1994) represents a clear summary of much of the thinking on phase-oriented treatment of DID. A "rational model" is defined as one that "requires clear and specific treatment objectives . . . [and] chart[s] the course of treatment from beginning to end" (p. 290). The three overall stages follow the emerging consensus: (1) stabilization, (2) integration, and (3) post-integrative treatment. While it would be redundant to discuss the treatment methods and goals of each stage once again, the reader may review the Horevitz and Loewenstein paper as a good synthesis of current thinking about phase-oriented treatment of DID.

In *Healing the Divided Self* Phillips and Frederick (1995) present a detailed "step-by-step, practical guide" (p. xvii) to the treatment of posttraumatic and dissociative disorders. Their phase-oriented treatment model is known as the SARI model, which stands for "safety and stabilization; accessing the trauma and related resources; resolving traumatic experiences and restabilization; and personality integration and the creation of a new identity" (p. 36). As the book title implies, their work emphasizes the important role of dissociation in response to trauma. Dissociation plays a central role in traumatic memory processing and also in the development of a spectrum of clinical conditions following traumatization. Dissociation also makes an important contribution to treatment in the form of hypnotic ego state techniques (Watkins, 1992). Both "traditional and Ericksonian hypnotherapeutic approaches" are the foundation for "healing the divided self" (pp. 18–19). Hypnotherapy methods are set within the context of a trusting, well-bounded treatment relationship.

Different hypnotic techniques are recommended for each stage in the overall SARI treatment model. For example, hypnotic ego strengthening techniques are used for safety and stabilizaton, especially those that mobilize the patient's inner resources and strengths. During the stabilization phase of treatment a variety of hypnotic methods are used to help the patient learn "to initiate or stop internal experience at will" (p. 46), manage addictions and self-destructive tendencies, curtail spontaneous regressions and abreactions, master intrusive traumatic symptoms, and enhance positive experiences and strengths.

Hypnotic ego state therapy plays a major role in accessing dissociative states and in reconstructing dissociated traumatic experiences. The goal is to build a treatment alliance with each ego state or dissociated part of the self, and to foster internal cooperation and harmony among the dissociated parts. Great care is given to pacing. "Emerging memories should never be allowed to overwhelm the ego state" (p. 77). "[T]he most effective pacing of reconstructing or uncovering traumatic material occurs when initiated by the patient herself" (p. 42). Uncovering memories is useful only if it "is helpful in resolving his current symptoms and difficulties" (p. 121). The goal of reconstructing traumatic memories is not to ascertain historical truth regarding abuse but to help integrate the dissociate aspects of the traumatic memory and self. "The assignment of truth and meaning to this material belongs to the patient and not to the therapist" (p. 119). The therapist helps to patient organize the fragmented dissociated traumatic memories and to reassociate the various somato-sensory, affective, and behavioral components of the traumatic memory that have previously been dissociated. Hypnotic fractionation methods (but not abreaction) are used for resolving traumatic experiences. Titrating the work is important because of the great potential for the patient to become destabilized during memory processing (p. 42).

The overall goal is to "heal the divided self" (p. 18), i.e., to achieve a new identity. Personality integration takes place over a number of stages: recognizing dissociated ego states; developing communication with the ego states; fostering empathy for other ego states; encouraging cooperation, sharing interiority across ego states; developing co-consciousness and maintaining co-consciousness; and developing a new identity (pp. 167–169).

A COMPARISON OF PHASE-ORIENTED TREATMENT MODELS

The phase-oriented treatment models that we have just reviewed share a number of similarities. Despite differences in the terms used and the number of stages described across these models, there is overwhelming consensus that trauma treatment unfolds in three broad stages—an initial stabilization stage, a middle stage addressing the integration of traumatic memories, and a post-integrative stage addressing engagement with everyday life and facilitating ongoing development. Every phase-oriented model describes each of these three fundamental stages in some form or another.

Despite this basic similarity about the main stages of treatment, there is great diversity regarding what is emphasized at each stage. For example, the methods and goals of stablization are "multidimensional" (James, 1989). Some experts emphasize building the therapeutic relationship (Briere, 1992; Courtois, 1988; Davies & Frawley, 1994; Herman, 1992; Meichenbaum, 1994; Pearlman & Saakvitne, 1995; Ross, 1989; Scurfield, 1985). Others emphasize attenuation of hyperarousal (Parson, 1984), containment of intrusive reexperiencing symptoms (Horowitz, 1976; Horowitz & Kaltreider, 1979), establishing safety (Brown & Fromm, 1986; Herman, 1992), enhancing self development (McCann & Pearlman, 1990), or facilitating coping with current life problems (Meichenbaum, 1994). The underlying theme of stabilization across these models is *mastery* (Brown & Fromm, 1986; Rice-Smith, 1993).

Likewise, while experts clearly agree that the second phase of treatment addresses integration of traumatic memories, there are differences in emphasis regarding handling trauma and abuse reports that are always remembered or are forgotten for some period of time. Some experts emphasize the therapeutic importance of acknowledging and validating abuse that the patient continuously remembers at the onset of phase-oriented treatment (Courtois, 1988; Herman, 1992; Sgroi, 1989). They also emphasize the value of enhancing the memory where the patient is partially or fully amnestic for the trauma or abuse (Brown & Fromm, 1986; Courtois, 1991, 1992a,b; Herman, 1992; Parson, 1984; Phillips & Frederick, 1995; Sgroi, 1989). Others emphasize dissolving dissociative amnestic barriers in DID patients when different alters contain respective fragments of the memory for the trauma (Steele & Colrain, 1990; van der Hart et al., 1993).

Furthermore, while trauma experts overwhelmingly agree that post-integrative treatment is necessary, different treatment foci are emphasized across these models. Experts emphasize self development (Brown & Fromm, 1986; McCann & Pearlman, 1990), relational development (Courtois, 1991, 1992a; Davies & Frawley, 1994; Herman, 1992; Pearlman & Saakvitne, 1995), or adaptation to everyday life (Meichenbaum, 1994). All of these goals are important, yet self development may be the primary focus with one patient and relational development with another.

If we adopt a critical perspective regarding the existing phase-oriented treatment models, it becomes obvious that certain important treatment approches are significantly underrepresented across these models. (1) With the exception of Meichenbaum's integrative cognitive-behavioral model, most of the available cognitive-behavioral treatment studies describe short-term anxiety management and exposure-based procedures limited to PTSD symptoms but do not integrate these procedures into a comprehensive phase-oriented model. (2) Most of the models we have reviewed fail to give adequate emphasis to the intial treatment frame, especially with difficult-to-manage patients (for exceptions cf. Briere, 1992; Kluft, 1993a; Pearlman & Saakvitne, 1995; Ross, 1989). (3) The vicissitudes of transference and countertransference manifestations at each of the three main stages of treatment are described in detail in only a few works (Davies & Frawley, 1994; McCann & Pearlman, 1990; Salter, 1995), and only one major work is devoted to that topic (Pearlman & Saakvitne, 1995). (4) The importance of integrating internalized perpetrator representations is seriously underrepresented across the literature (for exceptions cf. Brown & Fromm, 1986; Crowder, 1995; Davies & Frawley, 1994; Parson, 1984; Salter, 1995). (5) Few of the models adequately present criteria marking recovery (for exceptions cf. Kluft, 1982, 1993b; Lebowitz et al., 1993). (6) Only a few of the treatment models address the value of helping the patient transform the chronic victim self representation into a self representation revolving around normalcy (cf. Crowder, 1995; Meichenbaum, 1994; Sgroi, 1989). (7) Only a few of the available phase-oriented treatment models make a clear distinction between differences in treatment for patients with simple, single-incident versus complicated, cumulative traumatization (Brown & Fromm, 1986; Courtois, 1991, 1992a; Herman, 1992; Parson, 1984).

A PROPOSAL FOR A COMPREHENSIVE PHASE-ORIENTED TREATMENT OF TRAUMA

In this section we will attempt our own synthesis of the literature on phase-oriented trauma treatment, which attempts to address the differences in emphasis and shortcomings of the currently available phase-oriented trauma treatment models. The phase-oriented model presented herein is a refinement of work reported a decade ago on phase-oriented hypnotherapy for trauma (Brown & Fromm, 1986) and its subsequent development into a general model for trauma treatment, specifically applicable to chronic, complicated PTSD. Our assumption is that chronic PTSD, with or without significant dissociation, is typically associated with cumulative relational-based traumatization. For single incident trauma, like accident victimization or rape, a shortened version of the same treatment model can be used, one that addresses primarily the stabilization and memory integration work, but less so the latter stages of treatment described below. We are presenting the extended model in detail simply because a great deal of the trauma memory debate has focused on childhood sexual abuse and DID, where the lengthier verson is most relevant. Our hope is that this section will summarize current thinking on trauma treatment into a cohesive and comprehensive model of treatment.

We recognize, however, that in the current context of a heated controversy surrounding memory and trauma treatment, no model for trauma treatment will satisfy all the critics on both sides of the debate. It is our hope that the reader will interpret this synthesis simply as *one* viewpoint on our current understanding of treatment, albeit a viewpoint clearly informed by a detailed review of *both* the memory research and the professional trauma treatment literature.

The Treatment Frame

In the past decade it has become increasingly clear that a significant portion of patients with chronic PTSD carry a comorbid borderline or other personality disorder diagnosis. It is well documented that these patients often engage in remarkable "self-defeating behaviors" in therapy, so that treatment outcomes are often negative (Beutler & Clarkin, 1990). In response to these failures, a great deal of attention has been focused on establishing effective interventions for the self-defeating patient. Most of the emerging work addresses managment of the treatment frame in borderline (Linehan, 1993) and DID patients (Kluft, 1993a) through the establish-

ment of clear treatment contracts. In the best sense, patients need to demonstrate their ability to tolerate outpatient psychotherapy by meeting a number of goals. The patient may be given a time-limited pre-treatment trial, the goal of which is to meet whatever criteria are deemed necessary to commence therapy. Linehan (1993) uses a written behavioral contract that specifies target problem behaviors. The patient is expected to consistently focus on addressing these problems within a reasonable time frame, say, six months to year. If the patient succeeds he or she may negotiate a therapy contract. If the patient fails, the treatment is terminated.

Linehan's prerequisite criteria are arranged along a hierarchy. (1) Pre-treatment must first focus on stopping suicidal and other self-destuctive behaviors, like self-mutilation. We would add to this list the cessation of other-destructive behaviors like the perpetration of abuse or episodic dyscontrol. (2) Next, the pre-treatment addresses a variety of "therapy-interfering behaviors," such as coming late or not showing for the treatment session, failing to pay the bill, excessive requests for extra-therapeutic time through "emergency" phone calls, or maintaining a continuous crisis-orientation that distracts from mutually established treatment foci. Each of the problem behaviors becomes a target of the pre-treatment. The patient must learn to reduce their occurrence and thereby demonstrate an ability to tolerate outpatient treatment. (3) Finally, the pre-treatment addresses lifestyle issues that impact on treatment, such as mismanagement of financial resources, significant addictive behaviors, lack of social supports or the presence of destabilizing social systems, etc.

Kluft (1993a), likewise, has emphasized the necessity of establishing a clear treatment frame with DID patients, the only difference being that the contract includes an agreement from the respective alters in the personality system. The main objective of these contractual interventions is to help the patient settle into treatment and to prevent the occurrence of significant acting out or treatment disruption midway into the work by establishing absolutely clear communications about what is expected of the patient and what will or will not be tolerated in treatment. While such interventions serve to settle down the majority of patients who might otherwise act out in treatment, a minority are incapable of meeting the contractual agreements and may not be ready for outpatient treatment.

The Stabilization Phase

There is a remarkable consensus within the professional trauma treatment literature that rapid exploration or uncovering of trauma in most circumstances is contraindicated. Such an approach may serve only to further destabilize a patient already suffering from intrusive PTSD, dissociative, and other symptoms. Instead, most experts agree that the initial phase of treatment should focus on stabilization. The overall stabilization phase of treatment can be viewed from two perspectives, one focusing on coping enhancement and symptom stabilization, the other on areas of relationship dysfunction.

A Relational-Based Approach to Stabilization

In this era of managed care, with its increasing emphasis on applying clearly delineated treatment procedures to the treatment of specific symptoms of diagnosable conditions, it is easy to lose sight of a very important statistic: nearly half of the people who seek outpatient treatment do not seek help for *DSM* diagnosable conditions, but rather for long-term relational dysfunction and self pathology, i.e., "V codes" in *DSM* (Beutler & Clarkin, 1990). A very considerable emphasis of psychotherapy in general, trauma treatment being no exception, is the chronic, repetitive dysfunctional patterns that occur in patients' relationships. Identifying "core conflict relational themes" (Luborsky, 1984; Strupp & Binder, 1984) and other areas of interpersonal dysfunction (e.g., Klerman et al., 1984) that can be addressed directly and worked through as they become manifest in the transference relationship to the therapist, and providing an "emotionally corrective relationship" (Alexander & French, 1946) to serve as the foundation for establishing healthier, less dysfunctional relational patterns are proven treatment approaches for addressing significant relational pathology.

Patients presenting with trauma histories are no exception. That a significant portion of trauma survivors typically present with significant relational disturbance both subsequent to and sometimes pre-

dating the trauma is well established. The etiology of this relational disturbance is more controversial. Some trauma therapists have assumed that this relational disturbance is a consequence of trauma (e.g., Herman, 1992; Parson, 1984). Some false memory proponents have argued that the causal relationship between trauma and adult life relational problems has not been scientifically established (Dawes, 1994). Our position is that relational disturbance is commonly present in trauma survivors; some may be related specifically to the trauma and some is not.

The attachment literature has made a major contribution to our understanding of disturbances in attachment behavior and adult relational dysfunction. This work began with Ainsworth et al.'s (1978) now classic developmental studies using the strange situation paradigm. In this experimental design the interaction between a mother and her three- to six-month-old child is observed and videotaped behind a one-way mirror in the laboratory playroom. A stranger then enters the room. The mother leaves, then returns. The stranger leaves, then the mother leaves. In the 30-minute sequence child experimentalists have the opportunity to observe the mother and child in interaction, the child interacting with a stranger, the child with both a stranger and the mother, and the child alone. From such observations, Ainsworth and colleagues discovered two main categories of attachment behavior—secure and insecure. Insecure attachment manifested itself in two forms—anxious attachment characterized by clinging behavior and impulsiveness, and avoidant attachment characterized by avoidance of attachment and failure to show preference for the caregiver over the stranger. Subsequent researchers demonstrated that these forms of attachment behavior are remarkably consistent across developmental periods from infancy (Ainsworth, 1989) through the toddler years (Sroufe, 1983) and on into adulthood (Crittenden & Ainsworth, 1989).

Subsequent researchers identified another important type of insecure attachment behavior, known as disorganized attachment (Main & Solomon, 1986). Disorganized attachment shows extreme shifts between elements of anxious attachment, e.g., clinging, and elements of avoidant attachment, e.g., distancing. This "cyclical" defensive style has been described as central to personality disorder like borderline relational dynamics (Beutler & Clarkin,

1990). Gartner and Gartner (1988) remind us that families at risk for incest manifest significant family pathology (boundary diffusion, parentification, pathological triangulation, etc.) that interferes with the normal resolution of the separation-individuation crisis *prior to* the acts of incest. Thus, it becomes difficult to determine which adult incest-related symptoms are attributable to the incestuous acts per se and which are attributable to the wider context of family pathology of which incest is just one specific manifestation.

In their now classic volume, *Child Maltreatment*, Cicchetti and Carlson (1989) demonstrated that nearly 80% of children who grow up in families where some form of child maltreatment occurs—neglect, physical abuse, and/or sexual abuse—show *insecure attachment behavior* in adulthood, especially the disorganized type. The developing "pattern" of disorganized attachment is usually well established during infancy, i.e., usually *well* before the maltreatment or abuse.

In a more recent study addressing attachment disturbance and PTSD symptoms in adult women with a history of childhood sexual abuse, Alexander (1993) found that the greater portion of the variance of disorganized attachment behavior in adult survivors of incest was explained by early parent-child interactional disturbances that typically occurred prior to the sexual abuse, while the greater portion of the variance of symptoms (PTSD, dissociative, and depressive symptoms) was accounted for by the the sexual abuse per se. The weakness in the study is that Alexander assessed only attachment pathology, not other forms of relational disturbance that might have been more specifically related to the incest. The value of Alexander's work, nevertheless, is that it demonstrates that disorganized attachment behavior, in particular the cycling between intense clinging and detachment characteristic of personality disorder, is likely a function of the wider context of parent-child interactional disturbances that are established in infancy, typically well before physical and sexual abuse occur.

On the other hand, Alexander's work should not be interpreted to mean that trauma or abuse fails to make a signficant contribution to chronic relational disturbance in trauma survivors. A number of trauma experts have described the reenactment of trauma in relationships (Courtois, 1988; Hegeman,

1995; Herman, 1992; Spiegel, 1986; van der Kolk, 1987). In *Treating the Adult Survivor of Childhood Sexual Abuse*, Davies and Frawley (1994) have developed the most detailed account of trauma-specific relational pathology resulting from childhood sexual abuse. According to Davies and Frawley's clinical observations, "severe and chronic" sexual abuse results in "pervasive developmental arrests" including a disturbance in the "organization of self and object representations" (p. 43). Trauma results in often contradictory "dissociated systems of self and object representations" (p. 45), which have a definite symbolic and implicit influence on ongoing relationships and which become "activated" as the treatment unfolds. Some implicit influences "are enacted rather than verbally identified and processed" (p. 167). According to Davies and Frawley, this dissociation accounts for the "juxtaposition of what appears to be rather primitive, intrusive, and disruptive symptomatology in otherwise functional, often highly successful individuals" (p. 49).

As treatment unfolds the patient regressively reenacts these early patterns of relational disturbance in the form of specific transference-countertransference matrices. Davies and Frawley have identified "four relational matrices" that can be commonly observed in incest survivors. These include (1) the unseeing, uninvolved parent and the unseen, neglected child; (2) the idealized, omnipotent rescuer and the entitled child; (3) the sadistic abuser and the helpless, impotently enraged victim; and (4) the seducer and the seduced. Davies and Frawley are careful to point out that each pole of the respective matrix can be manifest in either the patient or therapist, in the transference or countertransference, at given points along the treatment.

These relational matrices become the primary focus of treatment, so that through interpretation these relational patterns can become reconfigured "and ultimately provide a pathway for the internalization of an entirely new object-related experience" (p. 59). As Davies and Frawley make clear:

> Abreaction and symbolization of memories, as described in much of the trauma literature, seem insufficient in accomplishing the kind of change necessary. It is only when such abreaction and symbolization occur within the containing and holding context of a new therapeutic relationship, when that

relationship becomes the vehicle for untangling and verbally encoding distorted, fragmented, and dissociated experiences of self in relation to other . . . that therapeutic work can be internalized in a meaningful and permanent way (pp. 60–61). . . . However, although such recovery of traumatic memory is necessary, it is barely sufficient to accomplish the necessary character changes in interpersonal functioning and inner harmony which we seek. Our position remains that traumatic abuse results in the dissociation not only of memories but of the entire system of complicated self and object representations associatively linked to those chronic abusive circumstance (p. 213). . . . Traumatic memories can be abreacted but abusive relationships cannot be so easily excised. (p. 214)

Their "relational treatment model" (p. 3) presumes the:

co-creation of a transitional space in which therapist and patient together are free to reenact, create context and meaning, and ultimately recreate in newly configured forms the central, organizing relational matrices of the patient's early life. (p. 3)

Addressing relational disturbances as part of stabilization and in other phases of the overall treatment is not simply a question of *whether* but *which* specific types of adult relational disturbances are or are not causally related to earlier trauma. The available data demonstrate that *disorganized, cyclical relational dynamics*—the intense shifts between clinging and avoidance characteristic of the relationships of most patients with a diagnosis of personality disorder are associated with parent-child attachment pathology (insecure, disorganized type) well established prior to the episodes of trauma and abuse. However, the available data also demonstrates that specific types of *dissociated relational pathology that is implicitly reenacted* are causally related to the trauma, e.g., chronic vulnerability to boundary-violating relationships and pathological dependency (Briere, 1992), traumatic bonding (Herman, 1992), preoccupation with themes of betrayal, shame, and powerlessness (Coffey et al., 1996), and specific types of trauma-related transference reenanctments, e.g., omnipotent rescuer/entitled child, failed protector, unseen child, victim/perpe-

trator, and seduced/seduced (Davies & Frawley, 1994).

No matter what portion of the overall variance of relational disturbance is contributed by preexisting parent-child interactional disturbances and by specific traumatic acts, the resulting relational disturbance is likely to be substantial in survivors of cumulative abuse and so serve as a major focus of treatment. Thus, it is not surprising that some trauma therapists have put the primary treatment emphasis squarely on relational disturbance (e.g., Davies & Frawley, 1994; Gelinas, 1995; Hedges, 1994; Hegeman, 1995; Pearlman & Saakvitne, 1995). Thus, among the numerous goals of stabilization there are a number of relational-based treatment foci. These include:

1. A consistent focus through treatment frame contracts and transference interpretation on the cyclical anxious and avoidant (personality disordered) attachment behaviors as they become manifest in the transference and in current life relationships.

2. A consistent focus on dissociation-related disconnection within the treatment relationship, or difficulty establishing a relationship (Davies & Frawley, 1994; Hegeman, 1995; Spiegel, 1986).

3. A consistent focus on the identification and working through of core conflict relational themes, or difficulty *within* relationships (Luborsky, 1984; Strupp & Binder, 1984) that may or may not be related to trauma.

4. A consistent focus on and working through of the trauma-related vulnerability to repeat boundary-violating relationships, to establish pathological dependency within the treatment relationship, or to repeat traumatic bonding (Briere, 1992).

5. A consistent focus on helping the trauma survivor work through trauma-related mistrust and establish a working treatment alliance (or, with DID patients, alliances) (Braun, 1986; Courtois, 1988; Herman, 1992; Meichenbaum, 1994; Rice-Smith, 1993; Ross, 1989; Scurfield, 1985).

In addition, the stabilization phase somewhat, and certainly the later phases of treatment, typically address the issue of trauma-related relational reenactments, such as traumatic bonding (Herman, 1992), and the specific transference-countertransference relational positions described by Davies and Frawley (1994) that need to be identified and worked through in the treatment relationship. Thus, since addressing relational disturbance is the foundation of treatment as well as an important treatment issue at every major phase of the overall treatment, it is not surprising that some trauma experts have emphasized a relational-based approach to trauma treatment (e.g., Davies & Frawley, 1994; Hedges, 1994; Hegeman, 1995; Herman, 1992; Pearlman & Saakvitne, 1995).

In *Trauma and the Therapist: Countertransference and Vicarious Traumatization in Psychotherapy with Incest Survivors*, Pearlman and Saakvitne (1995) describe "two paradigm shifts in the field of mental health" (p. 3), namely, an appreciation for the role of trauma in psychopathology and a shift to a "relational model" of treatment. While the book is primarily devoted to an understanding of countertransference and vicarious traumatization in the therapist, it clearly emphasizes the quality of the treatment relationship as the foundation of trauma treatment:

> The primary healing of psychotherapy with adult survivors of childhood sexual abuse occurs in the context of the therapeutic relationship. (p. 15)

Pearlman and Saakvitne stress "the therapeutic relationship, rather than a more limited focus on transference (i.e., the client)" (p. 15), since ". . . it is within this new relationship that opportunities emerge to rework and heal damage done in the context of early, trusting relationships" (p. 16). According to them, "the management of transference differs somewhat in therapies with survivors of severe abuse from that with other clients" (p. 20), in that it often entails working with dissociated aspects of the self, including the malevolent, internalized perpetrators. These powerful transferences "must be handled carefully in the therapeutic relationship" (p. 102), because such transferences "evoke particularly powerful and complicated countertransference responses" (p. 24), which the therapist must recognize and match with an ability to tolerate strong affect, maintain a sense of connection with others, and maintain a positive sense of self.

The patient's capacity for dissociation makes management of the transference and countertransference even more problematic. Dissociation means the "need to separate from the interpersonal relationship" (p. 137), so the therapist faces special difficulties maintaining the treatment alliance. Dissociation of self and object representations results in the manifestation of frequently shifting states and therefore a great variety of transference and countertransference reactions within a single treatment session.

A Problem-Focused Approach to Stabilization

There is a strong consensus in the professional trauma treatment literature that stabilization is the first major task in the treatment of the trauma survivor. We view the early work in terms of *skill development*. The patient must learn a variety of prerequisite skills in order to demonstrate the capacity for outpatient treatment, stabilize symptoms, and be capable of tolerating processing the trauma at a later point in the overall treatment.

There is a remarkable consensus that stabilization begins with the *establishment of a sense of safety*. If a particular patient is at risk for retraumatization, the first level of intervention is environmental (e.g., removal from the risk situation, supervised contact, etc.), so that external safety can be provided. The main intervention for all trauma patients involves establishing an internal sense of safety and safety in the treatment relationship. Of course, clarity about the treatment frame already contributes to safety in treatment. A structured inquiry about the sense of safety or structured imagery pertaining to safe places and safe situations in relationships as a consistent focus of treatment helps to develop an internal sense of safety as the foundation of the treatment relationship (Brown & Fromm, 1986; Hammond, 1990a).

Additional structured imagery protocols may focus on establishing a greater *sense of connection* in relationship and on *regulating the closeness and distance* in relationships. Another skill addressed early in treatment is self-soothing, e.g., imagining scenes that entail a sense of comfort or soothing, which leads over time to internalization of self-soothing capacities. Developing the *skill of self-soothing* is especially indicated in patients who lack the capacity to tolerate certain affects or who are vulnerable to depression (Brown, 1993) and therefore typically feel worse after they talk about issues in treatment. Structured imagery protocols and hypnotic ego-strengthening suggestions can also be used for *self-esteem enhancement* (Brown & Fromm, 1986; Hammond, 1990). The goal is for the patient to know at least something about how to feel good about him/herself, strong, and in control as a foundation of the treatment.

A major focus of stabilization work is *core PTSD symptoms.* According to *DSM-IV*, these include (1) physiological reactivity, (2) intrusive re-experiencing, and (3) generalized numbing and phobic avoidance. Since it is well established that dissociative symptoms are commonly present during and subsequent to traumatization (Spiegel & Cardena, 1991) and may predict chronicity of PTSD (Bremner et al., 1992; Cardena & Spiegel, 1993; Holon, 1993; Koopman, Classen, & Spiegel, 1994; Marmar et al., 1994; Shalev et al., 1996), dissociative symptoms are also best considered to be core PTSD symptoms. Reducing the frequency and severity of dissociative symptoms is an important objective of stabilization (Krystal et al., 1995).

Two kinds of *physiological reactivity* occur subsequent to traumatization—chronic hyperarousal and physiological reactivity to specific trauma stimuli. The physiological consequences of traumatization are both continuous (hyperarousal) and discontinuous or episodic (reactivity to stimuli). It may be difficult to address many of the other symptoms associated with trauma as long as as the patient remains in a chronic state of heightened arousal and or physiological reactivity. Moreover, it is especially important to address physiological reactivity because physiological overreactivity has been shown to be a significant predictor of chronicity of PTSD (Breslau & Davis, 1992).

One of first tasks of treatment may be to reduce the patient's *chronic hyperarousal* and hypervigilance through medication or regular practice of relaxation-based interventions. Anxiety management skill training has been used to manage hyperarousal in: combat veterans (Hickling et al., 1986; Peniston & Kulkosky, 1991), rape victims (Blanchard & Abel, 1976; Frank & Stewart, 1984; Kilpatrick, Veronen, & Resick, 1982; Resick et al., 1988; Veronen & Kilpatrick, 1983), torture victims (Basoglu, 1992),

and victims of severe, repetitive abuse (Hammond, in press, b). Hammond (1990a) recommends the use of methods of profound calming, including prolonged, deep, meditative hypnosis.

Through behavioral self-monitoring (e.g., Kazdin, 1974) the patient learns to identify very specific risk situations that trigger *episodes of physiological reactivity and intrusive re-experiencing symptoms.* Since intrusive reexperiencing is typically accompanied by physiological arousal (Wickramasekera, 1994), these symptoms are treated together. Intrusive reexperiencing symptoms include spontaneous trauma-related thoughts, images, dreams, nightmares, flashbacks, affect storms, somato-sensory symptoms, and spontaneous reenactments. Systematic desensitization using a hierarchy of trauma triggers has been used with combat veterans (Bowen & Lambert, 1986), rape victims (Celluci & Lawrence, 1978; Schindler, 1980; Wolff, 1977), and accident victims (Fairbank, DeGood, & Jenkins, 1981; Muse, 1986). Hypnotic cue utilization procedures (Brown & Fromm, 1986; Hammond, 1990a) have also been used. A relaxation cue is paired with recognition of the onset of the particular intrusive symptom. Whenever the patient begins to notice an intrusive shift or an accompanying physiological change, he or she is reminded of the relaxation cue and evokes the relaxed or safe state until calm is achieved. Foa and her associates (Foa, Steketee, & Rothbaum, 1989; Foa, Rothbaum, et al., 1995) have demonstrated in their research that the combination of relaxation-based interventions and exposure-based interventions is more effective than either alone, since posttraumatic response typically entails *both* chronic hyperarousal and arousal to specific trauma triggers. From a relational-based perspective, the "holding function" of the therapist also contributes to containing the hyperarousal (Davies & Frawley, 1994, p. 58).

For the negative symptoms of trauma, namely, *generalized numbing* of affective responsiveness, behavioral and cognitive *avoidance* of trauma stimuli, and agoraphobia secondary to trauma, exposure-based interventions are indicated. Prolonged exposure training, for example, has been used extensively with veterans (Fairbank, Gross, & Keane, 1983; Johnson, Gilmore, & Shenoy, 1982; Keane & Kaloupek, 1982). Helping the patient develop alternative coping strategies to avoidance of PTSD recollections may be particularly important, since Hyer et al. (1996) have demonstrated that utilization of predominantly escape-avoidance coping strategies subsequent to traumatization was a strong predictor of chronicity of PTSD.

McCann and Pearlman (1990) appropriately have emphasized the importance of addressing *cognitive distortions* early in treatment and of making cognitive work a main focus of stabilization work. Meichenbaum (1994) has developed a more elaborate protocol for correcting cognitive distortions in trauma survivors. Cognitive interventions focus on two levels of cognitive distortion: (1) moment-by-moment cognitive distortions such as negative self-talk and worry; and (2) distortions in relatively enduring cognitive structures, namely, beliefs. It is particularly important to identify specific beliefs that may have been shattered by traumatization (Janoff-Bulman, 1992; McCann & Pearlman, 1990), as well as new, pathological beliefs that may have been internalized as a consequence of the trauma (Roth & Lebowitz, 1988). The goal of the interventions is to identify and modify very specific trauma-related cognitive distortions that may otherwise significantly affect treatment response and outcome.

A great deal of the focus of the early stabilization work is on *management of current symptoms and problems*, not all of which will seem related to the trauma. Any given patient may present a wide range of current life symptoms. Anxiety-related symptoms (generalized anxiety, panic, specific phobias, obsessive-compulsive symptoms, agoraphobia) and depression are common presenting complaints that accompany a trauma history. Depression, for example, can be causally related to an early history of trauma and abuse (Widom & Morris,1997). Other current life symptoms may include disturbances in initiating or maintaining sleep, acute somatic distress, chronic pain, sexual dysfunction, and complicated grief. Addictive behaviors can include eating disorders, chemical dependency, and sexual compulsivity, which may (Widom & Morris, 1997) or may not (Pope & Hudson, 1992) be causally related to an early history of trauma or abuse. Other current life issues that become a major focus of stabilization treatment include a variety of chronic relational dysfunctions, self pathology, work and school performance problems, and self-defeating behaviors and/or substantial interpersonal difficul-

ties that are associated with personality disorder.

Nonhypnotic cognitive-behavioral and hypno-projective methods can be used to discover and enhance *coping resources* for each symptom or problem reported by the patient, such as anxiety, depression, grief, insomnia, acute somatic distress, pain, etc. (Brown & Fromm, 1986). Behavioral problem-solving methods are also useful (Meichenbaum, 1994). Psychopharmacological interventions are often indicated, especially those targeted toward very specific symptoms. Highly structured treatment manuals are available for a variety of these symptoms (Barlow, 1989): anxiety (Barlow, 1988), depression (Beck et al., 1979; Klerman et al., 1984), sleep disorders (Brown & Fromm, 1987), psychophysiological disorders (Brown & Fromm, 1986), and sexual dysfunction (Kaplan, 1974; Leiblum & Rosen, 1989). Sophisticated multimodal treatment protocols are also available that address chemical dependency (Brower et al., 1989; Brown & Fromm, 1987; Pomerleau & Pomerleau, 1977), eating disorders (Brownell, 1989; Garner & Garfinkel, 1985), and sexual compulsivity (Schwartz & Masters, 1993). Outcome research has also demonstrated that psychodynamic psychotherapy with a consistent focus on interpreting "core conflict relational themes" as they are reenacted in the transference to the therapist is an effective treatment for chronic relational dysfunction (Luborsky, 1984; Strupp & Binder, 1984). Recently, a variety of behavioral (Linehan, 1993) and psychodynamic (Kernberg et al., 1989) treatment manuals have described effective approaches for the interpersonal difficulties associated with personality disorder.

Stabilization primarily focuses on *current life functioning*. In this sense, the goals of stabilization extend far beyond specific trauma-related symptoms and problems. Where traumatization has affected major lines of development, like self, relational, or affect development, a good deal of the initial focus of treatment may be on helping the patient develop self-observational skills, identification and communication of feelings and needs, social skills and social supports, and affect regulatory skills. With respect to daily functioning, treatment may need to address performance in work or school, problems in intimate and peer relationships, and a variety of lifestyle issues, such as finances, social supports, outside interests, stress management, etc. Viewing stabilization solely in terms of safety represents an unfortunate oversimplification of our increasingly sophisticated understanding of stabilization. The reader can perhaps best appreciate the complexity of stabilization treatment by referring to Table 13.1, which summarizes the signs indicating that the patient has achieved the diverse goals of stabilization and is ready to proceed to the integration phase of treatment.

Dissociative identity disorder (DID) patients require special considerations during the stabilization phase (Phillips & Frederick, 1995). While it is necessary to establish all of the above-mentioned skills, DID patients necessitate "multi-leveled" interven-

TABLE 13.1
Signs of Stabilization

Skill in feeling sense of safety and safety-in-relationship

Skill in feeling a sense of connection, at least in therapy

Skill in self-soothing, and in applying this skill when needed

Evidence of enhanced self-esteem

Skill in effectively coping with and having a sense of mastery over a variety of ancillary current life problems:

symptoms (anxiety, depression, sleep disturbance, pain, etc.)

addictive behaviors such as chemical dependency, eating disorders, or sexual compulsivity

relational difficulties (diminished conflict or attachment problems)

work/school problems (better performance)

Skill in effectively alleviating core PTSD symptoms such as:

Physiological arousal

Reduced chronic hyperarousal

Reduced episodic reactivity to trauma triggers

Intrusive re-experiencing symptoms

Numbing and avoidance

Identification of and partial modification of trauma-related shattered and pathologically internalized beliefs about self and world

For DID patients additional benchmarks of progress in stabilization include:

Signs of accessing, identifying, and establishing a treatment alliance with respective alters in the personality system

Consistent evidence of skill in inter-alter communication and negotiation

Evidence that uncooperative alters have become part of the treatment alliance and have reduced their blocking and/or acting-out behaviors

tions. Since DID patients do not have a unitary self representational system, it is necessary for the therapist to establish a treatment alliance with every alter personality and to consider the specific treatment needs concurrently and even-handedly for each alter within the entire alter personality system. Thus, while one treatment objective may be to establish an internal sense of safety, the treatment approach must address establishing a sense of safety for each and every alter within the entire system, not just for the host personality.

When compared to non-DID PTSD patients, DID patients require additional special interventions to complete the goals of stabilization. These include procedures for *contacting* the alters *identifying* the characteristics and functions of each alter and mapping the alter personality system, teaching the respective alters *stabilization skills*, encouraging *inter-alter communication*, and teaching the alters *negotiation and other conflict-resolution skills*. DID patients also typically manifest a number of special treatment problems that must be addressed during stabilization. It may be necessary to focus on having the host and alter personality system learn skills to curtail and control spontaneous trauma-related re-enactments (sometimes called *spontaneous abreactions*, e.g., Putnam, 1989), *involuntary shifts* in state of consciousness, or *uncontrolled or dysphoric switching* between alters (Kluft, 1983; Putnam, 1989). A variety of hypnotic methods have been used to accomplish these goals, such grounding and containment techniques (Peterson, 1991), suggestions for increased control, and hypnotic depth-adjustment methods that help the patient gain increased voluntary control over shifts in state. *Uncooperative and blocking alters* that disrupt the treatment, battle for dominance, or act out in ways that jeopardize the treatment present a great challenge to the therapist, who must build a treatment alliance with such alters through empathic understanding and positive reframing of their problem behaviors.

Subjectively, the patient knows he or she has accomplished many of the goals of stabilization when the fear and reactivity to unfolding experience characteristic of posttraumatic response are transmuted into a curiosity about, a sense of mastery over, and self-efficacy about a range of current symptoms and problems. Above all, the patient feels in control and much more settled than at the onset of treatment. Out of this emerging confidence about dealing with whatever comes into unfolding experience, the patient shows a psychological readiness to proceed with the task of processing and integrating the trauma.

The Integration Phase

General Considerations

None of the professional trauma treatment literature we have reviewed has presented treatment narrowly as a "form of memory recovery therapy" per se. There is a remarkable consensus within this treatment literature that, with respect to memory, trauma recovery is best viewed in terms of *memory integration*. Recovery of memories is not about gathering information about the past. It is about mastery over what has been unclear or avoided in memory, making meaning out of one's personal history, and achieving integation (Waites, 1997). The integration phase of trauma treatment can be subdivided into two subphases: (1) *memory integration* and (2) *representational integration*. The first pertains to the integration of the previously dissociated fragments of narrative memory for trauma into a coherent memory and its integration within the consciously available autobiographical memory system (reversal of primary dissociation), as well as to the integration of the BASK components of the traumatic memory (reversal of secondary dissociation). The latter subphase pertains to the integration of dissociated representational fragments, e.g., the abuser self and failed protector self and object representations, into the consciously available self representational system, as well as to the integration of the narrative trauma memory within the unified self representational system (reversal of tertiary dissociation). Once the narrative memory for trauma is integrated as an aspect of the self and is no longer disavowed, the trauma becomes transformed. It takes on new meaning as part of the individual's current and ongoing autobiographical memory. It also takes on new meaning as the trauma narrative is disclosed, told, and retold as part of a socially shared autobiographical history. Van der Hart and Nijenhuis (1995; in press, a) have referred to these three goals of the integration phase as the reversal of primary, secondary, and tertiary dissociation.

Some recent empirical studies have lent support to the concepts of primary and secondary dissociation and the need to address these in treatment. At the earlier stages of treatment traumatic memory often manifests itself in a non-narrative, fragmented, or incomplete narrative form (Roe & Schwartz, 1996; van der Kolk & Fisler, 1995), and primarily in an "unsymbolized" somato-sensory or affective form (Davies & Frawley, 1994; van der Kolk & Fisler, 1995) and in the form of implicit influences on everyday behavior, notably, relational behavior (American Psychiatric Association, 1994; Davies & Frawley, 1994; Terr, 1988, 1994; Waites, 1997). Thus, related goals of treatment are to facilitate greater organization of the narrative memory for trauma (Foa et al., 1995; Waites, 1997), as well as integration of the dissociated BASK components of the traumatic memory (Braun, 1986; Phillips & Frederick, 1995). These studies have shown that, as the narrative memory for the trauma is processed in treatment over time, it is likely to become more complete, both with respect to number of details and length of the narrative report, more organized, and more personally meaningful, with respect to both the quality of emotions and the beliefs about the traumatic experiences (Foa, Rothbaum, et al., 1995; Roe & Schwartz, 1996; van der Kolk & Fisler, 1995).

Memory integration entails a process of "translating" (Harber & Pennebaker, 1992; van der Kolk & Fisler, 1995) or "*verbally encoding*" heretofore "unsymbolized" trauma-related symptoms and implicit behavioral reenactments into a coherent narrative (Krystal et al., 1995), as well as a process of "*making meaning*" (Horowitz, 1973; Waites, 1997) and "*realization*" (van der Hart et al., 1993) of the trauma as part of the personal history of the self.

The Special Case of Memory Enhancement— Indications and Contraindications

While trauma experts agree that memory integration is the main goal of the integration phase of trauma treatment for all traumatized patients, most experts also acknowledge that a clinically important subpopulation of trauma patients enter treatment with a relatively incomplete narrative memory for the trauma. These fully or partially amnestic patients present a special challenge, in that recovery or enhancement of their incomplete memory may be a necessary prerequisite to memory integration. We disagree with false memory advocates who claim that memory recovery should *never* be done, or who claim that *all* treatment that addresses recollections of trauma is memory recovery and not memory integration. We recognize, however, that some false memory advocates will strongly disagree with our position and interpret it as justification for memory recovery, at least under certain circumstances.

Our position, which is supported by the professional trauma literature, is that memory recovery has a legitimate place within the overall trauma treatment plan, provided that memory recovery, in the narrow sense, is restricted to those patients in whom full or partial amnesia for trauma is fundamental clinical problem. In this sense, memory recovery is well matched to the problem. Avoidance of memory enhancement in certain instances is an avoidance of clinical responsibility. Waites (1997) makes a similar argument:

> Where the subversion of memory is a primary complaint . . . therapy that evades the question is unlikely to be very helpful.
>
> From a practical standpoint, too, many clients expect therapy to help them confront and correct the subversion of memory for actual events, not just to supply a coherent narrative about the past. Sometimes differentiating between fact and fantasy is necessary for important and far-reaching decisions. . . .
>
> Where records are suspect and memory incomplete, it is often tempting to search for an omnipotent other who can provide all the answers. This search is itself a legacy of infantile helplessness and dependency. Psychotherapy that shifts the focus from reliance on received truths to an exercise in independent thinking will not yield definite answers to all hard questions. But it will free the client to consider possibilities that were formerly foreclosed by the systematic subversion of memory. (pp. 158–159)

Nevertheless, we wish to emphasize that memory recovery in most instances does not require special memory recovery techniques (e.g., Reviere, 1996). The main contraindication to memory enhancement is that certain memory enhancement methods that

might increase the memory error rate must be avoided, especially for the minority of patients who possess the trait of high memory suggestibility (cf. also Krystal et al., 1995, p. 162, for a discussion of the merits and risks of "guided recollection strategies").

In chapter 4 we reviewed a number of studies on hypermnesia and in chapter 10 we reviewed studies on hypnotic hypermnesia. These studies consistently demonstrated that repeated waking or hypnotic efforts to recall information about a target event resulted in a significant increase in the total amount of information recalled over time. This hypermnestic effect was not necessarily accompanied by an increase in the memory error rate provided that the waking or hypnotic interview method approximated free recall. In chapter 9 we learned, conversely, that repeated waking recall when accompanied by the systematic introduction of misinformation by the interviewer is accompanied by a remarkable increase in the memory error rate. In other words, hypermnesia following repeated recall is a well-established phenomenon, but whether the information retrieved is accurate or inaccurate is largely a function of how the interview is conducted.

Repeated inquiry that most closely approximates the condition of free narrative recall, wherein the interviewer refrains from supplying leading or misleading information, is likely to maximize the hypermnestic effect while minimizing the memory error rate. In this sense, the best "technique" for memory recovery is no technique, other than free recall. The therapist who follows the cardinal rule of psychoanalysis, namely, to instruct the patient to "say whatever comes to mind" within and across treatment sessions, is engaging in the kind of free narrative recall that is likely to yield a significant increase in the information about a past event without necessarily increasing the memory error rate. Frequently, further details become clear over time without any demand to recollect the trauma and often even without any structured inquiry into such past events.

What false memory proponents fail to realize in their criticisms of "memory recovery therapy" (e.g., Loftus & Ketcham, 1994; Ofshe & Watters, 1994) is that free recall is how most good trauma treatment is conducted. There is a vast difference between therapy in which additional memory details are recovered over time, largely through free narrative recall, and memory recovery therapy, in the sense of implying a technique to recover memories. Recent research has shown that additional narrative details of early traumatic memories are indeed likely to be reported over time both within and outside of treatment and that the overall extent of the narrative trauma memory increases and becomes more organized over time (Foa, Molnar, et al., 1995; van der Kolk & Fisler, 1995).

Setting aside the issue of free narrative recall, it is now becoming clear that additional narrative details about past trauma are likely to emerge at very precise moments in treatment, namely, in reaction to transference interpretations (Dalenberg, 1996; cf. also Waites, 1997, p. 223) and in reaction to reestablishing a context by which to understand past experience. Price (1995) asserts that dissociated memories that were never linguistically encoded are reported in therapy because of "the creation of a context and a discourse that recognizes and acknowledges such traumas" (p. 300). Waites (1997) defines the therapeutic context as providing a relationship in which it is safe to remember. Since much of the memory for trauma is retained as an implicit rather than explicit memory (American Psychiatric Association, 1994), which is reenancted in the transference, additional narrative details regarding the trauma typically follow transference interpretations that draw the patient's attention to these implicit reenactments (Davies & Frawley, 1994).

Whether these additional details are more or less historically accurate is a matter of controversy. Hedges (1994) and Spence (1982), for example, have warned that all transference interpretations are reconstructions, largely inaccurate. Hegeman (1995) doubts that the recollections are completely historically accurate, but nevertheless are "an effort at representing and communicating real experience" (p. 199). The only data-based study to test this hypothesis failed to support a radically nihilistic position. Dalenberg (1996) found that trauma recollections specifically recovered in response to transference interpretations in treatment were significantly more accurate than trauma recollections that were retrieved under other conditions in treatment, such as state-dependent retrieval.

In conclusion, good psychodynamic treatment, which combines free narrative recall with intrepretation of transference reenactments over time, is typically sufficient in and of itself to reverse full or partial amnesia for trauma. Are special memory recovery strategies, then, necessary? For the most part, no. When are they indicated? Certainly in a forensic context, like that associated with the trauma of experiencing or witnessing a crime (McConkey & Sheehen, 1995), or in the investigation of child abuse allegations (Hoorwitz, 1992), special memory recovery techniques have their use.

In the clinical setting, however, using specialized memory recovery strategies has become a matter of great controversy. False memory advocates oppose the use of specialized memory recovery strategies under *any* conditions. In our review of the professional trauma literature it becomes clear that trauma experts advocate their *qualified* use, i.e., for a subpopulation of amnestic patients at a certain point in the overall treatment. However, our review of the professional trauma literature also reveals that trauma experts are not always in agreement about what specific memory recovery strategies to recommend and are not always cognizant of the effect of these strategies on memory error rates. The great majority agree that imagery in the context of free recall is particularly useful (e.g., Brown & Fromm, 1986; Herman, 1992). Many agree that certain hypnotic procedures in the context of free recall may be useful in certain situations (Brown & Fromm, 1986; Herman, 1992; McCann & Pearlman, 1990; Phillips & Frederick, 1995; van der Hart et al., 1993), although others strongly advise against the use of hypnotic methods (e.g., Briere, 1992; Sgroi, 1989) or find their use unnecessary (Davies & Frawley, 1994).

We learned in chapters 10 and 11 that, contrary to the false memory claim, both imagery and hypnotic methods, properly conducted, lead to an increase in the completeness of a memory without sacrificing its overall accuracy, although some potential for memory distortion exists, especially for a subgroup of highly suggestible patients and/or when accompanied by unduly suggestive interview procedures. Otherwise, these procedures, in and of themselves, are not problematic. Our opinion, which not everyone will agree with, is that such specialized memory recovery techniques are sometimes indicated when: (1) the patient is suffering from a more pervasive or extreme amnesia for trauma, and

(2) that has not been reversed by the previous methods designed to minimize memory accuracy errors, such as free narrative recall. Under these very specific conditions the clinician may consider using *specific memory recovery strategies* while carefully weighing their benefits against the potential increase in the memory error rate.

In this sense, clinicians can learn from recent advances in the procedures for conducting child abuse investigations, namely, the use of the *step-wise approach* to inquiry about abuse (Bull, 1995; Hoorwitz, 1992; Yuille, 1988). In the step-wise approach the child abuse interviewer utilizes a hierarchy of methods from those with the lowest known memory error rate to those with the highest. If the desired material is not retrieved using the method with the lowest error rate, the method with the next lowest error rate is used, and so forth, keeping in mind that each step increases the error rate and thereby decreases the confidence that can be assigned to the evidence. Since each step is carefully documented, the court is able to evaluate the totality of the evidence and assign the recollections more or less credibility depending on what interviewing steps were used and what the likelihood of memory inaccuracy might be.

There no reason why clinicians could not utilize a similar step-wise approach to the problem of amnesia for trauma. The currently available data from the memory sciences suggest the hierarchy shown in Table 13.2 for increasing recollections about target events, from lowest to highest memory error rates.

We agree with Kluft (1996) that "the therapist should treat trauma 'from the top down,' working with consciously available material first, because the best approach to uncovering unavailable material without leading the patient is the resolution of presenting concerns" (p. 106). Beyond that careful adherence to free recall is advised. We believe that the problem of amnesia for trauma will be reversed for the majority of patients over the course of treatment by letting the patient freely recall whatever comes to mind, combined with attention to transference reenactments and their interpretation (levels 1 and 2 in Table 13.2) *before* utilizing any specific memory recovery strategies. The clinician is best advised to next utilize *context-reinstatement strategies* (level 3). Having the patient focus on and wonder about the period of his or her life in question

TABLE 13.2
A Step-Wise Approach to the Treatment of Amnesia for Trauma

Minimal Memory Error Rates
  1. free narrative recall

Mild Increase in Memory Error Rates
  2. transference interpretation combined with free recall (Dalenberg, 1996)
  3. context reinstatement combined with free recall (e.g., the Cognitive Interview [Fisher & Geiselman, 1992])

Mild-to-Modest Increase in Memory Error Rates
  4. state dependent recall (Bowers, 1981; Dalenberg, 1996)

Modest Increase in Memory Error Rates
  5. specialized memory recovery techniques (combinations of the above methods without supplying misinformation in the interview)

High Increase in Memory Error Rates
  6. interrogatory and coercive interviewing (systematically supplying misinformation within and across interviews combined with other interrogatory and coercive methods)

constitutes a kind of context-reinstatement strategy, like those that have been used in a forensic setting to increase the completeness of the memory without necessarily increasing its inaccuracy (Fisher et al., 1987). However, compared to free recall, context reinstatement introduces a mild increase in the error rate.

For those patients who persist with pervasive amnesia and for whom memory enhancement is a legitimate treatment objective, *state reinstatement strategies* (level 4) may be introduced. Often, free recall of past experience leads over time to increased awareness of the emotions associated with those events. When therapy helps the patient safely contain and increasingly tolerate affects of greater intensity, further narrative details of the memory are likely to return spontaneously as the affective states tolerated in the treatment are similar to the affective states and their intensity at the time of the original traumatization (Bower, 1981). Selectively focusing the inquiry on the affect or introducing techniques to amplify the affect is likely to increase the information about the target event but also modestly increase the memory error rate (Dalenberg, 1996).

As we learned in chapter 5, state- and context-reinstatement strategies are consistent with the two main ways that narrative autobiographical memory is tagged, namely, through affective associations and temporal referencing. While these methods increase the yield of total information about the target event, some of the detail information (less so the gist information) may contain inaccuracies.

Specialized memory recovery techniques typically refer to combinations of the previously mentioned methods such as hypnotic age regression, which combines free recall with context and state reinstatement. We learned in chapter 10 that age regression can yield significant increases in personally meaningful material about a target event without necessarily increasing the memory error rate, depending on how the interview is conducted. The problem is that such methods often convey unrealistic expectations to both patient and therapist and/or are used in combination with suggestive interviewing techniques that increase the error rate. Insofar as the therapist is fully cognizant of the risks and is especially careful to minimize suggestive factors in the interview, such methods have their place (cf. McConkey & Sheehan, 1995, for a discussion of risks and pitfalls).

Substages of Memory Integration Where Memory Is a Treatment Focus

Several recent studies have addressed the question of how the narrative memory for trauma is recollected over time, both within and outside of therapy (Brown, 1993; Foa, Molnar, et al., 1995; van der Kolk & Fisler, 1995). Studying recovery from acute PTSD caused by rape and from complicated PTSD caused by cumulative relational abuse, Foa et al. (1995), and Brown (1993), respectively, have independently described the distinct shifts in cognitive organization of the narrative memory for trauma at various points in treatment. Brown described three substages or shifts in narrative memory organization occurring during the integration stage of trauma treatment: (1) the initial occurrence of memory fragments; (2) organization of fragments into coherent accounts of single episodes of trauma; and (3) organization across episodes into a trauma story or narrative. Each successive change represents a new, increasingly complex level of cognitive

organization of the narrative memory. Each level, in turn, signifies a distinct subphase of treatment. We refer to these as the early, middle, and late subphases of memory integration.

EARLY MEMORY INTEGRATION During the stabilization phase the patient develops a variety of skills, e.g., self-soothing and safety and containment skills, and shows a reduction in PTSD (hyperarousal, intrusive, and numbing) symptoms and the frequency of dissociative shifts in state and/or switching personality systems. One consequence of successful stabilization is that the patient no longer approaches the prospect of recollecting traumatic events with fear, reactivity, and avoidance behaviors but with a curiosity, equanimity, and motivation to explore.

Prior to the early memory integration subphase patients who have a continuous memory for at least the gist of previous traumatization are nonetheless often somewhat avoidant of recollecting the trauma. Patients who suffer partial or full amnesia for the trauma, in addition to being avoidant, retain a relatively incomplete and highly fragmented narrative memory for the trauma and its details. Sometimes the amnesia also includes the gist of critical traumatic events. In either case, stabilization establishes the internal conditions through which the patient's *fear of remembering* the trauma, along with the *associated avoidant behaviors*, begins to subside.

As the patient makes a gentle and natural transition from fear to greater curiosity about the trauma, increased recall of details, and sometimes of more complete events, often spontaneously occurs. These narrative details often appear as fragments and are often followed by an intense reaction to the recalled material in the form of negative affect (van der Kolk & Fisler, 1995), increased physiological reactivity (Wickramasekera, 1994), or other psychological "aftershocks" (Frederickson, 1992).

The objectives of therapy during the early integration phase are (1) to help the patient reduce avoidance of and aftershocks about narrative trauma recollections and (2) to foster the free recall conditions within the treatment relationship where further narrative information about the trauma can be recollected in a way that minimizes memory commission errors. Subtle or obviously persistent pressure to recall past trauma on the part of the therapist increases not only the iatrogenic risk of memory commission errors but also the risk of greater "phobia to remembering" (van der Hart & Nijenhuis, 1995a), as well as the aftershock distress of having remembered more details. Encouraging free narrative recall minimizes both negative reaction to the memory material and the memory error rate. Following the cardinal rule of psychoanalysis, patients "say whatever comes to mind" without pressure (Menninger & Holzman, 1973). As the patient reports recollections, the therapist refrains from inquiry about content or detail but simply encourages the patient to go on. Otto Fenichel was once asked about the process of a good analytic hour. He answered that the main thing he said in the hour was, "and then . . . and then . . . and then . . . and then" (personal communication, Joel Shor, 1988).

As the patient explores free narrative recollections of past trauma, the narrative information about the trauma is often reported in a quite fragmented manner (Terr, 1994; van der Kolk & Fisler, 1995). One task of therapy is to help the patient identify memory fragments and to initiate the often difficult task of learning to discriminate between memory elements and fantasy productions. Most recollections at first contain a mixture of accurate and inaccurate elements.

For patients who have always remembered their trauma, free narrative recall is usually sufficient to help the patient recollect the memory, and sometimes to increase recollected details of narrative information about the trauma in a manner that is relatively free of avoidance or aftershocks over time. The goals of early integration are achieved when (1) the patient demonstrates a relative decrease in reactivity to, avoidance of, or aftershocks in reponse to traumatic recollections; (2) narrative details predominate over disguised symbolizations and implicit reenactments associated with traumatic experiences, and specifically for amnestic patients; and (3) there is a notable increase in narrative, albeit fragmented, details pertinent to traumatic recollections.

MIDDLE MEMORY INTEGRATION Middle integration begins when the patient's reactivity to traumatic recollections has markedly diminished and when the amnestic patient has sufficient fragments of the narrative memory consciously available so that themes become clear. Dissociation is the hallmark

of the middle integration phase. While narrative elements of the trauma memory show increasing detail and organization, these narrative recollections remain highly dissociated from the other BASK components of the trauma memory (secondary dissociation). Yet, the incidence of these *dissociated BASK components* of the trauma memory significantly increase during middle integration, even in the face of an increasingly clear narrative recollection of the trauma. A common example of such secondary dissociation is that the patient reports the narrative memory for the trauma with increasing detail and clarity while remaining highly dissociated from any emotions. Yet, at another point in the same session, the patient will report an intense affect with little or no content associated with it. Moreover, the increasing detail and organization of the narrative memory remain dissociated from the consciously available self representational system. Examples of such primary dissociation are that the patient is likely to have low confidence in the recollection as a memory per se or may complain that the trauma could not have happened to him or her.

The integration work generally proceeds utilizing simply free narrative recall. The patient usually will become aware of clear narrative trauma themes over time. At some point a *new level of memory organization* is achieved. The benchmark of this new organization is the report of relatively complete single episodes of traumatization, in which various previously reported fragments of memory for a single incident of trauma held by the person (or by various alter personalities in the case of DID) show increasing organization until the patient begins to report well-organized narrative memories that capture both the gist of the incident as well as details about it. During middle integration, however, the narrative memories for single trauma episodes are not yet organized *across*, only *within*, episodes. The goal of middle integration is to help the patient achieve an organization of the emerging narrative trauma fragments into a relatively cohesive recollection for single episodes of traumatic experiences.

Many patients who are partially or fully amnestic for trauma, as well as those who have always remembered at least the gist of the trauma, can achieve this goal of middle integration using free narrative recall alone. Some, patients, however, remain partially amnestic well into this phase so that context-

and state-reinstatement or other specialized memory enhancement methods are sometimes indicated, as long as the therapist has sufficiently allowed for free recall and has weighed the benefits of using these methods against the risks of memory commission errors. As we learned in chapter 11, these risks do not necessarily prohibit the use of such methods for selected patients. Potential contraindications occur when the patient is very highly suggestible, the therapist is unduly suggestive in interviewing style, or the case has potential legal ramifications that might make recollections inadmissible as evidence.

Because the patient is intensely aware of the pervasiveness of his or her own dissociative processes during middle integration the transference is also heavily colored by dissociative operations. Patients typically report feeling "disconnected" both within themselves and from the therapist, in a manner that appears much more extreme that previously in treatment. The therapist faces the challenge of how to help the patient feel that he or she is there along with the patient. In addition to this sensed disconnectedness, the patient struggles with vulnerability to and fear of dependency upon the therapist. Chronic trauma victims at this stage of treatment reveal a melancholic longing for a corrective relationship, one that is kind instead of violent and well-bounded instead of violating.

A number of problems are characteristic of middle uncovering, including: (1) fear of becoming "overwhelmed" because recall of narrative trauma information is not well paced; (2) reenactment of a "conspiracy to silence" (Butler, 1978), in which the patient recollects many aspects of the trauma clearly but is hesitant or unwilling to report these recollections out of fear that harmful consequences will be reenacted in the transference; and (3) activation of "invisible loyalties," in which the patient activates an intense, albeit pathological, loyalty to the abuser, fails to keep the harm of the abuse in perspective, fears further disclosure will threaten that bond, and therefore refuses to proceed with narrative recollection of the abuse and/or intensifies the pathological bond with the abuser.

Provided the clinician helps the patient work through the transference and other problems characteristic of middle integration, the patient is likely to achieve the main goals of this phase. For patients with a unitary personality, these include: (1) con-sistently reported coherent narratives of single abuse or trauma incidents replete with the memory for the gist of the traumatic action, sufficient plausibly verifiable detail, and appropriate location in time and context; and (2) a relative absence of reported feared consequences to self or others as a result of the recollections. For patients with DID there is an additional goal: (3) getting alter personalities, each of which holds a fragment of the memory for the event, to work together to synthesize the fragmented recollections of trauma incidents into a coherent narrative. This may require such methods as suggested cross-communication, suggested clustering (Kluft, 1988b, 1989b), sharing memory information across alters and with the host personality, and rebalancing the personality system in case certain alters have aftershock reactions to what is shared. By the end of middle phase the narrative trauma recollections of non-amnestic and previously partially or fully amnestic patients are fairly similar.

LATE MEMORY INTEGRATION It is important to emphasize that most of middle integration pertains to the *organization of narrative memory* per se, from fragments into coherent recollections of single episodes of traumatization. For victims of cumulative or repeated trauma resulting in chronic PTSD, late integration is characterized by another shift in narrative memory organization, namely, the capacity to organize a number of coherent single episodes of trauma into a larger organizational system, i.e., a *coherent trauma narrative or story*. As the patient continues to remember the trauma, he or she shows an increasing ability to organize these recollections across episodes. What dawns upon the patient is a "comprehensive picture of the trauma" (Frederickson, 1992) or "realization" of the trauma's impact (Janet, 1889; van der Hart et al., 1993). Again, most of this organization occurs spontaneously over time as a consequence of free recall, without the aid of special memory recovery techniques. We believe that the report of an increasingly organized trauma narrative is the outcome of a shift to a more complex level of cognitive organization. Another consequence of the cognitive complexity manifest at this stage of the treatment is the increased capacity to link the trauma story with current symptoms and problems.

With respect to memory content, a number of

new types of memories are typically reported by chronic PTSD patients during late uncovering. *Coping memories* refer less to memory for an abusive action per se than to the recollection of the various coping strategies used by the patient at the time of the abuse, such as leaving one's body, struggling, etc. *Aftermath memories* are memories not of the trauma or abuse incidents themselves but of the immediate or extended consequences. Thus, instead of recollecting an episode of sexual abuse in which the father comes to the child's room at night and molests her, the patient at this point reports what it felt like to eat breakfast with father the next morning or what she felt like in school thereafter.

The increased report of coping and aftermath memories during the late integration work implies a *progressive interiorization* of the phenomenology of the narrative memory. During the earlier stabilization and early integration work narrative memory for trauma is reported from the outside-in ("this is what he did to me . . . and then he did . . ."). During late uncovering the narrative memory is reported from the inside-out ("while he was doing that I did . . . and then I tried to deal with it by . . . and I felt . . . and believed that . . ."). In other words, awareness of internal reactions predominates over reports of trauma actions per se (cf. also Foa, Molnar, et al., 1995, regarding the increased reports of thoughts and feelings about acute rape experience as treatment progresses).

The other major feature of late integration is the increased capacity to organize previously dissociated BASK components of the trauma memory into an integrated memory for trauma. Up to this point, the behavioral reenactments, the range of affects, and somato-sensory experiences associated with the original traumatic event(s) have remained highly dissociated from the increasingly organized narrative memory for trauma. The primary task of late integration is to integrate the BASK components of the trauma memory with each other, thereby eradicating secondary dissociation. With DID patients the activity of child alters plays a critical role in this phase of recovery, since child alters often contain the intense affects dissociated at the time of traumatization.

Integration of the narrative trauma memory and the affects associated with the original trauma is not easy. For many patients free narrative recall over

the course of treatment is sufficient to accomplish this goal. For some patients specific memory integration techniques may be indicated. Unfortunately, these are often the same techniques that false memory advocates have considered to be memory recovery techniques, although most trauma experts use them more for BASK integration and less for memory uncovering per se. For example, affect intensification methods and even hypnotic techniques like the affect bridge and age regression (Watkins, 1971) have a legitimate role if the clinical goal at this stage of treatment is the integration of affect and memory, assuming that the content of the narrative memory for trauma is already available. Nash (1988) found that hypnotic age regression does not contribute to accurate recall but that it does facilitate greater awareness of affects and self representations associated with the recalled time or event in childhood. Since the objectives of late memory integration include linking the narrative trauma memory to affects and the self representational system, age regression is well matched to this goal. Thus, such methods are useful insofar as the clinician understands their appropriate contribution to integration and their problematic role in accurate recall. Fractionated abreaction and planned synthesis methods likewise have been used extensively with DID patients to accomplish BASK integration, not to recover memories per se (Kluft, 1983, 1989a; Sachs, van der Hart et al., 1993; Steele & Colrain, 1988).

Yet another major feature of late integration is that the patient at least begins to consider the trauma narrative to be an aspect of his or her personal history. A primary task of late integration is to integrate the narrative memory for trauma with the conscious self representation. The patient must "own" the narrative as part of the autobiographical memory. As Freud once said, "Where it was, I shall be." The narrative memory for trauma is no longer disavowed.

The benchmarks of accomplishing the goals of late integration are: (1) evidence of organization of the narrative memory for trauma across episodes into a comprehensive narrative or story about the trauma; (2) ability to set the narrative memory into context, i.e., time and place in personal history; (3) realization of impact of the event on one's personal history; (4) working through the "existential crisis" in meaning caused by this realization (van der Hart & Nijenhuis, in press, a); (5) integrating the narrative and other BASK components of the trauma memory, especially the range intense affects associated with the original trauma; (6) beginning integration of the narrative trauma memory with the conscious self representation.

Representational Integration

Full integration of the narrative trauma memory with the conscious self representation is rarely completed during the late memory integration phase. The reason for this is that the self representational system itself remains dissociated, at least in victims of severe, cumulative interpersonal trauma (Brende, 1984; Brown & Fromm, 1986; Davies & Frawley, 1994; Parson, 1984; Phillips & Frederick, 1995; van der Hart & Nijenhuis, in press, a). Full integration of the narrative trauma memory with the self representational system cannot be accomplished until the self representational system itself has achieved integration. The goal of the *representational subphase* of integration is to facilitate integration of the dissociated trauma-related self representations into the conscious self representational system. In patients who have had a relatively unitary conscious self representation, the task is to bring into consciousness and integrate trauma-related dissociated representations or introjects, especially the abuser self and the failed protector self representations. For patients with a history of DID, who may have never had a unified self representational system, the task is to integrate all alters and the host personality into a relatively stable, unified self system. For both categories of patients, at least some aspects of the overall self representational system have been dissociated.

Davies and Frawley (1994) consider memory integration to be merely a precursor to the more important goal of representational integration:

Recovery of the traumatic event(s) is merely one aspect of the clinical work that must be accomplished. Because we view these traumatic experiences as embedded in the entire constellation of the patient's internal object world and concomitant aspect of self experience, we view the emergence, containment, encoding, and integration of this entire split-off aspect of experience to represent the overriding therapeutic goal. (p. 64)

If s/he does not achieve representational integration, the patient will fail to fully integrate the narrative trauma memories or to achieve full unification of the personality, and will remain arrested along the lines of self and relational development.

Unfortunately, most of the PTSD treatment literature (less so the DID literature) has developed a blind spot. So much emphasis has been given to memory integration in general, and to memory enhancement for amnestic patients, that the importance of representational integration has been neglected as an absolutely critical goal of the overall treatment. A common misconception among some clinicians is that trauma treatment is, for the most part, complete when the patient integrates the narrative memory content and affects associated with the trauma. Were these patients to terminate treatment at that point, a very critical piece of the work would be left undone, and the clinician would have done no more than collude with the patient's fear of addressing seemingly "toxic" dissociated self representations that remain unacceptable to the consciousness personality system (cf. the "abusing other" as an example of a toxic dissociated representation—Davies & Frawley, 1994, p. 71). As has been commonly said, "There is nothing more dangerous than a good victim." Until the survivor of chronic, cumulative relational abuse can face his or her own internalization of the abuser, s/he will remain fearful of him/herself and of him/herself in relationship to others.

Most of the professional trauma literature fails to address the pathological internalization of trauma-related self and object representations under conditions of heightened fear arousal and/or the expression of extreme aggression. There are some exceptions. Brende (1984) and Parson (1984) have described how some combat veterans form "killer self" introjects during the conditions of extreme fear arousal and rampant release of aggression characteristic of active combat. Brown and Fromm (1986) have described the internalization of abuser and failed protector self representations as a consequence of extreme physical and/or sexual abuse. Sgroi (1989) speaks of the internalized pattern of self-abuse that must be addressed at the right point in recovery. Similarly, Herman (1992) and Crowder (1995) briefly speak about the "revenge fantasies" of victims. Davies and Frawley (1994) describe the "reactivation" of dissociated self and object representational systems in the transference/countertransference patterns in the treatment of adult incest survivors, such as the seducer and seduced, perpetrator and victim. Salter (1995) has written in some detail on the "internalized offender" in many victims and has noted important differences in the internalization pattern depending on whether the offender is sadistic or nonsadistic. Each of these trauma authorities is describing trauma-induced development of a type of pathological self or object representation (called a "released introject" [Bychowski, 1952] or "bad object" [Guntrip, 1961] in the early psychoanalytic literature).

Many types of pathological self representations can conceivably develop as a consequence of traumatization, and they have very important consequences for the patient's subsequent life. First, these pathological self representations are dissociated from the consciously available overall sense of self (Brown & Fromm, 1986; van der Hart & Nijenhuis, in press, a). Second, conscious acceptance of these dissociated representations and the intense aggression-related affects associated with them are strongly defended against. Third, following the trauma, these dissociated representations endure as part of the individual's inner psychic structure. Fourth, these dissociated representations carry on a quasi-autonomous existence from the rest of the conscious personality system and can exert a sometimes powerful implicit influence over unfolding conscious experience and/or everyday behavior, especially interpersonal behavior. Fifth, under certain conditions such dissociated representations become activated. The result is a remarkable shift in state, wherein the dissociated self representation significantly increases its often destructive or regressive influence over unfolding conscious experience or behavior. Conscious experience is marked by episodes of intrusive reexperiencing or dissociative symptoms and/or by the potential for abuse or outright episodic dyscontrol (activated abuser representation) or remarkable insensitivity to one's own or another's suffering (activated failed protector representation). Perhaps the most horrifying discovery for any victim is the realization that he or she has the poten-

tial to be as violent and dehumanizing or as insensitive and unprotective to others as the abuser was to him or her. Merely entertaining the notion of becoming an abuser or failed protector in any way is typically so reprehensible that the impulse is thoroughly defended against. As one patient aptly described her experience of an activated abuser self representation during this subphase of treatment, "It is very hard to fight the enemy when they have established an outpost in your own head!" Few victims of abuse wish to acknowledge the extent to which they have internalized the perpetrator and possess at least the potential for abuse. Many will never act out this potential in a way that has serious consequences; some, of course, do.

Under certain conditions dissociated trauma-induced self representations can become activated or triggered, much as intrusive reexperiencing symptoms are triggered: (1) current situations directly or indirectly remind the victim of the original trauma; (2) the current physiologial and/or emotional state is similar to that of the original trauma; or (3) developmental transitions or stress destabilize psychological defensive operations so that the dissociated representations exert more influence than normally would be the case. For example, the normal developmental intensification of aggression in his toddler might trigger a Vietnam veteran father and create the need to distance himself from his son for fear of losing control to the influence of a killer self introject.

Abuser and failed protector self representations also become activated at certain points in the overall course of therapy as a consequence of shifts in defensive operations. Where they become activated early in treatment, further stabilization is indicated. If relative stablization has been achieved, these representations typically become activated late in the integration phase of treatment. The increased manifestation of dissociated self representations at this point in the overall treatment could be understood as a consequence of the intense existential crisis that memory integration precipitates (Steele & Colrain, 1990; van der Hart et al., 1993). It could also be understood as a consequence of the progressively heightened awareness of the self over the course of the integration phase.

At some point the contents of the self—feelings, self talk, and beliefs—and perceptions of one's own coping and defensive stategies increasingly come into awareness. Even later the sense of self itself becomes the object of awareness ("I feel like I'm fragmented . . . in parts . . . don't feel whole"). At a critical point even the non-DID patient begins to discover and report the extent to which dissociative mechanisms have contributed to fragmenting what was previously taken to be a unitary sense of self. As the dissociated self representation(s) come into awareness, the patient becomes acutely aware of the disavowed parts and the consequent disruption of the unity of consciousness. In psychoanalytic terms, we might say that attention cathexis over the course of the integration phase is progressively attuned to self experience. We call this shift in awareness *progressive interiorization*. Awareness progressively shifts from the external traumatic event or action, to the internal content of experience of that event, and finally to the sense of self itself (i.e., reflexive awareness of the self representation) during the overall course of the integration phase of treatment.

For the most part, these dissociated representations are so rigidly defended against that signs of their activation in treatment can be observed only indirectly through shifts in defensive operations and symptom manifestations, through their implicit and often subtle influence on everyday behavior, and through the regressive swings of the transference. However, as a natural consequence of interiorization, these dissociated representations come increasingly into awareness over the course of therapy, often resulting in dramatic shifts in the treatment process, which mark the transition between the memory integration and representational subphases of the integration stage of treatment. Some common signs of their activation in the course of treatment are a sudden increase in suicidality or depression, increased self-mutilation or episodic dyscontrol, a marked increase in dissociation, or a significant increase in somatization after these clinical problems have for the most part subsided. Other signs of activation include: clinical evidence of splitting, a marked increase in manifest aggression in the transference, and the non-DID patient's report of a strong subjective sense of fragmentation or being "in parts" that had not been reported previously. In the DID patient, the perpetrator alters play a very active role in this phase of the overall treatment.

Three main strategies have been described in the professional trauma treatment literature to facilitate representational integration. Dissociated trauma-induced self representations like the abuser self and the failed protector self can be viewed from two perspectives: (1) from the perspective of the representation and (2) from the perspective of the impulses and affects associated with that representation. Thus, two essential strategies used for integrating these representations include: (1) those that work with the representations directly and (2) those that work with the associated impulses and affects.

(1) At least three kinds of representational strategies have been reported. (a) Strategies based on studies of *projective identification* (Grotstein, 1981) assume that the aggressive and sadistic content of the self system has been "translocated" out of the self into the object. The goal of therapeutic interventions with respect to a dissociated perpetrator self is to get the patient to relocate the intense aggression back within the self representation, i.e., increasingly to "own" the potential or real acts of aggression and abuse against others.

(b) Strategies based on *ego state therapy* reframe the adaptive function of the perpetrator part(s) and foster communication across ego states with conflictual views, the outcome of which is, at the least, resolution of conflicts across these separate states of the entire personality system and, at best, integration of them. The therapist uses ego state methods much as if he or she were conducting group therapy with the various dissociated representations and the everyday conscious self representation (Watkins & Watkins, 1979–80, 1981).

(c) Imagery and visualization techniques have been used in which the patient imagines these dissociated representations blending together (Kluft, 1993b). *Fusion techniques* are designed to actively structure directly bringing together the dissociated representations at the right point in the overall treatment.

(2) Strategies that focus on the aggressive impulse itself largely center on *revenge fantasies*. Abuse patients typically find it very difficult to acknowledge consciously their own aggressive and especially their own sadistic fantasies. "Justifiable aggression" in fantasy, i.e., against the perpetrator, is sometimes acceptable to the patient. Thus, consistently focusing on revenge fantasies at the appropriate point in

treatment is sometimes the only way that the abuse patient can gain access to his or her aggression and begin the task of owning the aggressive and sadistic impulses as a dimension of the conscious sense of self. As aggression and the dissociated trauma-related self representations become integrated into the overall self representational system, the aggression is transmuted from a potentially destructive force into the strength and assertiveness of a healthy and unified sense of self.

The third method to facilitate integration of dissociated representations is through interpretation of their implicit manifestations in the form of transference reenactments (Davies & Frawley, 1994). According to Davies and Frawley as "these unsymbolized memories begin to emerge . . . the patient often feels besieged" (p. 149). These implicit transference reenactments "have to be made explicit, so that the patient can begin to tame and integrate currently disowned self representations and identifications" (p. 175).

New trauma-related memories are often reported during the representional integration phase, although memory retrieval is rarely the focus of this stage of treatment. These new memories are highly specific in content. The themes revolve around sadistic aggression, dehumanization, and extreme moral conflicts associated with certain types of traumatic or abusive situations. In other words, as the extreme destructive aggression that was heretofore defended against as if it were not part of the self no longer needs to be disavowed, state reinstatement increases the likelihood that memories for the extreme experiences of sadistic violation and moral compromise associated with this aggression will also come into consciousness. With DID patients, the perpetrator alters become especially active at this phase of treatment, because they typically hold the dissociated recollections for the most horrible aspects of the trauma story. Once these recollections are integrated there is typically little need to maintain dissociative defenses across the self representational system, except for the fact that dissociation has been overlearned and has taken on a life of its own.

There are a number of signs of representational integration in non-DID abuse patients: (1) ownership of the potential perpetrator self and one's own capacity for sadism; (2) ownership of the failed protector self and one's own capacity to be insensitive or indifferent to others; (3) acceptance of and taking responsibility for realistic harm caused to others, past and present; (4) themes of increased mastery over aggression in fantasy; (5) increased behavioral assertiveness concomitant with a decreased fear of one's own potential destructiveness both in treatment and outside; (6) a marked decrease in the utilization of dissociative defenses; and (7) a marked increase in the frequency of reported fusions of previously dissociated representations.

Greaves (1989) has described a number of markers in DID patients moving toward integration, such as increased interpersonality communication, cooperation from previously malevolent alters, increased co-presence and co-consciousness, and reported spontaneous fusions. Kluft (1982, 1993b) has reported a number of signs of achieving integration in DID patients. These include (1) continuity of narrative memory, (2) absence of overt signs of multiplicity, (3) a subjective sense of a unitary sense of self, (4) absence of alter behavior under hypnotic exploration, (5) transference consistent with a unitary self representation, and (6) acknowledgment of attitudes and resources once manifest only in particular alters.

The outcome of *representational integration* is a fusion of any and all dissociated self representations with each other and with the consciously available self representational system, i.e., the achievement of a genuinely cohesive sense of self (Kohut, 1971) that is relatively resistant to subsequent "fragmenting shifts" (Lichtenberg, 1975), and that has integrated aggression, including the potential for sadistic aggression, with the self representation. With DID patients the subjective experience of achieving integration is often dramatic, although those who have studied the process remind us that integration typically occurs gradually (Greaves, 1989) and once achieved is relatively unstable over the next few years (Kluft, 1988b, 1993b).

Post-integrative Self and Relational Development

Early Post-integration Work

STABILIZING INTEGRATION DID patients who first achieve unification of the self representational system need additional treatment time to allow for their emotional reactions to unification, to blend their respective resources, and to consolidate the respective transferences of each alter personality into the single transference of a unitary personality toward the therapist (Kluft, 1988b, 1993b). In this sense, Kluft (1993b) views the patient's subjective achievement of unification as only a signpost of what eventually becomes genuine and stable integration. The early post-integration phase is characterized by relapses into fragmentation and by an unusual unevenness in skills and resources and recollections, until those of previously dissociated alters are fully blended with the conscious unitary sense of self. The patient must now learn to live in this world with this new personality system. As Kluft reminds us, "many therapists find that unification is the $^2/_3$ point of their treatment of the MPD patient" (1988b, p. 225).

In both DID and non-DID patients the central goal of the post-integration phase of treatment is *self and relational development*. Severe traumatization typically causes an arrest along several lines of development (Brown & Fromm, 1986; Davies & Frawley, 1994; McCann & Pearlman, 1990; Parson, 1984;). Now that the patient has become free from fixation on the trauma and has achieved memory and representational integration, he or she is able to continue progress along the various major lines of development, i.e., self (e.g., Lichtenberg, 1975), relational (e.g., Greenberg & Mitchell, 1983), and affective development (Brown, 1993).

SELF DEVELOPMENT With respect to self development, the burden of childhood abuse and also the parentification that accompanies some forms of child abuse like incest (Gelinas, 1983) interfere with the child's normally playful exploration of the world. As play is the vehicle of self development in later childhood, abuse often results in a *significant arrest in self development*. A common sign of arrested self development is *"impaired self reference,"* which Friedrich (1995) defines as "the absence of an internal base or model for behavior; for example, the victim's relative inability to be aware of his internal personal process and existence" (p. 163). In the severely traumatized adult the continuing self fragmentation can likewise cause arrested self development (Brown & Fromm, 1986; McCann & Pearlman, 1990; Parson, 1984).

During the early post-integrative phase the patient shows increasing signs of *self-awareness* of a wider range of internal experience beyond trauma recollections per se. Self-observational capacity is now more continuous than discontinuous (Bach, 1977) and the patient shows increasing skill in reflexively becoming aware of and formulating unfolding experience (Brown, 1993). Major foci of treatment are the quality of self experience and enhancement of self development (Kahn, 1972). The patient must *actively mourn* the victim or damaged self-image and must make the transition from survivor to thriver (Crowder, 1995). Overidentification with a victim or survivor self-image at this point may severely limit self development. The patient must also actively mourn the "bad" or "damaged goods" self-image to clear the way for the development of a balanced self-image that shows integration and acceptance of both positive and negative qualities of the self. The treatment typically also includes methods that actively enhance self-esteem. The therapist encourages the patient to actively imagine a healthy, non-damaged self and to work through the fear of the unfamiliarity of being normal.

With the maturation of self development the evolving self is seen by the patient to exist within more and more complex contexts (Kegan, 1982). The self's increasing context-sensitivity naturally leads to a greater awareness of how others' actions have affected the self and how the self has affected others.

As a consequence of this aspect of post-integration self development, the patient is able to *contextualize the trauma and appropriately assign responsibility* for its occurrence. For victims of child abuse this entails a greater appreciation of familial and transgenerational factors that might have contributed to the perpetration of abuse. Understanding the offender's psychology does not necessarily mean forgiveness, however. An incest victim, for example, may come to the realization of what motivated her father to sexually molest her and yet still wish to hold him accountable for the fiduciary obligation he has to her as a parent. A Vietnam veteran who participated in Operation Pheonix and was trained to assassinate villagers, many of whom were women and children, may come to realize the seriously flawed policy-making that led to such intelligence operations and still hold himself partially accountable for his role in the perpetration of atrocity. Parson (1984) has referred to this dimension of trauma recovery as "deresponsibilitizing." At this phase of treatment, but not before, negotiations with perpetrators or family members about previous abuse are sometimes, but not always, indicated. Disclosure is no longer necessarily motivated out of a need to remember more, to seek validation for abuse recollections, to act out the revenge of a dissociated perpetrator self, or other inappropriate reasons. Presumably, these motives have been worked through during the previous integration phase of treatment.

As part of post-integration self development the patient must also begin to overcome a long-standing pattern of *self inhibition*. The therapist helps the patient identify a range of new interests and aspirations, explore new possibilities, discover previously unrecognized talents and human potentials, and playfully experiment by engaging in a variety of new activities, until the patient can better discern which qualities, talents, potentials, interests, and activities seem most identified with core aspects of the self and which do not. In the context of these engagements the patient learns to discriminate what is "me" and what is "not me." The therapist helps the patient rehearse in fantasy potential areas of self exploration and to project him or herself into the future to imagine scenes of fulfilment in a life free of the after-effects of traumatization (Brown & Fromm, 1986). Beyond fantasy engagement, the patient must come to actually engage life in a new way. Overcoming self inhibition entails facing what one patient called "being scared of life and scared to hope." Self exploration in trauma survivors can also lead at this phase to the discovery of new values, life priorities, a central purpose to guide life, or enhanced moral development (Frankl, 1963; Wilson, 1989).

In addition to fantasy exploration of possibilities for the self, the patient is actively encouraged to embrace everyday life in a new way. The treatment focus shifts from "then and there" to "here and now" (Salter, 1995). Using behavioral exposure methods, the patient is given progressive assignments to engage in activities previously avoided out of fear and lack of self-confidence. With respect to work, the therapist helps the patient discover hidden resources and skills (McCann & Pearlman, 1990). With respect to daily stressors, the therapist helps the patient develop a wider and more effective range of adaptive coping resources and problem-solving skills (Lazarus, 1966).

RELATIONAL DEVELOPMENT Another major focus of the post-integration phase is *relational development* or what Herman (1992) has called "reconnection." The patient must learn to modify his or her object choice, i.e., change the maladaptive internal representation of relationship and the repetitive involvement in unhealthy relationships or avoidance of involvement based on this pattern. The patient must come to a realization of the subtle and not so subtle damage caused by staying in destructive relationships or avoiding relationships altogether. The therapist helps the patient keep the focus on examining factors that contribute to any one of a number of types of *relational disturbance* such as insecure attachment (Alexander, 1993; Cicchetti & Carlson, 1989; Crittenden & Ainsworth, 1989; Friedrich, 1995), repetition of traumatic attachments (Davies & Frawley, 1994; Miller, 1994), isolation and disconnection (Herman, 1992), or the repetition of core conflict relational themes across relationships (Strupp & Binder, 1984). The goal of this aspect of post-integrative work is to help the patient work through long-standing maladaptive patterns in his or her relational life both within the transference and in current life relationships outside of treatment.

A equally important goal is to help the patient establish healthy relational patterns. Ending destructive relationships and working through the internal object representational patterns that predispose the patient to relational disturbance in itself do not by themselves necesarily lead to *healthy relational behavior*. Many survivors of chronic relational-based trauma lack elaborate internal representations of healthy relationships. Encouraging the patient to rehearse healthy relationships in fantasy (Brown & Fromm, 1986) and to practice positive self-talk about healthy involvements (Meichenbaum, 1994) as a consistent focus of treatment can lead over time to the formation of stable, healthy internal representations of relationships that can serve as the basis for healthy attachments in everyday life. Complementing the work on internal relational representations and beliefs, the therapist helps the patient address everyday relational behavior by examining the quality of existing friendships and intimate relationships and encouraging the patient to explore new, healthy involvements. Another goal is to help the patient develop a healthy social support system, i.e., to reconnect with the wider community.

MODULATION OF IMPULSES AND AFFECTS

Sexual and physical abuse dysregulates impulse life. Victims experience sexual and/or aggressive impulses in the extreme—too much or too little—and find it difficult to stay aware of the impulse within a tolerable range. For victims of sexual abuse sexual desire disorders range from sexual compulsivity (too much) to inhibited sexual desire (too little). For victims of violence aggression ranges from chronic passivity (Morrier, 1984) to chronic irritability (Hoppe, 1962) or episodic dyscontrol (*DSM-IV*, 1994). For victims of sexual abuse, post-integration work entails helping the patient *work through any lasting sexual difficulties*, typically including sexual desire disorders—inhibited sexual desire (sexual aversion, dissociation, emotional numbing, or intrusive reexperiencing during sex) or sexual compulsivity (Schwartz, 1992)—and sometimes including problems with arousal and climax. For victims of violence, the work entails developing assertiveness skills and appropriate sublimatory channels for aggression.

For a variety of affects, likewise, dysregulation ranges from generalized numbing to vulnerability to affect storms. From a developmental perspective, these patients lack the capacity to tolerate and regulate impulse and affect states (Brown, 1993). The goal of this aspect of treatment is to help the patient learn the appropriate skills to modulate affective states, to develop the capacities to both experience a wide range of affects without numbing and tolerate the intensity of these affective states within some optimal range (Brown, 1993). In the transference the patient is likely to express considerable fear about the consequences of feeling certain emotions or having certain sexual or aggressive impulses, namely, that the therapist would abandon or criticize the patient for feeling such things. In working through the transference, the patient comes to realize that experiencing particular affects or impulses does not necessarily lead to rejection or ridicule.

PSYCHOPHYSIOLOGICAL STABILIZATION

For many patients with complicated PTSD, chronic, sustained hyperarousal and startle sensitivity persist throughout the stabilization and integration phases of treatment. If the work in the previous stages has been successful, intrusive reexperiencing symptoms and dissociated memory components and representations are remarkably absent from the post-integration treatment. Since the emergence of intrusive reexperiencing and dissociated symptoms is accompanied by physiological reactivity (Wickramasekera, 1994), the very conditions that sustain this physiological reactivity are now absent. Thus, complete eradication of the hyperarousal and startle sensitivity is possible. An appropriate objective at this point in the overall treatment is to help the patient re-train his or her psychophysiological system. Regular practice of relaxation training, with or without biofeedback, specifically reduces chronic hyperarousal, while prolonged exposure to startle stimuli under conditions of relaxation specifically reduces the startle sensitivity. Hammond (in preparation) particularly recommends prolonged, deep, meditative hypnosis and electroencephalographic biofeedback (theta brainwave training) (Peniston & Kulkosky, 1991) as non-medication stabilization and reconditioning procedures for overcoming conditioned autonomic hyperarousal. The overall goal of the psychophysiological training is stabilization and normalization of psychophysiological reponse patterns, so that the body stops reacting as if it were responding to trauma when trauma is no longer occurring.

COGNITIVE RESTRUCTURING

Within the trauma literature two perspectives have emerged on how trauma affects beliefs: (1) Since the pioneering work of Janoff-Bulman (1985) it has been well established that trauma "shatters" fundamental assumptions or stable core beliefs about self and world. Depending on the specific type of trauma, any given traumatic event may significantly damage one or more beliefs related to the sense of safety in the world (Janoff-Bulman, 1985), meaningfulness (Janoff-Bulman, 1985), causality (McCann & Pearlman, 1990), trust and dependency (Epstein, 1973, 1991), autonomy and independence (McCann & Pearlman, 1990), the sense of the future (Lifton, 1967; Terr, 1981, 1983a), the sense of belonging (Lifton, 1967), intimacy (McCann & Pearlman, 1990), locus of control (Rotter, 1966), and the distribution of power (McCann & Pearlman, 1990). (2) Specific traumatic events may also contribute to the development of new trauma-related beliefs or schemas, typically pathological schemas, such as beliefs about being permanently damaged or intrinsically "bad" (Roth & Lebowitz, 1988; Summit, 1983). Sometimes trauma contributes to the development of positive schemas, a renewed sense of ethics and spiritual meaning (Frankl, 1963; Wilson, 1989).

There is an evolving consensus in the professional trauma literature that a major focus of the post-integrative work must involve restructuring trauma-related beliefs. Many trauma experts also agree that addressing cognitive distortions is a consistent focus during each of three main phases of treatment. Addressing core beliefs, for example, is at the heart of McCann and Pearlman's stabilization work (1990). Identifying and working through the distorted beliefs of alter personalities are central to the treatment of DID patients during the integration phase of treatment (Fine, 1989a). However, most trauma experts agree that fundamental and stable changes in core beliefs are not likely until the post-integration phase of treatment, after intrusive reexperiencing and dissociative symptoms have subsided and the individual has achieved stable integration of the self representational system (Ross, 1989). Effective restructuring of beliefs presumes a unitary sense of self and a self no longer preoccupied with the intrusive past or the vicissitudes of symptoms, so that the focus is squarely on current and unfolding life experience.

Cognitive treatment consists of first identifying core beliefs that have been shattered or formed by traumatization, recognizing the irrational or distorted aspect of the belief, and then restructuring the belief (Hammond & Stanfield, 1977). McCann and Pearlman (1990) have described this process in detail with respect to PTSD patients. Ross (1989) has described a similar cognitive restructuring method for use with the various distorted beliefs of alter personalities in DID patients (pp. 260–266). Roth and Newman (1991) have described the process of transformation of beliefs in great detail. According to their analysis, the first task of cognitive therapy is to help the traumatized patient see that certain beliefs may have been affected by the trauma. Once a link is established between the distorted

belief and the traumatizing event, the patient is better able to see the extent to which this trauma-induced belief has become generalized to other situations to which it does not apply. The next step is to help the patient resolve this discrepancy and develop a more appropriate belief relevant to everyday nontraumatic experience. A similar procedure is followed for each trauma-related distorted core belief. Patients are also encouraged to view the trauma as a "meaning opportunity" (Frankl, 1963), as a vehicle to discover new meaning in life, new positive values, or a sense of purpose (Wilson, 1989).

Late Post-integration Work and Termination

The late post-integration work, consistent with adult development, focuses on the curiosity involved in discovering and formulating unfolding internal experience or the joy in mastering experiences in the everyday world (Brown, 1993). The patient shows an increased desire to understand unconscious motivations, distorted beliefs, and affective reactions to specific situations. Based on a greatly improved capacity for self-reference and reflexive self-awareness, the patient is now capable of analyzing his or her response to specific situations in a highly refined manner. At some point the patient realizes that he or she has internalized a set of skills for understanding and coping with everyday life situations. At that point the patient knows that the work of therapy can continue without treatment and discussion of termination begins.

CONCLUSIONS

This detailed discussion of phase-oriented trauma treatment is meant to convey to the reader the remarkable consensus that exists within the professional trauma literature about treatment of acute and chronic PTSD and DID. Experts in the trauma field have more or less adopted Janet's three-phase model of treatment: (1) stabilization, (2) integration, and (3) post-integration development. There are important differences in the literature about the emphasis at each stage of treatment. For example, some clinicians see stabilization primarily in terms of trauma-related symptoms, while others focus on the entire range of current symptoms and life problems. During the memory integration phase different clinicians see affective intensification as more or less necessary to achieve integration of the narrative trauma memory and associated affects (Peterson, 1991; van der Hart & Brown, 1992). During the post-integrative work some have emphasized relational development (Herman, 1992) and others self development (Brown & Fromm, 1986; McCann & Pearlman, 1990). Despite these differences in emphasis, it is clear that distinct stages of treatment can be identified, and within each of these stages clear treatment goals can be established. A variety of interventions currently exists to achieve these goals, and clear benchmarks of progress can be identified. It is also clear that a narrow view of professional trauma treatment as a form of "memory recovery therapy" is an unfortunately misleading and remarkably uninformed stereotype. This is not to say that a narrow form of memory recovery therapy is not sometimes practiced. Bad therapy certainly exists. But sophisticated phase-oriented trauma treatment cannot be reduced to a form of memory recovery therapy. The use of specialized memory enhancement procedures with select patients at a particular time in the overall treatment for a particular treatment goal does not mean that the diversity and sophistication of phase-oriented trauma treatment can be overlooked.

14

||||||||||||||||||||

Trauma Treatment and the Standard of Care

THE STANDARD OF CARE

In a malpractice suit the plaintiff bears the burden of proof to show that an alleged substandard treatment directly caused harm. How are we to define standard and substandard treatment? There is no simple or single answer to this question. Therefore, the courts generally have relied on several sources in defining the standard of care.

First, the standard of care has been defined by professional peer definitions of standard care. A practitioner is expected to provide a quality of treatment at least equal to the treatment provided by the average practitioner within the community of mental health professionals. Thus, professionals who are cognizant of their peers' treatment and whose own treatment does not differ essentially from generally accepted peer treatment are within the standard of care. Those who seek consultation and supervision from peers are, by virtue of their having sought to bring their treatment in line with that of their peers, well situated within the standard of care, even when there may be reasonable differences within the professional community about the best approach to a given treatment. Practitioners who work in isolation from their peers and whose treatment is markedly different from that of their peers are more at risk than the average practitioner of providing substandard care.

Second, the standard of care is defined in terms of regulatory and ethical guidelines within each professional discipline. Licensed practitioners across each discipline—psychiatry, psychology, social work, marital and family therapy, and psychiatric nursing— are constrained in their practice by state mental health laws and codes of ethics so that they are reasonably guaranteed to offer treatment that places priority on the patient's welfare and the needs of the wider community over harmful, self-serving interests. Third, the standard of care is defined by the experts within a given clinical domain, such as trauma treatment, i.e., by the authoritative clinical-scientific literature on trauma treatment, for example, and also by expert testimony on such treatment given in the courts.

Therefore, a practitioner's treatment of the allegedly traumatized patient is likely to meet any reasonable definition of a standard of care if he or she meets the following criteria: (1) occasionally or regularly seeks independent consultation or supervision, practices within a professional group or clinic where cases are periodically reviewed, or practices without peer consultation but sufficiently documents treatment so that a determination of its falling within the average of peer treatment can be made; (2) secures licensure and membership in his/her respective professional organization, and familiarizes him/herself with the state mental laws and code of ethics of his/her discipline; and (3) familiarizes him/herself with the evolving professional literature on trauma treatment (and memory) and/or participates in ongoing continuing education within the area of trauma treatment and related areas.

Substandard treatments usually are defined by one or a number of the following: (1) failure to secure consultation or supervision; (2) practice in isolation, the quality of which significantly departs from the the quality of practice generally accepted by the peer community; (3) failure to adequately document the treatment; (4) failure to demonstrate knowledge of and adherence to mental health law and ethical principles; and/or (5) failure to demonstrate knowledge of or ability to utilize in treatment the available authoritative clinical and scientific literature on trauma treatment.

The standard of care is not a static concept. As our understanding of trauma treatment, for example, evolves, *the standard of care is also constantly evolving.* Therefore, from a legal perspective, the defendant practitioner in a malpractice suit is judged by the standard of care at the time of treatment and not by the most recent standard. Thus, for example, malpractice suits against clinicians who practiced in the 1980s and early 1990s who currently are being sued for allegedly practicing "memory recovery therapy" and allegedly "implanting memories of abuse that never happened" (Loftus & Ketcham, 1994; Ofshe & Watters, 1994) fall outside of the usual definition of malpractice claims, since explicit knowledge of the risks of memory distortion and memory suggestion did not appear in the professional literature until the seminal papers by Loftus (1993), Ofshe and Watters (1993), and many since. Those who currently practice without taking heed of the literature on memory fallibility and suggestibility are at risk of future malpractice claims.

Substandard treatment should not be confused with quality care represented by a significant minority of practitioners within the wider professional community of practitioners. The courts have generally permitted the health professions to allow for reasonable disagreements about assessment and treatment, under the assumption that health and mental health issues are sufficiently complex to permit legitimate debate about different perspectives on, say, trauma diagnosis and treatment. Poole et al. (1995), for example, surveyed American and British practitioners listed in the respective national registers of highly qualified health service providers. They found, contrary to claims made by false memory advocates, that the vast majority of practitioners did not report a narrow focus on memory recovery in their treatments. However, "the majority indicated that it was important for clients with such histories to remember the abuse" (p. 430). However, the survey did show that "only a minority of therapists indicated a strong focus on helping clients recover suspected memories of csa [childhood sexual abuse]" (p. 434).

The fundamental issue here, in terms of malpractice law, is whether the practice represented by this "minority" is indeed substandard or whether it represents a reasonable professional debate about the value of memory recovery at least with the subpopulation of trauma patients who are fully or partially amnestic for their trauma. While this issue will ultimately be decided in the courts, it can not be readily assumed that all memory recovery, even as a primary focus of treatment, represents substandard care, although in some cases it may. The value of the Poole et al. survey is that it clearly corrects the false memory stereotype that all trauma treatment is about memory recovery. Moreover, it demonstrates that the wider community of professionals generally accepts the view that it is "important for clients with such [abuse] histories to remember the abuse" (p. 430), and that, for those who do not at all or only partially remember the abuse, memory recovery, within the context of broad-based treatment foci, is well within the current standard of care.

The debate centers upon those treatments where memory recovery is the primary or sole focus of treatment: can the professional community allow differences in opinion about the degree of emphasis on memory recovery within a given treatment, or is a narrow focus on memory recovery necessarily an issue of substandard care and therefore of malpractice? While this book may not resolve the debate, we believe that the reader will profit from a review of the current standard of care in trauma treatment, including what the professional trauma literature says about the role of memory recovery within the overall goals of trauma treatment. Consistent with the Poole et al. survey, the trauma treatment literature reviewed in the last chapter illustrated that memory recovery per se is rarely the sole or primary focus of trauma treatment, although it certainly has an important place in the treatment of certain allegedly traumatized individuals.

Our position has been that *phase-oriented trauma treatment* currently represents the standard of care for treating traumatized individuals, and that the integration of memory components, and sometimes the recovery of memories, plays a role within this overall treatment frame. In this chapter we will translate what we have learned from the previous chapters into a set a principles to guide the evolving standard of care in trauma treatment. The reader is also referred to other guidelines for treatment that have recently appeared (Brown, 1995a; Nagy, 1994). Our intention is to make it clear to clinicians what practices to avoid and how to minimize risks to clients as well as liability to the practitioner. In this sense, the false memory controversy is useful, in that it is helping the profession evolve a better standard of care for traumatized patients.

ETHICS AND PROFESSIONAL PRACTICE ISSUES

Training and Licensure

Those who conduct trauma treatment need to be qualified to do so. At a minimum, professional practice entails meeting the *requirements for licensure* as a health service provider at an independent level, according to the respective requirements of the state(s) in which the provider practices. Usually, this means that the practitioner has fulfilled the minimum requirements of successfully completing an accredited organized clinical training program toward an advanced clinical degree and a program including in its requirements participation in a number of supervised clinical practica, an intensive clinical internship, residency, and/or post-doctoral fellowship. While licensure requirements vary across states, the essential point is that practitioners licensed at an independent level have a broad familiarity with the field and have sufficient direct clinical experience, experience that has been carefully scrutinized by a variety of mentors and supervisors so as to minimize mistakes and excesses in practice that would otherwise lead to substandard care.

Licensure also means that the practitioner has become familiar with and adheres to the codes of ethics in his/her respective discipline and also with the state mental health laws regulating practice. Those who are not yet licensed at an independent level are expected to practice under the supervision of licensed professionals who have clinical and legal responsibility for their cases. While some false memory advocates have argued that licensure does not at all lead to competency but rather to a false view of competency (Dawes, 1994), we disagree with the nihilistic implication of such arguments. Until a better system evolves, training and practica requirements for licensure, however imperfect, represent a reasonable and generally accepted attempt to handle the problem of clinical competency and ensure at least a minimal standard of care. We are not convinced that giving mostly untrained trauma therapists within the trauma self-help movement freedom to practice is a better solution, especially those who have established practices without any or with only minimal formal training or direct supervision, and who are largely unfamiliar with the broader domain of assessment, treatment procedures, and clinical process beyond the narrow area of abuse treatment. The critical question is: how does the consumer come to know the training and competence of any given professional or lay practitioner so as to make an informed choice about entering treatment?

In most states licensure also requires that the practitioner demonstrate competence in one or a number of *specialty areas* within the mental health field and that he or she not practice outside of these areas of competence. Thus, practitioners have a duty to their clients to get specific training in trauma treatment before offering such treatment. Courtois (1995b) has remarked that courses on trauma treatment were rarely integrated into graduate-level clinical training programs until the last few years. Thus, for the current generation of clinicians knowledge about posttraumatic stress and dissociative disorders has come primarily from continuing education seminars and workshops.

Clinicians who utilize hypnotic procedures with trauma patients have a duty to get adequate training. Hypnosis should be used only by licensed health and mental health professionals with advanced degrees, within their area of expertise. Lay persons using these techniques with potentially traumatic material may be illegally practicing psychotherapy. Prior to using these procedures, licensed professionals should have received thorough training in hypnosis, meeting at least the minimum standards set forth in the ASCH *Standards of Training in Clinical Hypnosis* (Hammond & Elkins, 1994) for certification, or similar standards developed by the Society of Clinical and Experimental Hypnosis, Division 30 of the American Psychological Association, or the training standards on hypnosis established by the American Medical Association. Hypnotic uncovering techniques should only be used by health professionals with systematic training in hypnosis (Hammond & Elkins, 1994), who in addition have psychotherapeutic and hypnotherapeutic training in working with victims of abuse or trauma. Therapists using hypnosis, even in purely clinical contexts, should also be familiar with the most current legal rulings in their jurisdiction regarding the admissibility of hypnotically refreshed recollection.

Moreover, practitioners have a duty to their clients to *keep current on new developments*, both within the evolving standard of phase-oriented trauma treatment (including hypnotherapy where relevant) and within memory science. This book is designed to familiarize the practitioner with current knowledge. Chapters 4 through 7 and 11 review memory science. Chapters 8, 9, and 10 review the science of suggestibility. Chapter 13 reviews our current understanding of phase-oriented trauma treatment. While our hope is that the reader can keep abreast of these respective areas by reading a single source, we also hope that the reader will use the reference list to procure and read the original material as it pertains to issues in his/her clinical practice. Loftus (1993), Lindsay and Read (1994), and Brown (1995a) present reviews of the main issues in the trauma/memory debate. Van der Kolk and van der Hart (1991) and van der Kolk and Sapaorta (1993) are succinct summaries of clinically relevant hypotheses about trauma memory. Christianson (1992a) is good reference book on the emotion and memory literature, as is the shorter review (Christianson, 1992b). Loftus (1979a) is a basic introduction to misinformation suggestion. Gudjonsson (1992) is a detailed summary of work on interrogatory suggestibility. Pettinati (1988) is a good introduction to the work on hypnotic pseudomemory production. Brown (1995a) is a review and integration of works

on various types of suggestion. Herman (1992), McCann and Pearlman (1990), Parson (1984), and Phillips and Frederick (1995) are examples of reference works on phase-oriented trauma treatment. Brown and Fromm (1986), Hammond (1990a), and Watkins (1992) are standard texts on hypnotherapy. Pope and L. Brown (1996) review the main areas within which a therapist should have a working knowledge prior to doing trauma treatment: developmental theory, models of memory, suggestibility, trauma theory, dissociation, psychopathology, and assessment. While we can give only a few examples from a vast literature, our point is that practitioners have a duty to their clients to know the available literature, at least to overcome naive misunderstandings that may be inadvertently passed on to patients (e.g., that memory is like a tape recorder, or that trauma treatment means rapid uncovering and catharsis).

Informed Consent

A therapist has a duty to sufficiently inform a prospective client about the nature of the treatment to be provided, especially about its limitations and risks (Kluft, 1996; Knapp & VandeCreek, 1996; Nagy, 1994; Pope & L. Brown, 1996). With *informed consent* the accent is on "informed," not on simply getting written consent to cover liability. What should the patient be informed about? First, the patient should be given a general understanding of the treatment and what to expect. Second, if the trauma treatment potentially may involve enhancement of memory or the integration of memory components, the therapist should provide the patient with detailed and accurate information about memory. This information should correct myths, for example, that recovered memories are necessarily accurate. The patient needs to know that memory is imperfect, that most memories contain a mixture of accurate and inaccurate information, and that some memories, however emotionally compelling, may be quite inaccurate with respect to historical truth. It is advisable to inform the patient that emotionality about, vividness of detail about, and confidence in any given memory have little relationship to its accuracy or inaccuracy. Moreover, patients should know about common errors in memory, such as detail reconstruction, source misattribution, dating errors, and filling in the gaps. Third, if specialized memory enhancement techniques are used, the benefits and risks should be discussed (Nagy, 1994).

Patients should also be given sufficient information about suggestive influences potentially operative within and outside of treatment. If hypnosis is used, both therapist and patient alike need to be aware that hypnosis is not a truth serum or like the public image of a polygraph (which has likewise been found to be imperfect and is nonadmissible in court)—patients may lie, confabulate, or fantasize in hypnosis, and this should be conveyed to the patient as part of education concerning myths about hypnosis. As we saw in chapter 10, the problem has less to do with hypnotic techniques than with the context of hypnosis, i.e., the expectations that are part of the treatment relationship. Thus, it is better to correct misunderstandings about hypnosis and to set expectations accurately before proceeding (Kluft, 1996; McConkey & Sheehan, 1995).

Patients also need to be sufficiently informed about trauma treatment. Both therapist and patient are advised to understand the treatment in terms of a variety of broad-based treatment goals, but to keep a central focus on the chief complaint motivating the patient to enter treatment. To narrowly focus treatment or ignore the patient's reasons for entering therapy runs the risk of practicing substandard treatment. We believe that patients should know something about phase-oriented treatment, so that they do not have unrealistic expectations about uncovering and emotional catharsis. If the treatment is innovative or deviates substantially from generally accepted phase-oriented treatment, the patient needs to be informed about the experimental nature of the treatment. Whatever the nature of the treatment, the patient needs to be informed about limitations and foreseeable risks.

If a patient intends to make a legal complaint based on recovered memory, the clinician is strongly advised to inform the patient that the current state of the memory and forensic sciences is limited, in that it is difficult to guarantee the veracity of a memory based on the memory report alone, and that, if there is no independent corroboration, such a complaint is likely to be challenged in an adversarial legal system. Patients who enter treatment with a dual agenda of taking legal action based on a prior history of abuse and concurrently getting

treatment for the abuse are best advised that the legal and clinical agenda may work at cross purposes: taking legal action may destabilize the patient sufficiently to cancel out the treatment goal of stabilization, and proceeding with treatment while a legal action is pending, especially if hypnosis is used, may compromise the legal action in making memory claims potentially impeachable on the grounds of undue suggestion. Such informed consent is designed to protect the rights of patients to testify in court.

Several lines of research within memory science have suggested *strategies to inform clients that reduce memory distortion*. Research has shown that giving explicit warnings that not all of what is remembered is true significantly reduces misinformation suggestibility (Green et al., 1982; Mulder & Vrij, 1996; O'Sullivan & Howe, 1995; Warren et al., 1991). Thus, such warnings incorporated into informed consent procedures are directly designed to minimize memory distortion. In another study, children were not only warned but were given explicit instructions "to tell only what they really remembered" (Saywitz & Moan-Hardie, 1994, p. 413; cf. Warnick & Sanders, 1980, but negative results were also reported by Moston, 1987). With children some protocols have included instructions on how to answer questions with "I don't know" . . . "I don't want to say" . . . "I'm too scared to answer" . . . and "I don't understand what you're saying" (Hoorwitz, 1992). Saywitz and Moan-Hardie (1994) supplemented similar verbal instructions with visual aids, e.g., a picture of a child shrugging his shoulders. They also discussed with the children the "cost of error," namely, that the wrong person would be punished if they gave the wrong answers. Mulder and Vrij (1996) specifically told the children in their study that the interviewers did not necessarily know the answers. Van der Hart (in press) also developed a hypnotic cue conditioning method to help very highly suggestible patients to resist external misinformation suggestive influences. The implication of these studies is that explicitly including warnings that memory is imperfect and permission to give a range of responses to memory inquiry in informed consent is likely to contribute to increasing resistance to memory suggestions effects (cf. also Saywitz, 1995), especially if a combination of such methods are used (Mulder & Vrij, 1996). O'Sullivan and Howe (1995) say, "belief in memory vulnerability and suggestibility increases vigilance, which increases the probability of detecting misinformation" (pp. 106–107).

It is advised that the therapist discuss the information about memory and treatment in detail with the patient, creating an opportunity to answer the patient's questions and clarify points that remain unclear. We advise closing this discussion by giving the patient a written summary of the main points about memory fallibility and suggestibility, trauma treatment, and the legal implications of the treatment.

Duties Owed

Generally speaking, the therapist owes a duty primarily to the patient in treatment or previously in treatment with him or her. As we have seen, this duty means providing treatment with awareness of the standard of care, maintaining a concern for the patient's welfare over all other concerns, and keeping abreast of current developments in the field that are relevant to the treatment provided. The question yet to be resolved is whether or not the therapist has a duty to parties other than the patient(s) directly in treatment. The courts have tended to be conservative about dual duties. The rulings regarding duty to warn and duty to protect are largely constrained to issues of dangerousness to self and others. In such extreme situations therapists have been found by the courts to have a duty to parties outside of the limited domain of treatment, namely, to a specifically threatened person and sometimes to a community placed at danger. As a challenge to this conservative interpretation of therapist dual duty, a number of recent malpractice claims have appeared in which plaintiff family members have attempted to sue therapists, arguing that the therapist has a duty to the patient's family, not simply to the patient in treatment, even though the family member or members were not directly in treatment with the therapist. It is too early to tell how the courts ultimately will interpret third-party dual duty claims. Of course, the success of such claims is crucial to legal and political agendas of false memory advocacy groups. Meanwhile, practitioners are advised not create unnecessary dual duty liability.

First, therapists should refrain from telling patients to cut off relationships with family members. In cases where the family is dangerous to the patient, the therapist's goal is to help the patient understand the risk from, as well as the loyalty to, the harmful party, so that the patient can make an informed decision about the best course of action. In extreme cases of dangerousness, consultation with clinical and forensic experts is strongly advised. Apart from these exceptional cases, we advise therapists to take a neutral stance regarding their patient's wish to continue or cut off relationships with allegedly abusive family members.

Second, we strongly advise therapists to think carefully before occasionally bringing other family members into treatment sessions with their client. The therapist may have the view that he or she is simply treating the client in question, and that having other family members occasionally come to treatment sessions does not constitute a treatment contract with the other family members. As we will see in chapter 15, this gray area should be avoided wherever possible. Some malpractice suits have included the argument that once family members come to any treatment session, even though they are not in ongoing treatment, the therapist owes a duty to them. Some courts recently have made a determination against the therapist in favor of the third party, although this has been more the exception than the rule (*Ramona v. Ramona*).

If a patient does decide to confront an alleged abuser, it is critically important for the therapist to clarify in writing that the confrontation does not create any type of therapeutic relationship between the therapist and alleged abuser. This should take the form of a written release by the patient that acknowledges that the confrontation may be emotionally distressing to both the alleged abuser and the patient. Informed consent documents should not be signed by the alleged abuser because that would create an appearance of a professional relationship.

It is inappropriate and goes beyond proper therapeutic roles and boundaries to encourage patients to institute litigation. Therapists should caution adult patients against impulsive actions of any kind based on information uncovered in psychotherapy or hypnotherapy, encouraging them to thoughtfully and critically evaluate this material for a substantial period of time, as well as consider potential negative consequences of confrontation or disclosure of this information. Frankel (personal communication, 1994) says,

What is essential to the clinical work is that the product of the inquiry remains in the treatment context; it is not essential that veridicality be established. When the content is taken out of the clinical office into the home of aging parents 20–30 years after an alleged trauma, or into the courts, the situation becomes complicated and is in fact beyond the competence of many clinicians.

In working with children, therapists may be bound by law to report allegations of child abuse, but there is no increased credibility of a child's statement over that of an adult, and it should be conveyed to authorities that the account was based on psychotherapeutically or hypnotically elicited recall and that the allegation is of unknown veracity.

Documentation of Therapeutic Work

The more serious or unusual the memories and allegations of a patient, the more thorough the treatment notes should be. Intake chart notes should document discussions of memory, issues of accuracy and completeness of memory, suggestibility, informed consent, the maintenance of a stance of neutrality and the avoidance of offering definite opinions in the absence of corroborating evidence, the chief complaint, the history of the present illness, the personal and family history, the diagnosis, and the formulation and treatment plan. Ongoing treatment notes should reflect a summary of the content of each treatment session; the treatment foci, procedures, and goals; and criteria that assess progress toward these goals. Where memory enhancement or integration is done, the notes should document efforts to encourage critical evaluation of therapeutically elicited material, minimize suggestive influences, discourage confrontation with alleged perpetrators, and explore the potential negative ramifications of such confrontation. Notes should include the patient's recollections before, during, and after any memory recovery session (Knapp & VandeCreek, 1996).

When specific techniques like hypnosis are used explicitly for memory enhancement we recommend even more detailed documentation. Here are some examples:

Note Prior to First Hypnotic Experience:
Elicited and clarified patient expectations concerning the nature of hypnosis. Educated pt. re: hypnosis, myths and misconceptions. Talked re: the imperfection of memory, that memory is not like a tape recorder, re: confabulation, re: hypnosis and memory, and obtained informed consent. Patient read and signed informed consent, and had no further questions.

Note Prior to Conducting Exploratory Hypnosis:
Before hypnotic exploration, sought to establish neutral expectations concerning whether further information would be uncovered, and re: the accuracy or validity of information that might be elicited.

Note Following Hypnotic Elicitation of a Memory:
Out of hypnosis, again discussed the imperfection of memory, and the inability to know what is accurate, confabulated, or partially accurate without independent corroboration. Helped pt. process out of hypnosis factors supporting or not supporting the potential accuracy or inaccuracy of memory. Actively discouraged pt. from confronting any alleged perpetrator without independent corroborating evidence.

Assessment

The intake interview should be conducted in a neutral, nonleading manner. The patient's expectancies, goals, and perceptions of treatment should be explored. If the patient is requesting hypnosis the patient's understanding of hypnosis needs to be evaluated. If the patient has beliefs that abuse may have occurred, carefully evaluate how the patient came to hold these beliefs, since they may influence therapeutic productions. Referral source expectations and their potential contaminating influences should also be considered.

The primary goal of the intake evaluation is to conduct a *comprehensive assessment* toward the development of an *integrated treatment plan* (Beutler & Clarkin, 1990; Hammond, 1990b). Outcome research has consistently demonstrated that treatment plans that are both broad-based and yet consistently adhere to well-defined treatment foci, which include the chief complaint, have the best success. Therefore, the intake evaluation needs to be comprehensive enough to gather sufficient information to frame these treatment objectives. The information needs to include assessment of: the chief complaint; history of the present illness; personal and family history; trauma history; signs, symptoms, and behavioral problems; developmental problems related to self, relational and affect development; cognitive distortions; personality problems; medical problems; ego strength and coping resources; current level of functioning; and current stressors.

Where allegations of abuse become a question, we strongly recommend that the practitioner conduct a *formal assessment of suggestibility*. As we learned in chapters 8–11, suggestibility is not a unitary personality trait. At least two types of suggestibility need to be assessed: (1) hypnotizability and (2) memory suggestibility. It is recommended in working with potential victims of abuse and other types of trauma that therapists evaluate hypnotic responsivity, even when the therapist is not necessarily anticipating the therapeutic use of hypnosis, since hypnotizability is a significant risk factor for pseudomemory production. Consequently, it may be advisable for all psychotherapists, not just hypnotherapists, to consider obtaining a formal measure of hypnotic responsivity, e.g., the Stanford Hypnotic Clinical Scale, the Stanford Hypnotic Susceptibility Scale, Form C, or the Harvard Group Scale of Hypnotic Susceptibility (see Hilgard & Hilgard, 1983; Shor & Orne, 1962; Weitzenhoffer & Hilgard, 1962) and the Hypnotic Induction Profile (see Spiegel & Spiegel, 1978/1987), to document the level of hypnotizability and determine potential risk of pseudomemory production. At a minimum, therapists should elicit hypnotic phenomena of a known difficulty level to ascertain hypnotic capacity.

Benefits of obtaining a formal measure of hypnotizability include the following. If someone is highly hypnotizable, the absence of an induction ceremony does not mean that spontaneous trances have not taken place (e.g., Frankel, 1975), for example, during interrogation, interviews, or through the use of imagery techniques that elicit hypnotic responses in high-hypnotizable individuals, even though a clinician did not use the word "hypnosis." In fact, under motivated or pressured conditions, highly hypnotizable persons may be more prone to enter a hypnotic state (H. Spiegel, 1974, 1980). Conversely, the fact that an induction ceremony was conducted does not mean that the person was hypnotized. Finally, some have argued that we may need to work more carefully with highly hypnotizable persons due to their potential to accept ideas uncritically and to confabulate (e.g. Orne, 1979). Because high-hypnotizable persons appear to be the population most likely to manifest dissociative phenomena, therapists may need to work extra cautiously with these patients. Standardized procedures with norms and known psychometric properties will become especially important in the forensic setting because they comply with Daubert ruling criteria for something testable, repeatable, and falsifiable (*Daubert v. Merrell Dow Pharmaceuticals, Inc.*, 125 L.Ed.2d 469, 1993).

Awareness of the level of hypnotic responsivity of a patient also alerts the clinician to those individuals who may have greater potential vulnerability for pseudomemory production in or out of hypnosis. In situations involving allegations that therapists have encouraged the production of false memories, documentation that the patient scored low in hypnotizability may provide some supportive corroboration that the patient was not someone who would be anticipated to have a high likelihood for developing pseudomemories. In someone with low suggestibility, there is little likelihood that misleading therapeutic suggestions would be accepted. Thus, in *People v. Caro* (1988) a low hypnotizability score was found to be evidence that even though a hypnotic induction ceremony had been performed, the witness was not hypnotized.

The practitioner is also advised to formally assess memory suggestibility using the Gudjonsson Suggestibility Scale (Gudjonsson, 1984a, 1987a, 1992). We advise giving the GSS passage at the beginning of an intake session, followed by an immediate memory test. Then, the patient's delayed memory for the passage can be assessed again at the end of the intake session (50-minute delay) followed by the 20 interrogatory questions, the negative feedback instructions, and the 20 interrogatory questions again. The entire procedure takes about 15 minutes, 5 minutes at the beginning of the hour and 10 minutes at the end. Then, the clinician has a formal assessment of vulnerability to suggestive influences, such as supplying the patient with repeated misinformation or emotionally manipulating the patient. Patients' measuring high on the GSS Total score or on either the Yield or Shift scores are more likely to be vulnerable to suggestive interpersonal influences than those who score low. The therapist must carefully document the therapeutic interaction with this risk population. When the assessment shows that a given individual is in the high range of suggestibility, specifically memory suggestibility, the therapist needs to properly inform the patient of this vulnerability. With such patients we recommend that therapists avoid memory recovery. When memory recovery cannot be avoided, we recommend that the therapist explicitly discuss the patient's memory vulnerability with him or her and secure appropriate informed consent that the patient understands that any of his or her memories, recovered or not, are significantly vulnerable to external suggestive influences. Van der Hart (1987) has developed a cue utilization procedure to reduce suggestibility in patients "too susceptible to sugestions," but it is too early to tell if this method is effective in increasing resistance to memory suggestion in vulnerable patients. We also recommend that treatment sessions be videotaped, so that if subsequent allegations of undue therapeutic suggestion arise an independent assessment can be made of alleged claims.

It is very important, however, that the capacity for accepting hypnotic or interrogatory suggestions not be considered to be directly correlated with the likelihood that a particular memory is true or false. In other words, the fact that a person scores high on an hypnotic or interrogative suggestibility scale does not prove that his/her memories are false. At the opposite end of the continuum, people with low suggestibility should not be assumed to have only real memories. No matter what the susceptibility level, there is no substitute for independent corroboration. Performance on suggestibility scales is most useful in assessing in probabilistic terms the possibility of a suggestion having been accepted. It has nothing to do with whether an alleged memory is actually true or false. Such procedures simply demonstrate that the practitioner has carefully considered the question of suggestibility according to the best procedures currently available, and thus has sincerely attempted to meet an adequate standard of care.

As part of the diagnostic procedure the practitioner should be alert to diagnoses that research has shown to be associated with memory distortion.

Memory-vulnerable diagnoses include dissociative disorders, hysteria, and depression. Amnesia or dissociated memory has been consistently associated with a diagnosis of a dissociative disorder (Spiegel & Cardena, 1991). Likewise, false memory claims historically and currently have been associated with a diagnosis of hysteria (Kihlstrom, 1994b). Moreover, memory distortions have been well documented in depressive patients (Teasdale, Taylor, & Fogarty, 1980; Williams, 1992), although the nature of the memory distortion in depressive patients may differ at least qualitatively from that of trauma patients (except where dual diagnoses occur). Depressive patients have difficulty accessing primarily positive memories, while trauma patients have difficulty accessing mainly memories associated with negative affects. Depressive patients give general outlines of a memory but have difficulty reporting specific details, while trauma patients often give fragments and details of memories without a comprehensive picture of the abuse memory. Any controversial diagnosis should follow a careful standard of assessment, such as a standard structured interview like the SCID.

With the respect to the *evaluation of abuse allegations* the clinician is advised to view abuse-related memories along a *continuum of amnesia* from full awareness to partial amnesia to full amnesia (Courtois, 1992b; Harvey & Herman, 1994). For those patients who may have only a partial memory for previous abuse or trauma, and where there is any potential for future litigation we strongly recommend that the clinician conduct a videotaped interview as part of the intake, in which the patient is asked to produce a detailed free recall narrative of whatever he or she remembers about the previous abuse (cf. McConkey & Sheehan, 1995). The interview should include specific details of the abuse actions, located in time and context, as well as information about recovered memories and the circumstances under which the memories were retrieved. This videotape is kept as part of the medical record and stands as a statement of what the patient remembered at the onset of treatment, and is therefore untainted by allegations of subsequent suggestive therapeutic influence. In this way the therapist protects the legal rights of the patient by minimizing the likelihood that the pre-therapy record of memory for abuse would be inadmissible as evidence in a subsequent lawsuit.

There is a growing consensus that most patients do not initiate treatment to recover memories. Many patients fully or partially remembered the abuse all along. These patients seek treatment to alleviate their symptoms of distress, and with respect to their memories of abuse, to get a more complete understanding of these experiences. Nearly always this involves integrating previously dissociated affects and memories and making meaning out of the trauma. Sometimes the process will entail remembering additional details of incidents of abuse.

Other patients enter treatment because they have recently recovered memories of previous trauma outside of therapy, and are significantly distressed by this discovery. Usually they complain of intrusive reexperiencing, one of the symptoms of posttraumatic stress disorder. For such patients, the clinician is advised to assess and document intrusive and other acute posttraumatic stress symptoms, as well as to document the exact conditions under which the patient began to remember the abuse, to determine whether the patient has done any reading, viewed films, attended classes or groups, or associated with persons who have reported similar abuse that may have provided a contaminating influence that the therapist must be cautious not to reinforce. Although such experiences may provide possible contamination, we must at the same time objectively consider the possibility that events such as viewing a television program or reading a book about abuse may simply have provided a contextual cue eliciting a valid memory.

The assessment of *external suggestive influences* is critical when the patient's chief complaint is a suspicion of abuse without accompanying memory. In such cases the patient may not have an actual abuse history and the suspicion may represent contamination by external suggestive influences. In such cases the patient may also have a genuine abuse history and the suspicion may represent a memory for abuse that has been stored primarily as a behavioral memory, rather than as a narrative memory. External contaminating influences to assess include previous individual psychotherapy, referring sources, group psychotherapy, self-help groups, reports to the patient by others about their abuse-related therapy, discussions with family and peers about abuse, and exposure to television, movies, and reading material about abuse. We agree with Shapiro (1995), who places less confidence in patient's abuse memories recovered through prior therapies or self-help programs and more confidence in those that tentatively yet progressively are reported in current non-suggestive treatment.

A smaller group of patients enter treatment with no apparent memory of previous trauma. This group presents a particular challenge, in that the clinician must avoid both false positive and false negative determinations of abuse (Nash, 1994). It is certainly true that some of these patients manifest a "disguised presentation" of genuine abuse (Gelinas, 1983). It is also true that some of these patients were never abused. In such cases we must keep an open mind to both possibilities. Assessment of potential abuse in their history is necessarily probabilistic. We can say that certain signs and symptoms or certain risk factors are consistent with an abuse history and therefore raise our *index of suspicion,* but in the absence of specific memories and corroborative evidence no absolute determination can be made. Responses to checklists of signs and symptoms of abuse may raise our index of suspicion about genuine abuse, and in that sense they are useful in avoiding a false negative assessment of abuse (e.g. Briere, 1988, 1992; Courtois, 1988). On the other hand, false memory advocates have been correct in pointing out that symptom checklists have been misused, and their warnings help us to avoid a false positive assessment of abuse. The long-term effects of childhood sexual abuse are especially variable (Brown, 1990; Kendall-Tackett, Williams, & Finkelhor, 1993); the checklists of signs and symptoms of childhood sexual abuse are too general to make a definitive determination of abuse. In the current climate the practitioner is best advised to walk the middle path between the extremes of false negative and false positive diagnoses by thinking of all abuse assessment in probabilistic, not absolutist, terms.

Another approach to abuse assessment is based not on signs and symptoms but on risk factors present or absent in the history (Finkelhor, 1980). Finkelhor conducted research on a large number of hypothesized risk factors within the family history to see which ones were significantly associated with sexual abuse. The results demonstrated that children are at higher risk of sexual abuse if any number of the following risk factors are present: low socioeconomic status, social isolation of the family, imbalance in the educational level or power between the mother and father, marital dysfunction, little demonstrated affection in the marriage, conservative family values, having a stepfather, the father or stepfather shows little affection to child, mother shows little affection to the child, mother is absent or unavailable for a period of time, or mother is sexually punitive of the child. The results showed that:

> . . . among the children with none of the factors presenting their backgrounds, victimization was virtually absent. Among those with five factors, two-thirds had been victimized. The presence of each additional factor increased a child's venerability somewhere between 10 and 20%. The relationship is fairly linear and quite dramatic. . . . It must be remembered that even though the factors here suggest some ability to predict sexual victimization, only a small proportion of the variance (10%) is really "explained." (p. 272)

Finkelhor's *risk factor assessment* is a nice complement to the appropriate use of *checklists of signs and symptoms*. Like the use of checklists Finkelhor cautions us that risk factor assessment is necessarily probabilistic. However, the clinician who uses both approaches is likely to develop a more informed assessment of the index of suspicion of abuse.

If the index of suspicion remains high across approaches, the practitioner is advised to conduct two additional assessments to be discussed shortly: (1) The patient's *dissociative capacity* needs to be evaluated, since amnesia for abuse is typically associated with dissociation. (2) The patient's *suggestibility* needs to be assessed to rule out the likelihood that subsequent recovery of abuse memories is a function of suggestibility. Thus, our confidence level in suspecting genuine abuse is raised when the patient presents with: signs and symptoms consistent with abuse; five or greater family history risk factors associated with abuse; clear evidence of dissociation; and no evidence of being in the high range of hypnotic or memory suggestibility. Conversely, our confidence level is lowered when one of more of these four criteria cannot be met.

Regardless of the index of suspicion established through such assessment procedures, a practitioner needs to exercise great caution about what he or she communicates to the patient about his or her suspicions of abuse. As false memory advocates have pointed out, a clinician who first raises the possibility of abuse to the patient, prior to the patient's recovering any memories of abuse, may be suggesting abuse to the patient with no genuine abuse history (Yapko, 1994a). However, the clinician need not go to the other extreme of never saying anything about suspected abuse to a patient. In our opinion, the problem is more *how* it is communicated than *whether* it is communicated. As discussed in chapter 12, probabilistic communication of risk, say, for developing a medical condition in the future, or risk of developing complications to a medical procedure, is common is medical practice, and may retain a place in trauma treatment at least under certain conditions.

A practitioner should avoid two mistakes: (1) giving an "abuse diagnosis" or a "repressed memory diagnosis," because abuse, technically speaking, is not a *diagnosis*. Assessment of the index of suspicion of abuse is the correct term. (2) Communicating an index of suspicion of abuse to a patient should *never* be done prior to a formal assessment of suggestibility. If the patient is found to be highly hypnotizable or highly memory suggestible (according to the GSS), then an index of suspicion of abuse should never be communicated to the patient.

However, if upon formal prior assessment of suggestibility the patient is found to be in the low or average range of hypnotic or memory suggestibility, probabalistic communication about an index of suspicion of abuse is not precluded, depending on *when* and *how* it is communicated. Certainly no such communication should occur before the completion of a comprehensive intake evaluation, which includes the four criteria listed above. After such an evaluation, if it is the clinician's judgment that communicating his or her index of suspicion is in the patient's best interest, then the discussion should include appropriate qualifications. The practitioner needs to raise the question in probabilistic terms and must say that there is no way of determining with absolute certainty from signs and risk factors that genuine abuse had occurred. We advised that the clinician and patient also raise questions in their discussion about factors in the patient's history other than abuse that might account for some of the patient's symptoms. In other words, communicating an index of suspicion about abuse is best done as one of a number of hypothesis, not as the only or central idea. Such communication is consistent with some research on suggestion effects, which has shown that memory suggestibility is significantly decreased when misinformation is logically subordinate and increased when the information is a central part of the message (Baker & Wagner, 1987).

When making a formal diagnosis, the clinician needs to guard against under- and over-diagnosis. To stay within the standard of care practitioners should adhere to the diagnostic criteria described in *DSM-IV* (American Psychiatric Association, 1994). While PTSD might be the appropriate diagnosis for traumatized patients, the clinician should guard against making the diagnosis of PTSD when criterion A in *DSM-IV* has not been fulfilled, i.e., an identifiable traumatic stressor that would cause symptoms in almost anyone. The problem of making a PTSD diagnosis occurs for patients who fulfill the other three criteria but who have no memories for trauma or abuse. False memory advocates are correct in claiming that making a PTSD diagnosis in the absence of abuse memories is suggestive, in that it implies that abuse has occurred.

Technically speaking, PTSS (posttraumatic stress symptoms) is the appropriate diagnosis if there are intrusive, numbing, and physiological symptoms but no known stressor. In cases where the diagnosis of PTSD might be controversial or where there is a potential for litigation, we advise using a more formal structured interview in making the diagnosis. The posttraumatic stress disorder (PTSD) and disorders of extreme stress (DESNOS) sections of the Structured Clinical Interview for Diagnosis (SCID; Spitzer & Williams, 1986) and Clinically Administered PTSD Scale (Blake et al., 1990) are particularly useful. The MMPI-2 has three PTSD scales associated with it (e.g., Slenger & Kulka, 1989). The MMPI-2 has the added advantage of report distortion scales (L, F, K, VRIN, TRIN). Thus, greater confidence can be placed in the PTSD diagnosis if the patient measures high on the respective PTSD subscales of the MMPI-2 and measures low on the report distortion scales.

Self-report scales assessing trauma are also useful: the Impact of Events Scale (Horowitz, Wilner, & Alvarez, 1979), the civilian version of the Mississippi Scale (Keane, 1989; Keane, Caddell, & Taylor, 1988), and the Cincinnati Stress Response Schedule (Green, 1993). Most of these do not take a great deal of the clinician's time to administer. In chapter 17 we will see that physiological profiling can be an objective way to assess for PTSD criterion D in *DSM-IV*, namely, the degree of physiological reactivity associated with symptoms (Wickramasekera, 1994). The use of any of all or these procedures demonstrates the clinician's carefulness to diagnosis within the standard of care.

The clinician also has to guard against making an under- or over-diagnosis of dissociative identity disorder (DID). The Dissociative Experience Scale (DES, Bernstein & Putnam, 1986), while not a diagnostic instrument, alerts the clinician to the presence of significant dissociative symptoms at least in probabalistic terms. We recommend that a formal structured clinical interview be given to those patients who score high on the DES. Examples of structured interviews useful in diagnosing DID are the Dissociative Disorders Interview Schedule (Ross, 1989) and the SCID-D (Steinberg, 1993). The former has the advantage of being shorter to administer; the latter has the advantage of greater diagnostic validity.

The diagnosis of DID has become highly controversial. While DID is generally accepted in that it appears in *DSM-IV*, a vocal minority of clinicians has argued that DID is not a valid diagnosis (Merskey, 1992). Alleging that the diagnosis of DID does not exist except in being iatrogenically suggested by therapists has recently been a strategy in malpractice claims initiated or encouraged by false memory interest groups. Therefore, even where evidence for a DID diagnosis seems unequivocal, we recommend that practitioners carefully document how they arrived at a DID diagnosis and include evidence from objective psychological testing and structured interviews in their assessment and documentation.

EVALUATING PATIENT AND THERAPIST EXPECTATIONS AND BELIEFS ABOUT TREATMENT

The therapist should gather information from both the patient and prior therapists about all *previous treatments*, especially about what the patient felt was especially helpful or unhelpful about each. In order to gather information about what to expect about the unfolding treatment alliance and transference the therapist needs to ask detailed questions about how the patient perceived the relationship with each therapist. If the patient has been in previous treatment, there is no need to reinvent the wheel. Inquiring about what worked and what failed from both the patient's and previous therapist's perspective allows the new therapist to avoid the same pitfalls and design a treatment that enhances what is likely to work. Especially when the patient has a borderline and dissociative identity disorder diagnosis, the new therapist must be alert to a previous history of "therapy-interfering behaviors" (Linehan, 1993) or "self-defeating behaviors" (Beutler & Clarkin, 1990), most of which are based upon negative self-talk and maladaptive beliefs about treatment and human relationships. To reduce the risk that the patient will enter into an unproductive or destructive treatment relationship, it is critical that the therapist identify the pattern of self-defeating beliefs and have a sufficient understanding of the kind of therapy-interfering behaviors that might occur, like missing appointments, coming late, making excessive demands for extra-therapeutic contact, failing to pay the bill, or establishing a continual crisis orientation that distracts from treatment goals (Linehan, 1993).

We recommend that the therapist also evaluate the patient's *motivation* for treatment and the "*stage-of-change*" (Prochaska & DiClemente, 1984). According to the stage-of-change model each stage—precontemplation, contemplation, action, and maintenance—requires a different set of interventions. Most patients enter treatment during the contemplative phase, when they are disturbed by their problems and actively seeking a solution to them. The most problematic group of patients are those who seek treatment in the precontemplative stage. They are not disturbed enough by their problems to seek change, and often either drop out of treatment or continue to go through the motions without working towards change. Assessment tools are now available to identify stage-of-change characteristics (Rustin & Tate, 1993). Using such instruments, the clinician is able to identify precontemplative patients at the onset of treatment, so as to design interventions to work through resistance to treatment and/or to enhance motivation

for change in treatment. The evaluating therapist needs to be alert to patient *hidden agendas*, i.e., reasons for entering therapy other than treatment, such as the wish to get out of a relationship, the wish to get disability insurance, the wish to find an expert witness for litigation, or the wish to appear favorable to the court determining sentencing or parole.

We advise carefully evaluating the patient's *expectations and beliefs* about his or her condition and the treatment he or she is currently seeking. We advise learning about the patient's own explanatory model for the illness. Getting information about the theory of illness is especially important in dealing with cross-cultural clients. Included in the patient's general understanding of the illness is a more specific understanding of the nature of trauma and abuse. In cases where abuse is merely suspected by the patient, who has no memories of abuse, it is critical that the therapist inquire in detail about how the patient came to develop the belief that he or she was abused. Moreover, the therapist should find out the specific ways the patient believes the abuse has affected his or her life, both in the past and currently. With respect to treatment, the evaluating therapist should inquire about the patient's expectations about the current treatment, both realistic and unrealistic. Where hypnosis is requested by the patient, it is especially important to identify unrealistic expectations about what hypnosis will and will not do. Included in the patient's general expectations about treatment is an assessment of the patient's beliefs about memory and expectations about memory recovery.

The objectives of evaluating the patient's expectations and beliefs are: (1) to *correct unrealistic expectations and cognitive distortions* that might interfere with treatment progress; (2) to ground the treatment in *realistic and neutral expectations* about memory; and (3) to establish *realistic hopefulness* about the treatment. As part of the informed consent discussion previously reviewed, the clinician has the opportunity to correct misunderstandings and provide accurate information about the patient's condition, the nature of abuse and its effects, the nature of trauma treatment, hypnosis and hypnotherapy, and the nature of memory and memory recovery. For example, when increased confidence in memories occurs following memory recovery in psychotherapy or hypnotherapy, it is often due to unrealistic expectations of accurate recall on the part of the patient and/or therapist. It is critical that the therapist establish neutral expectations about memory recovery—neither falsely guaranteeing that recovered memories are usually accurate nor nihilistically emphasizing memory inaccuracy. Patients are best told that most recovered memories contain a mixture of accurate and inaccurate information, that recovered memories for salient emotional experiences, including trauma, are sometimes quite accurate for the gist of the experience, and that recovered memories for such experiences are sometimes quite inaccurate in detail and sometimes inaccurate even for the gist of the past experience. They are also best told that it is difficult to discriminate between accurate and inaccurate elements in any recollection based on the memory report itself. Apart from the issues about memory, there is an appropriate time and place for a therapist to confidently engender expectancies that the patient will get better.

Therapists must honestly assess their own *beliefs and potential biases* specifically about trauma. As advocates of the false memory position have correctly pointed out, therapists who can see trauma *only* as the primary etiology of the range of current signs and symptoms, and who zealously and narrowly pursue memory uncovering from the beginning of treatment with a complete disregard for stabilization, are at considerable risk to produce false beliefs in patients about past experiences. Pope and L. Brown refer to this phenomenon as a "premature cognitive commitment" to the abuse hypothesis (1996, pp. 116–117). They add that a therapist must be willing to observe and correct his/her own "cognitive distortions" about the patient and the treatment, especially if the therapist has an abuse background. Yet, a therapist who is equally aware of the fact that real trauma sometimes presents in a disguised manner, and also that harmful false beliefs about abuse that never happened sometimes manifest in psychotherapy, is likely to conduct therapy with a kind of careful scrutiny justified by the complexity of the task. Above all, the therapist should guard against expectations about remembering abuse that might place a demand or response bias upon the patient to come up with memories, mostly through guessing, that are therefore mostly historically inaccurate.

There have been a number of attempts to conduct research on therapists' beliefs (Garry, Loftus, & Brown, 1994; Poole et al., 1995; Yapko, 1994b). Most of this research has been conducted by advocates of the false memory position in an attempt to illustrate widespread distorted beliefs held by therapists about repression, naive realism about memory, enthusiasm for memory recovery, etc. Some of these surveys have serious sampling biases. Rather than being surveys of professional practitioners, for example, the Garry et al. survey was conducted with "graduate students" and the Yapko survey primarily with master's-level practitioners. Many of the questions on these surveys are constructed in a way to create response bias. Some questions force therapists to endorse extreme views, while no option is provided to endorse less extreme views (e.g., "The mind is like a computer, accurately recording events as they occurred" [Yapko, 1994b]).

The Poole et al. study corrects for some of the more blatant design flaws in the other studies. Our interpretation of the results is that the great majority of professional therapists do not hold extreme views about memory, suggestion effects, rates of child abuse, the role of abuse in the etiology of symptoms, the importance of remembering abuse in treatment, or the specific role of memory recovery techniques in treatment. The Poole et al. survey suggests that some minority of professional practitioners may have more extreme views. However, what some false memory advocates wish to interpret as "extreme views" sometimes represent reasonable disagreements within the field between advocates of the false memory and trauma accuracy positions, such as the belief that traumatic memories can be pushed out of awareness or that relatively accurate memories can sometimes be recovered (Garry et al., 1994).

Clinicians who wish to find out whether or not their treatment-related beliefs are in line with or deviant from the beliefs generally held by the majority of the wider professional community are advised to take the Poole et al. survey and compare their responses to individual items to the group responses.

Therapists who have their own abuse history have a special duty to their trauma patients not to let their abuse background interfere with the treatment. They should exercise particular caution to ensure that their own abuse issues have been adequately resolved. Such individuals should take extra care to monitor their own countertransference reactions and expectations that may be conveyed while providing psychotherapy and hypnosis services (Pearlman & Saakvitne, 1995). Having an abuse background is both an asset and liability to treatment. On the one hand, the therapist who has sufficiently worked through his or her own abuse background has the potential to be especially empathic to the abuse patient. On the other hand, the therapist must be on guard not to overidentify with the patient in any way. Some common forms of *overidentification* include overconfidence in memory accuracy and the reality of abuse reports, overzealous memory recovery, and focus on trauma-related themes at the expense of other legitimate treatment goals. The reader is referred to Pearlman and Saakvitne (1995) for a detailed review of working with countertransference with traumatized clients.

THE TREATMENT RELATIONSHIP

The treatment relationship should be well grounded in professionalism and ethical consideration of the patient's welfare (Pope & L. Brown, 1996). Above all else, abused patients need good *boundaries* in the treatment relationship (Knapp & VandeCreek, 1996). Unfortunately, however, the majority of patients who are victims of minor or major boundary violations in treatment, like sexual misconduct, have previous trauma histories (Schoener et al., 1989). Therapists who have personal histories of trauma need to be especially mindful of establishing good boundaries and not overidentifying with their patients, although recent research has shown that "a personal trauma history does not appear to negatively impact the therapist's response to trauma work" (Follette, Polusny, & Milbeck, 1994, p. 281). Trauma patients have an uncanny ability unconsciously to select therapists who have poor boundaries and thus manage to repeat their victimization. The best treatment for a patient who has been a victim of previous boundary violations is one that adheres to impeccable boundaries (Peterson, 1992). If a therapist is unaware of the range of potential boundary violations that could be damaging in treatment, he or she is advised to become familiar with

recent work in this area (e.g., Milgrom, 1992).

A therapist working with trauma patients needs to be especially sensitive to power dynamics in the treatment relationship. Most abuse, both physical and sexual, involves abuse of power. Most intrafamilial childhood sexual abuse occurs in a family wherein there is a significant discrepancy in the power distribution between the two parents (e.g., Finkelhor, 1980). Thus, treatments based on a large discrepancy in the power distribution between therapist and client are at risk of repeating the relationship dynamics of abuse. Therapists who are particularly authoritarian and those who establish rigid hierarchical relationships with their patients will inevitably have difficulty providing abused patients with just the right relational conditions for recovery. Therapists who establish a more egalitarian treatment relationship are in a better position to help their abused patients (Pope & L. Brown, 1996).

Being more egalitarian than hierarchical does not mean that the frame of the therapist-patient relationship is in any way compromised. It does mean that the relationship is based on an open, mutual exchange or dialogue about the assumptions and information guiding treatment, collaborative participation in defining treatment foci, and a genuine respect on the part of the therapist for the patient's decision-making capacity. Reciprocity in the treatment relationship, sensitivity to power dynamics, and basic human decency do not need to be at the expense of good boundaries. Moreover, an *open exchange* within the treatment relationship is best established in the wider context of the therapist's open exchange with his or her professional community. Therapists who readily and freely consult with colleagues about their work (while respecting confidentiality) and are open to new developments through continuing education already exemplify the principle of open exchange in their professional lives, making it easier to provide that in turn to their patients.

An important foundation of treatment with trauma patients is enhancement of the patient's sense of *autonomy* both within and outside of the treatment. Every attempt is made to explore and discover the patient's own resources for recovery. Stabilization and the other stages of phase-oriented treatment are built upon coping enhancement and through that providing the patient with a sense of mastery. If we have learned anything from painful treatment failures in the trauma field over the last two decades it is that treatments that foster undue dependency rarely succeed and are often harmful. Therapists who allow abuse victims to take a vacation from life to do memory recovery run the risk of fostering a harmful regression in their patients. Some experts who have consulted on many treatments at impasse now take the position that demonstration of the ability to maintain an adequate level of daily functioning, including meaningful work and supportive relationships, is not only a prerequisite to treatment but also a necessary requirement for continuation of treatment. A written treatment contract makes explicit the expectation that signs of a harmful regression or a deterioriation in daily functioning is grounds for termination and that both the patient and therapist are expected to proceed in a manner that enhances, not regresses, everyday functioning (Kluft, 1993a).

Another foundation of the treatment relationship is safety. *Safety in relationships* is painfully absent from the lives of trauma survivors, and thus is a fundamental ingredient in any healing relationship (Brown & Fromm, 1986; Herman, 1992). A safe relationship is one in which the relationship itself is not perceived as stressful. A safe relationship is also perceived as generally supportive of the patient's growth and confident in the patient's abilities. Treatment relationships founded on these principles not only foster recovery from trauma but also minimize memory distortion.

Overall, the relational conditions described here closely approximate the model of permissive hypnosis developed by Fromm (Fass & Brown, 1990). Yet, the model of a permissive treatment relationship need not be restricted to hypnotherapy. The same principles apply to the psychotherapy relationship: good professional boundaries; a collaborative, egalitarian relationship; a consistent focus on the patient's coping ability, inner resources and strengths, sense of mastery, and autonomy; a consistent focus on providing support and self-efficacy.

Providing a less hierarchical, more egalitarian, and open treatment relationship also reduces the risk of memory suggestion. Relationships that are more formal than informal have been found to significantly increase hypnotic pseudomemory production (Barnier & McConkey, 1992). High-status interviewers of children, namely, adult authority figures, are associated with significantly more memory commission errors than peer interviewers, at least in younger children (Ceci, Ross, et al., 1987; Goodman et al., 1990). McConkey et al. (1990) found that establishing rapport reduced the risk of hypnotic pseudomemory production. Young children provided with "substantial encouragement" and "considerable support" during interviews made significantly fewer memory commission errors specifically to abuse-related questions than did children who did not receive such support (Goodman et al., 1990, pp. 277–278). Moreover, children who made "self-statements to promote confidence" made significantly fewer memory commission errors in response to misleading questions than those who did not (Saywitz & Moan-Hardie, 1994, p. 415).

Closed social interactions are essential to the high number of memory commission errors characteristic of interrogatory suggestion (Gudjonsson, 1992; Gudjonsson & Clark, 1986). Conversely, treatment based on an open relationship would be likely to substantially reduce the risk of memory commission errors. The characteristics of this open relationship are: (1) a two-way exchange of information (no information control) between patient and therapist and an open exchange of information within the wider context of the patient's life and the therapist's professional life (no isolation); (2) minimization of the power differential between patient and therapist, yet in a well-bounded relationship; (3) a treatment based on encouragement of the patient's autonomy (no undue dependency); and (4) a treatment that reduces the stress of interviewing about the past (no interrogatory exploitation of stress as a means to pressure the interviewee about past events).

THE FRAME OF TREATMENT

In chapter 13 we learned of the range of patient management difficulties associated with the treatment frame. Patients with borderline or other personality disorder diagnoses, which often overlap the diagnosis of PTSD and or DID, often engage in a variety of self-destructive and/or therapy-interfering behaviors. The evolving standard of care is to use informed consent procedures and written behavioral contracts that clearly spell out the expectations of treatment and what types of behaviors will and will not be tolerated to continue treatment (e.g., Linehan, 1993). The emphasis of these procedures is on assisting the patient in reducing self- and therapy-defeating behaviors and to hold the patient responsible for demonstrating ongoing ability to tolerate a working outpatient treatment. Therapists are advised to familiarize themselves with recent developments regarding the treatment frame, so as to minimize dangerous management problems that might jeopardize the treatment, especially the management of boundary problems with trauma patients (Pearlman & Saakvitne, 1995).

TREATMENT PLANNING

There are a number of signs that the profession of psychotherapy has been moving in the direction of *integrative psychotherapy* (Beutler & Clarkin, 1990; Norcross & Goldfried, 1992). An integrative approach to psychotherapy is not limited to a particular approach or theoretical orientation but systematically selects the treatment approach and procedures or combination of approaches and procedures that best fit the givens of the clinical situation. A similar integrative approach to hypnotherapy has been described (Hammond, 1990b). An integrative approach to complex problems (Beutler & Clarkin, 1990) like trauma is best defined in terms of broad-based treatment goals, well-defined treatment objectives, a series of clear treatment foci, and a set of criteria by which to assess progress toward these goals. Practice within the best standard of care represents this integrative perspective.

Within the wider context of integrative psychotherapy, most trauma-related treatment adheres to a phase-oriented treatment approach, as described in chapter 13. A good standard of care is based on the development of a phase-oriented treatment plan with sufficient details for each of the three divisions in the overall treatment (stabilization, integration, and post-interation self and relational development), and with an adequate rationale for the the role of memory integration in general and memory enhancement in particular within this overall plan.

Hypnotherapy, like psychotherapy, adheres to an integrated, phase-oriented treatment plan (Brown & Fromm, 1986; Hammond, 1990b; Phillips & Frederick, 1995). A parsimonious, short-term suggestive approach to hypnosis is often the initial treatment of choice in treating less complex clinical conditions, such as single-incident, adult-onset PTSD. Tentative selection criteria for brief suggestive hypnosis include a history of relatively adequate functioning and adjustment prior to the current traumatization, symptoms that are perceived as egodystonic, good motivation to make changes, focal problems that are circumscribed and specific, the capacity to follow through with homework (e.g., self-hypnosis), and the ability to establish an unambivalent and positive therapeutic alliance, to cooperate, and to trust the therapist. When two to four sessions of suggestive hypnosis in a hypnotically responsive patient who meets these criteria do not seem to produce encouraging changes or symptom improvement, the therapist should explore the reasons for the resistance and shift to a more insight-oriented hypnotic strategy.

When a patient presents with long-standing and complex symptoms that have generalized to a large number of life areas, when the initial assessment suggests that adaptive functions and conflicts may be associated with the patient's problems, and when the patient's present life stressors and relationships do not seem to adequately account for symptomatic complaints, insight-oriented hypnotic techniques seem reasonably indicated as part of treatment. Hypnotic uncovering seems most compatible with patients who possess adequate impulse control and ability to tolerate affect involved in exploration, who are psychologically minded, verbal, and intelligent, who have the capacity for insight, who enter treatment with the expectation that insight will be curative, and who wish to pursue a therapeutic goal of self-awareness.

Age regression should not be done with a patient who does not give permission for the procedure. In more severely disturbed patients (e.g., those with serious borderline conditions, psychosis, or chemical dependency in addition to trauma) and where patient's ego strength is more fragile and regression potential is great, therapists must exercise considerable caution in using hypnosis for age regression or exploration, as contrasted with suggestive hypnosis and the use of self-hypnosis for symptom management and ego-strengthening. When a patient demonstrates an inability to organize material, extreme emotional lability, or spontaneous abreactions and frequent dissociative episodes, hypnotic uncovering techniques that loosen already tenuous control should generally be delayed until further stabilization has occurred. When these techniques are used with such patients they must be used with caution and only by very experienced hypnotherapists. These hypnotic methods must also be used with discretion in medically impaired patients, where the strain of recalling potentially traumatic material may endanger physical health. While therapists should be cautious about distortions to which more seriously disturbed patients may be prone, they should also realize that psychiatric disturbance does not necessarily compromise the validity or reliability of patient memories (Brewin, Andrews, & Gotlib, 1993), except under certain conditions (Dalenberg, 1995). Finally, in the event that issues arise in the therapy with legal ramifications, forensic guidelines should be followed.

False memory advocates have criticized the use of "specific memory recovery techniques" like hypnosis (Lindsay & Read, 1994; Loftus, 1993; Ofshe & Watters, 1993) on the grounds that such methods encourage confusion between memory and fantasy. The Task Force on Clinical Hypnosis and Memory of the American Society of Clinical Hypnosis (Hammond et al., 1995) has refuted these claims. In addition to the comprehensive guidelines recommended by the American Society of Clinical Hypnosis, Yapko (1994a) and Bloom (1994) have offered similar, though less detailed, suggestions for the conduct of therapy involving memories of abuse. The implicit message in some false memory arguments is that the introduction of memory recovery techniques like hypnosis represents substandard care. We disagree. Hypnotic methods have a long and generally accepted history in trauma treatment. Hypnotic procedures have a wide range of applicability for each stage in phase-oriented trauma treatment (Brown & Fromm, 1986; Phillips & Frederick, 1995). Only a small fraction of these hypnotic procedures are used specifically for memory enhancement at the appropriate phase of treatment with certain patients.

Even age regression may have an appropriate place. While age regression remains a controversial method to recover historically accurate memories, it is a useful method for enhancing affects and accessing self representations associated with childhood events (Nash, 1988). Also, as we learned in chapter 10, age regression can lead to retrieval of new, otherwise inaccessible information without compromising the accuracy of the memory. Thus, in the late integration phase age regression has a legitimate use if the treatment goal is to foster the integration of affects and memories, or of dissociated self representations and memories of abuse, provided that the abuse has been remembered all along or previously recovered by other means that do not pose a risk for having the patient mistake the compelling affects as evidence of historically genuine abuse.

The problem with the false memory argument it that is confounds hypnotizability, the use of specific hypnotic procedures for treatment goals other than memory enhancement, and hypnotic procedures specifically used for memory enhancement. The main issue is not whether or not hypnosis can be used, but how it is used, under what conditions, in what type of treatment relationship, for what type of treatment goal. The hypnotherapist whose use of hypnosis is informed by available scientific research about appropriate uses and limitations, who has carefully considered this information in the treatment plan, and who carefully documents these variables or videotapes the hypnotic treatment sessions, has made every effort to practice within the standard of care.

A similar false memory argument has been made about other so-called memory recovery methods, like guided imagery and journaling. Yet, the hypothesis that guided imagery per se contributes to memory distortion has not been supported by the scientific data. In fact, we have seen that imagery techniques have led to an increase in retrieved information without a decrease in memory accuracy in both adults and children. As with hypnosis, the potential problem with guided imagery has less to do with the use of imagery per se than with how it is used or misused. The same holds true for journaling. We do not recommend journaling as a memory recovery method, as has sometimes been advocated in the self-help literature (Bass & Davis, 1988). Yet, journaling as a means to integrate and make meaning out of discoveries in therapy is a legitimate use at the appropriate phase in the overall trauma treatment (van der Hart, Boon, & van Everdingen, 1990).

THE CONDUCT OF THERAPY

Interviewing Style

Therapists should conduct interviews in a manner that minimizes suggestion effects, especially those elements of suggestion that we learned in chapter 9 represent the higher end of the suggestion continuum, such as (1) psychophysiological destabilization, (2) information control, (3) repetition of misleading suggestions both within and across interviews, (4) emotional manipulation, and (5) interrogatory bias. Nonsuggestive interviewing, at a minimum, represents the opposite of each of these five elements of suggestion.

In suggestive interviewing the interviewer does everything possible to make the patient feel comfortable during the interview. If the patient reports feeling distressed by the interview, the therapist adopts stress reduction procedures prior to proceeding with the inquiry. Conducting an intentional stress interview departs significantly from this *principle of reducing the stress of inquiry.*

The therapist establishes an atmosphere in which the patient perceives the freedom to discover. Internally, the patient experiences the freedom to "say whatever comes to mind" (Menninger & Holzman, 1973), to explore spontaneous thoughts and fantasies, and to formulate experience as it unfolds. Externally, the patient brings this attitude of discovery into the domain of relationships, work, whatever he or she reads, etc. The patient learns to wonder about his or her reactions to various experiences and to bring these reactions into treatment for further exploration. The *principle of freedom to discover*, both within and outside of therapy, is as far from information control as is possible.

Quality interviewing is grounded in a deep sense of the patient's unfolding experience. The patient is encouraged to engage in an open-ended exploration of whatever comes into experience. Having established this attitude, the therapist is not to interfere with the patient's unfolding experience. Sys-

tematic leading and misleading on the part of the therapist represent a serious deviation from this *principle of not interfering with unfolding experience.*

The therapist has a duty to monitor his or her own ongoing reactions to the patient's verbalizations, so as to adopt a neutral stance toward the patient's productions. Apart from appropriate support to discover, encouragement to formulate, and empathic attunement, skilled therapists stay clear of bringing their own reactions to the patient's productions into the treatment hour, especially obviously manipulative reactions such as praise or blame, rewards or threats. These forms of emotional manipulation represent harmful departures from the *principle of neutrality.*

The therapist tries to listen to the patient's unfolding experience with "even-hovering attention" (Menninger & Holzman, 1973), i.e., with a curiosity free from biased preconceptions or therapist agendas. Both therapist and patient put the emphasis on the patient's, not the therapist's, understanding of unfolding experience. The skilled therapist tries to help the patient arrive at his or her own interpretation of experience before making interpretations. The task of the therapist is to assist the patient in formulating internal experience for the first time (Stern, 1985). Davies and Frawley (1994) make it quite clear why the therapist must refrain from communicating beliefs about abuse to the patient:

> . . . either the patient prematurely "accepts" the therapist's experience of reality as her own and begins to construct incest "memories" in a transferential need to please the therapist; or, as is more often the case, the patient becomes uncomfortable exploring her own trauma-related images and memories, because the therapist's certainty about their meaning forecloses on her own psychic elaboration of these thoughts. Here the therapist treads dangerously close to the parent who superimposed his view of reality onto that of the child during the original abuse. In either of these scenarios, something is being forcefully inserted into the experience of the child. (p. 110)

Therapists who operate with a confirmatory bias (Dawes, 1994) or a strong interrogatory bias (Gudjonsson, 1992) fail to understand the *principle of unbiased curiosity* about the patient's own ways of interpreting unfolding experience and jump to premature conclusions (Pope & L. Brown, 1996). Each of these principles can be found within any treatment that has a solid foundation in psychodynamic and psychoanalytic theory.

Memory Enhancement

General Principles

The majority of professional practitioners agree that remembering abuse is important in therapy (Poole et al., 1995). As we reviewed in chapter 7, there is abundant and compelling evidence for amnesia (full or partial) in certain patients across all types of trauma. Even some advocates of the false memory position have acknowledged that "forgotten knowledge, or the original memory, may nonetheless continue to influence the person's experience, thought, and action in the form of implicit [consciously amnestic] memory" (Kihlstrom & Barnhardt, 1993, p. 115).

For patients who have full or partial amnesia for abuse, assisting in remembering the abuse is a legitimate objective of treatment, well within the standard of care, regardless of whether the recollections represent more historical or more narrative truth (Spence, 1982). Remembering, integrating, and making sense out of previous traumatic experiences has a kind of "clinical utility" apart from the issue of memory accuracy (Nash, 1994). Memory enhancement certainly is within the standard of care when: (1) the patient's problem specifically is full or partial amnesia for trauma; and (2) when memory enhancement is set within the context of phase-oriented treatment, i.e., as one of a number of goals during the integration phase of treatment. We do not agree with those advocates of the false memory position who would have clinicians abandon memory enhancement altogether (e.g., Loftus, 1993; Ofshe & Watters, 1994). The issue is not *whether* it is done but *how* it is done. To put it another way: *the task of memory enhancement is to decrease memory ommission errors without increasing memory commission errors.* Following certain principles makes this possible.

First, memory enhancement that reduces the risk of distortion begins with the attitude of the therapist. We recommend that the therapist bring the general principles of interviewing outlined above into the specific situation of memory enhancement. The therapist must have *faith in the patient's own ability to remember,* and not prematurely demand or directly suggest that the memory will become increasingly clear. Pope and Brown remind us:

> Therapists can empower clients in a number of ways at this point in the therapy process. Clients can be reminded that they are free to make their own decisions about what appears to them in images or dreams or flashbacks, and that the therapist will not push them in particular directions. . . . The therapist can also support clients in searching for corroboration if this is what the client chooses to do. (1996, p. 197)

Otherwise, the therapist runs the risk of defining the patient's reality in the transference, much as the incestuous parent redefined the child-victim's reality (Davies & Frawley, 1994). Instead of repeating a "relationship of domination," the therapist and patient work to restore an intersubjective reality where the patient develops his/her own sense of the historical past (Grand, 1995a). In other words, memory enhancement is guided by the patient's freedom to discover and by the therapist's unbiased curiosity, non-interference, and neutrality. We know that *self-efficacy* correlates with successful outcome in many areas of treatment. There is good reason to believe that self-efficacy is important also in memory retrieval. Pope and Brown add, "the hallmark of competent response to a client in this circumstance is respect for the client's thoughtful consideration, questioning, and choices" (p. 200).

Second, the skilled therapist helps the patient to *tolerate ambiguity* and uncertainty about past experiences. In chapters 8 and 9 we learned that uncertainty about past events is a critical factor in vulnerability to both misinformation and interrogatory suggestibility. When uncertain, the patient is more likely to accept post-event misinformation and/or accept the interrogatory hypotheses of an overzealous interviewer. To reduce to risk of memory suggestion, both patient and therapist must learn to tolerate uncertainty about past experience, instead of pushing for "disambiguation" about the past (Gheorghiu et al., 1989). The therapist who pressures the patient to make his or her recollections less ambiguous, or who seeks premature closure about these recollections, will increase the risk of memory commission errors. Under such conditions the therapist has introduced a response bias that encourages the patient to guess or fill in the gaps. One way to help the patient learn to tolerate ambiguity is to explicitly teach the patient how to say, "I don't know" . . . "I don't remember" . . . or "I don't understand your question" (Hoorwitz, 1992; Saywitz & Moan-Hardie, 1994). Sometimes it is advisable to have patients practice responding to nonleading, leading, and misleading questions, so that they learn to discriminate among these types of inquiry. Patients should be helped to discriminate between questions asked or comments made, on the one hand, and suggestions given, on the other hand. When questions are asked more than once by the interviewer, patients should know that repetition of a question does not mean that the previous answer was wrong. Moreover, if they do not have an answer to a question, they need to know that this is a clearly acceptable response. The therapist must be careful to remain non-leading (Mutter, 1984).

Apart from these general attitudes about memory enhancement, the therapist needs to understand the differences among types of memory retrieval strategies. As we learned in chapter 3, there are four kinds of recall strategies: (1) free narrative recall, (2) cued recall, (3) leading recall, and (4) misleading recall. Numerous laboratory studies have made it quite clear that memory commission errors are significantly lower when a free recall retrieval strategy is used, and increase progressively along a continuum from cued, to leading, and then to misleading retrieval. Moreover, numerous laboratory studies have demonstrated that free recall over repeated interviews leads to a significant increase in the amount of information recalled without necessarily substantially increasing memory errors (Dent & Stephenson, 1979; Dunning & Stern, 1992; Geiselman et al., 1985; Malpass & Devine, 1981; Scrivner & Safer, 1988; Turtle & Yuille, 1994). Thus, the therapeutic process that most closely approximates *free narrative recall* is least likely to result in false beliefs about past trauma. Suggestions that supply content to the patient and misleading information are to be scrupulously avoided.

Clinicians should allow the patient to engage in relatively free recall, with minimal questioning concerning the content of the memory, for a sufficient duration of the treatment, until the meaning has been thoroughly elaborated by the patient. Questions about specific content and details should only follow the completion of a free narrative report by the patient. During the initial recall, therapists may wish to ask specific but nonleading questions about the feelings the subject is experiencing. Likewise, the therapist may sometimes simply repeat patient phrases verbatim to acknowledge hearing the statement of the patient, or may offer comments that encourage the patient to continue (e.g., "Um-hmm," "Yes," "Go on," "What are you aware of?" "Are you aware of anything else?" "Does anything else occur?"). Prior to questioning about content or initiating working-through techniques, patients may also be asked to return to the beginning of the event and to quietly review it for several minutes (Mutter, 1990). Be aware that information retrieved may not be veridical, but simply what the patient believes to be true.

Specific Memory Enhancement Strategies

While free narrative recall minimizes memory commission errors, it is not always successful as a retrieval strategy. Therefore, additional memory enhancement strategies may be utilized, provided the therapist weighs the goals against the potential increase in memory error rate. We recommend that the therapist carefully document attempts to utilize free recall prior to drawing upon memory enhancement methods. *Context- and state-dependent retrieval strategies* should be tried next. A common reason for failure to retrieve recollections under the condition of free recall is state dependence. Thus, methods that gently enhance the experience of affects (but not necessarily the expression of those affects, as in abreactive treatment) may increase retrieval (Bowers, 1981; Eich, 1980). Moreover, context-reinstatement techniques, i.e., those that ask the patient to focus on the time and place associated with the event in question, have been shown to increase the completeness of the memory without a corresponding increase in memory commission errors (Geiselman et al., 1985).

Even when minimally suggestive retrieval strategies like free narrative recall and state- and/or context-dependent retrieval strategies are utilized, some patients still fail to remember. Under no conditions should a therapist resort to coercive tactics or emotional manipulation or otherwise pressure the patient to remember. Communicating that the patient is "in denial" is substandard care. Blocks to memory are not uncommon in traumatized patients. However, sometimes blocks do not signify amnesia for trauma. They may signify ordinary forgetting or an assumption about a past event that never really occurred (Loftus, Garry, & Feldman, 1994). The problem is this: the more difficult retrieval is, the greater the likelihood that very specific memory enhancement methods may be used, and thus, the greater the likelihood that memory commission errors will occur. This is not to say that specific memory enhancement methods lead to false memories, but only that the therapist must be alert for greater memory distortion and inaccuracy.

Hypnosis represents a well-documented example of a specific memory enhancement method. As we learned in chapter 10, the issue is not *whether* hypnosis is used but *how* it is used. Numerous studies have shown that hypnotic memory enhancement increases the recollection of both accurate and inaccurate information (Hammond et al., 1995; Pettinati, 1988). Further, depending on the context of the hypnotherapy relationship, material can sometimes be retrieved that is not retrievable by other means and yet quite accurate (e.g., Reiser, 1980), and at other times quite inaccurate (e.g., Sanders & Simmons, 1983). For example, if a hypnotherapist suggests that the patient's "memory will now increase," that "everything has been recorded in your mind, nothing has been forgotten, and it will now be freely accessible and you can and will clearly remember everything," this will be anticipated to potentially increase both the volume of information produced and patient's confidence in what is "remembered." Such contaminating effects may be controlled considerably when neutral expectations are created prior to hypnosis, during hypnotic induction, and when essentially free narrative recall, state-dependent, and context-dependent retrieval strategies are utilized in trance. This neutrality should structure patient expectations to the effect that further information may or may not be forthcoming, and may or may not be accurate. Through such measures, errors of increased confidence are more likely to be minimized or eliminated.

Yet, when a therapist suggests, "You can and will recall everything," patients are given a motivated authorization to guess.

Hammond (1990a) has described a number of hypnotic procedures referred to as *dissociative regression techniques*. Such methods have been used to assist patients in recalling and integrating traumatic material of an intense emotional nature, but in a manner that titrates affect and avoids overwhelming the patient. These methods include techniques such as viewing a traumatic event from a distance or on a screen, the fractionated abreaction (wherein the full event is processed gradually in a start-stop-start-stop manner) (Kluft, 1982, 1985b; Phillips & Frederick, 1995; van der Hart et al., 1993), dissociating affect and content, giving suggestions for time distortion to speed up the recall of a memory and minimize patient suffering, and the affect bridge (Watkins, 1971) and age regression methods.

Ideomotor signals are likewise sometimes used to inquire about the emotions involved in or beliefs about an event, prior to remembering it, to ease a patient closer to potentially intense material. Another method uses structured inquiry along with ideomotor signals in a careful, nonleading manner to identify potential content associated with a memory prior to age regression. For example, someone may be asked, "Was there anyone else present with you at the time of this event? Was there more than one other person? Was it a male? Was it a female? Was it someone you knew? Was it a member of your immediate or extended family?"

Hypnotic dissociative regression techniques have an important place in the integration of the BASK components of memory, where the content of the traumatic memory is already available. We urge caution in using these methods as primary means to enhance memory unless the interviewer is exceptionally knowledgeable about the differences between suggestive and nonsuggestive interviewing methods. They should be used for memory enhancement only very conservatively, and only in certain situations, when less potentially suggestive retrieval strategies have previously been attempted.

It is not known definitively what degree of distortion may be introduced by the use of dissociative regression techniques, but we believe that such methods have some potential to alter a memory at least to some degree with certain individuals. We must await research to determine whether and how much distortion is encouraged by such methods in a clinical population with traumatic memories. But, when a screen or television technique is used, for example, patients are being asked to use their imagination and see an event differently. This has the inherent risk or potential of altering a memory in ways currently unspecified by research.

While awaiting such clinically relevant research, we recommend that therapists and patients collaboratively make decisions about the use of these methods, balancing the patient's emotional well-being with the need for historical accuracy. The benefits of retrieving additional trauma-relevant material must be weighed against the harm of increasing memory commission errors. In some cases (e.g., where a court case is not pending or anticipated, an alleged perpetrator is already in prison or deceased, or the patient already remembers the traumatic event that remains to be worked through), dissociative regression techniques may be very appropriate and therapeutic. But, when screen techniques are used, it should not be implied that the mind remembers everything as if recorded on a videotape, and should not, therefore, be suggested that the person can "zoom in" and will be able to see or hear anything that occurred. Such an approach creates demands on the patient and provides permission to imaginatively fantasize and confabulate information that may have never been recorded in memory.

We learned in chapter 10 that hypnotically enhanced memory is sometimes associated with a significant increase in the *confidence in the memory*, irrespective of its accuracy. The confidence displayed by subjects in material retrieved under hypnosis can influence the therapist's belief in the accuracy of the information. There is thus a reciprocal influence process. Therapists must be warned that confidence on the part of the patient or affective intensity does not mean that recalled material is accurate and should not lead to the acceptance of the information reported as veridical in nature. Events that are imagined in hypnosis may stir emotions and have a quality of reality and genuineness, especially if they meet the preconceptions or satisfy the emotional needs of the patient, and if they are reinforced by the therapist. Likewise, when something is remembered with partial accuracy but in a somewhat fuzzy manner that may not be entirely

comprehensible, it is possible that subjects may reconstruct or add to this material in ways of which they are not aware in an effort to make it meaningful, understandable, complete, or consistent.

Evaluating Retrieved Memories

Treatment of traumatic memories involves more than simply bypassing traumatic amnesia. Information elicited must be critically examined outside hypnosis and integrated in an ego-syntonic way. When a patient retrieves new memory material in the integration phase of treatment, it is often accompanied, at least early on, by *intense emotional distress*, by remarkable numbing, or by intrusive re-experiencing symptoms. The therapist helps the patient to better cope with his or her reactions to the emerging recollections. In chapter 9 we learned that a high state of stress or distress in an interrogatory interview significantly contributes to the rate of memory commission errors. Thus, the therapist's first goal in managing new recollections is reduction of the stress or distress associated with them.

Most psychodynamically trained clinicians understand that emerging recollections are often disguised and presented to consciousness in a *symbolized* form, due to the operation of psychologically motivated defenses (Ross, 1991). Therefore, therapists operating within the standard of care rarely take emergent recollections as a reflection of historical truth. Such recollections, as we have seen, are likely to contain mixtures of historically accurate and inaccurate material. Adler (1920/1969) originated the technique of obtaining the conscious, earliest recollections from patients—not in the belief that the memories were veridical, but because he believed that they reflected the basic perceptions of self, people, and the world that were held by the patient. He reported one of his own early childhood recollections about a path to school that led through a cemetery. He recalled being frightened to walk through the cemetery like other children. Finally, tired of his lack of courage, he decided to overcome his fear. He ran back and forth across the cemetery a dozen times until he felt that he had mastered his fear. However, he wrote:

Thirty years after that I met an old schoolmate and we exchanged childhood reminiscences. . . .

He insisted there never had been a cemetery on the way to our school. Then I realized that the story . . . had been but a poetic dress for my longing to overcome the fear of death. (p. 180)

Therapists must realize that a memory may be potentially distorted internally by the operation of wishes and defenses, and externally by leading influences of the media, reading, friends, family, and therapists. Thus, recollections may at times have great dynamic meaning and be of psychological import and value in treatment, even though they may not possess historic accuracy.

The therapist must find just the right *stance* toward the emerging recollections. A stance of silence or uninvolved impartiality may be perceived as rejection by patients. Perceived rejection by a therapist has been found to be associated with destructive effects (Lieberman, Yalom, & Miles, 1973). As helping professionals, we do not want to harm victims of alleged abuse by being perceived as rejecting and disbelieving their productions, particularly when at least the broad outlines of what they recall (with or without hypnosis) might be genuine. There is abundant evidence that abuse is widespread and that memory for at least the gist of abuse experiences is often accurate. At the same time, however, no one would wish to harm innocent people through encouraging impulsive or premature accusation where there is an absence of confirming evidence. Thus, in the interest of not causing harm to either the patient or other parties, we need to demonstrate a balance between supportiveness and empathic understanding, while at the same time assisting the patient to critically evaluate the material elicited in therapy or hypnotherapy. We must simultaneously convey openness and support, while still assuming a stance that memory is frequently imperfect and that rarely will all the details of any recollection be fully accurate. Since we were not actually present ourselves at the original situation being recalled, we cannot guarantee to patients that what was remembered is accurate.

We should believe in our patients and express faith in their developing better ways of knowing the truth, while remembering that having faith in a patient is not synonymous with always believing everything a patient believes or produces. We call this balanced stance *empathic neutrality*, empathic

in the sense of resonating with the patient's emotional reactions to emerging recollections, and neutral (or better, appropriately humble) with respect to the degree of accuracy and inaccuracy contained within the recollection. Overzealous acceptance of the recollection as fully accurate historical truth is to be avoided in that it may undermine the patient's emerging ability to discern reality for him/herself and destructively repeat in the treatment relationship the redefinition of reality by an authority figure experienced by the abused child (Davies & Frawley, 1994). Both therapist and patient should regard material elicited in psychotherapy or under hypnosis as simply one more source of information—information that cannot be relied on as superior to or more accurate, or necessarily inferior to or less accurate, than material already in conscious awareness. It is simply additional information to be weighed along with data and feelings already consciously available to the patient.

The therapist is advised to help the patient develop a *critical attitude* toward emerging recollections. The skilled therapist conveys faith in the patient's ability to learn ways to better distinguish between accurate and inaccurate elements of memory as the treatment unfolds, while tolerating ambiguity and avoiding or even *challenging premature closure* (Wells & Leippe, 1981). The skilled therapist facilitates the patient's epistemological development through which the patient learns to relinquish relying solely on external or internal sources of knowing historical truth in favor of balancing self-knowledge with objective analysis (Grand, 1995b). Both patient and therapist are advised to adopt what Fromm and French (1974) once described as necessary for dream interpretation, namely, a "*scientific attitude.*" In the spirit of the ongoing inquiry about what happened in the past, both therapist and patient alike continuously check and recheck their hypotheses about the events in question, while at the same time trying to identify their own biases and presuppositions. In this spirit each should remain open to evidence that might disconfirm hypotheses made about the past events. Therapists should maintain an openness to potential alternative explanations for the production of a "memory," including family or personal dynamics or possible secondary gains (e.g., as ways to save face, or revenge). Patients who firmly ground their ongoing inquiry in a scientific attitude sometimes report increased ability over time to recognize inaccurate elements in their recollections, and so to "edit out" at least bizarre, obviously inaccurate, and extraneous elements that were originally included due to the operation of psychological defenses or external contamination (e.g., Frederickson, 1992).

In cases where the abuse memory may potentially affect the lives of others, the therapist is advised to at least explore the question of *external corroborative evidence* with the patient. However, we do not agree with some advocates of the false memory position who believe that therapists have a duty to seek external corroboration of abuse allegations. Imposing such a duty upon trauma therapists would result in a dual role conflict. We advise, when abuse memories may affect the lives of others and certainly when litigation or other complaints are involved, that the therapist seek consultation from an independent forensic examiner regarding an evaluation of the available evidence. Within the courts there is a long tradition of evaluating evidence according to different standards, depending on the complaint in question. Likewise, within science we learn to place differing degrees of confidence in an interpretation depending on the nature of evidence that does and does not support it. We advocate that therapists and clinicians do the same, namely, critically evaluate recollections of abuse along a continuum from less to more confidence placed in the recollection depending on the nature and types of evidence that are available.

INTEGRATING AND MAKING SENSE OF MEMORIES FOR TRAUMA AND ABUSE

While memory enhancement may be an appropriate treatment objective, at least for the subpopulation of traumatized patients who have full or partial amnesia for trauma, it is *not* the primary treatment objective for the majority of patients during the integration phase of trauma treatment. The primary goal of the integration phase is, as the name implies, *integration*—first, of the dissociated BASK

components of memory, and second, of the dissociated introject or internalized abuse-related representations. Therefore, it is well within the standard of care to utilize clinical procedures specifically designed to enhance the integration of the affect and the memory content associated with traumatic experiences. These methods include several methods that false memory advocates have misclassified as "memory recovery techniques" (Lindsay & Read, 1994; Loftus, 1993; Ofshe & Watters, 1993). Structured waking imagery, hypnotic imagery, and hypnotic affect regulatory methods are not simply memory recovery methods. They have been used extensively during the integration phase of trauma treatment to foster integration of affect and other dissociated BASK components of traumatic memory (Brown & Fromm, 1986; Hammond, 1990a; van der Hart et al., 1993).

Moreover, abreactive and dissociative regression techniques sometimes have their place in the late memory and representation integration subphases of the integration phase, when the treatment goal is integration of the dissociated BASK components of memory and not memory recovery per se, although we agree with van der Hart and Brown (1992) that the term abreaction is unfortunate, since most abreactive procedures as currently used are not narrowly focused on affect, but more on integration of BASK components, correcting cognitive distortions, and making sense of the traumatic material (Fine, 1989a; van der Hart et al., 1993). However, the therapist must understand that the majority of trauma experts use abreactive and dissociative methods nearly always *after* the main content of the trauma memory has already been established, either because the patient always remembered it or because it was recalled in another manner prior to the introduction of abreactive or dissociated techniques. Planned abreaction is a method that presumes the patient already has a good working understanding of traumatic event (Steele & Colrain, 1990; van der Hart et al., 1993). However, the therapist who utilizes such powerful affect intensification methods has a duty to ensure that the patient is capable of tolerating the procedure without undue regression or dissociation.

One important goal of the integration phase of treatment is to help the patient make sense of the previous trauma history. The symptoms that initially brought the patient into treatment generally subside once the patient develops a coherent explanatory model for the illness (Frank, 1961). The patient must develop a "comprehensive view of the trauma" (Frederickson, 1992) or a "trauma narrative" (van der Hart et al., 1993), and in so doing must confront the "existential crisis" that comes with the full realization of the violation, evil, or other moral transgressions associated with the trauma. While the skilled clinician helps the patient bear the pain of this existential crisis, he or she must also realize that the trauma narrative is a construction, woven in part out of the threads of genuine trauma and violation and in part out of defensive distortion, the therapeutic dialogue, and the patient's current needs, not the least of which is to have a neat and tidy, coherent story about the trauma. Genuine accounts of abuse are rarely neat and tidy. While the patient may have a legitimate need to transcend "messy reality" (Rogers, 1993) in the service of ending treatment with a coherent explanatory model for the trauma, both therapist and patient must realize that such trauma stories are rarely an exact statement of historical truth, and while they often accurately portray the gist of the abuse in a way that will never again be forgotten, and may be told time and again as a socially shared reality, they are at best a mixture of genuine trauma recollections, inaccuracies, and embellishments.

PRESENTING PROBLEMS THAT MERIT CAUTION

Hammond et al. (1995) have described a number of situations that should perhaps raise a "red flag" in a therapist's mind concerning the possible validity of a recovered memory, encouraging extra circumspection before embarking on treatment. These situations are best regarded as situations where we encourage cautiousness on the part of therapists, and not as circumstances where it is impossible that a recalled memory has validity:

1. A patient with a history of switching therapists or doctor shopping. It may be wise to have such patients provide a detailed history of prior therapy in their own handwriting and to provide a release of information for all prior therapists. A patient unwilling to do this may not want unfavorable information in prior treatment records to be available.

2. When the possibility of litigation is raised, especially early in therapy or when an attorney has been consulted prior to the onset of therapy. Similarly, when the patient demonstrates overfamiliarity with psychological terminology and litigation concepts, it implies substantial prior experience that should be explored by the therapist.

3. In the treatment of highly manipulative patients with characterological issues.

4. A patient coming for treatment to "confirm" that he/she was abused in the past. The therapist cannot make that determination without independent factual corroboration. The therapist cannot act as a judge or jury.

5. A previous therapist has suggested that abuse may have occurred.

6. When uncovered memories are from before the age of three.

7. In persons remembering amnestic memories from adolescence or adulthood, or who claim to have a lack of memories for significant blocks of time after the middle of childhood, but who do not demonstrate evidence of a dissociative disorder on objective evaluation (e.g., with the Dissociative Experiences Scale and the SCID-D) (Bernstein & Putnam, 1986; Steinberg, 1994; Steinberg, Cicchetti, Buchanan, Hall, & Rounsaville, 1993).

8. In instances where the past relationship with the alleged perpetrator was an entirely positive one, not associated with ambivalent feelings, aloofness, or conflicts.

9. When patients have previously seen unlicensed therapists or lay hypnotists. Likewise, extra caution is indicated when a previous therapist has used nontraditional forms of therapy, such as (but not limited to) crystals, energy balancing, muscle testing, reading auras, past life therapy, or expelling entities from the patient. In such circumstances, we believe the potential for patients to be inappropriately influenced in their expectations and to misunderstand and misinterpret therapeutic techniques is high.

10. When patients have participated in lay support or self-help groups that are unsupervised by licensed professionals, and where a topic of discussion is often trauma, sexual abuse, or incest. Likewise, extra caution is indicated when the patient's memories are subject to contamination because the patient has participated in seminars on abuse, read literature on abuse, or viewed television or video presentations on abuse.

11. When the therapist has a personal history similar to the patient, potentially leading to the increased possibility of unconscious bias, misinterpretation, and countertransference. (pp. 34–35)

15

|||||||||||||||||||

Suing Therapists

For virtually all of the twentieth century, psychiatrists, psychologists, and other mental health professionals have been able to practice their professions without fear of being sued. Lawsuits against mental healers have been extraordinarily rare, especially in comparison with physical healers, lawyers, accountants, and other professionals (Trent & Muhl, 1975). As Cohen (1979) noted in the most comprehensive review at the time:

> Mental health professionals have remained relatively unscathed by claims of malpractice. Suits brought against psychologists, psychiatrists, and others have been relatively few in number, and relatively low dollar amounts have been paid in damages. It has been observed that the average American psychiatrist is sued once for every 50 to 100 years of practice, whereas the average neurosurgeon can expect to be sued once for every two years of practice. (p. 8)

Many of the legal actions filed have been "nuisance" suits, rather than legitimate malpractice claims, brought for fee disputes or brought by disgruntled patients hoping for a quick cash settlement from an insurance company. Cohen (1979) reports a study conducted in 1978 that showed that the majority of complaints filed against therapists involved fee disputes (p. 10).

Beginning in the mid–1960s, however, judges began an extensive expansion of the law of torts (White, 1980). New causes of action were recognized in areas such as tenants' rights, consumers' rights, environmental rights, women's rights, etc. Old rules on proof of causation were weakened or broadened to allow injured plaintiffs easier access to deep-pocket insurance coverage (Glannon, 1995). New duties were created and the types of situations for which damages would be awarded were increased (Kionka, 1992). In this manner, the underlying philosophy guiding the direction of the law of torts underwent a radical shift. Up until the 1960s, the general philosophy and purpose of tort law was to determine blame and award compensation. Beginning in the 1960s, however, courts viewed the law of torts as a mechanism for the social redistribution of losses. Emphasis on fault decreased as judges expanded the concept of blame or did away with it entirely.

In this increasingly litigious climate, the number of lawsuits filed against professionals also expanded. Despite this expansion of the law of torts in general, mental health professionals still enjoyed a relative immunity from liability.

In this chapter we will examine the modern law related to professional liability. This modern law is being tested and challenged in a wave of recent cases. The false memory controversy has generated legal actions attempting to change the way in which professional liability should be treated. The current attack on therapists, and therapy, is very widespread, with estimates ranging as high as several thousand potential lawsuits against practicing mental health professionals. More conservative estimates acknowledge that the number of cases presently in the legal system against therapists may be closer to one thousand. Whatever the number of such suits, it is clear that at no time in its history has the mental health professional community been under as severe a legal assault.

Professionals must understand that the standard of care to which their conduct must conform is not static. Rather, it grows with each new development and each new discovery in diagnosis and treatment. The relative immunity that "talking cures" have enjoyed up through the early 1990s should not be grounds for complacency. There is never a substitute for being adequately and currently informed and well prepared in one's vocational activities.

Before we begin, one note is necessary about understanding legal rules. In state legal cases, trial judges help settle individual disputes but they do not settle general rules of law. Appellate judges, hearing cases that have already been tried or responding to rulings made by trial judges, establish the law that is applicable in the particular state. The written opinion of the appellate judges is binding on trial judges in that jurisdiction; state trial judges generally do not write opinions, nor are their rulings binding on other courts. For this reason, lawyers generally cite and argue the opinions of appellate courts. Rulings by state trial judges are very difficult to research, while opinions of appellate judges are carefully collected and universally circulated. In federal cases, however, district judges, who are trial judges, also may write influential opinions, but these opinions are not binding on other district judges and are not binding on appellate judges. In the discussion that follows, we will usually refer to appellate cases, rulings, opinions, or judges because it is from these courts that the general rules that bind professionals are issued.

The modern attack on therapists and therapy generally has involved four different fact patterns based upon who is suing whom: (1) patients (recanters/retractors) suing therapists, (2) third-party (nonclient) lawsuits against therapists, (3)

accuser suing alleged perpetrator for past abuse, and (4) repressed memories as evidence in criminal cases. We will consider the first two patterns in this chapter and the final two in the next one.

PATIENTS (RECANTERS/RETRACTORS) SUING THERAPISTS

The law has no difficulty in recognizing that psychologists, psychiatrists, and other licensed mental healers owe their patients (1) a tort duty to exercise reasonable care under the circumstances, (2) a contractual duty to perform the promised services with competence, and (3) a fiduciary duty of loyalty and preservation of confidences. In almost all cases of suits against mental health professionals, where the quality of the care provided is the issue, the patient is the plaintiff.

Malpractice Law

Malpractice is negligence committed by a professional. Scholars have traced suits for malpractice as far back in legal history as 1354, and earlier cases may well exist (Sandor, 1957). Because malpractice is negligence committed by a "professional," unlicensed persons cannot be sued for malpractice (Cohen, 1979). As noted by Harris (1973), "Those people who practice outside the law are either quacks or non-professionals not yet under the state's statutory umbrella. Since no standards are established for their reputed professions, someone injured by their 'care' will have to rely on tort theories other than malpractice" (p. 409).

Unlicensed practitioners may not be sued for malpractice, but they certainly may be sued for negligence. The difficulty that plaintiffs face when they sue unlicensed practitioners is establishing the appropriate standard of care. For example, if a person sees a lay hypnotist for help with losing weight, what training or experience must this lay hypnotist have acquired? There are no established standards in such cases (*Johnson v. Gerrish*, 1986).

Because negligence and malpractice are essentially identical, the California Supreme Court recently noted that there is no separate category of malpractice apart from the general rules of negligence (*Flowers v. Torrance Memorial Hospital Medical Center*, 1994). While it may be very difficult to establish an appropriate standard of care that must be practiced by unlicensed persons, for licensed professionals the standard of care is usually established by expert testimony about prevailing customs and practices.

Negligence consists of conduct that is unreasonable under the circumstances and which causes harm to the party suing. All states recognize negligence as the largest body of the law of torts, which regulates civil (as opposed to criminal) wrongdoing apart from breach of contract. All therapists, licensed or not, must answer to the standards set by the law of negligence.

The law of negligence in all states recognizes that there are four elements that the person suing, the plaintiff, must prove. First, that a *duty* to exercise reasonable care was owed to the plaintiff. This element is no problem for a patient or client who hires a mental health professional because, by agreeing to perform professional services for the patient or client, the mental health professional is also promising to exercise reasonable care in treating that person. The duty requirement, however, is a major obstacle to third parties suing therapists, as we shall later discuss.

The second element of a malpractice cause of action is a *breach* of duty. The plaintiff must show that the mental health professional violated the duty owed. In order to prove that this duty was violated, the plaintiff must prove that the care given fell below the standard of care exercised by competent professionals in that geographical area at that time. Where the violation is obvious, such as a sexual assault of the patient or failing to observe obvious signs of potential suicide, expert testimony is not needed to establish the standard of care. Where matters are not so clear, the plaintiff must introduce expert testimony about what the proper practice should have included. The professional, of course, may bring in other experts to disagree or to define the standard of care quite differently. The breach of duty element, which defines the standard of care, assumes that there is a line of competent practice below which no professional should descend. The jury will be instructed to determine where that line is and whether it had been crossed in the particular case.

It should be noted that the standard of care is not necessarily uniform across the country, or even in one state. Rural practitioners with fewer available resources may not be required to practice at the level of urban healers with greater local resources. Also, the standard of care is not uniform over time. As the knowledge base increases about physical illness, mental illness, and social maladjustment, the standard of care may increase accordingly. As new developments occur, the standard must absorb and accommodate them. Consider the first doctor asked to treat the AIDS virus. This disease had never been seen before. Almost anything the doctor might do would, in retrospect, be in error. But the standard of care takes into consideration the fact that the disease is not one about which practitioners had information. But as more information about diagnosis and treatment of AIDS develops, the standard of care will require healers to know this information and to adjust their practices accordingly.

The third element of a malpractice claim is *causation*. The plaintiff must prove that the professional's breach of the standard of care was the actual cause of the harm suffered. Causation issues can be quite simple, such as where a surgeon does a poor job stitching up a wound and the area becomes badly infected, or where a psychiatrist prescribes the wrong drug and the patient suffers the expected adverse side effects. Most times, however, causation issues are very complex, especially in cases where the person claiming injury has a preexisting mental or physical condition. In suits against mental health professionals, patients may have difficulty establishing that the therapist caused emotional harm apart from the emotional harm that was likely to occur from the continuation of the patient's existing mental or social difficulties.

The fourth and final element of malpractice is *damages*. The plaintiff must allege and prove that the unreasonable conduct of the mental health professional caused actual harm for which the plaintiff is seeking compensation. The hardest of these cases deals with how to put a money price tag on the loss of a limb, the loss of sight or hearing, pain or suffering, or the loss of some aspect of the quality of life. When the harm is purely emotional, there is no scientific way to quantify a monetary remedy. It is no surprise, therefore, that juries often award multimillion-dollar verdicts in emotional distress cases.

Malpractice cases have not been as frequent

against mental health professionals as against medical and other professionals. Cassidy (1974) has speculated that lawsuits against mental health professionals are not brought because of several factors: (1) the patient often regards the therapist as a helping friend, (2) transference issues make the patient not likely to sue the therapist because it would be like suing a parent, (3) the patient may feel shame about past or present behaviors, and may want to protect his or her privacy, and (4) therapists are skilled at defusing negative feelings and dissuading patients from bringing lawsuits. To this list we might also add that proving a case of malpractice against a psychiatrist is not easy. Experts must be found who will testify against their fellow professionals. Furthermore, the law protects errors of judgment if they are reasonable, and the law does not require that the patient be cured, or even helped. In addition, because of the diverse opinions held in the therapeutic community—Simon (1992), for example, notes that there are "currently over 450 different schools of psychotherapy" (p. 481)—courts allow wide latitude regarding how therapy may be practiced.

Successful malpractice cases against therapists have generally fallen into several well recognized categories: (1) sexual misconduct with patients, (2) physical harm caused to patients, (3) physical methods, including medication, used on patients, or (4) suicide by the patient. Before the 1950s, the administration of electroconvulsive treatment "created the highest risk of liability for the therapist" (Perlin, 1994, p. 418; Sarno, 1979).

Cases involving sexual conduct with a therapist have held that patients may recover in malpractice actions. In *Richard H. v. Larry D.* (1988), a husband and wife went to the defendant-psychiatrist for marital counseling. After the defendant began having an affair with the wife, the husband sued for breach of duty. The defendant-psychiatrist argued that the husband could not recover because of California's Anti-Heartbalm statute (California Civil Code section 43.5), which prohibits the bringing of a cause of action for (1) alienation of affection, (2) criminal conversation, or (3) seduction of a person over the age of legal consent. The California Court of Appeals addressed the question of whether the Anti-Heartbalm statute, which lists no exceptions, applied to therapy settings. The court found in favor of the husband:

Section 43.5 was enacted to eliminate a class of lawsuits which were often fruitful sources of fraud and extortion and easy methods "to embarrass, harass, and besmirch the reputation of one wholly innocent of wrongdoing." (*Ikuta v. Ikuta* (1950) 97 Cal.App.2d 787, 789, 218 P.2d 854); . . . A review of the decisional law, however, reveals that section 43.5 does not create a blanket immunization from liability for conduct which, although technically within the constraints of section 43.5, breaches a duty of care independent of the causes of action barred therein.

For instance, a physician who engages in sexual relations with a patient may be liable for professional negligence if his conduct constitutes a "breach of the duty of care owed to the patient by the physician within the scope of the patient-physician relationship." (*Atienza v. Taub* (1987) 194 Cal.App.3d 388, 392, 239 Cal.Rptr. 454.)

* * *

. . . We do not think the statute was intended to lower the standard of care which psychiatrists owe their patients, nor to permit them to avoid liability for breach of their professional and fiduciary responsibilities, or commit fraud.

Deciding who is a patient and who is not one is not always easy when therapists permit family members to join therapy sessions. For example, in the recent case of *Smith v. Pust* (1993), a therapist had sexual intercourse with a patient. The patient's husband, who had attended two therapy sessions, was not permitted to recover against the therapist because he was not a patient. His attendance at the two sessions was to assist in the therapy of his wife. At no time did he consider himself to be a patient, and at no time did the therapist treat him as if he were a patient.

On the other hand, in *Marlene F. v. Affiliated Psychiatric Medical Clinic, Inc.* (1989), parents were allowed to recover from a therapist who molested their children, but only because the parents were also held to be patients of the therapist, who was counseling the entire families, not just the children.

Patients sometimes sue therapists on the grounds of misdiagnosis or failure to properly diagnose an illness. Patients usually do not recover. As Perlin (1994), one of the most respected legal commentators, has noted, "Courts have been fairly lenient in cases involving psychiatric misdiagnosis, because of the inherently inexact nature of such diagnosis, and because the diagnoses' reliability depends to a significant extent on the adequacy of the information communicated to the physician by the patient" (pp. 416–417). Therapists who demonstrate that they have acted reasonably and conscientiously in arriving at their conclusions are generally not held liable for errors in diagnosis and treatment. In *Wogelius v. Dallas* (1987), an Illinois appellate court held that the psychotherapist was not negligent where the therapist did not contact the patient's prior therapist. The court did note, however, that the patient claimed the prior therapist had not been good.

If the therapist is sued for using a verbal therapy, the case will be "especially problematic and difficult to sustain" (Perlin, 1994, p. 420). Tancredi (1986) is even more direct: "Throughout the history of psychiatric malpractice cases there has not been a reported decision of an American appellate court that has established psychiatric malpractice based on improper conduct of psychotherapy alone" (p. 13).

As of mid-1997, a few appellate cases permit holding a therapist liable for utilizing a "talking cure." It is difficult to estimate how many lawsuits are currently pending across the country requesting that courts find negligence in the way some therapists have conducted "talking cures." By mid-1995, the estimate was that approximately 800 such cases were filed (Weidlich, June 12, 1995). Patients hope that while juries are often respectful of the therapist, they will be more sympathetic to the patient's suffering. Further, the fact cannot be disregarded that jurors know that doctors, lawyers, and therapists carry insurance, so that a verdict for the patient will not be paid out of the pocket of the professional. This "loss shifting" to a "deep pocket," which spreads accident costs across the whole society, has been the hallmark of the growth of tort law, especially since the early 1960s (Keeton, 1984). It is the conservative backlash against this trend of expanding tort liability that has been the major force shaping tort law since the 1980s.

The conservative backlash is fueled by two forces, one economic and the other social. The economic force is the insurance carriers and businesses that are the most frequent targets of negligence lawsuits. Their costs of doing business have risen substantially, and, they argue, noncompetitively, because they have to price their goods and services to include the likelihood of lawsuits. The social force is the moral outrage at the assault on responsibility. With risk-shifting formulas, and "deep pocket" liability theories, the dreaded "abuse excuse" heard in criminal cases has also come to roost in civil cases. Tort law diminished the concept of individual responsibility in order to distribute losses, and thereby compensate victims. Moralists have been arguing that this disrespect for individual responsibility weakens the social fabric. They point to cases where drunk drivers cause injuries, but the bartender who sold the drink, or the social host who provided it, is held responsible, not the driver. They also point out that the law says that employers are liable for the acts of their employees, even if those acts had been expressly forbidden (Keeton, 1984), and that landlords may be liable for the conduct of criminals who enter their property and harm tenants.

For the first two-thirds of this century tort law favored the social policy of compensating victims. Law during this period rapidly expanded, thereby imposing a larger number of duties and an increasingly higher level of standard of care. Since the 1980s, however, the conservative backlash has turned the trend in tort law back toward more individualized liability. The recent wave of lawsuits against therapists hopes to reverse this backlash and return tort law to the days when it was liberally shifting losses to insurance deep pockets. This wave of lawsuits filed against therapists will precipitate appellate decisions in the next few years, thereby providing guidance on the standard of care to be practiced in verbal therapies. Nevertheless, it is already clear, as we shall later see, that juries are having little difficulty finding against therapists, especially in recovered memory and dissociative disorder cases.

By way of summary, patients are owed a duty of competent treatment by their therapists. Honest mistakes of judgment are not to be used as the basis of liability, and the fact that the patient got no better, or even got worse, is not determinative of malpractice. In *Sewell v. Internal Medicine and Endocrine Associates* (1992), the Supreme Court of Alabama upheld a jury instruction as an accurate statement of the law. The jury instruction stated, in part:

The Court charges the jury that untoward events may occur during medical treatment for which no one is liable. No presumption of evidence or liability arises from the fact that Patricia Sewell died. That is to say the question in this case is not whether the diagnosis or treatment rendered by the defendants was successful; rather, the question is whether the plaintiff has proved by substantial evidence that in rendering—in performing such treatment or rendering such diagnosis the plaintiff—the defendants, rather, breached the applicable standard of care. That is to say, again, your focus is not on the result, rather, your focus is whether or not the defendants have been proved to have failed to have abided by the applicable standard of care in their treatment of Mrs. Sewell. I further charge you that a physician is not an insurer or a guarantor of the successful diagnosis or treatment of a patient. Perfection is not required of a physician; rather, it is required that he meet the standard of care which I have defined. The fact that the care and treatment may not have produced good results does not in and of itself establish that the physician was negligent. I charge you that where there are various recognized methods of treatment which meet the standard of care a physician is at liberty to follow the one he thinks best, and is not liable for malpractice because an expert witness may give an opinion that some other method would have been preferable.

The court noted that "the jury should focus on the circumstances surrounding the defendant's conduct, rather than on the outcome, when determining whether the defendant's conduct was negligent. . . . To hold otherwise would be to hold that a defendant doctor is the insurer of satisfactory results of medical treatment, and such a result is expressly prohibited by [statute]."

The growth of modern cases against therapists suggests that therapists would be wise to seek the most training they can in the areas in which they practice. Given the litigious climate in general, and the "open season" against therapists stemming from recent false memory and dissociative disorder issues, therapists are advised to increase the level of their knowledge and skills. Unfortunately, the bad apples in any profession taint all the practitioners of that profession. There are a small number of therapists who conduct the astonishingly awful therapy often seen depicted in news exposés (Singer & Lalich, 1996). These few may be giving psychotherapy a black eye, but their conduct should be used as an inducement to other therapists to be more knowledgeable about the science upon which their own practice is based.

A special problem arises with therapeutic or medical practices that are unorthodox or innovative, which are generally called "experimental" treatments by the American Psychological Association. "Unorthodox" practices are procedures or techniques that are not generally followed by a majority of practitioners. "Innovative" practices are ones that have just been invented so they have not had a chance yet to establish their value in the larger therapeutic community. How, then, is a standard of care to be determined for unorthodox or innovative therapies?

Early law had a simple rule for healers using innovative or unorthodox therapies—deviate at your peril (Shapiro & Spece, 1981). In *Jackson v. Burnham* (1895), it was stated that "when a particular mode of treatment is upheld by a consensus of opinion among the members of the profession, it should be followed by the ordinary practitioner; and if a physician sees fit to experiment with some other mode, he should do so at his peril." Other state courts were in agreement (*Allen v. Voje*, 1902). During a less litigious era this harsh rule did not deter bold experimenters whose innovations are essential for progress. Modern litigiousness, however, could serve as a deterrent to the evolution of new therapeutic techniques, especially if any deviation automatically results in a form of strict liability (liability without fault). Until a technique is fully tested, who may judge whether it was reasonable to use it? What is the standard of care for something previously untried and untested?

Virtually all of the legal cases attempting to set a standard of care for innovative or unorthodox therapies have involved the practice of medicine, not psychiatry. Those cases that do involve psychiatric treatments have also involved the use of physical force, thereby triggering battery theories and raising additional issues of informed consent. No appellate cases have been found where the therapist was successfully sued for a therapy that did not involve some physical element.

Unorthodox Therapies

Medicine, psychiatry, and psychology all have mainstream practitioners as well as avant garde theorists. This latter group raises a legal issue as to the proper standard of care for practitioners who utilize minority, or unorthodox, therapies. As we have already noted, early common law forced the unorthodox practitioner to deviate at his or her own risk from mainstream doctrine. Modern law is more lenient.

If a therapy is conventional, it is tested by the prevailing standard of care (Shea, 1978). Experts must explain the nature of this standard to the judge and/or jury. If, however, a therapy is not conventional, it may still be regarded as acceptable to a "respectable minority" of practitioners and will be tested by this standard. The *"respectable minority" doctrine* is part of the *"two schools of thought" rule*, which forbids testing the conduct of a practitioner of one school by the standards established by another school of professional thought. In order to be a "school," a practice must be followed by a "respectable minority."

The "two schools of thought" rule has a venerable history. Statutes enacting its terms were in code books in many states by the middle 1800s. In 1848, the Iowa Supreme Court (*Bowman v. Woods*) acknowledged the right of healers to practice according to different schools. The healer agreed to abide by the recognized standard of care of that school (*Patten v. Wiggin*, 1862), and failure to conform to the beliefs or standards of another school did not constitute malpractice (*Ennis v. Banks*, 1917).

The "two schools of thought" doctrine was considered so important that many states added it to their statutes in the last century (*Crane v. Johnson*, 1917; *People v. Jordan*, 1916; *State v. Mylod*, 1898). These statutes generally prohibited discrimination against a recognized school of thought.

The impact of the "two schools of thought" doctrine is to serve as an absolute defense to a malpractice action. As part of this defense, the doctrine prohibits experts from one school testifying against proponents of another school. For example, in *Force v. Gregory* (1893), an expert from the allopathic school could not testify against a practitioner of the homeopathic school, and in *Swanson v. Hood* (1918), an osteopathic physician could not testify against an allopathic physician. Furthermore, patients were

presumed to have selected the physician because of the school in which the physician practices (*Van Sickle v. Doolittle*, 1918). Today, some states are likely to reject the presumption and look instead to the state's requirements of informed consent.

The purpose of the rule that followers of one acceptable school of medicine or therapy should not be judged by the standards of another acceptable school has not been challenged by courts, commentators, or legislators for the last century. The wisdom of the rule is easy to understand. In *Chumbler v. McClure* (1974), a plaintiff who was injured in an electrical explosion was treated by Dr. McClure, a neurosurgeon, with the female hormone estrogen, which was produced and marketed commercially as Premarin. Plaintiff claimed that the drug treatments caused him injury and that prescription of Premarin in this case fell below the appropriate standard of care. The record showed that there was "a division of opinion in the medical profession regarding the use of Premarin in the treatment of cerebral vascular insufficiency, and that Dr. McClure was alone among neurosurgeons in Nashville in using such therapy." The court held that the plaintiff could not recover:

> The test for malpractice and for community standards is not to be determined solely by a plebiscite. Where two or more schools of thought exist among competent members of the medical profession concerning proper medical treatment for a given ailment, each of which is supported by responsible medical authority, it is not malpractice to be among the minority in a given city who follow one of the accepted schools. . . .
>
> Were this not true, an anomaly might occur where nine neurosurgeons in Memphis, Tennessee, prescribed Premarin for cerebral vascular insufficiency and where nine neurosurgeons in Nashville prescribed other treatment. Should one Memphis neurosurgeon move to Nashville and continue to prescribe Premarin, he might be liable for malpractice. Such a result would impose a standard of practice upon the medical profession which would be totally unsupported by logic and unreasonable in concept. . . .

The most thorough judicial analysis of the "two schools of thought" rule is found in *Jones v. Chidester*

(1992), where the Pennsylvania Supreme Court noted that a "medical practitioner has an absolute defense to a claim of negligence when it is determined that the prescribed treatment or procedure has been approved by one group of medical experts even though an alternate school of thought recommends another approach, or it is agreed among experts that alternative treatments and practices are acceptable." The issue before the court was whether a school of thought must be advocated by a "considerable number" of experts or by "respective, reputable and reasonable" practitioners. As the court observed, the "former test calls for a quantitative analysis, while the latter is premised on qualitative grounds."

The court admitted that the law in Pennsylvania, and across the country, vacillated between these two standards:

> In *Borja v. Phoenix General Hospital, Inc.*, 151 Ariz. 302, 727 P.2d 355 (1986), the court [held] that the doctrine requires only support by a "respectable minority." California has defined its standard as one where "a physician chooses one of alternative accepted methods of treatment, with which other physicians agree." *Meier v. Ross General Hospital*, 69 Cal.2d 420, 434, 71 Cal.Rptr. 903, 445 P.2d 519 (1968). Florida has adopted the "respectable minority" test in *Schwab v. Tolley*, Florida App., 345 So.2d 747 (1977), while Arkansas accepts the doctrine when any alternative "recognized method" is employed by the physician. *Rickett v. Hayes*, 256 Ark. 893, 511 S.W.2d 187 (1974). Louisiana courts have favored an "acceptable alternative treatment" test. *Reid v. North Caddo Memorial Hospital*, La.App., 528 So.2d 653 (1988). The most recent Connecticut decision exonerates a practitioner who employed a treatment which was "one of choice among competent physicians." *Wasfi v. Chaddna*, 218 Conn. 200, 588 A.2d 204 (1991).
>
> In a similar vein, other states also have refused to adopt a quantitative test. *Gruginski v. Lane*, 177 Wash. 121, 30 P.2d 970 (1934) ("respectable minority"); *Walkenhorst v. Kesler*, 92 Utah 312, 67 P.2d 654 (1937) ("approval of at least a respectable portion of the profession"); *Holton v. Burton*, 197 Wis. 405, 222 N.W. 225 (1928) ("two accepted or recognized methods of treatment").

After examining the law across the country, the Pennsylvania Supreme Court adopted a blended test requiring "a considerable number of recognized and respected professionals in [the] given area of expertise" to satisfy the "two schools of thought" complete defense to malpractice. The defendant must bring in expert testimony that a considerable number of respected professionals would have followed the procedures he or she used, and then the jury may decide whether two legitimate schools really exist. A concurring judge forcefully argued that the court, not the jury, must make this decision.

It should be noted that the Pennsylvania Supreme Court's new test is more difficult for healers to meet because both of the older tests ("respected members" and "considerable numbers") must now be satisfied. It is for this reason, and others, that commentators, while expressing support for the "two schools" doctrine, have been critical of its interpretation. For example, D. R. Brown (1993) has argued that the Pennsylvania Supreme Court has now created a debate over "what constitutes a considerable number" (p. 233) of healers. Brown believes the court should have followed the qualitative standard used in Texas (*Hood v. Phillips*, 1977). Under the Texas test, if the healer can show that a "reasonable and prudent doctor" would have treated the patient in the same manner, then the healer is not liable for malpractice. According to Brown, this approach is preferable because

> it allows for the use of experimental methods of treatment. By quantifying medical acceptance, the "considerable number" and "respectable minority" standards unfairly bias the jury against medical situations that demand experimentation. The *Hood* standard properly focuses the issue on whether the physician acted appropriately under the circumstances. (pp. 232–233)

Newbold (1993) also criticizes *Jones v. Chidester* because of the excessive vagueness in defining a "school of thought," and because of its conclusion that whether a school exists is a question of fact for the jury rather than a question of law for the court, as the dissent adamantly insisted. Dailey (1994) has also suggested that *Jones v. Chidester's* conclusion "may inhibit the use of medically innovative procedures in Pennsylvania" (p. 713) and may unnecessarily interfere with obtaining a patient's informed consent.

As commentators predicted, the debate has continued in Pennsylvania concerning the proper definition of a "school of thought." In *Tesauro v. Perrige* (1994), the Superior Court of Pennsylvania provided some guidance in a case where the defendant, a dentist, had used a procedure described in a 1975 text. The only other reference to the procedure was to be found in a very brief mention in a 33-year-old manual that the court said "is clearly out of date." No other book, article, or expert endorsed the procedure. The court denied the application of the "two schools of thought" doctrine by holding that "the writings and teachings of one individual are inadequate factual support for the proposition that a considerable number of professionals agree with this treatment." It did not help the defendant that all of the experts he called on his behalf testified that they never used, and never would use, that procedure.

Bonavitacola v. Cluver (1993) also involved a dentist, but this time only one expert supported defendant's position and the court held that this was not enough to create a second school of thought. In *Jones v. Chidester*, the defendant produced three experts who testified in his favor. It may be that, unless these experts can be shown to be virtually the entire class of experts adopting their position, as was true in the United States Supreme Court decision in *Daubert v. Merrell Dow Pharmaceuticals, Inc.* (1993), three experts will be enough to support the defense.

Despite the essential importance of the "two schools of thought" doctrine to the repressed memory debate, medical malpractice defense lawyers have generally been unaware of the doctrine's existence or surprisingly reluctant to assert it as a complete defense. The doctrine, however, was designed for controversies precisely like the repressed memory legal disputes where two powerful groups of thought oppose each other's main principles. In such cases, experts from one group should not be permitted to testify against proponents of the other group. In *Cool v. Legion Insurance Company* (1996), attorneys filed a Motion in Limine to prohibit experts opposed to MPD from testifying against experts who do support that diagnosis. Ironically, because MPD, now DID, has been recognized since

DSM-III (1980), this motion involves a *majority* school of thought under attack from a relatively small *minority*. The motion was denied.

Unorthodox therapies thus have their own standard of care. If a therapist is able to show that the techniques or procedures he or she followed are supported by a respectable minority, the malpractice claim against the therapist automatically fails. Naturally, if the therapist violates the principles followed by the respectable minority, the malpractice action will succeed.

Innovative Therapies

Before a therapeutic treatment gets to be unorthodox, it must first be innovative. In other words, it must be invented, and then tested. Some pioneer must take the first step, but at what risk? Unlike unorthodox therapies, which have at least proved themselves attractive to a respectable minority, innovative therapies initially have few adherents beyond their creators. Who is available to judge them?

If a therapy practice or technique is neither conventional nor followed by a respectable minority, what standard of care should be met by the innovators who have not yet had time to attract followers? These therapies must involve experimentation before successes can be claimed. Instead of a success, however, what if the therapist's new technique results in a failure? Should the therapist be strictly liable because of the experimental deviation from even a respectable minority? Would the informed consent of the patient immunize the therapist from liability?

Interestingly, the law has provided no clear answers to these significant questions. The legal cases that have raised the issues have all involved physical violence inflicted on the patient. For example, the best-known legal case on innovative therapies involved the psychiatrist John Rosen and his "direct analysis" therapy (Rosen, 1953). Rosen, in the 1950s, was considered to be one of the most brilliant and innovative young psychiatrists in the country. His work was very well received, he was the recipient of many awards, and a favorable novel was published about his methods (Brand, 1968).

In *Hammer v. Rosen* (1959), a schizophrenic patient had previously been treated with "radical psychiatric care," including over 150 electric shock treatments, with no apparent improvement. When she became Rosen's patient, his "direct analysis" treatment made initial improvements in her condition, but the improvements did not last. The jury found that Rosen had not guaranteed a cure and had not committed fraud. The court noted, in reference to the malpractice claim, that "it was not shown that the treatment given by defendant was not consistent with good standards of professional judgment addressed to the patient's psychiatric problem." The dissenting judge noted that Rosen received $55,000 over a seven-year period of time to make the patient better, yet, after seven years under Rosen's treatment, she was actually worse. Evidence supported the fact that patients were beaten and bruised during their sessions with Rosen. Although there was evidence that Rosen had justified the beatings as part of the therapy, at the trial he claimed the marks were inflicted in self-defense. Inconsistently, however, he also claimed that the patient's family had given informed consent to the assaults as part of the therapy. The dissent noted that Rosen's methods were not a recognized method of treatment and no informed consent exists when the consenter is unaware that an experimental procedure is being used.

On appeal, the patient succeeded in reversing the judgment preventing her from recovering in malpractice against Rosen. In *Hammer v. Rosen* (1960) New York's highest court held that the patient had a right to present her malpractice case to the jury because "the very nature of the acts complained of bespeaks improper treatment and malpractice. . . ." The physical beatings alone, extended over time and justified as part of the therapy, were sufficient proof of malpractice. Rosen could attempt to explain the beatings as therapeutic, but it would be difficult to persuade a jury. The case was most likely settled out of court because no further record of it appears in case records. Masson (1988) has written a devastating portrait about Rosen's sexual activities with patients and the violence he inflicted on them.

In *Abraham v. Zaslow* (1975), psychologist Robert Zaslow developed a technique he called "rage reduction therapy" or "Z-therapy." As used on Ms. Abraham, the injured plaintiff, the therapy consisted of a 12-hour, all-night session during which time Abraham was "held down" on her back on the laps

of eight to twelve people who were sitting on a sofa. She claimed that she was "choked, and tortured and beaten" and was prevented from leaving. After the session, her physical problems included tears in her mouth and temporary renal failure. A psychiatrist testified that the session triggered an incipient schizophrenia into a full-blown paranoid schizophrenia, and also caused other mental damage. Zaslow raised three defenses: (1) experts would testify that his procedure helped people, (2) Abraham had consented, and (3) no expert was qualified to speak against his treatment unless that expert had tried it. On this last point, the court stated that Zaslow's position "assumes that rage reduction therapy is an accepted method of treating schizophrenic patients and that the decision on whether defendant was liable for malpractice depends upon whether he performed rage reduction therapy according to the standard of others also performing such therapy." Experts were permitted to express the opinion that this therapy, which caused physical and mental damage to patients, "did not conform to the standards of the community." Unfortunately, as in the *Hammer v. Rosen* cases, the court did not articulate how an innovative therapy is to be evaluated. Zaslow's license had earlier been revoked (*Zaslow v. State Board of Medical Examiners*, 1971) in a special hearing attended by all nine members of the Psychology Examining Committee. The Committee wanted to make it clear that its decision should not set a precedent "which would inhibit the employment of innovative techniques which meet the ethical and legal standards of the community" (American Psychological Association *Monitor*, 1973; Note, 1974).

Another unusual therapy in an unusual case may be found in *Rains v. Superior Court (Center Foundation)* (1984) where a group of patients sued the Center Foundation and its therapists for practicing a form of residential group psychiatric treatment program that involved physical beatings, which the court referred to as "sluggo therapy." The patients argued that their consent was not informed because they had been led to believe that the beatings were essential to the therapy. Instead, the patients alleged, the beatings were part of a sophisticated mind-control program that used "coercive persuasion" to turn patients into loyal and dedicated followers of the Center Foundation. The court held that the plaintiffs were entitled to present their case to a jury and were not bound by their signed statements of consent. The court's opinion discusses only issues of consent and whether the plaintiff could recover for battery based upon the physical contact. There is no discussion about evaluating innovative therapies. Hochman (1984) studied the Center Foundation and noted that in its prime there were 350 patients and therapists all living in the same section of Los Angeles, though hundreds of other patients lived elsewhere. Hochman considered the Center Foundation to be a "therapy cult." In the end, after ten years of existence (1971–1981), the Center Foundation was closed down because at least 50 patients filed over a dozen lawsuits requesting in excess of $300 million in damages from eleven different insurance companies. All of the cases settled in 1986, though the litigation among the insurance companies continued into the 1990s (*Center Foundation v. Chicago Insurance Company*, 1991).

In *Hood v. Phillips* (1977), Texas Supreme Court briefly reviewed the various options available for innovative therapies and reached the following conclusions:

> This review of the various standards reveals most courts have not attempted to articulate a distinction among "experimental," "outmoded," "rejected," and "accepted" surgical procedures. Instead, the majority of courts have attempted to draw a line between the reasonable and prudent physician who, as a last resort, turns to an "experimental" or a "rejected" treatment in the hope of assisting the patient and the individual practitioner who attempts to beguile his patient with false or distorted promises. These courts have recognized, as we do, that physicians should be allowed to exercise their professional judgment in selecting a mode or form of treatment. Further, physicians should be allowed to experiment in order that medical science can provide greater benefits for humankind. Consequently, we reject the "any variance" [results in strict liability] standard.
>
> The "respectable minority" standard . . . and "considerable number" test could convey to a jury the incorrect notion that the standard for malpractice is to be determined by a poll of the medical profession. Accordingly, these standards are rejected.
>
> . . . We are of the opinion that the statement of

the law most serviceable to this jurisdiction is as follows: A physician who undertakes a mode or form of treatment which a reasonable and prudent member of the medical profession would undertake under the same or similar circumstances shall not be subject to liability for harm caused thereby to the patient. The question which conveys to the jury the standard which should be applicable is as follows: Did the physician undertake a mode or form of treatment which a reasonable and prudent member of the medical profession would not undertake under the same or similar circumstances?

Simon (1993) has observed that therapies involving "physical or sexual abuse of patients are negligent *per se*" (p. 473), but other innovators who operate at the fringe are in some danger because there is "a nebulous boundary" between acceptable practice or legal liability. Simon concludes that "the fear of legal liability remains a real threat to stifle innovation in psychiatry" (p. 473). Because the law is not yet clear on the assessment of innovative therapies, that fear of innovation will remain, intensified in recent years by the increasing litigiousness against therapists.

Although the cases do not provide guidance concerning the evaluation of innovative therapies, some commentators have sensibly suggested that an experimental deviation from the acceptable community practices should be judged by a standard of care that asks two fundamental questions (Hampton, 1984): (1) Is the experimental deviation ethical? and (2) Are experts available to testify that the deviation was reasonably based upon current knowledge? As Freiberg (1978) correctly observes, because an experimental deviation represents "a greater risk to the patient," it must be justified in terms of (1) "the patient's needs," (2) "some foundation in psychiatric learning," and (3) the "unsuccessful" nature of conventional therapies and treatments (pp. 525–526).

Simon (1993) has suggested that "most clinicians are innovators, attempting novel treatment interventions according to the clinical needs of patients" (p. 473). For that reason he concludes that all but the most "egregious" therapies will fall into the respectable minority rule.

Is there such a thing as "recovered memory therapy"? Is "recovered memory therapy" an innovative or unorthodox treatment? Is the use of hypnosis to refresh recollection a "new" therapy? These brief questions require extensive answers. Unfortunately, the courts have not been uniform in addressing these concerns, and the law has proceeded to issue rulings without the benefit of good science to support those rulings.

Recanters/Retractors

In the modern controversy, recanters, also called retractors, are people who at first believe something about their past (such as they had been sexually abused decades earlier, or had been in Satanic cults), or something about their present (they suffer from multiple personality disorder, now called DID), but who now believe that these "memories" of the past were false or that the diagnosis of dissociative disorder led them to play the role of a person with DID. In recent years, many recanters have decided or been persuaded that they should sue their therapists (Simpson & Baker, 1994). Several malpractice grounds have been argued, including the claims that (1) the therapists used dangerous, unorthodox, and/or experimental procedures without first obtaining the patient's informed consent, (2) the "memories" of childhood sexual abuse were negligently or recklessly implanted by careless therapists who then further persuaded the patients that these memories were accurate, (3) the therapists negligently reinforced these "memories" as true even if they did not implant them, and (4) the therapists failed to do sufficient investigation to determine the accuracy of the "memories" no matter how they were recalled.

Recanting is not a new issue in psychiatry. Our current concern about repressed memories and recanting in forensic settings was anticipated by Erickson in 1938 in an article entitled "Negation or Reversal of Legal Testimony." The paper is a fascinating account of two different instances of provable, fully documented, physical and/or sexual abuse, which was later denied (recanted) by the victims. In the first report, two young girls, nine and eleven years of age, were found in a brothel run by their parents when it was raided by police. The girls freely gave detailed descriptions of what had happened to them in the brothel. Their accounts were corroborated by available evidence. After the passage of some months, their memories began to fade. Gradu

ally, they claimed they had no memories of ever being in a brothel, and they became annoyed at people who suggested that they had been in such an awful place or who suggested that their loving parents would ever do such a hideous thing to them.

According to Erickson, during the first interview the girls were interested in having a sympathetic listener. By the second interview, two months later, they no longer had a need to tell their story and the details became vague and contradictory. The "repugnance" associated with the first interview was replaced by the girls with "resentment" about their current physical condition, which included venereal disease.

By the third interview, the girls' medical problems had been cured, they had adjusted to their surroundings, and they were focused on immediate matters. Consequently, they denied much of the story and made only vague statements about their past. The final interview, conducted six months after the initial interview, was the most difficult because the girls resented talking about the past and trivialized the whole experience ("some bad men came to the house, but nothing bad happened"). The girls expressed warmth for their parents and disgust that the state authorities had invaded their lives.

Erickson found that once their confidence had been obtained, with careful questioning the girls could provide much of the initial detail, but they now claimed that the information they first gave to the police and others was untruthful. However, Erickson noted that "they seemed to have no real recollection of the whole experience as an actual happening in their own lives."

The second case involved a woman who was spending a racy evening with a criminal when they had a serious automobile accident. The criminal made no effort to rescue the young woman, and she was severely burned before rescuers came to save her. At the trial of the criminal, the young woman testified "with much bitterness and hatred" and her story was corroborated by the rescuers and by the criminal himself. Eight months after the conviction, the young woman attempted to have the case reversed on the grounds that she had lied. The criminal claimed that she had in fact told the truth and that he did not want his relatively short sentence reversed for a new trial that could produce a longer sentence, especially because he had already admitted his guilt. The young woman now sincerely believed that the criminal had exerted every effort to save her, efforts which she described in full, though they never occurred.

Erickson wrote that these cases of recanting forensic witnesses were not unknown to psychiatry in 1938. They represent:

> the not unusual legal situation in which a female, after sexual usage, testifies first against the offending male and then, after a period of suffering, reverses her beliefs and attitudes to testify sincerely in his behalf. This identity is manifest primarily in: (1) the highly pleasurable, exciting initial development of the experience; (2) the sudden complete transformation of this pleasurable situation into one of extreme terror, physical helplessness, and pain; and (3) the final evolution into a situation of long-continued suffering and general helplessness.

According to Erickson, these cases have a fundamental relationship to everyday repression of unpleasant or disagreeable experiences. He concluded that "in all probability the initial psychic dynamism in these cases, as in instances occurring in daily life, was the primary repression of the unpleasant affects arising not only from the traumatic aspects of the experience but from the girls' own guilty pleasurable participation."

False Recanters

Erickson's (1938) article suggests that normal psychodynamic forces might account for recanting where the underlying facts are true. An additional recent explanation for such recanting may be found in the social influence literature. Not surprisingly, just as therapists may succeed in persuading patients to believe in false memories, the same influence processes may be used by third parties, such as lawyers, families and/or other recanters, to persuade ex-therapy patients to recant true memories.

An example of social influences causing false recanting generally begins with patients who have been in treatment, either inpatient or outpatient, for a number of years. The chief complaint rarely involves issues of memory. Multiple diagnoses are typically given by the clinicians: major depression, posttraumatic stress disorder, borderline personality, some sort of dissociative disorder, and often chemical dependency or some other addictive behavior. Over the course of the treatment with the primary therapist, and often many collateral therapists, the patient progressively recovers memories of childhood sexual abuse, and may also recover ritual abuse memories. Also over the course of the treatment, the dissociative symptoms increase and DDNOS or DID is given as a diagnosis. Typical self-defeating and therapy-defeating behaviors emerge over the course of the treatment. Self-destructive behaviors and threats to others persist and become a central focus of the treatment, along with the focus on integration and alleviation of the dissociative symptoms through phase-oriented treatment. Treatment length is on the upper end of the continuum of duration. Nevertheless, a clear termination is reached, with or without complications, and the patient retains a relatively positive view of the therapist, at least for some aspects of the overall treatment. Sometime after termination the patient encounters a particular event(s) that causes a significantly negative reappraisal of the treatment. Sometime after that, the patient actively seeks information to support the reappraisal and becomes a retractor, following which a malpractice lawsuit is initiated.

Because malpractice suits for allegedly implanting false memories originally were handled by a small number of attorneys who disseminated their strategies widely, the architecture of these malpractice complaints tend to contain similar features. Also, these attorneys work closely with the False Memory Syndrome Foundation (FMSF), which provides them with four major benefits. First, the Foundation is an excellent source of up-to-date extensive information concerning the legal cases, legal arguments, and other legal developments around the country and abroad. Second, the FMSF data files are available to target disfavored therapists and to identify the patients of these therapists. Third, a small group of FMSF Scientific Advisory Board members appear as expert witnesses for these attorneys in many of the major cases involving recanters. Fourth, the FMSF has extraordinary access to the popular media, thereby allowing the possibility of pretrial publicity favorable to the recanter's pending case.

In false recanter cases the ex-patient is not deliberately lying in order to achieve a high jury verdict, and the attorneys have not brainwashed ex-patients into submission. Though there may be cases where either of these two things has happened, those cases are fraudulent and the conduct of the attorneys would be clearly unethical. The false recanter cases instead involve more subtle influence, in which the recanter now truly believes, incorrectly, that his or her former memories were false.

The malpractice claims contain relatively standard allegations such as misdiagnosis, failure to use appropriate informed consent, conducting treatment that is below the standard of care, conducting treatments that are experimental and hazardous, fostering undue dependency, and causing harm to the patient and/or third parties. The unique feature of these suits is their emphasis on the alleged experimental treatment offered: regardless of the nature of the psychotherapy offered, including solid psychodynamic treatment and/or phase-oriented trauma treatment, the treatment is characterized, or mischaracterized, as "memory recovery therapy." The use of relaxation, guided imagery, journaling, or hypnosis, irrespective of how it is used, is automatically taken as proof of a reckless and unduly suggestive memory recovery technique. Any focus on the patient's report of past experiences may also be taken as evidence for reckless memory recovery practices. The therapist is also alleged to be negligent for failing to seek independent corroboration of the abuse recollections (Scheflin, 1997a).

An additional and vital element of the false recanter cases is the exposure of the ex-patient to groups of recanters, to people who do not believe in repressed memory, to a literature that encourages recanters to sue, and to the lure of millions of dollars from a jury verdict. Under these intensive and suggestive conditions, ex-patients may be persuaded to disavow "memories" that are actually true and come to believe that their memories were false and were implanted by the therapist. Just as social influences may create false memories for accusers, so, too, may they create false recanters. As Beahrs, Cannell, and Gutheil (1996) have noted, "false memories are more likely to arise from social influence, either inside or outside of hypnosis or psychotherapy; intrinsic suggestibility (especially interrogative) and dissociative potential; and less so, simply from being hypnotized"

(p. 50). The mere fact that a patient disavows formerly held beliefs does not mean that the recanting is automatically the truth.

On the other hand, recanters may in fact be telling the truth. Under the influence of suggestion and social influence, some patients may come to believe sincerely in events that never occurred. When later removed from the sphere of influence, and given a neutral opportunity to shed the suggestions, a person's beliefs may undergo a dramatic change. The mere fact that a recanter is now saying something entirely different from what he or she said before should not automatically detract from the authenticity of the new testimony. This point also applies to persons who have recovered memories. Previously, no memory was available; now it is clear and traumatic. The person with recovered memories is in precisely the same situation as the recanter—each must explain why what was previously believed should be discounted as false, and why its opposite should now be accepted as truth.

Observers, including judges and juries, should search for truth by closely observing the arenas of influence and suggestion. If the recanter or the accuser has been in an environment that can be shown to be *unduly* suggestive over an extended period with *high* social influence factors present, and if the recanter or accuser can be shown by objective testing to be highly subject to influence and suggestion, doubt may be cast on the veracity of the current beliefs. The story might still be true, but there are strong reasons not to believe it. If the patient can overcome these two hurdles, suggestion and social influence, there is reason to believe the truth of his or her current beliefs.

Cases involving false recanters inevitably make certain arguments in support of the malpractice allegations. Unfortunately, the scientific studies generally fail to validate these crucial points.

First, the experts for the recanters argue that there is no scientific evidence for repression or for dissociated amnesia. As we initially described in Scheflin and Brown (1996), and more fully describe in chapter 7, there are currently 30 studies specifically on amnesia for childhood sexual abuse, including three prospective studies. Whitfield (in press) has recently reported an additional three or four studies also reaching the same conclusion. These studies make it clear that there is overwhelming scientific support for the existence of repressed or dissociated memory.

Second, the experts for the recanters always assume that recovered memories are necessarily inaccurate. Contrary to this claim, however, there are two recent data-based studies which show that recovered memories for trauma are no more or less accurate than continuous memories for trauma, including memories recovered specifically in therapy (Dalenberg, 1996; Williams, 1995).

Third, experts for the recanters argue either that (1) the patient had a personality trait of high memory suggestibility, or (2) the therapy was unduly suggestive. As a consequence, recollections of abuse or other horrors were implanted, reinforced, and expanded by the defendant therapist, wittingly or unwittingly. It is extremely rare that experts testifying on behalf of recanters have tested the recanters for memory suggestibility or hypnotizability. Leavitt (1997) has shown that, contrary to false memory claims, women reporting recovered memories of abuse were significantly less memory suggestible than other psychiatric patients or other populations for whom norms of memory suggestibility have been established. Gudjonsson (1992) has determined that one indication of the accuracy or inaccuracy of recanters is their trait of memory suggestibility. Objective testing in recovered memory and recanter cases would therefore seem highly advisable, if not essential.

On this third point, caution is merited. There are no studies on suggestion in psychotherapy per se. All of the available evidence is drawn from other areas of suggestion that have been the object of research, such as studies on misinformation suggestion and interrogatory suggestion. Patients most at risk for making false reports about past events are those who have a trait of high memory suggestibility and who have experienced a continous and exhaustive pattern of systematic interrogatory suggestion. Such extreme interviews must include (1) a high ratio of misinformation supplied by the interviewer, (2) the absence of warnings about the limitations of memory and of therapeutic retrieval techniques, and (3) elements of emotional manipulation. Fortunately for patients and therapists, most psychotherapy conducted within the standard of care does not represent this extreme, especially if the therapist encourages free recall in a neutral context.

Under certain conditions false information may be accepted by the patient, but typically for plausible events. As we have seen in chapter 8, studies that experimentally manipulate the type of information that may be the basis of a false report have shown that misinformation suggestion typically occurs for peripheral, not central, details and for plausible, not improbable, information. Such research fails to support the view that bizarre ritual abuse memories can easily be implanted in therapy. It is also useful to note that Ken Lanning (1992b), the F.B.I.'s specialist on child abuse matters, has written "I believe that the majority of victims alleging 'ritual' abuse are in fact victims of some form of abuse or trauma" (p. 39).

Ex-patients may have strong motivations falsely to recant. Some recanters have yielded to significant pressure from family members to retract sex abuse or other allegations under the promise of reestablishing contact with cut-off family members. Attorneys may supply strong motivation in the promise of jury awards in the millions of dollars. Recanters who have been successful in court may be used to help persuade ex-patients to authorize suit against a former therapist. Publicity may motivate recanters, as it has accusers, to appear on local and national talk shows.

The point is that such remarkable post-therapeutic suggestive influences must be carefully considered in weighing the evidence of these malpractice claims: to argue that suggestive influences *in therapy* have distorted the memory for childhood abuse is also to concede the possibility that similar suggestive influences *after therapy* may have distorted the memory once again, and to acknowledge that this post-therapy influence may have shaped the retraction misbelief and the malpractice allegations that arise from it.

Historically, there is a parallel with the research on child abuse investigations. Within the general population, false accusations run around 4–8%. Within the context of custody disputes, however, they run around 28–35%. Over the past decade, the rise of false allegations of abuse in the context of custody disputes clearly illustrates the sad fact that false allegations have increasingly been used as a strategy to win an advantage in custody hearings. Likewise, whereas earlier reports of false memories in therapy may have contained a larger portion of legitimate claims, more recent implanted false memory allegations are increasingly being used as a strategy in malpractice disputes, and thus the incidence of "false" false memory allegations is expected to rise.

While the evolving science has failed to support the majority of the false memory claims, malpractice cases based on allegations of implanting false memories are likely to increase. Therefore, practitioners in the trauma field are best advised to become familiar with the evolving scientific data on memory for trauma and on suggestive influences.

True Recanters

The existence of a class of false recanters makes matters worse for the class of true recanters who, like any other patient, may sue therapists for malpractice. If the treatment by the therapist has been substandard, liability will ensue. It is absolutely wrong to conclude that, from the mere fact that false memories occur in therapy, the therapist should automatically be liable for implanting them. It will still be necessary to show that the false memories are a product of negligent conduct by the therapist. Therapists using suggestive techniques are at risk here, though it would be unwise for courts to conclude that suggestive techniques are inherently substandard. As Beahrs, Cannell, and Gutheil (1996) have observed, "suggestive therapies are probably indicated for some patients" (p. 51).

Aside from the few unusual twists just discussed, cases of recanters suing therapists are no different from ordinary malpractice actions.

Breach of Contract

Patients who receive inadequate treatment may sue their therapist for breach of contract (*Stewart v. Rudner*, 1957). Very few cases exist, however, because the remedy for breach of contract does not include compensation for emotional distress. At best, the patient would recover either (1) the return of fees paid to the therapist or (2) a money award equal to the cost of receiving substitute therapy. The only advantage to suing for breach of contract is the longer statute of limitations. Thus, if the lawsuit is not brought in time in a tort case, the contract remedy may still be available.

Most therapists realize that it is foolish to promise or guarantee a cure. If a promise or guarantee of an outcome is given, however, the promise is binding and the therapist would have to pay what is called "expectation" damages; that is, the difference between the condition the patient was promised and the patient's present condition (*Hawkins v. McGee*, 1929). Calculating these damages would be immensely difficult, but not impossible. Although cases involving therapists do not appear to exist, a surprising number of "guarantee" cases may be found involving surgeons promising that sterilization procedures would be completely effective (*Christensen v. Thornby*, 1934; *Shaheen v. Knight*, 1957). The cases make it clear, however, that hope, optimism, and encouragement do not constitute a guarantee. The law recognizes a certain amount of "puffing" as therapeutic.

Breach of Fiduciary Responsibility

The therapy relationship includes a duty of loyalty on behalf of the therapist toward the patient (Frankel, 1983). Because the relationship is primarily one of trust and confidence, rather than the mere sale of goods or services, therapists must refrain from conduct that violates the fiduciary responsibility. Fiduciary relationships exist between "lawyers and clients, guardians and wards, and doctors and patients, to name but a few" (Cohen, 1979, p. 41). In general, the fiduciary duty mandates that therapists and others refrain from (1) revealing patient confidences and secrets unless permitted or required by law, (2) using the patient's confidential information to obtain an advantage or a benefit, or (3) dividing the therapist's loyalty between a patient and a third party.

In his excellent chapter "The Psychiatrist as a Fiduciary: Avoiding the Double Agent Role," Simon (1992) notes that "in psychiatry, double agentry occurs when a psychiatrist has a conflict of interest that interferes with the fiduciary responsibility to act solely in the best interests of the patient to whom a duty of care is owed" (p. 25). Conflicts generally arise in one of several ways.

First, there may be a conflict between the patient and the therapist. Sexual exploitation is one such conflict, business deals between patients and therapists is another (a dual relationship). Any situation where the therapist may obtain an advantage from confidential information of the patient is an additional illustration of patient-therapist conflicts. For example, in 1989, "a psychiatrist was charged with unlawful trading in the stock of BankAmerica Corp., based on inside information he allegedly received from a patient" (Cohen, 1989, p. B3). The psychiatrist, who faced 46 counts of securities and mail fraud, was treating the wife of a businessman who planned to become the CEO of BankAmerica. To accomplish that goal, the businessman arranged for a $1 billion investment to be made in BankAmerica if he should become its CEO. The psychiatrist confided the information to his broker, who purchased for him the BankAmerica stock in 23 transactions. The broker also told two of his friends, who also invested on the basis of this inside information. The psychiatrist made a $27,475 profit 40 days later when the plan became public. The District Court judge who denied the psychiatrist's request to have the indictment dismissed held that the misappropriation of confidential patient information constitutes a violation of the fiduciary relationship. When that confidential information is used to acquire stocks, federal securities laws are broken (*United States v. Willis*, 1990). The psychiatrist argued that the patient had suffered no harm, but the judge disagreed by noting that the patient had an economic interest in preserving the confidentiality of the information because disclosure might have jeopardized her husband's opportunity to become CEO. Furthermore, the judge also noted that the patient had a property interest in the continuing course of the therapy, which itself depends upon maintaining confidences and secrets. As the judge observed:

> Dr. Willis' disclosures jeopardized the psychiatrist-patient relationship and put at risk the patient's financial investment in psychiatric treatment, either by provoking the termination of the relationship and increasing the cost of treatment by requiring that she find a new psychiatrist, or by requiring additional treatment time to discuss the impact of his disclosures on their relationship.

Another form of conflict occurs when a therapist allows the interests of third parties to interfere with the undivided loyalty owed to the patient (Weinstein, 1992). Simon (1992) notes that such conflicts may arise when the therapist works for an agency or institution:

> For example, for the military psychiatrist, the loyalty to the soldier (patient) versus the military's best interests poses a potential double agent role. Prison psychiatrists are often confronted with the choice of having to serve the interests of their prisoner patients, prison officials, or society. School psychiatrists must balance the interests of the student, the parents, and the school administration. Psychiatrists working in mental institutions must manage the conflicting duties to their patients with those of the institution and society. (p. 25)

Unless the psychiatrist informs the patient otherwise and obtains informed consent, or unless a provision of law dictates otherwise, these conflicts must always be resolved with complete devotion to the protection of the patient's interests.

Therapist-third party conflicts also include issues between therapists and individuals, rather than agencies or institutions. Codes of ethics for attorneys contain extensive, detailed, and intricate rules for the avoidance of conflict of interest (American Bar Association, 1983). It is impermissible for an attorney, or any fiduciary, to permit someone to interfere with the independent judgment exercised on behalf of a client (Wolfram, 1986). Professionals who are in a fiduciary relationship must not divide loyalties between the patient and a third party. One of the reasons it has been so difficult for third parties successfully to sue therapists is because the creation of a duty owed to a third person necessarily harms the undivided loyalty owed to the patient (*MacDonald v. Clinger*, 1982).

THIRD-PARTY (NONCLIENT) LAWSUITS AGAINST THERAPISTS

Should therapists be liable to persons with whom they have no contractual ties? For example, should family members of a patient be able to sue a therapist for their own harm, even if the patient declines to sue? The answer to the question of "who may sue" has not been easy in the history of the law of torts. Over several centuries, the law has evolved crucial distinctions depending upon whether the negligent conduct caused physical harm, economic harm, or emotional harm.

Physical Harm

Early tort law was based on causation, not fault (Keeton, 1984). Causation was viewed quite narrowly, essentially requiring direct contact. In a famous historical example, if a man tossed a brick off a roof, causation would be found if it hit another man, but not if it landed in front of the other man who then tripped over it. Eventually, even these "indirect" physical injuries began to be acknowledged. Tort law today recognizes recovery for indirectly caused physical harm. Naturally, some limitation must be found because "indirect causation" is too vast a basis for liability. Many states follow a "foreseeability" limitation, which says that the defendant is responsible only for the physical harm that a reasonable person could foresee as likely to occur as a consequence of the negligent act. Other states are willing to extend causation beyond foreseeability, but only in very limited circumstances.

Therapists have little occasion negligently to cause physical harm to third parties. The failure to warn of dangerous side effects of drugs provides an illustration. For example, a bystander hit by the automobile driven by the patient who was not told the pills would make her sleepy will be able to bring a third-party liability action against the therapist. Because physical harm is involved, the therapist owed a duty to everyone threatened by his or her failure to warn the patient before the patient drove away.

In general, therapists who practice talking cures have not been sued for physical harm because no risk of physical harm to a third party is created. Liability could be imposed upon a *Tarasoff* theory of duty to protect if the therapist is unreasonable in assessing the patient's potential dangerousness, especially if that dangerousness is directed toward an identified, or identifiable, third person, such as a parent, relative, or girlfriend/boyfriend. According to the California Supreme Court in *Tarasoff v. Board of Regents of the University of California* (1976), when a patient makes a threat of death or serious bodily harm against a particular person, that person is entitled to protection. A moral duty to protect the innocent gives rise to a legal duty on the therapist

to provide protection, usually by warning the third person and/or the police (Felthous, 1989). The legal duty to maintain the confidences of the patient is not absolute (Scheflin, 1996) when human life is at stake (Douard & Winslade, 1990). Protection of threatened third parties is one instance where the preservation of human life is deemed superior to the keeping of patient secrets (Dietz, 1990; Slovenko, 1990). Because the therapist can foresee the potential for harm to the third party, the therapist is placed under a duty to protect that third party by committing the potentially violent patient, or by warning the potential victim and the police. Serious clinical issues are involved in *Tarasoff* cases (Beck, 1990).

Courts have traditionally permitted third-party lawsuits where physical harm was foreseeable. In *Myers v. Quesenberry* (1983), a California Court of Appeals court held that a duty was owed to a "foreseeable but not readily identifiable" third party when a doctor failed to warn the patient not to drive because of her diabetic condition enhanced by severe stress. Several other states have reached the same result as *Myers* (*Gooden v. Tips*, 1983; *Joy v. Eastern Maine Medical Center*, 1987; *Kaiser v. Suburban Transportation System*, 1965; *Welke v. Kuzilla*, 1985; *Wilschinsky v. Medina*, 1989).

In *DiMarco v. Lynch Homes-Chester County* (1990), a blood technician (Viscichini) was accidentally punctured while taking a blood sample from a patient. When Viscichini learned the patient had hepatitis, she immediately sought treatment from two physicians, both of whom told her that, if she remained symptom- free for six weeks, it would mean she had not been infected by the hepatitis virus. Although she was not told to refrain from sexual relations for any period of time, she did so until eight weeks after exposure. Because she had remained symptom-free during that time, she then resumed sexual relations with her boyfriend (DiMarco). Three months after exposure, Viscichini developed Hepatitis B and, three months after that, DiMarco was diagnosed as having the same disease. DiMarco sued Viscichini's doctors, claiming they were negligent in not warning Viscichini that if she had sexual relations within six months of exposure she could infect her sexual partner. In affirming the existence of a duty owed to DiMarco, the court explained that when

a physician treats a patient who has been exposed

to or who has contracted a communicable and/or contagious disease, it is imperative that the physician give his or her patient the proper advice about preventing the spread of the disease. Communicable diseases are so named because they are readily spread from person to person. Physicians are the first line of defense against the spread of communicable diseases, because physicians know what measures must be taken to prevent the infection of others. The patient must be advised to take certain sanitary measures, or to remain quarantined for a period of time, or to practice sexual abstinence or what is commonly referred to as "safe sex."

Such precautions are taken not to protect the health of the patient, whose well-being has already been compromised, rather such precautions are taken to safeguard the health of others. Thus, the duty of a physician in such circumstances extends to those "within the foreseeable orbit of risk of harm." . . . If a third person is in that class of persons whose health is likely to be threatened by the patient, and if erroneous advice is given to that patient to the ultimate detriment of the third person, the third person has a cause of action against the physician, because the physician should recognize that the services rendered to the patient are necessary for the protection of the third person.

A dissenting judge in *DiMarco* suggested the rules limiting an attorney's duty to his client, and those refusing to extend an attorney's duty to third persons, ought to be applied in the medical context, but the majority disagreed by stating that the "harm caused by a lawyer to a third party cannot possibly equal the harm that a physician can do to society at large by negligently failing to act to halt the spread of contagious and communicable diseases."

It is important to note, however, that the law permits third-party liability in these cases solely because of the social policy of avoiding *physical* harm. As we shall see, the law is far more reluctant to require duties to third persons when the harm threatened is economic or emotional.

Economic Harm

Tort law has been hesitant to require professionals to answer to third parties for negligently caused economic losses. The law's concern is that the amount of liability may greatly exceed the fault. For example, an accounting firm hired to do the books of a major corporation makes a negligent error about the company's net worth. Investors pour money into the corporation's stock and ultimately lose their investments. The accounting firm is certainly liable to the corporation for the economic losses caused by the negligence, but should thousands of investors, all unknown to the accounting firm and none having contracts with it, be allowed to recover hundreds of millions of dollars from the firm?

To protect against such potentially ruinous third-party liability, the law imposed what was called a "privity" barrier, which limited recovery only to those parties in "privity" with each other, meaning those parties with contracts between them. In the example just discussed, the accounting firm is liable to the corporation with whom it has a contract, but not to the investors with whom it has no contracts. Only the corporation is in "privity" with the accounting company.

The leading case establishing the privity rule in economic cases is *Ultramares Corp. v. Touche, Niven & Co.* (1931), which contains a brilliant analysis by Judge Cardozo that has kept generations of first-year law students burning the midnight oil. Cardozo rejected liability to third persons by noting in oft-quoted words that "if liability for negligence exists, a thoughtless slip or blunder, the failure to detect a theft or forgery beneath the cover of deceptive entries, may expose accountants to a liability in an indeterminate amount for an indeterminate time to an indeterminate class. The hazards of a business conducted on these terms are so extreme as to enkindle doubt whether a flaw may not exist in the implication of a duty that exposes to these consequences" (p. 422).

Over the years the privity barrier has been slightly lowered regarding third-party suits against professionals, but only where the professional knew of the existence of the third party, and, most importantly, knew that the client was intending the transaction to benefit this third party (*Bily v. Arthur Young & Company*, 1992). For example, suppose a client asks an attorney to draft a will so that the client's favorite charity will receive $10,000. The lawyer is negligent in drafting the will and the charity receives nothing. Should the charity, which is not the attorney's client, be allowed to sue the attorney for the $10,000? It is a general rule, established more than a century ago by the United States Supreme Court, that lawyers are not liable to third parties who are economically harmed by a lawyer's negligence in handling the client's affairs (*National Savings Bank v. Ward*, 1879).

Beginning with the seminal case of *Lucas v. Hamm* (1961), however, which was the first case in the country to permit a third-party economic loss suit against a lawyer, courts have permitted such suits where the client intends the third party to be a beneficiary under the client's will, but the attorney's negligence in drafting the will prevents the third party from receiving the bequest. Courts permit recovery in these cases because the client intended to confer a benefit on the third party and this fact was known to the lawyer. Thus, in the example, the charity would be permitted to sue the attorney for the $10,000. It is important to note that the interests of the client and the interests of the charity are not in conflict. In fact, their interests are identical—the charity wants the $10,000 and the client wants the charity to have it. The lawyer had been hired by the client *for the purpose of conferring this benefit on the charity*. The client communicated to the attorney the fact that the client intended the lawyer to facilitate the charity's reception of the money. Thus, the lawyer was not being asked to divide his or her loyalties between the client and the third-party charity. The third party had no interests adverse to the interests of client.

Some courts have moved a step further in permitting third-party suits. In *Home Budget Loans, Inc. v. Jacoby & Meyers Law Offices* (1989), the California Court of Appeal stated the rule as follows: "An attorney advising a client owes no duty to third persons affected by that advice 'in the absence of any showing that the legal advice was foreseeably transmitted to or relied upon by [the third party] plaintiffs or that [third party] plaintiffs were intended beneficiaries of a transaction to which the advice pertained.' (*Goodman v. Kennedy* (1976) . . .)." This statement of the rule appears to invite a foreseeability analysis, which would permit any foreseeable third party to sue and recover. Because of the importance of foreseeability in the current attempts to expand the law, we will take a moment to describe "a foreseeability analysis."

Remember the story about Mrs. O'Leary's cow?

According to history, the great Chicago fire began when Mrs. O'Leary placed a lit lantern in her cow barn. A cow knocked over the lantern and set the barn on fire. The fire in the barn ignited a neighboring building, which also began to burn. That building ignited the building next to it, which then ignited the building next to it, and so on. Eventually, a large portion of the entire city was ablaze. Mrs. O'Leary's act of placing the lit lantern in the barn where the cow could kick it over is clearly negligent conduct. Why is it negligent? Because a reasonable person could *foresee* that the cow was likely to knock it over and the fire would then ignite the straw setting the barn ablaze. Now that we know that Mrs. O'Leary is negligent, to whom must she pay damages?

Courts wrestling with this problem have generally chosen one of two different approaches: (1) the direct causation test, whereby Mrs. O'Leary would be liable to anyone who is harmed directly by her conduct, regardless of whether that person or that particular harm was foreseeable, or (2) the foreseeability test, whereby Mrs. O'Leary would be liable only to those persons, and for that harm, that a reasonable person would foresee as likely to result from the negligent act. Because the spread of the fire was direct, like dominoes falling in a row, the direct causation test would require Mrs. O'Leary to pay for the rebuilding of the entire city. Under the foreseeability analysis, however, Mrs. O'Leary might be liable only to her immediate neighbors, and perhaps even to the owners of the building after that, but she would not be responsible to everyone injured by the fire, even though her negligent act directly caused them harm. Thus, under a foreseeability analysis, the dangers to be foreseen determine whether someone is negligent and also toward whom they have a duty to act reasonably.

The foreseeability analysis, if applied to professionals, might permit third parties to recover from therapists if a reasonable person could foresee that negligent treatment of the patient would cause harm to these third parties. The problem with a foreseeability analysis under these circumstances is that it is always foreseeable that the patient's friends, relatives, workmates or classmates, neighbors, and others might be emotionally distressed if the patient is negligently treated. Under a foreseeability analysis, the therapist would always owe a duty to some, and indeed many, third parties.

Despite the language in *Goodman v. Kennedy* (1976) quoted above about foreseeability, the courts have refused to drop the privity barrier that low. Instead, in every case in which a third party is permitted to sue, the facts must show that the third party was someone the client was trying to benefit, or someone the client was seeking to obtain a benefit from, such as an investor. The cases involving attorneys make it clear that an attorney must have known about this person's role, and, most importantly, the third person's interests are not in conflict with the interests of the client. Many commentators have expressly warned about the dangers of dividing the loyalties of an attorney between a client and a third party (Cifu, 1989; Fiebach, 1988; Samet, Walker, Meehan, & Lubega, 1991).

The one exception to the rule that the lawyer owes undivided loyalty only to the client occurs in what Hazard (1987) has called "triangular relationships." For example, suppose a lawyer represents a conservator or a guardian. The conservator or guardian is in a fiduciary relationship with the conservatee or ward. If the attorney learns that the conservator or guardian is cheating the conservatee or ward, some states hold that the attorney owes a duty to the third party (conservatee or ward) that is superior to the duty owed to the client (*Fickett v. Superior Court*, 1976). This exception, however, requires that (1) the lawyer be in a fiduciary relationship with the client, which is always the case, and (2) the client be in a fiduciary relationship with a vulnerable third party.

Until the last two or three years, there has been no body of legal commentary applying third-party liability analysis to therapists. Most likely, however, courts would apply the rules developed for lawyers because each profession is bound by strict codes of loyalty and each profession works with intimate feelings and confidential information. Lowering the privity barrier in cases involving therapists and lawyers would require a rewriting, and substantial weakening, of the conflict of interest rules. The most recent American Psychological Association's Code of Ethics has strengthened these obligations, particularly in regard to dual relationships. The American Bar Association's Model Rules of Professional Responsibility (1983) has also broadened and strengthened the loyalty owed to clients. Third-party lawsuits against therapists or lawyers would reverse this ethical trend.

Emotional Harm: The "Bystander Theory"

In early common law, English courts refused to permit recovery where the plaintiff had suffered emotional distress unaccompanied by "physical" impact (Keeton, 1984). Thus, in one of the more famous cases, a driver of a team of horses was negligent and the horses galloped up to the plaintiff, stopping right next to her. Plaintiff, who was pregnant at the time, suffered severe emotional distress and also a miscarriage. It was held that, because the horses never actually touched her, she could not recover.

American courts adopted a similar rule. In a Pennsylvania case, a bull was negligently permitted to gallop after the plaintiff. It stopped a few bare inches from her. The Pennsylvania Supreme Court declined to allow recovery for plaintiff's emotional distress because there was no physical contact (*Bosley v. Andrews*, 1958).

This rule, called the "physical impact" rule, was designed to permit courts to have a clear "bright line" guide to when liability might be imposed. Without such a guide, it was feared that the courts would be flooded with claims of emotional distress based on what might have happened. As legal commentators have pointed out, if I am driving my car and I hit someone, I will know it. But how can I defend against the charge that I merely *scared* someone with my driving?

These concerns have been summarized by the Wisconsin Supreme Court in the recent case of *Bowen v. Lumbermens Mutual Casualty Company* (1994):

> While courts are willing to compensate for emotional harm incident to physical injury in a traditional tort action, they have been loath to recognize the right to recover for emotional harm alone. The common law historically distrusted emotion. Emotional suffering was deemed genuine and compensable only if it was associated with a provable physical injury claim in an accepted tort cause of action.

* * *

. . . Courts have historically been apprehensive that psychological injuries would be easy to feign and that suits would be brought for trivial emotional distress more dependent on the peculiar emotional sensitivities of the plaintiff than upon the nature of the tortfeasor's conduct. People should not, courts reasoned, be able to sue for everyday minor disturbances. Furthermore courts feared that opening the courts to claims for negligent infliction of emotional distress would open the floodgates of litigation and lead to unlimited liability for a negligent tortfeasor.

Nevertheless courts have acknowledged that justice requires recognition of some claims for negligently inflicted emotional harm. Courts have devised various criteria to balance a plaintiff's compensatory interests for emotional distress with the interests of the judicial system in authenticating claims and preventing unlimited liability of the tortfeasor.

Judges became dissatisfied with the "impact" rule after many cases arose where justice required compensation, but no "impact" could be proven. In order to deliver just verdicts within the impact rule, judges began to trivialize the nature of the impact required, such as where the only physical contact was some smoke in the eyes, or a slight impact with the car in which the plaintiff was seated.

The first Restatement of Torts, sec. 313 (American Law Institute, 1934), which was drafted by the country's most eminent scholars, judges, and practitioners to serve as a guide for the development of tort law, proposed no rule regarding recovery for emotional distress and resulting physical injury to a parent or spouse who witnessed the injury-causing negligent act. The Restatement provided in part:

Caveat: The [American Law] Institute expresses no opinion as to whether an actor whose conduct is negligent as involving an unreasonable risk of causing bodily harm to a child or spouse is liable for an illness or other bodily harm caused to the parent or spouse who witnesses the peril or harm of the child or spouse and thereby suffers anxiety or shock which is the legal cause of the parent's or spouse's illness or other bodily harm.

The refusal to state a position in these situations

or, more importantly, the refusal to state that there should always be no recovery in these "bystander" cases involving whether a duty is owed to people who are not themselves in harm's way (in the zone of physical danger) served as encouragement for judges to experiment with a variety of different approaches.

One year later, in 1935, a new rule began to emerge that was crafted by the Wisconsin Supreme Court in the leading case of *Waube v. Warrington* (1935). Under this "zone of danger" test, a plaintiff could recover even though not physically touched, provided the plaintiff was within the zone of actual danger of being physically injured. Thus, the negligent driver of the car that narrowly misses me may still be answerable for my emotional distress.

The "zone of danger" rule was based on tort law's familiar concepts of duty and foreseeability, especially as articulated by Judge Benjamin Cardozo in the famous case of *Palsgraf v. Long Island Railroad* (1928), which continues to torment the analytical abilities of first-year law students. In essence, *Palsgraf* said that a person who acts negligently is liable only to those who could be foreseen to be within a "zone of foreseeable risk" created by that conduct. A defendant's duty to act reasonably is owed only to those within that artificial zone. The *Waube* judges used this idea to say that a person owes a duty "to use ordinary care to avoid physical injury to those who would be put in physical peril." No duty is owed to persons outside the zone of actual physical danger.

The "zone of danger" test has proven to be a popular rule. Since its inception in 1935, it has become the law in most jurisdictions and is the rule adopted in the influential Restatement (Second) of Torts, sec. 313(2) (American Law Institute, 1965). But what about persons outside the zone of danger? Suppose a mother watches from the safe haven of the sidewalk or a bedroom window while a negligent driver hits her child in the street. Should the mother, who is not in danger herself, be allowed to recover for the emotional distress of seeing her child injured or killed? The Wisconsin Supreme Court in *Waube* (1935), the case that began the "zone of danger" test, rejected the mother's claim because she was outside the zone of physical danger and did not fear for her own safety.

Despite the popularity of the "zone of danger"

test, it too had problems similar to those of the "impact" rule. As the Wisconsin Supreme Court recently noted in *Bowen* (1994):

> Th[e] history of the . . . decisions in negligent infliction of emotional distress cases demonstrates the problem with the zone of danger doctrine: while it appears to allay the court's apprehension of opening the doors to trivial or fraudulent claims and to unlimited liability for a negligent tortfeasor, its rigid application prevents redress in deserving cases. Its companion rules of fear for one's own safety and physical manifestation of emotional distress have the same effect.

* * *

The nearly 60 years of court decisions since *Waube* demonstrate that rigid doctrinal limitations on liability to bystanders produce arbitrary, incongruous and indefensible results. Plaintiffs in substantially the same position have been treated differently. These defects have led the court to sow confusion in the law by circumventing the rules. . . .

By the late 1960s, judges had become more sensitized to the interests of injured plaintiffs. Throughout the entire law of torts, older decisions favoring vested interests were being overthrown in favor of increased consumer protection. Plaintiffs were expanding the boundaries of liability in many areas of the law, including negligence. The law of negligent infliction of emotional distress was not exempt from these judicial reform movements. Liberal courts were responding to the social pressures in the 1960s to recognize increasing rights of plaintiffs and increasing responsibilities of defendants. Beginning in the late 1960s, and lasting almost two decades, judges gave the ordinary citizen the most protection, and the greatest opportunity for recovery, that has ever been recognized. As we shall see later, however, conservative judges gradually have been undoing many of these reforms.

In *Dillon v. Legg* (1968), the California Supreme Court became the first court in the country to allow a bystander to sue for emotional distress where the bystander was not in "the zone of [physical] danger." In that landmark case, a mother in a position of safety watched a negligently driven automobile strike her child. *Dillon* based its conclusion that the

mother should be able to recover for her emotional distress on the foreseeability of such emotional distress to an observing relative, and the Court suggested three guidelines to be used by courts in assessing such foreseeability: (1) temporal proximity—the bystander was present at the time the accident occurred, (2) spatial proximity—the bystander witnessed or observed the accident, and (3) relational proximity—the bystander is a close relative of the accident victim.

The California Supreme Court was clear that these guidelines were not intended as rigid rules, but only as signposts that could be flexibly applied as principles of "foreseeability" in each case. In other words, the court was telling judges that they could expand the law even further in appropriate cases because "foreseeability" itself is an ever expanding idea. For example, I can foresee that if I negligently drive my car and strike a child, the parents of that child who witness the accident will suffer emotional distress. But I can also foresee that the child's friends, and indeed anyone, who witnesses the accident will be emotionally affected. Should everyone who was a witness be permitted to sue me?

The concept of foreseeability does not move backward. Once something is foreseeable, it never becomes unforeseeable. Because the foreseeability concept always moves forward, once something new becomes foreseeable, the door is opened a little wider to still other things being foreseeable. For example, I can also foresee that if I negligently drive my car and hit a child, relatives who were not present will also suffer emotional distress. So, too, will the child's classmates and playmates. Foreseeability is like the stone thrown in the water—from that center point, waves will radiate out in ever expanding circles.

After twenty years of expansion in favor of permitting plaintiffs to recover, the law was altered dramatically by newly elected conservative judges on the California Supreme Court in *Thing v. La Chusa* (1989). The judges held that the *Dillon* guidelines were now to be observed as strict limitations. Unless their conditions were precisely met, plaintiff-bystanders could not recover.

California courts have made it clear that negligent infliction of emotional distress is not a separate tort, but rather a part of the general law of negligence. In order to recover, plaintiffs must prove that a duty was owed to them by the defendant to refrain from negligently causing them emotional distress. Whether a duty exists is a question of law decided by the judge and not a question of fact to be decided by the jury. *Dillon*, as well as the cases which follow it, says that the duty is owed only to bystanders who meet the terms of the guidelines.

For example, in 1994, the Wisconsin Supreme Court formally rejected the "zone of danger" test and replaced it with the approach pioneered by California's *Dillon* decision. In *Bowen v. Lumbermens Mutual Casualty Company* (1994), the court noted that the tort of negligent infliction of emotional distress was not intended to provide compensation for "all traumas of everyday life," but only those terrible tragedies that involve the direct observance of serious harm to loved ones:

> Historically, the tort of negligent infliction of emotional distress has raised two concerns: (1) establishing authenticity of the claim and (2) ensuring fairness of the financial burden placed upon a defendant whose conduct was negligent. A court deals with these concerns by exploring in each case such public policy considerations as: (1) whether the injury is too remote from the negligence; (2) whether the injury is wholly out of proportion to the culpability of the negligent tortfeasor; (3) whether in retrospect it appears too extraordinary that the negligence should have brought about the harm; (4) whether allowance of recovery would place an unreasonable burden on the negligent tortfeasor; (5) whether allowance of recovery would be too likely to open the way to fraudulent claims; or (6) whether allowance of recovery would enter a field that has no sensible or just stopping point. The court has stated these public policy considerations that may preclude liability in capsule form as follows: When it would shock the conscience of society to impose liability, the courts may hold as a matter of law that there is no liability.

> Three factors, taken together, help assure that the claim in this case is genuine, that allowing recovery is not likely to place an unreasonable burden upon the defendant, and that allowance of recovery will not contravene the other public policy considerations we have set forth.

> First, the victim was seriously injured or killed. . .

> Second, the plaintiff was the victim's . . . spouse, parent, child, grandparent, grandchild or sibling. . . .

> We agree that emotional trauma may accompany the injury or death of less intimately connected persons such as friends, acquaintances, or passersby. Nevertheless, the suffering that flows from beholding the agony or death of a spouse, parent, child, grandparent, grandchild or sibling is unique in human experience and such harm to a plaintiff's emotional tranquility is so serious and compelling as to warrant compensation. Limiting recovery to those plaintiffs who have the specified family relationships with the victim acknowledges the special qualities of close family relationships, yet places a reasonable limit on the liability of the tortfeasor.

> Third, the plaintiff observed an extraordinary event. . . . Witnessing either an incident causing death or serious injury or the gruesome aftermath of such an event minutes after it occurs is an extraordinary experience, distinct from the experience of learning of a family member's death through indirect means. Thus it is an appropriate place to draw the line between recoverable and non-recoverable claims.

The Court held that a bystander who was not in the "zone of danger" could sue for negligence. Three judges wrote a special concurring opinion to express concern that "the majority's approach virtually assures that every claim for negligent infliction of emotional distress will go to the jury." These judges would require "that in order to survive a motion for summary judgment, plaintiffs have the burden of producing some extrinsic, verifiable evidence to support their claims" of emotional injury:

> Take the case of a person who claims that while crossing the street, they were nearly struck by a passing motorist, and that the fright occasioned by this near miss has caused them great emotional distress. If, as the majority instructs, the standard elements of negligence apply to this claim, the plaintiff will almost certainly survive a motion for summary judgment. I do not think this is appropriate. The potential for fraud is simply too great.

> Life in our society is full of near misses, as anyone who has run the gauntlet of rush-hour traffic can attest. These experiences can be extremely distressing. Nevertheless, people should not be able to convert such occurrences into a source of monetary recovery.

Most states still follow some version of the "zone of danger" test, but a number of states now have adopted a version of the *Dillon* guidelines approach, which allows recovery for bystanders not threatened with physical harm themselves. In addition to Wisconsin's move in *Bowen* to permit more people to sue for negligent infliction of emotional distress, the New Jersey Supreme Court has also opened wider the doors to recovery in *Dunphy v. Gregor* (1994), when it permitted recovery by a nonrelative, the deceased's fiancée (Podgers, 1995).

Under either test, however, therapists have never been held liable to bystanders for the obvious reason that no severe physical harm is done to the patient while a third party observes the event. Thus, for nonpatients who want to sue therapists for emotional distress, failure to be in the "zone of physical danger," or to have observed physical harm to a loved one, will defeat any cause of action. No appellate case in the United States has permitted a recovery against a therapist on bystander grounds for emotional distress, even though emotional harm to the nonpatient is foreseeable if negligent treatment is provided to the patient.

A more pro-plaintiff approach, followed by a few courts in the 1970s and early 1980s, might have permitted recovery based primarily on the foreseeability of the harm. For example, in *Chatman v. Millis* (1975), a divorced wife became concerned that her ex-husband was molesting their infant son during the father's visitations. The wife consulted a therapist, who heard her story and then met with the child. The therapist wrote a letter to the wife's attorney suggesting that unsupervised visits by the husband be ended. The husband sued the therapist for defamation and malpractice. The Arkansas Supreme Court did not reach the defamation claim, but it did hold that no duty was owed to the husband because of many factors—the therapist made no examination of the husband, the husband was not a patient, the diagnosis was not made for the purpose of benefitting the husband, and the husband did not rely on the diagnosis to his detriment. The dissenting judge argued that a foreseeability analysis should have been used to determine whether a duty was owed to the husband. In conclusion, the dissent noted:

> . . . it would border on absurdity to say that [the therapist] could not reasonably have foreseen that

a misdiagnosis of homosexuality would harm [the husband]. The fact that the diagnosis was made without [the therapist's] having known, seen or interviewed [the husband] or having administered any tests to him would seem, in and of itself, to be malpractice, but whether it is or not is a matter of evidence when the case is tried on its merits. It certainly is a sufficient allegation to state a cause of action. As a matter of fact, the only flaw the majority perceives in the complaint is the fact that [the husband] was not a patient of [the therapist]. I submit that reason and logic do not support the majority opinion. I would remand this case for further proceedings.

This liberal approach has lost favor with conservative judges, however, and though it was never the law in the first place, it is not likely to be resurrected with any frequency during a time when tort law in general is under highly successful attacks by business and insurance company interests. Since the 1980s, the law across the country has undergone a severe "tort reform" movement that has rolled back protections previously available to plaintiffs. Nevertheless, as we shall discuss below, a few recent cases have raised the possibility that liability may be based solely on a foreseeability analysis.

In California, the Supreme Court in the *Thing* case expressly disapproved the use of a foreseeability approach in cases involving negligent infliction of emotional distress. While foreseeability is the main guide in assisting judges in imposing liability where defendant's negligence causes *physical* harm, it provides little help in cases involving *emotional* harm, in part because, as California law-scholar Bernard Witkin has observed, "on a clear day some courts can foresee forever" (*Bro v. Glaser*, 1994, p. 904). In other words, it can always be foreseen that harm to a loved one will cause emotional distress.

Even if such third-party liability were to be considered by a court on its own merits, ethical rules that prohibit professionals from weakening their fiduciary duty of loyalty to their patients/clients and ethical restrictions on serving conflicting interests should be strong enough to prevent any such third-party liability from being imposed. The same considerations that courts have applied to limit third-party recovery of economic harm have also been applied in emotional harm cases.

In *Lamare v. Basbanes* (1994), a father fled the country with his two children after losing custody of them in a divorce brought by the mother because she suspected the father of molesting the children. One child was recovered and returned to the mother, but the other child had not been found. The mother claimed that the husband's lawyer's negligence was to blame because the lawyer knew that the husband would abscond with the children. The Court held that the lawyer owed no duty to the mother or the children:

> It is undisputed there was no attorney-client relationship between the [lawyer] and the [mother and children]. Absent an attorney-client relationship, the court will recognize a duty of reasonable care if an attorney knows or has reason to know a nonclient is relying on the services rendered. . . . However, the court will not impose a duty of reasonable care on an attorney if such an independent duty would potentially conflict with the duty the attorney owes to his or her client. . . . To impose a duty of care where there is the potential for conflicting interests would be inconsistent with [the ethical duties of attorneys as promulgated by the Supreme Court of Massachusetts].
>
> The rule is founded on the realization that, if a duty was owed to the adversary of an attorney's client, an unacceptable conflict of interest would be created, and because it would be inimical to the adversary system for an adverse party to be allowed to rely on an opposing party's attorney. . . . It is well-established that attorneys owe no duty to their client's adversary. . . .

The court found that the mother's interests were adverse to the father's interests, and also that the children were adverse parties as well:

> In this case, at all relevant times the [lawyer] represented the children's father. The children were represented by their guardian ad litem during the care and protection proceedings. Moreover, separate counsel had been appointed to represent the children with regard to the allegations of sexual abuse. It is clear from the allegations of sexual abuse alone that a potential conflict existed. Furthermore [the father] sought different visitation rights from those recommended by the guardian ad litem, thus

> putting the [lawyer] at further odds with the children. Accordingly, the [lawyer] owed no duty to the children.

As a final hope, the mother argued that a Massachusetts statute provided protection for children. The court dismissed this argument by noting that because there was no indication that the Legislature intended "to impose such a duty on an attorney representing a parent when the parent's interest may conflict with the child's interest," the court "will not infer such a duty."

A California court has suggested, but did not hold, that the protection of children from being molested is so important that it may require the attorney to owe a greater duty to the child, who is not the client, than is owed to the parent who is the client. In *Tushinsky v. Arnold* (1987), a wife hired an attorney to obtain a dissolution of her marriage to her husband, whom she accused of having molested their 12-year-old daughter during the last five years. The wife asked the attorney to make sure that the husband was not criminally prosecuted. The attorney, in disregard of these instructions, advised the wife to file a petition under the Domestic Violence Prevention Act (DVPA), knowing that the district attorney had "no choice" but to investigate the allegations. If the issue of whether the daughter had been molested had been left to the civil courts as part of the dissolution proceedings, no criminal accusation would have arisen. The wife followed the attorney's advice and filed a DVPA petition as well as a dissolution action against the husband. Meanwhile, the attorney, in the hopes of improving the dissolution case, had the daughter hypnotized to discover information about the alleged molestations. The District Attorney's office began an investigation of the husband, but was forced to terminate it because the fact that hypnosis had been used automatically tainted the most significant witness, the daughter. California law does not permit previously hypnotized witnesses to testify unless there is a recorded prehypnosis statement. The testimony is limited to what is contained in the statement. The falsely accused husband sued his wife for malicious prosecution and recovered a 6.15 million dollar verdict after proving that the wife had knowingly lied about the sexual molesting. The wife then sued the attorney for malpractice.

The *Tushinsky* court had little trouble finding that the wife's lies were the cause of her problems. Consequently, the court did not address whether the attorney's conduct in having the child hypnotized, and thus rendered legally incompetent to testify, was actionable malpractice. Had the sexual abuse charges against the husband been true, the attorney might have been found liable for malpractice by authorizing the daughter to be hypnotized. The court also discussed the proper resolution of the ethical conflict of interest facing the attorney:

> Given our conclusion that [the wife] was the sole proximate cause of the charges of child molestation being prosecuted against [the husband], and given the finding of the jury in the malicious prosecution case that the charges were false, the issue of whether [the attorney's] alleged hypnotism of the child was a proximate cause of the dismissal of the criminal charges is irrelevant. Regardless of the negligence involved, dismissal of criminal charges cannot serve as a basis for a malpractice action where the charges dismissed were false and the individual asserting both the criminal charges and the malpractice action knew the charges to be false when made.

We note that attorneys are often faced with a seemingly irresolvable dilemma of choosing between the perceived welfare of a child and the rights of its parents. When confronted with allegations of child molestation, a parent may establish several goals, all of equal value to the family involved. The parent may assert, as does [the wife] in her complaint, that her "immediate" concern is to exclude the alleged abuser from the family home in order to protect the child and to permit investigation of the charges. Often, the distraught family is adamant that it does not want the molester criminally prosecuted. Rather, the primary goal is often to protect the integrity of the family unit by dealing with the matter of sexual abuse of a child by seeking psychiatric care. The state does not, however, view the area of sexual abuse of children in the same manner. Nor does it establish the same priorities. "In the area of sexual abuse of children by adults, the law . . . has three objectives: to punish the abuser, to identify and protect his victims and to cure him in order to protect future potential victims." (*People v. Stritzinger* (1984) 34 Cal.3d

505, 523, 194 Cal.Rptr. 431, 668 P.2d 738 (conc. and dis. opn. of Kaus, J.).) Thus, an attorney's primary duty, when confronted with accusations such as those made by [the wife] against [the husband], is to act promptly to protect the child. We believe that an attorney can meet this responsibility by filing a petition for restraining orders, either in a dissolution action or under the DVPA. An attorney who files such a petition after being advised by his client that a third party, who is not a client of the attorney, has sexually abused a child, cannot be liable for any damages unless he does so with the knowledge that the facts contained within the petition are false.

Tushinsky provides no support for third-party liability against therapists because the case recognizes a superior duty only to abused or threatened children. Thus, in the absence of special legislation, third-party liability of therapists for negligent infliction of emotional distress is not likely, unless, as suggested by *Tushinsky*, the third party is an abused child.

California's "Direct Victim" Theory

The California Supreme Court, in a ruling not followed in other states, has provided third parties an additional avenue of recovery beyond the bystander theory discussed above. Known as the "direct duty" rule, this alternative way to prove negligent infliction of emotional distress began with *Molien v. Kaiser Foundation Hospitals* (1980). In *Molien*, a wife went to a doctor who negligently diagnosed her as having a venereal disease (syphilis). The doctor advised the wife to tell her husband so that he could be diagnosed and receive treatment, if necessary. The wife assumed that her husband was the source of the disease and, not surprisingly, the marriage soon fell apart. When it was later discovered that the doctor had made an error, the husband sued him. The Supreme Court held that the risk of harm to the husband was reasonably foreseeable and that the doctor's tortious conduct "was directed to him as well as to his wife." The husband was thus held to be a "direct victim" to whom a duty of due care is owed. According to the court, once the doctor directed that the husband be informed of the wife's diagnosis, with the foreseeable consequence that it could disrupt the marriage, the doctor "assumed a duty to convey accurate information and the husband accordingly was a 'direct victim' of the doctor's negligence" (*Marlene F. v. Affiliated Psychiatric Services*, 1989, p. 590).

Since *Molien*, which was decided during the Court's liberal days, the new conservative California Supreme Court has made two points about it: First, the opinion is overly broad and thoroughly unclear. While the Court has come close to overruling *Molien* twice, first in *Thing* (1989) and then in *Burgess* (1992), it instead has chosen to severely limit its application.

Second, *Molien's* language about foreseeability is not to be used as a means of extending the duty owed. As the Supreme Court's opinion in *Huggins v. Longs Drug Stores California* (1993) notes: "That duty did not arise simply because the doctor's misdiagnosis 'necessarily involved him directly'. . . , but because the doctor directed his patient, the wife, to advise the plaintiff [husband] of the diagnosis."

Huggins provides a good illustration of how narrowly the courts will construe the "direct duty" rule. A doctor prescribed a medicine for a two-month-old infant. The parents took the prescription to a pharmacist who negligently wrote directions to administer five times the dosage ordered by the doctor. The parents sued on a theory of negligent infliction of emotional distress. The Court held the parents could not recover, even though they themselves administered the medicine to their infant:

> If a child is seriously injured by erroneous medical treatment caused by professional medical negligence, the parent is practically certain to suffer correspondingly serious emotional distress. But even if it were deemed reasonably foreseeable to a pediatrician, or a pharmacist, that a parent's realization of unwitting participation in the child's injury would by itself be a source of significant emotional distress from guilt, anxiety, or otherwise, that foreseeability would not warrant our establishing a new right of recovery for intangible injury.

In *Burgess v. Superior Court* (1992), decided the year before *Huggins*, a mother was allowed to recover when a doctor inflicted permanent brain damage upon her child by depriving the child of oxygen during childbirth. However, liability was based on the duty owed to the mother as the doctor's patient.

The Court specifically noted that a father would not be permitted to recover under a "direct victim" theory in this case, despite the inevitability and foreseeability of his grief.

Very few plaintiffs are successful in demonstrating that they are "direct victims." In a thorough review of every case decided after *Molien*, a California Court of Appeals, in *Bro v. Glaser* (1994), noted that plaintiffs usually lose the argument that they are "direct victims."

In regard to medical and psychotherapy cases, the Court of Appeals correctly noted in *Martinez v. County of Los Angeles* (1986), that when the plaintiff is *not* the doctor's patient, "courts have not extended the *Molien* direct-victim cause of action. . . ."

Bro noted that in non-bystander cases, a plaintiff cannot win unless the plaintiff is a "direct victim." To be a direct victim, a plaintiff must show (1) a preexisting, consensual relationship between the plaintiff and the defendant, and (2) that defendant's conduct was sufficiently outrageous to trigger, as a matter of public policy, an obligation to compensate the plaintiff.

After *Bro* was decided, the "direct victim" issue again arose in *Underwood v. Croy* (1994). In this case, a wife had been seeing a licensed therapist. One day, the wife never came home, leaving her husband and two minor children to worry about what happened to her. The husband discovered that the wife and therapist were having an affair, and that the affair was the reason the wife walked out. The court had no difficulty holding that the husband and minor children were not "direct victims."

In its analysis, the *Underwood* court provided the clue to analyzing the California cases by noting that the old foreseeability approach, which had been popular with judges and juries in the 1970s, has now been replaced with a "duty" analysis that must be made by the courts. Clearly, California judges shifted the power to decide these cases from juries to themselves. It has always been clear in the law that juries decide issues of foreseeability, whereas judges decide questions involving to whom a duty may be owed. By holding that "direct victim" questions are a matter of duty, not foreseeability, California judges made it clear they did not want the law extended beyond those to whom some contractual duty or undertaking already existed. As the trial judge in the *Underwood* case sagely observed:

The bottom line is that the question of duty, a matter of law, is an issue of public policy. Our appellate courts may wish to extend public policy to find a duty of care is owed by a marriage counselor to his patient's various relatives when his sexual exploitation of the patient destroys the marriage which he was retained to help preserve. Such is not the law under existing authority.

In an extremely difficult emotional case, *Schwarz v. Regents of the University of California* (1990), a California Court of Appeals held that a father could not sue a psychotherapist on a direct-victim theory where the father had retained the therapist to treat his son but the therapist instead "facilitated and concealed" the mother's removal of the child to England. Even though the father had participated in counseling sessions with the therapist to improve family communications, the Court held that the son was the only patient. The Court further noted that the existence of a contract between the father and the caregiver for the caregiver to provide treatment for a child does not "impose on the caregiver a duty of care owed to the parent."

California's *Smith v. Pust* (1993) case, discussed above in reference to patients suing therapists, involved a therapist who had sexual intercourse with a patient. The patient's husband was held not be a patient, and was also held not to be a "direct victim" despite his attendance at some therapy sessions.

The most important, and most publicized, attempt by a third party to sue a therapist on "direct victim" grounds was partially successful. Because of its importance, the first *Ramona* case will be discussed in some detail, even though it is not an appellate decision and is therefore not binding on any other court or any other judge.

The First *Ramona* Case: Father v. Therapist

Gary Ramona was the Vice President for Marketing and Sales, and also the Chief Executive Officer of one of the satellite wineries, of the Robert Mondavi Wineries. He had spent 20 years of hard work achieving those positions, which paid a salary of almost $500,000 a year. He was married to Stephanie, and had three daughters—Holly, Kelli, and Shawna. Gary used the medical benefits from his job for his daughter, Holly, who at the time was suffering from depression and an eating disorder (bulimia). Arrangements were initially made by Stephanie, and, after Holly's approval, Holly began seeing Marche Isabella, a marriage, family, and child counselor (California M.F.C.C. license) who was in private practice in Irvine, California.

Therapy for the eating disorders began in late 1989. The first four months of therapy did not involve any issues of sex or abuse. At that point, Holly, who was 19 years old, began having flashes of memory, not flashbacks because she did not feel that she was immediately immersed in the recollection, outside of therapy. Several weeks later, these flashes of memory were discussed in the therapy sessions. At no time did Holly recover any memories in an actual therapy session. Holly reported sexual abuse by her father, which began when she was a child approximately five years of age, and which continued until she was about ten. As the therapy continued, now more focused on the abuse, memories emerged outside of therapy of several instances in which Holly was sexually assaulted by her father. After the therapy had ended, Holly had additional memories of abuse up until the age of 16.

One of the contested legal issues involved whether her therapist should be liable for memories that arose after the therapy had terminated. The judge ruled in favor of such potential liability, calling it the "timebomb" issue, by which he meant that Gary Ramona would be allowed to produce evidence that the alleged conduct of the therapist in implanting memories created a "timebomb" for additional memories to go off at a later time.

A psychiatrist hired by Stephanie and by Gary contacted Isabella because he believed that Gary should be directly confronted. The psychiatrist claimed he feared that there might be potential violence by Gary. In response to this contact from the family psychiatrist, Isabella decided to affiliate a psychiatrist, Richard Rose, on Holly's therapy to perform a psychiatric evaluation. The evidence is in dispute concerning whether Isabella also wanted the psychiatrist to conduct a sodium amytal interview to help confirm or disconfirm the authenticity of the memories. Stephanie filed for divorce two weeks before the amytal interview.

On March 15, 1990, Gary was invited by Holly to attend a meeting with Holly and her therapists.

Isabella was against a confrontation until after Holly was hospitalized in a facility where she would be safe. Holly persisted in favor of the confrontation and, once she was in Western Medical Center in Anaheim, Isabella and Rose agreed to the meeting. Holly's invitation to her father stated that the meeting would take place at Western Medical. When Gary arrived, the day after the amytal interview, Holly surprised her therapists by having her mother present. Holly accused her father of multiple sexual assaults. Isabella was present to monitor Holly's condition and to answer any medical question Gary might raise. Rose was not present at the meeting, though he had agreed that Holly was stable enough to handle it if she wanted it to occur. Contrary to some reports in the media, Isabella insists that at no time did she suggest to Gary that it would be best if he confessed. Her therapeutic stance had been uniformly against confrontation.

Stephanie, about two weeks before the amytal interview, was told by Holly about what Holly called the "rapes" committed upon her by her father. Stephanie believed Holly and remembered events from the past that she believed provided some support for Holly's story. Stephanie made a list of 28 reasons, based on past events, that supported her belief that her daughter's memories were true.

In March 1990, Stephanie, acting on the advice of her family psychiatrist for the protection of her daughters, told Kelli, 17, and Shawna, 12, about Holly's memories of their father's sexual conduct. She also told several of her closest friends, including the wife of one of Gary's business associates. Stephanie also called a reporter for a local paper to try to stop any reporting of the story. She succeeded, because it was never reported by the paper. Meanwhile, also in March 1990, Holly filed a child abuse report against Gary for herself, and Isabella, based on discussions with Holly and Shawna, filed a child abuse report on behalf of the younger daughters. These case investigations were later closed, apparently for lack of evidence, though the scope or extent of the investigations has not been disclosed.

In May 1990, Gary accepted a leave of absence for nine months (called by Robert Mondavi a "sabbatical") with full pay from his job to handle his personal matters, including the divorce and acting as the contractor on the building of his multimillion-dollar home. The Mondavi Winery at this time underwent a major corporate reorganization in which the sons became co-CEOs. Gary was offered several different other positions with the winery and, after rejecting all of them, he was fired. Robert Mondavi wrote the letter terminating Gary, and his sons testified against Gary at the trial. Gary sued the winery for wrongful termination and negotiated a $500,000 sealed settlement.

In December 1990, after substantial opposition from Isabella, Rose, and Stephanie, Holly filed suit against her father for the abuse. She had previously sought assistance from the Los Angeles District Attorney, but she received no satisfaction. In response, Gary brought a lawsuit against his daughter's two therapists, and the hospital, for negligent treatment of his daughter, and for intentional and negligent infliction of emotional distress on him.

Gary, in his Verified Second Amended Complaint (*Ramona v. Ramona*, 1991), alleged that the therapists breached their duty of due care to him by negligently treating his daughter. In particular, Gary alleged that defendants failed in their duty, in part by:

- taking advantage of Holly's condition of extreme suggestibility caused by her major depression and bulimia, extreme anxiety, reduced self-esteem, and despair to subject her to the unwarranted and speculative suggestion that her condition must have been caused by childhood sexual abuse by her father
- administering to Holly the sedative sodium amytal, which has been demonstrated to lead to disorientation, misidentification, and other errors and hallucinations
- misrepresenting to Holly that the fantasies and hallucinations caused by suggestion and administration of sodium amytal somehow corresponded to reality
- failing to warn Holly and obtain her informed consent to the "therapy" embarked upon by defendants without advising her that there is no scientific evidence that the so-called "therapy" reduced the major depression, reduced the bulimic behavior, or otherwise benefitted the persons subject to such "therapy"
- urging Holly to confront her father, her mother, and her sisters with her baseless fantasies and hallucinations that she had been sexually abused as a child by her father

- facilitating, hosting, and participating in these confrontations between Holly and the plaintiff urged on Holly by the defendants.

Gary alleged that, as a consequence of defendants' conduct, he lost his wife, his lucrative job, and contact with all three daughters. In addition, he was sued by Holly and continued to be the subject of slanderous remarks. He claimed damages for severe mental and emotional distress, as well as for lost income and loss of his good reputation and his "happy" family.

Gary's version of the facts differs significantly from that of the defense. For example, at the trial, Stephanie, Kelli, and Shawna all testified that the family, in the past and through to the present, had not been "happy." Testimony by Stephanie about the spousal abuse she claimed to have endured surprisingly was excluded by the judge. Although Stephanie was one of the original defendants sued by Gary, on charges of defamation, she was dropped as a defendant before the case went to trial.

More significantly, according to Gary's version, he was invited to the hospital meeting and was confronted by Isabella, who told him that he would be wise to confess to the abuse (Margolin, 1996). This point is important, because, as the trial transcript demonstrates, the judge was of the opinion that the plaintiff would have to prove "something that differentiates this case from a case in which the plaintiff wasn't summoned to a confrontational meeting, because . . . it's my view that if the plaintiff had not been summoned to a confrontational meeting, there would be no cause of action" (*Ramona v. Ramona*, May 3, 1994). The judge then noted that there were only two available avenues for recovery in California for negligent infliction of emotional distress—the "bystander theory" and the "direct victim theory." As the judge observed, "If you're not there watching it or you're not brought into it, you don't have a case in California" (*Ramona v. Ramona*, May 3, 1994).

It was clear that the "bystander theory" would not work in this case because Gary did not see any tragic physical accident involving Holly and because the treatment of Holly did not create a duty owed to Gary. As Judge Snowden observed during discussions with the lawyers concerning jury instructions (*Ramona v. Ramona*, May 3, 1994):

The way the law exists right now, a health care provider may, with impunity, proceed along dealing with memories that may or may not be accurate memories, may facilitate, encourage, do whatever they want in dealing with this patient as long as when the question comes up, "Well, doctor, should I confront my father about this?"

The health care provider says, "That's really a decision that's outside of the assistance I can provide you. I can try to help you. I can't tell you how to relate to other people. You'll have to make that decision yourself." (p. 10)

At a later point in the discussion the judge noted that, as long as therapy is confined to the patient and therapist, there is no third-party liability. To trigger such liability, according to the judge, the therapist "must undertake some kind of affirmative act to bring into the process the person who allegedly committed the act. That's the significance of the restrictions on [*Molien*] that the Supreme Court has placed" (pp. 11–12).

The judge's response prompted Dr. Rose's lawyer to note that because Rose was not at the meeting, and because he had not summoned Gary to it, he should be dropped from the case. Judge Snowden responded that it was sufficient that he "was a participant in the decision to summon" (p. 12). The judge pointed to a chart entry that generally said that "If there's a confrontational family meeting it's going to be under controlled circumstances" (p. 12). That was enough, Judge Snowden stated, for Rose's "being here," meaning in court on trial for tortious conduct.

Judge Snowden's reasoning raises serious questions concerning how therapy should be practiced. Holly was insisting on a confrontation; her therapists were arguing against it. First and foremost, the therapists had to make sure that Holly's mental and physical health was protected. Under the judge's analysis, Rose and Isabella would have had to decline to be present, thus leaving Holly to confront her father with her therapists not there to watch out for her. Holly was insistent that the meeting take place. It could be argued that Isabella's presence was the lesser of two evils. Better to protect than to abandon her highly vulnerable patient.

Indeed, had the therapist not been there, patient

abandonment charges might have been filed against her. Thus, Rose and Isabella faced a "damned-if-you-do" and "damned-if-you-don't" situation. Their absence could be construed as abandonment and their presence could be construed as colloboration. Judge Snowden was not sensitive to this vital issue.

Judge Snowden's reasoning also chills the therapeutic practice of inviting other family members into a therapy session, as was done in *Smith v. Pust* (1993), which held contrary to Judge Snowden's position. Defense lawyers attempted to explain to the judge that mere summoning was not sufficient under *Molien*. Instead, the summoning had to be because Gary would understand that he was receiving some kind of treatment or benefit. Judge Snowden rejected the argument by stating that:

> I think if he were simply summoned there for a confrontation and told what a horrible person he was for having raped his daughter, he would have a cause of action. So, I'm not inclined to instruct the jury that it had to be for his good and that if it wasn't there was no cause of action." (*Ramona v. Ramona*, Reporter's Transcript, May 3, 1994, p. 9)

Thus, the liability of the defendants hung on the slender reed of *Molien's* direct-victim theory. Did these defendants, who treated the daughter, owe a duty of due care to the father? Judge Snowden (*Ramona v. Ramona*, Order of May 12, 1993), had already held that a duty was owed in this case. According to Judge Snowden, though Gary was summoned to a meeting with his daughter and her therapists, at which meeting he was accused of having molested her years earlier, no cause of action existed for medical malpractice because Gary "was not . . . in any sense a patient; neither he nor anyone else viewed him as such or treated him as such."

On the other hand, Judge Snowden held that a duty did exist to support a cause of action for negligent infliction of emotional distress, by stating that "the facts of the instant case are at least as compelling as those of *Molien*. . . ." According to Judge Snowden, in footnote 1 of his Order:

> Plaintiff argues that his presence at the confrontational meeting of March 15 makes him a bystander-observer of injury to his daughter. Although such a cause of action could theoretically be stated, he would be able to sue for no more than a distraught father who heard his daughter falsely accuse the gardener of molesting her. Plaintiff, however, seeks to sue for a lot more than that.

Molien involved a husband whose wife was a patient of the doctor, but the husband was not a patient of the doctor. In *Molien*, as here argued by plaintiff, the duty is created when the healthcare practitioner "advises the patient to communicate the diagnosis to the 'direct victim'" (p. 2) (*Ramona v. Ramona*, Plaintiff's Opposition to Motion for Reconsideration, December 29, 1993).

It should be noted that, if Judge Snowden is correct about his interpretation of the law, the crucial fact in the case, upon which the duty issue is resolved, is whether the therapist either invited Gary to the hospital or accused him once he was there. These are matters of fact that the jury had to decide. As we shall see, the Special Verdict questions left to the jury failed to ask them about either of these points (invitation and accusation). Reversal could be based upon the judge's failure to properly instruct the jury.

Furthermore, a secondary question required either a specific legal ruling or the jury's factual determination. Suppose the jury found that Isabella did not confront Gary at the hospital. Gary's only basis for recovery would then be the invitation. Isabella claimed that she did not invite Gary, that Holly did. Isabella was left with two choices, either attend the meeting or not be present. She claimed that she made the decision to attend the meeting based upon her concerns for the mental health of her patient. The judge should have done one of two things: either rule, as a matter of law, that once Isabella agreed to let Holly invite Gary to the hospital, Isabella had met the *Molien* "direct victim" requirement; or asked the jury to make a specific finding concerning whether it was negligent for Isabella to be present at the meeting.

Judge Snowden also addressed the issue of whether Holly Ramona could testify after receiving a sodium amytal treatment. He ruled that "a narcotized witness would be disqualified in a criminal proceeding just as a hypnotized witness is." The fact that the sodium amytal was for treatment rather than for forensic purposes was irrelevant, especially because in this case the drugs were used to refresh memory. Judge Snowden brushed aside defendant's argument that the rules in criminal proceedings should not be imported into civil actions. "This may be correct," he noted, but it was not necessary to go that far; Holly's testimony was admissible because

> . . . a central part of plaintiff's case is that the administration of sodium amytal was a cause of Holly's having false memories that he molested her. This makes this case quite different from one where narcosis is employed to supposedly enhance or recover a memory of some material fact; here, the very fact of the narcosis is a major element of plaintiff's lawsuit. Holly's testimony is in the nature of demonstrative evidence and it is evidence that the jury ought to be able to evaluate. Thus the court's ruling will be that the testimony of a narcotized witness should be admitted into evidence in a civil action where the plaintiff is suing over the narcosis itself and the memories allegedly engendered by it.

On May 13, 1994, the judge left the jury a Special Verdict (*Ramona v. Ramona*, 1994), which means the jury was asked to answer a series of specific questions rather than just deliver a general verdict of "liability" or "no liability." Question Number 1 was "Were any of the defendants negligent in providing health care to Holly Ramona by implanting or reinforcing false memories that plaintiff had molested her as a child?" The jury answered "yes" regarding defendants Isabella, Rose, and Western Medical Center Anaheim. The jury also found that the same defendants caused the plaintiff "to be personally confronted with the accusation that he had molested Holly Ramona."

After settling the issue of liability and acknowledging that Gary suffered injury caused by the defendants, the jury dealt with damages. According to their Special Verdict, they awarded Gary no money for past or future pain, suffering, or inconvenience, but did award him $250,000 for past loss of earnings and $250,000 for future lost earnings.

The final issue addressed by the jury was apportioning the fault of all the parties. California law recognizes comparative negligence whereby the jury must assess the percentage of responsibility of each party. In this case, the jury decided the parties were negligent as follows:

Plaintiff (Gary)	5%
Isabella	40%
Rose	10%
Western Medical	5%
All other persons	40%

The $500,000 award to Gary was thus reduced by 5% to $475,000.

Meanwhile, post-verdict interviews with jurors show that their verdict was *not* based on false memory issues. Jury foreman Thomas Dudum told the press (Butler, 1994):

> We all get rather disturbed when Mr. Ramona captured the headlines by claiming a victory of sorts, when we knew the case did not prove that he did not do it. I want to make it clear that we did not believe, as Gary indicates, that these therapists gave Holly a wonder drug and implanted those memories. It was an uneasy decision and there were alot of unanswered questions. . . . It was apparent from the beginning that Mr. Ramona was a wonderful salesman for Mondavi, and he was selling us a story. . . . A lot of it was very difficult to swallow, and we were not fooled for a minute by his convenient act of tearing up.

Dudum also stated that the jurors generally believed that Holly had her first memories outside of therapy and that those memories were not induced or implanted by Isabella. Where Isabella went wrong, according to the jurors, was in reinforcing the memories by undue suggestion, and in sending Holly to an eating disorders therapy group that contained mostly victims of childhood sexual abuse. Dudum noted that Holly had entered therapy for an eating disorder and depression, but the therapy moved to other areas. As he told reporters after the verdict, "I say, let's work out the bulimia and depression and then move on to the other things" (Ayres, 1994).

The *Ramona* case was widely reported in the media as a victory in the fight against therapists' implanting false memories, though the jury appears to have rejected the position that implanting had occurred. Defense lawyers met with five jurors after the case. According to Isabella (personal communication with Alan W. Scheflin, June 1, 1996), they reached the following conclusions:

> . . . these five assured us that they felt that this case was not intended to be a victory for Gary Ramona. They felt that the jury instructions were so confusing and restrictive that they were basically forced to find in favor of the plaintiff, even though "the therapists were only just doing their job.". . . The jury felt that the defendants did not *implant* any memories, but that they did negligently reinforce a pre-existing false memory. The negligence was in the constant reassurance to Holly that she was telling the truth. They also felt (under the second part of the instruction) that the defendants didn't *cause* the confrontation, but that they did "act affirmatively" in the events leading to the confrontation.

The *Ramona* case was not appealed, according to Isabella and correspondence between the lawyers and the insurers, because since the verdict against the multiple defendants was so low, the costs of the appeal alone, not counting the new trial if the appeal were successful, would have been several times what the defendants had been found to owe. The appeal was not economically defensible. Had the case been appealed, however, there is a very strong likelihood that it would have been reversed on any one of several grounds.

Judge Snowden's belief that a cause of action could be stated on a bystander theory would be seriously questioned on appellate review because there was no significant physical harm to Holly observed by Gary. The reason for permitting the third-party relatives to recover is that they have witnessed an excruciating personal tragedy, usually loss of life or serious bodily injury to a loved one. The damages are measured by their special emotional pain and suffering caused by directly witnessing the horrible event. If a parent and a stranger both witness a negligent driver's car smash into a young child, both will suffer emotional distress. The extra distress of the parent, however, is the basis for recovery of damages. The stranger would be denied recovery. Research has failed to unearth a single case that provided a remedy on a fact pattern similar to *Ramona*.

Judge Snowden's ruling that the "direct victim" theory of the *Molien* case permitted Gary's cause of action to proceed also would be severely tested by appellate review. *Molien* involved a negligent diagnosis; *Ramona* did not (McKee, 1994). *Molien* involved a doctor who told his patient to tell her husband about the diagnosis; *Ramona* involved therapists who urged the patient not to confront her father. *Molien* involved the negligent diagnosis in reference to a dangerous physical illness; *Ramona* involved no physical condition and no physical danger. In *Molien* the facts were all admitted and the issue was their legal significance; in *Ramona* the parties disagreed entirely concerning the facts.

A third ground for the likely reversal of the judgment may be found in the wording of the special verdict questions left to the jury. By offering the jurors only the option of finding the defendants negligent of implanting memories, it could be argued that Judge Snowden unduly restricted their freedom of deliberation. As we have seen, many of the jurors expressed their concern that the verdict was required under the instructions given to them by the judge.

The absence of an appeal closes the door on Gary's case against Holly's therapists. Commentary on the case, however, is only just beginning. A recent book tells the story from Gary's point of view (Johnston, 1997).

The Second *Ramona* Case: Daughter v. Father

Holly's own case against her father has not yet gone to trial. Because sodium amytal had been used for memory retrieval, the original trial judge dismissed Holly's case against her father. Holly's new attorney, Gloria Allred, was no stranger to these sexual abuse, repressed memory issues. In an earlier case involving another client, Allred obtained a recovery of $500,000 based on the client's repressed memories. The victory was made possible after the legislature changed the law to allow victims who have repressed memories to sue after the buried recollections are recovered (Williams, 1996).

Putting their first judicial rejection aside, Holly and her attorney refiled the case in another court, this time relying on Holly's *pre*-amytal memories. This second suit was dismissed on the grounds that the abuse issue had been decided against Holly in the *Ramona* case. In essence, the judge ruled that Holly's personal case against her father was identical to her therapist's defense against her father, which had been rejected by the jury.

Holly appealed this summary judgment dismissal, claiming that the abuse issue had not been decided in the *Ramona* case because the issues and the evidence were not the same. The Court of Appeals opinion in *Ramona v. Ramona* (1995) made it clear that the central issue was whether the two cases were indeed close enough: "the question before us is privity. The issue, therefore, is whether the relationship between Holly . . . and her doctors . . . is 'sufficiently close' to bar Holly's action against Ramona" (p. 3). Contrary to the trial judge's view, the unanimous opinion of the appellate judges was that there was no "privity" between Holly's interests and her therapists' interests. Her case had not therefore been presented by her therapists. The fact that Holly actually testified for her therapists was found to be of no significance by the judges: "There is no evidence that the doctors' lawyers consulted with Holly or her lawyers about trial strategy or that they gave any consideration at all to Holly's interests in their efforts to avoid malpractice liability" (p. 5). The court, in the final paragraph of its brief, unpublished opinion, addressed the repressed memory issue:

> Finally, we agree that there is a connection between the two lawsuits—in the Napa action, [Gary] Ramona had to (and did) persuade the jury that Holly's memories of childhood molestation were false, and in this action Holly is asserting that the molestation she remembers did occur—that is simply not enough to extend the concept of privity to a relationship which no longer exists and which no court has ever found sufficient to create privity. (p. 6)

Holly was awarded her costs of appeal. The way was not cleared for a jury trial on the merits of Holly's allegations that her recovered memories of her father molesting her years earlier were accurate. As of mid–1997, Holly's case against her father is still pending. The Ramona women remain supportive of Holly, and Holly remains supportive of her therapist Marche Isabella, who is preparing a book about her experience in these cases.

Other Cases of Therapist Third-Party Liability

Many lawsuits are pending across the country challenging the privity barrier that has protected therapists from third-party lawsuits. The false memory movement and the continuing complaints about the specific interviewing techniques and the general procedures of child protective services have led to an increased interest in lawsuits against therapists and child protective service agencies by persons who are not their patients or clients. In most states, child protective services enjoy a governmental immunity from liability. Individual therapists, however, do not have immunity, except when they report suspected child abuse under mandated reporting statutes. Most courts continue to hold the line against creating conflicting duties to patients and nonpatients, but a small number of lower court judges have been swayed to cast their vote in favor of a remedy for those who claim to have been falsely accused of heinous offenses. As of mid-1997, some appellate courts have permitted third-party lawsuits to succeed, and some appellate courts have specifically disapproved of them.

In *Bird v. W.C.W.* (1994), the Texas Supreme Court emphatically rejected a therapist's duty to third parties in childhood sexual abuse cases. A psychologist diagnosed a child as having been sexually abused by his father, and she signed an affidavit to that effect. The affidavit was used by the child's mother in a custody battle. Eventually, all charges and allegations against the father were dropped. He sued the psychologist. In a strongly worded opinion, the unanimous court held that "as a matter of law there is no professional duty running from a psychologist to a third party to not negligently misdiagnose a condition of a patient" (p. 768). The judges were painfully aware of the risk of false allegations and the devastating consequences they cause. But they found a stronger public policy in the protection of children:

> Because they are dealing with such a sensitive situation, mental health professionals should be allowed to exercise their professional judgment in diagnosing sexual abuse of a child without the judicial imposition of a countervailing duty to third parties. (p. 769)

The court noted that a duty to third parties may be available in cases where physical harm is threatened and the utility of the therapist's conduct is minimal. For example, the therapist who forgets to tell the patient not to drive after taking a prescribed medication is negligent and creates a foreseeable risk to whomever is unfortunate enough to be injured in a car accident with the patient. The reasoning by which a duty is imposed in this latter situation, however, does not apply to the child abuse cases, according to the court, because "there is little social utility in failing to warn patients about known side-effects of a drug, but there is great social utility in encouraging mental health professionals to assist in the examination and diagnosis of sexual abuse" (p. 770). Although the court was unanimous in its rejection of a duty to third parties, two justices concurred in a two-paragraph opinion gently warning therapists to raise their standard of care or the court will do it for them.

Some lower court judges have bent the rigid "no duty" rule to permit third-party lawsuits to go to juries. *Montoya v. Bebensee* (1988) involved an *unlicensed* therapist who diagnosed child abuse by the father, reported the abuse to the state agency, and advised the mother to disobey the court order granting the father visitation rights. The therapist saw the child briefly on two occasions, but did not administer any psychological tests. She relied on "a method of analysis that she termed 'the technique of the non-verbal,' i.e., the child's body language" (p. 287). A social worker and other therapists contacted by the unlicensed therapist all disagreed with her diagnosis, but their opinions were ignored. Psychological tests of the child demonstrated that she had serious difficulty separating fantasy from reality. The Colorado Court of Appeals stated a broad rule that "a mental health care provider owes a duty to any person, who is the subject of any public report or other adverse recommendation by that provider, to use due care in formulating any opinion upon which such a report or recommendation is based" (p. 289).

Given the presence of gross negligence in the *Montoya* case, the court did not have to state so broad a rule, especially when the conduct was not that of a licensed professional. Having concluded that a duty was owed, however, the court then noted that the statutory immunity for reporting child abuse covers all good-faith actions taken according to the requirements of the statute. Thus, third parties could recover only if they could prove either (1) that the report was made in bad faith, or (2) that some of the therapist's conduct was not covered by the statutory immunity. Thus, the therapist's advising the mother to deny the father visitation rights granted to him by court order was not protected by the immunity. The court sent the case back for a trial and also permitted the father to sue a licensed therapist for negligently supervising the unlicensed therapist.

A federal district court judge went one step further in *Sullivan v. Cheshier* (1994) by permitting a case to go to trial where the plaintiff-third party was not the alleged sexual abuser, but rather his parents. During a hypnosis session conducted by an *unlicensed* psychologist, a patient remembered being sexually abused by her older brother. In the presence of the psychologist, the patient told her parents, who are now suing the psychologist. The parents filed a "healing arts malpractice affidavit from a psychiatrist who based his opinion solely on the statements made by the [parents]" (p. 657). The court noted that this is poor practice, but excusable here because the parents did not have access to the therapist's records. The malpractice action, however, was unavailable because the therapist was unlicensed. Third parties could, however, sue on a theory of nuisance, which the Illinois Supreme Court had earlier said was the appropriate action against unlicensed therapists (*Corgan v. Muehling*, 1991). The judge noted that in this case, it was alleged that the therapist

> specifically directed his actions, in part, against the parents and their interests, that he imposed a false memory in [the patient], instructed her to break contact with her parents if they dissented from her memory and prevented the parents from taking some reasonable steps to inquire into the validity of the memory. (p. 660)

Both the therapist and the patient vehemently denied that any memories were implanted. The court concluded that a jury could find that the use of hypnosis, the absence of prior memories, the absence of any corroborating evidence, and the refusal to allow the family to meet and discuss the issue could be reckless or intentional conduct and could be the basis for a finding of implanted memory. A later ruling in this case by another judge permitted the parents access to the therapy records because the therapist was not licensed and therefore did not fall within the class of persons entitled to preserve confidences (*Sullivan v. Cheshier*, 1995).

The *Sullivan* case went to trial at the end of March, 1997. Michael Yapko, Ph.D., provided expert opinion supporting the plaintiffs' argument that the therapist had used hypnosis in a manner which implanted false memories in his patient. Defense expert David Spiegel, M.D., ultimately proved to be more persuasive in his rejection of the false memory argument applied to this case. The defense was also aided by the fact that a close relative of the plaintiffs' voluntarily testified against them, thereby providing essential corroborating evidence in support of the accuracy of the repressed memories. Even though the trial judge limited the patient's testimony concerning what she had remembered, it took the jury only 90 minutes to return a verdict in favor of the therapist, rejecting the argument that false memories had been implanted (Lalley, 1997).

After the news stories on the *Sullivan* case appeared, Cynthia Bowman (1997), a Northwestern University law professor and leading expert on third-party lawsuits, addressed the result the jury reached:

Research shows that repressed memories do exist and lawsuits may provide a useful remedy for some abuse victims. But lawsuits brought by alleged abusers against their victims' therapists do more harm than good.

* * *

Third-party lawsuits like Sullivan vs. Cheshier —that is, lawsuits in which a non-party to the psychotherapeutic relationship is allowed to sue a therapist over the wishes of the patient—should not be allowed. Such lawsuits have a devastating effect not only upon adult survivors of childhood abuse but also upon the availability of therapy for survivors.

* * *

Whether the memories recovered are accurate, inaccurate or a mixture of the two, what happens if alleged abusers or other members of the patient's family are allowed to sue the therapist over the patient's objections? First, the child's relationship to her therapist is disrupted and her privacy shattered. Second, therapists treating sexual abuse survivors and their malpractice insurers will respond with alarm. Therapists may be deterred from taking on similar cases. No matter how satisfied the patient may be with her therapy, it is accompanied by the threat of a malpractice suit by a third party.

A third-party suit is not the appropriate remedy for problems of therapist malpractice. Bad therapists can be sued directly by their patients. The family has other legal remedies for damages suffered from false allegations of abuse. They may sue the child directly for defamation, for intentional infliction of emotional distress or, if the child has filed suit and failed to sustain the allegations of abuse, for malicious prosecution. By contrast, suing the therapist over the head of an adult, competent patient avoids direct confrontation with the adult child and shifts the blame to a non-family member.

The limits of placing such potential liability upon therapists are difficult to define. Whenever an individual enters psychotherapy, emotional disruption is likely to result and spill over onto other members of the patient's family. Should therapists be subject to suit, for example, when therapy results in a patient choosing to end a marriage? Whenever a child becomes alienated or estranged from parents during the course of therapy? Even if the claims of abuse are not accurate, family unity is unlikely to be promoted by the intervention of a lawsuit.

Finally, if the allegations of abuse are accurate, allowing the family to sue the therapist over the objections of an adult patient hands abusers the perfect preemptive weapon. When confronted with allegations of abuse, the abuser may move to sue the victim's therapist, thus intimidating his victim into not pressing charges against him. Many victims of childhood sexual abuse have been warned by their abusers never to tell anyone about what has happened or they will be punished. Suing the therapist to whom the adult child has turned for help fulfills this prophecy, once again violating the autonomy of the abuse victim. It also takes away her voice, which has been silenced for too long.

In *Sullivan*, the therapist won a jury victory against third-party liability. In *Lindgren v. Moore* (1995), a father, brother, and sister all brought suit against an *unlicensed* therapist and her licensed supervisor, claiming what the court called "false memory syndrome" and "recovered memory therapy." The federal trial judge, interpreting Illinois law, concluded that "Illinois law provides that a doctor owes no duty of care to a third party absent the existence of a 'special relationship' between the party and the patient" (p. 1187). The judge further found that the only "special relationship" recognized in Illinois giving rise to malpractice liability was that "between a fetus and his or her mother" (p. 1187). The *Sullivan* opinion was criticized on the grounds that the judge in that case confused negligence with intentional or reckless conduct. The federal judge in *Lindgren* declined to permit third-party liability for a

> more fundamental reason than has yet been advanced. The primary reason why doctors and psychiatrists should not be held to have a duty to third party, non-patients is simple: doctors should owe their duty *to their patient* and not to anyone else. (p. 1189, emphasis in original)

Had the patient complained about the therapy, the judge continued, "the question would be closer" (p. 1189). In a significant paragraph, the court concluded that

> The practice of medicine is fraught with legal potholes, and doctors should not have to navigate over new crevasses created by a heavy-handed judiciary. For purposes of standing to assert a malpractice claim, doctors should be free to recommend a course of treatment and act on the patient's response to the recommendation free from the possibility that someone other than the patient might complain in the future. Even if the patient is so injured as a result of the injury [sic—therapy?] that she cannot complain later, any action should be brought on behalf of the patient. (p. 1189)

Plaintiffs in *Lindgren* were not left without a possible remedy. The judge permitted them to continue the case on three tort theories: (1) intentional infliction of emotional distress, (2) direct interference with filial relationships with recovery for loss of so-

ciety of the family member, and (3) public nuisance. Neither of the first two theories, however, has been officially accepted in Illinois. No definitive cases support either intentional infliction in the medical malpractice context or direct interference with family relationships in any context. The third theory had been recognized as appropriate where the patient was the plaintiff, but only *Sullivan* permitted this theory for non-patient plaintiffs. Thus, Illinois courts might still reject this theory as well. In order to recover on this third theory, however, plaintiffs will have to win on the basis of one of the two others as well in order to show they have been harmed.

The cases just discussed all involved *unlicensed* therapists. In other cases permitting third-party lawsuits, the behavior of the licensed therapist was so irresponsible as to constitute gross negligence or intentional misconduct. In *Wilkinson v. Balsam* (1995), a father was permitted to sue a psychiatrist who diagnosed him as the abuser of his son, who was the psychiatrist's patient. The court found sufficient evidence to justify a jury's concluding that the psychiatrist had not acted in good faith. According to the court, the psychiatrist confused his roles as therapist, as evaluator, and as advocate, he used poor technique in interviewing the child, he ignored data that reached conclusions opposite from his own, he urged one person not to report information to the proper authorities, and he offered his opinions to persons not listed in the statute as privileged to receive that information. The court broadly stated that if a psychiatrist's conduct will foreseeably harm a third party, a duty is owed to that third party.

This conclusion reached in *Wilkinson*, however, is not binding on Vermont courts or on federal courts. Because the federal judge was speculating on how Vermont courts would answer the legal issue, Vermont courts are free to follow or reject this interpretation. Because the judge was not settling federal law issues, the ruling is not binding in federal cases.

In *Doe v. McKay* (1997), by contrast, an Illinois appellate court permitted a father to sue his daughter's therapist after several therapeutic sessions attended by the father resulted in his being accused by the therapist of molesting his daughter many years earlier. The father claimed that his daughter told him that the therapist arranged the joint meetings in the hopes of shocking the father into a confession. At these sessions, the therapist told the father that both he and his daughter had repressed their memories of the abuse. The father's complaint against the therapist was dismissed by the trial judge, but the appellate court found room for the suit to continue:

> Generally, a nonpatient third party cannot maintain a malpractice action absent a direct physician-patient relationship between the doctor and the patient or a special relationship between the patient and the third party under the doctrine of transferred negligence. . . . In this appeal, plaintiff argues that defendants owed him a duty because of his relationship with his daughter and because defendants directly involved plaintiff in his daughter's treatment.

* * *

> Similarly, we find transferred negligence to be applicable to the unique circumstances here. Key to this finding is the special relationship plaintiff shares with his daughter and the therapist's action to bring plaintiff into the treatment process. At defendant McKay's direction, during the daughter's therapy sessions, plaintiff's daughter accused plaintiff of sexually abusing her, and McKay repeatedly suggested to plaintiff's daughter that plaintiff might further harm her. As we must take this allegation as true, McKay's orchestrated accusations directly involved plaintiff in the treatment process. Once plaintiff was immersed in his daughter's treatment process, as a quasi-patient himself, it was not only reasonably foreseeable, but a virtual certainty, that McKay's conduct would harm plaintiff's relationship with his daughter. . . . Thus, we find that defendants' duty to use reasonable care in the treatment of their patient extended to plaintiff.

> . . . The risk and magnitude of harm to our society, namely, tearing a family apart without regard to the manner in which false accusations of sexual abuse are made, is so significant that it requires the protection of our law. A therapist's allegedly erroneous conclusion that a patient has been sexually abused by a parent endangers the parent-child relationship, but where the therapist draws the accused parent into the patient-child's treatment, accusations of sexual abuse are unde-

niably devastating and may not be made with impunity and disregard of the therapist's obligation of reasonable care. The therapist is in the best position to avoid such harm and is solely responsible for handling the treatment procedure. Defendants could have warned plaintiff and his daughter of the controversial nature of repressed memory therapy in separate sessions. We therefore hold that in a case such as this involving repressed memories of sexual abuse, where the parent is brought into the treatment process by the therapist, a therapist's duty to the patient to use reasonable care in the treatment process is extended to the parent.

The appellate court found that Illinois law permits a cause of action for negligent or intentional infliction of emotional distress where the conduct in question involves a direct intereference with a parent-child relationship. For example, Illinois allowed a father to sue his ex-wife and a psychiatrist for brainwashing his son against him (*Dymek v. Nyquist*, 1984). The fact that all of the previous cases involved minor children and visitation or custody rights was not considered by the court to be important.

Some cases have announced broad rules without commenting on how they are to be obeyed. In *Caryl S. v. Child & Adolescent Treatment Services, Inc.* (1994), a suit was brought by grandparents against a therapist who diagnosed the grandmother as having sexually abused her grandchild, who was the therapist's patient. The court noted that the strength of the plaintiff's claims "are dependent upon the core issue of whether there was, in fact, a negligent misdiagnosis by defendants of sexual abuse." Noting that the issue had never been decided before in any New York case, the court concluded that the therapist owed a duty to the third person who is falsely accused:

> Particularly where the claim of abuse arises in connection with other, highly charged disputes (such as divorce or custody and visitation proceedings), the determination that sexual abuse occurred is fraught with added dangers: "More and more allegations of incest and [child] sexual abuse by husbands are being made by their wives during custody disputes. If the allegations are proven, the perpe-

trator, usually the husband/father, is excluded from contact with his children. . . . Child psychiatrists are frequently used by both sides to evaluate the child and make a determination about the authenticity of the charges. . . . *A mistake might jeopardize a child's future or destroy a man's family life and career.*" (Green, True and False Allegations of Sexual Abuse in Child Custody Disputes, *Journal of the American Academy of Child Psychiatry*, vol. 25, 449–456, at p. 449 [1986], emphasis added).

And, regardless of the setting where the claim arises, there is also the danger, where it is not the child himself or herself who specifically makes the abuse charge, that unfounded allegations of sexual abuse can have a permanent detrimental effect upon the child. . . .

Given the foregoing, it should be readily apparent that when a professional becomes involved in a case where child sexual abuse is suspected, care must be taken in investigating and evaluating such a claim and in reaching the conclusion that such abuse did take place. Where the professional is involved in a therapeutic relationship with the child, it requires little imagination to see the harm that might result from a negligently and erroneously formed conclusion that sexual abuse had occurred, with subsequent treatment based on that "misdiagnosis." In such a situation there would be no dispute that a cause of action for malpractice (or ordinary negligence) would exist on the child's behalf against the professional. . . .

Where, however, the alleged abuser is not also involved in the therapeutic relationship with the child and his or her treating professional, the question arises, as here, whether that professional owes any duty of care to such an abuser. In that situation, a determination must initially be made by the professional that sexual abuse in fact occurred, and this determination is made not only about the child but also about the suspected abuser. When, based upon that determination, a course of action is thereafter embarked upon by the professional, it is intended to, and necessarily does, affect both the child and his or her abuser, especially where a family relationship is involved. A suspected abuser surely has the right to a reasonable expectation that such a determination, touching him or her as profoundly as it will, will be carefully made and will not be reached in a negligent manner.

The possible harm to a child from a professional misdiagnosis in such circumstances has already been noted. The potential harm to the alleged abuser is equally great. In *Rossignol v. Silvernail*, 185 A.D.2d 497, 499, 586 N.Y.S.2d 343, the Appellate Division, Third Judicial Department, referred to being labeled a child abuser as "one of the most loathsome labels in society," and pointed out the "physical and psychological ramifications" that may be "attendant to * * * addressing, defending and dealing with" such accusations. Rossignol also noted that, once made, "such charges are difficult to escape." (id., p. 500, 586 N.Y.S.2d 343)

Although the court permitted the case to go to trial, many questions are left unanswered by the court's conclusion. Will the therapist always be liable if later events show that the therapist was incorrect? The court could not have expected that therapists will be infallible. Also, it would be unfair automatically to permit lawsuits against therapists in cases where the charges against the alleged perpetrator are dropped or dismissed because those legal actions do not constitute proof that the alleged perpetrator is innocent of the charges.

It is not clear what the court means by "investigating and evaluating" the abuse claim. Should the therapist be required to search out leads or corroboration for the allegations? In the face of child abuse claims, must the therapist turn detective? Moen (1995), an attorney defending families from allegedly false claims of sexual abuse, argues that therapists cannot hide behind the excuse of narrative truth when forensic issues are involved in the therapy. Moen, however, fails to present any discussion of how he expects therapists to be "detectives," and his brief paper does little more than suggest that therapists have to be held accountable for false accusations made by their patients. This suggestion, of course, would require strict liability. It would also give attorneys easy victories in malpractice cases against therapists. Therapists would have to hope that their patients will prevail in court; if their patients do not, the therapists will be liable for failing to know historical truth. Slovenko (1995b) makes the same argument for accountability as did Moen, but he also fails to articulate the nature of the detective role and its consequences on the therapy.

Neither Moen nor Slovenko even hints at how these proposals would address the following small number of crucial issues that would necessarily arise if the demand that therapists also be detectives were accepted:

1. Should the patient be told that the therapist is conducting an investigation?
2. How does the therapist investigate without breaking the patient's confidentiality?
3. How thorough an investigation must be conducted?
4. Should the therapist interview other family members, or go through old medical records, or check police files, etc.?
5. What should the therapist tell the patient about the ongoing investigation?
6. What should the therapist do if the therapist reasonably concludes that the patient is telling the truth?
7. What should the therapist do if the therapist reasonably concludes that the patient is not telling the truth?
8. What should the therapist do if the investigation fails to determine historical truth because the evidence is inconclusive? Will the therapist be liable for, by hindsight, having made the wrong choice?
9. Should therapists receive training in investigation? Should graduate schools in the mental health professions offer mandatory courses in detective work?
10. How may therapists simultaneously meet their fiduciary duty of undivided loyalty to the client and their newly imposed reasonable care duty to third parties who may be injured if the therapist is wrong about historical truth?
11. How can therapists avoid violating conflict of interest rules when they must, on the one hand, mistrust the patient to the point of conducting an outside investigation, and, on the other hand, be answerable to the very people the patient has come to therapy to discuss?
12. Who pays for the expenses of investigation?

Scheflin (1997a) argues that it is a very bad idea to claim therapists should be detectives. Requiring therapists to become detectives invites a dangerous dual role conflict, which could easily be avoided by utilizing an independent forensic evaluator to assess abuse allegations.

The idea that clinicians should be investigators and not just therapists has appeared in a few legal matters. In a licensing revocation proceeding in Washington, the panel concluded that a therapist committed malpractice by "validating" the client's childhood sexual abuse memories "without either seeking to confirm by any other means or exploring alternative explanations or interpretations for the memories" (*In the Matter of the Disciplinary Action Concerning the Counselor Registration of Linda Rae MacDonald*, 1995).

At least two cases have gone to trial with nonpatient plaintiffs' emerging victorious. In *Althaus v. Cohen* (1994), a 19-year-old daughter went to a psychiatrist after having made accusations to the police of being molested by her parents. The psychiatrist listened to her story and conducted therapy. The therapist testified that some of what the daughter-patient told her was clearly unbelievable, and therefore not true. According to an Associated Press report (1994), "Some of the girl's claims were discounted immediately. She claimed her grandmother flew about on a broom, she was tortured with a medieval thumbscrew device, she bore three children who were killed, and she was raped in view of diners in a crowded restaurant." The daughter recanted and joined her parents in a lawsuit against Dr. Cohen for treating the daughter as if the stories she told were true.

But Dr. Cohen did not believe these things to be true, and she did not conduct therapy as if they were true. Furthermore, as Gutheil (personal communication, November 17, 1995) has noted, "Dr. Judith Cohen did not say that she was treating her patient as if the abuse was true. She said she was treating [the] symptoms she was showing and whatever cause there might be and I think that is a rather important notion. You treat symptoms; you don't treat causes in the usual sense of the word."

The jury held in favor of the parents and the daughter, and they voted 1–2 to award the parents and daughter a verdict of $272,000. But what did Dr. Cohen do wrong? Perhaps that she failed to say to the patient, "That's a lot of nonsense. I don't believe you." Had she said this, of course, she could have destroyed any trust in her that the patient might have developed.

Althaus has been cited by Slovenko (1995b) as an illustration of why therapists, who are narrative truth-seekers in the therapy room, should be forced to become detectives answerable in the courtroom to a standard of historical truth. But Dr. Cohen did not believe her patient and did not implant memories in her. The patient had already filed charges against her parents before she came to therapy, so real detectives had concluded that the abuse story, though not all of the details, contained historical truth. Furthermore, Dr. Cohen did not accept the full story her client told her, and she did not encourage the client to sue her parents or take any outside action against them. If she were to act as a detective, what should she have done? What would have changed in the therapy? Indeed, the ultimate fear, and irony, of *Althaus* is expressed by Gutheil (personal correspondence, 1995):

> What was so interesting was the claim that the doctor, Cohen, should have been a detective. But in this particular case it becomes fairly clear by the documents that it was the detectives who had planted the false memories in their repeated interviews of the patient. So in a funny way, while the actual detectives are implanting the false memory, the doctor is told that, for *not* being a detective, she must be blamed for the false memory. It was a perfect triangle.

In *Althaus*, it appears that the therapist was successfully sued by the patient who joined with her family claiming that it was wrong for the therapy to be conducted according to the narrative developed by the patient, rather than the alleged historical truth, which the therapist should have known by completely disbelieving her patient and totally ignoring her claims and expressed needs.

In *Khatain v. Jones* (1993), the father and mother who had been accused in therapy by their daughter (the patient) sued the therapist-psychiatrist for defamation and for negligent and intentional infliction of emotional distress. After the patient told her psychiatrist that her father had sexually abused her when she was a child, the psychiatrist conducted an "amytal interview" and one of patient's multiple personalities stated that the abuse had occurred and that the mother had been aware of it at the time it occurred. When the patient's husband discovered the abuse

allegations, he joined a session with his wife to obtain the psychiatrist's advice about an upcoming family marriage of the patient's daughter where everyone would be present. The patient feared that, because her parents were to be present, she would lose control and spoil the wedding for her daughter. The psychiatrist suggested that the patient, her daughters, and her husband, have a combined session. Family members had participated in patient's therapy from time to time in the past. At this particular session, which was held in a conference room in the psychiatric unit at Richardson HCA Medical Hospital, the psychiatrist "both conveyed information and facilitated the flow of information. [Defendant] told the daughters that their grandfather . . . had sexually abused Patient over a period of years [and that] their grandmother . . . had observed the acts of sexual abuse. Patient and Husband also revealed information to the daughters." The plaintiffs somehow learned of the allegations and filed suit based on the conversations that occurred in this session. The trial judge rejected the plaintiffs' claims on the grounds that the defendant had a qualified privilege to make the statements to the family.

Meanwhile, the Texas Supreme Court, in *Boyles v. Kerr* (1993), eliminated negligent infliction of emotional distress as a basis for tort liability, thus striking one of the major theories available to the non-patient plaintiffs. The appellate court in *Khatain* permitted these plaintiffs to go forward with their lawsuit because the qualified privilege enjoyed by the therapist might have been abused by defendant. In general, a qualified privilege permits the utterance of information that would otherwise be defamatory where the utterance is necessary to protect the interests of third parties, such as the family members in this case. The privilege is qualified, rather than absolute, because it may be lost by negligence or malice. The court focused on the applicable comments of the therapist, which was the sole basis upon which any liability could be found:

> At the conference, [defendant] said he believed Patient's account of sexual abuse. He also stated, however, that there was no way to be sure that the sexual abuse actually occurred. [Defendant] told those present at the conference that Patient's account of sexual abuse could be based in (i) truth; (ii) fantasy; (iii) a nightmare; or (iv) "whatever."

The deposition excerpt also indicates that [defendant] did not discuss Patient's disclosure with the [plaintiffs] before the conference. He said that he could not contact the [plaintiffs] without the permission of Patient and Husband.

... [Defendant] told those present at the conference that he believed Patient because (i) Patient had suggested vague feelings of guilt or shame during the course of her treatment; (ii) Patient's account was consistent with "the clinical picture that was becoming increasingly known sort of in American psychiatry"; and (iii) Patient's revelation "seemed to be real." [Defendant] also said, however, that "you can't rely on an Amytal interview . . . " and that he found the disclosure to be "quite shocking."

During the deposition, [Defendant] agreed a possibility existed that the [plaintiffs] could be psychologically destroyed by accusations of sexually abusing their daughter. He also said that he had not treated any patients with multiple personalities before his treatment of Patient.

Excerpts from the deposition of one of Patient's daughters were attached to the [plaintiffs'] response. The daughter stated that Patient had revealed the sexual abuse to [defendant] during the Amytal interview. She also said that ten-year-old "Sukinos," one of Patient's multiple personalities, disclosed the sexual abuse to [defendant].

After reciting these facts, the court concluded that "the record before us does not conclusively demonstrate that [defendant] was not negligent in making the complained-of communications during the June 3, 1990 conference." No other analysis is presented, and the court failed to identify which language might be proven to be negligent. Furthermore, the court of appeals did not discuss the issue of whether third parties could sue therapists under Texas law, a lawsuit that appears to be prohibited under the *Bird* (1994) ruling.

A case pending in California's Fourth District Court of Appeals may push the law even further, because the complaint requests that a therapist be held to have a duty to foreseeable third parties who may be harmed by the therapist's diagnosis of sexual abuse, even though the therapist did nothing to confront the third party with the claims alleged by the patient (*Trear v. Sills*, 1995).

Legal and Mental Health Commentary on Therapist Third-Party Liability

At a conference sponsored by the False Memory Syndrome Foundation, Slovenko (1995a) commented that following *Ramona*, "The door is open to litigation, which may discourage irresponsible therapy" (p. 393). He bases his view on the assumption that the defendant therapists practiced substandard "revival of memory" therapy (p. 399) and that "the therapists operated on the basis of unsupported beliefs and urged the patient to blame someone for her problems . . . [without] external validation" (p. 395). However, Slovenko's legal commentary is not supported by a detailed analysis of the therapy provided by the defendants or by a delineation of the science by which such therapy practices are alleged to be substandard.

A far more convincing legal commentary concerning the *Ramona* case can be found in the *Harvard Law Review* by law professors Cynthia Grant Bowman and Elizabeth Mertz (1996). Their review included an extensive analysis of the relevant background science and also the most formidable policy examination yet written on third-party liability of therapists. They conclude that *Ramona* sets a dangerous and erroneous precedent if courts should choose to follow it, even though it is not binding on any other court. Bowman and Mertz find no support for the liability of therapists to third parties in history, policy, science, ethics, or analysis. They leave open the question, however, of whether third-party liability might be permitted in those cases where the patient has recanted, thereby eliminating conflict of interest and confidentiality issues.

In reaching their conclusions, Bowman and Mertz review the scientific literature, both psychological and biochemical, concerning memory and dissociated amnesia. Their understanding of this literature, and the conclusions they draw from it, are quite close to our own perspective. They find evidence for a separate memory-processing system with traumatic events, and they conclude that "repressed" memory is indeed a real phenomenon. Of great significance to their analysis is their presentation of how the media has been used to distort science and policy issues in this hotly debated field. They doubt that the public, because of these rampant media distortions, is hearing the "more balanced message" (p. 622).

Of particular concern to Bowman and Mertz (1996) is the fact that third-party liability suits disrupt the therapeutic relationship itself, contrary to the wishes of the patient and the therapist. Because this disruption inevitably sidetracks, if not derails, the therapy, it constitutes a gross interference with a fiduciary relationship. No public or social policies are found by Bowman and Mertz (1996) to be strong enough to have this devastating impact. As they point out, the sanctity of the relationship, and the laws of confidentiality and privilege that shield it, were erected for the purpose of protecting the patient's interests. Every case of therapy is likely to involve some complaint about a third person. If that person could lawfully invade the sanctity of the therapy relationship and fish through the therapist's records for incriminating matter to support a lawsuit, private therapy would become impossible. Aggrieved third parties may suffer emotional and economic harm, but the therapist-patient relationship was not designed to protect these parties, nor could it function if a duty were owed to them.

Bowman and Mertz (1996) are willing to leave the door open for third-party lawsuits where the patient has become a recanter and the third party joins the patient's malpractice action against the therapist. Once the patient has determined that the relationship has produced negligently caused distress, and files a lawsuit against the therapist, third parties who are also aggrieved may join. If the law accepts this suggestion, however, we caution that the opportunities for collusion are very great. Patient and family members, under an offer from a lawyer to get them millions of dollars in a lawsuit, may find the offer extremely attractive. With knowledge that the insurance company, not the therapist, will foot the bill, and with knowledge that there is a strong likelihood of a settlement to protect the therapist's reputation, the offer might appear irresistible. Moreover, we learned in chapter 9 that recanters are likely to be highly suggestible individuals whose memory reports should be subjected to severe scrutiny before being believed.

Appelbaum and Zoltek-Jick (1996) have also raised grave concerns about the application of the "direct victim" theory as the judge construed it in

Ramona. They note that even the existence of legal uncertainty about the reach of *Ramona* will have a devastating impact on therapy. For example, therapists now do not know (1) whom will be held to be a "direct victim," (2) what duties will be owed to these victims, (3) what therapies are likely to trigger such liability, (4) how therapists can protect themselves, and (5) what impact these suits will have on confidentiality and privilege. Because third-party liability suits are not specifically limited to sexual abuse cases involving the validity of memories, the "direct victim" concept "may be applicable to a wide range of psychotherapeutic situations" (p. 464). Courts, they urge, "should be extremely cautious about imposing duties to third parties on therapists on the basis of the direct victim standard" (p. 464).

Student legal commentators have expressed a variety of opinions on third-party liability. Rock (1995) favors such liability as a "quality control tool" for psychotherapists. Her analysis, however, is based upon a factually inaccurate and distorted presentation of the *Ramona* case, as well as a severely limited understanding of the memory literature. Yamini (1996), by contrast, suggests that such suits be rejected, but also believes that therapists should be liable for intentional infliction of emotional distress if the therapist has "acted with the requisite degree of outrageous conduct to warrant liability" (p. 553). Once again, however, the research on basic memory issues is too superficial. Furthermore, the type of conduct courts generally demand to sustain claims of intentional infliction of emotional distress requires a particularly obnoxious degrading or disgusting personal insult to the victim (Keeton, 1984). It is not likely that the conduct of therapists will sink to this level.

As of mid-1997, no law journal article has presented a reasoned argument in support of third-party liability of therapists. The burden is on proponents of such liability because the current law in the states and in the federal courts rejects their viewpoint. To sustain their burden, proponents of third- party liability must deal with the difficult issues enumerated in the discussion earlier in this section. Conflict of interest loyalties are especially important to consider thoughtfully and in detail. It must also be remembered that any rules favoring third-party liability will have consequences on the issue of third-party liability for other professionals, such as accountants, lawyers, and members of the clergy. Well-developed arguments must therefore consider the broader questions of third-party liability in all professional settings.

The issue of third-party liability is a matter of law for judges to decide. The determination of whether to accept or reject such liability should also turn on an accurate understanding of the relevant science relating to memory, suggestion, influence, and hypnosis, at minimum. To date, courts in general have not been adequately apprised of what science says. Judges have heard much opinion and belief, but legal questions as important as that of third-party liability should be firmly grounded on fact, not fantasy. The debate about third-party liability is only just beginning. We hope that the path it takes will be securely grounded in the science of memory and that the contours of the legitimate practice of therapy will be respected. The detailed review of memory science and trauma treatment in this book was written out of that hope.

Proposed Legislation

Beyond efforts to challenge restrictions on third-party liability in the courts, a second assault on the privity barrier is in the process of being waged in state legislatures and the United States Congress. This legislation, if enacted, would (1) permit third-party suits against therapists, (2) outlaw the use of any therapy technique that cannot meet rigorous scientific standards, and (3) prohibit the use of hypnosis with memory work in therapy. It is estimated that in the next few years, battles concerning this legislation will be waged in at least half the states and in Congress.

In August 1994, a document was circulated by the Illinois FMS Society, the Texas Friends of FMS, the Florida Friends of FMS, Ohio Parents Falsely Accused, and the Minnesota Action Committee bearing the title "A Proposal to Finance Preparation of Model Legislation Titled *Mental Health Consumer Protection Act*." The proposal contains a preface stating that "patients across America are being subjected to experimental and dangerous forms of 'psychotherapy,' including 'memory retrieval/enhancement' therapy, at taxpayer expense." This therapy, the preface continues, constitutes a

"fraud" on patients and insurance carriers, including Medicare and Medicaid, costing "billions of tax dollars" for reimbursement to therapists who use "experimental, controversial, unproven and hazardous 'psychotherapy' procedures such as 'memory retrieval' or 'memory enhancement' therapies."

The solution suggested is legislation to accomplish the following goals: (1) require full disclosure to the patient of all risks and hazards of the therapy before it begins, (2) ban all funding for psychotherapy procedures that fail to meet "stringent tests for safety and effectiveness," (3) "permit third party (family) lawsuits against therapists who engage in willful and reckless acts such as 'memory retrieval' therapy," (4) criminalize fraudulent practices, which include the "willful or reckless induction of false accusations of abuse," (5) ban pseudoscience testimony from court, including any therapy procedure "that has not been validated and accepted by a substantial majority of the scientific (not the psychotherapy) community," and (6) create a Model Licensing Act for psychotherapists, which would require the maintenance of detailed therapy records and which would lengthen the statute of limitations for suits against therapists.

The proposal is a solicitation to raise funds, which would allow false memory "friends" to draft and publish a Mental Health Consumer Protection Act as a step toward state and federal passage.

The Act begins by stating that "the false memory syndrome, or 'recovery' of false memories in therapy" would not have "destroyed thousands of family relationships" if an appropriate regulatory program had been in existence to exercise control over "the practice of psychotherapy." The Model Legislation drafted to correct this omission has the six goals listed above. We will comment upon each goal in the order presented.

1. Informed Consent

The Act states that although informed consent is rigorously enforced in physical medicine, it is almost universally neglected in mental medicine. The presumption that the therapist "knows best" has been "disproved by the thousands of families destroyed by false memory allegations implanted by therapist bias" (p. 5). The Model Legislation mandates written informed consent before therapy begins. To be fully informed, the patient must be told about "all known risks and hazards of the therapy" and any "alternative treatments and procedures." All informed consent sessions must be audio- and/or videotaped.

This provision has some merit. In fact, the idea that patients should be told about the benefits and risks of a therapy and about alternative treatments is in conformity with the American Society of Clinical Hypnosis' *Clinical Hypnosis and Memory: Guidelines for Clinicians and for Forensic Hypnosis* (Hammond, et al., 1995).

There are one theoretical and several practical objections to this provision, however. From the theoretical point of view, Zeig (1985) has raised challenging objections to the wisdom of informed consent:

> . . . The patient has a right to successful treatment. Psychotherapy cannot be tailored to the Procrustean bed of antiquated ethical strictures that are impossible to follow.
>
> It is ill-advised to require psychologists to fully inform consumers and/or to require overt consent. Requiring overt consent does not have sufficient scope to cover modern strategic and Ericksonian approaches. Providing full information and demanding direct consent can intrude into the clinical situation.

Zeig does accept the patient's right to receive some information to make responsible choices, but he notes the danger of a fully informed consent:

> However, the patient's right to self-determination cannot be compromised. Patients must be afforded freedom of choice. While fully informing patients of the nature of treatment is impossible and based on an antiquated linear conception of human functioning, patients should generally be informed of inherent risks of treatment.
>
> In the courts, the primary purpose of the doctrine of informed consent is to maintain the patient's right to self-determination by providing information about inherent risks of procedures. . . . To reflect that philosophy, the APA Code of Ethics could be amended to state, "Psychologists *inform consumers*

as to the inherent risks of an evaluation, treatment, educational or training procedure. . . ." This wording provides a concept that can be operationalized, researched and applied.

The doctrine of informing the patient of risks cannot be applied indiscriminately, because a therapist will not be merely providing information; he or she will also be influencing the patient. . . .

For example, if the therapist tells the patient that the potential risk of treatment is divorce, not only is a fact being stated, a suggestion is also being made. As experts in communication, therapists should be sensitive to the multilevel structure of communication and responsible for its effect in all aspects of the therapy, including those involving ethics.

As psychologist Michael Yapko (1983) has noted, "maneuvering the client into a position of accepting offered suggestions is evidence of the skilled use of hypnosis." This point is quite important. Just as a patient needs to be made ready for surgery, a patient also needs preparation for effective psychotherapy. This preparation is often outside the awareness of the patient.

The effectiveness of what Zeig calls "covertly eliciting unconscious processes" has been noted by Alan Mitchell (1960), a British psychiatrist:

> My main mistake was over-eagerness to tell the patient what was wrong with him. For instance, if I believed the paralysis of his arm was caused by hostile impulses I would say so immediately. But the secret of successful treatment is entirely the reverse. It is better, even if many hours are required, to give the patient sufficient clues, so that, eventually, he will suggest the cause himself. (p. 60)

This point is well illustrated by a comment made by the late Adrian Fisher in the late 1960s, when he was Dean of the Georgetown University Law Center. Dean Fisher, who negotiated treaties with the Soviet Union on behalf of the United States government, observed that the secret of international negotiations was "to get the other side to make an offer you could accept." If the offer came from those on the other side, they were much more likely not to break it. The trick is to maneuver the other side into making the right offer. A definition of "diplomacy" found on a T-shirt makes the same point, though rather more bluntly: "Diplomacy is the ability to let someone else have your way."

As Yapko (1983) has observed, "direct approaches increase the likelihood of arousing resistance to therapeutic maneuvers. . . . By dealing directly with a client's fears, doubts, and self-esteem, the risk of threatening the person is high and may arouse the need for some defense—'resistance.'"

If Zeig's point is persuasive, with what can we replace the informed consent model as a standard of control? Alexander and Scheflin (1997; Scheflin, 1997b) have proposed the possibility of basing a new standard on the "fiduciary" nature of the doctor-patient relationship. The value of this "fiduciary" approach is that it gives to the patient a more realistic form of protection. The informed consent standard gives the patient knowledge, but not wisdom. Thus, as with most informed consent cases in physical medicine, the patient tells the doctor to do what the doctor thinks best because the patient cannot really make as good a choice as the doctor. The patient receives more protection when the doctor or therapist is forced to show that every decision and every choice made was done for the benefit of the patient within the prevailing professional standards.

Because it is based on an informed consent model exclusively, the Act appears to run contrary to modern cognitive psychology, which emphasizes the unconscious and nonconsensual aspects of decision-making (Bornstein & Pittman, 1992; Uleman & Bargh, 1989).

Zeig (1980), in an article describing some indirect techniques, has written, "If a patient is going to follow suggestions, then indirection is not necessary. In general, the amount of indirection necessary is directly proportional to the anticipated resistance."

While this point makes sense, it also raises the question about how a client can communicate "no" when the therapist sees every resistance as a force to be overcome. Paradoxically, the more the client might *really want to resist*, the more hidden from awareness the therapeutic procedures become. The fiduciary model forces the therapist to be able to justify every therapeutic decision, technique, and procedure as supportive of "the best interests of the patient."

In addition to the theoretical dispute, there is one aspect of this informed consent provision that requires comment. If this section were to be enacted, it would serve as a defense for therapists who have carefully explained the risks and benefits to the patients. Under the autonomy model that informed consent requirements adopt, and that this provision seeks to protect, the patient can give consent to "recovered memory" therapy or any other nonsexual or nonphysical therapy. Thus, this section would permit the continuation of precisely the therapies the Act wants to condemn. In order to be consistent, the Act would have to state that patients cannot give meaningful informed consent to certain therapies. Consumers generally resist having their freedom of choice diminished, as we know from Laetrile and other experimental treatments.

2. Banning Harmful Treatments

The Act laments the absence of any control "to prevent the introduction of any bogus and/or harmful new approach or to prevent the extension of existing approaches so that they become harmful." The solution is for a prohibition on state and federal funding for any therapy that "has not been scientifically proven safe and effective in numerous research investigations."

The standard for scientific safety advocated is found in the Federal Food, Drug, and Cosmetic Act. On November 8, 1990, President Bush signed into law some amendments to the Federal Food, Drug, and Cosmetic Act to confirm the FDA's authority to regulate health claims on food labels and in food labeling. The amendments added a provision establishing a scientific standard certain health claims must meet. The purposes for the amendments were (1) to help consumers maintain healthy dietary practices, and (2) to protect consumers from unfounded health claims. The scientific standard adopted by Congress to regulate labeling and advertising about food claims is the following (Federal Food, Drug, and Cosmetic Act, 1995):

> The Secretary shall promulgate regulations authorizing [labeling or advertising] claims . . . only if the Secretary determines, based on the totality of publicly available scientific evidence (including

evidence from well-designed studies conducted in a manner which is consistent with generally recognized scientific procedures and principles), that there is significant scientific agreement, among experts qualified by scientific training and experience to evaluate such claims, that the claim is supported by such evidence.

The minimal legal materials cited in support of the Act concern the issue of whether Congress intended the FDA to apply a different standard for dietary supplements than is applied for other food items (Food and Drug Administration, 1994). But none of the FDA material involves the regulation of therapy, a function Congress did not assign to the FDA. Interestingly, the Food and Drug Administration (1996) has recently issued new guidelines in an area far closer to the Act's concerns—experimental treatments in emergency settings. Contrary to the Act's approach, however, the FDA chose to "make it easier to carry out experiments on patients who are unable to give their consent because they are unconscious or undergoing emergency treatment" (Hilts, 1995). The purpose of the new regulations is to make it legally safer for doctors to conduct experiments on patients in emergency settings (*Medical Ethics Advisor*, December 1996).

Curiously, the Act fails to cite either of the two major legal tests for the admissibility of expert opinion—the *Frye* rule and the *Daubert* rule. These standards are currently being used by courts to evaluate scientific claims about therapeutic techniques. Why borrow a food labeling standard when two judicially tested rules already are in place to regulate therapy? The Act generally makes a fundamental error in failing to distinguish between a bad therapy and a good therapy used badly. As we have seen, very few therapies are considered bad without some physical or sexual contact with the patient (Scheflin, 1997b). Because there is no "recovered memory" therapy, there is no therapy to condemn. Of course, some therapists are too suggestive in their interactions and too quick to believe what they hear from patients. But these therapists are usually practicing a reasonable therapy badly, not a bad therapy. For well over one hundred years psychiatrists, and alienists before them, probed memory for childhood recollections. Does the Act really accept as fact that the

past has no relevance to the present or future?

The Act also makes another fundamental mistake in believing that laboratory experiments mirror real world events. While scientists may be able to study the effects of food in the laboratory, and feel comfortable that those results generalize to the outside world, the same assumption cannot be made about therapy, particularly trauma therapy. In the *Hamanne v. Humenansky* (1995) case, Ofshe (1995) testified, we believe correctly, that:

> . . . the study of influence and decision making, as it can be done in laboratories, establishes the basic principles through which these things operate. But one cannot do in scientific research, in laboratory-based research, the kinds of extreme things that can happen in police interrogation or in psychiatric hospitals or in cult groups. And the only way to study these things and show how this understanding of manipulation and influence works in the real world when important things are up for grabs, is to study the real settings in which it happens. (p. 119)

The Act does not reveal how scientifically to test real world phenomena. But even assuming that the laboratory experiments were relevant to the real world of trauma therapy, the laboratory actually supports the position maintained by trauma therapists (Scheflin & Brown, 1996), and it does not support the Act's overstated, oversimplified, and sometimes erroneous views about memory, hypnosis, and trauma.

3. Permitting Third-Party Lawsuits

The Act favors lawsuits "by third parties injured by negligent therapy." This potential liability is broader than any judicial opinion has been willing to go. The Act would permit malpractice suits for "all reasonably foreseeable victims of the willful and/or reckless use of hazardous therapy techniques or procedures. . . ." This confusion of negligence, which would be covered by insurance, with intentional conduct, which would not be covered, makes the statute contradictory.

The Act specifically targets "recovered memory" therapy, yet it provides no definition of that therapy and no proof that it is harmful. It then suggests that third-party lawsuits be screened by a panel consisting of one citizen, one lawyer, and one licensed therapist "to insure against frivolous suits." How this panel could provide such protection is not explained. Putting aside the serious constitutional issues that the Act probably violates the First Amendment right to petition the government for redress of grievances (the right of access to the courts), and that it probably violates the separation of powers provision by removing the right of judges to determine what cases they will hear, the Act would require the expenditure of state money to set up such panels, as well as the expenditure of time and money to try cases before the panels in order to win the right to try the case all over again in court. Such a proposal is costly, ill-conceived, and unnecessary.

Under the Act, a therapist would owe a duty to the patient and also to a third party with vastly conflicting interests, thus posing insurmountable ethical dilemmas. Nowhere does the Act explain how therapists may maintain confidentiality when sued by a third party. Perhaps confidentiality should not be protected, as Shuman and Weiner (1982) have suggested in their discussion of eliminating confidentiality and privilege. Thus, a satisfied patient would lose all privacy because a dissatisfied relative disagrees with the nature of the therapy (*Sullivan v. Cheshier*, 1995). This incursion into the privacy of therapy and therapy records runs counter to the United States Supreme Court's opinion in *Jaffee v. Redmond* (1996), where the Court *expanded* protection of therapy records by expanding the psychotherapist-patient privilege.

It should be pointed out that the attempt to destroy confidentiality and privilege hardly coincides with "consumer protection" legislation. How are consumers protected by knowing that their innermost secrets, beliefs, feelings, emotions, fears, and concerns are available for the voyeuristic amusement of the people whose conduct may have sent them into therapy in the first place?

The third-party liability provision may appear to benefit family members who are harmed by therapists, but the group that truly benefits are the lawyers because of the potential to intrude into any therapy session in the country provided they find one disgruntled family member. Of course, liability extends beyond family members under the Act to anyone who is "foreseeable." Does this mean that friends, schoolmates, workmates, and others are also entitled to sue, to obtain the confidential records, and to recover?

Finally, suppose that "recovered memory" therapy existed and that a therapist explained it fully to the patient. The patient was also told about alternatives. The patient consents to the therapy and is happy with the therapy. May a third party sue and recover despite the consent and satisfaction of the patient?

4. Banning Pseudoscience from the Courtroom

While the goal is beneficial, the law already has established tests, the *Frye* (1923) and *Daubert* (1993) rules, to accomplish it, as we shall see in the next chapter. Additional legislation would be confusing and unnecessary.

The Act would appear to exclude all memory from the courtroom, according to the provision that "there is clearly enough evidence to demonstrate that memory recovery and memory enhancement is [*sic*] sufficiently unreliable that they should also not be allowed in the courtroom." This, frankly, is the inevitable conclusion that false memory advocates must reach (Scheflin, 1997c). If memory itself is so malleable as to be untrustworthy, and if it is untrustworthy because (1) it is always reconstructive, and (2) it is always being influenced, then memory itself fails to meet the appropriate scientific test for reliability. The manner in which memories are retrieved may, at most, further contaminate memory, but memory is untrustworthy on its own. Memory, of course, is the basis of all testimony.

The Act would also ban from the courtroom "untested, unproven therapies and their results, unless the procedures have been validated and accepted by a substantial majority of the scientific (not the psychotherapy) community." This extraordinary provision can be tested by briefly raising several points. In the first place, how is it possible to have "untested, unproven therapies" and also have their "results"? Second, if the procedure is validated, it is no longer "untested and unproven." Third, the standard used to evaluate the therapy, the "substantial majority" test, contradicts the standard already selected by the Act from the FDA in provision 2. It also differs from the prevailing *Frye* (1923) and *Daubert* (1993) rules, as we shall see in the next chapter. Fourth, most, if not all, states reject a respectable minority test based exclusively on a nose count. Why should they then accept a nose count for a majority test? Fifth, exclusion of the psychotherapeutic community from evaluating psychotherapy is a gross violation of the venerable and correct "two schools of thought" doctrine, which is universally recognized and applied by judges. Sixth, how is a "*substantial majority* of the scientific community," excluding therapists, going to be able to test and evaluate therapeutic practices? Seventh, what "scientific community" does the Act mean? If therapists are excluded, who is included—physicists, mechanical engineers, dentists, astronomers, etc.? Even if the answer is doctors, the Act would be asking them to speculate outside their field of competence and expertise. As we learned in chapter 12, sociologists of science remind us that there is no "scientific community," but rather a variety of diverse and conflicting scientific interest groups. There is a real danger that one scientific interest group, defined as the "substantial majority" in this Act, would be given legislative authority to suppress opposing schools of thought within the wider clinical-scientific community. Furthermore, what is the wisdom of excluding therapists when they are the ones who will develop, test, and use the new procedure or technique?

5. Criminalize Fraudulent Practices

The Act singles out two types of fraud that should be criminalized: (1) "the willful or reckless induction of false accusations of abuse should carry specific criminal penalties," and (2) "the fraud associated with accepting payments from federal, state or insurance sources for improper procedures needs to be clearly delineated" in order to apply criminal penalties.

Substantial drafting problems again interfere with giving a sensible interpretation of the Act. Does the Act mean to criminalize (1) the willful *implanting* of false memories of child abuse, or (2) the willful *filing* of charges of sexual abuse known to be false? Although criminal statutes require more clarity than this provision contains, the idea of criminalizing ei-

ther of these two types of conduct merits discussion. A criminal penalty would apply only if it could be proven that either (1) the therapist *knew and intended* to implant false memories, or (2) the therapist filed charges *knowing* that they were false. Mere negligence would not be sufficient. In the vast array of false/repressed memory cases filling courtroom dockets, very few, if any, charge that the therapist maliciously intended to cause harm by deliberately and intentionally implanting false memories. Rather, the argument is precisely the opposite—that the therapists were so naive and incompetent as to be thoroughly unaware that they were implanting these memories by suggestion.

The second illustration concerns accepting payments for "improper procedures." The idea is too vague. In order to criminalize the acceptance of money, the therapist will have to be shown to have knowingly entered into an illegal transaction. The therapist would have to know that the therapy technique is "improper," and the therapist must have intended to use it anyway. Again, this is not the conduct typically complained of in the false memory controversy, though one of the Act's stated goals is to develop "a legal analysis comparing fraudulent and politicized psychotherapists to drunk drivers." The Act fails to provide such an analysis.

6. Create a Model Licensing Act

A proposed Model Licensing Act would cover two distinct issues: (1) unlicensed "therapists" who are not governed by "any coherent body of law and principles," and (2) licensed practitioners who should be required to maintain detailed records and acquire malpractice insurance. In addition, the Model Act would lengthen the statute of limitations "for suits against therapists."

The basic idea of regulating some nonlicensed therapists is worth considering (Scheflin & Alexander, 1997). Under current law, these therapists have no legal standard of care and are not covered under the privilege and confidentiality laws. There are no minimal education requirements, and, except for the avoidance of fraud or deception, they are under no legal duty to disclose their inadequate training (Hammond, 1992). Some "schools" that train lay hypnotherapists have even been granted the authority to confer M.A. and Ph.D. degrees on their graduates, thereby creating further consumer danger and confusion.

Among licensed therapists, the maintenance of detailed records is already part of the standard of care, and most therapists do obtain malpractice insurance. Mandating these as requirements would change very little.

Extending the statute of limitations for suits against therapists would parallel the activity of courts and legislatures in half the states that have applied lengthened statutes or delayed discovery doctrines to cases of childhood sexual abuse where memories of that abuse have been repressed (Williams, 1996). We examine these legal developments in the next chapter. The wisdom of protecting abuse victims whose memories return later is self-evident. Assume that a child is repeatedly sexually molested by her father. Her memory of these events is repressed as part of her mental self-protection. It is grossly unfair to say that when her memories do return, she has already lost her day in court. Because the repression was a natural and involuntary response to the molesting, the perpetrator should not be able to take advantage of the harm he or she has caused to avoid legal responsibility (Scheflin, 1997c).

The wisdom of extending the statute of limitations for suits against therapists is not obvious. In general, the statute begins to run after the harm has been discovered, not after it was committed. Thus, from the time the patient is aware of the mistreatment, the patient generally has several years to bring a malpractice action. For this entire century, the statute of limitations has provided patients more than enough time to file malpractice actions.

In our view, the proposal is generally ill-conceived and it is certainly poorly drafted. It is billed as a Consumer Protection Act; the one class of consumers who will most benefit from it are the lawyers. The provisions allowing any "foreseeable" person a lengthy period of time to sue a therapist who is mandated to have malpractice insurance will send lawyers scrambling for their business cards. Litigating attorneys will especially be beneficiaries of this proposal because it opens up the insurance coverage of thousands and thousands of therapists.

The bottom line, however, is that this proposal's draconian features are built upon a foundation of false science. As we have shown in this book, the laboratory studies and the clinical data generally do not support the extreme remedies the Act mandates because the Act is mistaken in its assumptions about "recovered memory" therapy and about repression. Certainly there are therapists who are practicing below the prevailing standard of care. That is true in every profession. The better solution has always been to educate them or weed them out, not to weaken the entire profession because of the few bad apples.

In early 1995, the Consumer Protection Act was redrafted and retitled "The Truth and Responsibility in Mental Health Practices Act" [TRMHPA]. In this redrafted form, the proposed statute was introduced into the legislatures of New Hampshire, Illinois, and Missouri, with other states also targeted. Proponents of TRMHPA are encouraging the United States Congress to pass federal legislation that would require each State to pass TRMHPA as a condition to receiving federal money for health care funding (Saunders, Bursztajn, & Brodsky, 1995).

Under the revised provisions, the same targets are under attack. According to the TRMHPA, "the tax dollars of hard working American citizens" are funding "the widespread use of unproven, ineffective and even dangerous mental health practices" because "current reimbursement systems fail to distinguish between effective, scientifically validated treatments and untested, hazardous mental health practices." Furthermore, in courts across the country, "unscientific testimony by mental health practitioners has become distressingly common" and "such deceptive, 'junk science' testimony is an unacceptable danger to individual and family liberty" as well as a "growing stain" on "the integrity of the American legal system."

The TRMHPA continues to propose the same old solutions. Therapists must obtain written "informed consent" from patients after (1) explaining the proposed treatment, (2) giving the patient "scientific journal citations" demonstrating that the treatment has been "proven" reasonably safe and effective "by reliable and valid scientific research studies including treatment outcome research comparing the proposed treatment to alternative treatments and control (no treatment) subjects," (3) listing foreseeable risks and hazards of the treatment, as well as benefits, and (4) listing alternative treatments with their risks and benefits. These forms must be used and submitted for the therapist to obtain financial reimbursement.

"Junk science" testimony in court is outlawed, although the TRMHPA never defines what "junk science" is or is not. The old attack on hypnosis is still present, coupled with the citation to the American Medical Association's 1985 Research Council statement about forensic hypnosis. Whereas the AMA had intended for hypnotists to be cautious and careful when doing memory work, authors of the TRMPHA appear to read the AMA statement far more broadly as condemning hypnosis and rejecting memory retrieval. Current research makes it clear that the AMA statement is inconsistent with the latest scientific literature and was based upon insufficient data when it was issued (Frischholz, 1996, in press; Scheflin, 1997c).

Reaction to TRMHPA has been consistently negative. The American Psychological Association (1995b) issued a strong resolution against it and noted that it "creates a bureaucracy and unnecessary barriers that interfere with consumer access to mental health services and fails to protect consumers." Saunders, Bursztajn, and Brodsky (1995), after a detailed and thorough medical and legal analysis of the provisions of TRMHPA, concluded:

> This legislation is an unworkable concoction of unconsidered reactions to real personal suffering and the vested interests of managed care under the ideology of "science." Many of its provisions would be difficult to interpret and implement without destroying existing structures of professional and statutory regulation and legal procedure. In the rush to stop iatrogenic, or clinically caused harm, HB 236 would itself inflict a kind of critogenic, or legally mandated harm. It would be the kind of radical surgery from whose very "success" the patient would bleed to death.

Simon (1995) observed that the TRMHPA would severely curtail the delivery of mental health services to consumers and would considerably hamper survivors of childhood sexual abuse from obtaining needed relief. In essence, Simon continues, "these 'reforms' sponsored by individuals accused of sex crimes would provide an indirect means by which offenders could silence their victims and avoid accountability" (p. 19).

Commentators seem agreed on several points. First, the clear impact of the TRMHPA would be to seriously hamper the practice of psychotherapy, especially with trauma patients. Second, the TRMHPA appears to be a monumental overreaction to a problem that is best handled in less drastic ways. Third, the TRMHPA destroys confidentiality and therefore sacrifices the trust necessary and essential to build a healing relationship. Fourth, the TRMHPA would be tremendously costly and bureaucratic to administer. Fifth, the TRMHPA would create a lawyer feeding-frenzy, which would bring thousands of meritless cases into an already overclogged legal system.

Indeed, apart from making it far easier for lawyers to sue therapists, the Act would be a consumer nightmare. Malpractice insurance rates would shoot through the ceiling, or else coverage would be denied entirely, as is already beginning to occur. Talented healers would be driven from the profession to avoid the talons of avaricious lawyers hoping for easy settlements. Because of the increased invasion of privacy and breach of confidentiality included in the proposed legislation, settlements to avoid embarrassing disclosures are more likely even though no tortious conduct occurred. Innovative and unorthodox therapies would be completely curtailed, and experimenters would hesitate to introduce new techniques for fear of absolute liability.

CONCLUSION

In this chapter we have examined traditional legal theory in regard to the issue of lawsuits against therapists. The present rules do not satisfy false memory advocates, who feel that therapists should be held more accountable, especially to nonclients. Beginning in 1986, with the first case of repressed memory, the law has been pushed, pulled, and pressured to find satisfactory solutions to intensely difficult scientific and social issues. The fate of therapists, patients, and families hangs in the balance. In the next chapter we will explore the recent litigation concerning repressed memory issues. These cases pose additional unique challenges to the courts, and the solutions have a major impact on individuals, families, and mental health professionals. As noted by Scheflin (1994c):

> The bitter turmoil about trauma therapy and repressed memory is causing anxious parents to ask, "If my child goes into therapy, will I be accused as a molester?" Anxious real victims of child abuse are asking, "Will anyone believe my story is true now that so many accusations are false?" Anxious therapists are asking, "Why should I take trauma clients when to do so makes it more likely for me to be sued?" The challenge for the law in the next decade will be to accommodate the valid claims of all three sides.

16

‖‖‖‖‖‖‖‖‖‖‖‖‖‖‖‖‖‖

Repressed Memory and the Law

Although the concept of "repressed" memory has a long history in psychiatry, it has a relatively short history in law. We will refer to "repressed" memory in this chapter rather than the generally accepted clinical terms, *traumatic amnesia* or *dissociative amnesia*, because much of the law is written in terms of "repressed" memory.

There are several reasons why repressed memory issues have only recently appeared in courts and legislatures. First, societal recognition of the extent of childhood sexual abuse and of its traumatizing consequences is itself a recent phenomenon. Laws to protect children from this abuse are mostly the product of the 1970s and afterward (Kalichman, 1993), though early legislation appeared in the 1960s in a few states. Even today, accurate statistics are difficult to obtain on the amount of child abuse, sexual and physical, that occurs in families. One of the major reasons statistics on child abuse, including child sexual abuse, are difficult to compile, besides the obvious point that these offenses occur in private and the young victims are threatened if they talk, is the inability of experts, officials, and lawmakers to agree on a satisfactory definition of the basic terms. The wider the definition, the higher the statistical report.

For example, in *People v. Deskins* (1996), the defendant was driving under the influence of alcohol when his car collided with another car occupied by a woman and four children. As a result of the collision, three of the children were killed and the woman and one child sustained serious injuries. A majority of justices on the Supreme Court of Colorado held that this conduct constituted "child abuse" within the meaning of the criminal statute (Colorado Statutes, 1986) because the standard for reckless child abuse does not require that the defendant be aware that the potential victim may be a child.

Second, immunity laws in most states prohibited one family member from suing another family member. The elimination of these immunities is also a post-1970 development (Keeton, 1984).

Third, the growth of cognitive psychology, the interest in practical applications of memory and memory error, the use of hypnosis in court cases, the study of the fallibility of eyewitness testimony and memory, and research on the credibility of child testimony, have all become matters of scientific scrutiny in the post-1970 era.

As we noted in the previous chapter, there are four types of lawsuits that have been presented to courts involving repressed memory issues:

1. Patients (recanters/retractors) suing therapists
2. Third-party (nonclient) lawsuits against therapists
3. Accuser suing alleged perpetrator for past abuse

4. Repressed memories as evidence in criminal cases

Central to these four types of lawsuits are two underlying questions: (1) is repressed memory real? and (2) should evidence or testimony based on repressed memory be admissible in courts of law as "scientific" evidence? The first question addresses science; the second question, which is obviously dependent upon the answer to the first question, addresses opinion and social policy.

In this chapter we will examine the last two types of lawsuits and the two central questions. Chapter 15 discussed the first two lawsuit types, and chapter 17 will inquire into any procedures or tests that may help to determine whether alleged abuse memories are true or false.

ACCUSER SUES ALLEGED PERPETRATOR FOR PAST ABUSE

Cases involving repressed memory began in the mid-1980s (*Tyson v. Tyson*, 1986). An adult plaintiff files a lawsuit against an alleged perpetrator, accusing him or her of having sexually abused the adult decades earlier when the adult was just a child. Because of the exceedingly long delay between the commission of the acts and the filing of the suit, the statute of limitations ordinarily will have run its course, thereby prohibiting the suit from being tried in court. The statute of limitations is generally passed by legislatures to limit the amount of time during which a lawsuit may be brought. Thus, breach of contract actions must usually be brought within four to six years, whereas tortious acts, such as battery, assault, negligence, etc., must be brought within one to four years. Once the statutory time period has expired, the lawsuit may not be brought no matter how much proof the plaintiff has to support the case. Legislatures enact statutes of limitation to encourage prompt filing of suits while the evidence is on hand and memory is relatively fresh. Suits brought after several years are harder to defend because the evidence may no longer be available and memories have become stale.

If a plaintiff wants to bring a lawsuit after the statutory time has expired, the plaintiff must have a valid legal argument to overcome the running of the statute of limitations in order to reach trial (Williams, 1996). Adults who sue for abuse that occurred decades earlier when they were children will find that the statutory time period has run. Theoretically, therefore, repressed memory cases would never get to court.

Plaintiff-accusers in repressed memory cases have thus found that before they can get to trial and put on their proof, they must formulate an argument that will permit them to get into court. These plaintiff-accusers must convince judges that the statute of limitations should not bar their claims.

The repressed memory cases therefore fall into two categories: (1) the cases that argue that the statute of limitations should not bar the claims, and (2) the cases that have succeeded in removing the statute of limitations barrier and are now in court deciding the merits of plaintiffs' claims.

The Statute of Limitations

The statute of limitations begins to run when the plaintiff knew of, or should have learned of, the existence of all of the necessary elements of the cause of action to pursue against the defendant. If there is a good reason why the plaintiff has not learned of all the elements of the cause of action, the running of the statute will be delayed. For example, most states "toll" the statute if the injury occurs to a minor. The statute will begin to run once the age of majority has been reached. The new adult then will generally have one to three years within which to bring the case.

Another illustration of "tolling" the statute is the "delayed discovery" doctrine, which is followed in the majority of states. This judicially created rule protects plaintiffs who experience unavoidable delays in discovering the harm done to them. For example, in the most traditional case, a sponge is left in the body of plaintiff during an operation. It may be several years before the sponge causes sufficient harm to alert the plaintiff to its existence. Under the delayed discovery doctrine, the statute of limitations will begin to run from the time plaintiff could reasonably know of the presence of the sponge. The delayed discovery doctrine has usually been applied to cases of personal injury, latent disease or harm, and medical malpractice, although there is also support for its application to psychiatric malpractice (*Simmons v. United States*, 1986).

The application of the delayed discovery doctrine to toll the statute of limitations in cases where the plaintiff psychologically represses memories of childhood sexual abuse developed from the judicial recognition that a cause of action does not begin until the victim discovers, or reasonably should have discovered, the harm or injury and its wrongfulness.

The first case to discuss the issue of whether repressed memory would trigger the application of the delayed discovery doctrine was *Tyson v. Tyson* (1986), a Washington Supreme Court opinion that answered the following question:

Does the discovery rule, which tolls the statute of limitations until the plaintiff discovers or reasonably should have discovered a cause of action, apply to intentional torts where the victim has blocked the incident from her conscious memory during the entire time of the statute of limitations?

In *Tyson*, a woman alleged that she had been sexually abused by her father during her childhood. She brought a civil action at the age of 26, several years after the statute of limitations had expired. The plaintiff alleged that the assaults caused her to suppress any memory of the acts until she entered therapy. Once the memories began to return, she filed suit within the appropriate time limit required by the delayed discovery doctrine.

The majority opinion refused to apply the delayed discovery rule to an incest case based on alleged recollection of events that were repressed from consciousness unless the plaintiff found a means of independently verifying the allegations. The medical malpractice sponge cases were distinguished from cases involving psychological repression of memories by noting that the source of injury in the former cases is objectively verifiable—the sponge is found in the body.

To this point about objective verifiability the majority added an additional twist—an attack on the subjectivity of psychotherapy:

. . . Psychology and psychiatry are imprecise disciplines. Unlike the biological sciences, their methods of investigation are primarily subjective and most of their findings are not based on physically

observable evidence. The fact that plaintiff asserts she discovered the wrongful acts through psychological therapy does not validate their occurrence. Recent studies by certain psychoanalysts have questioned the assumption that the analyst has any special ability to help the subject ascertain the historical truth. See generally Wesson, Historical Truth, Narrative Truth, and Expert Testimony, 60 Wash.L.Rev. 331 (1985). These studies show that the psychoanalytic process can even lead to a distortion of the truth of events in the subject's past life. The analyst's reactions and interpretations may influence the subject's memories or statements about them. The analyst's interpretations of the subject's statements may also be altered by the analyst's own predisposition, expectations, and intention to use them to explain the subject's problems. . . . Thus, the distance between historical truth and psychoanalytic "truth" is quite a gulf. From what "really happened" to what the subject or patient remembers is one transformation; from what he remembers to what he articulates is another; from what he says to what the analyst hears is another; and from what the analyst hears to what she concludes is still another. . . . While psychoanalysis is certainly of great assistance in treating an individual's emotional problems, the trier of fact in legal proceedings cannot assume that it will produce an accurate account of events in the individual's past.

The purpose of emotional therapy is not the determination of historical facts, but the contemporary treatment and cure of the patient. We cannot expect these professions to answer questions which they are not intended to address.

Application of the discovery rule in cases of repressed memory is ill-advised, according to the majority, because the "potential for spurious claims would be great and the probability of the court's determining the truth would be unreasonably low." The majority concluded that:

It is proper to apply the discovery rule in cases where the objective nature of the evidence makes it substantially certain that the facts can be fairly determined even though considerable time has passed since the alleged events occurred. Such circumstances simply do not exist where a plaintiff brings an action based solely on an alleged recollection of events which were repressed from her consciousness and there is no means of independently verifying her allegations in whole or in part.

The *Tyson* opinion contained a strong dissent, which focused on the reality of childhood sexual abuse. The majority had only a single sentence about child sexual abuse: "We recognize that child sexual abuse has devastating impacts on the victim" (p. 227). The dissent objected to "the summary manner in which [the majority] dismisses the enormous problem of child sexual abuse" and offered some extensive and sobering facts, quoted here at length:

Although definitions vary, child sexual abuse can be defined as "contacts or interactions between a child and an adult when the child is being used as an object of gratification for adult sexual needs or desires" [citation omitted]. It has been estimated that as much as one-third of the population has experienced some form of child sexual abuse [citations omitted]. Much of the sexual abuse of children occurs within the family [citation omitted]. In one study of 583 cases of child sexual abuse, the offender was a family member in 47 percent of the cases; otherwise, an acquaintance of the child in 42 percent, and a stranger in only 8 percent. Note, Testimony of Child Victims in Sex Abuse Prosecutions: Two Legislative Innovations, 98 Harv.L.Rev. 806, 807 n. 14 (1985). Of this high percentage of cases of abuse among family members, it has been estimated that 75 percent involve incest between father and daughter. Coleman, Incest: A Proper Definition Reveals the Need for a Different Legal Response, 49 Mo.L.Rev. 251, 251 n. 1 (1984). Both the high incidence of father/daughter incestuous abuse and the special problems of such incest victims have led to much commentary [citations omitted]. Because incestuous abuse is so pervasive and because the instant case involves father/daughter incest, I have focused on this type of sexual abuse.

Incestuous abuse begins, in the average case, when the daughter is 8 or 9 years old, although sexual relations and even intercourse may begin even earlier. . . . In order to ensure his daughter's availability to him and provide a cover for his conduct, the father demands secrecy from the child.

Often he frightens her into secrecy with threats of harm. . . . Because the victim is thus sworn to secrecy, she is forced to deal with the situation alone. Because she must cope alone, she is likely to internalize her self-blame, anger, fears, confusion, and sadness resulting from the incest. This internalization results in what has been referred to as "accommodation." . . . In accommodating herself to an intolerable situation, the victim often "blocks out" her experience for many years. . . . This "blocking out" is a coping mechanism. A victim will cope in this fashion because "some things are literally so difficult to deal with if remembered that your choices are to go crazy or to forget them." . . .

As the incest victim becomes an adult, she will often begin to exhibit signs of incest trauma. The most common are sexual dysfunction, low self esteem, poor capacity for self protection, feelings of isolation, and an inability to form or maintain supportive relationships. . . . At this time, the daughter may know she is injured. However, until such time as she is able to place blame for the incestuous abuse upon her father, it will be impossible for her to realize that his behavior caused her psychological disorders. . . . Often it is only through therapy that the victim is able to recognize the causal link between her father's incestuous conduct and her damages from incest trauma. . . . Once the victim begins to confront her experiences and link her damages with her father's incestuous conduct, she has taken a step as a survivor of childhood incestuous abuse.

The need for maturity of the survivor before she can confront her childhood incest experience results in a general lack of ability to file suit within the statutory period. . . . As has been seen, the maximum age at which an adult survivor of incest may file suit in this state is 21. Since many survivors are simply incapable of discovering a cause of action by the time they are 21 years old, they are effectively denied a legal remedy unless they are given the benefit of the discovery rule.

The dissent rejected the majority's negative perception of mental health expertise. In contrast, the dissent observed that courts use expert mental health testimony in a wide variety of cases. Furthermore, the distinction between narrative truth and historical truth adopted by the majority is of no consequence because, in the law review article cited by the majority, Professor Wesson

> suggests that any problems which may be created by the mental health professional's inability to substantiate detailed "truth" may be remedied. She recommends three solutions: (1) juries should be instructed that psychotherapists are experts whose testimony may be accepted or rejected; (2) parties should call their own mental health professionals as experts and conduct effective cross examinations; (3) more use should be made of the hypothetical question, which would allow the jury to discern the truth of the premises which underlie the opinion given by the expert. Wesson, 60 Wash.L.Rev. at 351–53. Far from advocating the nonuse of this type of expert testimony, the author identifies some problems and offers solutions. Yet it was this lone article on which the majority rested its premise that the testimony of mental health professionals is inherently unreliable in assisting the trier in the search for truth.

The dissent concluded by stating that because "it is unfair to deny adult survivors of childhood sexual abuse a legal remedy," the delayed discovery rule should apply to repressed memory cases where the jury finds that "the plaintiff has repressed all conscious memory of such abuse during the entire period of the statute of limitations."

Both the majority and the dissent in *Tyson* wrote powerful opinions that have shaped the law that has followed in its wake. To this day, courts continue to cite the reasoning of the majority or the dissent in reaching their conclusions.

The *Tyson* case was a defeat for the concept of repressed memory, but the decision so aroused the Washington legislature that it was superseded by statute in 1988. The legislature specifically noted its support for the dissenting view, which favored recognizing the validity of repressed memories (Washington Revised Code, 1995). This pattern, first judicial denial and then legislative acceptance of repressed memory, has been repeated in several states.

In *Johnson v. Johnson* (1988), a federal district court standardized a distinction between "Type 1 Plaintiffs" and "Type 2 Plaintiffs." In *Johnson*, the plaintiff alleged that she had repressed memories of

being sexually abused by her father over a ten-year period during her childhood. Twenty years later, at age 32, she brought a civil action after suddenly remembering the incest during psychotherapy, and after discovering its causal link to her present emotional harm. Thus, *Johnson* was a repressed memory case, not a continuing memory case.

The *Johnson* court divided childhood sexual abuse cases into two categories, depending on the claims made by the plaintiff:

Type 1 Plaintiffs are those who remember the sexual assaults at or before the age of majority, but are unaware that other physical and psychological problems they suffer as adults may have been caused by the prior sexual abuse until this becomes clear usually, but not necessarily, because of their involvement in therapy or some other intervention after the limitations period has expired.

Type 2 Plaintiffs are those who claim that, because of the trauma of the experience, they have had absolutely no recollection of the sexual abuse until shortly before filing suit.

The *Johnson* court found that the plaintiff was in the latter category and held that the delayed discovery doctrine applied to Type 2 Plaintiffs. Limiting its holding to the specific facts before it, the court did not address the issue of whether the discovery rule would apply to Type 1 Plaintiffs.

Should the delayed discovery doctrine apply to plaintiffs with continuing memories of the abuse? Because they had memories throughout their lives, it is easy to claim that they should have known of the legal cause of action and filed suit within the statutory limit.

Continuous Memories vs. Repressed Memories

In order to persuade courts that the statute of limitations should be delayed, plaintiffs with continuous memories have argued (1) that they did not equate the childhood abuse with the physical and/or mental problems they suffered as adults, (2) that they felt too guilty, too ashamed, too scared, too weak, or too insecure to file suit earlier, or (3) that they did not have sufficient memory until later to understand fully what had happened in the past.

The Canadian Supreme Court judges have authored some of the most carefully considered opinions on child abuse and delayed reporting of continuous memory. In the first crucial case, the Court directly addressed the issue of the psychological damage suffered by victims of child abuse (*R. v. L. (W.K.)*, 1991):

> For victims of sexual abuse to complain would take courage and emotional strength in revealing those personal secrets, in opening old wounds. If proceedings were to be stayed based solely on the passage of time between the abuse and the charge, victims would be required to report incidents before they were psychologically prepared for the consequences of that reporting.

That delay in reporting sexual abuse is a common and expected consequence of that abuse has been recognized in other contexts. In the United States, many states have enacted legislation modifying or extending the limitation period for the prosecution of sexual abuse cases, in recognition of the fact that sexual abuse often goes unreported, and even undiscovered by the complainant, for years. . . . Establishing a judicial statute of limitations would mean that sexual abusers would be able to take advantage of the failure to report which they themselves, in many cases, caused. This is not a result which we should encourage.

One year later, the Supreme Court of Canada found the opportunity to turn its expressed sympathy and support for incest victims into legal protection for them. In *K.M. v. H.M.* (1992), a young girl was molested by her father. She made several attempts to tell people, but her father forced her to recant the allegations. Other disclosures did not bring any changes in her father's sexual activity with her. After attending a self-help group for incest victims, she realized that her adult psychological problems were caused by the childhood incest. Therapy gave her the self-esteem to realize that "it was her father rather than herself who was at fault." Although a jury found in favor of the plaintiff, the trial judge concluded that the action was barred by the statute of limitations. Three issues were raised before the Canadian Supreme Court: "(1) whether incest is a separate and distinct tort not subject to any limitation period; (2) whether incest constitutes a breach of fiduciary duty by a parent not subject to any limitation period; and (3) if a limitation period

applies, whether it is postponed by the reasonable discoverability principle."

The judges found that incest was not a separate tort, but that it was a breach of fiduciary duty on the part of her father. In a breach of fiduciary duty, there is no statutory limit placed on when the action may be brought. This conceptualization of incest as a breach of fiduciary responsibility is fully consistent with psychologist Jennifer Freyd's (1993, 1994, 1996) "betrayal trauma theory," which notes that when the betrayer who causes severe trauma is someone a child needs to depend on, the trauma is much worse psychologically. According to Handler (1987), the long-term consequences that are reasonably foreseeable from the childhood sexual abuse include "depression, self-mutilation and suicidal behavior, eating disorders and sleep disturbances, drug or alcohol abuse, sexual dysfunction, inability to form intimate relationships, tendencies towards promiscuity and prostitution and a vulnerability towards revictimization" (pp. 716–717).

Legal commentators, almost unanimously, initially argued that the delayed discovery rule should be applied in all cases of childhood sexual abuse as a way of permitting alleged victims their day in court. For example, Gallagher (1993) concludes:

> It must be acknowledged that memory is a fragile thing, and the possibility of false memories does exist. Therefore, the risk of false accusations increases if the statute of limitations is tolled until such time as a memory is triggered. Such an accusation may be made by one who actually believes the abuse took place. While this concept is quite disturbing, it is not a sufficient reason to preclude all putative victims of childhood sexual abuse from seeking recovery. . . . At the risk of sounding glib, one must have faith in our legal system and assume that those who are wrongly accused will be exonerated.

On the other hand, some commentators have argued against the application of the delayed discovery rule on the grounds that the repressed memories are unreliable. Loftus and Rosenwald (1995) argue:

> Because corroborating evidence is usually difficult to establish for distant events, the classic repressed

memory trial is a credibility contest between accuser and accused. . . . Uncritical acceptance of every single recovered memory of sexual abuse, no matter how bizarre, benefits neither the client, the family, the mental health profession, nor the precious human facility of memory; and it trivializes genuine memory of abuse. (p. 358)

The disagreement between the day-in-court and unreliability of repressed memory positions centers around the confidence legal commentators have in the court's ability to evaluate the evidence. The great majority of legal commentators for the first few years overwhelmingly supported the day-in-court position, and favored a cause of action for both Type 1 and Type 2 Plaintiffs (Bickel, 1991; Cook & Millsaps, 1991; Kanovitz, 1992; Lamm, 1991; Napier, 1990; Snelling & Fisher, 1992; Thomas, 1991; Whitehead, 1992). Hagen (1991) has argued that permitting a day in court for all victims of childhood sexual abuse "provides the adult plaintiff with the opportunity to redress the wrongs done to the child's body." As Rodgers (1992) has observed:

Society has seemingly allowed incest perpetrators to commit perfect crimes. They violate all principles of morality by sexually abusing children. Yet, unless the child is astute enough to recognize that what has occurred is wrong and is brave enough to disclose the abuse to someone willing to help, the perpetrator may go unpunished because of the current law's insistence on protecting the perpetrator from a "stale claim."

Since 1986, when *Tyson* became the first appellate case on point, approximately 100 appellate opinions have discussed repressed memory issues. The majority of courts have been receptive to repressed memory claims, and those that have not have often been overruled by legislation or criticized by legal commentators. Because courts clearly favor repressed memory over continuous memory, Type 2 Plaintiffs will win more cases than Type 1 Plaintiffs. Lawyers are aware that clients without complete repression are not likely to prevail and they will explain this point to their clients. As a consequence, courts that reject Type 1 Plaintiff claims may be unintentionally encouraging false claims of repression as a ticket of entry into the courtroom. As we

have noted, most legal commentators have expressed the belief that fairness requires the application of the delayed discovery rule in childhood sexual abuse cases to both Type 1 and Type 2 Plaintiffs.

Why have commentators supported the delayed discovery doctrine's application in these childhood sexual abuse cases? An appellate case from Michigan reflects the sentiment of many judges and legislators who have struggled with the repressed memory/delayed discovery issue. The plaintiff in *Lemmerman v. Fealk* (1993) alleged repressed memories from nearly 50 years earlier. The plaintiff also alleged that when she confronted her father, he confessed. The Michigan Court of Appeals allowed application of the delayed discovery rule. The court noted that these cases always involve a delicate balance between harm to the defendant who must stand trial if the claim is stale and harm to the plaintiff denied a day in court if the facts are true. What tips the balance?

We agree with those jurisdictions which initially consider as more weighty the harm to the plaintiff denied a remedy than the harm to the defendant confronted with a stale claim. . . . The fact that sexual molestation of children exists, is extensive and leaves deep scars on its victims can no longer be seriously questioned. Adults who have repressed child sexual abuse bring to the courts unusual circumstances and injuries not readily conforming to the ordinary constructs on which periods of limitations are imposed.

In essence, as the court later specifically states, "to protect parents or relatives at the expense of the children works an intolerable perversion of justice."

Lemmerman applied the delayed discovery rule in favor of the alleged victim, but the case was reversed on appeal. In *Lemmerman v. Fealk* (1995), the Michigan Supreme Court refused to apply the discovery rule to any type of repressed memory case and cited the majority reasoning in *Tyson*, even though that case had been specifically rejected by the legislature. The Michigan justices also rejected the plaintiff's other attempt to delay the statute—the use of the insanity disability provision. In essence the plaintiff had argued that during the time the memories were repressed, she was "insane" and therefore disabled from bringing a lawsuit. The return of the memories removed the disability. Michigan statutes allow an insanity disability, but the Supreme Court, in line with most cases that have addressed this specific issue, declined to define repressed memory in terms of insanity. The court made it clear that it was not against repressed memories, but rather it felt that the discovery rule and the insanity disability were not designed to deal with the sex abuse/memory issues:

> Our decision should not be read as an expression of opinion that assault-based tort actions that plaintiffs have allegedly been unable to commence because of memory repression should never be recognized. We hold only that the devices presently available to this Court to allow actions beyond the statutory limitation period are inappropriate vehicles by which to allow these claims to survive a statute of limitations challenge. Neither the discovery rule nor the insanity disability grace period contemplates the situations presented to us by plaintiffs' claims. (p. 703)

While the court deferred to the legislature in repressed memory cases, it also held that if the defendant confesses to or admits the abuse, the plaintiff can pursue the claim. If the plaintiff has "objective and verifiable evidence" of the abuse, but not a confession or admission, the plaintiff is not entitled to pursue the claim, unless the legislature decides otherwise. In this case, there was no proof of the confession other than the plaintiff's claim that it occurred.

The Michigan legislature had previously addressed childhood sexual abuse claims by passing a statute in 1987 that extended the period of time such claims could be brought, and legislation was pending to provide additional protection to sexual abuse victims. The Michigan Supreme Court justices did not want to interfere with the total scheme of legislation on this subject. They did note that only about five states have no express legislation to extend the statute of limitations in childhood sexual abuse cases. Given the clear intention of the Michigan legislature to protect victims of childhood sexual abuse, it is likely that legislation will be passed to permit at least Type 2 Plaintiffs to bring their cases to court.

Judges permitting plaintiffs to have their day in court make a point of noting that the plaintiff still has the burden of proving the case before judge or jury. If corroborating evidence is unavailable, plaintiffs are likely to have great difficulty in prevailing. Critics of these actions have rejected the idea that repressed memories are reliable, and they have argued that plaintiffs with continuous memories should have brought legal action within the statutory time.

An examination of a series of Texas cases demonstrates how judges throughout the country have struggled with repressed memory/delayed discovery issues. In *Sanchez v. Archdiocese of San Antonio* (1994), a 57-year-old woman filed an action claiming that she had been sexually, physically, and emotionally abused by a nun more than 50 years earlier. She claimed that she reported the repeated abuses to two different priests at two different times but neither priest did anything to help her. She repressed all memory of the incidents until after several months in therapy. The nun is now deceased, the two priests are deceased, and there are no available witnesses. Should she have her day in court absent any item of corroborative evidence? The Texas Court of Appeals said no. This was the first case in which the court was asked to apply the discovery rule to child sexual abuse cases. Interestingly, the court makes a point of stating that the plaintiff in this case "knew of the abuse when it occurred and for some time later" (p. 90). The court went on to note that "We recognize that other jurisdictions have applied the discovery rule in childhood sexual abuse cases. However, we have been pointed to no case applying the discovery rule where the knowledge of the wrongfulness of the sexual abuse was known at the time of its occurrence" (p. 91). The court was influenced by the fact that no other evidence existed except plaintiff's recovered memory, and, given the "inordinate lapse of time, . . . the imprecise art of psychology and psychiatry, coupled with the figments of imagination enlarged by the passage of time and the uncertainty of the present memories of past events" (p. 92), applying the delayed discovery rule would not be fair. A simpler line of argument would have been that plaintiff's ancient memories, without anything else, are not sufficient to meet the burden of proof that what she remembered was more likely than not what actually happened.

One month after *Sanchez* was decided, however,

another Texas Court of Appeals, in an unpublished case (*L.C. v. A.K.D.*, 1994), decided that the delayed discovery rule does apply to childhood sexual abuse cases "where psychological defense mechanisms prevent discovery." The next month, the same Texas Court of Appeals reached the same conclusion in a published opinion (*Vesecky v. Vesecky*, 1994). The majority said that *Sanchez* involved a woman who knew at the time that the act was wrong and had reported it to others, whereas in *Vesecky* the woman had no memories at all until shortly before filing the suit. Texas courts have not explained why reporting the incident should make a difference, especially if the reports went unheeded. If, in both cases, there was no memory during the running of the statutory time, then the delayed discovery doctrine should apply.

In early 1996 the Texas Supreme Court issued an opinion on repressed memory that the court has not yet authorized for publication (*S.V. v. R.V,* 1996). Nevertheless, because the opinion represents the thinking of the judges, and because it will probably become law, it is important to consider the reasoning. A 21-year-old daughter intervened in the divorce proceedings between her parents to claim that her father had repeatedly molested her until she was 17 years old. According to the applicable statute of limitations governing claims based on sexual abuse, she had two years to file her lawsuit after her eighteenth birthday. She missed the deadline by four months. It was not possible to file within the deadline, she claimed, because she had totally repressed all memories of the abuse until one month after she reached 20. She claimed that the discovery rule permits her to file within two years of the return of her memories.

The trial judge rejected her claim that the discovery rule applied, but the appellate court reversed it in her favor. The Texas Supreme Court, in a lengthy and detailed opinion, concluded that the discovery rule would not apply.

The majority began its analysis by stating that the delayed discovery rule applies when two factors are present: (1) "the nature of the injury incurred is inherently undiscoverable," and (2) "the evidence of injury is objectively verifiable." Turning to the first factor, the majority noted that it had previously decided "a fiduciary's misconduct to be inherently undiscoverable." Though the prior cases on this point did not involve parents, the majority was willing to give the plaintiff the benefit of the rule:

> . . . given the special relationship between a parent and child, and the evidence reviewed in detail below that some traumas are by nature impossible to recall for a time, we assume without deciding that plaintiff can satisfy the inherent undiscoverability element for application of the discovery rule.

The majority then turned to the other factor by noting that the only evidence supporting plaintiff's claim of sexual abuse is (1) her own testimony, (2) her behavior traits and conduct, and (3) the testimony of experts. The court observed that her testimony alone was insufficient to prove that the abuse occurred, and her behavior traits could have many causal explanations besides sexual abuse, as the experts admitted. While the court of appeals seemed willing to accept the testimony of experts as satisfactory objective verification, the majority here rejected that conclusion. Expert testimony may support other physical evidence, but it cannot be used as the sole basis for meeting the second factor of objective verification.

What physical evidence would support the objective verification factor? The majority listed:

> a confession by the abuser, . . . a criminal conviction, . . . contemporaneous records or written statements of the abuser such as diaries or letters; medical records of the person abused showing contemporaneous physical injury resulting from the abuse; photographs or recordings of the abuse; an objective eyewitness's account, and the like.

Furthermore, the court left the door open for expert opinion alone to suffice for objective verification in cases where the experts were "near consensus." In this case, however, the plaintiff's own experts acknowledged the difficulties inherent in knowing whether memories reflect real events. As the court noted:

> Procedural memory could therefore play a role in tending to confirm or belie an accusation of abuse. The problem, of course, is that a certain type of procedural memory, like gagging, may indicate

child abuse, but the fact that a person gags does not indicate why; it does not eliminate all other possible causes except abuse. Thus, procedural memories may be misinterpreted by a patient or a therapist, and that misinterpretation may solidify into "truth."

The court had no difficulty rejecting the extreme false memory position. According to the majority, "there is overwhelming consensus that repression exists." The majority further noted that repression differs from "simple forgetting" and that there is a debate in the scientific community about whether amnesia "stems from repression or simple forgetting." The court also made it clear that it understood repression to be an unconscious mechanism not under the volitional control of the individual.

In essence, the court concluded that because there is no truth versus falsity gauge for "recovered" memories, they alone cannot meet the objective verifiability factor.

The facts of this case clearly influenced the majority's opinion. The plaintiff had become interested in sexual abuse and incest as a paper topic in high school. She also did additional research on this subject in college. Shortly after her parents separated, she learned that her mother had been molested as a child. When plaintiff went into therapy, she saw a therapist who claimed that none of her patients had ever made an untrue allegation of sexual abuse. The therapist further claimed that she did not think it was possible to make false allegations, but that it was possible to recover memories of abuse from the age of three. Referring to these beliefs as "confirmatory bias," the majority stated that plaintiff could easily have been influenced by them. We agree that the therapist's beliefs in this case contaminated the plaintiff's ability to succeed in a lawsuit, assuming the events were accurately remembered by her. We also agree that the therapist's beliefs may have influenced the development of false allegations of sexual abuse, if such events never occurred. We do not know, however, how strongly the therapist's beliefs were expressed to the plaintiff, nor do we know whether the plaintiff was highly susceptible to such influence. It is clear, however, that the therapist's beliefs, as described by the court, do not accord with the scientific facts about memory and childhood sexual abuse.

The Texas Supreme Court also concluded that the therapist used what the court considered to be suggestive techniques, including relaxation and guided imagery. Finally, it is clear that the court had difficulty believing that the plaintiff repressed memories of abuse that happened only three years earlier.

In conclusion, the majority made two points. First, its opinion applies only to application of the discovery rule. If plaintiff had brought her lawsuit within the statutory framework, she could have had her case resolved by the jury, even without the extra objective verification. This additional element of verification, however, applies when the discovery rule is requested.

Second, the court indicated that the issues involved depended upon the appropriate scientific knowledge:

> In sum, the literature on repression and recovered memory syndrome establishes that fundamental theoretical and practical issues remain to be resolved. These issues include the extent to which experimental psychological theories of amnesia apply to psychotherapy, the effect of repression on memory, the effect of screening devices in recall, the effect of suggestibility, the difference between forensic and therapeutic truth, and the extent to which memory restoration techniques lead to credible memories or confabulations. Opinions in this area simply cannot meet the "objective verifiability" element for extending the discovery rule.

At the end of its opinion, the court makes it clear that it has not addressed the significant issue of whether expert testimony about repressed memory is or is not admissible under the United States Supreme Court test formulated in *Daubert v. Merrell Dow Pharmaceuticals, Inc.* (1993), which Texas adopted in 1995 (*E.I. du Pont de Nemours and Company v. Robinson*, 1995). Resolution of that issue must await another day. We will discuss the *Daubert* test later in this chapter.

A concurring opinion raised two points. First, the judge wondered how the plaintiff could bring a negligence action for sexual abuse when such abuse is an intentional, not an inadvertent, thoughtless, or inattentive, act. The reason for the negligence action is the availability of homeowners insurance policies to cover the claims (*Boyles v. Kerr*, 1993), but the conduct itself does not fall within the meaning of "negligence." Defendant, however, did not challenge plaintiff's negligence theory.

The question of whether childhood sexual abuse is the tort of negligence or the intentional tort of battery is more than a semantic issue. Public policy in all states prohibits the obtaining of insurance for intentional acts, but permits people to insure against their own negligent ("unreasonable") conduct. Thus, a plaintiff suing on a theory of negligence may have access to insurance carried by the defendant. The same factual claims brought under the intentional tort of battery would not be covered by insurance and plaintiff would be able to recover only the personal assets owned by the defendant. Also, under the intentional tort theory, the insurance company probably would not have to supply legal counsel to the defendant and would not have to pay the costs of litigation. It is therefore to the advantage of the plaintiff to bring a negligence theory. But it is also to the defendant's advantage for the plaintiff to sue for negligence rather than battery because then the insurance company pays the bills, not the defendant. Perhaps that is why the defendant in this case did not object to the negligence action even though technically the judge is correct that sexual abuse is not negligence, but, rather, is clearly an intentional tort.

The concurring judge's second point involved expert testimony. The judge concluded that plaintiff's experts should not be permitted to testify about repressed memory theory because it cannot be empirically tested, because the potential error rate for such memories is high, because repressed memory diagnosis relies heavily on subjective interpretations of experts, and because repressed memory theory has not been generally accepted within the scientific community. Thus, "expert testimony regarding repressed memory is the type of junk science that should be kept out of our courtrooms. . . ."

Another concurring judge agreed that repressed memory theory would be inadmissible as scientific evidence under the prevailing test adopted after *Daubert*, but the judge noted that the *Daubert* test is particularly difficult regarding social and behavioral science because of the test's requirements of "falsifiability" and "error rates." Indeed, as this judge suggested but does not directly state, virtually all psychological and psychiatric testimony on issues

of mental state, dangerousness, competence, insanity, commitment, malingering, etc., is now in danger of being inadmissible under the *Robinson* (1995) case's acceptance of *Daubert*. In other words, *Daubert* might prohibit mental health testimony on any legal issue. This judicial viewpoint is, however, at odds with how courts in other states have interpreted *Daubert*.

A lengthy dissent rejected the majority's singling out repressed memories as requiring objective evidence when the identical problems occur with ordinary memories. The legislature in 1995 extended the period of time in which sexual abuse suits may be filed from two years to five years, thereby indicating a social policy favoring the granting of relief to victims of such crimes. The majority opinion reversed this social policy and pointed it in the opposite direction. Requiring the extra degree of evidence, because the victim is not to be believed, was initially part of rape law until the discriminatory nature of that policy was reversed.

In another portion of the dissent, the judge argued that repressed memory is no different from ordinary memory or eyewitness testimony. Under the majority analysis, memory and eyewitness testimony would need objective verification, and under the concurring opinions, expert testimony on these subjects would be inadmissible.

Finally, the dissent objected to the usurpation of the jury function of deciding issues of fact. In this case, the plaintiff was prepared to testify, her experts were available, and she and her experts were available for cross-examination. The defense was ready with its experts and its evidence. This is a typical case where factual matters in dispute must be resolved, not by an appellate court who sees and hears none of the witnesses, but rather by a jury drawn from the community.

S.V. v. R.V. (1996) nicely reflects the diverse views held by judges on the complicated repressed memory issues brought before them. Perhaps the most significant aspect of the case is the conclusion that more science needs to be presented to the courts. We completely agree.

Those courts that, as in *S.V. v. R.V.*, refuse to extend the delayed discovery rule to Type 2 Plaintiffs have not yet had to address the constitutional argument that the ruling violates the constitutional right, under the 14th Amendment, to equal protection, and also the constitutional right not to be punished because of status. Suppose we have a child molester who abuses child A and child B. Child A always remembers part of the abuse, whereas child B represses all memories until after the statute of limitations has run. Child B is at a significant disadvantage despite the fact that she had no control over the fact that her memories of the abuse were repressed. Most courts have recognized this unfairness and opted for additional protection for these Type 2 Plaintiffs. Texas, by penalizing sexual abuse victims who have repressed memories, might be violating their constitutional rights.

S.V. v. R.V. (1996) represents a developing judicial concern about repressed memory as a scientific concept. This concern has been shared by other courts. In *Blackowiak v. Kemp* (1995), plaintiff alleged that when he was 11 years old in 1970, the defendant, his school counselor, had oral and anal sex with him. Plaintiff claims to be unable to remember other incidents of molesting, though he feels they must have happened. The evidence shows that, at the time of the events, plaintiff told his friend to "watch out for" the defendant to avoid being abused, and plaintiff told his mother. Plaintiff admits that then, and thereafter, he has not directly discussed the abuse because of shame and guilt. Plaintiff claimed that, although he had always been aware of the fact of the sexual abuse, he had not been aware that it had caused him psychological and social problems. The applicable Minnesota statute (1992), stated that a lawsuit for damages caused by "sexual abuse" must be brought within six years "of the time the plaintiff knew or had reason to know that the injury was caused by the sexual abuse."

Plaintiff argued that the literal wording of the statute supported his position that the statute begins to run only when he knew, or reasonably should have known, about the *consequences* of the abuse, not the *fact* of the abuse itself. The only Minnesota case relevant to the issue was *ABC v. Archdiocese of St. Paul* (1994), where the plaintiff was found to have had knowledge that she was a victim of sexual abuse. The court of appeals in *ABC* held that this knowledge triggered the statute of limitations to run. By contrast, the plaintiff in *Blackowiak* never denied knowledge of the fact of the abuse. Rather, he contended that the statute is triggered by knowledge of the consequences of the abuse and not by the fact

of it. The court of appeals in *Blackowiak v. Kemp* (Minn.App. 1995), accepted this distinction and found in favor of the plaintiff. The Minnesota Supreme Court (*Blackowiak v. Kemp*, 1996) reversed the court of appeals, claiming the lower court had misread the statute:

> As we have observed, the nature of criminal sexual conduct is such that an intention to inflict injury can be inferred as a matter of law. . . . Accordingly, concepts of sexual abuse and injury within the meaning of this statute are essentially one and the same, not separable—as a matter of law one is "injured" if one is sexually abused. While perhaps the court of appeals was misled by the phrasing of the statute itself, we view the language as simply a legislative pronouncement that "personal injury caused by sexual abuse," as opposed to personal injury caused by any other activity, is entitled to a different limitation period because of its uniqueness and because of the difficulties attendant on the victim's often repressed recollections. . . .
>
> To construe the statute as the court of appeals has here is to inject a wholly subjective inquiry into an individual's unique circumstances, e.g., when did the victim "acknowledge" or "appreciate" the nature and the extent of the harm resulting from the abuse.

Because plaintiff had knowledge of the abuse earlier, the statute began to run at that time.

A forceful dissent rejected the majority's semantic approach. The crucial phrase in the statute was that plaintiff knew or should have known that "the injury was caused by the sexual abuse." The majority argued that the phrase meant that plaintiff must know that the wrongful act was sexual abuse and not some other tortious act. Because plaintiff knew he had been sexually abused, he knew that his injury was caused by the sexual abuse. The dissent, by contrast, argued that the statute meant something quite different— plaintiff must know that the sexual abuse was the cause of injury to him. As the dissent points out:

> The majority, by its decision today, would have us equate a moral knowledge of wrongdoing with the legal concept of knowledge of causation of injury. The [plaintiff] knew, as any child would, that the actions of appellant were wrong—morally wrong.

But that knowledge, based on upbringing, cannot be equated to an understanding of causation of a personal injury, especially an injury which did not manifest itself until many years later.

The dissent argued that it was not knowledge of the sexual abuse, or knowledge of the personal injury, that triggered the statute—it was the "link between them, the causation, one of the other," which determines whether a lawsuit is within the statutory period. Beyond misreading the literal language of the statute, the dissent accused the majority of violating the policy of the statute, which sought to protect children whose shame and guilt prevented them from appreciating the "link to the emotional injury which manifested itself later in life." The majority deprived a jury of the right to determine when plaintiff should have known that the emotional injuries he suffered were caused by the earlier acts of sexual abuse.

By way of summary, the law concerning the delayed discovery rule in cases involving childhood sexual abuse generally supports plaintiffs who claim repressed memories. Plaintiffs who have had lingering memories have had a much more difficult time having their day in court. Courts and legislators have not been fully sensitive to their pleas, though most legal commentators have been persuaded to support them. Adults suing alleged perpetrators have made other arguments to trigger the application of the delayed discovery doctrine.

Incapacity—Insanity

In some states, the courts or the legislatures have provided a trigger for the application of the delayed discovery rule based upon the mental disability of the plaintiff during the period of time in question. If the plaintiff is mentally disabled, the statute does not run. In acknowledging this exception, judges and legislators were mindful of limiting the exception to mental problems that were serious. "Insanity" is the term most often used, and the question addressed in recent repressed memory cases is whether a person who has repressed memories is "insane" or "mentally incapacitated." Thus, plaintiffs in repressed memory cases in some states have argued that they were "insane" during the period when the memories were repressed.

Pennsylvania's statutes specifically state that insanity cannot be used to extend the statute of limitations or delay its running. Thus, courts in that state have refused to apply the delayed discovery rule when plaintiffs have argued that their repressed memories should be considered a form of mental incapacity.

In *Pearce v. Salvation Army* (1996), the plaintiff filed suit for assault and battery, claiming that more than 21 years earlier, when the plaintiff was between 12 and 16, the defendant, who was then an agent with the Salvation Army, sexually molested her. She claimed to have repressed her memory of the molesting until she entered therapy. The plaintiff requested that the delayed discovery doctrine be applied to toll the running of the statute of limitations. The court noted that the statute begins to run when the plaintiff knows or should reasonably have known that (1) she has been injured, and (2) the injury was caused by the defendant's fault. In essence, the statute begins to run when a reasonable person would be suspicious enough to begin to investigate whether another person's conduct may have produced legally compensable harm.

The Pennsylvania Superior Court denied plaintiff's request for application of the delayed discovery rule. The court stated that its ruling was required because the statute precluded applying the discovery rule. The Judicial Code sections 5501 and 5533 specifically state that "insanity . . . does not extend the time" for the statute to begin to run. In the crucial passage, the court held that:

> . . . the legislature . . . pronounced that mental incapacity, whether by virtue of a diagnosed mental illness such as multiple personality disorder, or repression, does not operate to extend the limitations period because a "reasonable" person would have discovered the injury.

The court concluded by noting that any complaints about the legislative policy holding that people with mental incapacities have the ability to know that they were injured and could sue should be addressed to the legislators and not the courts.

An opposite result was reached in *Jones v. Jones* (1990). In this case, the statute expressly provided that insanity could toll the running of the statute until "coming . . . of sane mind." The court held that the mental trauma resulting from the plaintiff's abuse by her father for a ten-year period beginning when she was 11 could constitute "insanity" within the meaning of the statute. Summary judgment for the defendant was reversed, and the case was sent back for trial.

State Law on Delayed Discovery in Repressed Memory Cases

As of mid-1997, 31 states have passed laws extending the period of time in which childhood sexual abuse actions may be brought (Williams, 1996; Bowman, personal correspondence with A.W. Scheflin, March 12, 1997). Twenty-six of these statutes permit some form of delayed accrual of the action (Alaska, Arkansas, California, Colorado, Florida, Illinois, Iowa, Kansas, Maine, Massachusetts, Minnesota, Missouri, Montana, Nevada, New Jersey, New Mexico, Oklahoma, Oregon, Rhode Island, South Dakota, Utah, Vermont, Virginia, Washington, Wisconsin, Wyoming), while five statutes provide an extended period of time to sue with no delayed accrual (Connecticut, Georgia, Idaho, Louisiana, Texas).

Of the twenty states (including the District of Columbia) having no specific statute concerning childhood sexual abuse, four states have applied discovery accrual by judicial rulings to at least some survivor actions (District of Columbia, *Farris v. Compton*, 1994; North Dakota, *Osland v. Osland*, 1989; Ohio, *Ault v. Jasko*, 1994; New Hampshire, *McCollum v. D'Arcy*, 1994).

Another two states have used other means to fashion limited exceptions favoring victims of childhood sexual abuse (Indiana, *Fager v. Hundt*, 1993; North Carolina, *Leonard v. England*, 1994).

Thus, 37 states have either legislatively or judicially provided an extension of time for at least some childhood sexual abuse legal actions by adult survivors.

REPRESSED MEMORIES AS EVIDENCE IN CRIMINAL CASES

Only a few cases in the United States have involved criminal convictions based largely or in part on testimony from a repressed memory. *People v. Franklin* (1993) made legal history by being the first instance in which a repressed memory was used as the centerpiece for a criminal prosecution (Spiegel & Scheflin, 1994).

On September 22, 1969, eight-year-old Susan Nason did not return home after running a brief errand. Her mother became increasingly worried. After a massive search and hundreds of hours of police work, Susan's decomposed body was discovered by accident three months later. Considerable publicity and an intensive police investigation failed to find anyone to charge with the ghastly murder. Time passed, but clues did not surface and investigative leads all resulted in dead ends. Gradually, the case faded from the news and out of the "active" file for continued police investigation.

Twenty years later, in November of 1989, a young woman named Eileen Franklin-Lipsker contacted the police and, with hesitation, reported that she had suddenly had a memory that her father, George Franklin, Sr., had murdered her best friend Susan Nason. This sudden memory, containing information she claimed to have had no awareness of during the interim, led police to investigate the case once again. Satisfied that Eileen's memories were accurate, the police arrested her father, George Franklin, Sr., for the crime of murder. The highly publicized murder trial pitted expert psychiatrists and psychologists against one another on subjects never before addressed in courts of law. Contested issues included debate over the possibility that such memories could be dissociated and kept out of consciousness, the possible effects of such dissociated memories on behavior, and the varying means of verifying recollections.

Eileen Franklin-Lipsker grew up in a troubled household, one of five children born to an alcoholic father. She reported that her father was physically and sexually abusive to her siblings and to herself. Other members of the family confirmed these reports. Additional confirmation of her father's perverted sexual interest in young children was found in the police questioning of two sisters who were babysitters in the Franklin household. Both told police that whenever they were alone with George Franklin, he would make improper sexual advances toward them (Franklin & Wright, 1991).

Eileen also recalled seeing her father hold a gun

to her mother's head. Eileen later testified that her mother was aware of what was happening in the family but did nothing about it. Even worse, her mother was an emotional nonentity who failed to supply love and nurturing, much less protection. As she grew older, Eileen began using drugs, became sexually promiscuous, and was eventually arrested for prostitution. She managed to rid herself of these practices and eventually married and had children.

Eileen maintained a surprisingly cordial relationship with her father, taking a long trip with him to Hawaii shortly before she allegedly had the memory that resulted in her report to the police that he was a murderer. However, she testified that one day, as she was watching her six-year-old child play, the child's gaze and her eyes suddenly locked and she had an image of her little friend Susan. A detailed memory emerged in which she recalled inviting her friend to come with her and her father for a ride in their Volkswagen van. She then had an image that she crawled into the passenger seat of the van while her father climbed on top of Susan and began moving his hips. She then recalled his picking up a rock and hitting Susan in the head. Little Susan's hand was bloodied and her ring dented as she tried vainly to protect herself from the blows. Eileen said that her father told her that it was her fault since she had invited the child, and that he would kill her if she told anyone.

Eileen returned to school after the death of her friend, and her life seemed to continue fairly normally. She went on other trips in that same van with her father, including a long one to Mexico, did well in school, and showed no outward sign of significant distress immediately after the murder. The relationship was not, however, devoid of subsequent tension. She alleges that her father held her down when she was nine years old and allowed a man to rape her in exchange for drugs, and that her father also raped her sister, Janice.

Eileen continued to maintain a relationship with her parents after their divorce. Five years before this memory came back to her, her sister Janice had gone to the police with an accusation that her father had been a murderer. This stirred no memories in Eileen, and she made no statement at that time to the police.

The Franklin case called into stark relief the plausibility and veracity of dissociated memory. Is it plausible that an individual could have witnessed so horrifying an event and yet have no conscious recollection of it? The everyday sense of memory suggests the opposite—that we remember emotionally salient and important events but forget the routine and emotionally unimportant details of life. Nonetheless, as we have seen in chapter 7, the trauma and dissociation literature for over a century fully documents that emotionally salient events may be kept out of conscious awareness. Breuer and Freud's early studies in hysteria (1895) illustrated this point, as did Morton Prince's descriptions of dissociative fugue and multiple personality disorder (Prince, 1906). Modern research continues to support the existence of dissociated memory for crucial information about a person's history, relationships, drives, emotions, and motivations (Schacter & Tulving, 1994; Singer, 1990; Spear & Riccio, 1994; Whitfield, 1995b).

Dr. Lenore Terr, a clinical professor of psychiatry at the University of California, San Francisco, testified as the expert for the prosecution. Her field of expertise is childhood trauma and memory. Perhaps her best-known work was with the children of Chowchilla, who were buried alive in a school bus before digging themselves out. These children had no repressed memories, but they also were constantly in the limelight; the crime perpetrated upon them was a public, not a private event; and the crime was not sexual in nature and was not committed by a trusted family member or friend.

Terr testified that repressed memories are real, the result of unconscious defense mechanisms associated with trauma. There are two types of psychic traumas, Terr told her jurors. Type I is caused by a single act, such as the Chowchilla kidnapping and burial. Type II involves multiple, repeated acts of traumatization. (Please note that this distinction between types of traumas differs from the courts' distinction between Type 1 and Type 2 Plaintiffs.) In Terr's view, type II traumas cause dissociative responses. The child who knows trauma is coming mentally removes herself from it.

But, if this were true, Eileen Franklin would be a type I trauma victim because she only saw her father kill her friend on one occasion. Thus, Terr's position implies that Eileen should not have repressed her memories. Terr responded to this point by noting that, although there may have been only one extremely traumatic event, it was coupled with betrayal by a primary caregiver (her father), threats of violence toward her from him if she told anyone, continued molesting of her by him, and lack of support from other caregivers (her mother). Under these conditions, Terr concluded, repression was not surprising.

When a memory is recovered, Terr was asked, how do we know whether it is true or false? Terr listed three factors that differentiate true memories from false ones. First, the person's symptoms cause that person to experience responses to the memory even though there is no conscious awareness of the memory. Second, a true memory is rich in detail as compared to a false memory, which would be more like a story outline devoid of sights, sounds, smells, feelings, etc. Finally, a true memory would have the appropriate accompanying emotion and body responses.

Will the recovered memory be accurate? Terr testified that it is apt to be more accurate than ordinary memory because it is sealed away, as a fly in amber, from suggestive and reconstructive influences.

Terr was very effective in her testimony and the jury believed her. The defense cross-examination did little to shake her testimony or credibility (MacLean, 1993).

The defense offered two experts to counter Terr's position. Elizabeth Loftus testified that memory is inherently untrustworthy because of suggestion and reconstruction. When memories are acquired under severe emotional conditions, she argued, they are less detailed and often inaccurate. Furthermore, memories decay over time and so become less trustworthy. Creating or implanting false memories is quite easy, whereas telling the difference between true and false memories is exceptionally difficult.

MacLean (1993) has reported that the prosecutor's cross-examination of Loftus was quite successful. It began by getting Loftus to admit that while she had testified in 133 criminal cases, she had never once testified for the prosecution. Furthermore, Loftus was compelled to admit that she had no clinical practice; had done very few experiments with children and their memories; had not worked with real, as compared to simulated, trauma situations; and had not done any studies involving repressed memory.

Stanford psychiatrist David Spiegel also testified for the defense. Spiegel identified four crucial elements in the case that helped him form his testimony: (1) the possibility of dissociated memory, (2) what observable effects were available of traumatic memories that were not in consciousness, (3) an evaluation of Eileen's credibility, and (4) whether there was any independent corroboration.

Spiegel concluded that dissociated memory is a genuine phenomenon. As he later wrote (Spiegel & Scheflin, 1994):

> Is it possible to dissociate, i.e., to lose conscious awareness of an event as traumatic as this one for a period of 20 years? Indeed, such a fact is possible. There is evidence that dissociation serves as a defense against trauma and that memories of trauma may be kept out of conscious awareness. . . . Content and affect are intertwined in memory . . . , so that one means of controlling painful affect is to limit the availability of content in memory. Furthermore, dissociative symptoms are more frequent in individuals who report histories of trauma in childhood. . . .

Interestingly, the defense also accepted the reality of repressed memory, though denying its existence in this case. In papers filed with the court after the case, the defense stated they do "not claim that [sexual abuse by a parent] and subsequent repression is impossible, *no responsible person would make that assertion*" (Petition for Review, 1993, emphasis added; but see Ofshe & Singer, 1994).

Spiegel noted that some researchers have shown that children who are exposed to violent trauma inevitably suffer immediate consequences, which include (1) identifying the event as a stressor, (2) suffering intrusive imagery, (3) fearing a recurrence of the trauma, (4) losing interest in ordinary activities, (5) avoiding reminders of the event, and (6) having upsetting thoughts about the trauma event. Spiegel was struck by the absence of these factors in Eileen immediately after the murder. He concluded that it was not likely that she had witnessed the murder because she was not mentally or behaviorally affected by it.

On the second point, Spiegel looked for evidence that the traumatic event, though dissociated from conscious awareness, nevertheless still exerted some implicit influence, as it must. According to Spiegel and Scheflin (1994): "Despite the absence of conscious recollection, the victim with traumatically induced dissociative amnesia nonetheless acts like someone who was traumatized, with numbing and hyperarousal symptoms suggestive of the event." Spiegel rejected the idea that Eileen could have traumatic amnesia and yet no troubling symptoms.

The third point, Eileen's credibility, also led Spiegel to conclude that Eileen had not witnessed the murder. Eileen told four different stories about how she ultimately recovered her memory. First, she "remembered" the killing in a dream sequence, then in a survivor group, and next she told her brother that the memory had come into her head as a result of hypnosis. Later, she told him not to tell anyone she had mentioned hypnosis. California courts exclude hypnotically refreshed recollection from testimony (*People v. Shirley*, 1982; *People v. Guerra*, 1984; Scheflin & Shapiro, 1989; Spiegel, 1987). At trial, she explained that the memory returned after gazing into her daughter's eyes. This continual shifting of stories led Spiegel to believe that her testimony was untrustworthy.

The final point, independent physical corroboration, is crucial for the evaluation of the veracity of dissociated or hypnotically induced memory retrieval (Diamond, 1980; Orne et al., 1985; Spiegel, 1980), as it is to all forms of memory and memory retrieval procedures, especially when the consequences of the retrieved memory include conviction for murder. The corroboration component included two elements for Spiegel. First, were memories that had been repressed likely to have been contaminated, or are they more apt to be accurate? Dr. Terr, the psychiatric expert testifying for the prosecution, held that memories kept out of conscious awareness are relatively pristine when they reemerge. Her opinion was that a memory thus kept out of consciousness is less likely to be altered than a memory kept in consciousness all those years (Terr, 1994). Spiegel and Loftus disagreed with Terr and testified that these memories could indeed be influenced and altered even though kept out of conscious awareness. Distortion could enter through subsequent information acquired about the crime, changes in Eileen's relationship to her father, the means by which the memories were retrieved, and various reinforcements that came as a result of the

memory retrieval. Memories kept so far out of awareness could be subjected to modification without the benefit of conscious scrutiny and analysis. Indeed, suggestibility, one of the hallmarks of hypnosis, is vulnerability to social input. It derives in part from the suspension of critical judgment that is typical of the hypnotic state (Spiegel, 1988). Conscious scrutiny allows us to minimize damage to memory stores by subjecting memories to critical evaluations for plausibility after they are retrieved. While conscious attention can contaminate them—for example, Loftus' observations that the nature of questioning influences response (Loftus 1975, 1979a,b,c; Loftus & Loftus, 1980; Loftus et al., 1978)—it can also provide an evaluative defense against memory contamination. Indeed, repeated recollection trials improve rather than damage memory retrieval (Erdelyi & Kleinbard, 1978). Thus, the absence of conscious scrutiny is hardly reassurance that memory stores will not be contaminated.

Corroboration also involves the availability of additional evidence supporting the memory. Eileen testified as to a great number of details, but the defense pointed out that all of the details had been written up in the newspaper and magazine articles about the killing. Thus, Eileen's memories might be accurate or they might be remembered news stories. Every fact that Eileen testified to was widely available in the press and, therefore, she could have obtained this information in other ways than by being an eyewitness.

Eileen testified compellingly and the jury believed her story. Her father was convicted of first-degree murder. She has since written a book about her experience (Franklin & Wright, 1991) and other books have been written as well (MacLean, 1993). The case rested entirely on her ability as a witness to convince the jury, which she did. The defense attempted to portray her as someone who was indeed angry at her father with good reason: his abusive, drunken behavior. The defense contended that this anger led her to make a false accusation that he murdered Susan Nason. The jury did not accept this interpretation.

The possibility that Eileen Franklin-Lipsker's story about her repressed memory may have been fabricated in part, as well as the fact that she may have been dishonest about certain aspects of her memory retrieval (MacLean, 1993), does not absolutely refute the possibility that her father actually committed the murder and that Eileen was present at the time to witness it. George Franklin, Sr., according to available evidence, had sexual contact with his daughters during their childhoods, was often violent, sexually abused other young children, kept an extensive child pornography collection, had episodes of intense alcoholism, and expressed no surprise when arrested for the murder. Members of his immediate family had harbored suspicions for years that he was, in fact, the killer.

After the worldwide notoriety of the trial ended, the defense lawyers crafted an appeal. In a long opinion, the California Court of Appeals, though admitting federal error occurred at trial, upheld the life imprisonment sentence. The opinion is unpublished, which is quite surprising given the media interest in the trial itself and also in the scientific and forensic issue of repressed memories. Why was the opinion not published? As noted by Spiegel and Scheflin (1994):

> Prosecutor Elaine Tipton believes the opinion was not published because it did not add anything new to the law. . . . Defense attorney Douglas Horngrad believes it was not well reasoned. . . . Appellate counsel Dennis Riordan essentially agreed, believing that the Court did not want to set future precedent with its opinion, and it also did not want to overturn a conviction in a case of such high visibility that a made-for-TV movie based on its facts had already aired.

When the California Supreme Court declined to hear the case in 1993, the attorneys for George Franklin decided to pursue federal relief in early 1994. They expected that the issue of repressed memory would play a pivotal role in the federal appeal (Riordan, personal communication, 1993). In fact, however, it played no role at all. Federal District Court Judge Lowell Jensen (*Franklin v. Duncan*, 1995a) reversed Franklin's conviction because of three constitutional errors made by the trial judge: (1) Franklin's Fifth Amendment due process rights were violated when Eileen was permitted to testify that when she visited her father in jail to try to obtain a confession, he remained silent; (2) Eileen's visit to her father in jail with the "blessing" of the prosecutor violated Franklin's Sixth Amendment

rights; and (3) the trial judge's exclusion of the newspaper articles showing that Eileen could have learned of the facts about which she testified by reading the articles and not from witnessing the murder violated due process. Concerning "recovered" or "repressed" memory, Judge Jensen specifically noted the following:

> This is a "recovered memory" case, in that Franklin-Lipsker explained that twenty years after the event, one afternoon in early 1989 after looking at her daughter, she first remembered what she had seen in 1969. There has been a great deal of review and reflection in the mental health field on this subject in recent times. Petitioner cites several recent articles critical of the notion of "recovered memory." This developing body of thought, however, is not of controlling effect in this case. The judicial task of this Court is to determine whether or not the petitioner was actually prejudiced by trial conduct in violation of the United States Constitution. It was clear at the time of the trial, as it is today, that reliance by a jury on "recovered memory" testimony does not, in and of itself, violate the Constitution. Then as now, such testimony is admitted into evidence and is then tested as to credibility by the time-honored procedures of the adversary system. Admissibility of the memory is but the first step; it does not establish that the memory is worthy of belief. In this regard mental health experts will undoubtedly, as they must, continue their debate on whether or not the "recovered memory" phenomenon exists, but they can never establish whether or not the asserted memory is true. That must be a function of the trial process.
>
> By definition, trials are based on memories of the past. The recognition that memory grows dim with the passage of time is part and parcel of the trial system. Jurors are instructed that in assessing credibility they are to consider the ability of the witness to remember the event with the implicit assumption that asserted memories of events long past must be subject to rigorous scrutiny. From the common sense perspective of the trial process, then, a memory which does not even exist for a long passage of time and then is "recovered" must be at least subject to that same rigorous scrutiny. This case, then, may be described as a "recovered

memory" case, but in reality it is a "memory" case like all others. After direct and cross examination, after consideration of extrinsic evidence that tends to corroborate or to contradict the memory, the focus must be on the credibility, the believability, the truth of the asserted memory.

Judge Jensen's reversal of Franklin's conviction was immediately appealed by the prosecutor. Meanwhile, Franklin requested that he be permitted to leave jail on bond pending the outcome of the appeal. A hearing was held on May 3, 1995, and advocates on both sides of the false memory issue were present to express their views in confrontations inside and outside the courtroom. Judge Jensen ruled one month later (*Franklin v. Duncan*, 1995b) that Franklin would have to post a bond for one million dollars in order to be released. Franklin, unable to meet that amount, remained in prison. Two of the experts in the *Franklin* case, Terr (1994) and Loftus (Loftus & Ketcham, 1994), published books containing additional information about their involvement in the case.

On October 19, 1995, a panel of three judges from the federal Court of Appeals for the Ninth Circuit heard arguments about why the conviction should stand or why it should be reversed. Lawyers for Franklin stressed that he had been denied his constitutional rights and that the case turned on repressed memory. One judge commented that repressed memory was simply a variation of general memory, no different from other legal issues involving memory. The Ninth Circuit upheld the reversal of the conviction (*Franklin v. Duncan*, 1995c), not on repressed memory issues, however, but rather on the errors involving Eileen's prison visit and the failure to permit the defense to introduce into evidence all of the news articles about the case to show that Eileen had no memories apart from what had already been reported. The prosecution admitted that some errors did occur in the trial, but that the trial was ultimately fair and the verdict was correct. In June of 1996, after Judge Jensen finalized the reversal of Franklin's conviction, Franklin was released from jail and the prosecution had to decide whether to retry the case.

Several months later, the decision was made not to retry the case because several factors had developed raising serious questions about the prosecution's ability to obtain a conviction (Hansen, 1996). These factors included additional evidence that Eileen had undergone hypnosis, which would disqualify her testimony, additional "memories" from Eileen concerning other crimes her father committed that turned out to be false, and a dwindling of support from Eileen's family. George Franklin, Sr., is now a free man. In July 1997, he filed a multi-million-dollar lawsuit against the prosecutors, Eileen, and others.

In *Commonwealth v. Crawford* (1996), a defendant was put on trial more than twenty years after the crime. A witness testified that he had talked to the murder victim shortly before she was killed and learned that the victim was afraid of the defendant. Shortly thereafter, the witness testified, he saw the defendant throw the victim's body into the river. The witness never reported observing these events until 21 years later when he saw a young girl who looked like the victim. He claimed that he had no memory from after the crime until he reported it to his wife and then the police. Although other evidence corroborated parts of the story, the prosecution case rested squarely on the witness's testimony.

At trial, the witness was not permitted to testify about, or make reference to, "repressed" memory. The trial judge excluded a defense expert who was prepared to testify as follows:

> . . . Dr. Himmelhoch stated that the following criteria must be present in part or in full to determine whether the memory is an accurate recovered memory rather than psychiatric confabulations, hallucinations and/or lies: 1) the truthfulness of the memory is in direct proportion to the ability of the person to remember it accurately and in detail; 2) the presence of a history of alcohol and/or drug abuse significantly detracts from reliability and adds the possibility of chemically induced memories; 3) repressed memories always exact a psychological price in terms of interval psychopathology, i.e. usually anxiety symptoms such as panic attacks, social anxiety or hysterical conversions; 4) all verified cases of long-term repressed memories more than ten years are associated with massive, longer-term psychic trauma such as the Holocaust and the Buffalo Creek Dam disaster; they do not occur very often after a single acute traumatic event;

5) the presence of learning disabilities and/or a low IQ strongly decreases the likelihood that returned, repressed memories are accurate; 6) character structures that are simple and impressionable are much more likely to serve as a basis for a simple, if earnest, person to become entangled in triggered ideas and to elaborate extensively.

It is quite clear that Dr. Himmelhoch is mistaken in his beliefs about repressed memory. Nevertheless, the issue before the appellate court was not whether he was right, but whether he should have been permitted to testify and be cross-examined. Himmelhoch was also prepared to testify that the witness had a weak memory in general, had abused alcohol and drugs to the degree where his memory would be affected, had a borderline personality with learning disabilities, was vulnerable to being responsive to suggestions, and had not suffered any major psychiatric symptoms.

The appellate court reversed the conviction on the grounds that repressed memory was a subject esoteric enough to require expert testimony to enlighten the jurors. The trial judge considered repressed memory no different from ordinary memory and excluded the expert testimony on the grounds that it was really a comment on the credibility of the witness. Pennsylvania law, consistent with the law in other states, prohibits experts from commenting on whether the jury should believe a witness. The appellate court concluded that repressed memories are stored and retrieved differently from ordinary memory. The court noted that sixteen states allow prosecution for child sexual abuse based upon repressed memories, and noted that a commentator has suggested that experts be permitted to testify in all repressed memory cases (Hayes, 1994). In its concluding remarks, the court hints that repressed memory might not survive a *Frye* or *Daubert* analysis, in which case the witness will not be able to testify at all. If the witness is permitted to testify, however, experts are essential to assist jurors in understanding repressed memory.

In *State v. Quattrocchi* (1996), the Rhode Island Supreme Court reversed a conviction where the main testimony of sexual assault alleged to have been committed by the defendant was the product of flashbacks and repressed recollections of his former stepdaughter. The court noted the serious debate about repressed memories raging in the scientific community, but its holding was not directed to resolving that dispute or to choosing sides. Instead, the court reversed the conviction on the grounds that the trial judge admitted the repressed recollections and the expert testimony about it without first holding "a preliminary evidentiary hearing outside the presence of the jury in order to determine whether such evidence is reliable and whether the situation is one on which expert testimony is appropriate" (p. 884). A dissenting judge disagreed with the reversal in this case because the defendant had been tried once before a jury. That trial resulted in a mistrial. Defendant was convicted at the second trial so the trial judge had already seen and evaluated the evidence from the first trial.

The other major criminal case in which "robust" repression appears is the case of Father James Porter, who was sentenced to prison in November 1993 after admitting that he molested around 100 young boys and girls. The case against Porter began when one of his victims, Frank Fitzpatrick, suddenly recovered long-buried memories of the sexual abuse decades after it had occurred. Fitz-patrick began recovering the memories without therapy, hypnosis, or any other specialized memory retrieval technique. Fitzpatrick placed an advertisement in a newspaper, which asked "Remember Father Porter?" The reader was requested to call a phone number. To his astonishment, Fitzpatrick received many calls. He began an extensive investigation, which ultimately unearthed dozens of additional victims. While some of Father Porter's victims retained vivid memories, or parts of memories, others did not have any memories at all until something triggered their retrieval. Father Porter's confessions validated the veracity of the repressed memories (Berry, 1992; Burkett & Bruni, 1993). Porter admitted to sexual acts involving dozens and dozens of young boys and girls. He is now in prison after conviction for his crimes.

The failure of some of Father Porter's victims to have conscious recollection of significant sexual abuse transcends ordinary forgetting. Fitzpatrick himself considers his memories as having been "repressed" and not "forgotten."

The problem in the courtroom, as in therapy, is that it does a terrible disservice to the victims of trauma to disregard or disbelieve their recollections when the events they recite really occurred. Likewise, it is a terrible disservice to falsely accuse family members and others of crimes they did not commit. Partisans on either side of the false memory issue would like a simple answer, a general litmus test of truth. They hope that if the memory is there, the abuse was there, or, on the other side, that repressed memories are always false because they have been contaminated by expectation, suggestion, and sometimes hypnosis. However, discovering the truth in life is not so simple. Each case must be examined on its own merits.

Criminal cases that turn exclusively on repressed memory will be hard for prosecutors to win, unless the repressed memory provides details not previously reported or known, thereby authenticating the veracity of the memory. The presence of additional evidence supporting the repressed memory will always be helpful, and, in many if not most cases, will likely be necessary.

THE LEGAL TEST FOR THE ADMISSION OF EXPERT TESTIMONY

The *Frye* Rule

For 70 years, an old case involving a predecessor of the lie detector has been the prevailing test in federal and state courts for determining whether to admit expert opinion testimony about new or novel scientific matters. Under the famous *Frye* rule (*Frye v. United States*, 1923), when an expert bases an opinion upon a scientific technique, instrumentality, modality, or procedure, "the thing from which the deduction is made must be sufficiently established to have gained general acceptance in the particular [scientific] field in which it belongs."

The *Frye* rule for the admissibility of expert testimony was intended to leave the issue of admission to the scientists, not the judges. If the relevant scientific community believes a technique is reliable enough for an expert to base an opinion on its results, the expert's opinion is admissible in court. If the scientists point thumbs down, the expert cannot testify. The emphasis was on the *reliability* of a scientific instrumentality, not on its *relevance*. By "reliability," the law generally means what social

scientists would call "validity," that is, the instrumentality's relationship to truth.

The *Daubert* Case

In a surprising decision that caught court observers off guard, the United States Supreme Court, in the *Daubert v. Merrell Dow Pharmaceuticals, Inc.* (1993) case, unanimously concluded that the *Frye* rule would no longer govern federal trials. In its place, the Federal Rules of Evidence, particularly Rules 402 and 702, substitute a far more expansive approach that favors "relevancy" over "reliability." The Congressional intent behind the Federal Rules expressly states the goal of allowing more evidence to come before judges and juries. Political conservatives, including judges, had been arguing that the rules of evidence are too restrictive. "Let juries hear it all and filter the evidence as they see fit" became a rallying cry. Congress responded with a set of rules that keeps less evidence from the jury.

Whereas the old *Frye* rule left the issue of admission of expert testimony to the scientific community, *Daubert* makes the judge the official "gatekeeper." Because "general acceptance" is no longer an absolute prerequisite to the admissibility of expert testimony, the scientific community has far less control over what counts as good science or bad science.

Judges have not been too pleased with this additional responsibility, especially because the United States Supreme Court left no explicit test for the judges to use when acting as "gatekeepers" of scientific information.

Although the Supreme Court left no explicit test, the justices did suggest that scientific opinions and theories must be "verifiable and falsifiable." Declining to draw up a checklist, the Court did, however, suggest four loosely applied "guidelines" trial judges may use to determine whether a theory or opinion is "scientific": (1) testing, (2) peer review and publication, (3) the known or potential rate of error in the case of particular scientific techniques, and (4) whether the technique, theory, or opinion is "generally accepted."

As of April 1997, 23 states have been persuaded to follow some variation of the federal "relevancy" or *Daubert* model (Alabama, Arkansas, Delaware, Idaho, Indiana, Iowa, Kentucky, Louisiana, Massachusetts, Montana, New Hampshire, New Mexico, North Carolina, Ohio, Oklahoma, South Carolina, South Dakota, Texas, Utah, Vermont, West Virginia, Wisconsin, and Wyoming), while 15 states and the District of Columbia have chosen some version of the *Frye* "reliability" test (Alaska, Arizona, California, District of Columbia, Florida, Hawaii, Illinois, Kansas, Maryland, Minnesota, Nebraska, New Jersey, New York, Pennsylvania, Tennessee, and Washington). A few states have chosen to follow their own specially crafted evidentiary rules (Colorado, Connecticut, Nevada, Oregon, Rhode Island, and Virginia) and some states have not yet directly addressed the issue of which test to adopt (Georgia, Maine, Michigan, Mississippi, Missouri, and North Dakota).

How does "repressed memory" fare under the *Daubert* test? In cases involving the issue of whether to apply the delayed discovery rule when the plaintiff claims repressed memory, the court decides whether or not the plaintiff will have a day in court. But once the plaintiff is in court, what may the plaintiff prove? Will *Daubert* permit evidence on repressed memory? Let us now turn to this subject.

Is "Repressed Memory" Scientific?

From the perspective of science, the answer is clearly "yes." From the perspective of law, however, the issue is more complex. The proper use of the *Frye* test leads to the following conclusions. First, the test should not apply to witnesses who have repressed memories that have returned. Second, the test should not apply to experts because there is nothing new or novel about memory, repressed or otherwise. Third, expert testimony should be permissible to challenge memory in general, repressed memories in particular, and memory retrieval techniques in or out of therapy.

If the *Frye* test is nevertheless applied to repressed memory issues, it should be clear that "repressed memory" has been recognized by most medical, psychological, and mental health professional organizations. Though there are ideological destractors their disagreements do not interfere with the "general acceptance" in science of repressed memory or, more appropriately, dissociative amnesia. The world literature has validated this concept for over a century. Accepting the criticisms of the destractors

would be like deciding that the earth is not round because there is a Flat Earth Society that disagrees. Scientific knowledge does not have to be unanimous to be "generally accepted."

If the *Daubert* ruling is used, evidence from repressed memory should be admissible because it is both relevant and scientific. How has the law treated repressed memory? As we have seen, legislatures overwhelmingly, and judges usually, accept repressed memory as a valid reason to extend the statute of limitations. When the issue is the scientific nature of repressed memory, however, not all courts have reached a uniform agreement. The following profile of the most significant recent cases indicates that courts are not in agreement regarding how to apply the *Frye* or *Daubert* tests to repressed memory issues.

State v. Hungerford (1995)

A recent judicial opinion by a New Hampshire trial judge is, in our view, seriously mistaken concerning the law and science of memory. In *State v. Hungerford* (1995), criminal indictments were dismissed by trial judge William Groff because the victims recovered their memories after psychotherapy. The judge applied the *Frye* test and ruled that the victims could not testify "because the phenomenon of memory repression, and the process of therapy used in these cases to recover the memories, have not gained general acceptance in the field of psychology, and are not scientifically reliable."

Prosecutors correctly pointed out that expert opinion was not involved in the case and so *Frye* had no application. Judge Groff rejected this argument by noting that many courts have applied *Frye* to cases where hypnosis had been used to refresh memory. He found those cases analogous to the situation where repressed memories are retrieved in therapy. As we have already seen, *Frye* applies to *novel* techniques. There is nothing novel about therapy or about repressed memory.

Judge Groff determined that the *Frye* test applied to repressed memory because it had already been applied in hypnosis cases. However, equating hypnosis with any type of therapy is an error of science. Hypnosis is simply a medium, method, or procedure used in conjunction with many different approaches to treatment. Dr. Edward J. Frischholz (1995), the ºeditor-in-chief of the *American Journal of Clinical Hypnosis*, wrote a special editorial to clarify this point:

> First, the word "hypnotherapy" should be avoided whenever possible. . . . I do not believe that "hypnosis" is a form of "therapy" or "treatment" in its own right.

Furthermore, equating hypnotically refreshed recollection with repressed memory has no basis in science. Repressed memories may be retrieved without hypnosis and without therapy. There are no scientific studies evaluating or comparing hypnotically refreshed recollection with repressed memories. Judge Groff's simple assertion of their similarity is not supportable. According to Judge Groff:

> The concept of repressed memory and its recovery through therapy are clearly scientific processes. The recovery of a victim's repressed memory through therapy is not the same as a simple refreshed recollection under ordinary circumstances.

Judge Groff gives no explanation for this conclusion. Instead, he repeats the concept in an even more remarkable fashion:

> A jury can most assuredly understand the infirmities of memories and the motives that shape them in the normal course of their experience. The jurors are completely capable of evaluating the accuracy of the memory and the credibility of the person testifying from it, by virtue of the ordinary knowledge, common sense, and practical experience by which we all make such determinations in our everyday lives.
>
> However, the very concept of a "repressed" memory, that is, that a person can experience a traumatic event, and have no memory of it whatsoever for several years, transcends human experience. There is nothing in our development as human beings which enables us to empirically accept the phenomenon, or to evaluate its accuracy or the credibility of the person "recovering" the memory. The memory and the narration of it are severed from all the ordinary human processes by which memory is commonly understood.

As we have seen in chapter 7, *every* study conducted

on the topic supports the validity of amnesia for trauma in general and specifically of amnesia for childhood sexual abuse. Not a single one of the more than 30 relevant studies on amnesia for childhood sexual abuse has found otherwise. It is significant that Judge Groff states that "While all studies indicate amnesia for certain details of a traumatic event, few present any evidence of total amnesia for the event itself." As we have seen, this point is not true. *Every* study finds that some percentage of traumatized individuals do not have adult memories of the event itself for a significant duration of time unless those memories subsequently return in or out of therapy. Not a single study supports Judge Groff's view. Judge Groff cites four studies, all of which find amnesia for childhood sexual abuse. He criticizes them on the grounds that they contain methodological flaws. He then decides that the *opposite* of the conclusion they reach must therefore be the truth. As Spiegel and Scheflin (1994) have pointed out, this is a serious error of logic.

Furthermore, Judge Groff cites no studies supporting his personal viewpoint against the reality of traumatic amnesia or repressed memory. Yet, he rejects, without a single comment, Dr. Bessel van der Kolk's highly significant PET scan studies, which Groff admits "represent the 'cutting edge' of present traumatic memory research."

At another point in his opinion, Judge Groff states:

> Finally, the falsifiability of the phenomenon of repressed memories cannot be dismissed. Every expert that has testified in this case, and probably every researcher and professional involved in this issue, will concede that there is absolutely no ability, absent independent corroboration or confirmation, to determine whether a particular "repressed memory" is false or true. The potential of such false memories and the inability to identify them has readily been acknowledged since this controversial issue of memory repression surfaced one hundred years ago. The very question of whether a "repressed" memory exists is simply a question of whether what is remembered is true or not. It is either a memory, i.e. an actual recollection of an actual traumatic event, or it is a false memory, i.e. a manufactured narrative of an event which never happened. Furthermore, it must be acknowledged

that "false" memories do occur. This is known by the existence of cases in which it is impossible that the events remembered occurred, such as in cases of remembered alien abductions. A further indication of the potential for false memories are the recantation of a growing number of those who once claimed recovered memories.

It is clear that everything Judge Groff says about "repressed memory" is true of "memory" in general, as Loftus and others have testified for over a decade.

Judge Groff states that "the reliability of the victim's testimony of her recovered repressed memory depends on the reliability of the phenomenon of 'repressed memory' itself and upon the reliability of the process used to recover it." Thus, it is clear that he believes that any memory that first appears in therapy, *any kind of therapy*, is *automatically* unreliable. As he stated, "the victims had no memory of the assaults in these cases for several years and . . . their memories were recovered through the process of psychotherapy." Apparently, this is enough to prevent them from testifying. At one point Judge Groff refers to "memory retrieval," by which he means that "a specific purpose of [the] psychotherapy . . . was in part to retrieve or recover memories of possible or suspected sexual abuse." Most therapies, except those that are behaviorally based, necessarily involve memories. Behaviorally based therapies, however, are not beneficial for every psychological ailment. Whenever a therapy includes talk, Judge Groff's negative views about psychotherapy would be triggered. It is difficult to avoid the conclusion that the *Hungerford* opinion is based predominantly on the judge's bias against therapy rather than on an accurate reading of the science or the law.

We agree with Judge Groff's statement that "While a therapist should be successful in allowing the client to talk about an experience, the focus of the therapy is upon the experience, not the act of remembering it. Memory recovery is not a major focus of psychotherapy." Judge Groff is not specific about how "memory retrieval" was done in this case, which is the crucial point, except for noting that at one session there was a "visualization" of a bathroom. It should be obvious that when people start to remember, they often do so by visualizing a past

event. Would Judge Groff condemn all memories?

In *McCollum v. D'Arcy* (1994), the plaintiff alleged that the defendant had sexually abused her 35 years earlier and that her memories of the abuse had just returned during therapy. The New Hampshire Supreme Court found in favor of the plaintiff by applying the delayed discovery rule. The Court ordered an evidentiary hearing to evaluate the plaintiff's repressed memory and the process by which it was recovered. The Court also stated that "The plaintiff still carries the burden to substantiate her allegations of abuse and if challenged, to validate the phenomenon of memory repression itself and the admissibility of the evidence flowing therefrom." Judge Groff misinterprets this sentence, which merely notes that, as in every case, the plaintiff has the burden of proving the elements of the case. Judge Groff concludes that the Supreme Court intended that:

> Before any evidence flowing from the phenomenon of memory repression can be admitted, the validity of the phenomenon itself must be validated. If nothing else, *McCollum* indicates a recognition by the Court that such a phenomenon is subject to the *Frye* rule and the requirement of scientific reliability.

This interpretation does not appear to be sound. If the New Hampshire Supreme Court had serious doubts about repressed memory, the Court would have sent the case back for a hearing on that issue. Instead, the Court ruled that the delayed discovery doctrine applies in *all* cases where the plaintiff can prove repressed memory. This is the same conclusion reached by attorney Suzanne Groff (1994) in her carefully researched article in the *New Hampshire Bar Journal* about the *McCollum* case. It is hardly likely that the New Hampshire Supreme Court wanted to change the law to favor repressed memory, only to be compelled to rechange it the next year if repressed memory was shown to *never* be valid. The question in *McCollum* was whether to apply the delayed discovery rule to a case of "civil sexual assault." The Court, after noting that it had never addressed that issue before, found in favor of applying the rule in repressed memory cases. According to the Court, in a crucial passage Judge Groff failed to quote:

The plaintiff's interest in being compensated for injuries caused by the defendants' acts, especially where the abuse and its causal connection to the plaintiff's injuries were discovered decades after the abuse took place, outweighs any interest the defendants have alleged in putting such claims to rest.

Even more compelling is the Supreme Court's additional ruling rejecting the idea that the delayed discovery rule should be applied only "if there is independent corroborative evidence of sexual abuse." The Court noted that if the Legislature wanted to require such corroboration, they could do so. Thus, *McCollum* clearly articulates a right of recovery in repressed memory cases where the plaintiff can prove the memory was repressed. The justices would hardly create such a rule if they expected a trial judge to rule that repressed memory is *never* actionable.

In an important passage, Judge Groff states:

> There are no studies indicating that false memories have ever been implanted by the therapy process. However, therapy is recognized to be inherently suggestive. It is universally recognized that the processes involved in interactions such as psychotherapy are highly complex and undue suggestion may result. Suggestion has been found to be multi-dimensional, and may be influenced by the "hypnotizability" of the subject, the providing of misinformation, social persuasion, and interrogation. The significance of these factors in any given case will depend on the manner of inquiry, the credibility of the source, or the perceived power differential in the therapeutic relationship. Any significant false recollection usually requires an environment in which these factors are able to operate at a relatively high level. Nonetheless, because of the potential for suggestion the validity of the recovered memory is a source of concern. Studies have indicated that false memories may be created in subjects by the use of misinformation and other techniques, although there is a dispute as to the mechanism by which such false memories are implanted and their stability.

If therapy is "inherently suggestive," as Judge Groff states, then the law would have to exclude all state-

ments and identifications made during or after a therapy session. In other words, the *per se* exclusion rule adopted by most states regarding the use of hypnosis to refresh recollection, discussed in chapter 18, would be extended to therapy. Judge Groff's view that therapy is "inherently suggestive" fails to take into account that it is quite possible for people to be in therapy and yet not be influenced. The crucial variables are the suggestible nature of the patient and the use of suggestive interviewing by the therapist. Therapy itself is the wrong target.

At one point in his opinion Judge Groff appears to notice the universal nature of suggestion:

> Since suggestion is always an issue in therapy, it is the danger of undue or unreasonable suggestion that is of concern. It is generally agreed that in order to create a false memory, a fairly high level of suggestion is required. When psychotherapy has been conducted in a highly suggestive manner, there is a significant danger that the memory recovered is unreliable.

If the therapy was highly suggestive, that point can be raised by expert testimony at trial. It is clear that even highly suggestive therapy will not affect nonsuggestible patients. The issue of undue suggestion is one for the finders of fact, the jury, and not for the judge to decide as a matter of law. Judge Groff makes a correct factual point, but he makes an error of law in the manner in which he applies his observation.

Judge Groff runs the risk of setting the standard of care for how therapy should be practiced and what therapies should not be practiced. He says:

> Certain psychotherapy techniques raise universal questions of suggestion and thus the reliability of the recovered memory. It is often difficult to establish a concrete definition of certain psychotherapy techniques utilized in the field of psychology, and whether a particular technique has been or is being employed in a specific instance appears to be often a matter of degree. Use of so-called guided imagery, a process by which a therapist directs a client's visualization, is considered highly suggestive. Age regression therapy, by which a patient is encouraged to return to an appropriate time in his or her childhood and to experience

an event as that child would, is considered suggestive. Furthermore, a therapy by which a therapist communicates to his or her client a belief or confirmation of the client's beliefs or memories can be highly suggestive.

It is clear that a therapist must be careful not to repudiate or confront a client regarding his or her experience because such confirmation may be counter productive to the creation of a confidential environment. However, it is equally clear that the therapist must retain his or her neutrality. He or she must suspend judgment, listen, and try to understand. The therapist must not confirm, reinforce or validate the client's experience. It is inappropriately suggestive for a therapist to communicate to a client his or her belief that a dream or a flashback is a representation of a real life event, that a physical pain is a "body memory" of sexual abuse, or even that a particular memory recovered by a client is in fact a real event. Therapists are trained not to communicate subtle messages to their clients. A therapist must remain neutral in these matters, and guard against such confirmation by his or her conduct.

Judge Groff fails to note that suggestive influences apply across all life experiences, not just in the therapy room. While the therapist should avoid *undue* suggestion, especially in matters with forensic implications, it is not possible to avoid *all* suggestion. Furthermore, an important issue is not suggestion, as Judge Groff believes, but suggestibility. Individual differences are a very significant factor in whether suggestions are accepted or refused. Judge Groff is wrong to assume that all of the techniques he condemns are unduly suggestive to every patient.

Judge Groff fails to distinguish "disagreements" from "general acceptance." He notes that there is no uniformity in the psychology and psychiatry professions about "repressed memory." From that he concludes that it is not generally accepted in the scientific community. This reasoning would eliminate the *"two schools of thought" doctrine*, discussed in chapter 15, and, even worse, would eliminate any aspect of science in which there is some disagreement, a point clearly noted in *Freyd v. Whitfield* (1997). The American Psychiatric Association, the American Medical Association, the American Psychological Association, and the British Psychological Society all have acknowledged the existence of repressed memory, though they differ somewhat in their descriptions of it. All of the studies prove that it exists. The fact that the Australian Psychological Society and a relatively small group of influential researchers disagree is insufficient to say that the concept of repressed memory lacks general acceptance under *Frye*.

Judge Groff emphatically states that "It is true that psychotherapy has no duty to investigate the reality of a client's experience in a forensic sense. A psychotherapist is not a private investigator." Yet, in the very next sentence, he states that "a therapist must be concerned about the accuracy of a client's information, and it is common, even in a clinical setting, to take steps to verify to some extent a client's experience. It is inappropriate to be unconcerned with the truth of a client's experience during psychotherapy." Is the clinician a detective or not? Judge Groff appears to want to have it both ways. Furthermore, what does Judge Groff expect the therapist to do to verify the accuracy of what the patient reports? Would investigating the truth by snooping in the patient's life build the trust and confidence necessary to continue the therapy? Is it even ethical for the therapist to do this snooping? Would he have the therapist enter into an unethical dual relationship as therapist and clinical detective? (Scheflin, 1997a).

In our view, Judge Groff should have reached a different conclusion. If his ruling is to accord with science, he should have found that repressed memories do exist, but that the plaintiff must always show, with the assistance of expert testimony, (1) that the memories were truly repressed, (2) that the therapy or other influences were not unduly suggestive, and (3) that the plaintiff is or is not responsive to suggestion. The defense may rebut or disprove these elements and may introduce experts to show that the accuracy of any particular memory, repressed or otherwise, is subject to challenge.

State of New Hampshire v. Walters (1995)

Judge Groff's ruling in *Hungerford* was made after some of the nation's leading experts provided an exceptionally full record exploring the relevant issues on both sides. This extensive trial record was later reexamined by another New Hampshire trial judge in another criminal case involving the admissibility of recovered memories. In *State v. Walters* (1995), Presiding Judge Linda Dalianis, contrary to Judge Groff, found that (1) the alleged victim's spontaneously recovered memory was admissible, (2) expert testimony concerning repressed memory was admissible, (3) expert testimony concerning the reliability of recovered memories was admissible, and (4) expert opinion concerning the truth of the particular alleged memories was not admissible. These holdings were made under both the *Frye* test and New Hampshire's version of the *Daubert* approach.

Judge Dalianis first analyzed the issue of the reliability of recovered memories in general. She began by noting that the experts introduced by the defendant were *unable to cite any data* challenging the reliability of recovered memories. All the experts agreed that the reliability of memory itself could not be tested for veracity. There is no scientific procedure or technique that will determine whether a particular memory is true or false. The problem is further complicated by the fact that, as prosecution expert Daniel Brown testified, memory accuracy is often confused with memory completeness. Just as there is no litmus test for the veracity of any ordinary memory, there is no such test for the truth of recovered memories, as defense expert Elizabeth Loftus testified. In an extremely important passage, Judge Dalianis concluded, in our view correctly:

> Because the objective truth of memory cannot be scientifically determined, lay testimony of allegedly recovered memories cannot be barred on the basis that there has been no preliminary showing of its reliability. Even if the Court were to find that the rules governing the admissibility of proffered scientific evidence apply to lay testimony of a recovered memory, the Court would admit this testimony because there is no evidence that this type of evidence is inherently unreliable or even that it is less reliable than the typical memory evidence upon which the courts of this State must rely on a regular basis.

In reaching this conclusion, the court found that there were no scientific studies showing that recovered memories are *less* reliable than ordinary memories or are unreliable in general. Indeed, the court turned to defense expert Loftus's testimony to support this point:

> The most that the defense expert Loftus could assert to challenge the reliability of allegedly recovered memories is that if there is a lot of suggestion involved in their recovery, the alleged memories are less reliable than otherwise. . . . Even Dr. Loftus noted, however, that the fact that a long time has passed in which a person does not have a memory does not mean that the memory is not real.

In concluding this portion of the opinion, the court found, based on the scientific studies, that there was no reason to treat recovered memories any differently than any other type of memory:

> Absent some evidence, not speculation, that an allegedly recovered memory is less reliable than a "regular" memory, the Court will not bar lay witness testimony regarding an allegedly recovered memory.

Once admitted, the credibility of the memory is up to the jury as the finders of fact. In making this assessment, juries will need the guidance of experts about traumatic amnesia, repression, memory in general, and other scientific issues. Experts cannot, however, express an opinion as to the reliability of any particular memory. The court went one step further and concluded that because there were, at that time, no studies concerning the reliability of recovered memories in general, expert opinion on that point would also be inadmissible. Concerning the lay witness testimony based on recovered memories, the court found that this was not "scientific" evidence mandating a *Frye* or *Daubert* hearing. Rather, it is the witness's firsthand experience, no different from the perceptual recollections of any other lay witness. The court distinguished hypnotically refreshed recollection on the grounds that a scientific procedure was used to help recover the memories, thus triggering the requirement that the scientific procedure be one that is reliable. The court then extended this analysis by noting:

> The reliability of a recovered memory not the product of therapy or hypnosis is not dependent upon the reliability of an underlying scientific process,

however, because it is a spontaneous product of the brain just like any other memory.

The defendant proposed two additional arguments concerning the admissibility of lay witnesses' recovered memories, each of which was rejected by the Court. First, the defendant claimed that a lay witness might have excessive self-confidence in a false recovered memory. While this argument has succeeded with courts in hypnosis cases, it failed here because Judge Dalianis observed that a witness may also have an excessive self-confidence in a false ordinary memory, a point equally applicable to hypnosis cases. Second, the defendant claimed that the period of amnesia rendered the witness incompetent to testify once the memories returned. The court had little trouble observing that because the witness has recovered the memories, and therefore has a present ability to "remember and narrate the alleged events," the witness is now competent to testify.

Having fully dealt with the issue of lay witness testimony, the court turned its attention to the admissibility of expert opinion. In a carefully worded ruling, the court held that:

> expert evidence will be admitted at trial only to explain the phenomenon of traumatic amnesia, the data that supports the notion that a person may lose a memory as a result of psychological trauma, and to define the difference between the term "traumatic amnesia" which is a state, and "repression" which is a mechanism by which one might achieve an amnestic state for a traumatic event. The Court will not allow expert evidence regarding either the process of or the plausibility of "recovering" an allegedly repressed memory, because experts have not offered any data either supporting or refuting any theory of how or whether a "lost" memory might be recovered. Finally, because no data has been cited distinguishing the reliability of allegedly recovered memories from that of other types of memories, the experts may not single out allegedly recovered memories as especially reliable or unreliable.

The court focused directly on the issue of "repressed" memory by observing that, while it is a mental mechanism that has aroused controversy, the state of "traumatic amnesia" that it allegedly produces is without controversy. Quoting extensively from prosecution expert Daniel Brown, the court accepted his conclusion that even if one puts aside the mechanism of repression, there is no doubt of the existence of the state of traumatic amnesia. To focus, therefore, on repression is to miss the point. Furthermore, to test the repression hypothesis, it would be necessary to torture or traumatize people in the laboratory in order to study the effects. For this reason, repression cannot be scientifically studied like other laboratory-replicable phenomena. From this point the court concluded that experts cannot testify as to the reliability of repressed memory because this issue cannot be the basis of scientific study. On the other hand, because traumatic amnesia has been studied extensively, expert opinion on that topic is admissible. The court defined "traumatic amnesia" as "the phenomena by which one can lose memory for a traumatic event even in the absence of physiological force/trauma." On this topic the court found that there was general acceptance in the scientific community. After extensive quotation from prosecution experts Drs. Bessel van der Kolk, Daniel Brown, and Jon Conte, the court concluded by noting that even defense expert Elizabeth Loftus:

> conceded on cross-examination that the APA [American Psychological Association] policy which she helped to create notes that it is possible for memories of abuse that have been forgotten for a long period of time to be remembered. . . . The language of the APA report indicates that the challenge to recovered memories which is included therein concerns the mechanism by which delayed recall occurs, rather than the fact of its occurrence. . . . Furthermore, Dr. Loftus acknowledged that dissociation from a traumatic event is a recognized phenomenon.

Two defense experts, Drs. Paul McHugh and James Hudson, testified that traumatic amnesia is not generally accepted in the scientific community, but the court found their testimony was not supported by the scientific literature. Noting that traumatic amnesia "has been referenced in psychological works and studies for over one hundred years," and that the concept is also referenced in *DSM-IV* and "utilized by all experts in the area of psychiatry," the court had little difficulty rejecting the defense expert's position "until there is solid data which is disseminated which suggests that it should be questioned."

Judge Dalianis concluded:

> The Court will also admit expert testimony regarding the phenomenon of traumatic amnesia. Furthermore, the experts may testify about repressed memory in the sense of explaining the term and what it is understood to mean, but cannot offer an opinion as to the truth of the victim's testimony because no basis for such an expert opinion has been presented to this Court. The experts may testify as to the reliability of memory in general, but absent some offer of proof may not present the opinion that allegedly recovered memories are either reliable or unreliable.

In our view, Judge Dalianis, working from one of the most thorough transcripts available of expert evidence on both sides of the issues, has authored the most scientifically accurate and legally sensible opinion on the subject of recovered memory.

In State v. Hungerford (1997), the New Hampshire Supreme Court, ignoring the *Walters* opinion and most of the available scientific studies, upheld the dismissal of the criminal indictments. Despite serious flaws in the court's opinion, it correctly held that (1) repressed memory exists, and (2) every case involving repressed memory must be decided on an individual basis rather than by an automatic rule, such as the one used in many of the hypnosis cases discussed in chapter 18.

Isely v. Capuchin Province (1995)

In *Isely*, a former seminary student brought suit against the seminary, claiming that years earlier he had been sexually molested while there as a pre-Novitiate. In motions before a federal district court judge, the seminary argued that "repressed memory is not sufficiently recognized within the field of psychology (i.e., that it lacks scientific reliability and validity) such that expert testimony may be taken on it." The judge rejected this proposal, using a *Daubert* analysis. Under this analysis, the "general

acceptance" of the relevant scientific community "is not an absolute prerequisite to admissibility," and scientific validity may be shown if the expert has "good grounds, based on what is known." The court noted that, as of March 1995, only five appellate courts had addressed the application of the *Daubert* standards to "expert psychological testimony concerning allegations of childhood sexual abuse and post-traumatic stress disorder, repressed memory or traumatic amnesia." One of those cases, *State v. Alberico* (1993), established the appropriate test in repressed memory cases. First, the expert must be qualified by education and training to express an opinion. Second, the expert must demonstrate personal experience in treating people who have had repressed memories. Third, the expert must be prepared to testify that his or her theories about repressed memory "have some degree of scientific validity and reliability." Based upon this test, the Federal District Court judge in *Isely* concluded that the expert in the case could testify about repressed memory. The expert explained that repressed memory is validated by the studies and widely accepted in the clinical community. She acknowledged that it was not listed, as "repressed memory," in *DSM-IV*, and that there are "detractors who do not accept the theory [such as] Elizabeth Loftus. . . . However, Loftus's work has been countered by others in the field." The expert concluded that repressed memory has adherents in the field of psychology, but that acceptance "is not universal." The greatest controversy, according to the expert, "is specifically in the area of elicitation of repressed memories, not with the concept itself."

The *Isely* judge found in favor of the admission of testimony about the scientific nature of repressed memories. The expert will be permitted to testify (1) about repressed memory, (2) about her opinions concerning repressed memory, (3) whether, in her belief, the plaintiff "experienced or suffers from" repressed memory, (4) that the plaintiff's behavior and conduct are consistent with that of people who have experienced repressed memory, and (5) that the plaintiff's behavior and conduct are consistent with that of people who have experienced abuse. The judge also found that the defense could cross-examine to attempt to show that the "plaintiff's symptoms are also consistent with somebody who fantasizes about such events and believes them himself, or is susceptible to having 'memories' implanted in his subconscious. . . ."

The judge in *Isely* correctly dealt with *Daubert* and repressed memory issues. It hardly makes any sense for the legislature to say that the statute of limitations will be delayed because of repressed memories, only to have trial judges say that no expert or other testimony is admissible about repressed memories.

Eisenberg (1995) has arrived at a similar conclusion. In his view, in cases involving repressed memory with or without hypnosis, courts should use a "totality of the circumstances" test to determine the admissibility of expert testimony involving recovered memories.

Shahzade v. Gregory (1996)

In this case the sexual acts involved took place almost 50 years before the filing of the lawsuit. Plaintiff alleged complete repression of the memories and a hearing was held to determine whether repressed memory theory meets the *Daubert* test for admissibility of scientific evidence. The court had no difficulty in finding that repressed memory theory was generally accepted in the relevant scientific community of clinical psychiatrists, and that "the reliability of the phenomenon of repressed memory has been established." Judge Harrington accepted the expert testimony of Dr. Bessel van der Kolk, noting that he is "one of the country's most renowned psychiatrists in this field." Van der Kolk explained the applicable studies and noted that clinicians for over a century have accepted repressed memory theory. The repressed memory concept became controversial, he testified, only when sexual abuse, and not other traumatic stresses, was involved. Van der Kolk concluded that the debate about "repressed memories is not a scientific controversy, but merely a political and forensic one."

Judge Harrington easily dismissed the two experts for the defense. Dr. Bodkin "did not claim that the theory of repressed memory was invalid"; he instead claimed that the 52 studies relevant to the issue suffered from methodological flaws and therefore could not be used to validate the theory. Dr. Ofshe was readily dismissed on the grounds that he was not a clinical psychiatrist and, in any event, he supported van der Kolk's point that the prob-

lem was the malleability of memory in general.

The court noted that the proper term for repressed memory is "dissociative amnesia" and concluded that the accuracy of the plaintiff's specific memories was not the issue before the court. Rather, the issue was whether the theory itself was valid. On this point, the court unhesitatingly acknowledged that repressed memory theory is scientifically valid.

The *Shahzade* case was settled in 1997. We have already noted that another major appellate opinion, the Texas Supreme Court decision in *S.V. v. R.V.* (1996), conceded that repressed memory theory was valid.

Doe v. Maskell (1996)

In *Doe v. Maskell* (1996), the plaintiff claimed repressed memories and requested application of the delayed discovery rule that would permit bringing a cause of action after the statute of limitations period has expired. In denying the plaintiff's request, the court found that the crucial question is whether there is a difference between repressing and forgetting. Mere forgetting would be insufficient to toll the application of the statute of limitations. But the plaintiffs in this case claimed that they had not "forgotten," but rather had "repressed" the memories and "recovered" them much later in time. The heart of the court's analysis is contained in this excerpt, reprinted at length because of the importance of the arguments raised:

> To aid in an understanding of plaintiffs' argument, we have extracted two implicit assumptions: 1. That there is a qualitative and quantitative difference between "repression" and mere "forgetting"; and 2. that this difference is of a sufficient quality to compel us to find that plaintiff is excused by operation of the discovery rule and had no reason to have known about the existence of her cause of action.
>
> . . . We begin by attempting to understand what repression is. Even defining the term is not easy; it originated with Sigmund Freud who used the term differently and sometimes contradictorily throughout his career. David S. Holmes, The Evidence for Repression: An Examination of Sixty Years of Research, in *Repression and Disassociation: Implications for Personality, Theory, Psychopathology and Health*

85, 85–86 (J. Singer, ed. 1990) [hereinafter "The Evidence for Repression"]. Holmes chooses to adopt a definition of repression based on the manner in which the term is conventionally used: "It is my belief that in its general use the concept of repression has three elements: (1) repression is the selective forgetting of materials that cause the individual pain; (2) repression is not under voluntary control; and (3) repressed material is not lost but instead stored in the unconscious and can be returned to consciousness if the anxiety that is associated with the memory is removed. The assertion that repression is not under voluntary control differentiates repression from suppression and denial, with which it is sometimes confused. . . ." The Evidence for Repression at 86.

The plaintiffs have provided us with several studies purporting to validate the diagnosis of repression. [The court here cites the four studies discussed by Pope and Hudson. It does not cite or discuss any of the other 26 studies available.]

The defendants have also offered significant scientific information tending to discredit the concept of repression and its application in this setting. These arguments against repression take several forms.

First, the adversaries of repression stress that there is no empirical, scientific evidence to support the claims that repression exists. The studies purporting to validate repression theory are justly criticized as unscientific, unrepresentative, and biased. See e.g. Harrison G. Pope, Jr. & James I. Hudson, Can memories of childhood sexual abuse be repressed?, 25 Psychol. Med. 121 (1995); The Evidence for Repression at 96–99. The reason for the failure of repression enthusiasts to obtain empirical evidence may be the nature of the process itself. As Dr. Jason Brandt of the Johns Hopkins University School of Medicine testified:

"There are clear cases of people who claim that they don't remember things that happened in their past for whom no neurologic cause can be found. They don't have brain damage. They have nothing organically wrong that can account for [the claimed memory loss]. The question whether they remember or not, whether they truly have the mental state of a memory or not is impossible to determine."

"We know what they are reporting, we don't know what they are experiencing. Furthermore, I believe that it is virtually impossible to distinguish psychogenic amnesia from faking, from malingering since the distinction between the two hinges on how conscious it is to the person and how willful it is, how intentional it is. And how conscious somebody is and how willful they're being, are things that in spite of what we may say, we really don't have any way of assessing."

Just because there is so far no empirical validation for the theory of repression is not alone sufficient reason to discount the concept, yet it does cast some doubt.

Second, critics of repression theory point out that the scientific, and specifically, the psychological community has not embraced repression theory, and that, in fact, serious disagreement exists. [T]he existence of consensus (or lack thereof) in the scientific community is a . . . useful measure for this Court to evaluate the acceptance, and acceptability of a scientific theory.

Finally, critics of repression theory argue that the "refreshing" or "recovery" of "repressed" memories is more complicated than repression proponents would have us believe. This argument takes two forms: (1) that memories refreshed with the assistance of a mental health professional are subject to manipulations reflecting the biases of the treating professional; and (2) that a repressed memory cannot be retrieved whole and intact from the cold storage of repression. Despite the defendants attempts to characterize this case as one of assisted or enhanced memory recovery, this is simply not a situation in which the plaintiffs' memories have been manipulated by one or more mental health professionals acting in the guise of treatment. Nonetheless, in crafting a rule we must consider the apparently very real dangers of iatrogenic (therapist created) memories of sexual child abuse. . . .

After reviewing the arguments on both sides of the issue, we are unconvinced that repression exists as a phenomenon separate and apart from the normal process of forgetting. Because we find these two processes to be indistinguishable scientifically, it follows that they should be treated the same legally. Therefore we hold that the mental process of repression of memories of past sexual abuse does not activate the discovery rule. The plaintiffs' suits are thus barred by the statute of limitations. If the General Assembly should wish to rewrite the law, that is its prerogative and responsibility.

The *Doe* opinion contains many serious flaws, only a few of which will be dealt with at this time. First, the court exclusively relies on one article by Pope and Hudson and one chapter by Holmes to support its conclusion.

In citing the chapter by Holmes, the court ignores the other 17 chapters in the book, all of them written in support of the concept of repression. Thus, the Holmes position does not represent the prevailing scientific view. Indeed, Holmes himself notes in his chapter that his severely critical position is a distinctly minority viewpoint. He writes that when he asked why he had been invited to participate, he was told that the book was intended to contain "the entire spectrum of points of view concerning repression and that my view was certainly 'different' from those of most of the participants" (1990, p. 85). Thus, Holmes was honest in acknowledging that his anti-repression position is at odds with mainstream mental health thinking. The *Doe* court also bypasses the obvious point that the reason why it is possible to say that there is no laboratory proof of repression is because repression cannot be studied in the laboratory. Ethical codes prohibit the traumatization of human subjects used in experiments, especially when those subjects are young children and when the experiment involves their sexual molestation. As Pope and Hudson have noted in their two articles (1995a, 1995b), the only relevant studies are those that involve actual traumatization of children. This traumatization cannot be duplicated in the laboratory.

Finally, Gleaves (1996a) has effectively dismantled any legitimate reliance on the Holmes position.

The court cites the Pope and Hudson (1995b) article to support the view that no credible studies exist supporting repression. Yet, ironically, it fails to notice that the article itself distinguishes between "repression" and "forgetting" by making this distinction one of the criteria for evaluating the scientific studies. In other words, Pope and Hudson require that the traumatic events studied be the kind that

are not likely to be forgotten. If they are "forgotten," then, "repression" must exist. According to Pope and Hudson (1995a):

> . . . the burden of proof rests on those who hypothesize that human beings can actually expel traumatic memories from consciousness.
>
> This required proof may be simply stated: To reject the null hypothesis and demonstrate "repression," one need only exhibit a series of individuals who display clear and lasting amnesia for known experiences too traumatic to be normally forgettable.

Indeed, as Pope and Hudson (1995a) themselves correctly point out, in the studies where the traumatic abuse is known to have occurred, and where the trauma is so severe that "no one would be reasonably expected to forget it, the postulated mechanism of the amnesia—whether it be called 'repression,' 'dissociation' or 'traumatic amnesia'—is unimportant."

Thus, repression, for Pope and Hudson, is lack of recall for precisely those situations one would be expected never to forget. Most traumas for most people fall into the category of "it was so terrible I will never forget it." Constant intrusive thoughts and dreams of the trauma are one of its major consequences. Some traumas, however, like childhood sexual abuse, where the victim is molested and betrayed by a primary caregiver (J. Freyd, 1996), are so severe that, for some people, repressing recollection of it is essential to survival. Is this really so surprising? Not to mental health professionals. Janet and Freud were well aware of repression and dissociative phenomena a century ago, and Erickson in 1938 was writing about the psychological and legal dynamics of repression, and also about "the not unusual legal situation in which a female, after sexual usage, testifies first against the offending male and then, after a period of suffering, reverses her beliefs and attitudes to testify sincerely in his behalf." Clinicians have reported memory loss in patients throughout the century. Even in trauma studies where some memory of the trauma has remained, a robust finding has been that some victims of all types of traumatization will suffer memory distortion and impairment (Hammond et al., 1995). Dollinger (1985) found that two of the 38 children studied after watching lightning strike and kill a playmate had no memory of the event, and Weine et al. (1995) noted that some of the Bosnian refugees fleeing from "ethnic cleansing":

> demonstrate a profound capacity for not knowing about traumatic events that they have reportedly experienced. Not yet 1 year after the war, some refugees question whether or not it happened at all.

One final semantic point. The concept of "forgetting" in common parlance is a generic term that includes all forms of not remembering, including repression, dissociation, amnesia, etc. Therefore, it is not unusual for people who cannot recall to say they forgot. But the mechanisms for being unable to recall may be very different. In some instances, it may be a retrieval problem, while in others it may be an encoding or a storage problem. Technically, however, repression is different than ordinary forgetting, and Pope and Hudson (1995a,b) have identified an important difference—traumas not likely to be forgotten may be repressed.

The *Doe* court's conclusion that severe childhood sexual abuse sustained over a long period of time was merely "forgotten," and therefore was not worth legally recognizing, in effect wipes amnesia, dissociation, and repression from the psychiatric record books. Such a conclusion violates common sense, laboratory science, and human compassion. Nevertheless, the faulty *Maskell* analysis has already served as precedent for another Maryland case involving childhood sexual abuse.

In early 1997, the Maryland Court of Special Appeals was asked to decide when the statute of limitations begins to run in a case where the plaintiff, who had been an altar boy, recovered memories of repeated sexual molestings by several priests. The trial judge in *Doe v. Archdiocese of Washington* (1997) concluded that repressed memory does not exist. She said, "The Court sees no conceivable way that a person couldn't be cognizant of an actionable injury[,] where something like this occurred[,] for a period of seventeen years." Accordingly, she held that the statute of limitations accrued (began to run) from the time the plaintiff reached his majority. The Court of Special Appeals affirmed this ruling by holding that the child sexual abuse cause of action against the priests accrued upon the day the plain-

tiff attained majority, regardless of when he first appreciated the wrongfulness of the priests' alleged actions. The court also held that (1) the plaintiff's alleged failure to appreciate the wrongfulness of the priests' alleged misconduct did not rise to the level of the "mental incompetence" necessary to toll the running of the statute of limitations; and (2) the failure to disclose the knowledge that one of the priests was a child molester did not rise to the level of fraudulent concealment of the kind sufficient to toll the statute of limitations on plaintiff's claims against the archdiocese.

The court compared the plaintiff in this case to the plaintiff in the earlier case of *Doe v. Maskell*:

> We observe that the Complaint states that the sexual acts were "non-consensual." Apparently, [plaintiff] retreated from that position at the motion hearing. There, counsel argued that while Doe was aware of the priests' conduct, he did not appreciate the offensiveness of the contact or realize that he had been harmed until he reached the age of thirty-three. Rather, at the time of the abuse, because of his age and his relationship to the priests, [plaintiff] believed that the priests' conduct was "right and natural," and he thus did not know that he had been battered. Consequently, [plaintiff] argued that none of his claims against the priests accrued until 1994, when his marriage "deteriorated [and] he discovered that [the priests'] conduct had injured him." Counsel for [plaintiff] explained: [The defendant priests] used their position of power and trust and the confidence that was generated by that relationship to consistently, and in furtherance of their own sexual pleasure, take advantage of this boy. These people were charged with responsibility for knowing right from wrong and serving as examples to society and this boy. They obscured those notions of right and wrong and they transformed wrong into right, making this child believe that what was happening to him was natural and an ordinary course of events in his life. Now, this isn't a case about repressed memory. It's a case about when you discover that you have been injured. A battery is an offensive touching. If you reasonably believe that you have not been offensively touched and have not been injured, you do not know that there has been a battery. . . .

[I]f you are consistently taken advantage of because of your youth and the relationship between yourself and this priest and the series of priests, over a period of time, and you're told that this is right and you're told that it's natural and you're told that it's part of what—something that should go on in your life and part of your growing process, which you and I, sitting here today, know to be rationally irrational and wrong and morally decadent, and this conduct goes over time for a period of five or six years, you begin to think that it's right and natural. . . .

* * *

The repression theory posits two models of repression: "serial" repression, in which the memory of a traumatic event is repressed soon after it occurred, and "collective" repression, in which all the memories are repressed at the same time, perhaps many years after the occurrence of the last episode of abuse. . . . The Court noted that, even if it were to recognize the repression theory, in a case of "collective" repression, "if [the victims] had not yet repressed the memories of the sexual assault by the defendants by even the day after their attaining majority, the statute of limitations barred these claims three years after their eighteenth birthdays. . . ." Therefore, under a repression theory, the repression itself would have had to occur while the victim was protected by the disability of infancy. If, however, any memory of sexual abuse suffered during childhood survives into adulthood, the statute of limitations begins to run when the victim reaches the age of majority and the disability of infancy is lifted. Nevertheless, the Court ultimately held that even if no memory at all survives into adulthood, the limitations period still begins to run on the date the victim reaches the age of majority.

In contrast to the victims in *Maskell*, Doe concedes that he retained memories of the underlying conduct throughout his adulthood, although he denies that he knew the conduct was actionable or wrongful. Because the Court in *Maskell* refused to allow an exception that would delay the accrual date of a cause of action for situations in which the victim has no recollection whatsoever of abuse, we decline to fashion a lesser exception for a victim who was aware of the acts but did not appreci-ate at the time that they were wrong, or did not realize until years later that he was harmed.

CONCLUSION

Despite the recent rulings in Maryland, most courts are finally recognizing the reality of repressed memory—or, better, traumatic or dissociative amnesia. This frees them to turn to the more difficult issue of assessing whether, in any particular case, the memories are valid.

In general, recent trial cases across the country have supported different sides of the false memory issue. Victories and losses abound. In St. Paul, Minnesota, in the summer of 1995, a jury accepted the false memory argument and awarded a former patient $2.6 million (*Hamanne v. Humenansky*, 1995). A few weeks later, in neighboring Minneapolis, a jury rejected a false memory defense and awarded patients $4.5 million against a psychiatrist they claimed had sexually abused them (*Slavik v. Routt*, 1995). Adults have been successful in suing parents for childhood sexual abuse and in having those cases upheld on appeal (*Hoult v. Hoult*, 1995), and recanting patients have been successful in suing therapists for implanting memories (*Althaus v. Cohen*, 1994). Therapists have won lawsuits brought by patients and their families, and they have lost such suits. Patients have won some suits and lost others. The brief filed by the False Memory Syndrome Foundation in cases across the country contains a useful appendix listing major decisions and settlements favoring the false memory argument. We are not aware of any comparable list available to researchers of cases that have been dropped, settled, or won by plaintiffs or defendants arguing against the false memory position. We personally are aware of many such cases.

As should be the situation, each case must stand or fall on its own merits, including a proper understanding of the relevant science involved. It is a safe bet to predict that legal cases against therapists for talking cures that involve memory issues or dissociative disorders will continue to be brought. The inevitability of these cases should inspire therapists to upgrade their knowledge of these various fields and to upgrade the delivery of mental health services.

It is quite clear that (1) parents may expect more lawsuits based on repressed memories, (2) therapists may expect more lawsuits on the grounds that they implanted false memories of abuse, (3) therapists will be held to a higher standard of care in regard to work involving trauma, stress, memory, and hypnosis, and (4) courts and legislatures will be asked to continue to resolve these scientific, factual, and policy disputes. Because full discussion and debate on the science, the politics, and the law appropriate to these issues will inevitably continue, it is to be hoped that all sides will see the wisdom of acting less as adversaries and more as collaborators. No one is arguing in favor of implanting vicious and spiteful false memories, and no one is arguing in favor of poor therapy. Antagonism in this field has distorted the

science and thereby made solutions more difficult.

At bottom, the frustration in the repressed memory field is over the lack of a trustworthy mechanism to help us determine whether memories are more likely true or more likely false. Scheflin (1997c) has addressed this as the "Buridan's Ass" dilemma, referring to a centuries-old logic puzzle depicting a hungry jackass that was given two equal bales of hay placed at an equidistance, one on his left and one on his right. The ass died of starvation, finding no greater reason to choose one bale over the other.

If only science could find some litmus test to tell the difference between true and false memories, these problems might disappear. Are there any indicators to help us in this process? That is the topic for the next chapter.

17

IIIIIIIIIIIIIIIIIIIIII

Distinguishing Between True
and False Memories

FALSE ALLEGATIONS OF
CHILD SEXUAL ABUSE

The literature on child abuse investigations contains base rate data on true and false allegations of child sexual abuse. It is well established within the child abuse investigatory literature that the base rates for false negatives generally far exceed the base rates for false positives (Lawson & Chaffin, 1992; Kuehnle, 1996; Sorensen & Snow, 1991). Nondisclosure, partial disclosure, and delayed disclosure are quite common among children for whom abuse can be independently corroborated (Sorensen & Snow, 1991). Kuehnle correctly reminds us, "disclosure tends to be a process rather than a single event, with children disclosing further pieces of information over time" (1996, p. 21).

Within the last decade there has been increasing attention given to false positive cases of child and adult allegations of childhood sexual abuse. The source of false positives intensively studied were cases in which the allegation of sexual abuse arose for the first time within the context of a heated custody dispute. The more recent source of alleged false positives have implicated suggestive interviewing techniques used to support allegations of sexual abuse.

It is impossible to determine accurate base rates

for false negative and false positive allegations of sexual abuse in both children and adult survivors. Within the child investigatory literature the base rate of false reports within the overall population generally runs around 5–6% and ranges from 2% to 8%. In the most widely cited study, Jones and McGraw (1987) analyzed 576 allegations made to the Denver Department of Social Services in 1983. They classified reports as either "founded" (53%) or "unfounded" (47%). The unfounded cases consisted of 24% of all the cases where there was "insufficient information," another 17% where suspicions of abuse remained but could not be substantiated, and another 6% of "fictitious" cases. They qualify the study by saying:

> The definition of fictitious used in this study was that professionals did not consider that abuse had occurred. This is subject to error (p. 38). . . . We do not have an absolutely reliable test of the occurrence of child sexual abuse. (p. 31)

Subtracting those cases (n=137) where there was insufficient information to tell one way or the other, Jones and McGraw analyzed the remaining 439 cases. Among these a total of 30 were considered by the case workers to be fictitious. This represents an 8% rate of false cases. Other studies report similar false reporting rates (Everson & Boat, 1989—

5%; Faller, 1988b—3%; Goodwin et al., 1982—7%; Horowitz et al., 1985—5%; Peters, 1979—6%).

However, Ceci and Bruck (1995) interpret these data differently:

> Further analyses of the unfounded cases [23% in Jones & McGraw (1987)] revealed that these could be categorized as either deliberate/malicious attempts to make a false accusation (6% of all cases) or reports made in good faith but that turned out to be wrong (17% of all cases). On the basis of these data, some commentators have concluded that only a small proportion of reports (around 6%) are false. However, this is a misunderstanding of the data because the percentage of false reports is the entire 23%, 6% are deliberate lies, but the other 17% are just as baseless as the lies, even though they may be honest mistakes. (p. 31)

However, Ceci and Bruck are aware that the 17% pertains to cases "where there is not enough evidence" in their words (p. 30), so it is incorrect for them to conclude that the 17% "turned out to be wrong." Everson and Boat (1989) have argued the opposite, "There is reason to believe that the rate of false allegations obtained in the current study is inflated" (p. 235). In our view, one cannot conclude anything about these 17% of cases. Jones and McGraw considered the cases as "unsubstantiated suspicion" (p. 30), because the investigators believed the cases to be genuine abuse cases but could not get the level of evidence needed to prosecute the cases. Ceci and Bruck consider these same cases to be "false reports" (p. 30). Both points of view are speculative. While Ceci and Bruck may be correct in pointing out that the base rate of false reporting may be higher than 6–8%, they are not correct in assuming that *all* 17% of cases are false reports and that the base rate is as high as 23%, insofar as the 17% of unsubstantiated cases does not provide enough evidence to make a determination one way or another. The general consensus is that rates of false reporting run around 5–8% in the overall sample of child sexual abuse allegations (cf. Everson & Boat, 1989), if we take false reports to mean that the totality of the evidence failed to establish the credibility of the allegation.

We get a very different perspective on base rates of false reports of child sexual abuse when we look at allegations of sexual abuse that occur *for the first time* in the context of a custody dispute. These rates range from 28–36% (Benedek & Schetky, 1985—35%; Green, 1986—36%; Jones & Seig, 1989—28%; Thoennes & Tjaden, 1990—33%). These higher rates are primarily the result of the child's vulnerability to systematic suggestive influences by one parent as a strategy to win custody of the child from the accused parent. Because of the intense loyalty conflict that a child experiences with disputing parents, the child is more dependent on both, and therefore more vulnerable to parental influence (Benedek & Schetky, 1987a,b). Both parents and children regress in the midst of a heated custody dispute, which contributes to misperception (Schuman, 1986). Sometimes these false allegations arise out of "honest error" (Mantell, 1988, p. 621), when one parent misinterprets a child's report of nonabusive touch or behavior as sexual abuse (Benedek & Schetky, 1987b). Sometimes these false allegations involve "deceit" (Mantell, 1988). The nature of the social pressure can also include a parent's coaching the child to make false allegations against the other parent (Brant & Sink, 1984; Green, 1986; Tate et al., 1992).

These higher rates specifically in custody disputes are important because they illustrate the contribution of largely intrafamilial suggestive influences in increasing false reports of child sexual abuse. Ceci and Bruck (1995) have reviewed research where extrafamilial influences, namely, suggestive interviewing on the part of child abuse investigators, can likewise significantly increase the rate of false reports of child sexual abuse. False memory proponents have made similar arguments with respect to adults who recover memories of childhood sexual abuse in the context of psychotherapy where memory recovery techniques are used (Loftus & Ketcham, 1994).

With all of the controversy surrounding the veracity of child and adult claims of abuse, most researchers concede that we do not have an absolutely valid and reliable test to distinguish between true and false claims. Such a test is sorely needed, especially in the current climate, where there has been a remarkable escalation of false reports of child sexual abuse occurring in the context of heated custody disputes and claims of an increase in false reports of child sexual abuse in adults who have recovered memories within and outside of psychotherapy. While no such test yet exists, scientists have recently focused their attention on developing guidelines that might answer this need. The remainder of this chapter will examine the emerging research designed to develop methods to distinguish between true and false reports of abuse in children and adults.

PERSPECTIVES ON EVALUATING THE EVIDENCE

Developing a Scientific Approach to Evaluating the Evidence

How do we distinguish between true and false memories of childhood trauma recovered by adults spontaneously or in the context of psychotherapy? Likewise, how do we determine whether or not allegations of sexual abuse made by children are genuine or fabricated? These questions are by no means easy to answer, nor are they impossible to answer. While most of the work distinguishing between true and false allegations of sexual abuse has been done on claims made by children and not on adult recovered memories of childhood sexual abuse, this chapter will review whatever approaches are currently available that suggest ways to address this difficult question.

We have already seen in chapter 9 the difficulty even trained professionals have in discriminating between true and false claims. Recall the now well-known Mousetrap Study (Ceci & Bruck, 1995; Ceci, Leichtman, & White, in press). Ceci et al. showed videotaped transcripts of genuine and fabricated memories reported by the children to forensic and mental health experts. The experts were not told which of the reports were genuine or fabricated. They were asked to categorize the reports into those more likely to be genuine and those more likely to be fabricated. Experts trained in evaluating evidence were incorrect in distinguishing true from false reports in about two-thirds of the cases. Presumably, those with less training would do much worse. It has also been suggested that training may make the matter worse because training "may give a false sense of 'objective' security" (Ney, 1995, p. 9).

On the other hand, recent research on the cred-

ibility of interviewing has demonstrated that trained observers may not have difficulty distinguishing between suggestive and non-suggestive elements of an interview, or judging the overall credibility of an interview. Conte et al. (1991) surveyed professionals about the validation procedures used to investigate child sexual abuse allegations. They found "considerable agreement" in the abuse criteria used by professionals to evaluate allegations (p. 436). This is known as the *indicators approach* (Kuehnle, 1996). Interview guidelines are now available from the American Academy of Child and Adolescent Psychiatry and the American Professional Society on the Abuse of Children. Since an increasing number of child abuse investigators are aware of these guidelines, there is a growing consensus about what constitutes a credible interview. This is known as the *standards approach* (Kuehnle, 1996).

Research on investigative interviewing is just beginning to appear. Wood et al. (1996) used a coding system to evaluate videotaped interviews of high-risk cases where child sexual abuse was suspected. All interviews were conducted by the same experienced interviewer, who was blind to the purpose of the study. Results were evaluated in terms of the type of questions asked, the kind of support provided to the child, and the type of information provided. Over the course of 55 videotaped interviews, the type of inquiry consisted primarily of free recall (41%) and open-ended questions (34%), with 25% closed questions or questions that were leading. Non-abuse information was supplied 15% of the time and abuse-related information was given 10% of the time. Empathy and encouragement were prevalent in 96% of all interviews and emotional pressure (mainly praise) was scored in only 2% of the interactions across all 55 interviews.

The researchers conclude that the interviewer "did engage in so-called leading behaviors" (p. 81), in that the interviewer at times "direct[ed] and focus[ed] the responses of the child toward abuse-related disclosures" (p. 84). However, it should also be noted that these interviews were remarkably devoid of the constellation of interrogatory suggestive factors (e.g., emotional pressure, systematically supplying misinformation within and across sessions) that would be expected to significantly increase the reporting error rate. Wood et al. also note, "No interviewer behaviors were related to interview credibility" (p. 89). While most human interactions involve suggestive elements, it is the overall pattern of a high magnitude of suggestive (interrogatory and coercive) factors that significantly increases false reporting rates.

Unfortunately, research like the Ceci et al. study has led some false memory proponents to adopt a *nihilistic* position with respect to distinguishing genuine from fabricated allegations of abuse (Ceci, Leichtman et al., in press; Kihlstrom, 1993; Loftus, 1993; Spence, 1982, 1994a). There is no "Pinocchio test" (Ceci et al., in press) or "litmus test" (Kihlstrom, 1993) currently available to reliably distinguish between genuine and false allegations. They assert that there is simply no way to tell which reports are genuine and which are not, based on the memory report itself. Without independent corroboration, an allegation based on a memory alone is considered worthless.

Some trauma advocates have adopted the position of *naive realism* (e.g., Fredrickson, 1992). They have virtually ignored the research on inaccuracy in memory and have assumed that adult trauma victims who have recovered memories or children who make abuse allegations are seldom motivated to lie or to otherwise distort their memory report. They also believe that reasonably accurate memories for childhood abuse can be reconstructed in therapy. Others have taken a middle-ground position that most abuse reports contain a mixture of accurate and inaccurate information and that trained individuals can, within reason, assess the overall credibility of an abuse allegation.

We advocate a middle ground between the extremes of nihilism and naive realism. With respect to memory, we agree with the conclusion of the Working Group on Recovered Memories of the British Psychological Society (1995), namely, that most memories contain a mixture of accurate and inaccurate elements, and that the evidence for false memories, in an absolute sense, is rare. We also agree with the emerging data-based studies, which fail to support the false memory assumption that all recovered memories are inaccurate. These studies show that spontaneously recovered memories (Williams, 1995), as well as memories recovered in psychotherapy (Dalenberg, 1996), are no more or less accurate than continuous memories for trauma. With recovered memories as with ordinary memory,

the problem of distinguishing historically accurate from inaccurate elements is substantial.

With respect to developing a scientific approach to discriminating between genuine and fabricated allegations of abuse, we agree with Ross (1991) that clinicians, forensic experts, and memory scientists ought to learn from the historians. Historians do not concede that we can never know about past events. Nor do they believe that it is easy to reconstruct an accurate account of past events based on often sparse evidence. Historians have found the middle way between nihilism and naive realism by developing a scientific methodology and evidentiary standards for reconstructing the past. These methods are generally accepted within the community of historians, and various confidence levels can be assigned to a particular historical reconstruction based on the type of evidence available as well as on the methods used in the reconstruction. While most historians would readily concede that we can never "know" the past in an absolute sense, they might assert that the available historical methods at least allow us to reconstruct a reasonable approximation of a past event, an approximation that a community of scientists holds as plausible and places reasonable confidence in.

The assessment of true and false allegations of abuse is indeed a young science, but it is a science nonetheless. Like the historians, forensic experts need to develop a more sophisticated methodology for distinguishing between genuine and fabricated claims. The very intensity of the memory debate demands that we develop such a methodology. In response to this demand there have been some promising new developments. One is a volume that has recently appeared on the topic. *True and False Allegations of Child Sexual Abuse: Assessment and Case Management* (Ney, 1995) is one example of how scientists are beginning to brainstorm about developing methods to better discriminate true from false claims.

Invalid Criteria for Distinguishing Genuine and Fabricated Abuse Allegations

Before reviewing available and newly developing methods to discriminate between genuine and fabricated abuse allegations, let us remind the reader that both child abuse investigators and clinicians treating adult clients who may have been abused all too often utilize invalid criteria to assess the accuracy of abuse allegations or recovered memories, respectively. These invalid methods include (1) lists of signs and symptoms and (2) evaluating the nature of the memory report without consideration of its context.

Traditionally, many clinicians have relied on *general lists of signs of symptoms* assumed to be indicative of abuse (Bass & Davis, 1988; Briere, 1988, 1992; Burgess & Holmstrom, 1980; Courtois, 1988; Frederickson, 1992; MacFarlane, 1978; Sgroi, Porter, & Blick, 1982). As we saw in chapter 12, one problem is that these lists of signs and symptoms are often too general. They overlap substantially signs and symptoms of other conditions. Moreover, many studies have shown that the long-term signs and symptoms subsequent to sexual abuse are quite variable (Beitchman et al., 1992; Briere, 1988, 1992; Brown, 1990; Kendall-Tackett et al., 1993). While such signs and symptoms may raise the index of suspicion about abuse, their presence does not guarantee that genuine abuse has occurred. At best these signs and symptoms alert the clinician to investigate more thoroughly:

> . . . if a child displays any number of concurrent behaviors that are on indicator lists, there is legitimate cause for concern that something is wrong. A proper investigation must be made either to confirm or rule out sexual abuse. (Yuille, Tymofievich, & Marxsen, 1995, p. 25).

Other clinicians have relied on *specific indicators* of abuse. They argue that while lists of signs and symptoms are indeed too general, certain indicators, such as a history of persistent nightmares, perceptual distortions (Ellenson, 1986), or sexualized behavior (Browne & Finkelhor, 1986; Friedrich, 1993; Yates, 1982) are more reliable. Yuille et al. warn, however, that "Some experts have taken indicator lists at face value and have used them as a partial or complete basis of their opinion in court cases" (cited in Ney, 1995, p. 25). While nightmares and sensed visitations in the nighttime may indicate that something disturbed the child during sleep, they do not indicate specific abuse events by particular offenders and may indicate a disturbance other than sexual

abuse. Likewise, while highly sexualized behavior inappropriate to developmental age is "a clear indication of something sexual in the child's history" (Ney, 1995, p. 25), it may reflect a variety of sexualized or nonsexualized peer or familial activities other than sexual abuse. "Sexualized behavior by a child should always be given careful attention, but it may not, in itself, demonstrate abuse" (Ney, 1995, p. 25).

Clinicians have also relied too heavily on the *nature of the memory report* given by clients. In chapter 3 we learned that the emotionality accompanying a recovered memory has very little relationship to its accuracy. We also learned that the vividness of reported details has very little relationship to accuracy. In fact, richly embellished memories may be less, not more, accurate. Moreover, we learned that, except under certain conditions, the degree of confidence the client has in the genuineness of the memory has little relationship to its accuracy. Clients can have high confidence in memories that are largely inaccurate, and so may convince themselves, their therapists, and sometimes juries to believe in essentially false claims. On the other hand, clients can doggedly persist in their doubt about the genuineness of recovered memories of real abuse. Clinicians who have been informed by memory research understand that emotionality associated with, vividness of detail of, and confidence about a reported memory tell us virtually nothing valid about the memory report.

Forensic evaluators and clinicians need to appreciate that, as we learn more about memory, we have come to understand that we have to some extent looked in the wrong places to assess the validity of abuse allegations. There are, however, a number of newer and more promising areas of investigation being developed.

Available Valid Criteria and New Developments for Distinguishing Genuine and False Abuse Allegations

The Phenomenology of Memory

Some memory scientists have begun to investigate whether or not genuine and fabricated memories can be distinguished on the basis of the *phenomenology of the memory report*. These studies are based on *comparative* memory performance between those subjects genuinely abused and those non-abused or those falsely reporting abuse. Conceivably, genuine and fabricated recollections may differ from each other in important respects.

In chapter 7 we reviewed several recent studies comparing the phenomenology of abuse and non-abuse memories. These studies show that abuse-related memories, as compared to non-abuse memories, contain more sensory and perceptual information (van der Kolk & Fisler, 1995). As compared to ordinary narrative autobiographical memory, abuse-related memories are more likely to contain vague overgeneralizations (Kuyken & Brewin, 1995), are likely to be more fragmented and disorganized (Tromp et al., 1995), and are likely to emphasize the past and de-emphasize the role of the self (Klein & Janoff-Bulman, 1996). While comparative memory performance between abused and non-abused groups holds great promise, the studies are only just beginning to appear, so it is too early to draw firm conclusions about phenomenological differences between normal and trauma-related narrative memory.

Several studies also have investigated *phenomenological differences between ordinary memory and memory distorted by misinformation suggestion.* Schooler, Gerhard, and Loftus (1986) examined the memory reports from typical misinformation suggestion studies. The misinformation study included the three phases of the original Loftus paradigm as described in chapter 8. In the first phase subjects saw a slide show about a car accident (the red Datsun slide sequence). In the second phase experimental subjects read a narrative about the slide sequence that included misleading information about the original slide sequence (e.g., a suggested yield sign that was not part of the original slide sequence). In the third phase subjects responded to a yes/no memory test. Transcripts were prepared of both the genuine and "unreal" memories and criteria were developed to compare the real and unreal recollections. Results demonstrated that the mean number of words used by subjects to describe both the real and unreal memories was a valid way to discriminate between the reports. Descriptions of unreal memories that were the result of post-information suggestion were significantly longer than those of real memories.

Next, a number of criteria were used to examine the quality of the respective recollections: (a) sensory attributes; (b) awareness of context, e.g., the position of the car relative to the sign, the trees, etc.; (c) cognitive processes, i.e, mention of what the subject was thinking about while viewing the target stimuli; (d) the function of the yield sign; and (e) the use of verbal hedges, e.g., "I think . . . I believe." While contextual information failed to discriminate between real and unreal memories, the other four categories did discriminate. Real memories were characterized by significantly more sensory details. Unreal memories were characterized by significantly more references to what the subject was thinking and what he or she thought the yield sign was as well as by significantly more verbal hedges. Subsequent experiments replicated the results for different memory stimuli. Schooler et al. conclude:

> we observed that compared to descriptions of real memories, descriptions of suggested memories contained more words, were more likely to mention cognitive processes, and were more frequently qualified by verbal hedges. In addition, descriptions of real memories included more references to the sensory attributes of the critical item. . . . These studies constitute compelling evidence that the two kinds of memory descriptions can differ in systematic ways. (p. 176)

In another series of experiments, Schooler et al. randomly gave these real and unreal memory descriptions first to untrained and then to trained "judges" (volunteer college students). Untrained judges "had a slight but consistent ability to discriminate the suggested- and real-memory descriptions above what would be expected by chance" (p. 176). When "judges" were provided with accurate information about the phenomenological differences between real and unreal memory descriptions, their ability to discriminate between the genuine and fabricated reports significantly increased.

A very different strategy draws upon the tradition of *simulator methodology.* Simulator controls have been used extensively in hypnosis research (Orne, 1959). Subjects measuring extremely low in hypnotizability, who are essentially nonhypnotizable, are asked to fake being hypnotized. They are used as control subjects along with high-hypnotizable subjects in research wherein the experimenter is blind to which subjects are genuinely hypnotized and which are simulating. By examining the differential performance of genuine and simulating subjects, it is possible to determine which portion of the variance of the overall hypnotic performance is due to hypnotic talent and which is due to demand characteristics and other contextual effects.

In chapter 7 we reviewed Belicki et al.'s (1994) study on adult reports of childhood sexual abuse. They found that simulated abuse reports were indistinguishable from abuse reports in certain respects, but in other respects were different. In another study specifically designed to investigate simulated reports, Koopman, Marshall, et al. (1994) asked 30 women with no history of childhood sexual abuse to simulate abuse. The simulating subjects were asked to fill out a series of questionnaires about abuse by "pretend[ing] that you do have memories of having been sexually abused in childhood." Another 30 women with a documented history of childhood sexual abuse matched for demographic characteristics also filled out the same questionnaires. The response of genuinely abused versus simulating subjects significantly differed in many respects. The simulating subjects reported significantly *more* emotional distress, more dissociative experiences, and more negative perceptions of perpetrators when they imagined themselves to have been sexually abused than did the women who genuinely had been abused. The results are consistent with what is generally known about sexual abuse survivors in terms of a general numbing of emotional responsiveness, as well as an ambivalent relationship (and often an invisible loyalty) to the perpetrator. Koopman et al. conclude that the simulator design "appears to be useful in helping to identify possible criteria for evaluating the accuracy of reported memories of sexual abuse."

The Schooler et al. study (1986) is more than a decade old. Unfortunately, there has been little research along this promising line since. Nevertheless, the Schooler et al. study demonstrates that "subtle differences exist between perceived and suggested memories" (p. 171), which could serve as the foundation for a much more elaborate line of research, research that offers at least the hope that one day we may be able to validly and reliably distinguish between genuine and false memories based on differences in how each is described. The

Schooler et al. study and the Belicki et al. and Koopman et al. studies offer two differing perspectives on the same task of discriminating genuine from fabricated memories. The former study pertains to false recollections that subjects unwittingly took to be real but were the product of suggestion. The latter two studies pertain to false recollections intentionally fabricated by subjects. Both studies break new ground in their presentation of ways to discriminate between genuine and fabricated reports based on phenomenological differences in reports.

Corroborative Evidence

Many false memory advocates have argued that recovered memories of childhood sexual abuse cannot be taken seriously unless supported by external corroborative evidence (Frankel, 1993; Yapko, 1994a). Trauma advocates in turn have pointed to a number of independent studies on amnesia for childhood sexual abuse that have included corroborative evidence for the abuse (Burgess et al., 1995; Feldman-Summers & Pope, 1994; Herman & Schatzow, 1987; Kristiansen et al., 1995; Roe & Schwartz, 1996; van der Kolk & Fisler, 1995; Widom & Morris, 1997; Williams, 1994a). Coons and Milstein (1986; cf. Coons, 1994a, for follow-up) reported on 25 consecutive cases of dissociative disorder; about 60% of the patients had significant amnesia for childhood events, although amnesia was rarely the presenting problem. In a retrospective chart review corroborative evidence of abuse was found for most of the cases.

While we agree that corroborative evidence is vital to the discrimination between genuine and fabricated allegations of abuse in many instances, neither the false memory proponents nor the trauma accuracy advocates have offered detailed enough criteria as to what constitutes adequate external corroborative evidence (Dawes, 1994, pp. 172, 177). Much more research needs to be conducted on the nature and types of corroborative evidence used to test abuse allegations.

Schoener et al. (1989) have developed a set of criteria to evaluate sexual misconduct allegedly perpetrated by mental health and religious professionals. As with childhood sexual abuse, the evidence supporting allegations of professional sexual misconduct is often limited to the victim's allegations and the perpetrator's denial. Schoener et al. developed five criteria by which to evaluate these claims: (1) *admission or confession* of guilt by the alleged perpetrator; (2) *additional allegations* made by independent parties and/or convictions obtained for these allegations; (3) medical and *physical evidence* (e.g., victim's knowledge of the perpetrator's body characteristics like scars, circumcision, etc.); (4) *witnesses* to the event or at least to the context of the event (e.g., secretary validates that professional was in his office for an unusual length of time with the accusing client); and (5) *other sources of supporting evidence* such as love letters, photographs, etc.

With slight modifications these criteria are applicable to the evaluation of childhood sexual abuse allegations. In child sexual abuse cases the physical evidence sought is often based on medical examination of the genital and anal area. Witness support of the context of the event usually means that other family members or peers validate that the victim and alleged perpetrator probably were alone together for the alleged period of time. Witness support of the event usually means that other family members actually recall and validate the alleged sexual abuse. Other sources of supporting evidence usually mean family photographs from childhood, diaries, etc. In other words, there is a growing consensus at least on the types of corroborative evidence that should be sought.

Whitfield (1995b) developed a list of corroborative criteria specifically for evaluating abuse claims. It includes (1) external corroboration by the alleged perpetrator or other family members, (2) witness reports, (3) allegations by other victims, (4) information in letters and diaries, (5) photographs, (6) medical records, and (7) internal verification, such as the presence of PTSD symptoms, evidence of behavioral reenactments of the trauma, or certain characteristics of the memories themselves.

Alpert (1995a) presented a list of criteria she uses in her psychoanalytically oriented treatment of childhood sexual abuse survivors to evaluate abuse allegations. These include (1) validation by external sources, (2) establishing the character and opportunity of the alleged perpetrator, (3) the credibility of abuse details in light of memory research, (4) initial strong conviction about the abuse, (5) evidence of shutting out, down, and off, (6) evidence of inappropriate and boundary-violating be-

havior, (7) lapses in reality testing with respect to the body, and (8) phobias, compulsions, prohibitions, sexualized behaviors, and posttraumatic and dissociative symptoms consistent with the abuse hypothesis. Moreover, Alpert (1995b) believes that genuine abuse inevitably will be reenacted in the transference:

> The abuse hypothesis becomes even more plausible when we see repetition of the incest-related phenomena in life and in the analytic hour. (p. 385)

Utilization of various types of corroborative evidence is not, however, without complications. Adams (cited in Ney, 1995) has critically evaluated the use of medical evidence in support of sexual abuse allegations. She warns against the "over reliance on the medical examination, which is expected to show 'evidence' of abuse" (Ney, 1995, p. 233), because of the danger of false positives and false negatives. With respect to false positives she shows that unusual genital or anal findings sometimes occur when there is no history of abuse, and that these findings may readily be mistaken as proof of sexual abuse. With respect to false negatives, she says that in three studies where the perpetrators pleaded guilty "77% of the victims will have normal or nonspecific findings on examination" (p. 237). The reason, of course, is that many acts legally and clinically defined as sexual abuse include sexual fondling and genital touching but not necessarily genital penetration. Moreover, genital penetration can occur without damage to the hymen.

Faller (1988a) has described a continuum of admission of guilt by a perpetrator. The continuum ranges from denial, to indirect confession, to partial confession, to full confession. Therefore, seeking an admission of guilt by an alleged perpetrator in an absolute sense (did or did not do it) is too simple.

We do not intend, by discussing the problems inherent in relying on external corroborative evidence to dismiss the evaluation of corroborative evidence as part of an overall assessment of abuse allegations. Our hope is that further research will lead to a more comprehensive set of categories, as well as to refinement of a test of adequacy for each type of corroborative evidence considered. Nevertheless, while corroborative evidence is sometimes critical to the evaluation of allegations, we disagree with false memory advocates who see external corroborative evidence as a panacea to the problem of assessing memories of abuse.

The Development of Forensic Criteria

In recent years forensic experts have increasingly been called upon to render opinions about the veracity of allegations of child abuse made by children or recovered memories of child abuse made by adults (McGough, 1994). No generally accepted professional standard of examination currently exists to guide the forensic interview, the analysis of the data, or the formulation of an opinion. We agree with Rogers (1993), who says:

> . . . rendering expert opinion on the validity or invalidity of a particular recovered memory is probably premature. The best that an expert can do is to educate the trier of fact about what is or is not known about factors that may impact what is remembered, what is forgotten, and what is reported. (p.2)

Experts sometimes go beyond their role, and beyond the available science, in offering opinion about the truth or falseness of a given allegation. Nevertheless, while we wish that some experts had more constraint about the kind of testimony they offer, we also wish to avoid the extreme of nihilism. Our view is that forensic examination, when properly conducted, is a very useful method to aid the court in making a determination between genuine and fabricated abuse allegations. We also agree with McGough (1994) that the legal system has the capacity both to protect child witnesses from emotional damage while giving testimony and to ensure the reliability of their accounts.

As the demand for forensic evaluation of abuse allegations has grown enormously over the last five years, so has the sophistication of examination procedures, at least with respect to abuse claims made by children. A number of interview guidelines have appeared (Gardner, 1991; Hoorwitz, 1992; Jones, 1988; Kuehnle, 1996; McGough, 1994; Morgan, 1995; Ney, 1995; Rogers, 1993, 1994, 1995). Some of these guidelines address how to gather information and make recommendations about what to look

for in an interview (Kuehnle, 1996; Ney, 1995) and how to conduct an interview that minimizes error (Hoorwitz, 1992; Jones, 1988; Morgan, 1995; Yuille, 1988). Others specifically identify the factors to consider in making an assessment (Rogers, 1993, 1994, 1995). Still others present criteria or "indicators" that help to distinguish between genuine and fabricated claims when analyzing the data (Faller, 1988a; Gardner, 1992; M. Rogers, 1993, 1994, 1995; R. Rogers, 1988). Other works offer guidelines for each phase of the process—interviewing, data analysis, and formulating an opinion (Hoorwitz, 1992; Jones, 1988; Kuehnle, 1996; Morgan, 1995). The evolving consensus is that a "comprehensive model" that assesses multiple sources of information provides the most reliable tool for assessing abuse claims (Kuehnle, 1996).

While recent attempts to develop *forensic criteria or "indicators" of true and false abuse allegations* hold great promise, the results are still quite preliminary. The list of guidelines cannot be used as a checklist. No single indicator or set of indicators has met the test of adequacy or has unequivocally proven itself in making the determination between true and false claims. Nevertheless, the reader should be cognizant of what is currently available. And some promising attempts have been made to validate sex abuse criteria (Faller, 1988a).

Guidelines now exist for conducting a forensic interview. Examiners have moved away from the precarious position of interviewing only the accuser. Hoorwitz (1992) for example, recommends interviewing "everyone of relevance" (p. 36), including social service personnel and therapists. Gardner (1992) strongly recommends that accuser and accused both be interviewed so that the evaluation not be one-sided. Kuehnle (1996) advocates a comprehensive model in which the accusing child, the accused offender, and all relevant family and non-familial parties are interviewed.

Moreover, there is a growing consensus that interviews with children be conducted in a *step-wise manner*. Yuille (1988; cf. Yuille et al., 1993) advises that suggestive interviewing can be minimized if free narrative recall is introduced prior to an interview stage that includes cued questions and a more structured interview. The evolving consensus is that the intial focus should emphasize building rapport and introducing strategies to minimize suggestion. The next focus, on getting the details about the abuse allegation, emphasizes free narrative recall. Subsequent interviewing follows a set of steps, each of which may yield more information but also more memory error. Along a hierarchy from less to more memory commission errors the subsequent interviewing includes each successive step: open-ended questions; specific but nonleading questions; closed questions; and if necessary, leading questions (Jones, 1995). The fundamental assumption of the step-wise approach is that each step will yield more information about the target event yet may increase the error rate. Thus, with each step the reliability of the report is reduced and less confidence is placed in that piece of the overall evidence. A "driven interview" that is characterized by substantial leading and misleading would not serve as very reliable testimony in the current court climate (Jones, 1995).

A number of detailed step-wise protocols have been described in the literature. Hoorwitz (1992) lists nine steps in making an assessment: (1) establishing the purposes of the interview, (2) discussing the limits of confidentiality, (3) teaching the child how to answer questions in a way that minimizes suggestive distortion, (4) establishing rapport, (5) assessing mental status, development, and current functioning, (6) eliciting a description of the alleged abuse, (7) evaluating the effects of the alleged abuse, (8) exploring possible reasons for making false statements, and (9) helping the interviewee feel settled at the end of the process (p. 46).

Kuehnle (1996) lists 17 steps in her comprehensive step-wise approach to interviewing children alleging abuse: (1) assess the professional's competency, (2) and (3) define the professional's role to parents and attorneys, respectively, (4) obtain court order regarding the evaluation, (5) obtain written agreements, releases, etc., (6) schedule parent interviews, (7) obtain history, (8) review available records, (9) conduct all collateral interviews, (10) conduct intial interview with child with emphasis on building rapport, assessing language and conceptual development, (11) conduct a free recall interview with the child that also includes strategies to minimize suggestion, (12) continue the interview with focused questions, (13) use anatomical dolls, (14) observe the child and the alleged offender in interaction, (15) conduct comprehensive psychological testing, (16) evaluate all sources of data and

draw conclusions that include the strengths and weaknesses of the evidence and that illustrate how alternative hypotheses were considered, and (17) create a written report.

These guidelines contain valuable recommendations for instructing interviewees on how to answer questions in a manner that minimizes suggestive influences. The interview defines the interview goals in language appropriate to the interviewee. Some time is devoted to establishing the interviewee's basic understanding of who, what, where, and how, as well as a basic understanding of time, frequency, position, measurement, number, causal relationship, and perspective in order to establish the child's developmental baseline (Kuehnle, 1996; Morgan, 1995). These interviews contain strategies explicitly designed to increase resistance to suggestion. The child interviewee is explicitly given permission to say, "I don't know" . . . "I don't want to say" . . . "I don't understand the question." Disagreement and differences of opinion and talking in a safe way are encouraged. The interviewee practices answering neutral questions in these ways prior to conducting the abuse-related interview (Hoorwitz, 1992). The interviewee is told that if an interviewer repeats a question it does not imply that the previous answer to that question was incorrect (Kuehnle, 1996). The guidelines also contain recommendations for establishing a mutual understanding of the goals of the investigation, getting sufficient details, avoiding interrogatory interviewing, clarifying vague statements, and determining hidden agendas.

With the growing demand for guidelines for distinguishing between true and false reports of abuse in children and adults an number of criteria-based approaches have appeared in the literature. Faller (1988a) identified eight criteria useful in discrimnating between true and false reports of child abuse: (1) the context and timing of the disclosure, (2) the use of developmentally appropriate language, (3) the developmental appropriateness of the child's sexual knowledge, (4) the quantity and quality of the reported details about the abuse, (5) the external and internal consistency of the abuse allegation over time, (6) whether or not the described perpetrator behavior is characteristic of what is known about offenders, (7) the plausibility of the abuse allegations, and (8) the emotional reaction and symptomatic behavior of the child during the interview. Since this pioneering work a number of additional criteria-based approaches have been described (Benedek & Schetky, 1987b; Corwin, 1988; Gardner, 1992; Heiman, 1992; Kuehnle, 1996; Raskin & Esplin 1991; Wehrspann et al., 1987).

Some of these criteria-based approaches have been translated into guidelines for gathering information. Ney (1995), for example, has developed a series of guidelines for systematically gathering information in an interview. These are reproduced in Table 17.1.

These comprehensive guidelines were developed so that the interviewer remains "open to many possibilities" and avoids the pitfall of becoming "single-minded" about his or her hypotheses about the abuse allegations (p. 13).

Other forensic guidelines have been developed for analyzing the data collected through the interview process. The growing consensus is that certain *indicators* are more suggestive of genuine abuse claims, and others more suggestive of fabricated claims. Hoorwitz (1992) recommends enumerating the number of "confirmable and unconfirmable statements" manifest in the reports. Unconfirmable statements "contained qualifications that ruled out the possibility of confirming that it actually occurred.... While true statements cannot always be confirmed, they tend to be made in a manner that offers the potential for confirmation. When unconfirmable statements

TABLE 17.1
Ney's Guidelines for Gathering Information in an Interview

Identifying and Clarifying the Problem

Who originally made the report?

How was this dealt with?

What is the allegation(s)?

Who is involved?

How are the various individuals involved?

What meaning does the allegation have for various individuals?

How did the allegation first occur?

What has been the consistency of the child's report over time?

Has the allegation as reported by others remained consistent over time?

What are the behaviors of all parties who are associated with this allegation?

When do these behaviors occur?

How frequent are these behaviors?

What is the duration of these behaviors?

What are the unmet needs of those involved?

What are the various individuals' emotional reactions to the problem?

How have the various parties attempted to cope with the allegation of abuse?

What skills do various parties require to deal with this problem?

What are the skills/strengths of individuals related to the problem?

Individuals Involved and Their Personal Characteristics

Emotional

Physical health

Cognitive

Judgment

Values and beliefs

Self-concept

Characteristics of the Context

What were the prevalent conditions at the time of the child's original report?

What were the circumstances under which the initial report of concern was made?

How many times has the child been questioned?

Who has questioned the child?

What are the hypotheses of those who have interviewed the child?

What kinds of specific questions were asked of the child?

Was the child's disclosure made in a nonthreatening, nonsuggestive atmosphere?

Was the disclosure made after repeated interviews?

Were any of the adults who have had access to the child before assessment motivated to distort the child's recollection?

What is the functioning capability of the child and key individuals, interpersonal subsystems?

What is the motivation of the child/parents to work on specified target problems?

Are there cultural problems embodied in the problem system, such as cultural norms and language?

What are the interpersonal and communication dynamics involved in the spousal and family systems?

Are there environmental factors that may affect various individuals?

From Ney, 1995, pp. 11–12

begin to pile up, the story becomes increasingly suspect" (p. 154). Hoorwitz also includes a number of additional criteria: (1) presence or absence of a reason for disclosing the abuse, (2) presence or absence of abuse symptoms, (3) scenarios typical of or atypical of abuse, (4) abundance of confirmable vs. unconfirmable statements, (5) consistency vs. inconsistency between statements, (6) invariant sequencing in time and positioning in space, (7) congruence vs. incongruence between time reported and time required for abuse, (8) coherent and redundancy of detail vs. confabulation, (9) tidy fiction vs. messy reality, (10) first-hand vs. second-hand information, (11) congruence vs. incongruence of messages (pp. 200–201).

In chapter 7 we reviewed a list of 30 indicators that Gardner (1992) in *True and False Allegations of Child Sexual Abuse* developed to aid in distinguishing true from false abuse allegations. Although, to our knowledge, no reliability and validity data have been reported using this list, it may nevertheless serve as a guideline to the type of thinking that might go into developing valid criteria lists. A child's report is more likely to be genuine if it includes a number of the following indicators: (1) hesitancy regarding disclosure, (2) fear of retaliation, (3) guilt over consequences to accused, (4) guilt over participation in the sexual act, (5) specificity of detail, (6) credibility of report, (7) stability of report over time, (8) advanced sexual knowledge for age, (9) sexual excitation and preoccupation, (10) attitude toward genitals, (11) posttraumatic play, (12) threats and bribes, (13) invisible loyalty to accused, (14) spontaneous, non-rehearsed report, (15) lack of "borrowed" elements to story, (16) depression, (17) withdrawal, (18) pathological compliance, (19) psychosomatic disorders, (20) regressive behavior, (21) sense of betrayal, (22) sleep disturbance, (23) chronicity of symptoms, (24) seductive behavior, (25) pseudomaturity, (26) acting-out behavior, (27) poor school attendance or performance, (28) anxiety and fears, (29) history of running away, and (30) evidence of severe psychopathology. These indicators were developed to scrutinize claims made in custody disputes or in the context of abuse allegations arising in a day care center. According to Gardner, these criteria are not to be used as a checklist, but merely as guidelines. Gardner adds that presence of

a large number of these indicators raies the index of suspicion about abuse (pp. 181, 229), but there is no absolute number or cut-off point by which one can say with certainty that abuse did or did not genuinely occur.

Martha Rogers (1993, 1994, 1995) developed a list of variables to aid in distinguishing between genuine and fabricated allegations of childhood sexual abuse made by adults who either always remembered the abuse or recovered memories of the abuse and then made a complaint. The allegations are likely to be genuine when the variables in Table 17.2 are present and fabricated when they are not present.

In addition to these guidelines for discriminating between genuine and fabricated claims, Hoorwitz (1992) has provided guidelines for formulating and presenting a forensic opinion about the allegation. Included in his recommendations is a sample report. Since the truth or falseness of a given claim can never really be known in an absolute sense, Hoorwitz cautions that forensic opinions must be guided by the principle "that you help more than hurt" (p. 204) all the parties involved. Kuehnle (1996) recommends that the final report explicitly include a discussion of the strengths and weaknesses of the evidence and a discussion of alternative hypotheses considered.

The value of these several examples of evolving forensic guidelines is that none of them is one-sided. They represent balanced attempts to discover criteria to aid in distinguishing between genuine and fabricated allegations of abuse made by children and adults. Our hope is that further research will enable us to refine these sets of criteria so that we are better able to know which criteria and sets of criteria have the greatest discriminatory power in making the determination between true and false allegations of abuse.

Statement Analysis

False memory advocates have generally assumed that it is very difficult if not impossible to separate genuine from fabricated recovered memory reports based on the reports themselves, and that external corroboration is necessary to the assessment of abuse allegations. In contrast, a very promising method to discriminate between true and false abuse allegations is based on an analysis of the abuse allegations themselves. This method is known as "statement reality analysis" or, simply, statement analysis (Arntzen, 1970; Esplin, Boychuk, & Raskin, 1988; Raskin & Yuille, 1989; Trankell, 1972; Undeutsch, 1967, 1982, 1984; Yuille, 1988). Statement analysis originated in Germany with the work of Udo Undeutsch. Undeutsch has been especially critical of the nihilistic position taken by Elizabeth Loftus in her work on eyewitness testimony (1979a). He says of her work:

> . . . wholesale discrediting of the reliability of eyewitness testimony will inevitably discourage criminal justice officials from actively pursuing the goals of criminal justice. (1982, pp. 27–28)

The psychology of eyewitness testimony must of-

TABLE 17.2
Rogers' Variables Indicative of Childhood Sexual Abuse

Victim Variables

Is the plaintiff a bona fide patient?

Reasons for entering therapy appear clearly related to painful/stressful events that the patient could not cope with.

The patient does not select or change therapists for non-therapeutic reasons (like seeking an expert witness to support litigation).

Legal opinions have not been sought prior to treatment.

Litigation does not become an issue early in treatment.

Patient is not attempting to resolve past financial problems through litigation.

Filing suit to resolve dynamic conflicts can be ruled out.

Were symptoms and/or psychological testing consistent with the allegation?

Symptoms are not exaggerated or faked.

No evidence of malingering on psychological testing.

Deteriorization in functioning related to clinical picture or stress of litigation and not designed to support litigation.

Symptoms consistent with current knowledge of abuse.

Were observed fluctuations in affect and dissociative processes consistent with overall history of the client?

Is affective numbing a consequence of abuse or the effect of repeated rehearsal of a fabricated story?

Memory Variables

At least some recall of abuse was always remembered prior to beginning therapy, although details may become clear in treatment.

Recovered memories occur independently of exposure to therapy or other potential suggestive influences.

Retrieval and nature of memory are consistent with current scientific understanding of memory.

Rule out overzealous search for memory.

Memories occur as a result of free narrative recall.

Content of memories consistent with what is known about autobiographical memories.

Pattern of amnesia consistent with PTSD or dissociative disorder diagnosis.

Patient had ability to discriminate the source and context of the situation leading to the recovery of the memories.

Specific triggers identifiable.

Patient knows difference between memories, dreams, fantasies, etc.

Rule out fantasy-prone personality.

Self-monitoring parameters of memory.

Clarity vs. vague memory detail.

Context of memory and contiguous events supplied.

Salience of sensory-perceptive vs. apperceptive-cognitive phenomenological features of memory.

Core aspects of memory do not change across time even though memory may be reconstructed and gaps filled in.

Therapist/Examiner Variables

Adequate training.

Adequate knowledge about abuse, memory, the population of patients being examined, and the specific patient in question.

Adequate diagnosis and treatment plan.

Orientation to treatment is appropriate.

Therapist is informed about and can reasonably rule out undue suggestive influences.

Adequate documentation.

Adequate informed consent about experimental treatments.

Rule out repeated suggestive questioning.

Rule out hypnotizability, guided imagery, sodium amytal.

Rule out regression and catharsis-based treatment.

Rule out other influences like readings, groups, etc.

Rule out conclusory opinions offered by therapist to patient.

Rule out biased therapist's beliefs.

Rule out external influences like media exposure, readings, and suggestive influences in family or peer relationships.

Evidential patterns

The fact pattern of the allegation is consistent with what is known about abuse claims.

Corroborative evidence has been considered.

Character evidence has been considered.

From Rogers (1993, 1994, 1995).

fer more than doubts about the child's testimony, otherwise its contribution to the criminal justice system is only one-sided, preventing false convictions. But a useful technique for the evaluation of eyewitness testimony ought to work in both directions: it should be as useful for the tracing of possible errors or falsehood as for the verification of a truthful and reliable account (Undeutsch, 1989, p. 103).

There are important differences between the American and German legal systems. The German system, unlike its American counterpart, is not adversarial. Expert witnesses are not retained by either the prosecution or the defense but rather by the court. Since a landmark 1954 Supreme Court decision in Germany, psychologist and psychiatrist expert witnesses must be utilized to determine the credibility of witness statements; therefore, experts play a central role as they conduct interviews outside the court within their area of expertise in order to determine the reliability of the evidence. In the assessment of child sexual abuse allegations, the German court rarely makes a determination without careful consideration of the report provided by an expert witness, typically a psychologist. The method most frequently used by psychologists in Germany to evaluate the credibility of child abuse allegations is *statement analysis*.

Undeutsch describes two components of the term *credibility*. One component pertains to the eyewitness's ability to remember and report what he or she observed. Loftus's *Eyewitness Testimony* (1979a) discusses this aspect of credibility assessment in great detail. The other component pertains to *"willingness to tell the truth"* (Undeutsch, 1989, p. 105). Statement analysis is a method specifically developed "for the scientific assessment of the truthfulness of statements" (Undeutsch, 1982, p. 38). It was designed especially for those cases where the only evidence consists of the statements of the plaintiff and defendant parties, like sex offense cases. Moreover, statement analysis does not necessarily rely on character evidence. It has been well established that sexual abuse frequently occurs in seemingly normal, not just in overtly dysfunctional, families. Therefore, character witnesses are often not especially helpful in the assessment of sexual abuse allegations. Thus, statement analysis was developed to make the determination of credibility based primarily on the statements of the alleged victim and offender. Undeutsch says:

> . . . it is not the veracity of the reporting person but the truthfulness of the statement that matters, and there are certain relatively exact definable, descriptive criteria that form a key tool for the determination of the truthfulness of statements. (1982, p. 42)

The *testimonial statement* is the fundamental unit of analysis. Essentially, statement analysis pertains to a scientific method for analyzing the texts produced by the alleged victims and offenders. The underlying assumption is that "truthful accounts differ significantly and noticeably from false (invented, fabricated, fictitious, distorted) accounts" (Undeutsch, 1989, p. 110). Undeutsch's original statement analysis consists of a set of empirically derived objective criteria for distinguishing genuine from fabricated statements. These criteria fall into two categories: (1) criteria derived from single statements, and (2) criteria derived from sequences of statements. Both sets of criteria pertain to analysis of the statements themselves (Undeutsch, 1967, 1982, 1989).

Steller (1989) developed an additional set of criteria called "statement validity assessment." Unlike the original criteria, which are based on a content-analysis of statements, statement validity assessment is "more subjective and less formalized" (Steller, 1989, p. 141) and draws upon other sources of information, such as the appropriateness of the knowledge, affect, and language associated with the statements; the motivation of the parties making the statements; the presence or absence of suggestive influences; and the consistency of the statement evidence with other sources of evidence.

Undeutsch's original criteria (1967) have undergone a number of revisions by a number of researchers working with the procedure. Recently, an attempt has been made to integrate what has been learned across the various versions of statement analysis (Steller & Koehnken, 1989). A summary of the 19 integrated criteria are given in Table 17.3.

The first set of criteria pertain to the "general characteristics of the statement" (Steller, 1989, p. 136). *Logical structure* refers to the internal consistency or coherence of the entire account. How well do the different details hang together? *Unstructured production* refers to the observation that genuine accounts are often told in a spontaneous, less structured manner with many tangential details, while fabricated accounts are often well-tooled, neat, precisely chronological accounts. *Quantity of details* refers to the fact that genuine accounts are more likely to contain sufficient information about the location, characteristics of the people, and specific actions that took place as part of the abuse, whereas fabricated accounts are likely to be represented by a paucity of *specific* information about the abuse. With respect to simple events, genuine accounts have "definiteness, distinctness, specification" (Undeutsch, 1989, p. 112), and with respect to complex events, genuine accounts contain a wealth of details. However, Steller's criterion regarding quantity of details presumes a continuous memory for the alleged abuse, and recent research has shown that a fragmented and overly general account, at

least with respect to recovered memories of abuse, may be indicative of genuine abuse (Kuyken & Brewin, 1995; Tromp et al., 1995; van der Kolk & Fisler, 1995).

The second and third sets of criteria pertain to the specific content of the account. *Contextual embedding* refers to locating the allegation "in the life context of the defendant and victim" (Undeutsch, 1989, p. 112), i.e., locating the story in a definite place and at a definite time. Moreover, the alleged time and place must "contain the potential for the development of sexual activity" (p. 112). False allegations are often nonspecific. In contrast, genuine accounts often contain *detailed descriptions of the interactions* between victim and offender, often *reproduce conversations* between them in considerable detail, and sometimes contain *unexpected complications* (e.g., interruptions, failed sexual acts) or chance happenings that are absent from well-tooled fabricated accounts. *Unusual and superfluous details* pertain to the "peculiarities of the criminal-victim relationship known to be typical for the respective type of sex offense" (p. 114) as well as to details that would be beyond the capacity for the victim to make up (e.g., justifications, specific threats, precautionary measures against discovery). Such genuine accounts have a flavor of "originality," in contrast to the stereotyped nature of fabricated accounts. Another indicator of a genuine report is a plausible *misinterpretation* of an accurate detail. For example, when a young victim says, "he showed me how to make ice cream" the account is more plausible than if the child says "he ejaculated." *Related external associations* refer to evidence about other relationships that are relevant to the pattern of the victim-offender relationships, such as accounts about sibs, the other parent, other sexual partners, etc. Comments about the victim's *own mental state* during and subsequent to the abuse, as well as *attributions about the offender's mental state* are common in genuine accounts, especially if the report contains a complicated variety of changing reactions to the abuse.

The next set of criteria pertains to the motivation of the alleged victim in making the report. Sometimes the account contains statements that reveal of accuser's underlying motivation. Therefore, *spontaneous corrections* made while giving the account, compliments or *excuses* made about the perpetrator's behavior, *self-deprecating remarks, rais-*

TABLE 17.3
Criteria for Distinguishing Genuine from Fabricated Statements

General Characteristics
1. Logical structure
2. Unstructured production
3. Quantity of details

Specific Contents
4. Contextual embedding
5. Descriptions of interactions
6. Reproduction of conversation
7. Unexpected complications during the incident

Peculiarities of the Content
8. Unusual details
9. Superfluous details
10. Accurately reported details misunderstood
11. Related external associations
12. Accounts of subjective mental state
13. Attribution of perpetrator's mental state

Motivation-Related Contents
14. Spontaneous corrections
15. Admitting lack of memory
16. Raising doubts about one's own testimony
17. Self-deprecation
18. Pardoning the perpetrator

Offense-Specific Elements
19. Details characteristic of the offense

Reprinted from Steller, 1989, p. 137.

ing doubts about one's own testimony, or *doubts about one's memory* all serve as potential indicators of false testimony.

The final criterion pertains to the *specific pattern of the alleged offense.* Are the details of the allegation consistent with what is actually known about the offense in question, such as the pattern of progressive involvement in childhood sexual abuse?

These 19 criteria refer to individual statements made by an alleged victim or perpetrator. The *criteria derived from sequences of statements* pertain to the "persistence of the statements of the witness under consideration over time and across different situations" (Undeutsch, 1989, p. 115). While most accounts show some variation in peripheral detail over time, central actions rarely vary in genuine accounts.

Steller (1989) has added "statement validity assessment" to the original statement analysis method. While Steller admits that this method is "more subjective and less formalized" (p. 141) than statement analysis itself, the procedure nevertheless adds another dimension to the validity of the statement analysis. It attempts to address where the allegations might have come from and whether they are realistic in terms of what is known about the victim and the acts in question. Steller's "validity checklist" is reprinted in Table 17.4.

The statement analysis method has been used in "tens of thousands of [forensic] cases" in Germany,

Sweden, and other countries (Undeutsch, 1989, p. 116). Undeutsch claims that the method is accurate in about 90% of cases, and is therefore "superior to a common sense evaluation of testimonies in both directions" (Undeutsch, 1982, p. 50). Steller (1989), however, has cautioned that statement analysis was not originally developed to detect fabricated allegations. While statement analysis has generally proven to be useful in European courts, the statement analysis procedure has also stimulated a program of outcome evaluation research. Essentially, two research strategies have been used to evaluate the usefulness of statement analysis—simulation studies and field studies.

Koehnken and Wegener (1982) had half of a subject sample view a film. The other half merely heard about the film but did not see it. The narratives collected from each group were scrutinized with the statement analysis procedure. Consistent with statement analysis principles, subjects who actually saw the film reported a greater number of details and gave a more coherent account than those who did not see it. Yuille (1988) asked children to either tell a story about an event that really occurred or to make up a story about a plausible event that didn't really happen. Blind evaluators were able to correctly classify 96% of the true and false narratives. Steller, Wellershaus, and Wolf (1988) asked a group of 98 children to tell two stories each, a story based on a real event and another story based on an event that never really happened. Parents were interviewed to determine which stories had actually been experienced as real events. The study attempted to test the Undeutsch hypothesis that significant differences exist between genuine and fabricated statements. Results demonstrated that the usefulness of statement analysis depended on the type of story told by the children. Genuine and fabricated medical stories (e.g., having an operation) differed significantly but other stories (e.g., getting attacked by a dog) did not. Further analysis done on the medical stories demonstrated that some of the statement analysis criteria had strong discriminatory power, while others did not. While most of the statement-related criteria significantly differentiated genuine from fabricated stories, the motivational criteria did not. Significantly more genuine and fabricated stories were correctly classified by the statement analysis procedure than by other means.

TABLE 17.4
Steller's Validity Checklist

Psychological Characteristics
    Appropriateness of language and knowledge
    Appropriateness of affect
    Susceptibility to suggestion
Interview Characteristics
    Suggestive, leading, or coercive questioning
    Overall adequacy of the interview
Motivation
    Motives to report
    Context of the original disclosure
    Pressures to report falsely
Investigative Questions
    Consistency with the laws of nature
    Consistency with other statements
    Consistency with other evidence

Reprinted from Steller, 1989, p. 140

A number of field studies have also been conducted using the statement analysis procedure. In these studies narratives of independently documented samples of abused and non-abused subjects are compared using statement analysis procedures. Lamers-Winkelman, Buffing, and van der Zander (1992) studied the statements made by 103 children whose abuse had been independently classified into substantiated, highly probable, and unfounded cases. Statement analysis was able to significantly discriminate each of the types of cases but only in older children, presumably because younger children's reports were too incomplete. Esplin, Boychuk, and Raskin (1988) analyzed the reports given by two groups of children. Twenty children had a history of sexual abuse that was confirmed by confession and/or medical evidence. The other 20 children had made allegations of sexual abuse that could not be confirmed and were strongly suspect. Most of the unconfirmed cases occurred in the context of custody disputes, where fabricated allegations are common. The statement analysis procedure differentiated between the two groups at a high level of significance. As with the Steller et al. (1988) research, the motivational criteria were not especially useful in discriminating between true and false allegations but most of the statement-related criteria had a high discriminatory power.

Research from both the simulation and field studies lends support to the usefulness of statement analysis as a procedure to discriminate between genuine and fabricated claims of abuse made by children. Whether or not statement analysis can discriminate between genuine and fabricated recovered memories of abuse in adults has not yet been demonstrated. The research demonstrates, however, that not all 19 criteria are equally useful, and that those based more on objective analysis of the statements themselves and less on motivational judgments have greater validity. The value of statement analysis is limited when there are relatively few details to the allegation, as is often the case with reports of young children. Statement analysis also requires extensive training to use properly. Nevertheless, statement analysis offers great promise as a method that could be refined and prove useful, especially in sexual abuse cases and other cases where the only available evidence is the statements from the alleged victim and accuser. It is our hope that the brief discussion of statement analysis included here will dispel the nihilistic overstatements sometimes made in the memory debate that it is impossible to tell the difference between genuine and fabricated memories of abuse. For further discussion of statement analysis the reader is referred to reviews by Bekerian and Dennett (1995) and Horowitz (1991).

Physiological Tagging

One of the authors (D.B.) has conducted psychological and psychophysiological forensic evaluations on refugees who have made their plea to the U.S. Immigration and Naturalization Services for political asylum based on an alleged history of torture in their country of origin. The evaluation includes structured clinical interviewing (SCID-DSM), objective psychological testing, and psychophysiological testing. The client is interviewed about a variety of nonstressful and stressful topics while heart rate (HR), striate muscle activity (frontalis EMG), and electrodermal response are continuously monitored. The interview includes neutral topics, indirect and direct reminders of torture and other atrocities, as well as instructions to facilitate coping with intrusive recollections. The results across subjects typically show three psychophysiological patterns: (1) an elevated physiological baseline associated with trauma-related sustained hypervigilance; (2) a marked increase in physiological reactivity across all physiological measures when the subject is indirectly or directly asked to remember torture or other traumatic experiences; and (3) a failure to habituate the physiological arousal (especially electrodermal activity) after a stressful episode in the overall interview, and even after explicit instructions to calm to subject. Figure 17.1 illustrates a typical physiological profile for a 22-year-old South Asian man who had been imprisoned and tortured daily for three months. His father had also been imprisoned and tortured in the same prison and died of a cardiac arrest subsequent to electroshock torture when too much electrical current had been applied. Note in Figure 17.1 how tonic electrodermal activity shows progressive elevation throughout the interview after the subject had been asked indirectly and directly about his and his father's torture experiences, and regardless of specific instructions to relax the subject at several points in the interview. This highly

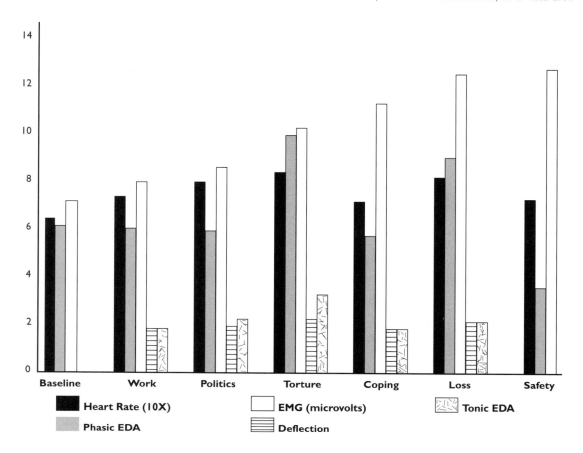

FIGURE 17.5

Psychophysiological Profile of a Torture Victim

specific pattern of physiological reactivity is characteristic of most of the alleged torture victims assessed by the author.

This observation raises an important question of whether the emergence of a trauma-related recollection in an interview is predictably accompanied by a specific pattern of physiological reactivity. According to *DSM-IV*, physiological reactivity is one of the four diagnostic criteria for PTSD. If we take the argument one step further, genuine trauma reports must necessarily be accompanied by physiological reactivity. In this sense, do we have a psychophysiological means to distinguish between genuine and fabricated allegations of abuse? These data predict that genuine recollections of abuse occurring spontaneously or in an interview are likely to be accompanied by a specific pattern of psychophysiological arousal, whereas fabricated recollections are not likely to be. In other

words, psychophysiological investigation may hold promise as a means to distinguish between genuine and fabricated recollections of abuse because genuine recollections may be *physiologically tagged*. Moreover, whereas lie detector evidence has generally been disallowed as testimony in many courts since the *Frye* rule in the 1920s, physiological profiling may be admissible not so much as a method to determine true or false claims but as a necessary component of the *diagnosis*, since the *DSM-IV* criteria for diagnosis include physiological reactivity. Thus, determination that a given subject was physiologically reactive to specific recollections may be admissible as part of the overall evidence examined by the court.

The data from a number of recent studies on the psychophysiology of trauma are consistent with our findings. A specific profile of psychophysiological measures has been used to accurately discriminate between combat veterans with and without PTSD in a number of studies (Blanchard et al., 1982, 1986; Malloy, Fairbank, & Keane, 1993; Pallmeyer, Blanchard, & Kolb, 1986; Pitman et al., 1987). With respect to the forensic relevance of this approach, other studies (Gerardi, Blanchard, & Kolb, 1989) have addressed the question of whether or not subjects can simulate this pattern of physiological reactivity. This study has demonstrated that some simulating subjects relative to genuinely traumatized individuals can produce an elevated physiological baseline and even elevated physiological response to specific trauma-related questions. However, none of the simulators was able to demonstrate failed habituation to the trauma-related stimuli. Thus, while certain components of the psychophysiological profile can be simulated, others cannot be, and simulation of the entire pattern appears to be highly improbable.

Psychophysiological tagging as a means to investigate abuse allegations has recently been reported in a pioneering case study by Ian Wickramasekera (in press). The patient, a 35-year-old married woman, presented with a variety of largely somatic complaints, including episodic vasovagal syncope, dizziness, headaches, tinnitus, flushing, sweating, blurred vision, and problems with sensorimotor coordination. She did not present with a diagnosable psychiatric condition and gave low scores on a general symptom checklist. As part of an intake evaluation of risk factors for somatization, a psychophysiological stress profile was administered along with testing on a High Risk Model of Threat Perception (Wickramasekera, 1979). The patient was found to have two of the five most common risk factors for somatization, namely, high hypnotizability and high covert negative affectivity or "repressed" neuroticism (p. 7). This patient did not show any initial elevated baseline physiological response. According to Wickramasekera, the combination of high hypnotizability and repressed neuroticism enabled the patient to "transduce" internal threats into somatic symptoms as well as to block the perception of that threat from consciousness (as evidenced by the low physiological baseline). The patient had a "general pattern of parasympathetic dominance" (p. 8). However, when asked about the circumstances when her somatic symptoms began the patient showed a significant drop in hand temperature, a constriction of blood pulse volume, and an elevation in electrodermal activity. Wickramasekera interpreted this specific physiological pattern as typical of "the perception of a threat" (p. 10) in response to the question posed by the therapist.

Later in the session the therapist used hypnotic age regression to have the patient return to the situation in which the somatic symptoms first occurred about a year earlier. As hypnosis was terminated the patient recovered a memory of herself "as a sad child in nursery school looking out of a window at other children playing in the yard, but confined to the classroom by a scary male principal" (p. 10). The therapist suggested outside of hypnosis that "other memories of her childhood might return." By the third treatment session the patient reported "several involuntary or intrusive vivid memories of sexual abuse by the male nursery school principal" (p. 11). She subsequently learned to use self-hypnosis both in the treatment sessions and at home to recover additional memories and details of the abuse, but often additional recollections would involuntarily intrude into her consciousness. Each intrusive recollection was accompanied by a specific and measurable pattern of sympathetic activation. As these memories were integrated into consciousness they were accompanied by significant changes in baseline heart rate, hand temperature, and electrodermal activity suggestive of "an elevated perception of threat" (p. 11). Her level of negative affect also increased over the course of the therapy sessions. Her somatic symptoms, however, disappeared and she ceased using medication after only three treatment sessions. These changes were observed up to a two-year follow-up interval. Moreover, the patient's mother corroborated the abuse memories by reporting that the principal had been convicted of child molestation based on independent testimony of three other children. Wickramasekera interprets the initial psychophysiological profile as biological evidence for "repressed memory" and the changes in physiological reactivity during treatment as evidence for the "transfer of unconscious or implicit memories of sexual abuse . . . into explicit or conscious memory" (p. 2).

This single case study is fascinating in that the treatment includes many of the ingredients that advocates of the false memory position warn against—the use of hypnosis with a highly hypnotizable patient, particularly hypnotic age regression, to discover the alleged cause of symptoms in past experiences. Nevertheless, a seemingly accurate and independently corroborated abuse memory was recovered. More importantly, the emergence of each memory fragment into consciousness was *physiologically tagged* by a specific pattern of sympathetic activation. While a single case study does not prove anything, the case generates an important hypothesis, namely, that *genuine recovered narrative trauma memories may be accompanied by specific physiological markers upon their emergence into consciousness, within and outside of therapy, while fabricated recovered memories would not be accompanied by such physiological tags.* Our hope is that Wickramasekera's case study opens an entire area of inquiry on physiological tags hypothesized to be associated with genuine trauma memories.

Allen et al. (1995) conducted a study on posthypnotic amnesia that raises the question of whether amnesia is also psychophysiologically tagged. The procedure utilized an event-related potential technology (ERP) in which subjects perform a task while EEG measurements are recorded to assess cortical electrical response to the specific task at a specified point in time. The EEG waveforms are subsequently analyzed with respect to five peak amplitudes: P1 (125–175 ms), N1 (175–225 ms), P2 (225–275 ms), N400 (275–475 ms), and LPC (350–700 ms). High- and low-hypnotizable subjects were used. A subgroup of low-hypnotizable subjects were asked to simulate hypnotic performance. The high-hypnotizable subjects consisted of two groups, with and without posthypnotic amnesia suggestions. All Ss learned serial word lists and then were given a word recognition task. Learned words appeared on one-third of the trials and unlearned words on two-thirds of the trials. In the experimental group some words were "covered" by amnesia. All groups showed larger LPC amplitudes to learned as compared to unlearned words, suggesting that recognition of learned words is accompanied by a specific psychophysiological response. As compared to other groups, the high-hypnotizable subjects who were given posthypnotic amnesia instructions to cover certain words, but not the simulators, exhibited a unique psychophysiological response to

covered words during amnesia, but altered this response when the cues was given to release the amnesia:

> . . . they had significantly smaller P1 . . . smaller N1 . . . larger N400 . . . and smaller LPC amplitudes than when they did not report amnesia. Simulation of hypnotic amnesia by low-hypnotizable participants is insufficient to produce amnesia-related changes in the ERP. (p. 428)

Allen et al. interpret these psychophysiological data to mean:

> These findings raise the possibility that at the earliest stages of information processing the HH-Amn [high-hypnotizable-amnestic] participants may attenuate or gate the stimulus input in a way that other individuals cannot. (p. 429)

Recently, Schacter (in press) reported an experiment in progress in which 12 subjects learned a list of 20 words. Later the subjects were asked to select the target words from a word list containing the original and decoy words that were conceptually related to the original words. PET activity was noted in the hippocampal region of the brain for both the original and decoy words. However, activity in the left temporal area occurred only when subjects selected the original but not the decoy words. This preliminary study raises important implications that true and false memories may be processed differently in the brain.

Taken together, these studies suggest the possibility that amnesia for trauma, and perhaps accurate and false memories, is associated with unique, subtle, but measurable psychophysiological and neurobiological patterns. Reversal of amnesia or recovery of the memory is accompanied by more obvious, gross psychophysiological indicators of physiological reactivity, which appear to persist. Since at least some of these features are absent in simulators, we are left with the very intriguing possibility that true and false allegations of abuse may someday be distinguishable based on psychophysiological response, and that the inadmissibility of "lie detector" evidence based on earlier, unsophisticated physiological studies may need to be reconsidered in light of the evolving science.

Hypnotic Ideomotor Signaling

While many authorities on hypnosis and memory scientists alike would readily agree that hypnosis is far from a reliable tool to investigate memory claims (e.g., Pettinati, 1988), the data, particularly on *ideomotor signaling,* may indicate otherwise. The hypnotic technique of ideomotor signaling (Cheek & LeCron, 1968; Hammond & Cheek, 1988), while not a lie detector or a direct line to the unconscious, has proven exceptionally useful in both clinical and investigative hypnosis in providing another useful source of information to be balanced with material already in conscious awareness (Erickson & Rossi, 1979).

Several experimental studies of chemically dissociated memory have provided support for the potential value of ideomotor signaling. As reviewed in chapter 10 Rath (1982) evaluated memory for suggestions given during surgeries under chemical anesthesia, for which patients had no conscious recall postsurgically. Patients listened to experimental and control messages, providing ideomotor finger signals indicating whether they had heard or not heard the intraoperative messages. Their ideomotor responses accurately discriminated at a significant level between messages they received versus those they did not receive. This evaluation is all the more significant because of the fact that Rath (1982) used a random sample (N=44), which although not tested for hypnotizability level, presumably included low-hypnotizable patients. Supporting this probability is the fact that the experiment produced a bimodal distribution of memory scores, such as we see in a hypnotizability distribution (Hilgard, 1965). In fact, one individual correctly recognized 20 of 22 items.

Levinson (1969) described how four of ten patients at an unusually deep plane of anesthesia correctly recalled, through the assistance of hypnotic ideomotor signaling techniques, a "crisis" during surgery. In this mock crisis, the anesthetist read a script with realism, suggesting the patient was "too blue" and that he was not satisfied with the patient's condition. Then, after a few moments of oxygenating the patient, he expressed satisfaction with the patient's condition and allowed the operation to continue. The four patients, in hypnotic age regression, "could repeat some of the actual words used by the anaesthetist. They could describe other inci-dents that had taken place during the operation" (p. 74). Four other patients, despite continuing amnesia, demonstrated an "alarm reaction" when the events were explored under hypnosis.

In two further studies, Bennett (1988) "used the ideomotor finger response . . . as a means of testing Cheek's claims. That verbatim hypnotic recall was at least partially obtained [for consciously amnestic material] through such means underlies the validity of the existence of memory systems that are highly resistant to verbal systems but accessible through nonverbal means" (p. 226). The latter studies included hypnotic suggestions given under anesthesia, for which there was no conscious recall but to which many subjects nonetheless made behavioral responses.

Thus, four experimental studies (two by Bennett, 1988; Levinson, 1969; and Rath, 1982) of chemically dissociated memory—a type of recall anticipated to have more ecological validity than examinations of "normal" memory—have provided support for the potential value of the ideomotor technique for accurately determining salient past experiences (cf. Rossi & Cheek, 1988). Clinical case reports also exist documenting the use of ideomotor signals to identify memories that were subsequently retrieved through hypnosis and afterwards independently corroborated (e.g., Hammond, in press a; Levinson, 1965). We know of no controlled experimental studies evaluating the utility or validity of other commonly used insight-oriented hypnotic exploration techniques (e.g., Brown & Fromm, 1986; Watkins, 1992; Wolberg, 1964). Clearly more relevant and practical research is needed concerning such techniques.

Concerning the technique of ideomotor signaling, the experience of an F.B.I. forensic hypnosis team that has worked on more than 130 F.B.I. investigations seems relevant. In their work, they found that the ideomotor signaling technique was the most useful single hypnotic method for providing valuable information (Garver, personal communication to D. C. Hammond, 1994).

It is vitally important to keep in mind, however, that leading or suggestive questions may be asked with this (or any other hypnotic technique), just as they may be in nonhypnotic interviews. Sometimes clinicians deliberately use suggestive questions in the process of promoting perceptual and symptomatic change. But when clinicians are working in an investigative or forensic context, or exploring past events of potential relevance to patient symptoms, they must be especially cautious not to phrase questions in a leading manner. Thus, in making recommendations for the use of hypnosis with memory, the ASCH task force on this topic (Hammond et al., 1995) recommended that it is less leading to use four ideomotor signals, as originally advocated by Cheek and LeCron (1968), for "yes," "no," "I don't want to say," and "I don't know, in case there is something that you not only don't know consciously, but you also don't know anything about it at any other level of awareness." Including a response option for "I don't know" avoids putting undue pressure on a patient to guess or implying that at some level he or she possesses further information. The fourth response option lessens the possibilities for confabulation or compliance with perceived therapist perceptions. However, as noted in chapter 10, an initial ideomotor response indicating that a past event is relevent to a current therapeutic concern should be followed by a free recall memory retrieval strategy rather than continued ideomotor questioning. Even non-leading, open-ended questions begin to increase the potential for memory commission errors.

Other Empirical Procedures

Leavitt and Labott (1996) used 13 Rorschach indicators, previously derived to distinguish between sexually abused and non-sexually abused women, to discriminate between authentic and false reports of abuse in women with recovered continuous memories for abuse. The study consisted of 29 women with continuous memory for childhood sexual abuse, 60 women who had recovered memories of CSA and who were inpatients on a dissociative disorders unit, and 85 women from psychiatric

units who did not report a history of sexual abuse. The group with recovered memories was divided into those with and those without a history of dissociative symptoms. Each subject was given the Rorschach. The Rorschach was scored in a number of ways, including for the 13 indicators of sexual abuse. A total of 12 of the 13 indicators significantly differentiated the abuse-reporting and non-abused groups. A total of 8 of these variables further significantly distinguished the dissociative from the non-dissociative recovered memory subgroups. Using a cut-off score of 2 of the 13 sexual abuse indicators, the indicators successfully classified 93% of the abuse-reporting group and 98% of the non-abused group. These indicators successfully classified 88% of those recovered memory subjects with dissociative symptoms but only 24% of those without dissociative symptoms. Leavitt and Labott conclude, "The results support the position that early sexual abuse produces lasting effects that are measurable on the Rorschach test" (p. 492). The authors attribute the unusual finding regarding the failure to correctly classify non-dissociative patients who had recovered memories to the fact that they reported abuse at very early ages (before age three).

CONCLUSION

While no "litmus test" currently exists to distinguish between true and false reports of abuse, scientists are responding to the heated controversy about abuse allegations by developing a number of procedures that might increase our precision in discriminating true from false allegations. While no one procedure has proven itself, our hope is that forensic experts will keep abreast of all these developing areas and draw upon the great variety of different methods currently available in making the determination between true and false reports.

18

||||||||||||||||||||

Hypnosis and the Law

WHERE HYPNOSIS AND THE LAW INTERSECT

There are four areas where the law takes notice of issues involving hypnosis. First, and most fundamentally, the law is concerned with the regulation of *who* may practice hypnosis and *how* hypnosis may be practiced. These issues involve the *regulation of hypnosis*. Statutes in half the states list hypnosis in the licensing definitions for physicians or psychologists (Hammond, 1992). Only a few states, such as California and Florida, have specific regulations concerning hypnosis (Scheflin & Alexander, 1997).

The second area of intersection concerns *hypnosis and advocacy* (Scheflin, 1997e). May attorneys use hypnotic techniques in their efforts to persuade judges and juries? Very little has been written on this intriguing subject, although some very famous lawyers, including F. Lee Bailey and Melvin Belli, have benefitted from training in hypnosis (Bryan, 1962, 1971).

The third area of forensic concern involves *hypnosis and antisocial conduct*. In this category are the questions about the abuse and misuse of hypnosis for the purpose of seduction or criminal conduct. The law's concern is with the responsibility of hypnotized subjects and hypnotizing influencers. No more than one or two dozen scattered cases on this subject have reached appellate courts in the last 150

years, thus making this subject of more theoretical than practical interest. Significant issues concerning the voluntariness of the subject and the resistability of the suggestions have remained unasked as well as unanswered. A recent outbreak of reported cases involving sex with hypnotists may revive these old controversies concerning the limits of hypnotic power.

The fourth, and most heavily litigated, area is *hypnosis for memory recall*, or, more accurately, the issue of whether a person who has previously been hypnotized is permitted to testify as a witness in court. It is this fourth area that will be the subject of discussion in this chapter.

THE DEVELOPMENT OF INVESTIGATIVE HYPNOSIS

Hypnosis was of little concern to American courts until 1968. Before that time, fewer than 50 appellate cases involving hypnosis had been decided in the entire country since the mid–1800s (Scheflin & Shapiro, 1989). In 1897, in a decision that purely by chance established the prevailing rule for two-thirds of the twentieth century, the California Supreme Court swept the entire field of hypnosis out of existence by tersely commenting that "The law of the United States does not recognize hypnotism"

(*People v. Ebanks*, 1897). The California Supreme Court pronouncement is not surprising considering the fact that no professional mental health organization had approved hypnosis for therapeutic purposes, or, indeed, for any purpose at that time, and none was to do so until 1955 when the British Medical Association (*British Medical Journal*, April 23, 1955) officially endorsed hypnosis as a therapeutic modality. The American Medical Association recognized hypnosis in 1958 (Council on Mental Health, AMA, 1958), the American Psychological Association did so in 1960 (Hilgard, 1965), and the American Psychiatric Association endorsed hypnosis in 1961 (American Psychiatric Association, 1961).

Although hypnosis was found medically and psychologically beneficial during World War I, it was not until World War II that serious attention was paid to its treatment possibilities. After World War II, hypnosis enjoyed a wave of respectability. By the mid–1950s, professional medical and psychological associations began recognizing the virtues of hypnosis as a therapeutic agent. Lay hypnotists began teaching police officers how to hypnotize, and the police gradually began incorporating hypnotic techniques into their investigation and interrogation procedures (Arons, 1967). Lay involvement in forensic hypnosis may still be found in many states (Hibbard & Worring, 1981; Kuhns, 1981; Monaghan, 1980; Reiser, 1980). But courts had slammed the door on admitting into courtroom testimony anything that was the product of hypnotic stimulation.

In 1968, however, a Maryland court permitted a witness who previously had been hypnotized to testify in court (*Harding v. State*, 1968). For the next 25 years, courts in almost every state, and legislatures in some, battled over the nature of forensic hypnosis and the appropriate legal rules to apply to it (Kline, 1983; Scheflin & Shapiro, 1989; Udolf, 1983). Other countries are also experiencing similar debates about the negatives and positives of hypnotically refreshed recollection (McConkey & Sheehan, 1995; Wagstaff, 1996).

Today, most of these heavily contested battles have ended, at least temporarily, and the courts across the country have articulated the following legal rules, discussed in detail in Scheflin and Shapiro (1989).

THE LAW OF FORENSIC HYPNOSIS

Admissibility of Statements Made in Trance

Virtually all courts refuse to permit the actual remarks a hypnotic subject makes while in a trance state to be admitted into evidence. Even if the subject's remarks are held admissible, the admission is not for the purpose of proving that the remarks are truthful. Thus, statements made by a crime victim in trance might be admitted into evidence to show something about the victim's mental functioning, but never admitted to prove that the statements are true (Giannelli, 1995).

Interestingly, this was the issue in the case that established the law of investigative hypnosis with one sentence, *People v. Ebanks* (1897). Defendant, who was accused of murder, complained that the trial judge did not let him put on the witness stand an expert hypnotist who was prepared to testify that the defendant's statements in trance proved that he was not guilty. *Ebanks* was correct in ruling that this evidence inadmissible. However, the broad sweep of the statement that "the law of the United States does not recognize hypnotism" had a deterrent effect on the use of hypnosis for memory recollection despite the warning given by a concurring justice in *Ebanks*, who urged that the court's ruling be limited to the specific facts. That warning went unheeded and the legal issue of the use of hypnotically refreshed recollection testimony remained dormant for over 70 years.

Experts generally are not permitted to testify as to what the subject said in hypnosis, though a court will occasionally make an exception (*State v. Turner*, 1970). Some courts permit the expert to repeat the remarks, not for the purpose of validating their truth or falsity, but rather to demonstrate what the expert relied upon to reach his or her conclusions (Scheflin & Shapiro, 1989).

Most trance statements are made out of court. In a very few cases, the question of whether to hypnotize a person in the courtroom has arisen. Courts are almost uniform in refusing to allow a witness to testify in a trance state. Perhaps the most significant, and unusual, decision has been *Dorsey v. State* (1992). In *Dorsey*, a young woman alleged that as a child, she was molested by her grandfather on a repeated basis. Her response was to dissociate into another personality, which carried the memories but kept them separate from the host personality. Memories of these events did not appear until her teenage years, when she felt something was wrong with her. To obtain relief she sought assistance from the female high school counselor. The counselor eventually coaxed the young woman into moving in with her and her husband, both of whom then began extensive sexual activity with the woman, which lasted for several years. At their criminal trial for rape and other sexual offenses, the counselor and her husband claimed the sexual activities were voluntary. A crucial legal issue before the court was whether the young woman should be permitted to testify in a dissociative state. The court noted that in Georgia, hypnotic and posthypnotic testimony is inadmissible in court. Should that rule bar the young woman's testimony?

The Georgia court, after noting that "we could find no law in any jurisdiction regarding the admissibility of testimony from a witness in a dissociative state," held that the woman would be permitted to testify in a dissociative state. The court accepted the position of one of the experts that the hypnotic state is voluntary, and therefore different from the nonvoluntary dissociative state. According to the court:

> The most important difference for our purposes is that hypnosis is a process a person voluntarily chooses to engage in yet which is externally imposed, while a dissociative state is involuntary and, although triggered by external stimuli, comes solely from within. We believe the nonvolitional nature of a dissociative state itself makes statements made while in such a state inherently more reliable than statements made in a hypnotic trance.

The court found an additional reason to support its conclusion to admit the testimony—that the reliability was greater in dissociative cases than in hypnosis cases:

> Moreover, unlike the statements made in the hypnosis and truth serum cases . . . , [in this case] the victim's testimony in a dissociative state could be tested for reliability. In the [hypnosis and truth serum cases which hold] that statements made in a hypnotic trance are inadmissible, the statements at issue were hearsay: the question presented was whether someone should be allowed to testify at trial regarding what was recalled and said by himself or another while in an artificially induced altered state of consciousness at an earlier time. Thus, in addition to concerns about the inherent reliability of the statement, those cases also involved concerns about the impossibility of testing that reliability due to the jury's inability to see the [witness] in the altered state making the statement and the opposing party's inability to cross-examine the [witness] in the state he was in at the time the statement was made.

Because in *Dorsey* the witness was permitted to testify in a dissociative state, this latter concern was not relevant. The jury and defense counsel would have an opportunity to observe her demeanor and hear her words while she was still in a dissociative condition. Cross-examination would take place while she was still dissociated. Accordingly, the Georgia court held that "the line of cases holding that statements made by a person in a hypnotic state are inadmissible does not control the admissibility of the victim's testimony in a dissociative state."

Dorsey will spark controversy in all directions. At the very least, it may open the door to the admissibility of testimony not previously allowed in court. For that reason alone, it will attract the attention of lawyers, jurists, and mental health experts.

Admissibility of Hypnotically Refreshed Testimony

1. The "Open Admissibility" Rule

When *Harding* (1968) opened the door to admissibility of hypnotically refreshed recollection, it ushered in the "*open admissibility*" rule. This rule states that posthypnotic testimony is always admissible, subject to the right of the adversary to discredit it by cross-examination or with contrary expert testimony. Hypnosis is treated no differently from any other form of memory retrieval. The jury can decide whether to believe it or not. But they get the right to hear it. From 1968 to 1978, the "open admissibility" rule was so popular with courts that it was the only rule applied by them.

Today, however, the rule has fallen into disfavor, and only a few states still adhere to the "open admissibility" rule. The reason for the rule's decline was the articulation by courts, beginning in the late 1970s, of dangers associated with hypnotic memory retrieval.

Another cause of disfavor is the leniency of the rule, best explained by a remarkable series of Wyoming Supreme Court cases. In the first case, *Chapman v. State* (1982), a city police officer performed the hypnosis despite his minimal training. The majority permitted the hypnosis subject to testify regarding posthypnotic recall. As the dissent observed:

> Stripped of its veneer, this case holds that a police officer who occasionally plays around with hypnotism can manipulate the recall of a witness and receive the blessing of this court. . . .

* * *

> The writer of this dissent knows the hypnotist personally. He is a well-qualified law enforcement officer and his honesty and integrity are not in question, but his skills as a hypnotist, and the reliability of the procedures used here, are totally deficient.

In the second case, *Gee v. State* (1983), even the prosecutor had difficulty in listing the qualifications of the hypnotist. The majority held that the hypnotist did not need any qualifications, thus prompting the dissent to note:

> It follows, therefore, that a hobo passing through town or a derelict in the county jail could hypnotize a potential witness, and the witness' testimony would be admissible at trial. . . .

* * *

There is a man in Oakland, California, who is the dean and and lone "professor" at "Croaker College." For the sum of $150 each, this man trains frogs to jump. . . . As part of his rigid training curriculum, the "professor" claims that he hypnotizes the frogs; while they are in their hypnotic trance, he plays an attitude-improvement tape to them.

Under our present standards the dean of "Croaker College" would be over-qualified as a hypnotist.

The dissent was prophetic for in the next case, *Haselhuhn v. State* (1986), the hypnotist was, in the words of the majority, "a non-professional with meager training in hypnotic techniques." We learn from the dissent that the "meagre training" was a 32-hour home course, and that the hypnotist was a maintenance man at the Pacific Power and Light Company. Once again, to the continuing astonishment of the dissent, the majority permitted the posthypnotic testimony to be introduced into evidence.

The "open admissibility" rule has been rejected in most states as too lenient, but it remains the law in Wyoming (*Prime v. State*, 1989) and perhaps a few other states. The "open admissibility" rule generally is not supported by hypnosis experts or by legal commentators.

2. The "Admissible with Safeguards" Rule

By 1978, courts began hearing that there were dangers lurking in posthypnotic recall. The possibility of (1) contamination by undue suggestion, (2) confabulation, (3) excess desire to please the hypnotist, and (4) increased self-confidence in the accuracy of the recalled material, led courts to reject the "open admissibility" rule and to provide a filter for admissible posthypnotic testimony. Orne suggested his now well-known guidelines as a precondition to admissibility (Laurence & Perry, 1988). These guidelines have been extremely important, especially after they were adopted and explained by the New Jersey Supreme Court in the *State v. Hurd* (1981) case:

> The fallibility of human memory poses a fundamental challenge to our system of justice. . . . Nevertheless, it is an inescapable fact of life that must be understood and accommodated. Rather than require historical accuracy as a condition for admitting eyewitness testimony, we depend on the adversary system to inform the jury of the inherent weaknesses of evidence. . . .
>
>   . . . [T]he experts who testified at trial indicated that in appropriate cases and where properly conducted the use of hypnosis to refresh memory is comparable in reliability to ordinary

recall. Therefore, we hold that testimony enhanced through hypnosis is admissible in a criminal trial if the trial court finds that the use of hypnosis in the particular case was reasonably likely to result in recall comparable in accuracy to normal human memory.

To provide an adequate record for evaluating the reliability of the hypnotic procedure, and to ensure a minimum level of reliability, we also adopt several procedural requirements based on those suggested by Dr. Orne. . . . Before it may introduce hypnotically refreshed testimony, a party must demonstrate compliance with these requirements.

First, a psychiatrist or psychologist experienced in the use of hypnosis must conduct the session. This professional should also be able to qualify as an expert in order to aid the court in evaluating the procedures followed. . . . In this way, the court will be able to obtain vital information concerning the pathological reason for memory loss and the hypnotizability of the witness. Furthermore, the expert will be able to conduct the interrogation in a manner most likely to yield accurate recall.

Second, the professional conducting the hypnotic session should be independent of and not regularly employed by the prosecutor, investigator or defense. This condition will safeguard against any bias on the part of the hypnotist that might translate into leading questions, unintentional cues, or other suggestive conduct.

Third, any information given to the hypnotist by law enforcement personnel or the defense prior to the hypnotic session must be recorded, either in writing or another suitable form. This requirement will help the court determine the extent of information the hypnotist could have communicated to the witness either directly or through suggestion.

Fourth, before inducing hypnosis the hypnotist should obtain from the subject a detailed description of the facts as the subject remembers them. The hypnotist should carefully avoid influencing the description by asking structured questions or adding new details.

Fifth, all contacts between the hypnotist and the subject must be recorded. This will establish a record of the pre-induction interview, the hypnotic session, and the post-hypnotic period, enabling a court to determine what information or suggestions the witness may have received during the session and what recall was first elicited through hypnosis. . . .

Sixth, only the hypnotist and the subject should be present during any phase of the hypnotic session, including the pre-hypnotic testing and the post-hypnotic interview. Although it may be easier for a person familiar with the investigation to conduct some of the questioning, the risk of undetectable, inadvertent suggestion is too great. . . . Likewise, the mere presence of such a person may influence the response of the subject.

This second rule, crafted after the "open admissibility" rule was found to be too permissive, is the "admissibility with safeguards" rule. It is now followed by a substantial number of states. Under this approach, before hypnotically refreshed recollection can be admitted into court, it must be shown to the judge's satisfaction that the guidelines in place have been met.

What if some, but not all, of the guidelines have been met? In other words, did failure strictly to meet the guidelines always prevent the posthypnotic testimony from being admitted into court? Many courts answered "no." These courts evolved a related rule, called the "totality of the circumstances" test. Courts that follow this approach do not require rigid adherence to strict guidelines. Rather, every case is judged on its own merits, with the trial judge deciding at a pre-trial hearing whether, considering "the totality of the circumstances," the manner in which the hypnosis sessions were conducted was likely to have contaminated the memory of the hypnotic subject to the point where those memories would be unreliable. If the totality of the circumstances showed no undue suggestion, the posthypnotic testimony was admissible.

A sizeable minority of states follow the *"admissibility with safeguards" rule*. The federal courts follow the *"totality of the circumstances" test* (*Borawick v. Shay*, 1995; Karlin & Orne 1996; Scheflin, 1996, 1997c).

3. The "Per Se Exclusion" Rule

As courts struggled to find an appropriate rule for the admissibility of hypnotically refreshed recollection, some hypnosis and memory experts and legal commentators began to argue that hypnosis always contaminates memory. The *"inevitability of contamination"* hypothesis is well stated by Kihlstrom (1993):

> Remembering is an act of reconstruction in which expectation and inference play major roles, whereas hypnosis is ultimately an act of the imagination in which normal reality testing is set aside. The hallucinating subject may believe he sees something, but there is nothing really out there; the age-regressed subject may believe she is five years old again, but she has not shrunk in the chair. Similarly, subjects given suggestions for hypermnesia may believe that they have recovered new memories, but this information may not be accurate. In the absence of objective corroborating evidence, there are no tests that can be applied to determine whether a memory is accurate. The situation is made worse by the fact that suggestion is central to hypnosis, raising the possibility that hypnotized eyewitnesses may be more vulnerable to leading questions and other postevent misinformation effects. Even when no new memories are produced, the popular belief in the efficacy of hypnosis may lead shaky eyewitnesses to become more confident in whatever it is that they do remember. (pp. 739–740)

By 1980, courts began to become more than cautious about hypnotically refreshed testimony. Indeed, the courts began to become alarmed about it, especially because hypnosis experts began to report clinical studies that demonstrated hypnotic alteration of memories. Orne changed his earlier view and now argued that hypnotically refreshed recollection should not be admissible in court (*State v. Peoples*, 1984). The guidelines, he said, were intended to be the minimum conditions necessary for experts to examine the hypnosis session in search of undue suggestion.

Beginning in 1980 with Minnesota's influential *Mack* case (*State v. Mack*, 1980), courts returned to the pre–1968 rule of automatic (*per se*) exclusion. The *Mack* case was not the first to raise questions about hypnotic procedures used with memory. The scientific reliability of hypnosis-induced evidence was doubted in *People v. Harper* (1969), where the court stated that "We see no reason to

equate examination under hypnosis and examination while under the influence of a drug having the effect of a 'truth serum' except to note that the scientific reliability of neither is sufficient to justify the use of test results of either in the serious business of criminal prosecution" (p. 7). The Virginia Supreme Court had, in *Greenfield v. Commonwealth* (1974), ruled hypnotic evidence not admissible in a criminal prosecution. *Mack* is, however, significant for two reasons. First, it is the first major state Supreme Court opinion containing a detailed analysis of problems raised with hypnotically refreshed memory. Second, it provides the foundation for the thinking that would later be used more broadly in the false memory controversy. Because so many courts have followed its reasoning, *Mack* will be discussed at length.

In *Mack*, the District Court certified to the Supreme Court "an important and doubtful question concerning the use of hypnotically-induced testimony in a criminal trial." Acknowledging that this was a case of first impression, the Supreme Court stated that the question certified is "whether a previously hypnotized witness may testify in a criminal proceeding concerning the subject matter adduced at the pretrial hypnotic interview." The Court held such testimony inadmissible.

Defendant was on trial for criminal sexual assault and for aggravated assault. The facts, as recited by the Minnesota Supreme Court, were as follows:

> At 2:19 A.M. on May 14, 1978, Marion J. Erickson was brought by ambulance from the Hi Lo Motel in Minneapolis to the Hennepin County Medical Center, bleeding profusely from her vagina. Defendant, who had met and danced with Ms. Erickson at the Spring Inn bar the evening before and had taken her to the motel on his motorcycle afterwards, had telephoned for an ambulance and told the ambulance drivers that he and Ms. Erickson "were engaged in sexual intercourse when she started bleeding." One of the drivers observed that Ms. Erickson was "quite drunk" and that her speech was unclear; she had difficulty walking but did walk from the motel room to the ambulance with defendant's assistance and insisted that "it wasn't (defendant's) fault." The other driver stated that defendant "seemed very concerned," and that

Ms. Erickson refused to give her name but asked defendant to go with her to the hospital.

At Hennepin County Medical Center Emergency Department, Ms. Erickson was attended by one intern who noted that she was in a "flat emotional state" and recorded that she told him she had been "engaged in sexual activity with fingers being placed in her vagina." Another intern who assisted in Ms. Erickson's treatment stated that she was suffering from a cut through the vaginal tissue into a muscle layer and that she believed she had been injured in a motorcycle accident. It was this intern's opinion that the injury could not have occurred during intercourse and that, because of its length and depth, it could not have been caused by a human fingernail. He said this type of injury could be the result of "tearing after childbirth."

After Ms. Erickson had been advised by the doctors concerning the nature of her injury and had been told by them that they did not believe she had been involved in a motorcycle accident, Ms. Erickson telephoned police on May 16 to report an assault. She told police she could remember nothing after the motorcycle accident until she awoke at the motel, bleeding from her vagina and lying in a pool of blood on the bed. She remembered saying, "David, don't leave me" and hearing someone assure her that he would not. She indicated that she had been suffering emotional problems, due to a serious relationship with a man that had recently ended, and that she had "blacked out" from drinking on other occasions.

At this point a police officer, some six weeks after the alleged assault, brought Ms. Erickson to Beauford Kleidon, "a self-taught lay hypnotist." Kleidon was told that he would be seeing "a witness with a memory block who had been hospitalized with a cut in her vagina." Kleidon, left alone with Ms. Erickson, tested her "hypnotic susceptibility with several standard tests, induced hypnosis with a standard fixation procedure, and, when he had determined that she had entered a deep hypnotic state, asked her permission for [two police officers] to enter the room." Ms. Erickson agreed and the police officers made an audiotape of the rest of the hypnosis session. The tape itself was lost, but a transcript was entered into evidence.

According to the Court:

The transcript reveals that Beauford Kleidon told Ms. Erickson that she would remember the events of May 13 and 14 as they actually occurred, but as though on a television screen and without emotion. Under hypnosis, Ms. Erickson reported that at the Hi Lo Motel David Mack "told me to get on the bed and take my clothes off. He said, 'I want to get even with you for running out on me.'" As the hypnotist assured her, "(y)ou will see it very plainly in your mind," but "you feel nothing," Ms. Erickson said, "oh, no, no, no * * *. He told me to spread my legs, * * *. He pulled out this switchblade and told me he was going to kill me * * * he kept sticking this knife up me and I remember screaming and screaming."

At the close of the session, Kleidon made the following statement, referred to at the hearing and in the briefs as a "post-hypnotic suggestion": "You are going to feel as if your body and your mind have been completely rejuvenized (sic) and you will be able to remember very clearly everything that has happened on the 13th and 14th. Now that memory is very clear in your mind. This does not disturb you."

The following day, Marion Erickson went to the police department and gave Lieutenant Weiss a typewritten statement recounting as her present memory the events of May 13, as she had reported them under hypnosis. On July 26, 1978, a complaint was issued, and David Mack was arrested on October 5, 1978.

The defendant argued that Ms. Erickson's "hypnotically-induced 'memory' of the alleged assault is not sufficiently reliable to merit admission and that permitting her to testify to this memory . . . would deny him his right to confrontation and to cross-examination under the Sixth and Fourteenth Amendments." By contrast, the prosecution argued that the testimony was her current memory, what the law calls "present recollection refreshed," and should be admitted "as long as certain safeguards can be established."

The Supreme Court held that the defendant's claim that the "hypnotically-prompted" recollection was unreliable must be tested by the *Frye* rule concerning the admissibility of scientific evidence. The Court said that "Although expert testimony deduced from the scientific discovery is admissible under far less stringent circumstances, 'the thing from which the deduction is made must be sufficiently established to have gained general acceptance in the particular field in which it belongs'" [citing *Frye*]. The *Frye* rule was adopted by the Minnesota Supreme Court in 1952 and has been applied to rule inadmissible the results of polygraph tests.

Technically, *Frye* should not apply to the admission of the testimony of ordinary witnesses, only to the opinions of *experts* who have relied on a *new* scientific apparatus or physical technique. The Court recognized this point but extended *Frye* to cover this factual setting:

> Under the Frye rule, the results of mechanical or scientific testing are not admissible unless the testing has developed or improved to the point where experts in the field widely share the view that the results are scientifically reliable as accurate. Although hypnotically-adduced "memory" is not strictly analogous to the results of mechanical testing, we are persuaded that the Frye rule is equally applicable in this context, where the best expert testimony indicates that no expert can determine whether memory retrieved by hypnosis, or any part of that memory, is truth, falsehood, or confabulation—a filling of gaps with fantasy. Such results are not scientifically reliable as accurate.

The Court utilized a questionable definition of hypnosis—"a highly suggestible state into which a willing subject is induced by a skilled therapist" (Coleman, 1960, p. 579). At the pretrial hearing, five experts on hypnosis and memory retrieval testified:

> The experts agreed initially that hypnosis is capable of releasing an emotional memory "block," and that historically valid memory can result from hypnotic recall. Hypnosis is used by trained psychiatrists and psychologists as a therapeutic tool. Several of the experts noted that for it to be therapeutically useful, it need not produce historically accurate memory. Thus, the historical or scientific accuracy of the memory adduced under hypnosis is not an ordinary subject of investigation or concern by its practitioners in the medical and psychological community.
>
> Expert testimony further indicated that a hypnotized subject is highly susceptible to suggestion,

even that which is subtle and unintended. Such suggestion may be transmitted either during the hypnotic session or before it by such individuals as, in this case, the doctors, who believed the wound was caused by a sharp instrument, and the policemen investigating the incident, who undoubtedly entertained their own theories regarding the cause of the injury. The hypnotized subject is influenced by a need to "fill gaps." When asked a question under hypnosis, rarely will he or she respond, "I don't know." Another factor, significant for this case, which can affect the "memory" produced under hypnosis is the subject's desire to please either the hypnotist or others who have asked the person hypnotized to remember and who have urged that it is important that he or she remember certain events. Most significantly, there is no way to determine from the content of the "memory" itself which parts of it are historically accurate, which are entirely fanciful, and which are lies.

In addition to its historical unreliability, a "memory" produced under hypnosis becomes hardened in the subject's mind. A witness who was unclear about his "story" before the hypnotic session becomes convinced of the absolute truth of the account he made while under hypnosis. This conviction is so firm that the ordinary "indicia of reliability" are completely erased, and hypnotic subjects have been able to pass lie detector tests while attesting to the truth of statements they made under hypnosis which researchers know to be utterly false. It would be impossible to cross-examine such a witness in any meaningful way. Such firm subjective conviction as could easily fool a juror is even more likely to result from a situation where the subject has been given a post-hypnotic suggestion like the one in this case: "You will remember very clearly everything that has happened on the 13th and 14th." Two of the experts testifying were convinced that such a suggestion would assure that the hypnotized person would remember what she had related under hypnosis as a memory of the events in question themselves. The subject's conviction of the truth of the "memory" could last indefinitely.

The Court was influenced by two nonscientific concerns raised by Orne. First, it noted that Orne had testified that he has seen an increase in the use of hypnosis by police to create more trustworthy witnesses:

> I've seen now several cases where this seemed to have happened * * *
>
> Typically, when a witness is a bad witness * * * you hypnotize (him) because * * *—the story goes all over the place every time he's asked something different—once you hypnotize (him), he consensually validates the story, and at that point it's fixed * * * you can take somebody who is a terribly bad witness and make [him] a very good witness, because you * * * convinced [him] not only of the reality, but that you believe in the reality, and as a consequence [he] become(s) (an) unshakable witness and that is a profound danger.

Second, the court was attentive to an argument based on judicial economy when it noted "the truth of Dr. Orne's observation that a case-by-case decision on the admissibility question would be prohibitively expensive. . . ."

Most important to the judges was the fact that in criminal cases, an admissibility rule had been used by other courts to reflect a pro-prosecution bias:

> There is today a tendency toward more liberal admission of testimony resulting in some way from hypnosis. It is significant, however, that this tendency clearly favors only the prosecution of criminal matters: In many of the reported cases in point, the accused was endeavoring to present to the jury hypnotic evidence of innocence; however, in others it was the prosecution which sought to place on the witness stand an individual whose testimony would be incriminating, but whose memory of the crimes had partially lapsed because of the passage of time, the consumption of drugs, or the trauma of being the victim of the unlawful events leading to the trial itself. While in the former instances the accused generally argued to little or no avail for the admissibility of the evidence, in the latter the defendant was unsuccessful in attempting to block introduction of the testimony. . . . The results of favoring hypnotically- induced testimony by prosecution witnesses but not by the accused are, as might be predicted, "no error" holdings; convictions are affirmed.

* * *

We recognize that there are two lines of cases regarding the admissibility of hypnotically-induced evidence: one line of cases where the exculpatory hypnotically-induced testimony of criminal defendants was excluded, and the other line of cases where the hypnotically-induced testimony of prosecution witnesses was admitted. . . . We follow the best scientific authority, however, in rejecting as artificial and unprincipled any distinction between hypnotically- induced testimony offered by the defense to exculpate and that offered by the prosecution to make its case. Regardless of whether such evidence is offered by the defense or by the prosecution, a witness whose memory has been "revived" under hypnosis ordinarily must not be permitted to testify in a criminal proceeding to matters which he or she "remembered" under hypnosis.

Why did the *Mack* judges reject hypnosis as a reliable technique for the retrieval of memories? According to the court:

> The crux of the problem is that hypnosis can create a memory of perceptions which neither were nor could have been made, and, therefore, can bring forth a "memory" from someone who cannot establish that she perceived the events she asserts to remember. Neither the person hypnotized nor the expert observer can distinguish between confabulation and accurate recall in any particular instance. After the hypnosis session, the hypnotically "retrieved" account differs in another way from ordinary human recall, to which the state seeks to liken it. Because the person hypnotized is subjectively convinced of the veracity of the "memory," this recall is not susceptible to attack by cross-examination.

In essence, the court articulated the following scientific reasons to reject hypnosis:

1. Hypnosis can create memories of events that never occurred or details that never existed.

2. Hypnotized subjects will confabulate and no person can tell what part of a hypnotically refreshed memory is true and what part is confabulation.

3. Hypnosis "hardens" the memory by giving the subject an increased confidence in its veracity, thereby impeding effective cross-examination.

4. Judges and juries may easily be unduly influenced, and, therefore, may give greater weight to the information dramatically recalled during hypnosis, even when instructed by the judge that these recollections might not be historically accurate.

The Court's rejection of hypnosis was not total. The judges did not entirely eliminate the police use of hypnosis:

We do not foreclose, by this opinion, the use of hypnosis as an extremely useful investigative tool when a witness is enabled to remember verifiable factual information which provides new leads to the solution of a crime. A witness under hypnosis may, for instance, bring forth information previously unknown to law enforcement authorities, such as a license plate number, which subsequently aids police in identification of a suspect. Experts see no reasonable objection to the use of hypnosis in this manner, provided the witness is willing, as long as the material remembered during hypnosis is not subsequently used in court as part of an eyewitness' testimony. Even where the use of hypnosis truly is to investigate a crime rather than to create a witness, adequate safeguards should be established to assure the utmost freedom from suggestion upon the hypnotized person's memory recall in the event he or she must later be called to testify to recollections recorded before the hypnotic interview.

In a footnote, the Court listed, but did not formally adopt, "the following safeguards recommended by the Orne Affidavit":

A. Hypnosis should be carried out by a psychiatrist or psychologist with special training in its use. He should not be informed about the facts of the case verbally; rather, he should receive a written memorandum outlining whatever facts he is to know, carefully avoiding any other communications which might affect his opinion. Thus, his

beliefs and possible bias can be evaluated. It is extremely undesirable to have the individual conducting the hypnotic sessions to have any involvement in the investigation of the case. Further he should be an independent professional not responsible to the prosecution or the investigators.

B. All contact of the psychiatrist with the individual to be hypnotized should be video taped from the moment they meet until the entire interaction is completed. The casual comments which are passed before or after hypnosis are every bit as important to get on tape as the hypnotic session itself. (It is possible to give suggestions prior to the induction of hypnosis which will act as posthypnotic suggestions.)

Prior to the induction of hypnosis, a brief evaluation of the patient should be carried out and the psychiatrist should then elicit a detailed description of the facts as the witness or victim remembers them. This is important because individuals often are able to recall a good deal more while talking to a psychiatrist than when they are with an investigator, and it is important to have a record of what the witness's beliefs are before hypnosis. Only after this has been completed should the hypnotic session be initiated. The psychiatrist should strive to avoid adding any new elements to the witness's description of his experiences, including those which he had discussed in his wake state, lest he inadvertently alter the nature of the witness's memories or constrain them by reminding him of his waking memories.

C. No other than the psychiatrist and the individual to be hypnotized should be present in the room before and during the hypnotic session. This is important because it is all too easy for observers to inadvertently communicate to the subject what they expect, what they are startled by, or what they are disappointed by. If either the prosecution or the defense wish to observe the hypnotic session, they may do so without jeopardizing the integrity of the session through a one-way screen or on a television monitor.

D. Because the interactions which have preceded the hypnotic session may well have a profound effect on the sessions themselves, tape recordings of prior interrogations are important to document that a witness had not been implicitly or explicitly cued pertaining to certain information which might then be reported for apparently the first time by the witness during hypnosis.

The Court was particularly aware that the facts in the case militated against the use of hypnosis. The Court noted that:

1. Hypnosis was unnecessary in identifying the defendant because he was the only person present with Ms. Erickson.
2. The hypnotist had no formal education and no scientific knowledge of memory, or of the impact of suggestion on memory.
3. The hypnotist was hired by the police "whose interest in the outcome of the hypnotic session might well have been communicated to Ms. Erickson. These interested parties, but no representative of the defendant, were, in fact, present at the hypnotic session, possibly cuing Ms. Erickson's memory by their facial expressions and gestures."
4. The hypnotic session occurred several weeks after the event and after Ms. Erickson "undoubtedly spoke to the physicians who treated her and entertained their own hypotheses regarding the origins of the injury, as well as to the police and her friends."
5. There was no corroboration of any of the facts recalled during or after hypnosis.
6. Portions of her recollection were clearly erroneous: "Although Ms. Erickson recalls the assault upon her as one of repeated stabbings, her hospital records indicate she had only a single deep cut inside her vagina and no injury to the labia or perineum. She described Mack's motorcycle as a black Yamaha, and stated that earlier in the day she had eaten lunch with her father at the Embers restaurant and had ordered pizza. However, defendant drove a maroon Triumph. Embers restaurants do not serve pizza."
7. The day after hypnosis, Ms. Erickson remembered having spent time with defendant before in the company of her friend Hazel. Hazel's description of the man Ms. Erickson was with did not match the defendant. (Hazel said the man was "around" 5'1", having

long, reddish-brown hair, and having a tattoo on his left arm." Defendant is 5'8" and has no tattoos on either arm.)
8. Ms. Erickson had been drinking—"It is not clear from the record before us that Ms. Erickson was not so drunk that she could not have remembered what had happened under any circumstances."

As the Court appropriately noted, "These circumstances support our holding that testimony of this previously hypnotized witness concerning the subject matter adduced at the pretrial hypnotic interview may not be admitted in a criminal proceeding." Because the hypnotically refreshed recollection of Ms. Erickson did not meet "ordinary standards of reliability for admission," the Court declined to hear defendant's constitutional challenges.

Two years after *Mack*, the California Supreme Court decided the influential *People v. Shirley* (1982) case, which adopted the *Mack* analysis but added a detailed examination of the hypnosis literature available at that time. Interestingly, *Shirley* was also a case involving a lay hypnotist, this time a district attorney, who was attempting, on the eve of trial, to hypnotize the alleged victim into telling one coherent story. The attempt failed, as noted by the majority opinion:

> The jury believed part of Catherine's story, as it convicted the defendant of rape; but it also apparently found that she was lying when she described in detail the alleged act of oral copulation, as it acquitted the defendant of that charge. The jury doubtless had a difficult task, since Catherine's performance as a witness was far from exemplary: the record is replete with instances in which her testimony was vague, changeable, self-contradictory, or prone to unexplained lapses of memory. Indeed, on occasion she professed to be unable to remember assertions that she had herself made on the witness stand only the previous day. (p. 245)

Thus, the hypnosis was *ineffective* in fabricating a coherent, consistent false story, and the jury was not awed by the use of hypnosis—they reached a reasoned approach, which accepted some parts of the hypnotically refreshed testimony and rejected other parts of it, as juries do with testimony that is not hypnotically refreshed.

The *Mack* and *Shirley* rulings sounded the death knell for forensic hypnosis in most states. Courts began to shut down the growing police practice of training police hypnotists. *Mack* and *Shirley*, and many cases that followed their lead, refused to admit into evidence the testimony of anyone who had previously been hypnotized for the purpose of memory retrieval.

This third rule, requiring *per se exclusion*, was so harsh that it was almost immediately modified to permit two major exceptions: (1) the posthypnotic testimony of defendants in criminal cases cannot be automatically excluded, according to the United States Supreme Court opinion in *Rock v. Arkansas* (1987), and (2) a person who has given a prehypnotic statement that was duly recorded could testify as to these prehypnotically recalled details, but not as to anything remembered during or after hypnosis. Similarly, a posthypnotic out-of-court or in-court identification was also impermissible if there had been no prehypnotic identification.

Today, a majority of states that have addressed the issue follow the *per se* exclusion rule as modified by the two noted exceptions (Perry, Orne, London, & Orne, 1996).

THE CURRENT FORENSIC HYPNOSIS DEBATE CONCERNING EXCLUSION

Most states have settled the issue of the admissibility of hypnotically refreshed recollection. The volume of litigation reaching appellate courts has dwindled substantially from the 1980s, when the legal rules were being formulated (Scheflin & Shapiro, 1989). It would be a mistake, however, to assume that forensic hypnosis has been suppressed because of the prevailing *per se* exclusion rule. From its ashes has arisen the beginning of a renewed challenge, which seeks to soften the harshness of the *per se* rule. The modern challenge begins with a fundamental disagreement with the validity of the science presented by experts to courts in the 1980s.

Courts a decade ago were told that hypnosis always contaminates memory and therefore should

never be used for memory refreshing, unless to develop investigative leads for police who would not present the hypnotized subject's testimony in evidence. The position that hypnosis always contaminates memory identifies several major concerns, all of which have been well stated by a legal analyst (Clemens, 1991):

The scientific consensus is that hypnosis does enhance recall. If this were the only factor to be considered, there would be no argument about its use. But the problems associated with hypnosis create the conflict. These problems lie in four major areas: suggestibility, confabulation, deliberate fabrication, and increased confidence.

Suggestibility is inherent in the hypnotic process. A hypnotic subject is intensely focused on the hypnotist and has an increased desire to please the hypnotist by complying with both implicit and explicit demands. Leading questions can imply the correct answer. However, the suggestions need not be verbal. The attitude, demeanor, and expectations of the hypnotist, coupled with tone of voice and body language, can convey suggestive messages to the subject. Most subjects will respond to these subtle hints and answer accordingly.

Often, the subject's desire to please will affect the truth of their statements. The subject may not be able to remember details which are being asked for by the hypnotist. The subject will then hallucinate or imagine the missing details. This pseudomemory will be remembered as being accurate. This fantasizing of information that seems plausible is called confabulation. The subject does not mean to lie, but the mind creates additional facts to make the story more logical.

The danger of someone deliberately lying while under hypnosis is minimal. The larger problem is that someone may pretend to be hypnotized and lie to enhance his version of the story. Only someone who has a working knowledge of hypnotic techniques could adequately fake the results. However, experiments in the area have shown that even the best in the field have difficulty distinguishing between those who are faking and those who are not. Feigned hypnosis presents the same problems as when a defendant commits perjury. The hypnotist can attempt to determine the veracity of the statements in the same manner that a jury would decide whether a witness was lying. Generally, the incentive for a witness to lie is much less than that of the actual defendant.

The last area of concern is the increased confidence that a subject has after hypnosis. The details that are confabulated are often assimilated by the mind and the subject believes that they are real memories. The amount of confidence that one has regarding the recalled materials is based on responsiveness to hypnosis rather than the accuracy of the information. This misplaced confidence creates a more credible witness, who is harder to cross-examine. The difficulty in testing the witness, when combined with the other concerns, provides the basis for the opposition to the use of hypnosis. However, the fact that hypnosis reveals relevant evidence can not be rebutted. (pp. 293–295)

The *per se* inadmissibility rule is based on the conception of hypnosis as an inevitable memory contaminator and confidence builder. If the science fails to support that position, as we have demonstrated in chapter 10, the rationale for automatic exclusion evaporates.

The modern debate about the *per se* centers around two major issues: (1) the continued wisdom of the *per se* exclusion rule based on what the scientific literature tells us, and (2) the application of the United States Supreme Court's decision in *Daubert v. Merrell Dow Pharmaceuticals, Inc.* (1993), which adopted a new standard for the admission of expert testimony in federal courts.

Objections to the Per Se Rule

Opponents of the present majority rule, which automatically disqualifies any posthypnotic recollection, contend that it is "unfair, unjust and unnecessary" (Scheflin, 1994b). They make several arguments: (1) the rule is unfair because it reaches results that are unjust, (2) the negative perception courts have about hypnosis is not supported by the scientific literature, (3) the existence of excellent new guidelines eliminate the dangers of the misuse of hypnosis, and (4) the United States Supreme Court's *Daubert* (1993) opinion about the admissibility of expert testimony may encourage a rejection of the *per se* rule (Eisenberg, 1995).

On the issue of fairness and justness, opponents point to the following consequences of the rule to help show the basic inequities in, and the fundamental unfairness of, the present prevailing *per se* disqualification rule.

Harm to Therapists

Courts following the *per se* exclusion rule have not considered the impact of this rule on therapists or their patients. The application of the *per se* rule has several negative effects on the practice of therapy, and no positive effects.

First, it violates equal protection by disenfranchising two classes of individuals: (1) people who have witnessed or been victims of crime or traumatic events and who have incomplete memories, and (2) people who have repressed memories of childhood sexual abuse and who need hypnosis to help recover those dissociated memories. In the first group, suppose a woman had been raped. She cannot fully recall the entire attack. Hypnosis, used according to specific guidelines, may help facilitate the recall. Why should this particular victim be denied access to the memories she may possess? For the second group, many states in recent years have passed legislation to protect the legal rights of persons with repressed memories (Williams, 1996). For example, in Minnesota, where the *Mack* opinion is still the law, the legislature enacted section 541.073, which expands the statute of limitations in sexual abuse cases. As the Minnesota Court of Appeals noted in *Blackowiak v. Kemp* (1995), "psychological injuries caused by sexual abuse are different from injuries suffered by victims of other torts."

Because some victims of sexual abuse will repress their memories by dissociating them from consciousness, hypnosis can be very valuable in retrieving these memories. Indeed, for some victims, hypnosis may provide the only avenue to the repressed memories. There is no scientific doubt that childhood sexual abuse has highly debilitating mental and physical consequences that manifest themselves in adult life. It is a natural consequence of the crime that these adult problems are likely, though not inevitable, and that some victims may be protected from the childhood trauma by repressing the memories. In Minnesota, and elsewhere, the *per se* exclusion rule is at odds with the Legislature's intent to protect victims of child abuse.

Consider the following actual case (Scheflin, 1997c):

> A four year old girl went to her mother and said "daddy's touching me in my private parts." The mother had a breakdown and was hospitalized. The child, now in the custody of daddy, learned not to talk about these things—look what happened to mommy when she was told. Several years pass and the molestings continued. Medical records of the child were consistent with molesting, but the child would not talk when asked. After a year of therapy, hypnosis was used and the child talked about the molesting. New York courts, which follow the *per se* rule, would not admit her posthypnotic testimony despite the fact that there was independent medical corroborating evidence that she was molested. Without her evidence, there was no proof that daddy was the molester. Daddy retained custody.

Can a *per se* exclusion rule be justified in this case where medical evidence is available to corroborate the child's posthypnotic statements?

Second, the *per se* exclusion rule puts in jeopardy every therapist who uses hypnosis for therapeutic purposes. Consider a case where a patient comes to a therapist for depression. There are no memories of abuse as a child and no discussion of the subject in therapy. Hypnosis is used as a relaxation technique. While in trance, the patient has a vivid and detailed recollection of having been abused years earlier. The therapist stops the hypnosis and it is not used again. Is it *always* true that this memory is so unreliable as to *never* be admissible in a court of law? Should any further memories she might have also be inadmissible? The *per se* rule excludes *all* posthypnotic recollections.

The threat to therapists and their patients was first pointed out by Scheflin and Shapiro in *Trance on Trial* (1989), which received the American Psychiatric Association's Manfred S. Guttmacher Award for alerting the hypnosis community to the potential legal danger. Scheflin and Shapiro (1989) note that, if a patient comes to a therapist for treatment and hypnosis is used, the patient may be disqualified from testifying about any memories that arise during or after hypnosis, even though the purpose of the hypnosis was not to discover memories

for investigative purposes. Because the use of hypnosis may have an adverse effect on the patient's legal rights, the patient must be informed that she must make a choice between those legal rights and her mental health.

Because restrictive rules on the admissibility of hypnotically refreshed recollections may ultimately disqualify the patient from testifying in court, important issues of informed consent were first raised by Scheflin (1993). Even though the therapist scrupulously followed all standards of professional competence, the therapist's failure to protect those rights could result in malpractice liability. The law is moving dramatically close to recognizing a client's cause of action against a therapist for deprivation of the patient's legal rights. So far, two of the following three steps have successfully been taken toward that possibility.

STEP 1: HYPNOTIZED PATIENT LATER DISQUALIFIED IN COURT   In *State v. Grimmet* (1990), a woman claimed she had been sexually abused by the defendant. A sexual assault counselor advised her to see a psychologist "to clarify her memory of the incident by hypnosis." The counselor felt that the use of hypnosis in this context would be therapeutic. The psychologist used hypnosis during all three of their sessions. When the victim was later called in court to testify against the defendant, the court ruled her posthypnotic testimony was inadmissible. The fact that the psychologist had used hypnosis solely for therapy, and not for investigative purposes, carried no weight with the Minnesota judges. According to the court, the therapeutic practice of hypnosis deprived the client of her legal right to testify.

In *State v. Mitchell* (1989), Patricia Tyrrell had been sleeping on the floor at a friend's house when a gunman burst in and started shooting. Tyrrell escaped, but others in the house were killed. Two months later, Tyrrell went to UCLA and was hypnotized. According to the Utah court, "She did this on her own and entirely independent of any action on the part of the police in an attempt to improve her memory so that she could identify the gunman. . . ." Tyrrell had had at least 20 in-person and telephone interviews with the police about the case before she was hypnotized. The police had shown her a picture of the defendant and they identified him as their prime suspect. As a result of the hypnosis, Tyrrell remembered many new details. The hypnosis session was videotaped. The night before appearing at a preliminary hearing, Tyrrell reviewed the videotape "four or five times."

The Utah Supreme Court followed its earlier *per se* exclusion rule and held Tyrell's hypnotically refreshed testimony inadmissible on the grounds of inherent unreliability. The Court took notice of the fact that the hypnosis had been Tyrrell's own act independent of police investigative requests, but this fact was not held to be important.

In *People v. Reese* (1985), a woman who had been sexually assaulted sought therapy for the purpose of restoring her memory for the event. Only after several hypnosis sessions was she able to recall what had happened. The defendant sought to suppress her testimony under Michigan's *per se* rule. In a crucial passage the Court noted:

On this appeal, the people argue that the [*per se*] holding should be limited to "forensic hypnosis" and not applied to the instant case involving "Therapeutic Hypnosis." We disagree. . . . While the dangers of suggestion may be dramatically reduced in nondirective therapeutic hypnosis in comparison to investigative hypnosis used by the police, there still remain the dangers that the subject may not have accurate recall and neither the subject nor the hypnotists can distinguish between the truth and confabulation.

The Court continued by noting that "The fact that therapeutic hypnosis is largely nonsuggestive may support a conclusion that prehypnotic testimony has not been tainted by the hypnosis." In this case, however, there was no prehypnotic recall.

In jurisdictions where the *per se* rule has not been adopted, on the other hand, courts have been more sympathetic to the interests of patients and therapists. In *Key v. State* (1983), a psychiatrist who failed to record the hypnosis sessions, but who met the other relevant guidelines, was held to be justified where he had not anticipated having to testify at trial because his use of hypnosis was solely "in a therapy context to help alleviate the victim's stress and trauma."

In *People v. McKeehan* (1986), the Colorado Court of Appeals was asked to admit the posthypnotic tes-

timony of a victim who had undergone hypnotic relaxation therapy by a mental health counselor before testifying. The "hypnosis" involved only "physical relaxation, deep breathing, and visualizing being in a pleasant place." The victim "was not questioned and no suggestions were made to her under hypnosis; rather, the sole purpose of the hypnosis was to allow her to relax and overcome her anxiety about testifying." The Colorado court held that the victim would be permitted to testify because the hypnosis did not involve techniques to enhance memory.

Even in some *per se* jurisdictions, the courts have chosen to soften the rigors of the rule, but only under very limited circumstances. The most extensive discussion is found in *McGlauflin v. State* (1993), where a young girl's mother wanted her to see a hypnotist for weight loss purposes. The young girl at first objected because "you have to tell [hypnotists] everything." When her mother asked what she meant, she said that she was afraid the hypnotist "would get out of me what [defendant] did to me." A witness testified that the young girl told her that "following hypnosis, she had remembered many details of the abuse that she had previously put out of her mind." The Alaska Court of Appeals found no error in the admission of the young girl's testimony, but the court reached this result only because it determined that (1) the girl had informed her mother, before any hypnosis, that defendant had molested her, (2) the hypnosis was conducted primarily for weight loss, (3) the hypnosis session was not intended for memory enhancement, (4) the hypnotist asked only two questions about the molesting—"Can you see the man who molested you?" and, after receiving a "yes" answer, "Do you want to say anything to him?"— the answer to which was "no," thereby ending the discussion, (5) the hypnotist testified that the only posthypnotic suggestion was for the girl to be more self-confident, and (6) the hypnosis session occurred before any legal action was contemplated.

Alaska, in the *Contreras v. State* (1986) case, had adopted a strict rule of excluding posthypnotic testimony. The question in *McGlauflin* was whether hypnosis performed for purely therapeutic reasons fell within the restrictions of *Contreras*. The Court of Appeals held that

Contreras applies to any situation in which a witness's memory has been enhanced or altered by hypnosis, regardless of the motive of the hypnotist. . . . [H]ypnosis performed for non-forensic purposes may also result in altered memory; and, when this is true, the *Contreras* rule should apply.

* * *

The *Contreras* rule is designed to insulate judicial decision-making from the false "memories" that can be created when it is employed to refresh or enhance a witness's recollection of events. But, . . . this danger does not arise from the simple experience of hypnosis itself. Rather, the danger is created when the hypnosis session is aimed at reviving or enhancing a witness's memories, or when (regardless of the hypnotist's subjective aim) the session is conducted in a manner that makes it likely that hypnosis has enhanced or altered the witness's memories of the events being litigated.

Thus, whenever hypnosis is used in therapy for the purpose of memory enhancement, retrieval, or refreshing, even if no forensic issue appears to be involved, the hypnotized subject will be disqualified from testifying at a later trial. In *McGlauflin*, because the hypnosis did not involve memory enhancement, and because the hypnosis did not focus on details of the molesting, the young girl who had been hypnotized was not disqualified from recounting details of the molesting she remembered after the hypnosis.

STEP 2: DISQUALIFIED WITNESS SUES HYPNOTIST

A woman from Illinois has taken the next step of suing the person responsible for having had her hypnotized, and thereby having had her disqualified from testifying. On the evening of September 2, 1982, a distraught Cathy Burns phoned the police to report that "an unknown assailant had entered her house, knocked her unconscious, and shot and wounded her two sons while they slept."

The officers assigned to the case began to suspect Burns even though she had passed a polygraph test and a voice stress test and had submitted exculpatory handwriting samples. Though Burns protested her innocence throughout, the officers theorized that Burns might have multiple personalities. Concerned about the legal consequences of using hypnosis on Burns, the officers asked the local prosecutor, Richard Reed, whether they should hypnotize her. Reed recommended hypnosis, though the police officers continued to harbor doubts that the technique would be found legal.

While undergoing hypnosis, Burns made some ambiguous statements that the officers interpreted as incriminating. She referred to both herself and the shooter as "Katie," which the police interpreted as support for their multiple personality theory. The prosecutor was again consulted and Reed told them that the hypnotic statements, though ambiguous, nevertheless constituted probable cause to arrest Cathy Burns.

Burns was arrested. The day after the arrest, at the probable cause hearing, one of the officers, in response to Reed's questioning, stated that Burns had "confessed" to shooting her children. The judge was not told, by the officer or by Reed, that the "confession" was ambiguous at best, was procured while Burns was undergoing hypnosis, and was inconsistent with Burns' repeated denials of guilt. As a consequence, Burns lost her job, was placed in a psychiatric ward for four months, was threatened with loss of custody of her two sons, and faced criminal prosecution.

Burns was successful, at a pretrial hearing, in suppressing the statements she made under hypnosis. Because this improper use of hypnosis on a suspect prevented prosecution, Reed dropped all charges against Burns. Reed told reporters, however, that he still believed Burns was guilty but liberal judges refuse to allow prosecutors to put criminals in jail (*Burns v. Reed*, 1990).

Burns filed a lawsuit against the police and Reed claiming that they had violated her civil and constitutional rights. The police settled before trial for $250,000, but Reed claimed absolute immunity for his acts, and also for the advice he gave to the police to hypnotize Burns. The Court of Appeal, affirming the district judge, held that the prosecutor was absolutely immune from liability.

When Burns' case was argued before the United States Supreme Court (*Burns v. Reed*, 1991), the issue to be decided was whether absolute prosecutorial immunity applied to Reed's (1) participation in the probable cause hearing (by eliciting false testimony from the officer), (2) legal opinion authorizing the police to use hypnosis, and (3) legal opinion as to the existence of probable cause based on Burns' hypnotically induced ambiguous statements.

The Supreme Court held that Reed's participation in the probable cause hearing was absolutely immune from civil liability. The legal advice he gave to the police, however, was held not "so intimately associated with the judicial phase of the criminal process" to warrant granting absolute immunity, either at common law or currently. In essence, as Justice Scalia expressly noted in his concurring opinion, "I agree that a prosecutor has absolute immunity for eliciting false statements in a judicial hearing, and that he has only qualified immunity for giving legal advice to police officers" (p. 1945). Thus, the path was cleared for Cathy Burns to have her day in court on her civil rights claims against Reed. Ultimately, however, she was unable to prevail.

In *Burns v. Reed* (1995), Cathy Burns was back to the Seventh Circuit Court of Appeals arguing that the District Attorney did not have a qualified immunity for (1) authorizing the interrogation of Burns "while she was under hypnosis," and (2) advising the police later that, "based primarily on the results of the hypnosis session," there was probable cause to arrest Burns. In order to succeed, Burns had to show that the District Attorney's conduct (1) violated a constitutional right and (2) the constitutional right was clearly established at the time the District Attorney made his decisions. Burns claimed that her constitutional rights were violated by the hypnosis session, and she cited to the court a string of cases involving the extraction of coerced confessions. She further argued that "psychological as well as physical pressure can overbear a suspect's will such that a resulting statement violates due process." The Seventh Circuit noted that many criminal interrogations contain "tactics that are at least arguably manipulative [as hypnosis] and by definition designed to extract information from recalcitrant suspects, while still falling within the boundaries of what is constitutionally permissible." The court stated that hypnosis

admittedly suffers from some unique defects—its known effects include increased suggestibility, a tendency to "confabulate" or fill in gaps with fictitious details, an inability to sift fantasy from fact

and an unwarranted boost in the subject's confidence in what he is relating.

The Seventh Circuit found that Burns was "allegedly subjected while in a vulnerable and highly suggestive hypnotic state to bullying and intimidation from the investigative officers, approved (and later concealed) by the [District Attorney]. This is a disturbing scenario that conceivably could skirt the edges of constitutional propriety."

Assuming Burns' constitutional rights had been violated, was it clear at the time of violation that she had that constitutional right? As the court noted, Burns "must offer more than the fact that federal case law clearly frowns on coercive interrogation; she must demonstrate that coercive interrogation clearly includes hypnosis, and did so at the time of the events in question." Burns failed to meet this burden. According to the court, "Our own search reveals that in 1982, the time of the complained-of conduct, courts were split on the validity of admitting confessions from suspects who complained that they had been hypnotized; but few, if any, courts posed the inquiry in constitutional terms—and several were unwilling to exclude statements from suspects who had been hypnotized." Has the hypnosis of a suspect become a violation of constitutional rights? The court does not answer this question, though the opinion notes that the United States Supreme Court decision in *Rock v. Arkansas* (1987) showed that no constitutional right existed as of that date. There are no developments after *Rock* that suggest hypnosis violates constitutional rights.

Burns lost her case against the District Attorney. The Seventh Circuit concluded that, although the District Attorney may have been in error in concluding the hypnosis information constituted probable cause, the mistake was reasonable and so the qualified immunity protects it. Therefore, regarding the authorization of the hypnosis session and the statement that it constituted probable cause, the qualified immunity protected the District Attorney for his conduct at that time.

Therapists, of course, do not enjoy any immunity. They are vulnerable to lawsuits from patients.

STEP 3: DISQUALIFIED PATIENT SUES THERAPIST The final step, a patient suing a therapist for violating his or her legal rights by using hypnosis therapeutically, is sure to follow, unless the therapist takes adequate precautions. Therapists from around the country have reported being threatened with such suits or narrowly avoiding them by asking specific prehypnosis questions about potential forensic matters that might arise. At least since the famous *Tarasoff* (1976) case, which required mental health officials to protect or warn third parties threatened by potentially violent clients, therapists have been aware that obedience to legal rules is a necessary aspect of the practice of therapy. With reference to the use of therapeutic hypnosis, the obligation to conform the practice of therapy to the mandate of law is even stronger because here the duty is owed directly to the patient, not to a third party.

The possibility that hypnotherapists might be sued for disqualifying their patients from testifying in court has been the subject of discussion in recent years at all major hypnosis conferences and many major mental health conferences. It is too late for therapists to argue in defense that they were unaware of the legal rules.

Therapists may take steps to protect themselves from this malpractice liability by drafting informed consent forms for their clients to sign. An example is provided in the American Society for Clinical Hypnosis' *Clinical Hypnosis and Memory: Guidelines for Clinicians and for Forensic Hypnosis* (Hammond et al., 1995). Because of this potential liability, an increasing number of therapists now report using informed consent forms before any hypnosis work is done.

It is important to note what the informed consent form is *not* intended to do: (1) it is not intended to protect therapists who use hypnosis when reasonable hypnosis specialists would agree that hypnosis should not have been used, and (2) it is not intended to protect therapists who use hypnosis when reasonable hypnosis specialists would agree that the hypnosis was performed below the legal standard of care, as, for example, if there is undue suggestion, leading questions, etc. The informed consent form accomplishes the following goals: (1) it alerts the patient to a potential legal problem so that the patient can make a fully informed choice, (2) it alerts therapists to the need to protect the legal rights of their patients, (3) it alerts therapists

to protect themselves from liability by delivering important information the patient needs to have in order to make an informed choice about the use of hypnosis, and (4) it reminds therapists to be extra cautious when using hypnosis with memory retrieval.

Advocates of the *per se* exclusion rule object to the use of informed consent forms on the grounds that (1) because, in their view, hypnosis always contaminates memory, hypnosis should never be used with memory in the first place, and (2) it may be illegal or unethical to obtain informed consent to have a person's memory permanently altered. Thus, the patient can never give an informed consent.

As we have seen in chapter 10, hypnosis does not always contaminate memory. Concerning the second objection, the law does permit informed consent for personality changing procedures (psychosurgery), memory altering procedures (electroshock therapy), and memory altering substances (alcohol and psychiatric drugs) (Shapiro & Spece, 1981). There seems little doubt that courts would permit a competent person *knowingly* to consent to a memory altering therapy. Such a case might involve a simple desire to obtain additional information about the past, even at the expense of potential contamination.

At the extreme, we can imagine the following case. Suppose a woman in her late twenties visits a therapist, complaining about severe depression as a consequence of having been molested by her father and ignored by her mother. The patient has tried many therapies, both organic and dynamic. None has relieved the depression. Should she be permitted to consent to having her memories altered in favor of a pleasant childhood?

Dr. Herbert Spiegel has described to us a case he handled during World War II. A soldier in combat saw his best friend shot and seriously wounded. The troop was retreating and the soldier was torn between staying with his injured friend or retreating to safety. He chose to retreat, but suffered severe symptoms as a consequence. Spiegel hypnotized him and implanted a false memory that he had seen his friend die. After the therapy, the soldier's symptoms disappeared and he actually went back into combat. Should the law have said that he had no right to consent to the falsehood?

Additional support for therapeutic false memory implantation may be found in Gravitz (1994), where the author defends the reconstruction of memory as a valid technique with severe trauma patients and notes that others have reported success with the technique (Lamb, 1985; Miller, 1986).

Courts generally test questions of consent by asking if the patient had the capacity to consent—in other words, sufficient understanding and judgment to make a choice based on full disclosure of potential consequences. If an adult has the capacity, the choice will be honored. Indeed, the California Supreme Court has held that criminal defendants are entitled to argue before juries that they should receive the death penalty (*People v. Bloom*, 1989; *People v. Stansbury*, 1993). If people can be competent to choose to die, they are likely to be competent in choosing how they want to live.

Provided there is a full disclosure, patients who are competent may consent to the use of hypnosis with memory, even if it were true that hypnosis always contaminates memory. Of course, the informed consent form would have to articulate the adverse consequences of using hypnosis for memory work.

Laboratory Experiments and Informed Consent

It should be noted that hypnosis laboratory researchers are also at risk for lawsuits based on negligence and breach of contract. The innocent subject who volunteers to participate in a laboratory experiment utilizing hypnosis, especially if memory work is involved, does not consent to lose his or her legal rights. Failure to explain to the subject, before the experiment, that hypnosis could disqualify the subject from testifying in court violates the subject's legal rights.

Ironically, the *per se* exclusion rule threatens especially those laboratory experiments designed to prove or disprove the rule's validity. Because of the judicial and legislative interest in forensic hypnosis issues in the 1980s, and because of the absence of real data on hypnosis and memory a decade ago (McCann & Sheehan, 1988), laboratory experiments on these topics have exploded in number. In the absence of informed consent, any of the research subjects who is adversely affected may sue the experimenters.

While the threat to therapists and experimenters can be handled with an informed consent form, the threat to patients is more severe. A judicial rule

should stand only for as long as it appears to be just and fair and necessary. In judging fairness, courts have been primarily concerned with the accuracy and reliability of hypnotically refreshed courtroom testimony. The right of the patient to be healed, and the right of the therapist to practice competent therapy, have been of virtually no concern to the courts because these factors have gone unmentioned. Many patients will be forced to choose between their health rights and their legal rights. If they choose hypnosis, they forfeit later court relief. If they do not choose hypnosis, they give up a valuable therapeutic agent. Opponents argue that the law should not force this harsh choice (Scheflin, 1997d).

Sex with Hypnotists

Suppose the therapist uses hypnosis to induce trance and then has illicit sexual relations with the patient. Unfortunately, many such cases are now pending in courtrooms across the country, and the participants are often paraded on national and local television talk shows. May the therapist argue that because of the hypnosis, the patient is disqualified from testifying? At least one court has held that the answer is "yes" (Spiegel, 1987) because the *per se* exclusion rule prohibits the introduction of memories that first appear during or after hypnosis.

Indeed, not only would the victims be disqualified from testifying, the police would be unable to obtain evidence by using undercover officers masquerading as potential customers. As soon as hypnotic techniques are used on these officers, they too would become disqualified as witnesses. The assaulter would become "investigative-resistant" and "conviction-proof." In these seduction cases, the *per se* inadmissibility rule becomes a license to rape (Scheflin, 1994a). Imagine a rapist who "hypnotizes" his victims immediately before assaulting them. Under a strict reading of the prevailing judicial rule, his victims could not testify against him.

Most courts are reaching a more sensible result by refusing to apply the *per se* exclusion rule in these cases. In *People v. Hughes* (1983), the New York Court of Appeals noted that "A criminal trial for rape or assault would present an odd spectacle if the victim was barred from saying anything, including the fact that the crime occurred, simply because he or she submitted to hypnosis sometime prior to trial to aid the investigation or obtain needed medical treatment." The Court therefore permitted the admission of prehypnotic recall.

In *Matter of Raynes* (1985), Raynes, a police officer with a longstanding exemplary record, opened a "private hypnosis service to aid people suffering from weight and smoking problems." Business prospered, but rumors began to spread of sexual advances made by Raynes toward his female clients. The Police Commission held a hearing to determine whether Raynes' activities violated the police code of conduct. Five women were permitted to testify that Raynes used hypnosis with them prior to initiating sexual contact. The hypnotic inductions themselves were filled with sexual images. The Supreme Court of Montana upheld Raynes' dismissal from the police force, but the court did not discuss the legal issue of the admission of posthypnotic testimony (Watkins, undated).

In *Hickey v. Askren* (1991), plaintiff alleged a series of torts committed by the defendant-therapist when he had sex with her while providing therapy. Unfortunately for her, the statute of limitations had run on all counts. The Georgia court noted that this was not a case of repressed memory and that there was "no evidence that [her] therapy included the use of drugs, hypnosis, or any other treatment whereby [she] may have incurred damage without her knowledge, so as to render this case analogous to situations which occur when a patient's injury has been concealed by the fraud of the tortfeasor." Thus, the court suggests that the statute of limitations would not run in a case where a defendant used hypnosis to seduce a patient. But, even if the statute would not bar plaintiff's claim, would plaintiff be permitted to testify about these posthypnotic events? The Georgia court was silent on this point.

In *People v. Sorscher* (1986), a Michigan court was more explicit on that point. The defendant, a dentist who used hypnosis on patients and friends, was accused of making sexual advances to males. He argued that the testimony of the alleged victims was inherently unreliable because it concerned events that occurred while the witnesses were in an hypnotic trance. Michigan followed a rule that hypnosis produces inherently unreliable results thereby tainting witnesses from providing admissible testimony (*People v. Gonzales*, 1982). Should the dentist

be permitted to suppress all the truthful testimony?

The court refused to apply the Michigan *per se* exclusion rule to this case:

> We perceive that the thrust of *Gonzales* is to exclude testimony which has been obtained through hypnosis as a method for improving a witness's memory. . . . In the case at bar, hypnosis was not used as a scientific technique to obtain evidence against defendant. Rather, it was used by defendant as an aid in the commission of a sexual assault.
>
> Moreover, we hold that, as a matter of public policy, a defendant should not be able to put a person under hypnosis, sexually assault that person and then claim that the person is incompetent to testify because the testimony is tainted by hypnosis.

It makes little judicial sense, and serves no cause of justice, to exclude posthypnotic recollections in these sex cases. But, once such testimony is admitted in these cases, is it fair to exclude posthypnotic testimony in *all* other types of cases?

Law Professor Paul C. Giannelli (1995), an expert on the rules of evidence and a supporter of the *per se* exclusion rule, acknowledges that the rule requires an exception in these cases, "Scheflin (1994a) makes a convincing argument for an exception in cases in which the crime occurs while the victim is hypnotized" (p. 222).

Perry, Orne, London, and Orne (1996), strong defenders of the *per se* rule, also acknowledge that an exception is inevitable in this situation:

> Scheflin (1994a) argues persuasively for the admission of evidence from a previously hypnotized crime victim, for instance, a female patient who alleges sexual relationships initiated by a therapist in the course of a hypnosis therapy session. Here there would appear to be no other course but to permit such a witness to testify; to do otherwise would be a clarion call to individuals wishing to engage in unconsenting sexuality without legal penalty by learning and applying hypnotic induction techniques. (p. 77)

Karlin (1997), arguing for a broader exception, notes that "if patients are abused in any way during hypnosis, the fact that they were hypnotized should not prevent them from testifying about the abuse" (p. 36). Thus, if a patient sues a therapist for hypnotically implanting false memories, this "abuse" during hypnosis will allow the patient to testify despite the fact that the recollections are all during or after hypnosis.

Self-Hypnosis

Suppose the victim of a violent crime buys and listens to a self-hypnosis relaxation tape. These tapes, many of which are admittedly of questionable value, are now available everywhere. Will this victim thereby be disqualified from testifying in court because she had been "hypnotized" by this tape? Technically, the answer is "yes," though no case has yet decided this precise issue.

In the Ohio case of *West v. Howard* (1991), the plaintiff's car and the defendant's car collided. The plaintiff brought suit but had no memory of the events leading up to the crash and no memory of the crash itself. The plaintiff sought the assistance of a social worker "trained in trance techniques," who taught plaintiff self-hypnosis and who supervised the gradual memory recall. The Ohio Supreme Court, in *State v. Johnston* (1988), had previously ruled that hypnotically refreshed recollection would be admissible provided the trial judge determines, by clear and convincing evidence, that under the totality of circumstances the testimony is reliable. The Orne guidelines are used as factors the trial judge may consider.

Would this ruling apply to self-hypnotic techniques? The Court of Appeals in *West* said yes:

> . . . this court is of the opinion that a hypnotic technique, such as the one used in the case before us, in which the patient or client herself controls the memory retrieval process could never meet the standard for reliability set forth in *Johnston*. . . . The guidelines and factors enunciated by the *Johnston* court require that the hypnosis session be conducted by a neutral qualified mental health professional and that the process of retrieval be documented so that it can be reviewed by the court for the dangers inherent in that process. The technique of self-hypnosis, as employed in this case, involves none of these safeguards and, because it is a learned technique, is subject to all of the dangers associated with hypnotic therapy. . . . That is, the suggestiveness involved in learning the technique and [plaintiff's] motivation for retrieving the memory render any subsequent memories refreshed through self-hypnosis inherently unreliable.

The *West* court was probably influenced by its view that although "self-hypnosis" is allegedly at issue, the social worker was "fully involved in the retrieval process and . . . there was considerable interaction" between plaintiff and the social worker. Furthermore, the plaintiff was encouraged to remember the accident "in order to relieve her emotional feelings" regarding the crash. Accuracy of the memory was thus less important than the emotional catharsis.

Another case that raises the issue of self-hypnosis as a means to refresh memory is *State v. Schreiner* (1991), which has a somewhat unusual fact pattern. Defendant Schreiner was tried for attempted murder and found not responsible because of a mental disease or defect, and he was sent to a psychiatric center. As part of his treatment, Schreiner received hypnotic therapy and was taught self-hypnosis. Both techniques were used for the purpose of relieving Schreiner's feelings of guilt and helping him remember whether he had committed other crimes.

After several years, doctors pronounced Schreiner cured and a hearing was scheduled concerning his transfer to another facility. Schreiner agreed to a psychiatric examination and was told that whatever he said would not be confidential and would be turned over to the prosecutor. Nevertheless, during the examination, Schreiner stated that several years earlier, following a "self-hypnotic episode," he "remembered" that he had killed Jamie Amsterdamer.

Schreiner is now on trial for the murder of Amsterdamer. He wants to suppress his statement as a product of hypnosis. Schreiner's therapist, to whom he had confessed the crime years before revealing it at the psychiatric examination, testified that although Schreiner "was not under hypnosis when he told her of these events, his statement resulted from the 'therapy or posthypnotic suggestion.'" Schreiner provided expert support for the claim that his statement had a "high probability of confabulation."

The New York Court of Appeals held that

> . . . the record supports no other inference than that defendant's statement was hypnotically induced. The evidence was that he initially thought he hadn't committed the Amsterdamer murder about which he had been questioned and that he "remembered" his involvement following an episode of self-hypnosis. The conclusion is thus inescapable that his recollection was the result of hypnotic therapy and posthypnotic suggestion. Because such recollections are inherently unreliable, the defendant's statement should not have been admitted into evidence against him.

The most recent case to raise this self-hypnosis issue is *People v. Sterling* (1992), a New York County Court decision. Defendant was the prime suspect in the murder of a 74-year-old woman whose testimony as a rape victim resulted in the conviction of defendant's brother for the offense. The defendant received full notification of his rights and was well aware that the police had focused their investigation on him.

Police officers picked up the defendant at 5:45 P.M. on the night of July 10, 1991, for more questioning. At that time the defendant agreed to submit to a polygraph, and he agreed to answer police questions. He was aware that he was not under arrest, and that he was free to stop talking or to leave whenever he wished.

At 11:20 P.M., Inspector Crough began questioning the defendant. Crough talked with the defendant about the defendant's "anger because his brother had been wrongfully accused and convicted of raping Viola Manville." Crough said he thought defendant had hurt Manville but did not mean to let things "go that far." Defendant requested hypnosis to help him remember the events of that night. The police refused to permit hypnosis.

At 12:45 A.M. the next morning, defendant again asked to be hypnotized and was again refused. Officer Sennett, who had no training in relaxation, just "winged it" when defendant asked for help to relax. Sennett "asked the defendant to lay down on the floor, to keep his feet up on the chair, and to take four deep breaths." Sennett held defendant's hand. After questions seeking memories of that evening, defendant responded that he saw himself

walking on the path and he saw, in the bushes, the naked body of "the lady with the white hair." When asked his feelings, defendant said, "Now, I'm feeling happy." Defendant then jumped up, saying, "This is all bullshit. I didn't do nothing." The defendant then threw his glasses against the wall.

Following "dinner" at 2:00 A.M., defendant's third request to be hypnotized was rejected. He was told that the police knew he did it and that he would feel a lot better if he would admit it. Crough and Sennett began massaging the defendant's back and shoulders, telling him, in a soft voice, that he must be in pain. They told him that he would feel better if he told the truth. Defendant confessed.

The court concluded that defendant was never under arrest, had been fully informed of his rights, had been made no false promises or representations, and had experienced no improper conduct or undue influence. Thus, the confession was voluntary.

Defendant argued that he had undergone a "self-hypnotic" experience, which resulted in his confession. An expert psychologist testified that the defendant "was highly responsive to hypnotic suggestion, and had an unusually high hypnotic capacity as measured by the Hypnotic Induction Profile, the Barber Suggestibility test, and the Barber Creative Imagination Scale." Thus, there was a "very high likelihood" that defendant "underwent a hypnotic event" while being questioned. The expert said it was "self-hypnosis in response to circumstances he was exposed to."

Defendant claimed that he had learned a hypnotic relaxation technique, similar to that used by the police who questioned him, from a friend, and that he still used the technique as a way to deal with stress.

Dr. Herbert Spiegel testified for the prosecution. After examining the defendant using the Hypnotic Induction Profile and "a cluster structural survey, i.e., a personality inventory test," Spiegel said that, though the defendant was in the top 25% of the population in ability to be hypnotized, there is no evidence that he actually was in hypnosis during the questioning. Relaxation is different from hypnosis, and no formal induction ceremonies for hypnosis were present. According to the judge, "even if this court dispensed with a showing that a defendant underwent a formal hypnotic event, the credible evidence does not support the defendant's contention that he underwent a self-hypnotic event when 'relaxed' by Officer Sennett. The court adopts the testimony of Dr. Spiegel and finds it credible."

Does the New York *per se* exclusion rule apply where there are no formal induction ceremonies? The court held it did not. Noting that all prior New York cases involved a formal induction process, here the fact that "a friend with no known training or expertise allegedly taught him a relaxation technique" is not a sufficient basis to say that defendant experienced a hypnotic event. Thus, "there was no hypnosis as defined in New York and no suggestion made in hypnosis that might infect his later statement." On appeal, the Appellate Division of the New York Supreme Court in *People v. Sterling* (1994) agreed by noting that the "defendant failed to prove that the state he achieved by use of a relaxation technique learned from a friend constituted hypnosis" (p. 449).

What ultimately is the rule for the admissibility of memories recovered after self-hypnosis? No court has answered this question with finality.

Nonhypnosis Hypnosis

Police, sensitive to the restrictive rulings involving hypnosis, are presently utilizing hypnotic techniques but refraining from calling such interrogations "hypnotic." Do the exclusionary rules pertaining to hypnosis also apply to "visualization," "guided imagery," or "relaxation"? So far, a rose by any other name is not, in the eyes of the law, a rose.

In *State v. Varela* (1991), a child was referred to a psychotherapist after suffering nightmares, mood swings, and other problems. At first the child revealed very little. The therapist used "relaxation therapy," which he described "as telling the child to take a few deep breaths, to begin to notice the sounds outside, and to think about what she was feeling" (p. 733). The therapist's supervisor said the technique was "Ericksonian hypnosis" but he also stated that practitioners of classical hypnosis would not label the technique as hypnosis. Both testified that there was minimal risk of suggestion and that the child made a first report after the relaxation about having been sexually abused by the defendant.

The child testified that the relaxation therapy did not bring back memories because she had not forgotten or repressed the sexual assaults. Because there was no pre-relaxation statement from the child, and the only testimony about the molestations was post-relaxation, the issue was raised of whether the child was disqualified from testifying under New Mexico's *State v. Beachum* (1981) decision, which had adopted the requirement that the "Orne guidelines" be followed before hypnotically refreshed recollection would be admissible.

The New Mexico court distinguished *Beachum* in two respects:

> First, *Beachum* involved the use of classical hypnosis; here Ericksonian hypnosis was used. There is evidence in the record that Ericksonian hypnosis does not create the same reliability problems as classical hypnosis.
>
> * * *
>
> The second distinction is that here the subject matter of the disclosure by the hypnotized witness was totally unanticipated by the hypnotist. This was not a case of hypnosis conducted for forensic purposes. . . . It is undisputed that the purpose of the hypnosis of the victim was therapy and no one present at the session, with the possible exception of the victim herself, had any reason to believe that the victim would disclose any allegations of sexual abuse. . . . The surprise was not in the matter of detail—such as the identity of the perpetrator of a crime—but of the very existence of an offense.

In a circumstance where "it is totally unanticipated that the hypnosis session will produce a disclosure relevant to litigation," the safeguards of *Beachum* are quite meaningless. That does not mean, however, that this "therapeutic" hypnosis is free of reliability problems. With *Beachum* inapplicable and the reliability problems present, what rule should be adopted?

The New Mexico court chose to put its faith in trial judges. In these "therapeutic" hypnosis cases where legally relevant disclosures are unexpected, trial judges should determine whether the prosecutor has shown, by clear and convincing evidence, that the use of hypnosis "was reasonably likely to result in recall comparable in accuracy to normal human memory." The court said that, because the child's revelations came as such a complete shock to the therapist, the trial judge "could properly determine that the possibility of improper suggestion at the session was sufficiently small that the victim's testimony should be admitted at trial. Indeed, the district court could find that the victim's recollection predated the session and was not refreshed by hypnosis."

The court did not decide whether separate rules should apply to Ericksonian hypnosis. Instead, the court noted that "the record in this case is inadequate for us to state definitively that the *Beachum* safeguards are unnecessary when Ericksonian hypnosis is used. We therefore do not rest our decision on that ground. We leave that issue to a future case."

The New Mexico result protects patients and therapists without unduly infringing upon the rights of defendants.

Colorado also has protected the victim in *People v. McKeehan* (1986). Here, the victim of an alleged sexual assault was treated by a mental health counselor with "hypnotic relaxation therapy," which consisted of "physical relaxation, deep breathing, and visualizing being in a pleasant place." According to the court, "[the victim] was not questioned and no suggestions were made to her under hypnosis; rather, the sole purpose of the hypnosis was to allow her to relax and overcome her anxiety about testifying." Defendant argued that the hypnosis disqualified the witness from testifying. The court disagreed. Because the hypnosis was not used to refresh the witness's memory, none of the prior restrictive rulings was applicable. Nothing in the record indicated that the victim was given suggestions, and nothing indicated that she made relevant remarks while in trance. Defendant claimed that "even if her memory were not refreshed, her hypnotic relaxation so affected her demeanor before the jury as to deny him due process of law." The Court rejected this argument by noting that the defendant was free to use the hypnotic relaxation to impeach the victim's credibility, but not to deny her the right to testify.

Murray v. State (1991) raised the interesting issue of whether the use of "progressive relaxation" techniques constitutes "hypnosis." The Court held it did not. In this case the victim underwent a hypnotic procedure that the psychologist called "progressive relaxation." In court the psychologist testified that this procedure "is an induction that you can use for hypnosis," but he stated that in his opinion the victim was not hypnotized: "I believe

[the victim] to be in a heavy state or a good solid state of relaxation. As far as trance state hypnosis, I do not believe that she reached a trance state of hypnosis." The court held that the victim was not hypnotized and therefore could testify.

In these cases courts must make a case-by-case analysis to determine whether undue suggestion occurred. Why should the name of the technique make any difference? The real issue is whether the evidence is reliable. In fact, although techniques of relaxation, guided imagery, and visualization may be used as a prelude to the induction of trance, they are not identical to hypnosis and should not automatically be treated as if the subject had entered an hypnotic state. Furthermore, these techniques have never been shown to be inherently unduly suggestive.

Again, the crucial issue is whether reliable and accurate information has been obtained, not what the technique was called. Application of a *per se* disqualification rule, or any rule, should not turn on a label.

False Confession Cases

A problem about the reach of the anti-hypnosis *per se* disqualification rule remains unresolved in cases of spontaneous hypnosis. Courts have generally seen hypnosis issues within the context of a formalized ritual of trance induction, deepening techniques, age regression or memory enhancement, and trance conclusion. However, as Beahrs (1989) has noted, "Both hypnotic phenomena and hypnotic transactions occur widely outside a professional setting, or in structured settings whose overt purpose is not to achieve or utilize hypnosis *per se*." What about cases where spontaneous trance occurs, such as in police interrogations?

Herbert Spiegel is credited with first raising this issue in 1976 in the famous *Reilly v. Connecticut* case, where the police talked a highly suggestible young man into confessing that he killed his mother (Connery, 1977).

Ofshe (1989, 1992) has recently provided detailed instances of false confessions in police interrogations that were not formal hypnosis sessions, but which, he alleged, utilized trance techniques. Gudjonsson (1992) has done extensive work in England on false confession cases. A detailed description of the use of trance techniques in police interrogations may be found in the briefs of the California Supreme Court case of *People v. Alcala* (1992).

Cases of spontaneous trance, as well as false confession cases, raise a larger problem about the role of suggestion in general, apart from formal trance procedures (Gheorghiu, Netter, Eysenck, & Rosenthal, 1989; Schumaker, 1991). It is senseless for the courts to maintain a rule that is easily avoided by not using the word "hypnosis" or is ignored where subjects go into trance unnoticed.

Civil Cases

Despite the hundreds of court rulings on forensic hypnosis in the last two decades, there is no general rule about hypnosis in civil cases. Karlin (1997) has recently noted that "as Scheflin and Shapiro (1989) predicted, we are seeing increasing use of hypnosis in the civil arena" (p. 35). Karlin and Orne (1996) state that they "know of two kinds of civil cases: those involving automobile accidents and those involving memories of child sexual abuse" (p. 82). In the former category, but including accidents without automobiles and also other civil actions, such as harassment, approximately 25 appellate legal decisions have been published, but no general rule may be extracted from them, other than it appears to be the case that whatever rule that state follows in criminal cases will be adopted in deciding civil cases.

Must amnesia caused by traumatic accidents persist because hypnosis cannot be utilized to offer relief? Three people are driving in a car when suddenly it swerves off the highway and plunges into a lake. Only one person, the car's owner, survives the tragedy. But he has no memory of either the accident or the events preceding it. Retrograde amnesia under these conditions of traumatic emotional shock is not unusual (Brunn, 1968; Loftus & Burns, 1982). The parents of one of the passengers sues the surviving owner. At issue is who was driving the vehicle—the deceased plaintiff or the surviving defendant/owner? If all other memory restoration techniques fail, may hypnosis be used to obtain an answer? The court in *Savin v. Allstate Insurance Company* (1991), faced this issue but did not resolve it.

Hughes (1991) notes that legal rules concerning the admissibility of hypnotically refreshed recollec-

tion have not been settled in civil cases in most states. In *Alsbach v. Bader* (1985), the Missouri Supreme Court adopted a *per se* exclusion rule. The court rejected the safeguards approach because

> such safeguards do not adequately address how a lay person, such as a trial judge or juror, will recognize when the hypnotized subject has lost his critical judgment and begun to credit "memories" that were formerly viewed as unreliable. Nor do safeguards provide a means for distinguishing between actual recall and confabulation invented and employed to fill gaps in the story.

The Supreme Court concluded that hypnotically refreshed recollection did not meet appropriate standards of reliability and accuracy.

The most recent civil cases have generally followed the same rule that the State follows in the criminal cases. Thus, Louisiana appears to admit hypnotically refreshed recollection in civil cases, and also in criminal cases. In *Carter v. Western Kraft Paper Mill* (1994), the Louisiana Court of Appeals noted that the issue of the admissibility of hypnotically refreshed recollection in civil cases was "unsettled," but the Court admitted the testimony and noted that the same rule applied in criminal cases.

In *Schall v. Lockheed Missles & Space Co.* (1995), a California Court of Appeals addressed the issue of the relevant rule in civil cases. The plaintiff alleged sexual harassment by her employer. The plaintiff had worked in a job requiring a security clearance. She violated the clearance and was transferred to a nonclassified job, which she never assumed because she took sick leave and then a vacation. Her harassment claim alleged that her former boss repeatedly made rude and insulting comments to the female employees. The plaintiff made no claim until after she had undergone therapy, which included hypnosis. She claimed that the hypnosis was not used for memory retrieval but rather to allow her to "access feelings" about what happened to her as a result of her employer's conduct. The plaintiff was unable to produce any corroboration of her allegations of harassment, and her therapist was unable to state unequivocally that the plaintiff had prehypnotic recall. The Court held that California's *per se* inadmissibility rule applied to civil cases. In all civil cases, the trial judge must hold a hearing to determine whether (1) the witness had been hypnotized, (2) the hypnosis was conducted to refresh memory, and (3) whether any proposed testimony is about events recalled and related to others prior to the hypnosis. Thus, the *per se* rule does not eliminate a pretrial hearing and does not save judicial resources.

This principle of symmetry, that the same rule must apply in civil and criminal cases, generally has been questioned by commentators (Imwinkelreid, 1990). Nevertheless, the current trend appears to be that courts will apply the same rules in civil cases that they apply in criminal cases. Thus, judges in states that have adopted a *per se* rule in criminal cases consider hypnosis equally dangerous in civil matters.

What might well turn out to be the largest group of civil cases involving hypnosis are the repressed memory cases referred to earlier by Karlin and Orne (1996). In general, three types of situations are likely to arise. First, an accuser sues an alleged perpetrator for childhood sexual abuse. The alleged perpetrator requests that the case be dismissed because the accuser had undergone hypnosis during therapy. In *per se* jurisdictions, this request will be granted.

For example, a recent Utah case, *Franklin v. Stevenson* (1996), involved allegations that the plaintiff was sexually assaulted by her cousin approximately 25 years earlier. The sexual abuse included threats against her and putting her in the carcass of a dead deer, with additional threats of what would happen to her if she told anyone. After the repressed memories returned and the plaintiff began telling others about them, she discovered that the Utah Juvenile Court had, in another case involving the cousin's own children, made a finding of fact that the cousin had sexually molested them. At the plaintiff's trial, the cousin's own daughter testified that she, too, had been sexually abused and had been placed in the carcass of a dead deer and told that her mother would be killed if she revealed anything that had occurred. The daughter testified that she had had these memories since the events occurred and had not repressed them.

A jury agreed with the plaintiff and awarded her $750,000 in damages. Finney (1996) examined the court record and concluded that the jury had reached the correct result. However, in a surprising move, trial judge Kenneth Rigtrup ordered the jury verdict to be replaced with his own ruling that the

case was barred by the fact that "relaxation" and other techniques had been used and therefore the plaintiff had been "hypnotized" (Rigtrup, 1996). The judge's order displays a fundamental misunderstanding of the entire memory and hypnosis literature. For example, the judge says that "in substance, there is no distinction between hypnotic suggestion or the use of communicating with metaphorical 'inner-children,' the use of journalling, the use of guided imagery, the use of relaxation and trance-work, and the use of writing with the non-dominant hand" (Rigtrup, 1996, p. 2). Thus the judge, on his own, without a hearing and without an examination of the relevant literature, decided to extend the *per se* exclusion rule to journaling, guided imagery, etc. What is startling, besides the judge's lack of knowledge about the scientific literature and the unfairness in not holding an evidentiary hearing, is the fact that in this case the memories he claims are unreliable were, in fact, corroborated. The case is currently (as of August 1997) on appeal to the Utah Supreme Court.

The second type of case is exactly like the first, but here the accuser sues the therapist for taking away his or her legal rights. This type of case, and the informed consent solution, were discussed earlier in this chapter. Interestingly, the therapist would most certainly argue that the *per se* rule prohibits such a lawsuit because all of the patient's memories are posthypnotic. Karlin's (1997) support for *per se* exclusion might prohibit these claims. He has argued for a broad exception that would apply "if patients are abused in any way during hypnosis, the fact that they were hypnotized should not prevent them from testifying about the abuse" (p. 36). Under his exception, the plaintiff would have to argue that he or she was "abused" when the therapist used hypnosis in the therapy.

The third type of repressed memory case involving hypnosis occurs when the patient and/or the alleged perpetrator sues the therapist for using hypnosis to obtain repressed memories. Plaintiffs will argue that (1) hypnosis is an experimental technique and no informed consent for its use was obtained, (2) hypnosis was used in an unduly suggestive manner, (3) the patient was never told that the memories might be false fantasies, (4) the therapist overly believed the memories were true and persuaded the patient of that fact, or (5) hypnosis should never be used with memories because it always contaminates them. This third type of case does not differ from those already discussed in chapter 15.

It should be noted that of all of the repressed memory cases decided at the appellate level, only a fraction of them, not more than 10%, appear to have involved hypnosis. Furthermore, as we have already seen, the science clearly shows that even when hypnosis is used, any memory distortions are likely to be the product of the inherent malleability of memory, social influence factors and the trait of hypnotizability, rather than of the hypnosis itself. As Beahrs, Cannell, and Gutheil (1996) have noted, "false memories are more likely to arise from social influence, either inside or outside of hypnosis or psychotherapy; intrinsic suggestibility (especially interrogative) and dissociative potential; and less so, simply from being hypnotized" (p. 50). Karlin (1997), writing about the alleged increase in confidence that hypnosis supposedly produces, admits:

> As research during the past decade has shown . . . , these factors are, in general, not unique to hypnosis. For example, it has been well known for 2 decades that repeated retrieval of a memory comprises an important learning experience. . . . Recently, Shaw (1996) has shown that events that increase ease of recall, such as repeated recall trials, increase confidence in correct and incorrect information. As in hypnosis, the increase in confidence is independent of the accuracy of the memory. (p. 33)

Clark and Loftus (1996) have reached the same conclusion:

> Social factors have been demonstrated in the laboratory as well. Luus and Wells (1994) showed that a witness's confidence in an inaccurate identification can be artificially inflated or deflated, depending on whether the witness is informed that another witness picked the same or a different person from the lineup. (p. 142)

The tendency to blame hypnosis for dangers that are not inherent to hypnosis is at the heart of the defense of the *per se* exclusion rule. It is because hypnosis does not *have* to contaminate memory, however, that guidelines for its use are possible.

Exceptions to the *Per Se* Rule

The purpose of the *per se* exclusion rule is to eliminate hypnosis issues in court. The rule is supposed to be automatic, yet exceptions to its harsh terms have proven unavoidable. The longer the list of exceptions, the less automatic the rule. With a string of exceptions, the rule permits, in an increasing number of cases, the introduction of testimony despite the hypnosis.

To date, the three exceptions universally adopted are:

1. Testimony is admissible concerning duly recorded prehypnosis statements.
2. Testimony is admissible about matters not discussed during hypnosis.
3. Defendants in criminal cases may testify despite previous hypnosis.

Giannelli (1995), a proponent of the *per se* exclusion rule, nevertheless suggests three additional exceptions:

1. The crime occurs while the victim is hypnotized, such as in hypnotic seduction cases.
2. The subject is not actually hypnotized.
3. Nonforensic hypnosis, where the person is hypnotized for therapy without memory work, or where the hypnosis was not for investigative purposes, is employed.

As noted earlier, commentators are united that an exception should be made for hypnotic seduction cases. It is reasonable to believe that courts will follow this advice.

With regard to hypnotic induction procedures that fail to result in trance states, courts that follow the *per se* rule are already accepting this exception. For example, the California Supreme Court has twice acknowledged that expert opinion testimony that the subject had not in fact been hypnotized may be used as a basis for the admission of the subject's testimony, even though the police used induction techniques, intending to induce trance (*People v. Caro*, 1988; *People v. Johnson*, 1988).

In cases where hypnosis is utilized for therapy rather than for investigative purposes, we have seen that the courts have been split on whether to provide an exception.

All of these exceptions, coupled with the likelihood of others based on problems with the *per se* rule, require pretrial evidentiary hearings. Why not simply require such a hearing in all hypnosis cases to test whether the hypnosis used was not unduly suggestive? In other words, because the *per se* rule is no longer automatic, and because a pretrial hearing about it is necessary anyway, the *per se* exclusion rule cannot be defended on the grounds that it saves judicial time. So the question arises, why not adopt the fairer view that hypnosis must withstand strict guidelines before hypnotically refreshed recollection will be admissible? With this rule, unreliable evidence will still be inadmissible, but nobody will automatically be denied access to courts of law before having had an opportunity to present his or her claim.

The only justification left for the *per se* exclusion rule is the argument that the scientific literature conclusively demonstrates that hypnosis is *always* the source of *unreliable* memories. Does the scientific literature reach this conclusion?

THE SCIENTIFIC LITERATURE AND JUDICIAL PERCEPTIONS OF THE DANGERS OF HYPNOSIS

The major objection to the "admissibility with guidelines" view is the belief that the scientific literature demonstrates that hypnosis has the dangers which courts have labeled. Modern laboratory research, however, challenges the basic negative attitudes courts hold about hypnosis.

In general, courts identify eight problems with the admissibility of hypnotically refreshed testimony. The eight problems fall into three general categories—suggestibility, reliability, and believability:

A. Suggestibility
   1. The subject becomes "suggestible" and may try to please the hypnotist with answers the subject thinks will be met with approval.
   2. The subject experiences a loss of critical judgment.
   3. The subject is highly responsive for the creation of pseudomemories.

B. Reliability
   4. The subject experiences "memory hardening," which gives him or her great confidence in both true and false memories, making effective cross-examination more difficult.
   5. The subject is likely to "confabulate," that is, to fill in details from the imagination, in order to make an answer more coherent and complete.
   6. The subject has source amnesia, which prevents properly identifying whether a memory occurred before or during hypnosis, or whether the memory is real or suggested.

C. Believability
   7. Juries will disproprtionately believe testimony that is the product of hypnosis.
   8. The subject can easily feign hypnosis and can be deceptive in trance.

As we saw in chapter 10, the suggestibility and reliability concerns are neither special nor unique to hypnosis and may be no more serious with hypnosis than without it. In other words, memory contamination is a function of *memory*—not of the use of *hypnosis* to facilitate recall.

Researchers have demonstrated that undue suggestion may be equally possible with clever interrogations and leading questions (Loftus, 1993). Undue suggestion is also prevalent in nonhypnotic situations, more so than has been previously believed. Spanos and his associates (1989) have concluded that there is no support for the notion that hypnotic interrogations facilitate the formation of pseudomemories (Spanos, Gwynn, Comer, Baltruweit, & de Groh, 1989).

Recent memory research has shown that confabulation is the natural way in which memory works (Loftus, 1980), rather than a by-product of hypnotic trance. Experiments with eyewitness testimony have conclusively demonstrated confabulation in nonhypnotic settings and have also demonstrated that hypnotically refreshed recollection is not necessarily confabulated (Loftus, 1979c; Wells & Loftus, 1984).

Judges generally believe that hypnosis will give the subject undue self-confidence in the accuracy of hypnotically refreshed recollections. This self-

confidence will be based on a genuine, sincere belief that the memories and pseudomemories are real
and true. As the court stated in *State v. Ture* (1984),
"effective cross-examination of a previously hypnotized witness is virtually impossible." This has been
labeled the "concreting" effect. Recent studies, however, contradict the assertion that hypnotically enhanced pseudomemories are more resistant to
cross-examination than pseudomemories produced
by skillful, suggestive interrogation (Spanos, Gwynn,
Comer, Baltruweit, & de Groh, 1989; Spanos,
Quigley, Gwynn, Glatt & Perlini, 1991). In *State v.
Dreher* (1991), the court correctly noted that:

> ... the defendant's argument that, because of the
> hypnosis session, [the hypnotized subject's] trial
> testimony was delivered with an aura of confidence
> which it would not otherwise have had is not per-
> suasive. The memory-hardening process is an in-
> trinsic part of a witness's preparation for trial.
> While ordinarily it takes the form of numerous pre-
> trial interviews and interrogations by counsel, the
> result is the same as that which defendant claims
> occurred here: a witness who testifies with con-
> viction and believability. The fact that the witness
> has been prepped to testify effectively does not
> disqualify his evidence so long as it has not been
> falsified. (pp. 220–221)

The scientific literature reviewed in chapter 10
demonstrates that the concern courts have had
about the dangers of hypnosis on the *suggestibility*
and *reliability* of memory are not well founded. With
regard to *believability* concerns, judges have stated
that restrictive admissibility rules regarding hypnotically refreshed recollection are essential to protect
against the inevitability that jurors will give significant weight to hypnosis as a truth-finder and accurate memory retrieval technique. Furthermore,
because the subject can simulate hypnosis without
detection, juries will be fooled into giving undue
weight to false testimony. For example, Udolf (1983)
has written that, when an expert states an opinion
based upon an hypnotic interview, "a jury may, in
spite of the court's cautionary instructions, be overly
impressed by the drama intrinsic in the [hypnotic]
procedure and regard such evidence as substantive
proof" (p. 69).

There is no proof that a jury will so act, and, of

course, the problem of jurors ignoring judicial instructions is not unique to hypnosis or inevitable
with regard to it. It is, in fact, more likely that, in
matters of science where jurors need professional
guidance, they will pay more—not less—attention
to judicial instructions. Indeed, Udolf (1983) recognizes this point and adds that the problem disappears because judges have discretion to refuse to
admit evidence that the jury might improperly evaluate. This discretion, Udolf continues, must be exercised at a pretrial hearing on a "case-by-case" basis
(p. 69).

It should be noted that Warner (1979), cited by
Wilson, Greene, and Loftus (1986) for the proposition that "testimony elicited by hypnosis may have
an untoward impact on the jury" (p. 110), actually
says the opposite:

> One of the greatest barriers to the expanded use
> of hypnosis in the courtroom has been the fear, on
> the part of the judiciary, that juries will be unduly
> influenced by the techniques and appearance of
> the hypnotic trance situation and be unable, as a
> consequence, to evaluate the testimony itself ob-
> jectively. It will be shown, later in the present pa-
> per, that such fears may very well have no basis in
> fact. (p. 421).

Warner (1979), a lawyer, actually was arguing for
an *expanded* role for hypnosis in the courts. Wilson,
Greene, and Loftus (1986) mistakenly identify him
as a "hypnosis researcher" and then cite him in favor of a *limited* role for forensic hypnosis. More importantly, Warner makes it clear that the argument
about believability initially comes from judges and
not directly from the hypnosis literature, which simply recycled the argument in articles disfavoring
hypnosis in the courts. Thus, the believability issue
is not one generated by science; rather, it was generated by a misperception of judicial attitudes.

This point is worth repeating. Today, judges use
the believability argument as a reason to refuse admission to hypnotically refreshed recollection. They
cite the hypnosis literature as evidence of this concern. Yet, when one explores the source of this concern in the hypnosis literature, it turns out that the
believability argument was generated as a speculation about how judges might react to hypnosis. We
thus have a self-fulfilling prophecy whereby an imag-

ined fear judges might have gets converted into an actual fear they claim is science-based.

When we turn to the science, we discover that the only studies on this point do not support the fear that jurors will have excessive zeal toward hypnotically refreshed recollection. A few anecdotal studies (McConkey & Jupp, 1985, 1985–86; Putnam, 1979; Wells, 1984;), which simply assessed student attitudes about hypnosis or forensic hypnosis, discovered a common belief that hypnosis could somewhat enhance accurate memory. These studies did not assess how this common belief would impact on performance as a juror in a legal case, nor did they involve the corrective instructions that would be given by a judge. The following three studies address these particular forensic concerns.

Wilson, Greene, and Loftus (1986) ran two studies to test the beliefs the public holds about hypnosis. The first study involved 347 college students who were generally unfamiliar with hypnosis. They were shown 13 statements and asked to evaluate how strongly they agreed or disagreed with each statement. The second study involved random telephone calls to potential jurors, a group of 238 registered voters who were residents of a specific county. They were contacted by telephone for twenty minutes before specific statements about hypnosis were read to them for their approval or disapproval. These statements were phrased in the negative, unlike the statements in the first experiment, which were positively framed.

The results from the two experiments were largely comparable, especially on the issue of the perception of hypnotically refreshed recollection. On this point, the study concluded that "approximately twice as many people reported that they would place less faith rather than more faith in the testimony of someone who had been hypnotized" (p. 118).

Furthermore, Wilson, Greene, and Loftus (1986), while clearly recognizing the limited nature of their study, and while suggesting caution in general regarding hypnosis, nevertheless concede that "the data do not provide evidence that the public wholeheartedly accepts that hypnosis produces accurate memories and jurors consistently react to hypnotically elicited evidence credulously" (p. 118).

In a later study, Greene, Wilson, and Loftus (1989) noted that their earlier study was relevant to the issue of "the faith that potential jurors *claim*

they would have in hypnotic testimony" (p. 64), but the study revealed "little about the faith jurors actually have in this type of testimony" (p. 64). This second study was designed to remedy this deficiency in the first study. Greene, Wilson, and Loftus (1989) prepared a script from an actual hypnosis case. They then prepared several versions of a film of a trial. The versions differed in reference to a crucial piece of information. The trial concerned a stabbing incident. In all three versions, a prosecution witness stated that the victim was seated and did not have a weapon. In the first version, a police officer testified that the witness recalled details of the stabbing immediately after it occurred ("immediate recall condition"). In the second version, the officer testified that the witness was unable to recall important details immediately, but spontaneously recalled them one week later during questioning ("delayed recall condition"). The third version involved the officer testifying that the witness was able to recall the details only after being hypnotized one week after the crime ("hypnotic recall condition"). Two groups of subjects were shown some version of the film. The first group comprised 108 university students who were also registered voters eligible for jury duty. The second group involved 162 jurors in Superior Court who were awaiting assignment to a case.

After viewing a version of the film, members of each group were asked about their predeliberation verdicts. The results showed no statistical difference among the students, who overwhelmingly favored conviction no matter what version of the film they saw. With reference to the real jurors, however, 100% who saw the "immediate recall condition" version voted for conviction, 79% of those who saw the "delayed recall condition" version voted for conviction, and 90% of the subjects who saw the "hypnotic recall condition" version favored conviction. These results were found to be statistically significant "between the immediate and delayed conditions" (p. 69).

When they turned to measuring the persuasiveness and believability of the police officer's testimony, Greene, Wilson, and Loftus (1989) reached the following significant conclusion:

> . . . it appears that hypnotic testimony may be viewed by jurors with a certain amount of skepticism. In some ways, its impact is comparable to

that of testimony based on delayed recall, and in other ways, it is given somewhat more credence than this delayed version. Rarely, however, does testimony from hypnosis seem to have as much impact as testimony from an immediate report. (p. 74)

* * *

When we evaluated believability of the prosecution witness across recall conditions, we found that subjects in the hypnotic recall condition seem to ride the middle ground. Both students and actual jurors rated the prosecution witness as less believable when she was hypnotized than when her testimony came immediately and spontaneously after the crime occurred, and actual jurors rated the witness as more believable when her testimony came from hypnosis than when her memory spontaneously returned one week after the incident. There is some indication then, that by varying the conditions under which a given event is recalled, the credibility of the source of the memory changes as well. (p. 75)

Greene, Wilson, and Loftus (1989) also compiled data to determine whether hypnosis would impact the believability of other prosecution witnesses who had not been hypnotized, such as the victim. They found that the victim was most believable in the immediate recall condition and least believable in the delayed recall condition. The hypnotic recall condition again found middle ground.

In conclusion, Greene, Wilson, and Loftus (1989) noted that "other indices lend support to the contention that hypnotic testimony is not blindly accepted as veridical" (p. 76) and "these findings corroborate other results: The hypnotic testimony did not have a disproportionately large impact on jurors' decision making" (p. 76).

An extension of the Greene, Wilson, and Loftus (1989) study was conducted by Spanos, Gwynn, and Terrade (1989), who wanted to determine whether jurors would weigh hypnotically refreshed testimony more heavily than the testimony of witnesses who had not been hypnotized. Two hundred seventy-one university undergraduates acting as mock jurors watched a videotape of an eyewitness who, under oath, "confidently" identified the defendant as the man who raped her. The jurors were informed that

the witness had initially given police only a fragmentary description. Jurors were then assigned to a control group or to one of three treatment groups. The control group was told that the witness, when questioned by police a few days later, provided a description that matched a suspect the police had already arrested. This suspect was then identified by the witness. Jurors who were assigned to the three treatment groups were in addition told that the questioning of the witness a few days later involved hypnosis used by a psychiatrist. Treatment group #1 then saw a videotape of an expert who discredited hypnosis when used with eyewitness testimony. Treatment group #2 saw a videotape of an expert who supported hypnosis in the recovery of repressed or traumatic memories. Treatment group #3 saw a videotape of a discrediting hypnosis expert and a supportive hypnosis expert.

Spanos, Gwynn, and Terrade (1989) concluded that, before the expert testimony was shown, "knowledge that the victim/witness's positive identification had been aided by hypnosis had no effect on jurors' ratings of the defendant's guilt" (p. 925). The jurors, before seeing the opinions of experts, were "not influenced by knowledge that the witness had been hypnotized" (p. 922). However, after hearing expert opinion, not surprisingly, it is clear that this opinion itself did have an impact on jury deliberations. The jurors who saw the unfavorable expert, and the jurors who saw both experts, tended to be influenced in a negative direction, whereas jurors who saw the positive expert were influenced favorably.

As with the Greene, Wilson, and Loftus (1989) study, Spanos, Gwynn, and Terrade (1989) did not supply information about the judge's instructions on hypnosis. Nevertheless, from all the available studies, we can conclude that jurors are not mesmerized by an artificial belief in the truth-productive powers of hypnosis. They do not concede to it the power to ascertain truth, and they listen and tend to follow the explanations of the experts, as in other cases where experts testify to aid the jurors' understanding of the facts. Careful instructions from the judge would appear to correct any possibility that unwarranted believability is a problem with forensic hypnosis.

It should be specially pointed out that from 1977 to 1983— the time the courts were first told about alleged distortions involving hypnotic retrieval of memories, distortions in the public perception of the veridicality of hypnotically retrieved information, and distortions in the hypnotic production of pseudomemories—there was virtually no literature directly on this topic. Indeed, there was virtually no literature at all. McCann and Sheehan (1988) have observed that by 1988, "only three studies . . . bear directly on the experimental creation of false memories in hypnotically responsive subjects" (p. 339). Those three studies, conducted from 1979 to 1986, which appeared to prove the ease with which hypnosis may be used to implant pseudomemories, clearly overstated their conclusions, as demonstrated by McCann and Sheehan's (1988) effective criticism of them. Indeed, the opposite of what they stated appears to be true. As noted by McCann and Sheehan (1988), "pseudomemory response, like other hypnotic responses, is clearly shaped and determined by psychological factors of influence. It appears also that pseudomemory response should not be viewed as a standard posthypnotic reaction" (p. 345). Sheehan (1996), after surveying the hypnosis and memory research publications from 1985 to 1996, has noted that "an important conclusion that has emerged from the literature is that memory contamination is a function of memory and influence and not a danger specific to the use of hypnosis. . . ." (p. 13).

In other words, it is not *hypnosis* that may contaminate memory, but rather *how* the hypnosis is conducted. If insufficient attention is given to the social influence factors at work with memory and its retrieval, then hypnosis, or any other method, may produce pseudomemories.

Because the scientific literature proves that judicial concerns with hypnosis, when it is properly used, are unfounded, the issue becomes detailing the guidelines that must be followed to protect against undue suggestion or social influence.

THE EMERGENCE OF DETAILED GUIDELINES

At the time courts were adopting the *per se* exclusion rule, only the general safeguards drafted by Martin T. Orne were available. His pioneering work has now been augmented by recently published,

carefully considered guidelines for the use of hypnosis with memory in clinical and in forensic settings. Practitioners who follow these guidelines will not be tampering with or contaminating memory. While no person can be sure that a hypnotically retrieved memory is accurate, no person can be sure that any memory is accurate. When properly used, hypnosis, or any method of memory retrieval, adds no further distortions to the memory.

The escalating scientific and forensic debate concerning false memory issues has encouraged many professional associations to examine fundamental questions concerning memory, hypnosis, and undue suggestion. On September 18, 1993, the Executive Committee of the American Society of Clinical Hypnosis voted to convene a Task Force on Hypnosis and Memory. The official charge of the Task Force was as follows (Ewin D. N., personal correspondence, October 27, 1993):

> To review current guidelines for the conduct of forensic hypnosis interviews and the 1985 AMA Report, and to then provide our own updated report and revised, expanded guidelines for the conduct of forensic hypnosis interviews.

> To create for the first time guidelines for clinicians in working with hypnosis and memory, especially where there is the possibility of uncovering potential memories of abuse. The latter guidelines, as you are aware, do not currently exist.

To fulfill its function, the task force studied the vast literature on memory, pseudomemory, trauma, childhood abuse, child testimony, eyewitness testimony, hypnosis, forensic hypnosis, and suggestion. Informal discussions and correspondence occupied several months until the Task Force met in Chicago on February 19, 1994, to draft guidelines for the proper conduct of forensic and clinical hypnotic interviews or memory retrieval sessions.

After a full day of intensive discussion and debate, two guidelines were prepared in a preliminary form. In early March 1994, these now annotated and expanded drafts were circulated to Task Force members for final revisions. Soon afterwards, copies of the draft were circulated to more than 70 major experts in all of the relevant fields for commentary. Special efforts were made to make sure that all viewpoints were represented, thereby providing the widest critical response. The Task Force received an enormous amount of exceptionally valuable feedback, almost entirely positive, but occasionally negative. This feedback led to extensive discussions and rewriting. After sometimes heated debate within the Task Force on a few issues, the final report received unanimous approval. The final product, *Clinical Hypnosis and Memory: Guidelines for Clinicians and for Forensic Hypnosis* appeared in February 1995.

The ASCH *Guidelines*, also discussed in chapter 10, should now be considered the current standard of care for the practice of hypnosis. In forensic settings, the *Guidelines* reject the *per se* inadmissibility rule.

McConkey and Sheehan (1995) have proposed guidelines for forensic hypnosis that are quite consistent with the ASCH *Guidelines*. McConkey and Sheehan, in agreement with the ASCH *Guidelines*, also reject the *per se* rule:

> Whereas the experimental evidence told us that significant distortion can often be expected to occur in hypnosis, it is not clear that hypnosis as such is inherently distorting. This, of course, means that our position on the forensic utility of hypnosis is not one that excludes the practice of hypnosis, but it is one that is cautious on several fronts. . . . (p. 210)

* * *

> Our position on the utility of hypnosis in the forensic setting is one of "admissibility with safeguards." (p. 211)

Gudjonsson (1992), one of the world's leading experts on interrogative suggestibility, has recently concluded that a *per se* exclusion rule is too harsh. In his definitive work on police interrogation methods and the production of false confessions, he notes:

> Investigative hypnosis seems to be most effective in very serious cases, such as murder, robbery, rape and terrorism, where the arousal created by the experience leads the mind to block out the painful emotional experience. The main conclusion one can draw from the anecdotal evidence is that hypnosis can be a highly effective tool in criminal investigations, even in cases where there has been no obvious psychological trauma. (p. 169)

When a person is questioned in order to discover the truth, knowledge of how that questioning may distort the truth is essential, as false memory advocates have correctly argued. But because a technique or procedure is capable of being abused or misused, it does not follow that it should never be used (Scheflin, 1997c).

The 1985 AMA Report

In 1985, an eight-member panel of the American Medical Association (AMA), led by Dr. Martin T. Orne, released a report on their study of hypnosis with memory. The AMA panel reached three important conclusions. First, the panel found no evidence of increased recollection by means of hypnosis for recall of memory for meaningless material. The experiments relied upon dealt with nonsense syllables or nonmeaningful word passages, learned under nonstressful conditions. The great bulk of the studies examined by the panel, where hypnosis was involved, fell into this category.

As the report noted, these studies are of questionable value to the forensic arena, where meaningful information obtained under traumatic conditions is usually involved. Witnesses are not generally asked to recite silly poetry on the witness stand. Memory for nonsense is generally weak without hypnosis because the information is not important enough to be stored in long-term memory. Hypnosis does not increase recall of this material; nor does anything else. This literature has been surveyed in chapter 10.

Second, the panel found no evidence of increased recollection by means of hypnosis for *recognition* memory.

Third, and most important, the panel found that when hypnosis is used for *recall* of meaningful past events, new information is often reported. Thus, significantly, the AMA acknowledged a hypermnesia effect with hypnosis for the recall of *meaningful* material. This conclusion alone justifies its use. The fact that the material remembered may include confabulations and pseudomemories as well as accurate information is also true of prodded memory without hypnosis. The AMA also found that in some cases pseudomemories may be the result of hypnosis transforming subjects' prior belief into thoughts or fantasies that they come to accept as memories. Furthermore, because hypnotized subjects tend to be more suggestible, they may become more vulnerable to incorporating any cues given during hypnosis into their recollections.

Several points are worth noting about these latter findings. Most importantly, the panel does conclude that hypnosis is capable of producing additional *truthful* information. The fact that the material produced might contain fantasies, confabulations, or imaginative generations is true of memory without hypnotic retrieval. The panel did not conclude that hypnosis was less effective than other memory retrieval techniques; nor did it conclude that hypnosis generates more fantasy, etc., than other techniques. Thus, the panel, in fact, concludes that, if used properly, hypnosis can retrieve unavailable truthful memories.

At the time the report was published, there was inadequate data to support the panel's negative concerns about pseudomemories. As McCann and Sheehan (1988) have observed after an examination of the relevant literature, "only three studies to date, however, bear directly on the experimental creation of false memories in hypnotically responsive subjects" (p. 339). In fact, in 1985, when the AMA report appeared, only *one study* was available. This study (Laurence and Perry, 1983, which was drawn from Laurence, 1982, and which is more fully discussed in Laurence, Nadon, Nogrady, and Perry, 1986), used a population of 27 high-hypnotizables and involved the creation of a pseudomemory of awakening in the night to the sound of loud noises. Bernheim (1891/1980), a century ago, had conducted this same experiment, and Orne in 1982 had demonstrated it before BBC cameras for a documentary on forensic hypnosis (Barnes, 1982).

The Laurence and Perry experiment was widely reported but little analyzed. The media reports about it, by contrast, were hyperbolic—hypnosis easily produces pseudomemories! The actual results were significantly more modest. Only 13 of the 27 highly hypnotizable subjects accepted the pseudomemory in a waking state. Thus, slightly less than half of the most vulnerable population were induced to accept a misinformation suggestion. On closer look, however, only 6 of the 13 subjects were "unequivocal in

their confidence that the suggested event had actually taken place" (McCann & Sheehan, 1988, p. 339). Thus, less than 25% of the most vulnerable population was willing to accept a pseudomemory of a "peripheral" detail in a "nontraumatic" setting.

A second study from the same Canadian laboratory appeared in 1986, one year after the AMA report. Labelle and Perry (1986) replicated the earlier study, but this time they added that imagery and absorption were significant predictors of the likelihood that subjects would accept created memories. This point is very important for two reasons. First, it suggests that the problem of memory creation is not a problem with hypnosis, but may be inherent in those people with traits of imagination and absorption. Thus, hypnosis is not the culprit; instead, we must look to individual differences. Second, this finding serves as a basis for using objective testing as a prelude to memory retrieval, including memory retrieval with hypnosis, just as the ASCH *Guidelines* require.

In addition to the paucity of reports available to the panel, there is the further problem that the initial Canadian study was not carefully examined. The exaggerated report of its results was used rather than a careful examination of its actual findings.

The third study referred to by McCann and Sheehan (1988), conducted by Spanos and McLean in 1986 also reported a high incidence of false memory acceptance in high-hypnotizables (nine out of eleven subjects), but when "hidden observer" instructions were given only two of the eleven subjects continued to adhere to their pseudomemories. According to McCann and Sheehan (1988):

> Spanos & McLean claimed that highly hypnotizable subjects exposed to the pseudomemory creation paradigm remain able to discriminate their pseudomemory imaginings accurately from actual memories and provide "memory" reports according to the expectations conveyed to them. Consequently, when the situation allows them to refute earlier pseudomemory reports while maintaining their self-presentation as deeply hypnotized, they can do so. (p. 340)

McCann and Sheehan (1988) further demonstrated that social influence context factors, not hypnosis, account for the acceptance of pseudomemories, thus disproving the Karlin and Orne (1996) thesis that hypnosis inevitably contaminates memory:

> Pseudomemory response, like other hypnotic responses, is clearly shaped and determined by psychological factors of influence. It also appears that pseudomemory response should not be viewed as a standard posthypnotic reaction. (p. 345)

When these social influence factors are controlled, as they are in the ASCH *Guidelines*, the production of suggested pseudomemories disappears as a problem, except for the general issue of the malleability of ordinary memory. Furthermore, again refuting the premise that hypnosis inevitably contaminates memory, McCann and Sheehan's (1988) studies show that (1) the pseudomemories are not really memories at all, and (2) contrary to the false memory position, the original memories do not get destroyed (see also McCann & Sheehan, 1987; McCloskey & Zaragoza, 1985):

> Results from the present study and this independent study both indicate that hypnotic pseudomemory can be breached by exposure to incontrovertible evidence relating to original events, and that pseudomemory elements are not irreversibly integrated with original memories. (McCann & Sheehan, 1988, p. 345 n. 4)

Thus, the AMA report suffers from at least two significant deficiencies. First, there were almost no relevant studies available from which to draw scientifically acceptable conclusions. Second, the single study that was available on pseudomemory production led the AMA researchers to incorrect conclusions about (1) the ease of hypnotically implanting memories, (2) the confidence in those memories, and (3) the issue of whether the original memories were retrievable or forever lost.

By contrast, the ASCH *Guidelines* had the advantage of an additional decade of experiments directly related to the central issues, as well as direct input from over 70 of the world's most significant authorities in the major fields of hypnosis, memory, social influence, and suggestion. Karlin (1997) states that he prefers the AMA report to the ASCH *Guidelines*, but Scheflin (1997c) has shown that Karlin's

analysis is seriously flawed and that Karlin has failed to cite even one single case where the ASCH *Guidelines* were followed and injustice resulted.

In 1994, the AMA reaffirmed its 1985 report (American Medical Association, 1994). Unfortunately, the 1994 report, which was not about hypnosis, failed to examine, analyze, discuss, or even cite *any* post–1985 scientific studies. Rather, the 1994 report on "Memories of Childhood Abuse" simply states that the 1985 report is still accurate and is reaffirmed. The 1994 AMA Committee must be seriously faulted for its scientific sloppiness in failing to discover that the earlier report was substantially in error. To reaffirm a scientifc document after a decade without checking and reporting on its continuing scientific validity is inherently misleading because it implies knowledge where there is none.

Three of the original eight members of the 1985 AMA report were members of the Task Force that wrote the ASCH *Guidelines*. At least one other member of the 1985 AMA group has also privately expressed substantial lingering doubts about the accuracy and viability of the 1985 AMA report. Thus, at least half of the original members of the 1985 AMA report now reject its conclusions! And they are not alone. Other critics have also found many additional serious flaws in the 1985 AMA report (Beahrs, 1988; Frischholz, 1996, in press; Reiser, 1986).

Given the paucity of research available when the 1985 AMA report was written, the widespread scholarly criticisms of it, and its repudiation by at least half of the original members, reliance on the 1985 AMA report is forensically unacceptable at this point.

The United States Supreme Court's *Daubert* Test

In the summer of 1993 the United States Supreme Court issued its significant decision in *Daubert v. Merrell Dow Pharmaceuticals, Inc.*, which changed the law in all federal courts and, as of the beginning of 1997, approximately two-thirds of the state courts, on the proper test for the admissibility of expert opinion testimony. The Court replaced the longstanding *Frye* (1923) reliability test based on general acceptance in the scientific community with a more complicated relevance test based on verifiability and falsifiability, which now requires trial judges to be "gatekeepers" concerning the admissibility of the expert opinions. Commentators generally acknowledge, and the Court specifically noted, that the intention of the new rule is to permit more expert testimony to reach juries, but they disagree on how lenient or strict trial judges should be when faced with the softer behavioral or social sciences compared to the physical sciences.

Of the several hundred judicial decisions issued since the *Daubert* ruling appeared, only a small fraction have involved the behavioral or social sciences. Of these opinions involving the behavioral or social sciences, very few have directly addressed hypnosis issues.

The *Daubert* (1993) decision in the United States Supreme Court has led several courts to hold that *per se* exclusion rules are no longer defensible. In two cases involving polygraph evidence, the United States Court of Appeals for the Fifth Circuit held that information obtained from a lie detector cannot automatically be excluded from evidence. In *United States v. Posado* (1995), the defendant in a drug trial was denied the opportunity to admit into evidence the results of a polygraph interview. The Fifth Circuit reversed this ruling:

> Our precedent, with few variations, has unequivocally held that polygraph evidence is inadmissible in a federal court for any purpose. . . . However, we now conclude that the rationale underlying this circuit's *per se* rule against admitting polygraph evidence did not survive *Daubert v. Merrell Dow Pharmaceuticals.* . . .

The *Posado* judges then took note that the United States Supreme Court had stated that it was replacing the "austere" *Frye* rule of general acceptance in the scientific community with the "flexible" inquiry based upon the Federal Rules of Evidence, which require that the trial judge make "initial determinations" that the evidence to be admitted is reliable ("as scientific, technical or other specialized knowledge" that is trustworthy) and relevant ("will it assist the trier of fact?"). A *per se* exclusion rule prohibits a judge from performing these tasks and is therefore indefensible under *Daubert*.

Of major significance is the fact that, as the court specially noted, "the government concedes

that a *per se* rule against admitting polygraph evidence, without further inquiry, is not viable after *Daubert*. . . ." Thus, if prosecutors agree that *per se* rules violate *Daubert*, their advocacy against such rules should carry great weight with the courts.

The *Posado* court also made a point of explaining that under *Daubert* the scientific evidence does not have to be absolute truth. The *Daubert* justices had written that the reliability element is satisfied when the evidence offered is "more than speculative belief or unsupported speculation. . . . Certainty is not required, but the knowledge asserted must be based on 'good grounds.'"

One year after its *Posado* decision, the Fifth Circuit again returned to the same issue and upheld its earlier ruling. In *United States v. Pettigrew* (1996), the facts closely parallel those in *Posado* because again a defendant in a criminal case sought to introduce polygraph evidence showing he had not intentionally deceived bank regulators. The Fifth Circuit reaffirmed the *Posado* rejection of *per se* exclusionary rulings and also reaffirmed the *Posado* court's reasoning that polygraph evidence could still be excluded, but not automatically. The trial judge in each individual case must "be guided by the twin precepts of [Federal Rules of Evidence] Rule 702: the scientific validity of the method, and ability to 'assist the trier of fact to understand the evidence or determine a fact in issue. . . .' "

In *United States v. Cordoba* (1996), the Ninth Circuit held that its *per se* exclusion rule against the admission of polygraph evidence was "effectively overruled" by the "flexible inquiry assigned to the trial judge by *Daubert*." The court further noted that other *per se* rules were equally as vulnerable to abolition and were being reversed. The Court of Military Appeals has also rejected a *per se* exclusion for polygraphs (*United States v. Scheffer*, 1996). The United States Supreme Court is scheduled to hear arguments in late 1997 on this issue (*United States v. Scheffer*, 1997), with commentators predicting that Daubert will be held to knock out *per se* rules (Reuben, 1997).

More directly on point, in *Rowland v. Commonwealth* (1995), a stepmother saw her stepson shoot her and her daughter in the back. The stepmother's physician diagnosed her as having posttraumatic stress disorder and recommended she see Dr. William Wester, a psychologist. Wester agreed with the diagnosis and decided to treat her with hypnosis. Before beginning the hypnosis treatment, Dr. Wester, a former president of the American Society of Clinical Hypnosis with extensive forensic hypnosis experience, took complete statements from the stepmother about the shooting incident. The first statement was audiotaped and the second statement was videotaped. Following the videotaping, Dr. Wester used hypnosis for the first time. The stepmother's statement while in trance was virtually identical to her recorded prehypnotic statements. The defendant requested that all testimony from the stepmother be suppressed, but the trial judge ruled "that the Commonwealth would be precluded from informing the jury that [the stepmother] had been placed under hypnosis. Further, he gave the defense leave to cross-examine her on this point, and ruled that, if the defense did so, then the Commonwealth would be allowed to introduce additional testimony to explain hypnosis." The defendant on appeal argued for a rule of *per se* inadmissibility. In a 4–3 decision, the Supreme Court of Kentucky held that a *per se* inadmissibility rule was inappropriate. The court cited the Court of Appeals decision, which noted that a *per se* exclusion might violate *Daubert*. The dissenting judges favored the *per se* exclusion because of their erroneous belief that hypnotically refreshed recollection "inherently involves dangerous problems with reliability."

Thus, the *Daubert* decision seems likely to erode the *per se* exclusion rule in one of two ways. First, some courts, as we have already seen, will decide that *Daubert* mandates the abolition of automatic exclusion. Second, other courts will not see the mandate, but will respond to the spirit of *Daubert*'s desire for flexibility by shifting from total exclusion to case-by-case analysis rules.

The era of *per se* exclusion may soon come to an end. When that happens, every person will at least be entitled to present his or her evidence to a judge and thereby have a day in court to be heard. Cases without merit will be immediately dismissed. Only cases in which the plaintiff is able to sustain the burden of proof will go forward to trial.

When used carelessly, hypnosis can assist in the creation of false memories. When used carefully, however, hypnosis is a valuable method for retrieving memories that can be proven to be accurate. As Kline (1983) noted many years ago:

When the context within which any procedure, particularly hypnosis, is so altered as to bring about coercion, pressure, and heightened suggestibility, then we are likely to be faced with confabulation or pseudomemories. When any interrogation procedure of investigative process, including hypnosis, is used carefully and is part of the total evaluation of mental process, the results relating to recollections and thoughts may offer a very different picture for evaluation and eventual presentation within the courtroom. (pp. 122–123)

THE RELEVANCE OF HYPNOSIS LAW TO THE FALSE MEMORY DEBATE

According to opponents, the *per se* exclusion rule stifles police investigations, threatens therapists with malpractice liability, and forces victims of violent crimes to choose between their mental health and their legal rights. According to its proponents, the *per se* rule protects memory from inevitable distortion, prevents innocent people from being falsely accused, and saves money and time by avoiding pretrial determinations of suggestibility and reliability. The central concern in this debate is the malleability of memory by hypnosis. The hypnosis cases and the judicial perceptions of hypnosis are directly relevant to the false memory debate, which also centers around the malleability of memory and the alleged ease by which inaccurate material may be hypnotically, or nonhypnotically, recovered.

In the last few years, as we have noted, a new type of case involving hypnosis has arisen, which courts have not yet fully addressed. These cases involve the use of hypnosis to uncover repressed memories. They differ from the investigative hypnosis cases because the latter involve a known crime and an attempt to obtain additional details about it, whereas the former involve the uncertainty of whether a crime was ever committed. In addition, there is a major temporal difference. With investigative hypnosis cases, the hypnosis is done shortly after the occurrence of the crime. With repressed memory cases, the hypnosis may occur decades after an alleged crime was committed.

False memory advocates are currently broadening their attack on therapy by extending their fears about the dangers of hypnosis in two expanding directions.

First, there is the claim that, even when hypnosis is not being utilized directly, its evil effects occur with techniques that are forms of "disguised" hypnosis. According to Perry (1995), disguised techniques are prevalent in stage hypnosis shows and have been acquired by "recovered memory" therapists. "Disguised" hypnosis, according to Perry, is any request for relaxation, imagination, etc. When famed mentalist Kreskin (1973, 1977) said he used suggestion, not hypnosis, in reality he was using "disguised" hypnosis. Perry writes about a student who discussed with her mother whether she should participate in an hypnosis experiment. On the morning of the experiment, the mother said that maybe the daughter should not participate because "you might never come out of it." This acted as a prehypnotic suggestion and the student had great difficulty coming out of the trance.

Of course, under this grossly expansive view, hypnosis becomes co-extensive with suggestion. Furthermore, because suggestion is everywhere—for example, in books, in the media, in conversations, and in therapy—it follows that everything is hypnosis (Rigtrup, 1996). Does Perry really believe that the mother "hypnotized" her daughter?

This is a dangerous viewpoint to take seriously. It is bad enough to equate hypnosis with all suggestion, thereby making the terms synonymous; it is even worse to equate it with all relaxation, as Perry does, and as Judge Rigtrup (1996) did in *Franklin v. Stevenson*. Does Perry think that therapists should keep their patients agitated in order to keep them out of trance? It should also be observed that *any* request for recall of the past is both suggestive and also the product of demand characteristics of wanting to please the questioner, etc. The request for information about the past also carries the implication that memory can reproduce prior events with accuracy. Logically, the false memory argument must thus eliminate *all memory* from evidence.

In addition, the argument against suggestion misses the point. Suggestion is an inevitable process of the communication and information processing systems central to expression. Judges, as well as therapists and experimenters, look for *undue* suggestion. This point was recognized in the invitation

extended by the Institute for Experimental Psychiatry Research Foundation to a reception during the False Memory Syndrome Foundation Conference held on April 16, 1993. The invitation said: "Mr. X is cordially invited to a Reception, in honor of the scientific speakers and families afflicted by the creation of false memories through the *misuse* of suggestion, . . ." (emphasis added). This phrasing is precise. It is when a phenomenon is *misused* or *abused* that *unacceptable* distortion occurs.

Another major point is missed when the discussion of hypnosis or suggestion is not specifically tailored to individual patients who vary in terms of their susceptibility. Very little research has been done on the issue of individual differences related to hypnotizability versus suggestibility scales. Many people may be suggestible and have memory contaminated without hypnosis, while others, even with hypnosis, may score very low on hypnotizability or suggestibility scales, so hypnotic influences will have no impact on their memories. It is likely that the malleability of memory is itself a function of individual differences—that there is a relationship beween hypnotizability and/or suggestibility and the ease of memory alteration or pseudomemory implantation/creation. Thus, the crucial issue is not whether hypnosis was used, but rather whether it was likely to have had an undue influence. The "totality of the circumstances" test is essential to make this determination. Otherwise we have the senseless rule in existence now, which automatically excludes hypnotically refreshed recollection whenever hypnosis is used, even though no more than 10% of the population are likely to be vulnerable high-hypnotizables.

Perry (1995) points to T. X. Barber's views that other processes explain hypnotic phenomena. Guided imagery, for Perry, is one "disguised" hypnosis technique. Perry argues that the "recovered memory" therapists picked up these techniques and added to them their "New Age ideology which argues that insight into the cause of symptoms leads to their alleviation." Does Perry doubt that this may be true in some cases?

Thus, under this first expansion of alleged hypnotic dangers, *even therapists who do not use hypnosis are using hypnosis.*

The second expansion is as unacceptable as the first. In two recent articles, the Ornes and their colleagues (Orne, Whitehouse, Dinges, & Orne, 1996;

Orne, Whitehouse, Orne, & Dinges, 1996) have argued that low-hypnotizables are also at risk from hypnosis. In other words, hypnotic consequences, especially bad ones, may affect people who, by definition, are not very responsive to hypnotic suggestion.

Thus, under this second expansion, *even those patients who are not very affected by hypnosis are affected by hypnosis.*

This second expansion has no support in the hypnosis literature, as we noted in chapter 10. In short, when used carelessly, hypnosis can assist in the creation of false memories. When used carefully, however, hypnosis is a valuable method for retrieving memories that can be proven to be accurate.

CONCLUSION

At the present time, patients risk not getting valid, competent, and beneficial hypnosis treatment, and mental health professionals, doctors, and dentists who use hypnosis risk malpractice liability. This situation must change.

As Scheflin (1997c) has noted, according to the *per se* exclusion rule:

> . . . a person who has been lobotomized could testify in court, a person who had received massive electroshock treatments could testify in court, a person who had taken enormous dosages of mind-altering psychiatric drugs or psychedelics could testify in court, a person who had suffered substantial organic brain damage could testify in court, but a person who had been competently hypnotized by an experienced professional who followed strict guidelines and avoided undue suggestions could not testify in court. Does that position make sense to you?

On the basis of laboratory experiments and the analysis of hard cases, the *per se* exclusion rule should be replaced with a pretrial hearing on the issue of undue suggestion.

Sheehan and McConkey (1993) are surely correct when they observe that "it seems extreme to take the view that all hypnotically obtained information should be ignored." Sadoff and Dubin (1990)

reach the same conclusion by observing that "the court must decide on a case by case basis about the admissibility of the hypnotic recall. We are opposed to the admissibility *per se* and the exclusion *per se* rules."

The three most formidable recent works on forensic hypnosis (Hammond et al., 1995; McConkey & Sheehan, 1995; Scheflin & Shapiro, 1989) and an increasing number of scientific (Gudjonsson, 1992) and legal (Clemens, 1991; Eisenberg, 1995; Scheflin, 1994a, 1996, 1997c) commentators are strongly concluding that the *per se* inadmissibility rule is unnecessary, unwise, and unjust.

The twin supports for the *per se* rule—scientific evidence of hypnotic contamination of memory and the absence of guidelines for using hypnosis in conjunction with memory work—are no longer in place. Since 1980, when the *Mack* case was decided, and since 1985, when the American Medical Association issued its report, a wealth of data from laboratories and clinical practice demonstrates that, when properly used, hypnosis can assist in the retrieval of accurate memories otherwise inaccessible. Furthermore, when used according to the guidelines now available, hypnosis is no more suggestive, contaminating, or unreliable than other methods of memory retrieval.

Wilson, Greene, and Loftus (1986) have stated that "evidence from laboratory research indicates that although hypnosis may increase the amount of information reported, it does not increase accuracy—some of the material recalled is confabulation, not fact" (p. 110). Other writers have expressed the same idea (Karlin, 1997; Karlin & Orne, 1996). What they fail to state is that no technique used to assist the retrieval of memory can guarantee accuracy, and all memory, hypnotically refreshed or otherwise, is partly a product of confabulation. As noted by Pamela Freyd (1995), co-founder and Executive Director of the False Memory Syndrome Foundation, "there is agreement" that

> Memory is a highly constructive process. People take bits and fragments that are stored, and they reconstruct a memory that makes sense to them in the here and now. There is a lot of filling in the blanks when people have a memory. . .
>
> . . . People misremember things all the time. (p. 18)

When properly used, hypnosis can result in more

information available for corroboration with no greater manipulation of memory than any other technique already legally approved.

If hypnosis is no worse than other forms of memory retrieval, and if it is capable of increasing the amount of information later proven to be true, why should it alone, among all forms of memory retrieval, be singled out for judicial condemnation? And if future scientific studies likewise demonstrate that psychotherapy is no worse than other forms of memory retrieval and is capable of increasing information without necessarily increasing the error rate, should we also repeat the same mistake of singling out psychotherapy for judical or legislative condemnation?

When courts first addressed hypnosis issues, few relevant studies were available and the experts preached that dire consequences would result if courts permitted hypnotically refreshed recollection to be introduced into evidence. Now that the science is available, it demonstrates that hypnosis is not the danger it was portrayed to be and that, when used properly, it can serve as an aid to the recall of accurate memories.

When courts first addressed repressed memory issues, the science was unavailable and the early experts again preached disaster. Now that the science has spoken, the early experts have been shown to be wrong once more.

The tension between science and law has been addressed by Reidinger (1996):

Science is about uncertainty, probability, convergence; it's a peer-driven conversation—largely consensual—of tentative theories, imperfect proofs, criticisms and revisions. Even a well-established scientific theory—such as evolution—a fact, for scientists—remains incomplete and subject to revision according to the discovery of new evidence.

Law, to the contrary, is about settling arguments *now*; it's an adversarial enterprise whose real goal is not truth so much as victory and closure with justice. (p. 59)

Great harm can be caused by judges when they rush to judgment in the absence of the relevant science. It is to be hoped that the United States Supreme Court's *Daubert* decision will toughen judicial responsibility in scientific matters.

It appears that the forensic hypnosis and the repressed memory controversies will follow Arthur Schopenaur's wise observation: "All truth passes through three stages. First, it is ridiculed. Second, it is violently opposed. Third, it is accepted as being self-evident" (quoted in *Jackson v. State*, 1989). With regard to both hypnosis and repressed memory, the manner in which the media was manipulated into reporting pseudoscience is now being recognized (Stanton, 1997, *Freyd v. Whitfield*, 1997; Bowman & Mertz, 1996), and scientists have now reached stage three of Schopenaur's prediciton. It is to be hoped and expected that the courts, the legislatures, the public, and the media will soon join them.

Bibliography

ABC v. Archdiocese of St. Paul. (1994). 513 N.W.2d 482 (Minn.App.).

Abelson, R.P., & Lesser, G.S. (1959). The measurement of persuasibility in children. In C.I. Hovland & I.L. Janis (Eds.), *Personality and persuasibility* (pp. 141–166). New Haven: Yale University Press.

Abernathy, E. (1940). The effect of changed environmental conditions upon the results of college examinations. *Journal of Psychology, 10*, 293–301.

Abraham v. Zaslow. (1975). 1 Civil 33219. California Court of Appeal, First Appellate District, Division Three. (Unpublished).

Adams, N. (1979). Disruption of memory functions associated with general anaesthetics. In J.F. Kihlstrom & F.J. Evans (Eds.), *Functional disorders of memory* (pp. 218–238). Hillsdale, NJ: Erlbaum.

Adler, A. (1920/1969). *The practice and theory of individual psychology.* Totowa, NJ: Littlefield, Adams.

Ahern, G. L., & Schwartz, G. E. (1985). Differential lateralization for positive and negative emotion in the human brain: EEG spectral analysis. *Neuropsychologia, 23*, 745–756.

Ainsworth, M.D. (1989). Attachments beyond infancy. *American Psychologist, 44*, 709–716.

Ainsworth, M.D., Blehar, M.C., Waters, E., & Wall, S. (1978). *Patterns of attachment: A psychological study of the strange situation.* Hillsdale, NJ: Erlbaum.

Akpinar, S., Ulett, G.A., & Itel, T.M. (1971). Hypnotizability predicted by computer-analyzed EEG pattern. *Biological Psychiatry, 3*, 387–392.

Albach, P., Moorman, P., & Bermond, B. (in press). Memory recovery of childhood sexual abuse. *Dissociation.*

Alexander, F., & French, T.M. (1946). *Psychoanalytic therapy: Principles and applications.* New York: Ronald Press.

Alexander, G.J., & Scheflin, A.W. (in press). *Law and psychiatry.* Durham, NC: Carolina Academic Press.

Alexander, P.C. (1993). The differential effects of abuse characteristics and attachment in the prediction of long-term effects of sexual abuse. *Journal of Interpersonal Violence, 8*, 346–362.

Allard, C.B., Kristiansen, C.M., Hovdestad, W.E., & Felton, K.A. (in press). *The retraumatizing impact of the recovered memory debate on adult survivors of child sexual abuse.*

Allen v. Voje. (1902). 114 Wis. 1, 89 N.W. 924.

Allen, J.J., Iacono, W.G., Laravuso, J.J., & Dunn, L.A. (1995). An event-related potential investigation of posthypnotic recognition amnesia. *Journal of Abnormal Psychology, 104*, 421–430.

Allison, R.B. (1974). A new treatment approach for multiple personalities. *American Journal of Clinical Hypnosis, 17*, 15–32.

Allodi, F., & Cowgill, G. (1982). Ethical and psychiatric aspects of torture: A Canadian study. *Canadian Journal of Psychiatry, 27*, 98–102.

Allyn, J., & Festinger, L. (1961). The effectiveness of unanticipated persuasive communications. *Journal of Abnormal and Social Psychology, 62*, 35–40.

Alpert, H.S., Carbone, H.A., & Brooks, J.T. (1946). Hypnosis as a therapeutic technique in the war neuroses. *Bulletin U.S. Army Medical Department, 5*, 315–324.

Alpert, J.L. (1995a). Criteria: Signposts toward the sexual abuse hypothesis. In J.L. Alpert (Ed.), *Sexual abuse recalled: Treating trauma in the era of the recovered memory debate* (pp. 363–396). Northvale, NJ: Jason Aronson.

Alpert, J.L. (1995b). Professional practice, psychological science, and the delayed memory debate. In J.L. Alpert (Ed.), *Sexual abuse recalled: Treating trauma in* the era of the recovered memory debate (pp. 3–28). Northvale, NJ: Jason Aronson.

Alpert, J.L. (1995c). *Sexual abuse recalled: Treating trauma in the era of the recovered memory debate.* Northvale, NJ: Jason Aronson.

Alpert, J.L. (1995d). Trauma, dissociation, and clinical study as a responsible beginning. *Consciousness and Cognition, 4,* 125–129.

Alsbach v. Bader. (1985). 700 S.W. 2d 823 (Sup.Ct.Mo.).

Althaus v. Cohen. (1994). No. 92–20893. Allegheny County Court of Common Pleas, Pennsylvania.

American Bar Association. (1983, as amended through 1996). *Model rules of professional conduct.* Chicago: American Bar Association.

American Law Institute. (1934). *Restatement of the law of torts.*

American Law Institute. (1965). *Restatement (second) of the law of torts.*

American Medical Association, Council on Scientific Affairs. (1985). Scientific status of refreshing recollection by the use of hypnosis. *Journal of the American Medical Association, 253,* 1918–1923.

American Medical Association, Council on Scientific Affairs. (1994). *Memories of childhood abuse.* CSA Report 5–A-94.

American Psychiatric Association. (February 15, 1961). Regarding hypnosis: A statement of position by the American Psychiatric Association.

American Psychiatric Association. (1980). *Diagnostic and statistical manual of mental disorders (DSM-III)* (3rd ed.). Washington, D.C.: American Psychiatric Press.

American Psychiatric Association. (1987). *Diagnostic and statistical manual of mental disorders (DSM-IIIR)* (3rd ed.). Washington, D.C.: American Psychiatric Press.

American Psychiatric Association. (1993). *APA Board of Trustees' Statement on Memories of Sexual Abuse.* Washington, D.C.: American Psychiatric Association.

American Psychiatric Association. (1994). *Diagnostic and statistical manual of mental disorders (DSM-IV)* (4th ed.).Washington, D.C.: American Psychiatric Association Press.

American Psychological Association. (March, 1973). Rage reduction therapy pioneer battles to keep California license. *APA Monitor, 4*(3), 5.

American Psychological Association. (August 10, 1995a). *APA board of directors statement on recovered memories.*

American Psychological Association. (February 18, 1995b). *APA resolution on "Mental Health Consumer Protection" acts.*

Anderson, K.J. (1990). Arousal and the inverted-U hypothesis: A critique of Neiss's "reconceptualizing arousal." *Psychological Bulletin, 107,* 96–100.

Anderson, J.R., & Bower, G.H. (1973). *Human associative memory.* Washington, DC: V.H. Winston & Sons.

Andrews, B., Morton, J., Bekerian, D.A., Brewin, C.R., Davies, G.M., & Mollon, P. (1995). The recovery of memories in clinical practice: Experiences and beliefs of British psychological society practitioners. *The Psychologist, 8,* 209–214.

Annas, G.J., & M.A. Grodin (Eds.). (1992). *The Nazi doctors and the Nuremberg code.* Oxford: Oxford University Press.

Anthony, D. (1990). Religious movements and brainwashing litigation: Evaluating key testimony. In T. Robbins & D. Anthony (Eds.), *In gods we trust: New patterns of religious pluralism in America* (2nd ed.) (pp. 295–344). New Brunswick, NJ: Transaction.

Anthony, D., & Robbins, T. (1992). Law, social science and the "brainwashing" exception to the first amendment. *Behavioral Sciences and the Law, 10,* 5–29.

Apkinar, S., Ulett, G. A., & Itil, T. M. (1971). Hypnotizability predicted by computer-analyzed EEG pattern. *Biological Psychiatry, 3,* 387–392.

Appelbaum, P.S., & Zoltek-Jick, R. (April 1996). Psychotherapists' duties to third parties: *Ramona* and beyond. *American Journal of Psychiatry, 153,* 457–465.

Archer, T., & Nilsson, L.-G. (Eds.). (1989). *Aversion, avoidance and anxiety.* Hillsdale, NJ: Erlbaum.

Archibald, H.C., & Tuddenham, R.D. (1965). Persistent stress reaction after combat. *Archives of General Psychiatry, 12,* 475–481.

Armstrong, L. (1978). *Kiss daddy goodnight: A speak out on incest.* New York: Hawthorne Books.

Armstrong, L. (1982). The cradle of sexual politics. In M. Kirkpatrick (Ed.), *Women's sexual experience: Explorations of the dark continent* (pp. 109–125). New York: Plenum.

Armstrong, L. (1994). *Rocking the cradle of sexual politics: What happened when women said incest.* Reading, MA: Addison-Wesley.

Arntzen, F. (1970). *Psychologie der Zeugenaussage [Psychology of witness testimony].* Gottingin: Verlag.

Arons, H. (1967). *Hypnosis in criminal investigation.* Springfield, IL: Charles C. Thomas.

Aronson, E., & Golden, B.W. (1962). The effect of relevant and irrelevant aspects of communicator credibility on opinion change. *Journal of Personality, 30,* 135–146.

As, A. (1962). The recovery of forgotten language knowledge through hypnotic age regression: A case report. *American Journal of Clinical Hypnosis, 5,* 24–29.

Associated Press. (December 18, 1994). Jury sides with family in sexual-abuse case.

Atkinson, R.C., & Shiffrin, R.M. (1968). Human memory: A proposed system and its control processes. In K.W. Spence (Ed.), *The psychology of learning and motivation: Advances in research and theory* (Vol. 2, pp. 89–195). New York: Academic Press.

Aubry, A.S., Jr., & Caputo, R.R. (1972). *Criminal interrogation* (2nd ed.). Springfield, IL: Charles C. Thomas.

Auerhahn, N.C., & Laub, D. (1984). Annihilation and restoration: Post-traumatic memory as pathway and obstacle to recovery. *International Review of Psychoanalysis, 11,* 327–344.

August, R.L., & Forman, B.D. (1989). A comparison of sexually abused and nonsexually abused children's behavioral responses to anatomically correct dolls. *Child Psychiatry and Human Development, 20,* 39–47.

Ault v. Jasko. (1994). 637 N.E.2d 870 (Ohio).

Averbach, E., & Coriell, A.S. (1961). Short-term memory in vision. *Bell Systems Technology Journal, 40,* 309–328.

Ayres, Jr., B.D. (May 14, 1994). Father who fought "memory therapy" wins damage suit. *The New York Times,* section 1, p. 1, col. 6.

Baars, B.J., & McGovern, K. (1995). Steps toward healing: False memories and traumagenic amnesia may coexist in vulnerable populations. *Consciousness and Cognition, 4,* 68–74.

Bach, S. (1977). On the narcissistic state of consciousness. *International Journal of Psychoanalysis, 58,* 209–233.

Baddeley, A.D., Lewis, V., & Nimmo-Smith, I. (1978). When did you last . . . ? In M.M. Gruneberg, P.E. Morris, & R.N. Sykes (Eds.), *Practical aspects of memory* (pp. 77–83). London: Academic Press.

Baddeley, A.D., & Wilson, B. (1979). Amnesia, autobiographical memory, and confabulation. In J. Kihlstrom & F.J. Evans (Eds.), *Functional disorders of memory* (pp. 225–251). Hillsdale, NJ: Erlbaum.

Bahrick, H.P., Bahrick, P.O., & Wittlinger, R.P. (1975). Fifty years of memory for names and faces: A cross-sectional approach. *Journal of Experimental Psychology: General, 104,* 54–75.

Baker, L., & Wagner, J. L. (1987). Evaluating information for truthfulness: The effects of logical subordination. *Memory & Cognition, 15,* 247–255.

Baker, R.A. (1982). The effect of suggestion on past-lives regression. *American Journal of Clinical Hypnosis, 25,* 71–76.

Baker, R.A., Haynes, B., & Patrick, B.S. (1983). Hypnosis, memory, and incidental memory. *American Journal of Clinical Hypnosis, 25,* 253–262.

Baker-Ward, L., Hess, T.M., & Flannagan, D.A. (1990). The effects of involvement on children's memory for events. *Cognitive Development, 5,* 55–69.

Bandura, A. (1977a). Self efficacy: Toward a unifying theory of behavioral change. *Psychological Review, 84,* 191–215.

Bandura, A. (1977b). *Social learning theory.* Englewood Cliffs, NJ: Prentice Hall.

Banks, W.P., & Pezdek, K. (1994). The recovered memory/false memory debate. *Consciousness and Cognition, 3,* 265–268.

Banyai, E. I. (1991). Toward a social-psychobiological model of hypnosis. In S. J. Lynn & J. W. Rhue (Eds.), *Theories of hypnosis* (pp. 564–598). New York: Guilford.

Barabasz, A.F., & Barabasz, M. (Eds.). (1993). *Clinical and experimental restricted environmental stimulation: New developments and perspectives.* New York: Springer-Verlag.

Barber, T.X. (1961). Experimental evidence for a theory of hypnotic behavior: II. Experimental controls in hypnotic age-regression. *International Journal of Clinical and Experimental Hypnosis, 9,* 181–193.

Barber, T.X. (1969). *Hypnosis: A scientific approach.* New York: Van Nostrand Reinhold.

Barber, T.X. (1978). Hypnosis, suggestions, and psychosomatic phenomena: A new look for the standpoint of recent experimental studies. *American Journal of Clinical Hypnosis, 21,* 13–27.

Barber, T.X., & Calverley, D.S. (1966). Effects of recall of suggested induction, motivational suggestions, and suggested regression: A methodological and experimental analysis. *Journal of Abnormal Psychology, 71,* 169–180.

Barber, T.X., Spanos, N.P., & Chaves, J.F. (1974). *Hypnotism, imagination, and human potentialities.* Elmsford, NY: Pergamon.

Barclay, C.R., & DeCooke, P. A. (1988). Ordinary everyday memories: Some of the things of which selves are made. In U. Neisser & E. Winograd (Eds.), *Remembering reconsidered: Ecological and traditional approaches to the study of memory* (pp. 91–125). New York: Cambridge University Press.

Barclay, C.R., & Wellman, H.M. (1986). Accuracies and inaccuracies in autobiographical memories. *Journal of Memory and Language, 25,* 93–103.

Barker, D. (1979). [Correspondence]. *Journal of Parapsychology, 43,* 268–269.

Barlow, D.H. (1988). *Anxiety and its disorders: The nature and treatment of anxiety and panic.* New York: Guilford.

Barlow, D.H. (1989). *Clinical handbook of psychological disorders: A step-by-step treatment manual* (2nd ed.). New York: Guilford.

Barlow, D.H., & Craske, M.G. (1989). *Mastery of your anxiety and panic.* Albany, NY: Graywind.

Barnes, M. (1982). *Hypnosis on trial.* London: British Broadcasting Company television program.

Barnier, A.J., & McConkey, K.M. (1992). Reports of real and false memories: The relevance of hypnosis, hypnotizability, and context of memory test. *Journal of Abnormal Psychology, 101,* 521–527.

Barrett, D. (1991). Deep trance subjects: the schema of two distinct subgroups. In R. Kuzendorf (Ed.), *Mental imagery* (pp. 101–112). New York: Plenum.

Barrett, D. (1992). Fantasizers and dissociaters: Data on two distinct subgroups of deep trance subjects. *Psychological Reports, 71,* 1011–1014.

Barrett, D. (1996). Fantasizers and dissociaters: Two types of high hypnotizables, two different imagery styles. In R. Kusendorf, N. Spanos, & B. Wallace (Eds.), *Hypnosis and imagination* (pp. 123–135). New York: Baywood.

Barrett, M.F. (1989–90). Pennsylvania's two schools of medical thought rule. *The Barrister, 20*(4), 15–19.

Barsalou, L.W. (1992). The context and organization of autobiographical memories. In U. Neisser & E. Winograd (Eds.), *Remembering reconsidered: Ecological and traditional approaches to the study of memory* (pp. 193–243). Cambridge, England: Cambridge University Press.

Bartlett, F.C. (1932). *Remembering.* New York: Cambridge University Press.

Basoglu, M. (1992). Behavioral and cognitive approach in the treatment of torture-related psychological problems. In M. Basoglu (Ed.), *Torture and its consequences:*

Current treatment approaches (pp. 402–429). Cambridge, England: Cambridge University Press.

Bass, E., & Davis, L. (1988). *The courage to heal: A guide for women survivors of child abuse.* New York: Harper & Row.

Bass, E., & Davis, L. (1994). *The courage to heal: A guide for women survivors of child abuse* (2nd ed.). New York: Harper & Row.

Bass, E., & Thornton, L. (Eds.). (1983). *I never told anyone: Writings by survivors of childhood sexual abuse.* New York: Harper-Collins.

Bastiaans, J. (1969). The role of aggression in the genesis of psychosomatic disease. *Journal of Psychosomatic Research, 13,* 307–314.

Baxter, J.S. (1990). The suggestibility of child witnesses: A review. *Applied Cognitive Psychology, 4,* 393–407.

Beahrs, J.O. (1988). Hypnosis cannot be fully nor reliably excluded from the courtroom. *American Journal of Clinical Hypnosis, 31,* 18–27.

Beahrs, J.O. (1989). Spontaneous hypnosis in the forensic context. *Bulletin of the American Academy of Psychiatry and the Law, 17,* 171–181.

Beahrs, J.O., Cannell, J.J., & Gutheil, T.G. (1996). Delayed traumatic recall in adults: A synthesis with legal, clinical, and forensic recommendations. *Bulletin of the American Academy of Psychiatry and Law, 24,* 45–55.

Beck, A.T., Rush, A., Shaw, B., & Emery, G. (1979). *Cognitive therapy of depression.* New York: Guilford.

Beck, F., & Godin, W. (1951). *Russian purge and the extraction of confession.* London: Hurst & Blackett.

Beck, J.C. (1990). Clinical aspects of the duty to warn or protect. In R.I. Simon (Ed.), *Review of clinical psychiatry and the law* (Vol. 1, pp. 191–204). Washington, D.C.: American Psychiatric Press.

Behlmer, G.K. (1982). *Child abuse and moral reform in england 1870–1908.* Stanford, CA: Stanford University Press.

Beitchman, J.H., Zucker, K.J., Hood, J.E., da Costa, G.A., Akman, D., & Cassavia, E. (1992). A review of the long-term effects of child sexual abuse. *Child Abuse and Neglect, 16,* 101–118.

Bekerian, D.A., & Bowers, J.M. (1983). Eyewitness testimony: Were we misled? *Journal of Experimental Psychology: Learning, Memory, and Cognition, 9,* 139–145.

Bekerian, D.A., & Dennett, J.L. (1995). Assessing the truth in children's statements. In T. Ney (Ed.), *True and false allegations of child sexual abuse: Assessment and case management* (pp.163–175). New York: Brunner/Mazel.

Bekerian, D.A., & Goodrich, S.J. (1995). Telling the truth in the recovered memory debate. *Consciousness and Cognition, 4,* 120–124.

Belicki, K., Correy, B., Boucock, A., Cuddy, M., & Dunlop, A. (1994). *Reports of sexual abuse: Facts or fantasies?* Unpublished manuscript. Brock University, St. Catherines, Ontario.

Belli, R.F. (1989). Influences of misleading postevent information: Misinformation interference and accep-

tance. *Journal of Experimental Psychology: General, 118,* 72–85.

Belli, R.F., Windschitl, P.D., McCarthy, T.T., & Winfrey, S.E. (1992). Detecting memory impairment with a modified test procedure: Manipulating retention interval with centrally presented event items. *Journal of Experimental Psychology: Learning, Memory, and Cognition, 18,* 356–367.

Benedek, E.P., & Schetky, D.H. (1985). Allegaions of sexual abuse in custody and visitation disputes. In E.P. Benedek & D.H. Schetky (Eds.), *Emerging issues in child psychiatry and the law* (pp. 145–156). New York: Brunner/Mazel.

Benedek, E.P., & Schetky, D.H. (1987a). Problems in validating allegations of sexual abuse. Part 1: Factors affecting perception and recall of events. *Journal of the American Academy of Child & Adolescent Psychiatry, 26,* 912–915.

Benedek, E.P., & Schetky, D.H. (1987b). Problems in validating allegations of sexual abuse. Part 2: Clinial evaluation. *Journal of the American Academy of Child & Adolescent Psychiatry, 26,* 916–921.

Benedikt, M. (1894). *Hypnotismus und Suggestion: Eine klinisch-psychologische Studie.* Leipzig, Germany: M. Breitenstein.

Bennett, H.L. (1987). Learning and memory in anesthesia. In M. Rosen & J.N. Lunn (Eds.), *Consciousness, awareness and pain in general anesthesia* (pp. 132–149). London: Butterworths.

Bennett, H.L. (1988). Perception and memory for events during adequate general anesthesia for surgical operations. In H.M. Pettinati (Ed.), *Hypnosis and memory* (pp. 193–231). New York: Guilford.

Bennett, H. L. (1990). Influencing the brain with information during general anaesthesia: A theory of 'unconscious hearing.' Chapter in B. Bonke, W. Fitch, & K. Millar (Eds.), *Memory and awareness in anaesthesia* (pp. 50–56). Amsterdam: Swets & Zeitlinger.

Bennett, H.L. (1993). Memory for events during anesthesia does occur: A psychologist's viewpoint. In P. S. Sebel, B. Bonke, & E. Winograd (Eds.), *Memory and awareness in anesthesia* (pp. 459–466). Englewood Cliffs, NJ: Prentice Hall.

Bennett, H.L., Davis, H.S., & Giannini, J.A. (1985). Nonverbal response to intraoperative conversation. *British Journal of Anesthesia, 57,* 174–179.

Bennett, H.L., DeMorris, R.N., & Willis, N.H. (1988). Acquisition of auditory information during different periods of anesthesia. *Anesthesia & Analgesia, 67,* S12.

Bennett, H.L., Sullivan, D.M., & Savelle, J.E. (1990). Neuroendocrine correlates of lower esophageal contractility and frontalis muscle activity. *Anesthesia and Analgesia, 70,* S20.

Berliner, L., & Williams, L.M. (1994). Memories of child sexual abuse: A response to Lindsay and Read. *Applied Cognitive Psychology, 8,* 379–387.

Bernet, C. Z., Deutscher, R., Ingram, R.E., & Litrownik, A.J. (November 1993). *Differential factors in the repression of memories of childhood sexual abuse.* Poster presented at the Annual Convention of the Association for the Advancement of Behavioral Therapy, Atlanta, GA.

Bernheim, H. (1888/1973). *Hypnosis and suggestion in therapy*. New York: Aronson.

Bernheim, H. (1891/1980). *New studies in hypnotism* (R.S. Sandor, Trans.). New York: International Universities Press.

Bernstein, E.M., & Putnam, F.W. (1986). Development, reliability, and validity of a dissociation scale. *Journal of Nervous and Mental Disease, 174,* 727–735.

Bernstein, M. (1956). *The search for Bridey Murphy*. New York: Doubleday.

Berry, J. (1992). *Lead us not into temptation: Catholic priests and the sexual abuse of children*. New York: Doubleday.

Best, H.L., & Michaels, R.M. (1954). Living out "future" experience under hypnosis. *Science, 120,* 1077.

Bethune, D. W., Ghosh, S., Gray, B., Kerr, L., Walker, I. A., Doolan, L. A., Harwood, R. J., & Sharples, L. D. (1993). Learning during general anaesthesia: Implicit recall following methohexitone or propofol infusion. In P. S. Sebel, B. Bonke, & E. Winograd (Eds.), *Memory and awareness in anesthesia* (pp. 57–63). New York: Prentice Hall.

Bethune, D.W., Ghosh, S., Walker, I.A., Carter, A., Kerr, L., & Sharples, L. (1993). Intraoperative positive therapeutic suggestions improve immediate postoperative recovery following cardiac surgery. Chapter in P.S. Sobel, B. Bonke, & E. Winograd (Eds.). *Memory and awareness in anesthesia* (pp. 154–161). Englewood Cliffs, NJ: Prentice Hall.

Bettinghaus, E.P., & Cody, M.J. (1994). *Persuasive communication* (5th ed.). New York: Harcourt Brace College Publishers.

Beutler, L.E., & Clarkin, J.F. (1990). *Systematic treatment selection: Toward targeted therapeutic interventions*. New York: Brunner/Mazel.

Bickel, L. (1991). Tolling the statute of limitations in actions brought by adult survivors of childhood sexual abuse. *Arizona Law Review, 33,* 427–453.

Biderman, A.D., & Zimmer, H. (Eds.). (1961). *The manipulation of human behavior*. New York: Wiley.

Bily v. Arthur Young & Company. (1992). 3 Cal.4th 370, 834 P.2d 745, 11 Cal.Rptr.2d 51, modified on denial of rehearing, Nov. 12, 1992.

Biomedical and Behavioral Research (1975). *Joint hearing before the Subcommittee on Health of the Committee on Labor and Public Welfare and the Subcommittee on Administrative Practice and Procedure of the Committee on the Judiciary, United States Senate*. Washington, D.C.: U.S. Government Printing Office.

Binet, A. (1896). *Alterations of personality* H.G. Galdwin (Trans.). London: Chapman & Hall.

Bird v. W.C.W. (1994). 868 S.W.2d 767 (Tex.Sup.Ct.).

Black, C. (1981). *It will never happen to me*. Denver, CO: MC Publishers.

Blackowiak v. Kemp. (1995). 528 N.W.2d 247 (Minn.App.).

Blackowiak v. Kemp. (1996). 546 N.W.2d 1 (Sup.Ct.Minn.).

Blake, D.D., Weathers, F.W., Nagy, L.N., Kalopek, D.G.,

Klauminser, G., Charney, D.S., & Keane, T.M. (1990). A clinician rating scale for assessing current and lifetime PTSD: The CAPS-1. *The Behavior Therapist, 18,* 187–188.

Blanchard, E.B., & Abel, G.G. (1976). An experimental case study of biofeedback treatment of a rape induced psychophysiological cardiovascular disorder. *Behavior Therapy, 7,* 113–119.

Blanchard, E.B., Kolb, L.C., Gerardi, R.J., Kolb, L.C., & Barlow, D.H. (1986). Cardiac response to relevant stimuli as an adjunctive tool for diagnosing post traumatic stress disorder in Vietnam veterans. *Behavior Therapy, 17,* 592–606.

Blanchard, E.B., Kolb, L.C., Pallmeyer, T.B., & Gerardi, R.J. (1982). The development of a psychophysiological assessment procedure for post-traumatic stress disorder in Vietnam veterans. *Psychiatric Quarterly, 54,* 220–229.

Bliss, E.L. (1980). Multiple personalities: A report of 14 cases with implications for schizophrenia. *Archives of General Psychiatry, 37,* 13881397.

Bloch, S. & Reddaway, P. (1977). *Psychiatric terror: How Soviet psychiatry is used to suppress dissent*. New York: Basic.

Block, E. (1976). *Hypnosis: A new tool in crime detection*. New York: David McKay.

Block, R. I., Ghoneim, M. M., Sum Ping, S. T., & Ali, M. A. (1991). Human learning during general anaesthesia and surgery. *British Journal of Anesthesia, 66,* 170–178.

Bloom, P.B. (1994). Clinical guidelines in using hypnosis in uncovering memories of sexual abuse. *International Journal of Clinical and Experimental Hypnosis, 42,* 173–178.

Blume, E.S. (1990). *Secret survivors: Uncovering incest and its aftereffects in women*. New York: Ballentine.

Boat, B.W., & Everson, M.D. (1993). The use of anatomical dolls in sexual abuse evaluations: Current research and practice. In G.S. Goodman & B.L. Bottoms (Eds.), *Child victims, child witnesses: Understanding and improving testimony* (pp. 47–69). New York: Guilford.

Boeke, S., Bonke,B., & Bouwhuis-Hoogerwerf, M. L. (1988). The effects of sounds presented during general anaesthesia on postoperative course. *British Journal of Anesthesia, 60,* 697–702.

Bohannon, J.N. III (1988). Flashbulb memories for the space shuttle disaster: A tale of two theories. *Cognition, 29,* 179–196.

Bohannon, J.N. III, & Symons, V.L. (1992). Flashbulb memories: Confidence, consistency, and quantity. In E. Winograd & U. Neisser (Eds.), *Affect and accuracy in recall: Studies of "flashbulb" memories* (pp. 65–91). London, England: Cambridge University Press.

Bohart, A. (1977). Role playing and interpersonal conflict resolution. *Journal of Counseling Psychology, 24,* 15–24.

Bohart, A. (1980). Toward a cognitive theory of catharsis. *Psychotherapy: Theory, Research, and Practice, 17,* 192–201.

Bohart, A., & Haskell, R. (April, 1978). *The ineffectiveness of a cathartic procedure for anger reduction.* Paper presented at the 158th Annual Convention of the Western Psychological Association, San Francisco, CA.

Bonavitacola v. Cluver. (1993). 619 A.2d 1363 (Pa.Super.).

Bonebakker, A. E., Bonke, B., Klein, J., Wolters, G., & Hop, W. C.J. (1993). Implicit memory during balanced anaesthesia. *Anaesthesia, 48,* 657–660.

Bonke, B., Schmitz, P. I. M., Verhage, F., & Zwaveling, A. (1986). Clinical study of so-called unconscious perception during general anaesthesia. *British Journal of Anesthesia, 58,* 957–964.

Bonke, B., Van Dam, M. E., Van Kleef, J. W., & Slijper, F. M. E. (1993). Implicit memory tested in children with inhalational anaesthesia. In P. S. Sebel, B. Bonke, & E. Winograd (Eds.), *Memory and awareness in anesthesia* (pp. 48–56). Englewood Cliffs, NJ: Prentice Hall.

Boon, S., & Draijer, N. (1993). *Multiple personality in the Netherlands.* Lissa: Swets & Zeitlinger.

Borawick v. Shay. (1994). 842 F.Supp. 1501 (D.Conn.).

Borawick v. Shay. (1995). 68 F.3d 597 (2nd Cir. (Conn.)), certiorari denied 116 S.Ct. 1869, 134 L.Ed.2d 966 (1996).

Bornstein, R.F., & T.S. Pittman (Eds.). (1992). *Perception without awareness.* New York: Guilford.

Bosley v. Andrews. (1958). 393 Pa. 161, 142 A.2d 263.

Bostrom, R.N. (1983). *Persuasion.* Englewood Cliffs, NJ: Prentice-Hall.

Bottoms, B., Shaver, P., & Goodman, G. (1993). *Profile of ritual abuse and religion-related abuse allegations in the United States.* Updated findings provided via personal communication from B. Bottoms. Cited in K.C. Faller (1994), Ritual abuse: A review of the research. *The American Professional Society on the Abuse of Children Advisor, 7, 1,* 19–27.

Bowart, W.H. (1978). *Operation mind control.* New York: Dell.

Bowen v. Lumbermens Mutual Casualty Company. (1994). 183 Wis.2d 627, 57 N.W.2d 432.

Bowen, G. R., & Lambert, J.A. (1986). Systematic desensitization therapy with post-traumatic stress disorder cases. In C.R. Figley (Ed.), *Trauma and its wake* (Vol. 2). New York: Brunner/Mazel.

Bower, B. (October 22, 1994). Stress hormones hike emotional memories. *Science News, 146,* 262.

Bower, G.H. (1981). Mood and memory. *American Psychologist, 36,* 129–148.

Bower, G.H. (1992). How might emotions affect learning? In S-A. Christianson (Ed.), *The handbook of emotion and memory: Research and theory* (pp. 3–31). Hillsdale, NJ: Erlbaum.

Bowers, K. S. (1976). *Hypnosis for the seriously curious.* Monterey, CA: Brooks/Cole.

Bowers, J.M., & Bekerian, D.A. (1984). When will postevent information distort eyewitness testimony? *Journal of Applied Psychology, 69,* 466–472.

Bowers, K.S., & Davidson, T.M. (1991). A neodissociative critique of Spanos's social-psychological model of hyp-

nosis. In S.J. Lynn & J.W. Rhue (Eds.), *Theories of hypnosis* (pp. 105–143). New York: Guilford.

Bowers, K.S., & Farvolden, P. (1996a). Revisting a century-old Freudian slip: From suggestion disavowed to the truth repressed. *Psychological Bulletin, 119,* 355–380.

Bowers, K.S., & Farvolden, P. (1996b). The search for the canonical experience: Reply to Pennebaker and Memon. *Psychological Bulletin, 119,* 386–389.

Bowers, K.S., & Hilgard, E.R. (1988). Some complexities in understanding memory. In H.M. Pettinati (Ed.), *Hypnosis and memory* (pp. 3–18). New York: Guilford.

Bowers, K.S., & Woody, E.Z. (1996). Hypnotic amnesia and the paradox of intentional forgetting. *Journal of Abnormal Psychology,105,* 381–390.

Bowman v. Woods. (1848). 1G. Greene 441 (Iowa Sup.Ct.).

Bowman, C.G. (April 8, 1997). Keep third-party malpractice suits against therapists out of court. *Chicago Tribune,* commentary section, p. 13.

Bowman, C.G., & Mertz, E. (1996). A dangerous direction: Legal intervention in sexual abuse survivor therapy. *Harvard Law Review, 109,* 549–639.

Bowman, L.L., & Zaragoza, M.S. (1989). Similarity of encoding context does not influence resistance to memory impairment following misinformation. *American Journal of Psychology, 102,* 249–264.

Boyles v. Kerr. (1993). 855 S.W. 2d 593 (Sup. Ct.Tex.).

Bradford, J. W., & Smith, S.M. (1979). Amnesia and homicide: The Padola case and a study of thirty cases. *Bulletin of the American Academy of Psychiatry and Law, 7,* 219–231.

Bradshaw, J. (1988). *Bradshaw on the family: A revolutionary way of self-discovery.* Deerfield Bech, FL: Health Communiations, Inc.

Brand, M. (1968). *Savage sleep.* New York: Crown Publishers, Inc.

Brant, R., & Sink, F. (October 12, 1984). *Dilemmas in court ordered evaluation of sexual abuse charges during custody and visitation proceedings.* Paper presented at the 31st Annual Meeting of the American Academy of Child Psychiatry, Toronto, Ontario.

Braude, S.E. (1995). *First person plural: Multiple personality and the philosophy of mind.* Lanham, MD: Rowman & Littlefield.

Braun, B.G. (1986). Issues in the psychotherapy of multiple personality disorder. In B.G. Braun (Ed.), *Treatment of multiple personality disorder* (pp. 3–28). Washington, D.C.: American Psychiatric Press.

Braun, B.G. (1988). The BASK model of dissociation: Part I. *Dissociation, 1,* 4–23.

Braun, B.G., & Sachs, R.G. (1985). The development of multiple personality disorder: Predisposing, precipitating, & perpetuating factors. In R. P. Kluft (Ed.), *Childhood antecedents of multiple personality* (pp. 37–64). Washington, D.C.: American Psychiatric Press.

Bremner, J.D., Krystal, J.H., Southwick, S.M., & Charney, D.S. (1995a). Functional neoroanatomical correlates of the effects of stress on memory. *Journal of Traumatic Stress, 8,* 527–553.

Bremner, J.D., Krystal, J.H., Charney, D.S., & Southwick, S.M. (1996). Neural mechanisms in dissociative amnesia for childhood abuse: Relevance to the current controversy surrounding the "false memory syndrome." *American Journal of Psychiatry, 153*(7), 71–82.

Bremner, J.D., Randall, P., Scott, T.M., Bronen, R.A., Seibyl, J.P. Couthwick, S.M., Delaney, R.C., McCarthy, G., Charney, D.S., & Innis, R.B. (1995b). MRI-based measurement of hippocampal volume in patients with combat-related posttraumatic stress disorder. *American Journal of Psychiatry, 152,* 973–981.

Bremner, J. D., Scott, T. M., Delaney, R. C., Southwick, S. M., Mason, J. W., Johnson, D. R., Innis, R. B., McCarthy, G., & Charney, D.S. (1993). Deficits in short-term memory in posttraumatic stress disorder. *American Journal of Psychiatry, 150,* 1015–1019.

Bremner, J.D., Southwick, S., Brett, E., Fontana, A., Rosenheck, R., & Charney, D.S. (1992). Dissociation and posttraumatic stress disorder in Vietnam combat veterans. *American Journal of Psychiatry, 149,* 328–332.

Brende, J.O. (1984). An educational-therapeutic group for drug and alcohol abusing combat veterans. *Journal of Contemporary Psychotherapy, 14,* 122–136.

Brende, J.O. & Benedict, B.D. (1980). The Vietnam combat delayed stress response syndrome: Hypnotherapy of "dissociative symptoms." *American Journal of Clinical Hypnosis, 23,* 34–40.

Brende, J.O., & McCann, I.L. (1984). Regressive experiences in Vietnam veterans: Their relationship to war, post-traumatic symptoms and recovery. *Journal of Contemporary Psychotherapy, 14,* 57–75.

Breslau, N., & Davis, G.C. (1992). Posttraumatic stress disorder in an urban population of young adults: Risk factors for chronicity. *American Journal of Psychiatry, 149,* 671–675.

Brett, E.A., & Ostroff, R. (1985). Imagery and posttraumatic stress disorder: An overview. *American Journal of Psychiatry, 142,* 417–424.

Breuer, J., & Freud, S. (1893–1895). Studies on hysteria. In J. Strachey (Ed. & Trans.), *The standard edition of the complete psychological works of Sigmund Freud* (Vol. 2). New York: Norton.

Brewer, W.F. (1986). What is autobiographical memory? In D.C. Rubin (Ed.), *Autobiographical memory* (pp. 25–49). New York: Cambridge University Press.

Brewer, W.F. (1988). Memory for randomly sampled autobiographical events. In U. Neisser & E. Winograd (Eds.), *Remembering reconsidered: Ecological and traditional approaches to the study of memory* (pp. 21–90). New York: Cambridge University Press.

Brewer, W.F. (1992). The theoretical and empirical status of the flashbulb memory hypothesis. In E. Winograd & U. Neisser (Eds.). *Affect and accuracy in recall: Studies of flashbulb memories* (pp. 274–305). New York: Cambridge University Press.

Brewin, C.M., Andrews, B., & Gotlib, I. (1993). Psychopathology and early experience: A reappraisal of retrospective reports. *Psychological Bulletin, 113,* 82–98.

Briere, J. (1988). The long-term clinical correlates of childhood sexual victimization. *Annals of the New York Academy of Sciences, 5528,* 327–334.

Briere, J. (1992). *Child abuse trauma: Theory and treatment of the lasting effects.* Newbury Park, CA: Sage.

Briere, J. (1995). Child abuse, memory, and recall: A commentary. *Consciousness and Cognition, 4,* 83–87.

Briere, J., & Conte (1993). Self-reported amnesia for abuse in adults molested in childhood. *Journal of Traumatic Stress, 6,* 21–31.

Briere, J., & Runtz, M. (1988). Multivariate correlates of childhood psychological and physical maltreatment among university women. *Child Abuse and Neglect, 12,* 331–341.

British Medical Journal. (April 23, 1955). Supplementary annual report of council, 1954–5. Supplement, 190–193.

British Psychological Society. (1995). *Report by the working group on recovered memories.* Leicester, England: The British Psychological Society.

Bro v. Glaser. (1994). 22 Cal.App.4th 1398, 27 Cal. Rptr.2d 894 (4th Dist.).

Broadbent, D.E. (1958). *Perception and communication.* London, England: Pergamon Press.

Broadbent, D.E. (1963). Flow of information within the organism. *Journal of Verbal Learning and Verbal Behavior, 2,* 34–39.

Brock, T.C. (1962). Cognitive restructuring and attitude change. *Journal of Abnormal and Social Psychology, 64,* 264–271.

Bromley, D. (in press). Folk narratives and deviance construction: Constructing tales as a response to structural tensions in the social order. In C. Sanders (Ed.), *Deviance in popular culture.*

Brower, K.J., Blow, F.C., & Beresford, T.P. (1989). Treatment implications of chemical dependency models: an integrative approach. *Journal of Substance Abuse Treatment, 6,* 147–157.

Brown, D. (1990). The long-term variable effects of incest. In M. Fass & D. Brown (Eds.), *Creative mastery in hypnosis and hypnoanalysis: A Festschrift for Erika Fromm* (pp. 199–229). Hillsdale, NJ: Erlbaum.

Brown, D. (1992). Clinical hypnosis research since 1986. In E. Fromm & M.R. Nash (Eds.), *Clinical hypnosis research* (pp. 427–458). New York: Guilford.

Brown, D. (June 11–12, 1993). *Psychodynamic approaches and hypnotherapy of trauma related disorders.* Presented at the Annual Trauma Conference, Harvard Medical School, Boston, MA.

Brown, D. (1995a). Pseudomemories, the standard of science, and the standard of care in trauma treatment. *American Journal of Clinical Hypnosis, 37,* 1–24.

Brown, D. (1995b). Sources of suggestion and their applicability to psychotherapy. In J.L. Alpert (Ed.), *Sexual abuse recalled: Treating trauma in the era of the recovered memory debate* (pp. 61–100). Northvale, NJ: Jason Aronson.

Brown, D., & Fromm, E. (1986). *Hypnotherapy and hypnoanalysis.* Hillsdale, NJ: Erlbaum.

Brown, D., & Fromm, E. (1987). *Hypnosis and behavioral medicine*. Hillsdale, NJ: Erlbaum.

Brown, D.R. (1993). Comment: Panacea or Pandora's box: The "two schools of medical thought" doctrine after *Jones v.Chidester*, 610 A.2d 964 (Pa. 1992). *Washington University Journal of Urban and Contemporary Law, 44*, 223–234.

Brown, J.A. (1958). Some tests of the decay theory of immediate memory. *Quarterly Journal of Experimental Psychology, 10*, 12–21.

Brown, J.A.C. (1963). *Techniques of persuasion: From propaganda to brainwashing*. Baltimore: Penguin.

Brown, L. (1995a). Not outside the range: One feminist perspective on psychic trauma. In C. Caruth (Ed.), *Trauma: Explorations in memory* (pp. 100–112). Baltimore, MD: Johns Hopkins University Press.

Brown, L. (1995b). The therapy client as plaintiff: Clinical and legal issues for the treating therapist. In J.L. Alpert (Ed.), *Sexual abuse recalled: Treating trauma in the era of the recovered memory debate* (pp.337–362). Northvale, NJ: Jason Aronson.

Brown, R., & Kulik, J. (1977). Flashbulb memories. *Cognition, 5*, 73–99.

Brown, R.W., & McNeill, D. (1966). The "tip of the tongue" phenomenon. *Journal of Verbal Learning and Verbal Behavior, 5*, 325–357.

Brown, W. (October 5, 1918a). The treatment of cases of shell shock in an advanced neurological centre. *Lancet, 15*, 505.

Brown, W. (October 5, 1918b). Hypnosis in hysteria [Letter to the editor]. *Lancet, 15*, 505.

Brown, W. (1919). Hypnosis, suggestion, and dissociation. *British Medical Journal, 191*, 734–736.

Brown, W. (1920–1921). The revival of emotional memories and its therapeutic value. *British Journal of Medical Psychology, 1*, 16–19.

Brown, W. (1938). Hypnosis, suggestibility and progressive relaxation. *British Journal of Psychology, 28*, 396–411.

Browne, A., & Finkelhor, D. (1986). Impact of childhood sexual abuse: A review of the research. *Psychological Bulletin, 99*, 66–77.

Brownell, K.D. (1989). *LEARN: The LEARN program for weight control*. Philadelphia, PA: University of Pennsylvania School of Medicine.

Brownfield, C.A. (1972). *The brain benders: A study of the effects of isolation* (2nd ed.). New York: Exposition Press.

Brownmiller, S. (1975). *Against our will: Men, women, and rape*. New York: Simon & Schuster.

Bruck, M., & Ceci, S.J. (1995). Amicus brief for the case of *State of New Jersey v. Michaels* presented by committee of concerned social scientists. *Psychology, Public Policy and Law, 1*, 272–322.

Bruner, J.S. (1986). *Actual minds, possible worlds*. Cambridge: Harvard University Press.

Brunn, J.T. (1968). Retrograde amnesia in a murder suspect. *American Journal of Clinical Hypnosis, 10*, 209–213.

Bryant, R.A. (1995a). Autobiographical memory across

personalities in dissociative identity disorder: a case report. *Journal of Abnormal Psychology, 104*, 625–631.

Bryant, R.A. (1995b). Fantasy proneness, reported childhood abuse, and the relevance of reported abuse onset. *International Journal of Clinical and Experimental Hypnosis, 43*, 184–193.

Bryant, R.A. (1996). Posttraumatic stress disorder, flashbacks, and pseudomemories in closed head injury. *Journal of Traumatic Stress, 9*, 621–629.

Bryan, W.J., Jr. (1971). *The chosen ones*. New York: Vantage Press.

Bryan, W.J., Jr. (1962). *Legal aspects of hypnosis*. Springfield, IL: Charles C. Thomas.

Buckhout, R., Apler, A., Chern, S., Silverberg, G., & Slomovits, M. (1974). Determinants of eyewitness performance on a lineup. *Bulletin of the Psychonomic Society, 4*, 191–192.

Bulik, C.M., Sullivan, P.F., & Rorty, M. (1989). Childhood sexual abuse in women with bulimia. *Journal of Clinical Psychiatry, 50*, 460–464.

Bull, R. (1995). Innovative techniques for the questioning of child witnesses, especially those who are young and those with learning disability. In M.S. Zaragoza et al. (Eds.), *Memory and testimony in the child witness* (pp. 179–194). Thousand Oaks, CA: Sage.

Burgess v. Superior Court. (1992). 2 Cal.4th 1064, 9 Cal.Rptr.2d 615, 831 P.2d 1197.

Burgess, A.W., & Clark, M.L. (1984). *Child pornography and sex rings*. Lexington, MA: Lexington Books.

Burgess, A.W., Hartman, C.R., & Baker, T. (1995). Memory presentations of childhood sexual abuse. *Journal of Psychosocial Nursing, 33*, 9–16.

Burgess, A.W., & Holmstrom, L.L. (1974). Rape trauma syndrome. *American Journal of Psychiatry, 131*, 981–986.

Burgess, A.W., & Holmstrom, L.L. (1980). Sexual trauma of children and adolescents: Pressure, sex, and secrecy. In L. Schultz (Ed.), *Sexual victimology of youths* (pp. 67–82). Springfield, IL: Charles C. Thomas.

Burke, A., Heuer, F., & Reisberg, D. (1992). Remembering emotional events. *Memory and Cognition, 20*, 277–290.

Burkett, E., & Bruni, F. (1993). *A gospel of shame: Children, sexual abuse, and the Catholic church*. New York: Viking.

Burns v. Reed. (1990). 894 F.2d 949 (7 Cir.).

Burns v. Reed. (1991). 500 U.S. 478, 111 S. Ct. 1934, 114 L.Ed.2d 547.

Burns v. Reed. (1995). 44 F.3d 524 (7 Cir.), rehearing and suggestion for rehearing en banc denied Feb. 6, 1995.

Butler, K. (June 26, 1994). A house divided. *Los Angeles Times Magazine*, 12.

Butler, L.D., Duran, R.E.F., Jasiukaitis, P., Koopman, C., & Spiegel, D. (1996). Hypnotizability and traumatic experience: A diathesis-stress model of dissociative symptomatology. *American Journal of Psychiatry, 153*, 42–63.

Butler, S. (1978). *Conspiracy of silence: The trauma of incest*. New York: Bantam.

Bybee, D., & Mowbray, C. (1993). An analysis of allegations of sexual abuse in a multi-victim day-care center case. *Child Abuse and Neglect, 17,* 767–783.

Bychowski, G. (1952). *Psychotherapy of psychosis.* New York: Grune & Stratton.

Cahill, L., Prins, B., Weber, M., & McGaugh, J.L. (October 20, 1994). B-adrenergic activation and memory for emotional events. *Nature, 371,* 702–704.

Caine, E. D., Weingartner, H., Ludlow, C. L., Cudahy, E. A., & Wehry, S. (1981). Qualitative analysis of scopolamine-induced amnesia. *Psychopharmacology, 74,* 74–80.

California v. Shirley. 458 U.S. 1125, 103 S.Ct. 13, 73 L.Ed.2d 1400, *cert. denied, California v. Shirley,* 459 U.S. 860, 103 S.Ct. 133, 74 L.Ed 2d 14.

Calof, D.L. (1994). From traumatic dissociation to repression: Historical origins of the "false memory syndrome" hypothesis. *Treating Abuse Today, 4,* 24–36.

Cameron, C. (April 1993). *Recovering memories of childhood sexual abuse: A longitudinal report.* Paper presented at the Western Psychological Association Convention, Phoenix, AZ.

Cameron, C. (1994). Women survivors confronting their abusers: Issues, decisions and outcomes. *Journal of Child Sexual Abuse, 3,* 7–35.

Cameron, C. (1996). Comparing amnesic and nonamnesic survivors of childhood sexual abuse: A longitudinal study. In K. Pezdek & W.P. Banks (Eds.), *The recovered memory/false memory debate* (pp. 41–68). New York: Academic Press.

Campbell, D.T., & Stanley, J.C. (1963). *Experimental and quasi-experimental designs for research.* Chicago: Rand-McNally.

Caplan, A.L. (Ed.). (1992). *When medicine went mad: Bioethics and the Holocaust.* Totowa, NJ: Humana Press.

Caplan, G. (1964). *Principles of preventative psychiatry.* New York: Basic.

Cardena, E. (1994). The domain of dissociation. In S.J. Lynn & R.W. Rhue (Eds.), *Dissociation: Theoretical, clinical and research perspectives* (pp. 15–31). New York: Guilford.

Cardena, E. & Spiegel, D. (1993). Dissociative reactions to the San Francisco Bay area earthquake of 1989. *American Journal of Psychiatry, 150,* 474–478.

Carter v. Western Kraft Paper Mill. (1994). 649 So.2d 541 (La.App.).

Cartwright, S.A. (1851). Report on the diseases and physical peculiarities of the Negro race. *New Orleans Medical and Surgical Journal, 7,* 691.

Caryl S. v. Child & Adolescent Treatment Services, Inc. (1994). 161 Misc.2d 563, 614 N.Y.S.2d 661 (Sup.Ct., Erie County).

Caseley-Rondi, G., Merikle, P. M., & Bowers, K. S. (1994). Unconscious cognition in the context of general anesthesia. *Consciousness & Cognition, 3,* 166–195.

Cassel, W.S. & Bjorklund, D.F. (in press). Developmental patterns of eyewitness memory and suggestibility: An ecologically based short-term longitudinal study. *Law and Human Behavior.*

Cassidy, P.S. (1974). The liability of psychiatrists for malpractice. *University of Pittsburg Law Review, 36,* 108–137.

Cavenar, J.O. & Nash, J.L. (1976). The effects of combat on the normal personality: War neurosis in Vietnam returnees. *Comprehensive Psychiatry, 17,* 647–653.

Ceci, S.J. (August, 1994). *Cognitive and social factors in children's testimony.* Paper presented at the Annual Meeting of the American Psychological Association.

Ceci, S.J. (1995). False beliefs: Some developmental and clinical considerations. In D.L. Schacter (Ed.), *Memory distortion: How minds, brains, and societies reconstruct the past* (pp. 91–128). Cambridge, MA: Harvard University Press.

Ceci, S.J. (November 14, 1996). [Remarks on ABC-TV's "Nightline"].

Ceci, S.J., & Bruck, M. (1993). Suggestibility of the child witness: A historical review and synthesis. *Psychological Bulletin, 113,* 403–439.

Ceci, S.J., & Bruck, M. (1995). *Jeopardy in the courtroom: A scientific analysis of children's testimony.* Washington, DC: American Psychological Association.

Ceci, S.J., Crotteau–Huffman, M.L.C., Smith, E., & Loftus, E.F. (1994). Repeatedly thinking about a nonevent: Source misattributions among preschoolers. *Consciousness and Cognition, 3,* 388–407.

Ceci, S.J., Lea, S.E.G., & Howe, M.J.A. (1980). Structural analysis of memory traces in children from four to ten years of age. *Developmental Psychology, 16,* 203–212.

Ceci, S.J., Leichtman, M., & White, T. (in press). Interviewing preschoolers: Remembrance of things planted. In D.P. Peters (Ed.), *The child witness in context: Cognitive, social, and legal perspectives.* The Netherlands: Kluwer.

Ceci, S.J., & Loftus, E.F. (1994). Memory work: A royal road to false memories? *Applied Cognitive Psychology, 8,* 351–364.

Ceci, S.J., Loftus, E.F., Leichtman, M.D., & Bruck, M. (1994). The possible role of source misattributions in the creation of false beliefs among preschoolers. *International Journal of Clinical and Experimental Hypnosis, 42,* 304–320.

Ceci, S.J., Ross, D.F., & Toglia, M.P. (1987). Suggestibility in children's memory: Psycholegal implications. *Journal of Experimental Psychology: General, 116,* 38–49.

Ceci, S.J., Toglia, M.P., & Ross, D.F. (Eds.). (1987). *Children's eyewitness memory.* New York: Springer.

Celluci, A.J., & Lawrence, P.S. (1978). The efficacy of systematic desensitization in reducing nightmares. *Journal of Behavior Therapy and Experimental Psychiatry, 9,* 109–114.

Center Foundation v. Chicago Insurance Company. (1991). 227 Cal. App.3d 547, 278 Cal.Rptr. 13 (2nd Dist., Div. 1).

Chadwick, D.L. (May 26, 1989). Book review of H. Wakefield & R. Underwager, *Accusations of child sexual abuse, Journal of the American Medical Association, 261,* 3035.

Chadwick, D.L. (1991). Book review of R. Underwager & H. Wakefield, *The real world of child interrogations*, *Child Abuse & Neglect*, 15, 602–603.

Chamberlain, D. (1987). The cognitive newborn: A scientific update. *British Journal of Psychotherapy*, 4, 30–71.

Chandler, C.C. (1991). How memory for an event is influenced by related events: Interference in modified recognition tests. *Journal of Experimental Psychology: Learning, Memory, and Cognition*, 17, 115–125.

Chapman v. State. (1982). 638 P. 2d 1280 (Sup.Ct.Wyo.).

Charcot, J.M. (1887). *Lecons sur les maladies du system nerveux faites a la salpetriere*, Tome III. Paris: Progres Medical and A. Delahaye & E. Lecrosnie.

Charney, D.S., Deutch, A.Y., Krystal, J.H., Southwick, S.M., & Davis, M. (1993). Psychobiologic mechanisms of posttraumatic stress disorder. *Archives of General Psychiatry*, 50, 294–305.

Chase, A. (1977). *The legacy of malthus: The social costs of the new scientific racism*. New York: Alfred A. Knopf.

Chase, T. (1987). *When rabbit howls*. New York: E.P. Dutton.

Chatman v. Millis. 1975. 257 Ark. 451, 517 S.W.2d 504.

Cheek, D. B.(1959). Unconscious perception of meaningful sounds during surgical anesthesia as revealed under hypnosis. *American Journal of Clinical Hypnosis*, 1, 101–113.

Cheek, D. B. (1964). Surgical memory and reaction to careless conversation. *American Journal of Clinical Hypnosis*, 6, 237–239.

Cheek, D. B. (1966). The meaning of continued hearing sense under general anesthesia. *American Journal of Clinical Hypnosis*, 8, 275–280.

Cheek, D. B. (1981). Awareness of meaningful sounds under general anesthesia: Considerations and a review of the literature 1959–1979. In H. J. Wain (Ed.), *Theoretical and clinical aspects of hypnosis* (pp. 87–106). Miami, FL: Symposia Specialists.

Cheek, D., & LeCron, L. (1968). *Clinical hypnotherapy*. New York: Grune & Stratton.

Cherry, E.C. (1953). Some experiments on the recognition of speech with one and two ears. *Journal of the Acoustical Society of America*, 25, 975–979.

Chertok, L., & de Saussure, R. (1979). *The therapeutic revolution: From Mesmer to Freud*. New York: Brunner/Mazel.

Christiaansen, R.E., & Ochalek, K. (1983). Editing misleading information from memory: Evidence for the co-existence of original and postevent information. *Memory and Cognition*, 11, 467–475.

Christensen v. Thornby. (1934). 192 Minn. 123, 255 N.W. 620.

Christianson, S-A.(1984). The relationship between induced emotional arousal and amnesia. *Scandinavian Journal of Psychology*, 25, 147–160.

Christianson, S-A. (1987). Emotional and autonomic responses to visual traumatic stimuli. *Scandinavian Journal of Psychology*, 28, 83–87.

Christianson, S-A. (1989). Flashbulb memories: Special, but not so special. *Memory and Cognition*, 17, 435–443.

Christianson, S-A. (1992a). Do flashbulb memories differ from other types of emotional memories? In E. Winograd & U. Neisser (Eds.), *Affect and accuracy in recall: Studies of "flashbulb" memories* (pp. 191–211). London, England: Cambridge University Press.

Christianson, S-A. (1992b). Emotional memories in laboratory studies versus real-life studies: Do they compare? In M.A. Conway, D.C. Rubin, H. Spinnler, & W.A. Wagenaar (Eds.), *Theoretical perspectives on autobiographical memory* (pp. 339–352). Dordrecht: Kluwer.

Christianson, S-A. (1992c). Emotional stress and eyewitness memory: A critical review. *Psychological Bulletin*, 112, 284–309.

Christianson, S-A. (1992d). *The handbook of emotion and memory: Research and theory*. Hillsdale, NJ: Erlbaum.

Christianson, S-A. (1992e). Remembering emotional events: Potential mechanisms. In S-A. Christianson (Ed.), *The handbook of emotion and memory: Research and theory* (pp. 307–340). Hillsdale, NJ: Erlbaum.

Christianson, S-A., & Fallman, L. (1990). The role of age on reactivity and memory for emotional pictures. *Scandinavian Journal of Psychology*, 31, 291–301.

Christianson, S-A., Goodman, J., & Loftus, E.F. (1992). Eyewitness memory for stressful events: Methodological quandaries and ethical dilemmas. In S-A. Christianson (Ed.), *The handbook of emotion and memory: Research and theory* (pp. 217–241). Hillsdale, NJ: Erlbaum.

Christianson, S-A., & Hubinette, B. (1993) Hands up! A study of witnesses' emotional reactions and memories associated with bank robberies. *Applied Cognitive Psychology*, 7, 365–379.

Christianson, S-A., & Loftus, E.F. (1987). Memory for traumatic events. *Applied Cognitive Psychology*, 1, 225–239.

Christianson, S-A., & Loftus, E.F. (1990). Some characteristics of people's traumatic memories. *Bulletin of the Psychonomic Society*, 28, 195–198.

Christianson, S-A., & Nilsson, L-G. (1984). Functional amnesia as induced by a psychological trauma. *Memory and Cognition*, 12, 142–155.

Christianson, S-A., & Nilsson, L-G. (1989). Hysterical amnesia: A case of aversively motivated isolation of memory. In T. Archer & L-G. Nilsson (Eds.), *Aversion, avoidance, and anxiety* (pp. 289–310). Hillsdale, NJ: Erlbaum.

Chu, J.A., & Dill, D.L. (1990). Dissociative symptoms in relation to childhood physical and sexual abuse. *American Journal of Psychiatry*, 147, 887–892.

Chu, J.A., Matthews, J., Frey, L.M., & Ganzel, B. (1996). The nature of traumatic memories of childhood abuse. *Dissociation*, 9, 2–17.

Chumbler v. McClure. (1974). 505 F. 2d 489 (6th Cir.).

Cialdini, R.B. (1984). *Influence: The new psychology of modern persuasion*. New York: Quill.

Cicchetti, D., & Carlson, V. (1989). *Child maltreatment:*

Theory and research on the causes and consequences of child abuse and neglect. New York: Cambridge University Press.

Cifu, D.A. (1989). Expanding legal malpractice to nonclient third parties: At what cost? *Columbia Journal of Law and Social Problems, 23,* 1–25.

Cipriani, D. (1988). *The role of initial recognition, type of postevent information, and source credibility in understanding the postevent information contamination effect.* Unpublished Master's thesis, Roosevelt University.

Claridge, K. (1992). Reconstructing memories of abuse: A theory-based approach. *Psychotherapy: Theory, Research, and Practice, 29,* 243–252.

Clark, S.E., & Loftus, E.F. (1996). The construction of space alien abduction memories. *Psychological Inquiry, 7,* 140–143.

Clarke-Stewart, A., Thompson, W., & Lepore, S. (May, 1989). *Manipulating children's interpretations through interrogation.* Paper presented at the biennial meeting of the Society for Research on Child Development, Kansas City, MO.

Clemens, B.A. (1991). Hypnotically enhanced testimony: Has it lost its charm? *Southern Illinois University Law Journal, 15,* 289–320.

Clevenger, N. (1991–1992). Statute of limitations: Childhood victims of sexual abuse bringing civil actions against their perpetrators after attaining the age of majority. *Journal of Family Law, 30,* 447–469.

Clifford, B.R., & Bull, R. (1978). *The psychology of person identification.* London: Routledge & Kegan Paul.

Clifford, B.R., & Hollin, C.R. (1981). Effects of the type of incident and the number of perpetrators on eyewitness memory. *Journal of Applied Psychology, 66,* 364–370.

Clifford, B.R., & Scott, J. (1978). Individual and situational factors in eyewitness testimony. *Journal of Applied Psychology, 63,* 352–359.

Coe, W.C., & Sarbin, T.R. (1991). Role theory: Hypnosis for a dramaturgical and narrational perspective. In S.J. Lynn & J.W. Rhue (Eds.), *Theories of hypnosis* (pp. 303–323). New York: Guilford.

Coffey, P., Leitenberg, H., Henning, K., Turner, T., & Bennett, R.T. (1996). Mediators of the long-term impact of child sexual abuse: Perceived stigma, betrayal, powerlessness, and self-blame. *Child Abuse and Neglect, 20,* 447–455.

Cohen, A. (1964). *Attitude change and social influence.* New York: Basic.

Cohen, E.A. (1953). *Human behavior in the concentration camp.* New York: Grosset & Dunlap.

Cohen, G. (1989). *Memory in the real world.* Hillsdale, NJ: Erlbaum.

Cohen, G., & Java, R. (1995). Memory for medical history: Accuracy of recall. *Applied Cognitive Psychology, 9,* 273–288.

Cohen, L.P. (July 27, 1989). Doctor is accused of inside trading on patient's data. *Wall Street Journal,* B3.

Cohen, N.J. (1996). Functional retrograde amnesia as a model of amnesia for childhood sexual abuse. In K.

Pezdek & W.P. Banks (Eds.), *The recovered memory/false memory debate* (pp. 81–94). New York: Academic Press.

Cohen, N.J., McCloskey, M., & Wible, C.G. (1990). Flashbulb memories and underlying cognitive mechanisms: Reply to Pillemer. *Journal of Experimental Psychology: General, 119,* 97–100.

Cohen, R.J. (1979). *Malpractice: A guide for mental health professionals.* New York: Free Press.

Cohen, R.L., & Harnick, M.A. (1980). The susceptibility of child witness to suggestion. *Law and Human Behavior, 4,* 201–210.

Cohler, B.J. (1994). Memory recovery and the use of the past: A commentary on Lindsay and Read from psychoanalytic perspectives. *Applied Cognitive Psychology, 8,* 365–378.

Cohn, D.S. (1991). Anatomical doll play of preschoolers referred for sexual abuse and those not referred. *Child Abuse and Neglect, 15,* 455–466.

Cole, C.B., & Loftus, E.F. (1987). The memory of children. In S.J. Ceci, M., Toglia, & D. Ross (Eds.). *Children's eyewitness memory* (pp.178–208). New York: Springer-Verlag.

Cole, W.G., & Loftus, E.F. (1979). Incorporating new information into memory. *American Journal of Psychology, 92,* 413–425.

Colegrove, F.W. (1899). Individual memories. *American Journal of Psychology, 10,* 228–255.

Coleman, J. (1960). *Abnormal psychology and modern life* (2nd ed.). Glenview, IL: Scott, Foresman & Company.

Collins, H.M. (1985). *Changing order: Replication and induction in scientific practice.* Newbury Park, CA: Sage.

Colorado Statutes. (1986). s 18–6–401(7) (a)(I), 8B C.R.S.

Colvin, R. (1992). *Evil harvest: The shocking true story of cult murder in the American heartland.* New York: Bantam.

Commonwealth v. Crawford. (1996). 452 Pa.Super. 354, 682 A.2d 323.

Conn, J.H. (1958). Meanings and motivations associated with spontaneous hypnotic regression. *International Journal of Clinical and Experimental Hypnosis, 6,* 21–44.

Connery, D.S. (1977) *Guilty until proven innocent.* New York: Putnam.

Conquest, R. (1990). *The great terror: A reassessment.* Oxford: Oxford University Press.

Conte, J.R. (1991). Child sexual abuse: Looking backward and forward. In M.Q. Patton (Ed.), *Family sexual abuse: Frontline research and evaluation* (pp. 3–22). Newbury Park, CA: Sage.

Conte, J.R., Sorenson, E., Fogarty, L., & Rosa, J.D. (1991). Evaluating children's reports of sexual abuse: Results from a survey of professionals. *American Journal of Orthopsychiatry, 61,* 428–437.

Contreras v. State. (1986). 718 P.2d 129 (Alaska).

Conway, F., & Siegelman, J. (1978). *Snapping: America's epidemic of sudden personality change.* New York: Dell.

Conway, M.A. (1988). *Vivid memories of novel, important,*

and mundane events. Unpublished manuscript.

Conway, M.A. (1992). *Autobiographical memory: An introduction.* Philadelphia: Open University Press.

Conway, M.A. & Bekerian, D.A. (1988). Characteristics of vivid memories. In M.M. Gruneberg, P.E. Morris, & R.N. Sykes (Eds.), *Practical aspects of memory: Current research and issues* (pp. 519–524). Chichester, England: John Wile.

Cook, C.W., & Millsaps, P.K. (1991). Redressing wrongs of the blamelessly ignorant survivor of incest. *University of Richmond Law Review, 26,* 1–40.

Cool v. Legion Insurance Company. (1996). Brief in Support of Motions in Limine—Alternate Schools of Thought. Case No. 94CV707, Medical Malpractice CH655-30104. Wisconsin Circuit Court, Outagamie County.

Coons, P.M. (1980). Multiple personality: Diagnostic considerations. *Journal of Clinical Psychiatry, 41,* 330–336.

Coons, P.M. (1986). Treatment progress in 20 patients with multiple personality disorder. *Journal of Nervous and Mental Diseases, 174,* 715–721.

Coons, P.M. (1994a). Confirmation of childhood abuse in child and adolescent cases of multiple personality and dissociative disorder not otherwise specified. *Journal of Nervous and Mental Disease, 182,* 461–464.

Coons, P.M. (1994b). Reports of satanic ritual abuse: Further implications about pseudomemories. *Perceptual and Motor Skills, 78,* 1376–1378.

Coons, P.M. & Milstein, V. (1986). Psychosexual disturbances in multiple personality: Characteristics, etiology, and treatment. *Journal of Clinical Psychiatry, 47,* 106–110.

Corgan v. Muehling. (1991). 143 Ill.2d 296, 158 Ill.Dec. 489, 574 N.E.2d 602.

Cork, R. C., Kihlstrom, J. F., & Schacter, D. L. (1993). Implicit and explicit memory with isoflurane compared to sufentanil/nitrous oxide. In P. S. Sebel, B. Bonke, & E. Winograd (Eds.), *Memory and awareness in anesthesia* (pp. 74–80). Englewood Cliffs, NJ: Prentice Hall.

Corrigan, J.D., Dell, D.M., Lewis, K.N., & Schmidt, L.D. (1980). Counseling as a social influence process: A review. *Journal of Counseling Psychology Monograph, 27,* 395–441.

Corwin, D. (1988). Early diagnosis of child sexual abuse: Diminishing the lasting effects. In G. Wyatt & G. Powell (Eds.), *The lasting effects of child sexual abuse* (pp. 251–269). Newbury Park, CA: Sage.

Council, J., Kirsch, I., Vickery, A.R., & Carlson, D. (1983). "Trance" vs. "skill" hypnotic inductions: The effects of credibility, expectancy, and experimenter modeling. *Journal of Consulting and Clinical Psychology, 51,* 432–440.

Council, J.R., & Huff, K. (1990). Hypnosis, fantasy activity, and reports of paranormal experiences of high, medium, and low fantasizers. *British Journal of Experimental & Clinical Hypnosis, 7,* 9–15.

Council, J.R., Kirsch, I., & Hafner, L.P. (1986). Expectancy versus absorption in the prediction of hypnotic responding. *Journal of Personality and Social Psychology, 50,* 182–189.

Council, L.J., Kihlstrom, J.F., Cork, R.C., Behr, S.E., & Hughes, S. (1993). Therapeutic suggestions presented during isoflurane anesthesia: Preliminary report. In P.S. Sebel, B. Bonke, & E. Winograd (Eds.), *Memory and awareness in anesthesia* (pp. 182–186). New York: Prentice Hall.

Council on Mental Health, American Medical Association. (1958). Medical use of hypnosis. *Journal of the American Medical Association, 186*–189.

Courtois, C. A. (1988). *Healing the incest wound: Adult survivors in therapy.* New York: Norton.

Courtois, C.A. (1991). Theory, sequencing, and strategy in treating adult survivors. In. J. Briere (Ed.), *New directions for mental health services* (Vol. 51, pp. 47–60). New York: Jossey-Bass.

Courtois, C.A. (1992a). The memory retrieval process in incest survivor therapy. *Journal of Child Sexual Abuse, 1,* 15–31.

Courtois, C.A. (1992b). Treatment of incest and complex dissociative traumatic stress reactions. In L. Vandecreek, S. Knapp, & T.L. Jackson (Eds.), *Innovations in clinical practice: A source book* (Vol. 13, pp. 37–54). Sarasota, FL: Professional Resource Press.

Courtois, C.A. (1995a). Assessment and diagnosis. In. C. Classen & I. D. Yalom (Eds.), *Treating women molested in childhood* (pp. 1–34). San Francisco, CA: Jossey-Bass.

Courtois, C.A. (1995b). Scientist-practitioners and the delayed memory controversy: Scientific standards and the need for collaboration. *Counseling Psychologist, 23,* 294–299.

Couture, L. J., Kihlstrom, J. F., Cork, R. C., Behr, S. E., & Hughes, S. (1993). Therapeutic suggestions presented during isoflurane anesthesia: Preliminary report. In P. S. Sebel, B. Bonke, & E. Winograd (Eds.), *Memory and awareness in anesthesia* (pp. 182–186). Englewood Cliffs, NJ: Prentice Hall.

Crabtree, A. (1992). Dissociation and memory: A two-hundred year perspective. *Dissociation, 5,* 150–154.

Crabtree, A. (1993). *From Mesmer to Freud: Magnetic sleep and the roots of psychological healing.* New Haven: Princeton University Press.

Craik, F.I.M., & Lockhart, R.S. (1972). Levels of processing: A framework for memory research. *Journal of Verbal Learning and Verbal Behavior, 11,* 671–684.

Crane, D. (1972). *Invisible colleges: Diffusion of knowledge in scientific communities.* Chicago: University of Chicago Press.

Crane v. Johnson. (1917). 242 U.S. 339, 37 S.Ct. 176, 61 L.Ed. 348.

Crasilneck, H.B., McCranie, E.J., & Jenkins, M.T. (1956). Special indications for hypnosis as a method of anesthesia. *Journal of the American Medical Association, 162,* 1606–1608.

Crawford, H.J. (1990). Cognitive and psychophysiological correlates of hypnotic responsiveness and hypnosis. In M.L. Fass & D. Brown (Eds.), *Creative mastery in hypnosis and hypnoanalysis* (pp. 47–54). Hillsdale, NJ: Erlbaum.

Crawford, H.J., & Allen, S.N. (1983). Enhanced visual memory during hypnosis as mediated by hypnotic responsiveness and cognitive strategies. *Journal of Experimental Psychology: General, 122*, 662–685.

Crawford, H.J., & Gruzelier, J.H. (1992). A midstream view of the neuropsychophysiology of hypnosis: Recent research and future directions. In. E. Fromm & M.R. Nash (Eds.), *Contemporary hypnosis research* (pp. 227–266). New York: Guilford.

Crittenden, P.M., & Ainsworth, M.D.S. (1989). Child maltreatment and attachment theory. In D. Cicchetti & V. Carlson (Eds.), *Child maltreatment: Theory and research on the causes and consequences of child abuse and neglect* (pp. 432–463). New York: Cambridge University Press.

Crombag, H.F.M., Wagenaar, W.A., & Van Koppen, P.J. (1996). Crashing memories and the problem of "source monitoring." *Applied Cognitive Psychology, 10*, 95–104.

Crouch, B., & Damphousse, K. (1991). Law enforcement and the Satanic crime connection: A survey of "cult cops," pages 191–204. In J.T. Richardson, J. Best, & D.G. Bromley, *The Satanism scare.* New York: Aldine De Gruyter.

Crovitz, H.F. & Schiffman, H. (1974). Frequency of episodic memories as a function of their age. *Bulletin of the Psychonomic Society, 4*, 517–518.

Crowder, A. (1995). *Opening the door: A treatment model for therapy with male survivors of sexual abuse.* New York: Brunner/Mazel.

Cushman, P. (1995). *Constructing the self, constructing America: A cultural history of psychotherapy.* Reading, MA: Addison-Wesley.

Cutler, B.L., Penrod, S.D., & Martens, T.K. (1987). The reliability of eyewitness identification: The role of system and estimator variables. *Law and Human Behavior, 11*, 233–258.

Cutshall, J., & Yuille, J.C. (1989). Field studies of eyewitness memory of actual crimes. In D. C. Raskin (Ed.), *Psychological methods in criminal investigation and evidence* (pp.97–124). New York: Springer.

Dailey, J.P. (1994). The two schools of thought and informed consent doctrines in Pennsylvania: A model for integration. *Dickinson Law Review 98*, 713–737.

Dale, P.S., Loftus, E.F., & Rathbun, L. (1978). The influence of the form of the question on the eyewitness testimony of preschool children. *Journal of Psycholinguistic Research, 7*, 269–277.

Dalenberg, C.J. (July 15–17, 1995). *The accuracy of continuous and recovered memories of trauma.* Presentation to the Society for Applied Research on Memory and Cognition.

Dalenberg, C.J. (1996). Accuracy, timing and circumstances of disclosure in therapy of recovered and continuous memories of abuse. *Journal of Psychiatry and Law, 24*, 229–275.

Dasgupta, A. M., Juza, D. M., White, G. M., & Maloney, J. F. (1995). Memory and hypnosis: A comparative analysis of guided memory, cognitive interview, and hypnotic hypermnesia. *Imagination, Cognition & Personality, 14*(2), 117–130.

Daubert v. Merrell Dow Pharmaceuticals, Inc. (1993). 509 U.S. 579, 113 S.Ct 2786, 125 L.Ed. 2d 469.

Davies, G. (1991). Research on children's testimony: Implications for interviewing practice. In C.R. Hollin & K. Howells (Eds.), *Clinical approaches to sex offenders and their victims* (pp. 93–115). New York: Wiley.

Davies, G., Tarrant, A., & Flin, R. (1989). Close encounters of the witness kind: Children's memory for a simulated health inspection. *British Journal of Psychology, 80*, 415–429.

Davies, J.M., & Frawley, M.G. (1994). *Treating the adult survivor of childhood sexual abuse: A psychoanalytic perspective.* New York: Basic.

Davis, P.J. (1990). Repression and the inaccessibility of emotional memories. In J.L. Singer (Ed.), *Repression and dissociation: Implications for personality theory, psychopathology, and health* (pp. 387–404). Chicago: University of Chicago Press.

Dawes, R.M. (1994). *House of cards.* Toronto: Maxwell Macmillan.

DeBenedittis, G., & Sironi, V.A. (1986). Depth cerebral electrical activity in man during hypnosis. *International Journal of Clinical and Experimental Hypnosis, 34*, 63–70.

DeBenedittis, G., & Sironi, V. A. (1988). Arousal effects of electrical deep brain stimulation in hypnosis. *International Journal of Clinical & Experimental Hypnosis, 38*, 125–138.

Deffenbacher, K.A. (1980). Eyewitness accuracy and confidence: Can we infer anything about their relationship? *Law and Human Behavior, 4*, 243–260.

Deffenbacher, K.A. (1983). The influence of arousal on reliability of testimony. In S.M.A. Lloyd-Bostock & B.R. Clifford (Eds.), *Evaluating witness evidence* (pp. 235–251). New York: Wiley.

Delboeuf, J. (1889). *Le Magnetisme Animal: A propos d' ulne visite a l'ecole de Nancy.* Paris: F.Alcan.

Delboeuf, J. (1893–4). Die verbrecherischen Suggestionen. *Zeitschrift für Hypnotismus,* 177–198, 221–240, 247–268.

deMause, L. (1988). *The history of childhood: The untold story of child abuse.* New York: Peter Bedrick.

deMause, L. (1994). Why cults terrorize and kill children. *Journal of Psychohistory, 21*, 505–518.

Dent, H.R. (1991). Experimental studies of interviewing child witnesses. In. J. Doris (Ed.), *The suggestibility of children's recollections* (pp. 138–146). Washington, D.C.: American Psychological Association.

Dent, H.R., & Stephenson, G.M. (1979). An experimental study of the effectiveness of different techniques of questioning child witnesses. *British Journal of Social & Clinical Psychology, 18*, 41–51.

DePascalis, V., & Penna, P.M. (1990). 40–Hz EEG activity during hypnotic induction and hypnotic testing. *International Journal of Clinical and Experimental Hypnosis, 38*, 125–138.

DePiano, F.A., & Salzberg, H.C. (1981). Hypnosis as an aid to recall of meaningful information presented under three types of arousal. *International Journal of Clinical and Experimental Hypnosis, 29,* 383–400.

Dershowitz, A.M. (1994). *The abuse excuse and other cop-outs, sob stories, and evasions of responsibility.* Boston: Little, Brown & Company.

de Sade, D.A.F. (1789/1987) *The one hundred twenty days of Sodom.* New York: Grune.

Dhanens, T.P., & Lundy, R.M. (1975). Hypnotic and waking suggestions and recall. *International Journal of Clinical and Experimental Hypnosis, 23,* 68–79.

Diamond, B.L. (1980). Inherent problems in the use of pretrial hypnosis on a prospective witness. *California Law Review, 68,* 313–349.

Dichter, E. (1960). *The strategy of desire.* Garden City, NY: Doubleday.

Dichter, E. (1964). *Handbook of consumer motivations: The psychology of the world of objects.* New York: McGraw-Hill.

Dichter, E. (1971). *Motivating human behavior.* New York: McGraw Hill.

Dietz, P.E. (1990). Defenses against dangerous people when arrest and commitment fail. In R.I. Simon (Ed.), *Review of clinical psychiatry and the law* (Vol. 1, pp. 205–219). Washington, D.C.: American Psychiatric Press.

Dillon v. Legg. (1968). 68 Cal.2d 728, 441 P.2d 912, 69 Cal. Rptr. 72.

DiMarco v. Lynch Homes-Chester County. (1990). 525 Pa. 558, 583 A.2d 422.

Dinges, D.F., Whitehouse, W.G., Orne, E.C., Powell, J.W. Orne, M.T., & Erdelyi, M.H. (1992). Evaluating hypnotic memory enhancement (hypermnesia and reminiscence) using multitrial forced recall. *Journal of Experimental Psychology: Learning, Memory and Cognition, 18,* 1139–1147.

Dobbs, D., & Wilson, W.P. (1960). Observations on the persistence of traumatic war neurosis. *Journal of Mental and Nervous Disorders, 21,* 40–46.

Dodd, D.H., & Bradshaw, J. M. (1980). Leading questions and memory: Pragmatic constraints. *Journal of Verbal Learning and Verbal Behavior, 19,* 695–704.

Doe v. Archdiocese of Washington. (1997). 114 Md.App. 169, 689 A.2d 634.

Doe v. Maskell. (1996). 342 Md. 684, 679 A.2d 1087.

Doe v. McKay. (1997). 286 Ill. App. 3d 1020, 222 Ill. Dec. 643, 678 N.E. 2d 50 (2nd Dist.).

Dollinger, S.J. (1985) Lightening-strike disaster among children. *British Journal of Medical Psychiatry, 58,* 375–383.

Domovitch, E., Berger, P.B., Wawer, M.J., et al. (1984). Human torture: Description and sequelae of 104 cases. *Canadian Family Physician, 30,* 827–830.

Donaforte, L. (1982). *I remembered myself: The journal of a survivor of childhood sexual abuse.* Ukiah, CA: Author.

Dorcus, R. M. (1960). Recall under hypnosis of amnestic events. *International Journal of Clinical & Experimental Hypnosis, 8*(1), 57–60.

Dorsey v. State (1992) 206 Ga. Ap. 709, 426 S.E. 2d 224.

Douard, J.W., & Winslade, W.J. (1990). *Tarasoff* and the

moral duty to protect the vulnerable. In R.I. Simon(Ed.), *Review of clinical psychiatry and the law* (Vol. 1, pp. 163–176). Washington, D.C.: American Psychiatric Press.

Draijer, N. (1990). *Seksuell misbruik van door verwanten: Een landelijk onderzoek naar de omvang, de aard, de gezinsachtergronded, de emotionele etekeniss en de psychische en psychosomatische gevolgen* [Sexual abuse of girls by relatives: A nation-wide survey of the nature, emotional signs and psychological and psychosomatic sequelae]. Den Haag: Ministerie van Sociale Zaken en Verkgelegenheid.

Dritsas, W.J., & Hamilton, V.L. (1977). *Evidence about evidence: Effects of presuppositions, item salience, stress, and perceiver set on accident recall.* Unpublished manuscript, University of Michigan.

Dubovsky, S.L., & Trustman, R. (1976). Absence of recall during general anesthesia: Implications for theory and practice. *Anesthesia & Analgesia, 55,* 969–701.

Dulles, A. (April 10, 1953). Address to Princeton alumni, Hot Springs, VA.

Dumas, L. (1964). A subjective report of inadvertent hypnosis. *International Journal of Clinical and Experimental Hypnosis, 12,* 78–80.

Duncan, E.M., Whitney, P., & Kunen, S. (1982). Integration of visual and verbal information in children's memory. *Child Development, 83,* 1215–1223.

Dunning, D., & Stern, L.B. (1992). Examining the generality of eyewitness hypermnesia: A close look at time delay and question type. *Applied Cognitive Psychology, 6,* 643–657.

Dunphy v. Gregor. (1994). 136 N.J. 99, 642 A.2d 372.

Dymek v. Nyquist. (1984). 128 Ill.App.3d 859, 83 Ill.Dec. 52, 469 N.E.2d 659 (1st Dist.).

Dywan, J. (1988). The imagery factor in hypnotic hypermnesia. *International Journal of Clinical and Experimental Hypnosis, 36,* 312–326.

Dywan, J., & Bowers, K. (1983). The use of hypnosis to enhance recall. *Science, 222,* 184–185.

Easterbrook, J.A. (1959). The effect of emotion on cue utilization and the organization of behavior. *Psychological Review, 66,* 183–201.

Ebbinghaus, H. (1885). *Über das Gedächtnis* [On memory]. Leipzig, Germany: Dunker.

Eberle, P., & Eberle, S. (1986) *Politics of child abuse.* Secaucus, NJ: Lyle Stuart.

Eberle, P., & Eberle, S. (1993) *The abuse of innocence: The McMartin preschool trial.* Buffalo, NY: Prometheus.

Edwards, B. (1988). *Drawing on the right side of the brain.* New York: St. Martins Press.

Edwards, P. (1987a). The case against reincarnation: Part 2. *Free Inquiry, 7*(1), 38–47.

Edwards, P. (1987b). The case against reincarnation: Part 3. *Free Inquiry, 7*(2), 38–49.

Ehrensaft, D. (1992). Preschool child sex abuse: The aftermath of the Presidio case. *American Journal of Orthopsychiatry, 62,* 234–244.

Eich, J.E. (1977). State-dependent retrieval of information in human episodic memory. In I.M. Birnbaum &

E.S. Parker (Eds.), *Alcohol and human memory* (pp. 141–157). Hillsdale, NJ: Erlbaum.

Eich, J.E. (1980). The cue-dependent nature of state-dependent retrieval. *Memory and Cognition, 8,* 157–173.

Eich, E. (1984). Memory for unattended events: Remembering with and without awareness. *Memory and Cognition, 12,* 105–111.

Eich, E., Reeves, J. L., & Katz, R. L. (1985). Anesthesia, amnesia, and the memory/awareness distinction. *Anesthesia & Analgesia, 64,* 1143–1148.

E.I. du Pont de Nemours and Co., Inc. v. Robinson. (1995). 923 S.W.2d (Tex. Sup.Ct.).

Eisen, M.L. (1996). The relationship between memory, suggestibility, and hypnotic responsivity. *American Journal of Clinical Hypnosis, 39,* 126–137.

Eisenberg, M.J. (1995). Recovered memories of childhood sexual abuse: The admissibility question. *Temple Law Review, 68,* 249–280.

Ellenson, G.S. (1986). Disturbances of perception in adult female incest survivors. *Social Casework, 67,* 149–159.

Elliott, D.M., & Briere, J. (1995). Posttraumatic stress associated with delayed recall of sexual abuse: A general population study. *Journal of Traumatic Stress, 8,* 629–647.

Elliott, D.M., & Fox, B. (1994). *Child abuse and amnesia: Prevalence and triggers to memory recovery.* Paper presented at the Annual Meeting of the International Society of Traumatic Stress Studies, Chicago, IL.

Ellis, B. (1991). Legend-trips and Satanism: Adolescents' ostensive traditions as "cult activity." In J.T. Richardson, J. Best, & D.G. Bromley, *The Satanism scare* (pp. 279–295). New York: Aldine De Gruyter.

El-Rayes, M. (1982). Traumatic war neurosis: Egyptian experience. *Journal of the Royal Army Medical Corps, 128,* 67–71.

Ennis v. Banks. (1917) 95 Wash.513.

Ennis, C.Z., McNeilly, C.L., Corkery, J.M., & Gilbert, M.S. (1995). The debate about delayed memories of child sexual abuse: A feminist perspective. *The Counseling Psychologist, 23,* 181–279.

Ensink, B.J. (1992). *Confusing realities: A study of child sexual abuse and psychiatric symptoms.* Amsterdam: VU University Press.

Epstein, G. (1981). *Waking dream therapy: Dream process as imagination.* New York: Human Sciences Press.

Epstein, S. (1973). The self-concept revisited, or a theory of a theory. *American Psychologist, 28,* 404–416.

Epstein, S. (1991). The self-concept, the traumatic neurosis, and the structure of personality. In D. Ozer, J.M. Healy, Jr., & A.J. Stewart (Eds.), *Perspectives on personality* (Vol. 3). Greenwich, CT: JAI Press.

Erdelyi, M.H. (1988). Hypermnesia: The effect of hypnosis, fantasy, and concentration. In H.M. Pettinati (Ed.), *Hypnosis and memory* (pp. 64–94). New York: Guilford.

Erdelyi, M.H. (1994). Hypnotic hypermnesia: The empty set of hypermnesia. *International Journal of Clinical and Experimental Hypnosis, 42,* 379–390.

Erdelyi, M.H., & Becker, J. (1974). Hypermnesia for pictures: Incremental memory for pictures but not for words in multiple recall trials. *Cognitive Psychology, 6,* 159–171.

Erdelyi, M.H., Finks, J., & Feigin-Pfau, M.B. (1989). The effect of response bias on recall performance, with some observations on processing bias. *Journal of Experimental Psychology: General, 118,* 245–254.

Erdelyi, M.H., & Frame, J.D. (1995). The case of Dr. John D. Frame's first memory: Historical truth and psychological distortion. *Consciousness and Cognition, 4,* 95–99.

Erdelyi, M.H., & Kleinbard, J. (1978). Has Ebbinghaus decayed with time? The growth of recall (hypermnesia) over days. *Journal of Experimental Psychology: Human Learning and Memory, 4,* 275–289.

Erickson, M.H. (1935). A study of an experimental neurosis hypnotically induced in a case of ejaculatio praecox. *British Journal of Medical Psychology, Part 1, 15,* 34–50.

Erickson, M.H. (November, 1936/1980). A clinical note on a word-association test. In E.L. Rossi (Ed.), *The collected papers of Milton H. Erickson, M.D.* (Vol. 3, pp. 289–291). New York: Irvington.

Erickson, M.H. (September, 1938). Negation or reversal of legal testimony. *Archives of Neurology and Psychiatry, 40,* 548–553.

Erickson, M.H. (1944). The method employed to formulate a complex story for the induction of an experimental neurosis in a hypnotic subject. *Journal of General Psychology, 31,* 67–84.

Erickson, M. H. (1963). Chemo-anaesthesia in relation to hearing and memory. *American Journal of Clinical Hypnosis, 6,* 31–36.

Erickson, M.H. (1967). Laboratory and clinical hypnosis: The same or different phenomena? *American Journal of Clinical Hypnosis, 9,* 166–170.

Erickson, M.H. (1980). *The collected papers of Milton H. Erickson, M.D.* (Vols. 1–4) E.L. Rossi (Ed.). New York: Irvington.

Erickson, M.H., & Kubie, L.S. (October, 1939/1980). The permanent relief of an obsessional phobia by means of communications with an unsuspected dual personality. In E.L. Rossi (Ed.), *The collected papers of Milton H. Erickson, M.D.* (Vol. 3, pp. 231–260). New York: Irvington.

Erickson, M.H., & Kubie, L.S. (1941). The successful treatment of a case of acute hysterical depression by a return under hypnosis to a critical phase of childhood. *Psychiatric Quarterly, 10,* 592–609.

Erickson, M.H., & Rossi, E.L. (1979). *Hypnotherapy: An exploratory casebook.* New York: Irvington.

Ernsdorff, G.M., & Loftus, E.F. (1995). Let sleeping memories lie? Words of caution about tolling the statute of limitations in cases of memory repression. *Journal of Criminal Law and Criminology, 84,* 129–176.

Ernst, S., & Goodman, L. (1985). *In our hands: A woman's book of self-help therapy.* Los Angeles: J.P. Tarcher.

Esplin, P.W., Boychuk, T., & Raskin, D.C. (June, 1988).

A field study of criteria-based content analysis of children's statements in sexual abuse cases. Paper presented at the NATO Advanced Study Institute on Credibility Assessmen, Maratea, Italy.

Eth, S. & Pynoos, R.S. (Eds.). (1985). *Post-traumatic stress disorder in children.* Washington, D.C.: American Psychoanalytic Association.

Evans, B.J., & Stanley, R.O. (Eds.). (1995). *Hypnosis and the law: Principles and practice.* Heidelberg, Victoria, Australia: Australian Society of Hypnosis.

Evans, C. (1973). *Cults of unreason.* New York: Dell.

Evans, C., & Richardson, P. H. (1988). Improved recovery and reduced postoperative stay after therapeutic suggestions during general anaesthesia. *Lancet, 2,* 491–493.

Evans, F.J. (1967). Suggestibility in the normal waking state. *Psychological Bulletin, 67,* 114–129.

Evans, F.J. (1979). Contextual forgetting: Posthypnotic source amnesia. *Journal of Abnormal Psychology, 88,* 556–563.

Evans, F.J. (1990). Sleep suggestion. In R.R. Bootzin, J.F. Kihlstrom, & D.L. Schacter (Eds.), *Sleep and cognition* (pp. 77–87). Washington, D.C.: American Psychological Association.

Evans, F.J., & Thorn, W.A.F. (1966). Two types of posthypnotic amnesia: Recall amnesia and source amnesia. *International Journal of Clinical & Experimental Hypnosis, 14,* 162–179.

Everson, M.D., & Boat, B.W. (1989). False allegations of sexual abuse by children and adolescents. *Journal of the American Academy of Child & Adolescent Psychiatry, 28,* 230–235.

Everson, M.D., & Boat, B.W. (1994). Putting the anatomical doll controversy in perspective: An examination of the major uses and criticisms of the dolls in child sexual abuse evaluations. *Child Abuse and Neglect, 18,* 113–129.

Ewin, D.M. (1990). Hypnotic technique for recall of sounds heard under general anaesthesia. In B. Bonke, W. Fitch, & K. Millar (Eds.), *Memory and awareness in anasthesia* (pp. 226–232). Amsterdam: Swets & Zeitlinger.

Executive Order. (1982). Exec. Order No. 12333, s. 2.10, 3 C.F.R. 213.

Eysenck, H.J. (1991). Is suggestibility? In J.F. Schumaker (Ed.), *Human suggestibility: Advances in theory, research, and application* (pp. 76–92). New York: Routledge.

Fager v. Hundt. (1993). 610 N.E.2d 246 (Ind.).

Fairbank, J.A., DeGood, D.E. & Jenkins, C.W. (1981). Behavioral treatment of a persistent post-traumatic startle response. *Journal of Behavior Therapy and Experimental Psychiatry, 12,* 321–324.

Fairbank, J.A., Gross, R.T., & Keane, T.M. (1983). Treatment of posttraumatic stress disorder: Evaluation of outcome with a behavioral code. *Behavior Modification, 7,* 557–568.

Faller, K.C. (1984). Is the child victim of sexual abuse telling the truth? *Child Abuse and Neglect, 8,* 473–481.

Faller, K.C. (1988a). Criteria for judging the credibility of children's statements about their sexual abuse. *Child Welfare, 67,* 389–401.

Faller, K.C. (1988b). The spectrum of sexual abuse in daycare: An exploratory study. *Journal of Family Violence, 3,* 283–298.

Faller, K.C. (1990). Sexual abuse of children in cults: A medical health perspective. *Roundtable, 2,* 2.

Faller, K.C. (1994). Ritual abuse: A review of the research. *The American Professional Society on the Abuse of Children Advisor, 7*(1), 19–27.

False Memory Syndrome Foundation. (December 5, 1992). *Newsletter,* 1.

False Memory Syndrome Foundation. (December 9–11, 1994). *Memory and reality: Reconciliation, scientific, clinical and legal perspectives.* Conference at Johns Hopkins University, Baltimore, MD.

Fancher, R.T. (1995). *Cultures of healing: Correcting the image of American mental health care.* New York: W.H. Freeman.

Farber, I.E., Harlow, H.F., & West, L.J. (1957). Brainwashing, conditioning and DDD. *Sociometry, 20,* 271–285.

Farris v. Compton. 1994. 652 A.2d 49 (D.C. App.).

Fass, M., & Brown, D. (1990). *Creative mastery in hypnosis and hypnoanalysis: A Festschrift for Erika Fromm.* NJ: Erlbaum.

Fazio, R.H., & Zanna, M.P. (1978). On the predictive validity of attitudes: The roles of direct experience and confidence. *Journal of Personality, 46,* 228–243.

Federal Food, Drug, and Cosmetic Act. (1995). 21 United States Code Annotated s. 343(r)(3)(B)(i).

Feiring, C., Taska, L., & Lewis, M. (1996). A process model for understanding adaptation to sexual abuse: The role of shame in defining stigmatization. *Child Abuse and Neglect, 20,* 767–782.

Feldman, G.C. (1993). *Lessons in evil, lessons from the light.* New York: Crown.

Feldman, G.C. (1995). Satanic ritual abuse: A chapter in the history of human cruelty. *Journal of Psychohistory, 22,* 340–357.

Feldman-Summers, S., & Pope, K.S. (1994). The experience of "forgetting" childhood abuse: A national survey of psychologists. *Journal of Consulting & Clinical Psychology, 62,* 636–639.

Felkin, R.W. (1890). *Hypnotism or psycho-therapeutics.* Edinburgh: Y.J. Pentland.

Fellows, B.J., & Creamer, M. (1978). An investigation of the role of hypnosis, hypnotic susceptibility and hypnotic induction on the production of age regression. *British Journal of Social and Clinical Psychology, 17,* 165–171.

Felthous, A.R. (1989). *The psychotherapist's duty to warn or protect.* Springfield, IL: Charles C. Thomas.

Felton, K., Kristiansen, C.M., Allard, C., & Hovdestad, W. (July, 1994). *Survivor's memory processes: Preliminary findings from a sample of 48 survivors of child sexual abuse.* Paper presented at the Annual Convention of the Canadian Psychological Association, Penticton, British Columbia.

Femina, D.D., Yeager, C.A., & Lewis, D.O. (1990). Child

abuse: Adolescent records vs. adult recall. *Child Abuse and Neglect, 14,* 227–231.

Ferenczi, S. (1916). *Sex in psychoanalysis* E. Jones (Trans.). Boston, MA: Richard G. Badger.

Ferenczi, S. (1932/1984). Confusion of tongues between adults and the child. In J. Masson, *The assault on truth* (pp. 283–295). New York: Farrar, Straus & Giroux.

Festinger, L. (1957). *A theory of cognitive dissonance.* Stanford, CA: Stanford University Press.

Fickett v. Superior Court. (1976). 27 Ariz. App. 793, 558 P.2d 988.

Fiebach, H.R. (1988). A chilling of the adversary system: An attorney's exposure to liability from opposing parties or counsel. *Temple Law Review, 61,* 1301–1322.

Figley, C.R., & McCubbin, H.I. (Eds.). (1984). *Stress and the family: Coping with catastrophe.* New York: Brunner/Mazel.

Fine, C.G. (1989a). Thoughts on the cognitive perceptual substrates of multiple personality disorder. *Dissociation, 1,* 5–10.

Fine, C.G. (1989b). Treatment errors and iatrogenisis across therapeutic modalities in MPD and allied dissociative disorders. *Dissociation, 2,* 77–82.

Finkelhor, D. (1979). *Sexually victimized children.* New York: Free Press.

Finkelhor, D. (1980). Risk factors in the sexual victimization of children. *Child Abuse and Neglect, 4,* 265–273.

Finkelhor, D. (1994). The "backlash" and the future of child protection advocacy: Insights from the study of social issues. In J.B. Myers (Ed.), *The backlash: Child protection under fire* (pp. 1–16). Thousand Oaks, CA: Sage.

Finkelhor, D., Williams, L., & Burns, N. (1988). *Nursery crimes: Sexual abuse in day care.* Newbury Park, CA: Sage.

Finney, L.D. (October, 1996). Sexual abuse and repressed memories in the landmark case of *Franklin v. Stevenson. Bender's Health Care Law Monthly,* 4–14.

Fish, V. (in press). *The delayed memory controversy in an epidemiological framework.*

Fish, V., & Scott, C. (in press). *Childhood abuse recollections in a non-clinical population: Forgetting, secrecy, dissociation, and absorption.*

Fishbein, M. (Ed.). (1967). *Readings in attitude theory and measurement.* New York: Wiley.

Fisher, C. (1943). Hypnosis in treatment of neurosis due to war and to other causes. *War Medicine, 4,* 565–576.

Fisher, C. (1945). Amnestic states in war neurosis: The psychogenesis of fugues. *Psychoanalytic Quarterly, 14,* 437–468.

Fisher, R.A. (1925). *Statistical methods for research workers.* Edinburgh, Scotland: Oliver & Boyd.

Fisher, R.P., & Geiselman, R. E. (1992). *Memory-enhancing techniques for investigative interviewing: The cognitive interview.* Springfield, IL: Thomas.

Fisher, R.P., Geiselman, R.E., & Amador, M. (1989). Field test of the cognitive interview: Enhancing the recol-

lection of actual victims and witnesses of crime. *Journal of Applied Psychology, 74, 722–727.*

Fisher, R.P., Geiselman, R. E., Raymond, D.S., Jurevich, L.M., & Warhaftig, M.L. (1987). Enhancing enhanced eyewitness memory: Refining the cognitive interview. *Journal of Police Science and Administration, 15,* 291–297.

Fisher, R.P., & McCauley, M.R. (1995). Improving eyewitness testimony with the cognitive interview. In M.S. Zaragoza, J.R. Graham, G.C.N. Hall, R. Hirschman, & Y.S. Ben-Porath (Eds.), *Memory and testimony in the child witness* (pp. 141–159). Thousand Oaks, CA: Sage.

Fisher, S. (1954). The role of expectancy in the performance of posthypnotic behavior. *Journal of Abnormal and Social Psychology, 49,* 503–507.

Fisher, S. (1962). Problems of interpretation and controls in hypnotic research. In G.H. Estabrooks (Ed.), *Hypnosis: Current problems* (pp. 109–126). New York: Harper & Row.

Fitzgerald, J.M., & Lawrence, R. (1984). Autobiographical memory across the life-span. *Journal of Gerontology, 39,* 692–698.

Fitzpatrick, F.L. (Spring, 1994). Joseph Cardinal Bernardin, Steven Cook, and personal responsibility. *The Survivor Activist, 2,* 2.

Fivush, R. (1994). Young children's event recall: Are memories constructed through discourse? *Consciousness and Cognition, 3,* 356–373.

Fivush, R., & Hammond, N.R. (1989). Time and again: Effects of repetition and retention interval on two year old's event recall. *Journal of Experimental Child Psychology, 47,* 259–273.

Fivush, R., & Hammond, N. (1990). Autobiographical memory across the preschool years: Toward reconceptualizing childhood amnesia. In R. Fivush & J.A. Hudson (Eds.), *Knowing and remembering in young children* (pp. 223–248). Cambridge, England: Cambridge University Press.

Fivush, R., & Hudson, N. (1990). *Knowing and remembering in young children.* Cambridge, England: Cambridge University Press.

Fivush, R., Hudson, J., & Nelson, K. (1984). Children's long-term memory for a novel event: An exploratory study. *Merrill-Palmer Quarterly, 30,* 303–316.

Fivush, R. & Shukat, J.R. (1995). Content, consistency, and coherence of early autobiographical recall. In M.S. Zaragoza et al. (Eds.), *Memory and testimony in the child witness* (pp. 5–23). Thousand Oaks, CA: Sage.

Fivush, R., & Schwarzmueller, A. (1995). Say it once again: Effects of repeated questions on children's event recall. *Journal of Traumatic Stress, 8,* 555–580.

Flowers v. Torrance Memorial Hospital Medical Center. (1994). 35 Cal. Rptr. 2d 685, 884 P. 2d 142.

Foa, E.B., Molnar, C., & Cashman, L. (1995). Change in rape narratives during exposure therapy for posttraumatic stress disorder. *Journal of Traumatic Stress, 8,* 675–690.

Foa, E.B., Rothbaum, B.O., & Molnar, C. (1995). Cognitive-behavioral treatment of post-traumatic stress disorder. In M.J. Friedman, D.S. Charney, & A.Y. Deutch (Eds.), *Neurobiological and clinical consequences of stress: From normal adaptation to post-tramatic stress disorder* (pp. 483–494). New York: Raven Press.

Foa, E.B., Rothbaum, B.O., Riggs, D.S., & Murdock, T.B. (1991). Treatment of posttraumatic stress disorder in rape victims: A comparison between cognitive-behavioral procedures and counseling. *Journal of Counseling and Clinical Psychology, 5,* 715–723.

Foa, E.B., Steketee, G., & Rothbaum, B.O. (1989). Behavioral/cognitive conceptualizations of post-traumatic stress disorder. *Behavior Therapy, 20,* 155–176.

Foenander, G., & Burrows, G.D. (1980). Phenomena of hypnosis: 1. Age regression. In G. Burrows & L. Dennerstein (Eds.), *Handbook of hypnosis and psychosomatic medicine* (pp. 67–83). Amsterdam: Elsevier/ North Holland Biomedical Press.

Follette, V.M., Polusny, M.M., & Milbeck, K. (1994). Mental health and law enforcement professionals: Trauma history, psychological symptoms, and impact of providing services to child sexual abuse survivors. *Professional Psychology: Research and Practice, 25,* 275–282.

Folsom, V.L., Krahn, D.D. Canum, K.K., Gold, L., & Silk, K.R. (1989). *Sex abuse: Role of eating disorder.* In New Research Program and Abstracts, 142nd Annual Meeting of the American Psychiatric Association, Washington, D.C.

Food and Drug Administration. (1994). Rules and regulations, Department of Health and Human Services, 21 CFR Parts 20 and 101, (Docket No. 85N-061D), RIN 0905– AB67, Food Labeling; General Requirements for Health Claims for Dietary Supplements, 59 Fed. Reg. 395, 400–405 (January 4).

Food & Drug Administration. (1996). 61 *Federal Regulations* (Oct. 2, 1996) 51,4971–51,531.

Force v. Gregory. (1893). 63 Conn. 167.

Forward, S., & Buck, C. (1978). *Betrayal of innocence: Incest and its devastation.* Los Angeles: J.P. Tarcher.

Frank, E., & Stewart, B.D. (1984). Depressive symptoms in rape victims. *Journal of Affective Disorders, 1,* 269–277.

Frank, J.D. (1961/1973). *Persuasion and healing.* Baltimore, MD: Johns Hopkins University Press.

Frankel, F.H. (1975). Physical symptoms and marked hypnotizability. *International Journal of Clinical and Experimental Hypnosis, 23,* 227–233.

Frankel, F.H. (1988). The clinical use of hypnosis in aiding recall. In H. Pettinati (Ed.), *Hypnosis and memory* (pp. 247–264). New York: Guilford.

Frankel, F.H. (1990). Hypnotizability and dissociation. *American Journal of Psychiatry, 14,* 823–829.

Frankel, F.H. (1993). Adult reconstruction of childhood events in the multiple personality literature. *American Journal of Psychiatry, 150,* 954–958.

Frankel, F.H. (1994). The concept of flashbacks in historical perspective. *International Journal of Clinical and Experimental Hypnosis, 42,* 321–336.

Frankel, F.H. (1996). Dissociation: The clinical realities.

American Journal of Psychiatry, 153, 64–70.

Frankel, T. (1983). Fiduciary law. *California Law Review, 71,* 795–836.

Frankl, V.E. (1963). *Man's search for meaning: An introduction to logotherapy.* New York: Washington Square Press.

Franklin, H.C., & Holding, D.H. (1977). Personal memories at different ages. *Quarterly Journal of Experimental Psychology, 29,* 527–532.

Franklin v. Duncan. (1995a). 884 F.Supp. 1435 (N.D.California, April 4).

Franklin v. Duncan. (1995b). 891 F.Supp. 516 (N.D. California, June 15).

Franklin v. Duncan. (1995c). 70 F. 3d. 75 (9 Cir. (CA)).

Franklin v. Stevenson. (1996). Civil No. 94–091779–PI in the Third Judicial District Court, Salt Lake County, Utah.

Franklin, E., & Wright, W. (1991). *Sins of the father.* New York: Ballantine.

Fredrickson, R. (1992). *Repressed memories: A journey to recovery from sexual abuse.* New York: Simon & Schuster.

Freiberg, J. (1978). The song is ended but the malady lingers on: Legal regulation of psychotherapy. *St. Louis University Law Journal, 22,* 519–533.

French, T.M., & Fromm, E. (1964). *Dream interpretation: A new approach.* New York: Basic.

Freud, S. (1896). The aetiology of hysteria. In J. Strachey (Ed. & Trans.). *The standard edition of the complete psychological works of Sigmund Freud* (Vol. 3, pp. 191–221). New York: Norton.

Freud, S. (1910). Five lectures on psychoanalysis. In J. Strachey (Ed. & Trans). *The standard edition of the complete psychological works of Sigmund Freud* (Vol. 11, pp. 1–56). New York: Norton.

Freud, S. (1905). Three essays on the theory of sexuality. In J. Strachey (Ed. & Trans.), *The standard edition of the complete psychological works of Sigmund Freud* (Vol. 7, pp. 135–243). New York: Norton.

Freyd, J.J. (August 7, 1993). *Theoretical and personal perspectives on the delayed memory debate.* Paper presented at the Center for Mental Health at Foote Hospital's Continuing Education Conference: Controversies around Recovered Memories of Incest and Ritualistic Abuse, Ann Arbor, MI.

Freyd, J.J. (1994). Betrayal-trauma: Traumatic amnesia as an adaptive response to childhood abuse. *Ethics and Behavior, 4,* 307–309.

Freyd, J.J. (1996). *Betrayal trauma: The logic of forgetting childhood abuse.* Cambridge, MA: Harvard University Press.

Freyd, J.J., & Gleaves, D.H. (1996). Remembering words not presented in lists: Relevance to the current recovered/false memory controversy. *Journal of Experimental Psychology: Learning, Memory, and Cognition, 22,* 811–813.

Freyd, P. (Spring, 1995). False memory syndrome phenomenon: Weighing the evidence. *American Judges Association Court Review,* 16–22.

Freyd, P. (November 25, 1996). *Tinker v. Tesson, M.D.* Circuit Court, Martin County, Florida. Number 93–29747 (25). Deposition of Pamela Freyd, Ph.D. Philadelphia PA.

Freyd, W. (April, 17, 1995). [Letter to WGBH-TV in Boston, MA].

Freyd v. Whitfield. (1997). Civil No. L–96–627 (D. Maryland, July 18).

Friedemann, V., & Morgan, M. (1985). *Interviewing sexual abuse victims using anatomical dolls: The professional's guidebook.* Eugene, OR: Shamrock Press.

Friedrich, W.N. (1993). Sexual victimization and sexual behavior in children: A review of the recent literature. *Child Abuse and Neglect, 17,* 59–66.

Friedrich, W.N. (1995). *Psychotherapy with sexually abused boys: An integrated approach.* Thousand Oaks, CA: Sage.

Frischholz, E.J. (1990). *Understanding the postevent information contamination effect.* Unpublished doctoral dissertation, University of Illinois at Chicago.

Frischholz, E.J. (July, 1995). [Editorial]. *American Journal of Clinical Hypnosis, 38,* 1.

Frischholz, E.J. (November 11, 1996). *Latest developments in forensic hypnosis and memory.* Paper presented at the 47th Annual Workshops and Scientific Program of the Society for Clinical and Experimental Hypnosis, Tampa, FL.

Frischholz, E.J. (in press). Hypnosis and memory: A critique of the 1985 A.M.A. Report. *American Journal of Clinical Hypnosis.*

Frischholz, E.J., Lipman, L.S., Braun, B.G., & Sachs, R.G. (1992). Psychopathology, hypnotizability, and dissociation. *American Journal of Psychiatry, 149,* 1521–1525.

Fromm, E. (1965). Hypnoanalysis: Theory and two case excerpts. *Psychotherapy: Theory, Research, and Practice, 2,* 127–133.

Fromm, E. (1970). Age regression with unexpected reappearance of a repressed childhood language. *International Journal of Clinical and Experimental Hypnosis, 18,* 79–88.

Fromm, E. (1992). An ego-psychological theory of hypnosis. In E. Fromm & M.R. Nash (Eds.), *Contemporary hypnosis research* (pp. 131–148). New York: Guilford.

Fromm, E., & French, T.M. (1974). Formation and evaluation of hypotheses in dream interpretation. In R.E. Woods & H.B. Greenhouse (Eds.), *The new world of dreams* (pp. 217–283). New York: Macmillan.

Frye v. United States. (1923). 54 App. D.C. 46, 293 F. 1013.

Fuchs, K., Paldi, E., Abramovici, H., & Peretz, B. A. (1980). Treatment of hyperemesis gravidarum by hypnosis. *International Journal of Clinical & Experimental Hypnosis, 28*(4), 313–323.

Fuller, L.L. (1967). *Legal fictions.* Stanford, CA.: Stanford University Press.

Furlong, M. (1990). Positive suggestions presented during anaesthesia. In B. Bonke, W. Fitch, & K. Millar (Eds.), *Memory and awareness in anaesthesia* (pp. 170–175). Englewood Cliffs, NJ: Prentice Hall.

Galanter, M. (Ed.). (1989a). *Cults and the new religious movements: A report of the American Psychiatric Association.* Washington, D.C.: American Psychiatric Association.

Galanter, M. (1989b). *Cults: Faith, healing, and coercion.* Oxford: Oxford University Press.

Galbraith, G.C., Cooper, L.M., & London, P. (1972). Hypnotic susceptibility and the sensory evoked response. *Journal of Comparative and Physiological Psychology, 80,* 509–514.

Galbraith, G. C., London, P., Leibovitz, M. P., Cooper, L. M., & Hart, J. T. (1970). EEG and hypnotic susceptibility. *Journal of Comparative & Physiological Psychology, 72,* 125–131.

Galin, D. (1974). Implications for psychiatry of left and right cerebral specialization: A neurophysiological context for unconscious processes. *Archives of General Psychiatry, 31,* 572–583.

Gallagher, B.D. (1993). Damages, duress, and the discovery rules: The statutory right of recovery for victims of childhood sexual abuse. *Seton Hall Legislative Journal, 17,* 505–540.

Galton, F. (1883). *Inquiry into human faculty and its development.* London, England: Macmillan.

Ganaway, G.K. (1989). Historical truth versus narrative truth: Clarifying the role of exogenous trauma in the etiology of MPD and its variants. *Dissociation, 2,* 205–220.

Ganaway, G.K. (1991) *Alternative hypotheses regarding satanic ritual abuse memories.* Paper presented at the 99th Annual Convention of the American Psychological Association, San Francisco, CA.

Ganaway, G.K. (1995). Hypnosis, childhood trauma, and dissociative identity disorder: Toward an integrative theory. *International Journal of Clinical and Experimental Hypnosis 43,* 127–144.

Gardner, M. (1957). *Fads and fallacies in the name of science.* New York: Dover.

Gardner, R.A. (1991). *Sex abuse hysteria: Salem witch trials revisited.* Cresskill, NJ: Creative Therapeutics.

Gardner, R.A. (1992). *True and false accusations of child sex abuse.* Cresskill, NJ: Creative Therapeutics.

Garner, D.M., & Garfinkel, P.E. (1985). *Handbook of psychotherapy for anorexia and bulimia.* New York: Guilford.

Garry, M., & Loftus, E.F. (1994). Pseudomemories without hypnosis. *International Journal of Clinical and Experimental Hypnosis, 42,* 363–378.

Garry, M., Loftus, E.F., & Brown, S.W. (1994). Memory: A river runs through it. *Consciousness and Cognition, 3,* 438–451.

Gartner, A.F., & Gartner, J. (1988). Borderline pathology in post-incest adolescents: Diagnostic and theoretical considerations. *Bulletin of the Menninger Clinic, 52,* 101–113.

Gauthier, L., Stollak, G., Messe, L., & Aronoff, J. (1996). Recall of childhood neglect and physical abuse as differential predictors of current psychological functioning. *Child Abuse and Neglect, 20,* 549–559.

Gee v. State (1983). 662 P. 2d 103 (Sup.Ct.Wyo.).

Geiselman, R.E., Fisher, R.P., MacKinnon, D.P., & Holland, H.L. (1985). Eyewitness memory enhancement in the police interview: Cognitive retrieval mnemonics versus hypnosis. *Journal of Applied Psychology, 70,* 401–412.

Geiselman, R.E.,& Machlovitz, H. (1987). Hypnosis in memory recall: Implications for forensic use. *American Journal of Forensic Psychology, 1,* 37–47.

Geiselman, R.E., & Padilla, J. (1988). Interviewing child witnesses with the cognitive interview. *Journal of Police Science and Administration, 16,* 236–242.

Gelinas, D.J. (1983). The persisting negative effects of incest. *Pychiatry, 46,* 312–332.

Gelinas, D.J. (1995). *Abuse with malevolent intent and the traumatic developmental context.* Unpublished manuscript.

Gelles, R.J. (1974). *The violent home: A study of physical aggression between husband and wives.* Beverly Hills, CA: Sage.

Gelles, R.J., & Straus, M.A. (1988) *Intimate violence.* New York: Simon & Schuster.

George, R. (1991). *A field and experimental evaluation of three methods of interviewing witness/victims of crime.* Unpublished manuscript, Polytechnic of East London.

Gerardi, R.J., Blanchard, E.B., & Kolb, L.C. (1989). Ability of Vietnam veterans to dissimulate a psychophysiological assessment for post-traumatic stress disorder. *Behavior Therapy, 20,* 229–243.

Gerber, S.R., & Schroeder, O. Jr., (Eds.). (1972). *Criminal investigation and interrogation.* Cincinnati, OH: W.H. Anderson Company.

Gerbert, B. (1980). Psychological aspects of Crohn's disease. *Journal of Behavioral Medicine, 3,* 41–58.

Gheorghui, V.A. & Kruse, P. (1991). The psychology of suggestion: An integrative perspective. In J.F. Schumaker (Ed.). *Human suggestability: Advances in theory, research, and application* (pp. 59–75). New York: Routledge.

Gheorghiu, V.A., Netter, P., Eysenck, H.J., & Rosenthal, R. (Eds.). (1989). *Suggestion and suggestibility: Theory and research.* Berlin: Springer.

Giannelli, P. (1995). The admissibility of hypnotic evidence in U.S. courts. *International Journal of Clinical and Experimental Hypnosis, 43,* 212–231.

Giaretto, H. (1976). The treatment of father-daughter incest: A psycho-social approach. *Children Today, 34,* 2–5.

Gibling, F., & Davies, G. (1988). Reinstatement of context following exposure to post-event information. *British Journal of Psychology, 79,* 129–141.

Gibson, J.J. (1966). *The senses considered as perceptual systems.* New York: Houghton Mifflin.

Gill, M. M., & Brenman, M. (1959). *Hypnosis and related states: Psychoanalytic studies in regression.* New York: International University Press.

Gisalson, I., & Call, J. (1982). Case report. Dog bite in infancy: Trauma and personality development. *Journal of the American Academy of Child Psychiatry, 21,* 203–207.

Gitelson, M.A. (1959). A critique of current concepts in psychosomatic medicine. *Bulletin of the Menninger Clinic, 23,* 165–178.

Glannon, J.W. (1995). *The law of torts.* Boston, MA: Little, Brown & Company.

Gleaves, D.H. (1994). On the reality of repressed memories. *American Psychologist, 49,* 440–441.

Gleaves, D.H. (1996a). The evidence for "repression": An examination of Holmes (1990) and the implications for the recovered memory controversy. *Journal of Child Sexual Abuse, 5,* 1–19.

Gleaves, D.H. (1996b). The sociocognitive model of dissociative identity disorder: A reexamination of the evidence. *Psychological Bulletin, 120,* 42–59.

Glenn, R.D. (1974). Standard of care in administering non-traditional psychotherapy. *University of California, Davis Law Review, 7,* 56–83.

Godden, D.R., & Baddeley, A.D. (1975). Context-dependent memory in two natural environments: On land and under water. *British Journal of Psychology, 66,* 325–331.

Gold, E., & Neisser, U. (1980). Recollections of kindergarten. *Quarterly Newsletter of the Laboratory of Comparative Human Cognition, 2,* 77–80.

Gold, S.N., Hughes, D., & Hohnecker, L. (1994). Degrees of repression of sexual abuse memories. *American Psychologist, 49,* 441–442.

Goldfeld, A.E., Mollica, R.F., Pesavento, B.H., & Farone, S.V. (1988). The physical and psychological sequelae of torture: Symptomatology and diagnosis. *Journal of the American Medical Association, 259,* 2725–2729.

Golding, J.M. (1995). *The fall 1995 Kentucky survey.* Unpublished data, University of Kentucky Survey Research Center.

Golding, J.M., Sanchez, R. P., & Sego, S.A. (1996). Do you believe in repressed memories? *Professional Psychology: Research and Practice, 27,* 429–437.

Goldmann, L. (1990). Cognitive processing and general anesthesia. In R. R. Bootzin, J. F. Kihlstrom, & D. L. Schacter (Eds.), *Sleep and cognition* (pp. 127–138). Washington, D.C: American Psychological Association.

Goldmann, L., & Levy, A. B. (1986). Orientating under anaesthesia. *Anaesthesia, 41,* 1056–1057.

Goldmann, L., Shah, M.V., & Hebden, M.W. (1987). Memory of cardiac anaesthesia. *Anaesthesia, 42,* 596–603.

Gooden v. Tips. (1983). 651 S.W.2d 364 (Tex.App.-Tyler).

Goodman v. Kennedy. (1976). 18 Cal.3d 335, 339, 134 Cal.Rptr. 375, 556 P.2d 737.

Goodman, G.S., & Aman, C. (1990). Children's use of anatomically detailed dolls to recount an event. *Child Development, 61,* 1859–1871.

Goodman, G.S., Aman, C., & Hirschman, J. (1987). Child sexual and physical abuse: Children's testimony. In S.J. Ceci, M.P. Toglia & D.F. Ross (Eds.), *Children's eyewitness memory* (pp. 1–23). New York: Springer.

Goodman, G.S., Bottoms, B.L., Schwartz-Kenney, B.M., & Rudy, L. (1991). Children's testimony about a stressful event: Improving children's reports. *Journal of Narrative and Life History, 1,* 69–99.

Goodman, G.S., & Clarke-Stewart, A. (1991). Suggestibility in children's testimony: Implications for sexual abuse investigations. In J. Doris (Ed.), *The suggestibility of children's recollections* (pp. 92–105). Washington, D.C: Amercian Psychological Association.

Goodman, G.S., Hirschman, J.E., Hepps, D., & Rudy, L. (1991). Children's memory for stressful events. *Merrill-Palmer Quarterly, 37,* 109–155.

Goodman, G.S., Qin. J., Bottoms, B.L., & Shaver, P.R. (1995). *Characteristics and sources of allegations of ritualistic child abuse.* Final report to the National Center on Child Abuse and Neglect.

Goodman, G.S., Quas, J.A., Batterman-Faunce, J.M., Riddleberger, M.M., & Kuhn, J. (1994). Predictors of accurate and inaccurate memories of traumatic events experienced in childhood. *Consciousness and Cognition, 3,* 269–294.

Goodman, G.S., & Reed, R.S. (1986). Age differences in eyewitness testimony. *Law & Human Behavior, 10,* 317–332.

Goodman, G.S., Rudy, L., Bottoms, B.L., & Aman, C. (1987). Children's concerns and memory: Issues of ecological validity in the study of children's eyewitness testimony. In R. Fivush & N.R. Hammond (Eds.), *Knowing and remembering in young children* (pp. 249–284). New York: Cambridge University Press.

Goodman, G.S., Rudy, L., Bottoms, B., & Aman, C. (1990). Children's concerns and memory: Issues of ecological validity in the study of children's eyewitness testimony. In R. Fivush & J. Hudson (Eds.), *Knowing and remembering in young children* (pp. 249–284). New York: Cambridge University Press.

Goodwin, J. (1985). Credibility problems in multiple personality disorder patients and abused children. In R.P. Kluft (Ed.), *Childhood antecedents of multiple personality* (pp. 2–19). Washington, D.C: American Psychiatric Press.

Goodwin, J. (1993). Human vector of trauma: Illustrations from the Marquis de Sade. In J. Goodwin (Ed.), *Rediscovering childhood trauma* (pp. 95–111). Washington, D.C: American Psychiatric Press.

Goodwin, J. (1994). Credibility problems in sadistic abuse. *Journal of Psychohistory, 21,* 479–496.

Goodwin, J., Sahd, D., & Rada, R.T. (1982). False accusations and false denials of incest: Clinical myths and clinical realities. In J. Goodwin (Ed.), *Sexual abuse: Incest victims and their families* (pp. 17–26). Boston, MA: John Wright.

Gosschalk, M.J., & Gregg, V.H. (1996). Relaxation and cognitive processing during memory retrieval. *Contemporary Hypnosis, 13,* 177–185.

Gould, C. (1987). Satanic ritual abuse: Child victims, adult survivors, system response. *California Psychologist,* 1–5.

Gould, C. (1995). Denying ritual abuse of children. *Journal of Psychohistory, 22,* 330–339.

Graf, P., Squire, L. R., & Mandler, G. (1984). The infor-

mation that amnesic patients do not forget. *Journal of Experimental Psychology, 10,* 164–178.

Graff, P., & Masson, M.E.J. (Eds.). (1993). *Implicit memory: New directions in cognition, development, and neuropsychology.* Hillsdale, NJ: Erlbaum.

Graffin, N.F., Ray, W.J., & Lundy, R. (1995). EEG concomitants of hypnosis and hypnotic susceptibility. *Journal of Abnormal Psychology, 104,* 123–131.

Grand, S. (1995a). Incest and the intersubjective politics of knowing history. In J.L. Alpert (Ed.), *Sexual abuse recalled: Treating trauma in the era of the recovered memory debate* (pp. 235–256). Northvale, NJ: Jason Aronson.

Grand, S. (1995b). Toward a reconceptualization of false-memory phenomena. In J.L. Alpert (Ed.), *Sexual abuse recalled: Treating trauma in the era of the recovered memory debate* (pp. 257–288). Northvale, NJ: Jason Aronson.

Grassian, S. & Holtzen, D. (1996). *Sexual abuse by a parish priest: I. Memory of the abuse.*

Gravitz, M.A. (1994). Memory reconstruction by hypnosis as a therapeutic technique. *Psychotherapy: Theory, Research, and Practice, 31,* 687–691.

Gravitz, M.A. (1995). Forensic hypnosis with children. *Journal of Police and Criminal Psychology, 10,* 2–6.

Gravitz, M.A. & Gerton, M.I. (1984). Origins of the term hypnotism prior to Braid. *American Journal of Clinical Hypnosis, 27,* 107–110.

Gray, J.T., & Fivush, R. (April 1987). *Memory in action: Contextual differences in two year old's memory performance.* Paper presented at the meetings of the Society for Research in Child Development, Baltimore, MD.

Greaves, G.B. (1980). Multiple personality: 165 years after Mary Reynolds. *Journal of Nervous and Mental Disease, 168,* 577–596.

Greaves, G.B. (1989). Precursors of integration in the treatment of multiple personality disorder: Clinical reflections. *Dissociation, 2,* 224–230.

Greaves, G.B. (1992) Alternative hypotheses regarding claims of Satanic cult activity: A critical analysis. In D.K. Sakheim & S.E. Devine (Eds.), *Out of darkness: Exploring Satanism and ritual abuse* (pp. 45–72). Paper presented at Trauma and Memory: An International Research Conference, Portsmouth, NH, July, 1996. New York: Lexington.

Green, A.H. (1980). *Child maltreatment: A handbook for mental health and child care professionals.* New York: Aronson.

Green, A.H. (1986). True and false allegations of sexual abuse in child custody disputes. *Journal of the American Academy of Child Psychiatry, 25,* 449–456.

Green, B.L. (1993). Identifying survivors at risk: Trauma and stressors across events. In J. Wilson & B. Raphael (Eds.), *International handbook of traumatic stress syndromes.* New York: Plenum.

Green, J. P., Lynn, S. J., Rhue, J. W., Williams, B., & Mare, C. (1989). *Fantasy proneness in highly hypnotizable subjects.* Paper presented at the annual meeting of the American Psychological Association, New Orleans, LA.

Green, J.P., Lynn, S.J., & Carlson, B.W. (1992). Finding the hypnotic virtuoso: Another look. *International Journal of Clinical and Experimental Hypnosis, 40,* 68–73.

Greenberg, J.R., & Mitchell, S.A. (1983). *Object relations in psychonalaytic theory.* Cambridge, MA: Harvard University Press.

Greenberg, L.S., & Safran, J.D. (1987). *Emotion in psychotherapy.* New York: Guilford.

Greenberg, R., Pearlman, C., Schwartz, W.R., & Grossman, H.Y. (1983). Memory, emotion, and REM sleep. *Journal of Abnormal Psychology, 92,* 378–381.

Greene, E., Flynn, M.S., & Loftus, E.F. (1982). Inducing resistance to misleading information. *Journal of Learning and Verbal Behavior, 21,* 207–219.

Greene, E., Wilson, L., & Loftus, E.F. (1989). Impact of hypnotic testimony on the jury. *Law and Human Behavior, 13,* 61–78.

Greenfield v. Commonwealth. (1974). 214 Va. 710, 204 S.E. 2d 414.

Greenleaf, E. (1969). Developmental-stage regression through hypnosis. *American Journal of Clinical Hypnosis, 12,* 20–36.

Greenleaf, M., Fisher, S., Miaskowski, C., & DuHamel, K. (1992). Hypnotizability and recovery from cardiac surgery. *American Journal of Clinical Hypnosis, 35*(2), 119–128.

Greenstock, J., & Pipe, M-E. (1996). Interviewing children about past events: The influence of peer support and misleading questions. *Child Abuse and Neglect, 20,* 69–80.

Gregg, V.H. (1993). Hypnosis and memory performance: Striking a balance between type I and type II errors. *Contemporary Hypnosis, 10,* 67–69.

Gregg, V.H., & Mingay, D.J. (1987). Influence of hypnosis on riskiness and discriminability in recognition memory for faces. *British Journal of Clinical and Experimental Hypnosis, 4,* 65–75.

Griffin, G.R. (1980). Hypnosis: Towards a logical approach in using hypnosis in law enforcement agencies. *Journal of Police Science and Administration, 8,* 385–389.

Griffiths, R. A., & Channon-Little, L. (1993). The hypnotizability of patients with bulimia nervosa and partial syndromes participating in a controlled treatment outcome study. *Contemporary Hypnosis, 10*(2), 81–87.

Grinker, R.R., & Spiegel, J.P. (1943). *War neuroses in North Africa: The Tunisian campaign.* New York: Josiah Macy Jr.

Grinker, R.R., & Spiegel, J.P. (1945). *Men under stress.* Philadelphia, PA: Blakiston.

Groen, J. (1957). Psychosomatic disturbances as a form of substituted behavior. *Journal of Psychosomatic Research, 2,* 85–96.

Groff, S.E. (June, 1994). Repressed memory or false memory: New Hampshire courts consider the dispute. *New Hampshire Bar Journal, 35*(2), 51–58.

Grosskurth, P. (1991). *The secret ring: Freud's inner circle and the politics of psychoanalysis.* New York: Addison-Wesley.

Grotstein, J.S. (1981). *Splitting and protective identification.* New York: Jason Aronson.

Grove, D.J., & Panzer, B.I. (1989). *Resolving traumatic memories: Metaphors and symbols in psychotherapy.* New York: Irvington.

Grunbaum, A. (1993). *Validation in the clinical theory of psychoanalysis: A study in the philosophy of psychoanalysis.* Madison, CT: International Universities Press.

Gruneberg, M.M., Morris, P.E., & Sykes, R.N. (Eds.). (1978). *Practical aspects of memory.* London: Academic Press.

Gruneberg, M.M., Moris, P.E., & Sykes, R.N. (Eds.). (1987). Practical aspects of memory: Current research and issues. *Memory in everyday life* (Vol. 1). Chichester: Wiley.

Gudjonsson, G.H. (1983). Suggestibility, intelligence, memory recall and personality: An experimental study. *British Journal of Psychiatry, 142,* 35–37.

Gudjonsson, G.H. (1984a). A new scale of interrogative suggestibility. *Personality and Individual Differences, 5,* 303–314.

Gudjonsson, G.H. (1984b). Interrogative suggestibility: Comparison between "false confessors" and "deniers" in criminal trials. *Medicine Science and the Law, 24,* 56–60.

Gudjonsson, G.H. (1986). The relationship between interrogative suggestibility and acquiescence: Empirical findings and theoretical implications. *Personality and Individual Differences, 7,* 195–199.

Gudjonsson, G.H. (1987a). The relationship between memory and suggestibility. *Social Behavior, 2,* 29–33.

Gudjonsson, G.H. (1987b). Historical background to suggestibility: How interrogative suggestibility differs from other types of suggestibility. *Personality and Individual Differences, 8*(3), 347–355.

Gudjonsson, G.H. (1988). Interrogative suggestibility: Its relationship with assertiveness, social-evaluative anxiety, state anxiety and method of coping. *British Journal of Clinical Psychology, 27,* 159–166.

Gudjonsson, G.H. (1989a). Compliance in an interrogative situation: A new scale. *Personality and Individual Differences, 5,* 535–540.

Gudjonsson, G.H. (1989b). The psychology of false confessions. *Medico-Legal Journal, 57,* 93–110.

Gudjonsson, G.H. (1990a). One hundred alleged false confession cases: Some normative data. *British Journal of Clinical Psychology, 29,* 249–250.

Gudjonsson, G.H. (1990b). The relationship of intellectual skills to suggestibility, compliance and acquiescence. *Personality and Individual Differences, 11,* 227–231.

Gudjonsson, G.H. (1991). Suggestibility and compliance among alleged false confessors and resisters in criminal trials. *Medical Science and the Law, 31,* 147–151.

Gudjonsson, G.H. (1992). *The psychology of interrogations, confessions and testimony.* New York: Wiley.

Gudjonsson, G.H., & Clark, N.K. (1986). Suggestibility in police interrogation: A social psychological model. *Social Behavior, 1*, 83–104.

Gudjonsson, G.H., & MacKeith, J.A.C. (1982). False confessions, psychological effects of interrogation. A discussion paper. In A. Trankell (Ed.), *Reconstructing the past: The role of psychologists in criminal trials* (pp. 253–269). Deventer, The Netherlands: Kluwer.

Gudjonsson, G.H., & MacKeith, J.A.C. (1988). Retracted confessions: Legal, psychological and psychiatric aspects. *Medical Science and the Law, 28*, 187–194.

Gudjonsson, G.H., Petursson, H., Skulasson, S., & Sigurdardottir, H. (1989). Psychiatric evidence: A study of psychological issues. *Acta Psychiatrie Scandinavica, 80*, 165–169.

Gudjonsson, G.H., & Sigurdsson, J.F. (1996). The relationship of confabulation to the memory, intelligence, suggestibility and personality of prison inmates. *Applied Cognitive Psychology, 10*, 85–92.

Guntrip, H. (1961). *Personality structure and human interaction*. New York: International Universities Press.

Gurvitz, T.V., Shenton, M.E., & Pitman, R.K. (1995). *Reduced hippocampal volume on magnetic resonance imaging in chronic posttraumatic stress disorder*. Paper presented at the Annual Meeting of the International Society of Traumatic Stress Studies, Miami, FL.

Guttmacher, M.S. (1955). *Psychiatry and the law*. New York: Grune & Stratton.

Haaken, J. (1994). *The recovered memory debate as psychodrama: A psychoanalytic feminist perspective*. Unpublished manuscript.

Haaken, J., & Schlaps, A. (1991). Incest resolution therapy and the objectification of sexual abuse. *Psychotherapy, 28*, 39–47.

Hacking, I. (1995). *Rewriting the soul: Multiple personality and the sciences of memory*. Princeton, NJ: Princeton University Press.

Hadfield, J.A. (1920). Hypnotism. In H.C. Miller (Ed.), *Functional nerve diseases: An epitome of war experience for the practitioner*. London: Hodder & Stoughton.

Hadfield, J.A. (1940). Treatment by suggestion and hypnoanalysis. In E. Miller (Ed.), *The neurosis of war* (pp.128–149). New York: Macmillan.

Hair, M. (June 1991). Courtroom views video of severed skull. *Detroit Free Press*, local news section, p. 1.

Hagen, A.M. (1991). Tolling the statute of limitations for adult survivors of childhood sexual abuse. *Iowa Law Review, 76*, 355–382.

Hale, N.G. Jr., (1995). *The rise and crisis of psychoanalysis in the United States: Freud and the Americans, 1917–1985*. Oxford, England: Oxford University Press.

Hall, R.C.W., Tice, L., Beresford, T.P., Wooley, B., & Hall, A.K. (1989). Sexual abuse in patients with anorexia nervosa and bulimia. *Psychosomatics, 30*, 73–79.

Halperin, D.A. (Ed.). (1983). *Religion, sect and cult*. Boston: John Wright-PSG Inc.

Hamanne v. Humenansky. (1995). No. C4–94–203 (Minn. Dist. Ct., Second Judicial Dist., County of Ramsey, Minn.).

Hammer v. Rosen. (1959). 7 A.D.2d 216, 181 N.Y.S.2d 805 (Sup.Ct., App.Div., First Dept.).

Hammer v. Rosen. (1960). 7 N.Y.2d 376, 165 N.E.2d 756, 198 N.Y.S.2d 65 (Ct.App.).

Hammersley, R., & Read, J.D. (1986). What is integration? Remembering a story and remembering false implications about the story. *British Journal of Psychology, 77*, 329–341.

Hammond, D.C. (1974). *Dimensions of helpfulness in saturation couples marathon group therapy in a prison setting*. Unpublished doctoral dissertation.,University of Utah.

Hammond, D.C. (1990a). (Ed.). *Handbook of hypnotic suggestions and metaphors*. Des Plaines, IL: American Society of Clinical Hypnosis Press.

Hammond, D.C. (1990b). Integrative hypnotherapy. In J.K. Zeig & W.M. Munion (Eds.), *What is psychotherapy? Contemporary perspectives* (pp. 406–412). San Francisco, CA: Jossey-Bass.

Hammond, D.C. (December, 1992). From the president's desk: Legislation to restrict lay hypnotists. *American Society of Clinical Hypnosis Newsletter, 33*, 3–4.

Hammond, D.C. (1994). *Medical and psychological hypnosis: How it benefits patients*. Des Plaines, IL: American Society of Clinical Hypnosis Press.

Hammond, D.C. (in press, a). Hypnotic exploration and abreaction of dissociated early childhood incest in a patient with psychogenic dyspareunia and Crohn's disease. In L. Handler, E. Baker & W.H. Smith (Eds.), *Hypnotherapy and sexual abuse*. New York: Guilford.

Hammond, D.C. (in press, b). Methods of profound calming in treating conditioned autonomic hyperarousal in victims of severe, repetitive abuse. *American Journal of Clinical Hypnosis*.

Hammond, D.C. (in press, c). The truism metaphor and positive age regression to experiences of mastery. In S. Krippner, L. Gray, & M. Bova (Eds.), *Healing stories*. New York: Irvington.

Hammond, D. C. (in preparation). *Integrative hypnotherapy: A comprehensive textbook*. New York: Norton.

Hammond, D. C., & Cheek, D. B. (1988). Ideomotor signaling: A method for rapid unconscious exploration. In D. C. Hammond (Ed.), *Hypnotic induction and suggestion: An introductory manual* (pp. 90–97). Des Plaines, IL: American Society of Clinical Hypnosis.

Hammond, D.C., & Elkins, G.R. (1994). *Standards of training in clinical hypnosis*. Des Plaines, IL: American Society of Clinical Hypnosis.

Hammond, D.C., Garver, R.B., Mutter, C.B., Crasilneck, H.B., Frischholz, E., Gravitz, M.A., Hibler, N.S., Olson, J., Scheflin, A.W., Spiegel, H., & Wester, W. (1995). *Clinical hypnosis and memory: Guidelines for clinicians and for forensic hypnosis*. Des Plaines, IL: American Society of Clinical Hypnosis Press.

Hammond, D.C., Hepworth, D.H., & Smith, V.G. (1977). *Improving therapeutic communication*. San Francisco, CA: Jossey-Bass.

Hammond, D.C., & Stanfield, K. (1977). *Multidimensional psychotherapy*. Champaign, IL: Institute for Personality & Ability Testing.

Hammond, N.R., & Fivush, R. (1990). Memories of Mickey Mouse: Young children recount their trip to Disneyworld. *Cognitive Development, 6*, 433–448.

Hampton, L.P. (1984). Malpractice in psychotherapy: Is there a relevant standard of care? *Case Western Law Review, 35*, 251–281.

Handler, C.B. (1987). Civil claims of adults molested as children: Maturation of harm and the statute of limitations hurdle. *Fordham Urban Law Journal, 15*, 709–742.

Hansen, M. (November, 1996). Repressed memory case unravels. *The American Bar Association Journal, 82*, 40.

Harber, K.D., & Pennebaker, J.W. (August, 1991). *The social impact of the Loma Prieta earthquake.* Paper presented at the American Psychological Association, San Francisco, CA.

Harber, K.D., & Pennebaker, J.W. (1992). Overcoming traumatic memories. In S-A. Christianson (Ed.), *Handbook of emotion and memory: Research and theory* (pp. 359–387). Hillsdale, NJ: Erlbaum.

Harding v. State (1968). 5 Md. App. 230, 246 A 2d 302, *cert. denied, Harding v. Maryland* 395 U.S.949, 89 S.Ct. 2030, 23 L.Ed. 2d 468 (1969).

Harris, A. (1996). False memory? False memory syndrome? The so-called false memory syndrome? *Psychoanalytic Dialogues, 6*, 155–187.

Harris, M. (1973). Tort liability of the psychotherapist. *University of San Francisco Law Review, 8*, 405–436.

Harris, M. (1974). *Cows, pigs, wars, and witches: The riddles of culture.* New York: Random House.

Harris, M. (1986). Are "past-life" regressions evidence of reincarnation? *Free Inquiry, 6*(4), 18–23.

Harris, T.G. (September, 1969). Sirhan B. Sirhan's bizarre paranoia: A conversation with Bernard L. Diamond. *Psychology Today,* 48–55.

Hart, J.T. (1965). Memory and the feeling-of-knowing experience. *Journal of Educational Psychology, 56*, 208–216.

Harvey, M.R., & Herman, J.L. (1994). Amnesia, partial amnesia, and delayed recall among adult survivors of childhood trauma. *Consciousness and Cognition, 3*, 295–306.

Haselhuhn v. State (1986). 727 P. 2d 280 (Wyo.Sup.Ct.), *certiorari denied, Haselhuhn v. Wyoming,* 479 U.S. 1098, 107 S.Ct. 1321, 94 L.Ed. 2d 174 (1987).

Hassan, S. (1988). *Combatting cult mind control.* Rochester, VT: Park Street Press.

Haugaard, J.J., Reppucci, N.D., Laird, J., & Nauful, T. (1991). Children's definitions of the truth and their competency as witnesses in legal proceedings. *Law and Human Behavior, 15*, 253–271.

Hawkins v. McGee. (1929). 84 N.H. 114, 146 Atl. 641.

Hayes, M.L. (1994). The necessity of memory experts for the defense in prosecutions for child sexual abuse based upon repressed memories. *American Criminal Law Review, 32*, 69–85.

Hazard, G.C. Jr., (1987). Triangular lawyer relationships: An exploratory analysis. *Georgetown Journal of Legal Ethics, 1*, 15–42.

Head, H. (1926). *Aphasia and kindred disorders of speech.* Cambridge, UK: Cambridge University Press.

Hebb, D.O. (1949). *The organization of behavior.* New York: Wiley.

Hechler, D. (1988). *The battle and the backlash: The child sexual abuse war.* Lexington, MA: Lexington Books.

Hedges, L.E. (1994). *Remembering, repeating, and working through childhood trauma: The psychodynamics of recovered memories, multiple personality, ritual abuse, incest, molest, and abduction.* Northvale, NJ: Jason Aronson.

Hegeman, E. (1995). Transferential issues in the psychoanalytic treatment of incest survivors. In J.L. Alpert (Ed.), *Sexual abuse recalled: Treating trauma in the era of the recovered memory debate* (pp. 185–214). Northvale, NJ: Jason Aronson.

Heiman, M.L. (1992). Annotation: Putting the puzzle together: Validating allegations of child sexual abuse. *Journal of Child Psychology and Psychiatry, 33*, 311–329.

Helfer, R.E., & Kempe, C.H. (1968). *The battered child.* Chicago: University of Chicago Press.

Helzer, J.E., Robins, L.N., & McEvoy, L. (1987). Post-traumatic stress disorder in the general population: Findings of the epidemilogical catchment area survey. *The New England Journal of Medicine, 317*, 1630–1634.

Hembrooke, H., & Ceci, S.J. (1995). Traumatic memories: Do we need to invoke special mechanisms? *Consciousness and Cognition, 4*, 75–82.

Henderson, J.L., & Moore, M. (1944). The psychoneurosis of war. *New England Journal of Medicine, 230*, 273–279.

Hendin, H., Haas, A.P., Singer, P., et al. (1984). The reliving experience in Vietnam veterans with posttraumatic stress disorder. *Comprehensive Psychiatry, 25*, 165–173.

Herman, J.L. (1981). *Father-daughter incest.* Cambridge, MA: Harvard University Press.

Herman, J.L. (1992). *Trauma and recovery.* New York: Basic.

Herman, J.L. (1994). Presuming to know the truth. *Nieman Reports, 48,*43–45.

Herman, J.L., & Schatzow, E. (1987). Recovery and verification of memories of childhood sexual trauma. *Psychoanalytic Psychology, 4*, 1–14.

Heuer, F., & Reisberg, D. (1990). Vivid memories of emotional events: The accuracy of remembered minutiae. *Memory and Cognition, 18*, 496–506.

Heuer, F., & Reisberg, D. (1992). Emotion, arousal, and memory for detail. In S-A. Christianson (Ed.), *The handbook of emotion and memory: Research and theory* (pp.151–180). Hillsdale, NJ: Erlbaum.

Hibbard, W.S., & Worring, R.W. (1981). *Forensic hypnosis.* Springfield, IL: Charles C. Thomas.

Hickey v. Askren. (1991). 198 Ga. App. 718, 403, S.E. 2d 225.

Hickling, E.J., Sison, G.F.F., & Vanderploeg, R.D. (1986). Treatment of post-traumatic stress disorder with relaxation and biofeedback training. *Behavior Therapy, 16*, 406–416.

Hicks, R.D. (1991). *In pursuit of Satan: The police and the* occult. Buffalo, NY: Prometheus Books.

Higbee, K.L. (1969). Fifteen years of fear arousal: Research on threat appeals: 1953–1968. *Psychological Bulletin, 72,* 426–444.

Hilgard, E.R. (1965). *Hypnotic susceptibility.* New York: Harcourt, Brace & World.

Hilgard, E.R. (1977/1986). *Divided consciousness: Multiple controls in human thought and action.* New York: Wiley-Interscience.

Hilgard, E.R. (1978). States of consciousness in hypnosis: Divisions or levels? In F.H. Frankel & H.S. Zamansky (Eds.), *Hypnosis at its bicentennial: Selected papers* (pp. 15–36). New York: Plenum.

Hilgard, E.R., & Bower, G.H. (1975). *Theories of learning* (4th ed.). Englewood Cliffs, NJ: Prentice Hall.

Hilgard, E.R., & Hilgard, J.R. (1983). Appendix B: The Stanford Hypnotic Clinical Scale. In E.R. Hilgard & J.R. Hilgard, *Hypnosis and the relief of pain* (revised ed.). Los Altos, CA: William Kaufmann.

Hilgard, J.R. (1970). *Personality and hypnosis.* Chicago, IL: University of Chicago Press.

Hill, S., & Goodwin, J. (1989). Satanism: Similarities between patient accounts and pre-Inquisition historical sources. *Dissociation, 2,* 39–44.

Hilts, P.J. (September 22, 1995). F.D.A. sets experimental-treatment rules. *The New York Times,* A9.

Hinkle, L.E., & Wolff, H.G. (1956). Communist interrogation and indoctrination of "enemies of the state." *American Medical Association Archives of Neurology and Psychiatry, 76,* 115–174.

Ho, B.T., Richards, B.W., & Chute, D.L. (Eds.). (1978). *Drug discrimination and state-dependent learning.* New York: Academic Press.

Hochman, J. (November, 1984). Iatrogenic symptoms associated with a therapy cult: Examination of an extinct "new psychotherapy" with respect to psychiatric deterioration and "brainwashing." *Psychiatry, 47,* 366–377.

Hoehn-Saric, R., Frank, J.D., & Gurland, B.J. (1968). Focused attitude change in neurotic patients. *Journal of Nervous and Mental Disease, 147,* 124–133.

Hoehn-Saric, R., Liberman, B., Imber, S.D., Stone, A.R., Frank, J.D., & Ribich, F.D. (1974). Attitude change and attribution of arousal in psychotherapy. *Journal of Nervous and Mental Disease, 159,* 234–244.

Hoehn-Saric, R., Liberman, B., Imber, S.D., Stone, A.R., Pande, S.K., & Frank, J.D. (1972). Arousal and attitude change in neurotic patients. *Archives of General Psychiatry, 26,* 52–56.

Hofling, C.K., Heyl, B., & Wright, D. (1971). The ratio of total recoverable memories to conscious memories in normal subjects. *Comprehensive Psychiatry, 12,* 371–379.

Holmes, D. (1990). The evidence for repression: An examination of sixty years of research. In J.L. Singer (Ed.), *Repression and dissociation: Implications for personality, theory, psychopathology, and health* (pp. 85–102). Chicago, IL: University of Chicago Press.

Holon, A. (1993). The North Sea oil rig disaster. In J.P.

Wilson & B. Raphael (Eds.), *International handbook of traumatic stress syndromes* (pp. 471–479). New York: Plenum.

Home Budget Loans, Inc. v. Jacoby & Meyers Law Offices. (1989). 207 Cal.App.3d 1277, 255 Cal.Rptr. 475.

Hood v. Phillips. (1977). 554 S.W.2d 160 (Tex.Sup.Ct.).

Hoorwitz, A.H. (1992). *The clinical detective: Techniques in the evaluation of sexual abuse.* New York: Norton.

Hoppe, K. (1962). Persecution, depression and aggression. *Bulletin of the Menninger Clinic, 26,* 195–203.

Hopwood, J.S., & Snell, H.K. (1933). Amnesia in relation to crime. *Journal of Mental Science, 79,* 27–41.

Horevitz, R., & Loewenstein, R.J. (1994). The rational treatment of multiple personality disorder. In S. J. Lynn & J. Rhue (Eds.), *Dissociation: Diagnosis, assessment, and treatment perspectives* (pp. 289–316). New York: Guilford.

Horowitz, J.M., Salt, P., Gomes-Schwartz, B., & Sauzier, M. (1985). *False accusations of child sexual abuse.* Unpublished manuscript.

Horowitz, M.J. (1973). Phase oriented treatment of stress response syndromes. *American Journal of Psychotherapy, 27,* 506–515.

Horowitz, M.J. (1974). Stress response syndromes: Character style and dynamic psychotherapy. *Archives of General Psychiatry, 31,* 768–781.

Horowitz, M.J. (1976). *Stress response syndromes.* New York: Aronson.

Horowitz, M.J., & Kaltreider, N.B. (1979). Brief therapy of the stress response syndrome. *Psychiatric Clinics of North America, 2,* 365–377.

Horowitz, M.J., & Reidbord, S.P. (1992). Memory, emotion, and response to trauma. In S.-A. Christianson (Ed.), *The handbook of emotion and memory: Research and theory* (pp. 343–358). Hillsdale, NJ: Erlbaum.

Horowitz, M.J., Wilner, N., & Alvarez, W. (1979). The impact of events scale: A measure of subjective stress. *Psychosomatic Medicine, 41,* 209–218.

Horowitz, S.W. (1991). Empirical support for statement validity assessment. *Behavioral Assessment, 13,* 293–313.

Hosch, H.H., & Bothwell, R.K. (1990). Arousal, description and identification accuracy of victims and bystanders. *Journal of Social Behavior and Personality, 5,* 481–488.

Hosch, H.H., & Cooper, D.S. (1982). Victimization as a determinant of eyewitness accuracy. *Journal of Applied Psychology, 67,* 649–652.

Hosch, H.H., Leippe, M.R., Marchioni, P.M., & Cooper, D.S. (1984). Victimization, self-monitoring, and eyewitness identification. *Journal of Applied Psychology, 69,* 280–288.

Hoult v. Hoult. 1995. 57 F.3d 1 (1st Cir., Mass.).

Hovdestad, W.E., & Kristiansen, C.M. (1996). A field study of "false memory syndrome": Construct validity and incidence. *Journal of Psychiatry and Law, 24,* 299–338.

Hovdestad, W.E., Kristiansen, C.M., Felton, K.A., & Allard, C.B. (in press). *An empirical study of the inci-*

dence of false memory syndrome.

Hovland, C.I., Janis, I.L., & Kelly, H. (1953). *Communication and persuasion.* New Haven, CT: Yale University Press.

Hovland, C.I., Lumsdaine, A., & Sheffield, F. (1949). *Experiments on mass communication.* Princeton, NJ: Princeton University Press.

Hovland, C.I., & Pritzker, H. (1957). Extent of opinion change as a function of amount of change advocated. *Journal of Abnormal and Social Psychology, 54,* 257–261.

Hovland, C.I., & Weiss, W. (1951). The influence of source credibility on communication effectiveness. *Public Opinion Quarterly, 15,* 635–650.

Howard, J. F. (1987). Incidents of auditory perception during anaesthesia with traumatic sequelae. *Medical Journal of Australia, 146,* 44–46.

Howe, M.L. (1991). Misleading children's story recall: Forgetting and reminiscence of the facts. *Developmental Psychology, 27,* 746–762.

Howe, M.L., Courage, M.L., & Peterson, C. (1994). How can I remember when "I" wasn't there? Long-term retention of traumatic experiences and emergence of the cognitive self. *Consciousness and Cognition, 3,* 327–355; Reprinted in K. Pezdek & W. P. Banks (Eds.), *The recovered memory/false memory debate* (pp. 121–149). New York: Academic Press. (1996).

Hudson, J.A., & Fivush, R. (1987). *As time goes by: Sixth graders remember a kindergarten experience.* (Report No. 13). Atlanta, GA: Emory Cognition Project.

Hudson, J.A., & Nelson, K. (1986). Repeated encounters of a similar kind: Effects of familiarity on children's autobiographical memory. *Cognitive Development, 1,* 253–271.

Huggins v. Longs Drug Stores California. (1993). 6 Cal.4th 124, 862 P.2d 148, 24 Cal. Rptr.2d 587.

Hughes, L.R. (1991). Hypnosis in the civil case: The problem of confabulating plaintiffs and witnesses. *Florida Bar Journal, 65,* 24–30.

Hull, C.L. (1933). *Hypnosis and suggestibility: An experimental approach.* New York: Appleton-Century Crofts.

Human drug testing by the CIA, 1977. (1977). Hearings before the Subcommittee on Health and Scientific Research of the Committee on Human Resources, United States Senate. Washington, D.C.: U.S. Government Printing Office.

Humes, E. (1991). *Buried secrets.* New York: Dutton.

Hunter, E. (1951). *Brainwashing in red China.* New York: Vanguard Press.

Huse, B. (1930). Does the hypnotic trance favor the recall of faint memories? *Journal of Experimental Psychology, 13,* 519–529.

Huston, P., Shakow, D., & Erickson, M. (1934). A study of hypnotically induced complexes by means of the Luria technique. *Journal of General Psychology, 11,* 65–97.

Hutchings, D. D. (1961). The value of suggestion given under anesthesia: A report and evaluation of 200 consecutive cases. *American Journal of Clinical Hypnosis, 4,* 26–29.

Hyer, L., McCranie, E.W., Boudewyns, P.A., & Sperr, E. (1996). Modes of long-term coping with trauma memories: Relative use and associations with personality among Vietnam veterans with chronic PTSD. *Journal of Traumatic Stress, 9,* 299–316.

Hyman, I.E., Husband, T.H., & Billings, F.J. (1995). False memories of childhood experiences. *Applied Cognitive Psychology, 9,* 181–197.

Imwinkelried, E.J. (1990). The case for recognizing a new Constitutional entitlement: The right to present favorable evidence in civil cases. *Utah Law Review, 1–* 46.

Inbau, F.E., Reid, J.E., & Buckley, J.P. (1986). *Criminal interrogation and confessions* (3rd ed.). Baltimore, MD: Williams and Wilkins.

Individual rights and the federal role in behavior modification. (1974). A Study Prepared by the Staff of the Subcommittee on Constitutional Rights of the Committee on the Judiciary, United States Senate. Washington, D.C.: U.S. Government Printing Office.

In re Goddell. (1875). 39 Wisc. 232.

Insko, C.A. (1967). *Theories of attitude change.* New York: Appleton-Century-Crofts.

International Society for the Study of Dissociation. (1994). *Guidelines for treating dissociative identity disorder.* Skokie, IL: ISS & D.

In the matter of the disciplinary action concerning the counselor registration of Linda Rae MacDonald. (1995). State of Washington Department of Health, RC 94012, "Agreed Findings, Conclusions of Law and Order."

Irving, B. (1980). *Police interrogation: A case study of current practice.* London: Research Studies No. 2, HMSO.

Irving, B. (1986). Interrogative suggestibility: A question of parsimony. *Social Behavior, 2,* 19–28.

Ito, Y., Teicher, M. H., Glod, C. A., Harper, D., Magnus, E., & Belbard, H.A. (1993). Increased prevalence of electrophysiological abnormalities in children with psychological, physical, and sexual abuse. *Journal of Neuropsychiatry and Clinical Neurosciences, 5,* 401–408.

Isely v. Capuchin Province. (1995). 877 F.Supp. 1055 (E.D.Mich.).

Jackson v. Burnham. (1895). 20 Colo. 532, 39 P. 577.

Jackson v. State. (1989). 553 So.2d 719 (Fla.Ct.App.4th Dist.).

Jacobs, R.C., & Campbell, D.T. (1961). The perpetuation of an arbitrary tradition through several generations of a laboratory microculture. *Journal of Abnormal and Social Psychology, 62,* 649–658.

Jacoby, L.L., Lindsay, D.S., & Toth, J.P. (1992). Unconscious influences revealed: Attention, awareness, and control. *American Psychologist, 47,* 802–809.

Jacoby, L.L., & Witherspoon, D. (1982). Remembering without awareness. *Canadian Journal of Psychology, 36,* 300–324.

Jaffee v. Redmond. (1996). 116 S.Ct. 1923, 135 L.Ed.2d 337.

James, B. (1989). *Treating traumatized children: New insights and creative interventions.* Lexington, MA: Lexington Books.

Jampole, L., & Weber, M.K. (1987). An assessment of the behavior of sexually abused and nonsexually abused children with anatomically correct dolls. *Child Abuse and Neglect, 11*, 187–192.

Janet, P. (1889). *L'automatisme psychologique* [Psychological automatism]. Paris: Felix Alcan.

Janet, P. (1901/1977). *The mental state of hystericals.* Washington, D.C.: University Publications of America.

Janet, P. (1904). Amnesia and the dissociation of memories by emotion. *Journal de Pschologie, 1*, 417–453.

Janet, P. (1907). *The major symptoms of hysteria.* New York: Macmillan.

Janet, P. (1925/1976). *Psychological healing.* New York: Arno.

Janet, P. (1928). *L'evolution de la memoire et la notion du temps.* Paris: Chachine.

Janis, I., & Feshbach, S. (1954). Effects of fear-arousing communications. *Journal of Abnormal and Social Psychology, 48*, 78–92.

Janis, I., & Field, P.B. (1959). A behavioral assessment of persuasibility: Consistency and individual differences. In C. I. Hovland & I.L. Janis (Eds.), *Personality and persuasibility* (pp. 29–54). New Haven: Yale University Press.

Janoff-Bulman, R. (1985). The aftermath of victimization: Rebuilding shattered assumptions. In C. Figley (Ed.), *Trauma and its wake: The study and treatment of posttraumatic stress disorder* (Vol. 1, pp. 15–35). New York: Brunner/Mazel.

Janoff-Bulman, R. (1992). *Shattered assumptions: Towards a new psychology of trauma.* New York: Free Press.

Jansen, C. K., Bonke, B., Klein, J. van Dasselaar, N., & Hop, W. C. J. (1991). Failure to demonstrate unconscious perception during balances anaesthesia by postoperative motor response. *Acta Anaesthesiologica Scandinavica, 35*, 407–410.

Johnson v. Gerrish. (1986). 518 A.2d 721 (Me.).

Johnson, C., & Scott, B. (September, 1976). *Eyewitness testimony and suspect identification as a function of arousal, sex of witness, and scheduling of interrogation.* Paper presented at the 75th Annual Convention of the American Psychological Association, Washington, D.C.

Johnson, C.H., Gilmore, J.D., & Shenoy, R.Z. (1982). Use of a flooding procedure in the treatment of stress-related anxiety disorder. *Journal of Behavior Therapy and Experimental Psychiatry, 13*, 235–237.

Johnson, M.K., & Lindsay, D.S. (1986). Despite McCloskey and Zaragoza, suggestibility effects may reflect memory impairment. Unpublished manuscript.

Johnson, M.K., Foley, M.A., Suengas, A.G., & Raye, C.L. (1988). Phenomenal characteristics of memories for perceived and imagined autobiographical events. *Journal of Experimental Psychology: General, 117*, 371–376.

Johnson, N.F. (1970). The role of chunking and organization in the process of recall. In G.H. Bower (Ed.), *The psychology of learning and motivation: Advances in research and theory* (Vol. 4, pp. 172–247). New York: Academic Press.

Johnson, V.E. (1980). *I'll quit tomorrow.* New York: Harper & Row.

Johnson v. Johnson. (1988). 701 F. Supp. 1363 (N.D. Ill.).

Johnston, M. (1997). Spectral evidence. New York: Houghton-Mifflin.

Johnston, J.C., Chajkowaski, J., DuBreuil, S.C., & Spanos, N. P. (1989). The effects of manipulated expectancies on behavioral and subjective indices of hypnotizability. *Australian Journal of Clinical and Experimental Hypnosis, 17*, 121–130.

Jones v. Chidester. (1992). 531 Pa. 31, 610 A2d 964.

Jones, D.P.H. (1995). *Interviewing the sexually abused child.* London: Gaskel, The Royal College of Psychiatrists.

Jones, D.P.H., & McGraw, J.M. (1987). Reliable and fictitious accounts of sexual abuse to children. *Journal of Interpersonal Violence, 2*, 27–45.

Jones, D.P.H., & Seig, A. (1988). Child sexual abuse allegations in custody or visitation cases: A report of 20 cases. In E.B. Nicholson & J. Bulkey (Eds.), *Sexual abuse allegations in custody and visitation cases* (pp. 22–36). Washington, D.C.: American Bar Association.

Jones v. Jones. (1990). 242 N.J.Super. 195, 576 A.2d 316, certification denied 122 N.J. 418, 585 A.2d 412.

Jonker, F., & Jonker-Bakker, P. (1991). Experiences with ritualist child sexual abuse: A case study from the Netherlands. *Child Abuse and Neglect, 15*, 191–196.

Jordening, H., & Pedersen, T. (1991). The incidence of conscious awareness in a general population of anesthetized patients. *Anesthesiology, 75*, A1055.

Joseph, R. (1988). The right hemisphere: Emotion, music, visual-spatial skills, body-image, dreams, and awareness. *Journal of Clinical Psychology, 44*, 630–673.

Joy v. Eastern Maine Medical Center. (1987). 529 A.2d 1364 (Me.)

Jung, C.G. (1906). *Diagnostiche Associationsstudien*, Part I. Leipzig, Germany: Barth.

Jung, C.G. (1921–1922). The question of the therapeutic value of "abreaction." *British Journal of Medical Psychology, 2*, 13–22.

Justice, B., & Justice, R. (1979). *The broken taboo: Sex in the family.* New York: Human Sciences Press.

Kafka, H. (1995). Incestuous sexual abuse, memory, and the organization of the self. In J.L. Alpert (Ed.), *Sexual abuse recalled: Treating trauma in the era of the recovered memory debate* (pp. 135–154). Northvale, NJ: Jason Aronson.

Kahaner, L. (1988). *Cults that kill: Probing the underworld of occult crime.* New York: Warner.

Kahn, M.M.R. (1972). *The privacy of the self: Papers on psychonalytic theory and technique.* New York: International Univesities Press.

Kail, R. (1990). *The development of memory in children* (3rd ed.). New York: Freeman.

Kaiser v. Suburban Transportation System. (1965). 65 Wash.2d 461, 398 P.2d 14.

Kalichman, Seth C. (1993).*Mandated reporting of suspected child abuse: Ethics, law, & policy.* Washington, D.C.: American Psychological Association.

Kalman, G. (1977). On combat neurosis. *International*

Journal of Social Psychiatry, 23, 195–203.

Kamisar, Y. (1961). Illegal searches or seizures and contemporaneous incriminating statements: A dialogue on a neglected area of criminal procedure. *University of Illinois Law Forum, 78,*147.

Kamisar, Y. (1980). *Police interrogation and confessions.* Ann Arbor, MI: University of Michigan Press.

Kandel, M., & Kandel, E. (May, 1994). Flights of memory. *Discover,* 32–38.

Kanovitz, J. (1992). Hypnotic memories and civil sexual abuse trials. *Vanderbilt Law Review, 45,* 1185–1262.

Kaplan, H.S. (1974). *The new sex therapy: Active treatment of sexual dysfunctions.* New York: Brunner/Mazel.

Kardiner, A. (1941). *The traumatic neuroses of war.* New York: Hoeber.

Kardiner, A., & Spiegel, H. (1947). *War, stress, and neurotic illness.* New York: Paul Hoeber.

Karlin, R.A. (1997). Illusory safeguards: Legitimizing distortion in recall with guidelines for forensic hypnosis. Two case reports. *International Journal of Clinical & Experimental Hypnosis, 45*(1), 18–40.

Karlin, R.A., and Orne, M.T. (1996). Commentary on *Borawick v. Shay:* Hypnosis, social influence, incestuous child abuse, and satanic ritual abuse: The iatrogenic creation of horrific memories for the remote past. *Cultic Studies Journal, 13,* 42–94.

Kartchner, F.D., & Korner, I.N. (1947). The use of hypnosis in the treatment of acute combat reactions. *American Journal of Psychiatry, 103,* 630–636.

Kassin, S.M., Ellsworth, P.C., & Smith, V.L. (1989). The "general acceptance" of psychological research on eyewitness testimony: A survey of the experts. *American Psychologist, 44,* 1089–1098.

Kassin, S.M., & McNall, K. (1991). Police interrogations and confessions. *Law and Human Behavior, 15,* 233–351.

Kassin, S.M., & Wrightsman, L.S. (1985). Confession evidence. In S.M. Kassin & L.S. Wrightsman (Eds.), *The psychology of evidence and trial procedures* (pp. 67–94). London: Sage.

Kaszniak, A.W., Nussbaum, P.D., Berren, M.R., & Santiago, J. (1988). Amnesia as a consequence of male rape: A case report. *Journal of Abnormal Psychology, 97,* 100–104.

Katchen, M.H. (1992). The history of Satanic religions. In D.K. Sakheim & S.E. Devine (Eds.), *Out of darkness: Exploring Satanism and ritual abuse* (pp.1–20). New York: Lexington.

Katchen, M.H., & Sakheim, D.K. (1992) Satanic beliefs and practices. In D.K. Sakheim & S.E. Devine (Eds.), *Out of darkness: Exploring Satanism and ritual abuse* (pp. 21–44). New York: Lexington.

Kater, M.H. (1989). *Doctors under Hitler.* Chapel Hill: University of North Carolina Press.

Kazdin, A.E. (1974). Self-monitoring and behavior change. In M.J. Mahoney & C.E. Thoreson (Eds.), *Self-control: Power to the person* (pp. 218–246). Monterey, CA: Brooks-Cole.

Keane, T.M. (1989). *Civilian Mississippi Scale of PTSD.* Unpublished manuscript, National Center for PTSD, Behavioral Science Division, V.A. Medical Center, Boston, MA.

Keane, T.M., Caddell, J.M., & Taylor, K.L. (1988). The Mississippi scale for combat-related PTSD: Three studies in reliability and validity. *Journal of Consulting and Clinical Psychology, 56,* 85–90.

Keane, T.M., & Kaloupek, D.G. (1982). Imaginal flooding in the treatment of post-traumatic stress disorder. *Journal of Consulting and Clinical Psychology, 50,* 138–140.

Kebeck, G., & Lohaus, A. (1986). Effects of emotional arousal on free recall of complex material. *Perceptual and Motor Skills, 63,* 461–462.

Keet, C.D. (1948). Two verbal techniques in a miniature counseling situation. *Psychological Monographs, 62,*(7, Whole No. 294).

Keeton, W.P. (Ed.). (1984). *Prosser and Keeton on the law of torts* (5th ed.). St. Paul: West Publishing.

Kegan, R. (1982). *The evolving self: Problem and process in human development.* Cambridge, MA: Harvard University Press.

Keiser, T.W., & Keiser, J.L. (1987). *The anatomy of illusion: Religious cults and destructive persuasion.* Springfield, IL: Charles C. Thomas.

Kelley, S.J. (1988). Ritualistic abuse of children: Dynamics and impact. *Cultic Studies Journal, 5*(2), 228–236.

Kelley, S.J. (1989). Stress responses of children to sexual abuse and ritualistic abuse in day-care centers. *Journal of Interpersonal Violence, 4,* 502–513.

Kelley, S.J. (1992). Stress responses of children and parents to sexual abuse and ritualisic abuse in day care centers. In A.W. Burgess (Ed.), *Child trauma, I: Issues and research* (pp. 231–257). New York: Garland Publishing.

Kelley, S.J. (1993). Ritualistic abuse of chldren in day care centers. In M. Langone (Ed.), *Recovery from cults* (pp. 340–351). New York: Norton.

Kelman, H., & Hovland, C.I. (1953). Restatement of the communicator in delayed measurement of opinion change. *Journal of Abnormal and Social Psychology, 48,* 327–335.

Kempe, C., Silverman, F., Steele, B., Droegemueller, W., & Silver, H. (July, 1962). The battered child syndrome. *Journal of the American Medical Association, 181,* 17–24.

Kempe, R.S., & Kempe, C.H. (1984). *The common secret: Sexual abuse of children and adolescents.* New York: W.H. Freeman.

Kendall-Tackett, K.A., Williams, L.M., & Finkelhor, D. (1993). Impact of sexual abuse on children: A review and synthesis of recent empirical studies. *Psychological Bulletin, 113,* 164–180.

Kenny, M.G. (1995). The recovered memory controversy: An anthropologist's view. *Journal of Psychiatry and Law, 23,* 437–460.

Kenyon-Jump, R., Burnette, M., & Robertson, M. (1991). Comparison of behaviors of suspected sexually abused and nonsexually abused preschool children using anatomical dolls. *Journal of Psychopathology and Behavioral*

Assessment, 13, 225–240.

Kernberg, O.F., Selzer, M., Koeningsberg, H., Carr, A., & Applebaum, A. (1989). *Psychodynamic psychotherapy of borderline patients.* New York: Basic.

Key v. State. (1983). 430 So.2d 909 (Fla.App.).

Khatain v. Jones. (1993). 1993 WL 240049 (Tex.App.-Dallas, 1993) (Not Published).

Kihlstrom, J.F. (1977). Models of posthypnotic amnesia. *Annals of the New York Academy of Sciences, 296,* 284–301.

Kihlstrom, J.F. (1978). Attempt to revive a forgotten childhood language by means of hypnosis. (Hypnosis Research Memorandum, 148). Stanford, CA: Laboratory of Hypnosis Research, Department of Psychology, Stanford University. Cited in Kihlstrom, J.F., & Barnhardt, T.M. (1993). The self-regulation of memory: For better & for worse, with and without hypnosis. Chapter in D.W. Wagner & J.W. Pennebaker (Eds.), *Handbook of mental control.* Englewood Cliffs, N.J.: Prentice Hall, pp. 88–125.

Kihlstrom, J.F. (1984). Conscious, subconscious, unconscious: A cognitive view. In K.S. Bowers & D. Meichenbaum (Eds.), *The unconscious reconsidered* (pp. 149–211). New York: John Wiley.

Kihlstrom, J.F. (1985). Hypnosis. *Annual Review of Psychology, 36,* 385–418.

Kihlstrom, J.F. (1987). The cognitive unconscious. *Science, 237,* 1445–1452.

Kihlstrom, J.F. (April 1993). *Exhumed memory.* Paper presented at the Joint Convention of the Rocky Mountain Psychological Association and the Western Psychological Association, Phoenix, AZ.

Kihlstrom, J.F. (1993). Review of Scheflin, A.W., and Shapiro, J.L., *Trance on trial. Contemporary Psychology, 38,* 739–740.

Kihlstrom, J.F. (1994a). Hypnosis, delayed recall, and the principles of memory. *International Journal of Clinical and Experimental Hypnosis, 42,* 337–345.

Kihlstrom, J.F. (1994b). One hundred years of hysteria. In S.J. Lynn, & J.W. Rhue. (Eds.), *Dissociation: Clinical and theoretical perspectives* (pp.365–394). New York: Guilford.

Kihlstrom, J.F. (1995). The trauma-memory argument. *Consciousness and Cognition, 4,* 63–67.

Kihlstrom, J.F., & Barnhardt, T.M. (1993). The self-regulation of memory, for better or for worse, with and without hypnosis. In D.M. Wegner & J.W. Pennebaker (Eds.), *Handbook of mental control* (pp. 88–125). Englewood Cliffs, NJ: Prentice-Hall.

Kihlstrom, J.F., & Hoyt, I.P. (1990). Repression, dissociation, and hypnosis. In J.L. Singer (Ed.), *Repression and dissociation: Implications for personality theory, psychopathology, and health* (pp. 66–109). Chicago, IL: University of Chicago Press.

Kihlstrom, J.F., & Schacter, D. (1990). Anaesthesia, amnesia, and the cognitive unconscious. In B. Bonke, W. Fitch, & K. Millar (Eds.), *Memory and awareness in anaesthesia* (pp. 21–44). Amsterdam: Swets & Zeitlinger.

Kihlstrom, J. F., Schacter, D. L., Cork, R. C., Hurt, C. A., & Behr, S. E. (1990). Implicit and explicit memory following surgical anesthesia. *Psychological Science, 1,* 303–306.

Kihlstrom, J.F., & Schacter, D.L. (1995). Functional disorders of memory. In A. Baddeley, B. Wilson & F. Watts (Eds.), *Handbook of memory disorders* (pp.337–364). Chichester, England: Wiley.

Kilpatrick, D.G., Veronen, L.J., & Resick, P. (1982). Psychological sequelae to rape: Assessment and treatment strategies. In D.M. Dolays & R.I. Meredith (Eds.), *Behavioral medicine: Assessment and treatment strategies* (pp. 423–497). New York: Plenum.

King, B., & Janis, I. (1956). Comparison of the effectiveness of improvised versus nonimprovised role-playing in producing opinion change. *Human Relations, 9,* 177–186.

King, M.A., & Yuille, J.C. (1987). Suggestibility and the child witness. In S.J. Ceci, M.P. Toglia, & D.F. Ross (Eds.), *Children's eyewitness memory* (pp. 24–25). New York: Springer-Verlag.

Kinnunen, T., Zamanski, H.S., & Block, M.L. (1994). Is the hypnotized subject lying? *Journal of Abnormal Psychology, 103,* 184–191.

Kinsey, A., Wardell, P.B., & Gebhard, P.H. (1953). *Sexual behavior in the human female.* New York: Pocket Books.

Kinscherff, R., & Barnum, R. (1992). Child forensic evaluation and claims of ritual abuse or satanic activity: A critical analysis. In D.K. Sakheim & S.E. Devine (Eds.), *Out of darkness: Exploring Satanism and ritual abuse* (pp. 73–107). New York: Lexington Books.

Kionka, E.J. (1992). *Torts.* St. Paul, MN: West Publishing.

Kirsch, I. (1991). The social learning theory of hypnosis. In S.J. Lynn & J. Rhue (Eds.), *Theories of hypnosis: Current models and perspectives.* (pp. 439–466). New York: Guilford.

Kirsch, I., Council J.R., & Mobayed, C. (1987). Imagery and response expectancy as determinants of hypnotic behavior. *British Journal of Experimental and Clinical Hypnosis, 4,* 25–31.

Kirsch, I., Silva, C.E., Carone, J.E., Johnston, J.D., & Simon, B. (1989). The surreptitious observation design: An experimental paradigm for distinguishing artifact from essence in hypnosis. *Journal of Abnormal Psychology, 98,* 132–136.

Klatzky, R.A. (1975). *Human memory: Structures and processes.* San Francisco: Freeman.

Klatzky, R.L., & Erdelyi, M. H. (1985). The response criterion problem in tests of hypnosis and memory. *International Journal of Clinical and Experimental Hypnosis, 33(3),* 246–257.

Klein, I., & Janoff-Bulman, R. (1996). Trauma history and personal narratives: Some clues to coping among survivors of child abuse. *Child Abuse and Neglect, 20,* 45–54.

Kleinsmith, L.J., & Kaplan, S. (1963). Paired-associative learning as a function of arousal and interpolated interval. *Journal of Experimental Psychology, 65,* 190–193.

Kleinsmith, L.J., & Kaplan, S. (1964). The interaction of arousal and recall interval in nonsense syllable paired-associate learning. *Journal of Experimental Psychology, 67,* 124–126.

Klerman, G.L., Rounsaville, B., Chevron, E., & Weissman, M. (1984). *Interpersonal psychotherapy of depression.* New York: Basic.

Kline, M.V. (1951). Hypnotic age regression and intelligence. *Journal of Genetic Psychology, 77,* 129–132.

Kline, M.V. (1956). *A scientific report on the search for Bridey Murphy.* New York: Julian Press.

Kline, M.V. (1958). *Freud and hypnosis.* New York: Julian Press and The Institute for Research in Hypnosis.

Kline, M.V. (1983). *Forensic hypnosis.* Springfield, IL: Charles C. Thomas.

Kluft, R.P. (1982). Varieties of hypnotic interventions in the treatment of multiple personality. *American Journal of Clinical Hypnosis, 24,* 230–240.

Kluft, R.P. (1983). Hypnotherapeutic crisis intervention in multiple personality disorder. *American Journal of Clinical Hypnosis, 26,* 73–83.

Kluft, R.P. (1984a). Aspects of the treatment of multiple personality disorder. *Psychiatric Annals, 14,* 5–55.

Kluft, R.P. (1984b). Treatment of multiple personality disorder. *Psychiatric Clinics of North America, 7,* 9–29.

Kluft, R.P. (1985a). (Ed.). *Childhood antecedents of multiple personality.* Washington, D.C.: American Psychiatric Press.

Kluft, R.P. (1985b). Using hypnotic inquiry protocols to monitor treatment progress and stability in multiple personality disorder. *American Journal of Clinical Hypnosis, 28,* 63–75.

Kluft, R.P. (1988a). On treating the older pateint with multiple personality disorder: "Race against time" or "make haste slowly." *American Journal of Clinical Hypnosis, 30,* 257–266.

Kluft, R.P. (1988b). The postunification treatment of multiple personality: First findings. *American Journal of Psychotherapy, 42,* 212–228.

Kluft, R.P. (1989a). Reflections on allegations of ritual abuse: Editorial. *Dissociation, 2,* 191–193.

Kluft, R.P. (1989b). Playing for time: Temporizing techniques in the treatment of multiple personality disorder. *American Journal of Clinical Hypnosis, 32,* 90–97.

Kluft, R.P. (1993a). Basic principles in conducting the psychotherapy of multiple personality disorder. In R.P. Kluft & C.G. Fine (Eds.), *Clinical perspectives on multiple personality disorder* (pp. 19–50). Washington, D.C.: American Psychiatric Press.

Kluft, R.P. (1993b). Clinical approaches to the integration of personalities. In R.P. Kluft & C.G. Fine (Eds.), *Clinical perspectives on multiple personality disorder* (pp. 101–133). Washington, D.C.: American Psychiatric Press.

Kluft, R.P. (1994). Editorial: Two jobs well done. *Dissociation, 7,* 201–202.

Kluft, R.P. (1996). Treating the traumatic memories of patients with dissociative identity disorder. *American Journal of Psychiatry, 153,* 103–110.

Kluft, R.P. (1997). The argument for the reality of the delayed recall of trauma. In P.S. Applebaum, L.A. Uyehara, & M. Elin (Eds.), *Trauma and memory: Clinical and legal controversies* (pp. 25–57). New York: Oxford University Press.

Kluft, R.P., & Fine, C. G. (1993). *Clinical perspectives on multiple personality disorder.* Washington, D.C.: American Psychiatric Press.

K.M. v. H.M. (1992). 96 D.L.R.4th 289, 36 A.C.W.S. (3d) 466 (Supreme Court of Canada).

Knapp, S., & VandeCreek, L. (1996). Risk manangement for psychologists: Treating patients who recover lost memories of childhood abuse. *Professional Psychology: Research and Practice, 27,* 452–459.

Knorr-Cetina, K.D., & Mulkay, M. (Eds.). (1983). *Science observed: Perspectives on the social study of science* (pp. 1–14). Newbury Park, CA: Sage.

Koehnken, G. & Wegener, H. (1985). Zum Stellenwert des Experiments in der forensischen Aussage-psychologie. *Zeitschrift für experimentelle und angewandte Psychologie, 32,* 104–119.

Koehnken, G., & Wegener, H. (1982). Zur glaubwürdigkeit von Zeugenausshen: Experimentelle überprüfung ausgeumehlter Glaubwuerdigkeit-skriterien. *Zeitschrift für experimentelle und angewandte Psychologie, 29,* 92–111.

Koestler, A. (1940). *Darkness at noon.* London: Cape.

Kohler, F. (1897). Experimentelle Studien auf dem Gebiete des hypnotischen Somnambulismus. *Zeitschrift für Hypnotismus, 6,* 357–374.

Kohut, H. (1971). *The analysis of self.* New York: International Universities Press.

Kolb, L.C. (1985). The place of narcosynthesis in the treatment of chronic and delayed stress reactions of war. In S.M. Sonnenberg, A.S. Blank, & J.A. Tabott (Eds.), *The trauma of war: Stress and recovery in Vietnam veterans* (pp. 211–226). Washington, D.C.: American Psychiatric Association Press.

Kolb, L. (1987). Neuropsychological hypothesis explaining posttraumatic stress disorder. *American Journal of Psychiatry, 144,* 989–995.

Kolb, L.C., & Multipassi, L.R. (1982). The conditioned emotional response: A subclass of chronic and delayed posttraumatic stress disorder. *Psychiatric Annals, 2,* 979–987.

Koopman, C., Classen, C., & Spiegel, D. (1994). Predictors of posttraumatic stress symptoms among survivors of the Oakland/Berkeley, Calif., Firestorm. *American Journal of Psychiatry, 151,* 888–894.

Koopman, C., Marshall, J., Abbott, B., Elliott, C., & Spiegel, D. (November 7, 1994). *Psychological effects of creating false memories of childhood sexual abuse.* Poster session at the Annual Meeting of the International Society of Traumatic Stress Studies, Chicago, IL.

Kopelman, M.D. (1987). Amnesia: Organic and psychogenic. *British Journal of Psychiatry, 150,* 428–442.

Korunka, C., Guttman, G., Schleinitz, D., Hilpert, M., Haas, R., & Fitzal, S. (1993). Effects of positive suggestions and music presented during anesthesia. In P.

S. Sebel, B. Bonke, & E. Winograd (Eds.), *Memory and awareness in anesthesia* (pp. 196–204). Englewood Cliffs, NJ: Prentice Hall.

Koss, M.P., Figueredo, A.J., Bell, I., Tharan, M., & Tromp, S. (1996). Traumatic memory characteristics: A cross-validated meditational model of response to rape among employed women. *Journal of Abnormal Psychology, 105,* 421–432.

Koss, M.P., Tromp, S., & Tharan, M. (1995). Traumatic memories: Empirical foundations, forensic and clinical implications. *Clinical Psychology: Science and Practice, 2,* 111–132.

Krafft-Ebing, R. von (1889). *An experimental study of the domain of suggestion.* New York: G.P. Putnam & Sons.

Kramer, T.H., Buckhout, R., Fox, P., Widman, E., & Tusche, B. (1991). Effects of stress on recall. *Applied Cognitive Psychology, 5,* 483–488.

Kranhold, C., Baumann, U., & Fichter, M. (1993). Hypnotizability in bulimic patients and controls: A pilot study. *European Archives of Psychiatry & Clinical Neuroscience, 242*(2–3), 72–76.

Kreskin. (1977). *Kreskin's mind power book.* New York: McGraw-Hill.

Kreskin. (1973). *The amazing world of Kreskin.* New York: Random House.

Kristiansen, C.M., Felton, K.A., Hovdestad, W.E., & Allard, C.B. (1995). *The Ottawa survivor's study: A summary of the findings.* Unpublished manuscript.

Kroger, W.S., & Douce, R.G. (1979). Hypnosis in criminal investigation. *International Journal of Clinical and Experimental Hypnosis, 27,* 358–374.

Kroll, N.E.A., & Timourian, D.A. (1986). Misleading questions and the retrieval of the irretrievable. *Bulletin of the Psychonomic Society, 24,* 165–168.

Krystal, J.H. (Ed.). (1968). *Massive psychic trauma.* New York: International Universities Press.

Krystal, J.H. (1993). Beyond *DSM-III-R:* Therapeutic considerations in posttraumatic stress disorder. In J.P. Wilson & B. Raphael (Eds.), *International handbook of traumatic stress syndromes* (pp. 841–854). New York: Plenum.

Krystal, J.H., Kosten, T.R., Southwick, S., Mason, J.W., Perry, B.D., & Giller, E.L. (1989). Neurobiological aspects of PTSD: Review of clinical and preclinical studies. *Behavior Therapy, 20,* 177–198.

Krystal, J.H., Southwick, S.M., & Charney, D.S. (1995). Post traumatic stress disorder: Psychobiological mechanisms of traumatic remembrance. In D.L. Schacter (Ed.), *Memory distortion: How minds, brains, and societies reconstruct the past* (pp.150–172). Cambridge, MA: Harvard University Press.

Kubie, L.S. (1943). Manual of emergency treatment for acute war neuroses. *War Medicine, 4,* 582–599.

Kubie, L.S. & Margolin, D. (1944). The process of hypnotism and the nature of the hypnotic state. *American Journal of Psychiatry, 100,* 611–622.

Kuehn, L.L. (1974). Looking down a gun barrel: Person perception and violent crime. *Perceptual & Motor Skills, 39,* 1159–1164.

Kuehnle, K. (1996). *Assessing allegations of child sexual abuse.* Sarasota, FL: Professional Resource Press.

Kuhn, T.S. (1962). *The structure of scientific revolutions.* Chicago, IL: University of Chicago Press.

Kuhns, B.W. (1981). *Hypnosis and the law.* Glendale, CA: Westwood Publishing.

Kumar, V.K., & Pekala, R.J. (1988). Hypnotizability, absorption, and individual differences in phenomenological experience. *International Journal of Clinical and Experimental Hypnosis, 36,* 80–88.

Kumar, V.K., & Pekala, R.J. (1989). Variations in phenomenological experience as a function of hypnosis and hypnotic susceptibility: A replication. *British Journal of Experimental & Clinical Hypnosis, 6,* 17–22.

Kuyken, W., & Brewin, C.R. (1995). Autobiographical memory functioning in depression and reports of early abuse. *Journal of Abnormal Psychology, 104,* 585–591.

Labelle, L., Bibb, B.C., Bryant, R.A., & McConkey, K.M. (1989). Suggested pseudomemory in hypnotic & nonhypnotic conditions: The influence of cognitive and social factors. Unpublished manuscript, Macquarie University, Sydney, Australia; Cited in Sheehan, P.W., Statham, D., & Jamieson, G.A. (1991). Pseudomemory effect & their relationship to level of susceptibility to hypnosis and state instruction. *Journal of Personality & Social Psychology, 60 (1),* 130–137.

Labelle, L., Laurence, J-R., Nadon, R., & Perry, C. (1990). Hypnotizability, preference for an imagic cognitive style, and memory creation in hypnosis. *Journal of Abnormal Psychology, 99,* 222–228.

Labelle, L., & Perry, C. (August 1986). *Pseudomemory creation in hypnosis.* Paper presented at the 94th Annual Convention of the American Psychological Association, Washington, D.C.

Lacey, J.H. (1990). Incest, incestuous fantasy, and indecency: A clinical catchment-area study of normal-weight bulimic women. *British Journal of Psychiatry, 157,* 399–403.

Ladavas, E., Nicoletti, R., Umilta, C., & Rizzolatti, G. (1984). Right hemisphere interference during negative affect: A reaction time study. *Neuropsychologia, 22,* 479–485.

Lakatos, I. (1970). Falsification and methodology of scientific research programmes. In I. Lakatos & A. Musgrave (Eds.), *Criticism and the growth of knowledge* (pp. 91–195). England: Cambridge University Press.

Lalley, H. (April 3, 1997). Doctor acquitted in repressed-memory case. *Chicago Tribune,* section 2, p. 8.

Lamare v. Basbanes. (1994). 418 Mass. 274, 636 N.E.2d 218 (Sup. Jud. Ct., Middlesex).

Lamb, C.S. (1985). Hypnotically induced deconditioning: Reconstruction of memories in the treatment of phobias. *American Journal of Clinical Hypnosis,28,* 56–62.

Lamers-Winkelman, F., Buffing, F., & van der Zanden, A.P. (September 1992). *Statement validity analysis in child sexual abuse cases: A field study.* Poster presented at the Third Conference of Law and Psychology, Oxford, England.

Lamers-Winkelman, F., van der Zander, A.P., & Buffing, F. (September 1992). *Interviews which did not lead to statements of sexual abuse*. Poster presented at the Third Conference of Law and Psychology, Oxford, England.

Lamm, J.B. (1991). Easing access to the courts for incest victims: Toward an equitable application of the delayed discovery rule. *Yale Law Journal, 100,* 2189–2208.

Langer, L.L. (1991). *Holocaust testimonies: The ruins of memory*. New Haven, CT: Yale University Press.

Langone, M.D. (Ed.). (1993). *Recovery from cults: Help for victims of psychological and spiritual abuse*. New York: Norton.

Lanning, K.V. (1991). Ritual abuse: A law enforcement view or perspective. *Child Abuse and Neglect, 15,* 171–173.

Lanning, K.V. (1992a). A law-enforcement perspective on allegations of ritual abuse. In D.K. Sakheim and S.E. Devine (Eds.), *Out of darkness: Exploring Satanism and ritual abuse* (pp. 109–146). New York: Lexington.

Lanning, K.V. (1992b). *Investigator's guide to allegations of "ritual" child abuse*. Behavioral Science Unit, National Center for the Analysis of Violent Crime, Federal Bureau of Investigation, Quantico, VA.

Lantos, J. (September 11, 1990). The first day of school: A primal terror returns. *Los Angeles Times,* B-7.

Larsen, S.F. (1988). Remembering without experiencing: Memory for reported events. In U. Neisser & E. Winograd (Eds.), *Remembering reconsidered: Ecological and traditional approaches to the study of memory* (pp. 326–355). New York: Cambridge University Press.

Larsen, S. F. (1992). Potential flashbulbs: Memories of ordinary news as the baseline. In E. Winograd & U. Neisser (Eds.), *Affect and accuracy in recall: Studies of flashbulb" memories* (pp. 32–64). London: Cambridge University Press.

Larson, E.J. (1995). *Sex, race, and science: Eugenics in the deep South*. Baltimore, MD: Johns Hopkins University Press.

Lashley, K.S. (1950). In search of the engram. *Symposia of the Society of Experimental Biology, 4,* 454–582.

Latour, B. (1987). *Science in action*. Cambridge, MA: Harvard University Press.

Latour, B. & Woolgar, S. (1979). *Laboratory life: The social construction of scientific facts*. Newbury Park, CA: Sage.

Laub, D.,& Auerhahn, N. (1993). Knowing and not knowing massive psychic trauma: Forms of traumatic memory. *International Journal of Psychoanalysis, 74,* 287–301.

Laurence, J-R. (1982). *Memory creation in hypnosis*. Unpublished doctoral dissertation, Concordia University, Montreal, Canada.

Laurence, J-R., Nadon, R., Nogrady, M., & Perry, C. (1986). Duality, dissociation and memory creation in highly hypnotizable subjects. *International Journal of Clinical and Experimental Hypnosis,34,* 295–310.

Laurence, J-R., & Perry, C. (1981). The "hidden observer" phenomenon in hypnosis: Some additional findings. *Journal of Abnormal Psychology, 90,* 334–344.

Laurence, J-R., & Perry, C. (1983). Hypnotically created memory among highly hypnotizable subjects. *Science, 222,* 523–524.

Laurence, J-R. & Perry, C. 1988. *Hypnosis, will, and memory: A psycho-legal history*. New York: Guilford.

Lausch, E. (1974). *Manipulation*. England: Aidan Ellis.

Lawson, L., & Chaffin, M. (1992). False negatives in sexual abuse disclosure interviews. *Journal of Interpersonal Violence, 7,* 532–542.

Lazarus, R.S. (1966). *Psychological stress and the coping process*. New York: McGraw-Hill.

L.C. v. A.K.D. (1994). No. 05–92–02867–CV (Ct.App.Tex.- Dallas, March 1).

Leavitt, F. (1994). Clinical correlates of alleged Satanic abuse and less controversial sexual molestation. *Child Abuse and Neglect, 18,* 387–392.

Leavitt, F. (1997). False attribution of suggestibility to explain recovered memory of childhood sexual abuse following extended amnesia. *Journal of Child Abuse & Neglect, 21*(3), 265–272.

Leavitt, F., & Labott, S.M. (1996). Authenticity of recovered sexual abuse memories: A Rorschach study. *Journal of Traumatic Stress, 9,* 483–496.

LeBaron, S., Zeltzer, L.K., & Fanurik, D. (1988). Imaginative involvement and hypnotizability in childhood. *International Journal of Clinical and Experimental Hypnosis, 36,* 284–295.

Lebowitz, L. Harvey, M.R., & Herman, J.L. (1993). A stage-by-dimension model of recovery from sexual trauma. *Journal of Interpersonal Violence, 8,* 378–391.

Lederer, L. (Ed.). (1980). *Take back the night: Women on pornography*. New York: William Morrow.

LeDoux, J.E. (1992). Emotion as memory: Anatomical systems underlying indelible neural traces. In S-A. Christianson (Ed.), *Handbook of emotion and memory* (pp. 269–288). Hillsdale, NJ: Erlbaum.

LeDoux, J.E. (1994). Emotion, memory and the brain. *Scientific American, 270,* 50–57.

Lee, K.A., Vaillant, G.E., Torrey, W.C., & Elder, G.H. (1995). A 50–year prospective study of the psychological sequelae of World War II combat. *American Journal of Psychiatry, 152,* 516–522.

Leiblum, S.R., & Rosen, R.C. (1989). *Principles and practice of sex therapy: Update for the 1990s*. New York: Guilford.

Leichtman, M.D., & Ceci, S.J. (1995). The effects of stereotypes and suggestions on preschoolers' reports. *Developmental Psychology, 31,* 568–578.

Leippe, M.R. (1980). Effects of integrative memorial and cognitive processes on the correspondence of accuracy and confidence. *Law and Human Behavior, 4,* 261–274.

Leippe, M.R., Romanczyk, A., & Manion, A.P. (1991). Eyewitness memory for a touching experience: Accuracy differences between child and adult witnesses. *Journal of Applied Psychology, 76,* 367–379.

Leippe, M.R., Wells, G.L., & Ostrom, T.M. (1978). Crime seriousness as a determinant of accuracy in eyewitness identification. *Journal of Applied Psychology, 63,* 345–351.

Leitch, A. (1948). Notes on amnesia in crime for the general practitioner. *Medical Press, 219*, 459–463.

Lemmerman v. Fealk. (1993). 507 N.W. 2d 226 (Mich. App.).

Lemmerman v. Fealk. (1995). 449 Mich. 56, 534 N.W.2d 695.

Leonard, J.R. (1963). *An investigation of hypnotic age-regression.* Unpublished doctoral dissertation, University of Kentucky.

Leonard v. England. (1994). 445 S.E.2d 50 (N.C. App.).

Lepore, S.J., & Sesco, B. (1994). Distorting children's reports and interpretations of events through suggestion. *Applied Psychology, 79*, 108–120.

Lesgold, A.M., & Petrush, A.R. (1977). *Do leading questions alter memories?* Unpublished manuscript, University of Pittsburgh.

Leuner, H. (1969). Guided affective imagery (GAI): A method of intensive psychotherapy. *American Journal of Psychotherapy, 23*, 4–22.

Leventhal, H. (1965). Fear communications in the acceptance of preventative health practices. *Bulletin of the New York Academy of Medicine, 41*, 1144–1168

Leventhal, H., Singer, R., & Jones, S. (1965). Effects of fear and specificity of recommendation upon attitudes and behavior. *Journal of Personality and Social Psychology, 2*, 20–29.

Levinger, G., & Clark, J. (1961). Emotional factors in the forgetting of word associations. *Journal of Abnormal and Social Psychology, 62*, 99–105.

Levinson, B. W. (1965). States of awareness during general anaesthesia. *British Journal of Anesthesia, 37*, 544–546.

Levinson, B.W. (1969). *An examination of states of awareness during general anaesthesia.* Unpublished thesis for the degree of Doctor of Medicine, University of Witwatersrand, South Africa.

Levinson, B. (1990). The states of awareness in anaesthesia in 1965. In B. Bonke, W. Fitch, & K. Millar (Eds.), *Memory and awareness in anaesthesia* (pp. 11–18). Amsterdam: Swets & Zeitlinger.

Levinson, B. (1993). Quo vadis. In P. S. Sebel, B. Bonke, & E. Winograd (Eds.), *Memory and awareness in anesthesia* (pp. 498–500). Englewood Cliffs, NJ: Prentice Hall.

Lewis, M. (1995). Memory and psychoanalysis: A new look at infantile amnesia and transference. *Journal of the American Academy of Child and Adolescent Psychiatry, 34*, 405–417.

Lewis, O. (1966). The culture of poverty. *Scientific American, 215*, 19–25.

Lewis, S. A., Jenkinson, J., & Wilson, J. (1973). An EEG investigation of awareness during anaesthesia. *British Journal of Psychology, 64*(3), 413–415.

Lichtenberg, J. D. (1975). The development of a sense of self. *Journal of the American Psychoanalytic Association, 23*, 453–483.

Lidz, B.T., Weathers, F.W., Monaco, V., Herman, D.S., Wulfsohn, M., Marx, B., & Keane, T.M. (1996). Attention, arousal, and memory in posttraumatic stress disorder. *Journal of Traumatic Stress, 9*, 497–519.

Lieberman, M.A., Yalom, E.D., & Miles, M.B. (1973). *Encounter groups: First facts.* New York: Basic.

Lief, H.I., & Fetkewicz, J.M. (1995). Retractors of false memories: The evolution of pseudomemories. *Journal of Psychiatry and Law, 23*, 411–435.

Liem, J.H., O'Toole, J. G., & James, J. B. (1996). Themes of power and betrayal in sexual abuse survivor's characterizations of interpersonal relationships. *Journal of Traumatic Stress, 9*, 745–761.

Lifton, R.J. (1956). "Thought reform" of Western civilians in Chinese prisons. *American Journal of Psychiatry, 110*, 732–739.

Lifton, R.J. (1961). *Thought reform and the psychology of totalism.* New York: Norton.

Lifton, R.J. (1967). *Death in life: Survivors of Hiroshima.* New York: Simon & Schuster.

Lifton, R.J. (1986). *The Nazi doctors: Medical killing and the psychology of genocide.* New York: Basic.

Lindemann, E. (1944). Symptomatology and management of acute grief. *American Journal of Psychiatry, 101*, 141–148.

Lindgren v. Moore. (1995). 907 F.Supp. 1183 (N.D.Ill.).

Lindsay, D.S. (1990). Misleading suggestions can impair eyewitnesses' ability to remember event details. *Journal of Experimental Psychology: Learning, Memory, and Cognition, 16*, 1077–1083.

Lindsay, D.S. (1994a). Contextualizing and clarifying criticisms of memory work in psychotherapy. *Consciousness and Cognition, 3*, 426–437.

Lindsay, D.S. (1994b). Memory source monitoring and eyewitness testimony. In D. F. Ross, J. D. Read & M. P. Toglia (Eds.), *Adult eyewitness testimony: Current trends and developments* (pp. 27–55). New York: Cambridge University Press.

Lindsay, D.S. (1995). Beyond backlash: Comments on Ennis, McNeilly, Corkery, and Gilbert. *The Counseling Psychologist, 23*, 280–289.

Lindsay, D.S., & Johnson, M.K. (1987). Reality monitoring and suggestibility: Children's ability to discriminate among memories from different sources. In S.J. Ceci, M.P. Toglia, & D.F. Ross (Eds.), *Children's eyewitness memory* (pp. 92–121). New York: Springer-Verlag.

Lindsay, D.S., & Johnson, M.K. (1989). The eyewitness suggestibility effect and memory for source. *Memory and Cognition, 17*, 349–358.

Lindsay, D.S., & Poole, D.A. (1995). Remembering childhood sexual abuse in therapy: Psychotherapists' self-reported beliefs, practices, and experiences. *Journal of Psychiatry and Law, 23*, 461–476.

Lindsay, D.S. & Read, J.D. (1994). Psychotherapy and memories of childhood sexual abuse: A cognitive perspective. *Applied Cognitive Psychology, 8*, 281–338.

Lindsay, R.C.L. & Wells, G.L. (1980). What price justice: Exploring the relationship of lineup fairness to identification accuracy. *Law and Human Behavior, 4*, 303–314.

Linehan, M.M. (1993). *Cognitive-behavioral treatment of*

borderline personality disorder. New York: Guilford.

Linton, C. P., & Sheehan, P. W. (1994). The relationship between interrogative suggestibility and susceptibility to hypnosis. *Australian Journal of Clinical and Experimental Hypnosis, 22*, 53–64.

Linton, M. (1975). Memory for real-world events. In D.A. Norman & D. E. Rumelhart (Eds.), *Explorations in cognition* (pp. 376–404). San Francisco, CA: Freeman.

Linton, M. (1978). Real-world memory after six years: An in vivo study of very long-term memory. In M. M. Gruneberg, P.E. Morris, & R.N. Sykes (Eds.), *Practical aspects of memory* (pp. 69–76). London: Academic Press.

Lipin, T. (1955). Psychic functioning in patients with undiagnosed somatic symptoms. *Archives of Neurology and Psychiatry, 73*, 329–337.

Lipowsky, Z.J. (1968). Review of consultation psychiatry and psychosomatic medicine. III: Theoretical issues. *Psychosomatic Medicine, 30*, 395–422.

Lipstadt, D. (1993). *Denying the holocaust*. New York: Harper-Collins.

List, J.A. (1986). Age and schematic differences in the reliability of eyewitness testimony. *Developmental Psychology, 22*, 50–57.

Liu, W. H. D., Standen, P. J., & Aitkenhead, A. R. (1992). Therapeutic suggestions during general anaesthesia in patients undergoing hysterectomy. *British Journal of Anesthesia, 68*, 277–281.

Liu, W. H. D., Thorp, T. A. S., Graham, S. G., & Aitkenhead, A. R. (1991). Incidence of awareness with recall during general anaesthesia. *Anaesthesia, 46*, 435–437.

Lloyd, R. (1976). *For money or love: Boy prostitution in America*. New York: Vanguard.

Loewenfeld, L. (1901). *Der Hypnotismus: Handbuch der Lehre von der Hypnose und der Suggestion, mit besonderer Berucksichtigung ihre Bedeutung für Medizin und Rechtspflege*. Wiesbaden: J.F. Bergmann.

Loewenstein, R.J. (1991). An office mental status examination for complex chronic dissociative symptoms and multiple personality disorder. *Psychiatric Clinics of North America, 14*, 567–604.

Loewenstein, R.J. (1997). Treatment of dissociative amnesia and dissociative fugue. In W. Reid (Ed.). *Treatment of DSM-IV psychiatric disorders*. (3rd ed.) (pp. 283–292). New York: Brunner/Mazel.

Loftus, E.F. (1975). Leading questions and the eyewitness report. *Cognitive Psychology, 7*, 560–572.

Loftus, E.F. (1979a). *Eyewitness testimony*. Cambridge: Harvard University Press.

Loftus, E.F. (1979b). The malleability of memory. *American Scientist, 67*, 312–320.

Loftus, E.F. (1979c). *The manipulative uses of language*. Audiotape No. 20234, A Psychology Today Cassette. New York: Ziff-Davis Publishing.

Loftus, E.F.(1980). *Memory*. Reading, MA: Addison-Wesley.

Loftus, E.F. (1992). Psi Chi/Frederick Howell Lewis Distinguished Lecture. Presented at the 100th Annual Convention of the American Psychological Association, Washington, D.C.

Loftus, E.F. (1993). The reality of repressed memories. *American Psychologist, 48*, 518–537.

Loftus, E.F., & Burns, T.E. (1982). Mental shock can produce retrograde amnesia. *Memory & Cognition, 10*, 318–323.

Loftus, E.F., & Coan. (in press). The construction of childhood memories. In D. Peters (Ed.), *The child witness in context: Cognitive, social, and legal perspectives*. New York: Kluwer.

Loftus, E.F., Feldman, J., & Dashiell, R. (1995). The reality of illusory memories. In D. L. Schacter (Ed.), *Memory distortion: How minds, brains, and societies reconstruct the past* (pp. 47–68). Cambridge, MA: Harvard University Press.

Loftus, E.F., Garry, M., & Feldman, J. (1994). Forgetting sexual trauma: What does it mean when 38% forget? *Journal of Consulting and Clinical Psychology, 62*, 1177–1181.

Loftus, E.F., & Hoffman, H.G. (1989). Misinformation and memory: The creation of new memories. *Journal of Experimental Psychology: General, 118*, 100–104.

Loftus, E.F., & Kaufman, L. (1992). Why do traumatic experiences sometimes produce good memory (flashbulbs) and sometimes no memory (repression)? In E. Winograd & U. Neisser (Eds.), *Affect and accuracy in recall: Studies of "flashbulb" memories* (pp. 212–223). London: Cambridge University Press.

Loftus, E.F., & Ketcham, K. (1991). *Witness for the defense: The accused, the eyewitness, and the expert who puts memory on trial*. New York: St. Martin's Press.

Loftus, E.F., & Ketcham, K. (1994). *The myth of repressed memory: False memories and allegations of sexual abuse*. New York: St. Martin's Press.

Loftus, E.F., Korf, N.L., & Schooler, J.W. (1989). Misguided memories: Sincere distortions of reality. In J.C. Yuille (Ed.), *Credibility assessment* (pp. 155–173). New York: Kluwer.

Loftus, E.F., Levidow, B., & Duensing, S. (1992). Who remembers best? Individual differences in memory for events that occurred in a science museum. *Applied Cognitive Psychology, 6*, 93–107.

Loftus, G.R., & Loftus, E.F. (1976). *Human memory: The processing of information*. Hillsdale, NJ: Erlbaum.

Loftus, E.F., & Loftus, G.R. (1980). On the permanence of stored information in the human brain. *American Psychologist, 35*, 409–420.

Loftus, E.F., Miller, D.G., & Burns, H.J. (1978). Semantic integration of verbal information into a visual memory. *Journal of Experimental Psychology: Human Learning and Memory, 4*, 19–31.

Loftus, E.F., & Palmer, J.C. (1974). Reconstruction of automobile destruction: An example of the interaction between language and memory. *Journal of Verbal Learning and Verbal Behavior, 13*, 585–589.

Loftus, E.F., & Pickrell, J.E. (1995). The formation of false memories. *Psychiatric Annals, 25*, 720–725.

Loftus, E.F., Polonsky,S., & Fullilove, M.T. (1994). Memories of childhood sexual abuse: Remembering and repressing. *Psychology of Women Quarterly, 18,* 67–84.

Loftus, E.F., & Rosenwald, L.A. (1995). Recovered memories: Unearthing the past in court. *Journal of Psychiatry and Law, 23,* 349–361.

Loftus, E. F., Schooler, J. W., Loftus, G. R., & Glauber, D. T. (1985). Memory for events occurring under anesthesia. *Acta Psychologica, 59,* 123–128.

Loftus, E.F., & Zanni, G. (1975). Eyewitness testimony: The influence of the wording of a question. *Bulletin of the Psychonomic Society, 5,* 86–88.

London, P. (1969). *Behavior control.* New York: Harper & Row.

Longino, H.E. (1990). *Science as social knowledge: Values and objectivity in scientific inquiry.* Princeton, NJ: Princeton University Press.

Los Angeles County Commission for Women. (1989). *Ritual abuse.* Unpublished report of the Ritual Abuse Task Force.

Lotto, D. (1994). On witches and witch hunts: Ritual and Satanic cult abuse. *Journal of Psychohistory, 21,* 373–396.

Luborsky, L. (1984). *Principles of psychoanalytic psychotherapy: A manual for supportive-expressive treatment.* New York: Basic.

Lucas v. Hamm. (1961). 56 Cal.2d 583, 15 Cal. Rptr. 821, 364 P.2d 685.

Luria, A.R. (1932). *The nature of human conflict* W. Horsley Gantt (Trans.). New York: Liveright.

Luria, A.R. (1979). *The making of mind.* Cambridge, MA: Harvard University Press.

Luus, C.A.E., & Wells, G.L. (1994). The malleability of eyewitness confidence: Co-witness and perseverance effects. *Journal of Applied Psychology, 714–723.*

Lynn, S.J., & Kirsch, I.I. (1996). Alleged alien abductions: False memories, hypnosis, and fantasy proneness. *Psychological Inquiry, 7*(2), 151–155.

Lynn, S.J., Milano, M., & Weekes, J.R. (1991). Hypnosis and pseudomemories: The effects of prehypnotic expectancies, *Journal of Personality and Social Psychology, 60,* 318–326.

Lynn, S., Milano, M., & Weekes, J.R. (1992). Pseudomemory and age-regression: An exploratory study. *American Journal of Clinical Hypnosis, 35,* 129–137.

Lynn, S.J., & Pezzo, M. (1994). *Close encounters of a third kind: Simulated hypnotic interviews of alien contacts.* Paper presented at the annual meeting of the American Psychological Association.

Lynn, S.J., & Rhue, J. (Eds.). (1991). *Theories of hypnosis.* New York: Guilford.

Lynn, S.J., & Rhue, J.W. (1988). Fantasy proneness: Hypnosis, developmental antecedents, and psychopathology. *American Psychologist, 43,* 35–44.

Lynn, S.J., & Rhue, J.W. (Eds.). (1994). *Dissociation: Clinical and theoretical perspectives.* New York: Guilford Press.

Lynn, S.J., Rhue, J.W., Myers, B.P., & Weekes, J.R. (1994). Pseudomemory in hypnotized and simulating subjects, *International Journal of Clinical and Experimental Hypnosis, 42,* 118–129.

Lynn, S.J., Weekes, J.R., & Milano, M.J. (1989). Reality versus suggestion: Pseudomemory in hypnotizable and simulating subjects. *Journal of Abnormal Psychology, 98,* 137–144.

Lyon, L.S. (1985). Facilitating telephone number recall in a case of psychogenic amnesia. *Journal of Behavior Therapy and Experimental Psychiatry, 16,* 147–149.

Lytle, R.A., & Lundy, R.M. (1988). Hypnosis and the recall of visually presented material: A failure to replicate Stager and Lundy. *International Journal of Clinical and Experimental Hypnosis, 36,* 327–335.

MacDonald v. Clinger. (1982). 84 A.D.2d 482, 446 N.Y.S.2d 801.

MacFarlane, K. (1978). Sexual abuse of children. In J. Chapman & M. Gates (Eds.), *The victimization of women* (pp. 81–109). Beverley Hills, CA: Sage.

MacLean, H.N. (1993). *Once upon a time: A true story of memory, murder, and the law.* New York: Harper Collins.

McCann, L., & Pearlman, L. (1990). *Psychological trauma and the adult survivor: Theory, therapy, and transformation.* New York: Brunner/Mazel.

McCann, T., & Sheehan, P.W. (1987). The breaching of pseudomemeory under hypnotic instruction: Implications for original memory retrieval. *British Journal of Experimental and Clinical Hypnosis, 4*(2), 101–108, 112–114.

McCann, T., & Sheehan, P.W. (1988). Hypnotically induced pseudomemories: Sampling their conditions among hypnotizable subjects. *Journal of Personality & Social Psychology, 54,* 339–346.

McCann, T., & Sheehan, P.W. (1989). Pseudomemory creation and confidence in the experimental hypnosis context. *British Journal of Experimental and Clinical Hypnosis, 6,* 151–159.

McCauley, M., & Fisher, R. (March 1992). *Improving children's recall of action with the cognitive interview.* Paper presented at the meeting of the American Psychology and Law Society, San Diego, CA.

McClelland, J.L. (1995). Constructive memory and memory distortions: A parallel distribution processing approach. In D.L. Schacter (Ed.), *Memory distortion: How minds, brains, and societies reconstruct the past* (pp. 69–90). Cambridge, MA: Harvard University Press.

McCloskey, M. (1992). Special versus ordinary memory mechanisms in the genesis of flashbulb memories. In E. Winograd & U. Neisser (Eds.), *Affect and accuracy in recall: Studies of "flashbulb" memories* (pp. 227–235). New York: Cambridge University Press.

McCloskey, M., Wible, C.G., & Cohen, N.J. (1988). Is there a special flashbulb-memory mechanism? *Journal of Experimental Psychology: General, 117,* 171–181.

McCloskey, M., & Zaragoza, M. (1985). Misleading postevent information and memory for events: Arguments and evidence against memory impairment hypotheses. *Journal of Experimental Psychology: General,* 1–16.

McCollum v. D'Arcy. (1994). 138 N.H. 285, 638 A.2d 797.

McConkey, K.M. (1992). The effects of hypnotic procedures on remembering: The experimental findings and their implications for forensic hypnosis. In E. Fromm & M.R. Nash (Eds.), *Contemporary hypnosis research* (pp. 405–426). New York: Guilford.

McConkey, K.M., & Jupp, J.J. (1985). Opinions about the forensic use of hypnosis. *Australian Psychologist, 20,* 283–291.

McConkey, K.M., & Jupp, J.J. (1985–86). A survey of opinions about hypnosis. *British Journal of Experimental and Clinical Hypnosis, 3,* 87–93.

McConkey, K.M., & Kinoshita, S. (1988). The influence of hypnosis on memory after one day and one week. *Journal of Abnormal Psychology, 97,* 48–53.

McConkey, K.M., Labelle, L., Bibb, B.C., & Bryant, R.A. (1990). Hypnosis and suggested pseudomemory: The relevance of test context. *Australian Journal of Psychology, 42,* 197–205.

McConkey, K.M., Roche, S.M., & Sheehan, P.W. (1989). Reports of forensic hypnosis: A critical analysis. *Australian Psychologist, 24,* 249–272.

McConkey, K.M., & Sheehan, P. W. (1995). *Hypnosis, memory, and behavior in criminal investigation.* New York: Guilford.

McCormak, P.D. (1979). Autobiographical memory in the aged. *Canadian Journal of Psychology, 33,* 118–124.

McDougall, W. (1920–1921). The revival of emotional memories and its therapeutic value (III). *British Journal of Medical Psychology, 1,* 23–29.

McDougall, W. (1926). *An outline of abnormal psychology.* London: Methuen.

McElroy, S.L., & Keck, P.E. (1995). Recovered memory therapy: False memory syndrome and other complications. *Psychiatric Annals, 25,* 731–735.

McEwan, N.H., & Yuille, J.C. (1981). *The effects of training and experience on eyewitness memory.* Presented at the 42nd Annual Conference of the Canadian Psychological Association, Toronto, Ontario.

McFall, M.E., Murburg, M., Grant, N.K., et. al. (1990). Autonomic responses to stress in Vietnam combat veterans with posttraumatic stress disorder. *Biological Psychiatry, 27,* 1165–1175.

McFall, M.E., Murburg, M., Roszell, D.K., & Veith, R.C. (1989). Psychophysiologic and neuroendocrine findings in posttraumatic stress disorder. *Journal of Anxiety Disorders, 3,* 243–257.

McFarlane, A.C. (1988) The longitudinal course of postraumatic morbidity: The range of outcomes and their predictors. *Journal of Nervous and Mental Disease, 176,* 30–39.

McGaugh, J.L. (1983). Hormonal influences on memory. *Annual Review of Psychology, 34,* 297–323.

McGaugh, J.L. (1989). Psychoneuroendocrinology of stress: A psychobiological perspective. In R.B. Brush & L. Levine (Eds.), *Psychoendocrinology* (pp. 305–339). New York: Academic Press.

McGaugh, J.L. (1992). Affect, neuromodulatory systems, and memory storage. In S-A Christianson (Ed.), *Hand-book of emotion and memory* (pp. 245–268). Hillsdale, NJ: Erlbaum.

McGaugh, J.L., & Gold, P.E. (1989). Hormonal modulation of memory. In R.B. Brush & S. Levine (Eds.), *Psychoendocrinology* (pp. 305–339). New York: Academic Press.

McGeoch, J.A. (1932). Forgetting and the law of disuse. *Psychological Review, 39,* 352–370.

McGlauflin v. State. (1993). 857 P.2d 366 (Alaska App.).

McGough, L.S. (1991). Commentary: Sexual abuse and suggestibilty. Commentary: Assessing the credibility of witnesses' statements. In J. Doris (Ed.), *The suggestibility of children's recollections* (pp. 115–117, 165–167). Washington, D.C.: American Psychological Association Press.

McGough, L.S. (1994). *Child witnesses: Fragile voices in the American legal system.* New Haven, CT: Yale University Press.

McGuire, W. (1960). Cognitive consistency and attitude change. *Journal of Abnormal and Social Psychology, 60,* 345–353.

McHugh, P.R. (1993). Do patients recovered memories of sexual abuse constitute a "false memory syndrome"? *Psychiatric News, 28,* 18.

McHugh, P.R. (1992). Psychiatric misadventures. *The American Scholar, 61,* 497–510.

McHugh, P.R. (1993). Psychotherapy awry. *The American Scholar, 63,* 17–30.

McIver, W., Wakefield, H., & Underwager, R. (1989). Behavior of abused and non-abused children in interviews with anatomically correct dolls. *Issues in Child Abuse Accusations, 1,* 39–48.

McKee, K. (July/August, 1994). The NAPA repressed memory case. *The California Therapist, 6,* 24–26.

McLeod, C. C., Corbisier, B., & Mack, J. E. (1996). A more parsimonious explanation for UFO abduction. *Psychological Inquiry, 7*(2), 156–168.

McLintock, T. T. C., Aitken, H., Downie, C. F. A., & Kenny, G. N. C. (1990). Postoperative analgesic requirements in patients exposed to positive intraoperative suggestions. *British Medical Journal, 301,* 788–790

McNally, R.J., English, G.E., & Leipke, H.J. (1993). Assessment of intrusive cognition in PTSD: Use of the modified Stroop paradigm. *Journal of Traumatic Stress, 6,* 33–41.

McNally, R.J., Kaspi, S.P., Rieman, C., & Zeitlin, S.B. (1990). Selective processing of threat cues in posttraumatic stress disorder. *Journal of Abnormal Psychology, 99,* 398–402.

Madakasira, S., & O'Brien, K.F. (1987) Acute posttraumatic stress disorder in victims of a natural disaster. *Journal of Nervous and Mental Disease, 175,* 286–290.

Mal, F.M. (1995). Psychiatrists' attitudes to multiple personality disorder: A questionnaire study. *Canadian Journal of Psychiatry, 40,* 154–157.

Main, M., & Solomon, J. (1986). Discovery of an insecure-disorganized/disoriented attachment pattern. In T. Brazelton & M.W. Yogman (Eds.), *Affective devel-*

opment in infancy (pp. 95–124). Norwood, NJ: Ablex Publishing.

Malinoski, P.T., Lynn, S.J., Martin, D., Aronoff, J., Neufeld, J., & Gedeon, S. (August 11, 1995). *Individual differences in early memory reports: An empirical investigation.* Paper presented at the Annual Meeting of the American Psychological Association, New York, NY.

Malloy, P.F., Fairbank, J.A., & Keane, T.M. (1993). Validation of a multimethod assessment of post-traumatic stress disorders in Vietnam veterans. *Journal of Consulting and Clinical Psychology, 51,* 488–494.

Malpass, R.S., & Devine, P.G. (1981). Guided memory in eyewitness identification. *Journal of Applied Psychology, 66,* 343–350.

Mannheim, K. (1946). *Ideology and utopia: An introduction to the sociology of knowledge.* New York: Harcourt Brace.

Mantell, D.M. (1988). Clarifying erroneous child abuse allegations. *American Journal of Orthopsychiatry, 58,* 618–621.

Marche, T.A,. & Howe, M.L. (1995). Preschoolers report misinformation despite accurate memory. *Developmental Psychology, 31,* 554–567.

Margolin, E. (January/February, 1996). A lawyer's view of invented memory: The Ramona case. *The Champion,* pp. 24–25, 62–64.

Marin, B. V., Holmes, D.L., Guth, M., & Kovac, P. (1979). The potential of children as eyewitnesses. *Law and Human Behavior, 3,* 295–306.

Marks, G., & Miller, N. (1987). Ten years of research on the false-consensus effect: An empirical and theoretical review. *Psychological Bulletin, 102,* 72–90.

Marks, J. (1988). *The search for the "Manchurian Candidate": The CIA and mind control.* New York: Dell.

Marlene F. v. Affiliated Psychiatric Medical Clinic, Inc. (1989). 48 Cal. 3d 583, 257 Cal. Rptr. 98, 770 P. 2d 278.

Marmar, C.R., Weiss, D.S. Metzler, T.J., Ronfeldt, H.M., & Foreman, C. (1996). Stress responses of emergency services personnel to the Loma Prieta earthquake Interstate 880 freeway collapse and control traumatic incidents. *Journal of Traumatic Stress, 9,* 63–85.

Marmar, C.R., Weiss, D.S., Schlenger, W.E., Fairbank, J.A., Jordan, K., Kulka, R.A., & Hough, R.L. (1994). Peritraumatic dissociation and posttraumatic stress in male Vietnam theater veterans. *American Journal of Psychiatry, 151,* 902–907.

Marshall, J. (1966). *Law and psychology in conflict.* New York: Bobbs-Merrill.

Martinez v. County of Los Angeles. (1986). 186 Cal. App. 3d 884, 231 Cal. Rptr 96 (2nd Dist), review denied, 1987.

Martinez-Taboas, A. (1996). Repressed memories: Some clinical data contributing toward its elucidation. *American Journal of Psychotherapy, 50,* 217–230.

Masserman, J. (1994). *Sexual accusations and social turmoil.* Oakland, CA: Regent Press.

Masson, J.M. (1984). *The assault on truth: Freud's suppression of the seduction theory.* New York: Farrar, Straus & Giroux.

Masson, J.M. (1988). *Against therapy.* New York: Athenaeum.

Matter of Raynes. (1985). 215, Mont. 484, 698 P. 2d 856.

Matthews, W.J., Kirsch, I., & Allen, G.J. (1984). Posthypnotic conflict and psychopathology: Controlling for the effects of posthypnotic suggestions. *International Journal of Clinical and Experimental Hypnosis, 32,* 362–365.

Mayer, R.S. (1991). *Satan's children: Case studies in multiple personality.* New York: G.P. Putnam's Sons.

Mazor, A., Gampel, Y., Enright, R.D., & Orenstein, R. (1990). Holocaust survivors: Coping with post-traumatic memories in childhood and 40 years later. *Journal of Traumatic Stress, 3,* 1–14.

Meares, A. (1961). *A system of medical hypnosis.* Philadelphia, PA: Saunders.

Medical Ethics Advisor. (December 1996). Can you waive informed consent? Sometimes. *Medical Ethics Advisor, 12*(12), 136–138.

Meerloo, J.A.M. (1956). *The rape of the mind.* New York: Grosset & Dunlap.

Meichenbaum , D. (1994). *A clinical handbook/practical therapist manual for assessing and treating adults with post-traumatic stress disorder (PTSD).* Waterloo, Ontario: Institute Press.

Meiselman, K.C. (1978). *Incest: A psychological study of cause and effects with treatment recommendations.* San Francisco, CA: Josey-Bass.

Melchert, T.P. (1996). Childhood memory and a history of different forms of abuse. *Professional Psychology: Research and Practice, 27,* 438–446.

Memon, A., Cronin, O., Evans, R., & Bull, R. (September, 1992). *An empirical test of the mnemonic component of the cognitive interview: Can they explain the apparent memory enhancing effects of the CI?* Paper presented at the Third European Law and Psychology Conference, Oxford, England.

Memon, A., & Vartoukian, R. (1996). The effects of repeated questioning on young children's eyewitness testimony. *British Journal of Psychology, 87,* 403–415.

Menninger, K.A., & Holzman, P.S. (1973). *Theory of psychoanalytic technique.* New York: Basic.

Merskey, H. (1992). The manufacture of personalities: The production of multiple personality disorder. *British Journal of Psychiatry, 160,* 327–340.

Mertin, P. (1989). The memory of young children for eyewitness events. *Australian Journal of Social Issues, 24,* 23–32.

Merton, R.K. (1973). *The sociology of science.* Chicago, IL: University of Chicago Press.

Mesel, E., & Ledford, F.F. Jr. (1959). The electroencephalogram during hypnotic age regression (to infancy) in epileptic patients. *Archives of neurology, 1,* 516–521.

Meyer, D.E. (1970). On the representation and retrieval of stored semantic information. *Cognitive Psychology, 1,* 242–300.

Michigan Statutes. (1987). M.C.L. sec. 767. 24(2).

Milgrom, J. (1992). *Boundaries in professional relationships.* Minneapolis, MN: Walk-In Counseling Center.

Millar, K., & Watkinson, N. (1983). Recognition of words presented during general anaesthesia. *Ergonomics, 26,* 585–594.

Miller, A. (1986). Brief reconstructive hypnotherapy for anxiety reactions: Three cases. *American Journal of Clinical Hypnosis, 28,* 138–146.

Miller, D. (1994). *Women who hurt themselves: A book of hope and understanding.* New York: Basic.

Miller, D.G., & Loftus, E.F. (1976). Influencing memory for people and their actions. *Bulletin of the Psychonomic Society, 7,* 9–11.

Miller, G.A. (1956). The magical number seven, plus or minus two: Some limits on our capacity for processing information. *Psychological Review, 63,* 81–96.

Miller, T.W., Kraus, R.F., Tatevosyan, A.S., & Kamenchenko, P. (1993). Post-traumatic stress disorder in children and adolescents of the Armenian earthquake. *Child Psychiatry and Human Development, 24,* 115–123.

Mineka, S., & Nugent, K. (1995). Mood-congruent memory bias in anxiety and depression. In D.L. Schacter (Ed.), *Memory distortion: How minds, brains, and societies reconstruct the past* (pp. 173–196). Cambridge, MA: Harvard University Press.

Mingay, D.J. (1986). Hypnosis and memory for incidentally learned scenes. *British Journal of Experimental and Clinical Hypnosis, 3,* 173–183.

Minnesota Statutes. (1992). Minn.Stat. s. 541.073, subd. 2(a).

Miranda v. Arizona. (1966). 384 U.S. 436, 86 S.Ct. 1602, 16 L.Ed.2d 694.

Mishkin, M. (1982). A memory system in the monkey. *Philosophical Transactions of the Royal Society of London [Biology], 298,* 85–92.

Mitchell, A. (1960). *Harley Street psychiatrist.* London: G.G. Harrop.

Mitchell, M.B. (1932). Retroactive inhibition and hypnosis. *Journal of Genetic Psychology, 7,* 343–359.

Moen, S.P. (1995). Consequences of the therapist's claim "I'm not a detective." *The Journal of Psychiatry and Law, 23,* 477–484.

Molien v. Kaiser Foundation Hospitals. (1980). 27 Cal. 3d 916, 167 Cal. Rptr. 831, 616 P. 2d 813.

Moll, A. (1902). *Hypnotism.* New York: Charles Scribner's Sons.

Moll, A. (1989/1958). *The study of hypnosis.* New York: Julian Press.

Moloney, J.C. (1955). Psychic self-abandon and extortion of confession. *International Journal of Psycho-analysis, 36,* 53–60.

Monaghan, F.J. (1980). *Hypnosis in criminal investigation.* Dubuque, IA: Kendall/Hunt Publishing.

Montoya v. Bebensee. (1988). 761 P.2d 285 (Colo. Ct. App.).

Morgan, M. (1995). *How to interview sexual abuse victims.* Thousand Oaks, CA: Sage.

Morrier, E.J. (1984). Passivity as a sequel to combat trauma. *Journal of Contemporary Psychotherapy, 14,* 99–113.

Morton, J. (1994). Cognitive perspectives on memory recovery. *Applied Cognitive Psychology, 8,* 389–398.

Morton, J., Hammersley, R.H., & Bekerian, D.A. (1985). Headed records: A model for memory and its failure. *Cognition, 20,* 1–23.

Moscovitch, M. (1992). Memory and working-with-memory: A component process model based on modules and central systems. *Journal of Cognitive Neuroscience, 4,* 257–267.

Moston, S. (1987). The suggestibility of children in interview studies. *First Language, 7,* 67–78.

Mulder, M.R., & Vrij, A. (1996). Explaining conversation rules to children: An intervention study to facilitate children's accurate responses. *Child Abuse and Neglect, 20,* 623–631.

Mulhern, S. (1994). Satanism, ritual abuse, and multiple personality disorder: A sociohistorical perspective. *International Journal of Clinical and Experimental Hypnosis, 42,* 265–288.

Mulkay, M. (1979). *Science and the sociology of knowledge.* London: Allen & Unwin.

Mullen, P.E., Anderson, J.C., Romans, S.E., & Herbison, G.P. (1996). The long-term impact of the physical, emotional, and sexual abuse of children: A community study. *Child Abuse and Neglect, 20,* 7–21.

Muller, I. (1991). *Hitler's justice: The courts of the Third Reich.* Cambridge, MA: Harvard Uiversity Press.

Muller, R. J. (1992). Is there a neural basis for borderline splitting? *Comprehensive Psychiatry, 33,* 92–104.

Munglani, R., & Jones, J.G. (1994). Information processing during sleep and anaesthesia. *Anaesthesia Review, 10,* 107–130.

Munsterberg, H. (1908). *On the witness stand.* New York: Doubleday.

Murdock, B.B., Jr. (1961). The retention of individual items. *Journal of Experimental Psychology, 62,* 618–625.

Murdock, B.B., Jr. (1962). The serial position effect of free recall. *Journal of Verbal Learning and Verbal Behavior, 64,* 482–488.

Murdock, B.B., Jr. (1967). Recent developments in short-term memory. *British Journal of Psychology, 58,* 421–433.

Murray v. State. (1991). 804 S.W. 2d 279 (Tex. App.).

Murray, E.J., Lamnin, A., & Carver, C.S. (1988). *Psychotherapy versus written confession: A study of cathartic phenomena.* Unpublished manuscript, University of Miami, Coral Gables, FL.

Murray, J.M.K. (1995). Repression, memory, and suggestibility. *University of Colorado Law Review, 66,* 477–522.

Murrey, G.J., Cross, H.J., & Whipple, J. (1992). Hypnotically created pseudomemories: Further investigation into the "memory distortion or response bias" question. *Journal of Abnormal Psychology, 101,* 75–77.

Muse, M. (1986). Stress-related, posttraumatic chronic pain syndrome: behavioral treatment approach. *Pain, 25,* 389–394.

Mutter, C.B. (1984). The use of hypnosis with defendants. *American Journal of Clinical Hypnosis, 27* 42–51.

Mutter, C.B. (1990). The use of hypnosis with defendants:

Does it really work? *American Journal of Clinical Hypnosis, 32,* 257–262.

Myers, C.S. (February 13, 1915). A contribution to the study of shell-shock. *Lancet,* 316–320.

Myers, C.S. (January 8, 1916). Contributions to the study of shell-shock. *Lancet,* 65–69.

Myers, C.S. (1920–21). The revival of emotional memories and its therapeutic value. *British Journal of Medical Psychology, 1,* 20–22.

Myers, C.S. (1940). *Shell shock in France 1914–18.* Cambridge, England: Cambridge University Press.

Myers, F.W.H. (1909). *Human personality and its survival of bodily death.* London: Longmans, Green.

Myers. J.E. (Ed.). (1994). *The backlash: Child protection under fire.* Thousand Oaks, CA: Sage.

Myers, J.E.B. (1990). The child sexual abuse literature: A call for greater objectivity. *Michigan Law Review, 88,* 1709–1733.

Myers v. Quesenberry. (1983). 144 Cal.App.3d 888, 193 Cal.Rptr. 733.

Nadel, L. (1994). Multiple memory systems: What and why, an update. In D.L. Schacter & E. Tulving (Eds.), *Memory systems 1994* (pp. 39–63). Cambridge, MA: M.I.T. Press.

Nader, K., Pynoos, R., Fairbanks, L., & Frederick, C. (1990). Children's PTSD reactions one year after a sniper attack at their school. *American Journal of Psychiatry, 147,* 1526–1530.

Nadon, R., D'Eon, J. L., McConkey, K. M., Laurence, J.-R., & Perry, C. (1988). Posthypnotic amnesia, the hidden observer effect, and duality during hypnotic age regression. *International Journal of Clinical and Experimental Hypnosis, 36,* 19–37.

Nagy, T.F. (July/August, 1994). Repressed memories: Guidelines and directions. *The National Psychologist, 3*(4), 8–9.

Napier, C.W. (1990). Civil incest suits: Getting beyond the statute of limitations. *Washington University Law Quarterly, 68,* 995–1020.

Nash, M.R. (1987). What if anything, is regressed about hypnotic age regression? A review of the empirical literature. *Psychological Bulletin, 102,* 42–52.

Nash, M.R. (1988). Hypnosis as a window on regression. *Bulletin of the Menninger Clinic, 52,* 383–403.

Nash, M.R. (1991). Hypnosis as a special case of psychological regression. In S.J. Lynn & J. Rhue (Eds.), *Theories of hypnosis: Current models and perspectives* (pp. 171–194). New York: Guilford.

Nash, M.R. (1994). Memory distortion and sexual trauma: The problem of false negatives and false positives. *International Journal of Clinical and Experimental Hypnosis, 42,* 346–362.

Nash, M.R., Drake, S.D., Wiley, S., Khalsa, S., & Lynn, S.J. (1986). Accuracy of recall by hypnotically age-regressed subjects. *Journal of Abnormal Psychology, 95,* 298–300.

Nash, M.R., Hulsey, T.L., Sexton, M.C., Harralson, T.L., & Lambert, W. (1993). Long-term sequelae of childhood sexual abuse: Perceived family environment, psychopathology, and dissociation. *Journal of Consulting and Clinical Psychology, 61,* 276–283.

Nash, M.R., Johnson, L.S., & Tipton, R.D. (1979). Hypnotic age regression and the occurrence of transitional object relations. *Journal of Abnormal Psychology, 88,* 547–555.

Nash, M.R., Lynn, S.J., Stanley, S., Frauman, D.C., & Rhue, J. (1985). Hypnotic age regression and the importance of assessing interpersonally relevant affect. *International Journal of Clinical and Experimental Hypnosis, 33,* 224–253.

Nash, M.R., Lynn. S.J., & Givens, D.L. (1984). Adult hypnotic susceptibility, childhood punishment, and child abuse: A brief communication. *International Journal of Clinical and Experimental Hypnosis, 32,* 6–11.

National Savings Bank v. Ward. (1879). 100 U.S. 195, 25 L.Ed. 621.

Neiderland, W.G. (1968). An interpretation of the psychological stress and defenses in concentration-camp life and its late after-effects. In H. Krystal (Ed.), *Massive psychic trauma* (pp. 60–72). New York: International Universities Press.

Neiss, R. (1988). Reconceptualizing arousal: Psychological states in motor performance. *Psychological Bulletin, 103,* 345–366.

Neiss, R. (1990). Ending arousal's reign of error: A reply to Anderson. *Psychological Bulletin, 107,* 101–105.

Neisser, U. (1962). Cultural and cognitive discontinuity. In T.E. Gladwin & W. Sturtevant (Eds.), *Anthropology and human behavior* (pp. 54–71). Washington, D.C.: Anthropological Society of Washington.

Neisser, U. (1967). *Cognitive psychology.* Englewood Cliffs, NJ: Prentice Hall.

Neisser, U. (1976). *Cognition and reality: Principles and implications of cognitive psychology.* San Francisco, CA: Freeman.

Neisser, U. (1978). Memory: What are the important questions? In M.M. Gruneberg, P.E. Morris, & R. N. Sykes (Eds.), *Practical aspects of memory* (pp. 3–19). New York: Academic Press.

Neisser, U. (1981). John Dean's memory: A case study. *Cognition, 9,* 1–22.

Neisser, U. (1982a). *Memory observed: Remembering in natural context.* New York: Freeman.

Neisser, U. (1982b). Snapshots or benchmarks? In U. Neisser (Ed.), *Memory observed: Remembering in a natural context* (pp. 43–48). New York: Freeman.

Neisser, U., & Harsch, N. (1992). Phantom flashbulbs: False recollections of hearing the news about *Challenger.* In E. Winograd & U. Neisser (Eds.), *Affect and accuracy in recall: Studies of "flashbulb" memories* (pp. 9–31). New York: Cambridge University Press.

Neisser, U., Winograd, E., & Weldon, M. S. (November 24, 1991). *Remembering the earthquake: "What I experienced" vs. "How I heard the news."* Paper presented at the Annual Meeting of the Psychonomic Society, San Francisco, CA.

Nelson, K. (1986). *Event knowledge: Structure and function in development.* Hillsdale, NJ: Erlbaum.

Nelson, K. (1988). The ontogeny of memory for real events. In U. Neisser & E. Winograd (Eds.), *Remembering reconsidered: Ecological and traditional approaches to the study of memory* (pp. 244–276). New York: Cambridge University Press.

Nelson, K., & Gruendel, J. (1986). Children's scripts. In K. Nelson (Ed.), *Event knowledge: Structure and function in development* (pp. 21–46). Hillsdale, NJ: Erlbaum.

Nelson, T.O. (1984). A comparison of current measures of the accuracy of feeling-of-knowing predictions. *Psychological Bulletin, 95,* 109–133.

Newbold, M.S. (1993). Medical malpractice law. Pennsylvania's "two schools of thought" doctrine revisited: Definition and application clarified, underlying goal thwarted—*Jones v. Chidester,* 610 A.2d 964 (Pa. 1992). *Temple Law Review, 66,* 613–628.

Newman, L.S., & Baumeister, R.F. (1996). Toward an explanation of the UFO abduction phenomenon: Hypnotic elaboration, extraterrestrial sadomasochism, and spurious memories. *Psychological Inquiry, 7*(2), 99–126.

Ney, T. (1995). *True and false allegations of child sexual abuse: Assessment and case management.* New York: Brunner/Mazel.

Nijenhius, E.R.S., & van der Hart, O. (1994). Dissociatieve stoornissen [Dissociative disorders]. In S. Mass et al. (Red.). *Handboek Klinische Psychologie* [Handbook of clinical psychology]. Houten: Bohn Stafleu Van Loghum.

Nilsson, L-G, & Archer, T. (1992). Biological aspects of memory and emotion: Affect and cognition. In S-A. Christianson (Ed.), *Handbook of emotion and memory* (pp. 289–306). Hillsdale, NJ: Erlbaum.

Nizer, Louis. (1966). *The jury returns.* Garden City, NY: Doubleday.

Noble, J., & McConkey, K.M. (1995). Hypnotic sex change: Creating and challenging a delusion in the laboratory. *Journal of Abnormal Psychology, 104,* 69–74.

Noel, B., with Watterson, K. (1992). *You must be dreaming.* New York: Poseidon Press.

Nogrady, H., McConkey, K.M., Laurence, J.-R., & Perry, C. (1983). Dissociation, duality, and demand characteristics in hypnosis. *Journal of Abnormal Psychology, 92,* 223–235.

Nogrady, H., McConkey, K.M., & Perry, C. (1985). Enhancing visual memory: Trying hypnosis, trying imagination, trying again. *Journal of Abnormal Psychology, 94,* 195–204.

Norcross, J.C., & Goldfried, M.R. (Eds.). (1992). *Handbook of psychotherapy integration.* New York: Basic.

Noyes, R., & Kletti, R. (1977). Depersonalization in reponse to life-threatening danger. *Comprehensive Psychiatry, 18,* 375–384.

Nurcombe, B., & Unutzer, J. (1991). The ritual abuse of children: Clinical features and diagnostic reasoning. *Journal of the American Academy of Child and Adolescent Psychiatry, 30,* 272–276.

Oates, K., & Shrimpton, S. (1991). Children's memories for stressful and non-stressful events. *Medicine, Science and the Law, 31,* 4–10.

Ochsner, J.C., & Zaragoza, M. (March, 1988). *Children's eyewitness testimony: Accuracy and suggestibility of a memory for a real event.* Paper presented at the Biannual Meeting of the American Psychology and Law Society, Miami, FL.

O'Connell, B.A. (1960). Amnesia and homicide. *British Journal of Delinquency, 10,* 262–276.

O'Connell, D.N., Shor, R.E., & Orne, M.T. (1970). Hypnotic age regression: An empirical and methodological analysis. *Journal of Abnormal Psychology, 76,* 1–32.

O'Connor, G.W. (1972). Interviewing and interrogation. In S.R. Gerber & O. Schroeder, Jr. (Eds.), *Criminal investigation and interrogation* (pp. 358–369). Cincinnati, OH: W.H. Anderson.

Odgers, S.J. (1988). Evidence law and previously hypnotized witnesses. *Australian Journal of Clinical and Experimental Hypnosis, 16,* 91–102.

Ofshe, R. (1989). Coerced confessions: The logic of seemingly irrational action. *Cultic Studies Journal, 6,*1–15.

Ofshe, R. (1991). Coercive persuasion and attitude change. In E. Borgatta & M. Borgatta (Eds.), *The encyclopedia of sociology* (pp. 212–224). New York: Macmillan.

Ofshe, R. (1992). Inadvertent hypnosis during interrogation: False confession due to dissociative state; misidentified multiple personality and the Satanic cult hypothesis. *International Journal of Clinical and Experimental Hypnosis, 40,* 125–156.

Ofshe, R. (July 6, 1995). Transcript of trial testimony. *Hamanne v. Humenansky.* No. C4–94–203 (Minn. Dist. Ct., Second Jud. Dist.).

Ofshe, R., & Singer, M.T. (1986). Attacks on peripheral versus central elements of self and the impact of thought reforming techniques. *Cultic Studies Journal, 3,* 3–24.

Ofshe, R., & Singer, M.T. (1994). Recovered-memory therapy and robust repression: Influence of pseudomemories. *International Journal of Clinical and Experimental Hypnosis, 42,* 391–410.

Ofshe, R., & Watters, E. (March/April, 1993). Making monsters. *Society,* 4–16.

Ofshe, R., & Watters, E. (1994). *Making monsters: False memories, psychotherapy, and sexual hysteria.* New York: Charles Scribner's Sons.

Ohman, A. (1991). Orienting and attention: Preferred preattentive processing of potentially phobic stimuli. In B.A. Campbell, R. Richardson, & H. Hayne (Eds.), *Attention and information processing in infants and adults: Perspectives from human and animal research* (pp. 263–295). Hillsdale, NJ: Erlbaum.

O'Keefe, J., & Nadel, L. (1978). *The hippocampus as a cognitive map.* Oxford, England: Clarendon Press.

Olio, K.A. (1989). Memory retrieval in the treatment of adult survivors of sexual abuse. *Transactional Analysis Journal, 19,* 93–100.

Olio, K.A. (1993). Comparing apples and oranges. *Raising Issues, 1,* 3–4.

Olio, K.A. (1994). Truth in memory. *American Psycholo-*

gist, 49, 442–443.

Olio, K.A. (1996). Are 25% of clinicians using potentially risky therapeutic practices? A review of the logic and methodology of the Poole, Lindsay et al. study. Journal of Psychiatry and Law, 24, 277–29.

Olio, K.A., & Cornell, W. (1994). The Paul Ingram case: Pseudomemory or pseudoscience? Violence Update, 4, 3–5.

Olson, L. (1992). Book review of R. Underwager and H. Wakefield, The real world of child interrogations, Social Work, 37, 276.

Oppenheimer, R., Howells, K. Palmer, R.I., & Chaloner, D.A. (1985). Adverse sexual experience in childhood and clinical eating disorders: A preliminary description. Journal of Psychiatric Research, 19, 357–361.

Orne, M.T. (1951). The mechanisms of hypnotic age regression: An experimental study. Journal of Abnormal and Social Psychology, 46, 213–225.

Orne, M.T. (1959). The nature of hypnosis: Artifact and essence. Journal of Abnormal and Social Psychology, 58, 277–299.

Orne, M.T. (1962). On the social psychology of the psychological experiment: With particular reference to demand characteristics and their manipulation. American Pychologist, 17, 776–783.

Orne, M.T. (1977). The construct of hypnosis: Implications of the definition for research and practice. In W.E. Edmonston (Ed.), Conceptual and investigative approaches to hypnosis and hypnotic phenomena. Annals of the New York Academy of Sciences, 296, 14–33.

Orne, M.T. (1979). The use and misuse of hypnosis in court. International Journal of Clinical & Experimental Hypnosis, 27, 311–340.

Orne, M.T. (1980). On the construct of hypnosis: How its definition affects research and its clinical application. In G.D. Burrows & L. Dennerstein (Eds.), Handbook of hypnosis and psychosomatic medicine (pp.29–51). Amsterdam: Elsevier/North-Holland.

Orne, M.T., Axelrad, D., Diamond, B.L., Gravitz, M.A., Heller, A., Mutter, C.B., Spiegel, D., & Spiegel, H. (1985). Scientific status of refreshing recollection by the use of hypnosis. Journal of the American Medical Association, 253, 1918–1923.

Orne, M.T., & Bates, B. (1993). Reflections on multiple personality disorder: A view from the looking glass of hypnosis past. In A. Kales et. al. (Eds.), Mosaic of contemporary psychiatry in perspective (pp. 247–260). New York: Springer-Verlag.

Orne, M.T., Soskis, D.A., Dinges, D.F., & Orne, E.C. (1984). Hypnotically induced testimony. In G.L. Wells & E.F. Loftus (Eds.), Eyewitness testimony: Psychological perspectives (pp. 171–213). Cambridge, England: Cambridge University Press.

Orne, M.T., Whitehouse, W.G., Dinges, D.F., & Orne, E.C. (1988). Reconstructing memory through hypnosis: Forensic and clinical applications. In H.M. Pettinati (Ed.), Hypnosis and memory (pp. 21–63). New York: Guilford.

Orne, E.C., Whitehouse, W.G., Dinges, D.F., & Orne, M.T. (October, 1996). Memory liabilities associated with hypnosis: Does low hypnotizability confer immunity? International Journal of Clinical and Experimental Hypnosis, 44, 354–367.

Orne, M. T., Whitehouse, W. G., Orne, E. C., & Dinges, D. F. (1996). "Memories" of anomalous and traumatic autobiographical experiences: Validation and consolidation of fantasy through hypnosis. Psychological Inquiry, 7(2), 168–172.

Ornstein, P.A. (1995). Children's long-term retention of salient personal experiences. Journal of Traumatic Stress, 8, 581–605.

Ornstein, P.A., Gordon, B.N., & Larus, D.M. (1992). Children's memory for a personally experienced event: Implications for testimony. Applied Cognitive Psychology, 6, 49–60.

Osgood, C.E., Soci, G.J., & Tannenbaum, P. (1957). The measurement of meaning. Champaign, IL: University of Illinois Press.

Osland v. Osland. (1989). 442 N.W.2d 907 (N.D.).

O'Sullivan, J.T., & Howe, M.L. (1995). Metamemory and memory construction. Consciousness and Cognition, 4, 104–10.

Overton, D.A. (1964). State-dependent or "dissociated" learning produced with pentobarbital. Journal of Comparative Physiological Psychology, 57, 3–12.

Overton, D.A. (1966). State-dependent learning produced by depressants and atropine-like drugs. Psychopharmacologia, 10, 6–31.

Overton, D.A. (1972). State-dependent learning produced by alcohol and its relevance to alcoholism. In B. Kissin & A. Begleiter (Eds.), The biology of alcoholism: Physiology and behavior (Vol. 2). (pp. 193–217). New York: Plenum.

Overton, D.A. (1973). State-dependent learning produced by addicting drugs. In S. Fisher & A.M. Freedman (Eds.), Opiate addiction: Origins and treatment (pp. 61–75). Washington, D.C.: Winston.

Packard, V. (1957). The hidden persuaders. New York: David McKay.

Paivio, A. (1969). Mental imagery in associative learning and memory. Psychological Review, 76, 241–263.

Pallmeyer, T.P., Blanchard, E.B., & Kolb, L.C. (1986). The psychophysiology of combat-induced post-traumatic stress disorder in Vietnam veterans. Behavioral Research and Therapy, 24, 645–652.

Palmer, S., Schreiber, C., & Fox, C. (November 24, 1991). Remembering the earthquake: "Flashbulb" memory for experienced vs. reported events. Paper presented at the annual meeting of the Psychonomic Society, San Francisco, CA.

Palsgraf v. Long Island Railroad. (1928). 248 N.Y. 339, 162 N.E. 99.

Parfitt, D.N., & Carlyle-Gall, C.M. (1944). Psychogenic amnesia: The refusal to remember. Journal of Mental Science, 379, 519–531.

Parson, E. R. (1984) The reparation of the self: Clinical and theoretical dimensions in the treatment of Vietnam combat veterans. *Journal of Contemporary Psychotherapy, 14,* 4–56.

Parwatikar, S.D., Holcomb, W.R., & Menninger, K.A., II. (1985). The detection of malingered amnesia in accused murderers. *Bulletin of the American Academy of Psychiatry and the Law, 13,* 97–103.

Patten v. Wiggin. (1862). 51 Me. 594.

Pattie, F.A. (1956). The genuineness of some hypnotic phenomena. In R.M. Dorcus (Ed.), *Hypnosis and its therapeutic applications* (pp. 1–18). New York: McGraw-Hill.

Pavlov, I.P. (1923). The identity of inhibition with sleep and hypnosis. *Scientific Monthly, 17,* 603–608.

Payne, D.G. (1987). Hypermnesia and reminiscence in recall: A historical and empirical review. *Psychological Bulletin, 101,* 5–27.

Pear, T.H. (1961). *The molding of modern man: A psychologist's view of information, persuasion and mental coercion today.* London: George Allen & Unwin.

Pearce v. Salvation Army. (1996). 1996 WL 181401 (Pa.Super.).

Pearlman, L.A., & Saakvitne, K. (1995). *Trauma and the therapist.* New York: Norton.

Pearson, R. E. (1961). Response to suggestions given under general anesthesia. *American Journal of Clinical Hypnosis, 4,* 106–114.

Pekala, R.J., & Forbes, E.J. (1988). Hypnoidal effects associated with several stress management techniques. *Australian Journal of Clinical and Experimental Hypnosis, 16,* 121–132.

Pekala, R.J., Forbes, E.J., & Contrisciani, P.A. (1988–89). Assessing the phenomenological effects of several stress management strategies. *Imagination, Cognition, and Personality, 8,* 265–281.

Penfield, W. (1958). Some mechanisms of consciousness discovered during electrical stimulation of the brain. *Proceedings of the National Academy of Sciences, 44,* 51–66.

Peniston, E.G., & Kulkosky, P.J. (1991). Alpha-theta brainwave neuro-feedback for Vietnam veterans with combat-related post-traumatic stress disorder. *Medical Psychotherapy, 4,* 1–14.

Pennebaker, J.W. (1987). Confession, inhibition and disease. *Advances in Experimental Social Psychology, 22,* 211–244.

Pennebaker, J.W., & Beall, S.K. (1986). Confronting a traumatic event: Toward an understanding of inhibition and disease. *Journal of Abnormal Psychology, 95,* 274–281.

Pennebaker, J.W., Colder, M.L., & Sharp, L.K. (1990). Accelerating the coping process. *Journal of Personality & Social Psychology, 58,* 528–537.

Pennebaker, J.W., & Hoover, C.W. (1985). Inhibition and cognition: Toward an understanding of trauma and disease. In R.J. Davidson, G.E. Schwartz, & D. Shapiro (Eds.), *Consciousness and self-regulation* (Vol. 4, pp. 107–136). New York: Plenum.

Pennebaker, J.W., Kielcolt-Glaser, J.K., & Glaser, R. (1988). Disclosure of traumas and immune function:

Health implications for psychotherapy. *Journal of Consulting & Clinical Psychology, 56,* 239–245.

Pennebaker, J.W., & O'Heeron, R.C. (1984). Confiding in others and illness rate among spouses of suicide and accident death victims. *Journal of Abnormal Psychology, 93,* 473–476.

Pennebaker, J.W., & Memon, A. (1996). Recovered memories in context: Thoughts and elaborations on Bowers and Farvolden (1996). *Psychological Bulletin, 119,* 381–385.

Pennebaker, J.W., & Susman, J.R. (1988). Disclosure of traumas and psychosomatic processes. *Social Science and Medicine, 26,* 327–332.

Penrod, S., Loftus, E.F., & Winkler, J. (1982). The reliability of eyewitness testimony: A psychological perspective. In N.L. Kerr & R.M. Bray (Eds.), *The psychology of the courtroom* (pp. 119–168). New York: Academic Press.

People v. Alcala. (1992). 4 Cal. 4th 742, 4 Cal 4th 1115A, 842 P.2d, 1192, 15 Cal. Rptr. 2d, 432.

People v. Bloom. (1989). 48 Cal.3d 1194, 774 P.2d 698, 259 Cal.Rptr. 669.

People v. Caro. (1988). 46 Cal. 3d 1035, 251 Cal. Rptr. 757, 761 P.2d 680.

People v. Deskins. (1996). 927 P.2d 368 (Colo.).

People v. Ebanks. (1897). 117 Cal. 652, 49 P. 1049, 40 L.R.A., 269.

People v. Franklin. (1993). San Mateo Superior Court, No. C-24395.

People v. Gonzales. (1982). 415 Mich. 615, 329 N.W. 2d 743, modified 417 Mich. 968 (1983).

People v. Guerra. (1984). 37 Cal.App.3d 385, 208 Cal.Rptr. 162, 690 P.2d 635.

People v. Harper. (1969). 111 Il App.2d 204, 250 N.E. 2d 5

People v. Hughes. (1983). 59 N.Y.2d 523, 453 N.E. 2d 484, 466 N.Y.S.2d 255.

People v. Johnson. (1988). 47 Cal.3d 576, 253 Cal.Rptr. 710, 764 P.2d 1087.

People v. Jordan. (1916). 172 Cal. 391, 156 Pac. 451.

People v. McKeehan. (1986). 732 P.2d 1238 (Colo. App.).

People v. McKeehan. (1986). 732 P.2d 1238 (Colo.App.), *certiorari dismissed,* 753 P.2d 243 (Colo. 1990).

People v. Reese. (1985). 149 Mich. App. 53, 385 N.W.2d 722.

People v. Shirley. (1982). 31 Cal. 3d 18, 723 P.2d 1354, 181 Cal. Rptr. 243, *stay denied, California v.Shirley,* 458 U.S. 1125, 103 S.Ct. 13, 73 L.Ed.2d 1400, *cert. denied, California v. Shirley,* 459 U.S. 860, 103 S.Ct. 133, 74 L.Ed.2d 114.

People v. Sorscher. (1986). 151 Mich. App. 122, 391 N.W. 2d 365.

People v. Stansbury. (1993). 4 Cal.4th 1017, 846 P.2d 756, 17 Cal.Rptr.2d 174.

People v. Sterling. (1992). Ind. #624/91 (County Court, Monroe County, New York, August 7).

People v. Sterling. (1994). 209 A.D.2d 1006, 619 N.Y.S.2d 448 (Sup.Ct., App.Div.).

Perlin, M.L. (1994). *Law and mental disability.* Charlottesville: Michie.

Perloff, R.M. (1993). *The dynamics of persuasion*. Hillsdale, NJ: Erlbaum.

Perry, C. (1995). The false memory syndrome (FMS) and "disguised" hypnosis. *Hypnos, 22,* 189–197.

Perry, C., Laurence, J-R., D'Eon, J. & Tallant, B. (1988). Hypnotic age regression techniques in the elicitation of memories: Applied uses and abuses. In H. Pettinati (Ed.), *Hypnosis and memory* (pp. 128–154). New York: Guilford.

Perry, C., Orne, M.T., London, R.W., & Orne, E.C. (1996). Rethinking per se exclusions of hypnotically elicited recall as legal testimony. *International Journal of Clinical and Experimental Hypnosis, 44,* 66–80.

Perry, C., & Walsh, B. (1978). Inconsistencies and anomalies of response as a defining characteristic in hypnosis. *Journal of Abnormal Psychology, 87,* 547–577.

Perry, J.C., & Jacobs, D. (1982). Overview: Clinial applications of the amytal interview in psychiatric emergency settings. *American Journal of Psychiatry, 139,* 552–559.

Peters, D.P. (1987). The impact of naturally occurring stress on children's memory. In S.J. Ceci, M.P. Toglia, & D.F. Ross (Eds.), *Children's eyewitness memory* (pp. 122–141). New York: Springer-Verlag.

Peters, D.P. (1991). The influence of stress and arousal on the child witness. In J. Doris (Ed.), *The suggestibility of children's recollections* (pp. 60–76). Washington, D.C.: American Psychological Association.

Peters, J.J. (1979). Children who are victims of sexual assault and the psychology of offenders. *American Journal of Psychotherapy, 30,* 598–642.

Peterson, J.A. (November 1991). *Hypnotic techniques recommended to facilitate the processing of memories retrieved by patients: Abreaction.* Paper presented at the 8th International Conference on Multiple Personality/Dissociative States, Chicago, IL.

Peterson, J.A. (1993). Reply to van der Hart/Brown article [Letter to the editor]. *Dissociation, 6,* 74–75.

Peterson, L.R., & Peterson, M.J. (1959). Short-term retention of individual verbal items. *Journal of Experimental Psychology, 58,* 193–198.

Peterson, M.R. (1992). *At personal risk: Boundary violations in professional-client relationships.* New York: Norton.

Petition for Review. (1993). *People v. Franklin,* Court of Appeal, No. AO52683.

Pettinati, H.M. (Ed.). (1988). *Hypnosis and memory.* New York: Guilford.

Pettinati, H.M., Horne, R.L., & Staats, J.M. (1985). Hypnotizability in patients with anorexia nervosa and bulimia. *Archives of General Psychiatry, 42,* 1014–1016.

Pettit, F., Fegan, M., & Howie, P. (September, 1990). *Interviewer effects on children's testimony.* Paper presented at the International Congress on Child Abuse and Neglect, Hamburg, Germany.

Petty, R.E., & Cacioppo, J.T. (1986). *Communication and persuasion: Central and peripheral routes to attitude change.* New York: Springer-Verlag.

Pezdek, K. (1994). The illusion of illusory memory. *Applied Cognitive Psychology, 8,* 339–350.

Pezdek, K., & Banks, W.P. (1996). *The recovered memory/false memory debate.* New York: Academic Press.

Pezdek, K., Finger, K., & Hodge, D. (in press). *Planting false childhood memories: The role of event plausibility. Psychological Science.*

Pezdek, K., & Roe, C. (1994) Memory for childhood events: How suggestible is it? *Consciousness and Cognition, 3,* 374–387.

Pezdek, K., & Roe, C. (1995). The effect of memory trace strength on suggestibility. *Journal of Experimental Child Psychology, 60,* 116–128.

Pezdek, K., & Roe, C. (1997). The suggestibility of children's memory for being touched: Planting, erasing, and changing memories. *Law and Human Behavior, 21,* 95–106.

Phelan, P. (1987) Incest: Socialization within a treatment program. *American Journal of Orthopsychiatry, 57,* 84–92.

Phillips, M., & Fredrick, C. (1995). *Healing the divided self: Clinical and Ericksonian hypnotherapy for post-traumatic and dissociative conditions.* New York: Norton.

Phillips, R.G., & LeDoux, J.E. (1992). Differential contribution of amygdala and hippocampus to cued and contextual fear conditioning. *Behavioral Neuroscience, 2,* 274–285.

Piaget, J. (1962). *Play, dreams and imitation in childhood.* New York: Norton.

Pierce, R.A., Nichols, M.P., & DuBrin, J.R. (1983). *Emotional expression in psychotherapy.* New York: Gardner.

Pillemer, D.B. (1984). Flashbulb memories of the assassination attempt on President Reagan. *Cognition, 16,* 63–80.

Pillemer, D.B. (1992). Preschool children's memories of personal circumstances: The fire alarm study. In E. Winograd & U. Neisser (Eds.), *Affect and accuracy in recall: Studies of "flashbulb memories"* (pp. 121–137). London: Cambridge University Press.

Pillemer, D.B., Rinehart, E.D., & White, S.H. (1986). Memories of life transitions: The first year of college. *Human Learning, 5,* 109–123.

Pillemer, D.B., & White, S.H. (1989). Childhood events recalled by children and adults. In H.W. Reese (Ed.), *Advances in child development and behavior* (Vol. 21, pp. 297–340). San Diego, CA: Academic Press.

Piper, A. (1994). Multiple personality disorder. *British Journal of Psychiatry, 164,* 600–612.

Pirolli, P.L., & Mitterer, J.O. (1984). The effect of leading questions on prior memory: Evidence for the co-existence of inconsistent memory traces. *Canadian Journal of Psychology, 38,* 135–141.

Pitman, R.K. (May, 1994). *Hormonal modulation of traumatic memory.* Paper presented at the Annual Meeting of the American Psychiatric Association, Philadelphia, PA.

Pitman, R.K., Orr, S.P., Laforgue, D., deJong, J.B., & Claiborn, J.M. (1987). Psychophysiology of PTSD imagery in Vietnam combat veterans. *Archives of General Psychiatry, 44,* 970–976.

Pitman, R.K., Orr, S., Laforgue, D. et al. (1990). Psychophysiologic responses to combat imagery of Vietnam veterans with posttraumatic stress disorder versus other anxiety disorders. *Journal of Abnormal Psychology, 99,* 49–54.

Pitman, R.K., van der Kolk, B.A., Orr, S.P., & Greenberg, M.S. (1990). Naloxone-reversible analgesic response to combat related stimuli in posttraumatic stress disorder. *Archives of General Psychiatry, 47,* 541–547.

Pitts, M., & Heaps, M. (1996). Memory and depth of processing in "hypnotized" and nonhypnotized subjects. *Contemporary Hypnosis, 13,* 129–136.

Podgers, J. (January 1995). Witnesses to tragedy. *American Bar Association Journal, 81.* 44–45.

Polanyi, M. (1958). *Personal knowledge.* London: Routledge.

Polusny, M.M., & Follette, V.M. (1996). Remembering childhood sexual abuse: A national survey of psychologist's clincal practices, beliefs, and personal experiences. *Professional Psychology: Research and Practice, 27,* 41–52.

Pomerleau, O.F., & Pomerleau, C.S. (1977). *Break the smoking habit: A behavioral program for giving up cigarettes.* Champaign, IL: Research Press.

Pomerantz, J. (in progress). *Memories of abuse: Women sexually traumatized in childhood.* Unpublished manuscript, The Center for Trauma and Dissociation, Denver, CO.

Poole, D.A., & Lindsay, D.S. (1995). Interviewing preschoolers: Effects of nonsuggestive techniques, parental coaching, and leading questions on reports of nonexperienced events. *Journal of Experimental Child Psychology, 60,* 129–154.

Poole, D.A. & Lindsay, D.S., Memon, A. & Bull, R. (1995). Psychotherapy and the recovery of memories of childhood sexual abuse: U.S. and British practitioners' beliefs, opinions, practices, and experiences. *Journal of Consulting and Clinical Psychology, 63,* 426–437.

Poole, D.A. & White, L.T. (1991). Effects of question repetition on the eyewitness testimony of children and adults. *Developmental Psychology, 27,* 975–986.

Poole, D.A., & White, L.T. (1995). Tell me again and again: Stability and change in the repeated testimonies of children and adults. In M.S. Zaragoza et al. (Eds.), *Memory and testimony in the child witness* (pp. 24–43). Thousand Oaks, CA: Sage.

Pope, H.G., & Hudson, J.I. (1992). Is childhod sexual abuse a risk factor for bulimia nervosa? *American Journal of Psychiatry, 149,* 455–463.

Pope, H.G., & Hudson, J.I. (1995a). Can individuals "repress" memories of childhood sexual abuse? An examination of the evidence. *Psychiatric Annals, 25,* 715–719.

Pope, H.G., & Hudson, J.I. (1995b). Can memories of childhood sexual abuse be repressed? *Psychological Medicine, 25,* 121–126.

Pope, H.G., & Hudson, J.I. (1995c). Does childhood sexual abuse cause adult psychiatric disorders? Essentials of methodology. *Journal of Psychiatry and Law, 23,* 363–381.

Pope, K.S. (1995). What psychologists better know about recovered memories, lawsuits, and the pivotal experiment: Review of "The myth of repressed memories: False memories and allegations of sexual abuse" by Elizabeth Loftus and Katherine Ketcham. *Clinical Psychology: Science and Practice, 2,* 304–315.

Pope, K.S. (1996). Memory, abuse, and science: Questioning claims about the false memory syndrome epidemic. *American Psychologist, 51,* 957–974.

Pope, K.S., & Brown, L. (1996). *Recovered memories of abuse: Assessment, therapy, forensics.* Washington, D.C.: American Psychological Association Press.

Popper, K. (1959). *The logic of scientific discovery.* New York: Harper & Row.

Postman, L. (1961). The present status of interference theory. In C.N. Cofer (Ed.), *Verbal learning and verbal behavior* (pp. 152–179). New York: McGraw-Hill.

Power, D.J. (1977). Memory, identification and crime. *Medicine, Science, and the Law, 17,* 132–139.

Powers, S.M. (1991). Fantasy proneness, amnesia, and the UFO abduction phenomenon. *Dissociation, 4,* 46–54.

Price, D. de S. (1963). *Little science, big science.* New York: Columbia University Press.

Price, D.W.W., & Goodman, G.S. (1990). Visiting the wizard: Children's memory for a recurring event. *Child Development, 61,* 664–680.

Price, M. (1995). Knowing and not knowing: Paradox in the construction of historical narratives. In J.L. Alpert (Ed.), *Sexual abuse recalled: Treating trauma in the era of the recovered memory debate* (pp. 289–310). Northvale, NJ: Jason Aronson.

Prime v. State. (1989). 767 P.2d 149 (Wyo.Sup.Ct.).

Prince, M. (1906). *The dissociation of a personality: A biographical study in abnormal psychology.* New York: Longman.

Prince, M. (1924). *The unconscious* (2nd ed.). New York: Macmillan.

Prochaska, J.O., & DiClemente, C.C. (1984). *The transtheoretical approach: Crossing the traditional boundaries of therapy.* Homewood, IL: Dow Jones-Irvin.

Project MKULTRA, The CIA's program of research in behavioral modification (1977). Joint Hearing before the Select Committee on Intelligence and the Subcommittee on Health and Scientific Research of the Committee on Human Resources, United States Senate. Washington, D.C.: U.S. Government Printing Office.

Proposal to Finance Preparation of Model Legislation Titled "Mental Health Consumer Protection Act." (August, 1994).

Putnam, F.W. (1989). *Diagnosis and treatment of multiple personality disorder.* New York: Guilford.

Putnam, F.W. (1991) The Satanic ritual abuse controversy. *Child Abuse and Neglect, 15,* 175–179.

Putnam, F.W., Guroff, J.J., Silberman, E.K., Barban, L., & Post, R.M. (1986). The clinical phenomenology of multiple personality disorders: A preliminary report. *Archives of General Psychiatry, 42,* 591–596.

Putnam, F.W., Helmers, K., Horowitz, L.A., & Trickett,

P.K. (1995). Hypnotizability and dissociativity in sexually abused girls. *Child Abuse and Neglect, 19,* 645–655.

Putnam, F.W., & Teicher, M. (1994). Unpublished address. American Psychiatric Association, Philadelphia, PA.

Putnam, W.H. (1979). Hypnosis and distortions in eyewitness memory. *International Journal of Clinical & Experimental Hypnosis, 27,* 437–447.

Pyck, K. (1994). The backlash in Europe: Real anxiety or mass hysteria in the Netherlands? A preliminary study of the Oude Pekala crisis. In J.E.B Myers (Ed.), *The backlash: Child protection under fire* (pp.70–85). Thousand Oaks, CA: Sage.

Pye, E. (1995). Memory and imagination: Placing imagination in the therapy of individuals with incest memories. In J.L. Alpert (Ed.), *Sexual abuse recalled: Treating trauma in the era of the recovered memory debate* (pp. 15–184). Northvale, NJ: Jason Aronson.

Pynoos, R., Frederick, C., Nader, K., Arroyo, W., Steinberg, A., Eth, S., Nunez, F., & Fairbanks, L. (1987). Life threat and posttraumatic stress in school-age children. *Archives of General Psychiatry, 44,* 1057–1063.

Pynoos, R., & Nader, K. (1989). Case study: Children's memory and proximity to violence. *Journal of the American Academy of Child and Adolescent Psychiatry, 28,* 236–241.

Quillian, M.R. (1969). The teachable language comprehender: A simulation program and theory of language. *Communications of the Association for Computing Machinery, 12,* 459–476.

R. v. L. (W.K.). (1991). 64 C.C.C. 3d 321, 12 W.C.B. (2d) 706, Supreme Court Reporter, 1:1091. (Supreme Court of Canada).

Raginsky, B.B. (1969). Hypnotic recall of aircrash cause. *International Journal of Clinical and Experimental Hypnosis, 17,* 1–19.

Rainer, D. (1983). *Eyewitness testimony: Does hypnosis enhance accuracy, distortion, and confidence?* Unpublished doctoral dissertation, University of Wyoming.

Rains v. Superior Court (Center Foundation). (1984). 150 Cal.App.3d 933, 198 Cal.Rptr. 249 (Second Dist.).

Ramona v. Ramona. (September 12, 1991). Superior Court, County of Napa, California, Case No. 61898. Plaintiff's verified second amended complaint for slander per se, negligent infliction of emotional distress and intentional infliction of emotional distress.

Ramona v. Ramona. (May 12, 1993). Order of Judge W. Scott Snowdon. Case No. C61898.

Ramona v. Ramona. (December 29, 1993). Superior Court, County of Napa, California, Case No. 61898, Plaintiff's Opposition to Motion for Reconsideration.

Ramona v. Ramona. (May 3, 1994). Superior Court of the State of California, In and For the County of Napa, Case No. C61898, Reporter's Transcript of Proceedings.

Ramona v. Ramona. (1994). Superior Court of the State of California, In and For the County of Napa, Case No. C61898.

Ramona v. Ramona. (1995). B091052, Super. Ct. No. KC009493. California Court of Appeal, Second Appellate District, Division One.(Oct. 3). (Unpublished).

Raschke, C. (1990). *Painted black: Satanic crime in America.* San Francisco, CA: Harper & Row.

Raskin, D.C., & Esplin, P.W. (1991). Assessment of children's statements of sexual abuse. In J. Doris (Ed.), *The suggestibility of children's recollections* (pp. 153–164). Washington, D.C.: American Psychological Association Press.

Raskin, D.C., & Yuille, J.C. (1989). Problems in evaluating interviews of children in sexual abuse cases. In S.J. Ceci, D.F. Ross, & M.P. Toglia (Eds.), *Perspectives on children's testimony* (pp. 184–207). New York: SpringerVerlag.

Rasmussen, O.V., & Lunde, I. (1980). Evaluation of investigation of 200 torture victims. *Danish Medical Bulletin, 27,* 241–243.

Rath, B. (1982). *The use of suggestions during general anesthesia.* Unpublished doctoral dissertation, University of Louisville.

Rathus, S.A. (1973). A 30–item schedule for assessing assertive behavior. *Behavior Therapy, 4,* 398–406.

Rauch, S., van der Kolk, B.A., Fisler, R., Alpert, N.M., Orr, S.P., Savage, C.R., Fischman, A.J., Jenike, M.A., & Pitman, R.K. (1996). A symptom provocation study of posttraumatic stress disorder using positron emission tomography and script-driven imagery. *Archives of General Psychiatry, 53,* 380–387.

Rauschenberger, S.L., & Lynn, S.J. (1995). Fantasy proneness, DSM-III-R Axis I psychopathology, and dissociation. *Journal of Abnormal Psychology, 104,* 373–380.

Read, J.D., & Lindsay, D.S. (1994). Moving toward a middle ground on the "false memory debate": Reply to commentaries on Lindsay and Read. *Applied Cognitive Psychology, 8,* 407–435.

Read, J.D., Yuille, J.C., & Tollestrup, P. (1992). Recollections of a robbery: Effects of arousal and alcohol on person identification. *Law and Human Behavior, 16,* 425–446.

Ready, D.J., Bothwell, R.K., & Brigham, J.C. (1997). The effects of hypnosis, context reinstatement, and anxiety on eyewitness memory. *International Journal of Clinical and Experimental Hypnosis, 45*(1), 55–68.

Realmuto, G., Jensen, J., & Wescoe, S. (1990). Specificity and sensitivity of sexually anatomically correct dolls in substantiating abuse: A pilot study. *Journal of the American Academy of Child and Adolescent Psychiatry, 29,* 743–746.

Realmuto, G., & Wescoe, S. (1992). Agreement among professionals about a child's sexual abuse status: Interviews with sexually anatomically correct dolls as indicators of abuse. *Child Abuse and Neglect, 16,* 719–725.

Register, P., & Kihlstrom, J. F. (1986). Finding the hypnotic virtuoso. *International Journal of Clinical and Experimental Hypnosis, 34,* 84–97.

Register, P.A., & Kihlstrom, J.F. (1988). Hypnosis and

interrogative suggestibility. *Personality & Individual Differences, 9,* 549–558.

Reidinger, P. (September, 1996). "They blinded me with science!" *American Bar Association Journal,* 58–62.

Reiff, R., & Scheerer, M. (1959). *Memory and hypnotic age regression.* New York: International Universities Press.

Reilly v. Connecticut. (1976). 32 Conn. Supp. 349, 355 A2d 324 (Super Ct.).

Reis, B.E. (1995a). Time as the missing dimension in traumatic memory and dissociative subjectivity. In J.L. Alpert (Ed.), *Sexual abuse recalled: Treating trauma in the era of the recovered memory debate* (pp. 215–234). Northvale, NJ: Jason Aronson.

Reisberg, D., Heuer, F., McLean, J., & O'Shaughnessy, M. (1988). The quantity, not the quality, of affect predicts memory vividness. *Bulletin of the Psychonomic Society, 26,* 100–103.

Reisberg, D., Scully, J., & Karbo, W. (1993). *The laboratory creation of false memories: How generalizable?* Paper presented at the Annual Meeting of the Psychonomic Society, Washington, D.C.

Reiser, B.J., Black, J.B., & Abelson, R.P. (1985) Knowledge structures in the organization and retrieval of autobiographical memories. *Cognitive Psychology, 17,* 89–137.

Reiser, M. (1980). *Handbook of investigative hypnosis.* Los Angeles, CA: Lehi Publishing.

Reiser, M. (April, 1986). Reader's forum. *Division on Psychological Hypnosis Newsletter,* 5–6. Washington, D.C.: American Psychological Association.

Relinger, H. (1984). Hypnotic hypermnesia: A critical review. *American Journal of Clinical Hypnosis, 26,* 212–225.

Resick, P.A., Jordan, C.J., Girelli, S.A., Hunter, C.K., & Marhoefer-Dvoak, S. (1988). A comparative outcome study of behavioral group therapy for sexual assault victims. *Behavior Therapy, 19,* 385–401.

Reuben, R.C. (1997). Moment of truth: Justices may settle admissibility of lie detector tests once and for all. *American Bar Association Journal,* p. 38 (August).

Revelle, W., & Loftus, D.A. (1992) The implications of arousal effects for the study of affect and memory. In S-A. Christianson (Ed.), *The handbook of emotion and memory: Research and theory* (pp. 113–149). Hillsdale, NJ: Erlbaum.

Reviere, S.L. (1996). *Memory of childood trauma.* New York: Guilford.

Reyher, J. (1958). *Hypnotically induced conflict in relation to subscription, repression, antisocial behavior, and psychosomatic reactions.* Unpublished doctoral dissertation, University of Illinois.

Reyher, J. (1962). A paradigm for determining the clinical relevance of hypnotically induced psychopathology. *Psychological Bulletin, 59,* 344–352.

Reyher, J. (1963). Free imagery: An uncovering procedure. *Journal of Clinical Psychology, 19,* 454–459.

Reyher, J. (1967). Hypnosis in research on psychopathology. In J.E. Gordon (Ed.), *Handbook of clinical and ex-*

perimental hypnosis (pp.110–147). New York: Macmillan.

Reyher, J., & Smyth, L. (1971). Suggestibility during the execution of a posthypnotic suggestion. *Journal of Abnormal Psychology, 78*(3), 258–265.

Rhue, J.W., & Lynn, S.J. (1987). Fantasy proneness: The ability to hallucinate "as real as real." *British Journal of Experimental and Clinical Hypnosis, 4,* 173–180.

Rhue, J.W., Lynn, S.J., & Kirsch, I. (Eds.). (1993). *Handbook of clinical hypnosis.* Washington, D.C.: American Psychological Association Press.

Rhue, J.W., Lynn, S.J., & Sandberg, D. (1995). Dissociation, fantasy and imagination in childhood: A comparison of physically abused, sexually abused, and non-abused children. *Contemporary Hypnosis, 12,* 131–136.

Rice-Smith. E. (1993). Group psychotherapy with sexually abused children. In H.I. Kaplan & B.J. Sadock (Eds.), *Comprehensive group psychotherapy* (3rd. ed., pp. 531–550). Baltimore, MD: Williams & Wilkins.

Rich, C.L. (1990). Accuracy of adults' reports of abuse in childhood. *American Journal of Psychiatry, 146,* 1358.

Richard H. v. Larry D. (1988). 198 Cal. App. 3d 591, 243 Cal. Rptr. 807 (1st Dist.).

Richardson, H. (Ed.). (1980). *New religions and mental health.* New York: Edwin Mellen Press.

Richardson, J.T., Best, J., & Bromley, D.G. (1991). *The Satanism scare.* New York: Aldine de Gruyer.

Rieker, P.P., & Carmen, E. (1986) The victim-to-patient process: The disconfirmation and transformation of abuse. *American Journal of Orthopsychiatry, 56,* 360–370.

Rigtrup, K. (December 26, 1996). Order Granting Final Judgment Notwithstanding the Verdict, *Franklin v. Stevenson,* Civil No. 94–09017791PI, in the Third Judicial District Court, Salt Lake County, Utah.

Rivers, H.R. (February 2, 1918). The repression of war experience. *Lancet,* 173–177.

Robins, L.N. (1966). *Deviant children grown up: A sociological and psychiatric study of sociopathic personality.* Baltimore, MD: Williams & Wilkins.

Robinson, E.S. (1932). *Association theory today.* New York: Century.

Robinson, J.A. (1976). A sampling of autobiographical memory. *Cognitive Psychology, 8,* 578–595.

Robinson, J.A. (1986). Temporal reference systems and autobiographical memory. In D.C. Rubin (Ed.), *Autobiographical memory* (pp. 159–190). Cambridge, England: Cambridge University Press.

Rock, S.F. (1995). A claim for third party standing in malpractice cases involving repressed memory syndrome. *William and Mary Law Review, 37,* 337–379.

Rock v. Arkansas. (1987). 483 U.S.44, 107 S.Ct. 2704, 97 L.Ed. 2d 37.

Rodeghier, M. Goodpaster, J., & Blatterbauer, S. (1991). Psychosocial characteristics of abductees: Results from the CUFOS Abduction Project. *Journal of UFO Studies, 3,* 59–90.

Rodgers, K.E. (1992). Childhood sexual abuse: Perceptions on tolling the statute of limitations. *Journal of Contemporary Health Law and Policy, 8,* 309–335.

Roe, C.M., & Schwartz, M.F. (1996). Characteristics of previously forgotten memories of sexual abuse: A descriptive study. *Journal of Psychiatry and Law, 24,* 189–206.

Roediger, H.L., & McDermott, K.B. (1995). Creating false memories: Remembering words not presented in lists. *Journal of Experimental Psychology: Learning, Memory and Cognition, 21,* 803–814.

Ronis, D.L., Baumgardner, M.H., Leippe, M.R., Cacioppo, J.T., & Greenwald, A.G. (1977). In search of reliable persuasion effects: I. A computer-controlled procedure for studying persuasion. *Journal of Personality and Social Psychology, 35,* 548–569.

Roesler, T.A., & Wind, T.W. (1994). Telling the secret: Adult women describe their disclosures of incest. *Journal of Interpersonal Violence, 9,* 327–338.

Rogers, M.L. (December 3–5, 1993). *Variables to consider in assessing complaints by adult litigants of childhood sexual abuse.* Unpublished manuscript presented at Memories of Trauma, Clark University, Worcester, MA.

Rogers, M.L. (1994). Factors to consider in assessing adult litigant's complaints of childhood sexual abuse. *Behavioral Sciences and the Law, 12,* 279–298.

Rogers, M.L. (1995). Factors influencing recall of childhood sexual abuse. *Journal of Traumatic Stress, 8,* 691–716.

Rogers, R. (1988). *Clinical assessment of malingering and deception.* New York: Guilford.

Rogge, O.J. (1959). *Why men confess.* New York: Thomas Nelson.

Root, M.P.P., & Fallon, P. (1988). The incidence of victimization experiences in a bulimic sample. *Journal of Interpersonal Violence, 3,* 161–173.

Rosen, J. (1953). *Direct psychoanalysis.* New York: Grune and Stratton.

Rosen, V.H. (1955). The reconstruction of a traumatic childhood event in a case of derealization. *Journal of the American Psychoanalytic Association, 3,* 211–221.

Rosenberg, M.J., Hovland, C.I., McGuire, W.J., Abelson, R.P., & Brehm, J.W. (1960). *Attitude organization and change: An analysis of consistency among attitude components.* New Haven, CT: Yale University Press.

Rosenthal, B.G. (1944). Hypnotic recall of material learned under anxiety- and non-anxiety-producing conditions. *Journal of Experimental Psychology, 34,* 369–389.

Ross, B.M. (1991). *Remembering the personal past: Descriptions of autobiographical memory.* New York: Oxford University Press.

Ross, C.A. (1988a). Cognitive analysis of multiple personality disorder. *American Journal of Psychotherapy, 42,* 229–239.

Ross, C.A. (1988b). Techniques in the treatment of multiple personality disorder. *American Journal of Psychotherapy, 42,* 40–51.

Ross, C.A. (1989). *Multiple personality disorder: Diagnosis, clinical features and treatment.* New York: Wiley.

Ross, C.A. (1995). *Satanic ritual abuse: Principles of treatment.* Toronto, Ontario: University of Toronto Press.

Ross, C.A., Heber, S., Norton, G.R., & Anderson, G. (1989). Differences between multiple personality disorder and other diagnostic groups on structured interview. *Journal of Nervous and Mental Diseases, 177,* 487–491.

Ross, C.A., Norton, G.R., & Fraser, G.A. (1989). Evidence against the iatrogenesis of multiple personality disorder. *Dissociation, 2,* 61–65.

Ross, C.A., Norton, G.R., & Wozney, K. (1989). Multiple personality disorder: An analysis of 236 cases. *Canadian Journal of Psychiatry, 34,* 413–418.

Ross, K. (1977). *Evaluative study of the Los Angeles Police Department Hypnosis Project.* B.A. project, University of Redlands, CA.

Ross, L., Greene, D., & House, P. (1977). The "false consensus effect": An egocentric bias in social perception and attribution processes. *Journal of Experimental Social Psychology, 13,* 279–301.

Ross, T. A. (October 19, 1918). The prevention of relapse of hysterical manifestations. *Lancet,* 516–517.

Rossen, H. (1989). *Zedenangst, het verhaal van Oude Pekala* [Moral anxiety: The story of Oude Pekala]. Amsterdam: Swets & Zeitlinger.

Rossi, E.L. (1980). Introduction to section 7: Experimental neurosis. In E.L. Rossi (Ed.), *The collected papers of Milton H. Erickson , M.D.* (Vol. 3, p. 287). New York: Irvington.

Rossi, E.L. (1993). *The psychobiology of mind-body healing* (revised ed.). New York: Norton.

Rossi, E.L., & Cheek, D.B. (1988). *Mind-body therapy: Ideodynamic healing in hypnosis.* New York: Norton.

Roth, S., & Lebowitz, L. (1988). The experience of sexual trauma. *Journal of Traumatic Stress, 1,* 79–107.

Roth, S., & Newman, E. (1991). The process of coping with sexual trauma. *Journal of Traumatic Stress, 4,* 279–297.

Rotter, J.B. (1966). Generalized expectancies for internal versus external control of reinforcement. *Psychological Monographs, 80* (1 Whole No. 609).

Rowland v. Commonwealth. (1995). 901 S.W.2d 871 (Ky.Sup.Ct.).

Rubenstein, R., & Newman, R. (1954). The living out of "future" experiences under hypnosis. *Science. 119,* 472–473.

Rubin, D.C. (1982). On the retention function for autobiographical memory. *Journal of Verbal Learning and Verbal Behavior, 21,* 21–38.

Rubin, D.C. (1992). Constraints on memory. In E. Winograd & U. Neisser (Eds.), *Affect and accuracy in recall: Studies of "flashbulb" memories* (pp. 265–273). London: Cambridge University Press.

Rubin, D.C., & Kozin, M. (1984). Vivid memories. *Cognition, 16,* 81–95.

Rubin, D.C., Wetzler, S.E., & Nebes, R.D. (1986). Autobiographical memory across the lifespan. In D.C. Rubin (Ed.), *Autobiographical memory* (pp. 202–221). Cambridge, England: Cambridge University Press.

Rubin, L.J. (1996). Childhood sexual abuse: False accusations of "false memory"? *Professional Psychology: Research and Practice, 27,* 447–451.

Rudy, L., & Goodman, G.S. (1991). Effects of participation on children's reports: Implications for children's testimony. *Developmental Psychology, 27,* 527–538.

Rush, F. (1977). The Freudian cover-up. *Chrysalis,* 31–45.

Rush, F. (1980). *The best kept secret: Sexual abuse of children.* New York: McGraw-Hill.

Russell, D. (1975). *The politics of rape: The victim's perspective.* New York: Scarborough House.

Russell, D.E.H. (1986). *The secret trauma: Incest in the lives of girls and women.* New York: Basic.

Rustin, T.A., & Tate, J.C. (1993). Measuring the stages of change in cigarette smokers. *Journal of Substance Abuse Treatment, 10,* 209–220.

Ryder, D. (1992). *Breaking the circle of Satanic ritual abuse: Recognizing and recovering from the hidden trauma.* Minneapolis, MN: Coringcare Publishers.

Sabourin, M. (1982). Hypnosis and brain function: EEG correlates of state-trait differences. *Research Communications in Psychology, Psyciatry and Behavior, 7,* 149–168.

Sabourin, M.E., & Cutcomb, S.D. (October 1980). *EEG spectral analysis and hypnotic susceptibility.* Paper presented at the Annual Scientific Meeting, Society for Clinical and Experimental Hypnosis, Chicago, IL.

Sabourin, M.E., Cutcomb, S.D., Crawford, H.J., & Pribram, K. (1990). EEG correlates of hypnotic susceptibility and hypnotic trance: Spectral analysis and coherence. *International Journal of Psychophysiology, 10,* 125–142.

Sachs, R.G., Braun, B.G., & Shepp, E. (1988). Techniques for planned abreactions with MPD patients. In B.G. Braun (Ed.), *Dissociative disorders 1988: Proceedings of the Fifth International Conference on Multiple Personality/Dissociative States* (p. 85). Chicago, IL.

Sachs, R.G., Frischholz, E., & Wood, J.I. (1988). Marital and family therapy in the treatment of multiple personality disorder. *Journal of Marital and Family Therapy, 14,* 249–259.

Sachs, R.G., & Peterson, J.A. (1994). *Processing memories retrieved by trauma victims and survivors: A primer for therapists.* Tyler, TX: Family Violence and Sexual Assault Institute.

Sadoff, R.L., & Dubin, L.L. (1990). The use of hypnosis as a pretrial discovery tool in civil and criminal lawsuits. In C.H. Wecht (Ed.), *Legal medicine* (pp. 105–124). Salem, NH: Butterworth's.

Salter, A.C. (1988). *Treating child sex offenders and victims: A practical guide.* Newbury Park, CA: Sage.

Salter, A.C. (1991). *Accuracy of expert testimony in child sexual abuse cases: A case study of Ralph Underwager and Hollinda Wakefield.* Unpublished manuscript sponsored by the New England Commissioners of Child Welfare Agencies.

Salter, A.C. (1995). *Transforming trauma: A guide to understanding and treating adult survivors of child sexual abuse.* Thousand Oaks, CA: Sage.

Salter, S. (April 10, 1993). Debating the way memory works. *San Francisco Examiner,* A-1, A-18.

Samet, J.I., Walker, R.P., Meehan, K.A., & Lubega, S.K. (Winter 1991). The attack on the citadel of privity. *The Brief, 20*(2), 9–13, 40–41. (American Bar Association, Section of Tort & Insurance Practice).

Sanchez v. Archdiocese of San Antonio. (1994). 873 S.W.2d 87 (Ct.App.Tex.—San Antonio).

Sanders, G.S., & Simmons, W.L. (1983). Use of hypnosis to enhance eyewitness accuracy: Does it work? *Journal of Applied Psychology, 68,* 70–77.

Sanders, G.S., & Warnick, D.H. (1980). Some conditions maximizing eyewitness accuracy: A learning/memory analogy. *Journal of Criminal Justice, 8,* 395–403.

Sanders, S. (1969). The effect of hypnosis on visual imagery. *Dissertation Abstracts International, 30,* 293B.

Sandfort, T. (1982). *Retrospectie als methode van dataverzameling; een overzicht vanliteratuur met betrekking tot de vraag ofretrospectie valide en betroiwbare data op kan leveren.* Rijks Universiteit Utrecht: IKPP (internal publication).

Sandor, A.A. (1957). The history of professional liability suits in the United States. *Journal of the American Medical Association, 163,* 459–466.

Sanford, L.T (1980). *The silent children.* Garden City, NY: Anchor Press/Doubleday.

Sapolsky, R., Krey, L., & McEwen, B.S. (1984). Stress down-regulates corticosterone receptors in a site specific manner in the brain. *Endocrinology, 114,* 287–292.

Saporta, J.A., & van der Kolk, B.A. (1992). Psychobiological consequences of severe trauma. In M. Basoglu (Ed.), *Torture and its consequences* (pp. 151–181). New York: Cambridge University Press.

Sarbin, T.R. (1950). Mental age changes in experimental regression. *Journal of Personality, 19,* 221–228.

Sargeant, W. (1957). *Battle for the mind: A physiology of conversion and brain-washing.* London: Heinemann.

Sargant, W. (1973). *The mind possessed: A physiology of possession, mysticism and faith healing.* Philadelphia, PA: Lippincott.

Sargant, W., & Slater, E. (1941) Amnestic syndromes in war. *Proceedings of the Royal Society of Medicine, 34,* 757–764.

Sarno, G.G. (1979). Malpractice in connection with electroshock treatment. *American Law Reports 3,* 317–350.

Saunders, L.S., Bursztajn, H.J. & Brodsky, A. (Spring, 1995). Recovery memory and managed care: HB 236's post-*Daubert* "science" junket. *TBN, 17.*

Savin v. Allstate Insurance Company. (1991). 579 So. 2d 453 (La. App.).

Saywitz, K.J. (1987). Children's testimony: Age-related patterns of memory errors. In S.J. Ceci, M.P. Toglia, & D.F. Ross (Eds.), *Children's eyewitness memory* (pp. 36–52). New York: Springer-Verlag.

Saywitz, K.J. (1995). Improving childen's testimony: The question, the answer, and the environment. In M.S. Zaragoza et al. (Eds.), *Memory and testimony in the child witness* (pp. 113–140). Thousand Oaks, CA: Sage.

Saywitz, K.J., Geiselman, R.E. ,& Bornstein, G.K. (1992). Effects of cognitive interviewing and practice on children's recall performance. *Journal of Applied Psychology, 77*, 744–756.

Saywitz, K.J., Goodman, G.S., Nicholas, E., & Moan, S.F.(1991). Children's memories of a physical examination involving genital touch: Implications for reports of child sexual abuse. *Journal of Consulting and Clinical Psychology, 59*, 682–691.

Saywitz, K.J., & Moan-Hardie, S. (1994). Reducing the potential for distortion of childhood memories. *Consciousness and Cognition, 3*, 408–425.

Scammell, H. (1991). *Mortal remains: A true story of ritual murder*. New York: Harper Collins.

Schachtel, E. (1947). On memory and childhood amnesia. *Psychiatry, 10*, 1–26.

Schacter, D.L. (1982). *Stranger behind the engram: Theories of memory and the psychology of science*. Hillsdale, NJ: Erlbaum.

Schacter, D.L. (1986). Amnesia and crime: How much do we know? *American Psychologist, 41*, 286–295.

Schacter, D.L. (1992a). Implicit knowledge: New perspectives on unconscious processes. *Proceedings of the National Academy of Science, 89*, 11113–11117.

Schacter, D.L. (1992b). Understanding implicit memory: A cognitive neuroscience approach. *American Psychologist, 47*, 559–569.

Schacter, D.L. (1995). Memory distortion: History and current status. In D.L. Schacter, J.T. Coyle, G.D. Fishbach, M-M. Mesulam, & L.E. Sullivan (Eds.), *Memory distortion: How minds, brains, and societies reconstruct the past* (pp. 1–43). Cambridge, MA: Harvard University Press.

Schacter, D.L., Kagan, J., & Leichtman, M.D. (1995). True and false memories in children and adults: A cognitive neuroscience perspective. *Psychology, Public Policy, and the Law*, 411–428.

Schacter, D.L., Riemane, E., Currant, T., Yun, L.S., Bandy, D., McDermott, K.B., & Roedigger, H.L. (1996). Neuroanatomical correlates of veridical and illusory recognition memory: Evidence from positron emission tomography, *Neuron , 17*, 267–274.

Schacter, D.L., & Tulving, E. (1994). *Memory systems 1994*. Cambridge, MA: M.I.T. Press.

Schaef, A. W. (1986). *Co-dependence: Misunderstood-mistreated*. San Francisco, CA: Harper & Row.

Schafer, D.W., & Rubio, R. (1978). Hypnosis to aid the recall of witnesses. *International Journal of Clinical and Experimental Hypnosis, 26*, 81–91.

Schall v. Lockheed Missles & Space Co. (1995). 37 Cal.App.4th 1485, 44 Cal.Rptr.2d 191 (6 Dist.).

Scheffler, I. (1967). *Science and subjectivity*. Indianapolis: Bobbs-Merrill.

Scheflin, A.W. (1982). Freedom of the mind as an international human rights issue. *Human Rights Law Journal, 3*, 1–64.

Scheflin, A.W. (August, 1993). Avoiding malpractice liability. *American Society of Clinical Hypnosis Newsletter, 34*(1), 6.

Scheflin, A.W. (1994a). Forensic hypnosis: Unanswered questions. *Australian Journal of Clinical and Experimental Hypnosis, 22*, 23–34.

Scheflin, A.W. (1994b). Forensic hypnosis and the law: The current situation in the United States. In B.J. Evans and R.O. Stanley (Eds.), *Hypnosis and the law: Principles and practice* (pp. 25–48). Heideleberg, Victoria, Australia: Australian Society of Hypnosis.

Scheflin, A.W. (Fall, 1994c). The truth about false memory. *Et Al., 1*, 28–29.

Scheflin, A. W. (1995). The Menendez case: legal commentary on the diary. In H. Thornton (Ed.), *Hung jury* (pp. 131–164). Philadelphia, PA: Temple University Press.

Scheflin, A.W. (1996). Commentary on *Borawick v. Shay*: The fate of hypnotically retrieved memories. *Cultic Studies Journal, 13*, 26–41.

Scheflin, A.W. (1997a). Narrative truth, historical truth and forensic truth: Implications for the mental health professional in court. In L. Lifson & R.I. Simon (Eds.), *The mental health practitioner and the law: An essential guide*. Cambridge, MA: Harvard University Press.

Scheflin, A.W. (1997b). Ethics and hypnosis: Unorthodox or innovative therapies and the legal standard of care. In W. Matthews & J. Edgette (Eds.), *Current thinking and research in brief therapy: Solutions, strategies, narratives* (pp. 41–62). New York: Brunner/Mazel.

Scheflin, A.W. (1997c). False memory and Buridan's ass: A response to Karlin, R.A., and Orne, M.T. (1996), "Hypnosis, social influence, incestuous child abuse, and satanic ritual abuse: The iatrogenic creation of horrific memories for the remote past." *Cultic Studies Journal*.

Scheflin, A.W. (1997d). The evolving standard of care in the practice of trauma and dissociative disorder therapy. *Psychiatric Annals*.

Scheflin, A.W. (1997e). Ethics and hypnosis: A preliminary inquiry into hypnotic advocacy. In W. Matthews & J. Edgette, *Current thinking and research in brief therapy: Solutions, strategies, narratives* (Vol. 2). New York: Brunner/Mazel.

Scheflin, A. W. & Alexander., G.J. (1997). *The legal regulation of hypnosis*. Unpublished manuscript.

Scheflin, A.W., & Brown, D. (1996). Repressed memory or dissociative amnesia: What the science says. *Journal of Psychiatry and Law, 24*, 143–188.

Scheflin, A.W., & Opton, E.M., Jr. (1978). *The mind manipulators*. London: Paddington.

Scheflin. A.W., & Shapiro, L. (1989). *Trance on trial*. New York: Guilford.

Schein, E.H. (1956). The Chinese indoctrination program for prisoners of war: A study of attempted "brainwashing." *Psychiatry, 19*, 149–172.

Schein, E. (1962). Man against man: Brainwashing. *Corrective Psychiatry and Social Therapy, 8*, 90–97.

Schein, E.H., Schneier, I., & Barker, C.H. (1961). *Coercive persuasion: A socio-psychological analysis of the "brainwashing" of American civilian prisoners by the Chinese communists*. New York: Norton.

Schiffer, F., Teicher, M. H., & Papanicolaou, A. C. (1995). Evoked potential evidence for right brain activity during the recall of traumatic memories. *Journal of Neuropsychiatry and Clinical Neurosciences, 7,* 169–175.

Schilder, P. (1927/1956). *The nature of hypnosis.* New York: International Universities Press.

Schindler, F.E. (1980). Treatment of systematic desensitization of a recurring nightmare of a real life trauma. *Journal of Behavior Therapy and Experimental Psychiatry, 11,* 53–54.

Schmidt, S.R. & Bohannon, J.N. III (1988). In defense of the flashbulb-memory hypothesis: A comment on McCloskey, Wible, and Cohen (1988). *Journal of Experimental Psychology: General, 117,* 332–335.

Schoener, G.R., Milgrom, J.H., Gonsioek, J.C., Luepker, E.T., & Conroe, R.M. (1989). *Psychotherapists' sexual involvement with clients: Intervention and prevention.* Minneapolis, MN: Walk-in Counseling Center.

Schooler, J.W. (1994). Cutting towards the core: The issues and evidence surrounding recovered accounts of sexual trauma. *Consciousness and Cognition, 3,* 452–469.

Schooler, J.W., Gerhard, D., & Loftus, E.F. (1986). Qualities of the unreal. *Journal of Experimental Psychology: Learning, Memory, and Cognition, 12,* 171–181.

Schooler, J.W., & Loftus, E. F. (1986). Individual differences and experimentation: Complementary approaches to interrogatory suggestibility. *Social Behavior, 1,* 105–112.

Schoutrop, M., Lange, A., Durland, C., Bermond, B., Sporry, A., & de Goederen, A. (1995). *The effects of structured writing assignments in reprocessing traumatic events: An uncontrolled trial.* Unpublished manuscript, University of Amsterdam, The Netherlands.

Schrag, P. (1978). *Mind control.* New York: Pantheon.

Schreiber, F.R. (1973) *Sybil.* Chicago, IL: Regency.

Schreuder, J.N. (1996). Posttraumatic re-experiencing in older people: Working through or covering up? *American Journal of Psychotherapy, 50,* 231–242.

Schultz, D.P. (1965). *Sensory restriction: Effects on behavior.* New York: Academic Press.

Schumaker, J.F. (1991). *Human suggestibility: Advances in theory, research, and application.* New York: Routledge.

Schuman, D.C. (1986). False accusations of physical and sexual abuse. *Bulletin of the American Academy of Psychiatry and Law, 14,* 5–21.

Schwarz v. Regents of the University of California. (1990). 226 Cal. App. 3d 149, 276 Cal. Rptr. 470.

Schwartz, G.E. (1990). Psychobiology of repression and health: A systems approach. In J.L. Singer (Ed.), *Repression and dissociation: Implications for personality theory, psychopathology, and health* (pp. 405–434). Chicago, IL: University of Chicago Press.

Schwartz, G.E., Davidson, R.J., & Maer, F. (1975). Right hemisphere lateralization for emotion in the human brain: Interactions with cognition. *Science, 190,* 286–288.

Schwartz, M. (1992). Sexual compulsivity as post-traumatic stress disorder: Treatment perspectives. *Psychi-*
atric Annals, 22, 333–338.

Schwartz, M., & Masters, R. (1993). Integration of trauma-based, cognitive behavioral systemic and addiction approaches for treatment of hypersexual pairbonding. *Sexual Addiction and Compulsivity, 1,* 57–76.

Scrivner, E., & Safer, M.A. (1988). Eyewitnesses show hypermnesia for details about a violent event. *Journal of Applied Psychology, 73,* 371–377.

Scurfield, R.M. (1985). Post-trauma stress assessment and treatment: Overview and formulations. In C.R. Figley (Ed.), *Trauma and its wake: The study and treatment of post-traumatic stress disorder* (Vol. 1, pp. 219–256). New York: Brunner/Mazel.

Selye, H. (1976). *The stress of life.* New York: McGraw Hill.

Semon, R. (1904/1921). *Die Mneme* [The engram]. London: George Allen & Unwin.

Sewell v. Internal Medicine and Endocrine Associates, P.C. (1992). 600 So.2d 242 (Ala.).

Sgroi, S.M. (1975). Sexual molestation of children: The last frontier in child abuse. *Children Today, 44,* 18–21.

Sgroi, S. (1989). Stages of recovery for adult survivors of child sexual abuse. In S. Sgroi (Ed.), *Vulnerable populations* (Vol. 2, pp. 11–130). Lexington, MA: D.C. Heath.

Sgroi, S.M., Porter, F.S., & Blick, L.C. (1982). Validation of child sexual abuse. In S.M. Sgroi (Ed.), *Handbook of clinical intervention in child sexual abuse* (pp. 9–37). Lexington, MA: Lexington Books.

Shadish, W.R., Fuller, S., & Gorman, M.E. et. al. (1994). Social psychology of science: A conceptual and empirical research program. In W.R. Shadish & S. Fuller (Eds.), *The social psychology of science* (pp. 3–123). New York: Guilford.

Shaheen v. Knight. (1957). 11 Pa.D & C.2d 41.

Shahzade v. Gregory. (1996). 923 F.Supp. 286 (D.Mass.).

Shalev, A.Y., Peri, T., Caneti, L., & Schreiber, S. (1996). Predictors of PTSD in injured trauma survivors. *American Journal of Psychiatry, 53,* 219–224.

Shapiro, M.H., & Spece, R.G. Jr. (1981). *Bioethics and law.* St. Paul, MN: West Publishing.

Shapiro, S. (1995). Impact of validation of recovered memories on patient's treatment. In J.L. Alpert (Ed.), *Sexual abuse recalled: Treating trauma in the era of the recovered memory debate* (pp. 311–336). Northvale, NJ: Jason Aronson.

Share, L. (1994). *If someone speaks, it gets lighter: Dreams and the reconstruction of infant trauma.* Hillsdale, NJ: Analytic Press.

Shaul, R.D. (1978). *Eyewitness testimony and hypnotic hypermnesia.* Unpublished doctoral dissertation, Brigham Young University.

Shaw, J. (1996). Increases in eyewitness confidence resulting from postevent questioning. *Journal of Experimental Psychology: Applied, 2,* 126–146.

Shea, T.E. (1978). Legal standard of care for psychiatrists and psychologists. *Western State University Law Review, 6,* 71–99.

Sheehan, P.W. (1969). Artificial induction of posthypnotic

conflict. *Journal of Abnormal Psychology, 74*, 16–25.

Sheehan, P.W. (1979). Hypnosis and the process of imagination. In E. Fromm & R.E. Shor (Eds.), *Hypnosis: Developments in research and new perspectives* (2nd ed., pp. 381–411). New York: Aldine.

Sheehan, P.W. (1988). Memory distortion in hypnosis. *International Journal of Clinical and Experimental Hypnosis, 36*, 296–311.

Sheehan, P.W. (1991). Hypnosis, context, and commitment. In S.J. Lynn & J.W. Rhue (Eds.), *Theories of hypnosis* (pp. 520–541). New York: Guilford.

Sheehan, P.W. (1996). Contemporary trends in hypnosis research. State-of-the-Art Address presented at the 26th International Congress of Psychology, Montreal, Canada (August 17).

Sheehan, P.W., Garnett, M., & Robertson, R. (1993). The effects of cue level, hypnotizability, and state instruction on responses to leading questions. *International Journal of Clinical and Experimental Hypnosis, 41*, 287–304.

Sheehan, P. W., Green, V., & Truesdale, P. (1992). Influence of rapport on hypnotically induced pseudomemory. *Journal of Abnormal Psychology, 101*, 690–700.

Sheehan, P.W., & Grigg, L. (1985). Hypnosis, memory and the acceptance of an implausible cognitive set. *British Journal of Clinical and Experimental Hypnosis, 3*, 5–12.

Sheehan, P. W., Grigg, L., & McCann, T. (1984). Memory distortion following exposure to false information in hypnosis. *Journal of Abnormal Psychology, 93*, 259–265.

Sheehan, P. W., & McConkey, K. M. (1982). *Hypnosis and experience: The exploration of phenomena and process*. Hillsdale, NJ: Erlbaum.

Sheehan, P.W., & McConkey, K.M. (1993). Forensic hypnosis: The application of ethical guidelines. In J.W. Rhue, S.J. Lynn, & I. Kirsch (Eds.), *Handbook of clinical hypnosis* (pp. 719–738). Washington, D.C.: American Psychological Association Press.

Sheehan, P.W., Statham, D., & Jamieson, G.A. (1991a). Pseudomemory effects over time in the hypnotic setting. *Journal of Abnormal Psychology, 100*, 39–44.

Sheehan, P.W., Statham, D., & Jamieson, G.A. (1991b). Pseudomemory effects and their relationship to level of susceptibility to hypnosis and state instructions. *Journal of Personality & Social Psychology, 60*, 130–137.

Sheehan, P. W., & Tilden, J. (1983). Effects of suggestibility and hypnosis on accurate and distorted retrieval from memory. *Journal of Experimental Psychology: Learning, Memory & Cognition, 9*, 283–293.

Sheehan, P. W., & Tilden, J. (1984). Real and simulated occurrences of memory distortion in hypnosis. *Journal of Abnormal Psychology, 93*, 47–57.

Sheehan, P. W., & Tilden, J. (1986). Level of susceptibility to hypnosis and the occurrence of hypnotic memory distortion. *International Journal of Clinical and Experimental Hypnosis, 34*, 122–137.

Sherry, D.F., & Schacter, D.L. (1987). The evolution of multiple memory systems. *Psychological Bulletin, 94*, 439–454.

Sheingold, K., & Tenney, Y. J. (1982). Memory for a salient childhood event. In U. Neisser (Ed.), *Memory observed* (pp. 201–212). New York: Freeman.

Shields, E. W., & Knox, V. J. (1986). Level of processing as a determinant of hypnotic hypermnesia. *Journal of Abnormal Psychology, 95*, 350–357.

Shor, R.E. (1959). Hypnosis and the concept of the generalized reality-orientation. *American Journal of Psychotherapy, 13*, 582–602.

Shor, R.E., & Orne, E.C. (1962). *The Harvard group scale of hypnotic susceptibility, Form A*. Palo Alto, CA: Consulting Psychologists Press.

Shore, J.H., Tatum, E.L., & Vollmer, W.M. (1986). Psychiatric reactions to disaster: The Mount St. Helens experience. *American Journal of Psychiatry, 143*, 590–595.

Shorvon, H.J., & Sargant, W. (1947). Excitory abreaction: With special reference to its mechanism and the use of ether. *Journal of Mental Science, 93*, 709–732.

Shrimpton, S. (1990). Book Review of H. Wakefield and R. Underwager. *Accusations of child sexual abuse, Child Abuse & Neglect, 14*, 601–602.

Shubat, N. (1968). *The influence of state and relationship on the hypotic recall of previously presented material: A test of hypnotic hypermnesia*. Unpublished doctoral dissertation, University of Montana.

Shuman, D.W., & Weiner, M.S. (1982). The privilege study: An empirical examination of the psychotherapist-patient privilege. *North Carolina Law Review, 60*, 893–942.

Sifneos, P.E. (1973). The prevalence of alexithymic characteristics in psychosomatic patients. *Psychotherapy and Psychosomatics, 24*, 255–263.

Sifneos, P.E., Apfel-Savitz, R., & Frankel, F. (1977). The phenomenon of alexithymia. *Psychotherapy and Psychosomatics, 28*, 47–57.

Silver, S.M., & Kelly, M.D. (1985). Hypnotherapy of PTSD in combat veterans from WWII and Vietnam. In W.E. Kelley (Ed.), *Post-traumatic stress disorders and the Vietnam veteran* (pp. 211–233). New York: Brunner/Mazel.

Silverman, A.B., Reinherz, H.Z., & Giaconia, R.M. (1996). The long-term sequelae of child and adolescent abuse: A longitudinal community study. *Child Abuse and Neglect, 20*, 709–723.

Simmel, E. (1944). War neurosis. In L. Lorand (Ed.), *Psychoanalysis Today* (pp. 211–233). New York: International Universities.

Simmons v. United States. 1986. 805 F.2d 1363.

Simon, J. (Fall, 1995). The highly misleading "Truth and Responsibility in Mental Health Practices Act": The "false memory" movement's remedy for a nonexistent problem. *Moving Forward, 3*, 11–21.

Simon, R.I. (1992). *Clinical psychiatry and the law*. (2nd. ed.) Washington, D.C.: American Psychiatric Press.

Simon, R.I. (August, 1993). Innovative psychiatric therapies and legal uncertainty: A survival guide for clinicians. *Psychiatric Annals, 23*, 73.

Simpson, S. & Baker, J.K. (Fall, 1994). Causes of action

against health care providers by retractors of abuse allegations. *Shepard's Expert and Scientific Evidence Quarterly, 2*(2), 1–31.

Singer v. American Psychological Association. (1993). Memorandum and Order, August 9, 1993. 1993 WL 307782 (S.D.N.Y.).

Singer, J.L. (1990). *Repression and dissociation: Implications for personality theory, psychopathology, and health.* Chicago, IL: University of Chicago Press.

Singer, M.T., & Lalich, J. (1995). *Cults in our midst: The hidden menace in our everyday lives.* San Francisco, CA: Jossey-Bass.

Singer, M.T., & Lalich, J. (1996). *"Crazy" therapies: What are they? Do they work?* San Francisco: Jossey-Bass.

Singh, K.K., & Gudjonsson, G.H. (1984). Interrogative suggestibility, delayed memory and self-concept. *Personality and Individual Differences, 5,* 203–209.

Sisk, S., & Hoffman, C. (1987) *Inside scars: Incest recovery as told by a survivor and her therapist.* Gainsville, FL: Pandora Press.

Siuta, J. (1990). Fantasy-proneness: Towards cross-cultural comparisons. *British Journal of Experimental and Clinical Hypnosis, 7,* 81–92.

Slavik v. Routt. (1995). No. PI 93–006461, District Court, Fourth Judicial District, County of Hennepin, Minnesota.

Slenger, W.E., & Kulka, R.A. (1989). *PTSD scale development for the MMPI-2.* Research Triangle Park, NC: Research Triangle Institute.

Sloan, G., & Leichner, P. (1986). Is there a relationship between sexual abuse or incest and eating disorders? *Canadian Journal of Psychiatry, 31,* 656–660

Slovenko, R. (1990). *Tarasoff* and its progeny. In R.I. Simon (Ed.), *Review of clinical psychiatry and the law* (Vol. 1, pp. 177–190). Washington, D.C.: American Psychiatric Press.

Slovenko, R. (Fall, 1995a). The duty of therapists to third parties. *The Journal of Psychiatry and Law, 23,* 383–410.

Slovenko, R. (April 29, 1995b). *"I'm not a detective"* in *"revival of memory."* Paper presented at a Conference on Law, Science, and Society sponsored by the American Bar Association, Detroit, Michigan.

Smith v. Pust. (1993). 19 Cal. App. 4th 263, 23 Cal. Rptr. 2d 364 (4th Dist.).

Smith, B.S., Ratner, H.H., & Hobart, C.J. (1987). The role of cuing and organization in children's memory for events. *Journal of Experimental Child Psychology, 44,* 1–24.

Smith, C.M. (1994). Recovered memories of alleged sexual abuse. *Seattle University Law Review, 18,* 51–91.

Smith, G.M. (1937). Originating before the age of three: Cured with the aid of hypnotic recall. *Character and Personality, 5,* 331–337.

Smith, K., & Gudjonsson, G.H. (1986). Investigation of the responses of "fakers" and "non-fakers" on the Gudjonsson Suggestibility Scale. *Medicine, Science and the Law, 26,* 66–71.

Smith, M., & Pazder, L. (1980) *Michelle remembers.* New York: Congdon & Latters.

Smith, M. C. (1983). Hypnotic memory enhancement of witnesses: Does it work? *Psychological Bulletin, 94,* 387–407.

Smith, M.E. (1952). Childhood memories compared with those of adult life. *The Journal of Genetic Psychology, 80,* 151–182.

Smith, R.H. (1972). *O.S.S.: The secret history of America's first Central Intelligence Agency.* Berkeley: University of California Press.

Smith, V.L., & Ellsworth, P.C. (1987). The social psychology of eyewitness accuracy: Misleading questions and communicator expertise. *Journal of Applied Psychology, 72,* 294–300.

Smyth, L. D. (1982). Psychopathology as a function of neuroticism and a hypnotically implanted aggressive conflict. *Journal of Personality and Social Psychology, 43*(3), 555–564.

Snelling, T., & Fisher, W. (1992). Adult survivors of childhood sexual abuse: Should Texas courts apply the discovery rule? *South Texas Law Review, 33,* 377–415.

Softley, P. (1980). *Police interrogation: An observational study in four police stations.* Home Office Research Study, No. 61. HMSO: London.

Solomon, P., Kubzansky, P.E., Leiderman, P.H., Mendelson, J.H., Trumbull, R., & Wexler, D. (1965). *Sensory deprivation: A symposium held at Harvard Medical School.* Cambridge, MA: Harvard University Press.

Sommerschield, H., & Reyher, J. (1973). Posthypnotic conflict, repression, and psychopathology. *Journal of Abnormal Psychology, 82,* 278–290.

Sonnenberg, S.M., Blank, A.S., & Talbott, J.A. (1985). *The trauma of war: Stress and recovery in Vietnam veterans.* Washington, D.C.: American Psychiatric Press.

Sorenson, T., & Snow, B. (1991). How to tell: The process of disclosure in child sexual abuse. *Child Welfare, 70,* 3–15.

Southard, E.E. (1919). *Shell-shock and other neuropsychiatric problems.* Boston, MA: W.W. Leonard.

Southwick, S.M., Krystal, J.H., Morgan, C.A., Johnson, D., Nagy, L.M., Nicolaou, A., Heninger, G.R., & Charney, D.S. (1993). Abnormal noradrenergic function in posttraumatic stress disorder. *Archives of General Psychiatry, 50,* 266–274.

Sowder, B. J. (1985). *Disasters and mental health: Selected contemporary perspectives.* Rockville, MD: National Institute of Mental Health.

Snow, B., & Sorenson, T. (1990). Ritualistic child abuse in a neighborhood setting. *Journal of Interpersonal Violence, 5,* 474–487.

Spanos, N.P. (1986). Hypnotic behavior: A social psychological interpretation of amnesia, analgesia and trance logic. *Behavior and Brain Sciences, 9,* 449–467

Spanos, N.P. (1994). Multiple identity enactments and multiple personality disorders: A sociocognitive perspective. *Psychological Bulletin, 116,* 143–165.

Spanos, N.P., Brett, P.J., Menary, E.P., & Cross, W.P. (1987). A measure of attitudes toward hypnosis: Relationships with absorption and hypnotic susceptibility. *American Journal of Clinical Hypnosis, 30,* 139–150.

Spanos, N.P., & Bures, E. (1993–94). Pseudomemory responding in hypnotic task-motivated and simulating subjects: Memory distortion or reporting bias? *Imagination, Cognition, and Personality, 13,* 303–310.

Spanos, N.P., Burgess, C.A., & Burgess, M.F. (1994). Past-life identities, UFO abductions, and Satanic ritual abuse. *International Journal of Clinical and Experimental Hypnosis, 42,* 433–446.

Spanos, N.P., & Chaves, J.F. (1989). *Hypnosis: The cognitive-behavioral perspective.* Buffalo, NY: Prometheus.

Spanos, N. P., Cross, P., Dickson, K., & DuBreuil, S. (1993). Close encounters: An examination of UFO experiences. *Journal of Abnormal Psychology, 102,* 624–632.

Spanos, N.P., deGroot, H.P., & Gwynn, M.I. (1987). Trance logic as incomplete responding. *Journal of Personality and Social Psychology, 53,* 911–921.

Spanos, N.P., Gwynn, M.I., Comer, S.L., Baltruweit, W.J., & de Groh, M. (1989). Are hypnotically induced pseudomemories resistant to cross-examination? *Law and Human Behavior, 13,* 271–289.

Spanos, N.P., Gwynn, M.I., & Terrade, K. (1989). Effects on mock jurors of experts favorable and unfavorable toward hypnotically elicited eyewitness testimony. *Journal of Applied Psychology, 74,* 922–926.

Spanos, N.P., & McLean, J. (1985–1986). Hypnotically created pseudomemories: Memory distortions or reporting biases? *British Journal of Experimental Hypnosis, 3,* 155–159.

Spanos, N.P., Menary, E., Brett, P.J., Cross, W., & Ahmed, Q. (1987). Failure of posthypnotic responding to occur outside the experimental setting. *Journal of Abnormal Psychology, 96,* 52–57.

Spanos, N.P., Menary, E., Gabora, N.J., DuBreuil, S.C., & Dewherst, B. (1991). Secondary identity enactments during hypnotic past-life regression: A sociocognitive perspective. *Journal of Personality and Social Psychology, 61,* 308–320.

Spanos, N.P., Quigley, C.A., Gwynn, M.I., Glatt, R.L., & Perlini, A.H. (1991). Hypnotic interrogation, pretrial preparation, and witness testimony during direct and cross-examination. *Law and Human Behavior, 15,* 639–653.

Spanos, N.P., Weekes, J.R., & Bertrand, L.D. (1985). Multiple personality: A social psychological perspective. *Journal of Abnormal Psychology, 94,* 362–376.

Spear, N.E., & Riccio, D.C. (1994). *Memory: Phenomena and principles.* Boston, MA: Allyn and Bacon.

Spence, D.P. (1982). *Narrative truth and historical truth: Meaning and interpretation in psychoanalysis.* New York: Norton.

Spence, D.P. (1987). *The Freudian metaphor: Toward paradigm change in psychoanalysis.* New York: Norton.

Spence, D.P. (1988). Passive remembering. In U. Neisser & E. Winograd (Eds.), *Remembering reconsidered: Ecological and traditional approaches to the study of memory* (pp. 311–325). Cambridge, England: Cambridge University Press.

Spence, D.P. (1994a). Narrative truth and putative child abuse. *International Journal of Clinical and Experimental Hypnosis, 42,* 289–303.

Spence, D.P. (1994b). *The rhetorical voice of psychoanalysis: Displacement of evidence by theory.* Cambridge, MA: Harvard University Press.

Sperling, G. (1960). The information available in brief visual presentations. *Psychological Monographs, 74,* No. 11.

Spiegel, D. (1981). Vietnam grief work using hypnosis. *American Journal of Clinical Hypnosis, 24,* 33–40.

Spiegel, D. (1984). Multiple personality as a post-traumatic stress disorder. *Psychiatric Clinics of North America, 7,* 101–110.

Spiegel, D. (1986). Dissociation, double binds, and post-traumatic stress in multiple personality disorder. In B.G. Braun (Ed.), *Treatment of multiple personality disorder* (pp. 61–78). Washington, D.C.: American Psychiatric Press.

Spiegel, D. (1987). The *Shirley* decision: The cure is worse than the disease. In R.W. Rieber (Ed.), *Advances in forensic psychology and psychiatry* (Vol. 2, pp. 101–118). Norwood, NJ: Ablex.

Spiegel, D. (1988). Hypnosis. In R.E. Hales, S.C. Yudofsy, & J.A. Talbott (Eds.), *American psychiatric press textbook of psychiatry* (pp. 907–928). Washington, D.C.: American Psychiatric Press.

Spiegel, D. (1993). Hypnosis in the treatment of post-traumatic stress disorder. In J.W. Rhue, S.J. Lynn & I. Kirsch (Eds.), *Handbook of clinical hypnosis* (pp. 493–508). Washington, D.C.: American Psychological Association.

Spiegel, D. (1995). Hypnosis and suggestion. In D.L. Schacter (Ed.), *Memory distortion: How minds, brains, and societies reconstruct the past* (pp.129–149). Cambridge, MA: Harvard University Press.

Spiegel, D., & Cardena, E. (1991). Disintegrated experience: The dissociative disorders revisited. *Journal of Abnormal Psychology, 100,* 366–378.

Spiegel, D., & Scheflin, A.W. (1994). Dissociated or fabricated? Psychiatric aspects of repressed memory in criminal and civil cases. *International Journal of Clinical and Experimental Hypnosis, 42,* 411–432.

Spiegel, D., & Spiegel, H. (1987). Forensic uses of hypnosis. In I.B. Weinter & A.K. Hess (Eds.), *Handbook of forensic psychology* (pp. 490–507). New York: Wiley.

Spiegel, D., & Vermutten, E. (1994). Physiological correlates of hypnosis and dissociation. In D. Spiegel (Ed.), *Dissociation: Culture, mind, and body* (pp. 185–209). Washington, D.C.: American Psychiatric Press.

Spiegel, H. (1968). *Fact or fiction?* Private film, NBC-TV studios, New York.

Spiegel, H. (1974). The grade 5 syndrome: The highly hypnotizable person. *International Journal of Clinical and Experimental Hypnosis, 22,* 303–319.

Spiegel, H. (1980). Hypnosis and evidence: Help or hindrance? *Annals of the New York Academy of Sciences, 347,* 73–85.

Spiegel, H., & Greenleaf, M. (1992). Personality style and

hypnotizability: The fix-flex continuum. *Psychiatric Medicine, 10*, 13–24.

Spiegel, H., Shor, G. & Fischman, S. (1945). An hypnotic ablation technique for the study of personality development. *Psychosomatic Medicine, 7*, 272–278.

Spiegel, H., & Spiegel, D. (1978/1987). *Trance and treatment: Clinical uses of hypnosis.* Washington, D.C.: American Psychiatric Press.

Spielberger, C.D. (1969). *The state-trait anxiety inventory.* Palo Alto, CA: Consulting Psychologists Press.

Strentz, T. (1982).The Stockholm syndrome: Law enforcement policy and hostage behavior. In F.M. Ochberg & D.A. Soskis (Eds.), *Victims of terrorism* (pp. 149–163). Boulder, CO: Westview Press.

Spitzer, R.L., & Williams, J.B. (1986). *Structured clinical interview for DSM-III-R: Patient and non-patient versions.* New York: Biometrica Research Dept., New York State Psychiatric Institute.

Sroufe, L.A. (1983). Infant-caregiver attachment and patterns of adaptation in preschool: The roots of maladaptation and competence. In M. Permutter (Ed.), *Minnesota symposium on child psychology* (Vol. 16, pp. 41–91). Hillsdale, NJ: Erlbaum.

Squire, L.R. (1982). The neuropsychology of human memory. *Annual Review of Neuroscience, 5*, 241.

Squire, L.R. (1987). *Memory and the brain.* New York: Oxford University Press.

Squire, L.R. (1992). Memory and the hippocampus: A synthesis from findings with rats, monkeys, and humans. *Psychological Review, 99*, 143–145.

Squire, L.R. (1995). Biological foundations of accuracy and inaccuracy in memory. In D.L. Schacter (Ed.), *Memory distortion: How minds, and societies reconstruct the past* (pp.197–254). Cambride, MA: Harvard University Press.

Squire, L.R., & Zola-Morgan, S. (1991). The medial temporal lobe memory system. *Science, 253*, 1380–1386.

St. Clair, D. (1987). *Say you love Satan.* New York: Dell.

St. Jean, R. (1978). Posthypnotic behavior as a function of experimental surveillance. *American Journal of Clinical Hypnosis, 20*, 250–255.

Stager, G.L., & Lundy, R.M. (1985). Hypnosis and the learning and recall of visually presented material. *International Journal of Clinical and Experimental Hypnosis, 33*, 27–39.

Stalnaker, J.M., & Riddle, E.E. (1932). The effect of hypnosis on long-delayed recall. *Journal of General Psychology, 6*, 429–440.

Stanton, M. (1997). U-Turn on memory lane. *Columbia Journalism Review,* pp. 44–49 (July/August).

State v. Alberico. (1993). 116 N.M. 156, 861 P.2d 192.

State v. Beachum. (1981). 97 N.M. 682, 643 P. 2d 246 (Ct. App.), writ quashed, 98 N.M. 51, 644 P.2d 1040 (1982).

State v. Dreher. (1991). 251 N.J. Super 300, 598 A 2d 216 (NJ Super).

State v. Grimmet. (1990). 459 N.W.2d 515 (Minn. App.).

State v. Hungerford. (1995). 1995 WL 378571 (N.H. Super., May 23).

State v. Hungerford. (1997). 1997 WL 358620 (N.H. Sup. Ct., July 1).

State v. Hurd. (1981). 86 N.J. 525, 432 A. 2d 86.

State v. Johnston. (1988). 39 Ohio St. 3d 48, 529 N.E.2d 898.

State v. Mack.(1980). 292 N.W. 2d 764 (Minn).

State v. Mitchell. (1989). 779 P.2d 1116 (Utah).

State v. Mylod. (1898). 40 Atl. 753 (R.I.).

State v. Peoples. (1984). 311 N.C. 515, 319 S.E.2d 177.

State v. Quattrocchi. (1996). 681 A.2d 879 (R.I.Sup.Ct.).

State v. Schreiner. (1991). 77 N.Y. 2d 733, 570 N.Y.S. 2d 464, 573 N.E. 2d 552.

State v. Ture. (1984). 353 N.W. 2d 502, 45 A.L.R. 4th 575 (Minn.).

State v. Turner. (1970). 81 N.M. 571, 469 P.2d 720 (Ct.App.).

State v. Varela. (1991). 817 P.2d 731 (N.M. App.).

State v. Walters. (1995). Nos. 93–S-2111,-2112. Superior Court, Hillsborough, Southern District (New Hampshire).

Steblay, N.M., & Bothwell, R.K. (1994). Evidence for hypnotically refreshed testimony: The view from the laboratory. *Law and Human Behavior, 18*, 635–651.

Steele, K. (1989). A model for abreaction with MPD and other dissociative disorders. *Dissociation, 2*, 151–159.

Steele, K., & Colrain, J.(1990). Abreactive work with sexual abuse survivors: Concepts and techniques. In M.A. Hunter (Ed.), *The sexually abused male: Applications of treatment strategies* (Vol. 2, pp. 1–55). Lexington, MA: Lexington Books.

Steiger, H., & Zanko, M. (1990). Sexual traumata among eating-disordered, psychiatric and normal female groups. *Journal of Interpersonal Violence, 5*, 74–86.

Stein, M.B., Hannah, C., Koverola, C., Yehuda, R., Torchia, M., & McClarty, B. (December 15, 1994). *Neuroanatomical and neuroendocrine correlates in adulthood of severe sexual abuse in childhood.* Paper presented at the 33rd annual meeting of the American College of neuropsychopharmacology, San Juan, PR.

Stein, N.L. (1996). Children's memory for emotional events: Implications for testimony. In K. Pezdek & W.P. Banks (Eds.), *The recovered memory/false memory debate* (pp.169–196). New York: Academic Press.

Steinberg, M. (1993). *Structured clinical interview of DSM-IV dissociative disorders (SCID-D).* Washington, D.C.: American Psychiatric Press.

Steinberg, M. (1994). *Interviewer's guide to the structured clinical interview for DSM-IV dissociative disorders* (Revised ed.). Washington, D.C.: American Psychiatric Press.

Steinberg, M., Ciccheti, D., Buchanan, J., Hall, P., & Rounsaville, B. (1993). Clinical assessment of dissociative symptoms and disorders: The structured clinicalinterview for *DSM-IV dissociative disorders (SCID-D). Dissociation, 6*, 3–15.

Steinberg, M.E., Hord, A.H., Reed, B., & Sebel, P.S. (1993). Study of the effect of intraoperative suggestion on postoperative analgesia and well-being. In P.S. Sebel, B. Bonke, & E.Winograd (Eds.), *Memory and awareness in anesthesia* (pp. 205–208). Englewood Cliffs, NJ: Prentice Hall.

Steller, M. (1989). Recent developments in statement analysis. In J.C. Yuille (Ed.), *Credibility assessment* (pp. 135–154). The Netherlands: Kluver.

Steller, M., & Koehnken, G. (1989). Criteria based statement analysis. In D.C. Raskin (Ed.), *Psychological methods for criminal investigation and evidence* (pp. 217–245). New York: Springer.

Steller, M., Wellershaus, P., & Wolf, T. (June, 1988). *Empirical validation of criteria-based content analysis.* Paper presented at the NATO Advanced Study Institute on Credibility Assessment, Maratea, Italy.

Stephen, J.F. (1883). *History of the criminal law of England.* London: Macmillan.

Stern, D. (1985). *The interpersonal world of the infant.* New York: Basic.

Stewart v. Rudner. (1957). 349 Mich. 459, 84 N.W.2d 816.

Stiff, J.D. (1994). *Persuasive communication.* New York: Guilford.

Stoltzy, S., Couture, L.J., & Edmonds, H.L. (1986). Evidence of partial recall during general anesthesia. *Anesthesia & Analgesia, 65,* S154.

Stoltzy, S., Couture, L.J., & Edmonds, H.L. (1987). A postoperative recognition test after balanced anesthesia. *Anesthesiology, 67,* A377.

Stover, E., & Nightingale, E.O. (1985). *The breaking of bodies and minds: Torture, psychiatric abuse, and the health professions.* New York: W.H. Freeman.

Stratton, J. (1977). The use of hypnosis in law enforcement criminal investigations. *Journal of Police Science and Administration, 5,* 399–406.

Streiker, L.D. (1984). *Mind bending: Brainwashing, cults, and the deprogramming in the '80s.* Garden City, NY: Doubleday.

Strentz, J. (1982). The Stockholm syndrome: Law enforcement policy and hostage behavior. In. F.M. Ochberg & D.A. Soskis (Eds.), *Victims of terrorism* (pp. 149–163). Boulder, CO: Westview.

Strong., S.R. (1968). Counseling: An interpersonal influence process. *Journal of Counseling Psychology, 15,* 215–348.

Strupp, H.H., & Binder, J.L. (1984). *Psychotherapy in a new key: A guide to time-limited dynamic psychotherapy.* New York: Basic.

Stuart, G.W., Laraia, M.T., Ballenger, J.C., & Lydiard, R.B. (1990). Early family experiences of women with bulimia and depression. *Archives of Psychiatric Nursing, 4,* 43–52.

Sturm, C.A. (1982). *Eyewitness memory: A comparison of guided memory and hypnotic hypermnesia techniques.* Unpublished doctoral dissertation, University of Montana.

Sugar, M. (1992). Toddler's traumatic memories. *Infant Mental Health Journal, 13,* 245–251.

Sullivan v. Cheshier. (1993). 1993 WL 546407 (N.D. Ill).

Sullivan v. Cheshier. (1994). 846 F.Supp. 654 (N.D.Ill., E.D.).

Sullivan v. Cheshier. (1995). 895 F.Supp. 204 (N.D. Il., E.D.).

Summit, R. (1983). The child sexual abuse accommodation syndrome. *Child Abuse and Neglect, 7,* 177–193.

Summit, R.C. (1988). Hidden victims, hidden pain: Societal avoidance of child sexual abuse. In G.E. Wyatt & G.J. Powell (Eds.), *Lasting effects of child sexual abuse* (pp. 39–60). Newbury Park, CA: Sage.

Summit, R.C. (1994) The dark tunnels of McMartin. *Journal of Psychohistory, 21,* 397–416.

S.V. v. R.V. (1996). 39 Tex.Sup.Ct.J. 386, 1996 WL112206 (Tex.Sup.Ct.) (Not yet released for publication).

Swanson v. Hood. (1918). 99 Wash. 506.

Szasz, T.S. (1972). The sane slave: Social control and legal psychiatry. *The American Criminal Law Review, 10,* 337–356.

Tancredi, L.R. (1986). Psychiatric malpractice. In J.O. Cavenar, Jr. (Ed.), *Psychiatry* (revised ed., Vol. 3, pp. 1–16). Philadelphia, PA: Lippincott.

Tarasoff v. Board of Regents of the Univ. of Cal. (1976). 17 Cal.3d 425, 131 Cal. Rptr. 14, 551 P.2d 334.

Tart, C.T. (1975). *States of consciousness.* New York: Dutton.

Tata, P.R., & Gudjonsson, G.H. (1990). The effects of mood and verbal feedback on interrogatory suggestibility. *Personality and Individual Differences, 11,* 1079–1085.

Tate, C., Warren, A., & Hess, T. (1992). Adult's liability for children's "lie-ability": Can adults coach children to lie successfully? In S.J. Ceci, M.D. Leichtman, & M.E. Putnick (Eds.), *Cognitive and social factors in early deception* (pp. 69–87). New York: Macmillan.

Taub, S. (1996). The legal treatment of recovered memories of child sexual abuse. *Journal of Legal Medicine, 17,* 183–214.

Tayloe, D.R. (1995). The validity of repressed memories and the accuracy of their recall through hypnosis: A case study from the courtroom. *American Journal of Clinical Hypnosis, 37,* 25–31.

Taylor, P.J., & Kopelman, M.D. (1984). Amnesia for criminal offences. *Psychological Medicine, 14,* 581–588.

Taylor, W.S. (1923). Behavior under hypnoanalysis and the mechanism of the neurosis. *Journal of Abnormal Psychology, 18,* 107–124.

Teasdale, J.D., Taylor, R., & Fogarty, S.J. (1980). Effects of induced elation-depression on the accessibility of memories of happy and unhappy experiences. *Behavior Research and Therapy, 18,* 339–340.

Tebecis, A.K., Provins, K.A., Farnbach, R.W., & Pentany, P. (1975). Hypnosis and the EEG: A quantitative investigation. *Journal of Nervous and Mental Disorders, 161,* 1–17.

Teicher, M.H., Glod, C.A., Surrey, J., & Swett, C. (1993). Early childhood abuse and limbic system ratings in adult psychiatric outpatients. *Journal of Neuropsychiatry and Clinical Neurosciences, 5,* 301–306.

Tellegan, A. (1979). On measures and conceptions of hypnosis. *American Journal of Clinical Hypnosis, 21,* 219–236.

Terr, L. (1979). Children of Chowchilla: A study of psychic trauma. *Psychoanalytic Study of the Child, 34,* 552–623.

Terr, L. (1981). Psychic trauma in children: Observations following the Chowchilla school-bus kidnapping. *American Journal of Psychiatry, 138,* 14–19.

Terr, L. (1983a). Chowchilla revisited: The effects of psychic trauma four years after a school bus kidnapping. *American Journal of Psychiatry, 140,* 1543–1550.

Terr, L. (1983b). Life attitudes, dreams, and psychic trauma in a group of "normal" children. *Journal of the American Academy of Child and Adolescent Psychiatry, 22,* 221–230.

Terr, L. (1988). What happens to early memories of trauma? A study of twenty children under age five at the time of documented traumatic events. *Journal of the American Academy of Child and Adolescent Psychiatry, 27,* 96–104.

Terr, L. (1991). Childhood traumas: An outline and overview. *American Journal of Psychiatry, 148,* 10–20.

Terr, L. (1994). *Unchained memories: True stories of traumatic memories, lost and found.* New York: Basic.

Terr, L. (1996). True memories of childhood trauma: Flaws, absences, and returns. In K. Pezdek & W. P. Banks (Eds.), *The recovered memory/false memory debate* (pp. 69–80). New York: Academic Press.

Tesauro v. Perrige. (1994). 437 Pa.Super. 620, 650 A.2d 1079.

Tessler, M., & Nelson, K. (1994). Making memories: The influence of joint encoding on later recall by young children. *Consciousness and Cognition, 3,* 307–326.

Thoennes, N., & Tjaden, P.G. (1990). The extent, nature, and validity of sexual abuse allegations in custody/visitation disputes. *Child Abuse and Neglect, 14,* 151–163.

Thom, D.A., & Fenton, N. (1920) Amnesias in war cases. *American Journal of Insanity, 76,* 437–448.

Thomas, R.L. (1991). Adult survivors of childhood sexual abuse and statutes of limitations: A call for legislative action. *Wake Forest Law Review, 26,* 1245–1295.

Thompson, C.P. (1982). Memory for unique personal events: The roommate study. *Memory and Cognition, 10,* 324–332.

Thompson, C.P., & Cowan, T. (1986). Flashbulb memories: A nicer interpretation of a Neisser recollection. *Cognition, 22,* 199–200.

Thompson, K.F. (1970). Clinical and experimental trance: Yes, there is a difference. *American Journal of Clinical Hypnosis, 13,* 3–5.

Thorndike, E.L. (1931). *Human learning.* New York: Century.

Thornton, H. (1995). *Hung jury.* Philadelphia, PA: Temple University Press.

Thing v. La Chusa. (1989). 48 Cal. 3d 644, 771 P.2d 814, 257 Cal. Rptr. 865.

Tichenor, V., Marmar, C.R., Weiss, D.S., Metzler, T.J., & Ronfeldt, H.M. (1996). The relationship of peritraumatic dissociation and posttraumatic stress: Findings in female Vietnam theater veterans. *Journal of Consulting and Clinical Psychology, 64,* 1054–1059.

Tichner, A., & Poulton, E. (1975). Watching for people and actions. *Ergonomics, 18,* 35–51.

Tillman, J.G., Nash, M.R., & Lerner, P.M. (1994). Does trauma cause dissociative pathology? In S.J. Lynn (Ed.), *Dissociation: Clinical, theoretical and research perspectives* (pp. 395–414). Washington, D.C.: American Psychological Association Press.

Time. (May 24, 1968). Evidence: Hypnosis and the truth. *Time,* 59.

Timm, H.W. (1981). The effect of forensic hypnosis techniques on eyewitness recall and recognition. *Journal of Police Science & Administration, 9,* 188–194.

Timm, H.W. (1985). An examination of the effects of forensic hypnosis. In D. Waxman, P. Misra, M. Gibson, & M. Basker (Eds.), *Modern trends in hypnosis* (pp. 327–344). New York: Plenum.

Toglia, M.P. (1995). Repressed memories: The way we were? *Consciousness and Cognition, 4,* 111–15.

Tollestrup, P.A., Turtle, J.W., & Yuille, J.C. (1994). Actual victims and witnesses to robbery and fraud: An archival analysis. In D. Ross, D. Read & S. Ceci (Eds.), *Adult eyewitness testimony: Current trends and developments* (pp. 144–160). New York: Springer-Verlag.

Torrie, A. (1944). Psychosomatic casualties in the Middle East. *Lancet, 1,* 6283–6287.

Toulmin, S. (1972). *Human understanding: The collective use and evolution of concepts* (Vol. 1). Princeton, NJ: Princeton University Press.

Trankell, A. (Ed.). (1972). *Reliability of evidence.* Stockholm: Beckmans.

Treadway, M., McCloskey, M., Gordon, B., & Cohen, N.J. (1992). Landmark life events and the organization of memory: Evidence from functional retrograde amnesia. In S.-A. Christianson (Ed.), *The handbook of emotion and memory: Research and theory* (pp. 389–410). Hillsdale, NJ: Erlbaum.

Trear v. Sills. (1995). No. GO16875 (Cal.Ct.App., Fourth Dist.).

Treisman, A.M. (1960). Contextual cues in selective listening. *Quarterly Journal of Experimental Psychology, 12,* 242–248.

Trent, C.L., & Muhl, M.P. (1975). Professional liability insurance and the American psychiatrist. *American Journal of Psychiatry, 132,* 1312–1314.

Tromp, S., Koss, M.P., Figueredo, A.J., & Tharan, M. (1995). Are rape memories different? A comparison of rape, other unpleasant, and pleasant memories among employed women. *Journal of Traumatic Stress, 8,* 607–627.

True, R.M. (1949). Experimental control in hypnotic age regression states. *Science, 110,* 583–584.

Truth and Responsibility in Mental Health Practices Act. (1995).

Tucker, A., Mertin, P., & Luszcz, M. (1990). The effect of a repeated interview on young children's eyewitness memory. *Australian and New Zealand Journal of Criminology, 23,* 117–124.

Tully, B., & Cahill, D. (1984). *Police interviewing of mentally handicapped persons: An experimental study.* London: Police Foundation of Great Britain.

Tulving, E. (1969). Retrograde amnesia in free recall.

Science, 164, 88–90.

Tulving, E. (1972). Episodic and semantic memory. In E. Tulving & W. Donladson (Eds.), *Organization of memory* (pp. 381–403). New York: Academic Press.

Tulving, E. (1976). Ecphoric processes in recall and recognition. In J. Brown (Ed.), *Recall and recognition* (pp. 37–73). London: Wiley.

Tulving, E., & Donaldson, W. (Ed.). (1972). *Organization of memory.* New York: Academic Press.

Tulving, E., & Osler, S. (1968). Effectiveness of retrieval cues in memory for words. *Journal of Experimental Psychology, 77,* 593–601.

Tulving, E., & Pearlstone, Z. (1966). Availability versus accessibility of information in memory for words. *Journal of Verbal Learning and Verbal Behavior, 5,* 381–391.

Tulving, E., & Thompson, D.M. (1973). Encoding specificity and retrieval processes in episodic memory. *Psychological Review, 80,* 352–373.

Tureen, L.L., & Stein, M. (1949). The base section psychiatric hospital. *Bulletin of the U.S. Army Medical Department,* 9(Suppl.), 105–137.

Turtle, J.W., & Yuille, J.C. (1994). Lost but not forgotten details: Repeated eyewitness recall leads to reminiscence but not hypermnesia. *Journal of Applied Psychology, 79,* 260–271.

Tushinsky v. Arnold. (1987). 195 Cal.App.3d 666, 241 Cal.Rptr. 103 (2nd Dist.).

Tversky, B., & Tuchin, M. (1989). A reconciliation of the evidence on eyewitness testimony: Comments on McCloskey & Zaragoza (1985). *Journal of Experimental Psychology: General, 118,* 876–90.

Tyson v. Tyson. (1986). 727 P.2d 226 (Wash.Sup.Ct.). Superceded by statute in 1988, Wash. Rev. Code Ann. s. 4.16.340 (West 1995).

Udolf, R. (1983). *Forensic hypnosis.* Lexington, MA: Lexington Books.

Udolf, R. (1987). *Handbook of hypnosis for professionals.* New York: Van Nostrand Reinhold.

Uleman, J.S., & Bargh, J.A. (Eds.). (1989). *Unintended thought.* New York: Guilford.

Ulibarri v. Gerstenberger. (1993). 178 Ariz. 151, 871 P.2d 698 (Ariz.App., review denied, 1994).

Ultramares Corp. v. Touche, Niven & Co. (1931). 255 N.Y. 170, 174 N.E. 441.

Underwager, R., & Wakefield, H. (1990). *The real world of child interrogations.* Springfield, IL: Thomas.

Underwood v. Croy. (1994). 30 Cal. Rptr. 2d 504 (4th Dist.) (Ordered Not Published by the Supreme Court on October 13, 1994).

Underwood, B.J. (1948). Retroactive and proactive inhibition after five and forty-eight hours. *Journal of Experimental Psychology, 38,* 29–38.

Underwood, B.J. (1957). Interference and forgetting. *Psychological Review, 64,* 49–60.

Underwood, B.J. (1969). Attributes of memory. *Psychological Review, 76,* 559–573.

Undeutsch, U. (1967). Beurteilung der Glaubhaftigkeit von Zeugenaussagen [Assessing the validity of testimonial statements]. In U. Undeutsch (Ed.), *Handbuch der Psychologie: Forensische Psychologie* (Vol. 2, pp. 26–181). Gottingen: Verlag für Psychologie.

Undeutsch, U. (1982). Statement reality analysis. In A. Trankell (Ed.), *Reconstructing the past* (pp. 27–56). Deventer, The Netherlands: Kluwer.

Undeutsch, U. (1984). Courtroom evaluation of eyewitness testimony. *International Review of Applied Psychology, 33,* 51–67.

Undeutsch, U. (1989). The development of statement analysis. In J.C. Yuille (Ed.), *Credibility assessment* (pp. 101–119). Deventer, The Netherlands: Kluwer.

United States v. Cordoba. (1996). 104 F.3d 225 (9th Cir.).

United States v. Fishman. 1990. 743 F.Supp. 713 (N.D.Cal.).

United States v. Pettigrew. (1996). 77 F.3d 1500 (5 Cir.).

United States v. Posado. (1995). 57 F.3d 428 (5 Cir.).

United States v. Scheffer. (1996). 44 M.J. 442 (Ct.Mil.App.).

United States v. Scheffer. (1997). No.96–1133 (U.S.Sup.Ct.).

United States v. Willis. (1990). 737 F. Supp. 269 (S.D.N.Y.).

Usher, J. A., & Neisser, U. (1993). Childhood amnesia and the beginnings of memory for four early life events. *Journal of Experimental Psychology: General, 122,* 155–165.

U.S. News & World Report. (May 8, 1953). Brain warfare: Russia's secret weapon, 54.

Vaksberg, A. (1990). *The prosecutor and the prey: Vyshinsky and the 1930s Moscow show trials.* London: Weidenfeld and Nicolson.

Van Benschoten, S.C. (1990). Multiple personality disorder and Satanic ritual abuse: The issue of credibility. *Dissociation, 3,* 22–30.

VandenBos, G.R., & Bryant, B.K. (Eds.). (1987). *Cataclysms, crisis and catastrophes: Psychology in action.* Washington, D.C.: American Psychological Association.

van der Hart, O. (1991). *Trauma, dissociatie en hypnose.* Amsterdam: Swets & Zeitlinger.

van der Hart, O. (1987). Hypnosis for individuals too susceptible to suggestions. *Australian Journal of Clinical and Experimental Hypnosis, 15,* 11–19.

van der Hart, O., Boon, S., & van Everdingen, G.B. (1990). Writing assignments and hypnosis in the treatment of traumatic memories. In M.L. Fass & D. Brown (Eds.), *Creative mastery in hypnosis and hypnoanalysis: A Festschrift for Erika Fromm* (pp. 231–253). Hillsdale, NJ: Erlbaum.

van der Hart, O., & Brown, P. (1992). Abreaction re-evaluated. *Dissociation, 3,* 127–140.

van der Hart, O., Brown, P., & van der Kolk, B.A. (1989). Pierre Janet's treatment of post-traumatic stress. *Journal of Traumatic Stress, 2,* 379–395.

van der Hart, O., & Friedman, B. (1989). A reader's guide to Pierre Janet on dissociation: A neglected intellectual heritage. *Dissociation, 2,* 3–16.

van der Hart, O., & Friedman, B. (1992). Trauma, dissociation and triggers: Their role in treatment and emergency psychiatry. *Emergency Psychiatry Today,* 137–142.

van der Hart, O., & Horst, R. (1989). The dissociation theory of Pierre Janet. *Journal of Traumatic Stress, 2,* 397–412.

van der Hart, O., & Nijenhuis, E. (1995). Amnesia for traumatic experiences. *Hypnos, 22,* 73–86.

van der Hart, O., & Nijenhuis, E.R.S. (a). The psychological processing of traumatic memories.

van der Hart, O., & Nijenhuis, E.R.S. (b). The validity of child abuse in a case of dissociative identity disorder.

van der Hart, O., Steele, K., Boon, S., & Brown, P. (1993). The treatment of traumatic memories: Synthesis, realization and integration. *Dissociation, 6,* 162–180.

van der Kolk, B.A. (Ed.). (1984). *Post-traumatic stress disorder: Psychological and biological sequelae.* Washington, D.C.: American Psychiatric Press.

van der Kolk, B.A. (1987). *Psychological trauma.* Washington, D.C.: American Psychiatric Press.

van der Kolk, B.A. (1988). The trauma spectrum: The interaction of biological and social events in the genesis of the trauma response. *Journal of Traumatic Stress, 1,* 273–290.

van der Kolk, B. (1989). The compulsion to repeat the trauma: Re-enactment, re-victimization, and masochism. *Psychiatric Clinics of North America, 12,* 389–411.

van der Kolk, B. (1993). Biological considerations about emotions, trauma, memory and the brain. In S. Ablon, D. Brown, E. Khantzian, & J. Mack (Eds.), *Human feelings: Explorations in affect development and meaning* (pp. 221–240). Hillsdale, NJ: Analytic Press.

van der Kolk, B.A. (1994). The body keeps score: Memory and the evolving psychobiology of posttraumatic stress. *Harvard Review of Psychiatry, 1,* 253–265.

van der Kolk, B.A. (1996). Trauma and memory. In B.A. van der Kolk, A.C. McFarlane, & L. Weisaeth (Eds.), *Traumatic stress: The effects of overwhelming experience on mind, body, and society* (pp. 279–302). New York: Guilford.

van der Kolk, B.A., Brown, P., & van der Hart, O. (1989) Pierre Janet on post-traumatic stress. *Journal of Traumatic Stress, 2,* 365–379.

van der Kolk, B.A., & Ducey, C.P. (1989). The psychological processing of traumatic experience: Rorschach patterns in PTSD. *Journal of Traumatic Stress, 2,* 259–274.

van der Kolk, B.A., & Fisler, R. (1995). Dissociation and the fragmentary nature of traumatic memories: Overview and exploratory study. *Journal of Traumatic Stress, 8,* 505–525.

van der Kolk, B.A., Fisler, R.E., & Vardi, D.J. (1995). *Dissociation and the perceptual nature of traumatic memories: Background and experimental confirmation.* Unpublished manuscript.

van der Kolk, B.A., McFarlane, A.C., & Weisaeth, L. (1996). *Traumatic stress: The effects of overwhelming experience on mind, body, and society.* New York: Guilford.

van der Kolk, B.A., Pelcovitz, D., Roth, S., Mandel, F.S., McFarlane, A., & Herman, J.L. (1996). Dissociation, somatization, and affect dysregulation: The complexity of adaptation to trauma. *American Journal of Psychiatry, 153,* 83– 93.

van der Kolk, B.A., & Saporta, J. (1993). Biological response to psychic trauma. In J.P. Wilson & B. Raphael (Eds.), *International handbook of traumatic stress syndromes* (pp. 25–34). New York: Plenum.

van der Kolk, B.A., & van der Hart, O. (1989). Pierre Janet and the breakdown of adaptation in psychological trauma. *American Journal of Psychiatry, 146,* 1530–1540.

van der Kolk, B.A., & van der Hart, O. (1991). The intrusive past: The flexibility of memory and the engraving of trauma. *American Imago, 48,* 425–454.

van der Kolk, B.A., van der Hart, O., & Marmar, C.R. (1996). Dissociation and information processing in posttraumatic stress disorder. In B.A. van der Kolk, A.C. McFarlane, & L. Weisaeth (Eds.), *Traumatic stress: The effects of overwhelming experience on mind, body, and society* (pp. 303–327). New York: Guilford.

van der Kolk, B.A., Vardi, D.J., Eisler, R.E., Herron, N., Hostettler, A., & Zakai, A. (May, 1994). *Traumatic versus autobiographical memory.* Paper presented at the Annual Meeting of the American Psychiatric Association, Philadelphia, PA.

Vandermaas, M. (1994). Does anxiety affect children's reports of memory for a stressful event? *Applied Cognitive Psychology, 7,* 109–127.

Vandermaas, M.O., Hess, T.M., & Baker-Ward, L. (1993). Does anxiety affect children's reports of memory for a stressful event? *Journal of Applied Psychology, 7,* 109–128.

Van Sickle v. Doolittle. (1918). 184 Iowa 855.

Veronen, L.J., & Kilpatrick, D.G. (1983). Stress management for rape victims. In D. Meichenbaum & M.E. Jaremko (Eds.), *Stress reduction and prevention* (pp. 341–374). New York: Plenum.

Vernon, J. (1963). *Inside the black room: Studies of sensory deprivation.* New York: Clarkson N. Potter.

Vesecky v. Vesecky. (1994). 880 S.W.2d 804. (Ct.App.Tex.—Dallas).

Victor, J.S. (1991). The dynamics of rumor—Panics about Satanic cults, pp. 221–236. In J.T. Richardson, J. Best, & D.G. Bromley, *The Satanism scare.* New York: Aldine De Gruyter.

Victor, J.S. (1993). *Satanic panic: The creation of a contemporary legend.* Chicago: Open Court.

Victor, J.S. (1994). *Sources of Satanic ritual abuse memories in therapist-patient interaction.* Unpublished manuscript.

Villemur, C., Plourde, G., Lussier, I., & Normandin, N. (1993). Auditory processing during isoflurane anesthesia: A study with an implicit memory task and auditory evoked potentials. In P. S. Sebel, B. Bonke, & E. Winograd (Eds.), *Memory and awareness in general anesthesia* (pp. 99–106). Englewood Cliffs, NJ: Prentice Hall.

Vincent, R.H. (1897). *The elements of hypnotism.* (2nd ed.). London: Kegan Paul, Trench, Trubner & Co.

Wagenaar, W.A. (1986). My memory: A study of autobiographical memory over six years. *Cognitive Psychology, 18,* 225–252.

Wagenaar, W.A., & Boer, J.P.A. (1987). Misleading postevent information: Testing parametered models of integration in memory. *Acta Psychologia, 66,* 291–306.

Wagenaar, W.A., & Groeneweg, J. (1990). The memory of concentration camp survivors. *Applied Cognitive Psychology, 4,* 77–87.

Wagstaff, G.F. (1982). Hypnosis and recognition of a face. *Perceptual and Motor Skills, 55,* 816–818.

Wagstaff, G.F. (1991). Compliance, belief, and semantics in hypnosis: A nonstate, sociocognitive perspective. In S.J. Lynn & J.W. Rhue (Eds.), *Theories of hypnosis* (pp. 362–398). New York: Guilford.

Wagstaff, G.F. (1996). Should "hypnotized" witnesses be banned from testifying in court? Hypnosis and the M50 murder case. *Contemporary Hypnosis, 13,* 186–190.

Wagstaff, G.F. & Frost, R. (1996). Reversing and breaching posthypnotic amnesia and hypnotically created pseudomemories. *Contemporary Hypnosis, 13,* 191–197.

Wagstaff, G.F., & Maguire, C. (1983). An experimental study of hypnosis, guided memory and witness memory. *Journal of the Forensic Science Society, 23,* 73–78.

Wagstaff, G.F., & Mercer, K. (1993a). Does hypnosis facilitate memory for deep processed stimuli? *Contemporary Hypnosis, 10,* 59–66.

Wagstaff, G.F., & Mercer, K. (1993b). Hypnotic hypermnesia or experimental demands? In search of an explanation. *Contemporary Hypnosis, 10,* 70–71.

Wagstaff, G.F., Traverse, J., & Milner, S. (1982). Hypnosis and eyewitness memory: Two experimental analogues. *IRCS Medical Science, 10,* 894–895.

Waites, E.A. (1997). *Memory quest: Trauma and the search for personal history.* New York: Norton.

Wakefield, H. & Underwager, R. (1988). *Accusations of child sexual abuse.* Springfield, IL: Charles C. Thomas.

Wakefield, H., & Underwager, R. (1992). Recovered memories of alleged sexual abuse: Lawsuits against parents. *Behavioral Sciences and the Law, 10,* 483–507.

Wakefield, H., & Underwager, R. (1994). *Return of the Furies: An investigation into recovered memory therapy.* Chicago, IL: Open Court.

Waldfogel, S. (1948). The frequency and affective character of childhood memories. *Psychological Monographs, No. 291, 62*(4).

Walker, L. (1979). *The battered woman.* New York: Harper & Row.

Walker v. Superior Court. (1988). 47 Cal.3d 112, 253 Cal. Rptr. 1, 763 P.2d 852.

Wallace, A.F.C. (1956). Revitalization movements. *American Anthropologist, 58,,* 264–281.

Wallace, W.P. (1965) Review of the history: Empirical and theoretical status of von Restorff phenomenon. *Psychological Bulletin, 63,* 410–424.

Wang, S., Wilson, J.P., & Mason, J.W. (1996). Stages of decompensation in combat-related posttraumatic stress disorder: A new conceptual model. *Integrative Physiological and Behavioral Science, 31,* 237–253.

Warner, K.E. (1979). The use of hypnosis in the defense of criminal cases. *International Journal of Clinical and Experimental Hypnosis, 27,* 417–436.

Warnick, D.H., & Sanders, G.S. (1980). Why do eyewitnesses make so many mistakes? *Journal of Applied Social Psychology, 10,* 362–366.

Warren, A.R., Hulse-Trotter, K., & Tubbs, E.C. (1991). Inducing resistance to suggestibility in children. *Law and Human Behavior, 15,* 273–285.

Warren A.R., & Lane, P. (1995). Effects of timing and type of questioning on eyewitness accuracy and suggestibility. In M.S. Zaragoza et al. (Eds.), *Memory and testimony in the child witness* (pp. 4–60). Thousand Oaks, CA: Sage.

Warren, A.R., & Swartwood, J.N. (1992). Developmental issues in flashbulb memory research: Children recall the *Challenger* event. In. E. Winograd & U. Neisser (Eds.), *Affect and accuracy in recall: Studies of "flashbulb" memories* (pp.95–120). London: Cambridge University Press.

Washington Revised Code. (1995). Section 4.16.340 (West, added 1988).

Waterman, J., Kelly, R., Oliveri, M.K., & McCord, J. (1993). *Beyond the playground walls: Sexual abuse in preschools.* New York: Guilford.

Watkins, J.G. (1949). *Hypnotherapy of war neurosis.* New York: Ronald Press.

Watkins, J.G. (1971). The affect bridge: A hypnoanalytic technique. *International Journal of Clinical and Experimental Hypnosis, 19,* 21–27.

Watkins, J. G. (1989). Hypnotic hypermnesia and forensic hypnosis: A cross-examination. *American Journal of Clinical Hypnosis, 32*(2), 71–83.

Watkins, J.G. (1992). *Hypnoanalytic techniques.* New York: Irvington.

Watkins, J.G. (Fall 1993). Dealing with the problem of "false memory" in the clinic and court. *Journal of Psychiatry and Law, 23,* 297–317.

Watkins, J.G. (n.d.). *Further data on the unethical use of hypnosis.* Unpublished manuscript.

Watkins, J.G., & Watkins, H.H. (1979–80). Ego states and hidden observers. *Journal of Altered States of Consciousness, 5,* 3–18.

Watkins, J.G., & Watkins, H.H. (1981). Ego state therapy. In R. Corsini (Ed.), *Handbook of innovative psychotherapies* (pp. 252–270). New York: Wiley.

Watson, D., & Friend, R. (1969). Management and social evaluative scale. *Journal of Consulting and Clinical Psychology, 33,* 448–457.

Watson, P. (1978). *War on the mind: The military uses and abuses of psychology.* New York: Basic.

Waube v. Warrington. (1935). 216 Wis. 603, 258 N.W. 497.

Weekes, J.R., Lynn, S.J., & Myers, B. (1993). *Pseudomemory and hypnosis: The impact of stimulus factors.* Unpublished manuscript, Ohio University.

Weekes, J.R., Lynn, S.J., Green, J.P., & Brentar, J.T. (1992). Pseudomemory in hypnotized and task-motivated subjects. *Journal of Abnormal Psychology, 101,* 356–360.

Wehrspann, W., Steinhauer, P., & Klajner-Diamond, H. (1987). Criteria for assessing credibility of sexual abuse allegations. *Canadian Journal of Psychiatry, 32,* 615–623.

Weidlich, T. (January 23, 1995a). "Abused" parent-killers win clemency: Florida and Maryland shorten terms of parricides who say they were victims. *National Law Journal, 17*(21), A6.

Weidlich, T. (June 12, 1995b). Repressed memories: Unreliable? Judges in four cases reject them before trial starts. *National Law Journal, 17*(41), A7.

Weidlich, T. (November 13, 1995c). Court to hear priest-abuse megacase: Repressed memories, time bars among many issues in 28 Rhode Island suits. *National Law Journal, 18*(11), A16.

Weinberger, D.A. (1990). The construct of the repressive coping style. In J.L. Singer (Ed.), *Repression and dissociation: Implications for personality theory, psychopathology, and health* (pp. 337–386). Chicago, IL: University of Chicago Press.

Weinberger, N.M. (1995). Retuning the brain by fear conditioning. In M.S. Gazzaniga (Ed.), *The cognitive neurosciences* (pp. 1071–1089). Cambridge, MA: M.I.T. Press.

Weinberger, N.M., Gold, P.E., & Sternberg, D.B. (1984). Epinephrine enables Pavlovian fear conditioning under anesthesia. *Science, 223,* 605–607.

Weinberger, N.M. (1995). Retuning the brain by fear conditioning. In M.S. Gazzanga (Ed.), *The cognitive neurosciences* (pp. 1071–1089). Cambridge, MA: M.I.T. Press.

Weine, S.M., Becker, D.F., McGlashan, T.H., Laub, D., Lazrove, S., Vojvoda, D., & Hyman, L. 1995. Psychiatric consequences of "ethnic cleansing": Clinical assessments and trauma testimonies of newly resettled Bosnian refugees. *American Journal of Psychiatry, 152,* 536–542.

Weingardt, K.R., Toland, H.K., & Loftus, E.F. (1994). Reports of suggested memories: Do people truly believe them? In D. F. Ross, J.D. Read, & M.P. Toglia (Eds.), *Adult eyewitness testimony: Current trends and developments* (pp. 3–25). New York: Cambridge University Press.

Weinstein, H.C. (Section Ed.) (1992). Perspectives on dual loyalties in the practice of psychiatry. In Simon, R.I. (Ed.), *Review of clinical psychiatry and the law* (Vol. 3, pp. 153–155). Washington, D.C.: American Psychiatric Press, Inc.

Weiss, W,. & Fine, B.J. (1956). The effect of induced aggressiveness on opinion change. *Journal of Abnormal and Social Psychology, 52,* 109–114.

Weitzenhoffer, A.M. (1953). *Hypnotism: An objective study in suggestibility.* New York: Wiley.

Weitzenhoffer, A.M. (1989). *The practice of hypnotism* (Vols. 1 & 2). New York:Wiley.

Weitzenhoffer, A.M., & Hilgard, E.R. (1962). *Stanford hypnotic susceptibility scale, form C.* Palo Alto, CA: Consulting Psychologists Press.

Welke v. Kuzilla. (1985). 144 Mich.App. 245, 375 N.W.2d 403.

Wells, G.L. (1984). How adequate is human intuition for judging eyewitness testimony? In G.L. Wells & E.F. Loftus (Eds.), *Eyewitness testimony: Psychological perspectives* (pp. 256–272). Cambridge: Cambridge University Press.

Wells, G.L., & Leippe, M.R. (1981). How do people infer the accuracy of eyewitness identifications? Memory for peripheral detail can be misleading. *Journal of Applied Psychology, 66,* 682–687.

Wells, G.L., & Loftus, E.F. (1984). *Eyewitness testimony.* Cambridge: Cambridge University Press.

Wells, G. L., & Turtle, J.W. (1987). Eyewitness testimony research: Current knowledge and emergent controversies. *Canadian Journal of Behavioral Science, 19,* 363–388.

West v. Howard. (1991). 77 Ohio App. 3d 168, 601 N.E.2d 528 (Ohio App.).

West, L.J., & Martin, P.R. (1994). Pseudo-identity and the treatment of personality change in victims of captivity and cults. In S.J. Lynn & J.W. Rhue, (Eds.), *Dissociation: Clinical and theoretical perspectives* (pp. 268–288). New York: Guilford.

Westerhof, Y., Woertman, L., & van der Hart, O. (in press). Forgetting child abuse: Feldman-Summers & Pope's (1994) study replicated among Dutch psychologists. *Journal of Consulting and Clinical Psychology.*

Westmoreland, C., Sebel, P.S., Winograd, E., & Goldman, W.P. (1992). *Indirect memory during anesthesia: Effect of midazolam.* Paper presented at the Second International Symposium on Memory and Awareness in Anesthesia, Atlanta, Georgia.

Wexler, R. (1990). *Wounded innocents: The real victims of the war against child abuse.* New York: Guilford.

Whipple, G.M. (1909). The observer as a reporter: A survey of the "psychology of testimony." *Psychological Bulletin, 6,* 153–170.

White, G.E. (1980). *Tort law in America: An intellectual history.* Oxford: Oxford University Press.

White, R.T. (1982). Memory for personal events. *Human Learning, 1,* 171–183.

White, R.W. (1941). A preface to the theory of hypnotism. *Journal of Abnormal Psychology, 36,* 477–505.

White, R.W., Fox, G.R., & Harris, W.W. (1940). Hypnotic hypermnesia for recently learned material. *Journal of Abnormal and Social Psychology, 35,* 88–103.

White, S., Strom, G.A., Santilli, G., & Halpin, B.M. (1986). Interviewing young sexual abuse victims with anatomically correct dolls. *Child Abuse and Neglect, 10,* 519–530.

White, S.H., & Pillemer, D. (1979). Childhood amnesia and the development of a socially accessible memory system. In J.F. Kihlstrom & F.J. Evans (Eds.), *Functional disorders of memory* (pp. 29–73). Hillsdale, NJ: Erlbaum.

Whitehead, T.M. (1992). Application of the delayed discovery rule: The only hope for justice for sexual abuse survivors. *Law and Psychology Review, 16,* 153–170.

Whitehouse, W.G., Dinges, D.F., Orne, E.C., & Orne, M.T. (1988). Hypnotic hypermnesia: Enhanced memory accessibility or report bias? *Journal of Abnor-*

mal Psychology, 97, 289–295.

Whitehouse, W. G., Orne, E. C., Orne, M. T., & Dinges, D. F. (1991). Distinguishing the source of memories reported during prior waking and hypnotic recall attempts. *Applied Cognitive Psychology, 5*, 51–59.

Whitfield, C.L. (1995a). The forgotten difference: Ordinary memory versus traumatic memory. *Consciousness and Cognition, 4*, 88–94.

Whitfield, C.L. (1995b). *Memory and abuse: Remembering and healing the effects of trauma.* Deerfield Beach, FL: Health Communications.

Whitfield, C.L. (in press). Traumatic amnesia: The evolution of our understanding from a clinical and legal perspective.

Wicker, A.W., & Pomazil, R.J. (1971). The relationship between attitudes and behavior as a function of specificity of attitude object and presence of significant others during assessment conditions. *Representative Research in Social Psychology, 2*, 26–31.

Wickless, C., & Kirsch, I. (1989). The effects of verbal and experiential expectancy manipulations on hypnotic susceptibility. *Journal of Personality and Social Psychology, 57*, 762–768.

Wickramasekera, I. (1979). *A model of the patient at high risk for chronic stress related disorders: Do beliefs have biological consequences?* Paper presented at the Annual Convention of the Biofeedback Society of America, San Diego, CA.

Wickramasekera, I. (1994). Somatic to psychological symptoms and information transfer from implicit to explicit memory: A controlled case study with predictions from the high risk model of threat perception. *Dissociation, 7*, 153–166.

Wickramasekera, I., Pope, A.T., & Kolm, P. (1996). On the interaction of hypnotizability and negative affect in chronic pain: Implications for the somatization of trauma. *Journal of Nervous and Mental Disease, 184*(10), 628–635.

Widom, C.S. (1989). The cycle of violence. *Science, 244*, 160–166.

Widom, C.S., & Morris, S. (1997). Accuracy of adult recollections of childhood victimization: Part 2. Childhood sexual abuse. *Psychological Assessment, 8*, 412–421.

Widom, C.S., & Shepard, R.L. (1996). Accuracy of adult recollections of childhood victimization: Part 1. Childhood physical abuse. *Psychological Assessment, 9*, 34–46.

Wilbur, C.B. (1984). Treatment of multiple personality. *Psychiatric Annals, 14*, 27–31.

Wilkinson v. Balsam. (1995). 885 F.Supp. 651 (D.Vermont).

Wilkinson, C.B. (1983) Aftermath of a disaster: The collapse of the Hyatt Regency hotel skywalks. *American Journal of Psychiatry, 140*, 1134–1139.

Williams. J.M.G. (1992). Autobiographical memory and emotional disorders. In S. Christianson (Ed.), *The handbook of emotion and memory: Research and theory* (pp. 451–477). Hillsdale, NJ: Erlbaum.

Williams, L. M. (1992). Adult memories of childhood

abuse: Preliminary findings from a longitudinal study. *The Advisor, 5*(2), 19–21.

Williams, L.M. (October 27, 1993). *Recall of childhood trauma: A prospective study of women's memories of child sexual abuse.* Paper presented at the Annual Meeting of the American Society of Criminology, Phoenix, AZ.

Williams, L.M. (1994a). Recall of childhood trauma: A prospective study of women's memories of child sexual abuse. *Journal of Consulting and Clinical Psychology, 62*, 1167–1176.

Williams, L.M. (1994b). What does it mean to forget child sexual abuse? A reply to Loftus, Garry, and Feldman (1994). *Journal of Consulting and Clinical Psychology, 62*, 1182–1186.

Williams, L.M. (1995). Recovered memories of abuse in women with documented child sexual victimization histories. *Journal of Traumatic Stress, 8*, 649–673.

Williams, M.R. (1996). Suits by adults for childhood sexual abuse: Legal origins of the "repressed memory" controversy. *Journal of Psychiatry and Law, 24*, 207–228.

Wilschinsky v. Medina. (1989). 108 N.M. 511, 775 P.2d 713.

Wilson, I. (1982). *All in the mind.* Garden City, NY: Doubleday.

Wilson, J.P. (1989). *Trauma, transformation and healing: An integrative approach to theory, research, and post-traumatic therapy.* New York: Brunner/Mazel.

Wilson, L., Greene, E., & Loftus, E.F. (1986). Beliefs about forensic hypnosis. *International Journal of Clinical and Experimental Hypnosis, 34*, 110–121.

Wilson, S.C., & Barber, T.X. (1981). Vivid fantasy and hallucinatory abilities in the life histories of excellent hypnotic subjects ("somnambules"): Preliminary report with female subjects. In E. Klinger (Ed.), *Imagery: Concepts, results, and applications* (Vol. 2, pp.133–152). New York: Plenum.

Wilson, S.C., & Barber, T.X. (1983). The fantasy-prone personality: Implications for understanding imagery, hypnosis and parapsychological phenomena. In A.A. Sheikh (Ed.), *Imagery: Current theory, research and application* (pp.340–387). New York: Wiley.

Wilson, S.L., Vaughan, R.W., & Stephen, C.R. (1975). Awareness, dreams and hallucinations associated with general anesthesia. *Anesthesia and Analgesia, 54*, 609–616.

Wingfield, A., & Stine, E.A.L. (1992). Age differences in perceptual processing and memory for spoken language. In R.L. West & J.D. Sinnott (Eds.), *Everyday memory and aging* (pp. 101–123). New York: Springer-Verlag.

Wingfield, H.E. (1920). *An introduction to the study of hypnotism.* London: Balliere Tindall.

Winje, D. (1996). Long-term outcome of trauma in adults: The psychological impact of a fatal bus accident. *Journal of Consulting and Clinical Psychology, 64*, 1037–1043.

Winn, D. (1983). *The manipulated mind.* London: Octagon Press.

Winograd, E., & Killinger, W.A., Jr. (1983). Relating age at encoding in early childhood to adult recall: Development of flashbulb memories. *Journal of Experimental Psychology: General, 112,* 413–422.

White, S.H., Strom, G., Santill, G., & Halpin, B.M. (1986). Interviewing young sexual abuse victims with anatomically correct dolls. *Child Abuse and Neglect, 10,* 519–529.

Winograd, E., & Neisser, U.(1992). *Affect and accuracy in recall: Studies of "flashbulb" memories.* New York: Cambridge University Press.

Winograd, E., Sebel, P.S., Goldman, W.P., Clifton, C.L., & Lowden, J.D. (1991). Indirect assessment of memory for music during anesthesia. *Journal of Clinical Anesthesiology, 3,* 276– 279.

Wogelius v. Dallas. (1987). 152 Ill. App.3d 614, 504 N.E.2d 791.

Woititz, J. G. (1983). *Adult children of alcoholics.* Pompano Beach, FL: Health Communications.

Wolberg, L.R. (1964). *Hypnoanalysis* (2nd ed.). New York: Grune & Stratton.

Wolff, R. (1977). Systematic desensitization and negative practice to alter the aftereffects of a rape attempt. *Journal of Behavior Therapy and Experimental Psychiatry, 8,* 423–425.

Wolfner, G., Faust, D., & Dawes, R. (1993). The use of anatomical dolls in sexual abuse evaluations: The state of the science. *Applied and Preventative Psychology, 2,* 1–11.

Wolfram, C.W. (1986). *Modern legal ethics.* St. Paul, MN: West Publishing.

Woo, R., Seltzer, J. L., & Marr, A. (1987). The lack of response to suggestion under controlled surgical anaesthesia. *Acta Anaesthesiologica Scandinavica, 31,* 567–571.

Wood, B., Orsak, C., Murphy, M., & Cross, H.J. (1996). Semistructured child sexual abuse interviews: Interview and child characteristics related to credibility of disclosure. *Child Abuse and Neglect, 20,* 81–92.

Wright, D.B. (1994). Recall of the Hillsborough disaster over time: Systematic biases of "flashbulb" memories. *Applied Cognitive Psychology, 7,* 129–138.

Wright, D.B., Varley, S., & Belton, A. (1996). Accurate second guesses in misinformation studies. *Applied Cognitive Psychology, 10,* 13–21.

Wright, L. (1993). *Remembering Satan.* New York: Knopf.

Wrightsman, L.S., & Kassin, S.M. (1993). *Confessions in the courtroom.* Newbury Park, CA: Sage.

Wundt, W. (1903). *Grundzuge der physiolgischen Psychologie.* (3 vols.). Leipzig.

Yalom, I.D. (1970). *The theory and practice of group psychotherapy.* New York: Basic.

Yamini, R.J. (1996). Repressed and recovered memories of child sexual abuse: The accused as "direct victim." *Hastings Law Journal, 47,* 551–580.

Yapko, M. (April 1, 1983). A comparative analysis of direct and indirect hypnotic communication styles. *American Journal Clinical Hypnosis, 25,* 270.

Yapko, M.D. (1990). *Trancework: An introduction to the practice of clinical hypnosis.* New York: Brunner/Mazel.

Yapko, M.D. (1994a). *Suggestions of abuse.* New York: Simon & Schuster.

Yapko, M.D. (1994b). Suggestibility and repressed memories of abuse: A survey of psychotherapists' beliefs. *American Journal of Clinical Hypnosis, 36*(3), 163–171.

Yarmey, A.D., & Bull, M.P. III. (1978). Where were you when President Kennedy was assassinated? *Bulletin of the Psychonomic Society, 11,* 133–135.

Yates, A. (1982). Children eroticized by incest. *American Journal of Psychiatry, 39,* 482–485.

Yates, A., & Terr, L. (1988). Anatomically correct dolls: Should they be used as the basis for expert testimony? *Journal of the American Academy of Child and Adolescent Psychiatry, 27,* 254–257, 387–388.

Yehuda, R., Giller, E.L., Southwick, S.M., Lowy, M.T., & Mason, J.W.(1991). Hypothalamic-pituitary-adrenal dysfunction in posttraumatic stress disorder. *Biological Psychiatry, 30,* 1031–1048.

Yehuda, R., Keefe, R.S.E., Harvey, P.D., Levengood, R.A., Gerber, D.K., Geni, J., & Siever, L.J. (1995). Learning and memory in combat veterans with posttraumatic stress disorder. *American Journal of Psychiatry, 152,* 137–139.

Yerkes, R.M., & Dodson, J.D. (1908). The relation of strength of stimulus to rapidity of habit-information. *Journal of Comparative Neurology of Psychology, 18,* 459–482.

Young, P.C. (1925). An experimental study of mental and physical functions in the normal and hypnotic states. *American Journal of Psychology, 36,* 214–232.

Young, P. C. (1926). An experimental study of mental and physical functions in the normal and hypnotic states: Additional results. *American Journal of Psychology, 37,* 345–356.

Young, W.C., Sachs, R.G., Braun, B.G., & Watkins, R.T. (1991) Patients reporting ritual abuse in childhood: A clinical syndrome. Report of 37 cases. *Child Abuse and Neglect, 15,* 181–189.

Yuille, J.C. (1986). Meaningful research in the police context. In J.C. Yuille (Ed.), *Police selection and training* (pp. 225–243). Dordrecht, The Netherlands: Martinus Nijhoff.

Yuille, J.C. (1988). The systematic assessment of children's tesimony. *Canadian Psychology, 29,* 247–262.

Yuille, J.C. (1994). Personal correspondence to D. Corydon Hammond, August 9, 1994.

Yuille, J.C., & Cutshall, J.L. (1986). A case study of eyewitness memory of a crime. *Journal of Applied Psychology, 71,* 291–301.

Yuille, J.C., & Cutshall, J.L. (1989). Analysis of the statements of victims, witnesses and suspects. In J.C. Yuille (Ed.), *Credibility assessment* (pp. 175–191). Dordrecht, The Netherlands: Kluwer.

Yuille, J.C., Davies, G., Gibling, F., Marxsen, D., & Porter, S. (in press). Eyewitness memory of police trainees for realistic role plays. *Journal of Applied Psychology.*

Yuille, J.C., Hunter, R., Joffe, R., & Zaparniuk, J. (1993). Interviewing children in sexual abuse cases. In G.

Goodman & B. Bottoms (Eds.), *Understanding and improving children's testimony: Clinical, developmental and legal implications* (pp. 95–115). New York: Guilford.

Yuille, J.C., & Kim, C.K. (1987). A field study of the forensic use of hypnosis. *Canadian Journal of Behavioral Sciences Review, 19*, 418–429.

Yuille, J.C., & McEwan, N.H. (1985). Use of hypnosis as an aid to eyewitness memory. *Journal of Applied Psychology, 70*, 389–400.

Yuille, J.C., & Tollestrup, P.A. (1990). Some effects of alcohol on eyewitness memory. *Journal of Applied Psychology, 75*, 268–273.

Yuille, J.C., & Tollestrup, P.A. (1992). A model of diverse effects on emotion on eyewitness memory. In S. Christianson (Ed.), *The handbook of emotion and memory: Research and theory* (pp. 201–213). Hillsdale, NJ: Erlbaum.

Yuille, J.C., Tymofievich, M., & Marxsen, D. (1995). The nature of allegations of child sexual abuse. In T. Ney (Ed.). *True and false allegations of child sexual abuse: Assessment and case management* (pp.21–46). New York: Brunner/Mazel.

Zacks, R. T., Hasher, L., & Sanft, H. (1982). Automatic encoding of event frequency: Further findings. *Journal of Experimental Psychology: Learning, Memory, and Cognition, 8*, 106–116.

Zajonc, R.B. (1980). Feeling and thinking: Preferences need no inferences. *American Psychologist, 35*, 151–175.

Zaragoza, M.S. (1987). Memory, suggestibility, and eyewitness testimony in children and adults. In S.J. Ceci, M.P. Toglia, & D.F. Ross (Eds.), *Children's eyewitness memory* (pp. 53–78). New York: Springer-Verlag.

Zaragoza, M.S. (1991). Preschool children's susceptibility to memory impairment. In J. Doris (Ed.), *The suggestibility of children's recollections* (pp. 27–39). Washington, D.C.: American Psychological Association.

Zaragoza, M.S., Graham, J.R., Hall, G.C.N., Hirschman, R., & Ben-Porath, Y.S. (1995). *Memory and testimony in the child witness.* Thousand Oaks, CA: Sage.

Zaragoza, M.S., & Koshmider, J.W. (1989). Misled subjects may know more than their performance implies. *Journal of Experimental Psychology: Learning, Memory and Cognition, 15*, 246–255.

Zaragoza, M.S., McCloskey, M., & Jamis, M. (1987). Misleading postevent information and recall of the original event: Further evidence against the memory impairment hypothesis. *Journal of Experimental Psychology: Learning, Memory, and Cognition, 13*, 36–44.

Zaragoza, M.S., & Mitchell, K.J. (1995). Empirical psychology and the repressed memory debate: Current status and future directions, *Consciousness and Cognition, 4*, 116–119.

Zaslow v. State Board of Medical Examiners. (December 4, 1971). No. 665–667, Super.Ct. San Francisco County.

Zeig, J. (1980). Symptom prescription techniques: Clinical applications using elements of communication. *American Journal of Clinical Hypnosis, 23*, 23.

Zeig, J. (1985). Ethical issues in hypnosis: Informed consent and training standards. In J. Zeig (Ed.), *Ericksonian psychotherapy: Structures* (Vol. 1, pp. 459–473). New York: Bruner/Mazel.

Zeitlin, S.B., & McNally, R.J. (1991). Implicit and explicit memory bias for threat in posttraumatic stress disorder. *Behavior Research Therapy, 29*, 451–457.

Zelig, M., & Beidleman, W.B. (1981). The investigative use of hypnosis. *International Journal of Clinical and Experimental Hypnosis, 29*, 401–412.

Zimbardo, P.G. (1960). Involvement and communication discrepancy as determinants of opinion conformity. *Journal of Abnormal and Social Psychology, 60*, 86–94.

Zimbardo, P.G. (1967). The psychology of police confessions. *Psychology Today, 1*(2), 17–20, 25–27.

Zimbardo, P.G., & Leippe, M.R. (1991). *The psychology of attitude change and social influence.* New York: McGraw-Hill.

Zola-Morgan, S., Squire, L.R., & Amaral, D.G. (1986). Human amnesia and the medial temporal region: Enduring memory impairment following a bilateral lesion limited to field CA1 of the hippocampus. *Journal of Neuroscience, 6*, 2950–2967.

Zola-Morgan, S., Squire, L.R., & Ramus, S. (1994). Severity of memory impairment in monkeys as a function of locus and extent of damage within the medial temporal memory system. *Hippocampus, 4*(4), 483–495.

Zubek, J.P. (Ed.). (1969). *Sensory deprivation: Fifteen years of research.* New York: Appleton-Century-Crofts.

Zulawski, D.E., & Wicklander, D.E. (1993). *Practical aspects of interview and interrogation.* Boca Raton, FL: CRC Press.

Name Index*

Subject Index

memory (*continued*)
    hypnosis and, *see* separate entry
    iconic, 67–68, 75, 84
    integration of traumatic, *see* integration
    interference, 217–19, 229, 230, 231, 261
    learning and, *see* separate entry
    level of processing and, 302, 303
    long-term, *see* separate entry
    "malleability" of, 214, 323, 671, 672
    misinformation and, *see* separate entry
    models of organization and processing, 74–77 (figure),
        198, 382–83
    multiple (multidimensional) memory systems, 77–80, 138,
        200, 383, 385–87, 418, 437
    narrative, *see* separate entry
    naturally occurring, 73–74
    nondeclarative, 79
    nonretention, 224, 231
    organization of, *see* cognitive and memory science
    original, vs. post-event, 217, 218, 219, 220, 221, 222, 230,
        234, 236, 330, 335, 336, 339, 340, 668–69
    parental, in laboratory research, 283, 363
    performance, *see* memory performance
    personal, 10, 88, 116–139 (*see also* autobiographical;
        narrative)
    phenomenology/quality of, 83, 92, 168, 172, 187, 282–83,
        439, 617–19
    procedural, 207, 586–87
    recall, 257 (*see also* separate entry)
    recanters, *see* retractors
    recovered, *see* memory recovery
    reinterpretation of, 217
    "remarkable," 143, 146, 148
    repetitive, 136
    representation, 66–71, 234–35, 261–62, 284, 335, 354,
        362, 364, 374, 378, 385, 418
    repression of, *see* repressed memory
    research in, *see* cognitive and memory science
    retrieval, *see* separate entry
    therapeutic influence on, *see* psychotherapy, suggestive
    schema-based model of, 135, 438
    science of, *see* cognitive and memory science
    screen, 58, 91, 136, 320
    semantic, 77, 78, 79
    short-term, *see* separate entry
    social factors involved in, *see* social influences
    somatic, 206–7, 210–11
    span, 74
    as state dependent, *see* separate entry
    strength of, 94–95, 246, 248, 249, 345, 362, 373–74, 378,
        379
    suggestibility, *see* separate entry
    testing, strategies/context for, 360, 361, 362
    see also recall; recognition; retrieval
    trace, *see* memory trace
    traumatic, *see* traumatic memory
    types of, 130, 139, 201, 207
    unbidden, 136
    weakening, 234
    work, *see* memory work
    see also information processing
Memory and Abuse: Remembering and Healing the Effects of

    Trauma, 7
memory accuracy:
    accuser vs. parental/perpetrator's, 14, 16–17, 389
    adult recall, 2, 19, 38, 47, 135–36, 161–63, 368–370
    assessment of scientific literature on, 109–112, 114–15,
        432
    autobiographical memories, *see* separate entry
    base rates of, 45
    behavioral, *see* separate entry
    central action vs. peripheral details, *see* separate entry
    children's, *see* children
    completeness and/vs., *see* memory, completeness
    confidence and/vs., *see* separate entry
    in constructivist theories, 66, 68–69, 382–83
    dates, 131, 138
    defined, 81
    emotion and, *see* separate entry
    emotionality vs. 82, 83, 118, 390, 394, 501, 520, 617
    for events of impact, 141, 142, 143, 144, 145, 146
    in eyewitness testimony, *see* eyewitness
    flashbulb memories, *see* separate entry
    in general, 45
    historical, 638 (*see also* truth, historical)
    hypnosis and, *see* separate entry
    indicators of, 19, 23, 36, 82–83
    laboratory simulations measuring, 99–109, 317
    psychopathology and, 135–36, 178, 402
    relativity of measures of, 81
    retractor vs. recovered, 389
    stages of memory process and, 84
    therapeutic variables and, 412
    in trace theories, 66, 68–69 (*see also* memory trace)
    for trauma, *see* traumatic memory
Memory Attitude Questionnaire, 383
Memory Attitude Survey, 70
Memory Characteristics Questionnaire, 188
Memory for Childhood Sexual Abuse Inventory, 168
Memory of Childhood Trauma: A Clinician's Guide to the Litera-
    ture, 49
memory distortion:
    accuracy and, 82
    autobiographical memories, 128, 136–38, 139
    children's by adult communication, 150
    coercive persuasion and, 280 (*see also* separate entry)
    defense mechanisms affecting, 38, 39, 419, 420, 522
    factors causing, 49–50, 81
    false memory and, 52, 53, 81
    flashbulb memories, 126, 127
    hypnotic (vs. nonhypnotic), 293, 309, 324, 331, 353, 414,
        661
    misinformation effect and, *see* separate entry
    motivated, 203, 211, 383
    psychoanalytic explanations of, 136–38
    reconstruction causing, 70, 71, 85, 122
    ritual (Satanic) abuse and, 60, 65
    studies on, 45
    suggestibility and, 395, 410–411, 502 (*see also* separate
        entry)
    traumatic vs. nontraumatic conditions, 95, 216–17
Memory Distortion: History and Current Status, 45
"memory distrust syndrome," 261
memory enhancement, 51, 415 (table), 416